T0189069

Communications in Computer and Information Science 1333

More information about this series at http://www.springer.com/series/7899

Haiqin Yang · Kitsuchart Pasupa ·
Andrew Chi-Sing Leung ·
James T. Kwok · Jonathan H. Chan ·
Irwin King (Eds.)

Neural Information Processing

27th International Conference, ICONIP 2020
Bangkok, Thailand, November 18–22, 2020
Proceedings, Part V

 Springer

Editors
Haiqin Yang ⓘ
Department of AI
Ping An Life
Shenzhen, China

Andrew Chi-Sing Leung ⓘ
City University of Hong Kong
Kowloon, Hong Kong

Jonathan H. Chan ⓘ
School of Information Technology
King Mongkut's University
of Technology Thonburi
Bangkok, Thailand

Kitsuchart Pasupa ⓘ
Faculty of Information Technology
King Mongkut's Institute
of Technology Ladkrabang
Bangkok, Thailand

James T. Kwok ⓘ
Department of Computer Science
and Engineering
Hong Kong University of Science
and Technology
Hong Kong, Hong Kong

Irwin King ⓘ
The Chinese University of Hong Kong
New Territories, Hong Kong

ISSN 1865-0929   ISSN 1865-0937   (electronic)
Communications in Computer and Information Science
ISBN 978-3-030-63822-1   ISBN 978-3-030-63823-8   (eBook)
https://doi.org/10.1007/978-3-030-63823-8

This Springer imprint is published by the registered company Springer Nature Switzerland AG
The registered company address is: Gewerbestrasse 11, 6330 Cham, Switzerland

Preface

This book is a part of the five-volume proceedings of the 27th International Conference on Neural Information Processing (ICONIP 2020), held during November 18–22, 2020. The conference aims to provide a leading international forum for researchers, scientists, and industry professionals who are working in neuroscience, neural networks, deep learning, and related fields to share their new ideas, progresses, and achievements. Due to the outbreak of COVID-19, this year's conference, which was supposed to be held in Bangkok, Thailand, was organized as fully virtual conference.

The research program of this year's edition consists of four main categories, Theory and Algorithms, Computational and Cognitive Neurosciences, Human-Centered Computing, and Applications, for refereed research papers with nine special sessions and one workshop. The research tracks attracted submissions from 1,083 distinct authors from 44 countries. All the submissions were rigorously reviewed by the conference Program Committee (PC) comprising 84 senior PC members and 367 PC members. A total of 1,351 reviews were provided, with each submission receiving at least 2 reviews, and some papers receiving 3 or more reviews. This year, we also provided rebuttals for authors to address the errors that exist in the review comments. Meta-reviews were provided with consideration of both authors' rebuttal and reviewers' comments. Finally, we accepted 187 (30.25%) of the 618 full papers that were sent out for review in three volumes of Springer's series of *Lecture Notes in Computer Science* (LNCS) and 189 (30.58%) of the 618 in two volumes of Springer's series of *Communications in Computer and Information Science* (CCIS).

We would like to take this opportunity to thank all the authors for submitting their papers to our conference, and the senior PC members, PC members, as well as all the Organizing Committee members for their hard work. We hope you enjoyed the research program at the conference.

November 2020

Haiqin Yang
Kitsuchart Pasupa

Organization

Honorary Chairs

Jonathan Chan   King Mongkut's University of Technology Thonburi, Thailand

Irwin King   Chinese University of Hong Kong, Hong Kong

General Chairs

Andrew Chi-Sing Leung   City University of Hong Kong, Hong Kong

James T. Kwok   Hong Kong University of Science and Technology, Hong Kong

Program Chairs

Haiqin Yang   Ping An Life, China

Kitsuchart Pasupa   King Mongkut's Institute of Technology Ladkrabang, Thailand

Local Arrangements Chair

Vithida Chongsuphajaisiddhi   King Mongkut University of Technology Thonburi, Thailand

Finance Chairs

Vajirasak Vanijja   King Mongkut's University of Technology Thonburi, Thailand

Seiichi Ozawa   Kobe University, Japan

Special Sessions Chairs

Kaizhu Huang   Xi'an Jiaotong-Liverpool University, China

Raymond Chi-Wing Wong   Hong Kong University of Science and Technology, Hong Kong

Tutorial Chairs

Zenglin Xu   Harbin Institute of Technology, China

Jing Li   Hong Kong Polytechnic University, Hong Kong

Proceedings Chairs

Xinyi Le   Shanghai Jiao Tong University, China
Jinchang Ren   University of Strathclyde, UK

Publicity Chairs

Zeng-Guang Hou   Chinese Academy of Sciences, China
Ricky Ka-Chun Wong   City University of Hong Kong, Hong Kong

Senior Program Committee

Sabri Arik   Istanbul University, Turkey
Davide Bacciu   University of Pisa, Italy
Yi Cai   South China University of Technology, China
Zehong Cao   University of Tasmania, Australia
Jonathan Chan   King Mongkut's University of Technology Thonburi,
                             Thailand
Yi-Ping Phoebe Chen   La Trobe University, Australia
Xiaojun Chen   Shenzhen University, China
Wei Neng Chen   South China University of Technology, China
Yiran Chen   Duke University, USA
Yiu-ming Cheung   Hong Kong Baptist University, Hong Kong
Sonya Coleman   Ulster University, UK
Daoyi Dong   University of New South Wales, Australia
Leonardo Franco   University of Malaga, Spain
Jun Fu   Northeastern University, China
Xin Geng   Southeast University, China
Ping Guo   Beijing Normal University, China
Pedro Antonio Gutiérrez   Universidad de Córdoba, Spain
Wei He   University of Science and Technology Beijing, China
Akira Hirose   The University of Tokyo, Japan
Zengguang Hou   Chinese Academy of Sciences, China
Kaizhu Huang   Xi'an Jiaotong-Liverpool University, China
Kazushi Ikeda   Nara Institute of Science and Technology, Japan
Gwanggil Jeon   Incheon National University, South Korea
Min Jiang   Xiamen University, China
Abbas Khosravi   Deakin University, Australia
Wai Lam   Chinese University of Hong Kong, Hong Kong
Chi Sing Leung   City University of Hong Kong, Hong Kong
Kan Li   Beijing Institute of Technology, China
Xi Li   Zhejiang University, China
Jing Li   Hong Kong Polytechnic University, Hong Kong
Shuai Li   University of Cambridge, UK
Zhiyong Liu   Chinese Academy of Sciences, China
Zhigang Liu   Southwest Jiaotong University, China

Wei Liu   Tencent, China
Jun Liu   Xi'an Jiaotong University, China
Jiamou Liu   The University of Auckland, New Zealand
Lingjia Liu   Virginia Tech, USA
Jose A. Lozano   UPV/EHU, Spain
Bao-liang Lu   Shanghai Jiao Tong University, China
Jiancheng Lv   Sichuan University, China
Marley M. B. R. Vellasco   PUC of Rio de Janeiro, Brazil
Hiroshi Mamitsuka   Kyoto University, Japan
Leandro Minku   University of Birmingham, UK
Chaoxu Mu   Tianjin University, China
Wolfgang Nejdl   L3S Research Center, Germany
Quoc Viet Hung Nguyen   Griffith University, Australia
Takashi Omori   Tamagawa University, Japan
Seiichi Ozawa   Kobe University, Japan
Weike Pan   Shenzhen University, China
Jessie Ju Hyun Park   Yeungnam University, Japan
Kitsuchart Pasupa   King Mongkut's Institute of Technology Ladkrabang,
                           Thailand
Abdul Rauf   Research Institute of Sweden, Sweden
Imran Razzak   Deakin University, Australia
Jinchang Ren   University of Strathclyde, UK
Hayaru Shouno   The University of Electro-Communications, Japan
Ponnuthurai Suganthan   Nanyang Technological University, Singapore
Yang Tang   East China University of Science and Technology,
                           China
Jiliang Tang   Michigan State University, USA
Ivor Tsang   University of Technology Sydney, Australia
Peerapon Vateekul   Chulalongkorn University, Thailand
Brijesh Verma   Central Queensland University, Australia
Li-Po Wang   Nanyang Technological University, Singapore
Kok Wai Wong   Murdoch University, Australia
Ka-Chun Wong   City University of Hong Kong, Hong Kong
Raymond Chi-Wing Wong   Hong Kong University of Science and Technology,
                           Hong Kong
Long Phil Xia   Peking University, Shenzhen Graduate School, China
Xin Xin   Beijing Institute of Technology, China
Guandong Xu   University of Technology Sydney, Australia
Bo Xu   Chinese Academy of Sciences, China
Zenglin Xu   Harbin Institute of Technology, China
Rui Yan   Peking University, China
Xiaoran Yan   Indiana University Bloomington, USA
Haiqin Yang   Ping An Life, China
Qinmin Yang   Zhejiang University, China
Zhirong Yang   Norwegian University of Science and Technology,
                           Norway

De-Nian Yang	Academia Sinica, Taiwan
Zhigang Zeng	Huazhong University of Science and Technology, China
Jialin Zhang	Chinese Academy of Sciences, China
Min Ling Zhang	Southeast University, China
Kun Zhang	Carnegie Mellon University, USA
Yongfeng Zhang	Rutgers University, USA
Dongbin Zhao	Chinese Academy of Sciences, China
Yicong Zhou	University of Macau, Macau
Jianke Zhu	Zhejiang University, China

Program Committee

Muideen Adegoke	City University of Hong Kong, Hong Kong
Sheraz Ahmed	German Research Center for Artificial Intelligence, Germany
Shotaro Akaho	National Institute of Advanced Industrial Science and Technology, Japan
Sheeraz Akram	University of Pittsburgh, USA
Abdulrazak Alhababi	Universiti Malaysia Sarawak, Malaysia
Muhamad Erza Aminanto	University of Indonesia, Indonesia
Marco Anisetti	University of Milan, Italy
Sajid Anwar	Institute of Management Sciences, Pakistan
Muhammad Awais	COMSATS University Islamabad, Pakistan
Affan Baba	University of Technology Sydney, Australia
Boris Bacic	Auckland University of Technology, New Zealand
Mubasher Baig	National University of Computer and Emerging Sciences, Pakistan
Tao Ban	National Information Security Research Center, Japan
Sang Woo Ban	Dongguk University, South Korea
Kasun Bandara	Monash University, Australia
David Bong	Universiti Malaysia Sarawak, Malaysia
George Cabral	Rural Federal University of Pernambuco, Brazil
Anne Canuto	Federal University of Rio Grande do Norte, Brazil
Zehong Cao	University of Tasmania, Australia
Jonathan Chan	King Mongkut's University of Technology Thonburi, Thailand
Guoqing Chao	Singapore Management University, Singapore
Hongxu Chen	University of Technology Sydney, Australia
Ziran Chen	Bohai University, China
Xiaofeng Chen	Chongqing Jiaotong University, China
Xu Chen	Shanghai Jiao Tong University, China
He Chen	Hebei University of Technology, China
Junjie Chen	Inner Mongolia University, China
Mulin Chen	Northwestern Polytechnical University, China
Junying Chen	South China University of Technology, China

Chuan Chen	Sun Yat-sen University, China
Liang Chen	Sun Yat-sen University, China
Zhuangbin Chen	Chinese University of Hong Kong, Hong Kong
Junyi Chen	City University of Hong Kong, Hong Kong
Xingjian Chen	City University of Hong Kong, Hong Kong
Lisi Chen	Hong Kong Baptist University, Hong Kong
Fan Chen	Duke University, USA
Xiang Chen	George Mason University, USA
Long Cheng	Chinese Academy of Sciences, China
Aneesh Chivukula	University of Technology Sydney, Australia
Sung Bae Cho	Yonsei University, South Korea
Sonya Coleman	Ulster University, UK
Fengyu Cong	Dalian University of Technology, China
Jose Alfredo Ferreira Costa	Federal University of Rio Grande do Norte, Brazil
Ruxandra Liana Costea	Polytechnic University of Bucharest, Romania
Jean-Francois Couchot	University of Franche-Comté, France
Raphaël Couturier	University Bourgogne Franche-Comté, France
Zhenyu Cui	University of the Chinese Academy of Sciences, China
Debasmit Das	Qualcomm, USA
Justin Dauwels	Nanyang Technological University, Singapore
Xiaodan Deng	Beijing Normal University, China
Zhaohong Deng	Jiangnan University, China
Mingcong Deng	Tokyo University, Japan
Nat Dilokthanakul	Vidyasirimedhi Institute of Science and Technology, Thailand
Hai Dong	RMIT University, Australia
Qiulei Dong	Chinese Academy of Sciences, China
Shichao Dong	Shenzhen Zhiyan Technology Co., Ltd., China
Kenji Doya	Okinawa Institute of Science and Technology, Japan
Yiqun Duan	University of Sydney, Australia
Aritra Dutta	King Abdullah University of Science and Technology, Saudi Arabia
Mark Elshaw	Coventry University, UK
Issam Falih	Paris 13 University, France
Ozlem Faydasicok	Istanbul University, Turkey
Zunlei Feng	Zhejiang University, China
Leonardo Franco	University of Malaga, Spain
Fulvio Frati	Università degli Studi di Milano, Italy
Chun Che Fung	Murdoch University, Australia
Wai-Keung Fung	Robert Gordon University, UK
Claudio Gallicchio	University of Pisa, Italy
Yongsheng Gao	Griffith University, Australia
Cuiyun Gao	Harbin Institute of Technology, China
Hejia Gao	University of Science and Technology Beijing, China
Yunjun Gao	Zhejiang University, China

Xin Gao   King Abdullah University of Science and Technology,
                               Saudi Arabia
Yuan Gao   Uppsala University, Sweden
Yuejiao Gong   South China University of Technology, China
Xiaotong Gu   University of Tasmania, Australia
Shenshen Gu   Shanghai University, China
Cheng Guo   Chinese Academy of Sciences, China
Zhishan Guo   University of Central Florida, USA
Akshansh Gupta   Central Electronics Engineering Research Institute,
                               India
Pedro Antonio Gutiérrez   University of Córdoba, Spain
Christophe Guyeux   University Bourgogne Franche-Comté, France
Masafumi Hagiwara   Keio University, Japan
Ali Haidar   University of New South Wales, Australia
Ibrahim Hameed   Norwegian University of Science and Technology,
                               Norway
Yiyan Han   Huazhong University of Science and Technology,
                               China
Zhiwei Han   Southwest Jiaotong University, China
Xiaoyun Han   Sun Yat-sen University, China
Cheol Han   Korea University, South Korea
Takako Hashimoto   Chiba University of Commerce, Japan
Kun He   Shenzhen University, China
Xing He   Southwest University, China
Xiuyu He   University of Science and Technology Beijing, China
Wei He   University of Science and Technology Beijing, China
Katsuhiro Honda   Osaka Prefecture University, Japan
Yao Hu   Alibaba Group, China
Binbin Hu   Ant Group, China
Jin Hu   Chongqing Jiaotong University, China
Jinglu Hu   Waseda University, Japan
Shuyue Hu   National University of Singapore, Singapore
Qingbao Huang   Guangxi University, China
He Huang   Soochow University, China
Kaizhu Huang   Xi'an Jiaotong-Liverpool University, China
Chih-chieh Hung   National Chung Hsing University, Taiwan
Mohamed Ibn Khedher   IRT SystemX, France
Kazushi Ikeda   Nara Institute of Science and Technology, Japan
Teijiro Isokawa   University of Hyogo, Japan
Fuad Jamour   University of California, Riverside, USA
Jin-Tsong Jeng   National Formosa University, Taiwan
Sungmoon Jeong   Kyungpook National University, South Korea
Yizhang Jiang   Jiangnan University, China
Wenhao Jiang   Tencent, China
Yilun Jin   Hong Kong University of Science and Technology,
                               Hong Kong

Wei Jin	Michigan State University, USA
Hamid Karimi	Michigan State University, USA
Dermot Kerr	Ulster University, UK
Tariq Khan	Deakin University, Australia
Rhee Man Kil	Korea Advanced Institute of Science and Technology, South Korea
Sangwook Kim	Kobe University, Japan
Sangwook Kim	Kobe University, Japan
DaeEun Kim	Yonsei University, South Korea
Jin Kyu Kim	Facebook, Inc., USA
Mutsumi Kimura	Ryukoku University, Japan
Yasuharu Koike	Tokyo Institute of Technology, Japan
Ven Jyn Kok	National University of Malaysia, Malaysia
Aneesh Krishna	Curtin University, Australia
Shuichi Kurogi	Kyushu Institute of Technology, Japan
Yoshimitsu Kuroki	National Institute of Technology, Kurume College, Japan
Susumu Kuroyanagi	Nagoya Institute of Technology, Japan
Weng Kin Lai	Tunku Abdul Rahman University College, Malaysia
Wai Lam	Chinese University of Hong Kong, Hong Kong
Kittichai Lavangnananda	King Mongkut's University of Technology Thonburi, Thailand
Xinyi Le	Shanghai Jiao Tong University, China
Teerapong Leelanupab	King Mongkut's Institute of Technology Ladkrabang, Thailand
Man Fai Leung	City University of Hong Kong, Hong Kong
Gang Li	Deakin University, Australia
Qian Li	University of Technology Sydney, Australia
Jing Li	University of Technology Sydney, Australia
JiaHe Li	Beijing Institute of Technology, China
Jian Li	Huawei Noah's Ark Lab, China
Xiangtao Li	Jilin University, China
Tao Li	Peking University, China
Chengdong Li	Shandong Jianzhu University, China
Na Li	Tencent, China
Baoquan Li	Tianjin Polytechnic University, China
Yiming Li	Tsinghua University, China
Yuankai Li	University of Science and Technology of China, China
Yang Li	Zhejiang University, China
Mengmeng Li	Zhengzhou University, China
Yaxin Li	Michigan State University, USA
Xiao Liang	Nankai University, China
Hualou Liang	Drexel University, USA
Hao Liao	Shenzhen University, China
Ming Liao	Chinese University of Hong Kong, Hong Kong
Alan Liew	Griffith University, Australia

Chengchuang Lin	South China Normal University, China
Xinshi Lin	Chinese University of Hong Kong, Hong Kong
Jiecong Lin	City University of Hong Kong, Hong Kong
Shu Liu	The Australian National University, Australia
Xinping Liu	University of Tasmania, Australia
Shaowu Liu	University of Technology Sydney, Australia
Weifeng Liu	China University of Petroleum, China
Zhiyong Liu	Chinese Academy of Sciences, China
Junhao Liu	Chinese Academy of Sciences, China
Shenglan Liu	Dalian University of Technology, China
Xin Liu	Huaqiao University, China
Xiaoyang Liu	Huazhong University of Science and Technology, China
Weiqiang Liu	Nanjing University of Aeronautics and Astronautics, China
Qingshan Liu	Southeast University, China
Wenqiang Liu	Southwest Jiaotong University, China
Hongtao Liu	Tianjin University, China
Yong Liu	Zhejiang University, China
Linjing Liu	City University of Hong Kong, Hong Kong
Zongying Liu	King Mongkut's Institute of Technology Ladkrabang, Thailand
Xiaorui Liu	Michigan State University, USA
Huawen Liu	The University of Texas at San Antonio, USA
Zhaoyang Liu	Chinese Academy of Sciences, China
Sirasit Lochanachit	King Mongkut's Institute of Technology Ladkrabang, Thailand
Xuequan Lu	Deakin University, Australia
Wenlian Lu	Fudan University, China
Ju Lu	Shandong University, China
Hongtao Lu	Shanghai Jiao Tong University, China
Huayifu Lv	Beijing Normal University, China
Qianli Ma	South China University of Technology, China
Mohammed Mahmoud	Beijing Institute of Technology, China
Rammohan Mallipeddi	Kyungpook National University, South Korea
Jiachen Mao	Duke University, USA
Ali Marjaninejad	University of Southern California, USA
Sanparith Marukatat	National Electronics and Computer Technology Center, Thailand
Tomas Henrique Maul	University of Nottingham Malaysia, Malaysia
Phayung Meesad	King Mongkut's University of Technology North Bangkok, Thailand
Fozia Mehboob	Research Institute of Sweden, Sweden
Wenjuan Mei	University of Electronic Science and Technology of China, China
Daisuke Miyamoto	The University of Tokyo, Japan

Kazuteru Miyazaki	National Institution for Academic Degrees and Quality Enhancement of Higher Education, Japan
Bonaventure Molokwu	University of Windsor, Canada
Hiromu Monai	Ochanomizu University, Japan
J. Manuel Moreno	Universitat Politècnica de Catalunya, Spain
Francisco J. Moreno-Barea	University of Malaga, Spain
Chen Mou	Nanjing University of Aeronautics and Astronautics, China
Ahmed Muqeem Sheri	National University of Sciences and Technology, Pakistan
Usman Naseem	University of Technology Sydney, Australia
Mehdi Neshat	The University of Adelaide, Australia
Quoc Viet Hung Nguyen	Griffith University, Australia
Thanh Toan Nguyen	Griffith University, Australia
Dang Nguyen	University of Canberra, Australia
Thanh Tam Nguyen	Ecole Polytechnique Federale de Lausanne, France
Giang Nguyen	Korea Advanced Institute of Science and Technology, South Korea
Haruhiko Nishimura	University of Hyogo, Japan
Stavros Ntalampiras	University of Milan, Italy
Anupiya Nugaliyadde	Murdoch University, Australia
Toshiaki Omori	Kobe University, Japan
Yuangang Pan	University of Technology Sydney, Australia
Weike Pan	Shenzhen University, China
Teerapong Panboonyuen	Chulalongkorn University, Thailand
Paul S. Pang	Federal University Australia, Australia
Lie Meng Pang	Southern University of Science and Technology, China
Hyeyoung Park	Kyungpook National University, South Korea
Kitsuchart Pasupa	King Mongkut's Institute of Technology Ladkrabang, Thailand
Yong Peng	Hangzhou Dianzi University, China
Olutomilayo Petinrin	City University of Hong Kong, Hong Kong
Geong Sen Poh	National University of Singapore, Singapore
Mahardhika Pratama	Nanyang Technological University, Singapore
Emanuele Principi	Università Politecnica delle Marche, Italy
Yiyan Qi	Xi'an Jiaotong University, China
Saifur Rahaman	International Islamic University Chittagong, Bangladesh
Muhammad Ramzan	Saudi Electronic University, Saudi Arabia
Yazhou Ren	University of Electronic Science and Technology of China, China
Pengjie Ren	University of Amsterdam, The Netherlands
Colin Samplawski	University of Massachusetts Amherst, USA
Yu Sang	Liaoning Technical University, China
Gerald Schaefer	Loughborough University, UK

Nhi N.Y. Vo	University of Technology Sydney, Australia
Hiroaki Wagatsuma	Kyushu Institute of Technology, Japan
Nobuhiko Wagatsuma	Tokyo Denki University, Japan
Yuanyu Wan	Nanjing University, China
Feng Wan	University of Macau, Macau
Dianhui Wang	La Trobe University, Australia
Lei Wang	Beihang University, China
Meng Wang	Beijing Institute of Technology, China
Sheng Wang	Henan University, China
Meng Wang	Southeast University, China
Chang-Dong Wang	Sun Yat-sen University, China
Qiufeng Wang	Xi'an Jiaotong-Liverpool University, China
Zhenhua Wang	Zhejiang University of Technology, China
Yue Wang	Chinese University of Hong Kong, Hong Kong
Jiasen Wang	City University of Hong Kong, Hong Kong
Jin Wang	Hanyang University, South Korea
Wentao Wang	Michigan State University, USA
Yiqi Wang	Michigan State University, USA
Peerasak Wangsom	CAT Telecom PCL, Thailand
Bunthit Watanapa	King Mongkut's University of Technology Thonburi, Thailand
Qinglai Wei	Chinese Academy of Sciences, China
Yimin Wen	Guilin University of Electronic Technology, China
Guanghui Wen	Southeast University, China
Ka-Chun Wong	City University of Hong Kong, Hong Kong
Kuntpong Woraratpanya	King Mongkut's Institute of Technology Ladkrabang, Thailand
Dongrui Wu	Huazhong University of Science and Technology, China
Qiujie Wu	Huazhong University of Science and Technology, China
Zhengguang Wu	Zhejiang University, China
Weibin Wu	Chinese University of Hong Kong, Hong Kong
Long Phil Xia	Peking University, Shenzhen Graduate School, China
Tao Xiang	Chongqing University, China
Jiaming Xu	Chinese Academy of Sciences, China
Bin Xu	Northwestern Polytechnical University, China
Qing Xu	Tianjin University, China
Xingchen Xu	Fermilab, USA
Hui Xue	Southeast University, China
Nobuhiko Yamaguchi	Saga University, Japan
Toshiyuki Yamane	IBM Research, Japan
Xiaoran Yan	Indiana University, USA
Shankai Yan	National Institutes of Health, USA
Jinfu Yang	Beijing University of Technology, China
Xu Yang	Chinese Academy of Sciences, China

Jinghui Zhong	South China University of Technology, China
Junping Zhong	Southwest Jiaotong University, China
Xiaojun Zhou	Central South University, China
Hao Zhou	Harbin Engineering University, China
Yingjiang Zhou	Nanjing University of Posts and Telecommunications, China
Deyu Zhou	Southeast University, China
Zili Zhou	The University of Manchester, UK

Contents – Part V

Machine Learning

Neural Network Models

Robotics and Control

Time Series Analysis

Computational Intelligence

A Discriminative STGCN for Skeleton Oriented Action Recognition

Lin Feng[1], Qing Yuan[2], Yang Liu[1(✉)], Qianxin Huang[2], Shenglan Liu[1], and Yingping Li[2]

[1] School of Innovation and Entrepreneurship, Dalian University of Technology, Dalian 116024, Liaoning, China
ly@dlut.edu.cn
[2] Faculty of Electronic Information and Electrical Engineering, Dalian University of Technology, Dalian 116024, Liaoning, China

Abstract. Action recognition plays a fundamental role in many applications and researches, including man-machine interaction, medical rehabilitation and physical training. However, existing methods realize action recognition mainly relies on the background. This paper attempts to recognize the actions only through the motions. Hence, skeleton information is utilized to realize action recognition. To fully utilize the skeleton information, this paper proposes a discriminative spatio-temporal graph convolutional network (DSTGCN) for background independent action recognition. DSTGCN not only pays attention to the spatio-temporal properties of the motions, but focuses on the inner-class distributions of the actions. Experiments result on two motion oriented datasets validate the effectiveness of the proposed method.

Keywords: Action recognition · Graph convolutional network · Spatiotemporal analysis · Discriminative analysis

1 Introduction

Human action recognition, which is playing a significant role in many applications such as video surveillance, and man-machine interaction [2], has raised the great attention in recent years.

There are many approaches attempting to analysis that under the dynamic circumstance and complicated background. In lots of cases, background information deserved serious consideration. For example, when a person's hand moves to his mouth, it's difficult to distinguish what he's doing. The question will become easy if there is a cup in the person's hand, cause of additional information is provided by the background.

This study was funded by National Natural Science Foundation of Peoples Republic of China (61672130, 61972064), The Fundamental Research Funds for the Central Universities (DUT19RC(3)012, DUT20RC(5)010) and LiaoNing Revitalization Talents Program (XLYC1806006).

However, it would be not effective and even negative that putting the background information together in certain cases. For instance, in figure skating, a person shows a wide range of exaggerated movements for performing. The changing background will disturb the action analysis, therefore, skeleton data without background information is more appropriate in pure action recognition.

Earlier conventional methods [5, 15] treat skeleton data as vector sequences, which could not fully express the interdependency among the joints. Unlike recurrent neural networks (RNN) and convolutional neural networks (CNN), graph convolutional networks (GCN) treats skeleton data as graphs that could fully exploit the relationships between correlated joints.

GCN shows excellent performance in skeleton-based action recognition. However, most previous works [16, 19] pay little attention on feature maps output by the network and there's room for improvement on datasets with unbalanced categories. Therefore, we proposed a new approach to solve them. We use the focal loss [10] instead of the cross entropy (CE) loss to adapt unbalanced categories. The focal loss can give different weights to different categories according to difficulty of recognition. Above that, we added the center loss [18] working for feature maps to make better distinction and make the network more robust.

In this paper, 1) we modify the loss function from the CE loss to the focal loss to make network more adaptable to the datasets with unbalanced categories. 2) We add the center loss on deep features to make better distinction. 3) On two datasets for skeleton-based action recognition, our methods exceeds the state-of-the-art on both.

2 Related Work

2.1 RGB-D Based Action Recognition

RGB-D based human action recognition has attracted plenty of interest in recent years. Due to RGB-D sensors such as Kinect, RGB data and depth data, which encoding rich 3D structural information, could easy to be obtained. Previous works [8, 17, 20] leads the discovery of the information from visual features and depth features. Instead of considering two modalities as separate channels, SFAM [17] proposed the use of scene flow, which extracted the real 3D motion and also preserved structural information. [20] proposed a binary local representation for video fusion. BHIM [8] represents both two features in the form of matrix that including spatiotemporal structural relationships. Those RGB-D based methods focus on finding an appropriate way to fuse two features.

2.2 Skeleton Based Action Recognition

With the development of deep learning, lots of methods based on conventional networks have been proposed, which learn the features automatically. Some RNN-based methods [11, 15] and CNN-based methods [7, 12] have achieved high performance on action recognition. Unlike the above methods, GCN-based methods [9, 16, 19] treat skeleton data as graph which could exploit the relationships between correlated joints better. ST-GCN [19] is the first to apply GCN on skeleton-based action recognition. 2s-AGCN [16] is an approach to adaptively learn the topology of the graph. AS-GCN [9] made attempts to capture richer dependencies among nodes. Those GCNs automatically learning with information of node location and structure.

3   The Proposed Approach

3.1   Graph Construction

Depending on devices and algorithms, skeleton data are usually represented as the sequence of 2D/3D coordinates. A joint is established connection with others by the graph along both the spatial and temporal dimensions. We construct the graph with joints according to the method in ST-GCN [19]. As shown in the left sketch of Fig. 1, a spatiotemporal graph is composed of the node set N and the edge set E. The node set N contains all the joint coordinates in a sequence. And the edge set E, composed of the spatial edge set E_S and the temporal edge set E_F, represents that how the nodes connected with others. For the spatial dimension, nodes connected with others as their natural connections in a frame. For the second subset E_F, nodes make connections among frames. The temporal edges connect the same nodes between adjacent frames.

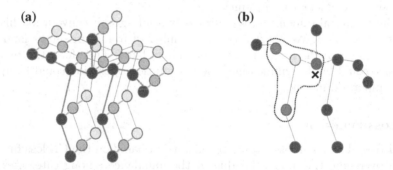

Fig. 1. (a) The spatiotemporal graph used. (b) The spatial configuration partitioning strategy.

3.2   Skeleton Oriented GCN

Deep graph convolutional network could be constructed based on the graph above. ST-GCN [19] consists of the ST-GCN blocks, which contains a spatial graph convolution and a temporal graph convolution.

The spatial graph convolution on node v_i could be formulated as [19]

$$f_{out}(v_i) = \sum_{v_j \in B_i} \frac{1}{Z_{ij}} f_{in}(v_j) \cdot w(l_i(v_j)) \tag{1}$$

where f_{out} denotes the output feature and f_{in} denotes the input feature. B_i denotes the set of nodes which connected with node v_i. w is the weight function, which is a little different from original convolutional operation, but both provide the weights for input. The difference is that the number of nodes in the neighbor set B_i is unfixed. To solve that, we use the spatial configuration partitioning strategy, proposed in ST-GCN [19]. As shown in the right sketch of Fig. 1, the block cross represents the gravity center of the skeleton. According to the distance to the block cross, the strategy divide the set B_i into three subsets. The normalizing term Z_{ij} denotes the cardinality of the subset which contains the node v_j. In fact, the feature map of the network could be represented as a $C \times T \times N$ tensor, where C denotes the number of channels and T denotes the length of frame sequences. N denotes the number of nodes in a frame. For the spatial configuration partitioning strategy, the Eq. 1 is transformed into

$$f_{out}(v_i) = \sum_j \Lambda_j^{-\frac{1}{2}} A_j \Lambda_j^{-\frac{1}{2}} f_{in} W_j \otimes M_j \tag{2}$$

where A_j, a $N \times N$ tensor, denotes the divided adjacency matrix. Note that $\sum_j A_j = A + I$, where A denotes the adjacency matrix, and I is an identity matrix. $\Lambda_j^{ii} = \sum_k (A_j^{ik}) + \alpha$ is a diagonal matrix designed for normalized. α is set as 0.001 to avoid Λ_j^{ii} being zero. W_j is the weight matrix, representing the w function. M_j is an attention matrix, which denotes the importance of nodes. $\otimes$ denotes the element-wise product.

In the temporal dimension, we can easily apply graph convolution like traditional convolution. We chose a certain number of frames before or later than the frame to make the number of the neighbors fixed. Therefore, the temporal kernel size could be determined and the convolution operation could be applied in the temporal dimension.

3.3 Loss Function

Focal Loss. The focal loss, an improved version based on the CE loss function, aims to overcome the difficulties due to the imbalance among categories. The formula for calculating the CE loss for binary classification is Eq. 3.

$$CE(p, y) = \begin{cases} -log(p) & if \quad y = 1 \\ -log(1-p) & otherwise, \end{cases} \tag{3}$$

and we define p_t as

$$p_t = \begin{cases} p & if \quad y = 1 \\ 1-p & otherwise, \end{cases} \tag{4}$$

and $CE(p, y)$ can be written as

$$CE(p_t) = -log(p_t) \tag{5}$$

Based on the CE loss, [10] proposed the focal loss:

$$L_F(p_t) = -\alpha_t(1-p_t)^\gamma log(p_t) \tag{6}$$

where α_t is a weighting factor to address the imbalance among categories. The factor $(1 - p_t)^\gamma$ could dynamically scale the loss. We set $\gamma > 0$, and the factor could automatically reduce the weight of easy examples and increase the weight of hard examples. Therefore, we considered that the focal loss is more suitable to the small-scale datasets, and our experiments proved that.

Center Loss. For making the deeply learned features more discriminative as shown in Fig. 2 and making network more robust, we add the center loss [18] in our work. The center loss, which could be formulated as Eq. 7, makes features discriminative by minimizing the intra class variance.

$$L_C = \frac{1}{2} \sum_{i=1}^{m} \|x_i - c_{y_i}\|_2^2 \tag{7}$$

Where c_{y_i} denotes the deep features center of the y_ith class, and c_{y_i} is dynamically updated based on mini-batch as the deep features changed. The center loss is proposed for face recognition task, due to separable features are not enough, discriminative features are needed. We considered that it will work for action recognition as well, and we proved that in our experiments.

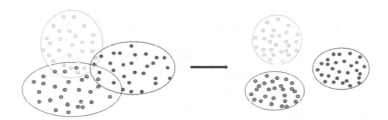

Fig. 2. The center loss function makes deep features more discriminative.

4   Experiments

In this section, we evaluate the performance of our approach and compare with some state-of-the-art methods on two human action recognition datasets: FSD-10 [14] and RGB-D human video-emotion dataset [13]. We evaluate the performance of approaches by top-1 classification accuracies on the validation set.

We use SGD as optimizer in all models, the batch size is set as 64. The learning rate is set as 0.1 and reduced by 10 in epoch 150 and 225. We use $L_S = L_F + \lambda L_C$ as loss function in our methods, and use the CE loss for comparison.

4.1   Evaluation on FSD-10

FSD-10. FSD-10 [14], a skating dataset consists of 1484 skating videos covering 10 different actions manually labeled. These video clips are segmented from performance videos of high level figure skaters. Each clip is ranging from 3 s to 30 s, and captured by the camera focusing on the skater. Comparing with other current datasets for action recognition, FSD-10 focuses on the action itself rather background. The information of background even bring negative effect. We divided FSD-10 into a training set (989 videos) and a validation set (425 videos). We train models on the training set and calculate the accuracy on the validation.

Comparisons and Analysis. For proving that the loss function $L_S = L_F + \lambda L_C$ is more suitable to FSD-10 than the CE loss, we run 2 groups of comparative experiments on FSD-10. The one is based on ST-GCN [19]: we first train ST-GCN with the CE loss, after getting the results, train it again with the loss function L_S. The other group is training on DenseNet [4] with the same operation. Besides, we compared the accuracy with the I3D [1], the STM [6] and the KTSN [14]. Table 1 give the result of our experiments. Both on ST-GCN and DenseNet, we see that the loss function L_S give a better performance than the CE loss on FSD-10.

Table 1. The result of our experiments on FSD-10.

Methods	Top-1 accuracy (%)
I3D (Resnet-50)	62.55
I3D (Resnet-101)	78.82
STM	66.25
KTSN	82.58
ST-GCN + CE loss	84.00
ST-GCN + L_S	87.52
DenseNet + CE loss	84.71
DenseNet + L_S	85.17

4.2   Evaluation on RGB-D Human Video-Emotion Dataset

RGB-D Human Video-Emotion Dataset. RGB-D human video-emotion data-set [13] consists of over 4 thousands RGB video clips and 4 thousands Depth video clips, covering 7 emotion categories. Each clip is around 6 s, containing the whole body of the actor. The background is green, without any information for recognition. The training set has 741 skeleton data, and the validation set has 644. We train models on the training set and calculate the accuracy on the validation.

Comparisons and Analysis. We performed our experiments on the video-emotion dataset for proving that the loss function L_S is suitable to the small-scale datasets for action recognition. Like the comparative experiments on FSD-10, we also run 2 groups of experiments based on ST-GCN [19] and DenseNet [4]. Besides, we compared the accuracy with the MvLE [13] and the MvLLS [3], the methods based on muti-view for recognition on this dataset. Table 2 give the result of methods. We see that the loss function is work on the video-emotion dataset as well, and our methods perform better than the state-of-the-art on this dataset.

Table 2. The result of our experiments on the video-emotion dataset.

Methods	Top-1 accuracy (%)
MvLE	41.00
MvLLS	37.97
ST-GCN + CE loss	54.96
ST-GCN + L_S	55.27
DenseNet + CE loss	52.32
DenseNet + L_S	53.72

5 Conclusion

In this paper, we adapted the center loss and the focal loss to the human action recognition. We use the focal loss aims to overcome the difficulties due to the imbalance among categories. And we consider it's more suitable to the small-scale datasets with unbalanced categories. We add the center loss to learn more discriminative features and to make better distinction on deep features. We performed our experiments on the FSD-10 [14] and the RGB-D human video-emotion dataset [13], and our methods achieved the state-of-the-art performance.

References

1. Carreira, J., Zisserman, A.: Quo vadis, action recognition? A new model and the kinetics dataset. In: proceedings of the IEEE Conference on Computer Vision and Pattern Recognition, pp. 6299–6308 (2017)
2. Duric, Z., et al.: Integrating perceptual and cognitive modeling for adaptive and intelligent human-computer interaction. Proc. IEEE **90**(7), 1272–1289 (2002)
3. Guo, S., et al.: Multi-view laplacian least squares for human emotion recognition. Neurocomputing **370**, 78–87 (2019)
4. Huang, G., Liu, Z., Van Der Maaten, L., Weinberger, K.Q.: Densely connected convolutional networks. In: Proceedings of the IEEE Conference on Computer Vision and Pattern Recognition, pp. 4700–4708 (2017)

5. Ji, S., Xu, W., Yang, M., Yu, K.: 3D convolutional neural networks for human action recognition. IEEE Trans. Pattern Anal. Mach. Intell. **35**(1), 221–231 (2012)
6. Jiang, B., Wang, M., Gan, W., Wu, W., Yan, J.: STM: spatiotemporal and motion encoding for action recognition. In: Proceedings of the IEEE International Conference on Computer Vision, pp. 2000–2009 (2019)
7. Ke, Q., Bennamoun, M., An, S., Sohel, F., Boussaid, F.: A new representation of skeleton sequences for 3D action recognition. In: Proceedings of the IEEE Conference on Computer Vision and Pattern Recognition, pp. 3288–3297 (2017)
8. Kong, Y., Fu, Y.: Bilinear heterogeneous information machine for RGB-D action recognition. In: Proceedings of the IEEE Conference on Computer Vision and Pattern Recognition, pp. 1054–1062 (2015)
9. Li, M., Chen, S., Chen, X., Zhang, Y., Wang, Y., Tian, Q.: Actional-structural graph convolutional networks for skeleton-based action recognition. In: Proceedings of the IEEE Conference on Computer Vision and Pattern Recognition, pp. 3595–3603 (2019)
10. Lin, T.Y., Goyal, P., Girshick, R., He, K., Dollár, P.: Focal loss for dense object detection. In: Proceedings of the IEEE International Conference on Computer Vision, pp. 2980–2988 (2017)
11. Liu, J., Shahroudy, A., Xu, D., Wang, G.: Spatio-temporal LSTM with trust gates for 3D human action recognition. In: Leibe, B., Matas, J., Sebe, N., Welling, M. (eds.) ECCV 2016. LNCS, vol. 9907, pp. 816–833. Springer, Cham (2016). https://doi.org/10.1007/978-3-319-46487-9_50
12. Liu, M., Liu, H., Chen, C.: Enhanced skeleton visualization for view invariant human action recognition. Pattern Recogn. **68**, 346–362 (2017)
13. Liu, S., Guo, S., Wang, W., Qiao, H., Wang, Y., Luo, W.: Multi-view laplacian eigenmaps based on bag-of-neighbors for RGB-D human emotion recognition. Inf. Sci. **509**, 243–256 (2020)
14. Liu, S., et al.: FSD-10: a dataset for competitive sports content analysis. arXiv preprint arXiv:2002.03312 (2020)
15. Shahroudy, A., Liu, J., Ng, T.T., Wang, G.: NTU RGB+ D: a large scale dataset for 3D human activity analysis. In: Proceedings of the IEEE Conference on Computer Vision and Pattern Recognition, pp. 1010–1019 (2016)
16. Shi, L., Zhang, Y., Cheng, J., Lu, H.: Two-stream adaptive graph convolutional networks for skeleton-based action recognition. In: Proceedings of the IEEE Conference on Computer Vision and Pattern Recognition, pp. 12026–12035 (2019)
17. Wang, P., Li, W., Gao, Z., Zhang, Y., Tang, C., Ogunbona, P.: Scene flow to action map: a new representation for RGB-D based action recognition with convolutional neural networks. In: Proceedings of the IEEE Conference on Computer Vision and Pattern Recognition, pp. 595–604 (2017)
18. Wen, Y., Zhang, K., Li, Z., Qiao, Y.: A discriminative feature learning approach for deep face recognition. In: Leibe, B., Matas, J., Sebe, N., Welling, M. (eds.) ECCV 2016. LNCS, vol. 9911, pp. 499–515. Springer, Cham (2016). https://doi.org/10.1007/978-3-319-46478-7_31
19. Yan, S., Xiong, Y., Lin, D.: Spatial temporal graph convolutional networks for skeleton-based action recognition. arXiv preprint arXiv:1801.07455 (2018)
20. Yu, M., Liu, L., Shao, L.: Structure-preserving binary representations for RGB-D action recognition. IEEE Trans. Pattern Anal. Mach. Intell. **38**(8), 1651–1664 (2015)

A Factorized Extreme Learning Machine and Its Applications in EEG-Based Emotion Recognition

Yong Peng[1,2,3]([✉]), Rixin Tang[2], Wanzeng Kong[2], and Feiping Nie[1]

[1] Center for OPTIMAL, Northwestern Polytechnical University, Xi'an 710072, China
yongpeng@hdu.edu.cn
[2] School of Computer Science, Hangzhou Dianzi University, Hangzhou 310018, China
[3] Provincial Key Laboratory for Computer Information Processing Technology,
Soochow University, Suzhou 215006, China

Abstract. Extreme learning machine (ELM) is an efficient learning algorithm for single hidden layer feed forward neural networks. Its main feature is the random generation of the hidden layer weights and biases and then we only need to determine the output weights in model learning. However, the random mapping in ELM impairs the discriminative information of data to certain extent, which brings side effects for the output weight matrix to well capture the essential data properties. In this paper, we propose a factorized extreme learning machine (FELM) by incorporating another hidden layer between the ELM hidden layer and the output layer. Mathematically, the original output matrix is factorized so as to effectively explore the structured discriminative information of data. That is, we constrain the group sparsity of data representation in the new hidden layer, which will be further projected to the output layer. An efficient learning algorithm is proposed to optimize the objective of the proposed FELM model. Extensive experiments on EEG-based emotion recognition show the effectiveness of FELM.

Keywords: Extreme learning machine · Factorized representation · Group sparsity · Emotion recognition · EEG

1 Introduction

ELM is an efficient training algorithm for single hidden layer feed forward neural networks (SLFNNs) in which the input weights are randomly generated and the output weights can be analytically obtained [6]. Compared with the back propagation-based network weights tuning methods, the tedious process of iterative parameter tuning is eliminated and the problems including slow convergence speed and local minima are avoided. From the perspective of model optimization, the consistency of ELM, SVM, least square SVM and proximal SVM has been fully investigated [5]. ELM provides us a unified solution to generalized SLFNNs, including but not limited to neural networks, support vector networks and regularized networks [5].

© Springer Nature Switzerland AG 2020
H. Yang et al. (Eds.): ICONIP 2020, CCIS 1333, pp. 11–20, 2020.
https://doi.org/10.1007/978-3-030-63823-8_2

In recent years, a lot of efforts have been made on ELM from perspectives of theory and application. Huang et al. proposed the incremental ELM to enhance the universal approximation performance of SLFNNs, which can randomly select hidden nodes and adjust the output weights accordingly [3,4]. Zong et al. applied ELM as a ranking algorithm from the pointwise and pairwise perspectives [12]. In order to reduce the influence of outliers, Horata et al. proposed a robust ELM [2]. A fuzzy ELM was proposed to make different contributions to the learning of output weights through inputs with different fuzzy matrices [11]. To simultaneously utilize the benefits of ℓ_1 and ℓ_2 norms, an elastic net regularized ELM was proposed to perform EEG-based vigilance estimation [10]. As a feature extraction model, the discriminative extreme learning machine with supervised sparsity preserving in which the constraints were imposed on the output weights to preserve the sparsity achieved promising performance in data classification [8]. Besides, ELM has been widely employed in diverse fields such as face recognition, human action recognition, speaker recognition and data privacy.

However, the random generation of input weights may cause some distortions to the ELM hidden layer data representation in comparison with the original structure information of data. Therefore, when given complicated data sets, it will be hard to obtain a well-formed output weight matrix to get good generalization performance. To this end, we propose a structured matrix factorized extreme learning machine (FELM) in this paper. Our FELM model acts as the matrix factorization on the output weight matrix by introducing another hidden layer in which we enforce the group sparsity representation of data to achieve local dependencies of hidden units. Particularly, the mixed-norm regularization (ℓ_1/ℓ_2 norm) is incorporated in the model to obtain the group sparsity. We verify the ability of FELM on EEG-based emotion recognition task. Experimental results demonstrate that it can obtain better performance than SVM and ELM.

2   The Proposed FELM Model

Our proposed FELM model keeps the randomly generated input weights and hidden biases unchanged as those of ELM. The difference between FELM and ELM is the introduction of another hidden layer between the original ELM hidden layer and the output layer, which works as partitioning the original output weight matrix into two matrices. Then, we can enforce the data representation in the newly added hidden layer to have desirable properties which are beneficial for improving the learning performance.

As shown in Fig. 1, FELM includes the input layer, hidden layer H1, hidden layer H2 and output layer. The hidden layer H2 is the newly added one. Let $\mathbf{X} = [\mathbf{x}_1, \cdots, \mathbf{x}_N] \in \mathbb{R}^{D \times N}$ represent the input data, where D is the number of features and N is the number of samples. The number of input units is D. $\mathbf{w}_i$ and b_i represent the input weights and hidden bias respectively. They are both randomly determined. Let $\mathbf{W} = [\mathbf{w}_1, \cdots, \mathbf{w}_P] \in \mathbb{R}^{D \times P}$ represent the input weight matrix. P is the number of units in the hidden layer H1. $\mathbf{a}_i$ indicate the input weights of the hidden layer H2, let $\mathbf{A} = [\mathbf{a}_1, \cdots, \mathbf{a}_P]^T \in \mathbb{R}^{P \times Q}$ represent the corresponding input weight matrix. $\mathbf{b}_j$ indicate the output weights of the hidden layer H2 and $\mathbf{B} = [\mathbf{b}_1, \cdots, \mathbf{b}_Q]^T \in \mathbb{R}^{Q \times C}$ represent the corresponding output weight matrix. Q is the number of units in the hidden layer H2. $f(\mathbf{X})$ indicate the output data. Let $\mathbf{T} = [\mathbf{t}_1, \cdots, \mathbf{t}_N] \in \mathbb{R}^{C \times N}$ indicate the expected output data. C represents the number of categories and the output units.

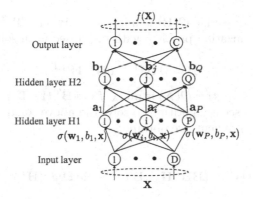

Fig. 1. Schematic diagram of the FELM model.

Specifically, the representation of the hidden layer H1 can be calculated as $\mathbf{h}(\mathbf{x}) = \sigma(\mathbf{w}_i, b_i, \mathbf{x}) = \sigma(\mathbf{w}^T\mathbf{x} + b)$, where $\sigma(a) = \frac{1}{1+e^{-a}}$ is the activation function in sigmoid form. The matrix form representation in H1 can be denoted as $\mathbf{H} = [\mathbf{h}(\mathbf{x}_1), \cdots, \mathbf{h}(\mathbf{x}_N)] \in \mathbb{R}^{P \times N}$. Then, the representation in hidden layer H2 can be obtained by $\hat{\mathbf{H}} = \phi(\mathbf{A}^T\mathbf{H})$. If $\phi(a) = a$ represents a linear function, equation (2) is equivalent to $\hat{\mathbf{H}} = \mathbf{A}^T\mathbf{H}$. The mapping relationship between the hidden layer H2 and the output layer is $f(\mathbf{X}) = \mathbf{B}^T\hat{\mathbf{H}}$.

For convenience, let $\mathcal{H} = \{1, 2, \cdots, Q\}$ denote the set of all units in the hidden layer H2. $\mathcal{H}$ can be partitioned into G groups and the gth group is represented by $\mathcal{G}_g$, where $\mathcal{H} = \cup_{g=1}^{G}\mathcal{G}_g$ and $\cap_{g=1}^{G}\mathcal{G}_g = \emptyset$. Therefore, $\hat{\mathbf{H}}$ can be expressed as $\hat{\mathbf{H}} = [\hat{\mathbf{H}}_{\mathcal{G}_1,:}; \cdots; \hat{\mathbf{H}}_{\mathcal{G}_g,:}; \cdots; \hat{\mathbf{H}}_{\mathcal{G}_G,:}]$. Therefore, the objective function of the FELM model can be expressed as follows:

$$\min_{\mathbf{A},\mathbf{B}} f = \|\mathbf{B}^T\hat{\mathbf{H}} - \mathbf{T}\|_F^2 + \alpha\Omega(\hat{\mathbf{H}}) + \beta\|\mathbf{B}\|_F^2, \quad (1)$$

where α is a regularization constant of the activation of the units in the hidden layer H2 and β is a regularization parameter of the hidden layer H2 output weight matrix $\mathbf{B}$. $\Omega(\hat{\mathbf{H}})$ represents the imposed penalty on sparse representations $\hat{\mathbf{H}}$.

Luo et al. [7] pointed out that group sparse representation can learn the statistical dependencies between hidden units, thereby improving model performance. Therefore, in order to implement the dependencies, we divide the units in the hidden layer H2 into non-overlapping groups on average to limit the dependencies within these groups and constrain the hidden units in a group to compete with each other. In addition, a mixed-norm regularization (ℓ_1/ℓ_2-norm) can achieve group sparse representation. So, we conduct the mixed-norm regularization $\Omega(\hat{\mathbf{H}}) = \sum_{g=1}^{G}\|\hat{\mathbf{H}}_{\mathcal{G}_g,:}\|_{1,2}$, where $\hat{\mathbf{H}}_{\mathcal{G}_g,:}$ is the representation matrix associated to the data within modality belonging to the gth group. The ℓ_1/ℓ_2-norm can be expressed as $\|\hat{\mathbf{H}}_{\mathcal{G}_g,:}\|_{1,2} = \sum_{i=1}^{N} \sqrt{\sum_{j \in \mathcal{G}_g} \hat{h}_{j,i}^2}$.

Objective (1) has two variables, $\mathbf{A}$ and $\mathbf{B}$. We can alternately optimize one with the other fixed.

1) Update $\mathbf{B}$. The objective $\mathcal{O}(\mathbf{B})$ is $\min_{\mathbf{B}} f = \|\mathbf{B}^T\hat{\mathbf{H}} - \mathbf{T}\|_F^2 + \beta\|\mathbf{B}\|_F^2$, which is a convex optimization problem with the closed-form solution as

$$\mathbf{B} = (\hat{\mathbf{H}}\hat{\mathbf{H}}^T + \beta\mathbf{I})^{-1}\hat{\mathbf{H}}\mathbf{T}^T. \tag{2}$$

2) Update $\mathbf{A}$. The objective $\mathcal{O}(\mathbf{A})$ is $\min_{\mathbf{A}} f = \|\mathbf{B}^T\hat{\mathbf{H}} - \mathbf{T}\|_F^2 + \alpha\Omega(\hat{\mathbf{H}})$. We can use a gradient descent algorithm to solve the above squared error objective. By deriving the gradient, we obtain

$$\frac{\partial f}{\partial \mathbf{A}} = 2\mathbf{H}[d\phi(\hat{\mathbf{H}}^T) \circ (\mathbf{BB}^T\hat{\mathbf{H}} - \mathbf{BT})^T] + 2\alpha\mathbf{H}[d\phi(\hat{\mathbf{H}}^T) \circ \hat{\mathbf{H}}^T \circ /\tilde{\mathbf{H}}^T], \tag{3}$$

where $\circ$ means element-wise multiplication, $\circ/$ means element-wise division. The element of $\tilde{\mathbf{H}}$ is denoted as $\tilde{h}_{j,i} = \sqrt{\sum_{j \in \mathcal{G}_g} \hat{h}_{j,i}^2}$. $d\phi(a)$ represents the gradient of the function $\phi(a)$. When it is a sigmoid function, $d\phi(a) = \sigma(a) \times (1 - \sigma(a))$ and when it is a linear function, $d\phi(a) = 1$. So in Eq. (3), $d\phi(\hat{\mathbf{H}}^T) = 1$. Equation (3) can be further simplified as

$$\frac{\partial f}{\partial \mathbf{A}} = 2\mathbf{H}(\mathbf{BB}^T\hat{\mathbf{H}} - \mathbf{BT})^T + 2\alpha\mathbf{H}(\hat{\mathbf{H}}^T \circ /\tilde{\mathbf{H}}^T). \tag{4}$$

So, the update rule of $\mathbf{A}$ using the gradient defined in (4) is $\mathbf{A} = \mathbf{A} - \epsilon\frac{\partial f}{\partial \mathbf{A}}$, where ϵ is a learning rate. We summarize the optimization of FELM in Algorithm 1.

Algorithm 1 The optimization to FELM objective in equation (1)

Input: Data $\mathbf{X}$, label $\mathbf{T}$, parameters $\theta = \{\alpha, \beta, P, Q, \epsilon, G\}$.
Output: The output weight matrix $\mathbf{A}$ in the hidden layer H1 and the output weight matrix $\mathbf{B}$ in the hidden layer H2.
1: Randomly initialize the input weights $\mathbf{w}_i$, bias b_i, $i = 1, 2, \ldots, P$, $\mathbf{A}$ and $\mathbf{B}$ and fix $\mathbf{w}_i$ and b_i.
2: **while** not converged **do**
3:    Update $\mathbf{B}$ according to (2);
4:    Update $\mathbf{A}$ according to $\mathbf{A} = \mathbf{A} - \epsilon\frac{\partial f}{\partial \mathbf{A}}$;
5: **end while**

The optimization of each variable in FELM is iterative. The objective function in terms of variable $\mathbf{B}$ is a convex function and the solution obtained to $\mathbf{B}$ is in closed-form. So the convergence of FELM mainly depends on the update rule of variable $\mathbf{A}$, which is based on the gradient descent method. As the number of iterations increases, the value of the objective function decreases along the gradient until it converges. We terminate the iteration when the objective function value $\frac{\|obj^{(t+1)} - obj^{(t)}\|_2}{\|obj^{(t)}\|_2} < 10^{-4}$ in the experiment.

The main complexity of FELM is the loop containing two blocks. The main cost lies in calculating the inverse of $Q \times Q$ matrices $\hat{\mathbf{H}}\hat{\mathbf{H}}^T + \beta\mathbf{I}$ for the updating of variable $\mathbf{B}$, which needs $O(Q^3)$ complexity in each iteration. For the updating to $\mathbf{A}$, we need $O(PQN)$ complexity to calculate in each iteration by a gradient descent method. As a whole, the complexity for FELM is $O(t(Q^3+PQN))$ where t is the number of iterations.

3 Experiments

In the experiments, we evaluate the effectiveness of FELM on emotion recognition from EEG signals. The publicly available three-class emotional EEG data set, SEED (http://bcmi.sjtu.edu.cn/~seed/), was used in our experiments. The differential entropy feature smoothed by the linear dynamic system is used due to its effectiveness in expressing the emotional effect [1,9]. The EEG data of each subject has three different sessions and there were about 3400 samples in each session. We perform experiments in three different paradigms, which are with-session and cross-session of the same subject, and cross-subject experiments.

We compare FELM with SVM and ELM in terms of the classification performance on the given EEG data. Linear kernel was used in SVM and the regularization parameter C was selected from 2^{-7} to 2^{10}. The regularization parameters α and β in FELM were chosen from 10^{-4} to 10^4. If the dimension of input data satisfied $D < 100$, the numbers of hidden units P and Q were searched from 100 to 500 with step size 100. If the dimension of input data satisfied $100 < D < 500$, P was chosen from 500 to 1000 and Q from 100 to 500. For simplicity, we set the learning rate ϵ to 0.01 and the group numbers G to 4. The input weights and bias in ELM were the same as FELM which has P hidden units.

A. Experimental Paradigm 1. In order to test the ability of FELM model to classify DE features on different frequency bands, we choose about 2000 samples from one session of each subject as training set, the rest within the same session as test set. Table 1 and 2 show the classification results of linear-SVM, ELM and FELM models using the differential entropy features of *delta, theta, alpha, beta* and *gamma* frequency bands as input, where the best results are highlighted in boldface. We can find that the classification accuracies of FELM are higher than those of ELM and SVM in most cases in Table 1. As shown in Table 2, the average classification accuracy of FELM in each of the five frequency bands is higher than that of ELM and SVM. In addition, the classification results on *beta* and *gamma* frequency bands are higher than those of other frequency bands, meaning that the variation of emotional states may be more closely related to these two frequency bands.

Table 3 shows the average confusion matrices of three models based on the 310-dimensional feature vector of all frequency bands. We can find that positive and neutral emotional states are easier to be identified than the negative state. The FELM model estimates the negative state more accurately than both SVM and ELM. The average classification accuracy of FELM for negative state is 60.31% which is much higher than those of ELM (55.43%) and SVM (58.73%).

Table 1. Emotion recognition accuracies for six subjects A, B, C, D, E and F.

A	Session 1			Session 2			Session 3		
	SVM	ELM	FELM	SVM	ELM	FELM	SVM	ELM	FELM
delta	49.93	53.76	**54.55**	37.57	**40.53**	**40.53**	46.75	48.84	49.64
theta	**60.26**	58.02	60.12	49.35	49.28	**51.66**	**58.31**	55.71	57.95
alpha	65.17	**66.62**	66.55	54.41	54.48	**56.58**	48.63	52.67	**58.16**
beta	**84.10**	81.29	81.00	**65.46**	63.08	64.96	57.15	63.08	**67.12**
gamma	81.50	83.02	**84.90**	67.27	68.06	**72.04**	59.54	60.77	**69.44**
Total	**82.59**	83.74	81.14	**75.65**	64.74	67.63	59.90	61.27	**65.39**
B	Session 1			Session 2			Session 3		
	SVM	ELM	FELM	SVM	ELM	FELM	SVM	ELM	FELM
delta	53.47	56.72	**57.15**	38.73	**48.12**	47.83	52.02	51.81	**52.75**
theta	57.59	60.12	**60.55**	55.92	57.15	**59.47**	52.38	59.18	**59.90**
alpha	72.83	82.01	**83.74**	65.75	64.45	**67.85**	65.10	70.30	**72.04**
beta	**90.17**	86.71	88.87	**69.44**	67.85	68.86	78.97	81.36	**82.01**
gamma	89.52	87.57	**91.26**	**70.66**	66.33	66.91	**77.24**	75.07	76.23
Total	**88.15**	85.84	87.79	65.82	70.01	**72.40**	71.82	73.63	**74.64**
C	Session 1			Session 2			Session 3		
	SVM	ELM	FELM	SVM	ELM	FELM	SVM	ELM	FELM
delta	50.79	54.26	**55.20**	35.77	39.38	**41.19**	44.73	**45.52**	42.34
theta	**69.44**	62.28	63.08	**49.57**	49.78	46.39	43.93	39.67	**46.60**
alpha	61.13	60.04	**63.15**	50.43	51.16	**53.32**	**49.21**	41.91	45.66
beta	**77.24**	70.38	72.25	90.03	**90.82**	90.39	58.60	47.83	**59.68**
gamma	76.37	72.04	**76.73**	**89.45**	85.04	89.38	59.18	53.61	**61.05**
Total	**76.52**	74.64	75.14	**91.11**	88.80	87.50	**61.20**	50.43	60.12
D	Session 1			Session 2			Session 3		
	SVM	ELM	FELM	SVM	ELM	FELM	SVM	ELM	FELM
delta	75.87	**77.67**	75.65	**60.33**	58.89	58.02	58.09	61.63	**63.08**
theta	**73.92**	69.22	69.94	56.00	57.88	**62.07**	55.78	54.62	**65.32**
alpha	70.16	80.78	**83.38**	80.56	76.01	**81.07**	80.27	**89.45**	87.79
beta	92.99	**96.10**	93.71	88.08	91.04	**95.38**	**97.18**	95.23	96.03
gamma	90.68	93.93	**95.23**	91.98	92.49	**94.58**	**96.32**	95.74	95.88
Total	96.68	96.10	**96.89**	91.04	**96.89**	**96.89**	97.25	**97.40**	95.30
E	Session 1			Session 2			Session 3		
	SVM	ELM	FELM	SVM	ELM	FELM	SVM	ELM	FELM
delta	**58.89**	51.16	50.65	**55.85**	55.06	53.97	48.70	49.28	**50.00**
theta	**66.47**	63.29	64.09	40.25	50.07	**58.53**	40.10	43.35	**43.79**
alpha	46.89	54.48	**59.39**	34.39	40.17	**44.15**	60.69	63.15	**66.40**
beta	67.12	71.53	**75.14**	53.90	65.97	**72.18**	63.08	67.34	**78.11**
gamma	76.59	77.60	**80.27**	70.66	70.88	**73.63**	63.29	**65.53**	64.60
Total	70.01	69.87	**72.18**	60.19	68.50	**69.51**	73.99	67.20	**76.81**
F	Session 1			Session 2			Session 3		
	SVM	ELM	FELM	SVM	ELM	FELM	SVM	ELM	FELM
delta	**69.65**	64.88	64.31	**45.16**	34.75	42.85	**55.85**	53.25	53.61
theta	**58.24**	**58.24**	57.73	46.82	49.78	**51.52**	**63.44**	60.62	60.26
alpha	60.48	**62.64**	62.57	**53.11**	48.55	52.24	66.84	65.53	**67.63**
beta	73.19	77.53	**78.54**	59.25	53.25	**61.56**	88.29	90.68	**90.97**
gamma	69.80	82.01	**85.26**	58.82	57.30	**61.05**	93.86	91.26	**95.30**
Total	73.19	76.30	**78.76**	56.50	**58.96**	58.24	87.50	89.23	**90.10**

"Total" means concatenating features from all the five frequency bands.

Table 2. Average performances of different algorithms in paradigm 1 (mean ± std%).

Frequency band	mean ± std (%)		
	SVM	ELM	FELM
delta	52.12 ± 10.46	52.53 ± 9.90	**52.96 ± 8.94**
theta	55.43 ± 9.46	55.46 ± 7.32	**57.72 ± 7.05**
alpha	60.34 ± 12.07	62.47 ± 13.70	**65.09 ± 12.84**
beta	75.24 ± 14.00	75.62 ± 14.44	**78.71 ± 11.84**
gamma	77.35 ± 12.25	76.57 ± 13.07	**79.65 ± 12.28**
Total	76.62 ± 13.12	76.31 ± 13.92	**78.14 ± 12.10**

Table 3. Confusion matrices of different algorithms in paradigm 1 (mean ± std%).

SVM	Positive	Negative	Neural
Positive	**90.62 ± 10.15**	6.58 ± 7.75	2.80 ± 4.08
Negative	17.11 ± 15.91	**58.73 ± 31.53**	24.16 ± 22.28
Neural	9.86 ± 9.52	10.97 ± 11.68	**79.17 ± 16.24**
ELM	Positive	Negative	Neural
Positive	**91.22 ± 9.80**	5.10 ± 6.45	3.68 ± 5.20
Negative	17.65 ± 18.88	**55.43 ± 28.36**	26.92 ± 19.22
Neural	9.61 ± 14.76	9.65 ± 11.17	**80.75 ± 18.12**
FELM	Positive	Negative	Neural
Positive	**88.95 ± 9.95**	7.53 ± 7.41	3.52 ± 5.03
Negative	13.76 ± 13.55	**60.31 ± 27.19**	25.93 ± 20.50
Neural	6.62 ± 7.79	9.53 ± 9.95	**83.85 ± 14.29**

B. Experimental Paradigm 2. In order to identify the stable emotional patterns across different times, we choose the EEG data from one session of one subject as training set and the data from another session of such subject as test set. This paradigm can be termed as 'cross-session' emotion recognition. Table 4 shows the recognition results of each subject respectively obtained by linear-SVM, ELM and FELM models whose average performances are presented in Table 5. Here A1-A1 means that all the training and test samples are from the same session; specifically, we used the former 2000 of total 3400 samples as training and the rest as test, which follows the pipeline in [9]. We can find from Table 4 that the recognition accuracies of FELM is the highest in most cases. Generally, the classification accuracies by respectively choosing training and test samples from different sessions are significantly lower than choosing both training and test samples from the same session. This is caused by the non-stationary property of EEG data even if it was collected from the same subject but at different times. The average FELM classification accuracy for all subjects in the experimental paradigm 1 is 78.14% while it is 67.44% in experimental paradigm 2. Nevertheless, 67.44% is still a relatively good result for the three-class emotion recognition task. This demonstrates that the transition of EEG patterns are stable among different sessions of the same subject.

Table 4. Emotion recognition accuracies (%) of different algorithms in paradigm 2.

		A1*	A2	A3		B1	B2	B3
SVM	A1	82.59	53.48	44.49	B1	**88.15**	32.62	54.10
ELM		**83.74**	**57.25**	**64.79**		85.84	59.75	57.75
FELM		81.14	55.24	57.04		87.79	**61.43**	**61.87**
SVM	A2	62.64	**75.65**	52.18	B2	65.09	65.82	67.47
ELM		59.66	64.74	47.53		59.05	70.01	**71.10**
FELM		**65.17**	67.63	**59.52**		**68.83**	**72.40**	69.51
SVM	A3	36.21	55.83	59.90	B3	**73.10**	44.49	71.82
ELM		55.42	50.65	61.27		65.91	62.32	73.63
FELM		**55.98**	**57.31**	**65.39**		71.66	**67.21**	**74.64**
ALG.s		C1	C2	C3		D1	D2	D3
SVM	C1	**76.52**	**80.41**	66.23	D1	96.68	80.55	83.50
ELM		74.64	80.32	66.82		96.10	82.20	**90.28**
FELM		75.14	78.99	**73.10**		**96.89**	84.00	82.12
SVM	C2	70.09	**91.11**	58.60	D2	**89.84**	91.04	**95.43**
ELM		70.86	88.80	**68.27**		85.50	**96.89**	91.54
FELM		**71.80**	87.50	63.20		84.03	**96.89**	93.64
SVM	C3	**79.29**	**81.35**	**61.20**	D3	**81.08**	**93.25**	97.25
ELM		56.48	72.04	50.43		79.17	87.71	**97.40**
FELM		78.61	78.34	60.12		78.99	88.80	95.30
ALG.s		E1	E2	E3		F1	F2	F3
SVM	E1	70.01	63.26	53.54	F1	73.19	**55.57**	**56.84**
ELM		69.87	59.78	48.26		76.30	54.71	53.89
FELM		**72.18**	**63.67**	**62.32**		**78.76**	51.94	53.95
SVM	E2	64.32	60.19	53.06	F2	61.82	56.50	69.27
ELM		46.32	68.50	**54.57**		**66.97**	**58.96**	65.00
FELM		**65.91**	**69.51**	52.83		61.14	58.24	**71.69**
SVM	E3	61.40	49.00	73.99	F3	43.69	52.53	87.50
ELM		43.25	44.61	67.20		59.58	49.18	89.23
FELM		**65.20***	52.86	**76.81**		**63.82**	**56.04**	**90.10**

"A1" is the first session of subject A. For example, the value 65.20 in bottom left corner is obtained by FELM in using E3 as training set and E1 as test set.

Table 5. Average performances of different algorithms in paradigm 2 (mean ± std%).

		Session 1	Session 2	Session 3
SVM	Session 1	81.19 ± 10.01	60.98 ± 18.20	59.78 ± 13.55
ELM		81.08 ± 9.44	65.67 ± 12.24	63.63 ± 14.75
FELM		**81.98 ± 9.06**	**65.88 ± 12.90**	**65.07 ± 10.59**
SVM	Session 2	68.97 ± 10.63	73.39 ± 15.15	66.00 ± 16.08
ELM		64.73 ± 13.20	74.65 ± 14.82	66.34 ± 15.20
FELM		**69.48 ± 7.98**	**75.36 ± 14.19**	**68.40 ± 14.12**
SVM	Session 3	62.46 ± 18.90	62.74 ± 19.75	75.28 ± 14.70
ELM		59.97 ± 11.97	61.09 ± 16.45	73.19 ± 17.55
FELM		**69.04 ± 9.06**	**66.76 ± 14.27**	**77.06 ± 13.65**

4   Conclusion

In this paper, we proposed an improved extreme learning machine model based on matrix factorization technique, termed as factorized ELM (FELM). This model performed matrix factorization on the ELM output weight matrix by adding an additional hidden layer between the hidden and output layers to mine the structured information of high-dimensional data. The group sparse representations was adopted to learn the local dependencies of hidden units. We applied FELM into emotion recognition from EEG signals. Based on the experimental results, we had three observations: 1) the EEG features from *beta* and *gamma* frequency bands might be more related to the transition of emotional states; 2) the positive emotional state is easier to recognize than the neutral and negative states; 3) there exist stable patterns in EEG features for performing cross-session recognition. In comparison with the baseline ELM and SVM, FELM obtained the best average classification performance.

Acknowledgments. This work was supported by NSFC (61971173,U1909202), Fundamental Research Funds for the Provincial Universities of Zhejiang (GK209907299001-008), Postdoctoral Science Foundation of China (2017M620470), Key Laboratory of Advanced Perception and Intelligent Control of High-end Equipment of Ministry of Education, Anhui Polytechnic University (GDSC202015) and Provincial Key Laboratory for Computer Information Processing Technology, Soochow University (KJS1841).

References

1. Duan, R.N., Zhu, J.Y., Lu, B.L.: Differential entropy feature for EEG-based emotion classification. In: NER, pp. 81–84 (2013)
2. Horata, P., Chiewchanwattana, S., Sunat, K.: Robust extreme learning machine. Neurocomputing **102**, 31–44 (2013)
3. Huang, G.B., Chen, L., Siew, C.K., et al.: Universal approximation using incremental constructive feedforward networks with random hidden nodes. IEEE Trans. Neural Netw. **17**(4), 879–892 (2006)

4. Huang, G.B., Li, M.B., Chen, L., Siew, C.K.: Incremental extreme learning machine with fully complex hidden nodes. Neurocomputing **71**(4–6), 576–583 (2008)
5. Huang, G.B., Zhou, H., Ding, X., Zhang, R.: Extreme learning machine for regression and multiclass classification. IEEE TSMC-B **42**(2), 513–529 (2012)
6. Huang, G.B., Zhu, Q.Y., Siew, C.K.: Extreme learning machine: theory and applications. Neurocomputing **70**(1–3), 489–501 (2006)
7. Luo, H., Shen, R., Niu, C., Ullrich, C.: Sparse group restricted Boltzmann machines. In: AAAI Conference on Artificial Intelligence, pp. 429–434 (2011)
8. Peng, Y., Lu, B.L.: Discriminative extreme learning machine with supervised sparsity preserving for image classification. Neurocomputing **261**, 242–252 (2017)
9. Peng, Y., Zhu, J.Y., Zheng, W.L., Lu, B.L.: EEG-based emotion recognition with manifold regularized extreme learning machine. In: EMBC, pp. 974–977 (2014)
10. Shi, L.C., Lu, B.L.: EEG-based vigilance estimation using extreme learning machines. Neurocomputing **102**, 135–143 (2013)
11. Zhang, W., Ji, H.: Fuzzy extreme learning machine for classification. Electron. Lett. **49**(7), 448–450 (2013)
12. Zong, W., Huang, G.B.: Learning to rank with extreme learning machine. Neural Process. Lett. **39**(2), 155–166 (2014)

A Literature Review of Recent Graph Embedding Techniques for Biomedical Data

Yankai Chen[1]([✉]), Yaozu Wu[2], Shicheng Ma[2], and Irwin King[1]

[1] Department of Computer Science and Engineering,
The Chinese University of Hong Kong, Shatin, Hong Kong
{ykchen,king}@cse.cuhk.edu.hk
[2] KEEP, The Chinese University of Hong Kong, Shatin, Hong Kong
yaozu279@gmail.com, shicheng@keep.edu.hk

Abstract. With the rapid development of biomedical software and hardware, a large amount of relational data interlinking genes, proteins, chemical components, drugs, diseases, and symptoms has been collected for modern biomedical research. Many graph-based learning methods have been proposed to analyze such type of data, giving a deeper insight into the topology and knowledge behind the biomedical data. However, the main difficulty is how to handle high dimensionality and sparsity of the data. Recently, graph embedding methods provide an effective and efficient way to address the above issues. It converts graph-based data into a low dimensional vector space where the graph structural properties and knowledge information are well preserved. In this paper, we conduct a literature review of recent graph embedding techniques for biomedical data. We also introduce important applications and tasks in the biomedical domain as well as associated public biomedical datasets.

Keywords: Graph embedding · Biomedical data · Biomedical informatics

1 Introduction

With the recent advances in biomedical technology, a large number of relational data interlinking biomedical components including proteins, drugs, diseases, and symptoms, etc. has gained much attention in biomedical academic research. Relational data, also known as the graph, which captures the interactions (i.e., edges) between entities (i.e., nodes), now plays a key role in the modern machine learning domain. Analyzing these graphs provides users a deeper understanding of topology information and knowledge behind these graphs, and thus greatly benefits many biomedical applications such as biological graph analysis [2], network medicine [4], clinical phenotyping and diagnosis [30], etc.

Although graph analytics is of great importance, most existing graph analytics methods suffer the computational cost drawn by high dimensionality

© Springer Nature Switzerland AG 2020
H. Yang et al. (Eds.): ICONIP 2020, CCIS 1333, pp. 21–29, 2020.
https://doi.org/10.1007/978-3-030-63823-8_3

and sparsity of the graphs. Furthermore, owing to the heterogeneity of biomedical graphs, i.e., containing multiple types of nodes and edges, traditional analyses over biomedical graphs remain challenging. Recently, graph embedding methods, aiming at learning a mapping that embeds nodes into a low dimensional vector space $\mathbb{R}^d$, now provide an effective and efficient way to address the problems. Specifically, the goal is to optimize this mapping so that the node representation in the embedding space can well preserve information and properties of the original graphs. After optimization of such representation learning, the learned embedding can then be used as feature inputs for many machine learning downstream tasks, which hence introduces enormous opportunities for biomedical data science. Efforts of applying graph embedding over biomedical data are recently made but still not thoroughly explored; capabilities of graph embedding for biomedical data are also not extensively evaluated. In addition, the biomedical graphs are usually sparse, incomplete, and heterogeneous, making graph embedding more complicated than other application domains. To address these issues, it is strongly motivated to understand and compare the state-of-the-art graph embedding techniques, and further study how these techniques can be adapted and applied to biomedical data science. Thus in this review, we investigate recent graph embedding techniques for biomedical data, which give us better insights into future directions. In this article, we introduce the general models related to biomedical data and omit the complete technical details. For a more comprehensive overview of graph embedding techniques and applications, we refer readers to previous well-summarized papers [7,14,33].

2   Homogeneous Graph Embedding Models

In the literature, homogeneous graphs refer to the graphs with only one type of nodes and edges. There are three main types of homogeneous graph embedding methods, i.e., *matrix factorization-based methods*, *random walk-based methods* and *deep learning-based methods*.

Matrix Factorization-Based Methods. Matrix factorization-based methods, inspired by classic techniques for dimensionality reduction, use the form of a matrix to represent the graph properties, e.g., node pairwise similarity. Generally, there are two types of matrix factorization to compute the node embedding, i.e., *node proximity matrix* and *graph Laplacian eigenmaps*.

For node proximity matrix factorization methods, they usually approximate node proximity into a low dimension. Actually, there are many other solutions to approximate this loss function, such as low rank matrix factorization, regularized Gaussian matrix factorization, etc. For graph Laplacian eigenmaps factorization methods, the assumption is that the graph property can be interpreted as the similarity of pairwise nodes. Thus, to obtain a good representation, the normal operation is that a larger penalty will be given if two nodes with higher similarity are far embedded. There are many works using graph Laplacian-based methods and they mainly differ from how they calculate the pairwise node similarity.

For example, BANE [44] defines a new Weisfeiler-Lehman proximity matrix to capture data dependence between edges and attributes; then based on this matrix, BANE learns the node embeddings by formulating a new Weisfiler-Lehman matrix factorization. Recently, NetMF [28] unifies state-of-the-art approaches into a matrix factorization framework with close forms.

Random Walk-Based Methods. Random walk-based methods have been widely used to approximate many properties in the graph including node centrality and similarity. They are more useful when the graph can only partially be observed, or the graph is too large to measure. Two widely recognized random walk-based methods have been proposed, i.e., DeepWalk [27] and node2vec [15]. Concretely, DeepWalk considers the paths as sentences and implements an NLP model to learn node embeddings. Compared to DeepWalk, node2vec introduces a trade-off strategy using breadth-first and depth-first search to perform a biased random walk. In recent years, there are still many random walk-based papers working on improving performance. For example, AWE [19] uses a recently developed method called *anonymous walks*, i.e., an anonymized version of the random walk-based method providing characteristic graph traits and are capable to exactly reconstruct network proximity of a node. AttentionWalk [1] uses the softmax to learn a free-form context distribution in a random walk; then the learned attention parameters guide the random walk, by allowing it to focus more on short or long term dependencies when optimizing an upstream objective. BiNE [13] proposes methods for bipartite graph embedding by performing biased random walks. Then they generate vertex sequences that can well preserve the long-tail distribution of vertices in original bipartite graphs.

Deep Learning-Based Methods. Deep learning has shown outstanding performance in a wide variety of research fields. SDNE [37] applies a deep autoencoder to model non-linearity in the graph structure. DNGR [8] learns deep low-dimensional vertex representations, by using the stacked denoising autoencoders on the high-dimensional matrix representations. Furthermore, Graph Convolutional Network (GCN) [20] introduces a well-behaved layer-wise propagation rule for the neural network model. Another important work is Graph Attention Network (GAT) [36], which leverages masked self-attentional layers to address the shortcomings of prior graph convolution-based methods. GAT computes normialized coefficients using the softmax function across different neighborhoods by a byproduct of an attentional mechanism across node pairs. To stabilize the learning process of self-attention, GAT uses multi-head attention to replicate K times of learning phases, and outputs are feature-wise aggregated, typically by concatenating or adding.

3   Heterogeneous Graph Embedding Models

Heterogeneous graphs mean that there are more than one type of nodes or edges within. The heterogeneity in both graph structures and node attributes makes it challenging for the graph embedding task to encode their diverse and rich information. In this section, we will introduce *translational distance methods* and *semantic matching methods*, which try to address the above issue by constructing different energy functions. Furthermore, we will introduce *meta-path-based methods* that use different strategies to capture graph heterogeneity.

Translational Distance Methods. The first work of translation distance models is TransE [6]. The basic idea of the translational distance models is, for each observed fact (h, r, t) representing head entity h having a relation r with tail entity t, to learn a good graph representation such that h and t are closely connected by relation r in low dimensional embedding space, i.e., $\mathbf{h} + \mathbf{r} \approx \mathbf{t}$, using geometric notations. Here $\mathbf{h}$, $\mathbf{r}$ and $\mathbf{t}$ are embedding vectors for entities h, t and relation r, respectively. To further improve the TransE model and address its inadequacies, many recent works have been developed. For example, RotatE [34] defines each relation as a rotation from the source entity to the target entity in the complex vector space. QuatE [45] computes node embedding vectors in the hypercomplex space with three imaginary components, as opposed to the standard complex space with a single real component and imaginary component. MuRP [3] is a hyperbolic embedding method that embeds multi-relational data in the Poincaré ball model of hyperbolic space, which can well perform in hierarchical and scale-free graphs.

Semantic Matching Methods. Semantic matching models exploit similarity-based scoring functions. They measure plausibility of facts by matching latent semantics of entities and relations embodied in their representations. Targeting the observed fact (h, r, t), RESCAL [26] embeds each entity with a vector to capture its latent semantics and each relation with a matrix to model pairwise interactions between latent factors. HolE [25] deals with directed graphs and composes head entity and tail entity by their circular correlation, which achieves a better performance than RESCAL. There are other works trying to extend or simplify RESCAL, e.g., DistMult [43], ComplEx [35]. Another direction of semantic matching methods is to fuse neural network architecture by considering embedding as the input layer and energy function as the output layer. For instance, SME model [5] first inputs embeddings of entities and relations in the input layer. The relation r is then combined with the head entity h to get $g_{left}(h, r) = M_1\mathbf{h} + M_2\mathbf{r} + \mathbf{b}_h$, and with the tail entity t to get $g_{right}(t, r) = M_3\mathbf{t} + M_4\mathbf{r} + \mathbf{b}_t$ in the hidden layer. The score function is defined as $f_r(h, t) = g_{left}(h, r)^T \cdot g_{right}(t, r)$. There are other semantic matching methods using neural network architecture, e.g., NTN [31], MLP [10].

Meta-path-Based Methods. Generally, a meta-path is an ordered path that consists of node types and connects via edge types defined on the graph schema, e.g., $A_1 \xrightarrow{R_1} A_2 \cdots \xrightarrow{R_{l-1}} A_l$, which describes a composite relation between node types A_1, A_2, $\cdots$, A_l and edge types R_1, $\cdots$, R_{l-1}. Thus, meta-paths can be viewed as high-order proximity between two nodes with specific semantics. A set of recent works have been proposed. Metapath2vec [11] computes node embeddings by feeding metapath-guided random walks to a skip-gram [24] model. HAN [41] learns meta-path-oriented node embeddings from different meta-path-based graphs converted from the original heterogeneous graph and leverages the attention mechanism to combine them into one vector representation for each node. HERec [29] learns node embeddings by applying DeepWalk [27] to the meta-path-based homogeneous graphs for recommendation. MAGNN [12] comprehensively considers three main components to achieve the state-of-the-art performance. Concretely, MAGNN [12] fuses the node content transformation to encapsulate node attributes, the intra-metapath aggregation to incorporate intermediate semantic nodes, and the inter-metapath aggregation to combine messages from multiple metapaths.

Other Methods. LANE [18] constructs proximity matrices by incorporating label information, graph topology, and learns embeddings while preserving their correlations based on Laplacian matrix. EOE [42] aims to embed the graph coupled by two non-attribute graphs. In EOE, latent features encode not only intra-network edges, but also inter-network ones. To tackle the challenge of heterogeneity of two graphs, the EOE incorporates a harmonious embedding matrix to further embed the embeddings. Inspired by generative adversarial network models, HeGAN [16] is designed to be relation-aware in order to capture the rich semantics on heterogeneous graphs and further trains a discriminator and a generator in a minimax game to generate robust graph embeddings.

4   Applications and Tasks in Biomedical Domain

In recent years, graph embedding methods have been applied in biomedical data science. In this section, we will introduce some main biomedical applications of applying graph embedding techniques, including *pharmaceutical data analysis*, *multi-omics data analysis* and *clinical data analysis*.

Pharmaceutical Data Analysis. Generally, there are two main types of applications, i.e., (i) *drug repositioning* and (ii) *adverse drug reaction analysis*. Drug repositioning usually aims to predict unknown drug-target or drug-disease interactions. Recently, DTINet [23] generates drug and target-protein embedding by performing random walk with restart on heterogeneous biomedical graphs to make predictions based on geometric proximity. Other studies over drug repositioning focused on predicting drug disease associations. For instance, Wang et al. [39] propose to detect unknown drug-disease interactions from the medical literature by fusing NLP and graph embedding techniques. An adverse drug reaction (ADR) is defined as any undesirable drug effect out of its desired therapeutic effects that occur at a usual dosage, which now is the center of drug development before a drug is launched on the clinical trial. Recently, inspired by translational distance models, Stanovsky et al. [32] propose a deep learning model to recognize ADR mentions in social media by infusing DBpedia.

Multi-omics Data Analysis. The main aim of multi-omics is to study structures, functions, and dynamics of organism molecules. Fortunately, graph embedding now becomes a valuable tool to analyze relational data in omics. Concretely, the computation tasks included in multi-omics data analysis are mainly about

(i) *genomics*, (ii) *proteomics* and (iii) *transcriptomics*. Works of graph embedding used in genomics data analysis usually try to decipher biology from genome sequences and related data. For example, based on gene-gene interaction data, a recent work [22] addresses representation learning for single cell RNA-seq data, which outperforms traditional dimensional reduction methods according to the experimental results. As we have introduced before, PPIs play key roles in most cell functions. Graph embedding has also been introduced to PPI graphs for proteomics data analysis, such as assessing and predicting PPIs or predicting protein functions, etc. Recently, ProSNet [40] has been proposed for protein function prediction. In this model, they introduce DCA to a heterogeneous molecular graph and further use the meta-path-based methods to modify DCA for preserving heterogeneous structural information. As for transcriptomics study, the focus is to analyze an organism's transcriptome. For instance, Identifying miRNA-disease associations now becomes an important topic of pathogenicity; while graph embedding now provides a useful tool to involve in transcriptomics for prediction of miRNA-disease associations. Li et al. [21] propose a method by using DeepWalk to embed the bipartite miRNA-disease network to make association prediction for miRNA-disease graphs.

Clinical Data Analysis. Graph embedding techniques have been applied to clinic data, such as electronic medical records (EMRs), electronic health records (EHRs) and medical knowledge graphs, providing useful assistance and support for clinicians in recent clinic development. To address the heterogeneity of EMRs and EHRs data, GRAM [9] learns EHR representation with the help of hierarchical information inherent to medical ontologies. ProSNet [17] constructs a biomedical knowledge graph to learn the embeddings of medical entities. The proposed method is used to visualize the Parkinson's disease data set. Conducting medical knowledge graph is of great importance and attention recently. For instance, Zhao et al. [47] define energy function by considering the relation between the symptoms of patients and diseases as a translation vector to further learn the representation of medical forum data. Then a new method is proposed to learn embeddings of medical entities in the medical knowledge graph, based on the energy functions of RESCAL and TransE [46]. Wang et al. [38] construct the objective function by using both the energy function of TransR and LINE's 2nd-order proximity measurement to learn embeddings from a heterogeneous medical knowledge graph to further recommend proper medicine to patients.

5   Conclusion

Graph embedding methods aim to learn compact and informative representations for graph analysis and thus provide a powerful opportunity to solve the traditional graph-based machine learning problems both effectively and efficiently. With the rapid development of relational data in the biomedical domain, applying graph embedding techniques now draws much attention in numerous biomedical applications. In this paper, we introduce recent developments of graph embedding methods. By summarizing biomedical applications with graph embedding methods, we provide perspectives over this emerging research domain for better improvement in human health care.

Acknowledgments. The work described in this paper was partially supported by The Chinese University of Hong Kong (CUHK 3133238, Research Sustainability of Major RGC Funding Schemes (RSFS)).

References

1. Abu-El-Haija, S., Perozzi, B., Al-Rfou, R., Alemi, A.A.: Watch your step: learning node embeddings via graph attention. In: NeurIPS, pp. 9180–9190 (2018)
2. Albert, R.: Scale-free networks in cell biology. J. Cell Sci. **118**, 4947–4957 (2005)
3. Balazevic, I., Allen, C., Hospedales, T.: Multi-relational poincaré graph embeddings. In: NeurIPS, pp. 4465–4475 (2019)
4. Barabási, A.L., Gulbahce, N., Loscalzo, J.: Network medicine: a network-based approach to human disease. Nat. Rev. Genet. **12**(1), 56–68 (2011)
5. Bordes, A., Glorot, X., Weston, J., Bengio, Y.: A semantic matching energy function for learning with multi-relational data. Mach. Learn. **94**(2), 233–259 (2013). https://doi.org/10.1007/s10994-013-5363-6
6. Bordes, A., Usunier, N., Garcia-Duran, A., Weston, J., Yakhnenko, O.: Translating embeddings for modeling multi-relational data. In: NeurIPS, pp. 2787–2795 (2013)
7. Cai, H., Zheng, V.W., Chang, K.C.C.: A comprehensive survey of graph embedding: problems, techniques, and applications. TKDE **30**(9), 1616–1637 (2018)
8. Cao, S., Lu, W., Xu, Q.: Deep neural networks for learning graph representations. In: AAAI (2016)
9. Choi, E., Bahadori, M.T., Song, L., Stewart, W.F., Sun, J.: GRAM: graph-based attention model for healthcare representation learning. In: SIGKDD (2017)
10. Dong, X., et al.: Knowledge vault: a web-scale approach to probabilistic knowledge fusion. In: SIGKDD, pp. 601–610 (2014)
11. Dong, Y., Chawla, N.V., Swami, A.: metapath2vec: scalable representation learning for heterogeneous networks. In: SIGKDD, pp. 135–144 (2017)
12. Fu, X., Zhang, J., Meng, Z., King, I.: MaGNN: metapath aggregated graph neural network for heterogeneous graph embedding. In: WWW, pp. 2331–2341 (2020)
13. Gao, M., Chen, L., He, X., Zhou, A.: BINE: bipartite network embedding. In: SIGIR, pp. 715–724 (2018)
14. Goyal, P., Ferrara, E.: Graph embedding techniques, applications, and performance: a survey. Knowl.-Based Syst. **151**, 78–94 (2018)
15. Grover, A., Leskovec, J.: node2vec: scalable feature learning for networks. In: SIGKDD, pp. 855–864 (2016)
16. Hu, B., Fang, Y., Shi, C.: Adversarial learning on heterogeneous information networks. In: SIGKDD, pp. 120–129 (2019)
17. Huang, E.W., Wang, S., Zhai, C.: VisAGE: integrating external knowledge into electronic medical record visualization. In: PSB, pp. 578–589. World Scientific (2018)
18. Huang, X., Li, J., Hu, X.: Label informed attributed network embedding. In: WSDM, pp. 731–739 (2017)
19. Ivanov, S., Burnaev, E.: Anonymous walk embeddings. arXiv:1805.11921 (2018)
20. Kipf, T.N., Welling, M.: Semi-supervised classification with graph convolutional networks. arXiv:1609.02907 (2016)

21. Li, G., Luo, J., Xiao, Q., Liang, C., Ding, P., Cao, B.: Predicting microrna-disease associations using network topological similarity based on deepwalk. IEEE Access **5**, 24032–24039 (2017)
22. Li, X., Chen, W., Chen, Y., Zhang, X., Gu, J., Zhang, M.Q.: Network embedding-based representation learning for single cell RNA-seq data. Nucleic Acids Res. **45**(19), e166 (2017)
23. Luo, Y., et al.: A network integration approach for drug-target interaction prediction and computational drug repositioning from heterogeneous information. Nat. Commun. **8**(1), 1–13 (2017)
24. Mikolov, T., Chen, K., Corrado, G., Dean, J.: Efficient estimation of word representations in vector space. In: ICLR (Workshop Poster) (2013)
25. Nickel, M., Rosasco, L., Poggio, T.: Holographic embeddings of knowledge graphs. In: AAAI (2016)
26. Nickel, M., Tresp, V., Kriegel, H.P.: A three-way model for collective learning on multi-relational data. In: ICML, vol. 11, pp. 809–816 (2011)
27. Perozzi, B., Al-Rfou, R., Skiena, S.: DeepWalk: online learning of social representations. In: SIGKDD, pp. 701–710 (2014)
28. Qiu, J., Dong, Y., Ma, H., Li, J., Wang, K., Tang, J.: Network embedding as matrix factorization: unifying DeepWalk, LINE, PTE, and node2vec. In: WSDM (2018)
29. Shi, C., Hu, B., Zhao, W.X., Philip, S.Y.: Heterogeneous information network embedding for recommendation. TKDE **31**(2), 357–370 (2018)
30. Shickel, B., Tighe, P.J., Bihorac, A., Rashidi, P.: Deep ehr: a survey of recent advances in deep learning techniques for electronic health record (EHR) analysis. IEEE J. Biomed. Health Inf. **22**(5), 1589–1604 (2017)
31. Socher, R., Chen, D., Manning, C.D., Ng, A.: Reasoning with neural tensor networks for knowledge base completion. In: NeurIPS, pp. 926–934 (2013)
32. Stanovsky, G., Gruhl, D., Mendes, P.: Recognizing mentions of adverse drug reaction in social media using knowledge-infused recurrent models. In: EACL (2017)
33. Su, C., Tong, J., Zhu, Y., Cui, P., Wang, F.: Network embedding in biomedical data science. Brief. Bioinf. **21**(1), 182–197 (2020)
34. Sun, Z., Deng, Z., Nie, J., Tang, J.: RotatE: knowledge graph embedding by relational rotation in complex space. In: ICLR (Poster). OpenReview.net (2019)
35. Trouillon, T., Welbl, J., Riedel, S., Gaussier, É., Bouchard, G.: Complex embeddings for simple link prediction. In: ICML (2016)
36. Veličković, P., Cucurull, G., Casanova, A., Romero, A., Lio, P., Bengio, Y.: Graph attention networks. arXiv:1710.10903 (2017)
37. Wang, D., Cui, P., Zhu, W.: Structural deep network embedding. In: SIGKDD, pp. 1225–1234 (2016)
38. Wang, M., Liu, M., Liu, J., Wang, S., Long, G., Qian, B.: Safe medicine recommendation via medical knowledge graph embedding. arXiv:1710.05980 (2017)
39. Wang, P., Hao, T., Yan, J., Jin, L.: Large-scale extraction of drug-disease pairs from the medical literature. J. AIST **68**(11), 2649–2661 (2017)
40. Wang, S., Qu, M., Peng, J.: Prosnet: integrating homology with molecular networks for protein function prediction. In: PSB, pp. 27–38. World Scientific (2017)
41. Wang, X., et al.: Heterogeneous graph attention network. In: WWW, pp. 2022–2032 (2019)
42. Xu, L., Wei, X., Cao, J., Yu, P.S.: Embedding of embedding (EOE) joint embedding for coupled heterogeneous networks. In: WSDM, pp. 741–749 (2017)
43. Yang, B., Yih, W.T., He, X., Gao, J., Deng, L.: Embedding entities and relations for learning and inference in knowledge bases. arXiv:1412.6575 (2014)

44. Yang, H., Pan, S., Zhang, P., Chen, L., Lian, D., Zhang, C.: Binarized attributed network embedding. In: ICDM, pp. 1476–1481. IEEE (2018)
45. Zhang, S., Tay, Y., Yao, L., Liu, Q.: Quaternion knowledge graph embeddings. In: NeurIPS, pp. 2731–2741 (2019)
46. Zhao, C., Jiang, J., Guan, Y., Guo, X., He, B.: EMR-based medical knowledge representation and inference via Markov random fields and distributed representation learning. Artif. Intell. Med. **87**, 49–59 (2018)
47. Zhao, S., Jiang, M., Yuan, Q., Qin, B., Liu, T., Zhai, C.: ContextCare: incorporating contextual information networks to representation learning on medical forum data. In: IJCAI, pp. 3497–3503 (2017)

Adaptive Ensemble Variants of Random Vector Functional Link Networks

Minghui Hu[1], Qiushi Shi[1], P. N. Suganthan[1]([✉]), and M. Tanveer[2]

[1] Nanyang Technological University,
50 Nanyang Avenue, Singapore 639798, Singapore
{minghui.hu,epnsugan}@ntu.edu.sg, qiushi001@e.ntu.edu.sg
[2] Indian Institute of Technology Indore, Simrol, Indore 453552, India
mtanveer@iiti.ac.in

Abstract. In this paper, we propose a novel adaptive ensemble variant of random vector functional link (RVFL) networks. Adaptive ensemble RVFL networks assign different weights to the sub-classifiers according to prediction performance of single RVFL network. Generic Adaptive Ensemble RVFL is composed of a series of unrelated, independent weak classifiers. We also employ our adaptive ensemble method to the deep random vector functional link (dRVFL). Each layer in dRVFL can be regarded as a sub-classifier. However, instead of training several models independently, the sub-classifiers of dRVFL can be obtained by training a single network once.

Keywords: Random vector functional link · Ensemble classifiers · Deep neural networks · Adaptive boosting

1 Introduction

In recent years, deep learning methods have become attractive because of their success in multiple areas. Convolutional neural networks (CNN) won lots of competitions with conventional methods in visual tasks, and recurrent neural networks (RNN) based models were good at processing sequential inputs [10]. These methods use gradient-based back-propagation (BP) learning algorithm to train a large number of parameters in their networks. Proposed by Hinton in [13], the main idea of BP algorithm is to tune the weights and biases following the gradient of the loss function. However, due to the large computational cost, some modern-day neural networks may need several weeks to finish the training step [11]. Moreover, overfitting [6] is another serious problem that can cause the model to perform well during the training while achieving poor performance when testing.

Meanwhile, some randomization based neural networks have been proposed to overcome the flaws of the BP-based models [14,15,17]. The weights and biases in these models are randomly generated and kept fixed during the training process. Only the parameters in the output layers are obtained by the close-form

H. Yang et al. (Eds.): ICONIP 2020, CCIS 1333, pp. 30–37, 2020.
https://doi.org/10.1007/978-3-030-63823-8_4

solution [16]. Random vector functional link network (RVFL) is a typical single-hidden-layer randomized neural network [12]. It has a direct link to convey the information from the input layer directly to the output layer. This is useful because the output layer contains both the linear original features and the non-linear transformed features. The newest version of this model was proposed in [8] and called ensemble deep random vector functional link network (edRVFL), the authors convert the single-hidden-layer RVFL to the deep version and employ the idea of ensemble learning to reduce the computational complexity. Similar to the conventional neural networks, the edRVFL network also consists of an input layer, an output layer, and several hidden layers. The hidden weights and biases in this network are randomly generated and do not need to be trained. The uniqueness of this frame is that each layer is treated as an independent classifier, just like a single RVFL network. Eventually, the final output is obtained by fusing all the outputs.

Ensemble learning methods are widely used in classification problems, they combine multiple models for prediction to overcome the weakness of each single learning algorithm [19]. Among them, bagging [1], boosting [4], and stacking [18] are the three most popular and successful methods. Adaboost was originally proposed to improve the performance of the decision trees [3]. This method intends to combine several weak classifiers to obtain a strong classifier. The misclassified samples in the previous classifiers will be given greater importance in the following classifiers. Furthermore, the classifier with higher accuracy will also be assigned a higher weight in the final prediction. In this paper, we introduce two novel methods using Adaboost to generate the ensemble model of RVFL and the deep version of RVFL. We called them adaptive ensemble random vector functional link networks (ada-eRVFL) and adaptive ensemble deep random vector functional link networks (ada-edRVFL). In ada-eRVFL, we treat each single RVFL network as the weak classifier in Adaboost. However, in ada-edRVFL, we treat every single layer as the weak classifier.

2 Related Works

2.1 Random Vector Functional Link Networks

Random vector functional link network (RVFL) is a randomization based single hidden layer neural network proposed by Pao [12]. The basic structure of RVFL is shown in Fig. 1.

Both the linear original features and the non-linearly transformed features are conveyed to the output layer through the direct link and the hidden layer, respectively. Therefore, the output weights β can be learned from the following optimization problem:

$$O_{RVFL} = \min_{\beta} ||D\beta - Y||^2 + \lambda ||\beta||^2 \qquad (1)$$

where D is the combination of all linear and non-linear features, and Y are the true labels of all the samples. λ denoted as the parameter for controlling

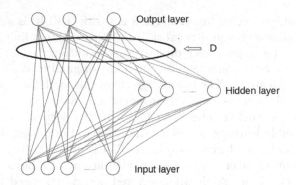

Fig. 1. The structure of RVFL network. The red lines are defined as the direct link which transfer the linear original features to the output layer. (Color figure online)

how much the algorithm cares about the model complexity. This optimization problem can be solved by ridge regression [7], and the solution can be written as follows:

$$PrimalSpace : \beta = (D^T D + \lambda I)^{-1} D^T Y \tag{2}$$

$$DualSpace : \beta = D^T (DD^T + \lambda I)^{-1} Y \tag{3}$$

The computational cost of training the RVFL network is reduced by suitably choosing between the primal or dual solution [15].

2.2   Ensemble Deep Random Vector Functional Link Networks

Inspired by other deep learning models, the authors of [8] proposed a deep version of the basic RVFL network. They also used ensemble learning to improve the performance of this model. The structure of edRVFL is shown in Fig. 2. Let n be the hidden neuron number and l be the hidden layer number. The output of the first hidden layer can be obtained by:

$$H^{(1)} = g(XW^{(1)}), \quad W^{(1)} \in \mathbb{R}^{d \times n} \tag{4}$$

where X denotes the input features, d represents the feature number of the input samples, and $g(\cdot)$ is the non-linear activation function used in each hidden neuron. When the layer number $l > 1$, similar to the RVFL networks, the hidden features in the previous hidden layer as well as the original features in the input layer are concatenated together to generate the next hidden layer. So Eq. 4 becomes, when $l > 1$:

$$H^{(l)} = g([H^{(l-1)} X]W^{(l)}), \quad W^{(l)} \in \mathbb{R}^{(n+d) \times n} \tag{5}$$

edRVFL network treats every hidden layer as a single RVFL classifier too. After getting predictions from all the layers via ridge regression, these outputs will be fused by ensemble methods to reach the final output.

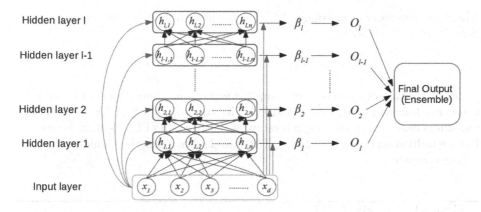

Fig. 2. The structure of edRVFL network. Each single layer is treated as an independent RVFL network. The final output is obtained by combing the predictions from all the classifier.

2.3 AdaBoost

Boosting has been proven to be successful in solving classification problems. It was first introduced by [3], with their algorithm called Adaboost. This method was originally proposed for the two-class classification problem and improving the performance of the decision tree. The main idea of Adaboost is to approximate the Bayes classifier by combining several weak classifiers. Typically, the Adaboost algorithm is an iterative procedure, it starts with using unweighted samples to build the first classifier. During the following steps, the weights of the misclassified samples in the previous classifier will be boosted in the next classifier. That means these samples are given higher importance during the error calculation. After several repetitions, it employs weighted majority voting to combine outputs from every classifier to obtain the final output.

In [5], the authors developed a new algorithm called Stagewise Additive Modeling using a Multi-class Exponential loss function (SAMME) which directly extended the Adaboost to the multi-class case without complicating it into multiple two-class problems.

3 Method

In this section, we proposed the adaptive ensemble random vector functional link networks (ada-eRVFL). ada-eRVFL is inspired by the adaptive boosting method. For a data set x, the weights α are assigned to the sub-classifiers according to the error function:

$$err^{(m)} = \sum_{i=1}^{n} \omega_i \mathbb{1}(c_i \neq R^{(m)}(x_i)) / \sum_{i=1}^{n} \omega_i \qquad (6)$$

where R represents the single RVFL classifier and ω is the sample weight described as the follows:

$$\omega_i \leftarrow \omega_i \cdot exp\left(a^{(m)} \cdot \mathbb{1}\left(c_i \neq R^{(m)}(x_i)\right)\right) \tag{7}$$

It is worth noting that the sample weights only contribute in computing the error function of the sub-classifier. The training phase of the weak RVFL-classifiers only utilizes the original samples. The weak RVFL classifiers for ensemble are individual and independent. The mis-classified samples would be assigned a larger weight.

Algorithm 1: ada-eRVFL

Input: A set of training data $x \in \{x_1, x_2, \ldots, x_n\}$.

Initialize the sample weights w_i and the classifier weight a_i;
for $m \leftarrow 0$ **to** M **do**

    Train an RVFL classifier $R^{(m)}(x)$ with the raw training data x;
    Compute the error of the classifier $R^{(m)}$;

$$err^{(m)} = \sum_{i=1}^{n} \omega_i \mathbb{1}(c_i \neq R^{(m)}(x_i)) / \sum_{i=1}^{n} \omega_i \tag{8}$$

    if $1 - err^{(m)} > 1/K$ **then**

        Compute the weight of the classifier;

$$a^{(m)} = log\frac{1 - err^{(m)}}{err^{(m)}} + log(K - 1) \tag{9}$$

        Set the sample weights as follows:

$$\omega_i \leftarrow \omega_i \cdot exp\left(a^{(m)} \cdot \mathbb{1}\left(c_i \neq R^{(m)}(x_i)\right)\right) \tag{10}$$

    else

        The classifier weight is 1 ;
        The sample weight are $1/N$;
    end

end
Output: The ensemble classifier C

$$C(x) = argmax \sum_{i=1}^{n} a^{(m)} \cdot \mathbb{1}(R^{(m)}(x_i) = k) \tag{11}$$

Another proposed variant is adaptive ensemble deep random vector functional link networks (ada-edRVFL). The deep RVFL network consists of a few hidden layers instead of single hidden layer in RVFL. Each hidden layer can

---

Algorithm 2: ada-edRVFL

Input: A set of training data $x \in \{x_1, x_2, \ldots, x_n\}$.

Initialize the sample weights w_i and the classifier weight a_i;
Train an deep RVFL classifier $D(x)$ with the training data x with L hidden layers.;
for $l \leftarrow 0$ **to** L **do**

    Compute the error of the sub classifier $R^{(l)}$;

$$err^{(m)} = \sum_{i=1}^{n} w_i \mathbb{1}(c_i \neq R^{(l)}(x_i)) / \sum_{i=1}^{n} w_i \tag{12}$$

    if $1 - err^{(l)} > 1/K$ **then**

        Compute the weight of the classifier;

$$a^{(l)} = log \frac{1 - err^{(m)}}{err^{(m)}} + log(K - 1) \tag{13}$$

        Set the sample weights as follows:

$$w_i \leftarrow w_i \cdot exp\left(a^{(l)} \cdot \mathbb{1}\left(c_i \neq R^{(l)}(x_i)\right)\right) \tag{14}$$

    else

        The classifier weight is 1 ;
        The sample weight are $1/L$;
    end
end
Output: The ensemble classifier C

$$D(x) = argmax \sum_{i=1}^{n} a^{(l)} \cdot \mathbb{1}(R^{(l)}(x_i) - k) \tag{15}$$

---

constitute a sub-classifier with the input layer, output layer and the direct link between them.

For both proposed ideas, we need to make sure the classifier weights α are positive, thus it is required that $1 - err^{(m)} > 1/K$.

4 Experiments

The experiments are performed on 9 classification datasets selected from UCI Machine Learning Repository [2], including both binary and multiple classification problems. Sample volume and feature dimensions are coverage from hundred to thousand. The details of the dataset are stated below. In the interests of a fair comparison, we use the exact same validation and test subsets and the same data pre-processing method as in [9].

For the RVFL based methods, the regularization parameter λ is set as $\frac{1}{C}$ where C is chosen from range $2^x\{x = -6, -4, \ldots, 10, 12\}$. Based on the size of the dataset, the hidden neuron number these methods can be tuned from $\{2^2, 2^3, \ldots, 2^{10}, 2^{11}\}$.

For the dRVFL based methods, the regularization parameter λ is set as $\frac{1}{C}$ where C is chosen from range $2^x\{x = -6, -4, \ldots, 10, 12\}$. Based on the size of the dataset, the hidden neuron number these methods can be tuned from $\{2^2, 2^3, \ldots, 2^{10}, 2^{11}\}$. Besides, the maximum number of hidden layers for the edRVFL based methods is set to 32, which is also the number of sub-classifiers in ada-edRVFL.

Table 1. Accuracy (%) and Average rank of variant approaches

Dataset names	Batch norm	ada Boost	Layer norm	High-way	RVFL	ResNet	ada-e RVFL	MSRA init	edRVFL	ada-ed RVFL
Led-display	62.8	67.8	64.8	70.4	71.6	71.6	72.6	72	71.6	**74.3**
Statlog-german-credit	75.2	74.4	74	**77.6**	74.1	77.2	75.7	72.8	75.6	76.69
oocytes4d	80.78	74.51	76.86	71.76	78.43	80	80.98	81.96	83.04	**83.92**
Haberman-survival	73.68	72.37	68.42	64.47	68.42	68.42	72.28	72.37	73.36	**74.01**
Contrac	45.38	51.3	45.92	50.54	50.06	51.36	50.2	51.36	51.36	**53.6**
Yeast	49.06	43.13	60.92	60.65	58.49	54.99	58.82	**61.73**	59.97	61.25
Heart-va	28	29	24	40	32	26	35	26	34.5	**37.5**
Pima	71.88	74.09	69.27	71.88	75.52	71.35	76.22	**76.56**	74.09	76.43
wine-quality-red	54.5	54.44	61	56.25	57.13	61.5	59.44	62.5	65.87	**66.5**
Teaching	50	51.97	**63.16**	52.63	51.61	55.26	52.63	60.53	51.97	55.92
Average accuracy	59.128	59.301	60.835	61.618	61.736	61.768	63.387	63.781	64.136	**66.012**
Average rank	7.55	7.25	7.2	6.05	6.8	5.8	4.6	3.95	4.1	**1.7**

From Table 1, the ada-dRVFL achieves the best performance on all datasets. On average, the accuracy of ada-edRVFL has an improvement of over two percentages. It suggests the proposed adaptive ensemble method can effectively boost the performance of weak classifiers, and this method make single RVFL network competitive with deep RVFL network.

5   Conclusion

We proposed an adaptive ensemble method of random vector functional link networks. Compared to the edRVFL, our framework outperforms the edRVFL's result. The proposed method can be employed to different RVFL based networks. After utilizing the proposed ensemble method, the performance of ensemble RVFL can compete with the deep RVFL networks. Specifically, we test the proposed method on 9 UCI classification task machine learning datasets. The experimental results show that the proposed ensemble variant is both effective and general.

References

1. Breiman, L.: Bagging predictors. Mach. Learn. **24**(2), 123–140 (1996)
2. Dua, D., Graff, C.: UCI machine learning repository (2017). http://archive.ics.uci.edu/ml
3. Freund, Y., Schapire, R.E.: A desicion-theoretic generalization of on-line learning and an application to boosting. In: Vitányi, P. (ed.) EuroCOLT 1995. LNCS, vol. 904, pp. 23–37. Springer, Heidelberg (1995). https://doi.org/10.1007/3-540-59119-2_166
4. Freund, Y., Schapire, R.E., et al.: Experiments with a new boosting algorithm. In: ICML, vol. 96, pp. 148–156. Citeseer (1996)
5. Hastie, T., Rosset, S., Zhu, J., Zou, H.: Multi-class adaboost. Stat. Interface **2**(3), 349–360 (2009)
6. Hawkins, D.M.: The problem of overfitting. J. Chem. Inf. Comput. Sci. **44**(1), 1–12 (2004)
7. Hoerl, A.E., Kennard, R.W.: Ridge regression: biased estimation for nonorthogonal problems. Technometrics **12**(1), 55–67 (1970)
8. Katuwal, R., Suganthan, P., Tanveer, M.: Random vector functional link neural network based ensemble deep learning. arXiv preprint arXiv:1907.00350 (2019)
9. Klambauer, G., Unterthiner, T., Mayr, A., Hochreiter, S.: Self-normalizing neural networks. In: Advances in Neural Information Processing Systems, pp. 971–980 (2017)
10. LeCun, Y., Bengio, Y., Hinton, G.: Deep learning. Nature **521**(7553), 436–444 (2015)
11. Livni, R., Shalev-Shwartz, S., Shamir, O.: On the computational efficiency of training neural networks. In: Advances in Neural Information Processing Systems, pp. 855–863 (2014)
12. Pao, Y.H., Takefuji, Y.: Functional-link net computing: theory, system architecture, and functionalities. Computer **25**(5), 76–79 (1992)
13. Rumelhart, D.E., Hinton, G.E., Williams, R.J.: Learning internal representations by error propagation. Technical report, California Univ San Diego La Jolla Inst for Cognitive Science (1985)
14. Schmidt, W.F., Kraaijveld, M.A., Duin, R.P., et al.: Feed forward neural networks with random weights. In: International Conference on Pattern Recognition, p. 1. IEEE Computer Society Press (1992)
15. Suganthan, P.N.: On non-iterative learning algorithms with closed-form solution. Appl. Soft Comput. **70**, 1078–1082 (2018)
16. Te Braake, H.A., Van Straten, G.: Random activation weight neural net (RAWN) for fast non-iterative training. Eng. Appl. Artif. Intell. **8**(1), 71–80 (1995)
17. Widrow, B., Greenblatt, A., Kim, Y., Park, D.: The no-prop algorithm: a new learning algorithm for multilayer neural networks. Neural Netw. **37**, 182–188 (2013)
18. Wolpert, D.H.: Stacked generalization. Neural Netw. **5**(2), 241–259 (1992)
19. Zhang, C., Ma, Y.: Ensemble Machine Learning: Methods and Applications. Springer, Heidelberg (2012). https://doi.org/10.1007/978-1-4419-9326-7

An Attention-Based Interaction-Aware Spatio-Temporal Graph Neural Network for Trajectory Prediction

Hao Zhou[1,4], Dongchun Ren[2], Huaxia Xia[2], Mingyu Fan[2,3], Xu Yang[4(✉)], and Hai Huang[1(✉)]

[1] National Key Laboratory of Science and Technology of Underwater Vehicle, Harbin Engineering University, Harbin 150001, China
`zhouhao94@yahoo.com, haihus@163.com`
[2] Meituan-Dianping Group, Beijing 100102, China
`{rendongchun,xiahuaxia}@meituan.com`
[3] School of Computer Science and Artificial Intelligence, Wenzhou University, Wenzhou 325035, China
`fanmingyu@wzu.edu.cn`
[4] State Key Laboratory of Management and Control for Complex System, Institute of Automation, Chinese Academy of Sciences, Beijing 100190, China
`xu.yang@ia.ac.cn`

Abstract. Pedestrian trajectory prediction in crowd scenes is very useful in many applications such as video surveillance, self-driving cars, and robotic systems; however, it remains a challenging task because of the complex interactions and uncertainties of crowd motions. In this paper, a novel trajectory prediction method called the Attention-based Interaction-aware Spatio-temporal Graph Neural Network (AST-GNN) is proposed. AST-GNN uses an Attention mechanism to capture the complex interactions among multiple pedestrians. The attention mechanism allows for a dynamic and adaptive summary of the interactions of the nearby pedestrians. When the attention matrix is obtained, it is formulated into a propagation matrix for graph neural networks. Finally, a Time-extrapolator Convolutional Neural Network (TXP-CNN) is used in the temporal dimension of the aggregated features to predict the future trajectories of the pedestrians. Experimental results on benchmark pedestrian datasets (ETH and UCY) reveal the competitive performances of AST-GNN in terms of both the final displace error (FDE) and average displacement error (ADE) as compared with state-of-the-art trajectory prediction methods.

Keywords: Trajectory prediction · Spatio-temporal prediction · Graph neural networks

1 Introduction

Pedestrian trajectory prediction in crowd scenes is important in many applications including robotic systems, video surveillance, and self-driving cars.

© Springer Nature Switzerland AG 2020
H. Yang et al. (Eds.): ICONIP 2020, CCIS 1333, pp. 38–45, 2020.
https://doi.org/10.1007/978-3-030-63823-8_5

Accurate trajectory prediction in surveillance systems is helpful for the identification of suspicious activities. When applied to robotics and self-driving cars,
it enables the controller to make intelligent strategies in advance of some critical
situations, such as emergency braking or collision avoidance.

Early pedestrian trajectory prediction methods, such as the Gaussian process regression method [14], the kinematic and dynamic method [16], and the
Bayesian network method [7], ignore the interactions among pedestrians and
are only able to make reasonable short-term predictions. As discussed in [1],
pedestrian trajectory prediction is a challenging task because of the complex
interactions among pedestrians, which are referred to as social behavior. Pedestrians tend to move in groups and avoid collisions when walking in the opposite directions, and their interactions are roughly driven by common sense and
social conventions. Because their destinations and possible paths are unknown,
the motion of multiple pedestrians in a crowd scene is generally randomly distributed. The GRIP method [9] proposes the use of a graph neural network
(GNN) for trajectory prediction. However, the graph is constructed via reference to the Euclidean distance between agents and is not the optimal choice
because all neighbors are treated equally.

Instead of the restriction of the local neighborhood assumption, the attention
mechanism is helpful for encoding the relative influences and the potential spatial
interactions among pedestrians due to the unequal importance of the neighboring pedestrians that contribute to the trajectory prediction. In this paper, the
use of the graph attention (GAT) [17] mechanism is proposed to capture the
interactions among pedestrians and then formulate the information into a propagation matrix for a GNN [18]. Because the GNN is able to define a normalized
weighted aggregation of features, it is a powerful tool with which to combine the
interactions and make a reasonable prediction. With the features aggregated by
the GNN, a Time-extrapolator Convolutional Neural Network (TXP-CNN) is
used as the decoder for prediction in the temporal dimension of data.

The remainder of this paper is organized as follows. A brief overview of related
work is provided in Sect. 2, and the proposed prediction model is defined and
presented in Sect. 3. Experimental comparisons with state-of-the-art methods on
the ETH [12] and UCY [8] pedestrian datasets are presented in Sect. 4. Finally,
some concluding remarks are given in Sect. 5.

2   Related Works

A recent study [1] indicates that the recurrent neural network (RNN) and its
variants, namely long short-term memory (LSTM) and gated recurrent units
(GRUs), are successful in trajectory prediction. Based on the multi-modal distribution assumption, Social-GAN [4] extends the social LSTM into an RNN-based
generative model. The CIDNN method [19] uses motion features extracted by
LSTM networks to encode the interactions among agents. Peek into the future
(PIF) [10] and Sophie [15] use deep convolutional neural networks (CNNs) to
extract the visual features from the scene and combines the motion features into

LSTMs for scene compliant trajectory prediction. Alternatively, [2] uses temporal convolutional networks to encode or decode the trajectories.

Many prediction methods propose the use of attention models to automatically assign importance to nodes. The social-BiGAT [6] method uses a graph attention model to capture the interactions between pedestrians and the surrounding scene. The STGAT method [5] first uses an LSTM to capture the trajectory information of each agent and applies GAT to model the interactions of multiple agents at every time step. Recently, the VectorNet method [3] has been proposed and utilizes a self-attention mechanism to aggregate all motion features of road agents. Social-STGCNN [11] defines a spatial graph by a Euclidean distance based kernel function. As compared with Social-STGCNN, the attention-based adaptive graph, rather than the distance-based graph [11], is used in the proposed method.

3   The Proposed Scheme

To overcome the weak graph representation issue of Social-STGCNN [11], the novel Attention-based Spatio-temporal GNN (AST-GNN) is proposed for pedestrian trajectory prediction in this section. The model is described in three parts, namely: (1) attention-based spatial graph representation, (2) the attention-based spatial GNN model, and (3) the time-extrapolator trajectory prediction model. The architecture of the proposed AST-GNN scheme is illustrated in Fig. 1.

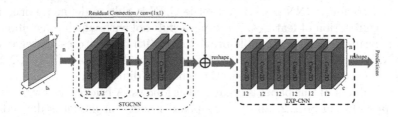

Fig. 1. The architecture of the proposed AST-GNN scheme.

3.1   Attention-Based Spatial Graph Representation

Input Representation of Pedestrian Prediction. The original trajectory data are sparse, so the raw data are first converted into a format that is suitable for subsequent efficient computation. Assuming that n pedestrians in a scene were observed in the past t time steps, this information is represented in a 3D array input with a size of $(n \times t \times c)$, where $c = 2$ denotes the coordinates (x_t^i, y_t^i) of a pedestrian.

Graph Representation of Pedestrian Prediction. The graph for pedestrian trajectory prediction is constructed in the spatial dimension. At time t, a spatial graph G_t is constructed that represents the relative locations of pedestrians in a scene at time step t. G_t is defined as $G_t = \{V_t, E_t\}$, where $V_t = \{v_t^i \mid \forall i \in \{1, ..., N\}\}$ is a node set of pedestrians in a scene. The feature vector of v_t^i on a node is the coordinates of th i-th pedestrian at time step t. $E_t = \{e_t^{ij} \mid \forall i, j \in \{1, ..., N\}\}$ is the edge set within graph G_t, e_t^{ij} denotes the edge between v_t^i and v_t^j.

To model how strongly two nodes influence each other, a weighted adjacency matrix is used to replace the normal adjacency matrix. In general, the distance relationship between pedestrians is used to build the weight of an adjacency matrix. However, the social network of a person is a complex problem, and cannot simply be decided by the distances between a pedestrian and the other. Thus, in this work, the GAT mechanism is used to adaptively learns the weighted adjacency matrix.

Graph Attention Mechanism. The GAT mechanism is used to calculate the weighted adjacency matrix A_t at time step t. The input of GAT mechanism $H_t = \{h_t^i \mid h_t^i \in \mathbb{R}^F, \forall i \in \{1, ..., N\}\}$ is the set of all feature vectors of nodes at time step t. To obtain sufficient expressive power to transform the input features into higher-level features, a learnable linear transformation $\mathbf{W} \in \mathbb{R}^{F' \times F}$ is used to transform feature vectors from $\mathbb{R}^F$ to $\mathbb{R}^{F'}$. Then, the self-attention mechanism is performed on the nodes:

$$\alpha_t^{ij} = \frac{exp(LeakyReLU(\mathbf{a}^{\mathbf{T}} \left[\mathbf{W}h_t^i \| \mathbf{W}h_t^j\right]))}{\sum_{k \neq i} exp(LeakReLU(\mathbf{a}^{\mathbf{T}} \left[\mathbf{W}h_t^i \| \mathbf{W}h_t^k\right]))}. \tag{1}$$

where α_t^{ij} measures the impact of the j-th node on the i-th node at time step t, $\mathbf{a} \subset \mathbb{R}^{2F'}$ is a weight vector, $\cdot^{\mathbf{T}}$ represents transposition, and $\|$ represents the concatenation operator. It should be noted that the activation function LeakyReLU uses the negative input slope $\alpha = 0.2$.

3.2 Attention-Based Spatial GNN Model

In the proposed AST-GNN model, the GAT mechanism is added to adaptively learn the weighted adjacency matrix. As described in Fig. 1, the AST-GNN consists of two parts, namely the spatial graph convolutional block and the temporal convolutional block. Moreover, a residual connection is used to connect the input and output to avoid significant information loss.

Spatial Graph Neural Networks. As described in Sect. 3.1, the input data format is $(n \times t \times c)$, and the attribute of each node is the coordinates of pedestrians. A convolutional layer with a kernel size 1 is first used to extract convolutional feature maps f_{conv}^t. Then, the attention-based graph representation operator presented in Sect. 3.1 is used to construct the weighted adjacency matrix A_t

using feature maps f_{conv}^t. The normalized weighted adjacency matrix A_t is then used to perform the graph operation by multiplication with f_{conv}^t as follow:

$$f_{graph}^t = \sigma(\Lambda_t^{-\frac{1}{2}} \hat{A}_t \Lambda_t^{-\frac{1}{2}} f_{conv}^t). \tag{2}$$

where f_{graph}^t is the graph feature map at time step t, $\hat{A}_t = A_t + I$, Λ_t is the diagonal matrix of $\hat{A}_t$, and σ is the activation function of the parametric ReLU (PReLU).

Time-Extrapolator Trajectory Prediction Model. The temporal convolutional block is used to model the graph information in the time dimension. First, the outputs of spatial graph convolutional blocks at different time steps are stacked into feature V with the format $(n \times t \times c_1)$, where $c_1 = 32$ is the feature dimension. Then, a convolutional layer with a kernel size of 1 is used to reduce feature dimension from c_1 to c_2 for subsequent efficient computation, where $c_2 = 5$. A convolutional layer with a kernel size of (1×3) is then used to process the graph feature along the temporal dimension. Finally, a residual connection between the input and output is used to produce the graph embedding $\widetilde{V}$.

3.3 Trajectory Prediction Model

As illustrated in Fig. 1, an encoder-decoder model is adopted to predict the trajectories of all pedestrians in a scene. The AST-GNN model is used as the encoder, and the Time-extrapolator Convolutional Neural Network (TXP-CNN) is the decoder. As presented in Fig. 1, the model first extracts the spatial node embedding $\widetilde{V}$ from the input graph. Then, the TXP-CNN receives $\widetilde{V}$ features and produces the predicted trajectories of pedestrians.

Time-Extrapolator Convolutional Neural Network. The TXP-CNN receives the graph embedding $\widetilde{V}$ and operates directly in the temporal dimension. The graph embedding $\widetilde{V}$ has a shape of $(n \times t \times c_2)$, we first reshape the features into the format $(n \times c_2 \times t)$. Then, five convolutional layers with kernel sizes of (3×1) are used to operator in the reshaped features, and PReLU activation function is added along every convolution operator. Next, a convolutional layer with kernel size of (3×1) is used to produce the output feature with format $(n \times c_2 \times t_f)$, where $t_f = 12$ is the expected prediction time steps. Finally, we reshape the output feature into format $(n \times c_2 \times t_f)$ and feed the reshaped feature into a GMM model for predicting future trajectories.

4 Experiments

4.1 Datasets and Metrics

In this section, the proposed method is evaluated on two well-known pedestrian trajectory prediction datasets: namely ETH [12] and UCY [8]. ETH contains two scenes respectively denoted as ETH and HOTEL, while UCY contains three scenes respectively denoted as ZARA1, ZARA2, and UNIV. The samples in both datasets were sampled at 0.4 s over 8 s. For a fair comparison with other methods, the experimental setups of the proposed method followed that of social-LSTM [1]. During training and evaluation, the first 3.2 s (8 frames) were used as the observed history and the remaining 4.8 s (12 frames) were considered as the prediction ground truth.

Two common metrics were used for evaluation, namely the average displacement error (ADE) [13] and final displacement error (FDE) [1]. The ADE measures the average prediction performance along the trajectory, while the FDE considers only the prediction precision at the end points.

4.2   Implementation Details

The PyTorch deep learning framework was used to implement the proposed network. The models were trained with an Nvidia Tesla V100 GPU. The stochastic gradient descent (SGD) algorithm was used as the optimizer. The model was trained for 250 epochs with a batch size of 128. The initial learning rate was set to 0.01 and the decay is set to 0.002 after 150 epochs.

4.3   Comparison with the State-of-the-art Methods

As exhibited in Table 1, the proposed method was compared with other state-of-the-art methods on the ETH and UCY dataset in terms of the ADE/FDE metrics. As can be seen, the proposed AST-GNN method achieved new state-of-the art performance and outperformed all existing state-of-the-art methods in terms of the FDE metric. This improvement is attributable to the added GAT mechanism. Regarding the FDE metric, the proposed method achieved an error of 0.74 with a 20% decrease as compared to the recent state-of-the-art method SR-LSTM-2 [21]. Regarding the ADE metric, the error of the proposed method was slightly greater than that of SR-LSTM-2 by 4%, but it was still one of the best results. More remarkably, the proposed method, which dos not use scene image information, outperformed methods that utilized image information, such as SR-LSTM, PIF and Sophie.

5   Conclusion

In this paper, a novel AST-GNN method was proposed that learns representative, robust, and discriminative graph embedding for pedestrians trajectory prediction. In the proposed method, the GAT mechanism is used to adaptively learn the weighted adjacency matrix, which enhances the graph representation ability. The results of experiments on the ETH and UCY datasets demonstrate that the proposed method outperformed existing pedestrian trajectory prediction methods. In the future, the GAT mechanism will be further used on a temporal graph of a pedestrian trajectory prediction model to enhance the representation ability.

Table 1. Comparison with state-of-the-art methods in term of the ADE/FDE metrics. The best performance for each dataset is highlighted in bold. * indicates non-probabilistic models.

Method	ETH	HOTEL	UNIV	ZARA1	ZARA2	AVG
Linear * [1]	1.33/2.94	0.39/0.72	0.82/1.59	0.62/1.21	0.77/1.48	0.79/1.59
SR-LSTM-2 * [21]	**0.63/1.25**	0.37/0.74	0.51/1.10	0.41/0.90	0.32/0.70	0.45/0.94
S-LSTM [1]	1.09/2.35	0.79/1.76	0.67/1.40	0.47/1.00	0.56/1.17	0.72/1.54
S-GAN-P [4]	0.87/1.62	0.67/1.37	0.76/1.52	0.35/0.68	0.42/0.84	0.61/1.21
Sophie [15]	0.70/1.43	0.76/1.67	0.54/1.24	0.30/0.63	0.38/0.78	0.54/1.15
PIF [10]	0.73/1.65	**0.30/0.59**	0.60/1.27	0.38/0.81	0.31/0.68	0.46/1.00
STSGCN [20]	0.75/1.63	0.63/1.01	0.48/1.08	0.30/0.65	**0.26**/0.57	0.48/0.99
GAT [6]	0.68/1.29	0.68/1.40	0.57/1.29	**0.29**/0.60	0.37/0.75	0.52/1.07
Social-BiGAN [6]	0.69/1.29	0.49/1.01	0.55/1.32	0.30/0.62	0.36/0.75	0.48/1.00
Social-STGCNN [11]	0.75/1.35	0.47/0.84	0.49/0.90	0.39/0.62	0.34/0.52	0.49/0.85
The proposed	0.69/1.27	0.36/0.62	**0.46/0.83**	0.32/**0.53**	0.28/**0.44**	**0.42/0.74**

Acknowledgments. This work is supported partly by the National Natural Science Foundation (NSFC) of China (grants 61973301, 61972020, 61633009, 51579053, 61772373 and U1613213), partly by the National Key R&D Program of China (grants 2016YFC0300801 and 2017YFB1300202), partly by the Field Fund of the 13th Five-Year Plan for Equipment Pre-research Fund (No. 61403120301), partly by Beijing Science and Technology Plan Project, partly by the Key Basic Research Project of Shanghai Science and Technology Innovation Plan (No. 15JC1403300), partly by Beijing Science and Technology Project. (No. Z181100008918018), partly by Beijing Nova Program (No. Z201100006820046), and partly by Meituan Open R&D Fund.

References

1. Alahi, A., Goel, K., Ramanathan, V., Robicquet, A., Li, F., Savarese, S.: Social LSTM: human trajectory prediction in crowded spaces. In: The IEEE Conference on Computer Vision and Pattern Recognition (CVPR), June 2016
2. Cui, H., et al.: Multimodal trajectory predictions for autonomous driving using deep convolutional networks. In: 2019 International Conference on Robotics and Automation (ICRA), pp. 2090–2096, May 2019
3. Gao, J., et al.: VectorNet: encoding HD maps and agent dynamics from vectorized representation. ArXiv abs/2005.04259 (2020)
4. Gupta, A., Johnson, J., Fei-Fei, L., Savarese, S., Alahi, A.: Social GAN: socially acceptable trajectories with generative adversarial networks. In: 2018 IEEE/CVF Conference on Computer Vision and Pattern Recognition, pp. 2255–2264, June 2018
5. Huang, Y., Bi, H., Li, Z., Mao, T., Wang, Z.: STGAT: modeling spatial-temporal interactions for human trajectory prediction. In: The IEEE International Conference on Computer Vision (ICCV), October 2019
6. Kosaraju, V., Sadeghian, A., Mart ın-Mart ın, R., Reid, I., Rezatofighi, H., Savarese, S.: Social-BiGAT: multimodal trajectory forecasting using bicycle-GAN and graph attention networks. In: Advances in Neural Information Processing Systems, vol. 32, pp. 137–146 (2019)

7. Lefevre, S., Laugier, C., Ibanezguzman, J.: Exploiting map information for driver intention estimation at road intersections. In: 2011 IEEE Intelligent Vehicles Symposium (IV), pp. 583–588, June 2011
8. Lerner, A., Chrysanthou, Y., Lischinski, D.: Crowds by example. Comput. Graph. Forum 26(3), 655–664 (2007)
9. Li, X., Ying, X., Chuah, M.C.: GRIP: graph-based interaction-aware trajectory prediction. In: 2019 IEEE Intelligent Transportation Systems Conference (ITSC), pp. 3960–3966 (2019)
10. Liang, J., Jiang, L., Niebles, J.C., Hauptmann, A.G., Fei-Fei, L.: Peeking into the future: predicting future person activities and locations in videos. In: 2019IEEE/CVF Conference on Computer Vision and Pattern Recognition (CVPR), pp. 5718–5727, June 2019
11. Mohamed, A., Qian, K., Elhoseiny, M., Claudel, C.: Social-STGCNN: a social spatio-temporal graph convolutional neural network for human trajectory prediction. arXiv e-prints arXiv:2002.11927 (2020)
12. Pellegrini, S., Ess, A., Schindler, K., van Gool, L.: You'll never walk alone: modeling social behavior for multi-target tracking. In: 2009 IEEE 12th International Conference on Computer Vision, pp. 261–268, September 2009
13. Pellegrini, S., Ess, A., Van Gool, L.: Improving data association by joint modeling of pedestrian trajectories and groupings. In: Daniilidis, K., Maragos, P., Paragios, N. (eds.) ECCV 2010. LNCS, vol. 6311, pp. 452–465. Springer, Heidelberg (2010). https://doi.org/10.1007/978-3-642-15549-9_33
14. Rasmussen, C.E., Williams, C.K.I.: Gaussian Processes for Machine earning (Adaptive Computation and Machine Learning). The MIT Press, Cambridge (2005)
15. Sadeghian, A., Kosaraju, V., Sadeghian, A., Hirose, N., Rezatofighi, H., Savarese, S.: SoPhie: an attentive GAN for predicting paths compliant to social and physical constraints. In: 2019 IEEE/CVF Conference on Computer Vision and Pattern Recognition (CVPR) (2019)
16. Toledo-Moreo, R., Zamora-Izquierdo, M.A.: Imm-based lane-change prediction in highways with low-cost gps/ins. IEEE Trans. Intell. Transp. Syst. 10(1), 180–185 (2009)
17. Velickovic, P., Cucurull, G., Casanova, A., Romero, A., Li, P., Bengio, Y.: Graph attention networks. In: International Conference on Learning Representations (2018)
18. Xu, K., Hu, W., Leskovec, J., Jegelka, S.: How powerful are graph neural networks? In: International Conference on Learning Representations (2019)
19. Xu, Y., Piao, Z., Gao, S.: Encoding crowd interaction with deep neural network for pedestrian trajectory prediction. In: The IEEE Conference on Computer Vision and Pattern Recognition (CVPR), June 2018
20. Zhang, L., She, Q., Guo, P.: Stochastic trajectory prediction with social graph network. arXiv preprint arXiv:1907.10233 (2019)
21. Zhang, P., Ouyang, W., Zhang, P., Xue, J., Zheng, N.: SR-LSTM: state refinement for LSTM towards pedestrian trajectory prediction. In: The IEEE Conference on Computer Vision and Pattern Recognition (CVPR), June 2019

An EEG Majority Vote Based BCI Classification System for Discrimination of Hand Motor Attempts in Stroke Patients

Xiaotong Gu and Zehong Cao[✉]

University of Tasmania, Hobart, TAS 7005, Australia
{xiaotong.gu,zehong.cao}@utas.edu.au

Abstract. Stroke patients have symptoms of cerebral functional disturbance that could aggressively impair patient's physical mobility, such as hand impairments. Although rehabilitation training from external devices is beneficial for hand movement recovery, for initiating motor function restoration purposes, there are still valuable research merits for identifying the side of hands in motion. In this preliminary study, we used an electroencephalogram (EEG) dataset from 8 stroke patients, with each subject conducting 40 EEG trials of left motor attempts and 40 EEG trials of right motor attempts. Then, we proposed a majority vote based EEG classification system for identifying the side in motion. In specific, we extracted 1–50 Hz power spectral features as input for a series of well-known classification models. The predicted labels from these classification models were compared and a majority vote based method was applied, which determined the finalised predicted label. Our experiment results showed that our proposed EEG classification system achieved $99.83 \pm 0.42\%$ accuracy, $99.98 \pm 0.13\%$ precision, $99.66 \pm 0.84\%$ recall, and $99.83 \pm 0.43\%$ f-score, which outperformed the performance of single well-known classification models. Our findings suggest that the superior performance of our proposed majority vote based EEG classification system has the potential for stroke patients' hand rehabilitation.

Keywords: Stroke rehabilitation · Hand motor attempts · EEG · Classification

1 Introduction

Stroke is the second most common cause of death worldwide and the third most common cause of disability. During the first year after a stroke occurs, a third of stroke patients have deficient or nonexistent hand function, and rare cases showed significant functional movement recovery in the following years [1]. Unfortunately, since impairments are often resistant to therapeutic intervention, even after extensive conventional therapies, the probability of regaining functions for the impaired hand is still low [2].

© Springer Nature Switzerland AG 2020
H. Yang et al. (Eds.): ICONIP 2020, CCIS 1333, pp. 46–53, 2020.
https://doi.org/10.1007/978-3-030-63823-8_6

A substantial amount of recent studies focusing on applying motor imagery (MI), the mental procedure of imagining body movements without physical actions [3], to post-stroke hand function restoration. Reviews of MI studies for post-stroke rehabilitation shows that MI may have value for patients recovering from stroke [4]. There are also researches in which MI is used for stroke patients to control robotic exoskeleton for hand rehabilitation [5]. When utilising MI for hand rehabilitation for stroke patients compared with healthy subjects, cautions must be taken related to the side of the affected hand [6]. Applying hand-in-motion classification to stroke patients' hand movements, cooperating with MI technique, could have better outcomes for rehabilitation.

Compared with traditional clinical brain signal measurement technology, the recently fast-growing non-invasive brain-computer interface (BCI) brain signal monitoring devices are more accessible and effective for daily post-stroke rehabilitation in the home environment to practice for hand function restoration [7]. Here, we consider the Electroencephalogram (EEG)-based BCI [8], one of the non-invasive neuro-feedback mechanisms, to detect hand movement with EEG devices and assist stroke patients during the rehabilitation stage. Currently, the EEG-based BCI studies have become a key approach for devising modern neuro-rehabilitation techniques [9], and demonstrated promising feasibility for assisting in multiple healthcare domains [10]. Abnormal EEG complexity of the brain, measured by entropy [11], found in patients with acute stroke, showed an increased mean entropy value [12]. Thus, we believe that the EEG-based BCI could be broadly used for hand movement detection and stroke rehabilitation clinically and in the home environment.

In this study, we explored a hand movement experiment and investigated the discrimination of hand motor attempts in stroke patients, by processing EEG signals collected from 8 stroke patients with impaired hand functions. The main contributions of our proposed majority vote based EEG classification system comprise the following three parts:

- The first study explored hand movement experiment of EEG signal for hand in motion attempts classification.
- The proposed majority vote based classification model achieved a comparatively high performance, which outperformed the performance of single well-known classification models.
- The proposed post-stroke hand-in-motion classification system is beneficial to be used in combined with MI technique for stroke patients' hand rehabilitation in future research and practice.

2   Materials and Method

2.1   Participant and EEG Data Recording

In this study, we used an EEG brain signal dataset[1] of 8 hemiparetic stroke patients who have impaired functionality with either by the left or right hand.

---

[1] Link: https://github.com/5anirban9.

This dataset also included hand trials from another two participants, the 'ground truth' labels, and some motion trails data of which were withheld for the WCCI 2020 competition. We do not have any affiliation to the competition and the data from these two participants were not included in our cross-subject classification task.

The EEG data were firstly collected when the subjects were requested to conduct unilateral motor attempts, and then the EEG signals were labelled as "left" or "right" indicating the side of subjects' motor attempts. Each participant conducted an equal number of left motor attempts as right motor attempts, as 40 left-hand trials and 40 right-hand trials. Each trial lasts for 8 s, with a sampling rate of 512 Hz. Each participant's data are divided into 80% training data and 20% testing data, as 32 (40 × 80%) left-hand trials and 32 (40 × 80%) right-hand trials were used for training and remaining 8 (40 × 20%) left-hand trials and 8 (40 × 20%) right-hand trials were used for testing. This is categorised as the cross-subject case.

The raw EEG data were transferred into power spectra, which were used for examining if significant differences of EEG power spectra between the left and right motor attempts exist. The EEG power features are the input for training classifiers. Figure 1 illustrates the procedure of the experiment, the analytical process of EEG data, and the applied classification models. The EEG signals of the motor attempts were recorded simultaneously from 12 channels (F3, FC3, C3, CP3, P3, FCz, CPz, F4, FC4, C4, CP4, and P4) according to the 10–20 international system as shown in Fig. 1-a.

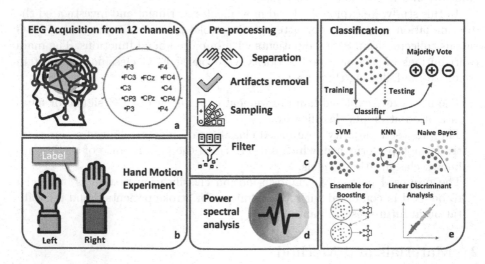

Fig. 1. Experiment and data analysis

2.2 EEG Data Analysis

All EEG data files were processed and analysed with EEGLAB in MATLAB software (The Mathworks, Inc.). EEGLAB is an extensible MATLAB toolbox for processing EEG and other electrophysiological signal data[2] that offers inter-active plotting functions, time/frequency transforms, artifact removal, and other extensions for EEG processing.

EEG Data Pre-processing. The raw EEG data files we processed are firstly labelled for each trial as number "1" representing "right motor attempt" or number "2" representing "left motor attempt" as shown in Fig. 1-b. Then, as shown in Fig. 1-c, the raw EEG data were separated as left or right motion data based on the labels and filtered through 1 Hz high-pass and 50 Hz low-pass finite impulse response filters as the recording sample rate is 512 Hz. The filtered data were then checked for any artifacts that need to be removed before being processed. Since no artifacts of visible muscle, eye-blink or other visible electromyography activity were detected, we proceeded processing on the filtered data. EEG sig-nals have weak time-frequency-spatial characteristics, non-stationary, non-linear, and weak intensity, so to extract adaptive features reflecting frequency and spa-tial characteristics, it is critical to adopt feature extraction methods [13]. For this study, we converted the time-domain EEG data into the frequency domain and extracted power spectral features for left and right side motor attempts, as shown in Fig. 1-d. We used the 256-point Fast Fourier Transforms (FFTs) win-dow, which was set at 256-point data length, and in each window, the segment was converted into frequency domain respectively.

Statistical Analysis. Before designing and applying classification models, since the EEG power spectra of each individual and cross-subjects are sufficient to con-duct statistical analysis to determine if there is a significant difference between left and right motor attempts, we applied paired t-test to each frequency and channel of single-subject EEG power to determine the mean difference between the two sides. The *p-value* of the paired t-test sets under 0.05, indicating the significant difference level of the left and right motor attempts of the stroke subjects.

3 Classification Models

Since EEG power has been labelled for each trial, we used supervised machine learning-based classification approaches, where one training sample has one class label, to train the motor attempt classifiers. With the cross-validation measure-ment, we set the three folds to randomly select two portions from each side motion features as the training set and the third portion from each side motion features as the testing set for the classifiers. The two training sets from left

---

[2] https://sccn.ucsd.edu/eeglab/index.php.

motions and the two training sets from the right motions were combined as the training sets for each classifier. The testing set from left motions and the testing set from the right motions were combined as the testing set to be applied to each classifier. The training data labels were attached to the determining feature sets and then applied to the train classifiers, as shown in Fig. 1-e.

In this study, we used five well-known classification methods as classifiers which are Support Vector Machine (SVM), k-nearest neighbours (KNN), Naive Bayes, Ensembles for Boosting, and Discriminant Analysis Classifier. Each side's training sets of extracted power spectral features were provided to each classifier for training. The performance of each classifier was evaluated by applying the testing set to the trained classifiers to obtain the accuracy results. We also employed precision, recall, and F-score performance metrics to assess the performance of each classifier.

Based on the results from the five classification models, we proposed a majority vote based classifier ensemble mechanism to improve the classification model. As shown in Table 1, a single If-Then rule that if x is A then y is B is applied as an assumption in the form. The top three accurate classifiers are ranked as 1st, 2nd, and 3rd. If the classifier with the highest accuracy rate states positive, then the majority vote-based label is positive, while in all other cases, the majority vote-based label is negative.

Table 1. A majority vote-based classifier

Predicted labels	Classifier	Classifier	Classifier	Vote-based labels
Ranking-Accuracy	1st	2nd	3rd	
	IF			THEN
Vote 1	Positive	Positive	Positive	
Vote 2	Positive	Positive	Negative	Positive
Vote 3	Positive	Negative	Positive	
Vote 4	Other cases			Negative

4   Results

For this study, we present two groups of findings which are the feature-based results of the EEG power spectra and the label classification performances of the five classifiers plus a majority vote-based classifier trained by the training sets and evaluated by the testing sets of 8 stroke patients. The results of this study are presented from two perspectives as power spectral feature-based and classifier-based.

We calculated the mean value of the significant difference of power spectra for each frequency and channel between left and right motor attempts in four frequency bands waves (delta, theta, alpha, and beta). For each of the 12 channels, the power spectra escalate rapidly and reach a peak at the frequency around 5 to 10 Hz, and maintained comparatively steady until surge to the highest power spectra level at 50 Hz. For 10 out of 12 channels (expect FC4 and P4), when the signal frequency is between approximately 10 to 40 Hz, the power spectra of left motor attempts and right motor attempts have the most significant differences ($p < 0.05$).

We separated and plotted the power spectra of left and right motor attempts to inspect if there are significant differences of EEG signals for left and right-hand motions. The tendency of power spectra mean value for the four frequency bands waves (delta, theta, alpha, and beta) of the 12 channels are shown in Fig. 2. For left and right motor attempts, on average, the most significant differences ($p < 0.05$) of power spectra mean value appear close to channel C4 in delta frequency range (3 Hz or lower), channel P3 in theta range (3.5 to 7.5 Hz), channel CPz in alpha range (7.5 to 13 Hz), and channel F4 in beta range (14 Hz to greater). The significant differences of the four frequency bands waves are demonstrated on brain scale map plotted with the 12 channel locations in Fig. 2, and the calculation is as follow, where P_Δ representing the significant difference (p < 0.05) of power spectra between left and right motion, movement of the left and right hands, P_R stands for power spectra of right motion, and P_L stands for power spectra of left motion. This finding verifies the conclusion in [14] that stroke patients present asymmetry in spectral power between hemispheres related to upper extremity motor function deficit.

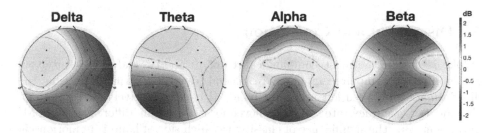

Fig. 2. Brain scale map plot of significant difference of power spectra between left and right motor attempts

The classifier results are demonstrated in Table 2 with the five well-known classifiers we used in this study for sub-results and the performance of a majority vote-based classifier we proposed as the improved results. Among the five trained existing classifiers, SVM performs the best in accuracy, precision, and F-score, while Linear Discriminant Analysis ranks the first for recall. Ensemble for Boosting classifier comes to third in accuracy, precision, and F-score, while KNN classifier ranks the third. Compared to the four top-ranking classifiers with performance above 98% in all categories, Naive Bayes ranks the lowest at approximately 80% for all four performance indicators. By employing a majority vote-based classifier we proposed in this study, we generally improved the proposed system's accuracy rate and the three performance metrics. Because the performance of most trained classifiers has an exceedingly high rate, for instance, SVM obtains $99.80 \pm 0.46\%$ in accuracy and $99.97 \pm 0.16\%$ in precision, the improvement rates of our proposed majority vote-based classifier are comparatively subtle. The experiment results show that our proposed majority vote-based EEG classification system can achieve $99.83 \pm 0.42\%$ accuracy, $99.98 \pm 0.13\%$ precision, $99.66 \pm 0.84\%$ recall, and $99.83 \pm 0.43\%$ f-score, and outperform the performance of single existing classification model.

$$P_\Delta(p < 0.05) = P_R - P_L$$

Table 2. Classification performance (left vs. right motor attempts)

Classifier (%)	Accuracy	Precision	Recall	F-score
SVM	99.80 ± 0.46	99.97 ± 0.16	99.64 ± 0.88	99.81 ± 0.46
KNN	98.33 ± 0.95	98.41 ± 1.37	98.28 ± 1.44	98.33 ± 0.95
Naive bayes	79.52 ± 2.95	78.55 ± 4.50	80.23 ± 3.53	79.30 ± 3.07
Ensemble for boosting	98.40 ± 1.06	98.75 ± 1.28	98.07 ± 1.51	98.40 ± 1.05
Linear discriminant analysis	99.73 ± 0.48	99.75 ± 0.53	99.72 ± 0.79	99.73 ± 0.48
A majority vote-based classifier	99.83 ± 0.42	99.98 ± 0.13	99.66 ± 0.84	99.83 ± 0.43

5   Discussion and Conclusion

Stroke is one of the most common causes of disability, and stroke survivors commonly suffer impaired mobility. In general, due to brain lateralisation, the discrimination between left and right hand MI is comparatively subtle, so high classification accuracy rate can be achieved for categorising different sides of MI movement. But the significance of classifying which side of hand is in motion via EEG signal processing can not be neglected for stroke rehabilitation.

In summary, in this study, we proposed a majority vote-based EEG classification system for categorising hand motor attempts in stroke patients. The experiment results show that our proposed majority vote-based EEG classification system exceeds the performance of many single classification models for left and right motor attempts classification, with an accuracy rate of 99.83%, precision rate of 99.98%, recall rate at 99.66%, and F-score rate at 99.83%. The results of this proposed classification system indicate its feasibility in facilitating further EEG-based BCI systems for stroke rehabilitation, and the possibly promising outcome for cooperating EEG-based BCI hand-in-motion classification model with MI for post-stroke rehabilitation.

References

1. Buch, E., et al.: Think to move: a neuromagnetic brain-computer interface (BCI) system for chronic stroke. Stroke **39**(3), 910–917 (2008)
2. Yue, Z., Zhang, X., Wang, J.: Hand rehabilitation robotics on poststroke motor recovery. Behav. Neurol. **2017**, 20 (2017). Article ID 3908135
3. Scott, M., Taylor, S., Chesterton, P., Vogt, S., Eaves, D.L.: Motor imagery during action observation increases eccentric hamstring force: an acute non-physical intervention. Disabil. Rehabil. **40**(12), 1443–1451 (2018)
4. Guerra, Z.F., Lucchetti, A.L., Lucchetti, G.: Motor imagery training after stroke: a systematic review and meta-analysis of randomized controlled trials. J. Neurol. Phys. Ther. **41**(4), 205–214 (2017)
5. Ferguson, P.W., Dimapasoc, B., Shen, Y., Rosen, J.: Design of a hand exoskeleton for use with upper limb exoskeletons. In: Carrozza, M.C., Micera, S., Pons, J.L. (eds.) WeRob 2018. BB, vol. 22, pp. 276–280. Springer, Cham (2019). https://doi.org/10.1007/978-3-030-01887-0_53
6. Kemlin, C., Moulton, E., Samson, Y., Rosso, C.: Do motor imagery performances depend on the side of the lesion at the acute stage of stroke? Front. Hum. Neurosci. **10**, 321 (2016)
7. Trujillo, P., et al.: Quantitative EEG for predicting upper limb motor recovery in chronic stroke robot-assisted rehabilitation. IEEE Trans. Neural Syst. Rehabil. Eng. **25**(7), 1058–1067 (2017)
8. Gu, X., et al.: EEG-based brain-computer interfaces (BCIs): a survey of recent studies on signal sensing technologies and computational intelligence approaches and their applications. arXiv preprint arXiv:2001.11337 (2020)
9. Cao, Z., Lin, C.T., Ding, W., Chen, M.H., Li, C.T., Su, T.P.: Identifying ketamine responses in treatment-resistant depression using a wearable forehead EEG. IEEE Trans. Biomed. Eng. **66**(6), 1668–1679 (2018)
10. Cao, Z., et al.: Extraction of SSVEPs-based inherent fuzzy entropy using a wearable headband EEG in migraine patients. IEEE Trans. Fuzzy Syst. **28**(1), 14–27 (2019)
11. Cao, Z., Ding, W., Wang, Y.K., Hussain, F.K., Al-Jumaily, A., Lin, C.T.: Effects of repetitive SSVEPs on EEG complexity using multiscale inherent fuzzy entropy. Neurocomputing **389**, 198–206 (2020)
12. Liu, S., et al.: Abnormal EEG complexity and functional connectivity of brain in patients with acute thalamic ischemic stroke. Comput. Math. Methods Med. **2016**, 9 (2016). Article ID 2582478
13. Kim, C., Sun, J., Liu, D., Wang, Q., Paek, S.: An effective feature extraction method by power spectral density of EEG signal for 2-class motor imagery-based BCI. Med. Biol. Eng. Comput. **56**(9), 1645–1658 (2017). https://doi.org/10.1007/s11517-017-1761-4
14. Saes, M., Meskers, C.G.M., Daffertshofer, A., de Munck, J.C., Kwakkel, G., van Wegen, E.E.H.: How does upper extremity Fugl-Meyer motor score relate to resting-state EEG in chronic stroke? A power spectral density analysis. Clin. Neurophysiol. **130**(5), 856–862 (2019)

An Evoked Potential-Guided Deep Learning Brain Representation for Visual Classification

Xianglin Zheng, Zehong Cao$^{(\boxtimes)}$, and Quan Bai

Discipline of ICT, University of Tasmania, Hobart, TAS 7001, Australia
{xianglin.zheng,zehong.cao,quan.bai}@utas.edu.au

Abstract. The new perspective in visual classification aims to decode the feature representation of visual objects from human brain activities. Recording electroencephalogram (EEG) from the brain cortex has been seen as a prevalent approach to understand the cognition process of an image classification task. In this study, we proposed a deep learning framework guided by the visual evoked potentials, called the Event-Related Potential (ERP)-Long short-term memory (LSTM) framework, extracted by EEG signals for visual classification. In specific, we first extracted the ERP sequences from multiple EEG channels to response image stimuli-related information. Then, we trained an LSTM network to learn the feature representation space of visual objects for classification. In the experiment, 10 subjects were recorded by over 50,000 EEG trials from an image dataset with 6 categories, including a total of 72 exemplars. Our results showed that our proposed ERP-LSTM framework could achieve classification accuracies of cross-subject of 66.81% and 27.08% for categories (6 classes) and exemplars (72 classes), respectively. Our results outperformed that of using the existing visual classification frameworks, by improving classification accuracies in the range of 12.62%–53.99%. Our findings suggested that decoding visual evoked potentials from EEG signals is an effective strategy to learn discriminative brain representations for visual classification.

Keywords: Visual classification · EEG · ERP · LSTM network

1 Introduction

Visual classification is a computer vision task that inputs an image and outputs a prediction of the category of the object image. It has become one of the core research directions of object detection and been developed rapidly with the discovery of Convolutional Neural Networks (CNN) in the last decades. CNN has been seen as a powerful network which is loosely inspired by human's visual architecture, however, some researchers are cognizant that there are still significant differences in the way that human and current CNN process visual information [4]. Particularly, the performance of recognition of negative images [8]

© Springer Nature Switzerland AG 2020
H. Yang et al. (Eds.): ICONIP 2020, CCIS 1333, pp. 54–61, 2020.
https://doi.org/10.1007/978-3-030-63823-8_7

and generalisation towards previously unseen distortions [4] have further shown the robustness of CNNs on object recognition are not at the human level.

For human beings, object recognition seems to be accomplished effortlessly in everyday life, because the advantage of visual exteroceptive sense is distinct. For example, someone usually directly looks at the objects they want to recognise to make full use of the foveal vision. It has always been a challenging issue in cognitive neuroscience to figure out the mechanisms that human employed for the visual object categorisation [12]. Researchers have investigated that the brain exhibits functions of feature extraction, shape description, and memory matching, when the human brain is involving visual cognitive processes [3]. Subsequent studies [6,15] have further revealed that analysing brain activity recordings, linkage with the operating human visual system, is possible to help us understand the presentational patterns of visual objects in the cortex of the brain. Inspired from the above visual neuroscience investigations, some recent work considered to process visual classification problems by analysing neurophysiology and neuroimaging signals recorded from human visual cognitive processes [1,7,9,10,16]. However, they are still limited to analyse the brain visual activities by using the raw physiological signals without extracting a more representative input during the signal preprocessing stage.

In addition, many existing visual classification studies have been focusing on electroencephalography (EEG)-based visual object discriminations as we explored above. EEG signals, featuring by a high temporal resolution in comparison with other neuroimaging, are generally recorded by electrodes on the surface of the scalp, which has been applied in developing several areas of brain-computer interface (BCI) classification systems [5], such as pictures, music, and speech recognitions [2]. However, the raw waveforms of EEG signals are the recorded spontaneous potential of the human brain in a natural state, which is difficult to distinguish the hidden event-related information during the visual cognitive process [3,11]. Thus, the event-related potential (ERP) was proposed to identify the real-time evoked response waveforms caused by stimuli events (e.g., specific vision and motion activities), which usually performed lower values than the spontaneous EEG amplitude [3] and extracted from the EEG fragments with averaged superposition in multiple visual trials.

2 Related Work

Decoding image object-related EEG signals for visual classification has been a long-sought objective. For example, the early-stage studies in [13,14] attempted to classify single-trial EEG responses to photographs of faces and cars. An image classification task [9] in 2015 considered a comprehensive linear classifier to tackle EEG brain signals evoked by 6 different object categories, and achieved the classification accuracy around 40%.

Afterwards, investigating the intersection between deep learning and decoding human visual cognitive feature spaces has increased significantly. In 2017, Sampinato et al. [16] proposed an automated visual classification framework to compute EEG features with Recurrent Neural Networks (RNN) and trained a CNN-based regressor to project images onto the learned EEG features. However, the recent two studies in 2018 and 2020 [1,10] brought force questions to Spampinato's block design [16] employed in the EEG data acquisition, where all stimulus of a specific class are presented together without randomly intermixed. In particular, the latest study in 2020 [1] replicated the Spampinato's experiment [16] with a rapid-event design and analysed the classification performance on the randomised EEG trials. In addition, we noted that a special structure recurrent neural network, Long Short-Term Memory (LSTM) network, is commonly used in these studies to learn the representations of brain signals, which have shown the feasibility to decode human visual activities and deep learning for visual classification.

However, most of current machine learning approaches for visual classification ignored to explore the EEG evoked potentials of spontaneous generation. Even now deep learning is still difficult to recognise distinctive patterns of evoked potentials from the raw waveforms of EEG signals with a visual stimulus, so we assume that excluding visual related evoked potentials could be a fundamental cause that leads to an uncertain feature representation space for visual classification and place a restriction on the improvement of classification accuracy.

Thus, in this study, our work was inspired from two assumptions: (1) the feature representations employed by human brains for visual classification will be more pronounced learned from the purer ERP which conveys image stimuli-related information; (2) the multi-dimensional ERPs can be decoded to obtain a one-dimensional representation using RNN and do not require pre-selection of spatial or temporal components. One special type of RNNs, the LSTM, presents the strong capability in recognising long-term and short-term feature representations from time-series EEG signals.

With the above two assumptions, in this study, we proposed the first visual evoked potential-guided deep learning framework, called ERP-LSTM framework, to learn the discriminative representations for visual classification. The ERP-LSTM framework is constituted by two stages: (1) acquiring the ERP waveforms from multiple EEG trials with averaged superposition; (2) a parallel LSTM network mapping the extracted ERPs into feature representation vectors and involving an activation layer that classifies the derived vectors into different classes.

3   Our Proposed Framework

The overview of our proposed ERP-LSTM framework is shown in Fig. 1, which is separated into two stages for visual classification. In Stage 1, we employed raw EEG signals recorded from the visual experiment and then extracted ERPs from the raw EEG data to secure the visual stimuli-related signals. In Stage 2, we trained an LSTM network to learn the representation space of the ERP sequences and followed a Softmax classification trained to discriminate the different classes of the images.

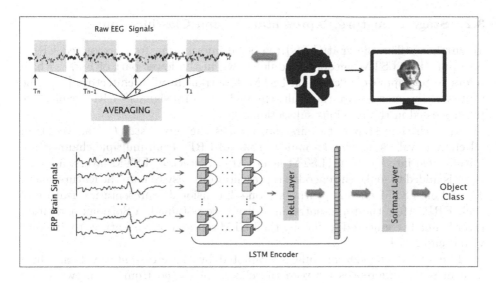

Fig. 1. The overview of the ERP-LSTM framework

3.1 Stage 1: ERPs Extractions from EEG

The representative features of EEG signals play an essential role in classifying image object categories. The first stage of our proposed framework aims to extract representative visual-related features of ERPs by increasing the signal-noise ratio (SNR) of the raw EEG signals with smooth-averaging measurement. A number of EEG segments with the same trials are averaged out to a fused waveform. In specific, during the averaging process, the consistent features of the segments (the ERPs) are retained, while features that vary across segments are attenuated (refer to the upper left corner of Fig. 1).

More formally, let $d_i^j = \left\{ T_1^j, T_2^j, \ldots, T_n^j \right\}$, $i \times n = N$, d_i^j is the i_{th} subset of the multi-channel temporal EEG signals, when one subject is viewing the j_{th} exemplar image. N is the number of EEG trials to be averaged, which contains n of EEG trials, where trial $T_n^j \in \mathbb{R}^c$ (c is the number of channels).

The averaging process is described by the following fomula:

$$e_i^j = \left(\sum T_n^j \right) / n, \quad T_n^j \in d_i^j \tag{1}$$

where e_i^j is the ERP sequence averaged from d_i^j.

Let E be the sum of extracted multi-channel ERPs, $E = \left\{ e_1^j, e_2^j, \ldots, e_i^j \right\}$, which will be the inputs of the LSTM encoder module we addressed in the next subsection to learn discriminative feature representations for visual classification.

3.2   Stage 2: Feature Representations and Classification

To further utilise the spatial and temporal information from extracted ERPs, we applied an LSTM encoder module shown in the lower part of Fig. 1, which refers to Spampinato's "common LSTM + output layer" architecture [16]. The inputs of the encoder are the multi-channel temporal signals - ERPs, which are preprocessed in the previous subsection.

At each time step t, the first layer takes the input $s(\Delta, t)$ (the vector of all channel values at time t), namely that all ERPs from multiple channels are initially fed into the same LSTM layer. After a stack of LSTM layers, a ReLU layer is added to make the encoded representations easy to map the feature space. The whole LSTM encoder outputs a one-dimensional representation feature of each ERP. After the representation vectors are obtained, a Softmax activation layer is finally connected to classify the LSTM representative features to different visual categories.

The LSTM encoder module is evaluated by the cross-entropy loss, which measures the differences between the classes predicted from the network and the ground-truth class labels. The total loss is propagated back into the neural network to update the whole model's parameters through gradient descent optimisation.

In the proposed ERP-LSTM framework, the LSTM encoder module is used for generating feature representations from ERP sequences, followed by a Softmax classification layer to predict the visual classes.

4   The Experiment

4.1   The Dataset

In this study, we evaluated our model on the dataset proposed in [9]. There are 51840 trials of EEG signal that were collected from 10 subjects viewed 72 images, where each subject completed 72 trials of each of the 72 images and conducted a total of 5,184 trials per subject. The 72 images belong to 6 different categories of images, which are Human Body, Human Face, Animal Body, Animal Face, Fruit Vegetable, and Inanimate Object. In this study, each of the trials was labelled to map the description of the visual evoked-related events, namely the corresponding image category or the image exemplar number. Note that, we excluded the associated dataset proposed in [16] because of the block design problem in EEG data acquisition as mentioned in Sect. 2.

4.2   Settings

In this study, we randomly segmented the 72 EEG trials into 6 sets, and each set contains 12 EEG trials. The trials in each set are averaged to extract an ERP sequence with the same image and category label. Then, we obtained 6 ERP sequences of each image and also achieved E, the ERP space of the overall extracted 124-channel ERP sequences. Of note, the ERP space E is split into the training set and the testing set with a proportion of 5:1, indicating that 80% ERP sequences for each image keep in the training set and the remaining 20% sequences are on the testing set. To further evaluate the performance of the classification framework, we performed two types of data classification: cross-subject and within-subject basis.

5 Results

5.1 Performance of Six-Category Visual Classification

As shown in Table 1, we presented the classification performance of the basic LSTM using raw EEG (EEG-LSTM) [16] and our proposed ERP-LSTM frameworks. It also illustrated the two types (cross-subject and within-subject) of classification performance. Our findings showed that our proposed ERP-LSTM framework could reach about 66.81% accuracy for cross-subject type of visual classification and achieve the highest classification accuracy of 89.06% for a single subject (subject 1). Both outcomes were outperformed that of EEG-LSTM framework, where the classification accuracy improved 30.09% across 10 subjects, 53.99% for subject 1, and 23.46% for averaged within-subject from 1 to 10.

Our findings suggested that the representation feature space encoded from the extracted ERPs is more discriminative to classify image objects compared to that of the raw EEG. Also, we suppose that the critical information for object cognition of the brain signals did not miss during the averaging process. On the contrary, the extracted ERPs have retained the spatial and temporal feature that is related to the visual evoked potentials.

Table 1. Performance of six-category visual classification

Accuracy	EEG-LSTM [16]	ERP-LSTM (our)	Improvement
Cross-subject	36.72%	66.81%	**30.09%**
Within-subject			
Subject 1	35.07%	89.06%	**53.99%**
Subject 2	35.30%	60.94%	**25.64%**
Subject 3	45.25%	71.88%	**26.63%**
Subject 4	35.88%	50.00%	**14.12%**
Subject 5	48.03%	65.62%	**17.59%**
Subject 6	47.80%	75.00%	**27.20%**
Subject 7	40.74%	62.50%	**21.76%**
Subject 8	31.37%	45.31%	**13.94%**
Subject 9	39.12%	60.94%	**21.82%**
Subject 10	47.45%	59.38%	**11.93%**

5.2 Performance of Exemplar-Level Visual Classification

Here, we further analysed the existing frameworks and our proposed ERP-LSTM framework at the exemplar image level. It removed the categories as the classification labels, and instead, it aims to identify a specific image as an exemplar. As shown in Table 2, we presented the existing two frameworks, Kaneshiro [9] and EEG-LSTM [16], to identify the exemplars with 72 classes across all 10 subjects. The findings showed that our proposed ERP-LSTM framework still could achieve the classification accuracy of 27.08% at the exemplar level, which outperformed 14.46% for Kaneshiro and 7.97% for EEG-LSTM. We also attached the results of six-category level classification to get insights into the difference between easy (category) and hard (exemplar) modes.

Table 2. Performance of category- and exemplar-level visual classification

Accuracy	Kaneshiro [14]	EEG-LSTM [16]	ERP-LSTM (our)
Categories (6 classes)	40.68%	36.72%	**66.81%**
Exemplars (72 classes)	14.46%	7.97%	**27.08%**

Thus, relative to the existing model, our work denoted that the representation feature decoded from the extracted ERPs is less confusion than raw EEG signals, which benefits to learn a more discriminative feature space for visual classification. Furthermore, our ERP-LSTM framework also achieved better performance than a recent work in 2020 [1] (in which the reported classification accuracy on 6 categories is 17.1%), even if we used the different data source. This suggested that the LSTM network is capable to encode the ERPs to obtain a representative feature space, as the advantages of LSTM network on tackling temporal dynamics of time-series EEG signals.

6 Conclusion

In this paper, we proposed an evoked potential-guided deep learning framework, called ERP-LSTM framework, for visual classification, which is separated into two stages: (1) extracting ERP sequences from multi-trial EEG segments; (2) a parallel LSTM network to encode a representation feature space for object categorisation as well as to classify EEG signal representations. Our proposed ERP-LSTM framework achieved better performance compared to existing frameworks both on the classification of 6 categories and 72 exemplar images. We believe our findings are presenting the feasibility to learn representational patterns of visual objects based on the recording of brain cortex activities, and an ERP-LSTM framework could learn characteristic features for visual classification.

References

1. Ahmed, H., Wilbur, R.B., Bharadwaj, H.M., Siskind, J.M.: Object classification from randomized EEG trials. arXiv preprint arXiv:2004.06046 (2020)
2. Bashivan, P., Rish, I., Yeasin, M., Codella, N.: Learning representations from EEG with deep recurrent-convolutional neural networks. arXiv preprint arXiv:1511.06448 (2015)
3. Gazzaniga, M., Ivry, R., Mangun, G.: Cognitive Neuroscience: The Biology of the Mind, 3rd ed., Chap. 6 (2008)
4. Geirhos, R., Temme, C.R., Rauber, J., Schütt, H.H., Bethge, M., Wichmann, F.A.: Generalisation in humans and deep neural networks. In: Advances in Neural Information Processing Systems (NIPS), pp. 7538–7550 (2018)
5. Gu, X., et al.: EEG-based brain-computer interfaces (BCIs): a survey of recent studies on signal sensing technologies and computational intelligence approaches and their applications. arXiv preprint arXiv:2001.11337 (2020)
6. Hanson, S.J., Matsuka, T., Haxby, J.V.: Combinatorial codes in ventral temporal lobe for object recognition: haxby (2001) revisited: is there a "face" area? Neuroimage **23**(1), 156–166 (2004)
7. Haynes, J.D., Rees, G.: Decoding mental states from brain activity in humans. Nat. Rev. Neurosci. **7**(7), 523–534 (2006)
8. Hosseini, H., Xiao, B., Jaiswal, M., Poovendran, R.: On the limitation of convolutional neural networks in recognizing negative images. In: 2017 16th IEEE International Conference on Machine Learning and Applications (ICMLA), pp. 352–358. IEEE (2017)
9. Kaneshiro, B., Guimaraes, M.P., Kim, H.S., Norcia, A.M., Suppes, P.: A representational similarity analysis of the dynamics of object processing using single-trial EEG classification. PLoS One **10**(8), e0135697 (2015)
10. Li, R., et al.: Training on the test set? An analysis of Spampinato et al. [31]. arXiv preprint arXiv:1812.07697 (2018)
11. Pascalis, V.D.: Chapter 16 - on the psychophysiology of extraversion. In: Stelmack, R.M. (ed.) On the Psychobiology of Personality, pp. 295–327. Elsevier, Oxford (2004)
12. Peelen, M.V., Downing, P.E.: The neural basis of visual body perception. Nat. Rev. Neurosci. **8**(8), 636–648 (2007)
13. Philiastides, M.G., Ratcliff, R., Sajda, P.: Neural representation of task difficulty and decision making during perceptual categorization: a timing diagram. J. Neurosci. **26**(35), 8965–8975 (2006)
14. Philiastides, M.G., Sajda, P.: Temporal characterization of the neural correlates of perceptual decision making in the human brain. Cereb. Cortex **16**(4), 509–518 (2005)
15. Simanova, I., Van Gerven, M., Oostenveld, R., Hagoort, P.: Identifying object categories from event-related EEG: toward decoding of conceptual representations. PLoS One **5**(12), e14465 (2010)
16. Spampinato, C., Palazzo, S., Kavasidis, I., Giordano, D., Souly, N., Shah, M.: Deep learning human mind for automated visual classification. In: Proceedings of the IEEE Conference on Computer Vision and Pattern Recognition (CVPR), pp. 6809–6817 (2017)

Cluster Aware Deep Dictionary Learning for Single Cell Analysis

Priyadarshini Rai[1], Angshul Majumdar[1(✉)], and Debarka Sengupta[1,2]

[1] Indraprastha Institute of Information Technology, New Delhi 110020, India
{priyadarshinir,angshul,debarka}@iiitd.ac.in
[2] Institute of Health and Biomedical Innovation,
Queensland University of Technology, Brisbane, Australia
https://iiitd.ac.in/

Abstract. The importance of clustering the single-cell RNA sequence is well known. Traditional clustering techniques (GiniClust, Seurat, etc.) have mostly been used to address this problem. This is the first work that develops a deep dictionary learning-based solution for the same. Our work builds on the framework of deep dictionary learning. We make the framework clustering friendly by incorporating a cluster-aware loss (K-means and sparse subspace) into the learning problem. Comparison with tailored clustering techniques for single-cell RNA and with generic deep learning-based clustering techniques shows the promise of our approach.

Keywords: Single cell clustering · Deep dictionary learning · Single cell analysis

1 Introduction

The problem of clustering is well known; there are many reviews (such as [1]) on this topic. The general topic of clustering studies the formation of naturally occurring groups within the data. The simplest (and still the most popular) approach for the same is perhaps K-means [2]. K-means segments the data by relative distances; samples near each other (pre-defined by some distance metric) are assumed to belong to the same cluster. Owing to the linear nature of the distance, the K-means was not able to capture non-linearly occurring groups. This issue was partially addressed by the introduction of kernel K-means [3]. Instead of defining the distance between the samples, a kernel distance was defined (Gaussian, Laplacian, polynomial, etc.) for clustering. Closely related to the kernel K-means is spectral clustering [3]. The later generalizes kernel distances to any affinity measure and applies graph cuts to segment the clusters.

K-means, kernel K-means, and spectral clustering are inter-related. A completely different approach is subspace clustering [4]. In the later, it is assumed that samples belonging to the same group/cluster will lie in the same subspace. There are several variants of subspace clustering, but the most popular one

H. Yang et al. (Eds.): ICONIP 2020, CCIS 1333, pp. 62–69, 2020.
https://doi.org/10.1007/978-3-030-63823-8_8

among them is the sparse subspace clustering (SSC) [5]. In SSC it is assumed that the clusters only occupy a few subspaces (from all possibilities) and hence the epithet "sparse".

So far, we have discussed generic clustering techniques. In the single-cell analysis, cell type identification is important for the downstream analysis. Therefore, clustering forms a crucial step in single-cell RNA expression analysis. Single-cell RNA sequencing (scRNA-seq) measures the transcription level of genes. But, the amount of RNA present in a single cell is very low due to which some genes did not get detect even though they are present and this results in zero-inated data. This data further gets compounded by trivial biological noise such as variability in the cell cycle specic genes. Also, a large number of genes are assayed during an experiment but only a handful of them are used for cell-type identification. This leads to high feature-dimensionality and high feature-redundancy in single-cell data. Applying clustering techniques directly on the high-dimensional data will cause suboptimal partitioning of cells.

This triggers the need for customized techniques. The existing state-of-the-art clustering techniques for single-cell data do not propose new algorithms for clustering per se but apply existing algorithms on extracted/reduced feature sets. One popular technique Seurat [6], instead of applying a distance-based clustering technique on all the genes, selects highly variable genes from which a shared nearest neighbor graph is constructed for segmentation. GiniClust [7] is similar to the former and only differs in the use of the Gini coefficient for measuring differentiating genes. Single-cell consensus clustering (SC3) [8] algorithm uses principal component analysis (PCA) to reduce the dimensions and then applies a cluster-based similarity partitioning algorithm for segmentation.

The success of deep learning is well known in every field today. What is interesting to note is that success has been largely driven by supervised tasks; there are only a handful of fundamental papers on deep dictionary learning-based clustering [9]. Deep dictionary learning is a new framework for deep learning. In the past, it has been used for unsupervised feature extraction [10], supervised classification [11], and even for domain adaptation [12]. However, it has never been used for clustering. This would be the first work on that topic. The advantage of deep dictionary learning is that it is mathematically flexible and can easily accommodate different cost functions. In this work, we propose to incorporate K-means clustering and sparse subspace clustering as losses to the unsupervised framework of deep dictionary learning.

2   Proposed Formulation

There are three pillars of deep learning - convolutional neural network (CNN), stacked autoencoder (SAE), and deep belief network (DBN). The discussion on CNN is not relevant here since it can only handle naturally occurring signals with local correlations. Moreover, they cannot operate in an unsupervised fashion, and hence is not a candidate for our topic of interest. Stacked autoencoders have been used for our purpose (deep learning-based clustering); the main issue with SAE is that it tends to overfit since one needs to learn twice the number of parameters (encoder and decoder) compared to other standard neural networks. However, SAE's are operationally easy to handle with good mathematical flexibility. DBN on the other hand learns the optimal number of parameters and hence does not overfit. However, the cost function DBN is not amenable to mathematical manipulations.

Deep dictionary learning keeps the best of both worlds. It learns the optimal number of parameters like a DBN and has a mathematically flexible cost function making it amenable to handle different types of penalties. This is the primary reason for building our clustering on top of the deep dictionary learning (DDL) framework. In our proposed formulation, we will regularize the DDL cost function with clustering penalties, where X is the given data (X – in our case single cells are along the columns and genes are along the rows), D is the dictionary learned to synthesize the data from the learned coefficients Z.

$$\min_{D_1,...D_N,Z} \|X - D_1\varphi(D_2\varphi(...\varphi(D_N Z)))\|_F^2 \tag{1}$$

The first clustering penalty will be with K-means.

$$\min_{D_1,D_2,D_3,Z,H} \underbrace{\|X - D_1 D_2 D_3 Z\|_F^2 \text{ s.t.} D_2 D_3 Z \geq 0, D_3 Z \geq 0, Z \geq 0}_{Dictionary Learning}$$

$$+ \underbrace{\left\|Z - Z H^T (HH^T)^{-1} H\right\|_F^2 \text{ s.t.} h_{ij} \in \{0,1\} \text{ and } \sum_j h_{ij} = 1}_{K-means} \tag{2}$$

Note that we have changed the cost function for dictionary learning. Instead of having activation functions like sigmoid or tanh, we are using the ReLU type cost function by incorporating positivity constraints. The reason for using ReLU over others is better function approximation capability [13]. The notations in the K-means clustering penalty has been changed appropriately.

In this work, we will follow the greedy approach for solving (2). In the dictionary learning part, we substitute $Z_1 = D_2 D_3 Z$. This leads to the greedy solution of the first layer of deep dictionary learning.

$$\min_{D_1,Z_1} |X - D_1 Z_1|_F^2 \text{ s.t.} Z_1 \geq 0 \tag{3}$$

The input for the second layer of dictionary learning uses the output from the first layer ($Z1$). The substitution is $Z_2 = D_3 Z$. This leads to the following problem

$$\min_{D_2,Z_2} \|Z_1 - D_2 Z_2\|_F^2 \text{ s.t.} Z_2 \geq 0 \tag{4}$$

For the third (and final) layer no substitution is necessary; only the output from the second layer is fed into it.

$$\min_{D_3,Z} \|Z_2 - D_3 Z\|_F^2 \text{ s.t.} Z \geq 0 \tag{5}$$

All the problems (3)–(5) can be solved by non-negative matrix factorization techniques; in particular, we have used the multiplicative updates [14]. Although shown here for three layers, it can be extended to any number.

The input to K-means clustering is the coefficients from the final layer (Z). This is shown as

$$\min_{H} \left\| Z - ZH^T (HH^T)^{-1} H \right\|_F^2 \text{ s.t.} h_{ij} \in \{0,1\} \text{ and } \sum_j h_{ij} = 1 \qquad (6)$$

The standard K-means clustering algorithm is used to solve it.

This concludes our algorithm to solve for the K-means embedded deep dictionary learning algorithm. Owing to the greedy nature of the solution, we cannot claim this to be optimal (owing to lack of feedback from deeper to shallower layers); however, each of the problems we need to solve (3)–(6) have well-known solutions.

Next, we show how the sparse subspace clustering algorithm can be embedded in the deep dictionary learning framework.

$$\min_{D_1, D_2, D_3, Z, C} \underbrace{\|X - D_1 D_2 D_3 Z\|_F^2 \text{ s.t.} D_2 D_3 Z \geq 0, D_3 Z \geq 0, Z \geq 0}_{Dictionary Learning}$$

$$+ \underbrace{\sum_i \|z_i - Z_{i^c} c_i\|_2^2 + \|c_i\|_1, \forall i \text{ in } \{1, ..., n\}}_{Sparse Subspace Clustering} \qquad (7)$$

The solution to the deep dictionary learning remains the same as before; it can be solved greedily using (3)–(5). Once the coefficients from the deepest layer are obtained (Z), it is fed into the sparse subspace clustering. This is given by

$$\min_{c_i's} \sum_i \|z_i - Z_{i^c} c_i\|_2^2 + \|c_i\|_1, \forall i \text{ in } \{1, ..., n\} \qquad (8)$$

Once (8) is solved, the affinity matrix is created and is further used for segmenting the data using Normalized Cuts.

3   Experimental Evaluation

3.1   Datasets

To evaluate the performance of the proposed method we used seven single-cell datasets from different studies.

Blakeley: The dataset consists of three cell lineages of the human blastocyst which are obtained using single-cell RNA sequencing (scRNA-seq). This scRNA-seq data of the human embryo gives an insight into early human development and was validated using protein levels. The study consists of 30 transcriptomes from three cell lines, namely, human pluripotent epiblast (EPI) cells, extraembryonic trophectoderm cells, and primitive endoderm cells [15].

Cell Line: Microfluidic technology-based protocol, Fluidigm, was used to perform scRNA-seq of 630 single-cells acquired from 7 cell lines. Each cell line was sequenced separately. Therefore, the original annotations were directly used. The sequencing results in 9 different cell lines, namely, A549, GM12878 B1, GM12878 B2, H1 B1, H1 B2, H1437, HCT116, IMR90, and K562. The cell lines GM12878 and H1 had two different batches [16].

Jurkat-293T: This dataset consists of 3,300 transcriptomes from two different cell lines - Jurkat and 293 T cells. The transcriptomes are combined in vitro at equal proportions (50:50). All transcriptomes are labeled according to the mutations and expressions of cell-type-specific markers, CD3D, and XIST [17].

Kolodziejczyk: This study reports the scRNA-seq of $\sim$704 mouse embryonic stem cells (mESCs) which are cultured in three different conditions, namely, serum, 2i, and alternative ground state a2i. The different culture condition of the cells results in different cellular mRNA expression [18].

PBMC: This dataset constitutes $\sim$68,000 peripheral blood mononuclear cell (PBMC) transcriptomes from healthy donors. They are annotated into 11 common PBMC subtypes depending on correlation with uorescence activated cell sorting (FACS)-based puried bulk RNA-Seq data of common PBMC subtypes. For this study, we randomly sampled 100 cells from each annotated subtype and retained the complete cluster in case the number of cells in it was less than 100 [17].

Usoskin: The data consists of 799 transcriptomes from mouse lumbar dorsal root ganglion (DRG). The authors used an unsupervised approach to cluster the cells. Out of 799 cells, 622 cells were classified as neurons, 68 cells had an ambiguous assignment and 109 cells were non-neuronal. The 622 mouse neuron cells were further classified into four major groups, namely, neurofilament containing (NF), non-peptidergic nociceptors (NP), peptidergic nociceptors (PEP), and tyrosine hydroxylase containing (TH), based on well-known markers [19].

Zygote: The RNA-sequencing data consists of 265 single cells of mouse preimplantation embryos. It contains expression proles of cells from zygote, early 2-cell stage, middle 2-cell stage, late 2-cell stage, 4-cell stage, 8-cell stage, 16-cell stage, early blastocyst, middle blastocyst, and late blastocyst stages [20].

3.2   Numerical Results

In the first set of experiments, we have compared the proposed algorithm with the two state-of-the-art deep learning techniques. The first technique is a stacked autoencoder (SAE) which comprises two hidden layers. The number of neurons in the first hidden layer of SAE is 20 and the nodes in the second layer are the same as the number of cell types in the single-cell data. The second method used as a benchmark is a deep belief network (DBN). Like SAE, DBN also has two hidden layers with 100 nodes in the first layer and the number of nodes in the second layer is the same as the number of clusters in the given dataset. For our proposed deep dictionary learning (DDL) the number of nodes in the first layer was 20 and those in the second one are the same as the number of cell types (similar to the configuration of SAE). These configurations yielded the best results. Both state-of-the-art techniques along with the proposed method use the K-means algorithm on the deepest layer of features to determine the clusters in the data.

To determine how SAE, DBN, and the proposed method can segregate different cell types using the respective deepest layer of features we employed two clustering metrics: adjusted rand index (ARI) and normalized mutual information (NMI), since the ground truth annotation (class) of each sample or cell is known apriori (Table 1).

Table 1. Clustering accuracy of the proposed method and existing deep learning techniques on single-cell datasets.

Algo	Metric	Blakeley	Cell line	Jurkat	Kolodziejczyk	PBMC	Usoskin	Zygote
DBN	NMI	.190	.567	.001	.032	.273	.015	.385
	ARI	.056	.430	.001	.171	.103	.007	.296
SAE	NMI	.181	.099	.925	.170	**.573**	.040	.107
	ARI	.011	.007	.958	.215	**.377**	.001	.006
Proposed method	NMI	**.933**	**.873**	**.974**	**.694**	.546	**.647**	**.639**
	ARI	**.891**	**.801**	**.989**	**.645**	.359	**.642**	**.359**

We see that the proposed method improves over existing deep learning tools by a large margin. Only in the case of PBMC are the results from SAE a close second.

In the next set of experiments, we used two well-known single-cell clustering methods, namely, GiniClust [7] and Seurat [6] as benchmark techniques. For both of our proposed methods (K-means and SSC) the configuration remains the same as before.

GiniClust could not yield any clustering results for the Cell Line dataset. It performs clustering by utilizing genes with a high Gini coefficient value. But, for this particular dataset, the technique could not identify any highly variable gene and hence could not cluster. Overall GiniClust almost always yields the worst results.

Among the proposed techniques (K-means and SSC), we find that K-means is more stable and consistently yields good results. Results from SSC fluctuate, yielding perfect clustering for Blakely to poor results in Kolodziejczyk, PBMC, and Usoskin. Only for the Kolodziejczyk and PBMC datasets does Seurat yield results comparable to Proposed + K-means; for the rest, Seurat is considerably worse than either of our techniques (Table 2).

Table 2. Clustering accuracy of the proposed method and single-cell clustering algorithms on single-cell datasets

Algo	Metric	Blakeley	Cell line	Jurkat	Kolodziejczyk	PBMC	Usoskin	Zygote
GiniClust	NMI	.277	–	.007	.214	.153	.061	.282
	ARI	.037	–	.000	.055	.030	.006	.025
Seurat	NMI	0	.717	.946	**.695**	**.585**	.447	.453
	ARI	0	.533	.974	**.710**	**.296**	.382	.123
Proposed + Kmeans	NMI	.933	.873	**.974**	.694	**.545**	**.647**	**.639**
	ARI	.891	.801	**.989**	.645	**.359**	**.642**	**.359**
Proposed + SSC	NMI	1	**.879**	.889	.522	.481	.492	.623
	ARI	1	**.814**	.821	.510	.303	.453	.317

4   Conclusion

This work proposes a deep dictionary learning-based clustering framework. Given the input (where samples/cells are in rows and features/genes are in columns) it generates a low-dimensional embedding of the data which feeds into a clustering algorithm. The low dimensional embedding represents each transcriptome; it is learned in such a manner that the final output is naturally clustered.

To evaluate the proposed method, we have compared against state-of-the-art deep learning techniques (SAE and DBN) and tailored single-cell RNA clustering techniques (GiniClust and Seurat). Our method yields the best overall results.

The current approach is greedy and hence sub-optimal; there is no feedback between the deeper and shallower layers. In the future, we would like to jointly solve the complete formulations (2) and (7) using state-of-the-art optimization tools.

References

1. Saxena, A., et al.: A review of clustering techniques and developments. Neurocomputing **267**, 664–681 (2017)
2. Jain, A.K.: Data clustering: 50 years beyond K-means. Pattern Recogn. Lett. **31**(8), 651–666 (2010)
3. Dhillon, I.S., Guan, Y., Kulis, B.: Kernel k-means: spectral clustering and normalized cuts. In: Proceedings of the Tenth ACM SIGKDD International Conference on Knowledge Discovery and Data Mining, pp. 551–556, August 2004
4. Vidal, R.: Subspace clustering. IEEE Signal Process. Mag. **28**(2), 52–68 (2011)
5. Elhamifar, E., Vidal, R.: Sparse subspace clustering. In: 2009 IEEE Conference on Computer Vision and Pattern Recognition, pp. 2790–2797, June 2009
6. Waltman, L., van Eck, N.J.: A smart local moving algorithm for large-scale modularity-based community detection. Eur. Phys. J. B **86**(11), 1–14 (2013). https://doi.org/10.1140/epjb/e2013-40829-0
7. Jiang, L., Chen, H., Pinello, L., Yuan, G.C.: GiniClust: detecting rare cell types from single-cell gene expression data with Gini index. Genome Biol. **17**(1), 144 (2016)
8. Kiselev, V.Y., et al.: SC3: consensus clustering of single-cell RNA-seq data. Nat. Methods **14**(5), 483–486 (2017)

9. Peng, X., Xiao, S., Feng, J., Yau, W.Y., Yi, Z.: Deep subspace clustering with sparsity prior. In: IJCAI, pp. 1925–1931, July 2016
10. Tariyal, S., Majumdar, A., Singh, R., Vatsa, M.: Deep dictionary learning. IEEE Access **4**, 10096–10109 (2016)
11. Mahdizadehaghdam, S., Panahi, A., Krim, H., Dai, L.: Deep dictionary learning: a parametric network approach. IEEE Trans. Image Process. **28**(10), 4790–4802 (2019)
12. Singhal, V., Majumdar, A.: Majorization minimization technique for optimally solving deep dictionary learning. Neural Process. Lett. **47**(3), 799–814 (2018)
13. Yarotsky, D.: Optimal approximation of continuous functions by very deep ReLU networks. arXiv preprint arXiv:1802.03620 (2018)
14. Lin, C.J.: On the convergence of multiplicative update algorithms for nonnegative matrix factorization. IEEE Trans. Neural Netw. **18**(6), 1589–1596 (2007)
15. Blakeley, P., et al.: Defining the three cell lineages of the human blastocyst by single-cell RNA-seq. Development **142**(18), 3151–3165 (2015)
16. Li, H., et al.: Reference component analysis of single-cell transcriptomes elucidates cellular heterogeneity in human colorectal tumors. Nat. Genet. **49**(5), 708 (2017)
17. Zheng, G.X., et al.: Massively parallel digital transcriptional profiling of single cells. Nat. Commun. **8**(1), 1–12 (2017)
18. Kolodziejczyk, A.A., et al.: Single cell RNA-sequencing of pluripotent states unlocks modular transcriptional variation. Cell Stem Cell **17**(4), 471–485 (2015)
19. Usoskin, D., et al.: Unbiased classification of sensory neuron types by large-scale single-cell RNA sequencing. Nat. Neurosci. **18**(1), 145 (2015)
20. Yan, L., et al.: Single-cell RNA-Seq profiling of human preimplantation embryos and embryonic stem cells. Nat. Struct. Mol. Biol. **20**(9), 1131 (2013)

Constrained Center Loss for Image Classification

Zhanglei Shi[1], Hao Wang[1], Chi-Sing Leung[1(✉)], and John Sum[2]

[1] Department of Electrical Engineering, City University of Hong Kong,
Kowloon, Hong Kong
zlshi2-c@my.cityu.edu.hk, wanghaocityu@gmail.com, eeleungc@cityu.edu.hk
[2] Institute of Technology Management, National Chung Hsing University,
Taichung, Taiwan
pfsum@nchu.edu.tw

Abstract. In feature representation learning, robust features are expected to have intra-class compactness and inter-class separability. The traditional softmax loss concept ignores the intra-class compactness. Hence the discriminative power of deep features is weakened. This paper proposes a constrained center loss (CCL) to enable CNNs to extract robust features. Unlike the general center loss (CL) concept, class centers are analytically updated from the deep features in our formulation. In addition, we propose to use the entire training set to approximate class centers. By doing so, class centers can better capture the global information of feature space. To improve training efficiency, an alternative algorithm is proposed to optimize the joint supervision of softmax loss and CCL. Experiments are performed on four benchmark datasets. The results demonstrate that the proposed scheme outperforms several existing architectures.

Keywords: Convolutional neural network (CNN) · Center loss (CL) · Image classification

1 Introduction

The neural network (NN) concept has been employed in many challenging tasks [1,2,6,10]. Especially, the convolutional neural network (CNN) has superiority in image-based recognition applications. One important reason is its powerful feature extraction capability. By stacking more layers, a network acquires more flexibility in feature representation. As a result, more robust features can be extracted and hence boosts the network performance.

The softmax loss bundled with deep structures is popular in feature learning [1,8,10]. During training, softmax has two roles. First, softmax acts as classifier and provides linear decision boundaries between classes [10]. The deep features from different classes become separate. Second, it enlarges magnitudes of deep features to boost its performance. Hence, the resultant features are pulled to fill the whole feature space [8].

© Springer Nature Switzerland AG 2020
H. Yang et al. (Eds.): ICONIP 2020, CCIS 1333, pp. 70–78, 2020.
https://doi.org/10.1007/978-3-030-63823-8_9

However, the feature magnitudes of all classes are not magnified equally and the deep features from the same class would have imbalanced magnitudes. As a result, the features may have large intra-class variation. The intra-class distance can be even larger than the inter-class distance for some cases. From the view of feature representation, large intra-class variation might significantly limit the NN discrimination ability [10].

Robust features are expected to have high intra-class similarity and large inter-class distance [8–11]. Center loss and its variants [9,10] aim at clustering same-class samples together around a learnable class center. The linear combination of softmax and center loss maximizes the intra-class compactness and inter-class separability simultaneously. Hence, the representation ability of deep features learned by using this joint supervision scheme can be enhanced. However, class center is expected to be the geometric center of that class to better characterize the feature distribution in feature space. Center loss treats the centers as free parameters and centers are optimized by stochastic gradient descent (SGD) approach. The centers will be iteratively updated from a random initialization using the training samples that belong to the corresponding class in every batch. The center update may lead to training instability [9].

In this paper, we propose a constrained center loss to improve the compactness within class and normalize the features simultaneously. Unlike the general center loss, the centers are learned analytically and directly from the deep features instead of training by gradient-based algorithms. To capture the global information of the feature space, we use the entire training set to estimate the centers. Since feeding forward the entire training samples is inefficient in every iteration. To improve the training efficiency, an alternative training approach is proposed. This approach contains two alternative steps. The first step is to estimate the class centers. Afterwards, we fix the class centers and then optimize the network parameters for a number of iterations. The alternative procedure is repeatedly applied until the network converges. Compared to some state-of-the-art approaches, the proposed method gives a better performance on several benchmark datasets.

The rest of this paper is arranged as follows. Section 2 presents the softmax loss and the general center loss. The proposed constrained center loss and the optimization algorithm are given in Sect. 3. Section 4 includes the experimental results. Finally, conclusions are presented in Sect. 5.

2 Softmax Loss and Center Loss

2.1 Softmax Loss

In supervised learning, the training set of N labeled pairs is expressed as $\mathcal{D} = \left\{ \{x_n, y_n\}_{n=1}^N : x_n \in \mathbb{R}^k, y_n \in \{1, ..., C\} \right\}$, where x_n is the nth training sample, its class label is denoted as y_n, and C is the number of classes. Deep learning aims at learning a nonlinear mapping function $\mathcal{F}(\Theta)$. This function maps the original input x into a deep feature space with d dimensions.

This paper considers the minibatch concept. Let m be the size of the current minibatch and let $\boldsymbol{f}_i$'s be the output vectors of the CNN for the current minibatch. Then we have the softmax loss to minimize:

$$\mathcal{L}_{\text{softmax}} = -\sum_{i=1}^{m} \log \frac{\exp(\boldsymbol{w}_{y_i}^{\mathrm{T}} \boldsymbol{f}_i)}{\sum_{j=1}^{C} \exp(\boldsymbol{w}_j^{\mathrm{T}} \boldsymbol{f}_i)}, \tag{1}$$

where $\boldsymbol{w}_j \in \mathbb{R}^d$ is the weight vector of class j in the top fully connected layer, y_i is the class label of the ith training sample.

2.2 Center Loss and Objective Function

The center loss (CL) approach [9,10] enhances the compactness of features from the same class by penalizing the distance between the samples and their centers

$$\mathcal{L}_{\text{intra}} = \frac{1}{2m} \sum_{i=1}^{m} \|\boldsymbol{f}_i - \boldsymbol{c}_{y_i}\|_2^2, \tag{2}$$

where $\boldsymbol{c}_{y_i} \in \mathbb{R}^d$ is its class center. The CL approach considers minimizing the objective: $\mathcal{L} = \mathcal{L}_{\text{softmax}} + \lambda \mathcal{L}_{\text{intra}}$. In the CL approach, all the parameters, including centers $\boldsymbol{c}_j$'s $(j = 1, \ldots, C)$, the interconnection weights of the CNN, and the softmax weight vectors $\boldsymbol{w}_j$ $(j = 1, \ldots, C)$, are simultaneously optimized by the SGD approach.

3 Constrained Center Loss and Our Approach

3.1 Constrained Center Loss

We enhance the compactness of features from the same class by penalizing the distance between the samples and their centers:

$$\mathcal{L}_{\text{intra}} = \frac{1}{2m} \sum_{i=1}^{m} \|\boldsymbol{f}_i - \boldsymbol{c}_{y_i}\|^2, \quad \text{s.t.} \quad \|\boldsymbol{c}_j\| = \alpha, \quad j = 1, \ldots, C. \tag{3}$$

Here, we restrict the norm of centers to be a target value α. We call the proposed loss in (3) as constrained center loss (CCL). Apart from intra-class compactness, the CCL also enhances the discriminative power of deep features from the view of feature normalization [8,11].

3.2 Update the Centers

Suppose that the interconnection weights of the CNN parts are fixed, i.e., $\boldsymbol{f}_i$'s are fixed. Then the problem stated in (3) can be decomposed into C individually constrained optimization problems. For simplicity, we focus on one specific Class y with center $\boldsymbol{c}_y$, where $y = 1, \cdots, C$. To maximize the similarities between the instances and their corresponding center, we have to minimize $\mathcal{L}_{\text{intra}_y}$ subject to $c_y^{\mathrm{T}} c_y = \alpha^2$.

Let m_y be the number of samples belonged to Class y in the current mini-batch, and let $\{f_{i,y}\}$ be the feature vectors of the training samples belonged to Class y. We introduce a Lagrange multiplier ζ. The Lagrangian of the objective function with respect to Class y is given by

$$\mathcal{L}(c_y, \zeta) = \frac{1}{2m_y} \sum_{i=1}^{m_y} \|f_{i,y} - c_y\|^2 + \zeta(\alpha^2 - c_y^{\mathrm{T}} c_y). \tag{4}$$

Differentiating the Lagrangian function with respect to ζ and c_y and setting the derivatives to zero, we will obtain

$$-\frac{1}{m_y} \sum_{i=1}^{m_y} (f_{i,y} - c_y) - 2\zeta c_y = 0, \tag{5}$$

$$c_y^{\mathrm{T}} c_y = \alpha^2. \tag{6}$$

From (5), we get $c_y = \frac{1}{(1-2\zeta)m_y} \sum_{i=1}^{m_y} f_{i,y}$. Defining $r = \sum_{i=1}^{m_y} f_{i,y}$, we can obtain $\frac{1}{(m_y - 2m_y\zeta)^2} r^{\mathrm{T}} r = \alpha^2$. Hence, $\zeta = \frac{1}{2}(1 - \frac{\|r\|}{\alpha m_y})$ and

$$c_y = \frac{1}{(1 - 2\zeta)m_y} r = \alpha \frac{r}{\|r\|} = \frac{\alpha \sum_{i=1}^{m_y} f_{i,y}}{\| \sum_{i=1}^{m_y} f_{i,y} \|}. \tag{7}$$

According to (7), the center for each class is updated approximately by the samples that belong to that class included in the current minibatch. This means centers updated from (7) only reflect the local distribution of feature. When the interconnection weights are fixed, a better idea is to seize the global distribution of the deep features by using **the entire training samples**. Hence, to obtain better centers during training, we propose to update the centers according to the following rule

$$c_j = \alpha \frac{\sum_{n=1}^{N} \delta(j, y_n) f_n}{\| \sum_{n=1}^{N} \delta(j, y_n) f_n \|}, \tag{8}$$

where $j = 1, \cdots, C$, and $\delta(j, y_n)$ is an indicator function. If $y_n = j$, then $\delta(j, y_n) = 1$. Otherwise, $\delta(j, y_n) = 0$.

3.3   Joint Supervision and Optimization

We combine $\mathcal{L}_{\text{intra}}$ with the softmax loss $\mathcal{L}_{\text{softmax}}$ to formulate a joint supervision loss. Inspired by [8,11], we assume that $\|w_j\| = 1$. The joint supervision optimization problem is given by

$$\min \mathcal{L} = \mathcal{L}_{\text{softmax}} + \lambda \mathcal{L}_{\text{intra}} = -\sum_{i=1}^{m} \log \frac{\exp(w_{y_i}^{\mathrm{T}} f_i)}{\sum_{j=1}^{C} \exp(w_j^{\mathrm{T}} f_i)} + \frac{\lambda}{2m} \sum_{i=1}^{m} \|f_i - c_{y_i}\|^2, \tag{9a}$$

$$\text{s.t. } \|c_j\| = \alpha, \quad \|w_j\| = 1, \quad j = 1, \ldots, C, \tag{9b}$$

where $\lambda > 0$ is the trade-off parameter that balances the importance of $\mathcal{L}_{\text{softmax}}$ and $\mathcal{L}_{\text{intra}}$. In this formulation, the complementary advantage of joint supervision is that $\mathcal{L}_{\text{softmax}}$ can separate different classes, while $\mathcal{L}_{\text{intra}}$ aims at explicitly encouraging the intra-class similarities. Hence, more discriminative features will be extracted by CNN.

In our model, there are three sets of parameters: the class centers c_j's, the parameters Θ of mapping function $\mathcal{F}(\Theta)$ (done by the CNN), and the classifiers w_j's. We adopt alternative strategy to learn these parameters. In the first step, we estimate class centers according to (8). Since the loss function $\mathcal{L}$ is differentiable. In the second step, the centers are fixed, and Θ and w_j's are optimized by the minibatch based SGD approach for a number of iterations. This alternative training process will be repeated until the network converges. We summarize the training algorithm in Algorithm 1.

Algorithm 1. Alternative Training Approach

1: **repeat**
2:     fix CNN and classifiers, and update centers $\{c_j\}$'s according to (8).
3:     fix centers, and train CNN and classifiers $\{w_j\}$'s via joint supervision (9) for some iterations.
4: **until** convergence

---

4   Experiments

4.1   Experiment Settings

We compare our proposed scheme with the original softmax, coco loss [8], vMF-A loss [11], and CL [10] on four benchmark datasets. The datasets are MNIST [4], Fashion-MNIST (FMNIST), CIFAR-10 [3] and CIFAR-100 [3]. The settings of training set and test set follow the common practice in these datasets. For CIFAR-10 and CIFAR-100, data augmentation [5] is utilized to learn robust features. For the proposed CCL, we use the original softmax loss to supervise the first several epochs as warm-start [7]. The SGD with weight decay of 0.0005 and momentum of 0.9 is adopted to optimize the model. For all experiments, the batch size is 256 and the class centers are updated every epoch (around 200 iterations).

We employ different CNN configurations listed in Table 1 for these datasets. The convolution units in our architecture may be stacked by several convolutional layers. For instance, the Conv1 unit of the architecture in the second column of Table 1 has 2 cascaded convolution layers with 32 filters of kernel size 5×5. In addition, the stride and padding are 1 and 2, respectively. To be short, we denote the Conv1 unit as $2 \times (5, 32)_{1/2}$. The max-pooling layer is denoted by Max, $2_{2/0}$. It denotes the grid is 2×2, where the stride is 2 and padding is 0. FC is the first fully-connected layer and its outputs are the deep feature vectors.

Table 1. CNN architectures for different datasets

Layer	MNIST	(F)MNIST	CIFAR-10	CIFAR-100
Conv0	–	$1 \times (3,64)_{1/0}$	$1 \times (3,64)_{1/0}$	$1 \times (3,96)_{1/0}$
Conv1	$2 \times (5,32)_{1/2}$	$3 \times (3,64)_{1/1}$	$4 \times (3,64)_{1/1}$	$4 \times (3,96)_{1/1}$
Pool1	Max, $2_{2/0}$			
Conv2	$2 \times (5,64)_{1/2}$	$4 \times (3,64)_{1/1}$	$4 \times (3,128)_{1/1}$	$4 \times (3,192)_{1/1}$
Pool2	Max, $2_{2/0}$			
Conv3	$2 \times (5,128)_{1/2}$	$3 \times (3,64)_{1/1}$	$4 \times (3,256)_{1/1}$	$4 \times (3,384)_{1/1}$
Pool3	Max, $2_{2/0}$			
FC	2	128	256	512

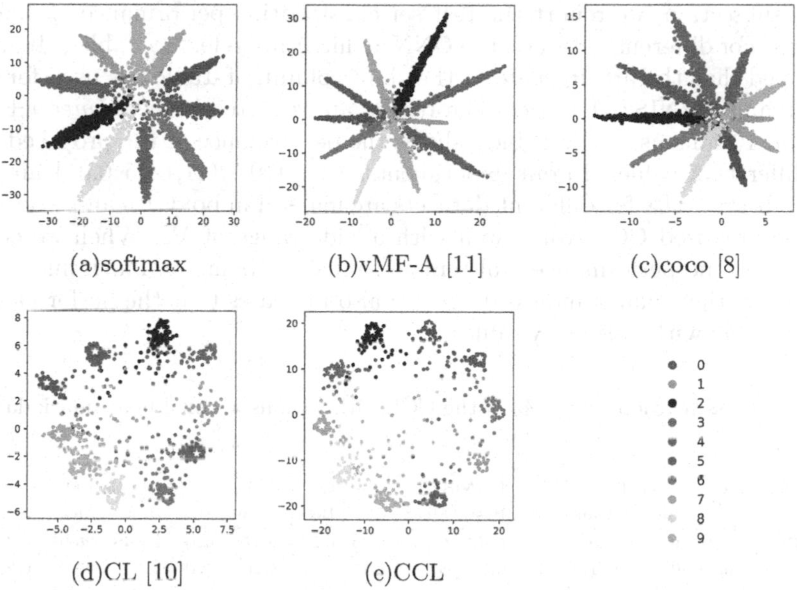

Fig. 1. Visualization of feature distribution and compactness learned by different losses on test set. The classes are distinguished by different colors. For CL and CCL, the class centers are marked by white stars.

4.2 Visualization of Feature Space

To visualize the feature vector distribution, we set the number of output in the FC layer to 2 [10]. The MNIST data set is considered and the CNN architecture for visualizing its feature space is shown in the second column of Table 1. The learned feature spaces of different losses are shown in Fig. 1. To be specific, the figure shows the scattering plots of the extracted deep feature vectors. The horizontal axis is the first component of the feature vector, while the vertical axis is the second component.

We can observe that, compared to softmax, coco and vMF-A lead to 'thinner' distribution for each class. Because these two losses focus on learning a better angular distribution. Hence, the feature samples are forced to be closer to their class weight vector in the angular distance. However, these two losses also ignore the intra-class compactness and the features are still pulled to fill in the space. That is, large intra-class variation still exists. On the contrary, CL and CCL largely improve the intra-class compactness. Feature samples are distributed around their class centers as shown in Fig. 1(d) and Fig. 1(e). In addition, the feature samples of CCL are distributed on the surface of a hypersphere. That is, CCL can provide normalization effect on balancing feature magnitude.

4.3   Classification Performance

In this subsection, we report the test set classification performance of different methods. For different datasets, the CNN architecture refers to Table 1. It should be noticed that the architecture in the third column of Table 1 is used for both MNIST and FMNIST datasets. The results are reported in '$best\ (mean \pm std)$' based on 10 runs as in [1]. Table 2 shows the performance of the proposed CCL with different λ values. In our experiments, $\lambda \in \{1, 0.5, 0.1, 0.05, 0.01\}$ and $\alpha = 40$. The best results for different datasets are marked in bold. It can be observed that the proposed CCL works well with a wide range of λ's. When we change the λ value, the performance still remain similar without too much fluctuation. In addition, the small standard deviation also indicates that the performance of CCL is stable with various λ values.

Table 2. Classification error (%) of the CCL with various λ's on 4 benchmark datasets

Method	λ	MNIST			FMNIST			CIFAR-10			CIFAR-100		
		Best	Mean	Std	Best	Mean	Std	Best	Mean	Std	Best	Mean	Std
CCL	1	**0.24**	0.30	0.04	**6.45**	6.76	0.20	6.22	6.47	0.18	**24.48**	25.09	0.30
	0.5	0.26	0.31	0.03	6.59	6.78	0.17	5.93	6.26	0.18	24.71	25.05	0.27
	0.1	0.29	0.33	0.03	6.72	6.91	0.14	6.00	6.16	0.10	24.88	25.37	0.29
	0.05	0.29	0.32	0.03	6.81	6.93	0.10	6.11	6.22	0.09	25.0	25.44	0.24
	0.01	0.26	0.33	0.04	6.76	7.03	0.16	**5.78**	6.13	0.20	25.0	25.52	0.30

Table 3 compares the **test set classification error** of different approaches. The best results are marked in bold, while the second-best results are marked in underline. For MNIST, the proposed CCL approach improves the best result from **0.26%** to **0.24%**. For FMNIST, the best performance are improved from **6.65%** to **6.45%**. The CIFAR-10 is more complex than MNIST and FMNIST. The CCL reduces the error rate of CL from **6.08%** to **5.78%**, which is **0.3%** improvement. Among all these datasets, CIFAR-100 is the most difficult dataset. For CIFAR-100, CCL can achieve more than **1.5%** improvements with all λ values. For the largest improvement, the best performance of vMF-A (**26.66%**), is improved to **24.48%**, with **2.18%** gains.

Table 3. Classification error (%) of different methods on 4 benchmark datasets

Method	MNIST			FMNIST			CIFAR-10			CIFAR-100		
	Best	Mean	Std	Best	Mean	Std	Best	Mean	Std	Best	Mean	Std
Softmax	0.28	0.35	0.03	6.86	7.19	0.19	6.20	6.43	0.21	30.06	30.81	0.56
Coco	0.38	0.44	0.04	6.93	7.20	0.15	6.58	6.87	0.19	27.67	28.27	0.36
vMF-A	0.34	0.41	0.04	6.65	6.96	0.16	6.11	6.47	0.19	26.66	26.92	0.13
CL	0.26	0.32	0.03	6.88	7.13	0.13	6.08	6.33	0.22	29.20	29.82	0.32
CCL	**0.24**	0.30	0.04	**6.45**	6.76	0.20	**5.78**	6.13	0.20	**24.48**	25.09	0.30

5 Conclusion

We propose a constrained center loss (CCL) for image classification. In our formulation, class center can be estimated analytically from the deep features. In addition, we propose to utilize the entire training set to update class centers. An alternative algorithm is proposed to optimize the structure. We conduct experiments on four benchmark datasets. The results showed that CNNs are able to extract compact and separate features with the CCL. In addition, the proposed CCL is superior to several state-of-the-art approaches.

Acknowledgments. The work presented in this paper is supported by a research grant from City University of Hong Kong (7005223).

References

1. He, K., Zhang, X., Ren, S., Sun, J.: Deep residual learning for image recognition. In: Proceedings of the IEEE Conference on Computer Vision and Pattern Recognition, pp. 770–778 (2016)
2. Huang, G.B., Learned-Miller, E.: Labeled faces in the wild: updates and new reporting procedures. Department of Computer Science, University of Massachusetts Amherst, Amherst, MA, USA, Technical report, pp. 14–003 (2014)
3. Krizhevsky, A., Hinton, G., et al.: Learning multiple layers of features from tiny images (2009)
4. LeCun, Y., Bottou, L., Bengio, Y., Haffner, P., et al.: Gradient-based learning applied to document recognition. Proc. IEEE **86**(11), 2278–2324 (1998)
5. Lee, C.Y., Xie, S., Gallagher, P., Zhang, Z., Tu, Z.: Deeply-supervised nets. In: Artificial Intelligence and Statistics, pp. 562–570 (2015)
6. Li, H., Liu, Y., Ouyang, W., Wang, X.: Zoom out-and-in network with map attention decision for region proposal and object detection. Int. J. Comput. Vis. **127**(3), 225–238 (2019)
7. Rippel, O., Paluri, M., Dollar, P., Bourdev, L.: Metric learning with adaptive density discrimination. arXiv preprint arXiv:1511.05939 (2015)
8. Wan, W., Zhong, Y., Li, T., Chen, J.: Rethinking feature distribution for loss functions in image classification. In: Proceedings of the IEEE Conference on Computer Vision and Pattern Recognition, pp. 9117–9126 (2018)
9. Wang, W., Pei, W., Cao, Q., Liu, S., Shen, X., Tai, Y.W.: Orthogonal center learning with subspace masking for person re-identification. arXiv preprint arXiv:1908.10535 (2019)

10. Wen, Y., Zhang, K., Li, Z., Qiao, Y.: A discriminative feature learning approach for deep face recognition. In: Leibe, B., Matas, J., Sebe, N., Welling, M. (eds.) ECCV 2016. LNCS, vol. 9911, pp. 499–515. Springer, Cham (2016). https://doi.org/10.1007/978-3-319-46478-7_31
11. Zhe, X., Chen, S., Yan, H.: Directional statistics-based deep metric learning for image classification and retrieval. Pattern Recogn. **93**, 113–123 (2019)

Deep Discriminative Embedding with Ranked Weight for Speaker Verification

Dao Zhou[1], Longbiao Wang[1(✉)], Kong Aik Lee[2], Meng Liu[1],
and Jianwu Dang[1,3]

[1] Tianjin Key Laboratory of Cognitive Computing and Application,
College of Intelligence and Computing, Tianjin University, Tianjin, China
{zhoudao,longbiao_wang,liumeng2017}@tju.edu.cn
[2] Institute for Infocomm Research, A*STAR, Singapore, Singapore
kongaik.lee@gmail.com
[3] Japan Advanced Institute of Science and Technology, Nomi, Ishikawa, Japan
jdang@jaist.ac.jp

Abstract. Deep speaker-embedding neural network trained with a discriminative loss function is widely known to be effective for speaker verification task. Notably, angular margin softmax loss, and its variants, were proposed to promote intra-class compactness. However, it is worth noticing that these methods are not effective enough in enhancing inter-class separability. In this paper, we present a ranked weight loss which explicitly encourages intra-class compactness and enhances inter-class separability simultaneously. During the neural network training process, the most attention is given to the target speaker in order to encourage intra-class compactness. Next, its nearest neighbor who has the greatest impact on the correct classification gets the second most attention while the least attention is paid to its farthest neighbor. Experimental results on VoxCeleb1, CN-Celeb and the Speakers in the Wild (SITW) core-core condition show that the proposed ranked weight loss achieves state-of-the-art performance.

Keywords: Speaker verification · Speaker embedding · Intra-class compactness · Inter-class separability

1 Introduction

Automatic speaker verification (ASV) is the process of automatically validating a claimed identity by analyzing the spoken utterance from the speaker. Speaker verification technology has been found important in various applications, such as, public security, anti-terrorism, justice, and telephone banking. Over the past few years, i-vector based representation [1], used in conjunction with a Probabilistic Linear Discriminant Analysis [2] backend, has been the state-of-the-art technique and has been deployed in most implementations.

© Springer Nature Switzerland AG 2020
H. Yang et al. (Eds.): ICONIP 2020, CCIS 1333, pp. 79–86, 2020.
https://doi.org/10.1007/978-3-030-63823-8_10

With the advancement in deep learning, performance of ASV has been greatly improved due to the large learning capacity of the deep neural network. In [3], a system based on convolutional neural network (CNN) outperforms the i-vectors/PLDA system. The aim of a speaker-embedding neural network [4] is to obtain a true representation (i.e., minimum intra-class differences) of a speaker's voice that is sufficiently different from other speakers (i.e., maximum inter-class differences). Apart from the neural network architecture, the loss function plays an important role to achieve this goal. In this regard, two types of loss functions, namely, metric-learning loss and classification loss, have shown to be effective for training speaker-embedding neural networks. Metric-learning loss [5,6] use pairwise or tripletwise training samples to learn discriminative features based on distance metric learning. Triplet loss [6] achieves both optimizations simultaneously by taking three training samples as input at one time.

The use of classification loss for speaker embedding neural network has been a major topic of interest. Classification loss, which includes softmax loss and its variants like angular softmax (A-Softmax) loss [7], additive margin softmax (AM-Softmax) loss [8] and additive angular margin softmax (Arc-Softmax) loss [9] have been proposed. A-Softmax loss and AM-Softmax loss introduce angular margin and cosine margin into the softmax loss respectively that tend to focus on encouraging intra-class compactness. Arc-Softmax loss incorporates the angular margin in an additive manner, that is different from the multiplicative angular margin in A-Softmax loss, to learn highly discriminative feature. These methods are not only simpler to implement compared to the triplet loss, but also give impressive performance in ASV tasks [10]. However, these variants of softmax loss have not paid special attention to inter-class separability. Very recently, [11] proposed the exclusive regularization to encourage inter-class separability for face verification and achieved outstanding performance.

In this paper, we present a ranked weight loss which explicitly encourages intra-class compactness and enhances inter-class separability simultaneously, which are achieved by paying the most attention and less attention to the target speaker and the speaker who is farther to the target speaker respectively during the neural network training process. The efficacy of the proposed ranked weight loss is validated on VoxCeleb1, CN-Celeb and SITW [3,12,13] corpora.

2   Prior Works

The proposed ranked weight loss is mainly inspired by the work of AM-Softmax loss [8] and exclusive regularization [11], we start with the definition of them.

2.1   AM-Softmax Loss

The traditional softmax loss is presented as:

$$L_S = \frac{1}{N} \sum_{i=1}^{N} -log \frac{e^{\mathbf{W}_{y_i}^T \mathbf{x}_i + b_{y_i}}}{\sum_{j=1}^{n} e^{\mathbf{W}_j^T \mathbf{x}_i + b_j}} \tag{1}$$

where N and n denote the batch size and the number of classes respectively, $\mathbf{x}_i$ is the feature vector of the i-th sample that belongs to class y_i and b is the bias term. $\mathbf{W}_j$ is the weight vector of class j. Here, $\mathbf{W}_{y_i}^T \mathbf{x}_i$ can be reformulated as $\|\mathbf{W}_{y_i}\| \|\mathbf{x}_i\| cos(\theta_{y_i,i})$.

However, the learned embeddings are not discriminative enough under the supervision of softmax loss. To address this issue, AM-Softmax loss [8,10] introduced an additive cosine margin into softmax loss to minimize intra-class distance. In AM-Softmax loss, the bias term b is discarded, weight $\mathbf{W}$ and feature x are normalized, and a hyperparameter s is introduced to scale the cosine values. AM-Softmax loss is given by:

$$L_{AM} = \frac{1}{N} \sum_{i=1}^{N} -log \frac{e^{s \cdot (cos(\theta_{y_i,i}) - m)}}{e^{s \cdot (cos(\theta_{y_i,i}) - m)} + \sum_{j=1;j \neq y_i}^{n} e^{s \cdot cos(\theta_{j,i})}} \tag{2}$$

in which m is a factor used to control the cosine margin.

2.2 Exclusive Regularization

Recently, [11] proposed the exclusive regularization to enlarge inter-class distance by penalizing the angle between a target class and its nearest neighbor. The formulation of exclusive regularization is defined as:

$$
\begin{aligned}
L_R &= \frac{1}{n} \sum_{y_i=1}^{n} \max_{j \neq y_i} cos(\psi_{y_i,j}) \\
&= \frac{1}{n} \sum_{y_i=1}^{n} \max_{j \neq y_i} \frac{\mathbf{W}_{y_i} \mathbf{W}_j}{\|\mathbf{W}_{y_i}\| \|\mathbf{W}_j\|}
\end{aligned}
\tag{3}
$$

where $\mathbf{W}_{y_i} \in \mathbb{R}^d$ is the y_i-th column of the weight matrix $\mathbf{W} \in \mathbb{R}^{d \times n}$, d represents the dimension of feature vectors and n is the number of classes. $\mathbf{W}_{y_i}$ can be regarded as the cluster center of class y_i, and $\psi_{y_i,j}$ is the angle between $\mathbf{W}_{y_i}$ and $\mathbf{W}_j$.

When applying the exclusive regularization to cooperate with AM-Softmax loss to supervise the model, the overall loss function (AME-Softmax loss) can be represented as:

$$L_{AME} = (1 - \lambda)L_{AM} + \lambda L_R \tag{4}$$

in which λ is the tradeoff between the AM-Softmax loss and the exclusive regularization.

3 Ranked Weight Loss

As stated in Sect. 2, AM-Softmax loss [8] achieves the promising performance in ASV tasks by encouraging intra-class compactness, and [11] further proposed the exclusive regularization to enhance inter-class separability. Nevertheless, the exclusive regularization only considers the impact of the target speaker's nearest neighbor and ignores the impact from other speakers.

We propose a ranked weight loss to encourage intra-class compactness and enlarge inter-class separability more fully. During the neural network training process, our method pays the most attention to the target speaker, while the corresponding attention is paid to its neighbors according to the inter-class distance. $\mathbf{W}_{y_i}$ is regarded as the cluster center of speaker y_i in our proposed method. For a training set with m speakers, the inter-class distance can be defined as:

$$d(y_i, j) = 1 - \frac{\mathbf{W}_{y_i} \mathbf{W}_j}{\|\mathbf{W}_{y_i}\| \|\mathbf{W}_j\|}, y_i \neq j \tag{5}$$

In addition, we set $d(y_i, y_i) = 0$, and rank the distances in accending order as follows:

$$d(y_i, y_i) < ... \leq d(y_i, j) \leq ... \leq d(y_i, m) \tag{6}$$

The ranked weights are then given by:

$$w'_j = \frac{1 - d(y_i, j)}{\sum_{k=1}^{m} (1 - d(y_i, k))^2} \tag{7}$$

In order to ensure that the ranked weights are positive so as not to affect the gradient direction of the loss function, we perform an exponential operation on the ranked weight function, the ranked weight function is redefined as:

$$w_j = e^{w'_j} \tag{8}$$

Therefore, the ranked weights are sorted in descending order as:

$$w_{y_i} > ... \geq w_j \geq ... \geq w_m \tag{9}$$

From Eq. (6) and Eq. (9), we observe that the target speaker y_i gets the most weight, while the smaller the inter-class distance, the greater the corresponding class weight. Finally, we introduce the ranked weight into AM-Softmax loss, leading to the ranked weight loss (RAM-Softmax loss), which is given by:

$$L_{RAM} = \frac{1}{N} \sum_{i=1}^{N} -log \frac{e^{w_{y_i} s \cdot (cos(\theta_{y_i,i}) - m)}}{e^{w_{y_i} s \cdot (cos(\theta_{y_i,i}) - m)} + \sum_{j=1; j \neq y_i}^{n} e^{w_j s \cdot cos(\theta_{j,i})}} \tag{10}$$

We see that the most weight and the corresponding weight are paid to increase the value of $cos(\theta_{y_i,i})$ and reduce the value of $cos(\theta_{j,i})$ respectively, which are inversely related to intra-class distance (i.e., cosine distance of feature-to-center) and inter-class distance, respectively.

4   Experimental Settings

4.1   Dataset

In our experiments, we validate the effectiveness of our proposed method on Vox-Celeb1 [3] and CN-Celeb [12] datasets that are collected 'in the wild'. CN-Celeb contains more genres and is more challenging than VoxCeleb1. Each utterance in VoxCeleb1 is no less than 3 s long, while more than 30% of the utterances are less than 2 s long in CN-Celeb. Both corpora are divided into development set and test set, respectively. The development set of VoxCeleb1, contains 148,642 utterances from 1,211 speakers, is used for model training, and the test set of VoxCeleb1 involves 4,874 utterances from 40 speakers. In CN-Celeb, 111,260 utterances from 800 speakers make up the first part CN-Celeb(T) (training set), and the second part CN-Celeb(E) (test set) consists of 18,849 utterances from 200 speakers. In addition, the SITW core-core condition is also used to evaluate the performance of the proposed ranked weight loss.

4.2 Implementation Details

In our experiments, the residual CNN (ResCNN) is used to training our model. The ResCNN contains 4 residual modules, which is simliar to the architecture in [6], but the depth of them are 2 instead of 3, then followed by an adaptive average pooling of size 4×1. The 1024-dimensional speaker embeddings are extracted from the fully connected layer.

During training, we randomly sample 3-s segments from each utterance to generate the input spectrograms through a sliding hamming window, window width and step are 20 ms and 10 ms respectively. The model is trained with a mini-batch size of 64. We used the standard stochastic gradient descent (SGD) as the optimizer. The initial learning rate is set to 0.1. And the additive cosine margin m is 0.2, while the angular margin terms are set to 2 and 0.2 in A-Softmax loss and Arc-Softmax loss respectively. Cosine similarity and equal error rate (EER) are used for back-end scoring method and performance evaluation metric, respectively.

5 Experimental Results

5.1 Exclusive Regularization Vs. Ranked Weight

To compare the performance of exclusive regularization and our proposed ranked weight, we conduct a series of experiments on CN-Celeb and VoxCeleb1. We follow [8] to set the scale factor s to 30, and the balance factor λ in AME-Softmax loss is set to different values (i.e., 0.1, 0.3 and 0.5) to show the effectiveness of exclusive regularization comprehensively. AM-Softmax loss is used as baseline method. Table 1 shows results of the above three methods. The ranked weight loss (RAM-Softmax loss) achieves the lowest EER compared with AM-Softmax loss and AME-Softmax loss. The relative reduction in EER amounts to 10.37% and 9.05% on VoxCeleb1 while 13.95% and 12.83% on CN-Celeb, respectively.

To explore the distribution of embeddings under different loss functions. We randomly sample 40 utterances for each speaker in the test set of VoxCeleb1, the distance information of these embeddings are illustrated in Table 2. Here, the intra-class distance refers to the average Euclidean distance from each sample to

Table 1. Verification performance of different loss function based systems on VoxCeleb1 and CN-Celeb. λ refers to the balance factor in AME-Softmax.

Dataset	Loss	λ	EER (%)
VoxCeleb1	AM-Softmax	–	4.82
	AME-Softmax	0.1	4.77
	AME-Softmax	0.3	4.75
	AME-Softmax	0.5	4.84
	RAM-Softmax	–	**4.32**
CN-Celeb	AM-Softmax	–	16.42
	AME-Softmax	0.1	16.21
	AME-Softmax	0.3	16.73
	AME-Softmax	0.5	16.33
	RAM-Softmax	–	**14.13**

the center of the corresponding class, while the inter-class distance refers to the average Euclidean distance between the centers of the classes. The center of class is computed by the average position of samples from that class. The proposed ranked weight loss achieves the largest inter-class distance and the smallest intra-class distance compared with AM-Softmax loss and AME-Softmax loss.

Table 2. The distance statistics under different loss functions. 'Intra' refers to intra-class distance, and 'Inter (Top-k)' refers to average distance between the target speaker and its k nearest neighbors.

	AM-Softmax	AME-Softmax	RAM-Softmax
Intra	7.94	7.70	**5.00**
Inter (Top-1)	13.68	14.12	**14.85**
Inter (Top-2)	15.78	15.96	**16.64**
Inter (Top-3)	17.38	17.35	**18.28**
Inter (Top-5)	20.25	20.27	**21.32**
Inter (Top-10)	26.31	26.72	**27.95**

Furthermore, we explore the performance of the above three methods on SITW core-core test set. Note that the speakers that overlap with the VoxCeleb1 *dev* (development set) were removed. Verification results are presented in Table 3. It is apparent that the proposed ranked weight loss achieves better performance than AM-Softmax loss and AME-Softmax loss.

Table 3. Verification performance on SITW core-core test set.

Training set	Loss	EER (%)
VoxCeleb1 *dev*	AM-Softmax	10.95
	AME-Softmax	10.72
	RAM-Softmax	**9.92**
CN-Celeb(T)	AM-Softmax	26.67
	AME-Softmax	26.81
	RAM-Softmax	**22.78**

5.2 Compared with Other Methods

Finally, we compare the performance of our ranked weight loss with the other state-of-the-art methods in Table 4. It is worth noticing that deep speaker systems perform better than traditional i-vector system on VoxCeleb1 while the i-vector system shows promising performance on CN-Celeb, which demonstrates that CN-Celeb is significantly different from VoxCeleb1. However, our proposed ranked weight loss achieves the best result on both datasets, it indicates that our method is more robust than i-vector and other loss functions.

Table 4. Verification performance of different ASV systems.

Dataset	Front model	Loss	Dims	Back-end scoring	EER (%)
VoxCeleb1	i-vector [3]	–	–	PLDA	8.80
	ResNet-34 [14]	A-Softmax	128	PLDA	4.46
	ResCNN	Softmax	1024	Cosine	6.44
	ResCNN	Arc-Softmax	1024	Cosine	4.64
	ResCNN	A-Softmax	1024	Cosine	4.43
	ResCNN	RAM-Softmax	1024	Cosine	**4.32**
CN-Celeb	i-vector [12]	–	150	LDA-PLDA	14.24
	TDNN [12]	Softmax	150	LDA-PLDA	14.78
	ResCNN	Softmax	1024	Cosine	16.85
	ResCNN	A-Softmax	1024	Cosine	15.91
	ResCNN	Arc-Softmax	1024	Cosine	15.41
	ResCNN	RAM-Softmax	1024	Cosine	**14.13**

6 Conclusions

We have presented a ranked weight loss, which explicitly enhances intra-class compactness and inter-class discrepancy simultaneously. This is achieved by paying the most attention to the target speaker and less attention to the speaker further apart from the target speaker during the neural network training process. Extensive experiments on VoxCeleb1, CN-Celeb and SITW Core condition corpora showed that the proposed ranked weight loss achieved the competitive performance compared with the current state-of-the-art methods.

Acknowledgments. This work was supported in part by the National Natural Science Foundation of China under Grant 61771333, the Tianjin Municipal Science and Technology Project under Grant 18ZXZNGX00330.

References

1. Dehak, N., Kenny, P., Dehak, R., Dumouchel, P., Ouellet, P.: Front-end factor analysis for speaker verification. IEEE Trans. Audio Speech Lang. Process. **19**, 788–798 (2011). https://doi.org/10.1109/TASL.2010.2064307
2. Prince, S., Elder, J.H.: Probabilistic linear discriminant analysis for inferences about identity. In: 2007 IEEE 11th International Conference on Computer Vision, pp. 1–8. IEEE (2007)
3. Nagrani, A., Chung, J.S., Zisserman, A.: VoxCeleb: a large-scale speaker identification dataset. In: Interspeech, pp. 2616–2620 (2017)
4. Snyder, D., Garcia-Romero, D., Sell, G., Povey, D., Khudanpur, S.: X-vectors: robust DNN embeddings for speaker recognition. In: 2018 IEEE International Conference on Acoustics, Speech and Signal Processing (ICASSP). IEEE, pp. 5329–5333 (2018). https://doi.org/10.1109/ICASSP.2018.8461375
5. Chung, J.S., Nagrani, A., Zisserman, A.: VoxCeleb2: deep speaker recognition. In: Interspeech, pp. 1086–1090 (2018)
6. Li, C., et al.: Deep speaker: an end-to-end neural speaker embedding system (2017)
7. Liu, W., Wen, Y., Yu, Z., Li, M., Raj, B., Song, L.: SphereFace: deep hypersphere embedding for face recognition. In: Proceedings of the IEEE Conference on Computer Vision and Pattern Recognition, pp. 212–220 (2017)
8. Wang, F., Cheng, J., Liu, W., Liu, H.: Additive margin softmax for face verification. IEEE Signal Process. Lett. **25**, 926–930 (2018)
9. Deng, J., Guo, J., Zafeiriou, S.: ArcFace: additive angular margin loss for deep face recognition. In: Proceedings of the IEEE Conference on Computer Vision and Pattern Recognition, pp. 4690–4699 (2019)
10. Liu, Y., He, L., Liu, J.: Large margin softmax loss for speaker verification. In: Interspeech, pp. 2873–2877 (2019)
11. Zhao, K., Xu, J., Cheng, M.M.: RegularFace: deep face recognition via exclusive regularization. In: Proceedings of the IEEE Conference on Computer Vision and Pattern Recognition, pp. 1136–1144 (2019)
12. Fan, Y., et al.: CN-CELEB: a challenging Chinese speaker recognition dataset (2020)
13. McLaren, M., Ferrer, L., Castan, D., Lawson, A.: The speakers in the wild (SITW) speaker recognition database. In: Interspeech, pp. 818–822 (2016)
14. Cai, W., Chen, J., Li, M.: Exploring the encoding layer and loss function in end-to-end speaker and language recognition system. In: Odyssey 2018 The Speaker and Language Recognition Workshop, pp. 74–81 (2018)

Disguising Personal Identity Information in EEG Signals

Shiya Liu, Yue Yao, Chaoyue Xing, and Tom Gedeon$^{(\boxtimes)}$

Research School of Computer Science, Australian National University,
Canberra, Australia
u6783346@alumni.anu.edu.au, {yue.yao,u6920870}@anu.edu.au,
tom@cs.anu.edu.au

Abstract. There is a need to protect the personal identity information in public EEG datasets. However, it is challenging to remove such information that has infinite classes (open set). We propose an approach to disguise the identity information in EEG signals with dummy identities, while preserving the key features. The dummy identities are obtained by applying grand average on EEG spectrums across the subjects within a group that have common attributes. The personal identity information in original EEGs are transformed into disguised ones with a CycleGAN-based EEG disguising model. With the constraints added to the model, the features of interest in EEG signals can be preserved. We evaluate the model by performing classification tasks on both the original and the disguised EEG and compare the results. For evaluation, we also experiment with ResNet classifiers, which perform well especially on the identity recognition task with an accuracy of 98.4%. The results show that our EEG disguising model can hide about 90% of personal identity information and can preserve most of the other key features. Our code is available at https://github.com/ShiyaLiu/EEG-feature-filter-and-disguising.

Keywords: EEG disguising model · EEG dummy identities · Grand average · Image translation

1 Introduction

Electroencephalography (EEG) is one of the most common methods of measuring brain electrical activities [17]. The signals contain complex information about the state of the human brain, which can be used to study brain functions, detect brain abnormalities and so on. Due to the uniqueness of the EEG signal from every individual, it can be a reliable source of biometric identification [4,13]; on the other hand, such personal information could be used for malicious purposes if not well protected. With increasing interest in and demand for research on EEG signals, there has been many EEG databases disclosed to the public. Therefore, there is a need to protect from exposure the personal identity information in the EEG signals of the experiment subjects, who will kindly contribute to such public EEG datasets in the future.

© Springer Nature Switzerland AG 2020
H. Yang et al. (Eds.): ICONIP 2020, CCIS 1333, pp. 87–95, 2020.
https://doi.org/10.1007/978-3-030-63823-8_11

Our key contribution is the creation of labelled EEG with dummy identities mimicking EEG signals from groups that have common features, but with averaged identity information. The EEG data with dummy identities helps disguise the identity information in the original EEG by composing a training set in the target domain, to which the original EEG is transformed. The experiment results suggest that the dummy identities effectively hide real identities in EEG, while our approach keeps the features of interest.

2   Related Works

Yao et al. proposed a feature filter to protect certain diseases from exposure [18]. There, the EEG signals with disease information are transferred to healthy EEG signals without such disease, so that the disease information can be effectively removed. The limitation of that approach is that it can only deal with the features from a limited number of categories (closed set), such that the EEG signals can be transferred from one class to another. For information that has potentially infinite classes (open set), such as personal identity, it is not feasible to find a class of EEG signals that has no identity information.

Instead of removing the information related to biometrics in EEG, this paper proposes an approach of disguising the identity information using a dummy identity, such that the EEG signal cannot be used for person recognition.

3   Methods

3.1   UCI EEG Dataset

The time-series data consists of EEG signals from two groups of subjects – alcoholic individuals and controls [2]. The dataset has three attributes: alcoholism, stimulus condition and subject identity. Each EEG signal contains 64 channels × 256 samples of data. The data within each subject is split into a training set (70%), a testing set (20%) and a validation set (10%), using the same within-subject train-test-validation splitting method as [9,18].

3.2   EEG Data Pre-processing

The raw time-domain EEG data is challenging to analyse due to its high dimensionality. We can extract prominent features from the frequency bands in EEG spectrum [11,15] for dimension reduction. We convert the EEG signals into the frequency domain using Fast Fourier Transform (FFT), which can capture most characteristics from stationary signals; and the short-term EEG signals in this work can be regarded as stationary [16].

To extract lower-level spectrum features, we adopt an approach proposed by Bashivan et al., which captures both spectral features and spatial information and represents them in images [1]. As in Fig. 1, with the spectrum features of the 64 channels and their corresponding electrode locations projected on a 2D plane, a

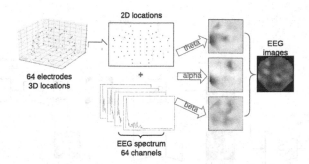

Fig. 1. Convert EEG spectrum into RGB EEG images [18]. Features from three frequency bands are extracted and used as red, green and blue channels of an image. (Color figure online)

feature matrix is calculated for each frequency band. we obtain color images by merging the feature matrix from three key frequency bands. As the EEG signals are collected from subjects as evoked by visual stimuli, we select the mid range frequency bands, i.e. bands θ (4–8 Hz), α (8–13 Hz) and β (13–30 Hz), which are less noisy and captures the most related information [12].

3.3   Disguised EEG Images Generation

Obtaining Labelled EEG Images with Dummy Identities. In neuroscience, grand averages of EEG signals across subjects is a common technique when statistically analysing EEG patterns in certain conditions [5,10,14]. The waveform of the grand mean of EEG signals can be regarded as a representative of a group and used to study their significant characteristics. A similar technique is also used in computer vision (CV) to investigate facial characteristics. E.g., Burt and Perrett generated composite face images by averaging the faces from different age groups, and those average faces can still be correctly recognized as faces in the corresponding age range [3].

We adopt this technique to generate average EEG images, which hold the characteristics of the common features of EEG signals in a certain group while having average biometric information. The averaged biometric information can be regarded as dummy identities. As the EEG dataset has 2 classes for the alcoholism attribute and 5 classes for stimulus condition attribute, we split the dataset into 10 groups corresponding to the 10 combinations of attributes. Then we take the grand average power of the EEG spectrums across each of several subjects within each group. The average EEG spectrums are converted into EEG images (see Sect. 3.2). This process is applied to the training dataset and the average EEG images are labelled as they are obtained within each group.

From Original to Disguised. We train a CycleGAN model [20] to generate the disguised EEG images that have the features which are consistent with the corresponding original images, but with dummy identity information instead of

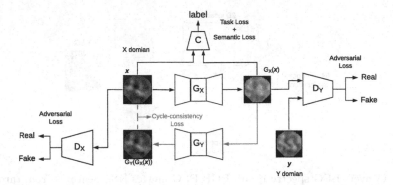

Fig. 2. The architecture of the image disguising model with task loss and semantic loss. G_X and G_Y denote the generators with real input images from X and Y domain respectively; D_X and D_Y denote the discriminator that distinguishes whether images are from X and Y domains respectively; x and y denote input images from X domain and Y domain. $G_Y(G_X(x))$ is a reconstructed image in X domain, which should be close to the corresponding real images x; C denotes the classifier that is used to add a further constraint to the model. For clearer illustration, only one direction of the cycle $(x \rightarrow G_X(x) \rightarrow G_Y(G_X(x)))$ is shown.

real identity information. For the training datasets, the source-domain data are the real EEG images and the target-domain data are the average EEG images with dummy identity obtained in Sect. 3.3.

The EEG images used in the model are labelled and we want them to be correctly classified to the original labels after translation to the target domain with dummy identities. Therefore, we need further constraints on our model to minimize the information loss in the most interesting features. We apply task and semantic loss in our model, as proposed by Hoffman et al. in their Cycle-consistent Adversarial Domain Adaptation (CyCADA) model [7,19].

We add an additional classifier C to our own CycleGAN-based model (Fig. 2) [7]. First, the classifier learns to make predictions on the labels of EEG images by minimizing the task loss during training. After the classifier is sufficiently trained to have relatively low task loss (<1.0), the model can take the semantic consistency into account, which means the label of a disguised EEG $G_X(x)$ predicted by the classifier should be consistent with the predicted label of the original EEG x, and similar to the other generator G_Y. The generators should learn to minimize the semantic loss during training.

3.4 Classification Tasks

To evaluate our model, we need to validate whether the personal identity information has been disguised such that it fails the person recognition task; also, we need to validate whether the information of interest is preserved, which means a disguised EEG image should be correctly classified to its original label. Therefore, we need to train classification models to predict the labels of the EEG data with respect to original subject identities, alcoholism and stimulus conditions.

ResNet Classifier. We could use a deep CNN model to extract high-level features from EEG images, which contains the low-level features we obtained from the EEG spectrum. Although deeper networks may give better results with higher-level features extracted, they also bring difficulties to optimization during the training and as a result degrade the performance in practice; this problem can be addressed by deep residual learning [6]. Thus, we implement ResNet models for the classifications which are essential to the evaluation step. To explore the impact of depth of ResNet models on our classification tasks, we will experiment with 18-layer, 34-layer and 50-layer ResNet models.

Joint Training. Since the average EEG images obtained in Sect. 3.3 are labelled data, we make use of them for joint training by combining them with the training dataset when training the classification model for alcoholism detection and stimulus classification tasks. This can add randomness and diversity to the training dataset thus improving the generalization of the classification model [8].

4 Experiment Results and Discussion

4.1 Evaluation Criteria

We aim for the disguised EEG images to fail the person recognition task while not sacrificing the performance on the alcoholism detection task and the stimulus classification task, and $accuracy = \frac{TP + TN}{TP + FP + TN + FN}$ is an important criterion when measuring those results. When classifying the subject identities of the disguised EEG, the accuracy should drop significantly compared with the results for original EEG images using the same classifier, while the accuracy of detecting alcoholism and classifying stimulus conditions of the disguised EEG images should be at the same level as that of the original EEG images.

Both the test dataset and validation dataset are imbalanced in the alcoholism label, so it is biased if accuracy is the only evaluation criterion. Thus, we also use $sensitivity = \frac{TP}{TP + FN}$ and $specificity = \frac{TN}{TN + FP}$ as additional evaluation criteria for the alcoholism detection task.

4.2 Performance of the Classification Models

To evaluate the performance of our EEG disguising model, we need to first train a classification model. We experiment with ResNet-based classification models with different numbers of layers. For comparison, we also trained an autoencoder-based classification model from Yao et al. [18].

As shown in Table 1, the ResNet-18 classification model performs well on alcoholism and personal identity recognition, with an accuracy of 92.5% and 98.4% respectively. In addition, the model achieves 91.1% sensitivity and 93.9% specificity in the alcoholism detection task, which is a balanced result. The testing results indicate that the ResNet-18 model has good generalization when classifying unseen samples. The model predicts the stimulus condition with an

Table 1. The testing results of classification models. Our Resnet based model outperfom autoencoder based model by 18.87% in terms of Identity accuracy.

	Alcoholism (%)			Stimulus (%)	Identity (%)
	Acc.	Sens.	Spec.	Acc.	Acc.
Yao et al.	87.84	88.16	84.42	51.67	79.53
ResNet-18	**92.49**	**91.13**	**93.85**	61.98	**98.40**
ResNet-34	91.88	90.78	92.99	**62.69**	97.26
ResNet-50	87.11	83.76	90.49	60.91	90.49

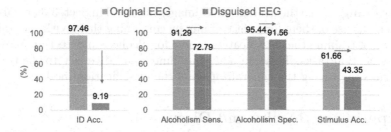

Fig. 3. Classification results: original EEG vs. disguised EEG. The disguised images generated by our method hides about 90% of personal identity information and can preserve most of the key features used for alcoholism and stimulus prediction.

accuracy of 62.0%, which is much higher than chance (20%) although it may not be optimal. The ResNet-34 classifier achieves similar results (slightly lower) compared to the ResNet-18 model and only the accuracy of stimulus condition prediction task (62.7%) is slightly higher, which indicates that the deeper network may contribute slightly to this task. However, the performance degrades when we explore deeper networks using a ResNet-50 classifier (Table 1).

The results in Table 1 show that the ResNet models outperform Yao et al.'s autoencoder-based model in general. With deeper network and more free parameters, the ResNet models are able to extract enough higher-level features for the classification tasks, especially the personal identity recognition, on which the ResNet models achieve the most improvement. Although the ResNet models benefit from deeper networks, the model with the most layers does not achieve the best results. The performance of the ResNet-50 model drops significantly. It indicates that the model is overly deep and has too many parameters for these EEG- related classification tasks, which causes overfitting.

4.3   Evaluation on the EEG Disguising Model

We use trained ResNet-18 models for the personal identity, alcoholism and stimulus condition classification tasks on both the original validation dataset and the corresponding disguised EEGs. In this experiment, we assume that the alcoholism information is of more interest; so during the training, the semantic loss and task loss come from the classifier's prediction on the alcoholism label.

Table 2. Classification results (%): disguised EEG with different semantic constraints. (a) Results with original EEG. (b) The 1st row (baseline) shows results without semantic constraints; the 2nd row (+ Alc.) shows results with the semantic constraint on the alcoholism feature; the 3rd row (+ Sti.) shows results with the semantic constraint on the stimulus feature; the 4th row (+ Alc. & Sti.) shows results with the semantic constraint on both of the alcoholism and stimulus feature.

(a) Original EEG

Original EEG	ID Acc.	Alcoholism Sens.	Alcoholism Spec.	Stimulus Acc.
	97.46	91.29	95.44	61.66

(b) Disguised EEG with Different Constraints

Constraint on	ID Acc. ↓	Alcoholism Sens. ↑	Alcoholism Spec. ↑	Stimulus Acc. ↑
Baseline	0.48	65.17	35.41	37.79
+ Alc.	**9.19**	72.79	**91.56**	43.35
+ Sti.	21.19	78.91	62.38	**52.61**
+ Alc. & Sti.	48.97	**93.47**	64.59	50.41

As shown in Fig. 3, when classifying the personal identity of the original EEG images, the accuracy is 97.5%; after those are disguised, the accuracy drops dramatically to 9.2%. It indicaes that the personal identity information in the original EEG is successfully hidden by our EEG disguising model and cannot be recognized by the classifier, which performs well on the original EEG data. For alcoholism detection, the classifier performs well on the original EEG images, achieves 91.3% sensitivity and 95.4% specificity; when using the same model to classify the disguised EEG images, the specificity only drops to 91.6%, while the sensitivity drops to 72.8%. For the stimulus condition classification task, although the accuracy drops from 61.7% to 43.4% when the task is performed on the disguised EEG, it is still much higher than chance (20%).

Although the decrease in the results of alcoholism and stimulus classification tasks show that there is some information loss in terms of the corresponding features, we do not see a sharp fall comparable with the results of the identity recognition task. It indicates that most of the alcoholism and stimulus features are preserved such that the classification model can still make similar predictions.

4.4 Ablation Study on the EEG Disguising Model

Ablation: Semantic Constraints on Stimulus Condition Feature. We also use the classifier in our EEG disguising model to impose a semantic constraint associated with the stimulus condition feature on the disguised EEG. Table 2 shows that the stimulus classification task on the disguised EEG achieves 52.6% accuracy, which is significantly higher than the counterpart result of using the classifier for alcoholism feature (43.4%). It implies that the classifier can effectively preserve more information of interest. Also, the results show that the performance of alcoholism detection task degrades, as the loss of alcoholism information increases without the constraint on it. Further, we find that the accuracy of personal identity task on disguised EEG also increases to 21.2%, which implies that the constraint may be too strong for the EEG disguising model so that more personal identity information is kept to reduce the semantic loss. A possible reason could be the classifier relies more on the identity information to predict the stimulus condition rather than the actual stimulus features.

Ablation: Semantic Constraints on both Alcoholism and Stimulus. We explore more restricted semantic constraints on the model by using the classifier to predict both the alcoholism and stimulus labels when calculating semantic loss. The results in Table 2 show the accuracy of the stimulus condition classification task (50.4%) and the sensitivity of the alcoholism task (93.5%) are higher, compared to the results of the models without semantic constraints on the stimulus or alcoholism features, respectively. However, the specificity of the alcoholism detection task is low, one possible reason is that the classifier may not be able to well handle the multi-label classification problem. The accuracy of personal identity increases as the constraint has become too strong.

Ablation: No Additional Semantic Constraints. We experiment with the model without the additional classifier that places semantic constraints on the disguised EEG. The results (Table 2) shows that the performance degrades on both the alcoholism and the stimulus condition classification task with the disguised EEG. It demonstrates that the semantic constraints are critical in our model to preserve the information of interests. Correspondingly, the accuracy of personal identity recognition (0.48%) drops significantly compared with the results of the model with the constraints. Without constraints, more identity information in the original EEG is disguised.

5   Conclusion and Future Work

Our EEG disguising model can be used to protect personal privacy, by hiding the personal identity information in EEG signals. The results demonstrate that the model is able to disguise 90% of the personal identity information in EEG signals with dummy identities while preserving most of the key information. In addition, we experiment with ResNet classifiers that can be used to perform different EEG classification tasks. From the results, we find that ResNet models are suitable for complex EEG signals, especially for the personal identity recognition, which requires more parameters and higher-level features to solve.

The information loss during the EEG disguising process should be improved, we may use a more complex classifier as the constraint. Also, we will validate our model on other EEG datasets to determine experimentally how well the model works in general. In addition, we will explore other techniques to improve the performance of the stimulus condition classification task. As an extension, we will also explore the possibility of decoding EEG signals at the feature level, one hypothetical approach could be gradually filtering out different key features in an EEG signal to see whether we can decode the EEG signal eventually.

References

1. Bashivan, P., Rish, I., Yeasin, M., Codella, N.: Learning representations from EEG with deep recurrent-convolutional neural networks. arXiv preprint arXiv:1511.06448 (2015)
2. Begleiter, H.: EEG database (1999)
3. Burt, D.M., Perrett, D.I.: Perception of age in adult caucasian male faces: computer graphic manipulation of shape and colour information. Proc. Roy. Soc. London Ser. B: Biol. Sci. 259(1355), 137–143 (1995)
4. Campisi, P., La Rocca, D.: Brain waves for automatic biometric-based user recognition. IEEE Trans. Inf. Forensics Secur. 9(5), 782–800 (2014)
5. Delorme, A., Miyakoshi, M., Jung, T.P., Makeig, S.: Grand average ERP-image plotting and statistics: a method for comparing variability in event-related single-trial eeg activities across subjects and conditions. J. Neurosci. Methods 250, 3–6 (2015)
6. He, K., Zhang, X., Ren, S., Sun, J.: Deep residual learning for image recognition. In: CVPR, pp. 770–778 (2016)
7. Hoffman, J., et al.: CyCADA: cycle-consistent adversarial domain adaptation. In: ICML (2018)
8. Krizhevsky, A., Sutskever, I., Hinton, G.E.: ImageNet classification with deep convolutional neural networks. In: NeurIPs, pp. 1097–1105 (2012)
9. Li, Y., Dzirasa, K., Carin, L., Carlson, D.E., et al.: Targeting EEG/LFP synchrony with neural nets. In: NeurIPs, pp. 4620–4630 (2017)
10. Marshall, P.J., Fox, N.A.: Infant EEG and ERP in relation to social and emotional development. In: Infant EEG and Event-Related Potentials, pp. 227–250 (2007)
11. McGrogan, N., et al.: Neural network detection of epileptic seizures in the electroencephalogram (1999)
12. Musha, T., Terasaki, Y., Haque, H.A., Ivamitsky, G.A.: Feature extraction from EEGs associated with emotions. Artif. Life Robot. 1(1), 15–19 (1997)
13. Palaniappan, R., Mandic, D.P.: Biometrics from brain electrical activity: a machine learning approach. IEEE TPAMI 29(4), 738–742 (2007)
14. Polich, J.: EEG and erp assessment of normal aging. Electroencephalogr. Clin. Neurophysiol./Evoked Potentials Sect. 104(3), 244–256 (1997)
15. Subasi, A.: Automatic recognition of alertness level from EEG by using neural network and wavelet coefficients. Expert Syst. Appl. 28(4), 701–711 (2005)
16. Tcheslavski, G.V., Gonen, F.F.: Alcoholism-related alterations in spectrum, coherence, and phase synchrony of topical electroencephalogram. Comput. Biol. Med. 42(4), 394–401 (2012)
17. Übeyli, E.D.: Combined neural network model employing wavelet coefficients for EEG signals classification. Digit. Signal Proc. 19(2), 297–308 (2009)
18. Yao, Y., Plested, J., Gedeon, T.: Information-preserving feature filter for short-term EEG signals. Neurocomputing (2020)
19. Yao, Y., Zheng, L., Yang, X., Naphade, M., Gedeon, T.: Simulating content consistent vehicle datasets with attribute descent. In: ECCV (2020)
20. Zhu, J.Y., Park, T., Isola, P., Efros, A.A.: Unpaired image-to-image translation using cycle-consistent adversarial networks. In: ICCV, pp. 2223–2232 (2017)

Fusioning Multiple Treatment Retina Images into a Single One

Irina Mocanu⍟, Loretta Ichim⍟, and Dan Popescu$^{(\boxtimes)}$⍟

University Politehnica of Bucharest, 060042 Bucharest, Romania
{irina.mocanu,loretta.ichim,dan.popescu}@upb.ro
http://www.upb.ro/

Abstract. Different retina diseases require laser treatment that is applied on retina images. For example, the treatment uses laser activation applied on the retina on different points. In this case, the treatment uses only a part of the fundus image, named retina treatment image. The scope of the paper is to combine all the retina treatment images in order to map all the treatment points on the whole fundus image. Thus an annotated fundus image with all treatment points is obtained. Thus, each treatment retina image is mapped on the corresponding fundus image in order to place the spot light on it. The spot light is similar as shape with the optic disc. The differentiation between them is made based on blood vessels - optic disc contains a high density of pixels from the blood vessels. Both blood vessel segmentation and detection of the spot light and optic disc are performed using convolutional neural network. Image alignment is performed using feature matching with homography computed using GMS (grid-based motion statistics). Evaluation was performed using different fundus images selected from public datasets. From each fundus image we generated different treatment retina images - cropped and rotated parts from the original image. The laser spot was simulated through a white circle placed in different positions on the retina treatment images.

Keywords: Convolutional neural networks · Image processing · Fundus image · Retina treatment image · Image alignment

1 Introduction

Vision is one of the most important senses that humans possess relying on it for almost every activity they do. Without vision, we cannot perform even the most basic actions such as walking or eating without someone help. All these aspects conduct to extensive studies for discovering vision impairment from the early stages in order to prevent loss of the complete vision.

Many people across the globe suffer from some form of visual impairment, that usually affects the retina [1, 2]. The analysis of retina images represents an important step for the diagnosis and treatment of eye diseases. The common

© Springer Nature Switzerland AG 2020
H. Yang et al. (Eds.): ICONIP 2020, CCIS 1333, pp. 96–103, 2020.
https://doi.org/10.1007/978-3-030-63823-8_12

eye diseases can be detected by analysing the aspect of retina blood vessels, the optic disc or presence of different lesions. They can indicate the presence of different retinal diseases such as diabetic retinopathy, glaucoma, age related macular disease.

In case of some retinal disease (e.g. diabetic macular edema, proliferative diabetic retinopathy) laser treatment is applied on retina images. The laser is activated on the retina by analysing the current treatment retina image, which represents a region from the whole fundus image. The point where laser is activated for treatment is recognized as the laser spot left on the acquired retina image.

The scope of the paper consists in mapping all the laser spots on the fundus image. The method can be useful in case of treatment performed on individual retina images using the laser spot. After, treatment, all these points are mapped on the fundus image. In future, by analyzing treatments from time to time it is possible to evaluate the evolution of the disease. Thus, a method for creating a composite image obtained by placing together on the fundus image all the detected treatment laser spots detected on the treatment retina images. It is out of scope to detect any eye disease or any evolution of it. Thus, both fundus and retina treatment images are processed in order to detect both optical disc and the laser spot. Two types of neural networks: U-Net and Attention U-Net convolutional neural network combined with image pre and post processing are used (selected based on their results). Laser spot must be differentiated from the optical disc that is located at the intersection of blood vessels. Thus, blood vessels from retina images are extracted using both two networks, too.

Since these two images are acquired from different positions (fundus image and retina treatment image), we need to find a correspondence between them. An alignment of the two images is needed. We use feature matching between two images using GMS (grid-based motion statistics) feature correspondence [15]. It removes motion inconsistent correspondences towards the high-accuracy matching. Using the computed features between two images, the homography is computed in order to find the correspondence for each point from one image to a point into the other image and the laser spot is placed on its corresponding position in the fundus image.

Tests were performed with images from public datasets from which we generated retina treatment images that were synthesized from fundus images through a number of transformations (transform to gray scale, crop a part of the image, rotate, and place a fictitious laser beam spot on this image), for obtaining a set of realistic retina treatment images to be matched to the corresponding fundus image.

The rest of the paper is organised as follows. Section 2 presents existing results for both vessel segmentation and optical disc detection. Proposed method is described in Sect. 3. Section 4 shows evaluation results. Conclusions and future work are given in Sect. 5.

2   Related Work

Paper [3] presents a Support Vector Machine (SVM) classifier with a linear kernel on a set of feature vectors learned for each pixel. The output score of the SVM indicates for each pixel if it is a pixel that represents a vessel or not. A threshold is used to create a binary vessel map.

Due to the increase in the size of the training datasets and the advancement of graphical processing units, deep learning-based methods started to obtain performances that outmatched the previous state-of-the-art approaches on different tasks, including image segmentation [4]. Convolutional neural networks have drawn attention for image classification and segmentation. The advantage of neural networks is that they can learn automatically features directly from the input data, without any manual feature engineering.

Paper [5] proposes a convolutional neural network for vessel segmentation from fundus images. This network consists of both an encoder and a decoder. The first half, encodes the information using pooling layers to summarize neighboring features, while the other half rebuilds the feature maps, in order to obtain the segmented output, which must have the same size as the input. The problem with pooling layers is that they discard information that could be useful for localisation. Localisation is important in segmentation because the segmented pixels must be mapped exactly to the corresponding pixels from the input image. In order to counteract this problem, skip connections are used to propagate low level features learned at the early layers and combine them with the high level features learned at the later layers. The obtained accuracy is around 96% on three public datasets.

A conditional generative adversarial network is proposed in [6] for optical disc detection. The network has an encoder-decoder architecture, while the discriminator consists of five convolutional layers. Tests were performed on two public datasets: DRISHTI GS1 [12] and RIM-ONE [14] obtaining accuracy of 0.96% and 0.98%.

3   Proposed Method

The paper presents a method for creating a composite image starting from a set of treatment retina images. The composite image is obtained by placing together on the fundus image the treatment laser spots from all the treatment retina images. Each retina treatment image must be aligned with the fundus image in order to obtain the position of the spot on the fundus image. Thus, the treatment retina image must be processed in order to detect the laser spot. Both laser spot and optic disc have circular shapes. First, detection of both elements (optic disc and laser spot) will be performed. There are situations in which both optical disc and laser spot are presented in the treatment retina image. In these cases, we must differentiate the spot laser between the optic disc. If both two elements are detected as part of the retina treatment image, blood vessel segmentation is applied on this image. Optic disc is the region that contains a high density of pixels associated with blood vessels. After that we can detect the laser spot. Then, image alignment is performed in order to map the laser spot on the fundus image. The following steps are used for mapping the laser spot from the treatment retina images on the fundus image: (1) laser spot detection from the retina treatment image: (1a) detect the optic disc and laser spot from the treatment retina images; (1b) eliminate optic disc from the retina treatment images through vessel segmentation and (2) retina treatment image is aligned with the fundus image in order to place the laser spot on the fundus image. Blood vessel segmentation and optic disc detection are performed in order to increase the accuracy for laser spot detection. After image alignment, the position of the laser spot must be mapped on the fundus image. If we performed only image alignment, we didn't have the position of the laser spot.

3.1 Laser Spot Detection from the Retina Treatment Images

First retina treatment images are processed in order to detect both optic disc and the laser spot. Detection of both optic disc and laser spot is performed using both U-Net and Attention U-Net convolutional neural networks [9] combined with image pre and post processing. Laser spot must be differentiated from the optic disc that is located at the intersection of blood vessels. Thus, blood vessels from retina images are extracted using Attention U-Net network, too. Second, optic disc is eliminated based on the blood vessels extracted from the retina image. Optic disc has a high density of pixels from the blood vessels.

U-Net [7] is a fully-convolutional network, composed of an encoder and a decoder. However, this high-level representation learned by the encoder is not enough for the semantic segmentation task. The network needs to learn about localization as well. This is accomplished by the second half of U-Net. This half represents the decoder, which is symmetric to the encoder, the only difference being that pooling layers are replaced by upsampling layers or transposed convolutions, which learn to reconstruct the feature maps. In order to enable precise localization, the low level features learned in the early layers from the encoder are concatenated with the high level representation learned in the later layers of the decoder. Then a convolutional layer is applied to the concatenation and learns to combine this information.

A further improvement was proposed in [9] in the form of an attention gate that can be used for medical images, in order to focus on specific areas of the image. This attention gate was incorporated in the Attention U-Net architecture at the concatenation step in the decoder. Its purpose is to extract only the relevant data that comes through the skip connection, removing the noise.

3.2 Vessel Segmentation from the Fundus Images

The quality of the images in the collected datasets may be affected by several conditions such as unbalanced illumination, motion blur, low contrast, noise. In addition, the images were acquired in different settings (from different screening programs, from different hospitals, with different devices) may further affect their quality. Thus, we perform the following pre-processing steps before blood vessel segmentation: (1) *Gamma correction* for improving the brightness of the image; (2) *Contrast enhancement* using adaptive histogram equalization; (3) *Extracting one color channel* we considered the green channel (we tested also to extract blood vessels from red and green channels using different factors – the best results were obtained from the green channel). As post-processing we used erosion and dilatation.

3.3   Alignment of the Fundus Image with Retina Treatment Image

Since these two images are acquired from different positions (fundus image and retina treatment image), we need to find a correspondence between them. An alignment of the two images is needed. We use feature matching between two images using GMS [15,16] in order to select corresponding points between two images. We selected this method because it is robust to various of image: viewpoint, scale, and rotation. It is also fast: it take only 1 or 2 ms in a single CPU thread while processing 50 K correspondences between two images. Using these corresponding points, the two images will be aligned. Thus the homography is computed in order to find the transformation from one image to another based on the corresponding points detected by GMS. After that, the laser spot is placed on its corresponding position in the fundus image.

In order to detect matches between two images: fundus image and retina treatment image, a set of feature mappings must be obtained. We test the features matching algorithm Features mapping using GMS descriptor that eliminates false matchings. We performed homography computation for image alignment. A homography can be computed when we have enough corresponding points in the two images. A homography is a 3×3 matrix - M, that can be used to map a point p - from the retina image – to the corresponding point p' into the fundus image. The homography can be computed based on matches detected by descriptors used for matching computation between two images.

4   Evaluation Results

The solution is implemented in Python. Image processing is performed using OpenCV. The training of the network is made on Google Collaboratory [8]. Evaluation was performed on images collected from the following public datasets: (1) The DRHAGIS: Diabetic Retinopathy, Hypertension, Age-related macular degeneration and Glacuoma ImageS database [13]; (2) The High-Resolution Fundus Image Database [12]; (3) Digital Retinal Images for Optic Nerve Segmentation Database [10]; (4) DRISHTI-GS [11,12]. From each fundus image we generated different treatment retina images (cropping and rotating parts from the original image). The laser spot is simulated through a white circle placed in different positions. We used 400 images for training and 100 images for testing.

4.1 Blood Vessel Segmentation

Results for blood vessel segmentation are the following: (1) accuracy: 0.9776 (U-Net)/0.9780 (AttU-Net); (2) sensitivity: 0.6402 (U-Net)/0.6742 (AttU-Net); (3) specificity: 0.9931 (U-Net)/0.9919 (AttU-Net).

We can see that the algorithm manages to segment properly most of the blood vessels as shown in Fig. 1 (on the left side). However it has difficulties in segmenting the more delicate vessels, even though contrast enhancement was applied in order to make them more visible. Figure 1 (on the right side) shows the worst results. The presence of lesions in some areas obstruct some of the vessels and the algorithm did not learn to interpolate the connection (in the ground truth image, there is no obstruction). In addition, the algorithm fails to segment the smallest vessels, as they are difficult to see even with the naked eye.

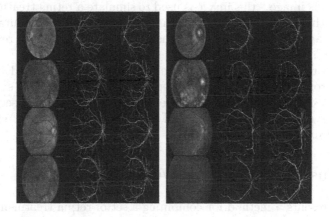

Fig. 1. Best results (left) and worst results (right) for blood vessel segmentation

4.2 Optic Disc Detection

Results for optic disc detection are the following: (1) accuracy: 0.9631 (U-Net)/0.9737 (AttU-Net); (2) sensitivity: 0.9543 (U-Net)/0.9245 (AttU-Net); (3) specificity: 0.9634 (U-Net)/0.9777 (AttU-Net).

Figure 2 shows both the best results (left) and the worst results (right) obtained on the test set. In the first image, only a small part of the optic disc is segmented. The presence of the blood vessels inside the optic disc may be a reason for this behaviour. In the second image, improper illumination caused the algorithm to segment a large part of the retina as the optic disc.

4.3 Image Alignment

We tested the image alignment process on pairs of images – fundus and retina treatment images – obtained by simulating laser spots on parts of processed

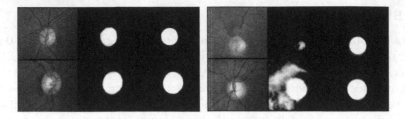

Fig. 2. Best results (left) and worst results (right) for optic disc detection

fundus images. The pairs of images we used for such testing are: (1) a fundus image (obtained from the datasets); (2) a region of the same image obtained by cropping, rotating and converting into a gray scale image – obtained from the previous fundus image – this image is used to simulate a retina treatment image.

Based on the correct computed matches, the homography computation allows for correct image alignment, and the transformation of points from retina images to the fundus image is correct.

The worst results for blood vessel segmentation and optic disc detection may cause an improper detection of the laser spot. Also, if the size of the spot is higher it can be detected as optic disc. In case of a good blood vessel segmentation, the optic disc is correctly detected and after that, also the laser spot will be correctly obtained.

5   Conclusions and Future Work

The paper presents a method for combining a set of retina treatment images in order to obtain a map of the laser treatment spots on the whole fundus image. Each treatment retina image is aligned with the corresponding fundus image for placing the spot light on it. Evaluation was performed using different fundus images from public datasets. From each fundus image we generated different treatment retina images - cropped and rotated parts from the original image. The laser spot is simulated through a white circle placed in different positions on the retina treatment images. Visual evaluation was performed on the laser spots mapping. As future work, evaluation with real retina image treatment and real spot lights will be made.

References

1. Abràmoff, M.D., Garvin, M.K., Sonka, M.: Retinal imaging and image analysis. IEEE Rev. Biomed. Eng. **3**, 169–208 (2010)
2. Zhang, X., Saaddine, J.B., Chou, C.F., et al.: Prevalence of diabetic retinopathy in the United States, 2005–2008. JAMA **304**, 649–656 (2010)
3. Strisciuglio, N., Azzopardi, G., Vento, M., Petkov, N.: Supervised vessel delineation in retinal fundus images with the automatic selection of B-cosfire filters. Mach. Vis. Appl. **27**(8), 1137–1149 (2016)

4. LeCun, Y., Bengio, Y., Hinton, G.: Deep learning. Nature **521**(7553), 436–444 (2015)
5. Oliveira, A.F.M., Pereira, S.R.M., Silva, C.A.B.: Retinal vessel segmentation based on fully convolutional neural networks. Expert Syst. Appl. **112**, 229–242 (2018)
6. Singh, V.K., Rashwan, H.A., Maaroof, N., Romani, S., Puig, D.: Retinal optic disc segmentation using conditional generative adversarial network. In: 21st International Conference of the Catalan Association for Artificial Intelligence (2018)
7. Ronneberger, O., Fischer, P., Brox, T.: U-net: convolutional networks for biomedical image segmentation. In: Navab, N., Hornegger, J., Wells, W.M., Frangi, A.F. (eds.) MICCAI 2015. LNCS, vol. 9351, pp. 234–241. Springer, Cham (2015). https://doi.org/10.1007/978-3-319-24574-4_28
8. Google Collaboratory. https://colab.research.google.com/. Accessed 17 Mar 2020
9. Oktay, O., et al.: Attention U-net: learning where to look for the pancreas (2018)
10. Carmona, E.J., Rincón, M., García-Feijoo, J., Martínez-de-la-Casa, J.M.: Identification of the optic nerve head with genetic algorithms. Artif. Intell. Med. **43**, 243–259 (2008)
11. Sivaswamy, J., Krishnadas, S.R., Chakravarty, A., Joshi, G.D., Tabish, A.U.S.: A comprehensive retinal image dataset for the assessment of glaucoma from the optic nerve head analysis. JSM Biomed. Imaging Data Papers **2**(1), 1004–1008 (2015)
12. Sivaswamy, J., Krishnadas, K.R., Josh, G.D., Madhulika, J., Tabish, A.U.S.: Drishti-GS: retinal image dataset for optic nerve head (ONH) segmentation. In: IEEE ISBI, Beijing (2014). https://doi.org/10.1109/ISBI.2014.6867807
13. Holm, S., Russell, G., Nourrit, V., McLoughlin, N.: DR HAGIS-a fundus image database for the automatic extraction of retinal surface vessels from diabetic patients. J. Med. Imaging Bellingham **4**(1), 014503 (2017)
14. Fumero, F., Alayon, S., Sanchez, J.L., Sigut, J., Gonzalez-Hernandez, M.: RIM-ONE: an open retinal image database for optic nerve evaluation. In: 2011 24th International Symposium on Computer-Based Medical Systems (CBMS), Bristol, pp. 1–6 (2011). https://doi.org/10.1109/CBMS.2011.5999143
15. Bian, J.-W., et al.: GMS: grid-based motion statistics for fast, ultra-robust feature correspondence. Int. J. Comput. Vis. (2020)
16. Bian, J.-W., et al.: An evaluation of feature matchers for fundamental matrix estimation. In: British Machine Vision Conference (2019)

Humidity Sensor Accuracy Improvement Based on Two Nested Kalman Filters for Commercial Cultivation of Tropical Orchids

Prachumpong Dangsakul[1], Nutchanon Siripool[2]($\boxtimes$),
Kraithep Sirisanwannakul[2], Rachaporn Keinprasit[1],
Khongpan Rungprateeptavorn[1], Suthum Keerativittayanun[1],
and Jessada Karnjana[1]

[1] NECTEC, National Science and Technology Development Agency,
112 Thailand Science Park, Khlong Luang 12120, Pathum Thani, Thailand
prachumpong.dan@nectec.or.th
[2] Sirindhorn International Institute of Technology, Thammasat University,
131 Moo 5, Tiwanon Rd., Bangkadi, Muang 12000, Pathum Thani, Thailand
{6022800245,6022792111}@g.siit.tu.ac.th

Abstract. Polymer dielectric-based humidity sensors used in the orchid greenhouse monitoring system usually have a problem concerning the accuracy when used continuously for some time. It is because those sensors are exposed to high humid conditions regularly. In a sense, data read from the humidity sensor is noisier than those from other sensors deployed in the greenhouse. Therefore, this paper proposes a simple data-driven technique based on two nested Kalman filters for sensor accuracy improvement. It aims to minimize the difference between humidity values read from a humidity sensor and those from the more-accurate sensor. The humidity values are estimated by a Kalman filter, of which its prediction is made based on another different Kalman filter. The inner Kalman filter delivers such the prediction by fusing information obtained from surrounded sensors. Experimental results show that this technique can improve measurement accuracy by 32.02%. This paper also discusses the possibility of applying the proposed scheme in the case that the sensor fails to operate normally, in which the Kalman gain will be adjusted so that the Kalman filter relies more on the prediction.

Keywords: Kalman filtering · Sensor accuracy improvement · Orchid greenhouse · Humidity sensor

1 Introduction

The value of the world orchid market is around 400 million US dollars in 2019, and most of the orchid are tropical ones [1]. Also, more than 69 nations worldwide have orchid markets in their countries, and significant exporters include

© Springer Nature Switzerland AG 2020
H. Yang et al. (Eds.): ICONIP 2020, CCIS 1333, pp. 104–112, 2020.
https://doi.org/10.1007/978-3-030-63823-8_13

Thailand, Japan, the United States, Vietnam, China, and India, which currently account for 68.28% of the total export [1]. Among those countries, Thailand is the world's biggest exporter of the cut orchid. In Thailand, most orchid farms are of traditional farming; that is, agriculture is done under opened and uncontrolled environment. Therefore, to increase the yield and to industrialize the farming, ICT and embedded system technologies have been suggested since 2003 [13]. Those technologies can be used in monitoring and controlling environmental parameters concerning the cultivation, and with them, the intensive farming is just a few steps ahead. The core idea of such monitoring and control systems is intuitive and straightforward, i.e., the environment should be controlled to match the plant's needs concerning current environmental factors [2,14]. For orchid farming, the factors that affect the quality and quantity of the product are temperature, humidity, nutrients, air quality, and light intensity [12]. One of the crucial and demanding factors in automatic monitoring is the air humidity since the humidity sensor tends to degrade when it is continuously exposed under a high humid condition [4]. As a consequence and in a sense, data read from the humidity sensor are quite noisy. Therefore, as the first step toward orchid greenhouse control, this work's focus is to improve the accuracy of the humidity sensor by using a data-driven approach.

One of the popular methods in sensor accuracy improvement is Kalman filtering. For example, A. Lesniak *et al.* applied a Kalman filter to magnetotelluric recordings to reduce noise in multichannel data and found that it is effortless and useful in practice [6]. The Kalman filter has been used not only to improve the accuracy of sensor data but also to extract a clean signal from a noisy one. M. Fujimoto *et al.* used a Kalman filtering algorithm to remove noise from speech signals and found that it worked comparably to traditional methods [3]. Besides noise reduction or accuracy improvement, the Kalman filter has been adopted in greenhouse control systems. For example, D. H. Park *et al.* used the Kalman filter to automatically control the greenhouse climate [9]. In their work, a feedback control system with a Kalman filter was used to maintain the temperature and humidity to the predefined values. Similarly, P. Shi *et al.* applied an extended Kalman filter for the same purpose [11]. According to their model, the temperature and humidity were controlled by controlling the heater, ventilation, and foggy machine. The result of this work is impressive. It could minimize the error between the values read from the sensors and those of the requirements. However, the focus of this work is different from ours since it did not aim to improve the accuracy of the sensor itself.

To the best of our knowledge, no work has yet to apply the Kalman filtering algorithm to improve the accuracy of the humidity sensor used in the orchid agriculture domain. Therefore, this paper aims to investigate such the application and to report experiments conducted to verify its effectiveness. This paper has also studied the possibility of applying it in the case that the sensor fails to operate normally. In this case, the Kalman gain will be adjusted so that the Kalman filter believes more in the prediction model.

2 Background

The overview of the monitoring system that was deployed to collect data used in this work and, for the completeness in itself, the one-dimensional Kalman filter, are introduced in this section.

2.1 Overview of an Orchid Greenhouse Monitoring System

The monitoring system for collecting data is installed at a commercial greenhouse of the size of 6 × 20 square meters, which is located in Ratchaburi, Thailand. The system consists of 21 humidity and temperature sensors, three dataloggers, a gateway, some fan and foggy controllers, and a weather station. Each humidity-temperature sensor is spatially separate to cover 2 × 2.5 square meters. Data read from it are to be sent to a datalogger, of which its function is to re-format the collected data and forward them to the gateway. The gateway then regularly send data from all loggers to a database through a GPRS network. The user can access those data via a web browser.

The humidity-temperature sensor used in the project is a digital sensor, called SHT31, of the Sensirion company. It operates based on the principle of capacitance measurement. According to the collected data under this project for more than a year, we found that some sensors work improperly after eight months. For example, data are noisier and drifted from the actual values. This is in part due to the environment under which they are exposed. For instance, spraying liquid such as water (for controlling humidity) or insecticide chemicals constantly for some time could cause failure in relative humidity measurement. In such a high humid condition, this problem with the polymer dielectric-based sensor has been broadly observed [4].

2.2 One-Dimensional Kalman Filtering

According to the Kalman filtering, we can describe any linear system in the steady-state by two equations: state equation and measurement equation [5–8, 10]. The state equation assumes that the state x_k of a system at time k is evolved from a linear combination of the previous state at time $k-1$, a control input u_{k-1}, and some zero-mean process noise w_{k-1} with a variance of Q. Thus,

$$x_k = Ax_{k-1} + Bu_{k-1} + w_{k-1}, \tag{1}$$

where A is a known state-transition factor that applies the effect of the previous state on the current state, and B is a control input factor that applies the effect of the input on the state.

The output y_k of the system that we can measure is assumed to be a linear combination of the state x_k that we want to estimate and some measurement white noise v_k with a variance of R. Thus,

$$y_k = Cx_k + v_k, \tag{2}$$

where C is an observation factor that relates the state x_k to the measurement y_k. In a nutshell, the Kalman filter estimates x_k, which is denoted by $\hat{x}_k$ and called *a posteriori estimate*, by combining a predicted state estimate $\hat{x}_k^-$ (*a priori estimate*) and the difference between the measurement y_k and a predicted measurement $\hat{y}_k$. That difference is sometimes called a *residual* or a *measurement innovation*. Thus, the state estimate can be expressed mathematically as

$$\hat{x}_k = \hat{x}_k^- + K(y_k - \hat{y}_k) = \hat{x}_k^- + K(y_k - C\hat{x}_k^-), \tag{3}$$

where K is a blending factor, called the *Kalman gain*. The Kalman filtering algorithm calculates the Kalman gain K such that the expectation of the square of the difference between the state x_k and the state estimate $\hat{x}_k$ is minimized. The difference (i.e., $x_k - \hat{x}_k$) is called *a posteriori estimate error*, and the expectation is *a posteriori error variance*, which is denoted by P_k.

The Kalman filtering algorithm consists of five steps as follows. First, given the previous state estimate $\hat{x}_{k-1}$, it projects the state ahead from the equation

$$\hat{x}_k^- = A\hat{x}_{k-1} + Bu_{k-1}. \tag{4}$$

Note that, for $k = 1$, we denote the previous state estimate $\hat{x}_{k-1}$ by $\hat{x}_0$, which is called the *initial state*.

Second, *a priori error variance* P_k^-, which is defined by the expectation of the square of the difference between the state x_k and the predicted state estimate $\hat{x}_k^-$, is projected ahead from the equation

$$P_k^- = AP_{k-1}A + Q, \tag{5}$$

where P_{k-1} is the previous (*a posteriori*) error variance. For $k = 1$, we denote the previous error variance P_{k-1} by P_0, which is called the *initial error variance*. In a sense, P_k^- is a measure of the uncertainty in the state estimate $\hat{x}_k$ due to a process noise and the propagation of the uncertainty of the previous predicted state estimate $\hat{x}_{k-1}^-$. The first two steps form the prediction stage of the algorithm.

Third, the Kalman gain K is computed by the equation

$$K = \frac{P_k^- C}{CP_k^- C + R}. \tag{6}$$

Fourth, the Kalman gain K is used to scale the measurement innovation (i.e., $y_k - C\hat{x}_k^-$), and the state estimate $\hat{x}_k$ is updated by adding the scaled measurement innovation to the predicted state estimate $\hat{x}_k^-$, i.e.,

$$\hat{x}_k = \hat{x}_k^- + K(y_k - C\hat{x}_k^-). \tag{7}$$

Last, the state error variance is updated by the equation

$$P_k = (1 - KC)P_k^-. \tag{8}$$

The steps from number three to number five form the measurement update stage of the Kalman filtering algorithm, and it can be seen that given some initial state estimate $\hat{x}_0$ and some initial error variance P_0, the Kalman filter can estimate the state x_k for any k.

3   Proposed Method

As mentioned in the previous section, the Kalman filtering algorithm calculates the Kalman gain to weigh its belief between the prediction and the measurement. In this work, the latter is data read from the humidity sensor at the location of interest. The former used to estimate a humidity value is constructed based on another Kalman filter. This second Kalman filter projects the humidity value by assuming that the data read from neighbour sensors are a sequence of measurements, and the predicted (*a priori*) state estimate is the previous state estimate.

Figure 1 shows the structure of the proposed method. As an instance, in our experiment, we want to accurately estimate the actual humidity value of the sensor no. 4. The other sensors that surround the sensor no. 4 are the neighbour sensors, as shown in Fig. 1(a). In this work, the state equation of the first Kalman filter is formulated as follows.

$$x_k = x_{k-1} + w_{k-1}, \tag{9}$$

where x_k is the humidity value at the location of the sensor no. 4 at time k and w_{k-1} is the process noise at time $k-1$. The measurement equation is

$$y_k = x_k + v_k, \tag{10}$$

where y_k is the data read from the sensor no. 4 at time k and v_k is the measurement noise at time k. The predicted (*a priori*) state estimate $\hat{x}_k^-$ is then computed by

$$\hat{x}_k^- = \hat{x}_{k-1}, \tag{11}$$

where $\hat{x}_{k-1}$ is the previous state estimate that is determined by the second Kalman filter, which is called the *inner* Kalman filter in this work. Hence, the first Kalman filter is the *outer* one.

The state equation and the measurement equation of the second Kalman filter are as follows.

$$x_l^p = x_{l-1}^p + w_{l-1}^p, \tag{12}$$

and

$$y_l^p = x_l^p + v_l^p, \tag{13}$$

where x_l^p is the humidity value at time l (and it is to be used as the previous state estimate $\hat{x}_{k-1}$ of the first Kalman filter), w_{l-1}^p is the process noise at time l of the second Kalman filter, x_0^p is the initial state estimate of the second Kalman filter, y_l^p is the measurement at time l of the second Kalman filter, and v_l^p is the measurement noise of the second Kalman filter. Similarly, the predicted (*a priori*) state estimate $\hat{x}_l^{p-}$ is computed by

$$\hat{x}_l^{p-} = \hat{x}_{l-1}^p, \tag{14}$$

where $\hat{x}_{l-1}^p$ is the previous state estimate and is assumed to be a constant for a given k, which is the average value of y_l^ps.

Let N be a set of indices of the neighbour sensors. For instance, in our experiment, $N = \{1, 2, 6, 7\}$, as illustrated in Fig. 1(a). The proposed method assumes that y_l^p for $l = 1$ to $n(N)$, where $n(N)$ is the cardinality of N, is a sequence of $y_{k,i}$, where $y_{k,i}$ is the data read from the neighbour sensor no. i for $i \in N$. Also, it assumes that the initial state estimate x_0^p is the average value of the humidity values of $y_{k,i}$ for all is.

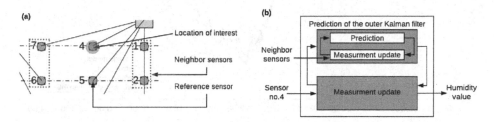

Fig. 1. Positions of sensors used in this paper and the diagram of nested Kalman filter.

4 Experiment and Results

4.1 Experimental Setup

In this work, humidity data are collected and sent to the database every 5 min. Therefore, there are 288 datapoints a day. In our experiment, the duration for data analysis is about 314 days, i.e., from 21 September 2018 to 31 July 2019. The aim of this work is to apply the proposed method to estimate the actual humidity value read by the sensor no. 4. Also, we assumed that that actual humidity value could be approximated by the humidity value read by the sensor no. 5. The reason for this assumption is that, according to our back analysis on variances and drifts of data from all sensors, we found that the sensor no. 5 was most stable and has the smallest drift. In addition, the sensors no. 4 and no. 5 are close to each other. As shown in Fig. 1, the neighbour sensors are sensors no. 1, no. 2, no. 6 and no. 7.

We compared the proposed method with the average model Kalman filter and interested sensor. The average model uses the average value from a nearby sensor instead of the inner Kalman filter to be used as the prediction state.

4.2 Experimental Result

Figure. 2 shows the estimated values of the proposed method, compared to data read from sensor no. 4, the average of data read from neighbour sensors, and values estimated a Kalman filter, of which its prediction is the average of data read from neighbour sensors (which is denoted by 'average model' in the figure).

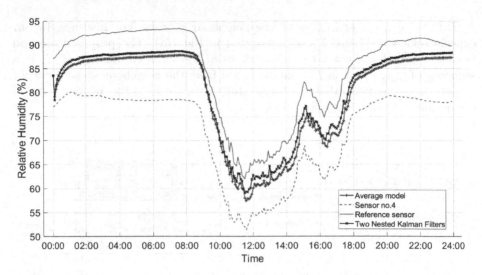

Fig. 2. Humidity data obtained from the proposed method in comparison with those obtained from other methods.

Table 1. Comparison of the RMSEs of the proposed method and other methods.

| | With Kalman filter | | Without Kalman filter | |
Date	Proposed method	Average model	Average value	Sensor no. 4
21 − 30 September 2018	1.25545	1.53920	1.24245	1.58278
1 − 31 October 2018	1.45087	1.66113	1.61453	1.85758
1 − 30 November 2018	1.51279	1.79340	1.39390	1.38452
1 − 31 December 2018	1.67796	1.84608	1.44386	1.88464
1 − 31 January 2019	2.02165	2.01123	1.81751	2.46357
1 − 28 February 2019	1.50797	1.67928	1.41362	1.64797
1 − 31 March 2019	1.99078	2.20287	1.78755	2.28450
1 − 30 April 2019	2.03453	2.21354	1.62406	2.52173
1 − 31 May 2019	1.94417	2.16628	1.98743	2.25142
1 − 30 June 2019	2.73336	3.25308	5.41979	6.32111
1 − 31 July 2019	3.76175	3.32243	8.50690	8.00316
Average RMSE	**1.99012**	**2.15350**	**2.56833**	**2.92754**

In this work, we use the root-mean-square error (RMSE) to evaluate the error between the reference sensor no. 5 and other methods. The comparison of the RMSEs among different methods is shown in Table 1.

When the nested Kalman filtering was deployed in improving the accuracy of the humidity measurement, the average RMSE dropped from 2.92754 to 1.99012, i.e., the average RMSE dropped approximately 32.02%. The average RMSE of the average model was 2.15350, which is 26.44% less than the average RMES of sensor no. 4. It can be noticed that the RMSE values obtained from the proposed method were less than the average model by approximately 7.59%. Therefore, the Kalman filtering with the proposed method could considerable improve the accuracy of the humidity sensors.

5 Discussion

The proposed method not only can improve the accuracy of sensor but also has a potential for estimating actual values when the sensor works improperly. For example when a sensor is malfunction, as shown in Fig. 3, we can adjust the variances of the measurement so that the Kalman filter relies more on the prediction. The result from the adjustment is shown in Fig. 3.

Note that this adjustment was done based on back analysis of the collected data by hand, not by automatic procedure, which is to be investigated further.

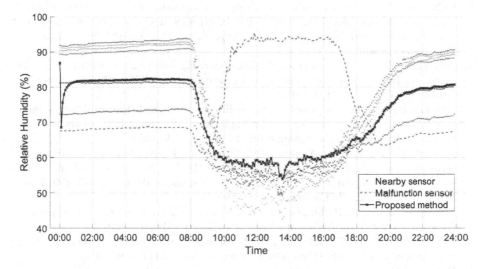

Fig. 3. Applying the proposed method to a malfunction sensor.

6 Conclusion

This paper proposed a method for accuracy improvement in humidity measurement by using two nested Kalman filters. The outer Kalman filter is used to estimate the actual values of humidity data read from one sensor, and the inner Kalman filter is used as the prediction model of the outer Kalman filter. The experimental results showed that this technique could improve the accuracy of the humidity measurement considerably.

Acknowledgments. This work is the output of an ASEAN IVO (http://www.nict.go. jp/en/asean_ivo/index.html) project, titled 'A Mesh-topological, Low-power Wireless Network Platform for a Smart Watering System,' and partially financially supported by NICT (http://www.nict.go.jp/en/index.html). The authors would like to express sincere gratitude to Thai Orchids Co., Ltd., for the experiment greenhouse. Also, the authors would like to express their sincere gratitude to Dr. Patchareeya Boonkorkaew of Kasetsart University for granting the authors permission to access and use data.

References

1. Department of international trade promotion homepage. https://www.ditp.go.th/contents_attach/539560/539560.pdf
2. Du, X., Wang, J., Ji, P., Gan, K.: Design and implement of wireless measure and control system for greenhouse. In: Proceedings of the 30th Chinese Control Conference, pp. 4572–4575 (2011)
3. Fujimoto, M., Ariki, Y.: Noisy speech recognition using noise reduction method based on Kalman filter. In: 2000 IEEE International Conference on Acoustics, Speech, and Signal Processing. Proceedings (Cat. No. 00CH37100), vol. 3, pp. 1727–1730 (2000)
4. Griesel, S., Theel, M., Niemand, H., Lanzinger, E.: Acceptance test procedure for capacitive humidity sensors in saturated conditions. In: WMO CIMO TECO-2012, Brussels, Belgium, pp. 1–7 (2012)
5. Kalman, R.E.: A new approach to linear filtering and prediction problems (1960)
6. Leśniak, A., Danek, T., Wojdyła, M.: Application of Kalman filter to noise reduction in multichannel data. Schedae Inf. **17**(18), 63–73 (2009)
7. Marselli, C., Daudet, D., Amann, H.P., Pellandini, F.: Application of Kalman filtering to noisereduction on microsensor signals. In: Proceedings du Colloque interdisciplinaire en instrumentation, C2I, 18–19 November 1998, pp. 443–450. Ecole Normale Supérieure de Cachan, France (1998)
8. Musoff, H., Zarchan, P.: Fundamentals of Kalman Filtering: a Practical Approach. American Institute of Aeronautics and Astronautics, Reston (2009)
9. Park, D.H., et al.: A study on greenhouse automatic control system based on wireless sensor network. Wirel. Pers. Commun. **56**(1), 117–130 (2011)
10. Rhudy, M.B., Salguero, R.A., Holappa, K.: A Kalman filtering tutorial for undergraduate students. Int. J. Comput. Sci. Eng. Surv. **8**(1), 1–9 (2017)
11. Shi, P., Luan, X., Liu, F., Karimi, H.R.: Kalman filtering on greenhouse climate control. In: Proceedings of the 31st Chinese Control Conference, pp. 779–784. IEEE (2012)
12. Stuckey, I.H.: Environmental factors and the growth of native orchids. Am. J. Bot. **54**(2), 232–241 (1967)
13. Waksman, G., Escriou, H., Gentilleau, G.: The situation of ICT in the French agriculture. In: European Scientific Association (EFITA) 2003 Conference, pp. 5–9 (2003)
14. Xing, X., Song, J., Lin, L., Tian, M., Lei, Z.: Development of intelligent information monitoring system in greenhouse based on wireless sensor network. In: 2017 4th International Conference on Information Science and Control Engineering (ICISCE), pp. 970–974 (2017)

Identification and Classification of Cyberbullying Posts: A Recurrent Neural Network Approach Using Under-Sampling and Class Weighting

Ayush Agarwal[1], Aneesh Sreevallabh Chivukula[2], Monowar H. Bhuyan[3], Tony Jan[4], Bhuva Narayan[5], and Mukesh Prasad[2(✉)]

[1] Department of Information Technology, Delhi Technological University, Delhi, India
[2] School of Computer Science, FEIT, University of Technology Sydney, Sydney, Australia
mukesh.prasad@uts.edu.au
[3] Department of Computing Science, Umea University, Umeå, Sweden
[4] School of IT and Engineering, Melbourne Institute of Technology, Sydney, Australia
[5] School of Communication, FASS, University of Technology Sydney, Sydney, Australia

Abstract. With the number of users of social media and web platforms increasing day-by-day in recent years, cyberbullying has become a ubiquitous problem on the internet. Controlling and moderating these social media platforms manually for online abuse and cyberbullying has become a very challenging task. This paper proposes a Recurrent Neural Network (RNN) based approach for the identification and classification of cyberbullying posts. In highly imbalanced input data, a Tomek Links approach does under-sampling to reduce the data imbalance and remove ambiguities in class labelling. Further, the proposed classification model uses Max-Pooling in combination with Bi-directional Long Short-Term Memory (LSTM) network and attention layers. The proposed model is evaluated using Wikipedia datasets to establish the effectiveness of identifying and classifying cyberbullying posts. The extensive experimental results show that our approach performs well in comparison to competing approaches in terms of precision, recall, with F1 score as 0.89, 0.86 and 0.88, respectively.

Keywords: Cyberbullying · Natural language processing · Under-sampling · Recurrent Neural Network · Social media

1 Introduction

There has been a dramatic increase in instances of online abuse and cyberbullying on web platforms such as Wikipedia, YouTube, Instagram, Reddit, Facebook, and Twitter in the recent years. Being able to comment or reply anonymously has further fuelled the growth of such instances. According to Chu et al. [1], 40% of people on the web have experienced bullying or harassment of some kind including sexual harassment, physical threats, etc. In extreme cases, cyberbullying can cause severe mental health

© Springer Nature Switzerland AG 2020
H. Yang et al. (Eds.): ICONIP 2020, CCIS 1333, pp. 113–120, 2020.
https://doi.org/10.1007/978-3-030-63823-8_14

issues as well. Manually filtering the comments or replies that qualify as cyberbullying can be a very tedious, if not an impossible task when there are hundreds of thousands of comments being posted every hour. Hence, there has been an increasing demand for developing ways to detect instances of cyberbullying automatically and filter them out without human intervention.

Due to increasing availability of annotated datasets from web platforms (e.g., Facebook, YouTube), we can leverage machine learning and natural language processing techniques for data-driven solutions to detect cyberbullying posts. Deep learning has also evolved as an efficient solution for such cyberbullying detection problems due to the availability of a large amount of labeled data for supervised learning. However, building highly accurate models for cyberbullying detection remains difficult for several reasons. As outlined by Wulczyn et al. [2], firstly, even though there is a definition for cyberbullying, there are no hard guidelines to determine if a piece of text may constitute a cyberbullying comment or not. This can often be highly dependent on the context of the comment. As observed in crowdsourced datasets, not every annotator has the same opinion about each comment, and the annotations are dependent on the annotator's bias. Secondly, publicly-available datasets are highly imbalanced and have a very small percentage of comments labeled as positive for bullying. Machackova et al. [23] discuss attack patterns of cyberbullying and coping strategies used by different groups. They measure the effect of cyberbullying in terms of the type of attack, length of cyber aggression, harm experienced by the person and how the user responds to the attack. Using crowdsourcing, Wulczyn et al. [2] released cyberbullying datasets over a large corpus of over 100k human-annotated comments on Wikipedia articles. The corpus is annotated to indicate if a comment indicates a personal attack. They have also performed a thorough analysis of the data to answer questions related to anonymity and patterns of attacks. This paper leverages the Wikipedia datasets in modelling evaluation.

Improving upon the approaches using Term Frequency-Inverse Document Frequency (TFIDF), Yin et al. [3] combined features like context, sentiment, and content for designing a supervised classification model in cyberbullying detection. Tokunga [4] provides a review of past research work on cyberbullying victimization. It discusses the evolving definition of the term Cyberbullying and provides research directions to better theorize the detection problem. Schrock and Boyd [5] list the major platforms where Cyberbullying may take place: chat-rooms, social media websites, blogs, and multiplayer online games. Warner and Hirschberg [6] present an annotated corpus for words that are commonly found in hate speech texts. This approach was to feed feature sets in an SVM classifier. Kwok and Wang [7] implement a binary Naïve Bayes classifier on a Twitter dataset for classifying tweets as racist and not racist. But their model did not achieve significant performance gains. Cheng et al. [8] present antisocial behavior analysis based on online forums and report an analysis of the commenting patterns of people who tend to get banned from these forums due to their behavior. Waseem and Hovy [9] propose a list of eleven conditions for annotating a tweet corpus created by them for studying hate speech. They experiment with variable length character n-grams used for performing a binary classification through logistic regression. Waseem [10] performs an analysis of annotator behavior on the corpus. They found that machine learning systems trained on annotations created by experts rather than amateurs were better at predicting hate speech.

Ross et al. [11] assess the reliability of annotations for detecting hate speech and cyberbullying. They used the definition of hateful comments provided by Twitter to see if it improved annotation quality which in their study did not. They motivate the need for a more pervasive definition of cyberbullying which would guide the annotator's behaviour towards creating more reliable annotations. Nobata et al. [12] propose a supervised approach for online abuse detection by extracting four types of features, namely, syntactic, distributed syntactic, linguistic and n-grams. They further performed a temporal analysis of the data to analyze its robustness.

Saleem et al. [13] bypass the annotation problem entirely by finding online communities that identify themselves as self-hate on Reddit. Their method performed better than the earlier keyword-based approaches even while using logistic regression for performing classification. Sahlgren et al. [14] propose a method for learning textual representations for abusive languages through three approaches, keywords, n-grams, and word embeddings. Their method was tested on the Wikipedia dataset using a logistic regression classifier. Aroyehun and Gelbukh [15] experiment with deep learning models like Recurrent Neural Networks (RNNs) and Convolutional Neural Networks (CNNs) for performing the classification on an aggression dataset. For performance improvement, they augmented the training dataset using round-trip translation. Chu et al. [1] assess the Wikipedia dataset with three different deep learning models, LSTM with word embeddings, CNN with word embeddings and CNN with character embeddings. They used glove vectors for initializing the embedding matrix of training data. Cheng et al. [8] propose another approach of using multi-task sentence embedding models using SVM Classifier for abuse and cyberbullying detection. Mishra et al. [16] derive a method for generating context-aware embeddings for out-of-vocabulary words. They then use bi-directional RNNs for performing the classification and posted their results on the Wikipedia dataset. Kumar et al. [17] employ a concatenated attention and bi-directional RNN model for modeling the semantic and contextual relations in the text.

The following are the major contributions of this paper:

- We propose a RNN-based approach to identify and classify the cyberbullying posts.
- We use the word embeddings from two different sources to initialize the model and uses max-pooling to reduce the sparseness of the data representation in an embedding layer.
- Then we use multiple Bi-LSTM layers along with attention for processing contextual information in the text.
- Finally we perform under-sampling and use class weighting to reduce the effect of class imbalance in the dataset on classification model's training loss and testing performance.

The rest of the paper is organized as follows: Sect. 2 explains the proposed approach, Sect. 3 describes the dataset and experimental results, and finally future research directions are given in the conclusion in Sect. 4.

2 Proposed Approach

The text input embeddings are initialized by performing a mean of 300-dimensional glove [24] vectors and 300-dimensional paragram [25] embedding for each word in the vocabulary. We use two different embeddings to accommodate the vocabulary of the Wikipedia dataset as 1/3 of the vocabulary of the dataset was not present in the glove word embeddings. Due to the varied length of comments and some uncommon vocabulary on Wikipedia, the embedding matrix was very sparse. After the text embedding layer, we propose a 1-dimensional max-pooling layer to reduce the sparseness of the embedding matrix by reducing the total number of values in the matrix by half (with window size = 2). This ensured that sparseness was reduced while losing minimum information because of the small window size.

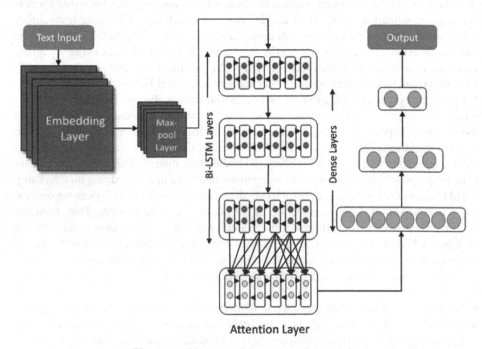

Fig. 1. Architecture of the proposed approach

Bidirectional LSTMs (Bi-LSTMs) [19] are an extension of traditional LSTMs. Bi-LSTMs train two LSTMs instead of one LSTM on the input sequence. The first LSTM is trained on the input sequence as-is and the second LSTM is trained from the opposite direction on a reversed copy of the input sequence. Hence, it is possible to capture the contextual information in a much better way as the information can be processed from both the previous and future time stamps. As a more efficient choice for understanding sequential information, our proposed architecture uses multiple blocks of bi-directional LSTM layers for capturing contextual features in the comments. The proposed model also contains a hierarchical attention layer for focusing on more important words. An input text may contain a lot of irrelevant words which is not important for classification. Attention mechanisms [20] allow us to attend to or focus on the more relevant words of such an input by giving them a higher importance in classification. With an attention mechanism, the full source sentence isn't encoded into a fixed-length vector. Rather, a decoder network is allowed to "attend" to different parts of the source sentence at each step of the output generation. Importantly, this lets the model learn what to attend to, based on the input sentence and what it has produced so far.

The proposed architecture of the model is shown in Fig. 1. The processed text input is sent to the Embedding Layer. Max pooling is applied to the output received from the Embedding Layer. The pooled output is sent to a stack of 3 Bi-directional LSTM Networks and an Attention Layer. The output received from this stack is sent to a network of dense layers. The output is then classified using a softmax classifier. Class weighting is applied to counter the imbalance in the data. Samples in each class are given different weights while calculating the training loss. These class weights are inversely proportional to the number of samples in the class. Thus we give more weightage to the minority class calculating the training loss. The loss function is thus penalized more for misclassifying a sample belonging to the minority class.

3   Performance Evaluation

3.1   Dataset

To establish the performance of the proposed approach, we use the Wikipedia dataset [2], which contains over 100k comments from the discussions in the talk pages of Wikipedia articles. The comments were labeled using crowdsourcing with 10 annotators. Of the 100k comments, 13,590 have been labeled as a personal attack, and rest as not containing any personal attack. The dataset was cleaned to remove white spaces, special characters, punctuation, digits, contractions and some common misspellings were also corrected. The comments were then tokenized. Table 1 is a summary of the Wikipedia dataset for cyberbullying detection. Figure 2 and Fig. 3 display a word cloud of the most frequent keywords in the non-personal attack and personal attack category of the dataset, respectively.

Table 1. Wikipedia dataset

Dataset	No. of posts	Max length of comments	95 percentile length of comments	No. of classes	Vocabulary size
Wikipedia	100,000	2846	231	2	55262

Under-sampling refers to a group of sampling techniques designed to balance the class distribution of an imbalanced dataset. They are generally used to reduce samples from the majority class to reduce or eliminate imbalance in classes in proportion to samples. In contrast, oversampling adds samples to the minority class to reduce the class

Fig. 2. Some of the top words from the comments labeled as a not a personal attack

Fig. 3. Some of the top words from the comments labeled as a personal attack

imbalance. However, over-sampling can often lead to overfitting due to the repetition of samples of the minority class.

In the Wikipedia dataset, the minority class was only a little more than 10% of the dataset. We use Tomek Link under-sampling method [21] to reduce this data imbalance. Tomek Link method is used for removing samples that lie on the borderline of pairs of classes. Given two instances x and y belonging to different classes and separated by a distance dist (x, y), (x, y) is called a Tomek link if there is no instance z such that dist (x, z) is less than dist (x, y) or dist (y, z) is in turn less than dist (x, y). Thus, Tomek Links Under-sampling method removes a sample (A) which satisfies this condition i.e. there is no other sample (B) who's distance from (A) is less than (A)'s distance from origin. Some of the top words from the comments labeled as a not a personal attack and personal attack are shown in Figs. 2 and 3, respectively.

3.2 Results

The dataset is divided into an 80–20 percentage split. The validation data is further divided into test data and validation data according to a 50–50 percentage split. We report the precision, recall and F1 score on the testing data for the proposed RNN model. Training loss is calculated using binary cross-entropy loss function performing the classification with a softmax classifier and an Adam optimizer [22]. Class weighting scheme, is also used to account for the imbalanced data, for further optimization of the training loss. The proposed model achieves 0.89 precision, 0.86 recall and 0.88 F1 score for the test data in Table 2. The performance is compared with the results achieved by Mishra et al. [16], Kumar et al. [17], Chu et al. [1] and Chen et al. [18] in Table 2. The experimental setup for data partition and calculation of precision, recall, F1-score, accuracy and validation approaches for the proposed approach is the same as other approaches with which the result has been compared.

In the proposed method, Tomek link under-sampling helps to remove data samples that may be ambiguous or borderline for the training algorithm to correctly classify. As the text length and vocabulary is highly varied, Max-pooling also reduces the sparseness of the embedding matrix. Bi-directional LSTM Layers make it possible to understand the contextual properties of the cyberbullying comments. Attention Layer helps in attending to the most important parts of the text.

Table 2. Performance comparison of the proposed approach with other methods on the test dataset

Methods	Precision	Recall	F1 score
Mishra et al. [16]	0.81	0.74	0.77
Kumar et al. [17]	0.83	0.77	0.79
Chu et al. [1]	–	–	0.71
Chen et al. [18]	–	0.82	–
The proposed approach	**0.89**	**0.86**	**0.88**

4 Conclusion and Future Work

In this paper, the challenges of detecting cyberbullying in online comments are addressed. The use of under-sampling and class weighting schemes in the training loss function reduces the effect of class imbalance in classifying the dataset. Multiple blocks of bi-directional LSTM and attention layers capture contextual and temporal information in the data. Max-pooling reduces sparseness of the embedding matrix representing cyber-bullying text. Proposed modelling elements combine together to increase classification performance in cyberbullying detection. The proposed approach performs significantly better than the approaches in the state-of-the-art ones on Wikipedia datasets. This method can be employed for the automatic detection of online cyberbullying. Next, we will experiment with sparse representation models and deep generative modelling on the embedding matrix, and explore attention mechanisms for imbalanced classification.

References

1. Chu, T., Jue, K., Wang, M.: Comment abuse classification with deep learning. Von https://web.stanford.edu/class/cs224n/reports/2762092.pdf. abgerufen (2016)
2. Wulczyn, E., Thain, N., Dixon, L.: Ex machina: personal attacks seen at scale. In: Proceedings of the 26th International Conference on World Wide Web, pp. 1391–1399 (2017)
3. Yin, D., Xue, Z., Hong, L., Davison, B.D., Kontostathis, A., Edwards, L.: Detection of harassment on web 2.0. In: Proceedings of the Content Analysis in the WEB, vol. 2, pp. 1–7 (2009)
4. Tokunaga, R.S.: Following you home from school: a critical review and synthesis of research on cyberbullying victimization. Comput. Hum. Behav. **26**(3), 277–287 (2010)
5. Schrock, A., Boyd, D.: Problematic youth interaction online: Solicitation, harassment, and cyberbullying. In: Computer-Mediated Communication in Personal Relationships, pp. 368–398 (2011)
6. Warner, W., Hirschberg, J.: Detecting hate speech on the world wide web. In: Proceedings of the Second Workshop on Language in Social Media, pp. 19–26. Association for Computational Linguistics (2012)
7. Kwok, I., Wang, Y.: Locate the hate: detecting tweets against blacks. In: Twenty-Seventh AAAI Conference on Artificial Intelligence (2013)
8. Cheng, J., Danescu-Niculescu-Mizil, C., Leskovec, J.: Antisocial behavior in online discussion communities. In: Ninth International AAAI Conference on Web and Social Media (2015)

9. Waseem, Z., Hovy, D.: Hateful symbols or hateful people? Predictive features for hate speech detection on Twitter. In: Proceedings of the NAACL Student Research Workshop, pp. 88–93 (2016)
10. Waseem, Z.: Are you a racist or am i seeing things? Annotator influence on hate speech detection on Twitter. In: Proceedings of the First Workshop on NLP and Computational Social Science, pp. 138–142 (2016)
11. Ross, B., Rist, M., Carbonell, G., Cabrera, B., Kurowsky, N., Wojatzki, M.: Measuring the reliability of hate speech annotations: the case of the european refugee crisis, arXiv preprint arXiv:1701.08118 (2017)
12. Nobata, C., Tetreault, J., Thomas, A., Mehdad, Y., Chang, Y.: Abusive language detection in online user content. In: Proceedings of the 25th International Conference on World Wide Web, pp. 145–153 (2016)
13. Saleem, H.M., Dillon, K.P., Benesch, S., Ruths, D.: A web of hate: tackling hateful speech in online social spaces, arXiv preprint arXiv:1709.10159 (2017)
14. Sahlgren, M., Isbister, T., Olsson, F.: Learning representations for detecting abusive language. In: Proceedings of the 2nd Workshop on Abusive Language Online (ALW2), pp. 115–123 (2018)
15. Aroyehun, S.T., Gelbukh, A.: Aggression detection in social media: using deep neural networks, data augmentation, and pseudo labeling. In: Proceedings of the First Workshop on Trolling, Aggression and Cyberbullying (TRAC-2018), pp. 90–97 (2018)
16. Mishra, P., Yannakoudakis, H., Shutova, E.: Neural character-based composition models for abuse detection, arXiv preprint arXiv:1809.00378 (2018)
17. Kumar, R., Ojha, A.K., Malmasi, S., Zampieri, M.: Benchmarking aggression identification in social media. In: Proceedings of the First Workshop on Trolling, Aggression and Cyberbullying (TRAC-2018), pp. 1–11 (2018)
18. Chen, H., McKeever, S., Delany, S.J.: The use of deep learning distributed representations in the identification of abusive text. In: Proceedings of the International AAAI Conference on Web and Social Media, vol. 13, no. 01, pp. 125–133 (2019)
19. Schuster, M., Paliwal, K.K.: Bidirectional recurrent neural networks. IEEE Trans. Signal Process. **45**(11), 2673–2681 (1997)
20. Vaswani, A., et al.: Attention is all you need. In: Advances in Neural Information Processing Systems, pp. 5998–6008 (2017)
21. Tomek, I.: Two modifications of CNN (1976)
22. Kingma, D.P., Ba, J.: Adam: a method for stochastic optimization, arXiv preprint arXiv:1412.6980 (2014)
23. Machackova, H., Cerna, A., Sevcikova, A., Dedkova, L., Daneback, K.: Effectiveness of coping strategies for victims of cyberbullying. Cyberpsychol.: J. Psychosoc. Res. Cyberspace **7**(3) (2013)
24. Pennington, J., Socher, R., Manning, C.D.: Glove: global vectors for word representation. In: Proceedings of the 2014 Conference on Empirical Methods in Natural Language Processing (EMNLP), pp. 1532–1543 (2014)
25. Wieting, J., Bansal, M., Gimpel, K., Livescu, K.: Towards universal paraphrastic sentence embeddings, arXiv preprint arXiv:1511.08198 (2015)

Knowledge-Experience Graph with Denoising Autoencoder for Zero-Shot Learning in Visual Cognitive Development

Xinyue Zhang[1], Xu Yang[1(✉)], Zhiyong Liu[1], Lu Zhang[1], Dongchun Ren[2], and Mingyu Fan[2]

[1] State Key Laboratory of Management and Control for Complex Systems, Institute of Automation, Chinese Academy of Sciences, Beijing 100190, People's Republic of China
{Zhangxinyue2020,xu.yang}@ia.ac.cn
[2] Meituan-Dianping Group, Beijing 100190, People's Republic of China
rendongchun@meituan.com

Abstract. Visual cognitive development is vital for intelligent robots to handle various types of visual tasks rather than predefined ones. It can transfer the classification ability from an original model to a novel task. However, the high reliance on large amounts of data hinders its development. The energy it costs to adjust to the novel tasks is also a tough problem. Thus we propose a model called knowledge-experience graph (KEG) to imitate the mechanisms of human brains. With the help of social knowledge stored in the knowledge graph, the novel classes can be easily added. The combination of the experience via denoising autoencoder (DAE) also takes the relationship in the visual space into account. With the propagation of information among the graph by graph convolutional network (GCN), KEG generates the classifier of the novel tasks effectively. Experiments show that KEG improves the classification accuracy of novel categories on zero-shot learning and accomplishes visual cognitive development to a certain extent.

Keywords: GCN · Zero-shot learning · Cross-task learning · Cognitive development · Image classification · Denoising autoencoder

1 Introduction

Visual cognitive development is important for intelligent robots. With the ever-growing development of computer vision, an intelligent robot has to face various types of visual tasks rather than deterministic and predefined ones. To adjust

This work is supported partly by the National Natural Science Foundation (NSFC) of China (grants 61973301, 61972020, 61633009, and U1613213), partly by the National Key R&D Program of China (grants 2016YFC0300801 and 2017YFB1300202), partly by the Beijing Science and Technology Plan Project, and partly by the Meituan Open R&D Fund.

© Springer Nature Switzerland AG 2020
H. Yang et al. (Eds.): ICONIP 2020, CCIS 1333, pp. 121–129, 2020.
https://doi.org/10.1007/978-3-030-63823-8_15

to this unstructured and dynamic environments, a robot needs to transfer the classification ability from an original model to a novel task, while the former ability is still reserved. Cognitive development not only focuses on the cross-task problem but also deals with the zero-shot learning task. The original model has to use the unlabeled samples to retrain itself, which means it learns a novel classifier with no need of human annotation. In this way, the time and energy it takes to adjust to the novel tasks may be cut down a lot and the intelligent robot may be applied to a much tough and complicated area.

The recently proposed graph convolutional network [2] has exhibited a powerful ability in transferring knowledge across tasks. It can propagate messages among the graph and take the structural information into account. To accomplish the visual cognitive development of robots, it is reasonable to set up a neural network evolving on its own just as human brains, which is accomplished mostly by transferring information from base categories with the help of supplementary information. There are two normal sources of this information. The first one is the social knowledge developed in society, and the second one is the experience obtained based on previous tasks, which is also called empirical knowledge.

Recent researches on zero-shot learning are mostly from two viewpoints. Social knowledge builds the relation map of different classes at the macro level. Wang et al. [1] build an unweighted knowledge graph combined with word embedding [3,4] upon the graph convolutional network [2] to handle zero-shot problem. Kampffmeyer et al. [5] improve upon this model and propose Dense Graph Propagation to prevent dilution of knowledge. As for the empirical knowledge, it is acquired by recalling the related experience of the recognition task [7,8]. Gidaris et al. [6] get the experience as CNN is trained to recognize the base classes and propose to implement the Denoising Autoencoder network to reconstruct general weights of both the base classes and novel classes. The main part of these models is to initialize the novel categories with few samples.

Though social knowledge makes it easy to add novel classes to the map, it ignores the relationship in visual space. Empirical knowledge on the other side considers the unique visual features of the datasets. However, as the visual features are extracted from images, it can not handle zero-shot problem. Thus we argue that both these methods are not ideal for visual cognitive development.

To tackle this problem, we propose to combine social knowledge and empirical knowledge to build the relation map. The key problem for zero-shot learning is to initialize the features of novel categories with no labeled samples available. An intuitive idea is to estimates the feature of novel ones from prestored social knowledge. Based on this idea, we propose a model called knowledge-experience graph (KEG). KEG makes use of social knowledge in form of knowledge graph. The knowledge graph shows the relationship between the categories with the structure of inheritance. Novel classes aggregate supplementary information from related classes to conduct knowledge inference along the edges. Furthermore, it uses a traditional recognition model to train the base classes and observes the classification weights of base classes. Combined with the estimated value of novel classes from social knowledge, these initial weights build up an unweighted graph with the relationship of similarity. By employing the graph convolution network, information of different nodes propagates along edges and aggregates on the novel classes iteratively. By taking the classification of base classes as ground truth, KEG finally gets the weights of novel classes and develops its cognitive ability on the novel task.

The main contributions of the paper can be summarized in three aspects. Firstly, KEG extracts social knowledge from the knowledge graph and makes it easier to add novel tasks to the original model. Secondly, based on the denoising autoencoder, the combination of the experience makes KEG focus more on the uniqueness of specific tasks. Thirdly, by introducing the graph convolutional network, the inter-cluster similarity and inter-cluster dissimilarity are taken into consideration at the same time. Thus it makes sense for KEG to deal with visual cognitive development for robots.

2   Methodology

2.1   Problem Definition

KEG focuses on visual cognitive development on the image classification task. Let C denotes all of the categories involved in the task which contains two parts novel classes C_{novel} and base classes C_{base}. The original model is trained on the C_{base} with the labeled samples, while novel classes refer to the task with no labels. According to zero-shot learning, the dataset contains two parts: the training set D_{train} with images from base classes and the testing set D_{test} with images from novel classes. Thus KEG learns from D_{train} to reconstruct a model available to D_{test} at the same time.

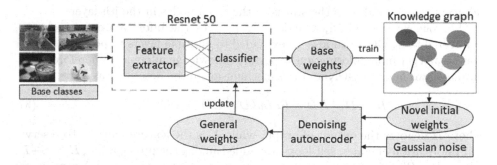

Fig. 1. Integrated framework of KEG which takes both the social knowledge and empirical knowledge into account.

2.2   Knowledge Inference Module

The knowledge graph well represents the relation map among different categories. Given an unweighted graph as $G = <V, E>$, where $V = \{v_1, v_2, ..., v_n\}$ represents the node-set of all classes, each node in it refers to a category.

$E = \{e_{i,j} = (v_i, v_j)\}$ is an edge set, if two node are related there will be an edge between them. KEG exploits the WordNet [10] as the knowledge graph to extract social knowledge. For every category, WordNet stores up its semantic description. Glove text model trained on the Wikipedia dataset is exploited to transfer the semantic description into a word embedding vector that can be operated. The feature matrix of knowledge denoted as $X_K \in R^{N \times S}$, where N is the total number of classes and S is the feature dimension of each class. For WordNet, the relationship is complicated, like hyponymy, meronymy, and troponymy. KEG builds the knowledge graph based on the hyponymy. The relationship between the nodes can be represented as

$$e_{(i,j)} = \begin{cases} 1, & \text{hyponymy(i,j)} \\ 0, & otherwise \end{cases} \tag{1}$$

The knowledge inference module works to build up the relationship among categories for zero-shot learning. The key problem is to initialize the classification weights of novel classes with no labeled samples. To gather information from related base classes to novel ones, KEG employs the graph convolutional network on the knowledge graph. For one layer of the graph neural network, a given node receives messages propagate from its neighbor along the edges and then aggregates this information combined with its status to update the class feature. The update process for a given node can be represented as

$$h^{i+1} = f(h^i, E) \tag{2}$$

where $f(x)$ refers to the mechanism of propagation and aggregation. E is the adjacent matrix and h^i is the status of the given nodes in the ith layer.

For one layer in GCN, a node only receives the information from classes connected to it. GCN can also be extended to multiple layers to perform deeper spread and get more information to perform knowledge inference. Therefore KEG employs two layer of GCN and the mechanism can be described as

$$H = \hat{D}^{-\frac{1}{2}} \hat{E} \hat{D}^{-\frac{1}{2}} ReLu(\hat{D}^{-\frac{1}{2}} \hat{E} \hat{D}^{-\frac{1}{2}} X K^{(0)}) K^{(1)} \tag{3}$$

where H denotes the output of graph, while X is the feature matrix. To reserve self information of nodes, self-loops are added among the propagation, $\hat{E} = E + I$, where $E \in R^{N \times N}$ is the symmetric adjacency matrix and $I \in R^{N \times N}$ represents identity matrix. $D_{ii} = \sum_j E_{ij}$ normalizes rows in E to prevent the scale of input modified by E. K^l is the weight matrix of the lth layer which GCN regulates constantly to achieve better performance.

During the training process, the goal is to predict the initial classification of novel classes. The graph is trained to minimize the predicted classification weights and the ground-truth weights by optimizing the loss

$$L = \frac{1}{2M} \sum_{i=1}^{M} \sum_{j=1}^{P} (W_{i,j} - W_{i,j}^k)^2, \tag{4}$$

where W^k refers to the output of base classes on GCN, which is a part of H, and W denotes the ground truth of classification weight obtained from the visual transfer model. M is the number of base classes and P is the dimensionality of the vector.

2.3   Visual Transfer Module

To take the visual feature into account, KEG learns the experience from the process the original model is trained. For an traditional classification model $C(F(\cdot|\theta)|w)$ based on CNN, it contains two parts: feature extractor $F(\cdot|\theta)$ and category classifier $C(\cdot|w^v)$ where θ and w^v indicate the parameters trained with $C_{train} = \{(\hat{x}_1, \hat{y}_1), ..., (\hat{x}_M, \hat{y}_M)\}$. $W^v \in R^{M \times P}$ refers to the classification weights that determines the classification score of each category. M is the total number of base categories and P is the length of classification weight. The goal of visual transfer module is to reconstruct a general version of classification with the framework of denoising autoencoder.

KEG also builds up a graph to represent the relationship among categories, i.e. $G^v = <X^v, E^v>$, where X^v is the node set and E^v represents the edge set. Each node refers to a category and has a visual feature X_i^v. For the base classes, the visual feature is the classification weights extracted from the original model while for the novel ones it is the initial classification from the knowledge inference model.

$$x_i^v = \begin{cases} w^v, & C_i \in C_{base} \\ w^k, & C_i \in C_{novel} \end{cases} \tag{5}$$

KEG exploits cosine similarity to generate propagation channels which are the set of edges$(i, j) \in E$ of the graph. With the boundary of cosine similarity, it can decide the density of the graph. If the visual feature of two classes are related their information can be propagated reciprocally by the edge.

$$e_{(i,j)} = \begin{cases} 1, & \frac{x_i^v \cdot x_j^v}{\|x_j^v\|\|x_j^v\|} > s \\ 0, & otherwise \end{cases} \tag{6}$$

It is worth noting that the edge is connected in terms of cosine similarity of the initial node features which is the vector before the injection of Gaussian noise. S refers to the boundary to the cosine similarity which decides the density of the graph.

To exploit the denoising autoencoder to generate the classification weights of novel classes, KEG injects Gaussian noise to the input

$$\hat{x^v} = x^v + G \tag{7}$$

G is the Gaussian noise with the same size as the node feature. Autoencoder is a neural network that generates the output by taking the input as the ground-truth. KEG uses the classification weights extracted from the original model as the ground-truth. By employing a two layers GCN on the graph, novel classes learn the mechanism of an end to end learning of classification model from the original one and generate more universal classification weights $\tilde{W} \in R^{N \times P}$. $\tilde{W}$ is applied to the last layer of the original model which is transferred to $C(F(\cdot|\theta)|\tilde{w})$. Note that differs from W^v, $\tilde{W}$ contains n rows of P, which means it represents the classification of the whole classes C.

With the knowledge inference module and visual transfer module, KEG develops the cognitive ability to novel tasks by generating more universal classification weights. Combined with the original classification model, KEG computes the classification score of every categories as $[s_1, s_2, ..., s_N] = \{z^T \tilde{w}_1, z^T \tilde{w}_2, ..., z^T \tilde{w}_N\}$. z refers to the visual features extracted from the original model. In other words, KEG learns a mapping network, which makes a good inference from the knowledge and experience space to visual space. With the general classification scores $s = z^T \tilde{w}$, KEG distinguishes novel classes with few samples and transfers the original model to other datasets efficiently.

3   Experiment

3.1   Datasets

As KEG focus on the transfer learning of models between different datasets, ImageNet [9] is used as the base classes and AWA2 [17] as the novel classes. Besides, WordNet represents the source for constructing a knowledge graph.

ImageNet. ImageNet is an image dataset constructed base on the hierarchical structure of WordNet. We use ImageNet 2012 as the training set for zero-shot learning, which contains 1000 categories. There are no more than half of the categories are animals. Besides it also contains other classes like daily necessities, buildings, foods, which is a general dataset.

Animals with Attributes 2. AwA2 contains images of 50 animal classes with pre-extracted feature for each image. However, as we try to learn the experience from base classes, we do not use the feature it provides, but the images only. There are about ten classes that are disjoint from ImageNet and they make up the testing set in the experiment to test the transfer ability of KEG.

3.2   Experimental Setting

The original recognition model is pre-trained on ResNet50 on ImageNet 2012. The final general classification weights will adjust to the last layer of it. The output dimension of KEG is set to 2049. The model is trained in 3000 epochs. We use Adam optimizer for the training process with the weight decay of 0.0005 and the learning rate of 0.001. The boundary of similarity is set to 0.6 to ensure the density of the graph is suitable. The information of every node is mixed with both experience and knowledge equably. The whole project is under the framework of PyTorch and operated on the Ubuntu system.

3.3   Comparison

Table 1. Top-1 accuracy (%) results for classification

Model	Accuracy
SGCN [5]	74.6
SSE [11]	61.0
DEM [12]	67.1
SAE [13]	61.0
RelationNet [14]	64.2
SYNC [15]	46.6
SJE [16]	61.9
KEG	77.8

From the experiment results posted in Table 1, KEG shows better performance on zero-shot learning. It increases the classification accuracy of novel tasks. Previous methods have to extract visual features from novel classes, KEG needs no sample on novel categories. KEG stores prior social knowledge with the structure of the knowledge graph. It can easily get information from the semantic description to support its visual inference. Thus with the help of social knowledge, the way exploits empirical information expands its application range.

On the other hand, the information from the social knowledge is lack of the feature from visual space. Empirical knowledge shows the connection between categories from a visual point. From the experiment, it shows there are obvious differences in the accuracy of specific categories between KEG and SGCN, for example, 'mole'. The direct neighbors of 'mole' from the inheritance and the visual space are different. From the relationship shown in Fig. 2, we notice that besides the relationship from biology, there is also a similarity in the visual feature. For example, the dolphin belongs to the mammal but it looks more like fish. Thus it is more reasonable to gather information from the visual side since the goal of the model is to classify the image correctly.

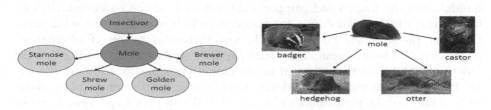

Fig. 2. The direct neighbor from the relationship of inheritance and the visual space.

3.4 Analysis of KEG

We perform ablation studies on modules of KEG to ensure that the choices we make have the best performance. Specifically, we examine the modules on the following. First, we test the similarity boundary of the connection mechanism to analyze the influence of the density of the graph. Then we use the best performance "similarity" and change the "DAE module" to ensure its importance for the increase of accuracy. The result of the ablation study is shown below.

Table 2. Top-1 accuracy results for classification

Similarity	0.8	0.6	0.5	0.4
Accuracy	76.3	77.8	73.3	73.96
DAE module	0	1		
Accuracy	74.6	77.8		

From the ablation study, we notice that a suitable similarity boundary is vital for accuracy. When the boundary is high, The similarity between categories is tight which results in a dense graph. However large boundary does not bring better performance which may be caused by dilution of information through the path. When the boundary is small, it means the relationship between the neighbor becomes further which results in a sparse graph. Since the given node can not get enough supplementary information from its neighbor the accuracy cuts down as well. Thus a suitable similarity boundary is vital for the performance. We also test the necessity of the model which shows that with the help of DAE the classification accuracy of zero-shot learning increases. The injected Gaussian noise indeed helps to reconstruct a general version of the classification weights.

4 Conclusion

In this paper, we address the problem of visual cognitive development from two parts: zero-shot learning and cross-task learning. The proposed model KEG stores social knowledge with the structure of the knowledge graph. Thus KEG builds a relation map, which supports the accession of the novel task. It also takes the feature relationship in the visual space into account with the information from the empirical knowledge. The mix of the two sources of information makes it suitable to accomplish visual cognitive development. During experiments, the ability of the proposed model outperforms previous state-of-the-art methods. In future work, we will devote to improving the mechanism of fusion to further improve the performance of our model. We also try to perform a better connection mode to avoid the attenuation of information.

References

1. Wang, X.L., Ye, Y.F., Gupta, A.: Zero-shot Recognition via Semantic Embeddings and Knowledge Graphs. In: CVPR (2017)
2. Kipf, T.N., Welling, M.: Semi-supervised classification with graph convolutional networks. In: ICLR (2017)
3. Frome, A., et al.: Devise: a deep visual-semantic embedding model. In: Advances in Neural Information Processing Systems, pp. 2121–2129 (2013)
4. Li, Y., Wang, D., Hu, H., Lin, Y., Zhuang, Y.: Zero-shot recognition using dual visual-semantic mapping paths. In: Proceedings of the IEEE Conference on Computer Vision and Pattern Recognition (2017)
5. Kampffmeyer, M., Chen, Y., Chen, Y.: Rethinking knowledge graph propagation for zero-shot learning. In: Conference on Computer Vision and Pattern Recognition (2019)
6. Gidaris, S., Komodakis, N.: Generating classification weights with GNN Denoising Autoencoders for few-shot learning. In: Conference on Computer Vision and Pattern Recognition (2019)
7. He, K., Ren, S., Sun, J.: Deep residual learning for image recognition. In: Proceedings of the IEEE Conference on Computer Vision and Pattern Recognition, pp. 770–778 (2016)
8. Krizhevsky, A., Sutskever, I., Hinton, G.E.: classification with deep convolutional neural networks. In: Advances in Neural Information Processing Systems, pp. 1097–1105 (2012)
9. Deng, J., Dong, W., Socher, R., Li, L.J., Li, K., Fei-Fei, L.:. Imagenet: a large-scale hierarchical image database. In Proceedings of the IEEE Conference on Computer Vision and Pattern Recognition, pp. 248–255 (2009)
10. Miller, G.A.: Wordnet: a lexical database for english. Commun. ACM **38**(11), 39–41 (1995)
11. Ziming, Z., Saligrama, V.: Zero-shot learning via semantic similarity embedding. In: Proceedings of the IEEE International Conference on Computer Vision, pp. 4166–4174 (2015)
12. Zhang, L., Xiang, T., Gong, S.: Learning a deep embedding model for zero-shot learning. In: Proceedings of the IEEE Conference on Computer Vision and Pattern Recognition, pp. 2021–2030 (2017)
13. Kodirov, E., Xiang, T., Gong, S.: Semantic autoencoder for zero-shot learning. In: Proceedings of the IEEE Conference on Computer Vision and Pattern Recognition, pp. 3174–3183 (2017)
14. Sung, F., Yongxin, Y., Li, Z., Xiang, T., Torr, P., Hospedales, T.M.: Learning to compare: Relation network for few-shot learning. In: Proceedings of the IEEE Conference on Computer Vision and Pattern Recognition, pp. 1199–1208 (2018)
15. Changpinyo, S., Wei-Lun, C., Boqing, G., Sha, F.: Synthesized classifiers for zero-shot learning. In: Proceedings of the IEEE Conference on Computer Vision and Pattern Recognition, pp. 5327–5336 (2016)
16. Akata, Z., Reed, S., Walter, D., Honglak, L., Schiele, B.: Evaluation of output embeddings for fine-grained image classification. In: Proceedings of the IEEE Conference on Computer Vision and Pattern Recognition, pp. 2927–2936 (2015)
17. Xian, Y., Lampert, C.H., Schiele, B., Akata, Z.: Zero-Shot learning - a comprehensive evaluation of the good, the bad and the ugly. IEEE Trans. Pattern Anal. Mach. Intell. **40**(8), 2251–2265 (2018)

Learning Higher Representations from Bioacoustics: A Sequence-to-Sequence Deep Learning Approach for Bird Sound Classification

Yu Qiao[1], Kun Qian[2(✉)], and Ziping Zhao[1(✉)]

[1] College of Computer and Information Engineering, Tianjin Normal University, Tianjin, China
jaderqiao@126.com, ztianjin@126.com
[2] Educational Physiology Laboratory, The University of Tokyo, Tokyo, Japan
qian@p.u-tokyo.ac.jp

Abstract. In the past two decades, a plethora of efforts have been given to the field of automatic classification of bird sounds, which can facilitate a long-term, non-human, and low-energy consumption ubiquitous computing system for monitoring the nature reserve. Nevertheless, human hand-crafted features need numerous domain knowledge, and inevitably make the designing progress time-consuming and expensive. To this line, we propose a sequence-to-sequence deep learning approach for extracting the higher representations automatically from bird sounds without any human expert knowledge. First, we transform the birds sound audio into spectrograms. Subsequently, higher representations were learnt by an autoencoder-based encoder-decoder paradigm combined with the deep recurrent neural networks. Finally, two typical machine learning models are selected to predict the classes, i.e., support vector machines and multi-layer perceptrons. Experimental results demonstrate the effectiveness of the method proposed, which can reach an unweighted average recall (UAR) at 66.8% in recognising 86 species of birds.

Keywords: Sequence-to-sequence learning · Bird sound classification · Bioacoustics · Deep learning · Internet of Things

This work was partially supported by the National Natural Science Foundation of China (Grant No. 61702370), P. R. China, the Key Program of the Natural Science Foundation of Tianjin (Grant No. 18JCZDJC36300), P. R. China, the Open Projects Program of the National Laboratory of Pattern Recognition, P. R. China, the Zhejiang Lab's International Talent Fund for Young Professionals (Project HANAMI), P. R. China, the JSPS Postdoctoral Fellowship for Research in Japan (ID No. P19081) from the Japan Society for the Promotion of Science (JSPS), Japan, and the Grants-in-Aid for Scientific Research (No. 19F19081) from the Ministry of Education, Culture, Sports, Science and Technology, Japan.

H. Yang et al. (Eds.): ICONIP 2020, CCIS 1333, pp. 130–138, 2020.
https://doi.org/10.1007/978-3-030-63823-8_16

1 Introduction

Bird sound recognition refers to the identification of bird species by a given audio. In recent years, the global climate has changed rapidly, and this drastic climate change will lead to a large number of species decrease, which will seriously affect the biological diversity. For this reason, people have come up with many ways to track endangered species. Nevertheless, most of them are expensive for human resources. For instance, observing birds through traditional telescopes can be easily influenced by the weather, which makes the observation of birds less accurate and inconvenient. To overcome the aforementioned challenges, the wireless acoustic sensor networks (WASN) can not only cover the unattended field and/or other places with harsh environment, but also alleviate the influence of weather on bird observation.

In the past decade, numerous efforts have been given to the field of bird sound classification. Many scholars began to use the information implied in bird sound to classify bird species, so as to determine the distribution of birds in a certain area. Large scale acoustic features feeding to an extreme learning machine was introduced in [1,2], which demonstrated an efficient and fast way for recognising bird species by using human hand-crafted features. For machine learning models, SVM was found efficient in previous work [3–5]. There are also applications of convolution neural networks to bird sound recognition. Piczak et al. used convolutional neural networks to do pure audio bird recognition [6]. Three different CNN models were trained according to the difference of time-frequency representations (TFRs): Mel-CNN, Harm-CNN, Perc-CNN. Also, trained a different deep learning framework SubSpectralNet (Subnet-CNN), which is employed to classify bird Sounds. Finally, experiments proved that the performance of classification can be improved by selectively combining the four models separately [7].

In this work, motivated by the success achieved in the field of *natural language processing*, we propose a sequence-to-sequence deep learning model based on recurrent neural network (RNN) for extracting higher representations from the bird sounds without any human domain knowledge. Originally, the sequential to-sequence model is used to deal with speech-to-speech or text-to-speech translation in [8,9]. Similar to the voice of the human, bird sound belongs to a kind of time sequence data, and contains a plenty of semantic information.

For above considerations, sequence-to-sequence structure is introduced to the higher representations learning of bird sounds. As show in Fig. 1, the specific steps include (a) Preprocessing: transform the raw bird sound audio data to spectrograms; (b) Autoencoder Training: the autoencoder-based RNN models is trained by continuously reducing the loss between the prediction sequence and the input sequence; (c) Higher Representations Extraction: the higher representations were learnt by autoencoder-based RNN models; (d) Classifiers Training: a classifier is selected for making the final prediction by the learnt representations. We select two typical machine learning models, i.e., support vector machine (SVM) and multi-layer perceptron (MLP) as the classifiers in this study. (e) Classification Predictions: outputting the results using different classifier.

The main contributions in this work are: Firstly, we introduce the unsupervised sequence-to-sequence deep learning approach to the field of learning higher representations from bird sound. Secondly, we investigate the effect by using different topologies of the deep neural networks. Finally, we analyze and discuss the deep learnt features' performances on recognising bird sounds. We hope this study can facilitate the relevant work in finding more robust and efficient acoustical features from the bioacoustics in future.

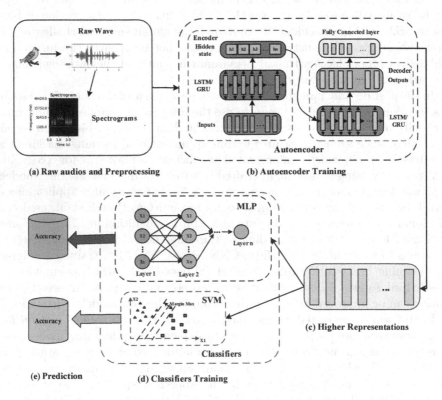

Fig. 1. The framework of proposed Seq2Seq based higher representation learning system for bird sound classification.

This paper is organized as follows: Firstly, we introduce the methods used in Sect. 2. Section 3 introduces experimental design, including description of the database, data preprocessing, experimental setting and results. And the discussion will be given Sect. 4. Finally, we conclude this study in Sect. 5.

2   Methods

2.1   Sequence-to-Sequence Deep Learning Approach

Sequence to Sequence (Seq2Seq) learning was firstly proposed by Kyunghyun Cho et al. [10], which has been demonstrated to be efficient in the field of machine translation and speech recognition [11].

Here, we will describe the underlying framework of RNN Encoder-Decoder briefly, which proposed by Sutskever et al. [12]. In the Encoder-Decoder framework, encoder readers input sequence and transform it into a vector v. Here, we assume $X = (x_1, x_2, ..., x_t)$ as input sequence, and $Y = (y_1, y_2, ..., y_t)$ as output sequence, then

$$h_t = f(x_t, h_{t-1}) \tag{1}$$

Where f is the nonlinear function of RNN hidden layer, h_t is the hidden state at time t, which is calculated by the input x_t at time t and the hidden state of the previous layer h_{t-1}.

$$v = q(h_1, h_2, ..., h_t) \tag{2}$$

Where in Eq. (2), encoder converts the hidden state at all moment into a vector v through a nonlinear function q, vector v contains the key information extracted from the input sequence.

The decoder is often trained to predict the output of next time y_t, which is obtain by vector v and all of the previous predictions $y_1, y_2, ..., y_{t-1}$, such as Eq. (3):

$$
\begin{aligned}
& p(y_1, y_2, ..., y_t | x_1, x_2, ..., x_t) \\
& = \prod_{t=1}^{t} p(y_t | x_1, x_2, ..., x_{t-1}, y_1, y_2, ..., y_{t-1}) \\
& = \prod_{t=1}^{t} p(y_t | v, y_1, y_2, ..., y_{t-1})
\end{aligned}
\tag{3}
$$

The decoder probability distribution at a given time can be expressed as

$$\prod_{t=1}^{t} p(y_t | v, y_1, y_2, ..., y_{t-1}) = g(h_t, y_{t-1}, v) \tag{4}$$

where g is a nonlinear, potentially multi-layered, function that outputs the probability of y_t, and h_t is the hidden state of the RNN.

Motivated by the success of Seq2Seq, we introduce and propose an autoencoder based RNN model in bird sound classification task.

The Mel spectrum is a time-dependent sequence of frequency vectors, which represents the amplitude of the MEL frequency band of a piece of audio. In the recurrent autoencoder, the Mel spectrum is fed to the multi-layer encoder RNN firstly, and then updates the hidden state of the encoder according to the input frequency vector. The final hidden state is reconstructed by a full connection layer that contains information about the entire input sequence. Finally, a multi-layer decoder RNN reconstructs the original input sequence utilizing the reconstructed features.

Here, we'll mainly train a Seq2Seq model for the extraction of the higher representations. Our aim is to extract the features of the full connection layer from the trained Seq2Seq model, which is the key for the later retraining of the classification model.

2.2 Evaluation Metrics Method

Considering the imbalanced distribution of the MNB database, we use the unweighted average recall (UAR) as the evaluation metrics for this study. UAR is defined as the averaged recall achieved by the model in recognising different classes. Compared to the conventionally used accuracy, UAR is more rigorous in the case of imbalanced data. For details of UAR, it can be referred to [13].

3 Experimental Design

3.1 Database

In this study, we use the database provided by the Museum für Naturkunde Berlin (MNB)[1], Berlin, Germany. To make an applicable training process, we eliminated the species which contain less than 20 audio recordings, which resulted in a database having 86 species in total (5 060 audio recordings with a whole length of approximately 4.0 h). We split the whole database into three sets, i.e., train (60%), development (20%), and test (20%), respectively. All the hyper-parameters of the classifiers will be tuned and optimised by the dev set, and applied to the final test set.

3.2 Preprocessing

Since the sample time in the database is different, before extracting the spectrograms, we found that the high frequency part of bird song could be included by converting the original audio into 4 s. Therefore, we adopted the following processing: if the time is less than 4 s, fill it according to the silence; instead, it only intercepts to 4 s.

In addition, because the sampling frequencies of bird sounds are not consistent, so according to Nyquist's sampling law: when the sampling frequency f_s is greater than 2 times of the highest frequency f_{max} in the signal, that is $f_s > 2f_{max}$, the sampled digital signal can completely retain the information in the original signal. Based on this law, when extracting the spectrograms, the

---

[1] http://www.animalsoundarchive.org/RefSys/Statistics.php.

highest frequency of all the audios are controlled to about half of the sampling frequency. In this way, the extracted spectrograms contain the information of the high-frequency part of the bird sound, so that the extracted features can contain more effective information, thus ensuring the accuracy of subsequent training.

In order to reduce the influence of noise on the classification results, when extracting the features of the spectrograms, we found that it was better to control the amplitude below −50 db.

To conclude, the raw audio data of bird sound will be transformed to spectrograms with the window width w = 0.08 s, the window overlap 0.5w = 0.04 s, and $N_{mel} = 128$ Mel frequency bands, with amplitude clipping below −50 db.

3.3 Experimental Setting

In the phase of Seq2Seq learning, we used the open source toolkit, i.e., AuDeep [14,15]. When investigating the topologies of the deep learning models, we firstly study the long short-term memory (LSTM) [12] and the gated recurrent unit (GRU) [16] based RNNs. Then, we compare the different Encoder-Decoder structures with the combinations of the unidirectional RNN and the bidirectional RNN (BiRNN). Additionally, we change the hidden layer numbers with 2, 3, or 4 to find the differences in capacity of learning higher representations. Our experiment is going to be performed for 64 batch size, learning rate 0.001 and 20% dropout.

When tuning the hyper-parameters of the models, we use a grid searching strategy in development set and apply the optimised values to the test set. For SVM, the kernels are selected from *linear, radical basis function (RBF), poly,* and *sigmoid*. The *Gama* and *C* values are all tunned from 10^{-5}, 10^{-4}, ..., 10^4, 10^5. For MLP, the *Alpha* value is tuned as the same grid as *Gama* and *C* values. The hidden layer structures are optimised from [(500, 500, 500), (600, 600, 600), (650, 650, 650), (700, 700, 700), (750, 750, 750), (800, 800, 800), (850, 850, 850), (900, 900, 900), (950, 950, 950), (1000, 1000, 1000), (1200, 1200, 1200)]. Both of the SVM and the MLP models are implemented in Python script based on the scikit-learn library [17]. To eliminate the effects of outliers, all of the features are standardised before fed into the classifiers.

3.4 Experimental Results

By adjusting the topologies of the autoencoder, network depth and various parameters of the classifiers, the best parameters of the final experiment are shown in the Table 1.

The results using LSTM and GRU based RNN models (two hidden layers) are shown in Table 2 and Table 3, respectively. In this study, a two hidden layer GRU (BiRNN-BiRNN as the Encoder-Decoder) based model can reach the best performance. In particular, when fed into a MLP classifier, the UAR can be reaching at 66.8% for recognising totally 86 species of birds.

Table 1. The parameters of final model.

Hyperparameter	Value
RNN cell	GRU
Encoder depth	2
Decoder depth	2
Encoder	Bidirectional
Decoder	Bidirectional
Kernel	*rbf*
C	100
Alpha	0.1
MLP hidden layers	(850, 850, 850)

Table 2. The results (UAR: %) achieved by two-layer LSTM RNN models.

Encoder	Decoder	SVM		MLP	
		Dev	Test	Dev	Test
RNN	RNN	33.2	33.7	34.6	31.9
BiRNN	RNN	27.8	30.3	25.7	26.9
BiRNN	BiRNN	55.1	**52.8**	49.0	**46.8**
RNN	BiRNN	22.8	22.6	29.3	25.3

Figure 2 illustrates the comparison between different topologies of the models. It is demonstrated that, a two-layer BiRNN-BiRNN structure can be the best option in this work.

4   Discussion

As a pilot study on using Seq2Seq deep learning approach to extract higher representations from the bird sounds, we can find that, it is feasible to build an efficient framework for recognising bird sounds without any human hand-crafted features. In addition, we may find that, the selection of the deep learning topologies can effect the final model's performances (see Table 2 and Table 3). Among the experimental results in this study, GRU based RNN can be superior to LSTM based RNN in learning higher representations from the bird sounds (a significance level at $p < 0.001$ by one-tailed z-test). When adding the hidden layers of the RNN models, we may find a decrease in final performance (see Fig. 2). It is reasonable to think that due to the current limited size of the database, the model seems to be vulnerable to be over-fitting. In future work, we will implement our approach in larger size bird sound databases. An interesting finding is that, when introducing the BiRNN structure, the performance can be improved (see Table 2 and Table 3). Similar to human speech, bird sound may also have the strong contextual information, which can be extracted not only

Table 3. The results (UAR: %) achieved by two-layer GRU RNN models.

Encoder	Decoder	SVM		MLP	
		Dev	Test	Dev	Test
RNN	RNN	62.0	60.3	60.9	58.9
BiRNN	RNN	64.4	62.4	60.6	58.9
BiRNN	BiRNN	68.0	**65.7**	63.3	**66.8**
RNN	BiRNN	62.3	62.2	62.4	62.1

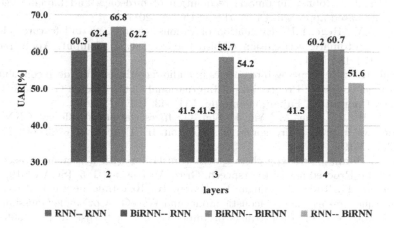

Fig. 2. The results (UARs: %) achieved by different topologies of the proposed model (GRU RNN) evaluated by test set.

from the *forward* direction, but also the *backward* direction. We should make efforts towards finding the contextual information through deeply understanding of the bird vocalisations. Finally, when comparing the classifiers' ability to make the final predictions, we find both of the two machine learning models, i.e., SVM and MLP, can be sufficient to fulfil the task.

5   Conclusion

In this work, we proposed a Seq2Seq deep learning approach for automatically extracting higher representations from bird sounds. The proposed method was demonstrated to be efficient to utilize longer term temporal information and achieved 66.8% of UAR. Moreover, we investigated the effects to the final classification performance by using different deep learning topologies. We found that, a BiRNN-BiRNN structure can reach the highest performance in this study. Future work can be given to the direction of combining the convolutional neural networks and autoencoders to extract more advanced features from the birds' vocalisation. In addition, it is our interest to contribute more to understand in depth about the relationship between the learnt representations and the birds' behaviour activities.

References

1. Qian, K., Zhang, Z., Ringeval, F., Schuller, B.: Bird sounds classification by large scale acoustic features and extreme learning machine. In: Proceedings of GlobalSIP, Orlando, Florida, USA, pp. 1317–1321. IEEE (2015)
2. Qian, K., Guo, J., Ishida, K., Matsuoka, S.: Fast recognition of bird sounds using extreme learning machines. IEEE Trans. Electr. Electron. Eng. **12**(2), 294–296 (2017)
3. Papadopoulos, T., Roberts, S.J., Willis, K.J.: Automated bird sound recognition in realistic settings (2018)
4. Kaewtip, K.: Robust automatic recognition of birdsongs and human speech: a template-based approach. Ph.D. thesis, UCLA (2017)
5. Bang, A.V., Rege, P.P.: Evaluation of various feature sets and feature selection towards automatic recognition of bird species. Int. J. Comput. Appl. Technol. **56**(3), 172–184 (2017)
6. Piczak, K.J.: Recognizing bird species in audio recordings using deep convolutional neural networks. In: Proceedings of International Conference on Genetic & Evolutionary Computing, Fujian, China, pp. 534–543. IEEE (2016)
7. Xie, J., Hu, K., Zhu, M., Yu, J., Zhu, Q.: Investigation of different CNN-based models for improved bird sound classification. IEEE Access **7**(8922774), 175353–175361 (2019)
8. Jia, Y., et al.: Direct speech-to-speech translation with a sequence-to-sequence model. In: Proceedings of Interspeech, Graz, Austria, pp. 1–5. ISCA (2019)
9. Okamoto, T., Toda, T., Shiga, Y., Kawai, H.: Real-time neural text-to-speech with sequence-to-sequence acoustic model and WaveGlow or single Gaussian WaveRNN vocoders. In: Proceedings of Interspeech, Graz, Austria, pp. 1308–1312. ISCA (2019)
10. Cho, K., et al.: Learning phrase representations using RNN encoder-decoder for statistical machine translation. In: Proceedings of EMNLP, Doha, Qatar, pp. 1724–1734. Association for Computational Linguistics (2014)
11. Cho, K., Van Merrinboer, B., Bahdanau, D., Bengio, Y.: On the properties of neural machine translation: encoder-decoder approaches. In: Proceedings of SSST-8, Doha, Qatar, pp. 103–111 Association for Computational Linguistics (2014)
12. Sutskever, I., Vinyals, O., Le, Q.V.: Sequence to sequence learning with neural networks. In: Proceedings of Proceedings of the 27th International Conference on Neural Information Processing Systems, Montreal, Canada, pp. 3104–3112. MIT Press (2014)
13. Qian, K.: Automatic general audio signal classification. Ph.D. thesis, Munich, Germany (2018). Doctoral thesis
14. Amiriparian, S., Freitag, M., Cummins, N., Schuller, B.: Sequence to sequence autoencoders for unsupervised representation learning from audio. In: Proceedings of the DCASE 2017 Workshop, Munich, Germany, pp. 17–21. IEEE (2017)
15. Freitag, M., Amiriparian, S., Pugachevskiy, S., Cummins, N., Schuller, B.: auDeep: unsupervised learning of representations from audio with deep recurrent neural networks. J. Mach. Learn. Res. **18**(1), 6340–6344 (2017)
16. Deng, Y., Wang, L., Jia, H., Tong, X., Li, F.: A sequence-to-sequence deep learning architecture based on bidirectional GRU for type recognition and time location of combined power quality disturbance. IEEE Trans. Industr. Inf. **15**(8), 4481–4493 (2019)
17. Pedregosa, F., et al.: Scikit-learn: machine learning in python. J. Mach. Learn. Res. **12**, 2825–2830 (2011)

Neural Network Including Alternative Pre-processing for Electroencephalogram by Transposed Convolution

Kenshi Machida$^{(\boxtimes)}$, Isao Nambu, and Yasuhiro Wada

Nagaoka University of Technology,
1603-1 Kamitomioka, Nagaoka, Niigata 940-2188, Japan
kmachida@stn.nagaokaut.ac.jp

Abstract. In the classification of electroencephalograms for a brain-computer interface (BCI), two steps are generally applied: preprocessing for feature extraction and classification using a classifier. As a result, combinations of a myriad of preprocessing and a myriad of classification method have disordered for each classification target and data. Conversely, neural networks can be applied to any classification problem because they can transform an arbitrary form of input into an arbitrary form of output. We considered a transposed convolution as a preprocessor that can set the window width and number of output features and classified it using a convolutional neural network (CNN). Using a simple CNN with a transposed convolution in the first layer, we classified the data of the motor imagery tasks of the BCI competition IV 2 dataset. The results showed that, despite not being among the best conventional methods available, we were still able to obtain a high degree of accuracy.

Keywords: BCI competition IV · Electroencephalogram · Neural network · CNN · Transposed convolution

1 Introduction

Most studies on electroencephalography (EEG) in this field have focused on the brain-computer interface (BCI). Further, numerous studies have applied EEG classification techniques to achieve such an interface. A typical example is a method using a dataset from a BCI competition, and the latest dataset is from the BCI Competition IV held in 2008, although methods with a higher classification accuracy have since been reported. For example, Ang et al. [1] applied a Filter Bank Common Spatial Pattern and conducted a classification using a naïve Bayesian Parzen window classifier. In addition, Gaur et al. [2] applied subject-specific multivariate empirical mode decomposition-based filtering and conducted a classification using the minimum distance to Riemannian mean method. As described above, when analyzing an EEG, a two-step process, namely, preprocessing followed by a classification, is generally applied. Hence,

© Springer Nature Switzerland AG 2020
H. Yang et al. (Eds.): ICONIP 2020, CCIS 1333, pp. 139–146, 2020.
https://doi.org/10.1007/978-3-030-63823-8_17

various combinations of pre-processing and classification methods have resulted in inconsistencies for each classification target. However, it remains unclear whether such methods have been applied to a BCI.

The most effective technique to achieve a BCI through modern technology is the use of a neural network. Neural networks convert any input into any output and can thus be applied to any classification problem. In addition, a processor specialized for neural network processing was developed [4] and has recently been actively incorporated into small devices, such as smartphones. The environment in which this approach can be implemented is becoming more popular now.

To date, EEG classification has been conducted in two stages: feature extraction through a preprocessing and classification using a classifier. A neural network may convert an input into any output, that is, a model obtaining a classification label should be used by entering an EEG directly. In this study, we demonstrate that a previously applied window analysis of the signals can be primitively reproduced on a neural network and that a high classification accuracy can be obtained.

2   Method

A neural network must have the flexibility to cope with various types of data, including images and time signals, and be able to arbitrarily adjust the degree of freedom of the calculation. Conversely, an overlearning is likely to occur, and depending on the network configuration, numerous hyperparameters must be adjusted. In addition, when learning, many techniques such as adjusting the learning rate and early stopping must be considered. However, such situations can be avoided by applying only a few techniques.

2.1   Batch Normalization

Batch normalization [5] is a method used to normalize the input to each layer of a neural network such that a mean of zero and a variance of 1 are achieved.

According to [6], the higher the learning rate that is set, the more regularized the regularization effect becomes because the amount of noise is increased, owing to the mini-batch selection. When not normalized, the mean and variance increase exponentially as the layer deepens, but they can be kept constant by applying batch normalization, thereby making the gradient highly dependent on the input. Furthermore, the error does not diverge even when a high learning rate is set.

2.2   Convolution Layer

A convolution layer is used for inputs with one or more dimensions of spatial features. A convolution is applied to the spatial feature directions using a kernel. In a convolution layer, the number of weighting parameters is smaller than the number of input–output features and, thus, is regularized. Because an EEG is a time signal, the necessity of considering the regularization parameter is reduced by using a convolution layer that applies a convolution in the time direction.

2.3 Transposed Convolution

A transposed convolution is a conversion applied opposite a convolution. If a convolution is an encoder, a transposed convolution behaves similar to a decoder. An up-sampling can be conducted in the spatial feature direction, and the feature map can be projected onto a higher dimensional space.

2.4 Network Structure

Two different network structures were applied in this study. One is a 1D CNN model that convolves the EEG only in the time-axis direction. In this case, global average pooling was conducted after the four convolution layers, and classification was applied using all connected layers. The other is a 2D CNN model that applies a convolution layer after transforming it into a form with 2D spatial features using a transposed convolution. There are several benefits to converting from 1D to 2D. For example, when a convolution layer is used, the ratio of the number of weight parameters to the number of inputs and outputs decreases; thus, the regularization effect is enhanced. In addition, because a 2D CNN model has many useful learned models, some of which have achieved high results in the ImageNet Large-Scale Visual Recognition Challenge, the model can be transferred. In general, during the process of transforming 1D spatial features into 2D spatial features through a transformed convolution, a window analysis is applied on the time signal, and the features are extended in the new axial direction. Thus, the calculation corresponding to the preprocessing performed thus far can be primitively reproduced by the neural network.

Although the input EEG has spatial features in two directions, namely, the time direction and the channel direction, the channel direction is arranged in order of the channel number of the EEG at the time of measurement and is not spatially a significant feature. The EEG channel direction is placed the unconstrained channel direction of the convolution layer.

Tables 1 and 2 show the specific configurations of the above two models:

Table 1. 1D CNN model structure

Layer	1D CNN model	
	Structure	Output shape
Input	–	(250, 1, 22)
1	Conv [3, 1] 22ch Batch Normalization Leaky ReLU(α = 0.2)	(248, 1, 22)
2	Conv [3, 1] 22ch Batch Normalization Leaky ReLU(α = 0.2)	(246, 1, 22)
3	Conv [3, 1] 32ch Batch Normalization Leaky ReLU(α = 0.2)	(244, 1, 32)
4	Conv [3, 1] 32ch Batch Normalization Leaky ReLU(α = 0.2)	(242, 1, 32)
5	Global Average Pooling	(32)
6	Dense [4] Softmax	(4)

Table 2. 2D CNN model structure

Layer	2D CNN model	
	Structure	Output shape
Input	–	(250, 1, 22)
1	Transposed Conv [8, 150] 8ch Batch Normalization	(257, 150, 8)
2	Conv [3, 3] 8ch Batch Normalization Leaky ReLU(α = 0.2)	(255, 148, 8)
3	Conv [3, 3] 16ch Batch Normalization Leaky ReLU(α = 0.2)	(253, 146, 16)
4	Conv [3, 3] 32ch Batch Normalization Leaky ReLU(α = 0.2)	(251, 144, 32)
5	Conv [3, 3] 32ch Batch Normalization Leaky ReLU(α = 0.2)	(249, 142, 32)
6	Global Average Pooling	(32)
7	Dense [4] Softmax	(4)

2.5   Dataset

The BCI competition IV 2a dataset [3] was used for the network evaluation. This dataset includes EEG signals recorded from nine subjects on four types of motor image tasks: right hand, left hand, tongue, and foot. A total of 22 EEG channels is applied, and the sampling frequency 250 Hz. A total of 288 training and test data trials are recorded for each subject, including missing parts and some excluded trials.

In this case, after replacing the missing values with zeros and applying a low-pass filter, the sampling frequency was down-sampled 63 Hz, which was approximately one-fourth of the original rate, and all trials including the excluded trials were applied. As the input, a 4s signal was used, for which a motor image was shown during the trial. The signal was normalized to achieve an average value of zero and a variance of 1 for each trial, as well as for each channel before being input into the neural network.

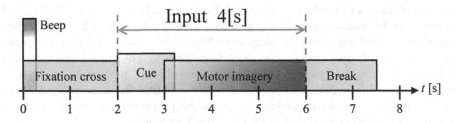

Fig. 1. Timing scheme of the paradigm

2.6   Training and Evaluation

The cross-entropy is used as the cost function. In addition, Adam [7] was used as the optimizer, the mini-batch size was 58, and the learning rate was 0.0001. The parameters were updated 1,000 times without changing the learning rate or stopping the learning early.

5-fold cross-validation was conducted for each subject 6 times using the training data, and the classification accuracy of the test data was observed 30 times.

3   Results

Table 3 shows the mean and standard deviation (std) of accuracy when the validation and test data were classified in the model after the parameter update. The classification accuracy of the 2D CNN model was higher than that of the 1D CNN model.

Table 4 shows the accuracy when converted into the kappa value and compared with the value from a previous study. The p-value has been computed using the Wilcoxon signed rank test. The neural network containing the Transposed Convolution achieved an mean kappa of 0.62, which is superior to all previously reported results.

Table 3. Accuracy validation and evaluation

Subject	5-fold cross-validation					Evaluation				
	1D CNN		2D CNN		2D-1D	1D CNN		2D CNN		2D-1D
	mean	std	mean	std		mean	std	mean	std	
1	70.41	± 5.97	84.91	± 4.24	14.50	75.61	± 2.40	86.79	± 2.10	11.18
2	51.17	± 7.13	64.09	± 7.34	12.92	39.44	± 2.85	46.84	± 3.10	7.40
3	81.99	± 5.08	89.71	± 3.67	7.72	81.79	± 1.86	90.76	± 1.04	8.97
4	48.83	± 7.32	68.83	+ 6.34	20.00	48.78	± 2.05	66.33	± 4.70	17.55
5	56.49	± 4.97	65.15	± 6.79	8.65	49.68	± 2.73	55.68	± 3.37	6.01
6	48.54	± 6.18	64.91	± 6.49	16.37	46.01	± 2.79	49.88	± 3.80	3.88
7	81.05	± 5.37	93.16	± 3.34	12.11	73.67	± 3.00	88.09	± 2.01	14.42
8	81.40	± 4.12	89.94	± 3.26	8.54	74.48	± 2.09	81.83	± 1.55	7.35
9	69.42	± 3.91	79.77	± 3.97	10.35	73.61	± 2.24	78.10	± 2.75	4.49
Average	65.48%		77.83%		12.35	62.56%		71.59%		9.03

4 Discussion

A high-level accuracy was obtained by extending an EEG into a 2D map using a transposed convolution. Using this method, a transposed convolution was applied to extend a signal with a fixed window width in a new axis direction. The best-known method for extending a signal to a 2D map during a conventional

Table 4. Evaluated kappa value comparison with previous studies

Subject	Kappa value			
	1D CNN	2D CNN	Method-[2]	Method-[1]
1	0.675	0.824	0.86	0.75
2	0.193	0.291	0.24	0.37
3	0.757	0.877	0.70	0.66
4	0.317	0.551	0.68	0.53
5	0.329	0.409	0.36	0.29
6	0.280	0.332	0.34	0.27
7	0.649	0.841	0.66	0.56
8	0.660	0.758	0.75	0.58
9	0.648	0.708	0.82	0.68
Average	0.501	0.621	0.60	0.52
p value	0.0039	–	0.5898	0.0391

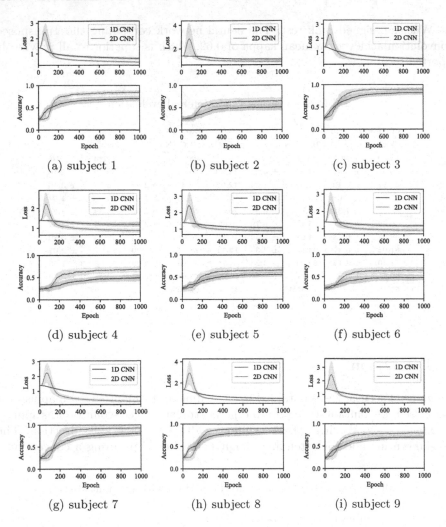

Fig. 2. Loss and accuracy curve of the validation data

analysis is a short-term Fourier transform (STFT). For example, when an STFT is used, the frequency axis is extended by the same number as the window width. However, only frequency information at equal intervals is extracted, and the validity of information is not guaranteed. Therefore, by incorporating the preprocessing into a neural network, the window width and number of expansions can be set arbitrarily, and learning is applied to extract features effective for classification. The idea here is that, by visualizing the parameters and the output of each layer, understanding of the EEG can be improved by analyzing the components of the source necessary for the classification that are included in the signal.

In this neural network, the learning rate can be an important parameter because batch normalization is used in each layer. Although the weight parameter does not diverge owing to the effect of such normalization, if the learning rate is too large, the regularization effect becomes stronger and the accuracy does not increase. Figure 2 shows the mean and std of learning curve for 6 times 5-fold cross-validation. When observing the transition of the validation loss, the loss continues to decrease near the end of learning. That is, the accuracy might be improved by adjusting the learning rate for each validation or according to the learning epoch.

5   Conclusion

We attempted to learn the transformation equivalent of a preprocessing with arbitrary window widths and spatial sizes by applying a transposed convolution to EEG signals, followed by using a network of simple structures to which a 2D CNN can be naturally applied. We showed that high accuracy can be achieved by replacing the complex preprocessing of EEGs with a neural network.

Acknowledgements. This work was partly supported by JSPS KAKENHI Grant Numbers 18K19807 and 18H04109, KDDI foundation, and Nagaoka University of Technology Presidential Research Grant. We would like to thank Editage (www.editage.com) for English language editing.

References

1. Ang, K.K., Chin, Z.Y., Wang, C., Guan, C., Zhang, H.: Filter bank common spatial pattern algorithm on BCI competition iv datasets 2A and 2B. Frontiers Neurosci. **6**, 39 (2012). https://doi.org/10.3389/fnins.2012.00039. https://www.frontiersin.org/article/10.3389/fnins.2012.00039
2. Gaur, P., Pachori, R.B., Wang, H., Prasad, G.: A multi-class EEG-based BCI classification using multivariate empirical mode decomposition based filtering and Riemannian geometry. Expert Syst. Appl. **95**, 201-211 (2018). https://doi.org/https://doi.org/10.1016/j.eswa.2017.11.007. http://www.sciencedirect.com/science/article/pii/S0957417417307492
3. Brunner, C., Leeb, R., Muller-Putz, G., Schlogl, A., Pfurtscheller, G.: BCI competition 2008-graz data set a. Institute for Knowledge Discovery (Laboratory of Brain–Computer Interfaces), Graz University of Technology (2008). http://bbci.de/competition/iv/desc_2a.pdf
4. Jouppi, N.P., et al.: In-datacenter performance analysis of a tensor processing unit. SIGARCH Comput. Archit. News **45**(2), 1-12 (2017). https://doi.org/10.1145/3140659.3080246
5. Ioffe, S., Szegedy, C.: Batch normalization: accelerating deep network training by reducing internal covariate shift. In: Bach, F., Blei, D. (eds.) Proceedings of the 32nd International Conference on Machine Learning. Proceedings of Machine Learning Research, Lille, France, 07–09 July 2015, vol. 37, pp. 448-456. PMLR (2015). http://proceedings.mlr.press/v37/ioffe15.html

6. Bjorck, N., Gomes, C.P., Selman, B., Weinberger, K.Q.: Understanding batch normalization. In: Bengio, S., Wallach, H., Larochelle, H., Grauman, K., Cesa-Bianchi, N., Garnett, R. (eds.) Advances in Neural Information Processing Systems, vol. 31, pp. 7694–7705. Curran Associates, Inc. (2018). http://papers.nips.cc/paper/7996-understanding-batch-normalization.pdf
7. Kingma, D.P., Ba, J.: Adam: a method for stochastic optimization. In: Bengio, Y., LeCun, Y. (eds.) 3rd International Conference on Learning Representations, ICLR 2015, San Diego, CA, USA, 7–9 May 2015, Conference Track Proceedings (2015). http://arxiv.org/abs/1412.6980

Neural Network Training Using a Biogeography-Based Learning Strategy

Seyed Jalaleddin Mousavirad[1]([⊠]), Seyed Mohammad Jafar Jalali[2]([⊠]),
Sajad Ahmadian[3], Abbas Khosravi[2], Gerald Schaefer[4], and Saeid Nahavandi[2]

[1] Faculty of Engineering, Sabzevar University of New Technology, Sabzevar, Iran
[2] Institute for Intelligent Systems Research and Innovation (IISRI),
Deakin University, Waurn Ponds, Australia
sjalali@deakin.edu.au
[3] Faculty of Information Technology, Kermanshah University of Technology,
Kermanshah, Iran
[4] Department of Computer Science, Loughborough University, Loughborough, UK

Abstract. The performance of multi-layer feed-forward neural networks is closely related to the success of training algorithms in finding optimal weights in the network. Although conventional algorithms such as back-propagation are popular in this regard, they suffer from drawbacks such as a tendency to get stuck in local optima. In this paper, we propose an effective hybrid algorithm, BLPSO-GBS, for neural network training based on particle swarm optimisation (PSO), biogeography-based optimisation (BBO), and a global-best strategy. BLPSO-GBS updates each particle based on neighbouring particles and a biogeography-based learning strategy is used to generate the neighbouring particles using the migration operator in BBO. Our experiments on different benchmark datasets and comparison to various algorithms clearly show the competitive performance of BLPSO-GBS.

Keywords: Neural network training · Optimisation · Particle swarm optimisation · Biogeography-based optimisation · Training

1 Introduction

Artificial neural networks (ANNs) have been extensively used to tackle complex machine learning tasks in different domains such as food quality [21] and medicine [10]. ANNs can deal with both supervised and unsupervised problems and benefit from properties such as learning capability and an ability to generalise [17,18].

Multi-layer feed-forward neural networks (MLFFNNs) are one of the most widely employed ANN architectures. In MLFFNNs, each connection has a weight, determining its strength. Training a MLFFNN means finding optimal weights to minimise the difference between the actual output and the predicted

© Springer Nature Switzerland AG 2020
H. Yang et al. (Eds.): ICONIP 2020, CCIS 1333, pp. 147–155, 2020.
https://doi.org/10.1007/978-3-030-63823-8_18

output. Gradient-based algorithms such as back-propagation (BP) are most commonly employed for this purpose but suffer from drawbacks such as a tendency to get stuck in local optima and sensitivity to initialisation.

To tackle these problems, a reliable alternative are population-based metaheuristic (PBMH) algorithms such as particle swarm optimisation (PSO) [12] and human mental search (HMS) [19]. In the literature, several PBMHs have been proposed for MLFFNN training including genetic algorithm (GA) [5], asexual reproduction optimization [1], artificial bee colony (ABC) [11], grey wolf optimiser (GWO) [3], imperialist competitive algorithm [17], and butterfly optimisation algorithm (BOA) [9].

PSO is a leading PBMH for neural network training. It updates each candidate solution based on its position, its personal best position, and the global best position. [7] compares PSO with back-propagation and indicates that PSO outperforms BP. In [16], a combination of PSO and gravitational search algorithm (GSA) is used for neural network training, while in [22], a partial opposition PSO (POBL-PSO), which also benefits from a local search based on difference-offsprings, is employed for MLFFNN optimisation.

In this paper, we propose a novel algorithm, BLPSO-GBS, for MLFFNN training. Our proposed algorithm integrates biogeography-based learning strategy (BLS) with PSO so that each particle updates itself based on its position, its personal best position and the personal best positions of other particles based on the migration operator in biogeography-based optimisation (BBO). In addition, we propose a global-best strategy for updating each particle to further improve the efficacy of the algorithm. Extensive experiments show that BLPSO-GBS yields very competitive performance for MLFFNN training.

2   Comprehensive Learning Particle Swarm Optimisation

Particle swarm optimisation (PSO) [12] is an effective PBMH which has shown good performance in solving complex optimisation problems. PSO starts with a set of random candidate solutions called particles. In each iteration, each particle is updated based on its position, its personal best position, and the global best position as

$$v_{t+1}^i = \omega v_t^i + c_1 r_1 (pbest_t^i - x_t^i) + c_2 r_2 (gbest_t - x_t^i), \tag{1}$$

and

$$x_{t+1}^i = x_t^i + v_{t+1}^i, \tag{2}$$

where x_t^i shows the position of the i-th particle in the t-th iteration, $pbest_t^i$ is the personal best position, and $gbest_t$ is the global best position. Also, r_1 and r_2 are two randomly generated vectors within $[0, 1]$, $c1$ and $c2$ are the acceleration coefficients and ω is the inertia weight.

Comprehensive learning particle swarm optimisation (CLPSO) [14] is a variant of PSO to overcome premature convergence in standard PSO algorithm. CLPSO updates the velocity term as

$$v_{t+1}^i = \omega v_t^i + c_1 r (pbest_{f_i(d)}^f - x_t^i), \tag{3}$$

where $f_i(d)$ signifies that in the d-th dimension particle i learns from a neighbouring particle's *pbest*. Each particle can learn from the *pbest* of different particles for different dimensions, with standard CLPSO employing a probability-based selection to determine the neighbouring particles.

3 BLPSO-GBS Algorithm

Neurons are the main components of MLFFNNs, and receive information from other neurons, carry out a weighted sum and create an output using an activation function. MLFFNNs have 3 types of layers, an input layer, hidden layers, and an output layer. Finding optimal values for connection weights and bias terms is a challenging task that determines the success of a training algorithm. In this paper, we propose our novel BLPSO-BGS algorithm for MLFFNN training.

For encoding strategy, our algorithm uses a 1-dimensional array whose length is equal to the total number of weights and biases.

Since in this paper, we focus on classification problems, we employ an objective function based on classification error and formulated as

$$E = \frac{100}{P} \sum_{p=1}^{P} \xi(\overrightarrow{p}), \tag{4}$$

with

$$\xi(\overrightarrow{p}) = \begin{cases} 1 & \text{if } \overrightarrow{y_p} \neq \overrightarrow{d_p} \\ 0 & \text{otherwise} \end{cases}. \tag{5}$$

The aim of MLFFNN training is to find weights and biases so that the difference between predicted output y_p and desired output d_p is minimised.

3.1 Biogeography-Based Learning Strategy

Biogeography-based optimisation (BBO) [23] is a PBMH algorithm where candidate solutions are known as islands and information is shared through migration between islands. Biogeography-based learning strategy (BLS) [6] is a scheme to generate neighbouring particles $f_i = [f_i(1), f_i(2), ..., f_i(D)]$ for PSO based on the BBO migration operator. It proceeds in the following steps:

1. Particles are ranked based on their *pbest*, i.e. for a minimisation problem as

$$fit(pbest_{s_1}) < fit(pbest_{s_2}) < ... < fit(pbest_{s_N}), \tag{6}$$

where s_1 is the particle with the best *pbest* and s_N the one with the worst.
2. The ranks for each particle are assigned as

$$rank(s_1) = N - 1, rank(s_2) = N - 2, ..., rank(s_N) = 0, \tag{7}$$

so that the particle with the best *pbest* has the highest rank, while the particle with the worst *pbest* yields the lowest rank.

3. Immigration and emigration rates for each particle are calculated as

$$\lambda(s_1) = (1 - \frac{N-1}{N}), \mu(s_1) = \frac{N-1}{N},$$

$$\lambda(s_2) = (1 - \frac{N-2}{N}), \mu(s_1) = \frac{N-2}{N}, ... \qquad (8)$$

$$\lambda(s_N) = (1 - \frac{N-N}{N}), \mu(s_1) = \frac{N-N}{N}.$$

so that particle x_{s_1} (with the best *pbest*) has the lowest immigration rate and the highest emigration rate.

4. The biogeography-based exemplar generation method detailed in Algorithm 1 is applied for particle i.

Input   : $rank(i)$: rank, λ_{rank_i}: immigration rate, μ_{rank_i}: emigration rate
Output: $f_i = [f_i(1), [f_i(2), ..., [f_i(D)]$: exemplar vector index

for $i \leftarrow 1$ **to** D **do**
  if $rand_j < \lambda_{rank_i}$ **then**
    Utilise a roulette wheel to select a particle with index j with probability μ_{rank_j};
    $f_i k \leftarrow j$;
  else
    $f_i k \leftarrow i$;
  end
end
if $f_i(k) == i, (i = 1, ..., D)$ **then**
  Randomly select a particle with index j;
  Randomly select a dimension l;
  $f_i l \leftarrow j$;
end

Algorithm 1: Biogeography-based exemplar generation algorithm for particle i

3.2   Global Best Strategy

BLPSO updates each particle using Eq. (3), while the global best solution has useful information that can enhance the performance of the algorithm. We therefore update the velocity by incorporating the global best particle to guide the particles, leading to

$$v_{t+1}^i = \omega v_t^i + c_1 r_1 (pbest_{f_i(d)}^f - x_t^i) + c_2 r_2 (gbest_t^i - x_t^i), \qquad (9)$$

where $gbest_t^i$ is the global best position in the t-th iteration.

3.3   Algorithm

Algorithm 2 summarises the working of our proposed BLPSO-GBS algorithm in pseudo code form.

Input : D: dimensionality of problem, MAX_{NFC}: maximum number of
function evaluations, N_P: population size, c_1: self-cognitive coefficient,
c_2: self-learning coefficient

Output: x^*: the best particle

Randomly generate the initial population Pop of size N_P;
Evaluate the fitness for each particle using Eq. (4);
Set $pbest_i$ as $pbest_i - Pop_i$;
Set $gbest$ as the best particle in the current population;
$NFE = N_P$;
while $NFE < MAX_{NFE}$ **do**
    for $i \leftarrow 1$ **to** N_P **do**
        Assign ranking values for all particles based on fitness of their $pbest$;
        Assign immigration and emigration rates for all particles;
        Generate exemplar vector index $f_i = [f_i(1), f_i(2), ..., f_i(D)]$ using
        Algorithm 1;
        Update velocity v_i using Eq. (9);
        Update position x_i using Eq. (2);
        Calculate objective function value of x_i ;
        if $f(x_i) < f(pbest_i)$ **then**
         | $pbest_i \leftarrow x_i$
        end
        if $f(x_i) < f(gbest)$ **then**
         | $gbest \leftarrow x_i$
        end
    end
end
$x^* \leftarrow$ the best candidate solution in Pop

Algorithm 2: BLPSO-GBS algorithm.

---

4   Experimental Results

To evaluate our proposed BLPSO-GBS algorithm, we carry out experiments on clinical classification benchmark datasets with varied characteristics from the UCI repository[1].

Upper and lower bounds for all algorithms are set -10 and $+10$, respectively. Since in this paper we do not focus on finding an optimal network structure, we follow [17,20] to determine the number of neurons in the hidden layer as $2N + 1$,

---

[1] https://archive.ics.uci.edu/ml/index.php.

where N is the number of input features. For comparison, we employ standard 10-fold cross validation, where the dataset is divided into 10 partitions, one partition is used as the test set while the others are used for training, and the process is repeated 10 times so that each partition is selected once for testing.

For evaluation, we compare our algorithm with various other algorithms including DE [8], ABC [11], GWO [15], DA [13], WOA [2], and SSA [4]. Since our algorithm is based on PSO, we also compare BLPSO-GBS with three PSO-based training algorithms including standard PSO, PSOGSA [16] as one of the state-of-the-art PSO-based trainers, and POBL-PSO [22] as one of the most recent PSO-based training algorithms. The number of function evaluations and population size for all PBMHs are set to 25000 and 50, respectively. For BLPSO-GBS, c_1 and c_2 are set to 2 and 2 respectively, while for other algorithms we employ defaults settings. The results for all algorithms and all datasets are given in Table 1.

Table 1. Classification results on all datasets.

		DE	ABC	GWO	DA	WOA	SSA	PSO	PSOGSA	POBL-GBS	BLPSO-GBS
BCW	mean	97.36	97.95	98.10	97.51	97.07	97.80	97.95	98.24	97.95	98.39
	std. dev.	2.06	1.03	1.39	1.83	1.96	2.42	1.72	1.52	1.85	1.89
	median	97.10	98.53	98.53	97.79	97.08	98.53	97.82	98.53	98.53	98.53
	max	100	98.55	100	100	100	100	100	100	100	100
	min	94.12	95.59	95.59	95.59	94.12	94.12	92.65	95.59	94.12	94.12
	rank	9	5	3	8	10	7	6	2	4	1
BTSC	mean	79.81	80.62	80.08	79.94	80.48	80.61	80.48	80.22	80.35	81.02
	std. dev.	4.48	4.06	3.14	4.52	3.07	2.65	3.35	3.80	4.25	4.02
	median	80.00	80.54	80.54	79.19	81.22	80.54	81.21	80.67	80.67	81.33
	max	89.33	88.00	84.00	89.33	84.00	84.00	85.33	84.00	86.67	85.33
	min	72.00	73.33	74.67	74.67	75.68	77.03	76.00	72.00	73.33	72.00
	rank	10	2	8	9	5	3	4	7	6	1
LD	mean	67.81	70.75	73.01	70.42	62.87	69.85	73.36	69.89	72.07	75.11
	std. dev.	8.21	6.47	9.74	7.01	6.40	7.78	6.28	7.51	10.24	6.70
	median	67.14	70.00	72.48	69.58	62.31	68.11	70.59	72.06	76.81	74.29
	max	82.86	80.00	85.29	82.86	71.43	82.86	85.29	80.00	82.86	88.24
	min	58.82	62.86	52.94	58.82	50.00	61.76	67.65	54.29	50.00	62.86
	rank	9	5	3	6	10	8	2	7	4	1
PID	mean	76.94	78.26	67.45	77.85	76.95	77.34	77.60	78.64	78.65	80.85
	std. dev.	4.97	4.45	2.79	5.40	3.65	6.50	3.24	6.22	3.81	4.22
	median	77.12	78.95	67.98	77.92	77.27	75.32	78.43	78.57	78.43	81.04
	max	84.42	84.42	71.43	85.71	83.12	93.51	81.82	88.31	87.01	88.31
	min	69.74	71.43	62.34	65.79	72.37	70.13	72.73	64.94	72.73	73.68
	rank	9	4	13	5	8	7	6	3	2	1
VC	mean	85.16	82.9	81.94	81.94	79.03	85.81	86.45	84.84	84.84	87.42
	std. dev.	5.31	5.70	7.93	5.31	10.99	7.16	8.02	8.34	6.09	5.15
	median	85.48	82.26	82.26	79.03	80.65	87.10	90.32	87.10	85.48	85.48
	max	93.55	93.55	93.55	90.32	93.55	93.55	96.77	93.55	93.55	96.77
	min	77.42	74.19	67.74	77.42	61.29	70.97	70.97	67.74	74.19	80.65
	rank	4	7	8.5	8.5	11	3	2	5.5	5.5	1

The Breast Cancer Wisconsin (BCW) dataset, collected by the University of Wisconsin, has 699 instances that classify as either benign or malignant. It contains 9 features including clump thickness, uniformity of cell size, and mitoses. MLPs of structure 9-19-1 are trained, and as a result, the problem has a dimensionality of 210. From the obtained results, we can see that BLPSO-GBS is top-ranked, followed by PSOGSA and GWO.

The Blood Transfusion Service Center (BTSC) dataset, taken from Hsin-Chu City in Taiwan, contains 748 samples and 4 features that classify an instance as donating blood and not-donating blood. MLPs of structure 4-9-1 are trained. The results show BLPSO-GBS to yield the highest accuracy.

The Liver Disorder (LD) dataset, from BUPA Medical Research Ltd., contains 345 instances with 6 clinical features and has 2 classes. MLPs with structure 6-13-1 are trained and therefore, the number of decision variables is 105. BLPSO-GBS again obtains the highest accuracy and with a considerable margin. The second rank goes to PSO, with our proposed algorithm increasing the accuracy from 73.36% to 75.11% and thus decreasing the classification error by more than 6%.

The Pima Indians Diabetes (PID) dataset is a challenging dataset indicating whether a patient has diabetes or not. It contains 768 instances with 8 features and 2 classes. ANNs of structure 8-17-1 are trained and therefore, the number of decision variables is 210. The obtained results clearly confirm that our proposed algorithm outperforms all other methods. POBL-PSO is placed in the second rank, whilst PSOGSA is ranked third. BLPSO-GBS improves the classification error by more than 10% compared to POBL-PSO.

The Vertebral Column (VC) dataset is a clinical dataset with 6 biomedical features. It contains 310 samples divided in 2 classes. As we can see from Table 1, BLPSO-GBS achieves the best classification accuracy of 87.42%, meaning that classification error is reduced by more than 7% compared to the next best approach.

5   Conclusions

In this paper, we have proposed a novel algorithm, BLPSO-GBS, for multilayer feed-forward neural network training based on particle swarm optimisation (PSO), biogeography-based optimisation (BBO), and a global-best strategy. Our proposed algorithm updates each candidate solution based on neighbouring particles with a biogeography-based learning strategy (BLS) responsible for generating the neighbours. In addition, a global-best strategy is introduced to further improve the performance of our proposed algorithm. In an extensive set of experiments on a variety of clinical classification benchmark datasets, we have demonstrated that BLPSO-GBS yields excellent neural network training performance and outperforms various other approaches. In future work, we intend to extend our algorithm to find weights and architectures simultaneously, while a multi-objective version of BLPSO-GBS is also under investigation.

References

1. Ahmadian, S., Khanteymoori, A.R.: Training back propagation neural networks using asexual reproduction optimization. In: 2015 7th Conference on Information and Knowledge Technology (IKT), pp. 1–6 (2015)
2. Aljarah, I., Faris, H., Mirjalili, S.: Optimizing connection weights in neural networks using the whale optimization algorithm. Soft. Comput. **22**(1), 1–15 (2016). https://doi.org/10.1007/s00500-016-2442-1
3. Amirsadri, S., Mousavirad, S.J., Ebrahimpour-Komleh, H.: A levy flight-based grey wolf optimizer combined with back-propagation algorithm for neural network training. Neural Comput. Appl. **30**(12), 3707–3720 (2018)
4. Bairathi, D., Gopalani, D.: Salp swarm algorithm (SSA) for training feed-forward neural networks. In: Bansal, J.C., Das, K.N., Nagar, A., Deep, K., Ojha, A.K. (eds.) Soft Computing for Problem Solving. AISC, vol. 816, pp. 521–534. Springer, Singapore (2019). https://doi.org/10.1007/978-981-13-1592-3_41
5. Bidgoli, A.A., Komleh, H.E., Mousavirad, S.J.: Seminal quality prediction using optimized artificial neural network with genetic algorithm. In: 9th International Conference on Electrical and Electronics Engineering (ELECO), pp. 695–699 (2015)
6. Chen, X., Tianfield, H., Mei, C., Du, W., Liu, G.: Biogeography-based learning particle swarm optimization. Soft. Comput. **21**(24), 7519–7541 (2016). https://doi.org/10.1007/s00500-016-2307-7
7. Gudise, V.G., Venayagamoorthy, G.K.: Comparison of particle swarm optimization and backpropagation as training algorithms for neural networks. In: IEEE Swarm Intelligence Symposium, pp. 110–117. IEEE (2003)
8. Ilonen, J., Kamarainen, J.K., Lampinen, J.: Differential evolution training algorithm for feed-forward neural networks. Neural Process. Lett. **17**(1), 93–105 (2003)
9. Jalali, S.M.J., Ahmadian, S., Kebria, P.M., Khosravi, A., Lim, C.P., Nahavandi, S.: Evolving artificial neural networks using butterfly optimization algorithm for data classification. In: Gedeon, T., Wong, K.W., Lee, M. (eds.) ICONIP 2019. LNCS, vol. 11953, pp. 596–607. Springer, Cham (2019). https://doi.org/10.1007/978-3-030-36708-4_49
10. Jalali, S.M.J., Karimi, M., Khosravi, A., Nahavandi, S.: An efficient neuroevolution approach for heart disease detection. In: 2019 IEEE International Conference on Systems, Man and Cybernetics (SMC), pp. 3771–3776. IEEE (2019)
11. Karaboga, D., Akay, B., Ozturk, C.: Artificial bee colony (ABC) optimization algorithm for training feed-forward neural networks. In: Torra, V., Narukawa, Y., Yoshida, Y. (eds.) MDAI 2007. LNCS (LNAI), vol. 4617, pp. 318–329. Springer, Heidelberg (2007). https://doi.org/10.1007/978-3-540-73729-2_30
12. Kennedy, J., Eberhart, R.: Particle swarm optimization (PSO). In: IEEE International Conference on Neural Networks, pp. 1942–1948 (1995)
13. Khishe, M., Safari, A.: Classification of sonar targets using an MLP neural network trained by dragonfly algorithm. Wireless Pers. Commun. **108**(4), 2241–2260 (2019)
14. Liang, J.J., Qin, A.K., Suganthan, P.N., Baskar, S.: Comprehensive learning particle swarm optimizer for global optimization of multimodal functions. IEEE Trans. Evol. Comput. **10**(3), 281–295 (2006)
15. Mirjalili, S.: How effective is the grey wolf optimizer in training multi-layer perceptrons. Appl. Intell. **43**(1), 150–161 (2015)
16. Mirjalili, S., Hashim, S.Z.M., Sardroudi, H.M.: Training feedforward neural networks using hybrid particle swarm optimization and gravitational search algorithm. Appl. Math. Comput. **218**(22), 11125–11137 (2012)

17. Mousavirad, S.J., Bidgoli, A.A., Ebrahimpour-Komleh, H., Schaefer, G.: A memetic imperialist competitive algorithm with chaotic maps for multi-layer neural network training. Int. J. Bio-Inspired Comput. **14**(4), 227–236 (2019)
18. Mousavirad, S.J., Bidgoli, A.A., Ebrahimpour-Komleh, H., Schaefer, G., Korovin, I.: An effective hybrid approach for optimising the learning process of multi-layer neural networks. In: International Symposium on Neural Networks, pp. 309–317 (2019)
19. Mousavirad, S.J., Ebrahimpour-Komleh, H.: Human mental search: a new population-based metaheuristic optimization algorithm. Appl. Intell. **47**(3), 850–887 (2017). https://doi.org/10.1007/s10489-017-0903-6
20. Mousavirad, S.J., Schaefer, G., Jalali, S.M.J., Korovin, I.: A benchmark of recent population-based metaheuristic algorithms for multi-layer neural network training. In: Proceedings of the 2020 Genetic and Evolutionary Computation Conference Companion, pp. 1402–1408 (2020)
21. Mousavirad, S., Akhlaghian, F., Mollazade, K.: Classification of rice varieties using optimal color and texture features and BP neural networks. In: 7th Iranian Conference on Machine Vision and Image Processing, pp. 1–5 (2011)
22. Si, T., Dutta, R.: Partial opposition-based particle swarm optimizer in artificial neural network training for medical data classification. Int. J. Inf. Technol. Decis. Making **18**(5), 1717–1750 (2019)
23. Simon, D.: Biogeography-based optimization. IEEE Trans. Evol. Comput. **12**(6), 702–713 (2008)

Perceived Image Reconstruction from Human Brain Activity via Time-Series Information Guided Generative Adversarial Networks

Shuo Huang, Liang Sun, Muhammad Yousefnezhad, Meiling Wang,
and Daoqiang Zhang$^{(\boxtimes)}$

College of Computer Science and Technology MIIT Key Laboratory of Pattern
Analysis and Machine Intelligence,
Nanjing University of Aeronautics and Astronautics, Nanjing, China
dqzhang@nuaa.edu.cn

Abstract. Understanding how human brain works has attracted increasing attentions in both fields of neuroscience and machine learning. Previous studies have used autoencoder and generative adversarial networks (GAN) to improve the quality of perceived image reconstruction from functional Magnetic Resonance Imaging (fMRI) data. However, these methods mainly focus on acquiring relevant features between stimuli images and fMRI while ignoring the time-series information of fMRI, thus leading to sub-optimal performance. To address this issue, in this paper, we develop a time-series information guided GAN method for reconstructing visual stimuli from human brain activities. In addition, to better measure the *modal difference*, we leverage a pairwise ranking loss to rank the stimuli images and fMRI to ensure strongly associated pairs at the top and weakly related ones at the bottom. Experimental results on real-world datasets suggest that the proposed method achieves better performance in comparison with several state-of-the-art image reconstruction approaches.

Keywords: Perceived image reconstruction · functional Magnetic Resonance Imaging (fMRI) · Long-Short Term Memory (LSTM) · Generative adversarial networks (GAN)

1 Introduction

"Reading minds" has been one of the most significant challenges in the field of neuroscience in the past for a long time [1,2]. To this end, an algorithm called the human brain encoding and decoding has been proposed, where the encoding part embeds information into neural activities, while the decoding part extracts

This work was supported by the National Key Research and Development Program of China (Nos. 2018YFC2001600, 2018YFC2001602) and the National Natural Science Foundation of China (Nos. 61876082, 61861130366 and 61732006), the Royal Society-Academy of Medical Sciences Newton Advanced Fellowship (No. NAF\ R1\180371).

© Springer Nature Switzerland AG 2020
H. Yang et al. (Eds.): ICONIP 2020, CCIS 1333, pp. 156–163, 2020.
https://doi.org/10.1007/978-3-030-63823-8_19

information from neural activities [3]. Functional Magnetic Resonance Imaging (fMRI) is one of the most popular tools for studying the human brain, using blood oxygen level dependence (BOLD) signals as a proxy for visual neural activity. The main idea is to use these measurements of neural activities to process cognitive state [4,5].

Recent years, several deep neural network based methods have been proposed for decoding the cognitive states in human brains. For instance, some studies use the outputs of DNN to reveal the neural activities in human visual cortex [6–8]. However, there are still some challenges for the perceived image reconstruction from human brain activity with fMRI. In particular, 1) fMRI data is usually high-dimensional with a lot of complex noises, which interferes with the mining of real brain activity and influences the reconstruction results; 2) the pairwise samples are treated as time point samples, which ignores the time-series information of the visual task; 3) the limited mapping between the stimuli images and the evoked brain avtivity patterns, which fails to correctly assess the correlation between the two cross-modal data.

To address these issues, in this paper, we propose a novel visual stimuli reconstruction method based on LSTM and GAN. Specifically, there are three components in our method to solve the challenges mentioned before. The first part is the stimuli images encoder, which is used for mapping the stimuli images to a latent space through deep neural network. The second part is a LSTM network, used for fMRI feature mapping to extract time-series information from fMRI. The last part is the discriminator for stimuli image generation, which generates the images as similar as the original input images. We also employ the pairwise ranking loss [9] to encourage the similarity of ground truth caption-image pairs to be greater than that of all other negative ones.

The major contributions of this paper are two folds. First, we propose a novel method to reconstruct the visual images from the evoked fMRI data. A time-series information guided GAN method is proposed to capture the time-series information in fMRI data via LSTM network and complete the task of stimuli image reconstruction through GAN. Second, we introduce a pairwise ranking loss to measure the relationship between the stimuli images and fMRI signals. This loss function ranks the stimuli images and fMRI that ensure strongly associated (corresponding) is at the top and weakly correlated at the bottom.

2 Proposed Method

2.1 Notations

Let N be the number of images which we used in the visual stimuli task, and D denotes the dimensions of stimuli images. Suppose $X = \{x_{pq}\} \in \mathbb{R}^{N \times D}, p = 1 : N, q = 1 : D$ denotes the stimuli images. At the same time, the preprocessed fMRI time series for S subjects is denoted by $Y = \{y_{mn}\} \in \mathbb{R}^{T_f \times V}, m = 1 : T_f, n = 1 : V$, where T_f is the number of time points in units of TRs (Time of Repetition), V is the number of voxels, and y_{mn} denotes the functional activity for the subject in the m-th time point and the n-th voxel. As the proposed

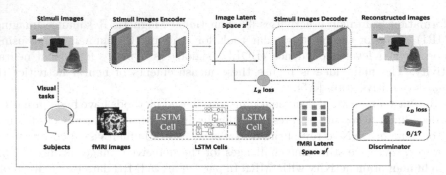

Fig. 1. The schematic diagram of time-series information guided GAN method

method is a cross-modal data reconstruction task, the samples are pairwise, which is saying that the number of the samples is T, and $T = N = T_f$. Here, for convenience, we let (x_t, y_t) be a pairwise sample at time point $t, t = 1, 2, \ldots, T$.

2.2   Time-Series Information Guided GAN

We develop a time-series information guided GAN method for modeling the relationship between the visual stimuli (images) and the evoked fMRI activity patterns. Our method generates two different modals from a shared latent space, via the two-view specific generative model and a discriminative model. The schematic diagram of the proposed method is shown in Fig. 1. There are three sub-networks in the proposed model, i.e., 1) a image encoder for mapping the stimuli images into latent space, 2) a LSTM generator for fMRI feature mapping, and 3) a discriminator for image reconstruction.

Stimuli Images Autoencoder: Due to only a small number of sample can be used to train the network for stimuli image reconstruction task, we pretrain an autoencoder to improve the performance. The pretrained encoder network is employed to map the stimuli images into a latent representation. Herein, in the cross-modal reconstruction model, the image encoder can map the features of visual stimuli into the image latent space z^i, where the latent feature $z_t^i = f_\theta(x_t)$. Here $f(\cdot)$ is the encoder function, θ is the parameters in the encoder. While the decoder network reconstructs the original input image $\hat{x}_t = g_\phi(z_t^i)$ by using the nonlinear function $g(\cdot)$, where ϕ is the parameters in the decoder. The loss function of the autoencoder can be defined as follows:

$$\min_{\theta,\phi} \frac{1}{T} \sum_{t=1}^{T} \|x_t - g_\phi(f_\theta(x_t))\|_F^2 , \tag{1}$$

LSTM Network for fMRI Feature Mapping: The fMRI generator produces an output image $\hat{y}_t$ given the corresponding neural response in sequential order $y_t, t \in 1 \cdots T$. Here, the generated image $\hat{y}_t$ is as similar as possible to the reconstructed image in the next step y_{t+1}. Therefore, the generator should be a sequential LSTM model, which produces the sequentially next image, $\hat{y}_t = \mathcal{L}(y_1, y_2, \cdots, y_t)$, $t = 1, 2, \ldots, T$. The LSTM network maps the fMRI signals into the fMRI latent space z^f, where the latent feature $\hat{y}_t = \mathcal{L}(y_t)$, $t = 1, 2, \ldots, T$. Here, $\mathcal{L}(\cdot)$ defines the LSTM network mapping.

Discriminator for Stimuli Image Generation: The discriminator in the model takes a reconstructed or original image as input, then a binary decision is made to decide whether the input is real or fake. We involve two loss components to compute the loss between the generated image x_t^{recon} and the original image x_t on the basis of features from the trained deep neural networks. The first component is feature reconstruction loss $\mathcal{L}_f$, which determines whether features are activated above a threshold at all. The feature reconstruction loss is obtained via mean absolute error, which is calculated between the generated image x_t^{recon} and the original image x_t. The feature reconstruction loss $\mathcal{L}_f$ can be determined as

$$\min \sum_{t=1}^{T} \sum_{q=1}^{D} |(x_t)^q - (x_t^{recon})^q|, \tag{2}$$

where D denotes the dimensions of stimuli images.

The second component of the losses is the discriminator loss $\mathcal{L}_d$. The discriminator discriminates the real sample. Here, to make the discriminative result close to 1, we let the generated image x_t^{recon} close to the real image x_t to fool the discriminator. The discriminator loss $\mathcal{L}_d$ can be defined as

$$\min_{G} \max_{D} V(D, G) = E_{x \sim p_{data}(x)}[\log(D(x))] + \\ E_{z \sim p_z(z)}[\log(D(1 - D(G(z))))]. \tag{3}$$

The hybrid loss function $\mathcal{L}_D$ combine the two loss components as

$$\mathcal{L}_D = \frac{1}{T}(\mathcal{L}_f + \mathcal{L}_d). \tag{4}$$

2.3 Ranking Loss for Cross-Modal Data Fusion

One of the most significant challenges for reconstructing the visual stimuli is how to model the relationship between the stimuli images and the evoked fMRI scans. Inspired by [9], we develop the rank loss from the image-textual reveral to visual stimuli reconstruction field for measuring the relationship between the two cross-madal data. We denote $(\hat{x}_t, \hat{y}_t)$ as the pairwise image-fMRI sample at time point t, which generated from the two specific generators of cross-modal data. We further denote the non-corresponding samples by using $\hat{x}_t'$ and $\hat{y}_t'$, where $\hat{x}_t'$ goes over stimuli images independent of $\hat{y}_t$, and $\hat{y}_t'$ goes over brain activities not evoked by $\hat{x}_t$. The objective function ensures that the groundtruth image-activity pairs at the top and weakly related ones at the bottom. Therefore, we optimize the ranking loss below:

$$\mathcal{L}_R = \frac{1}{T} \sum_{t=1}^{T} \mathcal{L}_{Rank}(\hat{x}_t, \hat{y}_t), \tag{5}$$

where the single pairwise sample ranking loss $\mathcal{L}_{Rank}$ is defined as follows:

$$\mathcal{L}_{Rank} = \sum_{\hat{x}_t'} [\alpha - s(\hat{x}_t, \hat{y}_t) + s(\hat{x}_t', \hat{y}_t)]_+ + \sum_{\hat{y}_t'} [\alpha - s(\hat{x}_t, \hat{y}_t) + s(\hat{x}_t, \hat{y}_t')]_+, \tag{6}$$

where α is a margin, $s(\hat{x}_t, \hat{y}_t) = -\parallel (\max(0, \hat{x}_t - \hat{y}_t)) \parallel^2$ is the order-violation penalty used as a similarity. Futher, $[x]_+$ represents $\max(x, 0)$.

The overall loss function is then given as follows:

$$\mathcal{L}_{loss} = \lambda_D \mathcal{L}_D + \lambda_R \mathcal{L}_R, \tag{7}$$

where λ_D, λ_R are hyper-parameters to balance the effects of the two loss functions. We randomly choose all the parameters from $\{0.01, 0.05, 0.1, 0.5, 1, 5, 10\}$. The values were determined via optimizing on the training set. Optimization specifically for each dataset may improve the results further.

3   Experimental Results

Datasets: In this paper, we employ two publicly available datasets to validate the proposed method, including, a) Open NEURO[1] dataset, and b) Handwritten digits dataset. For the Open NEURO dataset, we select the dataset numbered DS105 [2] in the Open NEURO Project. In DS105, 6 subjects were stimulated with grayscale images in 8 categories, and each subject underwent 12 runs of experiments. Among them, subject No.5 miss one run of data record, with only 11 runs of data. In this paper, we use a leave-one-out cross validation strategy to adjust the parameters and evaluate the effectiveness of the method we propose. In each phase, data from five subjects are used for training, while data from one subject is used during the test stage.

For the handwritten digits dataset, we use the same dataset as the experiment in [6]. There are one hundred gray-scale handwritten digit images (50 of digital "6" and the equal numbers of digital "9") in the dataset. The image resolution is 28×28. A 10-fold cross validation was performed (i.e. each category contained 45 training data and 5 test data for each experiment).

Experiment Settings: The proposed method is compared with four well-known methods, including 1) Bayesian canonical correlation analysis (BCCA) [10]: A multiview linear generative model designed for neural encoding and decoding. 2) Deep canonically correlated autoencoder (DCCAE) [11]: A cross-view representation model to learn the deep representations from multiview data. 3) Deep

---

[1] http://openneuro.org.

Table 1. Performances of compared methods on the $DS105$ dataset.

Model	Euc_dis↓	p-value	PCC↑	p-value	MSE↓	p-value
BCCA	0.787±0.153	1.3839e-14	0.561±0.159	9.8467e-11	0.208±0.062	8.2238e-9
DCCAE	0.751±0.196	1.6552e-10	0.584±0.193	8.5767e-10	0.171±0.104	2.0229e-7
DGMM	0.652±0.122	2.4369e-7	0.636±0.146	2.8228e-7	0.124±0.069	3.4167e-4
DCGAN	0.641±0.089	7.9318e-5	0.651±0.096	8.0966e-6	0.116±0.074	0.0055
Proposed	**0.609±0.061**	—	**0.689±0.063**	—	**0.091±0.051**	—

Table 2. Performances of compared methods on the handwritten digits dataset.

Model	Euc_dis↓	p-value	PCC↑	p-value	MSE↓	p-value
BCCA	0.679±0.155	1.1709e-10	0.423±0.139	1.6853e-22	0.119±0.023	1.8554e-20
DCCAE	0.631±0.064	9.5486e-9	0.529±0.047	5.0496e-20	0.077±0.018	3.3630e-11
DGMM	0.585±0.061	0.0025	0.801±0.061	0.0291	0.037±0.019	0.004
DCGAN	0.581±0.055	0.0238	0.799±0.057	0.0163	0.038±0.022	0.0096
Proposed	**0.568±0.037**	—	**0.812±0.059**	—	**0.033±0.015**	—

generative multiview model (DGMM) [6]: A deep generative multi-view learning model for reconstructing the perceive images from brain fMRI activities. 4) Deep convolutional generative adversarial network (DCGAN) [12]: A GAN framework used to generate arbitrary images from the stimuli domain (i.e., handwritten characters or natural gray scale images).

Three evaluation metrics are used to measure the reconstruction performance of different methods, including 1) Euclidean distance (Euc_dis), the smaller the value is, the more similar reconstructed result we obtained. 2) Pearson's correlation coefficient (PCC), which shows the correlation between the original and reconstructed images. 3) Mean squared error (MSE), which calculates the pixel-level error between the reconstructed image and the original image. The smaller the error, the more similar the reconstructed image is to the real image.

Quantitative Analysis: Performances of compared methods on two datasets were listed in Table 1 and 2. Table 1 shows the experimental results of dataset DS105, several observations can be drawn as follows. First, the proposed method obtains a considerably better performance compared with the other methods. Second, by comparing the proposed method with BCCA, a linear model for stimuli reconstruction, we can see that our method is always out-perform BCCA. These results show that our reconstruction method with deep network is better than linear model by extracting nonlinear features from visual images and fitting images. Third, compared with DCCAE, the proposed method shows significantly better performance. As a nonlinear cross reconstruction model, DCCAE achieves better performance than BCCA, but compared with our method, there is a lack of time-series information mining. Fourth, the performance of DGMM is moderate on both of the two datasets. This may be caused by the performance gap between

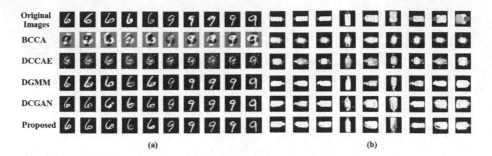

Fig. 2. Image reconstruction results of different methods on two datasets. (a) Handwritten digits dataset (b) *DS*105 dataset (category=bottles).

DGMM's deep network model and GAN's generative discriminant model. The last but not the least, compared with DCGAN, LSTM network in our method plays an important role in mining the correlation between the stimuli images and the brain activity patterns.

For the handwritten digits dataset, the results are shown in Table 2. The quantitative results on the three evaluation metrics are also at the best level. For the three campared methods of BCCA, DCCAE and DGMM, we refer to the experimental settings in [6], and also refer to their experimental results on MSE. And for Euc_dis and PCC here, we obtained similar results as which on DS105 dataset. The reason is as analyzed above. Compared with DCGAN, our method also takes the better results because of the use of LSTM network and the cross-modal ranking loss. In addition, p-values are also displayed in the tables to verify the significance of our experimental results.

Qualitative Analysis: The reconstructed results on two different datasets are shown in Fig.2(a)-(b), respectively. In each figure, the top row shows the presented visual images, while the following rows show the reconstructed results of all compared methods.

In Fig. 2(a), the reconstructed handwritten digits are very similar to the original images. Compared with our method, the performances of BCCA and DCCAE are not acceptable. The complex noises often influence the their reconstruction results and the results also lack of the basic features in the original images. Furthermore, the reconstruction results of DGMM and DCGAN are coarse too. Although their results are better than those of BCCA and DCCAE, they lost some information in details compared with our method, because they did not take the time-series information into account. The reconstructing results of DS105 (categories = "bottles") are shown in Fig. 2(b). As can be seen from the figure, our method produces better reconstruction results than the compared methods. Fig. 2(b) also indicates that the effect of our method is obviously better than other methods on the reconstruction of natural images. In particular, BCCA and DCCAE cannot provide acceptable performance in characterizing detailed contours, which may be related to their mapping capabilities. DGMM and DCGAN are better than the first two methods, but they are not as good as our method when describing image details, such as color.

4   Conclusion

In this paper, we present a time-series information guided GAN method for perceived image reconstruction from human brain activities. Our method is not only a generative model to model the relationship between the stimuli image and the evoked brain activities, but also take the time-series information of fMRI data into account. Furthermore, the pairwise ranking loss is introduced to measure the relationship between the stimuli images and the corresponding fMRI data, which ensures that the strongly associated pairs is at the top and the weakly related ones is at the bottom. Our reconstruction model can also achieve better performance in comparison with state-of-the-art reconstruction methods on both of the two publicly available fMRI datasets.

References

1. Smith, K.: Brain decoding: reading minds. Nature News **502**(7472), 428 (2013)
2. Haxby, J.V., Gobbini, M.I., Furey, M.L., Ishai, A., Schouten, J.L., Pietrini, P.: Distributed and overlapping representations of faces and objects in ventral temporal cortex. Science **293**(5539), 2425–2430 (2001)
3. Kay, K.N., Naselaris, T., Prenger, R.J., Gallant, J.L.: Identifying natural images from human brain activity. Nature **452**(7185), 352 (2008)
4. Brachman, R.J., Schmolze, J.G.: An overview of the KL-ONE knowledge representation system. Cogn. Sci. **9**(2), 171–216 (1985)
5. DiCarlo, J.J., Zoccolan, D., Rust, N.C.: How does the brain solve visual object recognition? Neuron **73**(3), 415–434 (2012)
6. Du, C., Du, C., Huang, L., He, H.: Reconstructing perceived images from human brain activities with Bayesian deep multiview learning. IEEE Trans. Neural Netw. Learn. Syst. **30**(8), 2310–2323 (2018)
7. Güçlütürk, Y., Güçlü, U., Seeliger, K., Bosch, S., van Lier, R., van Gerven, M.A.: Reconstructing perceived faces from brain activations with deep adversarial neural decoding. In: Advances in Neural Information Processing Systems, pp. 4246–4257 (2017)
8. Shen, G., Dwivedi, K., Majima, K., Horikawa, T., Kamitani, Y.: End-to-end deep image reconstruction from human brain activity. Front. Comput. Neurosci. **13**, 21 (2019)
9. Gu, J., Cai, J., Joty, S. R., Niu, L., Wang, G.: Look, imagine and match: Improving textual-visual cross-modal retrieval with generative models. In: Proceedings of the IEEE Conference on Computer Vision and Pattern Recognition. pp. 7181–7189 (2018)
10. Fujiwara, Y., Miyawaki, Y., Kamitani, Y.: Modular encoding and decoding models derived from bayesian canonical correlation analysis. Neural Comput. **25**(4), 979–1005 (2013)
11. Wang, W., Arora, R., Livescu, K., Bilmes, J.: On deep multi-view representation learning. In: International Conference on Machine Learning. pp. 1083–1092 (2015)
12. Seeliger, K., Güçlü, U., Ambrogioni, L., Güçlütürk, Y., van Gerven, M.A.: Generative adversarial networks for reconstructing natural images from brain activity. NeuroImage **181**, 775–785 (2018)

Protein-Protein Interactions Prediction Based on Bi-directional Gated Recurrent Unit and Multimodal Representation

Kanchan Jha[1(✉)], Sriparna Saha[1], and Matloob Khushi[2]

[1] Department of Computer Science and Engineering, Indian Institute of Technology Patna, Patna 801103, Bihar, India
jha.kanchan15@gmail.com, sriparna.saha@gmail.com
[2] School of Computer Science, The University of Sydney, Sydney, NSW, Australia
matloob.khushi@sydney.edu.au

Abstract. Protein-protein interactions (PPIs) are responsible for various biological processes and cellular functions of all living organisms. The detection of PPIs helps in understanding the roles of proteins and their complex structure. Proteins are commonly represented by amino acid sequences. The method of identifying PPIs is divided into two steps. Firstly, a feature vector from protein representation is extracted. Then, a model is trained on these extracted feature vectors to reveal novel interactions. These days, with the availability of multimodal biomedical data and the successful adoption of deep-learning algorithms in solving various problems of bioinformatics, we can obtain more relevant feature vectors, improving the model's performance to predict PPIs. Current work utilizes multimodal data as tertiary structure information and sequence-based information. A deep learning-based model, ResNet50, is used to extract features from 3D voxel representation of proteins. To get a compact feature vector from amino acid sequences, stacked autoencoder and quasi-sequence-order (QSO) are utilized. QSO converts the symbolic representation (amino acid sequences) of proteins into their numerical representation. After extracting features from different modalities, these features are concatenated in pairs and then fed into the bi-directional GRU-based classifier to predict PPIs. Our proposed approach achieves an accuracy of 0.9829, which is the best accuracy of 3-fold cross-validation on the human PPI dataset. The results signify that the proposed approach's performance is better than existing computational methods, such as state-of-the-art stacked autoencoder-based classifiers.

Keywords: Protein-protein interactions · Deep-learning · Multimodality · Bi-directional GRU

1 Introduction

Protein is the primary integrant of all living organisms. The interactions among proteins are responsible for various biological processes and molecular functions

H. Yang et al. (Eds.): ICONIP 2020, CCIS 1333, pp. 164–171, 2020.
https://doi.org/10.1007/978-3-030-63823-8_20

in the cell [1–3]. The study of PPIs is essential as it is not only the basis of many life functions but also is very helpful in exploring the growth and causes of several diseases and plays a significant role in targeting new drug discovery [4]. High throughput experimental methods and computational methods are two ways to identify PPIs. Yeast two-hybrid (Y2H) [5], tandem affinity purification (TAP) [6], and mass spectrometric protein complex identification (MS-PCI) [7] are some popular experimental techniques that have been used for PPI prediction. But these methods have high false positives, and false negatives as the output depends on the experimental environment and operational processes. Moreover, these methods are costly and time-consuming, which restrict them from exploring the whole PPI networks. Therefore, there is a need for designing the robust computational methods in conjunction with experimental techniques to predict PPIs more accurately.

Computational methods have to follow a two-stage approach when identifying protein interactions. Firstly, the protein representations (amino acid sequences and 3D structure) are converted into feature vectors containing numeric values. These feature vectors are then fed into models that can identify interactions more accurately. To obtain a feature vector for each protein, researchers use various protein information such as structural information, evolutionary information, and sequence-based information. With the successful adoption of deep-learning methodologies in various domains, computational biologists have recently started exploring deep-learning methods to solve various bio medical problems, such as the prediction of protein interactions and their functions. Sun et al. [8] have used the stacked autoencoder classifier in their work to predict labels for protein interactions. Du et al. [9] have utilized a deep learning classifier that employs two separate neural networks, one for each protein in a pair to analyze their input descriptions. Gonzalez-Lopez et al. [10] have used a deep recurrent neural network to process the input feature vectors of proteins in pairs. The computational approaches used to solve different problems in bioinformatics vary in their input representations and algorithms.

Earlier, researchers have utilized one type of information (unimodal) that represents proteins to classify protein interactions. Recent studies encourage the use of multimodal data to enhance the performance of the model. The features obtained from different modalities complement each other and improve the predictive capability of a classifier. In recent years, with the help of the latest technologies, multiple kinds of information are available to express proteins. This information can be structural information, evolutionary information, or sequence-based information. As deep-learning methods can capture non-linear features and can handle high-dimensional data, it is possible to utilize multimodal information to predict protein interactions.

In this paper, we propose a framework to identify PPIs that integrates two types of protein information. One is sequence-based information, and the other is 3D structural information of protein's atoms. Quasi-sequence-order (QSO) [11] is a sequence-based method that transforms the sequences of amino acids into feature vectors containing numeric values. To get the compact form of features obtained by QSO, we have used a stacked autoencoder with one hidden layer. The structural information includes 3D coordinates (x, y, z) of protein's atoms, which we have downloaded from RCSB Protein Data Bank (PDB; http://www.rcsb.org/pdb/). To visualize protein's tertiary structure using its coordinates, we have used a voxel-based representation. In the voxel-based description of an object, also known as volumetric representation [12], a binary voxel is used to discretize its structure spatially. The value of 1 represents the occupancy of the voxel, and 0 means the voxel is empty. As the binary volumetric depiction of proteins is about the shape only, we incorporate biological indicators such as hydropathy index, isoelectric point, and charge into these representation models. It means the occupied voxel represents the values of these attributes instead of 1. The values of these indicators describe the local properties of the protein's building block. By doing so, we get three more volumetric descriptions of proteins. So, we have four volumetric representations of proteins using structural information and biological descriptors of amino acids, as illustrated in Fig. 1. We have used a pre-trained ResNet50 model (a subclass of convolutional neural network) to extract features from these representations of proteins. Finally, these feature vectors from two different modalities (sequence and structural) of proteins are concatenated in pairs and used as inputs to the bi-directional GRU based classifier that predicts protein interactions.

2   Methodology

This section illustrates the working of the proposed method. Our approach to identify interactions between proteins involves two phases, i.e., feature extraction and supervised learning. The feature extraction phase employs multimodal information and deep learning algorithms to extract features from different modalities of proteins. In the supervised learning phase, these extracted features are used as input to a classifier. Below we have detailed each stage of the proposed framework with the corresponding inputs and outputs.

2.1   Quasi-Sequence-Order

Quasi-sequence-order (QSO) is one of the sequence-based methods that converts the symbolic representations of proteins into their numeric descriptions. It represents the distribution patterns of amino acid of specific physical-chemical properties along the protein sequences. To encode protein sequences, QSO is defined as

$$X_k = \frac{f_k}{\sum_{k=1}^{20} f_k + \omega \sum_{d=1}^{lag} \tau_d}, (1 \leq k \leq 20) \tag{1}$$

Here, f_k represents the normalized occurrence of amino acid of type k in the given protein sequence. In this experiment, ω is the weighting factor initialized at $\omega = 0.1$, and the default value of lag is 30. τ_d is defined as

$$\tau_d = \sum_{i=1}^{N-d} (d_{i,i+d})^2 \tag{2}$$

where, N is the length of the protein sequence, $d_{i,i+d}$ represents the distance between the two amino acids present at position i and $i + d$, respectively. The distance between two amino acids at different positions is derived from the distance matrix, which includes the Schneider-Wrede physical-chemical distance matrix and the Grantham chemical distance matrix. Using QSO as a protein sequence encoding method, each protein is represented as a feature vector with $100 \, [(20 + 30) \times 2]$ elements [11].

2.2   Voxel-Based Protein Structure

To get the volumetric representation of proteins, we need the 3D coordinates information of elements of which proteins are made up. These coordinates' information of protein's atoms are present in a text file with pdb extension. In binary volumetric representation, a voxel is the volume element that has to be fitted in a cube V of a fixed grid size l in the three dimensions. Nearest neighbor interpolation is used to obtain the continuity between voxels, such that for (i, j, k) $\in [0; l - 1]^3$, a voxel of vertices

$$(i + \delta x, j + \delta y, \delta k + z)|(\delta x, \delta y, \delta z) \in \{0, 1\}^3$$

takes the value 1 if the backbone of the enzyme passes through the voxel, and 0 otherwise. The volumetric representations of proteins consider only the backbone atoms (calcium, nitrogen, and carbon) of proteins and ignore their side chains. Before converting the 3D coordinates into voxel, some preprocessing steps are executed on these coordinates of proteins' atoms. These steps include the centering of coordinates to zero and their scaling. After converting coordinates to voxel, the voxel having no neighborhood is removed [13].

2.3   Deep-Learning-Based Approaches

Residual network [14], Bi-directional GRU [15] followed by attention layer [16] are some deep learning methods used in our work. Figure 1 depicts how these deep learning methods are utilized at each stage of the proposed approach to identify protein interactions. In the current context, we have used four images that depict the shape and local properties of protein sequences. We have used a pre-trained ResNet50 model to extract features from these images separately, which give a feature vector of 2048 elements. These feature vectors are then concatenated in pairs and passed through the bi-directional GRU layer, followed by the attention layer, as shown in Fig. 1. QSO is the sequence-based method to get a numeric representation of proteins. QSO method expresses each protein as a vector with 100 elements. So, each protein pair is represented as a feature vector with 200 elements. The representations of these protein pairs are then passed through stacked autoencoder having one hidden layer to get their compact information, as presented in Fig. 1. Finally, the features obtained from two modalities of proteins are merged and used as input to the sigmoid layer, predicting PPIs–the sigmoid layer's output varies between 0 and 1. Concerning a threshold value, if a value is higher than that threshold, it is interpreted as a positive pair otherwise negative pair.

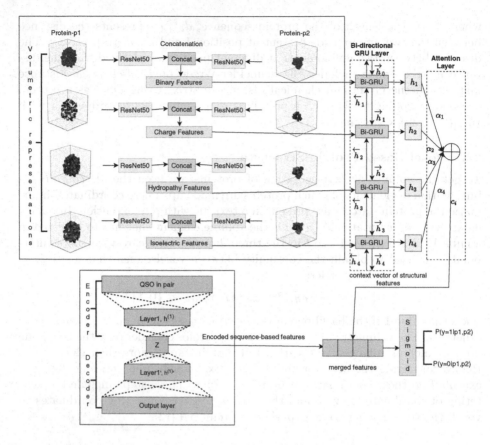

Fig. 1. The working of proposed methodology

3   Results

This section presents the description of the dataset used in this experiment, evaluation metrics to measure the performance of the model, and summarizes the obtained results. To evaluate model's performance, we have used accuracy, sensitivity, specificity, precision, and F-score as evaluation metrics. We have implemented the proposed model in Keras (python-based framework).

3.1   Dataset Description

In this experiment, we have used Pan's [17] PPI dataset. This dataset contains both positive samples and negative samples. The positive pairs are procured from the human protein reference database (HPRD, 2007 version). A removal of identical pairs and those having odd symbols like U and X is performed, after which 36,545 positive protein pairs are remained. To get negative protein pairs, proteins are paired from different subcellular locations. Information about the subcellular locations is procured from the Swiss-Prot database, version 57.3. Some preprocessing is done by eliminating proteins with more than one subcellular location or having fragmented annotations or having residues length less than 50. After preprocessing, we have a total of 2,184 proteins from different subcellular locations. A random coupling of proteins belonging to different subcellular locations is done, followed by the addition of negative pairs from [18]. This gives us a total of 36,480 negative pairs. On removing pairs with unascertained symbols like U and X gives a total of 36,323 negative pairs. The final tally of negative and positive pairs has a total of 36,545 positive pairs and 36,323 negative pairs.

Due to the unavailability of protein's tertiary structure information for all the proteins in the benchmark dataset (available only for 10,359 protein sequence), the total number of protein pairs is reduced to 25,493. Hence altogether, we are left with a dataset having 25,493 samples in a total of which 18,025 are positive pairs, and 7,468 are negative pairs.

3.2   Prediction Performance of Proposed Model

We have first trained the stacked autoencoder classifier used by Sun et al. [8] with input features obtained by the QSO method. Table 1 presents the results of this classifier using 3 fold cross-validation (CV). The results that we get are similar to the values obtained in [8]. The average accuracies using 3-fold cross-validation of stacked autoencoder classifier taking QSO and autocovariance based input features are {0.9346, 0.9300} with {0.9536, 0.9483} sensitivity at the specificity of {0.8887, 0.8860}, respectively.

Table 2 summarizes the results of the proposed model trained on merged features (sequence and structural). 0.9708 is the average accuracy of 3-fold cross-

Table 1. The 3-fold CV results on Human PPI dataset using stacked autoencoder-based classifier with Quasi-sequence-order feature vectors

Test set	Accuracy	Sensitivity	Specificity	Precision	F-measure
1	0.9346	0.9544	0.8867	0.9531	0.9538
2	0.9314	0.9502	0.8859	0.9526	0.9514
3	0.9377	0.9561	0.8935	0.9559	0.9560
Average	**0.9346**	**0.9536**	**0.8887**	**0.9539**	**0.9537**
Standard deviation	0.0025	0.0024	0.0034	0.0014	0.0018

Table 2. The 3-fold CV results on Human PPI dataset using Bi-directional GRU-based classifier that integrates structural features with Quasi-sequence-order

Test set	Accuracy	Sensitivity	Specificity	Precision	F-measure
1	0.9513	0.9551	0.9421	0.9755	0.9652
2	0.9781	0.9890	0.9518	0.9802	0.9846
3	0.9829	0.9902	0.9654	0.9857	0.9880
Average	**0.9708**	**0.9781**	**0.9531**	**0.9805**	**0.9793**
Standard deviation	0.0139	0.0162	0.0095	0.0041	0.0100

Table 3. Performance comparison between proposed and existing methods

Model	Accuracy	Sensitivity	Specificity	Precision	F-measure
SAE_AC [8]	0.9300	0.9483	0.8860	0.9530	0.9506
SAE_CT [8]	0.9083	0.9259	0.8656	0.9433	0.9345
Proposed approach	**0.9708**	**0.9781**	**0.9531**	**0.9805**	**0.9793**

validation with {0.9781, 0.9531} as average sensitivity and specificity, respectively. The obtained results justify the fact of using multimodal data to improve prediction performance of the classifier.

3.3   Comparison with Existing Method

We have compared our method with a state-of-the-art stacked autoencoder (SAE) based classifier [8]. SAE_AC and SAE_CT are the classifiers trained on input features obtained by autocovariance and conjoint triad sequence methods. Table 3 presents the values of performance metrics of both approaches (existing and proposed). To make this comparison fair, we have trained the SAE_AC and SAE_CT on the same dataset (with 25,493 samples), which is used to train our proposed model and reported the results in Table 3.

4   Conclusion

In this work, we have utilized two types of information that describe proteins, i.e., sequence information and structural information for predicting the protein interactions. The deep learning algorithms are employed in feature extraction tasks and to classify the protein interactions based on extracted features. The feature extraction stage in PPIs involves quasi-sequence-order as sequence-based information and volumetric representations incorporating fundamental properties (Hydropathy, Isoelectric, and Charge) of amino acids as structural information. The deep-learning models such as stacked autoencoder and ResNet50 are used to get compact, and relevant feature vectors from raw features set, respectively. These feature vectors are then concatenated in pairs and fed into the classifier that predicts labels. We have constructed a classifier with a bi-directional GRU layer followed by the attention layer and sigmoid layer. This model achieves an average accuracy of 0.9708 using 3-fold cross-validation. The proposed method's performance signifies its superiority compared to other existing methods such as state-of-the-art stacked autoencoder-based classifier.

Acknowledgement. Dr. Sriparna Saha would like to acknowledge the support of Science and Engineering Research Board (SERB) of Department of Science and Technology India (Grant/Award Number: ECR/2017/001915) to carry out this research.

References

1. Wang, L., et al.: Advancing the prediction accuracy of protein-protein interactions by utilizing evolutionary information from position-specific scoring matrix and ensemble classifier. J. Theor. Biol. **418**, 105–110 (2017)
2. Khushi, M., Clarke, C.L., Graham, J.D.: Bioinformatic analysis of cis-regulatory interactions between progesterone and estrogen receptors in breast cancer. PeerJ **2**, e654 (2014)
3. Khushi, M., Choudhury, N., Arthur, J.W., Clarke, C.L., Graham, J.D.: Predicting functional interactions among DNA-binding proteins. In: Cheng, L., Leung, A.C.S., Ozawa, S. (eds.) ICONIP 2018. LNCS, vol. 11305, pp. 70–80. Springer, Cham (2018). https://doi.org/10.1007/978-3-030-04221-9_7
4. You, Z.H., Lei, Y.K., Gui, J., Huang, D.S., Zhou, X.: Using manifold embedding for assessing and predicting protein interactions from high-throughput experimental data. Bioinformatics **26**(21), 2744–2751 (2010)
5. Ito, T., Chiba, T., Ozawa, R., Yoshida, M., Hattori, M., Sakaki, Y.: A comprehensive two-hybrid analysis to explore the yeast protein interactome. Proc. Natl. Acad. Sci. **98**(8), 4569–4574 (2001)
6. Gavin, A.C., et al.: Functional organization of the yeast proteome by systematic analysis of protein complexes. Nature **415**(6868), 141–147 (2002)
7. Ho, Y., et al.: Systematic identification of protein complexes in Saccharomyces cerevisiae by mass spectrometry. Nature **415**(6868), 180–183 (2002)
8. Sun, T., Zhou, B., Lai, L., Pei, J.: Sequence-based prediction of protein protein interaction using a deep-learning algorithm. BMC Bioinform. **18**(1), 277 (2017)
9. Du, X., Sun, S., Hu, C., Yao, Y., Yan, Y., Zhang, Y.: Deepppi: boosting prediction of protein-protein interactions with deep neural networks. J. Chem. Inf. Model. **57**(6), 1499–1510 (2017)
10. Gonzalez-Lopez, F., Morales-Cordovilla, J.A., Villegas-Morcillo, A., Gomez, A.M., Sanchez, V.: End-to-end prediction of protein-protein interaction based on embedding and recurrent neural networks. In: 2018 IEEE International Conference on Bioinformatics and Biomedicine (BIBM), pp. 2344–2350. IEEE (2018)
11. Chen, C., Chen, L.X., Zou, X.Y., Cai, P.X.: Predicting protein structural class based on multi-features fusion. J. Theor. Biol. **253**(2), 388–392 (2008)
12. Hegde, V., Zadeh, R.: Fusionnet: 3D object classification using multiple data representations. arXiv preprint arXiv:1607.05695 (2016)
13. Amidi, A., Amidi, S., Vlachakis, D., Megalooikonomou, V., Paragios, N., Zacharaki, E.I.: EnzyNet: enzyme classification using 3D convolutional neural networks on spatial representation. PeerJ **6**, e4750 (2018)
14. He, K., Zhang, X., Ren, S., Sun, J.: Deep residual learning for image recognition. In: Proceedings of the IEEE Conference on Computer Vision and Pattern Recognition, pp. 770–778 (2016)
15. Cho, K., et al.: Learning phrase representations using RNN encoder-decoder for statistical machine translation. arXiv preprint arXiv:1406.1078 (2014)
16. Bahdanau, D., Cho, K., Bengio, Y.: Neural machine translation by jointly learning to align and translate. arXiv preprint arXiv:1409.0473 (2014)
17. Pan, X.Y., Zhang, Y.N., Shen, H.B.: Large-Scale prediction of human protein-protein interactions from amino acid sequence based on latent topic features. J. Proteome Res. **9**(10), 4992–5001 (2010)
18. Smialowski, P., et al.: The negatome database: a reference set of non-interacting protein pairs. Nucleic Acids Res. **38**(suppl_1), D540–D544 (2010)

RipNet: A Lightweight One-Class Deep Neural Network for the Identification of RIP Currents

Ashraf Haroon Rashid[1], Imran Razzak[2(✉)], M. Tanveer[1],
and Antonio Robles-Kelly[2]

[1] Indian Institute of Technology Indore, Simrol, Indore 453552, India
{ashrafrashid,mtanveer}@iiti.ac.in
[2] School of Information Technology, Deakin University, Geelong, Australia
{imran.razzak,antonio.robles-kelly}@deakin.edu.au

Abstract. Rip or rip current is a strong, localized and narrow current of water flowing away from shore through the surf zone, cutting through the lines of breaking ocean waves. There are hundreds of deaths due to drowning and 85% of rescues missions on beaches are due to rip currents. Although, there are rare drowning between flags, however, we can not put and monitor enough flags. Automated rip current identification can help to monitor the coast however there are several challenges involved in development of automated rip current identification. In this work, we present an automated rip current identification based on fully convolutional autoencoder. The proposed framework is able to reconstruct the positive RIP currents images with minimal root mean square error (RMSE). Evaluation results on Rip currents dataset showed an increase in accuracy, specificity and sensitivity to 99.40% 99.134%, and 93.427% respectively in comparison to state of the art methods.

Keywords: Rip currents · Rip detection · CNN · Autoencoder · Anomaly detection

1 Introduction

Rip currents seem like the safest place to swim. However, it is a kind of 2–3 meters wide river inside ocean having speed of 2–3 meter per second, if not stronger. However, in rare cases, width can be up to 400 m with the speed of 6–10 meter per second. No matter what is the width and speed of rip currents, even the lowest speed of any width size can cause the death even of swimmer or pro surfer. One in four Australian aged between 16–69 has faced rip current at least once in his (her) life. Many of them have had non-fatal drowning incidents that have lifelong health complications, and many have suffered head, spinal and other life threatening injuries. Rip currents do not pull under water causing the people to drown, however, simply pull the people into the ocean (take away from the beach), often take back people into the wave zone eventually.

© Springer Nature Switzerland AG 2020
H. Yang et al. (Eds.): ICONIP 2020, CCIS 1333, pp. 172–179, 2020.
https://doi.org/10.1007/978-3-030-63823-8_21

The signs of rip currents are, deeper and darker color water, rippled surface surrounded by smooth water and seemingly calmer water between breaking waves, foamy or sandy water out beyond the wave or anything floating out to sea. Narrow and concentrated seaward flowing rip currents normally exist in most of the beaches in the world. There are only few drowning between the flags, however, we can not have enough flags and beach monitoring, thus there are many easily accessible beaches that are not monitored and patrolled. Restricting the people to swim in flagged areas and not to chose those beaches is challenging.

The Convolutional Neural Network (CNN) has become the methodology of choice for many automated tasks, following its tremendous success in routine computer vision applications such as object detection. CNN has the ability to create features from the data without any human intervention and has outperformed handcrafted features. Maryan et al. compared different methods such as Viola–Jones algorithm, convolution neural networks, and a meta-learner for rip current identification [5]. In comparison to deep learning method, meta-classifier consisting of SVM, neural network, decision tree, random forest, k-nearest neighbors, Naïve Bayes, bagging, and Ada-boost showed better performance. This may be due to imbalance dataset problem and small number of images. To improve the performance, in this work we present deep learning based anomaly detection by considering non-rip images as anomalies. The aim of this paper is to develop an efficient approach for rip current identification. To do so, we have preformed several experiments from classification to anomaly detection. We have compared the performance of one-class anomaly detection with other methods that shows that one-class anomaly detection is better than other methods. It might be due to the highly imbalanced nature of the dataset.

The **key contributions** of this work are:

- Unlike earlier work that focus on object detection, we consider the rip currents identification as anomaly detection problem that results in improving the performance by dealing with imbalance class problem simultaneously.
- In order to improve the identification performance, We solved the problem of rip current through one class approach using fully convolutional autoencoder.
- Experimental results on benchmark dataset showed that anomaly detection showed better performance in comparison to meta classifier.

2   Rip Currents Identification

In this section, we present deep anomaly detection for detection of rip currents. We considered rip currents detection problems as problem of anomaly detection rather than object detection/object classification. As discussed in earlier section, meta-classifier showed better performance than deep learning that may be due to the imbalance and small dataset that is challenging problem especially for binary class problem. Unlike Maryan et al. [5], in this work, we improved the deep learning performance for rip current identification through autoencoder based anomaly detection. Figure 1 shows the proposed framework for rip current identification.

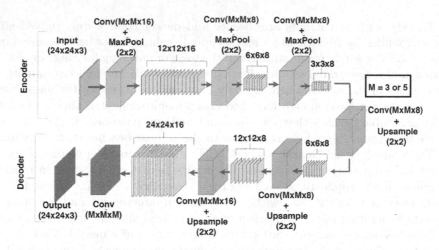

Fig. 1. The fully convolutional autoencoder architecture used in the experiments.

The images in the dataset are low in resolution and poor in quality. In addition to this, dataset is highly unbalanced with only about 13.5% positive samples in binary class problem. Thus, we specifically focus on the problem of RIP current identification from the perspective of one class classification (anomaly detection) as opposed to the methodology used by [5]. Considering it as anomaly detection solved the aforementioned challenges of imbalance and small dataset problem. We present fully convolutional autoencoder for rip anomaly detection. The fully convolutional autoencoder architecture used in the experiments is given in Fig. 1. The architecture is a light-weight seven layer fully convolutional autoencoder trained from scratch using only the positive RIP images. Since the dense fully connected layers constitute most of the parameters of a deep neural network [2], avoiding the fully connected layers helps the FCN-AE to have lesser amount of parameters. Inspired by the VGG16 architecture [7], we also use small 3×3 convolutions all throughout the network. The encoder consists of a 2×2 max-pooling layer after a convolution operation, whereas, the decoder consists of 2×2 up-sampling layer after a convolution operation. The penultimate layer of the decoder consists of a 3×3 convolution layer with 3 channels that combines the 16 channel 24×24 output into a $24 \times 24 \times 3$ channel output. This output is the reconstructed output that the decoder produces using information compressed in 8 channels of dimension 3×3 with 8 channels. This bottleneck feature layer is found after the third convolution operation. The padding operation helps the network to preserve the original input dimensions in every layer convolution layer. We also tested the FCN-AE with a convolution kernel of size 5×5 throughout the network.

The fully convolutional autoencoder is able to reconstruct the positive RIP images with minimal mean squared error (MSE) since it has only seen the RIP images during training. However, when a non-RIP image (negative image) is fed into the network, it reconstructs it with a high MSE error owing to the fact that it has not encountered a negative image during training. The FCN-AE banks on this difference in reconstruction error for detecting RIP images from non-RIP images. The non-RIP images can also be considered as anomalies that are dissimilar to images that the FCN-AE was trained on.

3   Experiments

In this section, we describe the experiment setup, results and comparative evaluation of proposed fully convolutional autoencoder based rip current identification. In order to evaluate the performance of proposed approach, we have used accuracy, sensitivity and specificity and performed hold-out crossvalidation on the RIP dataset. In this study, we use the small RIP dataset [4] consisting of 651 RIP positive images and 4794 non-RIP negative images. Notice that the dataset is highly unbalanced with only about 13.5% positive samples. We have divide the dataset into training dataset of 1190 images and testing dataset of 4065 images. The training dataset is further divided into training dataset of 184 RIP images and validation dataset of 1006 images (46 RIP images, 960 non-RIP images). All the images are of the resolution $24 \times 24 \times 3$ and two non-RIP images were discarded as they were not of the same resolution.

We have performed two experiments with two different model configurations:

- Using fully convolutional autoencoder (FCN-AE) architecture combined with simple thresholding.
- Using stacked one class support vector machine (OC-SVM) along with reconstruction error features generated from FCN-AE.

3.1   Parameter Setting

The FCN-AE architecture is developed through the help of hold-out cross-validation. We consider the following configurations for training the network: learning rate = 0.0001, optimizer = Adam, padding = 'same' in all the convolution layers, number of epochs = 750 and batch size = 8. We used 3×3 and 5×5 convolutions throughout the network. The encoder consists of a 2×2 max-pooling layer and the decoder consists of 2×2 up-sampling layer after a convolution operation. The penultimate layer consists of a 3×3 or a 5×5 convolution layer with 3 channels that combines the 16 channel 24×24 output into a $24 \times 24 \times 3$ channel output. For experiment-I, we experimented with various number of threshold values to understand their effect on final classification performance. The threshold value(s) can also be determined using the cross-validation procedure. For experiment-II, the following OCSVM parameters are determined using grid search: $\gamma = \{0.1, 0.01, 0.001, 1, 10, 100\}$, and $\nu = \{0.1, 0.01, 0.001, 0.3, 0.4, 0.5, 0.6, 0.7\}$. All the codes are implemented in the Python (version 3.7) [8] running on a workstation with Windows 10 OS, 64-bit, running on 2.30 GHz Intel ® Xeon processor, 128 GB RAM and Nvidia Quadro K1200 GPU with 4 GB memory. The FCN-AE is implemented in Keras (version 2.3.1) [3] with tensorflow backend (version 1.15) [1]. The OCSVM is implemented using scikit-learn (version 0.22) [6].

3.2 Results

In the following discussion, we describe the results of our experiments with different parameters values described in Sect. 4.1 . Table 1 describes the results of proposed rip current anomaly detection using fully convolutional autoencoder with different threshold values. Table 2 gives results of the stacked OCSVM with FCN-AE.

Table 1. Results for FCN-AE with simple thresholding

Kernel size	Threshold	Accuracy (%)	Sensitivity (%)	Specificity (%)
3 × 3	0.001	97.834	63.203	99.921
	0.002	94.832	84.847	99.634
	0.0025	94.022	89.177	99.034
	0.003	98.105	92.640	98.435
	0.0035	97.785	94.805	97.96
	0.004	97.17	96.969	97.18
	0.0045	96.309	98.268	96.191
	0.005	95.301	98.701	95.096
	0.0055	**94.587**	**99.134**	**94.314**
	0.006	93.8	99.567	93.453
	0.0065	92.349	100	91.888
5 × 5	0.001	97.908	63.6363	99.973
	0.002	98.597	84.8484	99.426
	0.0025	98.548	88.744	99.139
	0.003	98.031	90.909	98.461
	0.0035	97.490	93.073	97.756
	0.004	97.269	97.402	97.261
	0.0045	96.432	98.701	96.296
	0.005	95.621	98.701	95.435
	0.0055	94.710	99.134	94.444
	0.006	**99.400**	**99.134**	**93.427**
	0.0065	98.356	99.567	92.357

Experiment-I. In our first experiment, we applied fully convolutional autoencoder followed with a simple thresholding operator. The RMSE values of samples greater than the applied threshold are considered as out-of-class anomalies by the network. These anomalies are classified into the non-RIP category. The samples with RMSE values less than the threshold are classified as in-class positive-RIP images. Table 1 shows the results obtained RIP channel dataset using FCN-AE with simple thresholding. We performed several experiment with threshold values from 0.0065 to 0.001. We can observe that threshold within [0.0065, 0.001] achieved accuracy exceeding 90% especially 97.834% for threshold value 0.001. However, accuracy alone is not sufficient for an unbiased performance evaluation as dataset is highly unbalanced. Thus, our objective is to determine a threshold value that can provide us with an appropriate trade-off between sensitivity and specificity values.

We observe from Table 1 that the threshold of 0.001 has the worst sensitivity-specificity trade-off for both 3×3 and 5×5 kernels. As the threshold increases further to 0.002, we can observe a drastic change in the sensitivity as it jumps to about 84.84%. With further increase in the threshold value, the sensitivity increases whereas the specificity decreases. The threshold values of 0.004, 0.0045, 0.005 and 0.0055 provide the most appropriate sensitivity-specificity trade-off. Threshold values greater than 0.006 result in a sensitivity of 100% and a specificity of about 92%. The reduction in specificity values leads to an increase in false positive count (FP count) by classifying negative images as positive RIP images. Since the RIP currents pose grave danger to human lives, a highly sensitive RIP detection model might also prove beneficial. We also observe that the large size 5×5 kernel produces a very minor improvement in specificity values.

Experiment-II. Table 1 showed the results of experiment-2, wherein, one class support vector machine (OCSVM) was stacked with the fully convolutional autoencoder. The optimal parameters for OCSVM in both cases were found to be $\gamma = 1$ and $\nu = 0.01$ through hold-out crossvalidation. The OCSVM reaches a sensitivity of about 80% and a specificity of about 99%. We observe that the features produced by the network with 3×3 kernel produces marginally better FP count as compared to that of the network with 5×5 kernel. This is mostly due to the high dimensional nature of features input to the OCSVM. The OCSVM receives a training set of size 184×1728, where 1728 is the number of features and 184 is the number of samples. The usage of feature reduction techniques along with OCSVM can provide better results and is left as a future work.

Table 2. Results for FCN-AE with OCSVM

Kernel size	Accuracy (%)	Sensitivity (%)	Specificity (%)
3 × 3	**98.72**	**80.086**	**99.843**
5 × 5	98.696	80.086	99.817

3.3 Discussion

In this section, we evaluated the performance of proposed rip current identification and compared with state of the art methods. Up to our knowledge, Maryan et al. [5] on the only effort has been done for RIP channel detection.

Table 3 describes results of selected methods from [5] that are comparable to our work. All the methods mentioned in Table 3 approach the RIP identification problem through a binary classification perspective by training the models on RIP images as well as the non-RIP images. In contrast, the method used in this work uses only the RIP images for training the model. In the real world, there can be billions of diverse non-RIP (negative) images. Training each model on every possible negative image to attain a robust classifier for RIP images is not easily achievable. Hence, the FCN-AE provides a highly efficient and practical approach towards RIP identification.

We can observe from Table 1 that the threshold values of 0.004, 0.0045, 0.005, 0.0055 provide a good sensitivity-specificity trade-off. The positive identification rate of the RIP images are approximately 97%, 98%, 99% and 99% respectively for the 3×3 kernel, whereas, for the 5×5 kernel it is 97%, 98% and 98%. The corresponding false positive rates are approximately 108, 146, 188 and 218 for the 3×3 kernel, and, 105, 142, 175 and 213 for 5×5 kernel. For the highest threshold value of 0.0065, a positive identification rate of 100% is observed for both kernels along with a false positive value of about 311 and 293 respectively for 3×3 and 5×5 kernels.

Table 3. Comparision of Proposed RIP current Identification with state of the art methods.

Model	Detection rate (%)	FP count
Max distance from average	1	>400
SVM	98	>400
Viola-Jones	88	15
Meta-learner	85	8
SVM scaling and all Haar features	95	–
Meta-classifier on Haar features	85	8
Proposed FCN-AE with 3×3 kernel	**99.134**	218
Proposed FCN-AE with 5×5 kernel	**99.134**	213
Proposed FCN-AE + OCSVM with 3×3 kernel	80.086	7
Proposed FCN-AE + OCSVM with 5×5 kernel	80.086	7

We can observe that for most of the threshold values except 0.0065, the false positive identification rate is less than 300 for the 3×3 kernel. For the 5×5 kernel, all the threshold values produce a FP count of < 300. This is an improvement as compared to other methods mentioned in Table 3. Also, we obtained a very high positive RIP identification rates of >95% in most cases and almost 100% with the threshold >0.006. Comparing these results with the results of Table 3, we can observe that the FCN-AE clearly outperforms the methods mentioned in the Table 3. The FCN-AE with simple thresholding also outperforms the hybrid FCN-AE stacked with OCSVM. Another advantage of FCN-AE is that due to its convolution layer, it learns more diverse and abstract set of features based on the data. This generates more discriminative set of features as compared to the hand crafted Haar features generated in [5]. We also notice that our model is trained on just 230 RIP images as no data augmentation techniques are used to increase the size of the dataset. Yet, the FCN-AE is able to achieve a commendable performance of >95% sensitivity and <300 false positive rates in most of the cases. This again reinstates that the FCN-AE is a simple, lightweight yet, robust model for the problem of RIP identification.

However, the FCN-AE achieved comparatively similar performance as of stacking methods used in [5]. This is due to the fact that stacking reduces overfitting and increases model performance. The use of stacking and other ensemble techniques for improving the performance of FCN-AE is not in the scope of this work and is left as a future work.

4 Conclusions

We presented a novel lightweight deep architecture for the identification of RIP currents by leveraging the one-class learning approach. The proposed model learns to identify RIP currents from a very small number of RIP images. Unlike earlier work, we consider the rip currents identification problem as anomaly detection. The proposed model does not need additional negative samples during training, thereby, making it a very practical approach for the real world. The proposed model achieves high sensitivity with very less false positive classifications. A pitfall of the proposed model currently is that it is not a full fledged RIP channel detector due to limitation of datasets. In future, we will work on extension of dataset and will use of various ensemble techniques to reduce the false positive count.

References

1. Abadi, M., et al.: TensorFlow: Large-scale machine learning on heterogeneous systems https://www.tensorflow.org/. Software available from tensorflow.org (2015)
2. Cheng, Y., Wang, D., Zhou, P., Zhang, T.: A survey of model compression and acceleration for deep neural networks. arXiv preprint arXiv:1710.09282 (2017)
3. Chollet, F., et al.: Keras (2015). https://github.com/fchollet/keras
4. Martan, C., Hoque, M.: Dataset of rip current images 2018 [cited 2018 may, 5th]
5. Maryan, C., Hoque, M.T., Michael, C., Ioup, E., Abdelguerfi, M.: Machine learning applications in detecting rip channels from images. Appl. Soft Comput. **78**, 84–93 (2019)
6. Pedregosa, F., et al.: Scikit-learn: Machine learning in Python. J. Mach. Learn. Res. **12**, 2825–2830 (2011)
7. Simonyan, K., Zisserman, A.: Very deep convolutional networks for large-scale image recognition. arXiv preprint arXiv:1409.1556 (2014)
8. Van Rossum, G., Drake Jr, F.L.: Python reference manual. Centrum voor Wiskunde en Informatica Amsterdam (1995)

Road Traffic Injury Prevention Using DBSCAN Algorithm

Pattanapong Chantamit-o-pas$^{(\boxtimes)}$, Weerakorn Pongpum,
and Krisakorn Kongsaksri

Faculty of Information Technology, King Mongkut's Institute of Technology
Ladkrabang, Ladkrabang 10520, Bangkok, Thailand
{Pattanapong,59070163,59070005}@it.kmitl.ac.th
https://www.it.kmitl.ac.th

Abstract. Machine learning has been used in innovation research for the last two decades. It is widely applied in decision making such as clustering, analysis, predicting, evaluating prognosis, and recommendation. The car accident often causes death or disability in most countries. Road accident victims usually have poor quality of life because of serious illness, long-term disability, which is a huge burden to their families and some eventually died. The behavior of driving on road is a major risk factor to road traffic. This research develops a mobile application that can notify the driver when there is a risk nearby. It focuses on Thailand and it is applied only to local cases. The dataset comes from Thai Road Safety Collaboration (ThaiRSC), which is a non-governmental organization that records a lot of daily accident cases. It uses the DBSCAN algorithm, a clustering technique, for road traffic injury prevention applied on the ThaiRSC's dataset that focused on 3 districts of Bangkok, namely Ladkrbang, Pravet, Suan Lung, as well as all province in eastern Thailand. The outcomes of this research are beneficial in warning drivers if they are likely to encounter a road accident.

Keywords: Machine learning · DBSCAN · Clustering · Road accidents

1 Introduction

Road traffic injuries (RTIs) are a major cause of public health problem in most countries [1,2]. Road accident is a major problem in Thailand. The main causes of road accidents include speed violation, drinking, lack of rest and so on. So, the Government of Thailand established a Road Safety Operations Center that includes the government agencies concerned and non-government organizations such as JS-100 traffic radio station, Thai Road Safety Collaboration (ThaiRSC), and so on. The center announced legislations to reduce road traffic accidents and promoted some campaign such as 'Don't Drink and Drive' and 'You Drink I Driver' as well as introduced a campaign to encourage all drivers to ware

H. Yang et al. (Eds.): ICONIP 2020, CCIS 1333, pp. 180–187, 2020.
https://doi.org/10.1007/978-3-030-63823-8_22

safety helmets [1,3]. This research focuses on Thailand that it is applied only to local cases. The dataset comes from ThaiRSC, which is a non-governmental organization that records a lot of daily accident cases. This organization stores the road accidents information in its database and daily publishes the complied data on its website [4].

One of the problems in data mining in transaction of road accidents is that accidents data is voluminous, high-density and complex. The need for algorithms with very high accuracy is required as analysis is considered quite significant task that needs to be carried out precisely and efficiently. Most common technique used to introduce clustering technique from data set are Density-Based Spatial Clustering of Applications with Noise algorithm (DBSCAN) and k-Nearest Neighbor (k-NN) multiple imputation. DBSCAN is one of clustering algorithm that computes and groups abstract object into similarly classes [5]. Basically, it receives input from dataset, organizes the data into semantically consistent groups, based on a previously define similarity metric [6]. Most researchers applied DBSCAN algorithm to grouping high-density for mining large spatial databases [6–8]. The density of the road accidents datasets is high because accidents occur in similar locations in different type of accident. Some road accident involded people deaths. Szénási and Csiba [9] modified DBSCAN algorithm and GIS coordinate in order to find road accidents black spot. Furthermore, they applied GPU within DBSCAN to speed-up accident black sport localization. It can run parallel algorithm to finding each accidents data of a cluster [8]. Hegyi, Borsos and Koren [7] compared DBSCAN and Kernel Density Estimation (KDE) for searching possible accident black spot. They used Hungarian guideline to define the spot. The result show that DBSCAN found the greater number of road accidents than KDE algorithm. It has consumed a great deal of time and memory for processing.

In similarly study, Agrawal, Ruth, Nandini and Sravani [5] contributed to analysis of road accident locations in India. They developed an android application that used fragment to defined the accidents spot. It sends pop up message when user enter cluster area. Therefore, the Global Position System (GPS) is significant as it shows location of an accident or traffic [10,11]. This research used longitude and latitude value from data source. Significantly, our research illustrates more density of accident cases than those the previous research, that does not record cases between death and injury. If the new marker includes a death cases in the cluster, a red marker will shown in the map. So, drivers will drive more carefully. The color is important to take advantage of the wealth of knowledge hidden in these datasets and create a domain of previous accident case, which will lead to more preventive information to driver who are careless in driving.

The rest of this paper is organized as follows. Section 2 reviews DBSCAN algorithm. Section 3 discusses the DBSCAN algorithm on road accidents dataset. Section 4 discusses the road traffic injury prevention model on road accidents dataset with mobile application and the conclusion and future work are presented in Sect. 5 of this paper.

2   DBSCAN Algorithm

DBSCAN (Density- Based Spatial Clustering of Application with Noise), introduced by Ester, Kriegel, Sander and Xu [12], is designed to discover the clustering technique for spatial and non-spatial high dimensional dataset. This algorithm is defined a cluster or group data set as a connect each object that related to dense component and grows in any direction that density leads. It is computed and compared each object by a proximity radius between each pair of objects as neighborhood object. That given radius (Eps) has to contain at least a minimum number of point ($MinPts$). The density of the neighborhood has to exceed some threshold. The other objects are not reachable from any radius that classified as noise objects. Each set of objects related with center point determined a cluster [13] (see Fig. 1).

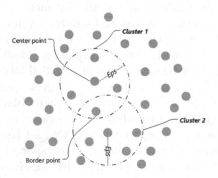

Fig. 1. Graphical presentation of defined each of object in cluster by DBSCAN.

3   DBSCAN Concept for Road Accidents Dataset

Clustering can be done by algorithms such as, k-Nearest Neighbour (k-NN), Mean-Shift clustering and many other techniques. These techniques categorize knowledge from large databases for crucial decision support. An unsupervised learning technique is applied to high density data for grouping data, and statistical data analysis. This algorithm consists of 2 functions for grouping road accidents spot. First algorithm, it created a cluster that calculated and put the spot in each cluster. The ExplandCoreCluster finding the spot discovered by radius.

We need to consider multiple output unit for clusters. Let e be an event of road accidents with its desired output a set of clusters. The number of point $e \in E$ within a given radius Eps as a eps-neighborhood of e, donate by $N_{Eps}(e_j)$. That $N_{Eps}(e_j) = \{e \in E | dist(e, i) < eps\}$, where $dist(e, i)$ is the distance function. An accident spot $e \in E$ is referred to as a core point if its eps-neighborhood contain at least a minimum of number of points ($MinPts$), i.e., $|N_{Eps}(e_j)| \geq MinPts$. An object of accident is a border object, e_{border}, if

$dist(e_{border}) < MinPts$ AND a core object exists so that $e_{border} \in N_{Eps}(e_{core})$; the border object e_{border} belong to the neighborhood of e_{core} and the local density is less than $MinPts$. This shown in Fig. 2 and 3 as below.

```
function DBSCAN returns A set of clusters
inputs: accidents, a set of road accidents data, each with input event of accident eᵢ ,distance threshold Eps, and the
minimum number of points per cluster MinPts. Output a set of cluster y set activation function ExplandCoreCluster
initial value : ClusterId = 1
repeat
    for eᵢ in accidents do
        if eᵢ UNCLASSIFIED
            ExplandCoreCluster (eᵢ, ClusterId)
            if ExpandCoreCluster successful
                ClusterId = ClusterId + 1
            endif
        endif
    end
until some stopping criterion is satisfied
return A set of clusters
```

Fig. 2. The DBSCAN algorithm applied in road accidents dataset [12, 14].

```
function ExpandCluster returns a nearness point with expansion success
inputs: accidentId, each with input event of road accidents e and ClusterId and output marker y set activation
function Retrieve_Neighors
        accidents = Retrieve_Neighor(eᵢ, Eps)
if |accidents| < MinPts
    marker eᵢ as noise object
    return without expansion success
else
    assign all objects in accidents list to ClusterId
    delete object eᵢ, from accidents list
for all eⱼ in examples do
    N_Eps(eⱼ) = Retrieve_Neighors(eⱼ,Eps)
    if |N_Eps(eⱼ)| > MinPts        ## eⱼ is a core object
        for all eₖ in N_Eps(eⱼ) do
            if eₖ is UNCLASSIFIED or is NOSIE
                if eₖ is UNCLASSIFIED
                    add eₖ to accidents list
                endif
                assign eₖ to ClusterId
            endif
        end
    endif
end
endif
return ExpandCluster
```

Fig. 3. The ExpandCluster algorithm for classified each object in cluster [12, 14].

4   Model Evaluation

4.1   Data Source

This research has applied DBSCAN algorithm on the road accidents dataset from Thai Road Safety Collaboration that an organization for road safety in Thailand

(a)   (b)

Fig. 4. (a) The original road accidents dataset from ThaiRSC [4] and (b) The graphical represented the new mark by using DBSCAN algorithm.(no death case in sample).

between January and April 2019 [4]. It has 56,746 records and 7 attributes per record that focused on 3 districts of Bangkok namely Ladkrbang, Pravet, Suan Lung, as well as all provinces in eastern Thailand. It contains AccidentId, Date and Time, Longitude, Latitude, Accident place description, Accident information, and Passed away case. These attributes are related to road accidents (see Fig. 4(a)). Green spot is an accident as normal cases. Red spot has death peoples in road accidents.

The original accident data of ThaiRSC shows a nearby spot. We need to create a new spot and group of each object as in a neighborhood. In terms of DBSCAN algorithm, it will be a defined object and create cluster or a group dataset and connect to others. It computes and compares each object by a proximity radius between each pair of objects as a neighborhood object. If we do not create a new spot in a map, the system will always be on alert to drivers. Furthermore, the radius value is important to spanning the neighborhood. So, it will classify the accident and shows the accident spot for the driver.

For data pre-processing, incompleted (missing) data were removed from the dataset in order to avoid the impact to the performance of scanning process. After pre-processing, the dataset attributes contain AccidentID, Date, Time, and accident information. These attributes will be presented in numeric format. The new dataset has smaller size and suitable for clustering process in mobile application. For DBSCAN algorithm, the system represented a new marker in green spot on GoogleMap. If a road accident had death cases, the marker will be changed to red spot. It indicated in the cluster (see Fig. 4(b)).

4.2   Model of Road Traffic Injury Prevention

In this research, we proposed a mobile application model. This model consists of 3 main steps. First step, cleaning data and reformat using Point of interest API. Second Step, it is loading data to the mobile application. Final, it is an application run all algorithm and show road accident areas to users (see Fig. 5).

The mobile application deployed by using KOTLIN programming language for android application. It is based on Java programming. It also used GoogleMap API and direction API for maps. Furthermore, the Global Position System technology used to identify the vehicles.

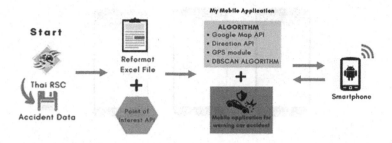

Fig. 5. The mobile application model for road traffic injury prevention.

4.3   Evaluation

Based on the data source, there are 56,746 accidental spots, which affect to the performance of the application. This paper attempts to decrease the number of spots in order to increase the accuracy in the system. We conducted a comparison of two algorithms between DBSCAN and K-Mean. K-Mean algorithm is clustering accidental cases from nearby area. It depends upon number of specified clusters. This research addresses 5,000 and 10,000 clusters. Then, the spot values are 5,000 and 10,000 respectively (see Table 1).

For DBSCAN, the radius are 200 and 400 m of the dataset. First experiment, we tested the algorithm from the source. We identified the radius parameter as 400 m. The result shows that an application shows accidental spots and achieve requirement (see Fig. 6(c)). However, it sends a wrong side voice message to drivers. For example, the driver is driving in left lane but the warning message comes from the right hand side. Second experiment, we reduced a radius parameter to 200 m to fixed a voice message error (see Table 1).

Table 1. Number of reduced spots between DBSCAN and K-Mean Algorithm of 56,746 spots

DBSCAN Algorithm		K-Mean Algorithm	
Eps = 200 m	Eps = 400 m	N = 5,000	N = 10,000
39,542	31,037	5,000	10,000

Table 2. Feature of Mobile Application by using DBSCAN Algorithm

Feature	Eps = 400m	Eps = 200m
Voice message for warning driver	✓	✓
Present a maker of road accidents	✓	✓
Identifies the destination	✗	✓
Represent route and destination	✗	✓

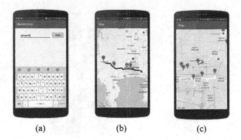

(a)   (b)   (c)

Fig. 6. Mobile application for road traffic injury prevention system. (a) Identified the destination (b) Presented a route of trip with marker and navigator and (c) Presented the marker of road accidents.

By using an application, we added destination feature. These processes of experiment starting process, based on the following steps:

- Step1: Setup the destination from driver (see Fig. 6. (a)).
- Step2: An application clustering data from source.
- Step3: Getting GPS of the vehicle and loading the marker of road accidents.
- Step4: Display route and accident's marker in map (see Fig. 6. (b)).
- Step5: Scanning the position of user's vehicle and accidents' markers that computed from the system.
- Step6: An application notifies by voice message when vehicle nearby markers.

Finally, we summarize features of mobile application (see Table 2).

5   Conclusion and Future Work

In this paper, the result shows that during clustering procedure to group the high-density in a map to define the relationship among different area. DBSCAN algorithm is better than K-Mean algorithm. The result of DBSCAN shows for all values lowest at 200 m of sample size. First experiment, it can achievement and find bug of warning system. The radius is too wide that is 400 meters. So, it has a problem to create markers in a map. In second experiment, we fixed and reduced radius parameter, as 200 m. It work better. This confirms that clustering technique is most suitable for grouping the high density and analysis road accidents.

World Health Organization shows evidence of road traffic injury (RTIs) prevention is significant to reduce the public health problem. Thailand has announced the legislation intervention for reduced road traffic. That covers speed limit, don't drive and drink, and You Drink I Drive. However, this policy is ineffective for people, if citizen are not aware of their drive on the road. Thus, technology is significant to support to drive when combining it into a multi-faceted approach. it is more effective significantly reducing road traffic fatalities and injuries as the voice message beneficial to crash and injury prevention.

Furthermore, this should enable us to reduce and prevent the road traffic injury in Thailand. One important key milestone is to use DBSCAN and Cluster to construct expectations of how attributes are related with the known cases. We hope that this pilot application could be used for evaluating a driver for full-scale implementation in the interim.

Acknowledgments. This research would not have been accomplished. Additionally, without support from the Thai Road Safety Collaboration. With this acknowledgement, we would like to express our sincere appreciation to them.

References

1. Peden, M., et al.: World report on road traffic injury prevention. World Health Organization, Geneva (2004)
2. Peden, M.: Global collaboration on road traffic injury prevention. Int. J. Inj. Contr. Saf. Promot. **12**, 85–91 (2005)
3. Staton, C., et al.: Road traffic injury prevention initiatives: a systematic review and metasummary of effectiveness in low and middle income countries. PLoS ONE **11**, e0144971 (2016)
4. ThaiRSC homepage. http://www.thairsc.com. Accessed 1 Nov 2019
5. Agrawal, K., Ruth, V.M., Nandini, Y., Sravani, K.: Analysis of Road Accident Locations Using DBSCAN Algorithm (2018)
6. Andrade, G., Ramos, G., Madeira, D., Sachetto, R., Ferreira, R., Rocha, L.: G-dbscan: A GPU accelerated algorithm for density-based clustering. Procedia Comput. Sci. **18**, 369–378 (2013)
7. Hegyi, P., Borsos, A., Koren, C.: Searching possible accident black spot locations with accident analysis and GIS software based on GPS coordinates. Pollack Periodica **12**, 129–140 (2017)
8. Szénási, S.: GPU implementation of DBSCAN algorithm for searching multiple accident black spots. In: 15th SGEM Geoconference on Informatics, Geoinformatics and Remote Sensing. pp. 647–652 (2015)
9. Szénási, S., Csiba, P.: Clustering algorithm in order to find accident black spotsidentified by GPS coordinates. In: 14th GeoConference on Informatics, Geoinformatics, and Remote Sensing. pp. 497–503 (2014)
10. Wu, Y., Wang, Y., Qian, D.: A google-map-based arterial traffic information system. In: 2007 IEEE Intelligent Transportation Systems Conference, pp. 968–973. (2007)
11. Verma, P., Bhatia, J.: Design and development of GPS-GSM based tracking system with Google map based monitoring. Int. J. Comput. Sci. Eng. Appl. **3**, 33 (2013)
12. Ester, M., Kriegel, H.-P., Sander, J., Xu, X.: A density-based algorithm for discovering clusters in large spatial databases with noise. In: Kdd, pp. 226–231. (1996)
13. Patwary, M.M.A., Palsetia, D., Agrawal, A., Liao, W., Manne, F., Choudhary, A.: A new scalable parallel DBSCAN algorithm using the disjoint-set data structure. In: SC 2012: Proceedings of the International Conference on High Performance Computing, Networking, Storage and Analysis, pp. 1–11. IEEE (2012)
14. Tran, T.N., Drab, K., Daszykowski, M.: Revised DBSCAN algorithm to cluster data with dense adjacent clusters. Chemom. Intell. Lab. Syst. **120**, 92–96 (2013)

Skeleton-Based Action Recognition with Dense Spatial Temporal Graph Network

Lin Feng[1], Zhenning Lu[2], Shenglan Liu[1(✉)], Dong Jiang[2], Yang Liu[1], and Lianyu Hu[2]

[1] School of Innovation and Entrepreneurship, Dalian University of Technology, Dalian 116024, Liaoning, China
[2] Faculty of Electronic Information and Electrical Engineering, Dalian University of Technology, Dalian 116024, Liaoning, China

Abstract. The skeleton information of human body can provide important information for human action recognition. In the field of action recognition based on skeleton, The graph convolutional network has achieved remarkable results. However, the classification methods cannot fully understand realistic and complex actions such as competitive sports. We propose a new spatiotemporal graph convolutional network named DSTG-Net. DSTG-Net optimizes the original graph convolutional network using the feature of dense structure. Our model is tested on two realistic and complex datasets, FSD-10 and video-emotion, and its effectiveness is validated.

Keywords: Action recognition · Graph convolution · Dense spatial temporal graph networks

1 Introduction

Action recognition is an essential part of human-computer interaction technology. However, it remains challenging to explore the field of action recognition [3, 21]. In recent years, convolutional network is applied to graph data by graph convolution, and many successful applications have been achieved [15]. Yan et al. [20] proposed ST-GCN to construct spatiotemporal graph convolutional network to recognize human action based on joint information. It is still a significant challenge to understand realistic and complexity actions by ST-GCN. In the traditional graph convolutional network, the order of adjacency matrix will gradually rise with the deepening of the number of layers, which will weaken the link information retained in adjacency matrix.

For solving the above all problems, this paper proposes a densely connected spatiotemporal graph convolutional network(DSTG-Net). We have done some

This study was funded by National Natural Science Foundation of Peoples Republic of China (61672130, 61972064), The Fundamental Research Funds for the Central Universities (DUT19RC(3)01) and LiaoNing Revitalization Talents Program (XLYC1806006), The Fundamental Research Funds for the Central Universities, No. DUT20RC(5)010.

H. Yang et al. (Eds.): ICONIP 2020, CCIS 1333, pp. 188–194, 2020.
https://doi.org/10.1007/978-3-030-63823-8_23

experiments on realistic and complex datasets. Our model achieves the best performance on datasets. The main contributions of this work lie in three aspects: (1) The skeleton points of datasets are extracted and central preprocessed, (2) In this paper, we propose an end-to-end densely connected spatiotemporal graph convolutional network, which improves ST-GCN with dense structure [6]. Using dense structure, the lower order information will always be preserved, better preserving the link information. (3) DSTG-Net is tested on two realistic and complex datasets, FSD-10 [14] and Video-Emotion [13], and is validated its effectiveness.

2 Related Work

2.1 Skeleton-Based Action Recognition

In recent years, with the significant breakthrough of deep learning technology and poor performance of traditional models on realistic and complex dataset, more and more skeleton-based action recognition methods using deep learning methods gradually appear. RNNs and CNNs are the most widely used models. RNNs vectorize and quantify the coordinates of skeleton information [4,11,17]. The method based on CNNs usually transforms skeleton data into RGB image first [7,10,12]. But the skeleton image information is different from the traditional regular RGB image, so the traditional CNNs model can not be used directly. Traditional CNNs and RNNs perform unsatisfactorily in the task of action classification and pose estimation driven by skeleton data. Yan et al. [20] proposed a spatiotemporal graph convolutional network(ST-GCN). In addition, ST-GCN can get better performance than traditional deep learning methods. Spatiotemporal features include temporal features and spatial features. In the video or the extracted human skeleton data can reflect the temporal and spatial information of human action. Zheng Xiao et al. [19] use the spatiotemporal cube to represent the joint point mode.

2.2 Graph Networks

In recent years, convolutional networks [9] have developed rapidly, but the traditional networks can only deal with Euclidean spatial data such as text and voice, it can't deal with Non-Euclidean spatial data such as graph data. Graph data and modeling are widely studied [1,5,8,16,18]. Researchers pay more attention to how to construct convolution operators on graphs when modeling convolutional networks. Gilmer et al. [5] proposed a message passing method to extract the isomorphism invariance of features from molecular graph for chemical prediction.

3 Dense Spatial Temporal Graph Network

3.1 Overview

The whole network model adopts the back-propagation method for end-to-end training. In this section, we will introduce the composition and operation principle of DSTG-Net.

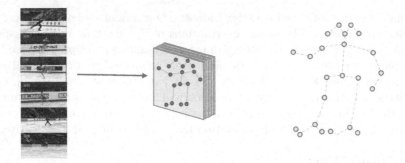

Fig. 1. The diagram of extracting skeleton points

As shown in Fig. 1, in terms of data, we use OpenPose [2] toolbox to extract the skeleton information of datasets. The extracted information includes 2D coordinates and confidence scores of the human joints. Joint coordinates of skeleton information are used as the input of the whole network.

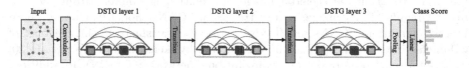

Fig. 2. The overview of DSTG-Net.

The structure of our proposed model is shown in Fig. 2. The whole network includes three DSTG layers. DSTG-Net keeps the connection between different layers of DenseNet, which makes full use of features and further alleviate the vanishing-gradient problem [6]. On the premise of optimizing the calculation, the high level of classification performance is guaranteed. DSTG-Net utilizes multi-level spatiotemporal convolution operation on the skeleton data to generate a higher-level feature map. Finally, SoftMax classifier is attached to get corresponding action type.

3.2 DSTG Layer

DSTG layer is the most important component in DSTG-Net. In Fig. 3, there are three DSTG layers in the whole network. In this section, the structure and operation principle of DSTG layer are described.

DSTG layer is composed of STGCN blocks. STGCN block contains some STGCN units which as shown in the Fig. 4. Each STGCN unit includes attention mechanism module(ATT), graph convolutional network module(GCN) and time convolution networks module(TCN). Through STGCN unit, GCN and TCN are used alternately to transform space and time dimension information.

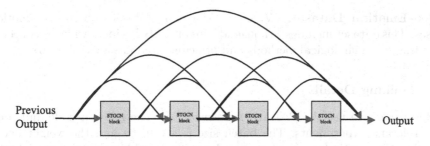

Fig. 3. Structure of DSTG layer

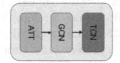

Fig. 4. Structure of STGCN unit

Each STGCN unit can be described as Eq. 1. In Eq. 1, f_{out} and f_{in} are corresponding to input and output data. Here W is weight matrix can be trained. $\Lambda^{-\frac{1}{2}}(A+I)\Lambda^{-\frac{1}{2}}$ are corresponding to standardized adjacent matrix. A and I are corresponding to adjacent matrix and identity matrix.

$$f_{out} = \Lambda^{-\frac{1}{2}}(A + I)\Lambda^{-\frac{1}{2}} f_{in} W \tag{1}$$

By using the features of dense structure, the underlying features can be reused. Dense structure avoids the vanishing-gradient problem caused by big and deep models. With the training of the origin graph convolutional network, the order of adjacency matrix A will gradually rise, which will weaken the link information retained in A. Using dense structure, the lower order information of A will always be obtained to be retained.

3.3 Data Augmentation

To prevent overfitting, enrich the training samples and improve the effect of deep network learning, we use different data augmentation techniques to train model. In the skeleton flow, the input coordinates are centralized.

4 Experiments

4.1 Datasets

FSD-10 Dataset. FSD-10 [14] is a dataset having a large collection of fine-grained figure skating actions, which includes ten action types. This dataset collects from worldwide figure skating professional competitions which are manually segmented by a team trained for this task for about 80 h. The dataset consists of 1484 figure skating videos, which range from 3 s to 30 s. FSD-10 datasets is used for figure skating action recognition task research.

Video-Emotion Dataset. Video-emotion [13] dataset contains 7 emotion classes. This dataset includes 4 thousand clips of RGB-D videos which is collected according to psychological methods and principles and has a length of 6 s.

4.2 Training Details

In this paper, we use the PyTorch framework to write relevant code and complete relevant experiments. The batch size is set to 64 and the weight decay is 0.0001. The optimization strategy adopts stochastic gradient descent(SGD) with Nesterov momentum(0.9). In addition, we choose cross-entropy as the loss function. The maximum number of frames in each sample is 256. We will repeat the sampling until it reaches 256 frames for samples with less than 256 frames. For samples with more than 256 frames, we will divide samples to 256 groups and select one frame from every group as same time interval. The initial learning rate is set as 0.1, divided by 10 in the 150th and 255th rounds, and trained in the 300th round.

4.3 Comparative Experiment

Some comparative experiments are conducted to validate the effectiveness and superior performance of the DSTG-Net with the central preprocessing method and partition strategy compared with other methods.

Table 1. Central comparative experiment.

Methods	Accuracy(%)
Remove Centralization	77.88
Centralization	86.82

As shown in Table 1, the performance of centralized DSTG-Net is higher than the method without centralization. In spatial tasks, the angle of camera is irregular. The results of this study show that centralization should be applied in realistic and complex datasets.

Table 2. Partition strategies experiment.

Strategy	Accuracy(%)
Uni-labeling	84.08
Distance partitioning	84.86
Spatial configuration partitioning	86.82

Three partition strategies are proposed in ST-GCN, which are uni-labeling, distance partitioning and spatial configuration partitioning strategy [20]. Three partition strategies are compared on the FSD-10 dataset by our proposed model. In Table 2, the comparative experimental results show that the third partition spatial configuration partitioning has the best performance. The senior partition strategy can improve the ability of additive modeling and recognition.

Table 3. Comparison of methods recognition accuracy(%) in FSD-10 dataset and video-emotion dataset.

Model	FSD-10	video-emotion
ST-GCN [20]	84.24	65.50
DenseNet [6]	84.71	53.00
DSTG-Net	86.82	68.44

With the central preprocessing method and spatial configuration partitioning strategy, the classification accuracy of DSTG-Net is compared with ST-GCN and DenseNet. In Table 3, the performance of DSTG-Net is better than the other two methods, which is proved that the dense structure can optimize the original ST-GCN. The origin graph convolutional network optimized by the dense structure can have better reuse features.

5 Conclusion

In this work, we propose a novel densely connected graph network (DSTG-Net) for skeleton-based action recognition. Dense structure is adopted to enhance feature propagation and reuse isolated features. Compared with ST-GCN and DenseNet, DSTG-Net achieves better classification performance on two datasets. Furthermore, future studies could fruitfully explore this issue further by graph optimization and RGB information.

References

1. Battaglia, P.W., et al.: Relational inductive biases, deep learning, and graph networks. arXiv preprint arXiv:1806.01261 (2018)
2. Cao, Z., Simon, T., Wei, S.E., Sheikh, Y.: Realtime multi-person 2d pose estimation using part affinity fields. In: Proceedings of the IEEE Conference on Computer Vision and Pattern Recognition. pp. 7291–7299 (2017)
3. Carreira, J., Zisserman, A.: Quo vadis, action recognition? a new model and the kinetics dataset. In: proceedings of the IEEE Conference on Computer Vision and Pattern Recognition. pp. 6299–6308 (2017)
4. Du, Y., Wang, W., Wang, L.: Hierarchical recurrent neural network for skeleton based action recognition. In: Proceedings of the IEEE conference on computer vision and pattern recognition. pp. 1110–1118 (2015)

5. Gilmer, J., Schoenholz, S.S., Riley, P.F., Vinyals, O., Dahl, G.E.: Neural message passing for quantum chemistry. In: Proceedings of the 34th International Conference on Machine Learning. vol. 70. pp. 1263–1272. JMLR. org (2017)

6. Huang, G., Liu, Z., Van Der Maaten, L., Weinberger, K.Q.: Densely connected convolutional networks. In: Proceedings of the IEEE Conference on Computer Vision and Pattern Recognition. pp. 4700–4708 (2017)

7. Kim, T.S., Reiter, A.: Interpretable 3d human action analysis with temporal convolutional networks. In: 2017 IEEE Conference on Computer Vision and Pattern Recognition Workshops (CVPRW). pp. 1623–1631. IEEE (2017)

8. Kipf, T., Fetaya, E., Wang, K.C., Welling, M., Zemel, R.: Neural relational inference for interacting systems. arXiv preprint arXiv:1802.04687 (2018)

9. LeCun, Y., Bottou, L., Bengio, Y., Haffner, P.: Gradient-based learning applied to document recognition. Proc. IEEE **86**(11), 2278–2324 (1998)

10. Liu, H., Tu, J., Liu, M.: Two-stream 3d convolutional neural network for skeleton-based action recognition. arXiv preprint arXiv:1705.08106 (2017)

11. Liu, J., Shahroudy, A., Xu, D., Wang, G.: Spatio-temporal lstm with trust gates for 3d human action recognition. In: Leibe, B., Matas, J., Sebe, N., Welling, M. (eds.) ECCV 2016. LNCS, vol. 9907, pp. 816–833. Springer, Cham (2016). https://doi.org/10.1007/978-3-319-46487-9_50

12. Liu, M., Liu, H., Chen, C.: Enhanced skeleton visualization for view invariant human action recognition. Pattern Recogn. **68**, 346–362 (2017)

13. Liu, S., Guo, S., Wang, W., Qiao, H., Wang, Y., Luo, W.: Multi-view laplacian eigenmaps based on bag-of-neighbors for rgb-d human emotion recognition. Inf. Sci. **509**, 243–256 (2020)

14. Liu, S., et al.: Fsd-10: A dataset for competitive sports content analysis. arXiv preprint arXiv:2002.03312 (2020)

15. Niepert, M., Ahmed, M., Kutzkov, K.: Learning convolutional neural networks for graphs. In: International Conference on Machine Learning. pp. 2014–2023 (2016)

16. Santoro, A., et al.: A simple neural network module for relational reasoning. In: Advances in Neural Information Processing Systems. pp. 4967–4976 (2017)

17. Shahroudy, A., Liu, J., Ng, T.T., Wang, G.: Ntu rgb+ d: a large scale dataset for 3d human activity analysis. In: Proceedings of the IEEE Conference on Computer Vision and Pattern Recognition. pp. 1010–1019 (2016)

18. Wang, X., Gupta, A.: Videos as space-time region graphs. In: Proceedings of the European Conference on Computer Vision (ECCV). pp. 399–417 (2018)

19. Xiao, Z., Mengyin, F., Yi, Y., Ningyi, L.: 3d human postures recognition using kinect. In: 2012 4th International Conference on Intelligent Human-Machine Systems and Cybernetics. vol. 1, pp. 344–347. IEEE (2012)

20. Yan, S., Xiong, Y., Lin, D.: Spatial temporal graph convolutional networks for skeleton-based action recognition. In: Thirty-second AAAI Conference on Artificial Intelligence (2018)

21. Yue-Hei Ng, J., Hausknecht, M., Vijayanarasimhan, S., Vinyals, O., Monga, R., Toderici, G.: Beyond short snippets: deep networks for video classification. In: Proceedings of the IEEE Conference on Computer Vision and Pattern Recognition. pp. 4694–4702 (2015)

Supervised Learning Algorithm for Spiking Neural Networks Based on Nonlinear Synaptic Interaction

Xianghong Lin[✉], Jiawei Geng, and Qian Li

College of Computer Science and Engineering, Northwest Normal University,
Lanzhou 730070, China
linxh@nwnu.edu.cn

Abstract. In biological nervous systems, the synaptic transmission of information is a complex process through the release of neurotransmitters. The input of multiple signals shows nonlinear interaction characteristics in synapses, so nonlinear synaptic interaction is considered as an important part of biological neural networks. At present, most artificial neural networks simplify synapses into a linear structure. Considering the nonlinear interaction of the input multiple signals of synapse, this paper proposes an online supervised learning algorithm for spiking neural networks based on nonlinear synaptic kernels, which can implement the complex spatio-temporal pattern learning of spike trains. The algorithm is successfully applied to learn sequences of spikes. In addition, different learning parameters are analyzed, such as synaptic kernel. The experimental results show that the proposed algorithm has high learning accuracy.

Keywords: Spiking neural networks · Nonlinear synaptic kernels · Supervised learning · Spike train learning

1 Introduction

Traditional artificial neural networks (ANNs) encode neural information by the spike firing rate of the biological neurons [1]. Spiking neural networks (SNNs) are composed of more biologically plausible spiking neurons, which can encode the neural information with precisely timed spike trains. SNN is an important research field in artificial intelligence. In recent years, the interest of many researchers has shifted to SNNs. This is because SNNs are more reasonable than ANNs in biology, more accurate in information processing, and have certain advantages in dealing with various spatio-temporal events [2]. SNNs are the third generation of ANNs, and they have a greater computing capacity. Maass et al. [3,4] proved that SNNs can simulate any forward Sigmoid neural network, and thus can realize the approximation of any continuous function. Their operation mode is closer to biological neurons, and their performance is better than traditional ANNs.

© Springer Nature Switzerland AG 2020
H. Yang et al. (Eds.): ICONIP 2020, CCIS 1333, pp. 195–203, 2020.
https://doi.org/10.1007/978-3-030-63823-8_24

SNNs are suitable tools for processing complex spatio-temporal information [5]. However, because of their intricately discontinuous and implicit nonlinear mechanisms, the formulation of efficient supervised learning algorithms for SNNs is difficult, and has become an important problem in this research field. Researchers have conducted many studies on supervised learning for SNNs and achieved some results [6]. Since the spike train is a discrete spike event set, to facilitate analysis and calculation, the convolution operations are used to convert the spike train to a unique continuous function. Recently, with the continuous deepening of researches, the supervised learning algorithm based on kernel function gradually formed a new direction [7–9]. Tapson et al. [10,11] describe a neural network synthesis method that generates synaptic connectivity for neurons which process time-encoded neural signals, and then solves for the optimal input-output relationship using computed dendritic weights.

Considering the nonlinear interaction of the input multiple signals of synapse, the SNNs in this paper consists of three layers: input layer, hidden layer and output layer. The hidden layer of the network consists of synapses. Each synapse implements a synaptic kernel function. The synaptic kernels are biologically inspired, being based on typical functions used to model the transfer functions in mammalian neurons. They are effectively filters which are defined in terms of their spike response [11]. The synaptic responses to input events are summed at the synapse and are also nonlinearly scaled. In this paper, we propose a new supervised learning algorithm for spiking neural networks based on nonlinear synaptic interaction. The method redefines the hidden layer into a more biologically significant synaptic layer, and uses new weight update rule for online learning.

2 Network Structure and Nonlinear Synaptic Kernel

2.1 The Structure of SNNs

Neurons in a multilayer feed-forward SNN are hierarchically arranged. The network structure in this paper can be simply expressed as the standard structure of input layer, nonlinear synapses and output layer. The difference between the nonlinear synapses and the general hidden layer is that the synaptic kernel is used instead of the general neuron. Compared with conventional feed-forward network structure, it has the following characteristics: (1) the hidden layer is usually much larger than the input layer; (2) the connections between the input layer and the synaptic layer is randomly generated and will not change during the training; (3) the weight from the synaptic layer to the output layer is optimal through learning adjustment; (4) the hidden layer in the learning algorithm is a nonlinear synapse.

Figure 1 shows the SNN structure based on nonlinear synaptic interaction. The network structure is composed of nonlinear synapses and standard neurons, where the function is $F_j(g, t)$ the function of the jth nonlinear synapse, and the input neuron is connected by nonlinear synapses to its dendritic branches and then to the output neuron. The weight $w_{ij}^{(1)}$ represents the presynaptic weight of the ith input neuron to the jth nonlinear synapse, which is randomly initialized at the beginning and then no longer changes, providing a supporting condition for the nonlinear connection of the later network and mapping it to a higher dimensional space. The weight $w_{jo}^{(2)}$ represents the postsynaptic weight of the jth nonlinear synapse to the output neuron. The weight will change according the learning rule. By constantly adjusting the weight to find the optimal solution, the postsynaptic weight of the connection between the nonlinear synapse and the output layer of the soma can be calculated. In the network, dendritic branches and nonlinear synapses echo each other and have nonlinear responses. Finally, the outputs from dendritic branches are summed in the soma of the output neuron.

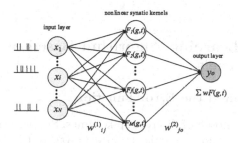

Fig. 1. SNN structure based on nonlinear synaptic interaction.

2.2 Nonlinear Synaptic Kernel

In the SNNs with the nonlinear synaptic interaction, the hidden nonlinear synaptic structure has three functions: (1) The axon signals from the presynaptic neurons are weighted and transmitted to the postsynaptic dendritic branches. (2) The axon signals are nonlinearly transformed. Synapses are implemented as filter elements which produce a nonlinear impulse response, in response to incoming spikes. (3) The axon signals are integrated by means of a nonlinear time-persistent filter. The sum of these converted signals represents the response of dendrites to their synaptic inputs. Dendritic signals are summed at the soma, and if they exceed a threshold, the axon hillock emits a spike. Many nonlinear synaptic kernel functions can be used in this paper, such as alpha synaptic function, damped resonant synaptic function, synaptic delay with alpha function, synaptic delay with Gaussian function, etc. Table 1 lists some typical synaptic functions in mathematical form.

In Table 1, t_i^f represents the fth spike emitted by the ith input neuron, τ is the time constant for the various kernel functions, ΔT is an explicit synaptic or dendritic delay, and w is the natural resonant frequency for a damped resonant synaptic function. Different nonlinear synapse functions are used for different dendritic branches.

Table 1. Typical nonlinear synaptic kernel functions.

Nonlinear kernel functions	Mathematical expression
Alpha synaptic function	$F_j(g,t) = tanh\left(\sum_{i=1}^{N}\sum_{f=1}^{F_i} w_{ij}^{(1)} \frac{t-t_i^f}{\tau} e^{-\frac{t-t_i^f}{\tau}}\right)$
Damped resonant synaptic function	$F_j(g,t) = tanh\left(\sum_{i=1}^{N}\sum_{f=1}^{F_i} w_{ij}^{(1)} e^{-\frac{t-t_i^f}{\tau}} sin(w(t-t_i^f))\right)$
Synaptic delay with alpha function	$F_j(g,t) = \begin{cases} tanh\left(\sum_{i=1}^{N}\sum_{f=1}^{F_i} w_{ij}^{(1)} \frac{t-t_i^f-\Delta T}{\tau} e^{-\frac{t-t_i^f-\Delta T}{\tau}}\right), & t-t_i^f \geq \Delta T \\ 0, & t-t_i^f < \Delta T \end{cases}$
Synaptic delay with Gaussian function	$F_j(g,t) = \begin{cases} tanh\left(\sum_{i=1}^{N}\sum_{f=1}^{F_i} w_{ij}^{(1)} \frac{1}{\sigma\sqrt{2\pi}} e^{-\frac{(t-t_i^f-\Delta T)^2}{2\sigma^2}}\right), & t-t_i^f \geq \Delta T \\ 0, & t-t_i^f < \Delta T \end{cases}$

3   Supervised Learning Algorithm Based on Nonlinear Synaptic Kernels

3.1   The Definition of the Error Function

The spike train is composed of discrete spike times. Suppose the simulation time interval is $\Gamma = [0, T]$, and the spike train $s = \{t^f \in \Gamma, f = 1, ..., F\}$ can be expressed as:

$$s(t) = \sum_{f=1}^{F} \delta(t - t^f) \tag{1}$$

where F is the number of spikes fired by the neuron in the time interval Γ, and t^f is the fth spike time. $\delta(t)$ is the Dirac delta function, $\delta(t) = 1$ if $t = 0$ and $\delta(t) = 0$ otherwise.

In order to facilitate calculation, it is necessary to transform discrete spike train into a continuous function [12]. We can choose a specific smoothing function h, the convolution of spike train s is expressed as:

$$f_s(t) = s * h = \sum_{f=1}^{F} h(t - t^f) \tag{2}$$

The synaptic weight adjustment rules aim to minimize the error function E, which is used for judging errors to update parameters, including synaptic weights and deviation values. By adjusting the synaptic weights, the actual output spike train is consistent with the desired output spike train. The error function at time t is defined as:

$$E(t) = \frac{1}{2} \sum_{o=1}^{N_o} [f_{s_o^a}(t) - f_{s_o^d}(t)]^2 \tag{3}$$

where s_o^a is the actual output spike train, s_o^d is the desired spike train, and N_o is the number of output layer neurons.

3.2   Learning Rule of Synaptic Weights

When adjusting the synaptic weights, the delta update rule is used to calculate the gradient. The weight adjustment amount $\Delta w_{jo}^{(2)}$ between the jth nonlinear synapse and the oth output neuron can be expressed as:

$$\Delta w_{jo}^{(2)}(t) = -\eta \nabla E_{jo}(t) \tag{4}$$

where η is the learning rate, and $\nabla E_{jo}(t)$ is the gradient calculation value of $E(t)$ for the weight $\Delta w_{jo}^{(2)}$. The calculation is as follows:

$$\nabla E_{jo}(t) = \frac{\partial E(t)}{\partial w_{jo}^{(2)}} = \frac{\partial E(t)}{\partial f_{s_o^a}(t)} \frac{\partial f_{s_o^a}(t)}{\partial w_{jo}^{(2)}} \tag{5}$$

The first partial derivative term $\partial E(t)/\partial f_{s_o^a}(t)$ in Eq. (5) can be calculated using Eq. (3):

$$\frac{\partial E(t)}{\partial f_{s_o^a}(t)} = \frac{\partial [\frac{1}{2} \sum_{o=1}^{N_o} [f_{s_o^a}(t) - f_{s_o^d}(t)]^2]}{\partial f_{s_o^a}(t)} = f_{s_o^a}(t) - f_{s_o^d}(t) \tag{6}$$

In order to establish the relationship between the input and output spike trains, we use the linear Poisson neuron model [13]. This neuron model outputs a spike train, which is a realization of a Poisson process with the underlying intensity function estimation. The instantaneous spike firing intensity of a neuron is determined by the instantaneous spike firing intensity of its presynaptic neurons:

$$f_{s_o^a}(t) = \sum_{j=1}^{N_j} w_{jo}^{(2)} F_j(g, t) \tag{7}$$

where $F_j(g, t)$ is a nonlinear synaptic kernel and $w_{jo}^{(2)}$ represents the weight between the jth nonlinear synapse and the oth output neuron.

Using Eq. (7), the second partial derivative term $\partial f_{s_o^a}(t)/\partial w_{jo}^{(2)}$ in Eq. (5) can be calculated as follows:

$$\frac{\partial f_{s_o^a}(t)}{\partial w_{jo}^{(2)}} = \frac{\partial [\sum_{j=1}^{N_j} w_{jo}^{(2)} F_j(g, t)]}{\partial w_{jo}^{(2)}} = F_j(g, t) \tag{8}$$

Then the calculated value of $\nabla E_{jo}(t)$ is:

$$\nabla E_{jo}(t) = \frac{\partial E(t)}{\partial w_{jo}^{(2)}} = (f_{s_o^a}(t) - f_{s_o^d}(t))F_j(g,t) \tag{9}$$

Finally, the weight learning rule between the nonlinear synapse on the dendritic branch and the soma output layer is:

$$\Delta w_{jo}^{(2)}(t) = -\eta \nabla E_o(t) = -\eta(f_{s_o^a}(t) - f_{s_o^d}(t))F_j(g,t) \tag{10}$$

In general, the weights in the feed-forward SNNs can be adjusted according to Eq. (10) in an online manner, that is, the weight $w_{jo}^{(2)}$ is updated when the output neuron fires an actual spike or a desired spike.

4   Experiments and Results

In this section, we use spike train learning experiments to prove the learning ability of the proposed supervised learning algorithm. First, we demonstrate the spike train learning process and then the parameter effects on the learning performance are analyzed, such as the type and number of synaptic kernel, and so on. At the same time, when one parameter is analyzed, all other parameters remain unchanged.

4.1   Simulation Parameter Settings

In the experiment, the parameter values of the Spiking Neuron Model used in the spike train learning are: the time constant of the postsynaptic potential $\tau = 2ms$, the time constant of the refractory period $\tau_R = 50ms$, the neuron threshold $\theta = 1$, and the length of the absolute refractory period $t_{ref} = 1ms$. The network structure are including: the number of input neurons is $N = 10$, the number of hidden synapses is $M = 100$, and number of output neurons $O = 1$. The range of synaptic weights is $[0, 0.5]$. Each input and desired spike train is randomly generated according to the Poisson process with rates 30 and 50 Hz in the time interval of $[0, T]$. We set $T = 200ms$, the learning rate is 0.01, and time step 0.1 ms. The results are averaged over 50 trials. In each experiment, the learning algorithm stops learning when it reaches a maximum of 100 learning epochs or until the network error $E = 0$. In order to evaluate the learning performance, we adopt the similar value C based on the correlation measurement [6].

4.2   Spike Train Learning Performance

Figure 2 shows the learning process of spike trains. Figure 2(a) shows that the learning accuracy increases rapidly at the beginning of learning in the 5 epochs, and it is very close to 1 after 10 learning epochs. Figure 2(b) shows the learning process under the $200ms$ simulation duration. In the Fig. 2(b), • is the actual output spike train for each iteration when iterating multiple times, Δ is the initial actual output spike train before learning, and ∇ is the desired spike train.

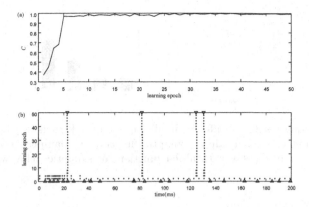

Fig. 2. The learning process of spike trains. (a) Learning accuracy. (b) Learning process.

4.3   Comparison of Different Nonlinear Synaptic Kernels

Figure 3 shows the learning results of different synaptic kernels. Figure 3(a) shows the learning accuracy for the different synaptic kernels. By comparing the performance differences, the most suitable synaptic kernel was found from the experimental results. It can be seen from the figure that the synaptic delay with alpha function has a higher learning accuracy. Figure 3(b) shows the average number of iterations when different nonlinear synaptic kernels reach the highest accuracy, and the learning epoch between different nonlinear synaptic kernels is somewhat different. This paper uses synaptic delay with alpha function with relatively high learning accuracy and small variance for calculation.

4.4   Parameter Changes and Analysis

Figure 4 shows the learning results of different numbers of nonlinear synaptic kernels. Figure 4(a) shows that as the number of synaptic kernels increases, the learning accuracy gradually increases, and when the number of synaptic kernels exceeds 700, it gradually stabilizes. From Fig. 4(b) we can see that the learning epochs of the algorithm tend to increase gradually with the increase of the nonlinear synaptic kernel numbers.

Figu5 shows the learning results of different frequencies of desired output spike trains. Figure 5(a) shows that when the desired output spike frequency increases, the learning accuracy tends to decrease. Figure 5(b) shows that the learning epoch when the learning accuracy reaches the highest.

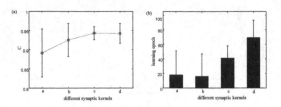

Fig. 3. The learning results of different nonlinear synaptic kernels. (a) Learning accuracy. (b) Learning epochs. a: alpha synaptic function; b: damped resonant synaptic function; c: synaptic delay with alpha function; d: synaptic delay with Gaussian function.

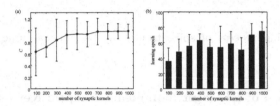

Fig. 4. The learning results of different numbers of nonlinear synaptic kernels. (a) Learning accuracy. (b) The learning epoch when the learning accuracy reaches the highest.

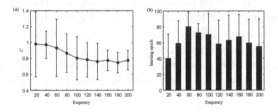

Fig. 5. The learning results of different frequencies of desired output spike trains after 100 learning epochs. (a) Learning accuracy. (b) The learning epoch when the learning accuracy reaches the highest.

5   Conclusions

In this paper, we proposes a supervised learning algorithm for spiking neural networks based on nonlinear synaptic interaction. The spiking neural network with nonlinear synapse is closer to the real biological nervous system, and it has good performance in information processing. We conducted experiments on the proposed algorithm and analyzed the learning performance of different nonlinear synaptic kernels, as well as the effects of various parameters on the learning performance. Experimental results show that the algorithm has high learning accuracy and efficiency. In the future, we can apply this algorithm to solve complex pattern recognition problems.

References

1. Prieto, A., Prieto, B., Ortigosa, E.M., et al.: Neural networks: an overview of early research, current frameworks and new challenges. Neurocomput. **214**, 242–268 (2016)
2. Ghosh-Dastidar, S., Adeli, H.: Spiking neural networks. Int. J. Neural Syst. **19**(4), 295–308 (2009)
3. Maass, W.: Networks of spiking neurons: the third generation of neural network models. Neural Netw. **10**(9), 1659–1671 (1997)
4. Maass, W.: Fast sigmoidal networks via spiking neurons. Neural Comput. **9**(2), 279–304 (1997)
5. Gerstner, W., Kistler, W.M.: Spiking Neuron Models: Single Neurons, Populations, Plasticity. Cambridge University Press, Cambridge (2002)
6. Wang, X., Lin, X., Dang, X.: Supervised learning in spiking neural networks: a review of algorithms and evaluations. Neural Netw. **125**, 258–280 (2020)
7. Mohemmed, A., Schliebs, S., Matsuda, S., et al.: SPAN: Spike pattern association neuron for learning spatio-temporal spike patterns. Int. J. Neural Syst. **22**(4), 1250012 (2012)
8. Lin, X., Wang, X., Hao, Z.: Supervised learning in multilayer spiking neural networks with inner products of spike trains. Neurocomput. **237**, 59–70 (2017)
9. Lin, X., Zhang, N., Wang, X.: An online supervised learning algorithm based on nonlinear spike train kernels. In: Huang, D.-S., Bevilacqua, V., Prashan, P. (eds.) ICIC 2015. LNCS, vol. 9225, pp. 106–115. Springer, Cham (2015). https://doi.org/10.1007/978-3-319-22180-9_11
10. Tapson, J.C., Cohen, G.K., Saeed, A., et al.: Synthesis of neural networks for spatio-temporal spike pattern recognition and processing[J]. Front. Neurosci. **7**(7), 153 (2013)
11. Tapson, J.C., Cohen, G.K., Schaik, A.V.: ELM solutions for event-based systems. Neurocomput. **149**, 435–442 (2015)
12. Park, I.M., Seth, S., Paiva, A.R.C., et al.: Kernel methods on spike train space for neuroscience: a tutorial. IEEE Signal Process. Magaz. **30**(4), 149–160 (2013)
13. Gütig, R., Aharonov, R., Rotter, S., et al.: Learning input correlations through nonlinear temporally asymmetric hebbian plasticity. J. Neurosci. **23**(9), 3697–3714 (2003)

Temporal EEG Neural Activity Predicts Visuo-Spatial Motor Sequence Learning

Raunak Swarnkar[✉][iD] and Krishna P. Miyapuram[iD]

Centre for Cognitive and Brain Sciences, Indian Institute of Technology
Gandhinagar, Palaj, India
{raunak.swarnkar,kprasad}@iitgn.ac.in

Abstract. Learning sequential movements has been foundational to intelligent behavior. How we do acquire a new motor skill and the corresponding neural representations of motor sequence learning have been already established for a standard visuo-spatial map where the object itself is the target of action. Initial stages involve learning an effector-specific representation that facilitates learning. However, the neural representations of how non-standard visuo-spatial mappings influence motor sequential learning have not been systematically understood. Using high temporal resolution of EEG, we used a modified version of the SRTT to control visuo-motor mappings by varying color and position. Subjects learnt sequential movements through trial-and-error over different visuo-spatial conditions. Behavioral results indicate significant differences between conditions, suggesting role of distinct cognitive processes. Further, ERP analysis revealed ERN in error trials and differential amplitude changes in lateral scalp electrodes suggesting the involvement of neural activity subservient to motor learning. Using scalp topography, we found differences in time course of activity between visuomotor learning over frontal, central, parietal and occipital scalp electrodes as learning progressed. This study further demonstrates the role of temporal neural activity as a predictor for visuomotor mappings and sequential motor learning driven by error feedback.

Keywords: Motor sequence learning · Visuospatial mapping · ERN · EEG

1 Introduction

Human behavior is very often concerned with learning a set of elements in some order, or what can be called a sequence. One can define a sequence as a list of elements that follow an order. In terms of motor sequences, learning a sequence would be followed by executing series of interrelated actions (specifically, motor movements) to accomplish a goal [5]. When a task concerns learning sequences that consist of movements, it is termed as motor sequence learning. Importantly, if there is learning, then there should be an improvement in performance in terms of lower reaction time (RT) and/or higher accuracy over time of course of execution of movements. Motor sequence learning has been difficult and complex to

© Springer Nature Switzerland AG 2020
H. Yang et al. (Eds.): ICONIP 2020, CCIS 1333, pp. 204–211, 2020.
https://doi.org/10.1007/978-3-030-63823-8_25

study owing to the involvement of many cognitive processes. In the Serial Reaction Time (SRT) Task, based on trial-and-error, participants learn the correct association between the visual stimulus and the keyboard response. Participants obtain a speed-accuracy trade-off, since they are required to respond as fast and as accurately as possible. Improvising performances in terms of reduced RT and improved accuracy over trials explain the sequence learning behavior in terms of motor execution.

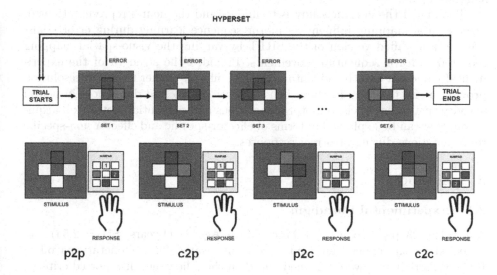

Fig. 1. Experimental design

Murray et al. (2000) describes standard visuomotor mapping where an object providing visual cue is itself the target of action, and a transformational mapping when an object's location has systematic spatial relationship with target action [11]. As opposed to these, an arbitrary visuomotor mapping does not have direct relationship with location of stimuli and the target action. Bapi et al. (2000a) have proposed that while learning, an effector-specific representation is acquired through pressing of the keys using hand movements, which later consolidates to effector non-specific representation and becomes automatic [1]. Bapi et al. (2000b) suggested that sequence learning is facilitated by visual representation in the early stage and consolidation of mo-tor representation occurs at a later stage [2]. This theory has found evidence based on activation of distinct network of brain areas at various stages of visuomotor sequence learning that sub-serve these representations. Evidence for differential neural activity corresponding to visuo-motor sequence learning corresponding to fronto-parietal network has been suggested in [4], and further distinction in activity was also found [9].

Since learning involves improved performance with decrease in error rate, it has not been investigated how error-related feedback activity distinguishes between different stages of sequential motor learning. Beaulieu and colleagues

(2014) used the SRTT to study if error feedback while learning sequences can elicit changes in EEG signals over the time course of learning [3]. Error Related Negativity (ERN) component was differentially averaged across early and late stages of learning. It was observed that ERN amplitude over fronto-central electrodes varied significantly in early and late sequence learning tasks, which also correlated with improved performance in terms of reaction time and accuracy. Evidence for changes in ERN and learning acquisition have also been previously suggested [7,8].

The aim of the current study is to understand the neural representations of visuo-spatial mapping influencing motor sequence learning during error trials. We use a modified version of the SRTT by varying the visuo-spatial mapping required to learn sequential movements. Provided the strength of the experimental paradigm and the advantage of EEG offering higher temporal resolution proving useful to study learning behavior, we aim to find differences in neural activity that underlie visuo-motor associations and sequential motor skill acquisition, that can be explained in terms of effector-specific and effector non-specific representations during incorrect responses.

2   Method

2.1   Experimental Paradigm

A total of 23 participants (11 Male, Mean Age 21.11 years, SD = 2.54) volunteered for the experiment and were compensated for a monetary payoff of Rs.100. Participants were screened based on the following self-reported criteria: right-handed, no previous history of neurological disorders, no previous history of brain injuries. The study was approved by the local ethics committee of Indian Institute of Technology Gandhinagar.

Table 1. Hypothesized representations

Display sequence	Pos	Col	Pos	Col
Keypad response	Pos	Pos	Col	Col
Abstract representation	×	✓	✓	×
Motor representation	✓	×	×	✓
Color map	×	×	✓	✓
Visuo-spatial map	✓	✓	×	×

Participants performed a modified version of the SRTT, a Visuo-motor Sequence Learning Task. The stimulus display consisted of 4 squares placed equidistantly from the centre of the screen. Participants were presented with a single-colored square in the follow task and two-colored squares in the main task based on the type of sequence, and were required to press keys on a numpad highlighted with color keys, with one and two keypresses respectively.

Participants learnt a fixed number of sets, called a hyperset. For each of the sequence conditions, participants performed consecutive 2 key-presses and learnt the corresponding type of sequence by trial-and-error. Response had to be provided within 3.5 s of the stimulus display consisting of a set of 2 colored squares at a time. Failure to provide the correct response resulted in resetting the trial sequence and the trial would begin again from the first set. On successfully learning all the sets of key-presses, the trial would end, and was followed by the next hyperset of the same sequence condition. Figure 1 summarizes the 4 conditions in the sequence tasks across combination of display sequences and keypad response.

2.2   EEG Data Acquisition and Analysis

Data was acquired using High Density 128 Channel EGI Geodesic Sensor Net. Data was recorded using NetStation Acquisition software, down-sampled at 250 Hz. 22 electrodes from the non-scalp area and 1 defective electrode were removed and Cz was used as reference electrode. We used Harvard Automated Pre-Processing Pipeline [6] for pre-processing. Bad-channels were detected using spectrum criteria using a 3 SD threshold. Wavelet-ICA was used to remove arte-factual IC components from the data by convolution methods with a level 5 coiflet wavelet and a threshold multiplier of 0.75. ICA was run on this cleaned data again to reject artefactual ICs using ICLabel in an automated fashion with a threshold probability of 0.5. The average rejected ICs was 9.6956 with a std. dev of 5.1029. Interpolation and re-referencing were performed as the next step. Epochs of 600 ms were extracted from trials of interest.

3   Results

3.1   Establishing Learning Behavior

As expected, learning across conditions was observed to vary differently with time. Error Rate across hypersets was taken as the behavioral measure to track subjects' performance (Fig. 2a). Error Rate was measured as the ratio of total success trials to total attempted trials. Repeated Measures ANOVA for Error Rate found main effects of Time to be of significance ($F(1,14) = 111.08$, $p < 0.02$). Error Rate was found to be lower for p2p and c2c where motor learning was involved due to effector-specific representations, as compared to p2c and c2p tasks that required arbitrary visuo-motor mapping. However, neither main effects of Condition, nor interaction effects were found to be significant. Repeated Measures ANOVA for Reaction Time found main effects of Time ($F(1,14) = 38,435$, $p < 0.05$) as well as Position-Color Condition ($F(1,14) = 102.505$, $p < 0.05$) to be of significance (Fig. 2b). RT was found to be higher for p2c and c2c where responses had to be given based on color map which had to be recalled before giving a response, as compared to p2p and c2p tasks that required only spatial

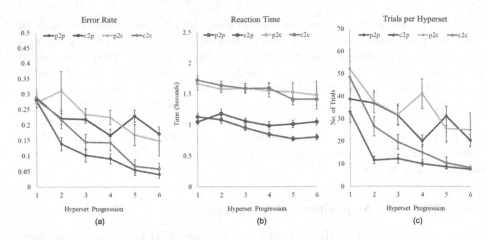

Fig. 2. Behavioral Results: (a) Decreasing trend of average Error Rate suggests that learning has occurred but more importantly,distinct learning behavior observed between conditions. (b) Reaction Time across conditions and hypersets (c) No. of trials attempted to complete each hyperset observed to be decreasing with hyperset progression. Error bars indicate standard deviation/sqrt(sample size).

position mapping. No interaction effect was found to be significant. Another measure to observe learning was to calculate total attempted trials to learn a hyperset for a corresponding sequence (Fig. 2c). Trials per hyperset were observed as below. Repeated Measures ANOVA for Trials Per Hyperset found main effects of Time to be of significance ($F(1,14) = 19.742$, $p < .05$). Importantly, this measure was found to be higher for p2c and c2p where abstract representations were acquired while learning, as compared to p2c and c2p tasks where motor learning was involved. However, no main effects of position-color condition were found to be significant. No interaction effects were found statistically significant.

3.2   Event-Related Potentials for Error Feedback

Since the experiment required subjects to provide response with the right-hand, we expected contralateral EEG activity over cortical areas found to be associated with motor learning. We observed significant differences in activity between F3, C3 and P3, and F4, C4 and P4, which lie on the frontal, central and parietal scalp regions. For error trials, Error-Related Negativity (ERN) was observed at frontal, central electrodes. ERN is characterized by a negative peak in the range of 50–150 ms. Further, differences in amplitudes were observed at 200, 300, 400 ms time points, suggesting lateralization of neural activity underlying error feedback being learnt distinctively. Time latencies over 300 ms were also found to be distinct between left and right scalp electrodes.

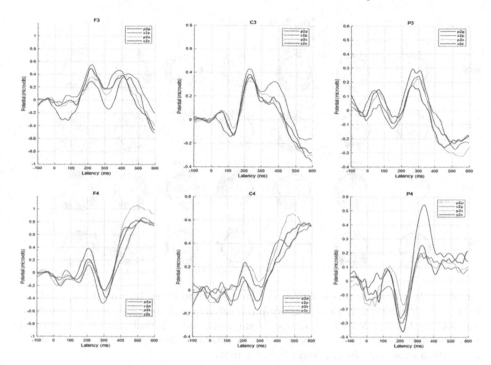

Fig. 3. Lateral differences in ERP between conditions: (A) Electrodes on the left scalp sites: Frontal F3, Central C3, Parietal P3 (B) right scalp sites Frontal F4, Central C4, Parietal P4

For error trials, topoplots revealed significant differences between conditions. p2p and c2p tasks show increased activity in the left electrode sites over central, parietal and occipital region. No such effects were observed for p2c and c2c tasks. Frontal activity over 400 ms latencies was observed in c2c and p2c tasks, which was different from p2p and c2p tasks which show increased activity over frontal as well as central areas.

4   Discussion and Conclusion

In this study, we investigated how sequence learning varies with visuomotor mappings. The learning paradigm consisted of performing sequential movements to be learnt through trial-and-error. The sequence to be learnt was controlled through two stimulus properties: color and position varied in terms of stimulus (or rather display) and response, constituting of four tasks (p2p, p2c, c2p and c2c). The experiment consisted of two modes of learning, that differed in terms of effector-specific and effector non-specific visuomotor mapping. Primarily, behavioral results indicate the role of different cognitive processes underlying arbitrary vs. transformational visuomotor mapping in sequence learning behavior. Reaction Time was found to vary distinctly for each condition of position

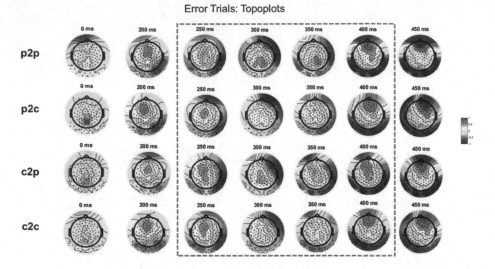

Fig. 4. Scalp topoplots reveal differences between conditions. Increased amplitude at 300 ms over left central, parietal and occipital region in p2p and c2p tasks was observed, but not in p2c and c2c tasks. Increase in amplitude over frontal, central and parietal sites was observed at over 400 ms latencies in p2p and c2p tasks, but not p2c and c2c tasks which show only frontal and central activity.

and color display-response variation, further suggesting the role of distinct cognitive processes underlying each of the condition. We also found that learning was consistent across hypersets as participants learnt the correct sequence through trial-and-error, hence suggesting that there was a learning behavior observed from the first to the last hyperset sequence. We further studied the neural representations underlying visuo-motor sequence learning behavior using EEG to study the temporal order of cognition. Using ERP of stimulus-locked and error trials, we suggest the role of differences in amplitude between contra and ipsilateral scalp electrodes over the motor cortex. Using scalp topoplots, we also found differential activity of change in amplitude across conditions over electrodes on the frontal, central and parietal brain areas. This finding is consistent with studies establishing the role of involvement of cortical areas such as Supplementary Motor Area (SMA), Premotor Cortex, Primary Motor Cortex (M1), Posterior Parietal Cortex, apart from subcortical structures such as the Basal Ganglia and Cerebellum [10,12]. If we assume that scalp-level topoplots reveal underlying temporal order of cognition, we then found corroborative evidence of involvement of these cortical areas in our sequence learning tasks, showing distinct activity in error trials for each condition. Since learning is reinforced with feedback, EEG activity observed for error trials substantiates the involvement of these cortical areas in understanding how sequence learning varies with different visuo-spatial characteristics.

One of the limitations of the current study is the inter-individual difference in learning across individuals, since there is a huge variance in terms of speed and accuracy of how a subject learns. This limits the analysis in terms of capturing a degree of learned behavior to be associated with the completion of every trial. With limitations of EEG in terms of spatial accuracy being subpar, it becomes a challenge to identify functional localization of neural activity within the brain, and thus applies to the current study. Although a source-level analysis can reveal the under-lying neural bases, our findings suggest that scalp topoplots and ERPs are a good predictor of visuo-motor sequence learning. With the advantage of higher temporal resolution using EEG, we show neural representations under-lying changes in neural activity while engaged in acquiring a motor skill and learning a visuo-spatial map.

References

1. Bapi, R., Doya, K., Harner, A.: Evidence for effector independent and dependent representations and their differential time course of acquisition during motor sequence learning. Exper. Brain Res. **132**, 149–162 (2000)
2. Bapi, R.S., Graydon, F.X., Doya, K.: Time course of learning of visual and motor sequence representations. In: Proceedings of Society for Neuroscience, USA (2000)
3. Beaulieu, C., Bourassa, M.È., Brisson, B., Jolicoeur, P., De Beaumont, L.: Electrophysiological correlates of motor sequence learning. BMC Neurosci. **15**(1), 102 (2014)
4. Pammi, V.S.C., Miyapuram, K.P., Samejima, K.B., Raju, S., Doya, K.: Changing the structure of complex visuo-motor sequences selectively activates the frontoparictal network. NeuroImage **59**(2), 1180–1189 (2011)
5. Dahms, C., Brodoehl, S., Witte, O.W., Klingner, C.M.: The importance of different learning stages for motor sequence learning after stroke. Hum. Brain Map. **41**(1), 270–286 (2020)
6. Gabard-Durnam, L.J., Mendez Leal, A.S., Wilkinson, C.L., Levin, A.R.: The harvard automated processing pipeline for electroencephalography (HAPPE): standardized processing software for developmental and high-artifact data. Front. Neurosci. **12**, 97 (2018)
7. van der Helden, J., Boksem, M.A., Blom, J.H.: The importance of failure: feedback-related negativity predicts motor learning efficiency. Cereb. Cortex **20**(7), 1596–1603 (2010)
8. Hikosaka, O., et al.: Parallel neural networks for learning sequential procedures. Trends Neurosci. **22**, 464–471 (1999)
9. Miyapuram, K.P., Pamnani, U., Doya, K., Bapi, R.S.: Inter subject correlation of brain activity during visuo-motor sequence learning. In: Loo, C.K., Yap, K.S., Wong, K.W., Teoh, A., Huang, K. (eds.) ICONIP 2014. LNCS, vol. 8834, pp. 35–41. Springer, Cham (2014). https://doi.org/10.1007/978-3-319-12637-1_5
10. Sakai, K., Hikosaka, O., Miyauchi, S., Sasaki, Y., Fujimaki, N., Putz, B.: Presupplementary motor area activation during sequence learning reflects visuo-motor association. J. Neurosci. **19**(10), 1–6 (1999)
11. Murray, E.A., Bussey, T.J., Wise, S.P.: Role of prefrontal cortex in a network for arbitrary visuomotor mapping. Exper. Brain Res. **133**(1), 114–129 (2000). https://doi.org/10.1007/s002210000406
12. Kawai, R., et al.: Motor cortex is required for learning but not for executing a motor skill. Neuron **86**(3), 800–812 (2015)

The Analysis of Relationship Between SSVEP and Visual Field Using a Circle-Form Checkerboard

Tsutomu Yoshida[✉] and Akitoshi Itai

Graduate School of Engineering, Chubu University, Aichi, Japan
tp20018-4309@sti.chubu.ac.jp, itai@isc.chubu.ac.jp

Abstract. A brain computer interface whose operation is transmitted by SSVEP is often investigated to control a wheelchair. The operation is generated by the user's attention to blinking visual stimulus. In order to avoid various accidents, the user needs to pay own attention to the surrounding situation and visual stimulus, simultaneously. Miura showed the relationship between the position of visual stimulus and the amount of SSVEP. In addition, the amount of SSVEP is rapidly decreased when the visual stimulus is located on the outside of the central visual field. However, a square visual stimulus used in the previous research is not suitable since the distance from eye-sight to visual stimulus is not constant. In this paper, we adopt the circle-form pattern reversal stimulus to clear the relationship between the visual field and SSVEP.

Keywords: SSVEP · Brain Computer Interface · Visual stimulus

1 Introduction

Recently, a Brain Computer Interface(BCI) using Steady-State Visual Evoked Potential(SSVEP) has attracted attention [1,2]. SSVEP is an electroencephalogram(EEG) evoked by attention to visual stimulus [3].

BCI is a technology that uses EEG to recognize intention and operate a wheelchair and computer, and so on. In the SSVEP based BCI, multiple flickering visual stimuli, which are connected to the user's will, are displayed in front of the user. The flickering frequency of these stimuli is different from each other. The user pays own attention to the one visual stimulus to control the BCI system. However, when the user controls a wheelchair using BCI, the user needs to pay own attention to the surrounding situation. This means that the visual stimulus should be displayed avoiding a line of sight. Therefore, it is an important task to know the placement of visual stimulus which enhances the SSVEP.

We showed that the SSVEP is decreased with an increasing of distance between a fixation point and visual stimulus [4,5]. On the other hand, the SSVEP is not decreased by the checkerboard placed on a fixation point, when the attention is not paid toward the visual stimulus [5]. Miura showed that the SSVEP

© Springer Nature Switzerland AG 2020
H. Yang et al. (Eds.): ICONIP 2020, CCIS 1333, pp. 212–219, 2020.
https://doi.org/10.1007/978-3-030-63823-8_26

is enhanced by the visual stimulus placed within 3 degrees from the gaze point [6]. This fact means the amount of SSVEP depends on the area of the visual stimulus reflected in the visual field.

The distance is defined as the angle between a fixation point and the center of the visual stimulus. However, the square visual stimulus applied to the conventional method is not suitable to stimulate a circle-form visual field uniformly. This means that the relationship between the visual field and SSVEP has not been correctly compared in previous studies. In this paper, we construct a virtual reality (VR) measurement system to stimulate a retina at an arbitrary angle around the gaze. The concentric pattern reversal/flash circular visual stimulus is adopted to project a stimulus onto the retina. We show the relationship between the location of two type visual stimuli and SSVEP.

2 SSVEP

2.1 Visual Stimulus

There are two types of visual stimuli to evoke SSVEP. The pattern reversal stimulus produces the second harmonic of the flickering frequency of the pattern image [7]. The pattern reversal consists of two different checkerboard patterns displayed in a liquid crystal monitor (Fig. 1). The flash stimulus yields SSVEP on a frequency using a blinking light such as LED (Light Emitting Diode) or boards (Fig. 2)[7].

Fig. 1. Checkerboard for pattern reversal stimulus   **Fig. 2.** Two boards for flash stimulus

2.2 SSVEP

The SSVEP is the periodic EEG response to a visual stimulus with a periodic blinking. The SSVEP is evoked by attention to a visual stimulus [8]. It is known that the visual stimulus of 15 Hz produces a greater SSVEP than other frequencies [9]. The amplitude spectrum of the EEG signal recorded by a 15 Hz pattern reversal stimulus is shown in Fig. 3. In this figure, the EEG signal includes peaks at 15 and 30 Hz. These are the first and second harmonics of flickering frequency. The amplitude spectrum of the EEG signal recorded by a 15 Hz flash stimulus is shown in Fig. 4. In this figure, the EEG signal includes peaks at 15 Hz. This is the first harmonic of flickering frequency. From these results, we use the visual stimulus of 15 Hz.

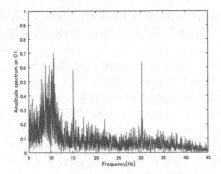

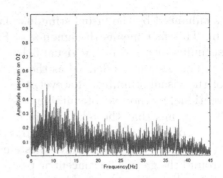

Fig. 3. Amplitude spectrum of EEG gazing 15 Hz pattern reversal stimulus

Fig. 4. Amplitude spectrum of EEG gazing 15 Hz flash stimulus

3 Experiment

The system consists of a VR based stimulus presentation and EEG recording. We introduce the detail of the presentation and recoding systems here.

3.1 The Proposed Visual Stimulus

The visual stimulus is displayed through the VR goggle of HTC VIVE Pro and is controlled by Unity [10,11]. The VR space is enclosed by gray backgrounds ((R, B, G) = (128, 128, 128)). In VR space, a transparent sphere with a radius of 5 cm is placed 55 cm ahead of the subject. The visual stimulus is projected into the sphere. Therefore, the visual stimulus is placed on 60 cm ahead of the subject.

We use a circle-form checkerboard and flashing circle as a visual stimulus. The square visual stimulus used in conventional researches is shown in Fig. 5. The retina and visual field is spread in a concentric circle (yellow circles). The angle θ of Fig. 5 is defined by the position of the fixation point and the center of visual stimulus. From Fig. 5, the square checkerboard pattern does not stimulate the retina at the same distance from the fixation point.

The proposed circle-form visual stimulus is drawn in Fig. 6. In Fig. 6, the stimulated area forms a circle. This area is the same as the form of a visual field. Therefore, the circle-form visual stimulus is suitable for our purpose.

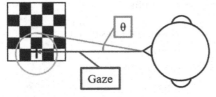 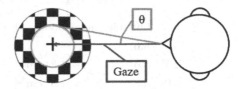

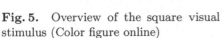

Fig. 5. Overview of the square visual stimulus (Color figure online)

Fig. 6. Overview of the circle visual stimulus

3.2 Visual Stimulus

The proposed circle-form pattern reversal stimulus is shown in Fig. 7. The angle is defined by the center of the circle and the edge of the inner circle. The checkerboard area is fixed as $21.6\,cm^2$ regardless of angle θ. This means the stimulated area of the retina is constant. Details of visual stimulus are shown Table 1. The outside angle is the angle from the gaze point to the outside edge of the visual stimulus. The radius of the inner and outside edge is the length from the gaze to the inner and outside edge of visual stimulus. The radius of inner edge for $\theta = 0.0°$ is written as g-h since there is no edge. The visual stimulus is created by clipping the inner radius area from the circle pattern reversal stimulus(Fig. 8). The grid size of the checker pattern is $1\,cm \times 1\,cm$. The circle-form pattern reversal stimulus of 7 angles is prepared to adjust the recording conditions of conventional research. In addition, the circle-form flash stimulus is also constructed.

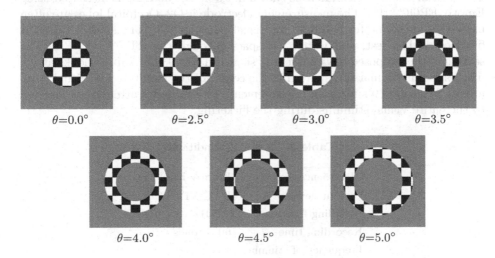

Fig. 7. 7 kind of pattern reversal stimulus

Table 1. The details of visual stimulus

θ	Outside angle	Radius of inner edge	Radius of outside edge
0.0°	5.0°	–	2.62 cm
2.5°	5.6°	1.31 cm	2.93 cm
3.0°	5.8°	1.57 cm	3.06 cm
3.5°	6.1°	1.84 cm	3.20 cm
4.0°	6.4°	2.10 cm	3.36 cm
4.5°	6.7°	2.36 cm	3.53 cm
5.0°	7.1°	2.62 cm	3.70 cm

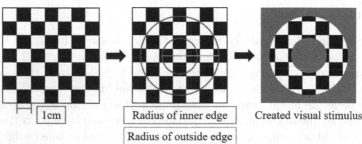

1cm | Radius of inner edge | Created visual stimulus
Radius of outside edge

Fig. 8. How to create the visual stimulus

3.3 Recording Conditions

The measurement environment is shown in Table 2. The EEG is measured using
Emotiv EPOC+[12]. The measurement electrode is O2. Occipital lobes are often
used to record a better response for visual stimulus [13]. The subject's head is
fixed on a chin rest, and watch VR space through the HTC VIVE Pro. The
setting of the proposed environment is shown in Fig. 9. The subject looks at the
fixation point (+ mark) displayed in the center of the monitor. The visual stimulus is flickering 60 s for each measurement. The subject's attention is directed
to the entire visual stimulus during the flickering.

Table 2. Recording conditions

Electroencephalograph	Emotiv EPOC+
Output device	HTC VIVE Pro
Sampling frequency	128 Hz
Recording time	60 seconds
Frequency of stimulus	15 Hz
The electrode	O2

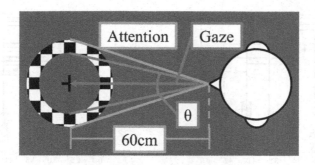

Fig. 9. Overview of VR space

4 Results

EEG is analyzed by the discrete Fourier transform. The amplitude spectrum at 15/30 Hz is used as an amount of SSVEP for flash/pattern reversal stimulus, respectively. To evaluate the performance of SSVEP, the T-test is applied to SSVEP measured by different angles. The number of the subject is 3. The EEG is measured 5 times at each angle for 2 subjects, 3 times at each angle for 1 subject. Therefore, the number of data is 13.

4.1 The Pattern Reversal Stimulus

In the pattern reversal stimulus, the amplitude spectrum at 30 Hz is used as SSVEP. The result of T-test is shown in Fig. 10. Color bars are the averaged amount of SSVEP, error bars are the standard deviation of SSVEP. The horizontal axis is the θ. * represents a significant difference of $p = 0.05$.

From Fig. 10, the SSVEP is significantly decreased from $\theta = 0.0°$ to $2.5°$. However, the SSVEP is increasing with θ until $\theta = 4.0°$.

4.2 The Flash Stimulus

In the flash stimulus, the amplitude spectrum of 15 Hz is used as the amount of SSVEP. T-test is also performed as Sect. 4.1. The averaged SSVEP and a result of T-test is drawn in Fig. 11. The axes, color bars, error bars and the number of data are the same as Fig. 10.

From Fig. 11, the SSVEP is decreased with θ increasing.

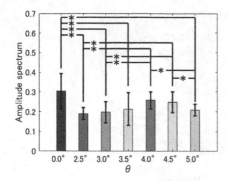
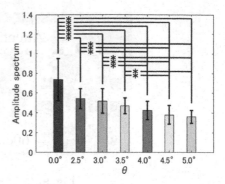

Fig. 10. SSVEP of pattern reversal stimulus

Fig. 11. SSVEP of flash stimulus

4.3 Discussion

From Fig. 11, the SSVEP for flash stimulus is decreased with increasing of the distance between a fixation point and visual stimulus. The decreasing trend is the same as conventional researches. This result shows that the SSVEP is evoked by the attention toward the circle-form visual stimulus correctly.

On the other hand, the SSVEP shown in Fig. 10 is not continuously decreasing. The SSVEP is rapidly decreased in 2.5° the same as [5]. The human recognition function is suppressed in the outside of the visual field [14]. Oyabu suggests that the amount of SSVEP is related visual recognition of checkerboard [15]. There is a possibility that the rapid decrease at 2.5° is the effect of visual recognition of the visual stimulus since the visual field is located at the 2.5° from the center of gaze. However, the SSVEP is increasing from 3.0° to 4.0°.

Now we focus on the checkerboard pattern of circle-form visual stimulus. Wakita suggests that the amount of SSVEP is related to the number of lattice of checkerboard [16]. From Fig. 7, one square size of the checkerboard is the same at all θ. However, the displayed checkerboard pattern is different since the thickness of the circle-form depends on the θ. These facts mean that the SSVEP shown in Fig. 10 includes the effect of lattice pattern of pattern reversal stimulus.

5   Conclusion

In this paper, we construct the recording environment to evaluate the relation of the SSVEP and visual field. The evaluation is performed by using the circle-form pattern reversal and flash stimulus. From results, the SSVEP evoked by the circle-form flash stimulus is decreased with increasing of angle θ. This means that the amount of the SSVEP depends on the distance from a fixation point to visual stimulus since the area of all stimuli is the same. On other hand, the SSVEP evoked by circle-form pattern reversal stimulus does not show the simple decreasing trend. There is a possibility that the amount of SSVEP was affected of lattice by Wakita report [16]. This means that circle-form pattern reversal stimulus is not showing correctly relationship between the location of visual stimulus and SSVEP. The future task is to develop other circle-form pattern reversal stimulus which does not affect the SSVEP.

References

1. Wolpaw, J.R., Birbaumer, N., McFarland, D.J., Pfurtscheller, G., Vaughan, T.M.: Brain computer interfaces for communication and control. Clin. Neurophys. **113**(6), 767–791 (2002)
2. Lebedev, M.A., Nicolelis, M.A.L.: Brain machine interfaces: past, present and future. Trends Neurosci. **29**(9), 536–546 (2006)
3. Regan, D.: Steady-state evoked potentials. J. Opti. Soc. Am. **67**(11), 1475–1489 (1977)
4. Itai, A., Sakakibara, T.: The relationship between a location of visual stimulus and SSVEP. Proceedings of International Symposium on Communications and Information Technologies, pp. 145–148 (2015)
5. Matsui, T., Matsui, M., Itai, A.: The characteristics of SSVEP related to sight and attention for flickering stimulus. In: Proceedings of International Workshop on Smart Info-Media Systems in Asia (SISA), pp. 193–196 (2017)
6. Miura, K., Itai, A.: Factor analysis of the range of SSVEP evoked by the pattern reversal stimulus. In: Workshop on Informatics 2017, PD-17 (2017)
7. Goto, Y., Hagiwara, K., Ikeda, T., Tobimatsu, S.: Visual evoked potentials and visual evoked cerebral magnetic fields. Clin. Neurophys. **40**(1) (2012)
8. Morgan, S.T., Hansen, J.C., Hillyard, S.A.: Selective attention to stimulus location modulates the steady-state visual evoked potential. Proc. Natl. Acad. Sci. USA **93**(10), 4770–4774 (1996)
9. Kus, R., et al.: On the quantification of SSVEP frequency responses in human EEG in realistic BCI conditions. PLoS One **8**(10), e77536 (2013)
10. HTC VIVE Pro. https://www.vive.com/jp/product/vive-pro-full-kit/. Accessed 21 June 2020
11. Unity Homepage. https://unity.com/ja. Accessed 21 June 2020
12. Emotiv EPOC+. https://www.emotiv.com/product/emotiv-epoc-14-channel-mobile-eeg/. Accessed 21 June 2020
13. Shibasaki, K.: Functional diagnosis of the brain by evoked potentials. Biomed. Eng. **1**(5) (1987)
14. Hatada, T.: Measurement of information receiving and visual field. Hum. Eng. **29**(Supplement), 86–88 (1993)
15. Oyabu, K., Funase, A., Itai, A.: An effect of eyesight and visual contact for SSVEP. ME Bio Cybern. **17**(15–41), 79–83 (2017)
16. Wakita, K., Funase, A., Takumi, I.: The relationship obetween a lattice size of checkerboard and SSVEP. Biomed. Eng. **53**(Supplement), S446–S449 (2015)

The Dynamic Travelling Thief Problem: Benchmarks and Performance of Evolutionary Algorithms

Ragav Sachdeva, Frank Neumann, and Markus Wagner[(✉)]

School of Computer Science, University of Adelaide, Adelaide, Australia
ragav.sachdeva@student.adelaide.edu.au,
{frank.neumann,markus.wagner}@adelaide.edu.au

Abstract. Many real-world optimisation problems involve dynamic and stochastic components. While problems with multiple interacting components are omnipresent in inherently dynamic domains like supply-chain optimisation and logistics, most research on dynamic problems focuses on single-component problems. With this article, we define a number of scenarios based on the Travelling Thief Problem to enable research on the effect of dynamic changes to sub-components. Our investigations of 72 scenarios and seven algorithms show that – depending on the instance, the magnitude of the change, and the algorithms in the portfolio – it is preferable to either restart the optimisation from scratch or to continue with the previously valid solutions.

Keywords: Dynamic optimisation · Multi-component problems

1 Introduction

Real-world optimisation problems often involve dynamic and stochastic components, and evolutionary algorithms have shown to be very successful for dealing with such problems. This is due to the very nature of evolutionary computing techniques that allows them to adapt to changing environments without having to restart the algorithm when the problem characteristics change.

In this paper, we investigate dynamic variants of the travelling thief problem (TTP). The TTP has been introduced in the evolutionary computation literature in [2] as a multi-component problem combining the classical travelling salesperson problem (TSP) and the knapsack problem (KP). The TTP comprises a thief stealing items with weights and profits from a number of cities. The thief has to visit all cities once and collect items such that the overall profit is maximised. The thief uses a knapsack of limited capacity and pays rent for it proportional to the overall travel duration. To make the two components (TSP and KP) interdependent, the speed of the thief is made non-linearly dependent on the weight of the items picked so far. The interactions of the TSP and the KP in the TTP result in a complex problem that is hard to solve by tackling the

© Springer Nature Switzerland AG 2020
H. Yang et al. (Eds.): ICONIP 2020, CCIS 1333, pp. 220–228, 2020.
https://doi.org/10.1007/978-3-030-63823-8_27

components separately. The TTP has gained significant attention in the evolutionary computation literature and several competitions organised to solve this problem have led to significant progress improving the performance of solvers.

In order to further extend the impact and significance of studies around the TTP, and to support research on the effects of dynamic changes to subcomponents of problems, we design two types of dynamic benchmarks. The first one relates to the KP where items in cities can become available and unavailable. This inevitably changes the options of items that can be collected. The second one relates to the TSP component of the problem where cities can be made available and unavailable modelling the change in availability of locations.

We design different scenarios for these dynamic settings and examine how evolutionary algorithms based on popular algorithmic components for the TTP can deal with such changes. In particular, we are interested in learning when one should continue with the optimisation by recovering from the previous solution, or when one should create a new solution from scratch as a starting point.

Note. The full version of this article is available at https://arxiv.org/abs/2004.12045 [7]. It contains, among other, a review of "TTP variants to date" in Sect. 2, a detailed description of the heuristics in Sect. 4, an investigation of single disruptive events in Sect. 5, and an outline of possible future work.

2   The Travelling Thief Problem

The TTP combines two well-known problems, namely, the Travelling Salesman Problem and the Knapsack Problem. The problem is defined as follows: we are given a set of n cities, the associated matrix of distances d_{ij}, and a set of m items distributed among these cities. Each item k is defined by a profit p_k and a weight w_k. A thief must visit all the cities exactly once, stealing some items on the road, and return to the starting city.

The knapsack has a capacity limit of W, i.e. the total weight of the collected items must not exceed W. In addition, we consider a renting rate R that the thief must pay at the end of the travel, and the maximum and minimum velocities denoted v_{max} and v_{min} respectively. Furthermore, each item is available in only one city, and $A_i \in \{1, \ldots, n\}$ denotes the availability vector. A_i contains the reference to the city that contains the item i.

A TTP solution is typically coded in two parts: the tour $X = (x_1, \ldots, x_n)$, a vector containing the ordered list of cities, and the picking plan $Z = (z_1, \ldots, z_m)$, a binary vector representing the states of items (1 for packed, 0 for unpacked).

To establish a dependency between the sub-problems, the TTP was designed such that the speed of the thief changes according to the knapsack weight. To achieve this, the thief's velocity at city c is defined as $v_x = v_{max} - C \times w_x$, where $C = \frac{v_{max} - v_{min}}{W}$ is a constant value, and w_x is the weight of the knapsack at city x. The total value of items is $g(Z) = \sum_m p_m \times z_m$, such that $\sum_m w_m \times z_m \leq W$. The total travel time is $f(X, Z) = \sum_{i=1}^{n-1} t_{x_i, x_{i+1}} + t_{x_n, x_1}$, where $t_{x_i, x_{i+1}} = \frac{d_{x_i, x_{i+1}}}{v_{x_i}}$ is the travel time from x_i to x_{i+1}. The TTP's objective is to maximise the total travel gain function, which is the total profit of all items minus the travel time multiplied with the renting rate: $F(X, Z) = g(Z) - f(X, Z) \times R$.

For a worked example, we refer to the initial TTP article by Bonyadi et al. [3].

3   Dynamic Travelling Thief Problem (DynTTP)

Broadly speaking, DynTTP is an extension of the classic TTP where the problem constraints can change during run-time. In this study, we investigate the introduction of dynamism in two different ways by flipping the availability status of $d\%$ of the (1) items and (2) cities uniformly at random, i.e. if an item/city is available, it is made unavailable and vice-versa. From here on, we will call the event when availabilities change a *disruption*, and the time span between two disruptions is called an *epoch* which is of duration z.

To allow for a meaningful investigation, both these dynamic changes are studied independently of one another. Furthermore, while "Toggling Items" the tour is kept fixed and similarly while "Toggling Cities" the packing list is not re-optimised. In addition, to guarantee that the solutions remain valid and to permit a fair analysis, we make the following design decisions:

Toggling Items: If an item is made unavailable, it is no longer in the current packing plan (if already picked) and cannot be picked again by the thief. On the other hand, if an item is made available again, it is available for the thief to steal but it is not automatically added to the current packing list (to prevent unintentionally exceeding the knapsack capacity).

Toggling Cities: If a city is made unavailable, it is removed from the current tour while maintaining the order of the remaining cities. Of course, this also implies that the items in this city are no longer available either. On the other hand, if a city is made available again, it is inserted back into the tour at the same position as it was before. Furthermore, toggling a city back in, also updates the knapsack to include the items from this city that were previously in the packing list. This is an acceptable thing to do because even if all the cities are toggled 'on', the knapsack will not exceed capacity as the packing plan would revert back to the initial solution at $t = 0$.

As it is often the case with dynamic optimisation (see Fig. 1), it depends on the magnitude of the change, on the available computational budget, and on the available algorithms whether it is preferable to restart the optimisation from scratch or to recover based on the previous solution.

Note that a dedicated random number generator is responsible for modifying the instances. This way, different algorithms observe the same set of conditions for a given instances, and thus we ensure that sequences of disruptions remain comparable, as otherwise instances would drift apart.

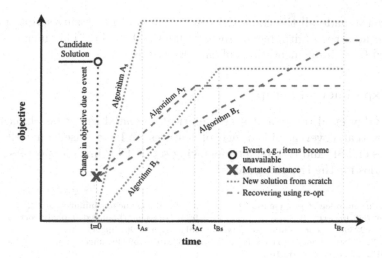

Fig. 1. Simplified DynTTP scenario: as time $t = 0$, an instance gets disrupted, and a decision maker has to decide (1) whether to employ algorithm A or algorithm B and (2) whether to recover from the previous solution R (marked X) or to optimise from scratch S. $t_{AS} \ldots t_{BR}$ denote the times needed by the different choices to converge.

4   Heuristics for the DynTTP

As the items/cities are toggled ensuing from the dynamic change, the objective value of the known TTP solution changes. At this point there are two choices: Re-build a TTP solution from scratch for, what is effectively a new TTP instance; or re-optimise the packing/tour for the previously known best solution.

To achieve this, we make use of a number of generic as well as problem-specific algorithmic building blocks.

For the different scenarios of the dynamically changing availability of items and cities, we combine the building blocks in the following seven ways.

Toggling Items – four approaches: 1. Re-optimise the mutated packing using BITFLIP [5]; 2. Re-optimise the mutated packing using REA$_m$ [4] with the population size of m, which is the number of items originally available; 3. Create a new packing plan from scratch using PACKITERATIVE [5]; 4. Create a new packing plan from scratch using PACKITERATIVE and then optimise it using BITFLIP;

Toggling Cities – three approaches: 1. Re-optimise the mutated tour using INSERTION [5]; 2. Create a new tour from scratch using CLK [1]; 3. Create a new tour from scratch using CLK and then optimise it using INSERTION.

5   Computational Investigation

In the following, we first describe our experimental setup and the 72 scenarios. Then, we present the results and highlight situations that we find interesting.

We have made all the code, the results, the and processing scripts publicly available at https://github.com/ragavsachdeva/DynTTP. This includes cross-validated C++ implementations of the algorithms.

5.1 Experimental Setup

Polyakovskiy et al. presented a systematically created set of benchmark TTP instances that cover a wide range of features and are based on well known instances of TSP and KP [6]. The following set of TTP instances covers a range of scenarios for the travelling thief:[1]

280_ n279_ bounded-strongly-corr_ 01	a280_ n1395_ uncorr-similar-weights_ 05
a280_ n2790_ uncorr_ 10	fnl4461_ n4460_ bounded-strongly-corr_ 01
fnl4461_ n22300_ uncorr-similar-weights_ 05	fnl4461_ n44600_ uncorr_ 10
pla33810_ n33809_ bounded-strongly-corr_ 01	pla33810_ n169045_ uncorr-similar-weights_ 05
pla33810_ n338090_ uncorr_ 10	

The numbers in each instance name are (from left to right) the total number of cities, the total number of items, and the knapsack size in that instance. For example, instance a280_ n2790_ uncorr_ 10 has 280 cities all of which (except the first) have 10 items each, totalling 2790 items, and it has the largest knapsack. In addition the terms uncorrelated, uncorrelated-similar-weights and bounded-strongly-correlated reflect the unique knapsack types as described in [6]. To facilitate readability, we will use the abbreviations A279, A1395, ..., P338090, which include the number of items in their names.

In our computational study of the DynTTP, we investigate disruptions of the following types: (1) instance feature $f \in \{$items, cities$\}$; (2) amount of disruption $d \in \{1\%, 3\%, 10\%, 30\%\}$; (3) period z (time between disruptive events).

As the disruptions to instances are random (modulo the determinism described in Sect. 3), we perform 30 independent runs of each scenario – a "scenario" is an instance, together with an instance feature f that is to be disrupted, an amount of disruption d, and a period z.

The initial solutions are created by CLK to generate a good TSP tour and then by PACKITERATIVE+BITFLIP to converge to a good TTP solution.

5.2 Multiple Disruptive Events

We investigate the performance over time for multiple disruptions. In particular, we observe 10 epochs and each lasts for a period of $z = m$ function evaluations (equal to the number of items in the original instance) or for 10 min, whichever comes first. Due to the high dimensionality of this study, (1) we use heatmaps to allow for a qualitative inspection of the results, and (2) we cut through the data in different ways and use statistical tests to compare the heuristic approaches.

---

[1] It has also been the subset used at the 2014/2015 and 2017 TTP competitions, e.g., https://cs.adelaide.edu.au/~optlog/TTP2017Comp/.

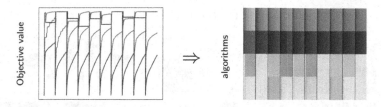

Fig. 2. *Average* performance of four algorithms for 10 epochs (F4460, $d = 30\%$). Time, as measured in the number of evaluations, passes from left to right; each period is of length $z = 4460$ evaluations. Within each epoch, the performance is normalised across all algorithms. The lighter the colour, the higher the performance. Algorithms: BITFLIP (green, 1st row), REA$_m$ (blue, 2nd row), PACKITERATIVE (black, 3rd row), PACKITERATIVE+BITFLIP (red, 4th row).

Heatmaps. Before moving on, we briefly explain the creation of each heatmap. First, we record for each of the 30 runs all TTP objective scores. Second, for each scenario and each epoch (as these are identical) we determine the minimum and maximum objective scores across all algorithms, and then linearly normalise the average of the 30 trajectories into $[0, 1]$. These scores are then visualised as coloured bars, from black (lowest value seen by any algorithm in this scenario and epoch), via red to a light peach (highest value seen by any algorithm). Figure 2 shows an example for four algorithms. To facilitate readability, we omit all labels, because the period is fixed (as defined above), and because the order of the four (respectively three) approaches is stated in the captions.[2]

Figure 3 shows all the results. While we will dig deeper in our following statistical analyses, it is obvious that some situations are "very clear". For example, for the *Toggling Items* scenarios and for P338090 (rightmost column of heatmaps), the bottom two approaches always perform best (these are PACKITERATIVE and PACKITERATIVE+BITFLIP, which both start from scratch) as they have the brightest colours. In contrast to this, the approaches that start from scratch for the *Toggling Cities* scenarios (with $d = 1\%$) perform the worst. We can also see that, as we move from left to right in this matrix of heatmaps, that patterns change and thus the ranking of the algorithms change – this is important for anyone making decisions: based on this qualitative analysis, it is already clear that different situations require conceptually different approaches.

Statistical Analyses. Given our high-dimensional dataset, we can cut through it in various ways and compare the performance of the different algorithms under various conditions. As inputs to these tests, we use the averaged (normalised) performance in two ways: (1) the final performance at the end of an epoch (END), and (2) the area-under-the-curve of the objective scores in an epoch (AUC), to consider the convergence speed as well as quality. We employ the pairwise, one-sided Mann-Whitney U test as a ranksum test that does not rely on normal-distributed data. Again, we will limit ourselves to interesting cases, and to those with p-values of less than 5%. In the following, we first provide a global

---

[2] The algorithm's order is also identical to the order listed in Sect. 4.

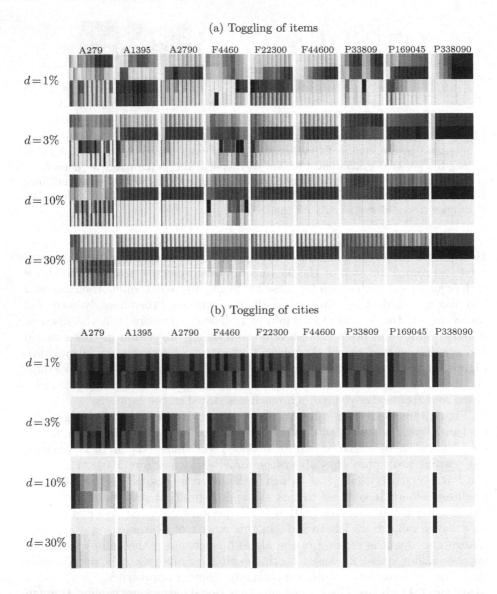

Fig. 3. DynTTP results of seven algorithms on 72 scenarios, and for a duration of 10 epochs each. The performance has been normalised across all algorithms (within each individual epoch and w.r.t. to all objective scores seen in this epoch) to allow for a relative performance comparison. **Part (a)** Toggling of items: BITFLIP (1st row), REA$_m$ (2nd row), PACKITERATIVE (3rd row), PACKITERATIVE+BITFLIP (4th row). **Part (b)** Toggling of cities: INSERTION (1st row), CLK (2nd row), CLK+INSERTION (3rd row). The lighter the colour, the higher the performance. **Example:** based on the heatmap in the top right corner of Part (a) (i.e., P338090 and $d = 1\%$), we can see that all algorithms perform comparatively at first, but then PACKITERATIVE and PACKITERATIVE+BITFLIP gradually perform better and better than the other two approaches.

picture, and then slice through the data along the four amounts of disruption d and along the nine instances. This results in 650 pair-wise statistical tests.

Global level (aggregated over all epochs, instances and values of d**).** (1) Toggling Items: Starting from scratch is preferred, as PACKITERATIVE+BITFLIP outperforms PACKITERATIVE, which outperforms BITFLIP and that in turn outperforms REA_m. (2) Toggling Cities: Recovering is preferred here, as INSERTION outperforms both CLK and CLK+INSERTION, which perform comparably. One of the reasons for this is that we do not optimise the packing in this case, and when we start from scratch the TSP is changed and the packing no longer is adequate with it. Moreover, the heuristics here are problem-independent, whereas PACKITERATIVE is TTP-specific.

Disruptions d **(aggregated over all epochs and instances):** (1) Toggling Items: We now see a few changes in the ranking when d=1%, i.e., BITFLIP now outperforms PACKITERATIVE as well (in addition to REA_m, but only in case of AUC) possibly because the change to the instance is very minor and recovering is better than risking the start from a solution from scratch that is of unknown quality. However, when $d \geq 3\%$ the disruption seems too big for BITFLIP to recover, and PACKITERATIVE again outperforms BITFLIP. (2) Toggling Cities: We observe only a single change from the global picture, i.e, CLK+INSERTION outperforms the other two when $d = 30\%$ (END).

Instances (aggregated over all epochs and values of d**).** (1) Toggling Items: A279 is a surprise in that REA_m outperforms all three in AUC; for the next four larger instances (up to F22300) this does not hold anymore and many comparisons are insignificant; for the largest five instances, the global picture holds and PACKITERATIVE+BITFLIP is the always significantly better. (2) Toggling Cities: There is never any deviation from the global picture, except for P338090, where there are not significant differences of all three approaches when the final performance (END) is considered.

To sum up, we observe that disruptive events have a major impact on the performance, which in turn significantly affect the relative rankings.

Acknowledgment. This work has been supported by the Australian Research Council through grants DP160102401 and DP200102364.

References

1. Applegate, D., Cook, W.J., Rohe, A.: Chained Lin-Kernighan for large traveling salesman problems. INFORMS J. Comput. **15**(1), 82–92 (2003)
2. Bonyadi, M.R., Michalewicz, Z., Barone, L.: The travelling thief problem: the first step in the transition from theoretical problems to realistic problems. In: IEEE Congress on Evolutionary Computation, pp. 1037–1044. IEEE (2013)
3. Bonyadi, M.R., Michalewicz, Z., Barone, L.: The travelling thief problem: the first step in the transition from theoretical problems to realistic problems. In: IEEE Congress on Evolutionary Computation, pp. 1037–1044. IEEE (2013)
4. Doerr, B., Doerr, C., Neumann, F.: Fast re-optimization via structural diversity. CoRR abs/1902.00304 (2019). http://arxiv.org/abs/1902.00304

5. Faulkner, H., Polyakovskiy, S., Schultz, T., Wagner, M.: Approximate approaches to the traveling thief problem. In: Genetic and Evolutionary Computation Conference, pp. 385–392. ACM (2015)
6. Polyakovskiy, S., Bonyadi, M.R., Wagner, M., Michalewicz, Z., Neumann, F.: A comprehensive benchmark set and heuristics for the traveling thief problem. In: Genetic and Evolutionary Computation Conference, pp. 477–484. ACM (2014)
7. Sachdeva, R., Neumann, F., Wagner, M.: The dynamic travelling thief problem: benchmarks and performance of evolutionary algorithms. CoRR abs/2004.12045 (2020). http://arxiv.org/abs/2004.12045

Using Applicability to Quantifying Octave Resonance in Deep Neural Networks

Edward Collier[1]([envelope]), Robert DiBiano[2], and Supratik Mukhopadhyay[1]

[1] Louisiana State University, Baton Rouge, LA 70803, USA
ecoll28@lsu.edu
[2] Ailectric, Baton Rouge, LA 70803, USA

Abstract. Features in a deep neural network are only as robust as those present in the data provided for training. The robustness of features applies to not just the types of features and how they apply to various classes, known or unknown, but also to how those features apply to different octaves, or scales. Neural Networks trained at one octave have been shown to be invariant to other octaves, while neural networks trained on large robust datasets operate optimally at only the octaves that resonate best with the learned features. This may still discard features that existed in the data. Not knowing the octave a trained neural network is most applicable to can lead to sub-optimal results during prediction due to poor preprocessing. Recent work has shown good results in quantifying how the learned features in a neural network apply to objects. In this work, we follow up on work in feature applicability, using it to quantify which octaves the features in a trained neural network resonate best with.

1 Introduction

Over the years, the performance of deep neural networks have improved leaps and bounds. One of the most well understood concepts in feature spaces is transferability [18]. Transferability refers to the practice of applying, or transferring, a learned feature space to a task that the feature space was not originally trained on. Within the same domain it has been shown that feature spaces generally have large areas of overlap. This overlap allows the learned features to be applied to many or even all tasks within the same domain [6].

The human brain also uses transfer learning to perform zero or one shot learning by using analogy. Humans can perform analogy selectively on problems by applying what they know to part or all of a problem. The human brain has the capability to learn representations and apply them to almost any scale. Features learned in a neural network apply specifically to the scale they were trained at, creating multiple clusters for the same feature at different scales, or octaves, in the feature space. Lower layer generic features have more scale invariance and greater cluster overlapping, but on the higher layers, the clusters will begin to have greater separation, the greater the scale difference is. To the best of our knowledge, there has been no metric proposed that can quantify how well the features resonate with varying scales within a trained neural network.

© Springer Nature Switzerland AG 2020
H. Yang et al. (Eds.): ICONIP 2020, CCIS 1333, pp. 229–237, 2020.
https://doi.org/10.1007/978-3-030-63823-8_28

In this paper, we make three key contributions. First, we measure feature applicability for an octave, which we refer to as octave resonance, at a standard scale. The second contribution is to measure the octave resonance for networks trained on large data sets with a distribution of octaves for features. Lastly, we take a similar approach to the authors in [6] and measure the layer octave resonance.

2   Related Work

For deep neural networks, regardless of domain, learning is done by fitting a distribution of features at each layer of the network [2,3,7], where the larger the dataset, the better fit the feature space is [1,14]. By transferring the learned weights from one domain to a similar one and performing moderate fine-tuning [10] on available data, a network can achieve convergence quickly and without a large dataset [16]. Transferring weights has found usage in diverse applications that involve image classification [19] and language processing [8].

One of the fascinating behaviors that transfer learning [17] utilizes is the generic to specific nature in which features are learned. It is known that the lower layers of neural networks pick up generic features, that are common to almost all inputs for a specific input type, such as images [18]. As the inputs make a forward pass up the network, the learned features become more and more specific to the domain and class of the input [18]. Applicability is a quantitative measure of transferability, or domain adaptability, measuring how well the features from a learned task apply to any other task, including the learned task [6].

3   Proposed Method

We present our proposed methodology in this section. In Sect. 3.1 we formulate applicability for a specific layer. We give our formulation for octave resonance across an entire network in Sect. 3.2. Next, we define the layer by layer octave resonance in Sect. 3.4.

3.1   Applicability

The formal definition of applicability for a trained layer is the degree to which a known class can be differentiated from all other classes, known or unknown, using learned features. Mathematically, applicability is presented in Eq. 2. For any neural network N, there are two overlapping sets; the sets of known classes that the model was trained on, and the set of all classes $un=\{un_0, un_1, un_2, ..., un_k\}$ for which applicability will be measured at each model layer n_i, where all layers before and including n_i are frozen. For an input x, the ability for a model to differentiate at layer n_i is the classification error between the two sets, expressed in Eq. 1.

$$\xi_j = N((x, un_j), n_i) \tag{1}$$

where un_j is the jth class in un. The applicability between one class and the rest in un is the average differentiability between x and all individual classes un_j in un. This is expressed in Eq. 2.

$$App_x = \frac{\sum_{j=1}^{a} \xi_j}{a} \tag{2}$$

where the total number of layers in the neural network the applicability is being averaged over is a.

3.2   Octave Resonance

Applicability, traditionally, has little concern for scale. To compute octave resonance, un must be split into subsets based on the octave where points in one cluster can be transformed into another via some common function $x \rightarrow z(x)$; in this case $z(x)$ is zooming in or out an octave. When checking for the octave resonance, it is not useful to check within the same set. Instead, the comparison is between one set and the rest. Keeping this in mind, octave resonance is then redefined as a trained neural network's ability to differentiate an input from one octave from inputs across all other octaves. The octaves that resonate best with the learned features will have the highest amount of differentiation between classes. This changes Eq. 1 to Eq. 3.

$$\xi_j = N((z_k(x), un_j), n_i) \tag{3}$$

where input x is transformed to the octave set k with transformation z, and compared to all classes in un. In this case, un still covers all the octave subsets.

3.3   Network Octave Variation

We hypothesize that in a trained model, containing only a single octave present within the training dataset, the applicability will drop-off more severely for images at varying octaves than if it were trained on a dataset with multiple octaves. Because neural networks have a finite number of trainable parameters, there is a cap on the amount that can be learned. For a neural network to have effectively learned an octave within its training set, it would have to fit to the distribution of the features for the octave that exist within the training dataset. Even over a large training set, a neural network will likely ignore the least common octaves, as those features would not be identified as important.

3.4   Layer Octave Resonance

While we have been measuring the octave resonance for the entire model, applicability can also be measured for individual layers. Layer applicability is identical to full model applicability, except every layer from the first layer through the layer being measured are frozen. Model applicability is then the layer applicability for the final layer of the model.

4 Experimental Evaluation

We present our experimental results in this section. In our experiments, we focus on datasets from two primary categories. The first are datasets which contain objects at only one scale, and the second are datasets that contain multiple scales. We show how the features resonate with various octaves across the two dataset types. Lastly, we measure the octave applicability layer by layer to show how the generic layers (i.e., layers that learn generic features) resonate better than specific layers (i.e., layers that learn specific features).

4.1 Datasets

We use four primary datasets in our evaluation; MNIST [13], Bangla Numeral [4,5,15], CIFAR10 [11], and ILSVRC2012 [12]. We separate the four datasets into two groups of two each. The first group consists of the MNIST and Bangla Numeral datasets which both have a consistent octave. The second group, CIFAR10 and **ILSVRC2012**, are datasets that cover multiple octaves.

There are an infinite number of octaves with which an octave can be compared against, we instead test over a finite, but representative range of octaves. Zero padding is used for all the images that have outward zooming. We have found during testing that the models have little meaningful variance for scale factors outside of range $z = (0.01, 6.0)$.

4.2 Octave Resonance Evaluation

Octave resonance at any layer is a neural network's average differentiability between one octave and all other octaves. To compute octave resonance, we finetuned a 1v1 neural network for all possible combinations of classes across all octaves, excluding identical pairs at different octaves, for each dataset. The layer(s) before and at which the applicability is being computed are frozen to preserve the learned features and octaves. The validation accuracy between the two classes, after convergence, is the differentiability metric between the two classes. The average differentiability metric for each octave is the applicability of that octave and the average differentiability for each class in each octave.

4.3 Constant Octave Model

For testing our constant octave models, we have trained models on two datasets that maintain a fairly consistent scale throughout, the MNIST dataset and the Bangla Numeral one [4,5,15]. For the MNIST and Bangla Numeral datasets, there were 170 1v1 neural networks trained. Figure 1 shows the class octave resonance across all the tested octave for the Bangla Numeral dataset. In Table 1, we present a numerical breakdown of octave resonance for each class, for select octaves, in the MNIST dataset.

Looking at both Fig. 1 and Table 1, we can see a clear applicability peak centered around the original octave. For all classes, the highest applicability

Table 1. MNIST Class octave resonance

Class	0.01	0.05	0.1	0.15	0.2	0.25	0.5	0.75	1.0	1.25	1.5	1.75	2.0	3.0	4.0	5.0	6.0
0	0.00	0.00	0.00	0.00	0.00	0.00	0.02	0.93	1.00	0.95	0.66	0.44	0.27	0.05	0.02	0.01	0.01
1	0.00	0.00	0.00	0.00	0.08	0.00	0.96	0.99	1.00	0.98	0.97	0.94	0.93	0.71	0.35	0.15	0.06
2	0.00	0.00	0.00	0.00	0.00	0.00	0.35	0.99	0.99	0.96	0.84	0.63	0.53	0.34	0.27	0.23	0.23
3	0.00	0.00	0.00	0.00	0.42	0.00	0.35	0.98	0.99	0.96	0.78	0.31	0.10	0.05	0.10	0.12	0.14
4	0.00	0.00	0.00	0.00	0.00	0.00	0.40	0.94	0.99	0.96	0.89	0.64	0.54	0.16	0.05	0.01	0.01
5	0.00	0.00	0.00	0.10	0.01	0.00	0.13	0.84	0.98	0.96	0.86	0.66	0.46	0.14	0.09	0.08	0.07
6	0.00	0.00	0.00	0.00	0.00	0.00	0.01	0.98	0.99	0.94	0.82	0.76	0.62	0.36	0.24	0.16	0.11
7	0.00	0.00	0.00	0.00	0.00	0.00	0.07	0.94	0.99	0.96	0.85	0.74	0.68	0.49	0.33	0.23	0.15
8	0.00	0.00	0.00	0.00	0.00	0.00	0.02	0.95	0.99	0.92	0.67	0.31	0.20	0.21	0.30	0.33	0.33
9	0.00	0.00	0.00	0.01	0.04	0.01	0.85	0.94	0.98	0.94	0.72	0.40	0.16	0.04	0.06	0.07	0.04

Class by class octave resonance for the MNIST dataset.

occurs at the original octave. This is corroborated by the fact that the models were trained on a fairly constant octave, in addition to the fact that the set of features under consideration are relatively simple. The mode of the applicability for the classes varies in length slightly, some lasting much longer, but in general the applicability for scales 0.75, 1, and 1.25 are above 0.9 before dropping off, sometimes drastically.

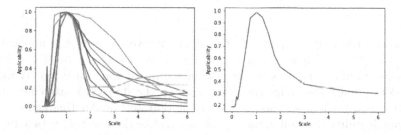

Fig. 1. *Left*: Prediction classes for MNIST for the down scale octaves with the lowest applicability. *Right*: Combined octave resonance for the Bangla Numeral dataset across all classes.

There are classes, like class 1 in MNIST, that have a less drastic applicability drop off when upscaling. This is likely a result of certain classes possessing scale invariant features. For example class 1 in MNIST is very simple and could possibly be defined by a vertical edge detection feature. This feature can exist regardless of scale and will lead to higher differentiability for larger scales than more complex scale variant features. This behavior also affects the accuracy of the low end features. When down scaling, the applicability has a much steeper drop-off before settling at close to 0.

4.4   Varying Octave Model

Similar to case of the constant octave models, we trained 170 1v1 models for both the CIFAR10 and ILSVRC2012 datasets. In the case of ILSVRC2012, we hand selected 10 classes from the dataset to test on. For the more complex models, we chose to use the ResNet model [9] for both the ILSVRC2012 and CIFAR10 datasets. On the *Right* side of Fig. 2, we present the octave resonance for the test classes in ILSVRC2012, on the left side, we present 10 class octave resonance from ILSVRC2012, while in Table 2, we provide numeric values for the octave resonance for the CIFAR10 classes.

Table 2. CIFAR10 Class octave resonance

Class	0.01	0.05	0.1	0.15	0.2	0.25	0.5	0.75	1.0	1.25	1.5	1.75	2.0	3.0	4.0	5.0	6.0
Bird	0.00	0.00	0.00	0.00	0.00	0.00	0.35	0.99	0.99	0.96	0.95	0.95	0.90	0.64	0.47	0.33	0.30
Cat	0.00	0.00	0.00	0.00	0.00	0.10	0.35	0.98	0.95	1.00	1.00	1.00	0.95	0.62	0.20	0.12	0.14
Deer	0.00	0.00	0.00	0.00	0.00	0.14	0.95	0.98	1.00	0.99	1.00	1.00	0.99	0.94	0.69	0.43	0.29
Dog	0.00	0.00	0.00	0.00	0.00	0.30	0.85	0.92	1.00	1.00	0.95	0.94	0.88	0.84	0.59	0.48	0.25
Frog	0.00	0.00	0.00	0.00	0.00	0.15	0.50	0.98	1.00	1.00	1.00	0.96	0.94	0.88	0.77	0.63	0.50
Horse	0.00	0.00	0.00	0.00	0.00	0.00	0.45	0.97	0.98	1.00	1.00	0.99	0.95	0.72	0.30	0.15	0.09
Ship	0.00	0.00	0.00	0.00	0.00	0.01	0.12	0.19	0.88	0.94	0.99	0.99	0.85	0.57	0.40	0.33	0.33
Truck	0.00	0.00	0.00	0.01	0.04	0.00	0.85	0.94	0.98	0.94	0.92	0.80	0.66	0.40	0.33	0.16	0.07

Class by class octave resonance for the CIFAR10 dataset.

It is notable that compared to the single octave datasets, the applicability peak lasts substantially longer and the drop-off for upscaling is much less drastic and more gradual. The opposite is true in the down scale direction. While the mode does persist longer for the down scaling, the drop-off is extreme, almost as if there is a point where no feature can fit that octave. Another cause for the rapid applicability drop-off is the 0 padding. Unlike the constant octave models, the training datasets images are RGB and not binary. The zero padding adds an unnatural artifact to the image that could be the cause of the applicability drop.

One of the more interesting behaviors, that we can see on the *Left* side of Fig. 1, is that the highest applicability is not centered around the original octave. This behavior can be best explained by looking at the applicability of an individual image. Because the scale of the inputs varies between all the images, the model will learn the features at the most common or important octaves. This will partially exclude some octaves from the feature set reducing the applicability for individual images on the periphery of the feature space.

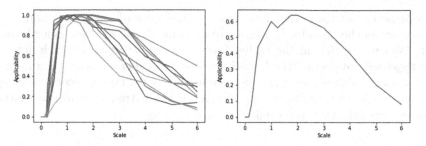

Fig. 2. *Left* 10 class octave resonance from ILSVRC2012. *Right* Model octave resonance for the ILSVRC2012 dataset.

4.5   Octave Resonance of Unknown Classes

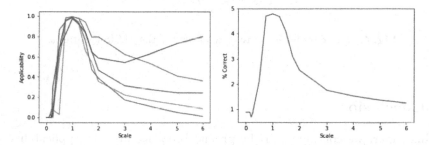

Fig. 3. *Left* octave resonance for unknown classes that only the output layer was trained on. *Right* Combined octave resonance across all unknown classes.

It is also valuable to observe how octaves react to classes that the features are not necessarily learned for. In Fig. 3, we present the applicability for classes that the model was not originally trained on. We split the MNIST and Bangla numeral datasets in half, and trained a neural network on the first half, which we will refer to the known set. We can see that comparing the unknown graphs (Fig. 3) to those in Fig. 1, the octave resonance is still centered around 1, the base applicability, as expected. The peak in the unknown set is much smaller with the applicability drop-off much more severe than for the known classes. Because the lower layers were frozen, the unknown classes are fitting themselves to features that might not necessarily apply perfectly to them.

4.6   Layer Octave Resonance

It has been shown that the applicability of earlier layers in a neural network is high for almost all classes in a domain, known or unknown [6]. Generic features are represented at the earlier layers of a neural network and have more applicability across the domain. In Fig. 4, we measure the octave resonance layer by layer. We can see that in the earlier layers, the applicability for each octave is close together, supporting the hypothesis that the generic features can resonate across octaves. The octave resonance diminishes as the layers become more specific, where, by the last layer the octaves on the extremes have substantially lower applicability than the original octave.

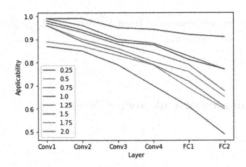

Fig. 4. Layer by layer octave resonance for the MNIST dataset.

5   Conclusion

In this paper, we continued on the ground breaking work in applicability [6] by computing, to the best of our knowledge, the first ever metric for octave resonance in neural networks using applicability. We demonstrated how shifting the octaves of images can cause considerable drop off in applicability even when the image is still recognizable to the human eye. We studied the resonance for neural networks that were trained on both one octave or many, and showed how the octave resonance is much more stable in the varying octave model. Lastly, we showed how octave resonance changes layer by layer. We showed that, consistent with layer applicability and transferability, the lower layers with generic features are more scale invariant than the higher layers.

References

1. Basu, S., Ganguly, S., Mukhopadhyay, S., DiBiano, R., Karki, M., Nemani, R.: Deepsat: a learning framework for satellite imagery. In: Proceedings of the 23rd SIGSPATIAL International Conference on Advances in Geographic Information Systems, p. 37. ACM (2015)
2. Basu, S., et al.: Learning sparse feature representations using probabilistic quadtrees and deep belief nets. Neural Process. Lett. **45**(3), 855–867 (2017)
3. Basu, S., et al.: Deep neural networks for texture classification – a theoretical analysis. Neural Netw. **97**, 173–182 (2018)

4. Bhattacharya, U., Chaudhuri, B.B.: Handwritten numeral databases of indian scripts and multistage recognition of mixed numerals. IEEE Trans. Pattern Anal. Mach. Intell. **31**(3), 444–457 (2008)
5. Bhattacharya, U., Shridhar, M., Parui, S.K., Sen, P., Chaudhuri, B.: Offline recognition of handwritten bangla characters: an efficient two-stage approach. Pattern Anal. Appl. **15**(4), 445–458 (2012)
6. Collier, E., DiBiano, R., Mukhopadhyay, S.: Cactusnets: layer applicability as a metric for transfer learning. arXiv preprint arXiv:1804.07846 (2018)
7. Collier, E., et al.: Progressively growing generative adversarial networks for high resolution semantic segmentation of satellite images. In: Tong, H., Li, Z.J., Zhu, F., Yu, J. (eds.) 2018 IEEE International Conference on Data Mining Workshops, ICDM Workshops, Singapore, 17–20 November 2018, pp. 763–769. IEEE (2018)
8. Glorot, X., Bordes, A., Bengio, Y.: Domain adaptation for large-scale sentiment classification: a deep learning approach. In: Proceedings of the 28th International Conference on Machine Learning (ICML-2011), pp. 513–520 (2011)
9. He, K., Zhang, X., Ren, S., Sun, J.: Identity mappings in deep residual networks. In: Leibe, B., Matas, J., Sebe, N., Welling, M. (eds.) ECCV 2016. LNCS, vol. 9908, pp. 630–645. Springer, Cham (2016). https://doi.org/10.1007/978-3-319-46493-0_38
10. Hinton, G.E., Salakhutdinov, R.R.: Reducing the dimensionality of data with neural networks. Science **313**(5786), 504–507 (2006)
11. Krizhevsky, A., Hinton, G., et al.: Learning multiple layers of features from tiny images (2009)
12. Krizhevsky, A., Sutskever, I., Hinton, G.E.: Imagenet classification with deep convolutional neural networks. In: Advances in Neural Information Processing Systems, pp. 1097–1105 (2012)
13. LeCun, Y., Bottou, L., Bengio, Y., Haffner, P.: Gradient-based learning applied to document recognition. Proc. IEEE **86**(11), 2278–2324 (1998)
14. Liu, Q., et al.: Deepsat v2: feature augmented convolutional neural nets for satellite image classification. Remote Sens. Lett. **11**(2), 156–165 (2020)
15. Liu, Q., Collier, E., Mukhopadhyay, S.: PCGAN-CHAR: progressively trained classifier generative adversarial networks for classification of noisy handwritten bangla characters. In: Jatowt, A., Maeda, A., Syn, S.Y. (eds.) ICADL 2019. LNCS, vol. 11853, pp. 3–15. Springer, Cham (2019). https://doi.org/10.1007/978-3-030-34058-2_1
16. Liu, Q., Mukhopadhyay, S.: Unsupervised learning using pretrained CNN and associative memory bank. In: 2018 International Joint Conference on Neural Networks, IJCNN 2018, Rio de Janeiro, Brazil, 8–13 July 2018, pp. 1–8. IEEE (2018)
17. Pan, S.J., Yang, Q.: A survey on transfer learning. IEEE Trans. Knowl. Data Eng. **22**(10), 1345–1359 (2010)
18. Yosinski, J., Clune, J., Bengio, Y., Lipson, H.: How transferable are features in deep neural networks? In: Advances in Neural Information Processing Systems, pp. 3320–3328 (2014)
19. Zhu, Y., et al.: Heterogeneous transfer learning for image classification. In: AAAI (2011)

Machine Learning

A Derivative-Free Method for Quantum Perceptron Training in Multi-layered Neural Networks

Tariq M. Khan$^{(\boxtimes)}$ and Antonio Robles-Kelly

Faculty of Science, Engineering and the Built Environment, Deakin University,
Waurn Ponds, VIC 3216, Australia
{tariq.khan,antonio.robles-kelly}@deakin.edu.au

Abstract. In this paper, we present a gradient-free approach for training multi-layered neural networks based upon quantum perceptrons. Here, we depart from the classical perceptron and the elemental operations on quantum bits, *i.e.* qubits, so as to formulate the problem in terms of quantum perceptrons. We then make use of measurable operators to define the states of the network in a manner consistent with a Markov process. This yields a Dirac–Von Neumann formulation consistent with quantum mechanics. Moreover, the formulation presented here has the advantage of having a computational efficiency devoid of the number of layers in the network. This, paired with the natural efficiency of quantum computing, can imply a significant improvement in efficiency, particularly for deep networks. Finally, but not least, the developments here are quite general in nature since the approach presented here can also be used for quantum-inspired neural networks implemented on conventional computers.

Keywords: Quantum perceptron · Derivative-free training methods for quantum-inspired neural networks · Measurable operators

1 Introduction

Quantum computing algorithms often exhibit significant increases in efficiency, in some cases exponentially, compared to their classical counterparts. This is particularly relevant to machine learning, which has had a growing importance in recent years. This is since machine learning methods tend to be computationally intensive. Thus, recently, there have been numerous research studies aiming to investigate the promise of quantum computers for machine learning [1–4].

Moreover, it has been suggested that quantum computers may be an ideal platform for the implementation of artificial neural networks [3]. In recent years ongoing attempts have been made to implement artificial neural networks (ANN) in quantum computers. Grover et al. [5] attempted to emulate quantum computation on classical computers to perform search quadratically faster than its

© Springer Nature Switzerland AG 2020
H. Yang et al. (Eds.): ICONIP 2020, CCIS 1333, pp. 241–250, 2020.
https://doi.org/10.1007/978-3-030-63823-8_29

classic equivalent in an unordered dataset. The computational power of quantum computing in terms of efficiency and effectiveness for ANNs as compared to that of classical computers has also been explored in [2]. Nonetheless, the incorporation of quantum computation into ANNs is still an open and challenging research direction [4].

This is further compelled by the fact that deep learning is an algorithmic class within the wider category of machine learning algorithms with their own practical and architectural properties. Deep nets are used primarily to classify patterns on a specific data set and/or to produce new data that imitates these patterns. At heart, there are three main components in neural network algorithms. Firstly, the model, comprised by a parametric functional hypothesis class, typically set up in a network of layered composition of simpler parametric functions. Secondly, a cost function, which determines how well the prediction based upon the input data fits a specific hypothesis. Thirdly, the optimizer. This is an algorithmic technique used to minimise the loss function based upon the parameters in the network. This is often done by backward error propagation, also known as the backpropagation algorithm. This is at the core of ANN training.

Moreover, the cost (error) function of ANNs is often purely a function of the network's output. The backpropagation algorithm is the most common method in both, quantum and classical computing to train ANNs [6]. This is used to train the network using the cost function gradient (in relation to the network parameters), beginning with the output layer going layer-by-layer towards the input one. In 1986, the backpropagation algorithm was proposed by Rumelhart and Mcllelland to solve the non-linear continuous function weight adjustment problems in the area of the neural multi-layer feedforward network as a back error method [7].

Since the development of the back-propagation method for neural networks, a lot of research has been carried out on the choice of activation function, design of structure parameters and characterise the loss function. A lot of research has also been carried out to improve the efficiency of the back-propagation methods in neural networks. Sun et al. [8] have developed an improved prediction model of back-propagation neural network and quantitatively researched related parameters. Xiao *et al.* [9] present a short-term load forecast method for Neural Network Prediction.

Here we note that, although the back-propagation algorithm is the most widely used one in artificial neural networks in both classical as well as quantum domains, it does exhibit the following drawbacks:

- It can fall into local extremum points if there are multiple points on the loss space with zero gradient [10].
- Its speed of convergence is dependent on two aspects. Firstly, the learning rate. Secondly, the magnitude of the gradient associated to the excitation function [11]. This can result in slow convergence rates. This is further complicated by the fact that the magnitude of the learning rate is not a straightforward parameter to set. If the learning rate is too large, the back propagation

solver will often suffer from "over shooting". If the learning rate is too small, the network may fail to converge at all.

– Its computational complexity is dependent on the network structure, increasing with the number of hidden layers and the number of neurons per layer.

In this paper, we turn our attention to the evaluation of the quantum perceptron as a means to tackle the drawbacks above in the training of neural networks. To do this, we depart from the concept of a single quantum bit, *i.e.* a qubit, and examine the strategies for evaluating the equivalent in quantum computing of the perceptron in machine learning. We then focus on measurable operators to model the evolution of an artificial neural network as the action of a unitary transformation on the network's present firing states. This has the advantage that, for training an artificial neural network, the forward pass is given by a measurement of the transformed state whereas the training can be effected using a gradient-free strategy whose complexity is devoid of the number of layers in the network. This, together with the natural efficiency of quantum neural nets, is a promising trait that can greatly speed up both training and testing of neural networks in quantum computing. This unitary transformation would, of course, have to include information on the probabilities of transition between each basic state.

2   Background

In this section, we briefly introduce the concepts of quantum computing that are necessary for the remainder of the paper. For a detailed introduction on quantum computing, we would like to remit the interested reader to [3].

2.1   Quantum Bits

As mentioned earlier, we depart from the concept of qubit. A quantum bit or qubit can be represented by a linear combination of two base states using the "Bra-ket" notation, *i.e.* the pairing of a linear function and complex vector in a Hilbert space, as follows $|0\rangle = [1,0]^T$ and $|1\rangle = [0,1]^T$, where, as usual, $[\cdot]^T$ is a column vector given by the transpose of a row vector. These are used to define the qubit as $|\psi\rangle = a|0\rangle + b|1\rangle = [\psi_0, \psi_1]^T$.

In the expression above, ψ_0 and ψ_1 are complex numbers, usually called probability amplitudes in the literature. This treatment leads, in a straightforward manner to the natural extension to a multi-qubit expression. To represent a system with multiple qubits, a tensor product, which yields a matrix representation can be employed without any loss of generality. To illustrate this, consider, for instance, the two-qubit case where the quantum bits are given by $|\psi\rangle = [\psi_0, \psi_1]^T$ and $|\phi\rangle = [\phi_0, \phi_1]^T$. Using this notation, their tensor product is given by $|\psi\rangle \otimes |\phi\rangle = [\psi_0\phi_0, \psi_0\phi_1, \psi_1\phi_0, \psi_1\phi_1]^T$. From this product, it becomes evident that the resultant output is a four-dimensional vector. Moreover, this can be extended to any pair of vector in an m and n dimensions, which would yield yet another $(m \times n)$-dimensional vector.

2.2 Classical Perceptron

Recall that a perceptron is a binary classification algorithm for supervised learning, which is the simplest type of neural network. Let the ith instance of the dataset be the input vector $\mathbf{x}_i$ to the perceptron. The output of the perceptron is based upon the vector $\mathbf{y}$ whose j^{th} entry is governed by $\langle \mathbf{w}_j, \mathbf{x}_i \rangle + b_j$, where b_j is a constant, $i.e.$ the bias, $\mathbf{w}_j$ is a vector of weights and $\langle \cdot, \cdot \rangle$ is the dot product as usual. The output of the perceptron is then given by a function $y_i = f(\mathbf{y})$ where each vector of weights $\mathbf{w}_j$ corresponds to a neuron. Thus, the output for the input instance $\mathbf{x}_i$ is given by

$$y_i = f\left(\sum_{j=1}^{N} \langle \mathbf{w}_j, \mathbf{x}_i \rangle + b_j \right) \tag{1}$$

where $f(\cdot)$ is known as the activation function, $\mathbf{W}$ is a matrix of weights whose j^{th} row corresponds to $\mathbf{w}_j^T$ and $\mathbf{b}$ is a vector whose entry indexed j is given by b_j.

3 Derivative-Free Training of a Quantum Perceptron

As mentioned earlier, the qubit is often represented using the Bra-ket notation. In this manner, following the notion that $\mathbf{x}_i$ can be represented using the notation $|x_1\rangle$, consider the training set written in the form $\{(|x_1\rangle, |y_1\rangle), \ldots, (|x_N\rangle, |y_N\rangle)\}$ where $|x_j\rangle$ is an input and $|y_j\rangle$ is the corresponding label.

Recall that, in order to obtain the weight vector $|w_j\rangle$, as suggested in [12], a tensor product can be used, which yields $W_i = |y_i\rangle \otimes \langle x_i|$. After calculating the vector of weights using the expression above, these can be added to get the final weight vector given by $\hat{W} = \sum_{i=1}^{N} W_i$. Note that the matrix $\hat{W}$ is, in general, not unitary. Thus, to preserve the quantum properties requiring a unitary matrix, $\hat{w}$ is decomposed into three unitary matrices using the singular value decomposition (SVD) given by $\hat{\mathbf{W}} = \mathbf{U\Sigma V}^*$.

As noted by Liu $et\ al.$ [12], the diagonal matrix $\mathbf{\Sigma}$ can be substituted, without any loss of generality, with a unitary matrix with ones in diagonal and zeros elsewhere, $i.e.$ an identity matrix. This yields, using the notation commonly employed in quantum machine learning texts where the unitary matrix $\mathbf{U}$ is denoted by $\hat{F}$, the quantum perceptron output given by $\hat{Y} = \hat{F}|x_j\rangle$. Here, we follow Zak and Williams [13], who viewed an n-neuron network as a dynamic system that obeys the differential equation given by

$$\tau_i \frac{\partial}{\partial t} Z_i = -Z_i + f\left(\sum_{j=1}^{N} W_j Z_j \right) \tag{2}$$

where τ_i is a positive time constant, Z_i is the activation of the ith neuron and W_j are synaptic weights analogue to those elaborated upon previously that feed the activation function of the neuron indexed j to the activation function $f(\cdot)$.

Equation 2 can be used to formulate the update of the quantum perceptron weights as follows

$$W^{new} = M\left\{U\hat{Y} - W^{old}\right\}$$ (3)

where W^{old} is the current, *i.e.* old, weights, U is a unitary matrix that acts on the state vector $\hat{Y}$, M is a measurable operator that project states of $U\hat{Y}$ into some eigenstate of M. The use of measurable operators naturally provides a link to statistics and quantum measurements. The Eq. 3 shows the update of the perceptron weights by using the state vector projected upon U (the orthonormal basis spanned by the SVD of the sum of outer products in $\hat{W} = \sum_{i=1}^{N} W_i$).

4 Measurable Operators

In this section, we examine closer the role of the measurable operator M. This is due to the fact that it can open-up several opportunities as related to the design of neural networks, specially as related to approaches elsewhere in the literature that employ backpropagation methods for training. Note that $U\hat{Y}$ can be viewed as a representation of a sequence of measurable states that define a Markov process with a transition probability matrix. Moreover, Quantum probability is a non-commutative extension of classical probability which represents random variables as self-adjoint operators that act on a complex Hilbert space whereby the underlying probability is measured by a unitary vector.

Furthermore, note that M is, by definition, a self-adjoint operator. In quantum mechanics, self-adjoint operators form a Dirac–Von Neumann formulation. Self-adjoint operators represent the physical observables such as spin, momentum, angular momentum and position on a Hilbert space. Recall that, by definition, probability distributions are non-negative and normalised to unity. Since self-adjoint operators are unitarily equivalent to real-valued multiplication operators, they can be easily generalised to theoretically unbounded operators on infinite-dimensional spaces. Here, we will also require M to be hermitian. This is important since then, by definition, has an orthonormal set of eignevectors $|\xi\rangle$ with real eigenvales λ_i.

Note that, if the elements of U are appropriately chosen, then any desired Markov chain can be simulated without a random number generator. This is possible due to the inherent randomness of quantum measurement processes. The modulus square of the probability amplitude represents the probability of a network in the jth transitions to the ith state. This can be expressed using the following expression

$$\Pr\left[Y^{new} = |i\rangle Y^{old} = |j\rangle\right] = ||u_{ij}||^2$$ (4)

where u_{ij} is the entry indexed i, j of U and we have used the notation Y^{new} and Y^{old} to denote the current and previous states of the network. It is worth noting in passing that, since U is a unitary matrix, there will be appropriate constraints on the possible values of $||u_{ij}||^2$ so as to avoid divergent behavior. We remit the interested reader to [13] for further reading on this.

5   Algorithm Properties

5.1   Complexity

It is worth noting that the complexity of the computations above will be far more efficient in a quantum computer than running an equivalent simulation on a classical computer. The reason being that quantum computers have the potential to be exponentially larger than classical computers, with the capacity to represent random stochastic states naturally [13].

Also, note the SVD is exponentially faster in quantum computers than on classical ones [14]. Rebentrost *et al.* [14] proposed quantum-SVD for non-sparse low rank matrices with complexity $O(poly \log N)$. Gyongyosi *et al.* [15] proposed an algorithm for quantum-SVD with complexity $O(N \log N)$. This complexity is similar to the standard Fourier transform complexity of $O(N \log N)$ [16]. On a classical computer, singular value decomposition of non-sparse low-rank matrices has a complexity, in general, and without further structural assumptions, of $O(N^3)$ [14]. Further, in quantum computing, the multiplication is much faster than the classical computing. The space complexity of Karatsuba multiplication for numbers of n bits in quantum spans from $O(n^{1.427})$ to $O(n)$ while maintaining a gate complexity of $O(n^{\log_2 3})$ [17], where log_2 denotes the binary logarithm. This is achieved by avoiding the need to store and compute intermediate results [17].

In terms of the actual quantum speedup, recall this is often either exponential or strong exponential [18]. In exponential quantum speedups, a quantum computer can solve a problem exponentially faster than a classical algorithm based upon the computational cost of the best known classical algorithm. In strong exponential quantum speedups, however, the reference is the classical complexity of the method itself. The method presented here can be measured in terms of a strong exponential speedup on the SVD given by

$$S_2 = \frac{classical\,complexity}{quantum\,complexity} = \frac{O(N^3)}{O(N \log N)} = O\left(\frac{N^2}{\log N}\right) \tag{5}$$

Note that the main difference between exponential and strong exponential speedups resides in the fact that computational cost is ever decreasing due to efficiency increments in memory, data structures, etc. For strong exponential speedups, it can always be asserted that a quantum computer can solve a problem exponentially faster than a classical algorithm. This is important since quantum feedback networks are exponentially faster than those on classical computers, but they can never attain a strong exponential quantum speedup [19]. This leaves as the only avenue to obtain strong exponential quantum speedup in quantum neural network as that of using evaluation strategies with strong exponential speedups. Moreover, despite quantum neural networks employing backpropagation methods can take advantage of these faster multiplication and efficient integration requirements, the evaluation strategy presented earlier replaces multiplication with a subtraction operation in its backward step. This is a significant improvement with respect to backpropagation, specially for large, very deep networks.

To appreciate this more clearly, recall that, in quantum computing, if the network consists of only one perceptron, then the complexity of our evaluation strategy presented earlier is consistent with that of back-propagation. This only applies for the one perceptron case since, when the number of hidden layers of the network increases, then the complexity of the back-propagation will increase significantly. On the other hand, the complexity of the evaluation strategy presented earlier will not increase with respect to the number of layers in the network. Therefore, the developments presented earlier open-up the door for the efficient evaluation and training of complex, multi-layered networks that can be prohibitively costly computationally with back-propagation approaches. As quantum computing also provides space-complexity advantages over classical methods, increasing the number of hidden layers does not impose large memory constraints. For instance, a quantum associative memory has an exponential gain in storage capacity as compared to classical associative memories [20].

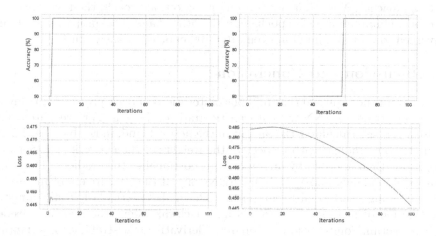

Fig. 1. Simulation results for a perceptron trained using our approach (left-hand column) and backpropagation (right-hand column). The top row show the error for the XOr gate whereas the bottom row shows the loss. In all the plots, the independent axis corresponds to the training index.

5.2 Simulation Results

We have followed standard practice for the proof of concept by implementing the XOr. This is since the XOr is a universal non-linear gate which is sufficient for all logic operations on a quantum computer that can be used to construct arbitrary unitary transformations. This is a classical problem in artificial neural network research. The problem is that of, given two binary inputs, predict the output of an exclusive or gate. An XOr gate returns a false value (a zero) if the inputs are equal and true (unity) if the inputs are not. In this case, we have used this simulation in order to illustrate the convergence rate and loss value of a quantum perceptron network with a hidden layer with two neurons and an $L - 1$ loss function trained using both, our approach and backpropagation.

In order to provide a plain field for training both networks, we have employed a sigmoid as the measurable operator in Eq. 3. In our implementation in order to optimize connection weights we chose the average error as an objective function. For measuring accuracy, 0.5 is used as a cut-off value between zero and one. Both networks are trained for 100 iterations, whereby, at each of these, the inputs are generated randomly. At each iteration, we verify the output with another, randomly generated testing instance pair of inputs. In the top row of Fig. 1 we show the error obtained using the instance input pair for both networks as a function of iteration number. The left-hand panel in Fig. 1 shows that backpropagation achieves 100% accuracy, i.e. delivers the correct XOr output for the corresponding inputs, after 58 iterations. Our method achieves the same accuracy after 2 iterations. Moreover, in the bottom row of Fig. 1 we show the loss function for both approaches. Note that, by training using our approach, the loss converged to a local minimum after 3 epochs. On the other hand, backpropagation didn't converged to a local minimum even after 100 epochs, as shown in Fig. 1.

6   Discussion and Conclusion

Note that it is not unusual that millions of iterations of back-propagation may be required to train an ANN with stochastic gradient descent. For every iteration, the forward pass calculates the output of the network and, in the backward pass, calculates the gradient with respect to the weights of the network. The network weights are then updated by an amount proportional to the gradient. This computational demands makes training ANNs one of the key drivers of increasing demand for high performance computing. This makes particularly compelling the investigation of methods for forward and backward steps that can be speeded up by quantum computations. Moreover, derivative-free strategies in quantum computing can remove some of these steps altogether. One of the advantages of using strategies like the one presented here is that they require a forward pass but does not involve a back-propagation step. This makes these methods 2 to 3 times faster than those based upon back-propagation in a traditional computer. Moreover, an additional advantage is that, by using these evaluation strategies, a large number of non-differentiable excitation functions can be explored.

This also applies to the objective functions of quantum networks, which can potentially be discontinuous or even non-compact in neural networks trained using back-propagation methods. The strategies such as that presented here can also be very effective when solutions are known to be within an elliptical domain, i.e. around a fixed point. Moreover, gradient descent, despite effective, can be inefficient, particularly if the choice of starting point is poor, whereby the training can easily converges to a local minimum which may be far from an ideal solution.

Quantum-inspired neural networks (QiNNs) and Quantum computing-based neural networks have been shown to be more effective and efficient as compared to conventional ANNs [21]. In addition, QiNN models are not limited to solely those that can only be implemented on quantum computers, rather there has been renewed interest in methods that can take advantage of QiNN traits while being implemented on conventional computers [21].

References

1. Lloyd, S., Mohseni, M., Rebentrost, P.: Quantum principal component analysis. Nat. Phys. **10**, 631–633 (2014)
2. Jeswal, S.K., Chakraverty, S.: Recent developments and applications in quantum neural network: a review. Arch. Comput. Methods Eng. **26**(4), 793–807 (2019)
3. Biamonte, J., Wittek, P., Pancotti, N., Rebentrost, P., Wiebe, N., Lloyd, S.: Quantum machine learning. Nature **13**, 195–202 (2017)
4. Chen, J., Wang, L., Charbon, E.: A quantum-implementable neural network model. Quantum Inf. Process. **16**(10), 1–24 (2017). https://doi.org/10.1007/s11128-017-1692-x
5. Grover, L.K.: A fast quantum mechanical algorithm for database search. In: Proceedings of the Twenty-Eighth Annual ACM Symposium on Theory of Computing, series STOC 1996, New York, NY, USA, pp. 212–219. Association for Computing Machinery (1996)
6. Wang, Y., Niu, D., Ji, L.: Short-term power load forecasting based on IVL-BP neural network technology. Syst. Eng. Procedia **4**, 168–174 (2012)
7. Rumelhart, D.E., Hinton, G.E., Williams, R.J.: Learning representations by back-propagating errors. Nature **323**, 533–536 (1986)
8. Sun, Z., Wang, X., Zhang, J., Yang, H.: Prediction and control of equiaxed α in near-β forging of TA15 Ti-alloy based on BP neural network: for purpose of tri-modal microstructure. Mater. Sci. Eng. A **591**, 18–25 (2014)
9. Xiao, Z., Ye, S.J., Zhong, B., Sun, C.X.: BP neural network with rough set for short term load forecasting. Expert Syst. Appl. **36**, 273–279 (2009)
10. Zhang, Y., Ruan, G.: Bernoulli neural network with weights directly determined and with the number of hidden- layer neurons automatically determined. In: Yu, W., He, H., Zhang, N. (eds.) ISNN 2009. LNCS, vol. 5551, pp. 36–45. Springer, Heidelberg (2009). https://doi.org/10.1007/978-3-642-01507-6_5
11. Xu, B., Zhang, H., Wang, Z., Wang, H., Zhang, Y.: Model and algorithm of BP neural network based on expanded multichain quantum optimization. Math. Prob. Eng. **2015** (2015)
12. Liu, W., Gao, P., Wang, Y., Yu, W., Zhang, M.: A unitary weights based one-iteration quantum perceptron algorithm for non-ideal training sets. IEEE Access **7**, 36 854–36 865 (2019)
13. Zak, M., Williams, C.P.: Quantum neural nets. Int. J. Theor. Phys. **37**(2), 651–684 (1998)
14. Rebentrost, P., Steffens, A., Marvian, I., Lloyd, S.: Quantum singular-value decomposition of nonsparse low-rank matrices. Phys. Rev. A **97**, 012327 (2018)
15. Gyongyosi, L., Imre, S.: An improvement in quantum Fourier transform (2012)
16. Eldar, Y.C., Forney, G.D.: Optimal tight frames and quantum measurement. IEEE Trans. Inf. Theory **48**(3), 599–610 (2002)
17. Gidney, C.: Asymptotically efficient quantum Karatsuba multiplication (2019)
18. Papageorgiou, A., Traub, F.J.: Measures of quantum computing speedup. Phys. Rev. A **88**(2) (2013)

19. Kerenidis, I., Landman, J., Prakash, A.: Quantum algorithms for deep convolutional neural networks. In: International Conference on Learning Representations (2019)
20. Trugenberger, C.A.: Probabilistic quantum memories. Phys. Rev. Lett. **87**(6), 067901 (2001)
21. Sagheer, A., Zidan, M., Abdelsamea, M.M.: A novel autonomous perceptron model for pattern classification applications. Entropy **21**(8), 1–24 (2019)

A Homogeneous-Heterogeneous Ensemble of Classifiers

Anh Vu Luong[1], Trung Hieu Vu[2], Phuong Minh Nguyen[3], Nang Van Pham[4],
John McCall[5], Alan Wee-Chung Liew[1], and Tien Thanh Nguyen[5(✉)]

[1] School of Information and Communication Technology, Griffith University,
Brisbane, Australia
[2] School of Electronics and Telecommunications,
Hanoi University of Science and Technology, Hanoi, Vietnam
[3] Department of Environmental Technology, Faculty of Environmental Sciences,
VNU University of Science, Vietnam National University, Hanoi, Vietnam
[4] School of Electrical Engineering, Hanoi University of Science and Technology,
Hanoi, Vietnam
[5] School of Computing, Robert Gordon University, Aberdeen, UK
t.nguyen11@rgu.ac.uk

Abstract. In this study, we introduce an ensemble system by combining homogeneous ensemble and heterogeneous ensemble into a single framework. Based on the observation that the projected data is significantly different from the original data as well as each other after using random projections, we construct the homogeneous module by applying random projections on the training data to obtain the new training sets. In the heterogeneous module, several learning algorithms will train on the new training sets to generate the base classifiers. We propose four combining algorithms based on Sum Rule and Majority Vote Rule for the proposed ensemble. Experiments on some popular datasets confirm that the proposed ensemble method is better than several well-known benchmark algorithms proposed framework has great flexibility when applied to real-world applications. The proposed framework has great flexibility when applied to real-world applications by using any techniques that make rich training data for the homogeneous module, as well as using any set of learning algorithms for the heterogeneous module.

Keywords: Ensemble method · Multiple classifiers · Combining classifiers · Random projection · Ensemble learning · Combining methods

1 Introduction

Classification is one of the most studied machine learning problems. Given a set of labeled observations called training set, classification algorithms exploit the knowledge from the features-label relationship so as to assign a class label to an unlabeled sample. Although many learning algorithms have been proposed, no algorithm is known to perform the best for all problems. A popular solution is to combine multiple algorithms in an ensemble system in order to achieve better

© Springer Nature Switzerland AG 2020
H. Yang et al. (Eds.): ICONIP 2020, CCIS 1333, pp. 251–259, 2020.
https://doi.org/10.1007/978-3-030-63823-8_30

performance than using any single algorithm. In ensemble learning, training different learning algorithms on the original training set to generate the base classifiers is known as heterogeneous ensemble, while training only one learning algorithm on many different training sets obtained from the original training data to generate the base classifiers is known as homogeneous ensemble [1].

In this study, we propose an ensemble system by combining homogeneous and heterogeneous ensembles into a single framework. Our work is based on the observation that random projection, a data transformation method, can create different projected data from the original data [2], thus making the new data available for many different learning algorithms to train base classifiers. In the proposed framework, the set of random projections is applied to the original training data to generate the new training sets (homogeneous module). Different learning algorithms then train on the new projected data to obtain base classifiers (heterogeneous module). The outputs of all the base classifiers are combined to get the final collaborated prediction for the sample. For the combining algorithm, we introduce four methods based on the two popular combining rules: Sum Rule and Majority Vote Rule [3]. In the first two combining algorithms, Sum Rule or Majority Vote Rule is directly applied to the outputs of all base classifiers. Meanwhile, in the remaining two combining algorithms, the two rules are combined by conducting the Sum Rule on the predictions associated with each random projection or associated with each learning algorithm first and then applying Majority Vote Rule on the outputs of the Sum Rule.

The structure of this paper is as follows. Section 2 presents background and related work in the ensemble system. Section 3 introduces a new ensemble framework consisted of a combination of homogeneous and heterogeneous ensemble and four combining methods to combine the outputs of the proposed ensemble. Experimental studies are presented in Sect. 4 in which we describe the settings for the experiments and the comparisons and discussions based on the experimental results. The conclusion is presented in Sect. 5.

2 Background and Related Work

In this section, we briefly introduce research approaches related to the ensemble system. First, there are approaches focusing on designing new architectures for the ensemble system. For example in [4], Zhang et al. used both random subspace and bootstrap sampling technique on the original training data to obtain the new training sets. The k Nearest Neighbor (kNN) algorithm is trained on these new training sets to obtain the EoC. In [5], an ensemble learning-based deep model was proposed in which learning model includes several layers of ensemble of classifiers. One layer receives input training data created by previous layer and then generates input training data for its next layer.

Besides, several combining algorithms have been introduced for classifiers' output aggregation as the better replacement for traditional combiners e.g. Sum Rule and Majority Vote. Nguyen et al. [6] used information granules to model predictions of the base classifiers in the form of vectors of intervals called granule prototypes. In this method, the combining algorithms were constructed by considering the distance between the predictions for a test sample and the granule prototypes. Kuncheva et al. [7] associated each class by a representation called decision template which is the average of the meta-data of training instances that belong to a class. The class that minimizes the distance between the corresponding decision template and the meta-data of the test sample is the final prediction. Nguyen et al. [8] proposed a Bayesian-based combining method in which the posterior probability that a sample belongs to a class label is computed by using the likelihood and the prior distribution. The likelihood distribution is approximated by the multivariate Gaussian.

Several modifications meanwhile focused on improving the performance of existing ensemble systems. Some approaches search for the weights of the base classifiers in the aggregation [2]. Several improvements for Boosting-based ensemble approach are RotBoost by combining Rotation Forest and AdaBoost in a single framework [9] and TotalBoost by adapting the constraints on the edges of all past hypotheses [10].

3   Proposed Ensemble System

In this study, we construct a new ensemble system by combining the homogeneous ensemble and the heterogeneous ensemble in a single framework. Briefly, we generate the new training sets from the original training data (the homogeneous module) and then train several different learning algorithms on these new training sets to obtain the base classifiers (the heterogeneous module). A class label is assigned to a test sample by combining the outputs of these base classifiers. By doing this, we can get rich diversity from the two types of ensembles: diversity from using different training sets and diversity from using different learning algorithms. Therefore, this is expected to perform better than either of the heterogeneous and homogeneous ensemble methods. There are two questions concerning the proposed ensemble (i) How to generate the new training sets used in the training of different learning algorithms to obtain the base classifiers? (ii) How to aggregate the base classifiers' outputs?

3.1   The Homogeneous-Heterogeneous Ensemble System

We use random projection [11, 12] to generate the new training sets since the projected data is significantly different compared to the original data [2]. Random projection is a projection from a p-dimensional space $\mathbb{R}^p$ (up-space) to a q-dimensional space $\mathbb{R}^q$ (down-space): $T : \mathbb{R}^p \rightarrow \mathbb{R}^q : \mathcal{D}_j = T[\mathcal{D}] \subset \mathbb{R}^q$. The projection T can be represented in the form of matrix R in which each element of the matrix is generated according to a specified random distribution.

During the training phase, K random matrices of size $(p \times q)$ denoted by $R_j (j = 1, ..., K)$ are generated. A random matrix is simply obtained by $R_j = \{r\}$ of size $(p \times q)$, where r are random variables such that $E(r) = 0$ and $Var(r) = 1$. After that, K new training sets $\mathcal{D}_j$ in the down-space (of size $(|\mathcal{D}| \times q)$ are generated from the original training set $\mathcal{D}$ (of size $|\mathcal{D}| \times p$) through the projection R_j from $\mathcal{D}$ to $\mathcal{D}_j$ which is given by:

$$\mathcal{D}_j = (\mathcal{D}R_j)/\sqrt{q} \tag{1}$$

The T different learning algorithms $\{\mathcal{K}_i\}i = 1, ..., T$ are then trained on each $\mathcal{D}_j$ to obtain the *base classifiers* $h_{i,j}(i = 1, ..., T; j = 1, ..., K)$.

We consider the prediction of the base classifiers $h_{i,j}; i = 1, ..., T; j = 1, ..., K$ on a set $\mathcal{V} = \{x_n, n = 1, ..., N\}$. Each instance x_n in $\mathcal{V}$ is first projected to the down-space by:

$$\tilde{x}_{n,j} = (x_n R_j)/\sqrt{q} \tag{2}$$

The projected data $\tilde{x}_{n,j}$ is fed into classifier $h_{i,j}$ to obtain the prediction. The predictions for the instances in $\mathcal{V}$ are given by:

$$L = \begin{bmatrix} P_{1,1}(y_1|x_1) \cdots P_{1,1}(y_M|x_1) \cdots P_{1,K}(y_1|x_1) \cdots P_{T,K}(y_M|x_1) \\ \vdots \qquad\qquad \ddots \qquad\qquad \vdots \\ P_{1,1}(y_1|x_N) \cdots P_{1,1}(y_M|x_N) \cdots P_{1,K}(y_1|x_N) \cdots P_{T,K}(y_M|x_N) \end{bmatrix} \tag{3}$$

in which $P_{i,j}(y_m|x_n)$ is the prediction that observation x_n belongs to class label y_m given by base classifier $h_{i,j}$. Each row of L is the concatenation of the predictions of all classifiers for one observation. The prediction matrix L (size of $N \times TKM$) is called the meta-data of $\mathcal{V}$.

3.2   Combining Methods

For the homogeneous ensemble, several hundred or thousand of classifiers are generated on the new training sets. Majority Vote rule on a large number of inputs, therefore, is effective for the combining purpose. This makes Majority Vote rule the most popular combining algorithm for the homogeneous ensemble. However, the Majority Vote rule is less effective on the heterogeneous ensemble as the majority on a small set of predictions is unreliable to obtain the final decision. In this study, we introduce four combining methods based on the Sum and Majority Vote rules to combine the output of base classifiers in the proposed ensemble system.

Sum rule: We compute the average on the predictions of all base classifiers given in (3). The Sum rule for the proposed ensemble method is given by:

$$x \in y_u \text{ if } y_u = \text{argmax}_{y_m, m=1,...,M} \frac{1}{TK} \sum_{i=1}^{T} \sum_{j=1}^{K} P_{i,j}(y_m|x) \tag{4}$$

Sum-Majority Vote rule 1: Sum rule is first applied to the predictions associated with each random projection. After this step, we obtain K predictions results for each class label. The Majority Vote rule then is used on these predictions to obtain the final decision.

$$x \in y_u \text{if} y_u = \text{argmax}_{y_m, m=1,...,M} \sum_{j=1}^{K} \Delta_{j,m}; \Delta_{j,s} = \begin{cases} 1 & \text{if} s = \text{argmax}_{m=1,...,M} \sum_{i=1}^{T} P_{i,j}(y_m|x) \\ 0 & \text{otherwise} \end{cases}$$

$$\tag{5}$$

Sum-Majority Vote rule 2: This is similar to the Sum-Majority Vote rule 1 except the order they are applied. Here Sum rule is used on the predictions associated with each learning algorithm to acquire the T predictions results for each class label. The Majority Vote rule then is used on these predictions to obtain the final decision.

$$x \in y_u \text{ if } y_u = \text{argmax}_{y_m, m=1,\ldots,M} \sum_{i=1}^{T} \Delta_{i,m}; \Delta_{i,s} = \begin{cases} 1 & \text{if } s = \text{argmax}_{m=1,\ldots,M} \sum_{j=1}^{K} P_{i,j}(y_m|x) \\ 0 & \text{otherwise} \end{cases}$$

(6)

Majority Vote rule: The Majority Vote rule applied to the prediction of all $(T \times K)$ base classifiers on the sample x is given by:

$$x \in y_u \text{ if } y_u = \text{argmax}_{y_m, m=1,\ldots,M} \sum_{i=1}^{T} \sum_{j=1}^{K} \Delta_{i,j,m}; \Delta_{i,j,s} = \begin{cases} 1 & \text{if } s = \text{argmax}_{m=1,\ldots,M} P_{i,j}(y_m|x) \\ 0 & \text{otherwise} \end{cases}$$

(7)

4 Experimental Studies

4.1 Experimental Settings

We selected 24 popular datasets from the UCI database for our experiments. To construct the homogeneous module, we used *Normal*-based random projections $\mathcal{N}(0,1)$ with $q = 2 \times [\log_2(p)]$ [13]. We used three different learning algorithms: Linear Discriminant Analysis, Naïve Bayes, and kNN (k is set to 5) to create the heterogeneous module.

We performed 10-fold Cross-Validation procedure in which each fold a data file is divided into the training data and testing data. The Cross-Validation procedure was run 3 times so that we obtained 30 test results on each dataset from which to calculate the mean and variance of classification error rate.

4.2 Influence of Parameters

Different Number of Random Projections. We examine the influence of using a different number of random projections on the performance of the proposed ensemble and which are the most suitable combining algorithms for the proposed ensemble. In this study, we used 10, 50, and 100 random projections in the homogeneous module (see Fig. 1). Some observations can be made:

- Sum-Majority Vote rule 2 is the poorest combining method in our experiment. Sum-Majority Vote rule 2 uses Sum rule on the outputs associated with random projections (up to hundred) and then uses Majority Vote rule on the outputs of Sum rule (only 3). Because of voting on a small set of results, the Majority Vote rule results in poor performance. In fact, the classification error rates of Sum-Majority Vote rule 2 are usually higher than those of the other combining methods.

– Majority Vote rule has average performance in the experiment. However, on some datasets like Iris and Fertility, this method obtains the lowest classification error rates among all four combining methods.
– Sum rule and Sum_Majority Vote rule 1 are the best combining methods for the proposed ensemble as their performance is usually better than those of the other combining methods.
– A common trend in this figure is the reduction of classification error rate when increasing the number of random projections in the homogeneous module. However, there are exceptional cases on datasets like Led7digit.

In the next section, we used Sum_Majority Vote rule 1 as the combining algorithm for the proposed ensemble (with 100 random projections and 3 learning algorithms to obtain 300 classifiers) when comparing to the benchmark algorithms.

4.3   Comparison to Benchmark Algorithms

We selected three homogeneous ensemble methods namely Random Subspace, TotalBoost, and RotBoost as the benchmark algorithms (using 300 base classifiers). For RotBoost, we used 10 Rotation Forest [9] and 30 classifiers in AdaBoost to create 300 classifiers. Besides, we chose one well-known combining algorithms for heterogeneous ensemble systems namely the Decision Template method [7] for the comparison. We used the Friedman test to compare the results of all methods on all experimental datasets. Since p-value of this test is smaller than the pre-selected significant level of 0.05, we rejected the null hypothesis that all methods perform equally. We then run the Nemenyi post-hoc test to perform pairwise comparison of all methods. Some observations can be made from the test results in Table 1 and Fig. 2.

– Random Subspace ranks the second with rank value 2.94. Random Subspace randomly selects features from the feature space and then generate new training data that is associated with the selected features. In fact, this method normally is outstanding for high dimensional datasets like Libras (90 features) and Sonar (60 features) in the experiment.
– Decision Template method has an average performance and is worse than the proposed method based on the Nemenyi test result. The study in [6] showed that Decision Template method may not provide good representation for the meta-data, resulting in poorly performance on some datasets.
– RotBoost and TotalBoost are two poorest methods in our experiment and are worse than the proposed ensemble based on the Nemenyi test result.
– The proposed ensemble ranks the first with rank values 1.7. In detail, the proposed ensemble ranks first on 9 datasets (37.5%) and ranks second on 14 datasets (58.33%).

We note that some different approaches can be used to construct the homogeneous module for particular problems. For example, we can use random subspace technique to produce new training sets when working with high-dimension data. The heterogeneous module meanwhile can be customized by changing the learning algorithms that are used to produce the base classifiers. By this way, the proposed framework has great flexibility when applied to real-world applications.

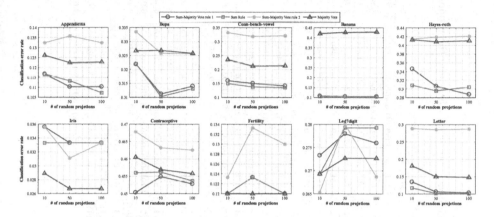

Fig. 1. The classification error rate of the proposed ensemble system with 4 combining algorithms on 10 datasets

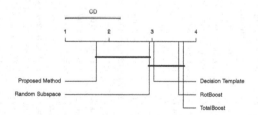

Fig. 2. The Nemenyi test result

Table 1. The mean and variance of classification error rates of the benchmark algorithms and the proposed ensemble

	Proposed ensemble		Decision template		Random Subspace		TotalBoost		RotBoost	
	Mean	Variance	Mean	Variance	Mean	Variance	Mean	Variance	Mean	Variance
Appendicitis	0.1103 (1)	7.79E-03	0.1297 (2)	8.24E-03	0.1418 (5)	8.14E-03	0.1358 (4)	6.40E-03	0.1324 (3)	6.41E-03
Artificial	0.2395 (2)	1.68E-03	0.2443 (3)	1.62E-03	0.2714 (4)	2.60E-03	0.2295 (1)	1.67E-03	0.3300 (5)	2.83E-03
Balance	0.1082 (2)	3.14E-04	0.0960 (1)	9.38E-04	0.2134 (5)	1.46E-03	0.1280 (3)	2.11E-03	0.1547 (4)	1.18E-03
Banana	0.1052 (1)	8.33E-05	0.1117 (2)	1.36E-04	0.3848 (5)	2.74E-03	0.1259 (4)	1.22E-04	0.1173 (3)	2.78E-04
Blood	0.2286 (2.5)	1.28E-03	0.2674 (4)	2.34E-03	0.2228 (1)	6.55E-04	0.3160 (5)	2.92E-03	0.2286 (2.5)	5.94E-04
Breast-Tissue	0.3600 (2)	1.20E-02	0.3858 (4)	1.07E-02	0.3333 (1)	6.75E-03	0.3752 (3)	1.34E-02	0.3955 (5)	1.76E-02
Bupa	0.3140 (1)	3.37E-03	0.3324 (3.5)	5.18E-03	0.3324 (3.5)	5.23E-03	0.3150 (2)	5.42E-03	0.3390 (5)	4.38E-03
Conn-bench-vowel	0.1414 (2)	2.43E-03	0.1938 (4)	2.50E-03	0.0594 (1)	8.83E-04	0.1655 (3)	2.40E-03	0.3611 (5)	6.28E-03
Contraceptive	0.4528 (1)	1.19E-03	0.4662 (3)	1.73E-03	0.4777 (4)	8.59E-04	0.5234 (5)	9.79E-03	0.4653 (2)	7.14E-04
Fertility	0.1200 (2)	1.60E-03	0.4200 (5)	2.29E-02	0.1200 (2)	1.60E-03	0.1767 (4)	5.23E-03	0.1200 (2)	1.60E-03
Haberman	0.2638 (1)	2.15E-03	0.3102 (4)	3.90E-03	0.2982 (3)	3.25E-03	0.3718 (5)	1.08E-02	0.2810 (2)	2.26E-03
Hayes-roth	0.2875 (2)	1.24E-02	0.4042 (5)	2.05E-02	0.3417 (3)	1.82E-02	0.1854 (1)	3.81E-03	0.3688 (4)	1.75E-02
Iris	0.0333 (1.5)	1.41E-03	0.0333 (1.5)	1.41E-03	0.0444 (4)	2.77E-03	0.0667 (5)	4.73E-03	0.0378 (3)	1.68E-03
Led7digit	0.2760 (2)	4.17E-03	0.2700 (1)	4.37E-03	0.4533 (5)	2.38E-03	0.2993 (3)	7.03E-04	0.2853 (3)	7.09E-03
Letter	0.1034 (2)	6.07E-05	0.1192 (3)	5.99E-05	0.0994 (1)	5.33E-05	0.3599 (5)	4.02E-03	0.1733 (4)	1.47E-04
Libras	0.2639 (2)	2.97E-03	0.2991 (4)	4.36E-03	0.2000 (1)	2.39E-03	0.2972 (3)	4.39E-04	0.4722 (5)	7.61E-03
Marketing	0.6662 (1)	1.29E-04	0.6978 (4)	2.00E-04	0.6705 (3)	1.16E-04	0.7083 (5)	7.28E-03	0.6701 (2)	2.14E-04
Sonar	0.1808 (2)	6.43E-03	0.2292 (4)	5.77E-03	0.1379 (1)	4.84E-03	0.1856 (3)	5.49E-05	0.2387 (5)	6.43E-03
Twonorm	0.0229 (2)	2.69E-05	0.0211 (1)	1.93E-05	0.0271 (3)	3.10E-05	0.0330 (4)	2.53E-03	0.0375 (5)	6.91E-05
Vertebral	0.1807 (1)	3.37E-03	0.1914 (4)	3.88E-03	0.2763 (5)	2.48E-03	0.1817 (2)	2.98E-04	0.1839 (3)	3.76E-03
Waveform_w_noise	0.1673 (2)	2.01E-04	0.1634 (1)	2.00E-04	0.1705 (3)	2.64E-04	0.1781 (5)	2.19E-04	0.1744 (4)	2.54E-04
Waveform_wo_noise	0.1568 (3)	3.98E-04	0.156 (2)	3.36E-04	0.1518 (1)	3.19E-04	0.1834 (5)	1.52E-03	0.1635 (4)	3.78E-04
Wine_red	0.4230 (2)	1.26E-03	0.5157 (5)	1.16E-03	0.3112 (1)	3.80E-04	0.4294 (4)	1.44E-03	0.4255 (3)	6.63E-04
Yeast	0.3971 (1)	8.78E-04	0.4182 (2)	7.85E-04	0.4926 (5)	1.96E-03	0.4771 (4)	1.44E-03	0.4499 (3)	2.67E-03
Average ranking	1.71		3.04		2.94		3.71		3.6	

*(·) indicates the ranking of a method on each dataset

5   Conclusions

In this work, we have introduced a design for ensemble systems by combining homogeneous module and heterogeneous module in a single framework by using random projections and different learning algorithms. The random projections are applied on the training set to generate many training set schemes. Several different learning algorithms then train classifiers on these new schemes. We proposed four combining algorithms to combine the outputs of these classifiers based on Sum Rule and Majority Vote Rule. Experiments on some well-known datasets show that the proposed ensemble system significantly outperformed several well-known benchmark algorithms. The proposed design is general, that means any techniques that make rich training data can be used for the homogeneous module, as well as any set of learning algorithms can be used for the heterogeneous module.

References

1. Nguyen, T.T., Liew, A.W.C., Tran, M.T., Pham, X.C., Nguyen, M.P.: A novel genetic algorithm approach for simultaneous feature and classifier selection in multi classifier system. In: IEEE CEC, pp. 1698–1705 (2014)
2. Nguyen, T.T., Dang, M.T., Liew, A.W.C., Bezdek, J.C.: A weighted multiple classifier framework based on random projection. Inf. Sci. **490**, 36–58 (2019)
3. Kittler, J., Hatef, M., Duin, R.P.W., Matas, J.: On combining classifiers. IEEE Trans. Pattern Anal. Mach. Intell. **20**(3), 226–239 (1998)
4. Zhang, Y., Cao, G., Wang, B., Li, X.: A novel ensemble method for k-nearest neighbor. Pattern Recogn. **85**, 13–25 (2019)
5. Nguyen, T.T., et al.: Deep heterogeneous ensemble. Aust. J. Intell. Inf. Process. Syst. **16**(1), 1–9 (2019)
6. Nguyen, T.T., Nguyen, M.P., Pham, X.C., Liew, A.W.C., Pedrycz, W.: Combining heterogeneous classifiers via granular prototypes. Appl. Soft Comput. **73**, 795–815 (2018)
7. Kuncheva, L.I., Bezdek, J.C., Duin, R.P.W.: Decision templates for multiple classifier fusion: an experimental comparison. Pattern Recogn. **34**, 299–314 (2001)
8. Nguyen, T.T., Nguyen, T.T.T., Pham, X.C., Liew, A.W.C.: A novel combining classifier method based on variational inference. Pattern Recogn. **49**, 198–212 (2016)
9. Zhang, C.X., Zhang, J.S.: RotBoost: a technique for combining rotation forest and AdaBoost. Pattern Recogn. Lett. **29**(10), 1524–1536 (2008)
10. Warmuth, M.K., Liao, J., Ratsch, G.: Totally corrective boosting algorithms that maximize the margin. In: Proceeding of ICML, pp. 1001–1008 (2006)
11. Dang, M.T., et al.: An ensemble system with random projection and dynamic ensemble selection. In: Proceeding of ACIIDS, pp. 576–586 (2018)
12. Johnson, W., Lindenstrauss, J.: Extensions of Lipschitz mapping into Hilbert space. In: Conference in Modern Analysis and Probability of Contemporary Mathematics, American Mathematical Society, vol. 26, pp. 189–206 (1984)
13. Pham, X.C., et al.: Learning from data stream based on random projection and Hoeffding tree classifier. In: Proceeding of DICTA (2017)

A Particle Swarm Optimization Based Joint Geometrical and Statistical Alignment Approach with Laplacian Regularization

Rakesh Kumar Sanodiya[1], Mrinalini Tiwari[2], Leehter Yao[1(✉)], and Jimson Mathew[2]

[1] National Taipei University of Technology, Taipei 10608, Taiwan
rakesh.pcs16@gmail.com, ltyao@ntut.edu.tw
[2] Indian Institute of Technology Patna, Patna, India
mrinalini.cse0206@gmail.com, jimson@iitp.ac.in

Abstract. Transfer Learning or Domain Adaptation is an emerging sub-field of Machine learning in which the source domain carrying ample amount of labeled data is employed to classify a diverse but inter-related target domain data. However, in primitive machine learning algorithms, there is a pre-assumption that training and test data belong to the same set of distributions. But in a real-world scenario, the source (or training data), as well as the target domain (or test data), has a diverse distribution of data. Also, the source domain is equipped with the labeled data information while the target domain has a scarcity of labeled data or has completely unlabelled data information. Although the existing transfer learning algorithms like Joint Geometrical and Statistical Alignment (JGSA) takes into account several objectives to reduce the geometrical shift and distribution shift simultaneously, still they lack in fulfilling objectives like Laplacian regularization and degenerate feature elimination. So, we proposed a novel approach called Particle Swarm Optimization based Joint Geometrical and Statistical Alignment approach with Laplacian regularization (PSO-JGSAL) which incorporates new objective with JGSA and also utilizes the PSO approach for selection of an optimum set of features for classification purposes. Rigorous experiments have been done on Office-Caltech datasets (with SURF Features and Decaf Features) and our proposed PSO-JGSAL shows promising results as compared to already existing primitive and domain adaptation methods.

Keywords: Unsupervised learning · Transfer learning · Domain adaptation · Classification · Feature selection · Particle swarm optimization

1 Introduction

Machine learning (ML) is an eminent field that focuses on gaining an insight of the human ability to learn things. Many day-to-day life problems like image

© Springer Nature Switzerland AG 2020
H. Yang et al. (Eds.): ICONIP 2020, CCIS 1333, pp. 260–268, 2020.
https://doi.org/10.1007/978-3-030-63823-8_31

recognition, medical imaging, etc. need the utilization of this technology. The classical ML techniques deal with the pre-assumption that the training and testing data relies on the same distribution. However, in a real-world scenario, as the distribution of data varies for the source as well as target domains, the classifier which is trained using source domain information is not able to classify the target domain information. To overpower these shortcomings of the primitive ML methods, Transfer Learning(TL) or Domain Adaptation(DA) comes into play. The main concern of TL/DA algorithms is to reduce the distribution gap between both domains. Based on the data accessibility, existing TL algorithms [4,11] can be grouped into two types: a) Semi-supervised [8], and b) Unsupervised [10]. Both the categories have sufficient amount of labeled information for the source domain, however, Semi-supervised TL has only a few labeled information while Unsupervised TL has no labeled information for the target domain.

One of the common approaches for TL is Feature-based [4] in which a common feature subspace is created between both domains for better classification of target domain data. However, the main problem with these current techniques [4,11] is that they consider original features from both domains, where some features are distorted. In the past, the amount of work [6] to eliminate distorted features has been considered, but the fitness function or objective function considered by them is not as strong as other methods [11]. Therefore, in order to overpower the limitations of existing TL methods, we propose a novel approach PSO-JGSAL that uses Particle Swarm Optimization [6] technique for choosing the best feature subset(or removing distorted features) from both domains by taking all the necessary objectives into a newly formulated fitness function. The main contributions of our approach are:

- In this work (PSO-JGSAL), we have taken into account all the relevant objectives that are being missed by the already existing TL algorithms in order to reduce the difference of distributions between the two domains.
- For demonstrating the efficiency of PSO-JGSAL, it is compared with several existing algorithms on the real-world DA datasets.
- From the results, it can be verified that the proposed PSO-JGSAL algorithm outperforms all of the already existing algorithms.

2   Related Work

The main aim of existing TL approaches is to keep the distributions discrepancy between the domains to a minimum. Many techniques have been developed for the same purpose. The technique Transfer Component Analysis (TCA) [7] utilizes the MMD approach to discover transfer components across domains by projecting the data from the two domains into a new space. Another technique, Joint distribution alignment (JDA) [4] upgrades the performance of TCA, by taking into account the conditional distribution also. Joint Geometrical and Statistical Adaptation (JGSA) [11] takes into account several objectives to diminish the distribution shift and geometrical shift simultaneously. But it does not take into account some of the objectives like Laplacian regularization and degenerate feature elimination. Although MEDA [10] removes the drawbacks of JGSA by taking into account the Laplacian regularization, still it does not eliminate distorted features in both the domains. Nguyen et al. [6] introduce a feature-based transfer learning method using particle swarm optimization (PSO), which selects good subset of features across both domains w.r.t to a new fitness function. However, its fitness function considers only Maximum Mean Discrepancy (MMD) objective function.

3   Framework for Visual Domain Adaptation:

3.1   Particle Swarm Optimization (PSO)

Eberhart and Kennedy, in 1995, proposed a population-based optimization algorithm,i.e. the Particle Swarm Optimization(PSO) that is based on simulating the behavior of birds/fishes/ants in a swarm/group. The birds/fishes/ants that are searching for the food are referred to as 'Particles'. The main focus of the PSO algorithm is to determine the optimal solution by iteratively improving the existing position (P_t) and velocity (V_t) of the particles. In our research, we have also utilized the PSO technique for choosing the best feature subset across both the domains(source and target). Each particle contains 2 fields: a)Position field, that inhibits the position of common feature subset across both the domains b) Fitness value field, that holds the fitness value(accuracy) corresponding to (a). Also, two particles, namely $Best_P$ and $Best_G$, where $Best_P$ holds a best particle among all the particles in current iteration and $Best_G$ holds a best particle among all the particles, which have been so far obtained. Initially, PSO starts with the random subset of features, then tries to optimize it by iteratively updating the position (P_t) and velocity (V_t) values depending on the values of $Best_P$ and $Best_G$ by the following formula:

$$V_{t+1} = w * V_t + c_1 * r_1 * (Best_P - P_t) + c_2 * r_2 * (Best_G - P_t) \tag{1}$$

$$P_{t+1} = P_t + V_{t+1} \tag{2}$$

where V_{t+1} and P_{t+1} are the velocity and position of particle at time t+1. $c_1, c_2 \in (0, 2)$ are the learning factors, $r_1, r_2 \in (0, 1)$ are the random numbers, and w is the initial weight.

3.2   Formulation of the Model

Source Domain Discriminative Information Preservation. We have incorporated the Linear Discriminant Analysis(LDA) technique into our fitness function that tries to increase the between-class (S_{bc}) and reduce the within-class (S_{wc}) variance as much as possible. These goals can be accomplished by a source domain projection vector matrix M as:

$$\underset{M}{\text{Max}} \ \text{Tr}(M^T S_{bc} M) \tag{3}$$

$$\underset{M}{\text{Min}} \ \text{Tr}(M^T S_{wc} M) \tag{4}$$

where $\text{Tr}(.)$ is the trace of $(.)$, and S_{bc} and S_{wc} can be calculated as follows: $S_{wc} = \sum_{c=1}^{C} \mathcal{X}_s^c H_s^c (\mathcal{X}_s^c)^T$, and $S_{bc} = \sum_{c=1}^{C} n_s^c (m_s^c - \bar{m}_s)(m_s^c - \bar{m}_s)^T$, respectively. Here, $\mathcal{X}_s^c$ is source domain data, m_s^c is the mean of data samples and n_s^c is the number of source domain data samples belonging to c^{th} class. H_s^c is the centering matrix of cth class, and $\bar{m}_s$ is the total mean of all the data samples.

Target Domain Variance (TDV) Maximization. By utilizing PCA, the target domain data will be cast on a new subspace such that the variation of data is maximum. Thus, with the help of target domain projection vector matrix N, the TDV can be maximized as follows:

$$\underset{N}{\text{Max}} \ N^T J_t N \tag{5}$$

where $J_t = \mathcal{X}_t^T H_t \mathcal{X}_t$ and H_t are scatter and centering matrices of target domain. $\mathcal{X}_t$ is the target domain data.

Distribution Divergence Minimization(DDM). The Maximum Mean Discrepancy (MMD) [4] approach is utilized to compare distributions based on RKHS (Reproducing Kernel Hilbert Space). The distributing mismatch (marginal distribution) between both domains can be computed as:

$$\underset{M,N}{\text{Min}} \left\| \frac{1}{n_s} \sum_{x_i \in \mathcal{X}_s} M^T x_i - \frac{1}{n_t} \sum_{x_j \subset \mathcal{X}_t} N^T x_j \right\|_F^2 \tag{6}$$

However, when the data follows the class-wise distribution, the conditional distribution will have to be considered too for reducing the gap between the domains. The conditional distribution is reduced by the formula:

$$\underset{M,N}{\text{Min}} \sum_{i=1}^{C} \left\| \frac{1}{n_s^i} \sum_{x_i \in \mathcal{X}_s^i} M^T x_i - \frac{1}{n_t^i} \sum_{x_j \in \mathcal{X}_t^i} N^T x_j \right\|_F^2 \tag{7}$$

where n_s and n_t number of labelled samples in source domain and unlabelled samples in target domain respectively. By combining Eqs. 6 and 7, the final joint distribution minimization term can be computed same as in JGSA [11] method.

Geometrical Diffusion on Manifolds(GDM). The prior knowledge of the geometry of the unlabeled data belonging to both domains is also considered, Thus, with $\mathcal{X}$(data of both the domains), we can construct a NN-nearest neighbor graph G to model the relationship between nearby data samples. Particularly, we draw an edge between data samples x_i and x_j if they are among NN-nearest neighbor of each other. Thus, the corresponding weight matrix W can be calculated as:

$$W_{ij} = \begin{cases} 1, & \text{if } x_i \in \mathcal{N}_{\text{NN}}(x_j) \mid x_j \in \mathcal{N}_{\text{NN}}(x_i) \\ 0, & \text{otherwise} \end{cases}$$

where, $\mathcal{N}_{NN}(x_i)$ and $\mathcal{N}_{NN}(x_j)$ depicts the set of NN nearest neighbours of x_j and x_i respectively. The Laplacian matrix is computed as $L = (D - W)$, where the column sum of W are the diagonal matrix D entries i.e. $D_{ii} = \sum_j W_{ij}$. Finally, the regularization term can be derived as:

$$R = \sum_{i,j} (x_i - x_j)^2 W_{ij} = 2\mathcal{X}L\mathcal{X}^T \tag{8}$$

Subspace Divergence Minimization(SDM). Bringing the subspaces of the domains closer can help in reducing the divergence between them. We can optimize the projection vectors M and N simultaneously, without utilizing a new matrix to project the two subspaces by using following equation:

$$\underset{M,N}{\text{Min}} \|M - N\|_F^2 \tag{9}$$

3.3 Newly Formulated Fitness Function

In this section, the newly formulated fitness function for the proposed PSO-JGSAL framework, by incorporating all the objectives listed in Subsect. 3.3, is described. The overall fitness function can be represented as:

$$\text{Max} \frac{\mu\{\text{TDV}\} + \beta\{S_{wc}\}}{\alpha\{\text{SDM}\} + \beta\{S_{bc}\} + \eta\{\text{GDM}\} + \{\text{DDM}\}}$$

where μ, β, α, and η are various trade-off parameters that equalize the significance of every term. Thus, the fitness function can be represented as:

$$\underset{M,N}{\text{Max}} \frac{\text{Tr}\left([M^T \ N^T] \begin{bmatrix} \beta S_{bc} & 0 \\ 0 & \mu J_t \end{bmatrix} \begin{bmatrix} M \\ N \end{bmatrix}\right)}{\text{Tr}\left([M^T \ N^T] \begin{bmatrix} B_s + \alpha I + \beta S_{wc} + \eta R & B_{st} - \alpha I + \eta R \\ B_{ts} - \alpha I + \eta R & B_t + (\alpha + \mu)I + \eta R \end{bmatrix} \begin{bmatrix} M \\ N \end{bmatrix}\right)}$$

where $I \in \mathbb{R}^{d*d}$ is the identity matrix. For optimizing the fitness function, we will use the same steps as proposed by the JGSA [11] method.

3.4 Overview of PSO-JGSAL Algorithm

The main aim of our proposed PSO-JGSAL algorithm in the TL framework is to choose the best feature subset across both the domains in order to reduce the risk of degenerated feature transformation. Our newly formulated fitness function governs PSO to choose the optimal subset of features across both the domains so that our proposed approach attains higher accuracy than the already existing methods. Following are the steps of our proposed PSO-JGSAL algorithm:

- **Step 1:** Set up the initial values of the parameters such as Population size (POP_{size}), selected number of features (Fea), maximum available features (Max_F), maximum iterations(I_{max}), iteration(i), c1, c2, w etc.

- **Step 2:** Every particle has two associated field values a) Position(pos) and Value(val), where pos consists of the positions for choosing the feature subset across the two domains and val consists of the computed accuracy from the fitness function corresponding to pos field. Both particles $Best_P$ and $Best_G$ also contains these two fields. VEL and POP_s is the velocity matrix and the position matrix consisting of all particle velocities and positions in the Population set POP. Initialize val field of VEL matrix to 0, POP_s matrix with randomly chosen values between $(1, Max_F)$ for selecting random feature subset across both the domains.
- **Step 3:** Here, the feature subset across both the domains is selected based on the values in the Position Matrix (POP_s) and corresponding Fitness value val is computed. These values are assigned to corresponding fields of the particle.
- **Step 4:** A particle having the maximum fitness value from the Population set POP will be assigned as the $Best_P$ Particle. If the val field of $Best_P$ particle has higher value than the val field of $Best_G$ particle (i.e., $Best_P.val > Best_G.val$), then $Best_G$ is assigned with the $Best_P$.
- **Step 5:** Depending on Step (5), update each particle velocity according to Eq. (1) and update the velocity matrix (VEL). Also, update each particle position according to Eq. (2) and update the position matrix (POP_s).
- **Step 6:** Repeat steps 3–5 until the number of iterations $<= I_{max}$.

In order to calculate the fitness value, all the objectives mentioned in Subsect. 3.3 are incorporated in the fitness function. Then, after the optimization of the fitness function, the data samples from both the domains are projected with the fitness vectors corresponding to highest eigenvalues. Finally, the fitness value is computed by applying k-NN classifier on the projected data.

4 Experiments

4.1 Benchmark Datasets

We have utilized the publicly available Office-Caltech object dataset for performing the experiments. This dataset comprises of images from four different domains: a) Caltech-256 (C), b) DSLR (D), c) Webcam (W) and d) Amazon (A).

At a time one of the four domains is treated as a source while another one as the target. So, a total of 12 combinations are used to calculate the average accuracy for the Office-Caltech dataset. We have considered two types of features for this dataset namely SURF and Decaf6.

4.2 Parameter Sensitivity Test

For determining the best values of parameters (α, β, η, μ, k and NN) to be used in our proposed PSO-JGSAL algorithm, we have conducted a parameter sensitivity test on different datasets. As we are incorporating JGSA objectives into our fitness function, we have taken the optimal values of the parameters

Table 1. Accuracy (%) of proposed PSO-JGSAL on different datasets

Office-Caltech dataset using SURF features.

Traditional Approaches										PSO-JGSAL (Proposed)
Tasks	GFK	TCA	CORAL	TJM	JDA	ARTL	SCA	JGSA	MEDA	
C→A	46.0	45.6	52.1	46.8	43.1	44.1	45.6	51.5	56.5	**60.50**
C→W	37.0	39.3	46.4	39.0	39.3	31.5	40.0	45.4	53.9	52.88
C→D	40.8	45.9	45.9	44.6	49.0	39.5	47.1	45.9	50.3	**53.50**
A→C	40.7	42.0	45.1	39.5	40.9	36.1	39.7	41.5	43.9	43.72
A→W	37.0	40.0	44.4	42.0	38.0	33.6	34.9	45.8	53.2	**57.28**
A→D	40.1	35.7	39.5	45.2	42.0	36.9	39.5	47.1	45.9	**54.77**
W→C	24.8	31.5	33.7	30.2	33.0	29.7	31.1	33.2	34.0	**38.02**
W→A	27.6	30.5	36.0	30.0	29.8	38.3	30.0	39.9	42.7	**44.15**
W→D	85.4	91.1	86.6	89.2	92.4	87.9	87.3	90.5	88.5	**94.90**
D→C	29.3	33.0	33.8	31.4	31.2	30.5	30.7	29.9	34.9	**37.13**
D→A	28.7	32.8	37.7	32.8	33.4	34.9	31.6	38.0	41.2	**44.15**
D→W	80.3	87.5	84.7	85.4	89.2	88,5	84.4	91.9	87.5	**96.27**
Average	43.1	46.2	48.8	46.3	46.8	44.3	45.2	50.0	52.7	**56.44**

Office-Caltech dataset using DeCaf6 features.

Traditional Approaches										PSO-JGSAL (Proposed)
Tasks	GFK	TCA	CORAL	TJM	JDA	ARTL	SCA	JGSA	MEDA	
C→	88.2	89.8	92.0	88.8	89.6	92.4	89.5	91.4	93.4	**93.7**
C→W	77.6	78.3	80.0	81.4	85.1	87.8	85.4	86.8	95.6	94.24
C→	86.6	85.4	84.7	84.7	89.8	86.6	87.9	93.6	91.1	**98.72**
A→C	79.2	82.6	83.2	84.3	83.6	87.4	78.8	84.9	87.4	86.9
A→W	70.9	74.2	74.6	71.9	78.3	88.5	75.9	81.0	88.1	86.1
A→D	82.2	81.5	84.1	76.4	80.3	85.4	85.4	88.5	88.1	**96.17**
W→	69.8	80.4	75.5	83.0	84.8	88.2	74.8	85.0	93.2	**89.0**
W→A	76.8	84.1	81.2	87.6	90.3	92.3	86.1	90.7	99.4	91.85
W→D	100.0	100.0	100.0	100.0	100.0	100.0	100.0	100.0	99.4	**100.0**
D→	71.4	82.3	76.8	83.8	78.1	87.3	78.1	86.2	87.5	**89.6**
D→	76.3	89.1	85.5	90.3	90.0	92.7	90.0	92.0	93.2	**93.5**
D→W	99.3	99.7	99.3	99.3	98.6	100.0	98.6	99.7	97.6	**100.0**
Average	81.5	85.6	84.7	86.0	88.2	90.7	85.9	90.0	92.8	**93.31**

α, β, μ, and k as indicated in the JGSA [11] work. Since we are adding an extra objective into our proposed fitness function, so for finding the optimal values of parameters η (Trade-off parameter for the Laplacian term) and NN (no. of nearest neighbors), we have done the parameter sensitivity test on both the datasets. We vary the value of η between 10^{-3} and 10^3 and found that the algorithm is performing better when η value is 10^{-1} for both the datasets. The value of NN is varied from 1 to 10 and our proposed algorithm is producing good results when NN value is 1 for both the datasets. For the PSO algorithm also, we have determined the appropriate value of the parameters. The algorithm is performing good when the value of $Pop_{size} = 100$, $I_{max} = 10$, $c_1 = c_2 = 2$, and $w = 0.5$ for both the datasets. Our proposed algorithm is giving better performance when the value of $Max_F = 750$ for the Office-Caltech dataset using SURF Features and $Max_F = 3000$ for the Office-Caltech dataset using Decaf Features.

5 Experimental Results and Discussion

The experiments were conducted on 2 real-world datasets namely, the Office-Caltech dataset with SURF Features, and the Office-Caltech dataset with Decaf6 Features. The results of experiments on these datasets are shown in Table 1. Our proposed PSO-JGSAL approach is compared with other existing state-of-the-art methods like: JDA [4], GFK [2], TCA [7], TJM [5], JGSA [11], CORAL [9], SCA [1], ARTL [3] and MEDA [10]. It achieves a mean accuracy of 56.44% for all combinations of the Office-Caltech dataset with SURF Features. Average accuracy of 93.31% is achieved by PSO-JGSAL for all combinations of the Office-Caltech dataset with Decaf Features. The results show that our proposed PSO-JGSAL approach is superior than all other existing approaches.

6 Conclusion

In this work, we have proposed a novel Particle Swarm Optimization based Joint Geometrical and Statistical Alignment approach with Laplacian Regularization (PSO-JGSAL) for visual domain adaptation. The proposed method incorporates all the relevant objectives into the fitness function which successfully instructs the PSO algorithm to choose best subset of features for the classification purpose. Experimental results analysis on two real-world datasets have indicated the superiority of our proposed PSO-JSGAL technique over existing approaches.

References

1. Ghifary, M., Balduzzi, D., Kleijn, W.B., Zhang, M.: Scatter component analysis: A unified framework for domain adaptation and domain generalization. IEEE Trans. Pattern Anal. Mach. Intell. **39**(7), 1414–1430 (2016)
2. Gong, B., Shi, Y., Sha, F., Grauman, K.: Geodesic flow kernel for unsupervised domain adaptation. In: 2012 IEEE Conference on Computer Vision and Pattern Recognition. pp. 2066–2073. IEEE (2012)
3. Long, M., Wang, J., Ding, G., Pan, S.J., Philip, S.Y.: Adaptation regularization: a general framework for transfer learning. IEEE Trans. Knowl. Data Eng. **26**(5), 1076–1089 (2014)
4. Long, M., Wang, J., Ding, G., Sun, J., Yu, P.S.: Transfer feature learning with joint distribution adaptation. In: Proceedings of the IEEE International Conference on Computer Vision. pp. 2200–2207 (2013)
5. Long, M., Wang, J., Ding, G., Sun, J., Yu, P.S.: Transfer joint matching for unsupervised domain adaptation. In: Proceedings of the IEEE Conference on Computer Vision and Pattern Recognition. pp. 1410–1417 (2014)
6. Nguyen, B.H., Xue, B., Andreae, P.: A particle swarm optimization based feature selection approach to transfer learning in classification. In: Proceedings of the Genetic and Evolutionary Computation Conference. pp. 37–44 (2018)
7. Pan, S.J., Tsang, I.W., Kwok, J.T., Yang, Q.: Domain adaptation via transfer component analysis. IEEE Trans. Neural Netw. **22**(2), 199–210 (2011)
8. Sanodiya, R.K., Mathew, J., Saha, S., Thalakottur, M.D.: A new transfer learning algorithm in semi-supervised setting. IEEE Access **7**, 42956–42967 (2019)

9. Sun, B., Feng, J., Saenko, K.: Return of frustratingly easy domain adaptation. In: Thirtieth AAAI Conference on Artificial Intelligence (2016)
10. Wang, J., Feng, W., Chen, Y., Yu, H., Huang, M., Yu, P.S.: Visual domain adaptation with manifold embedded distribution alignment. In: 2018 ACM Multimedia Conference on Multimedia Conference. pp. 402–410. ACM (2018)
11. Zhang, J., Li, W., Ogunbona, P.: Joint geometrical and statistical alignment for visual domain adaptation. In: Proceedings of the IEEE Conference on Computer Vision and Pattern Recognition. pp. 1859–1867 (2017)

Class-Dependent Weighted Feature Selection as a Bi-Level Optimization Problem

Marwa Hammami[1(✉)], Slim Bechikh[1], Chih-Cheng Hung[2,3], and Lamjed Ben Said[1]

[1] SMART lab, University of Tunis, ISG-Campus, Tunis city, Tunisia
marwaalhammami@gmail.com, slim.bechikh@fsegn.rnu.tn,
lamjed.bensaid@isg.rnu.tn
[2] Kennesaw State University, Kennesaw, USA
chung1@kennesaw.edu
[3] Anyang Normal University, Anyang, China

Abstract. Feature selection aims at selecting relevant features from the original feature set, but these features do not have the same degree of importance. This can be achieved by feature weighting, which is a method for quantifying the capability of features to discriminate instances from different classes. Multiple feature selection methods have shown that different feature subset can reduce the data dimensionality and maintain or even improve the classification accuracy. However, different features can have different abilities to distinguish instances of one class from the other classes, which makes the feature selection process a difficult task by finding the optimal feature subset weighting vectors for each class. Motivated by this observation, feature selection and feature weighting could be seen as a BLOP (Bi-Level Optimization Problem) where the feature selection is performed in the upper level, and the feature weighting is applied in the lower level by performing mutliple followers, each of which generates a set of weighting vectors for each class. Only the optimal feature subset weighting vector is retrieved for each class. In this paper, we propose a bi-level evolutionary approach for class-dependent feature selection and weighting using Genetic Algorithm (GA), called Bi-level Class-Dependent Weighted Feature Selection (BCDWFS). The basic idea of our BCDWFS is to exploit the bi-level model for performing upper level feature selection and lower level feature weighting with the aim of finding the optimal weighting vectors of a subset of features for each class. Our approach has been assessed on ten datasets and compared to three existing approaches, using three different classifiers for accuracy evaluation. Experimental results show that our proposed algorithm gives competitive and better results with respect to the state-of-the-art algorithms.

Keywords: Feature selection and weighting · Class-dependent features · Bi-level optimization · Evolutionary algorithms

1 Introduction

Classification is one of the important tasks in machine learning and data mining, which aims to classify each instance in the dataset into different classes based on its features. It is difficult to determine which features are useful without a prior knowledge. However,

© Springer Nature Switzerland AG 2020
H. Yang et al. (Eds.): ICONIP 2020, CCIS 1333, pp. 269–278, 2020.
https://doi.org/10.1007/978-3-030-63823-8_32

not all features are essential since many of them are redundant or even irrelevant which may significantly degrade the classification performance and reduce the quality of the feature set due to the large search space known as "the curse of dimensionality" [8].

Feature selection is the process of choosing a subset of the original features from data, which results in a fast and better classification process. Feature selection methods can be categorised into wrapper, filter or embedded approaches based on how a learning algorithm is involved in the feature selection process [3]. Finding the optimal feature subset is a diffiult task mainly due to the large search space, where the total number of possible solutions is 2^n for a dataset with n features. Not only the selection of features, but also the relative importance of features may improve the classifier performance. Often the differences in the scales of different features may cause distortion in the natural structure of the data. Therefore, it is important to rescale them to restore the original data structure. However, different features can have different abilities to distinguish different classes [1]. For example, a feature may be good at distinguishing samples of class A from those of class B, C and D, but may not be good at differentiating samples of class B from those of C and D. Therefore, it may be more difficult to select a better discriminating feature subset with the corresponding class-dependent weighting vector. Evolutionary Computation (EC) techniques have been used to address feature selection and feature weighting tasks. A range of research work has been done in this area [3–5,8,12,16]. A variety of feature selection approaches has been proposed, but the use of bi-level model for solving class-dependent feature selection and weighting problems has not yet been investigated except some recent studies that addressed the feature construction as a bi-level optimization problem [4,16]. Therefore, the development of a bi-level evolutionary approach for feature selection based on class-dependent feature weighting is still an open issue.

Bi-level optimization is an important research area of mathematical programming [2]. It has emerged as an important field for progress in handling many real life problems in different domains such as classification and machine learning [2]. A bi-level optimization problem (BLOP) is a hierarchy of two optimization tasks (upper level or leader, and lower level or follower problems). The lower level task appears as a constraint such that only an optimal solution to the lower level problem is a possible feasible candidate to the upper level one. In this context, the class-dependent weighted feature selection can be treated as a bi-level optimization problem. Finding the optimal subset of features with the corresponding class-relevant weighting vectors is expected to achieve a good performance. Motivated by this observation, the main goal of our paper is to propose an efficient bi-level evolutionary approach for class-dependent weighted feature selection using GA.

2 Proposed Approach: BCDWFS

2.1 Main Idea and Motivations

Most of the proposed feature selection methods are class-independent [3], where a subset of features is selected without focusing on any class of the problem. Therefore, finding the optimal feature subset with optimal weighting for each class is expected to improve the classification performance. In doing so, we propose an original bi-level evolutionary approach for weighted feature selection that aims at distinguishing instances of one class from the other classes. A schematic of BCDWFS for a three-class problem showing the interplay between the upper and the lower level, is shown in Fig. 1. The BLOP is applied to perform feature selection and consequently produces optimal weighting vectors for each class of the upper level feature subset. The proposed BCDWFS consists of two steps. In the upper level, an Evolutionary Feature Selection (EFS) algorithm is used to select a subset of features deemed most informative without sacrificing performance. These features are then fed to the lower level, where a Class-Dependent Feature Weighting (CDFW) algorithm is performed. Multiple followers are produced for the selected upper level feature subset, each of which corresponds to one class. In fact, each upper level feature subset (x_u) is associated with multiple follow-ers (x_l). The number of followers is the number of classes (c). Each follower produces nb weighting vectors. A sequence of c concatenated vectors including the feature sub-set optimal weights is hereafter submitted to the upper level to perform the evaluation process. Note that nb is the maximum number of generated weighting vectors for each class. The output of the proposed method is the optimal subset of features with the corresponding optimal weighting vectors for each class. The upper level seeks to opti-mize a combined filter-wrapper objective function including the number of features and the average classification accuracy, while the lower level optimizes one filter objective, namely the mutual information. Due to the high computational cost of bi-level optimiza-tion algorithms, we have used an existing efficient algorithm called CODBA [7,17] that was adapted to our BCDWFS proposed approach.

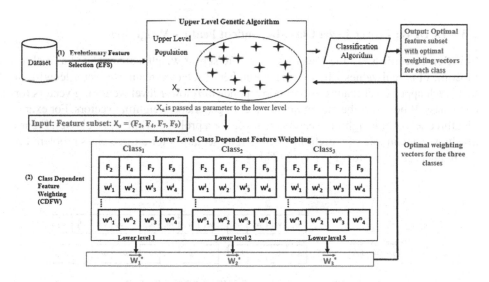

Fig. 1. General algorithmic scheme of BCDWFS for a three-class problem.

2.2 ULFS: Upper Level Feature Selection

Solution Encoding. In the upper level, a representation for candidate feature subset is encoded as a chromosome in such a way that each bit encodes a single feature: $S = F_1\, F_2\, F_3...F_i...F_n$. In fact, each individual in the population, i.e. a subset of features, is represented by a vector of n bits where each bit can takes the value of 1 or 0. Where n is the number of features. In Fig. 2a, "1" represents that the corresponding feature is selected and "0" otherwise.

Fitness Function. The upper level fitness function is represented in Eq. 1, which seeks to minimize the number of features and maximize the classification accuracy, where $|X|$ represents the number of selected features and $Avg(Acc)$ is the average classification accuracy for each feature subset. Each lower and upper level objective function is normalized in the range of [0,1]. The normalization function is defined in [16].

$$F_u(X) = |X| + \frac{1}{Avg(Acc)}$$ (1)

$Avg(Acc)$ is the average classification accuracy of nf feature subsets, where nf is the number of classes, Acc is the classification accuracy of the feature subset, and $\overrightarrow{W_i^*}$ is the optimal weighting vector for the class i. The $Avg(Acc)$ equation is the following:

$$Avg(Acc) = \frac{\sum_{i=1}^{nf}(Acc(\overrightarrow{W_i^*}))}{nf}$$ (2)

2.3 LCDFW: Lower Level Class-Dependent Feature Weighting

Solution Encoding. In the lower level, feature subset weights are encoded as a chromosome of w real values where w is the number of selected features (vector length). In fact, each upper level feature subset corresponds to n lower level weighting vectors for each class. Where n is the maximum number of generated weighting vectors. For example, three sets of n weighting vectors are given for a problem whith three classes. Figure 2b shows an example of weighting vectors representation for a three-class problem for the feature subset vector $[F_2, F_4, F_7, F_9]$.

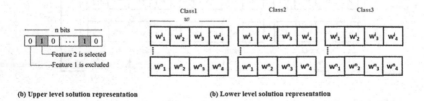

(b) Upper level solution representation   (b) Lower level solution representation

Fig. 2. Solution representation for upper and lower levels.

Fitness Function. The lower level fitness function is presented in Eq. 3, which aims to maximise the relevance between a feature subset X and the class label c. $I(x; c)$ means the mutual information [6] between the feature x and c. To perform feature weighting, a weight vector is associated to each dataset. We use the weighted dataset method as given in [5]. Note that the mutual information is normalized in the range of [0,1] based on a previous study [18].

$$F_l(X, c) = max(\sum_{x \in X} I(x; c)) \tag{3}$$

3 Experimental Study

3.1 Datasets

Ten datasets are used in the experiments. These datasets were chosen from the UCI Machine Learning Repository. The dataset description is given in Table 1. We used discretization for the biological datasets. For more details about discretization methods for biological data, please refer to [11].

Table 1. Datasets

Dataset	#Features	#Classes	#Instances	Class-Distribution
Low-dimensional Datasets				
Wine	13	3	178	33%-40%-27%
Inosphere	34	2	351	64%-37%
Splice	60	4	3190	20%-20%-30%-30%
Madelon	500	2	4400	45%-55%
High-dimensional Datasets				
Colon	2000	2	62	35% - 65%
DLBCL	5469	2	77	25% - 75%
CNS	7129	2	60	35% - 65%
Prostate	10509	2	102	50% - 50%
Leukemia1	5327	3	72	13%-35%-53%
SRBCT	2308	4	83	13%-22%-30%-34%

3.2 Competitor Algorithms and Parameter Setting

To evaluate the performance of BCDWFS, we compare the classification accuracy of the selected features with those selected by two class independent feature selection algorithms (named FW-NSGA-II [8] and RapidPSO [12]), and a weighted feature selection algorithm (named WFS [5]). For each low-dimensional dataset, the instances are randomly divided for each dataset into two sets: 70% as the training set and 30% as the test set such that the class distribution is approximately maintained [4]. For high-dimensional datasets, 10-fold cross validation (10-CV) [13] is used to test the performance of our proposed algorithm.

To ensure fairness of comparison, we use the same number of function evaluations, which is set to 6250000, for all the algorithms. The number of generations and populations is set to 50 for upper and lower levels. The tournament selection method is used with the tournament size = 7 and the elitism size = 1. In the upper level, two-point crossover and two-point mutation are applied. The mutation rate is $1/n$, where n is the number of available features and the crossover probability is 0.9. In the lower level, we have used the simulated binary crossover (SBX) [9] to combine two parents with a 0.9 probability. The polynomial mutation operator (PM) [10] for real-parameter GAs was also used with 0.1 probability. According to a previous study [15], we use $K = 5$ for the KNN classifier. For each dataset, all the algorithms have been conducted for 40 independent runs. We note that all algorithms are coded in Java programming language and all simulations are performed on 50 nodes [2]. [2] Wilcoxon test [14] is used in our case with the significance level of 0.05 to compare the classification accuracy achieved by using all the features for classification, and those selected by BCDWFS and the competitor algorithms.

4   Results and Discussions

Table 2 shows the experimental result of the BCDWFS selected features compared with Full (i.e. using the original feature set), WFS, RapidPSO, and FW-NSGA-II, where column "#F" shows the average size of each feature set. Columns of "B-K-NN", "B-NB", and "B-DT" represent the best results of K-Nearest Neighbor (K-NN), Naïve Bayes (NB), and Decision Trees (DT), respectively. All columns of "A $\pm$ Std-K-NN", "A $\pm$ Std-NB", and "A $\pm$ Std-DT" represent the average and the standard deviation of the accuracy. Each column of "A $\pm$ Std" was achieved through 30 independent runs obtained by K-NN, NB and DT using the full feature set "Full", the selected feature by WFS, RapidPSO, and FW-NSGA-II. The Wilcoxon significance test results for KNN, NB and DT are displayed in column S1, S2, and S3, respectively. Symbol "+" or "−" means that the result is significantly better or worse than the proposed algorithm and symbol "=" means they are similar. The numbers under the dataset name is the number of instances in the dataset.

4.1   Performance of the Selected Features

Table 2 shows the results of the selected features obtainted by BCDWFS compared to Full, WFS, RapidPSO, and FW-NSGA-II. It can be seen that the number of features selected by the BCDWFS is negligible compared with the original feature size. The " − " marks appeared in column S_1 of Table 2 show that the selected features help KNN achieve significantly higher accuracy than using full feature sets on all datasets.

---

[2] https://hpcdocs.kennesaw.edu/dokuwiki/ksu_hpc_nodes

Table 2. Best, average and std of the accuracy of the selected features. Best-values on each dataset are marked in bold.

Dataset	Subset	#F	B-K-NN	A±Std-K-NN	S_1	B-NB	A±Std-NB	S_2	B-DT	A±Std-DT	S_3
				low-dimensional Datasets							
Wine	Full	24	78.40	76.27±2.15	(−)	76.69	75.63±2.90	(−)	80.40	73.14±4.15	(−)
(178)	WFS	9	78.11	75.19±3.14	(−)	79.47	76.23±0.20	(−)	84.98	78.69±2.64	(−)
	RapidPSO	7	88.57	75.47±0.15	(−)	76.41	70.65±4.55	(−)	80.86	77.20±2.74	(−)
	FW-NSGA-II	5	82.00	72.63±1.18	(−)	79.14	78.17±2.40	(−)	80.90	76.08±1.97	(−)
	BCDWFS	6	**90.43**	**87.64±4.90**		87.77	86.74±1.29		90.11	89.28±2.35	
Inosphere	Full	128	86.59	75.99±1.44	(−)	79.47	78.17±2.90	(−)	80.93	79.16±2.08	(−)
(351)	WFS	7	89.00	88.15±1.28	(−)	89.65	88.92±3.25	(−)	92.47	90.01±3.24	(−)
	RapidPSO	12	92.50	90.48±1.15	(−)	89.11	88.67±2.65	(−)	87.55	86.99±2.53	(−)
	FW-NSGA-II	5	90.44	89.66±4.45	(−)	95.50	85.28±1.41	(−)	95.91	92.79±2.26	(−)
	BCDWFS	9	**95.08**	**93.15±3.30**		95.98	94.25±3.34		98.79	**95.10±0.25**	
Splice	Full	60	71.47	69.99±4.00	(−)	76.69	75.90±0.97	(−)	76.66	75.78±2.80	(−)
(3190)	WFS	11	82.08	73.48±4.14	(−)	70.98	68.41±0.20	(−)	85.69	74.04±3.92	(−)
	RapidPSO	8	80.78	75.73±4.15	(−)	80.09	79.71±2.11	(−)	82.07	78.73±2.45	(−)
	FW-NSGA-II	6	80.74	86.60±1.08	(−)	85.99	73.43±2.47	(−)	81.37	70.01±2.99	(−)
	BCDWFS	7	**97.58**	**90.27±2.30**		94.94	92.43±3.34		98.88	**97.99±2.45**	
Madelon	Full	500	79.21	78.96±1.90	(−)	89.25	86.90±1.07	(−)	87.37	86.47±1.45	(−)
(4400)	WFS	10	83.18	77.89±3.14	(−)	89.72	87.51±3.90	(−)	87.98	85.47±0.47	(−)
	RapidPSO	12	89.53	**85.72±0.35**	(+)	86.41	88.59±2.58	(−)	89.59	86.99±2.15	(−)
	FW-NSGA-II	6	90.49	82.09±0.27	(−)	85.14	74.12±2.22	(−)	84.90	78.42±1.29	(−)
	BCDWFS	7	**91.15**	83.84±1.37		97.89	96.98±2.57		90.60	**89.57±1.25**	
				High-dimensional Datasets							
Colon	Full	2000	73.27	72.20±1.00	(−)	72.80	71.80±2.00	(−)	74.42	74.42±0.00	(−)
(62)	WFS	30	83.42	75.30±4.02	(−)	84.03	74.28±3.18	(−)	85.95	84.96±4.66	(=)
	RapidPSO	21	83.68	74.45±3.30	(−)	78.45	71.36±0.23	(−)	87.25	**87.01±4.00**	(+)
	FW-NSGA-II	16	82.20	73.05±4.02	(−)	80.95	80.62±2.65	(−)	80.22	70.89±4.14	(−)
	BCDWFS	18	**95.43**	**80.92±1.30**		90.77	84.00±2.76		92.89	85.49±2.41	
DLBCL	Full	5469	84.36	81.35±2.00	(−)	81.23	81.23±0.00	(−)	89.12	88.22±0.00	(+)
(77)	WFS	34	87.54	80.31±0.10	(−)	96.25	83.23±3.42	(−)	95.75	83.94±5.16	(−)
	RapidPSO	33	95.07	81.77±2.54	(−)	90.58	85.95±2.13	(−)	97.55	86.00±3.47	(−)
	FW-NSGA-II	31	90.60	82.82±5.48	(−)	87.45	85.15±3.53	(−)	95.57	**93.22±3.41**	(+)
	BCDWFS	36	**98.92**	**97.99±2.85**		98.04	96.61±2.00		90.81	85.03±3.12	
CNS	Full	7129	59.12	58.12±2.00	(−)	57.93	59.93±1.00	(−)	72.03	71.03±0.00	(−)
(60)	WFS	41	70.56	70.16±3.28	(−)	70.53	60.87±3.34	(−)	72.76	60.34±5.27	(−)
	RapidPSO	52	74.23	56.37±2.42	(−)	64.98	60.83±2.37	(−)	70.72	59.22±4.60	(−)
	FW-NSGA-II	55	80.31	73.39±1.40	(−)	84.70	82.14±2.76	(−)	80.34	79.02±4.44	(−)
	BCDWFS	49	**87.77**	**87.53±0.18**		89.34	88.47±3.10		88.23	84.91±2.23	
Prostate	Full	10509	81.15	76.15±1.73	(−)	60.05	60.55±1.00	(−)	86.08	80.49±0.00	(−)
(102)	WFS	54	90.00	80.15±4.27	(−)	89.54	86.06±2.76	(−)	90.08	81.22±3.19	(−)
	RapidPSO	46	88.38	80.12±0.54	(−)	85.75	80.22±2.82	(−)	91.10	85.11±2.63	(−)
	FW-NSGA-II	46	90.99	84.62±2.86	(−)	86.88	76.31±2.25	(−)	80.78	74.32±3.29	(−)
	BCDWFS	38	**97.86**	**97.28±1.49**		97.98	97.93±1.15		99.69	**98.99±4.00**	
Leukemia1	Full	7129	88.03	76.03±1.00	(−)	90.96	90.96±0.00	(−)	91.21	90.21±5.00	(−)
(72)	WFS	69	92.00	79.31±3.27	(−)	95.25	85.42±3.42	(−)	91.15	81.04±5.87	(−)
	RapidPSO	85	95.57	83.24±2.16	(−)	90.57	84.95±1.56	(−)	90.17	82.15±3.87	(−)
	FW-NSGA-II	50	79.06	85.77±2.14	(−)	90.00	85.99±3.34	(−)	83.17	88.77±2.55	(−)
	BCDWFS	32	**98.99**	**98.40±4.47**		98.70	96.47±1.00		99.25	**96.11±1.47**	
SRBCT	Full	15154	89.07	88.07±1.73	(−)	85.05	82.05±2.00	(−)	98.77	**97.99±2.00**	(+)
(83)	WFS	66	98.40	88.75±0.16	(−)	96.22	93.35±0.23	(−)	98.12	91.29±1.63	(−)
	RapidPSO	71	90.84	86.20±1.79	(−)	94.62	79.61±0.22	(−)	90.20	80.16±0.11	(−)
	FW-NSGA-II	45	92.30	90.10±4.75	(−)	89.89	89.19±2.47	(−)	86.98	85.09±3.25	(−)
	BCDWFS	42	**100.00**	**97.79±2.28**		99.82	99.00±3.95		95.00	92.26±2.57	

B/A/Std: Best/Average/standard deviation of the accuracy; +/−/=: means that the result is significantly better/worse/similar than using all features.

Compared to the selected features by the WFS, the selected features by BCDWFS help K-NN, NB and DT obtain a significantly better results on almost all datasets. The highest improvement of 21% on average is found on Prostate using KNN. Similarly, the selected features by the BCDWFS obtain higher performance than that of RapidPSO on all datasets except for Madelon and Colon datasets with KNN and DT, respectively. But its best accuracy always higher than the best accuracy obtained by RapidPSO. BCD-WFS achieves better accuracy on almost all datasets than using those selected by FW-NSGA-II except for DLBCL dataset with DT. The best accuracy of BCDWFS is 32% increase on Prostate using DT compared with FW-NSGA-II. The results indicate that by performing class-relevant weights, thus narrowing the GA search space, BCDWFS can select more relevant features.

In general, over 30 comparisons with Full using the three learning algorithms on 10 datasets, BCDWFS wins 28 and loses 2 in terms of average accuracy. However, in term of the best accuracy, BCDWFS outperforms Full in all 30 cases except for the DT on SRBCT. Compared to WFS and FW-NSGA-II, BCDWFS outperforms WFS in all 30 cases and outperforms FW-NSGA-II in 29 cases. Comparing with RapidPSO, BCDWFS wins 28 in terms of average accuracy and loses 2 on Madelon and Colon datasets with KNN and DT, respectively. Results showed that BCDWFS can select a small number of features with high discrimination and generalised well to the three learning algorithms in most cases, with some dataset exceptions due to the same degree of their feature's importance which is equal to $1/n$ (n is the number of features).

To sum up, performance of the three learning algorithms show that BCDWFS with the bi-level model can help the upper level GA to better explore the search space than the competitive algorithms. It results in better discriminating power for almost all datasets and better average accuracy than that of the competitive algorithms. The out-performance of our algorithm over the three peer algorithms could be explained by the main distinction of our BCDWFS that consists in finding the optimal upper level feature subsets with the optimal lower level weighting vectors for each class; which is not the case for the three other algorithms that use a single level of optimization. Another component contributing to BCDWFS superior performance is the class-dependent feature weighting performed in the lower level, which helps GA to select relevant features.

5   Conclusion

The goal of this work is to propose a bi-level class-dependent feature selection method (BCDWFS) that selects optimal feature subsets with optimal weighting vectors for each class which improves the classification performance. The core novelty of this approach is to show the effectiveness of the bi-level model by handling upper level feature selection and lower level class-dependent feature weighting. Performances of the BCDWFS selected features are compared with those on the original set and those generated by a weighted feature selection algorithm (WFS) and two class independent feature selection algorithms (RapidPSO and FW-NSGA-II) using KNN, NB and DT. Results on the ten low- and high-dimensional datasets show that our proposal is very competitive compared with the existing algorithms. The proposed strategies in BCDWFS demonstrate that by taking into account class-dependency in weighted feature selection, the proposed method can achieve better performance than a class independent approach that uses a single level of optimization. This work can be extended in a number of ways. One of the promising directions for handling preprocessing techniques could be the use of an integrating approach to discretization and feature selection in a one stage to improve the classification performance, the computation time and the storage requirement. In addition, as the use of multiple followers in the lower level could incur a considerable computational cost, we believe that using surrogate models [19] could be a good choice to reduce this cost.

References

1. Wang, L., Zhou, N., Chu, F.: A general wrapper approach to selection of class-dependent features. IEEE Trans. Neural Netw. **19**(7), 1267–1278 (2008)
2. Colson, B., Marcotte, P., Savard, G.: An overview of bilevel optimization. Ann. Oper. Res. **153**(1), 235–256 (2007)
3. Xue, B., Zhang, M., Browne, W.N., Yao, X.: A Survey on evolutionary computation approaches to feature selection. IEEE Trans. Evol. Comput. **20**(4), 606–626 (2016)
4. Hammami, M., Bechikh, S., Louati, A., Makhlouf, M., Said, L.B.: Feature construction as a bi-level optimization problem. Neural Comput. Appl. **32**(17), 13783–13804 (2020). https://doi.org/10.1007/s00521-020-04784-z
5. Das, A., Das, S.: Feature weighting and selection with a Paretooptimal trade-off between relevancy and redundancy. Pattern Recogn. Lett. **88**(1), 12–19 (2017)
6. Shannon, C., Weaver, W.: The mathematical theory of communication. The University of Illinois Press, Urbana (1948)
7. Chaabani, A., Bechikh, S. Ben Said, L.: A co-evolutionary decomposition-based algorithm for bi-level combinatorial optimization. In: Proceedings of the IEEE Congress on Evolutionary Computation, pp. 1659–1666. IEEE (2015)
8. Hammami, M., Bechikh, S., Hung, C.C., Ben Said, L.: A Multi-objective hybrid filter-wrapper evolutionary approach for feature selection. Memetic Comput. **11**(2), 193–208 (2019)
9. Deb, K., Agrawal, R.B.: Simulated binary crossover for continuous search space. Complex Syst. **9**(2), 115–214 (1995)
10. Deb, K., Deb, D.: Analyzing mutation schemes for real-parameter genetic algorithms. Int. J. Artif. Intell. Soft Comput. **4**(1), 1–28 (2014)
11. Gallo, C.A., Cecchini, R.L., Carballido, J.A., Micheletto, S., Ponzoni, I.: Discretization of gene expression data revised. Briefings Bioinform. **17**(5), 758–770 (2015)
12. Butler-Yeoman, T., Xue, B., Zhang, M.: Particle swarm optimisation for feature selection: a hybrid filter-wrapper approach. In Proceedings of the IEEE Congress on Evolutionary Computation, pp. 2428–2435. IEEE (2015)
13. Statnikov, A., Aliferis, C.F., Tsamardinos, I., Levy, S.: A comprehensive evaluation of multi-category classification methods for microarray gene expression cancer diagnosis. Bioinform. **21**(1), 631–643 (2005)
14. Derrac, J., García, S., Molina, D., Herrera, F.: A practical tutorial on the use of nonparametric statistical tests as a methodology for comparing evolutionary and swarm intelligence algorithms. Swarm Evol. Comput. **1**(1), 3–18 (2011)
15. Xue, B., Zhang, M., Browne, W.N.: Particle swarm optimization for feature selection in classification: a multi-objective approach. IEEE Trans. Cybernet. **43**(1), 1656–1671 (2013)
16. Hammami, M., Bechikh, S., Hung, C.C., Ben Said, L.: Class dependent feature construction as a bi-level optimization problem. In Proceedings of the IEEE Congress on Evolutionary Computation, pp. 1–8. IEEE (2020)

17. Chaabani, A., Bechikh, S., Said, L.B.: A new co-evolutionary decomposition-based algorithm for bi-level combinatorial optimization. Appl. Intel. **48**(9), 2847–2872 (2018). https://doi.org/10.1007/s10489-017-1115-9
18. Estevez, P., Tesmer, M., Perez, C., Zurada, J.: Normalized mutual information feature selection. IEEE Trans. Neural Netw. **20**(2), 189–201 (2009)
19. Azzouz, N., Bechikh, S., Ben Said, L.: Steady state IBEA assisted by MLP neural networks for expensive multi-objective optimization problems. In Proceedings of the Annual Conference on Genetic and Evolutionary Computation, pp. 581–588. ACM (2009)

Classification of Multi-class Imbalanced Data Streams Using a Dynamic Data-Balancing Technique

Rafiq Ahmed Mohammed$^{(\boxtimes)}$, Kok Wai Wong, Mohd Fairuz Shiratuddin, and Xuequn Wang

The Discipline of Information Technology, Mathematics And Statistics, Murdoch University, Perth, Australia
{Rafiq.Mohammed,K.Wong,F.Shiratuddin,A.Wang}@murdoch.edu.au

Abstract. The performance of classification algorithms with imbalanced streaming data depends upon efficient re-balancing strategy for learning tasks. The difficulty becomes more elevated with multi-class highly imbalanced streaming data. In this paper, we investigate the multi-class imbalance problem in data streams and develop an adaptive framework to cope with imbalanced data scenarios. The proposed One-Vs-All Adaptive Window re-Balancing with Retain Knowledge (OVA-AWBReK) classification framework will combine OVA binarization with Automated Re-balancing Strategy (ARS) using Racing Algorithm (RA). We conducted experiments on highly imbalanced datasets to demonstrate the use of the proposed OVA-AWBReK framework. The results show that OVA-AWBReK framework can enhance the classification performance of the multi-class highly imbalanced data.

Keywords: Active learning · ARS · Imbalanced streaming data · Incremental learning · Multi-classification · One-vs-all · Racing Algorithm · Random Forest

1 Introduction

Due to the complexity with multi-class imbalanced data, we may lose performance in one class while trying to gain it on another class [1]. Also, the task of imbalanced learning becomes challenging with streaming multi-class data to achieve an efficiency of handling class concept changes [2]. Moreover, high Imbalance Ratio (IR) has a significant effect on the classification performance for highly imbalanced stream data learning [3]. Hence, the task of lowering IR in data streams would be imminent and a challenging task unless supported by a dynamic framework [4, 5]. Besides, in data streams, IR and concept frequently change for the class distribution. Also, it would be a challenge to select adaptive window sizes based on a threshold value to adjust windows sizes and capture minority class concept changes. Hence, the task of adaptive window size is a popular practical challenge for learning in the real-time data streams [6].

The use of Automated Re-balancing Strategy (ARS) in providing active learning for faster reduction of uncertainty with highly imbalanced data streams is still a research

© Springer Nature Switzerland AG 2020
H. Yang et al. (Eds.): ICONIP 2020, CCIS 1333, pp. 279–290, 2020.
https://doi.org/10.1007/978-3-030-63823-8_33

focus area in Machine Learning (ML). In streaming data, the imbalanced phenomenon is vital when one of its classes exhibits a higher representation over the other class [2]. Classification problems with multi-class are present and used in many real-world domains such as in bioinformatics, call logs, weather prediction, cancer detection and, heart rates [2, 7, 8]. Learning and improving multi-class predictions in the presence of highly imbalanced data is a challenging task. Researchers [4] applied a chunk-based strategy using the uncertainty of the paired ensemble, and OVA strategy to be able to adapt to dynamic multi-class ratios. The researchers [5] used a real-time class imbalance detection framework to reflect the IR in the learning process dynamically. Also, in addressing the challenges of imbalanced learning, re-sampling the data stream is one of the two popular strategies as compared with feature selection [9]. The re-sampling or re-balancing strategy should be based on active learning to handle multi-class imbalanced data streams [4].

Most of the multi-class classification algorithms face challenges with dynamic nature of imbalanced data streams. The reason lies with how well multi-class classifiers are utilised and the possibility of eliminating obsolete classifiers based on their overall accuracy on the recent chunks [10]. However, the literature suggests that most of ARS are available for static Batch data [11], i.e. when all data are available and re-balanced them as Batch. In online learning, data is not static, and the systems need to be adaptive to deal with imbalanced data streaming problems [9]. Similarly, multi-class systems need to adapt to OVA for data streams [12]. The application of adaptive measures such as dynamic window sizes [13], dynamic framework [4, 5], dynamic re-balancing [2], ARS [11], RA to reduce uncertainty in the learning process [14], and active learning [4] will make the classification technique to be adaptive to handle multi-class imbalanced data streams. This process will lower IR in data streams and also derive consistent prediction rates for the classifier.

The challenge of dynamic re-balancing multi-class data streams is not well studied. The application of ARS for imbalanced data streams has not been discussed much [11], and for multi-class data streams are not studied. Therefore, this paper aims to look into dynamically determining class imbalance status in data streams. It also aims to automatically apply a re-balancing technique that can lead classifiers to adapt to a class imbalance in the data streams effectively. In this paper, we investigate the multi-class imbalanced problems in data streams and develop a framework by addressing the needs of dynamically dealing with imbalanced data streams using batch-incremental processing. Results in the paper confirmed that the proposed framework could be used to provide consistent classification accuracies for multi-class imbalanced data streams.

2 Related Works

Multi-class decomposition is a promising technique to solve multi-class problems [9]. The most popular binarization techniques can be classified into two groups, called the OVA and One-Vs-One (OVO) [15]. OVA is popular because it requires less decomposition and is time-efficient [9]. When we are decomposing the multi-class imbalanced data streams to binary class, we need to select a suitable classifier and other relevant techniques to accommodate in the novel framework. Random Forest (RF) is a popular ensemble learner for imbalanced data stream classification problems to provide stable accuracy [8, 16]. The researchers [15] has implemented the OVA because of its innate features of needing only *"n–1"* for n classes with RF successfully for the first time and has shown its significance with static datasets. Moreover, novel re-balancing techniques were often combined with parallel based ensemble such as RF for data streams [9]. RF with Random Under-Sampling (RUS) re-balancing technique is scalable and capable of classification with highly imbalanced massive datasets [17]. RF has also shown prediction superiority in data streaming as compared to Neural Networks and SVM [11].

Considering the incremental frameworks for imbalanced data streams, the researchers [18] used the Adaptive Incremental Learning (ADAIN) framework for continuous stream data to represent the learning capability of each data chunk. The ADAIN captures previously acquired knowledge h_{t-1} (hypothesis at t-1) to apply to the new data chunk to improve the learning capability of misclassified instances. The selectively resampling procedure technique in [3] was used to preserve the minority samples of previous chunks, and this framework has demonstrated the effectiveness of unsupervised learning with imbalanced data streams. FLORA is a supervised accumulative learning technique that uses streaming windows of both positive and negative instances of the target class of data to track changes over time [19]. However, these techniques lack the capability of re-using the preserved minority and majority samples for multi-class supervised highly imbalanced data stream problems.

From our literature review, the ARS works with static batch data [20]. Besides, RA has the active learning features of providing a faster reduction of uncertainty to select an appropriate technique with imbalanced data [14]. However, an ARS is not yet implemented for the data streaming environment [11]. Hence, there is a need to examine further how well the incremental re-balancing is implemented in an automated strategy. There is also a lack of an appropriate framework that can address the needs of handling highly imbalanced multi-class data streams using dynamic and automated re-balancing strategy, which is stable and consistent. Therefore, this paper aims to propose a new framework to address this gap.

3 Proposed Framework

In this section, we present the proposed OVA-AWBReK framework for learning from imbalanced data streams. The OVA-AWBReK consists of two modules, i.e. (1) Incremental re-balancing module where it trains the classifier with incremental re-balancing data whereby it adaptively passes the previously learned knowledge as increments to the subsequent windows, and (2) Adaptive window module that dynamically adjusts window sizes with an IR threshold. The entire framework is designed for highly imbalanced data streams and offer resilience to challenges discussed in this paper – multi-class imbalanced problems in data streams, adaptive window sizes based on threshold value to adjust windows sizes, lowering IR in data streams, active learning to reduce uncertainty in the learning process.

3.1 OVA-AWBReK Methodology

The formulation of the OVA-AWBReK framework is derived in the following steps.

Step 1. In the OVA-AWBReK, the feature vectors instances ds_i, ds_{i+1},..., ds_n are received in a chunk of multi-class Data Stream DS_j at time j. As soon as we receive the data stream, we perform the OVA binarization, then for each binary class data split for training D_j and for test T_j from the set of instances from (ds_i, ds_{i+1},..., ds_n) DS at time j.

$$\text{Imbalance Ratio } IR_{(j,c,p)} \leftarrow \frac{sum\ of\ minority\ samples}{sum\ of\ majority\ samples} \tag{1}$$

Step 2. When the streams of data chunk DS_j, DS_{j+1} are highly imbalanced with high IR IR_j, IR_{j+1},..., as calculated by Eq. (1), we apply an ARS and select 'b' from the available re-balancing techniques, i.e., RUS, SMOTE, Random Over-Sampling (ROS), Tomek link, One Side Selection (OSS), Edited Nearest Neighbour (ENN), Condensed Nearest Neighbor (CNN), Neighbourhood Cleaning Rule (NCL), No Sampling [20]. The re-balancing technique 'b' is applied to the training dataset (D_j), as calculated by Eq. (2), of a specific stream of data chunk DS_j, and as a result, re-balanced data R_j at time j is derived.

Step 3. During the process of derivation, suitable re-balancing technique 'b' is selected using $\emptyset$, for the combined current D_j and previous stream R_{j-1}, using Eq. (4).

$$D_{ji} = \sum_{i=1}^{0.9n} ds_n \tag{2}$$

$$T_{ji} = \sum_{i=1}^{0.1n} ds_n \tag{3}$$

$$R_{(j,c,p)} = \emptyset_b\, (D_{(j,c,p)} + R_{(j-1,c,p)}) \tag{4}$$
$$\textit{where } b = 1,2, ..., 9,\ c = \text{'RF'}, p = \text{'AUC' or F1'}$$

$$M_{j,i} = f(D_{ji}) \tag{5}$$

$$PO_{j,i} = M_{j,i}(T_{j,i}) \tag{6}$$

$$R_{(j,c,p)} = S_{(j)}\,(\emptyset_b\, (D_{(j,c,p)} + R_{(j-1,c,p)}))$$
$$\textit{where } b = 1,2, ..., 9,\ c = \text{'RF'},\ p = \text{'AUC' or 'F1'},\ IR_{(j,c,p)} < IR_{CUT\,(j,c,p)},\ M_{j,i} = \tag{7}$$
$$f(D_{ji}),\ PO_{j,i} = M_{j,i}\,(T_{j,i}),\ \textit{and } PO_{j,i-1} < PO_{j,i} > PO_{j,i+1}$$

Where $\emptyset$ selects the most suitable re-balancing technique 'b' with minimum classification error '$\varepsilon \sim 0$' based on statistical significance using the Friedman test.

Step 4. The OVA-AWBReK adapts to data distribution IR IR_j, IR_{j+1},..., changes, along with changes to the re-balanced data value R_j, R_{j+1},..., within the data streams (training datasets) D_j, D_{j+1},...,. Also, the OVA-AWBReK dynamically adapts the window size to allow the instances to be processed for efficient learning. During the process of derivation, suitable window size W_j is selected using the process S_j at time j, as calculated by Eq. (7), and Step 7.

Step 5. Classification models M_j, M_{j+1},..., are generated by choosing a classification technique 'C' and the performance metric 'p' value for re-balanced data $R_{(j, c, p)}$ at time j. Select the model M_j with minimum classification error '$\varepsilon \sim 0$' using Eq. (5).

Step 6. We apply the model M_j on the test dataset T_j at time j, as calculated by Eq. (3), and calculate the prediction output PO_j for the performance metric 'p' using Eq. (6).

Step 7. The process S_j compares the IR of the stream of instances (ds_i, ds_{i+1},..., ds_n) with the IR_{cut} (cut-off threshold) for ds_i, ds_{i+1},..., ds_n. Moreover, the framework also compares Prediction Output (PO) result $PO_{j, i}$ at $D_{j, i}$ with the PO results of the subsequent data stream at $D_{j, i+1}$, and even the earlier stream's PO at $D_{j, i-1}$. Then based on maximum PO at either of timestamp, it either rolls back instances to $D_{j, i-1}$, when $PO_{j, i-1}$, is higher than $PO_{j, i}$ at time j and i^{th} data instances or slide window forward to subsequent stream if $PO_{j, i+1}$ is higher. Subsequently, the formulation in Eq. (4), incorporate the IR cut-off threshold, and adaptive windowing will become as in Eq. (7).

4 Experiments

We implemented the OVA-AWBReK framework to highlight the significance of incremental re-balancing, ARS as a quicker way to reduce uncertainty in the learning process and to adapt dynamically adjusted window sizes with IR threshold. In our experiments, we applied the OVA to both Covertype and Yeast datasets to reduce multi-class to a binary classification problem. After binarization, we get "$n-1$" binary datasets for n classes. When using OVA, the outputs from all the binary datasets needs to be combined to derive an average classification performance of the technique.

To demonstrate that OVA-AWBReK can handle multi-class imbalanced data streams effectively comparison experiments were carried with the AUC-ROC and F1 metrics which are commonly used to deal with similar problems. F1, which is the harmonic mean of precision and recall, is more appropriate for the successful separation between minority and majority [17, 21]. While AUC is evaluated for predict probability for each of the class, and then later used to evaluate overall classification performance. AUC is a suitable metric to deal with highly imbalanced datasets [11]. A highly imbalanced multi-class Forest Covertype and Yeast datasets [22] from UCI is used for the study to justify usability of OVA-AWBReK. We compared the performance of OVA-AWBReK with an amended FLORA for mining imbalanced data streams and a popular algorithm that is still currently being used for dealing with imbalanced data stream problems [19].

4.1 Datasets

We conducted experiments on two real-world datasets. Covertype [4, 8] and Yeast [12, 23] are often used as benchmark datasets for data streams. The Covertype dataset consists of 7 classes, 54 attributes and 581,012 instances. Since classes C1 and C2 are over-represented with combined 85.22%, we have re-sampled Covertype dataset (Table 1) to have a fair representation of all classes. The Yeast dataset consists of 10 classes, 8 attributes and 1,484 instances. The main intention is to show how the OVA-AWBReK framework works well with a highly imbalanced dataset, and also to show that the framework can provide comparable results with low imbalanced datasets.

Table 1. Data distribution of experimental data sets

Data Set	The ratio of Classes %										Instances
	C1	C2	C3	C4	C5	C6	C7	C8	C9	C10	
Yeast	31.20	28.91	16.44	10.98	3.44	2.96	2.36	2.02	1.35	0.34	1,484
Covertype (original)	36.46	48.76	06.15	0.47	1.63	2.99	3.53	–	–	–	581,012
Covertype (Re-sampled)	30.99	30.99	15.83	1.22	4.20	7.69	9.08	–	–	–	225,871

4.2 Dealing with Imbalanced Data

As discussed in Sect. 1 and 2, we have explored various re-balancing techniques and frameworks available to mitigate the problem of class imbalance. RUS [17, 24], ROS [24], Synthetic Minority Over-Sampling Technique [20, 25], Tomek link, CNN, OSS, ENN and NCL [20] are some of the re-balancing techniques. In our work, to deal with the imbalanced data problem for streaming data, we implemented ARS using RA technique, which was implemented as ARS for batch data [20].

4.3 Experimental Setup

For the streaming batch experiments on both Covertype and Yeast binary datasets, we distributed the entire dataset into eight windows. Later, we accumulate every window's data to a subsequent window to represent data streaming. The derivation of the optimal window size is based on the number of streams received each day. If there is an 'n' number of instances a day, and the window size 'wsize' should be n/w, where 'w' number of windows required for the framework. If we consider an example derivation, a fraud detection system has received 160,000 instances in a day [26]. Therefore, n = 160,000. If we want a classification system model to be updated every 3 hours, then the number of windows 'w' = 8. Hence, 'wsize' = 160,000/8 = 20,000. In this streaming batch process, each window of data will be distributed as 90% for training the RF model, and the rest 10% data used for the blind test [27]. We performed 3-fold cross-validation for generating the prediction models on each of the datasets.

4.4 Experimental Procedures

Since data in real-time is not static, we conducted the first set of experiments to simulate streaming batch data using benchmark FLORA technique on each of Covertype and Yeast datasets. It is noted that the FLORA does not perform data re-balancing during the training in the data streams. In addition to FLORA's accumulative learning features for streaming batch, we also use ARS and OVA for binarization of multi-class dataset. This technique is to ensure that the comparison is consistent. For this reason, we rename FLORA as the OVA - Accumulative re-balanced (AR) technique– streaming batch for our experiments. The ARS to select an appropriate re-balancing technique for streaming batch learning is a significant part of the OVA-AWBReK framework. For this reason, we explored RA, which has active learning feature is to remove uncertainty with imbalanced data streams [14]. For the second set of experiments, we used the OVA-AWBReK to show performance improvement with incremental re-balancing technique. We also study the impact of IR, which would assist in classifying data streams with imbalanced data distributions.

1) *Performance evaluation of classifiers*: For evaluating the classifier performance in data stream environment, the options to use the last batch score to capture the concept in the stream [28] and the average score to show the significance of average performance of the technique.

1) *OVA - Accumulative Re-balanced (OVA-AR) technique– streaming batch*

For the first set of streaming batch experiments using Yeast and Covertype datasets, we applied OVA to classify multi-class data. Later we applied automated re-balancing techniques using RA, and then RF to train and tested by each classification model.

2) *OVA - Adaptive Window re Balancing with Retain Knowledge (OVA-AWBReK)*

We conducted the second set of experiments using Yeast and Covertype datasets by OVA-AWBReK. For the OVA-AWBReK, we initially tried to improve the performance with incremental re-balancing technique. Later, we found that by also implementing adaptive windows with IR threshold has enhanced the performance of the technique when the IR is high and not stable in the class distribution of a dataset.

a) *Yeast dataset - Experiments and Discussions*

The classification performance in Table 2 and Fig. 1(a) shows the AUC metric of each class for both OVA-AR and OVA-AWBReK using Yeast dataset. In Table 2 and Fig. 1(b) shows the F1 metric of each class for both OVA-AR and OVA-AWBReK using Yeast dataset. The performance in Table 2 shows that OVA-AWBReK outperforms OVA-AR using AUC metric in terms of class average predictions, and almost for each class predictions. The results of AUC show improvement up by 4.57%, from 88.59% for OVA-AR to 92.64% for OVA-AWBReK. Moreover, when AUC of each class is compared, the

OVA-AWBReK improves the AUC of minority class significantly. The minority class for C1 (Class 1) increases up to 91.54% compared with, OVA-AR, 83.04%.

Table 2. AUC-ROC and F1 of each class for OVA streaming predications – yeast dataset

Class	Imbalance Ratio (%)	Accumulative Re-balanced (OVA – AR)– AUC-ROC	Incremental Re-balanced with Threshold (OVA – AWBReK) – AUC-ROC	Accumulative Rebalanced (OVA – AR) – F1	Incremental Re-balanced with Threshold (OVA – AWBReK) – F1
C1	5.08	0.8304	**0.9154**	0.6203	**0.8018**
C2	2.46	**0.8603**	0.8561	**0.6329**	0.6014
C3	2.21	0.7868	**0.8858**	0.5575	**0.6873**
C4	32.73	0.9805	**0.9990**	0.4922	**0.6226**
C5	28.10	0.9225	**0.9693**	0.2246	**0.5108**
C6	8.10	0.9874	**0.9929**	0.8188	**0.8951**
C7	41.40	0.9767	**0.9805**	0.3782	**0.6237**
C8	48.47	0.6742	**0.7287**	0.0285	**0.1756**
C9	73.20	0.8404	**0.9366**	0.6458	**0.7723**
C10	295.80	**1.0000**	**1.0000**	0.2083	**0.9583**
Prediction Average		0.8859	**0.9264**	0.4607	**0.6649**

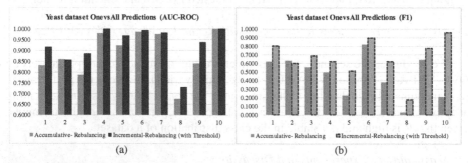

(a)   (b)

Fig. 1. Accumulative re-balanced & incremental re-balanced with Threshold AUC-ROC& F1 result for Yeast data stream

The performance in Table 2 and Fig. 1(b) shows that the OVA-AWBReK outperforms OVA-AR using F1 metric in terms of class average predictions, and almost for each class predictions. The results of F1 show the improvement up by 44.32%, from 46.07% for OVA-AR to 66.49% for the OVA-AWBReK. Moreover, when F1 of each class is compared, the OVA-AWBReK improves F1 of minority class significantly. The minority class for C1 (Class 1) increases up to 80.18% compared with the basic technique, OVA-AR, 62.03%. Furthermore, when the IR is higher for a class, the F1 metric is significantly higher for OVA-AWBReK as compared to OVA-AR. For the C10 (Class 10) with IR of 295.80, the minority class predictions increase up to 95.83% compared with the OVA-AR technique, 20.83% with a drastic improvement of 360.10%.

b) *Covertype dataset - Experiments and Discussions*

The classification performance in Table 3 and Fig. 2(a) shows the AUC metric of each class for both OVA-AR and OVA-AWBReK using Covertype dataset. In Table 3 shows the AUC metric of each class for both OVA-AR and OVA-AWBReK using Covertype dataset. The performance in Table 3 shows that OVA-AWBReK outperforms OVA-AR using AUC metric in terms of class average predictions, and for each class predictions. The results of AUC show improvement up by 1.00%, from 97.54% for OVA-AR 98.54% for OVA-AWBReK. Moreover, when the AUC of each class is compared, OVA-AWBReK improves the AUC of minority class significantly. The minority class for C1 (Class 1) increases up to 96.43% compared to OVA-AR, 94.89%. The performance in Table 3 and Fig. 2(b) shows that the OVA-AWBReK outperforms OVA-AR using F1 metric in terms of class average predictions, and almost for each class predictions. The results of F1 show the improvement up by 13.23%, from 71.79% for OVA-AR to 81.29% for the OVA-AWBReK. Moreover, when the F1 of each class is compared, the OVA-AWBReK improves the F1 of the minority class significantly. The minority class for C1 (Class 1) increases up to 87.03% compared with the basic technique, OVA-AR, 81.43%. Furthermore, when the IR is higher for a class, the F1 metric is significantly higher for OVA-AWBReK as compared to OVA-AR. For the C4 (Class 4) with IR of 81.22, the minority class predictions increase up to 68.88% compared with the OVA-AR, 34.11% with a drastic improvement of 101.93%.

c) *Discussions*

From our analyses, we can conclude that OVA-AWBReK is adaptive and achieved consistent and stable prediction average rates of F1 and AUC metric concerning highly imbalanced dataset. When using OVA-AR, we accumulated original data in the stream and applied suitable re-balancing technique. However, when using OVA-AWBReK, we retained re-balanced data of current window and incremented it to the subsequent stream, and thus we retained the concept of minority class has helped to improve the performance. Furthermore, when the IR is higher for a class in the data stream, OVA-AWBReK performed well using AUC, and significantly better with F1 metric, on both datasets as compared to OVA-AR technique. Also, adaptive windows when comparing IR of a stream with IR threshold has enabled to lower the IR in the stream. We want to highlight that the OVA-AWBReK work well for the highly imbalanced dataset.

Table 3. AUC-ROC and F1 of each class for OVA streaming predications – Forest Covertype dataset

Class	Imbalance Ratio (%)	Accumulative Rebalanced (OVA – AR)- AUC-ROC	Incremental Re-balanced with Threshold (OVA – AWBReK)- AUC-ROC	Accumulative Rebalanced (OVA – AR) – F1	Incremental Re-balanced with Threshold (OVA – AWBReK)- F1
C1	2.23	0.9489	**0.9643**	0.8143	**0.8703**
C2	2.23	0.9381	**0.9596**	0.7897	**0.8296**
C3	5.32	0.9844	**0.9934**	**0.8523**	0.8347
C4	81.22	0.9956	**0.9962**	0.3411	**0.6888**
C5	22.79	0.9837	**0.9936**	0.6895	**0.7824**
C6	12.01	0.9848	**0.9933**	0.6433	**0.7957**
C7	10.01	0.9926	**0.9973**	0.8953	**0.8891**
Prediction Average		0.9754	**0.9854**	0.7179	**0.8129**

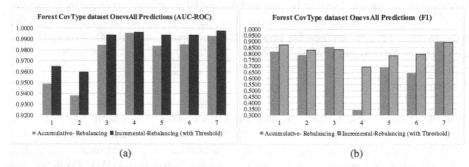

(a)   (b)

Fig. 2. Accumulative re-balanced& incremental re-balanced with Threshold AUC& F1 for Forest Covertype data stream

5   Conclusion

We implemented the OVA-AWBReK framework, an OVA-batch streaming technique for multi-class data that focussed on integrating four techniques, OVA for binarization of multi-class data, increments of re-balanced data, adaptive window with IR threshold and ARS. We focussed on a framework to handle the problem of imbalanced class distribution of large and small size data and with higher and lower IR class distribution.

The experiment results can demonstrate that functionality of OVA-AWBReK could achieve consistent and better F1 and AUC-ROC as compared to OVA-AR, which is an amended FLORA technique. Moreover, OVA-AWBReK is computationally efficient, the reason being ARS using RA runs for a subset (approximately 10%) of a given dataset. OVA-AWBReK with incremental re-balancing and ARS gives a faster reduction of uncertainty in the imbalanced data stream learning process to select a suitable re-balancing technique on the fly. We will consider the use of more datasets in future works to expand testing of OVA-AWBReK under vast operating conditions.

References

1. FernáNdez, A., et al.: Analysing the classification of imbalanced data-sets with multiple classes: Binarization techniques and ad-hoc approaches. Knowl.-Based Syst. **42**, 97–110 (2013)
2. Ancy, S., Paulraj, D.: Handling imbalanced data with concept drift by applying dynamic sampling and ensemble classification model. Comput. Commun. **153**, 553–560 (2020)
3. Ren, S., et al.: Selection-based resampling ensemble algorithm for nonstationary imbalanced stream data learning. Know-Based Syst. **163**, 705–722 (2019)
4. Zhang, H., et al.: Online active learning paired ensemble for concept drift and class imbalance. IEEE Access **6**, 73815–73828 (2018)
5. Wang, S., Minku, L.L., Yao. X.: A learning framework for online class imbalance learning. In: 2013 IEEE Symposium on Computational Intelligence and Ensemble Learning (CIEL). IEEE (2013)
6. Bifet, A., Gavalda, R.: Learning from time-changing data with adaptive windowing. In: Proceedings of the 2007 SIAM International Conference on Data Mining. SIAM (2007)
7. Sen, A., et al.: Binarization with boosting and oversampling for multiclass classification. IEEE Trans. Cybernet. **46**(5), 1078–1091 (2015)
8. Losing, V., Hammer, B., Wersing, H.: Incremental on-line learning: A review and comparison of state of the art algorithms. Neurocomput. **275**, 1261–1274 (2018)
9. Haixiang, G., et al.: Learning from class-imbalanced data: Review of methods and applications. Expert Syst. Appl. **73**, 220–239 (2017)
10. Siahroudi, S.K., Moodi, P.Z., Beigy, II.: Detection of evolving concepts in non-stationary data streams: A multiple kernel learning approach. Expert Syst. Appl. **91**, 187–197 (2018)
11. Dal Pozzolo, A., et al.: Learned lessons in credit card fraud detection from a practitioner perspective. Expert Syst. Appl. **41**(10), 4915–4928 (2014)
12. Hashemi, S., et al.: Adapted one-versus-all decision trees for data stream classification. IEEE Trans. Knowl. Data Eng. **21**(5), 624–637 (2014)
13. Kuncheva, L.I., Žliobaitė, I.: On the window size for classification in changing environments. Intell. Data Anal. **13**(6), 861–872 (2009)
14. Nguyen, V.-L., Destercke, S., Masson, M.-H.: Partial data querying through racing algorithms. Int. J. Approx. Reas. **96**, 36–55 (2018)
15. Adnan, M.N., Islam, M.Z.: One-vs-all binarization technique in the context of random forest. In: Proceedings of the European Symposium on Artificial Neural Networks, Computational Intelligence and Machine Learning (2015)
16. Zainudin, M.S., et al.: Activity recognition using one-versus-all strategy with relief-f and self-adaptive algorithm. In: 2018 IEEE Conference on Open Systems (ICOS). IEEE (2018)
17. Mohammed, R.A., Wong, K.-W., Shiratuddin, M.F., Wang, X.: Scalable machine learning techniques for highly imbalanced credit card fraud detection: a comparative study. In: Geng, X., Kang, B.-H. (eds.) PRICAI 2018. LNCS (LNAI), vol. 11013, pp. 237–246. Springer, Cham (2018). https://doi.org/10.1007/978-3-319-97310-4_27

18. He, H., et al.: Incremental learning from stream data. IEEE Trans. Neural Netw. **22**(12), 1901–1914 (2011)
19. Lazarescu, M.M., Venkatesh, S., Bui, H.H.: Using multiple windows to track concept drift. Intell. Data Anal. **8**(1), 29–59 (2004)
20. Dal Pozzolo, A., Caelen, O., Waterschoot, S., Bontempi, G.: Racing for unbalanced methods selection. In: Yin, H., et al. (eds.) IDEAL 2013. LNCS, vol. 8206, pp. 24–31. Springer, Heidelberg (2013). https://doi.org/10.1007/978-3-642-41278-3_4
21. Fisher, W.D.: Machine learning for the automatic detection of anomalous events. ProQuest Dissertations Publishing (2017)
22. Blake, C.L., Merz, C.J.: *UCI* Machine Learning Repository. Irvine, CA: University of California, School of Information and Computer Science (1998)
23. Abdi, L., Hashemi, S.: To combat multi-class imbalanced problems by means of over-sampling techniques. IEEE Trans. Knowl. Data Eng. **28**(1), 238–251 (2015)
24. Drummond, C., Holte, R.C.: C4. 5, class imbalance, and cost sensitivity: why under-sampling beats over-sampling. In: Workshop on learning from imbalanced datasets II. Citeseer (2003)
25. Chawla, N.V., et al.: SMOTE: synthetic minority over-sampling technique. J. Artif. Intell. Res. **16**, 321–357 (2002)
26. Dal Pozzolo, A., et al.: Credit card fraud detection: a realistic modeling and a novel learning strategy. IEEE Trans. Neural Netw. Learn. Syst. **29**(8), 3784–3797 (2018)
27. Shahparast, H., Mansoori, E.G.: An online fuzzy model for classification of data streams with drift. In: 2017 Artificial Intelligence and Signal Processing Conference (AISP). IEEE (2017)
28. Lichtenwalter, R.N., Chawla, N.V.: Learning to classify data streams with imbalanced class distributions. New Frontiers in Applied Data Mining. LNCS. Springer, Heidelberg (2009)

Data Reduction for Noisy Data Classification Using Semi-supervised Manifold-Preserving Graph Reduction

Li Zhang[1,2]([⊠]) [ID], Qingqing Pang[1], Zhiqiang Xu[1], and Xiaohan Zheng[1]

[1] School of Computer Science and Technology & Joint International Research Laboratory of Machine Learning and Neuromorphic Computing, Soochow University, Suzhou 215006, Jiangsu, China
zhangliml@suda.edu.cn, {20164227004,20184227056}@stu.suda.edu.cn
[2] Provincial Key Laboratory for Computer Information Processing Technology, Soochow University, Suzhou 215006, Jiangsu, China

Abstract. This paper investigates the issue of data reduction for noisy data classification in semi-supervised learning. A novel semi-supervised manifold-preserving graph reduction (Semi-MPGR) is proposed for data reduction in the framework of semi-supervised learning. In Semi-MPGR, the adjacent graph consists of three sub-graphs that are constructed by labeled samples, unlabeled ones, and both. In doing so, the role of label information is strengthened. On the basis of the defined graph, Semi-MPGR selects data points according to their connection strength. The retained data could maintain the manifold structure of data and be efficiently handled by semi-supervised classifiers. Experimental results on several real-world data sets indicate the feasibility and validity of Semi-MPGR.

Keywords: Classification · Adjacent graph · Semi-supervised learning · Data reduction

1 Introduction

As a technique of data preprocessing, data reduction has been a hot topic in machine learning and data mining [1,3]. Data reduction can be found in many situations. For example, if data contains noise, data reduction could be used to filter noise [2,4,5]. To make normal methods deal with large-scale data, data reduction could be used to pick up representative samples [6]. To fast train support vector machines (SVM), data reduction could be used to find potential support vectors to reduce the number of training samples [7–9]. For unbalance learning, data reduction could be used to reduce the number of data in the majority class to make a balance [10,11]. In summary, the main goal of data reduction is to find representative samples from the original data set. For different learning tasks, methods for data reduction are also different. This paper focuses on the task of noisy data classification in the framework of semi-supervised learning.

Supported by the Natural Science Foundation of the Jiangsu Higher Education Institutions of China under Grant No. 19KJA550002, the Six Talent Peak Project of Jiangsu Province of China under Grant No. XYDXX-054, and the Priority Academic Program Development of Jiangsu Higher Education Institutions.

H. Yang et al. (Eds.): ICONIP 2020, CCIS 1333, pp. 291–299, 2020.
https://doi.org/10.1007/978-3-030-63823-8_34

To implement data reduction, under-sampling and clustering are two kinds of common techniques. The random under-sampling (RUS) is the simplest way that randomly pick up a fixed number of samples [3]. By using a clustering algorithm, the original data can be partitioned into several groups in which the centers would be treated as representative samples [4,6]. Although these two kinds of methods can remove outliers and noisy samples to a certain extent, they cannot maintain the local structure of original data well. To preserve the manifold structure of data, a manifold-preserving graph reduction (MPGR) method was designed for data reduction [2]. MPGR first constructs a graph without considering the label information, and selects representative samples according to the connection strength of samples. In doing so, MPGR can maintain the local manifold structure of unlabeled data and delete possible outliers and noisy points. On the basis of MPGR, Xu and Zhang proposed a supervised MPGR (SMPGR) for supervised learning. SMPGR utilizes the label information to guide the construction of graph. Obviously, SMPGR is not suit for semi-supervised learning. Although MPGR can be applied to semi-supervised learning, MPGR is naturally a unsupervised method that ignores the label information in the original data. Thus, MPGR would lose the labeled samples, which are so rare and valuable that we do not want to reduce it any more.

To deal with data reduction for noisy data classification in semi-supervised learning, this paper presents a semi-supervised manifold-preserving graph reduction (Semi-MPGR) method based on MPGR. The goal of Semi-MPGR is to filter noise data and find representative samples for the subsequent processing. To construct the adjacent graph of all data, Semi-MPGR requires three sub-graphs that are constructed on labeled samples, unlabeled samples, and both. On the basis of the graph, the connection strength of samples is taken as a measurement. The greater the connection strength of a sample is, the more important the sample. In doing so, Semi-MPGR could find the representative samples that could maintain the manifold information. Extensive experiments are conducted on synthetic and real-world data sets. Experimental results indicate that Semi-MPGR is promising.

2   Semi-supervised Manifold-Preserving Graph Reduction

Although MPGR was designed for semi-supervised learning because there are a great number of unlabeled data in the semi-supervised case, MPGR cannot effectively utilize the limited label information that is valuable for semi-supervised learning. It is easy to find that MPGR hardly plays a good role in the two scenarios: When there exists a larger sample noise, the manifold structure is relatively unclear. The sample points selected by MPGR usually keep the same "unclear" structure. In particular, noise samples on the edge of the manifold structure cannot be removed. In addition, the labeled data could be excluded by MPGR. To remedy it, this section proposes Semi-MPGR by designing the weight matrix with label information.

2.1   Adjacent Graph

In the framework of the semi-supervised binary classification problem, there is a set of training sample-pairs $D = \{(\mathbf{x}_1, y_1), \cdots, (\mathbf{x}_m, y_m)\}$, where $\mathbf{x}_i \in X \subseteq \mathbb{R}^n$, X is the set of samples, $y_i \in Y = \{-1, 0, +1\}$ is the label information of $\mathbf{x}_i$, Y is the set of sample labels, n is the number of features, and m is the number of samples. Sample $\mathbf{x}_i$ is an unlabeled one when $y_i = 0$, while sample $\mathbf{x}_i$ belongs to one of classes when $y_i = -1$ or $y_i = +1$. Let X_L be the set of ℓ labeled samples and X_U be the set of u unlabeled ones. Thus, $X = X_L \cup X_U$ and $m = \ell + u$.

In fact, the weight matrix $\mathbf{W}$ can be partitioned as:

$$\mathbf{W} = \begin{bmatrix} \mathbf{W}^{LL} & \mathbf{W}^{LU} \\ \mathbf{W}^{UL} & \mathbf{W}^{UU} \end{bmatrix} \tag{1}$$

where $\mathbf{W}^{LL} \in \mathbb{R}^{\ell \times \ell}$ is the weight matrix of labeled samples, $\mathbf{W}^{UU} \in \mathbb{R}^{u \times u}$ is the weight matrix of unlabeled samples, $\mathbf{W}^{LU} = (\mathbf{W}^{UL})^T$ denotes the connection between labeled samples and unlabeled samples.

According to (1), we need to construct three sub-graphs to generate $\mathbf{W}$ using the k-nearest neighbor rule. In semi-supervised learning, we usually greatly trust samples with labels. Thus, the weights between labeled samples should be greater. For the set X_L, we connect the labeled neighbors of a labeled sample using a weight of 1. Namely,

$$W_{ij}^{LL} = \begin{cases} 1, & if \ \mathbf{x}_i \in N_L(\mathbf{x}_j) \ and \ \mathbf{x}_j \in N_L(\mathbf{x}_i) \ and \ \mathbf{x}_i, \mathbf{x}_j \in X_L \\ 0, & otherwise \end{cases} \tag{2}$$

where $N_L(\mathbf{x}_i) \subset X_L$ means the set of labeled nearest neighbors of $\mathbf{x}_i$. For the unlabeled samples, we can connect them using a heat kernel:

$$W_{ij}^{UU} = \begin{cases} \exp\left(-\frac{\|\mathbf{x}_i - \mathbf{x}_j\|}{2\sigma^2}\right), & if \ \mathbf{x}_i \in N_U(\mathbf{x}_j) \ and \ \mathbf{x}_j \in N_U(\mathbf{x}_i) \ and \ \mathbf{x}_i, \mathbf{x}_j \in X_U \\ 0, & otherwise \end{cases} \tag{3}$$

where $\sigma > 0$ is the parameter for constructing graph, and $N_U(\mathbf{x}_i) \subset X_U$ means the set of unlabeled nearest neighbors of $\mathbf{x}_i$. Obviously, both W^{LL} and W^{UU} are symmetric.

Now, we consider the construction of W^{UL}. It is intuitive to further observe the connection relationship of unlabeled samples with labeled ones. In other words, we find the labeled neighbors for unlabeled data. The i-th row and j-th column of $\mathbf{W}^{NL}$ is defined as:

$$W_{ij}^{UL} = \begin{cases} \exp\left(-\frac{\|\mathbf{x}_i - \mathbf{x}_j\|}{2\sigma^2}\right), & if \ \mathbf{x}_j \in N_L(\mathbf{x}_i) \ and \ \mathbf{x}_i \in X_U \ and \ \mathbf{x}_j \in X_L \\ 0, & otherwise \end{cases} \tag{4}$$

Clearly, $\mathbf{W}^{UL}$ is not symmetric. However, the weight matrix $\mathbf{W}$ of all data is symmetric because we make $\mathbf{W}^{UL} = (\mathbf{W}^{LU})^T$.

Remark 1: Why do we partition $\mathbf{W}$? First, we try to emphasize the connection between label samples and make the connection weight values greatest. Second, we want to observe the connection of unlabeled samples with labeled ones. If an unlabeled sample is closer to any of labeled samples, it would help to maintain the local structure around the label ones.

Remark 2: Why do we build unidirectional connections instead of bidirectional ones between labeled and unlabeled samples? As mentioned above, we hope to utilize the label information to aid the selection of unlabeled samples. Thus, it is unnecessary to consider the connection of labeled samples with unlabeled ones.

2.2 Algorithm Description

Once the weight matrix is determined, we can calculate the connection strength for a given sample x_i and select the most important sample among candidate samples using the following rule:

$$x^* = \arg \max_{x_i \in X_c} d(x_i) \tag{5}$$

where $X_c \subseteq X$ is the set of candidate samples. Note that Semi-MPGR iteratively selects an important sample from the set of candidate samples. Thus, X_c would be changed in each iteration.

Roughly speaking, Semi-MPGR has two main steps: constructing the weight matrix W and calculating the connection strength, which is similar to MPGR. Semi-MPGR has a different way for constructing the adjacent graph from MPGR. Given ℓ labeled and u unlabeled samples, the computational complexity of constructing the adjacent graph in Semi-MPGR is $O((\ell^2 + u^2 + \ell u)n)$. Let n_g be the maximum number of edges that are linked to the vertices in the original graph. Then, the complexity of calculating the connection strength is $O(rmn_g)$. Semi-MPGR has a similar computational complexity as MPGR because only the construction of the weight matrix is different.

3 Experiments

Semi-MPGR is designed for data reduction that is to select a part of data to represent the original data in a sense, say, manifold structure here. This section is to validate the effectiveness of Semi-MPGR and conduct experiments on a synthetic data set and UCI data sets [12].

Because we adopt the framework of semi-supervised learning, we take LapSVM as the subsequent classifier to measure the classification ability of retained data generated by Semi-MPGR or other compared methods including MPGR and random under-sampling (RUS). For LapSVM, we adopt the radial basis function (RBF) kernel $K(x_i, x_j) = \exp\left(-\|x_i - x_j\|^2/2\sigma^2\right)$ with the kernel parameter $\sigma > 0$. In constructing the adjacent graphs, we also need the parameter σ, see (3) and (4). For simplicity, the parameter σ in both the RBF kernel and the graph construction is the same and determined by using the median method [13]. Namely, we set σ as the median value in the set $\{\|x_i - \bar{x}\|^2\}_{i=1}^m$, where $\bar{x}$ is the mean of training samples.

The code of our algorithm is written in MATLAB R2013a on a PC with an Inter Core I7 processor with 8GB RAM.

3.1 Synthetic Data Set

We conduct experiments on the two-moon data set that is a classical synthetic data set for classification [2]. On the two-moon data set, we compare the distribution of retained samples obtained by MPGR and Semi-MPGR.

In this experiment, there are 2000 unlabeled training examples and 50 labeled ones for each class, as shown in Fig. 1 where symbols "o" and "□" denote samples in Class 1 and Class 2, respectively, and the symbol "·" denotes unlabeled samples. In fact, these unlabeled training examples have been corrupted by the Gaussian white noise with zero mean and 0.09 variance, which almost covers the manifold structure of data.

Let $r = 0.1m$ and $k = 2$ for both MPGR and Semi-MPGR. The distribution of retained data is shown in Fig. 2. Obviously, most labeled samples are ignored by MPGR, which results in an unclear structure as Fig. 1. However, Semi-MPGR can extract all labeled samples in this case and restore the manifold structure of labeled data, which supports the effectiveness of Semi-MPGR for utilizing the label information.

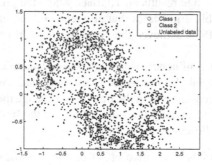

Fig. 1. Distribution of training samples in the two-moon data set.

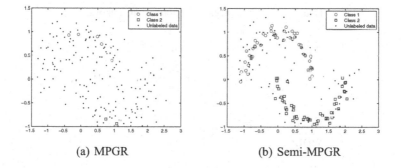

(a) MPGR   (b) Semi-MPGR

Fig. 2. Distribution of retained data obtained by (a) MPGR and (b) Semi-MPGR.

3.2 UCI Data

We conduct experiments on seven UCI data sets that are summarized in Table 1. These data sets cover a wide range of areas (including pathology, vehicle engineering, bioinformatics, and finance), with sample size ranging from 267 to 1473 and data features ranging from 9 to 34. We normalize all data sets so that features are scaled to $[-1, 1]$ before training. In the experimental procedure, each UCI data set is randomly divided into two subsets: 80% for training and 20% for test. On the training set, we randomly select 10% as labeled data, and the rest as unlabeled. We repeat 10 times for data partition.

Four methods are considered for comparison: None, RUS, MPGR and Semi-MPGR. The common parameter is r. Let r vary in the set $\{0.1\,m, \cdots, 0.8\,m\}$. For both MPGR and Semi-MPGR, k is also an important parameter. the selection range of k is from 6 to 14. The five-fold cross validation method is applied to choose the optimal r and k on the training set. The experimental results on the test sets are reported.

Table 2 shows the average results on 10 trials, where the greatest values are in bold type. Observation on Table 2 indicates that all preprocessing methods are effective on most data sets. Semi-MPGR achieves the best classification performance among four compared methods.

To further observe the influence of label noise on data reduction methods, we add 5%, 10%, 15% and 20% label noise to the labeled original data. In other words, 5%, 10%, 15% and 20% labeled samples in the training set change their labels. Experimental results are listed in Table 3, where the bold values are the best one among compared methods. We have the following conclusions.

- First, the label noise has a negative effect on the classification performance. The greater the label noise is, the worse the classification performance is for all methods on most data sets.

Table 1. Information of UCI data sets

Data	#Instances	#Attributes	#Categories
Australian	700	14	2
CMC	1473	9	2
German	1000	24	2
Ionosphere	351	34	2
Hearts	270	13	2
Spect	267	22	2
WDBC	569	14	2

Table 2. Classification accuracy (%) on UCI data sets without label noise

Dataset	None	MPGR	RUS	Semi-MPGR
Australian	85.00 ± 2.08	**85.87 ± 1.33**	85.49 ± 2.00	**85.87 ± 1.94**
CMC	54.74 ± 3.43	54.65 ± 2.19	54.96 ± 3.27	**55.35 ± 4.11**
German	64.00 ± 3.87	63.75 ± 6.00	64.35 ± 3.87	**64.70 ± 4.47**
Heart	82.41 ± 3.18	80.93 ± 3.60	82.41 ± 3.18	**82.59 ± 3.40**
Ionosphere	75.43 ± 7.93	82.29 ± 6.32	75.96 ± 7.18	**83.57 ± 4.63**
Spect	54.91 ± 9.52	55.85 ± 7.24	55.21 ± 8.31	**58.49 ± 9.86**
WDBC	90.89 ± 2.77	90.89 ± 2.89	90.89 ± 2.77	**91.33 ± 2.12**

Table 3. Classification accuracy (%) on UCI data sets with label noise

		(a) 5% label noise		
Dataset	None	MPGR	RUS	Semi-MPGR
Australian	85.22 ± 2.94	83.84 ± 4.96	85.22 ± 2.94	**85.58 ± 2.76**
CMC	54.39 ± 3.59	**55.48 ± 2.68**	54.29 ± 2.83	55.44 ± 4.05
German	**66.10 ± 4.90**	63.90 ± 5.23	**66.10 ± 4.90**	**66.10 ± 4.90**
Heart	78.52 ± 7.16	78.52 ± 6.60	78.52 ± 7.16	**78.70 ± 6.37**
Ionosphere	73.00 ± 6.98	74.71 ± 6.63	73.40 ± 6.79	**77.14 ± 7.62**
Spect	54.34 ± 7.95	58.30 ± 8.27	54.28 ± 5.12	**58.49 ± 9.29**
WDBC	90.80 ± 3.57	90.53 ± 3.34	90.80 ± 3.57	**91.68 ± 2.90**
		(b) 10% label noise		
Dataset	None	MPGR	RUS	Semi-MPGR
Australian	83.19 ± 3.24	**83.26 ± 3.75**	83.19 ± 3.24	**83.26 ± 3.30**
CMC	54.87 ± 2.84	54.78 ± 4.96	54.87 ± 2.84	**55.13 ± 2.85**
German	**62.35 ± 4.96**	61.55 ± 7.21	**62.35 ± 4.96**	**62.35 ± 4.96**
Heart	75.37 ± 6.71	73.33 ± 7.26	75.37 ± 6.71	**75.56 ± 5.51**
Ionosphere	69.86 ± 9.02	75.14 ± 6.97	70.40 ± 7.97	**76.71 ± 5.60**
Spect	53.77 ± 4.29	58.68 ± 4.91	55.26 ± 4.14	**58.87 ± 5.25**
WDBC	89.74 ± 3.47	90.00 ± 2.57	89.74 ± 3.47	**91.33 ± 2.82**
		(c) 15% label noise		
Dataset	None	MPGR	RUS	Semi-MPGR
Australian	**81.38 ± 4.52**	80.51 ± 5.88	**81.38 ± 4.52**	81.30 + 4.53
CMC	53.38 ± 2.64	53.47 ± 5.14	53.54 ± 3.06	**53.86 ± 3.28**
German	65.50 ± 4.75	65.70 ± 4.35	65.50 ± 4.75	**65.80 ± 4.76**
Heart	75.00 ± 5.40	73.52 ± 5.46	75.00 ± 5.40	**75.37 ± 6.93**
Ionosphere	72.14 ± 9.55	72.29 ± 8.25	72.14 ± 9.55	**74.00 ± 7.88**
Spect	56.04 ± 6.60	58.49 ± 3.88	56.06 ± 6.50	**59.43 ± 9.04**
WDBC	87.88 ± 4.87	89.12 ± 4.59	87.88 ± 4.87	**89.47 ± 5.20**
		(d) 20% label noise		
Dataset	None	MPGR	RUS	Semi-MPGR
Australian	83.91 ± 4.28	82.39 ± 5.24	83.91 ± 4.28	**83.99 ± 4.31**
CMC	54.87 ± 3.57	53.42 ± 4.09	54.87 ± 3.57	**55.26 ± 4.14**
German	63.10 ± 4.77	63.55 ± 4.97	63.10 ± 4.77	**64.25 ± 5.26**
Heart	**74.26 ± 7.43**	70.74 ± 9.55	**74.26 ± 7.43**	**74.26 ± 7.43**
Ionosphere	69.00 ± 5.13	72.43 ± 7.38	69.64 ± 5.20	**72.86 ± 7.16**
Spect	57.36 ± 6.36	57.55 ± 11.47	57.08 ± 5.11	**57.74 ± 6.11**
WDBC	84.69 ± 3.42	84.16 ± 6.67	84.69 ± 3.42	**85.40 ± 3.24**

– Under each level of label noise, Semi-MPGR is superior to compared methods at least on five out of six data sets. In other words, Semi-MPGR can assure its advantage even if existing label noise.

4 Conclusion

In this paper, we propose Semi-MPGR for data reduction of noisy data in semi-supervised learning. To fully take use of the label information, Semi-MPGR constructs two sub-graphs related to the labeled data and one sub-graph related to only unlabeled data. There is an assumption that the labeled data is correct and has a manifold structure. In such a case, Semi-MPGR performs well, which is supported by the experiments on the synthetic data set. Semi-MPGR can select all labeled data and keep the manifold structure of data. Moreover, experimental results on the UCI data sets show that LapSVM with data reduction can obtain better performance. Semi-MPGR outperforms other compared methods, even when there exists label noise in the training set.

From experiments, we can see the number of retained samples has a great effect on the performance of data reduction methods, including Semi-MPGR. It is worth finding a way to adaptively determine the value of this parameter in future.

References

1. Zhang, S., Zhang, C., Yang, Q.: Data preparation for data mining. Appl. Artif. Intell. **17**(5–6), 375–381 (1999)
2. Sun, S., Hussain, Z., ShaweTaylor, J.: Manifold-preserving graph reduction for sparse semi-supervised learning. Neurocomput. **124**(2), 13–21 (2014)
3. Madigan, D., Nason. M.: Data reduction: sampling. In: Handbook of Data Mining and Knowledge Discovery, pp. 205–208 (2002)
4. Barca, J.C., Rumantir, G.: A modified k-means algorithm for noise reduction in optical motion capture data. In: 6th IEEE/ACIS International Conference on Computer and Information Science in Conjunction with 1st IEEE/ACIS International Workshop on e-Activity, pp. 118–122 (2007)
5. Xu, Z., Zhang, L.: Supervised manifold-preserving graph reduction for noisy data classification. In: 11th International Conference on Knowledge Science, Engineering and Management. pp. 226–237. Changchun, China, August 17–19 (2018)
6. Nie, F., Zhu, W., Li, X.: Unsupervised large graph embedding. In: Proceedings of 31st AAAI Conference on Artificial Intelligence(AAAI), San Francisco, USA (2017)
7. Ou, Y.Y., Chen, C.Y., Hwang, S.C., Oyang, Y.J.: Expediting model selection for support vector machines based on data reduction. IEEE Int. Conf. Syst. **1**, 786–791 (2003)
8. Panda, N., Chang, E.Y., Wu, G.: Concept boundary detection for speeding up SVMs. In: 23rd International Conference on Machine Learning, pp. 681–688 (2006)
9. Zhang, L., Zhou, W., Chen, G., Zhou, H., Ye, N., Jiao, L.: Pre-extracting boundary vectors for support vector machine using pseudo-density estimation method. In: International Symposium on Multispectral Image Processing and Pattern Recognition, vol. 7496, pp. 74960J–74960J-7 (2009)
10. Kubat, M., Matwin, S.: Addressing the course of imbalanced training sets: one-sided selection. In: Proceedings of International Conference on Machine Learning, pp. 179–186 (1997)

11. Zhang, J., Mani, I.: KNN approach to unbalanced data distributions: A case study involing information extraction. In: Proceedings of Workshop on Learning from Imbalanced Datasets (2003)
12. Dheeru, D., Karra Taniskidou, E.: UCI machine learning repository (2018). https://archive.ics.uci.edu/ml
13. Yang, L., et al.: Kernel sparse representation-based classifier. IEEE Trans. Signal Process. **60**(4), 1684–1695 (2012)

Deep Convolutional Transform Learning

Jyoti Maggu[1], Angshul Majumdar[1(✉)], Emilie Chouzenoux[2],
and Giovanni Chierchia[3]

[1] Indraprastha Institute of Information Technology Delhi, New Delhi, India
{jyotim,angshul}@iiitd.ac.in
[2] CVN, Inria Saclay, Univ. Paris-Saclay, CentraleSupélec, Gif-sur-Yvette,
Paris, France
emilie.chouzenoux@centralesupelec.fr
[3] LIGM, ESIEE Paris, Univ. Gustave Eiffel, Noisy-le-Grand, Paris, France
giovanni.chierchia@esiee.fr

Abstract. This work introduces a new unsupervised representation learning technique called Deep Convolutional Transform Learning (DCTL). By stacking convolutional transforms, our approach is able to learn a set of independent kernels at different layers. The features extracted in an unsupervised manner can then be used to perform machine learning tasks, such as classification and clustering. The learning technique relies on a well-sounded alternating proximal minimization scheme with established convergence guarantees. Our experimental results show that the proposed DCTL technique outperforms its shallow version CTL, on several benchmark datasets.

Keywords: Transform learning · Deep learning · Convolutional neural networks · Classification · Clustering · Proximal methods · Alternating minimization

1 Introduction

Deep learning and more particularly convolutional neural networks (CNN) have penetrated almost every perceivable area of signal/image processing and machine learning. Its performance in traditional machine learning tasks encountered in computer vision, natural language processing and speech analysis are well assessed. CNNs are also being used with success in traditional signal processing domains, such as biomedical signal analysis [9], radars [14], astronomy [3] and inverse problems [22]. When large volumes of labeled data are available, CNNs can be trained efficiently using back-propagation methods and reach excellent performance [18]. However, training a CNN requires labeled data in a large quantity. The latter issue can be overcome by considering alternate learning

This work was supported by the CNRS-CEFIPRA project under grant NextGenBP PRC2017.

H. Yang et al. (Eds.): ICONIP 2020, CCIS 1333, pp. 300–307, 2020.
https://doi.org/10.1007/978-3-030-63823-8_35

paradigms, such as spiking neural network (SNN) [21] and the associated Hebbian learning [10], or alternate optimization strategies such as in [20]. However, none of those approaches can overcome the fundamental problem of neural networks, that is their limited capacity of learning in an unsupervised fashion. This explains the great recent interest in the machine learning community for investigating representation learning methods, that keep the best of both worlds, that is the performance of multi-layer convolutional representations and the unsupervised learning capacity [2,7,8,12,19].

In this work, we propose a deep version of the convolutional transform learning (CTL) approach introduced in [12], that we call deep convolutional transform learning (DCTL). A proximal alternating minimization scheme allows us to learn multiple layers of convolutional filters in an unsupervised fashion. Numerical experiments illustrate the ability of the method to learn representative features that lead to great performance on a set of classification and clustering problems.

The rest of the paper is organized into several sections. Section 1.1 introduces the transform learning paradigm and briefly reminds our previous CTL approach. The proposed DCTL formulation and the associated learning strategy are presented in Sect. 2. The experimental results are described in Sect. 3. The conclusion of this work is drawn in Sect. 4.

1.1 Convolutional Transform Learning

We proposed in [12] the CTL approach, where a set of independent convolution filters are learnt to produce some data representations, in an unsupervised manner. The CTL strategy aims at generating unique and near to orthogonal filters, which in turn produces good features to be used for solving machine learning problems, as we illustrated in our experiments [12]. We present here a brief description of this approach, as its notation and concepts will serve as a basis for the deep CTL formulation introduced in this paper.

We consider a dataset $\{x^{(m)}\}_{1 \leq m \leq M}$ with M entries in $\mathbb{R}^N$. The CTL formulation relies on the key assumption that the representation matrix T gathers a set of K kernels $t_1, \ldots, t_K$ with K entries, namely

$$T = [t_1 \mid \ldots \mid t_K] \in \mathbb{R}^{K \times K}. \tag{1}$$

This leads to a linear transform applied to the data to produce some features

$$(\forall m \in \{1, \ldots, M\}) \qquad Z_m \approx X^{(m)}T, \tag{2}$$

where $X^{(m)} \in \mathbb{R}^{N \times K}$ are Toeplitz matrices associated to $(x^{(m)})_{1 \leq m \leq M}$ such that

$$X^{(m)}T = [X^{(m)}t_1 \mid \ldots \mid X^{(m)}t_K]$$
$$= [t_1 * x^{(m)} \mid \ldots \mid t_K * x^{(m)}], \tag{3}$$

and $*$ is a discrete convolution operator with suitable padding. Let us denote

$$Z = \begin{bmatrix} Z_1 \\ \vdots \\ Z_M \end{bmatrix} \in \mathbb{R}^{NM \times K}. \tag{4}$$

The goal is then to estimate (T, Z) from $\{x^{(m)}\}_{1 \leq m \leq M}$. To do so, we proposed in [12] a penalized formulation of the problem, introducing suitable conditioning constraints on the transforms, and sparsity constraint on the coefficients. The learning of (T, Z) was then performed using an alternating minimization scheme with sounded convergence guarantees. The aim of the present paper is to introduce a multi-layer formulation of the CTL, in order to learn deeper representations, with the aim of improving the representation power of the features.

2   Proposed Approach

2.1   Deep Convolutional Transform Model

Starting from the CTL model, we propose to stack several layers of it to obtain a deep architecture. For every $\ell \in \{1, \ldots, L\}$, we will seek for the transform matrix

$$T_\ell = [t_{1,\ell} | \ldots | t_{K,\ell}] \in \mathbb{R}^{K \times K}, \tag{5}$$

where $t_{k,\ell} \in \mathbb{R}^K$ is the k-th kernel on the ℓ-th layer of the representation. The associated coefficients will be denoted as

$$Z_\ell = \begin{bmatrix} Z_{1,\ell} \\ \vdots \\ Z_{M,\ell} \end{bmatrix} \in \mathbb{R}^{NM \times K}, \tag{6}$$

with

$$(\forall m \in \{1, \ldots, M\}) \qquad Z_{m,\ell} = [z_1^{(m,\ell)} | \ldots | z_K^{(m,\ell)}] \in \mathbb{R}^{N \times K}. \tag{7}$$

The learning of $(T_\ell)_{1 \leq \ell \leq L}$ and $(Z_\ell)_{1 \leq \ell \leq L}$ will be performed by solving

$$\underset{(T_\ell)_{1 \leq \ell \leq L}, (Z_\ell)_{1 \leq \ell \leq L}}{\text{minimize}} \quad F(T_1, \ldots, T_L, Z_1, \ldots, Z_L) \tag{8}$$

where

$$F(T_1, \ldots, T_L, Z_1, \ldots, Z_L) = \sum_{\ell=1}^L \left(\frac{1}{2} \sum_{m=1}^M ||Z_{m,\ell-1}T_\ell - Z_{m,\ell}||_F^2 + \mu||T_\ell||_F^2 \right.$$

$$\left. - \lambda \log \det(T_\ell) + \beta||Z_\ell||_1 + \iota_+(Z_\ell) \right), \tag{9}$$

Here, we denote ι_+ the indicator function of the positive orthant, equals to 0 if all entries of its input have non negative elements, and $+\infty$ otherwise. Moreover, by a slight abuse of notation, we denote as $\log \det$ the sum of logarithms of the singular values of a squared matrix, taking infinity value as soon as one of those is non positive. The first layer follows the CTL strategy, that is $Z_{m,0} \equiv X^{(m)}$. Moreover, for every $\ell \in \{2, \ldots, L\}$, we introduced the linear operator $Z_{m,\ell-1}$ so as to obtain the compact notation for the multi-channel convolution product:

$$Z_{m,\ell-1}T_\ell = [Z_{m,\ell-1}t_{1,\ell} | \ldots | Z_{m,\ell-1}t_{K,\ell}] \tag{10}$$

$$= [t_{1,\ell} * z_1^{(m,\ell-1)} | \ldots | t_{K,\ell} * z_K^{(m,\ell-1)}]. \tag{11}$$

2.2 Minimization Algorithm

Problem (8) is non-convex. However it presents a particular multi-convex structure, that allows us to make use of an alternating proximal minimization algorithm to solve it [1,4]. The proximity operator [5] of a proper, lower semi-continuous, convex function $\psi : \mathcal{H} \mapsto]-\infty, +\infty]$, with $(\mathcal{H}, \|\cdot\|)$ a normed Hilbert space, is defined as[1]

$$(\forall \widetilde{X} \in \mathcal{H}) \quad \mathrm{prox}_{\psi}(\widetilde{X}) = \underset{X \in \mathcal{H}}{\mathrm{argmin}} \ \psi(X) + \frac{1}{2}\|X - \widetilde{X}\|^2. \tag{12}$$

The alternating proximal minimization algorithm then consists in performing iteratively proximity updates, on the transform matrix, and on the coefficients. The iterates are guaranteed to ensure the monotonical decrease of the loss function F. Convergence to a local minimizer of F can also be ensured, under mild technical assumptions. The algorithm reads as follows:

$$\begin{aligned}
&\text{For} \quad i = 0, 1, \ldots \\
&\left|\ \begin{aligned}
&\text{For} \quad \ell = 1, \ldots, L \\
&\left|\ \begin{aligned}
&T_\ell^{[i+1]} = \mathrm{prox}_{\gamma_1 F(T_1^{[i+1]}, \ldots, T_L^{[i]}, Z_1^{[i+1]}, \ldots, Z_L^{[i]})} \left(T_\ell^{[i]}\right) \\
&Z_\ell^{[i+1]} = \mathrm{prox}_{\gamma_2 F(T_1^{[i+1]}, \ldots, T_L^{[i]}, Z_1^{[i+1]}, \ldots, Z_L^{[i]})} \left(Z_\ell^{[i]}\right)
\end{aligned}\right.
\end{aligned}\right.
\end{aligned} \tag{13}$$

with $T_\ell^{[0]} \in \mathbb{R}^{K \times K}$, $Z_\ell^{[0]} \in \mathbb{R}^{NM \times K}$, and γ_1 and γ_2 some positive constants. We provide hereafter the expression of the proximity operators involved in the algorithm, whose proof are provided in the appendix.

Update of the Transform Matrix: Let $i \in \mathbb{N}$ and $\ell \in \{1, \ldots, L\}$. Then

$$\begin{aligned}
T_\ell^{[i+1]} &= \mathrm{prox}_{\gamma_1 F(T_1^{[i+1]}, \ldots, T_\ell^{[i]}, Z_1^{[i+1]}, \ldots, Z_L^{[i]})} \left(T_\ell^{[i]}\right), \\
&= \underset{T_\ell \in \mathbb{R}^{K \times K}}{\mathrm{argmin}} \ \frac{1}{2\gamma_1}\|T_\ell - T_\ell^{[i]}\|_F^2 \\
&\quad + \frac{1}{2}\sum_{m=1}^{M} \|Z_{m,\ell-1}^{[i+1]}T_\ell - Z_{m,\ell}^{[i]}\|_F^2 + \mu\|T_\ell\|_F^2 - \lambda \log \det(T_\ell) \\
&= \frac{1}{2}\Lambda^{-1}V\left(\Sigma + (\Sigma^2 + 2\lambda\mathrm{Id})^{1/2}\right)U^\top,
\end{aligned} \tag{14}$$

with

$$\Lambda^\top \Lambda = \sum_{m=1}^{M} (Z_{m,\ell-1}^{[i+1]})^\top (Z_{m,\ell-1}^{[i+1]}) + (\gamma_1^{-1} + 2\mu)\mathrm{Id}. \tag{15}$$

Here above, we considered the singular value decomposition:

$$U\Sigma V^\top = \left(\sum_{m=1}^{M} (Z_{m,\ell}^{[i]})^\top (Z_{m,\ell-1}^{[i+1]}) + \gamma_1^{-1}T_\ell^{[i]}\right)\Lambda^{-1}. \tag{16}$$

---

[1] See also http://proximity-operator.net/.

Update of the Coefficient Matrix: Let $i \in \mathbb{N}$. We first consider the case when $\ell \in \{1, \ldots, L-1\}$ (recall that $\mathcal{Z}_{m,0} = X^{(m)}$ when $\ell = 1$). Then

$$
Z_\ell^{[i+1]} = \text{prox}_{\gamma_2 F(T_1^{[i+1]}, \ldots, T_L^{[i]}, Z_1^{[i+1]}, \ldots, Z_L^{[i]})} \left(Z_\ell^{[i]} \right),
$$

$$
= \underset{Z_\ell \in \mathbb{R}^{MN \times K}}{\text{argmin}} \; \frac{1}{2\gamma_2} \| Z_\ell - Z_\ell^{[i]} \|_F^2
$$

$$
+ \frac{1}{2} \sum_{m=1}^{M} \| \mathcal{Z}_{m,\ell-1}^{[i+1]} T_\ell^{[i+1]} - Z_{m,\ell} \|_F^2 \tag{17}
$$

$$
+ \frac{1}{2} \sum_{m=1}^{M} \| \mathcal{Z}_{m,\ell} T_{\ell+1}^{[i+1]} - Z_{m,\ell+1}^{[i]} \|_F^2
$$

$$
+ \beta \| Z_\ell \|_1 + \iota_+(Z_\ell).
$$

Although the above minimization does not have a closed-form expression, it can be efficiently carried out with the projected Newton method. In the case when $\ell = L$, the second term is dropped, yielding

$$
Z_L^{[i+1]} = \text{prox}_{\gamma_2 F(T_1^{[i+1]}, \ldots, T_L^{[i+1]}, Z_1^{[i+1]}, \ldots, Z_{L-1}^{[i+1]}, \cdot)} \left(Z_L^{[i]} \right)
$$

$$
= \underset{Z_L \in \mathbb{R}^{MN \times K}}{\text{argmin}} \; \frac{1}{2\gamma_2} \| Z_L - Z_L^{[i]} \|_F^2 \tag{18}
$$

$$
+ \frac{1}{2} \sum_{m=1}^{M} \| \mathcal{Z}_{m,L-1}^{[i+1]} T_L^{[i+1]} - Z_{m,L} \|_F^2 + \beta \| Z_L \|_1 + \iota_+(Z_L).
$$

Here again, the projected Newton method can be employed for the minimization.

3 Numerical Results

To assess the performance of the proposed approach, we considered the three image datasets[2] *YALE* [6], *E-YALE-B* [11], and *AR-Face* [13]. These are well known small-to-medium size benchmarking face datasets. Owning to space limitations, we skip their descriptions.

In the first set of experiments, we want to show that the accuracy of deep transform learning indeed improves when one goes deeper. Going deep beyond three layers makes performance degrade as the model tends to overfit for the small training set. To elucidate, we have used a simple support vector machine (SVM) classifier. The results are shown in Table 1 for levels 1, 2, 3 and 4. It has already been shown in [12] that the single layer CTL yielded better results than other single layer representation learning tools, including dictionary learning and transform Learning. Therefore it is expected that by going deeper, we will improve upon their deeper counterparts. We do not repeat those baseline experiments here, by lack of space. We also skip comparison with CNNs because

---

[2] http://www.cad.zju.edu.cn/home/dengcai/Data/FaceData.html.

Table 1. Accuracy on SVM with layers

Dataset	CTL	DCTL-2	DCTL-3	DCTL-4
YALE 150 × 150	94.00	94.28	**96.00**	92.21
YALE 32 × 32	88.00	89.11	**90.00**	87.73
E-YALE-B	97.38	97.00	**98.00**	94.44
AR-Faces	88.87	92.22	**97.67**	82.21

Table 2. Classification accuracy using KNN

Dataset	Raw features	CTL	DCTL
YALE 150 × 150	78.00	70.00	**80.00**
YALE 32 × 32	**60.00**	58.85	**60.00**
E-YALE-B	71.03	84.00	**85.00**
AR-Faces	55.00	**56.00**	58.00

Table 3. Classification accuracy using SVM

Dataset	Raw features	CTL	DCTL
YALE 150 × 150	93.00	94.00	**96.00**
YALE 32 × 32	68.00	88.00	**90.00**
E-YALE-B	93.24	97.38	**98.00**
AR-Faces	87.33	88.87	**97.67**

Table 4. Convolutional transformed clustering: ARI

YALEB/Method	Raw features	DCTL-2	DCTL-3
K-means	0.785	0.734	**0.788**
Random	0.733	0.718	**0.738**
PCA-based	0.734	**0.791**	0.777

Table 5. Clustering time in sec

YALEB/Method	Raw features	DCTL-2	DCTL-3
K-means	2.28	0.45	**0.14**
Random	1.95	0.33	**0.08**
PCA-based	0.36	0.09	**0.03**

of its supervised nature, whereas the proposed technique is unsupervised. We only show comparison of our proposed technique with raw features and with CTL. We take extracted features from the proposed DCTL and perform classification using two classifiers, namely KNN and SVM. The classification accuracy is reported in Table 2 and Table 3. Then we perform clustering on the extracted features of DCTL and report the comparison of Adjusted Rank Index (ARI) in Table 4. We also report clustering time on extracted features in Table 5. It is worthy to remark that the time to cluster extracted features from the proposed methodology is comparatively less than others.

4   Conclusion

This paper introduces a deep representation learning technique, named Deep Convolutional Transform Learning. Numerical comparisons are performed with the shallow convolutional transform learning formulations on image classification and clustering tasks. In the future, we plan to compare with several other deep representation learning techniques, namely stacked autoencoder and its convolutional version, restricted Boltzmann machine and its convolutional version, discriminative variants of deep dictionary and transform Learning.

References

1. Attouch, H., Bolte, J., Svaiter, B.F.: Convergence of descent methods for semi-algebraic and tame problems: proximal algorithms, forward-backward splitting, and regularized Gauss-Seidel methods. Math. Program. **137**, 91–129 (2011)
2. Chabiron, O., Malgouyres, F., Tourneret, J.: Toward fast transform learning. Int. J. Comput. Vis. **114**, 195–216 (2015)
3. Chan, M.C., Stott, J.P.: Deep-CEE I: fishing for galaxy clusters with deep neural nets. Mon. Not. R. Astron. Soc. **490**(4), 5770–5787 (2019)
4. Chouzenoux, E., Pesquet, J.C., Repetti, A.: A block coordinate variable metric forward-backward algorithm. J. Glob. Optim. **66**(3), 457–485 (2016)
5. Combettes, P.L., Pesquet, J.C.: Proximal splitting methods in signal processing. In: Bauschke, H., Burachik, R., Combettes, P., Elser, V., Luke, D., Wolkowicz, H. (eds.) Fixed-Point Algorithms for Inverse Problems in Science and Engineering. Springer Optimization and Its Applications, vol. 69, pp. 185–212. Springer-Verlag, New York (2010). https://doi.org/10.1007/978-1-4419-9569-8_10
6. D.J.: The Yale face database (1997). http://cvc.yale.edu/projects/yalefaces/yalefaces.html. 1(2), 4
7. El Gheche, M., Chierchia, G., Frossard, P.: Multilayer network data clustering. IEEE Trans. Signal Inf. Process. Over Netw. **6**(1), 13–23 (2020)
8. Fagot, D., Wendt, H., Févotte, C., Smaragdis, P.: Majorization-minimization algorithms for convolutive NMF with the beta-divergence. In: Proceedings of the IEEE International Conference on Acoustics, Speech and Signal Processing (ICASSP 2019), pp. 8202–8206 (2019)
9. Hannun, A.Y., et al.: Cardiologist-level arrhythmia detection and classification in ambulatory electrocardiograms using a deep neural network. Nat. Med. **25**(1), 65 (2019)

10. Kempter, R., Gerstner, W., Van Hemmen, J.L.: Hebbian learning and spiking neurons. Phys. Rev. E **59**(4), 4498 (1999)
11. Lee, K., Ho, J., Kriegman, D.: Acquiring linear subspaces for face recognition under variable lighting. IEEE Trans. Pattern Anal. Mach. Intell. **5**, 684–698 (2005)
12. Maggu, J., Chouzenoux, E., Chierchia, G., Majumdar, A.: Convolutional transform learning. In: Cheng, L., Leung, A.C.S., Ozawa, S. (eds.) ICONIP 2018. LNCS, vol. 11303, pp. 162–174. Springer, Cham (2018). https://doi.org/10.1007/978-3-030-04182-3_15
13. Martinez, A.M.: The AR face database. CVC Technical Report24 (1998)
14. Mason, E., Yonel, B., Yazici, B.: Deep learning for radar. In: 2017 IEEE Radar Conference (RadarConf), pp. 1703–1708. IEEE (2017)
15. Ravishankar, S., Bresler, Y.: Learning sparsifying transforms. IEEE Trans. Signal Process. **61**(5), 1072–1086 (2013)
16. Ravishankar, S., Bresler, Y.: Online sparsifying transform learning - Part II. IEEE J. Sel. Topics Signal Process. **9**(4), 637–646 (2015)
17. Ravishankar, S., Wen, B., Bresler, Y.: Online sparsifying transform learning - Part I. IEEE J. Sel. Topics Signal Process. **9**(4), 625–636 (2015)
18. Rumelhart, D.E., Hinton, G.E., Williams, R.J.: Learning representations by back-propagating errors. Nature **323**(6088), 533–536 (1986)
19. Tang, W., Chouzenoux, E., Pesquet, J., Krim, H.: Deep transform and metric learning network: wedding deep dictionary learning and neural networks. Technical report (2020). https://arxiv.org/pdf/2002.07898.pdf
20. Taylor, G., Burmeister, R., Xu, Z., Singh, B., Patel, A., Goldstein, T.: Training neural networks without gradients: a scalable ADMM approach. In: International Conference on Machine Learning, pp. 2722–2731 (2016)
21. Van Gerven, M., Bohte, S.: Artificial neural networks as models of neural information processing. Front. Comput. Neurosci. **11**, 114 (2017)
22. Ye, J.C., Han, Y., Cha, E.: Deep convolutional framelets: a general deep learning framework for inverse problems. SIAM J. Imaging Sci. **11**(2), 991–1048 (2018)

Deep Denoising Subspace Single-Cell Clustering

Yijie Wang[1] and Bo Yang[2(✉)]

[1] School of Software Engineering, Xi'an Jiaotong University, Xi'an 710049, Shaanxi, China
wyj045000@stu.xjtu.edu.cn
[2] School of Computer Science, Xi'an Polytechnic University, Xi'an 710048, Shaanxi, China
yangboo@stu.xjtu.edu.cn

Abstract. The development of second-generation sequencing technology has brought a great breakthrough to the study of biology. Clustering transcriptomes profiled by single-cell Ribonucleic Acid sequencing (scRNA-seq) has been routinely conducted to reveal cell heterogeneity and diversity. However, clustering analysis of scRNA-seq data remains a statistical and computational challenge, due to the pervasive drop-out events obscuring the data matrix with prevailing "false" zero count observations. In this paper, we propose a novel clustering technique named Deep Denoising Subspace Single-cell Clustering (DDS²C) to improve the clustering performance of scRNA-seq data, by utilizing autoencoder and data self-expressiveness structures. The DDS²C incorporates the loss functions of network structures and data denoising in a unified manner. The validity of DDS²C is examined over benchmark datasets from four representative single-cell sequencing platforms. The experimental results demonstrate that DDS²C outperforms than some state-of-the-art scRNA-seq clustering methods in terms of accuracy efficiency and scalability.

Keywords: Deep learning · Clustering · Subspace

1 Introduction

Single-cell Ribonucleic Acid sequencing (scRNA-seq) is a rapidly growing and widely applying technology [1,2]. It can reveal the heterogeneity and diversity between cell populations and has helped researchers to better understand complex biological questions [3]. Clustering analysis has been routinely conducted in most scRNA-seq studies. Clustering is a classical unsupervised machine learning problem and has been studied extensively in recent decades. Because of the "curse of dimensionality", clustering could perform better on a small dimensionality than on a high one [4]. The simplest method is based on principal component analysis (PCA) [5]. As one of the popular methods for dimensionality reduction, PCA has been widely used in single-cell research for clustering.

© Springer Nature Switzerland AG 2020
H. Yang et al. (Eds.): ICONIP 2020, CCIS 1333, pp. 308–315, 2020.
https://doi.org/10.1007/978-3-030-63823-8_36

Considering the specificity of scRNA-seq data, ZIFA [7] uses a zero inflation factor to deal with missing events in scRNA-seq data.

Deep neural networks (DNNs) have demonstrated theoretical function approximation capability [8] and feature learning properties [9]. Specifically, DNNs can reduce the dimensions of scRNA-seq data in a supervised manner [6]. The main problem with clustering scRNA-seq data is that they are so sparse that most measurements are zero. Many technologies are particularly prone to dropout events due to the relatively shallow sequencing depth per cell [13]. The grouping of cell populations in the scRNA-seq dataset is still a statistical and computational challenge.

Different from the existing methods, we developed Deep Denoising Subspace Single-cell Clustering (DDS^{2}C), a deep learning method based on autoencoder and data self-expressiveness approaches, which can improve the clustering effect of scRNA-seq data through denoising the single-cell model. Our method aims to perform optimization clustering when performing dimensionality reduction and denoising the autoencoder.

2   Method

2.1   Architecture and Workflow

The architecture of Deep Denoising Subspace Single-cell Clustering is shown in Fig. 1. The workflow of our method consists of three steps, including data pre-processing, subspace self-expression, and data denoising. We describe the details of each step in the following.

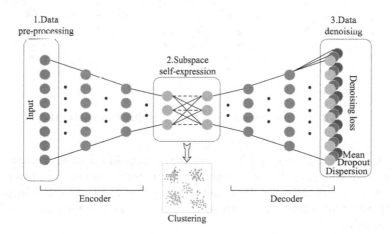

Fig. 1. The architecture of Deep Denoising Subspace Single-cell Clustering.

2.2 Data Pre-processing

Raw scRNA-seq read count data are pre-processed by the Python package SCANPY [14]. Genes with no count in any cell are filtered out. Size factors are calculated and read counts are normalized by library size, so total counts are same across cells. If we denote the library size (number of total read counts) of cell i as s_i, then the size factor of cell i is $s_i/median(s)$. We take the log transform and scale of the read counts, so that count values follow unit variance and zero mean. The pre-processed read count matrix is treated as the input for our deep neural network.

2.3 Subspace Self-expression

Sparse representation believes that each data point in the subspace union can be effectively represented as a linear or affine combination of samples belonging to the same subspace in the data set [16]. In order to achieve effective clustering, it is indispensable to reduce the dimensionality of the pre-processed data. We use an autoencoder to achieve the purpose of dimensionality reduction of scRNA-seq data [15]. As an excellent autoencoder, the architecture of Deep Subspace Clustering Networks [17] is depicted as Fig. 2, in which there are some encoder layers, one self-expressive layer, and some decoder layers.

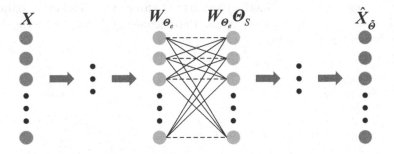

Fig. 2. Architecture of deep subspace clustering networks.

Let $X = [x_1, x_2, ..., x_N] \in \mathbb{R}^{D \times N}$ denote the data in the original input space, which is a collection of N data samples drawn from a union of multiple linear subspaces with dimension D. W denotes the output of the encoder. Inspired by the Deep Subspace Clustering Networks, we design the loss function of subspace self-expression as follows

$$L_S = \| \Theta_S \|_q + \frac{\lambda}{2} \| W_{\Theta_e} - W_{\Theta_e} \Theta_S \|_F^2 \quad s.t. \ diag(\Theta_S) = 0 \tag{1}$$

where Θ_e represents the encoder parameters, Θ_S represents the self-expressive layer parameters and Θ_d represents the decoder parameters. λ is the trade-off parameters. Different effects can be obtained by different choices of q. Typically, with the value of q decreasing from infinity toward zero, the sparsity of the solution increases. The parameters of the self-expressive layer Θ_S is used to instead of reconstruction coefficients C.

2.4   Data Denoising

Here, we apply the denoising autoencoder technique to map the input of read counts to an embedded space. In practice, we first corrupt the input with random Gaussian noise, then construct the autoencoder with regular fully connected layers. Formally, input is corrupted by noise

$$X^{noise} = X + b \qquad (2)$$

where b represents the random Gaussian noise. Note that the noise can be incorporated into every layer of the encoder, which is defined as a stacked denoising autoencoder [18]. We define the encoder function as $W = g_{\Theta_e}(X^{noise})$ and the decoder function $\hat{X} = f_{\Theta_d}(W_{\Theta_e}\Theta_S)$. The encoder and decoder functions are both fully connected neural networks with rectifier activation. Here Θ_e and Θ_d are the learned weights of the functions. The learning process of the denoising autoencoder minimizes the loss function

$$L_1\left(X, f_{\Theta_d}\left(g_{\Theta_e}\left(X^{noise}\right)\Theta_S\right)\right) \qquad (3)$$

where L_1 is the loss function.

In order to better capture the characters of scRNA-seq data, we continue to improve the autoencoder. Unlike the regular autoencoder, the loss function of the new autoencoder is the likelihood of a Zero Inflation Negative Binomial distribution [19]. It is applied to characterize the dropout events in scRNA-seq. The model is parameterized with the mean (μ), the dispersion (θ) of the negative binomial distribution and with an additional coefficient (π) that represents the weight of the point mass of probability at zero (the probability of dropout events):

$$A\left(X^{num}|\mu, \theta\right) = \frac{\Gamma(X^{num} + \theta)}{X^{num}!\Gamma(\theta)}\left(\frac{\theta}{\theta + \mu}\right)^{\theta}\left(\frac{\mu}{\theta + \mu}\right)^{X^{num}} \qquad (4)$$

$$B(X^{num}|\pi, \mu, \theta) = \pi\delta_0(X^{num}) + (1 - \pi)A(X^{num}|\mu, \theta) \qquad (5)$$

where X^{num} represents the raw read counts. The autoencoder estimates the parameters μ, θ and π. If $Y = f'_{\Theta_d}\left(g_{\Theta_e}\left(X^{noise}\right)\Theta_S\right)$ represents the last hidden layer of decoder, we append three independent fully connected layers to Y to estimate the parameters

$$M = diag(s_i) \times \exp(\Theta_\mu Y) \qquad (6)$$

$$P = \exp(\Theta_\theta Y) \qquad (7)$$

$$\Pi = sigmoid(\Theta_\pi Y) \qquad (8)$$

where M, P and Π represent the matrix form of estimations of mean, dispersion and dropout probability, respectively. The size factors s_i are calculated in the data pre-processing part and are included as an independent input to the deep learning model. The activation function chosen for mean and dispersion is exponential because the mean and dispersion parameters are non-negative values, while the activation function for the additional coefficient π is sigmoid, and represents the dropout probability. Dropout probability is in the interval of 0–1, so sigmoid is a suitable choice of activation function. The loss function of the autoencoder is the negative log of the B likelihood:

$$L_d = -\log(B(\boldsymbol{X}^{num}|\pi, \mu, \theta))$$ (9)

2.5 Loss Function

We pre-train the whole model before the clustering stage. Then learn the sparse representation matrix C from the self-expressive layer. We calculate the sample affinity matrix $\boldsymbol{Z}$ from C. Finally, we do spectral clustering for the scRNA-seq data on the basis of $\boldsymbol{Z}$. The loss function of the whole model includes two parts: the denoising part and the self-expression part. So the loss function of DDS^{2}C is

$$L = L_d + \gamma L_S$$ (10)

where L_d and L_S are the denoising loss and the self-expression loss, respectively, and $\gamma > 0$ is the coefficient that controls the relative weights of the two losses.

3 Experiments and Results

3.1 Datasets

We applied DDS^{2}C to four real scRNA-seq datasets to demonstrate its performance. The four datasets were generated from four representative sequencing platforms: PBMC 4k cells from the 10X genomics platform (10X PBMC) [11], mouse embryonic stem cells from a droplet barcoding platform (mouse ES cells) [12], mouse bladder cells from the Microwell-seq platform (mouse bladder cells) [13] and worm neuron cells from the sci-RNA-seq platform (worm neuron cells) [20], as summarized in Table 1.

Table 1. Details of four scRNA-seq datasets.

Dataset	Sequencing platform	Sample size (cell numbers)	No. of genes	No. of groups
10X PBMC	10X	4271	16449	8
Mouse ES cells	Droplet barcoding	2717	24046	4
Mouse bladder cells	Microwell-seq	2746	19079	16
Worm neuron cells	sci-RNA-seq	4186	11955	10

3.2   Results

We used the following three performance metrics to evaluate the consistency between the obtained clustering and the true labels: normalized mutual information (NMI) [21], adjusted Rand index (ARI) [22] and clustering accuracy (CA).

Table 2. Comparison of clustering performances of different methods on four datasets.

Methods	NMI	CA	ARI
10X PBMC			
DDS^{2}C	**0.723**	**0.665**	**0.534**
SIMLR	0.696	0.639	0.517
CIDR	0.640	0.653	0.523
PCA+k-means	0.653	0.560	0.401
DEC	0.609	0.612	0.522
Mouse ES cells			
DDS^{2}C	**0.891**	**0.917**	**0.874**
SIMLR	0.842	0.903	0.860
CIDR	0.716	0.763	0.729
PCA+k-means	0.877	0.869	0.836
DEC	0.740	0.759	0.640
Mouse bladder cells			
DDS^{2}C	**0.672**	**0.537**	**0.421**
SIMLR	0.641	0.513	0.394
CIDR	0.243	0.264	0.122
PCA+k-means	0.594	0.424	0.362
DEC	0.585	0.491	0.343
Worm neuron cells			
DDS^{2}C	**0.634**	**0.655**	**0.412**
SIMLR	0.610	0.634	0.397
CIDR	0.131	0.246	0.033
PCA+k-means	0.354	0.379	0.173
DEC	0.361	0.378	0.165

The ranges of NMI and CA are from 0 to 1, while the ARI can yield negative values. The three metrics are statistics of the concordance of two clustering labels; the higher the values, the higher concordance of the clustering. The three metrics of the clustering performance are visualized in Table 2, where the best scores are shown in bold fonts. We observe that the proposed deep learning method DDS^{2}C outperformed all the other methods, including SIMLR [23],

CIDR [24], PCA+k-means and DEC [10] in all four datasets. For the autoencoder of our method, there are five fully connected layers in both the encoding and decoding phases. We choose the learning rate is 0.001. Through experiments, we found that $\lambda = 64$, and $\gamma = 3$ achieve better performance for most cases.

4   Conclusion

In conclusion, an effective and efficient deep subspace clustering method called DDS^2C is presented for denoising and analyzing scRNA-seq data. DDS^2C first preprocesses the data of scRNA-seq, then adopts denoising autoencoder to achieve dimensionality reduction and denoise the data. In the training process of the model, we use the self-expressiveness approach to learn a data affinity matrix from the data. Finally, we apply spectral clustering on the affinity matrix to cluster scRNA-seq data. By comparing with several competing methods, we have proved that DDS^2C has excellent clustering performance on real datasets. As an ever-growing number of large-scale scRNA-seq datasets become available, we expect more applications of our method.

Acknowledgement. This work is supported by National Natural Science Foundation of China (NSFC) Grant (61806159); China Postdoctoral Science Foundation Grant (2018M631192) and Xi'an Municipal Science and Technology Program (2020KJRC0027).

References

1. Picelli, S., Faridani, O.R., Björklund, Å.K., Winberg, G., Sagasser, S., Sandberg, R.: Full-length RNA-seq from single cells using Smart-seq2. Nat. Protoc. **9**, 171–181 (2014)
2. Chen, X., Teichmann, S.A., Meyer, K.B.: From tissues to cell types and back: single-cell gene expression analysis of tissue architecture. Ann. Rev. Biomed. Data Sci. **1**, 29–51 (2018)
3. Shapiro, E., Biezuner, T., Linnarsson, S.: Single-cell sequencing-based technologies will revolutionize whole-organism science. Nat. Rev. Genet. **14**, 618–630 (2013)
4. Bellman, R.E.: Adaptive Control Processes: A Guided Tour. Princeton University Press, Princeton (2015)
5. Wold, S., Esbensen, K., Geladi, P.: Principal component analysis. Chemometr. Intell. Lab. Syst. **2**, 37–52 (1987)
6. Lin, C., Jain, S., Kim, H., Bar-Joseph, Z.: Using neural networks for reducing the dimensions of single-cell RNA-Seq data. Nucleic Acids Res. **45**, e156–e156 (2017)
7. Pierson, E., Yau, C.: ZIFA: dimensionality reduction for zero-inflated single-cell gene expression analysis. Genome Biol. **16**, 241 (2015)
8. Hornik, K.: Approximation capabilities of multilayer feedforward networks. Neural Netw. **4**, 251–257 (1991)
9. Bengio, Y., Courville, A., Vincent, P.: Representation learning: a review and new perspectives. IEEE Trans. Pattern Anal. Mach. Intell. **35**, 1798–1828 (2013)
10. Xie, J., Girshick, R., Farhadi, A.: Unsupervised deep embedding for clustering analysis. In: International Conference on Machine Learning, pp. 478–487. International Machine Learning Society, New York (2016)

11. Klein, A.M., et al.: Droplet barcoding for single-cell transcriptomics applied to embryonic stem cells. Cell **161**, 1187–1201 (2015)
12. Han, X., et al.: Mapping the mouse cell atlas by microwell-Seq. Cell **172**, 1091–1107 (2018)
13. Angerer, P., Simon, L., Tritschler, S., Wolf, F.A., Fischer, D., Theis, F.J.: Single cells make big data: new challenges and opportunities in transcriptomics. Curr. Opinion Syst. Biol. **4**, 85–91 (2017)
14. Wolf, F.A., Angerer, P., Theis, F.J.: SCANPY: large-scale single-cell gene expression data analysis. Genome Biol. **19**, 15 (2018)
15. Kingma, D.P., Welling, M.: Stochastic gradient VB and the variational auto-encoder. In: Second International Conference on Learning Representations, ICLR (2014)
16. Elhamifar, E., Vidal, R.: Sparse subspace clustering: algorithm, theory, and applications. IEEE Trans. Pattern Anal. Mach. Intell. **35**, 2765–2781 (2013)
17. Ji, P., Zhang, T., Li, H., Salzmann, M., Reid, I.: Deep subspace clustering networks. In: Advances in Neural Information Processing Systems, pp. 24–33. Long Beach (2017)
18. Vincent, P., Larochelle, H., Lajoie, I., Bengio, Y., Manzagol, P.-A.: Stacked denoising autoencoders: learning useful representations in a deep network with a local denoising criterion. J. Mach. Learn. Res. **11**, 3371–3408 (2010)
19. Eraslan, G., Simon, L.M., Mircea, M., Mueller, N.S., Theis, F.J.: Single-cell RNA-seq denoising using a deep count autoencoder. Nat. Commun. **10**, 1–14 (2019)
20. Cao, J., et al.: Comprehensive single-cell transcriptional profiling of a multicellular organism. Science **357**, 661–667 (2017)
21. Strehl, A., Ghosh, J.: Cluster ensembles – a knowledge reuse framework for combining multiple partitions. J. Mach. Learn. Res. **3**, 583–617 (2003)
22. Hubert, L., Arabie, P.: Comparing partitions. J. Classif. **2**, 193–218 (1985)
23. Wang, B., Zhu, J., Pierson, E., Ramazzotti, D., Batzoglou, S.: Visualization and analysis of single-cell RNA-Seq data by kernel-based similarity learning. Nat. Methods **14**, 414–416 (2017)
24. Lin, P., Troup, M., Ho, J.W.K.: CIDR: ultrafast and accurate clustering through imputation for single-cell RNA-Seq data. Genome Biol. **18**, 59 (2017)

Deep Detection for Face Manipulation

Disheng Feng, Xuequan Lu$^{(\boxtimes)}$, and Xufeng Lin

Deakin University, Geelong, Australia
sheldonvon@outlook.com, {xuequan.lu,xufeng.lin}@deakin.edu.au

Abstract. It has become increasingly challenging to distinguish real faces from their visually realistic fake counterparts, due to the great advances of deep learning based face manipulation techniques in recent years. In this paper, we introduce a deep learning method to detect face manipulation. It consists of two stages: feature extraction and binary classification. To better distinguish fake faces from real faces, we resort to the triplet loss function in the first stage. We then design a simple linear classification network to bridge the learned contrastive features with the real/fake faces. Experimental results on public benchmark datasets demonstrate the effectiveness of this method, and show that it generates better performance than state-of-the-art techniques in most cases.

Keywords: Deepfake detection · Digital forensics · Face manipulation

1 Introduction

Face manipulation has received considerable attention in recent years. Its detection or localization becomes more challenging with the rapid development of deepfake generation techniques. For example, Karras et al. [1] introduced a high-resolution full-forged image synthesis method by progressively adding layers to both the generator and discriminator. Thies et al. [2] introduced a deferred neural rendering technique that equips the traditional graphics pipeline with learnable components for synthesizing photo-realistic face images. The increasing appearance of such computer-generated face images or videos has cast serious doubts on the credibility of digital content, and potentially poses huge threats to privacy and security. Thus, it is essential to devise robust and accurate detection methods to identify face manipulations.

Some existing methods detect face manipulation based on the visual cues left by the manipulation methods, such as the abnormality of head pose [3], the frequency of eye blinking [4], and the face warping artifacts [5]. However, these methods are designed for specific visual disturbance caused by manipulation methods, which may fail as the manipulation technologies become more mature in the foreseeable future. Other detection approaches resort to deep learning techniques [6–10]. Nevertheless, these methods usually ignore the role of loss functions, which consequently hinders the improvement of detection performance. Furthermore, most deep learning models for face manipulation detection

© Springer Nature Switzerland AG 2020
H. Yang et al. (Eds.): ICONIP 2020, CCIS 1333, pp. 316–323, 2020.
https://doi.org/10.1007/978-3-030-63823-8_37

are trained and tested on the same dataset, which overlooks the cross-dataset adaption of the trained model and brings difficulties for other researchers to perform reasonable comparisons.

Given the above motivations, we introduce a novel face manipulation detection approach in this paper. Our key idea is to use a loss function for contrastive learning of three samples. We achieve this by resorting to the triplet loss [11]. Specifically, inspired by [11], we design three samples with two positive samples (one is anchor) and one negative sample, and then formulate the loss by minimizing the distance between one positive sample and the anchor and maximizing the distance between the anchor and the negative sample. We employ Xception [12] as the backbone, with certain modifications (Sect. 3.1). We further design a linear classification network to perform binary classification (0 and 1, corresponding to real and fake faces respectively), to bridge the learned contrastive features with the real or fake faces. In addition to the intra-dataset evaluation, we also conduct the cross-dataset evaluation (Sect. 4.4). Experiments validate our method and demonstrate that it outperforms state-of-the-art techniques in most cases, in terms of detection performance evaluated with AUC (Area Under the ROC Curve). We also conduct an ablation study showing that our contrastive learning enables substantial improvement in detection accuracy.

2   Related Work

In this section, we will review the works that are most related to our work. We first revisit the previous research on face manipulation methods and then cover the current feasible detection methods.

Face Image Manipulation Methods. The origin core mind of deepfake can be found in 2016, when Zhmoginov and Sandler [13] developed a gradient-ascent approach to effectively invert low-dimensional face embeddings to realistically looking consistent images, which is also based on GAN. This technique was later implemented in the well-known mobile phone application called FaceAPP [14] which contributes to some of the face forgery datasets. Thies et al. [2] introduced a deferred neural rendering method called Neural Texture which can synthesize face manipulate images in conjunction with a rendering network. Li et al. [15] proposed an enhanced DeepFake-based method to solve problems such as visible splicing boundaries, color mismatch and visible parts of the original face, which was used to generate the Celeb-DF dataset.

DeepFake Detection Methods. In recent years, some methods have been developed to detect the visual imperfections left by Deepfake algorithms. Li et al. [5] presented a detection method against the face-warping drawback of the Deepfake methods (caused by limited synthesis resolution). They proposed another method [4] to detect the eye blinking details which is a physiological signal that could be easily neglected by Deepfake methods. Yang et al. [3] proposed a detection approach using the inconsistencies in the head poses of the fake videos. Matern et al. [16] proposed a similar detection method regarding a variety of visual features. However, one obvious drawback is that those visual imperfections could be easily refined [15], and thus they could be invalid very soon. On the other hand, some deep learning methods are proposed to deal with the Deepfake detection problem. Zhou et al. [17] presented a method using a two-stream GoogLeNet InceptionV3 model [18] to achieve state-of-the-art performance. Afchar et al. [6] offered a feasible method called MesoNet, providing an important baseline for comparisons. Rössler et al. [9] presented high performance results using network structure based on depth-wise separable convolution layers with residual connections called Xception [12]. Some more recent methods such as Dang et al. [7] and Tolosana et al. [10] also utilized Xception as the backbone network. Nguyen et al. [8] used a capsule structure with a VGG19 as an embedded backbone network for DeepFake detection. Nguyen et al. [19] proposed to use a multi-task learning approach to simultaneously detect manipulated data and locate the manipulated regions for each query.

3 Our Method

Our method first learns features with the aid of a contrastive loss (i.e., triplet loss) which can metrically push the forgery faces away from the real faces. Then we design a simple linear classification network to obtain binary results.

3.1 Network Structure

Feature Extraction Network. We first introduce the feature extraction stage. We need to train a function $f(\theta) : \mathbb{R}^D \to \mathbb{R}^E$, mapping semantically different data $\mathbb{R}^D$ to metrically further points $\mathbb{R}^E$. Following the work [11], we construct a model satisfying

$$TripletNet(x, x^-, x^+) = \begin{bmatrix} \|Net(x) - Net(x^-)\|_2 \\ \|Net(x) - Net(x^+)\|_2 \end{bmatrix} \in \mathbb{R}^2_+, \tag{1}$$

where $Net(x) = Xception(x)$ and x is a randomly selected image (the anchor, could be manipulated image or pristine image). x^+ and x^- are images which are randomly selected from the same class as the anchor and a different class, respectively. We simply employ the Xception [12] as the backbone network, since it has been proved to be effective and powerful. To achieve this, we modify the last layer with a dropout layer in conjunction with a linear layer.

Classification Network. We devise a simple linear classification network that takes the output of the feature extraction network (2D points) as input and outputs a binary value (0 or 1) to indicate real or fake. The components of this network are as follows: Linear layer (size: 2), ReLu layer, Linear layer (size: 128), Linear layer (size: 256), ReLu layer, Linear layer (size: 128), ReLu layer, Linear layer (size: 2), Leaky ReLu layer.

3.2   Training and Inference

We first train the feature extraction network and use the well-tuned backbone network to extract the features from the images. We then train the linear classification network using those extracted features (2D points) as train data. Notice that this process is also used for the inference stage.

3.3   Implementation

Our networks are implemented in PyTorch on a desktop PC with an Intel Core i9-9820X CPU (3.30 GHz, 48 GB memory) and a GeForce RTX 2080Ti GPU (11 GB memory, CUDA 10.0). The SGD optimizer is used for training both the feature extraction and classification networks. Specifically, the former is trained with a learning rate of 4×10^{-4} and the batch size is typically set to 12 in our experiments. We observed that the loss became steady after 8 epochs. Therefore, the number of epochs is empirically set to 10. The classification network is trained with a learning rate and momentum of 3.0×10^{-3} and 1.0×10^{-1}, respectively.

4   Experimental Results

In this section, we will first introduce the datasets used in our experiments. We then report the results and analyze the effectiveness of our model by evaluating the triplet structure. In the end, we will compare our model with state-of-the-art methods in both intra-dataset setting and cross-dataset setting.

4.1   Datasets

A variety of face manipulation datasets have been proposed to facilitate the evaluation and benchmarking of image manipulation detection methods. In our experiments, we used the following datasets: *FaceForensics++ (FF++)* [9], *UADFV* [5] and *Celeb-DF* [15]. Note that, *FF++* includes DeepFake videos generated with four face manipulation methods (Deepfake [20], Neural Texture [2], faceswap [21] and face2face [22]). *Celeb-DF* is a large face forgery dataset with refined video synthesis solving common problems such as temporal flickering frames and color inconsistency in other datasets.

Similarly, the above datasets provide data in the format of videos. To train our network, we use the face detector in Dlib [23] to crop the video frames into a specific size. Detail information can be found in Table 1.

4.2   Extracted Features

In this section, we present the visual results of the extracted features. We only report the results on the FF++ dataset for illustration purpose. We generate one dataset for each method (Neural Texture, DeepFake, Face2Face and DeepFake), including real faces and corresponding manipulated faces.

Table 1. Image numbers in the split sets used in our experiments.

Datasets	Train (real)	Train (fake)	Test (real)	Test (fake)
FF++	115556	108935	20393	20473
UADFV	10100	9761	1783	1723
Celeb-DF	172187	165884	30386	29259

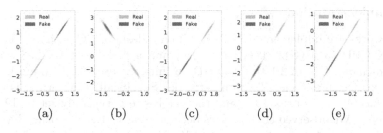

(a)   (b)   (c)   (d)   (e)

Fig. 1. (a)–(e) are the outputs of the feature extraction network tested on five datasets (Neural Texture, DeepFake, Face2Face, FaceSwap and Combination, respectively).

From Fig. 1, We observed that two different colors of points forming two distinct clusters. The results of the datasets using DeepFake and FaceSwap outperform the others.

In Table 2, we list the Area Under the ROC Curve (AUC) as well as the Equal Error Rate (ERR) tested on the test sets of different datasets. We can see an overall near-perfect performance with extremely low EERs.

Table 2. Comparisons of AUC (Area Under the ROC Curve) and EER (Equal Error Rate) on each dataset.

Datasets	DeepFake	Face Swap	Face2Face	Neural texture	Combination
AUC	99.99	99.99	99.99	99.99	99.96
ERR	9.47×10^{-4}	9.72×10^{-3}	1.12×10^{-1}	5.91×10^{-2}	8.55×10^{-1}

4.3   Ablation Study

We compare the Xception network and our proposed model (i.e., Xception network with the triplet loss), on four datasets generated in Sect. 4.2. Although the Xception network itself is highly competent to detect the manipulated face images (98.85%, 98.23%, 98.36%, 94.50% for DeepFake, FaceSwap, Face2Face and NeuralTexture respectively), our contrastive learning with triplet loss clearly enables the learning of more discriminative features and boost the detection accuracy (1%, 0.87%, 1.34% and 2.92% higher than the corresponding methods respectively).

4.4   Comparisons with State-of-the-Art Methods

In Table 3, we show the comparisons of our method and the state-of-the-art methods on the above mentioned three datasets in both intra-dataset and cross-dataset settings. Specifically, we separately trained our networks on the train set of each dataset and evaluate the detection performance on the test sets of all three datasets. Although the results of our method and other methods are not strictly comparable, it provides reasonable comparisons [7].

Table 3. AUC (%) on FF++, UADFV and Celeb-DF. Best results in intra-dataset setting are underlined, and best results for the cross-dataset setting are in bold.

Methods	Train data	FF++	UADFV	Celeb-DF
Two-stream [17]	Private	70.1	85.1	53.8
Meso4 [6]	Private	84.7	84.3	54.8
MesoInception4 [6]	Private	83.0	82.1	53.6
HeadPose [3]	UADFV	47.3	89.0	54.6
FWA [5]	UADFV	**80.1**	97.4	56.9
VA-MLP [16]	Private	66.4	70.2	55.0
VA-LogReg [16]	Private	78.0	54.0	55.1
Multi-task [19]	FF	76.3	65.8	54.3
Xception [9]	FF++	99.7	**80.4**	48.2
Capsule [8]	FF++	96.6	61.3	57.5
Xception [15]	UADFV	–	96.8	52.2
Xception+Reg. [7]	UADFV	–	98.4	57.1
Xception+Tri. (ours)	FF++	<u>99.9</u>	74.3	**61.7**
Xception+Tri. (ours)	UADFV	61.3	<u>99.9</u>	**60.0**
Xception+Tri. (ours)	Celeb-DF	60.2	88.9	<u>99.9</u>

For FF++, we achieved a 0.2% improvement comparing to the Xception [9] when testing the same dataset, reaching 99.9%. For the cross-dataset setting, while our method is weaker than Xception when testing UADFV, it boosts 13.5% on the Celeb-DF which is more representative than the UADFV in terms of quality, quantity and diversity.

Regarding the detectors trained with UADFV, one strong competitor is FWA [5], which is merely 2.5% and 3.1% less than our method when testing the UADFV and Celeb-DF datasets, respectively. However, FWA achieves an AUC 18.8% higher than our method on testing the FF++ dataset. It is worth mentioning that FWA is based on the observations that previous face forgery algorithms could only generate images with limited resolutions, which requires to warp the fake face to match the original face. In other words, these kinds of methods [3,5] detect the forgery faces based on the imperfections of the manipulation algorithms, which can easily be obsoleted. This disadvantage becomes significant on the Celeb-DF. In this regard, our method has a better generalization ability.

We also observe that when training on UADFV, method [7] ranks the 2nd and the 3rd place when testing on UADFV and Celeb-DF, respectively. We also show outstanding performance of our method on the Celeb-DF which is a relatively new, larger dataset in higher resolution with refined videos. Note that, it provides noticeably different information for the network to learn. When testing the other two datasets, the loss of such information may cause the variation on the performance. Our method outperforms state-of-the-art techniques, in terms of the intra-dataset setting (underlined numbers), and generates best results on testing the more challenging Celeb-DF in cross-dataset setting (bold numbers).

5   Conclusion

We have introduced a deep learning approach for the detection of face manipulation. It first learns the contrastive features which are then taken as input to a simple binary classification network. Results show that our method is effective, and outperforms state-of-the-art techniques in most cases. Since there are still noticeable space for improving the cross-dataset detection performance, we would like to design more effective face manipulation detection techniques with high generalization capability in the future.

Acknowledgement. This work is supported in part by Deakin University (Australia) internal grant (CY01-251301-F003-PJ03906-PG00447 and 251301-F003-PG00216-PJ03906).

References

1. Karras, T., Aila, T., Laine, S., Lehtinen, J.: Progressive growing of GANs for improved quality, stability, and variation. In: International Conference on Learning Representations (2018). https://openreview.net/forum?id=Hk99zCeAb
2. Thies, J., Zollhöfer, M., Nießner, M.: Deferred neural rendering: image synthesis using neural textures. ACM Trans. Graph. (TOG) **38**(4), 1–12 (2019)
3. Yang, X., Li, Y., Lyu, S.: Exposing deep fakes using inconsistent head poses. In: ICASSP 2019–2019 IEEE International Conference on Acoustics, Speech and Signal Processing (ICASSP), Brighton, United Kingdom, pp. 8261–8265 (2019). https://doi.org/10.1109/ICASSP.2019.8683164
4. Li, Y., Chang, M.C., Lyu, S.: In ictu oculi: exposing AI created fake videos by detecting eye blinking. In: 2018 IEEE International Workshop on Information Forensics and Security (WIFS), pp. 1–7. IEEE, December 2018
5. Li, Y., Lyu, S.: Exposing deepfake videos by detecting face warping artifacts. In: Proceedings of the IEEE/CVF Conference on Computer Vision and Pattern Recognition (CVPR) Workshops, June 2019
6. Afchar, D., Nozick, V., Yamagishi, J., Echizen, I.: MesoNet: a compact facial video forgery detection network. In: 2018 IEEE International Workshop on Information Forensics and Security (WIFS), Hong Kong, Hong Kong, pp. 1–7 (2018). https://doi.org/10.1109/WIFS.2018.8630761

7. Stehouwer, J., Dang, H., Liu, F., Liu, X., Jain, A.: On the detection of digital face manipulation. arXiv preprint arXiv:1910.01717 (2019)
8. Nguyen, H.H., Yamagishi, J., Echizen, I.: Capsule-forensics: using capsule networks to detect forged images and videos. In: ICASSP 2019–2019 IEEE International Conference on Acoustics, Speech and Signal Processing (ICASSP), pp. 2307–2311. IEEE, May 2019
9. Rössler, A., Cozzolino, D., Verdoliva, L., Riess, C., Thies, J., Niessner, M.: Face-forensics++: learning to detect manipulated facial images. In: 2019 IEEE/CVF International Conference on Computer Vision (ICCV), pp. 1–11 (2019)
10. Tolosana, R., Romero-Tapiador, S., Fierrez, J., Vera-Rodriguez, R.: DeepFakes evolution: analysis of facial regions and fake detection performance. arXiv preprint arXiv:2004.07532 (2020)
11. Hoffer, E., Ailon, N.: Deep metric learning using triplet network. In: Feragen, A., Pelillo, M., Loog, M. (eds.) SIMBAD 2015. LNCS, vol. 9370, pp. 84–92. Springer, Cham (2015). https://doi.org/10.1007/978-3-319-24261-3_7
12. Chollet, F.: Xception: deep learning with depth wise separable convolutions. In: 2017 IEEE Conference on Computer Vision and Pattern Recognition (CVPR), pp. 1800–1807 (2017)
13. Zhmoginov, A., Sandler, M.: Inverting face embeddings with convolutional neural networks. CoRRabs/1606.04189 (2016). http://arxiv.org/abs/1606.04189
14. Faceapp. https://www.faceapp.com/. Accessed 06 July 2020
15. Li, Y., Sun, P., Qi, H., Lyu, S.: Celeb-DF: a large-scale challenging dataset for DeepFake forensics. In: IEEE Conference on Computer Vision and Patten Recognition (CVPR), Seattle, WA, United States (2020)
16. Matern, F., Riess, C., Stamminger, M.: Exploiting visual artifacts to expose deep-fakes and face manipulations. In: 2019 IEEE Winter Applications of Computer Vision Workshops (WACVW), pp. 83–92. IEEE, January 2019
17. Zhou, P., Han, X., Morariu, V.I., Davis, L.S.: Two-stream neural networks for tampered face detection. In: 2017 IEEE Conference on Computer Vision and Pattern Recognition Workshops (CVPRW), pp. 1831–1839. IEEE, July 2017
18. Szegedy, C., et al.: Going deeper with convolutions. In: Proceedings of the IEEE Conference on Computer Vision and Pattern Recognition, pp. 1–9 (2015)
19. Nguyen, H.H., Fang, F., Yamagishi, J., Echizen, I.: Multi-task learning for detecting and segmenting manipulated facial images and videos. CoRR (2019)
20. Deepfakes github. https://github.com/deepfakes/faceswap. Accessed 06 July 2020
21. Faceswap github. https://github.com/MarekKowalski/FaceSwap/. Accessed 06 July 2020
22. Thies, J., Zollhofer, M., Stamminger, M., Theobalt, C., Nießner, M.: Face2face: real-time face capture and reenactment of RGB videos. In: Proceedings of the IEEE Conference on Computer Vision and Pattern Recognition, pp. 2387–2395 (2016)
23. King, D.E.: DLIB-ML: a machine learning toolkit. J. Mach. Learn. Res. 10, 1755–1758 (2009)

DeepEquaL: Deep Learning Based Mathematical Equation to Latex Generation

Ghaith Bilbeisi[1]([✉]), Sheraz Ahmed[2], and Rupak Majumdar[3]

[1] University of Kaiserslautern, Kaiserslautern, Germany
ghaith.bilbeisi@gmail.com
[2] German Research Center for Artificial Intelligence (DFKI),
Kaiserslautern, Germany
[3] Max Planck Institute for Software Systems, Kaiserslautern, Germany

Abstract. Document digitization is an active and important field of Machine Learning research that involves various Natural Language Processing tasks such as Optical Character Recognition and Machine Translation. One form of said digitization is the recognition and parsing of mathematical equations where structure, syntax, and smaller details are essential properties that must be preserved. More specifically, we focus this work around mathematical formula image to Latex generation, where we use input images of printed equations to predict the corresponding Latex code. We present an exploration of Deep Learning techniques that we believe could benefit existing state of the art models. We base our exploration on an attentional encoder-decoder architecture with a convolutional neural network to extract features from the input images. In our evaluations of the various modifications we also find and propose a model with two novel components, Max-Blur-Pooling and a Fine-Grained Feature map. Our proposed model outperforms state of the art models in all evaluation metrics.

Keywords: Image-to-latex generation · Optical character recognition · Deep Learning

1 Introduction

This paper investigates the nature and effectiveness of Deep Learning methods in generating accurate Latex markup from input images of mathematical equations. The problem at hand is relateable to any user of the Latex language, as it is known that generating math equations through the Latex markup syntax is no fun task. While it is not necessarily a difficult task for humans, it is relatively time consuming and laborious, especially when more complex equations are involved with matrices, symbols, and sub/super-scripts.

Optical Character Recognition (OCR) and Machine Translation (MT) are two of the most important Natural Language Processing (NLP) tasks being solved today. Although the two fields are a subset of the same general domain, they are often approached independently and are seldom seen within the same

© Springer Nature Switzerland AG 2020
H. Yang et al. (Eds.): ICONIP 2020, CCIS 1333, pp. 324–332, 2020.
https://doi.org/10.1007/978-3-030-63823-8_38

task. This is where our task is somewhat unique; it is at the face of it an OCR task since we simply need to identify each symbol and produce the corresponding character(s) from the vocabulary. Mathematical equations, however, are not so straightforward to parse. Interpreting each symbol independently (as is the case in most OCR models) will likely yield poor results. Consider an equation with a fraction for example; here, both the nominator and denominator must fall within the "\frac{}{}" brackets but looking at them independently, without considering the sequence structure, will result in a wrong prediction. Therefore, for accurate understanding of the content and layout of math equations, the context of each symbol within the equation in general must be factored into the parsing. With that in mind, the parallels between our task and MT tasks become apparent.

2   Background and Related Work

The problem of mathematical formula recognition has been the subject of research for quite some time. Going back as far as 1950 [3], researchers have been studying the structure of mathematical formulae in order to better understand them, and potentially identify them using machines. For this work, we focus on printed formulas in order to produce an accurate and reliable model which can potentially be further developed in the future to accommodate handwritten equations as well.

In [4], the authors combine CNNs, encoder-decoder LSTMs, and attention in their approach to generating markup from images of mathematical formulas. The CNN first produces a fine feature map out of the input image that is fed into the encoder. The encoder then produces the representation that is fed into the decoder which, with the use of attention, produces the final predictions. We present a more detailed overview of this model's architecture, which was partially adopted from [6], in the next section. At the time of its publication, this model was able to produce SotA results for the task of image to markup generation on the Im2latex-100K dataset which was published in the same work. The authors also use their approach to preform handwritten mathematical formula recognition. Results are competitive with all non-commercial systems they evaluated their model against and show promise for this approach in handwritten mathematical formula recognition. We use this model as the basis for our additions and experimentation, and our bench-marking, as we will present in the results and discussion sections.

More recently, an upgraded version of this model was proposed in [2] and was able to outperform its predecessor in all metrics. In this new model, the authors contributions are twofold; first, they modify the CNN architecture so that it produces a fine-grained feature map, and second, they make use of a fine-grained attention map which allows the model to focus on very small symbols in the input. At the time of this publication, the authors have yet to publish their code, therefore, we are limited to replicating their FGFE network and comparing our own against it.

3   Proposed Approach

Our proposed architecture is demonstrated in Fig. 1; First, a fine grained feature extraction CNN produces a $256 \times H/4 \times W/4$ feature map (see Sect. 3.2). Within this CNN architecture, we replace 2-strided max-pool layers with max-blur-pool layers (see Sect. 3.1). The feature map is then fed into an LSTM row-encoder which produces an encoded grid representation of the feature map. Finally, an attention based LSTM decoder produces the markup predictions using the feature grid produced by the encoder. This attention based encoder-decoder model is adopted from [4] with two encoder-decoder LSTM layers and is based on the very popular architecture of [6].

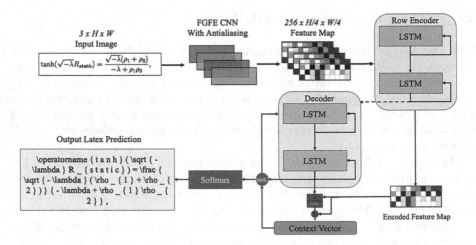

Fig. 1. Our proposed network structure. Each of the major components shown here is described in more detail in the following sections. Due to space restrictions the CNN had to be condensed into the block shown here but its details can be seen in Fig. 2. An example input image is shown from the test set, along with the output prediction produced by our model.

3.1   CNN Antialiasing

Invariance for geographical transformations of the input has been a topic of research and importance for as long as CNNs have gained prevalence. However, shift invariance seems to receive little attention and is usually overlooked. For our problem, symbols are often shifted within the image considering they rarely appear at the same position, making shift invariance valuable. Zhang [7] proposes a novel design to max-pooling in CNNs in which max-pooling, blurring, and sub-sampling are combined to provide reduced aliasing and thereby more resistance to shift variance. The author considers a 2 strided max-pool operation as consisting of two parts, first a single strided max evaluation and then the sub-sampling of those values. In the proposed max-blur-pool, these operations are supplemented with an $M \times M$ blur convolution in between. This results in a layer that first performs a 1 strided max operation, then applies the blur kernel to the results, and finally sub-samples from the resulting values. In our model, we replace the 2 strided max-pooling layer in both our base model and our fine grained features model with a max-blur-pool layer, and experiment with different sizes of the blur kernel (3, 5, and 7). Our findings indicate 7 to be the optimal size for the blur kernel. We also experiment with modifying and replacing the two remaining max-pool layers with (1, 2) and (2, 1), though neither of these modifications yielded positive results.

3.2   Fine Grained Feature Extraction

Another modification we made was to increase the depth of the CNN and reduce the number of filters and the amount of dimensionality reduction in order to extract finer features. This is a common technique used to produce finer feature maps in applications where closer attention to details is required. This is relevant in our case because mathematical formulas will often hold a lot of information in relatively small regions within the image. More specifically, fine grained feature maps are essential for identifying sub/super-scripts, fractions, and easily confused symbols or characters. In models with fine grained feature extraction, we split our CNN into three blocks, each followed by pooling (with strides of (2, 2), (2, 1), (1, 2) respectively) and batch normalization as demonstrated in Fig. 2.

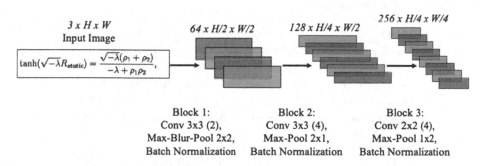

Fig. 2. Overview of the FGFE CNN architecture used in the DeepEquaL model.

4   Results and Evaluation

Following presenting our various results in this section, we will discuss their impact and possible implications in the next chapter. Table 1 shows the results of different variations of DeepEquaL in comparison to state of the art models, in both sequence and image evaluation metrics.

4.1 Training Parameters and Procedure

Our models were trained for 100K iterations each, and snapshots were created at every 10K iterations. All models were trained end-to-end using cross-entropy-loss, Stochastic Gradient Descent optimization, a batch size of 20, and a learning rate of 0.1 that decays by 0.5 every 10K iterations starting at iteration 50K. Each model also had a dropout rate of 0.3 for LSTM layers after the first in encoder and decoder configurations with more than one layer. We use beam search [1] with a beam size of 5 during testing to ensure the best performance for each model.

After the training of each model, we select the snapshot with the lowest perplexity and highest accuracy on the validation set to be evaluated using BLEU score and edit distance. Out of the 60+ evaluated models, the ones performing close to or higher than the base model were evaluated further using image accuracy and edit distance. The image-based evaluations are produced by using the predicted markup to generate a PDF document with Latex, which is then converted to an image and used for evaluation. The ground truth labels are also processed similarly to produce gold images for evaluations, instead of using the input image itself.

Table 1. Result comparison of our proposed model versus other state of the art models. Evaluation metrics are Image Edit Distance (IED$_w$), Image Accuracy (IA$_w$), Image Accuracy without white-spaces (IA), as well as the Combined Score (CS) which is the average of the five metrics.

Model	CS	BLEU	ED	IA	IA$_w$	IED$_w$
DeepEquaL (F:256, M:7)	89.37	89.05	91.6	87.74	86.11	92.35
DeepEquaL (F:256, M:3)	88.97	88.88	90.99	87.07	85.66	92.25
DeepEquaL (F:128, M:3)	88.894	88.87	91.07	86.87	85.44	92.22
DeepEquaL (F:128, M:7)	88.686	88.84	91.5	86.77	84.96	91.36
Fine Grained Feature Model F:128 (partial adaptation of [2])	88.59	88.96	91.04	86.46	84.96	91.53
Im2Tex [4]	85.47	87.45	90.39	81.07	78.93	89.51

4.2 Dataset

We used the im2latex-100K dataset [4] for all of our training and testing, using this dataset enables us to directly compare our results with the model that is the focus of our comparisons (Im2Tex [4]) since they reported their results on the same dataset. The dataset is composed of 100,000 images of labeled mathematical formulas, the labels consisting of the Latex markup corresponding to the image. The data is split into training, validation, and testing sets with 77K, 8K, and 10K images respectively.

4.3   Evaluation of Our Proposed Approach

Qualitative Analysis. In our analysis of the resulting images from our proposed model and the model of [4], we found three major areas of improvement, as shown in Fig. 3. For the first area of improvement, we found that the original model had difficulties in parsing repeating symbols. As demonstrated in example (a) of Fig. 3, the model exhibits a curious behavior when confronting repeating symbols, even when they are of no significant complexity. The second category for which we observed noticeable improvement was in small errors of small sized symbols (example b of Fig. 3). We noticed that the original model had a hard time identifying small symbols that occur regularly in mathematical equations, and often confused or completely overlooked them. The third significant improvement we found was when encountering dense equations spanning multiple lines, especially when the positioning of the lines differed. As shown in example (c) in Fig. 3, the original model does have some limited capacity for dealing with multiple lines, but fails to generalize this understanding to more than two or three lines, especially when symbol density is high in more complex equations.

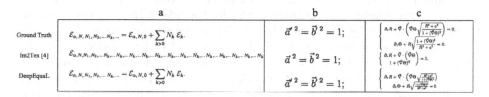

Fig. 3. Examples of the three major areas of quantitative improvement.

Quantitative Analysis. Moving on to quantitative analysis, we looked at the relationship between the length of the predicted Latex and its corresponding BLEU score.

Intuitively, we presumed that longer sequences correspond to more complex images and will, therefore, result in lower performance. As seen in Fig. 4, our assumption held true with the average BLEU score dropping significantly as the sequence length exceeded 100 symbols. Longer sequences remain

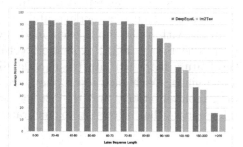

Fig. 4. Graph of the Average BLEU score against Latex sequence length.

a difficult problem to solve, and our additions did not, unfortunately, overcome it. Looking at the performance of the original model plotted alongside our proposed model in Fig. 4, we can see that there are significant improvements across all length groups, including the biggest ones. To evaluate the statistical significance of these results, we performed approximate randomization testing [5] (AR) with $N = 1000$ on the entire corpus and each of the bins in Fig. 4. We observe a significance value of ($p = 0.001$) for the entire corpus and each of the bins up to the 90–100 bin. This significance value is the minimum possible (indicating maximum significance) depending on the number of trials, and occurs when there are no random permutations of the data that result in a higher average difference in score than the actual results. As for the final three bins, the significance values are ($p = 0.118$, $p = 0.352$, $p = 0.125$) respectively, all of which are below the threshold of statistical significance. We note that these final three length bins have by far the least amount of data in the corpus, which resulted in such variance in reliability.

5   Discussion

5.1   DeepEquaL

In our qualitative analysis, we observed the model's ability to correctly predict equations with multiple lines of different positions. We believe that the credit for this development is shared, first by the added LSTM layers and the FGFE architecture for enhancing the ability to detect symbols in dense environments through more a detailed feature map and higher model complexity. And second by the Max-Blur-Pooling for adding shift in-variance which bolsters the model's ability to identify multiple lines even when they are positioned at shifted positions. As for the original model's strange behavior in repeating symbols indefinitely when facing a repetition of symbols in the input image, we believe our model was able to overcome this behavior due to the addition of a second LSTM layer to the encoder and decoder. Due to the deeper network, the model gained more complexity and was able to overcome the overly simplistic behavior of repeating symbols without properly parsing the input. We also observed our model's ability to correctly identify and predict small symbols within the input even in dense areas which we believe is, in major part, due to the FGFE 256 architecture. With this new CNN architecture, the feature maps fed into the encoder/decoder network is much more detailed and refined. With such input, the encoder is able to produce even more complex representations, and the attentional decoder is provided with additional information that allows it to accurately identify even the smallest symbols.

5.2   Ablation Study

Looking at Fig. 5 we can see the four models' BLEU scores across the different sequence length bins, side by side. As expected, all three of the new models outperform the original across the board, all with maximum AR significance ($p = 0.001$). More interestingly, we can see here the areas of impact each of the two additions (FGFE and Max-Blur-Pool) have relative to the ensemble method. Here, we can iden-

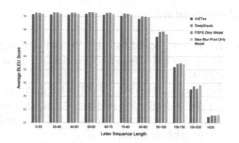

Fig. 5. BLEU Score comparison of our proposed model and the two models created by removing one of the two new features, as well as the original model of [4].

tify the FGFE as being responsible for the majority of the performance improvement, at times it even outperforms the ensemble model. We can also notice that the Max-Blur-Pool model is specifically helpful for the larger sequence lengths, albeit still struggling with sub 50 averages. Overall, however, the ensemble model is able to compound the benefits of the two techniques and provide the best performance.

6   Conclusion

The problem of mathematical equation image to Latex generation is an interesting task that borrows features from OCR and Machine Translation, and could improve the quality of life for any scientist working with Latex. In our work, we preformed an extensive search of possible techniques that we hypothesized could benefit models solving this problem. Through our implementations we trained and tested over 60 different models, exploring new techniques and various model parameters in an effort to find better performance. Our findings suggest that both antialiased convolutions and Fine-Grained Feature Extraction have a significant positive impact on performance, and are able to makeup for some of the weaknesses exhibited by prior models. We believe that some of our findings could provide real value to other applications outside of mathematical formula image to Latex generation, which share some of the same features as our problem. Looking ahead, one major area to explore is applying our model to handwritten formulas and studying its validity and the effects our modifications might have on a similar yet more difficult problem.

References

1. Abdou, S., Scordilis, M.S.: Beam search pruning in speech recognition using a posterior probability-based confidence measure. Speech Commun. **42**(3–4), 409–428 (2004)
2. Bender, S., Haurilet, M., Roitberg, A., Stiefelhagen, R.: Learning fine-grained image representations for mathematical expression recognition. In: International Conference on Document Analysis and Recognition Workshops (ICDARW), Sydney, pp. 56–61. IEEE (2019)
3. Bourbaki, N.: The architecture of mathematics. Am. Math. Monthly **57**(4), 221–232 (1950)
4. Deng, Y., Kanervisto, A., Ling, J., Rush, A.M.: Image-to-markup generation with coarse-to-fine attention. In: 34th International Conference on Machine Learning, Sydney, pp. 980–989. JMLR.org (2017)
5. Noreen, E.W.: Computer-Intensive Methods for Testing Hypotheses. Wiley, New York (1989)
6. Xu, K., et al.: Show, attend and tell: neural image caption generation with visual attention. In: 32nd International Conference on Machine Learning, Lille, pp. 2048–2057. JMLR.org (2015)
7. Zhang, R.: Making convolutional networks shift-invariant again. In: 36th International Conference on Machine Learning, Los Angeles, pp. 2048–2057. JMLR.org (2019)

Design and Implementation
of Pulse-Coupled Phase Oscillators
on a Field-Programmable Gate Array
for Reservoir Computing

Dinda Pramanta[✉] and Hakaru Tamukoh

Graduate School of Life Science and Systems Engineering, Kyushu Institute
of Technology, 2-4 Hibikino, Wakamatsu-ku, Kitakyushu, Fukuoka 808-0196, Japan
{dinda-pramanta,tamukoh}@brain.kyutech.ac.jp

Abstract. Reservoir computing (RC) has been viewed as a model of a
neurological system. The RC framework constructs a recurrent neural
network, which mimics parts of the brain, to solve temporal problems.
To construct a neural network inside a reservoir, we adopt the pulse-
coupled phase oscillator (PCPO) with neighbor topology connections on
a field-programmable gate array (FPGA). Neural spikes for the PCPO
are generated by the Winfree model. The low resource consumption of
the proposed model in time-series generation tasks was confirmed in an
evaluation study. We also demonstrate that on the FPGA, we can expand
a 3×3 PCPO into a 10×10 PCPO, generate spike behavior, and predict
the target signal with a maximum frequency of 418.796 MHz.

Keywords: FPGA · Pulse-coupled phase oscillator · RC · Winfree
model

1 Introduction

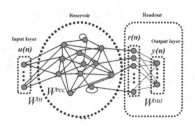

Fig. 1. Schematic of reservoir computing [1].

Supported by JSPS KAKENHI grant number 17H01798.

H. Yang et al. (Eds.): ICONIP 2020, CCIS 1333, pp. 333–341, 2020.
https://doi.org/10.1007/978-3-030-63823-8_39

Recent advances in neuroscience have roused growing interest in neuron-inspired communication architectures [2]. Reservoir computing (RC) as shown in Fig. 1, the *input layer* connects to an internal layer called the *reservoir*, in which the connections are spikes randomly and sparsely. The network structure and the connections are fixed and do not need to be trained. RC requires a large-size network [2] incurring a high computational cost, especially for the arithmetic logic unit that computes the interactions between units of the network.

Spiking neural networks are commonly modeled as pulse-coupled phase oscillator (PCPO) networks [3–7]. The communications among the oscillators are generated by the Winfree model [4]. When a single transition occurs during one spike timing, only one-bit signal lines are required between pairs of oscillators. These features allow for achieving hardware implementation with low-power intelligent information processing and high-speed performance, such as very large scale integration (VLSI) systems which constructed based on spike-based computation.

To demonstrate the effectiveness of spike-based computation features, researchers have proposed various analog VLSI circuits [8–10] and digital circuits using field-programmable gate arrays (FPGAs) [11,12]. Previously, we established that various sizes and interconnections of PCPO networks could be emulated in a parametrized FPGA design [12]. We also confirmed that spike-based computation could realize brain-like VLSI [13]. However, to design and implement a PCPO for adaptive RC, developing encoder and decoder are necessary.

Here we propose a novel RC model and its hardware architecture based on PCPOs. We have implemented on Xilinx Virtex6 ML605 hardware. In time-series generation tasks, we show that the model uses fewer resources than a competitive model [14].

2   Modeling PCPO

2.1   PCPO

The Winfree model [4] enables the efficient design of PCPO circuits. The fundamental equation of PCPOs is given by:

$$\frac{\partial \phi_i}{\partial t} = \omega_i + Z(\phi_i)Spk(t) \tag{1}$$

Here, $Spk(t)$ denotes the inputs from other oscillators, ϕ_i is the i-th phase variable with 2π periodicity, ω_i is the i-th natural angular frequency, and $Z(\phi_i)$ is the phase sensitivity function giving the response of the i-th oscillator. Spike inputs are expressed as follows:

$$Spk(t) = \frac{K_0}{N} \sum_{j=1}^{N} \sum_{n=1}^{\infty} \delta(t - t_j n) \tag{2}$$

where δ is the Dirac delta function representing the timing of input spikes with zero pulse width. In the hardware, the spike pulses have a definite width Δt, during which ϕ_i is updated depending on the value of $Z(\phi_i)$. From the (2) K_0 is the coupling strength, N is the number of oscillators, and $t_j n$ is the firing time. To implement the PCPO model in digital hardware, (1) and (2) are respectively discretized as follows:

$$\phi_i(t+1) = \phi_i(t) + \omega_i + \frac{K_0}{N} \sum_{j=1}^{N} Z(\phi_i) Spk_j(t) \tag{3}$$

$$Spk_j(t) = \begin{cases} 1, & if\phi_j(t) = \phi_{th} \\ 0, & otherwise \end{cases} \tag{4}$$

The discretized model given by (3) and (4) can be simply implemented in logic circuits [12]. The phase value at the next time step is calculated by adding the current phase, the natural angular frequency, and the summed products of the phase sensitivity function and input pulses. The natural angular frequency ω_i is assumed constant. The oscillator outputs a spike pulse when the phase variable reaches the threshold ω-th, and then resets to $\omega_i = 0$.

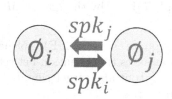

(a) Schematic of coupled network.

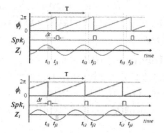

(b) Phase variables $((\phi_j)$ and $(\phi_i))$ and pulse inputs.

Fig. 2. Visualisation of pulse-coupled phase oscillators.

Two oscillators are coupled by spikes Spk_i and Spk_j. Figure 2 is a schematic of two pulse-coupled phase oscillators and a timing diagram explaining their updates. The phase sensitivity function is given by $Z(\phi_i) = -\sin(\phi_i)$. Spikes occur by updating the pulse timing. Each oscillator undergoes two update phases: positive updating and negative updating [15].

2.2 RC Based on a Leaky Integrator

According to the schematic of RC in Fig. 1, the leaky integrator (LI) based used for a time series generation task. States that a continuous-value unit of the reservoir in discrete-time system of $r(n)$, while $r(n) \in \mathbb{R}_r^N$ expressed as follows:

$$r(n+1) = r(n) + 1/\tau(-\alpha_0 r(n) + f_r((W^{in}u(n) + W^{rec}r(n))) \tag{5}$$

$n \in \mathbb{Z}$ is the discrete time, $u(n) \in \mathbb{R}_u^N$ is the input signal, α_0 is the leaking rate, τ is the time constant, and $f_r(x) = \tanh(x)$ is an activation function. The output layer $y(n)$ is defined as follows:

$$y(n) = f_y(W^{out}r(n)) \tag{6}$$

where W^{in} and W^{out} are the input and output recurrent matrices, $f_y(x) = \tanh(x)$. The output matrix W^{out} is computed by ridge regression as follows:

$$(W^{out})^T = (M^T M + \lambda E)^{-1} M^T G \tag{7}$$

The matrix M is collected from the $r(n)$ series of the reservoir, λ is a regularization parameter, E is the identity matrix, and G is a target matrix. The stepwise procedures are given below.

Run the Network: Using (5), run the network from $n = 0$ to $n = T_1$ with an input signal $u(n)$ and collect the series of the reservoir state $r(n)$ into matrix M. Next, collect the sigmoid-inverted target data sequence into matrix G.

Compute W^{out}, $y(n)$ and $z(n)$: Compute the output matrix $y(n)$ by (6), then transpose W^{out} for the ridge regression (7) that obtains the output $(W^{out})^T$. To obtain the real output signal system $z(n)$, multiply (W^{out}) by the matrix M of reservoir series.

Error Measurement: Determine the root mean square error (RMSE) (normalized into 0–1) of each signal by (8). The RMSE measures the deviation between the output $z(n)$ and the target signal y_{target}. The output and target signals are given as $\hat{y}i$ and yi respectively, and n is the data length.

$$RMSE = \sqrt{\frac{1}{n} \sum_{i=1}^{n} (\hat{y}i - yi)^2} \tag{8}$$

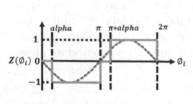

(a) Span parameter *alpha* (α).

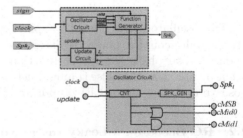

(b) Updating circuit (top) and oscillator circuit (bottom).

Fig. 3. Easy hardware implementation of the PCPOs.

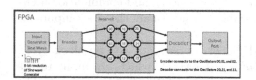

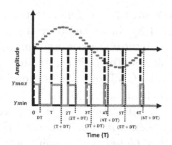

Fig. 4. Architecture of the proposed model.

Fig. 5. Activity during one period of a modulated sine wave.

Table 1. One-type variance of α ($\alpha = 3$).

Index of oscillators	Alpha (α)
(0, 0)	3
(0, 1)	3
(0, 2)	3
(1, 0)	3
(1, 1)	3
(1, 2)	3
(2, 0)	3
(2, 1)	3
(2, 2)	3

Table 2. Three-type variance of α ($\alpha = 1$, $\alpha = 2$, and $\alpha = 3$).

Index of oscillators	Alpha (α)
(0, 0)	1
(0, 1)	2
(0, 2)	3
(1, 0)	3
(1, 1)	2
(1, 2)	1
(2, 0)	2
(2, 1)	1
(2, 2)	3

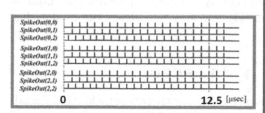

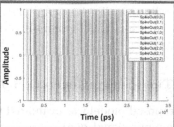

(a) in-phase synchronization mode based on Table 1.

(b) Random-like spiking mode based on Table 2.

Fig. 6. Initialization of 3×3 PCPO with the α-set.

To simplify the function shape of $Z(\phi_i)$ for the hardware implementation, we define the span parameter α during which $Z(\phi_i) = 0$ (see Fig. 3(a)) [12,15]. Setting $\alpha > \Delta t$, we can generate randomly behaved PCPOs without over-updating. Figure 3(b) shows the overall circuit comprising an *Oscillator Circuit*, a *Function Generator circuit*, and an *Update Circuit*. The *Oscillator Circuit* contains an n-bit counter (CNT), a spike generator (SPK_GEN), and combinational circuits. The CNT represents the phase variable ϕ_i and counts the clock inputs for implementing ω_i in (3) [16].

Each time step t in the discretized model corresponds to one clock cycle. It has been inferred from $cMSB$, $cMid0$, and $cMid1$, which are input to the *Function Generator* circuit, determine the shape of the function $Z(\phi_i)$. The *Function Generator* circuit combines the signals to generate the outputs Zp and Zn. The output from the *Update Circuit* receives Zp, Zn, and Spk_j. The other oscillators similarly provide their update signals to the main *Oscillator Circuit*.

Figure 4 shows the proposed architecture in the FPGA. We constructed a 3×3 of PCPOs with neighbor topology connections. The sine waves are generated in the FPGA with 8-bit resolution. The encoder and decoder parts apply pulse width modulation (PWM) [17]. Figure 5 shows the duty cycle parameter (D), the fraction of one period during which a signal or system is active. In this case, a counter reference was used (T). The modulation of the rectangular pulse varied the average value of the waveform as a single line binary wave. The decoder compares the current outputs with the modulated signal from the counter reference.

3   Experimental Results

3.1   Run the Network Without Input Generator

Tables 1 and 2 show the values of the parameter α selected for initialization. Figures 6(a) and (b) show the spiking activities in all networks initialized by the α values in Tables 1 and 2, respectively. Figure 6(a) shows the in-phase synchronization of the original model [11], and Fig. 8(b) shows the random-like mode.

3.2   Time-Series Generation Task of the PCPOs

The proposed model was evaluated in a time-series generation task. After encoding the input signal $u(n) = (u_1, ..., u_{Nu})$, we collected the series of the decoded reservoir state $r(n) = (r_1, ..., r_{Nr})$ and computed the output of matrix W^{out} by ridge regression, which matches the output $y(n)$ to the target time series y_{target} (*Target Signal*). In Figs. 7, 8, and 9, the *Input Signal* is an 8-bit-resolution sine wave and y_{target} has double the phase of the *Input Signal* with $(t-1)$, *Counter Internal State* represents the reservoir state, and the *Target and Output Signal* are presented by the dashed and solid blue lines in the bottom panels respectively. The networks successfully predicted the Target Signal with the RMSE computed by (8).

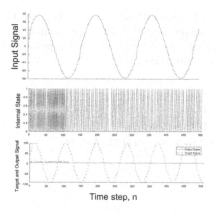

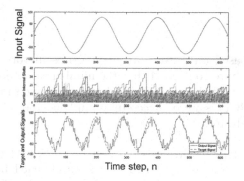

Fig. 7. Results of 3 readout channels of the 3×3 of PCPOs using the α values in Table 1.

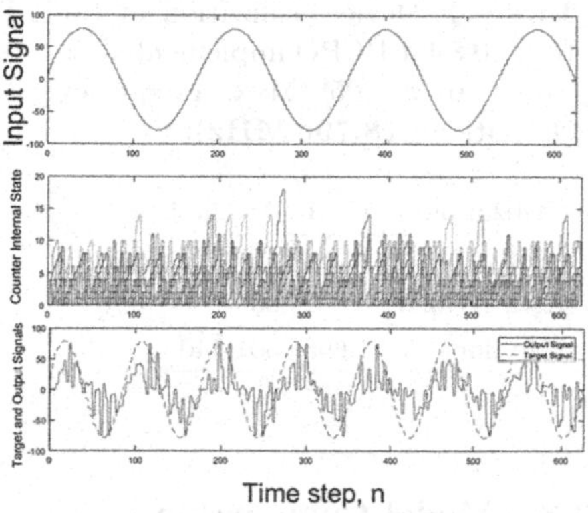

Fig. 8. Results of all 9 readout channels of the 3×3 of PCPOs using the α values in Table 2.

Fig. 9. Results of all 100 readout channels of the 10×10 PCPO for $\alpha = 1$, 2 and 3.

We expanded our 3×3 PCPO model (Figs. 7 and 8) to a 10×10 model (Fig. 9). The parameter α was again varied as 1, 2, and 3, and all 100 readout channels of the 10×10 PCPO were used. The RMSE results of the 3×3 and 10×10 PCPOs are listed in Table 3. Note that increasing the numbers of oscillators and readout channels, improves the accuracy of the output signal.

Table 3. RMSE results

Oscillator-set	Doubled-sine
3×3 (9 readout)	0.267
10×10 (100 readout)	0.145

Table 4. Device utilization of the 10×10 8-bit PCPO implemented on Virtex 6 ML605 (Max. Frequency Operation **418.796 MHz**).

Utilization	Used	Available
LUTs	2,283	150,720
RAM_B18E1	0	832
Flip-flops	1,695	301,440

Table 5. Device utilization of 2-100-2 32bit-ternary weight ESN FPGA Implemented on Zynq UltraScale+MPSoCZCU102 (operation frequency **200 MHz**) [14].

Utilization	Used	Available
LUTs	28,933	274,080
BRAM_18K	48	912
Flip-flops	44,021	548,160

3.3 Model Comparison

Comparison with ESN Model: Tables 4 and 5 compare the hardware implementations of look up tables (LUTs) and flip-flops. Note that our model consumes fewer resources and operates at higher speed than the existing model.

4 Conclusion

We proposed RC based on pulse-coupled phase oscillators which inspired by Winfree model. We have confirmed that the number of oscillators and readouts affecting the accuracy of the output signal and performed in a time-series generation task. The PCPOs were successfully implemented with low resource on ML605-Virtex6 hardware.

Acknowledgment. This research is supported by JSPS KAKENHI grant number 17H01798. This paper was partly based on results obtained from a project commissioned by the New Energy and Industrial Technology Development Organization (NEDO), Japan.

References

1. Tanaka, G., et al.: Recent advances in physical reservoir computing: a review. Neural Netw. **115**, 100–123 (2019)
2. Lukoševičius, M., Jaeger, H.: Reservoir computing approaches to recurrent neural network training. Comput. Sci. Rev. **3**(3), 127–149 (2009)
3. Kuramoto, Y.: Chemical oscillations, waves, and turbulence. Courier Corporation (2003)
4. Winfree, A.T.: The Geometry of Biological Time. Springer, New York (2001). https://doi.org/10.1007/978-1-4757-3484-3
5. Mirollo, R.E., Strogatz, S.H.: Synchronization of pulse-coupled biological oscillators. SIAM J. Appl. Math. **50**(6), 1645–1662 (1990)
6. Kuramoto, Y.: Collective synchronization of pulse-coupled oscillators and excitable units. Physica D **50**(1), 15–30 (1991)
7. Izhikevich, E.M.: Dynamical Systems in Neuroscience. MIT Press, Cambridge (2007)

8. Atuti, D., Kato, N., Nakada, K., Morie, T.: CMOS circuit implementation of a coupled phase oscillator system using pulse modulation approach. In: 2007 18th European Conference on Circuit Theory and Design, pp. 827–830. IEEE (2007)
9. Matsuzaka, K., Tohara, T., Nakada, K., Morie, T.: Analog CMOS circuit implementation of a pulse-coupled phase oscillator system and observation of synchronization phenomena. Nonlinear Theory Appl. IEICE **3**(2), 180–190 (2012)
10. Matsuzaka, K., Tanaka, H., Ohkubo, S., Morie, T.: VLSI implementation of coupled MRF model using pulse-coupled phase oscillators. Electron. Lett. **51**(1), 46–48 (2014)
11. Suedomi, Y., Tamukoh, H., Tanaka, M., Matsuzaka, K., Morie, T.: Parameterized digital hardware design of pulse-coupled phase oscillator model toward spike-based computing. In: Lee, M., Hirose, A., Hou, Z.-G., Kil, R.M. (eds.) ICONIP 2013. LNCS, vol. 8228, pp. 17–24. Springer, Heidelberg (2013). https://doi.org/10.1007/978-3-642-42051-1_3
12. Suedomi, Y., Tamukoh, H., Matsuzaka, K., Tanaka, M., Morie, T.: Parameterized digital hardware design of pulse-coupled phase oscillator networks. Neurocomputing **165**, 54–62 (2015)
13. Pramanta, D., Morie, T., Tamukoh, H.: Implementation of multi-FPGA communication using pulse-coupled phase oscillators. In: Proceedings of 2017 International Conference on Artificial Life And Robotics (ICAROB 2017), pp. 128–131 (2017)
14. Honda, K., Tamukoh, H.: A hardware-oriented echo state network and its FPGA implementation. J. Robot. Netw. Artif. Life (2020)
15. Pramanta, D., Morie, T., Tamukoh, H.: Synchronization of pulse-coupled phase oscillators over multi-FPGA communication links. J. Robot. Netw. Artif. Life **4**(1), 91–96 (2017)
16. Pramanta, D., Tamukoh, H.: High-speed synchronization of pulse coupled phase oscillators on multi-FPGA. In: Gedeon, T., Wong, K.W., Lee, M. (eds.) ICONIP 2019. CCIS, vol. 1143, pp. 318–329. Springer, Cham (2019). https://doi.org/10.1007/978-3-030-36802-9_34
17. Katori, Y., Morie, T., Tamukoh, H.: Reservoir computing based on dynamics of pseudo-billiard system in hypercube. In: International Joint Conference on Neural Networks (IJCNN 2019) (2019)

Element-Wise Alternating Least Squares Algorithm for Nonnegative Matrix Factorization on One-Hot Encoded Data

Zhuo Wu, Tsuyoshi Migita, and Norikazu Takahashi$^{(\boxtimes)}$ (iD)

Graduate School of Natural Science and Technology, Okayama University,
3-1-1 Tsushima-naka, Kita-ku, Okayama 700–8530, Japan
ps3m981k@s.okayama-u.ac.jp, migita@cs.okayama-u.ac.jp,
takahashi@okayama-u.ac.jp

Abstract. Matrix factorization is a popular technique used in recommender systems based on collaborative filtering. Given a matrix that represents ratings of items by users, one can obtain latent feature vectors of the users and the items by applying one of the existing matrix factorization algorithms. In this paper, we focus our attention on matrices obtained from categorical ratings using one-hot encoding, and propose an element-wise alternating least squares algorithm to obtain latent feature vectors from such matrices. We next show that the proposed algorithm has the global convergence property in the sense of Zangwill. We also show through experiments using a benchmark dataset that the proposed algorithm is effective for prediction of unknown ratings.

Keywords: Recommender systems · Nonnegative matrix factorization · One-hot encoding · Global convergence

1 Introduction

Recommender systems have been used in various domains such as music [7], movies [12], books [8], and so on, in order to provide personalized recommendations to users. There are two main approaches to building such systems: the content-based filtering and the collaborative filtering [6]. The former creates a profile for each user or item to characterize its nature, while the latter analyzes relationships between users and items based on past user behavior.

Matrix factorization is one of the most popular techniques for the collaborative filtering approach [2–4, 6]. Given a matrix that represents ratings of items by users, one can obtain latent feature vectors of the users and the items by applying a matrix factorization algorithm to it. Once the latent feature vectors for all users and items are obtained, one can predict the rating of an item by a user who has never had an interaction with the item, by computing the dot product of the corresponding latent feature vectors. In addition, one can use the prediction results to recommend items to users. This is the basic idea of recommender systems based on matrix factorization.

© Springer Nature Switzerland AG 2020
H. Yang et al. (Eds.): ICONIP 2020, CCIS 1333, pp. 342–350, 2020.
https://doi.org/10.1007/978-3-030-63823-8_40

Existing matrix factorization algorithms assume that ratings of items by users are numerical scores. However, it is often the case that ratings are categorical (e.g., 'like' or 'neutral' or 'dislike') rather than numerical. In order to apply matrix factorization algorithms to categorical data, we need to transform them to numerical data. A simple way to do this is to use a technique called one-hot encoding [1]. For example, if the categories are 'like', 'neutral' and 'dislike', they are expressed as one-hot vectors $(1,0,0)$, $(0,1,0)$ and $(0,0,1)$, respectively. Because matrices obtained from categorical data by using one-hot encoding are very sparse and have a special structure, it is important to develop matrix factorization algorithms suitable for those matrices and to see how they can improve the performance of recommender systems based on matrix factorization.

In this paper, we propose an element-wise alternating least squares algorithm for nonnegative matrix factorization on one-hot encoded data. The proposed algorithm is obtained from a mathematical programming problem. This problem is based on the one considered by He et $al.$ [2], but there are two main differences between these problems. One is that our problem has nonnegativity constraints for factor matrices. This is reasonable because matrices obtained by one-hot encoding are inevitably nonnegative. The other is that the objective function in our problem contains additional terms so that the product of factor matrices approaches to a matrix having the special structure mentioned above. We next show that the proposed algorithm has the global convergence property in the sense of Zangwill [11]. We also show through experiments using a benchmark dataset that the proposed algorithm is effective for prediction of unknown ratings.

2   Problem Formulation

Suppose that we are given a dataset $\mathcal{D}$ consisting of M instances. All instances have the same I categorical variables, and for each $i \in \{1, 2, \dots, I\}$ the i-th variable either takes one of N_i (≥ 2) possible values or does not have a value. We apply one-hot encoding to $\mathcal{D}$ to obtain a data matrix $\boldsymbol{R} = (r_{mn}) \in \{0, 1, \infty\}^{M \times N}$ with $N = \sum_{i=1}^{I} N_i$. Let $L_1 = 1$, $U_1 = N_1$, $L_i = \sum_{j=1}^{i-1} N_j + 1$ for $i = 2, 3, \dots, I$, and $U_i = L_i + N_i - 1$ for $i = 2, 3, \dots, I$. Then, for each pair $(m, i) \in \{1, 2, \dots, M\} \times \{1, 2, \dots, I\}$, $(r_{m,L_i}, r_{m,L_i+1}, \dots, r_{m,U_i})$ is either a one-hot vector, that is, a vector such that only one element takes 1 and all other elements take 0, or $(\infty, \infty, \dots, \infty)$ which corresponds to the case where the value of the i-th categorical variable of the m-th instance is not available.

We consider the problem of finding two nonnegative matrices $\boldsymbol{P} = (p_{mk}) \in \mathbb{R}_+^{M \times K}$ and $\boldsymbol{Q} = (q_{nk}) \in \mathbb{R}_+^{N \times K}$ such that $\boldsymbol{P}\boldsymbol{Q}^T$ is approximately equal to $\boldsymbol{R}$, where K is a positive integer less than $\min\{M, N\}$ and $\mathbb{R}_+$ denotes the set of nonnegative real numbers. If we find such nonnegative matrices $\boldsymbol{P}$ and $\boldsymbol{Q}$ then $\boldsymbol{p}_m = (p_{m1}, p_{m2}, \dots, p_{mK})^T$ and $\boldsymbol{q}_n = (q_{n1}, q_{n2}, \dots, q_{nK})^T$ can be considered as the latent feature vectors for the m-th row and the n-th column of $\boldsymbol{R}$, respectively. Furthermore, by using $\boldsymbol{P}\boldsymbol{Q}^T$, we can predict the values of those elements of $\boldsymbol{R}$ which take ∞. In particular, when $\boldsymbol{R}$ represents the evaluations of items made by users, we can recommend some items to each user by using the value of PQ^T. This is the basic idea of recommender systems based on matrix factorization.

In this paper, we propose to formulate the above-mentioned problem as the following mathematical programming problem:

$$
\begin{array}{cc}
\text{minimize} & J(P, Q) \\
\text{subject to} & P \geq 0, \quad Q \geq 0
\end{array}
\tag{1}
$$

where

$$
\begin{aligned}
J(P, Q) = & \sum_{(m,n) \in \mathcal{R}} w_{mn} \left(r_{mn} - p_m^T q_n\right)^2 + \sum_{(m,n) \notin \mathcal{R}} c_n (p_m^T q_n)^2 \\
& + \lambda \left(\sum_{m=1}^{M} \|p_m\|^2 + \sum_{n=1}^{N} \|q_n\|^2 \right) \\
& + \mu \sum_{m=1}^{M} \sum_{i=1}^{I} \left[\left\{ \sum_{\alpha=L_i}^{U_i} (p_m^T q_\alpha) - 1 \right\}^2 + \sum_{\alpha=L_i}^{U_i} \sum_{\substack{\beta=L_i \\ \beta \neq \alpha}}^{U_i} (p_m^T q_\alpha)(p_m^T q_\beta) \right].
\end{aligned}
\tag{2}
$$

with $\mathcal{R} = \{(m,n) \in \{1, 2, \ldots, M\} \times \{1, 2, \ldots, N\} \mid r_{mn} \in \{0, 1\}\}$, $w_{mn} \in \mathbb{R}_+$, $c_n \in \mathbb{R}_+$, $\lambda \in \mathbb{R}_{++}$, and $\mu \in \mathbb{R}_+$. Here $\mathbb{R}_{++}$ denotes the set of positive real numbers. This mathematical programming problem is based on the existing work [2]. In fact, if we set $\mu = 0$ and remove the nonnegativity constraints, the above problem is identical with that considered in [2]. Therefore, a key feature of our new objective function (2) is the term containing μ, which is designed so that $(p_m^T q_{L_i}, p_m^T q_{L_i+1}, \ldots, p_m^T q_{U_i})$ approaches to some one-hot vector. It is easy to see that the term takes the minimum value 0 if and only if $(p_m^T q_{L_i}, p_m^T q_{L_i+1}, \ldots, p_m^T q_{U_i})$ is a one-hot vector for all $m \in \{1, 2, \ldots, M\}$ and $i \in \{1, 2, \ldots, I\}$.

Let $\mathcal{F}$ be the feasible region of (1), that is, $\mathcal{F} = \mathbb{R}_+^{M \times K} \times \mathbb{R}_+^{N \times K}$. The first order necessary condition for $(P, Q) \in \mathcal{F}$ to be a local minimum point of (1) is that

$$
\frac{\partial J}{\partial p_{mk}} \begin{cases} = 0, & \text{if } p_{mk} > 0, \\ \geq 0, & \text{otherwise} \end{cases} \quad \forall (m, k) \in \{1, 2, \ldots, M\} \times \{1, 2, \ldots, K\}
\tag{3}
$$

and

$$
\frac{\partial J}{\partial q_{nk}} \begin{cases} = 0, & \text{if } q_{nk} > 0, \\ \geq 0, & \text{otherwise} \end{cases} \quad \forall (n, k) \in \{1, 2, \ldots, N\} \times \{1, 2, \ldots, K\}.
\tag{4}
$$

If $(P, Q) \in \mathcal{F}$ satisfies (3) and (4) then it is called a stationary point of (1).

3   Derivation of Update Rule

Although the objective function (2) is not jointly convex in $\boldsymbol{P}$ and $\boldsymbol{Q}$, it is strictly convex with respect to one variable. So if we select one variable and optimize it while treating the others as constants, the objective function value decreases or remains unchanged. Hence we may reach a local optimal solution of (1) by solving the $MK + NK$ one-variable optimization problems repeatedly. This technique is known as the element-wise Alternating Least Squares (eALS) [2] and has been widely used in the literature (see for example [5]). In what follows, we derive an update rule for p_{mk} and q_{nk} based on the eALS.

The partial derivative of J with respect to p_{mk} is given by

$$
\begin{aligned}
\frac{\partial J}{\partial p_{mk}} = {} & 2p_{mk} \sum_{n \in \mathcal{R}_{m*}} w_{mn} q_{nk}^2 - 2 \sum_{n \in \mathcal{R}_{m*}} w_{mn} \left(r_{mn} - \hat{r}_{mn}^k \right) q_{nk} \\
& + 2p_{mk} \sum_{n \notin \mathcal{R}_{m*}} c_n q_{nk}^2 + 2 \sum_{n \notin \mathcal{R}_{m*}} c_n \hat{r}_{mn}^k q_{nk} + 2\lambda p_{mn} \\
& + 2\mu p_{mk} \sum_{i-1}^{I} \sum_{\alpha = L_i}^{U_i} q_{\alpha k} \left(2 \sum_{\beta = L_i}^{U_i} q_{\beta k} - q_{\alpha k} \right) \\
& + 2\mu \sum_{i=1}^{I} \sum_{\alpha = L_i}^{U_i} q_{\alpha k} \left(2 \sum_{\beta = L_i}^{U_i} \hat{r}_{m\beta}^k - 1 \right)
\end{aligned}
$$

where $\mathcal{R}_{m*} = \{ n \in \{1, 2, \dots, N\} \mid r_{mn} \in \{0, 1\} \}$ for $m = 1, 2, \dots, M$, and $\hat{r}_{mn}^k = \sum_{j=1, j \neq k}^{K} p_{mj} q_{nj}$. By solving $\partial J / \partial p_{mk} = 0$ for p_{mk}, we have $p_{mk} = \phi_{mk}^p / \psi_{mk}^p$ where

$$
\begin{aligned}
\phi_{mk}^p = {} & \sum_{n \in \mathcal{R}_{m*}} \left[w_{mn} r_{mn} - (w_{mn} - c_n) \hat{r}_{mn}^k \right] q_{nk} - \sum_{j \neq k} p_{mj} s_{jk}^q \\
& - \mu \sum_{i=1}^{I} \sum_{\alpha = L_i}^{U_i} q_{\alpha k} \left(2 \sum_{\beta = L_i}^{U_i} \hat{r}_{m\beta}^k - 1 \right),
\end{aligned} \tag{5}
$$

$$
\psi_{mk}^p = \sum_{n \in \mathcal{R}_{m*}} (w_{mn} - c_n) q_{nk}^2 + s_{kk}^q + \lambda + \mu \sum_{i=1}^{I} \sum_{\alpha = L_i}^{U_i} q_{\alpha k} \left(2 \sum_{\beta = L_i}^{U_i} q_{\beta k} - q_{\alpha k} \right), \tag{6}
$$

respectively, and s_{jk}^q is the (j, k) element of the matrix $\boldsymbol{S}^q$ defined by $\boldsymbol{S}^q = \sum_{n=1}^{N} c_n \boldsymbol{q}_n \boldsymbol{q}_n^T$. If $\phi_{mk}^p / \psi_{mk}^p$ is nonnegative, this is the unique optimal solution of the one-variable optimization problem with respect to p_{mk}. Otherwise, $p_{mk} = 0$ is the unique optimal solution because the one-variable objective function is strictly convex as stated above. Therefore, the optimal solution is given by $p_{mk} = \max \{ 0, \phi_{mk}^p / \psi_{mk}^p \}$.

Similarly, the optimal solution to the problem of minimizing J with respect to q_{nk} subject to $q_{nk} \geq 0$ is given by $q_{nk} = \max\{0, \phi_{nk}^q / \psi_{nk}^q\}$ where

$$\phi_{nk}^q = \sum_{m \in \mathcal{R}_{*n}} \left[w_{mn} r_{mn} - (w_{mn} - c_n) \hat{r}_{mn}^k \right] p_{mk} - c_n \sum_{\substack{j=1 \\ j \neq k}}^{K} q_{nj} s_{jk}^p$$

$$- \mu \sum_{m=1}^{M} p_{mk} \left(\hat{r}_{mn}^k - 1 \right) - 2\mu \sum_{\substack{\alpha = L_{i(n)} \\ \alpha \neq n}}^{U_{i(n)}} \sum_{j=1}^{K} q_{\alpha j} s_{jk}^p, \tag{7}$$

$$\psi_{nk}^q = \sum_{m \in \mathcal{R}_{*n}} (w_{nm} - c_n) p_{mk}^2 + c_n s_{kk}^p + \lambda + \mu s_{kk}^p, \tag{8}$$

respectively, $\mathcal{R}_{*n} = \{m \in \{1, 2, \ldots, M\} \mid r_{mn} \in \{0, 1\}\}$ for $n = 1, 2, \ldots, N$, $i(n)$ is the value of i satisfying $L_i \leq n \leq U_i$, and s_{jk}^p is the (j, k) element of the matrix S^p defined by $S^p = \sum_{m=1}^{M} P_m P_m^T$.

4   Overall Algorithm and Its Global Convergence

The update rule for the elements of P and Q obtained in the previous section is formally described in Algorithm 1. Let $\{(P^{(t)}, Q^{(t)})\}_{t=0}^{\infty}$ be the sequence generated by repeated applications of Algorithm 1, where $(P^{(0)}, Q^{(0)})$ is the initial value of (P, Q) and $(P^{(t)}, Q^{(t)})$ with $t \geq 1$ is the value of (P, Q) after the t-th application of Algorithm 1. It is clear from the derivation of the update rule that $J(P^{(t+1)}, Q^{(t+1)})$ is less than or equal to $J(P^{(t)}, Q^{(t)})$ for all $t \geq 0$. Moreover, we can show that Algorithm 1 has the global convergence property in the sense of Zangwill [11].

Theorem 1. For any $(P^{(0)}, Q^{(0)}) \in \mathcal{F}$, the sequence $\{(P^{(t)}, Q^{(t)})\}_{t=0}^{\infty}$ generated by repeated applications of Algorithm 1 has at least one convergent subsequence and the limit of any convergent subsequence is a stationary point of (1).

Proof. We omit the proof because it is similar to [5, Theorem 1].

It follows from Theorem 1 that if a relaxed version of the first order necessary condition is used as the stopping condition then the finite termination of the algorithm is guaranteed [5,9,10]. In our algorithm, we use the stopping condition given by

$$\frac{\partial J}{\partial p_{mk}} \begin{cases} \in [-\delta_1, \delta_1], & \text{if } p_{mk} > \delta_2, \\ \geq -\delta_1, & \text{otherwise} \end{cases} \quad \forall (m, k) \in \{1, 2, \ldots, M\} \times \{1, 2, \ldots, K\} \tag{9}$$

and

$$\frac{\partial J}{\partial q_{nk}} \begin{cases} \in [-\delta_1, \delta_1], & \text{if } q_{nk} > \delta_2, \\ \geq -\delta_1, & \text{otherwise} \end{cases} \quad \forall (n, k) \in \{1, 2, \ldots, N\} \times \{1, 2, \ldots, K\}, \tag{10}$$

Algorithm 1. Update of P and Q

Require: $R \in \{0, 1, \infty\}^{M \times N}$, $(P, Q) \in \mathcal{F}$, $I, L_1, L_2, \ldots, L_I, U_1, U_2, \ldots, U_I \in \mathbb{N}$,
   $w_{mn} \in \mathbb{R}_+$ $(m = 1, 2, \ldots, M; n = 1, 2, \ldots, N)$, $c_n \in \mathbb{R}_+$ $(n = 1, 2, \ldots, N)$, $\lambda \in \mathbb{R}_{++}$,
   $\mu \in \mathbb{R}_+$
Ensure: Updated (P, Q)
 1: Set $\hat{r}_{mn} \leftarrow p_m q_n^T$ for all (m, n) such that $r_{mn} \neq \infty$.
 2: Set $S^q \leftarrow \sum_{n=1}^{N} c_n q_n q_n^T$.
 3: **for** $m = 1, 2, \ldots, M$ **do**
 4:     **for** $k = 1, 2, \ldots, K$ **do**
 5:         Set $\hat{r}_{mn}^k \leftarrow \hat{r}_{mn} - p_{mk} q_{nk}$ for $n = 1, 2, \ldots, N$.
 6:         Set $p_{mk} \leftarrow \max\{0, \phi_{mk}^p / \psi_{mk}^p\}$ where ϕ_{mk}^p and ψ_{mk}^p are defined by (5) and
         (6), respectively.
 7:         Set $\hat{r}_{mn} \leftarrow \hat{r}_{mn}^k + p_{mk} q_{nk}$ for $n - 1, 2, \ldots, N$.
 8:     **end for**
 9: **end for**
10: Set $S^p \leftarrow P^T P$.
11: **for** $n = 1, 2, \ldots, N$ **do**
12:     **for** $k = 1, 2, \ldots, K$ **do**
13:         Set $\hat{r}_{mn}^k \leftarrow \hat{r}_{mn} - p_{mk} q_{nk}$ for $m = 1, 2, \ldots, M$.
14:         Set $q_{nk} \leftarrow \max\{0, \phi_{nk}^q / \psi_{nk}^q\}$ where ϕ_{nk}^q and ψ_{nk}^q are defined by (7) and (8),
         respectively.
15:         Set $\hat{r}_{mn} \leftarrow \hat{r}_{mn}^k + p_{mk} q_{nk}$ for $m = 1, 2, \ldots, M$.
16:     **end for**
17: **end for**
18: Return (P, Q) and stop.

---

where δ_1 and δ_2 are positive constants.

The overall algorithm we propose in this paper is shown in Algorithm 2, and its finite termination property is stated in the next theorem.

Theorem 2. Algorithm 2 stops within a finite number of iterations.

Proof. We omit the proof because it is similar to [5, Theorem 2].

5   Experiments

In order to evaluate the effectiveness of the proposed algorithm, we conducted experiments using MovieLens Latest Dataset[1]. For the experiments, we constructed a very small dataset $\mathcal{D}$ by selecting the first 20 $(= M)$ movies in the movie list and 20 $(= I)$ users who had rated many of those 20 movies. We also converted numerical variables to categorical ones by considering all ratings lower than 2.0 as 'bad', between 2.0 to 4.0 as 'medium', and higher than 4.0 as 'good', and applied one-hot encoding to $\mathcal{D}$ to obtain the data matrix $R \in \{0, 1, \infty\}^{20 \times 60}$. In all experiments, we set $K = 10$, $w_{mn} = 1.0$ for all m and n, $c_n = 0.2$ for all

---

[1] https://grouplens.org/datasets/movielens/.

Algorithm 2. Proposed eALS algorithm

Require: $R \in \{0, 1, \infty\}^{M \times N}$, $(P, Q) \in \mathcal{F}$, I, $L_1, L_2, \ldots, L_I$, $U_1, U_2, \ldots, U_I \in \mathbb{N}$,
   $w_{mn} \in \mathbb{R}_+$ ($m = 1, 2, \ldots, M$; $n = 1, 2, \ldots, N$), $c_n \in \mathbb{R}_+$ ($n = 1, 2, \ldots, N$), $\lambda \in \mathbb{R}_{++}$,
   $\mu \in \mathbb{R}_+$, $\delta_1, \delta_2 \in \mathbb{R}_{++}$
Ensure: Updated (P, Q)
1: **while** (P, Q) does not satisfy (9) and (10) **do**
2:    Run Algorithm 1 to update (P, Q).
3: **end while**
4: Return (P, Q) and stop.

---

n, and $\lambda = 0.2$. Also, we used uniform random numbers between 0.0 and 0.1 for
the initial values of P and Q.

In the first experiment, for various values of μ, we updated P and Q 20
times by using Algorithm 1, and then constructed $\hat{R}^{OH}$ from PQ^T by converting $(p_m^T q_{L_i}, p_m^T q_{L_i+1}, \ldots, p_m^T q_{U_i})$ to a one-hot vector in such a way that the
maximum value in the former corresponds to 1 in the latter. Figure 1 shows
how the value of the objective function $J(P, Q)$ evolves as the number of iterations increases. It is clear that the value of the objective function decreases
monotonically and converges to some constant for all cases. Table 1 shows the
reconstruction accuracy a^r which is defined by

$$a^r = \frac{|\{(m, i) \mid (\hat{r}_{m,L_i}^{OH}, \hat{r}_{m,L_i+1}^{OH}, \ldots, \hat{r}_{m,U_i}^{OH}) = (r_{m,L_i}, r_{m,L_i+1}, \ldots, r_{m,U_i})\}|}{|\{(m, i) \mid (r_{m,L_i}, r_{m,L_i+1}, \ldots, r_{m,U_i}) \neq (\infty, \infty, \ldots, \infty)\}|}. \quad (11)$$

It is easy to see that the reconstruction accuracy decreases monotonically as the
value of μ increases.

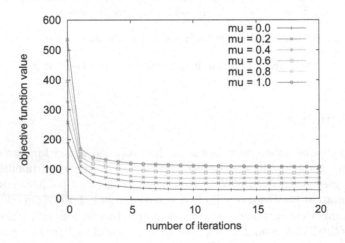

Fig. 1. Evolution of the objective function value.

Table 1. Reconstruction accuracy a^{r} of the proposed eALS algorithm.

μ	0.0	0.2	0.4	0.6	0.8	1.0
a^{r}	1.000	0.979	0.944	0.919	0.858	0.807

In the second experiment, for various values of μ, we evaluated the reconstruction and prediction accuracies of the proposed algorithm using the leave-one-out cross validation approach. For each (m, i) such that $(r_{m,L_i}, r_{m,L_i+1}, \ldots, r_{m,U_i}) \neq (\infty, \infty, \ldots, \infty)$, we replaced $(r_{m,L_i}, r_{m,L_i+1}, \ldots, r_{m,U_i})$ with $(\infty, \infty, \ldots, \infty)$ and constructed $\hat{R}^{\mathrm{OH}}$ in the same way as the first experiment. We then calculated the reconstruction accuracy a^{r}_{mi} using (11) and the prediction accuracy a^{p}_{mi} which is 1 if $(\hat{r}^{\mathrm{OH}}_{m,L_i}, \hat{r}^{\mathrm{OH}}_{m,L_i+1}, \ldots, \hat{r}^{\mathrm{OH}}_{m,U_i})$ is equal to the original $(r_{m,L_i}, r_{m,L_i+1}, \ldots, r_{m,U_i})$ and 0 otherwise. We finally computed the averages of a^{r}_{mi} and a^{p}_{mi} over all (m, i) such that $(r_{m,L_i}, r_{m,L_i+1}, \ldots, r_{m,U_i}) \neq (\infty, \infty, \ldots, \infty)$ to get the average reconstruction accuracy $a^{\mathrm{r}}_{\mathrm{ave}}$ and the average prediction accuracy $a^{\mathrm{p}}_{\mathrm{ave}}$. Table 2 shows the results of this experiment. As is expected from the results of the first experiment, the average reconstruction accuracy decreases monotonically as the value of μ increases. However, the average prediction accuracy increases with μ when $0.0 \leq \mu \leq 0.8$ and stays at the maximum value when $0.8 \leq \mu \leq 1.8$. This means that the term including μ of the objective function is effective in improving the prediction accuracy.

Table 2. Results of leave-one-out cross validation.

μ	0.0	0.2	0.4	0.6	0.8	1.0	1.2	1.4	1.6	1.8	2.0
$a^{\mathrm{r}}_{\mathrm{ave}}$	0.999	0.973	0.942	0.909	0.851	0.827	0.813	0.807	0.807	0.804	0.801
$a^{\mathrm{p}}_{\mathrm{ave}}$	0.690	0.711	0.751	0.802	0.807	0.807	0.807	0.807	0.807	0.807	0.802

6 Conclusions

We have proposed a novel element-wise alternating least squares algorithm for matrices obtained from categorical data by one-hot encoding. As shown in the experiments, the prediction accuracy of the recommender system based on the proposed algorithm increases as the value of the parameter μ increases from zero. This indicates that the terms including μ of the objective function play an important role for prediction of unknown ratings. However, it is not clear at this moment whether this claim holds true for other datasets. Thus further experiments using large datasets are needed to evaluate the performance of the proposed algorithm.

Acknowledgments. This research was partially supported by the STRADA (Studies on TRaffic Accident Data Analysis) project. The authors would like to thank the core members of this project: Makoto Maeda and Tadashi Koriki of TOSCO Corporation, Takafumi Komoto and Chihiro Egi of Okayama Prefectural Police, and Takayuki Shuku of Okayama University, for their valuable comments on one-hot encoding and nonnegative matrix factorization.

References

1. Cerda, P., Varoquaux, G., Kégl, B.: Similarity encoding for learning with dirty categorical variables. Mach. Learn. **107**(8–10), 1477–1494 (2018)
2. He, X., Zhang, H., Kan, M.Y., Chua, T.S.: Fast matrix factorization for online recommendation with implicit feedback. In: Proceedings of the 39th International ACM SIGIR Conference on Research and Development in Information Retrieva, pp. 549–558 (2016)
3. Hernando, A., Bobadilla, J., Ortega, F.: A non negative matrix factorization for collaborative filtering recommender systems based on a bayesian probabilistic model. Knowl.-Based Syst. **97**, 188–202 (2016)
4. Hu, Y., Koren, Y., Volinsky, C.: Collaborative filtering for implicit feedback datasets. In: Proceedings of 2008 Eighth IEEE International Conference on Data Mining, pp. 263–272. IEEE (2008)
5. Kimura, T., Takahashi, N.: Gauss-Seidel HALS algorithm for nonnegative matrix factorization with sparseness and smoothness constraints. IEICE Trans. Fund. Electr. Commun. Comput. Sci. **100**(12), 2925–2935 (2017)
6. Koren, Y., Bell, R., Volinsky, C.: Matrix factorization techniques for recommender systems. Computer **42**(8), 30–37 (2009)
7. Lee, S.K., Cho, Y.H., Kim, S.H.: Collaborative filtering with ordinal scale-based implicit ratings for mobile music recommendations. Inf. Sci. **180**(11), 2142–2155 (2010)
8. Núñez-Valdéz, E.R., Lovelle, J.M.C., Martínez, O.S., García-Díaz, V., De Pablos, P.O., Marín, C.E.M.: Implicit feedback techniques on recommender systems applied to electronic books. Comput. Hum. Behav. **28**(4), 1186–1193 (2012)
9. Takahashi, N., Hibi, R.: Global convergence of modified multiplicative updates for nonnegative matrix factorization. Computational Optimization and Applications **57**(2), 417–440 (2014)
10. Takahashi, N., Katayama, J., Seki, M., Takeuchi, J.: A unified global convergence analysis of multiplicative update rules for nonnegative matrix factorization. Computational Optimization and Applications **71**(1), 221–250 (2018)
11. Zangwill, W.: Nonlinear Programming. A Unified Approach. Prentice Hall, Englewood Cliffs (1969)
12. Zhou, Y., Wilkinson, D., Schreiber, R., Pan, R.: Large-scale parallel collaborative filtering for the netflix prize. In: Fleischer, R., Xu, J. (eds.) AAIM 2008. LNCS, vol. 5034, pp. 337–348. Springer, Heidelberg (2008). https://doi.org/10.1007/978-3-540-68880-8_32

Graph Learning Regularized Non-negative Matrix Factorization for Image Clustering

Xianzhong Long[1,2(✉)], Jian Xiong[3], and Yun Li[1,2]

[1] School of Computer Science and Technology, Nanjing University of Posts and Telecommunications, Nanjing 210023, China
{lxz,liyun}@njupt.edu.cn
[2] Jiangsu Key Laboratory of Big Data Security and Intelligent Processing, Nanjing 210023, China
[3] National Engineering Research Center of Communications and Networking, Nanjing University of Posts and Telecommunications, Nanjing 210003, China
jxiong@njupt.edu.cn

Abstract. The methods based on graph regularized non-negative matrix factorization have been extensively used in image and document clustering. However, these algorithms employed the fixed graph information and did not consider how to learn a graph automatically. For the sake of solving this problem, a kind of graph learning regularized non-negative matrix factorization (GLNMF) method is proposed in this paper. Specifically, self-representation regularized term is applied to generate weight matrix, which is updated iteratively during GLNMF optimization process. The final goal is to learn an adaptive graph and a good low dimensional representation. Furthermore, we derive the corresponding multiplicative update rules for our optimization problem. Image clustering experiments on three benchmark datasets indicate the significance of our proposed method.

Keywords: Non-negative matrix factorization · Graph learning · Image clustering

1 Introduction

Non-negative matrix factorization was first proposed in [1], which decomposes a matrix into two non-negative matrix multiplication forms. The non-negativity constraint results in a partial representation, because it only allows addition, not subtraction. Concretely, NMF employs a linear combination of basis vectors to represent the original data, where the basis matrix and coefficient matrix are non-negative. The methods based on NMF are applied in many application scenarios, including image clustering [2,3] and face recognition [4]. A series of methods based on NMF were summarized and were divided into four categories in [5], including constrained NMF, basic NMF, structured NMF and generalized NMF.

Many studies have shown that the high dimensional data usually have a potential nonlinear low dimensional manifold space. Consequently, many models

© Springer Nature Switzerland AG 2020
H. Yang et al. (Eds.): ICONIP 2020, CCIS 1333, pp. 351–360, 2020.
https://doi.org/10.1007/978-3-030-63823-8_41

based on manifold learning are proposed to discover the low dimensional embedding of data. Influenced by manifold learning, some NMF algorithms based on it are put forward for solving clustering or classification tasks [2]. However, the process of graph construction and NMF optimization procedure are independent in the above methods. In other words, once the graph is constructed in these algorithms, their graph structure will not be changed in the subsequent matrix decomposition process. However, previous studies have shown that the graph obtained by learning can achieve better performance than the fixed graph. In order to solve this problem, several algorithms have been proposed. For example, NMF with locality constrained adaptive graph was proposed in [6] and flexible NMF model with adaptively learned graph regularization was given in [7]. In these methods, the weight matrix of graph, basis matrix and coefficient matrix can be simultaneously learned during NMF iteration process.

Inspired by adaptive graph regularization, this paper gives a new algorithm called graph learning regularized non-negative matrix factorization (GLNMF), which explicitly integrates weight graph learning into NMF framework. Specifically, the weight matrix is obtained by self-expression learning and is updated during the NMF optimization process.

2   Related Work

$\mathbf{X} = [\mathbf{x}_1, \mathbf{x}_2, \cdots, \mathbf{x}_n] \in \mathbb{R}^{m \times n}$ is a data matrix and each column represents an image with m dimension. $\mathbf{W} \in \mathbb{R}^{m \times r}$, $\mathbf{U} \in \mathbb{R}^{n \times r}$ and $\mathbf{H} \in \mathbb{R}^{r \times n}$ ($r \ll \min(m, n)$). This section reviews the K-Means, NMF, GNMF, CF and LCCF algorithms.

2.1   K-Means

The aim of K-Means clustering is trying to divide the n samples into $r(r \leq n)$ sets $\mathbf{S} = \{S_1, S_2, \ldots, S_r\}$, in order to minimize the within-cluster sum of square error [8]. The corresponding optimization problem is as follows:

$$\min_{\mathbf{S}} \sum_{i=1}^{r} \sum_{\mathbf{x} \in S_i} \|\mathbf{x} - \mu_i\|_2^2 \tag{1}$$

Where μ_i is the average of all samples in the set S_i. After K-Means clustering, every sample is appointed to a sole center.

2.2   Non-negative Matrix Factorization

The NMF optimization problem using Euclidean distance to measure reconstruction error is as follows:

$$\min_{\mathbf{W}, \mathbf{H}} \|\mathbf{X} - \mathbf{W}\mathbf{H}\|_F^2$$
$$\text{s.t.} \, \mathbf{W} \geq 0, \mathbf{H} \geq 0 \tag{2}$$

2.3   Graph Regularized Non-negative Matrix Factorization

Based on the manifold learning theory, the GNMF model was given in [2], in which the adjacent data points in the high-dimensional space remain close neighbors in the low-dimensional manifold space. The optimization problem of GNMF is as follows:

$$\min_{\mathbf{W},\mathbf{H}} \|\mathbf{X} - \mathbf{WH}\|_F^2 + \lambda \mathrm{Tr}(\mathbf{HLH}^T)$$
$$\text{s.t.} \mathbf{W} \geq 0, \mathbf{H} \geq 0 \tag{3}$$

where λ is a non-negative regularization parameter and is employed to balance the reconstruction error and regularized term. $\mathbf{L}$ is the Laplacian matrix.

2.4   Concept Factorization

CF [9] decomposes a matrix $\mathbf{X}$ into a product of three matrices, i.e., $\mathbf{X} \approx \mathbf{XUH}$. CF solves the following optimization problem.

$$\min_{\mathbf{U},\mathbf{H}} \|\mathbf{X} - \mathbf{XUH}\|_F^2$$
$$\text{s.t.}\ \ \mathbf{U} \geq 0, \mathbf{H} \geq 0 \tag{4}$$

2.5   Locally Consistent Concept Factorization

Similar to GNMF, LCCF adds the the graph Laplacian regularized term into the standard CF objective function [10]. LCCF solves the following problem:

$$\min_{\mathbf{U},\mathbf{H}} \|\mathbf{X} - \mathbf{XUH}\|_F^2 + \lambda \mathrm{Tr}(\mathbf{HLH}^T)$$
$$\text{s.t.} \mathbf{U} \geq 0, \mathbf{H} \geq 0 \tag{5}$$

3   Graph Learning Regularized Non-negative Matrix Factorization

The weight matrices in the GNMF and LCCF are computed before multiplication update, and they do not consider how to learn an adaptive graph. However, the graph information is very important in manifold learning because it characterizes the neighborhood relationship of sample points in low dimensional representation space. In order to solve this problem, we devise a graph learning regularized NMF.

3.1   GLNMF Model

Inspired by the self representation learning method in subspace clustering, the affinity matrix is constructed by the obtained representation coefficient [11]. According to the affinity matrix (weight matrix), we further construct the Laplacian matrix and update it iteratively.

The optimization problem of GLNMF is as follows:

$$\min_{\mathbf{W},\mathbf{H},\mathbf{S}} \|\mathbf{X} - \mathbf{WH}\|_F^2 + \|\mathbf{X} - \mathbf{XS}\|_F^2 + \lambda \mathrm{Tr}(\mathbf{HLH}^T) + \beta \mathrm{Tr}(\mathbf{H}^T\mathbf{EH}) + \gamma\|\mathbf{S}\|_F^2$$
$$\mathrm{s.t.}\,\mathbf{W} \geq 0, \mathbf{H} \geq 0, \mathbf{S} \geq 0$$

$$(6)$$

where parameters λ, β and γ are three non-negative constants, $\mathbf{S} \in \mathbb{R}^{n \times n}$ is the learned self representation coefficient, $\mathbf{C} = (\mathbf{S} + \mathbf{S}^T)/2$ is an affinity matrix, and a diagonal matrix $\mathbf{B} \in \mathbb{R}^{n \times n}$ is obtained according to the affinity matrix $\mathbf{C}$. $\mathbf{B}_{jj}$ is the column (or equivalently row, since $\mathbf{C}$ is symmetrical) sum of the affinity matrix $\mathbf{C}$, i.e., $\mathbf{B}_{jj} = \sum_{i=1}^{n} \mathbf{C}_{ij}$. $\mathbf{L} = \mathbf{B} - \mathbf{C}$ is called Laplacian matrix and $\mathbf{L} \in \mathbb{R}^{n \times n}$. $\mathbf{E} = \overline{\mathbf{1}} - \mathbf{I}$, all elements of the matrix $\overline{\mathbf{1}} \in \mathbb{R}^{r \times r}$ are 1 and the matrix $\mathbf{I} \in \mathbb{R}^{r \times r}$ is an identity matrix. The regularized term $\mathrm{Tr}(\mathbf{H}^T\mathbf{EH})$ is used to reduce the correlation of row vectors in the coefficient matrix $\mathbf{H}$. The regularized term $\|\mathbf{S}\|_F^2$ is employed to avoid the invalid solution of $\mathbf{S}$ in the optimization process. In addition, in order to improve the robustness of our model, before using $\mathbf{S}$ to construct the weight matrix $\mathbf{C}$, only the largest t values are retained in each column of $\mathbf{S}$.

3.2   The Update Rules of GLNMF

Although the formula (6) is not jointly convex for $(\mathbf{W},\mathbf{H},\mathbf{S})$, when we fix other variables, it is convex for one of the variables in $(\mathbf{W},\mathbf{H},\mathbf{S})$. Therefore, we can get the multiplicative update rules of GLNMF. The objective function (6) can be written as:

$$
\begin{aligned}
J &= \mathrm{Tr}((\mathbf{X} - \mathbf{WH})(\mathbf{X} - \mathbf{WH})^T) + \mathrm{Tr}((\mathbf{X} - \mathbf{XS}) \\
&\quad (\mathbf{X} - \mathbf{XS})^T) + \lambda \mathrm{Tr}(\mathbf{HLH}^T) + \beta \mathrm{Tr}(\mathbf{H}^T\mathbf{EH}) + \gamma \mathrm{Tr}(\mathbf{SS}^T) \\
&= 2\mathrm{Tr}(\mathbf{XX}^T) - 2\mathrm{Tr}(\mathbf{XH}^T\mathbf{W}^T) + \mathrm{Tr}(\mathbf{WHH}^T\mathbf{W}^T) \\
&\quad -2\mathrm{Tr}(\mathbf{XS}^T\mathbf{X}^T) + \mathrm{Tr}(\mathbf{XSS}^T\mathbf{X}^T) + \lambda \mathrm{Tr}(\mathbf{HLH}^T) \\
&\quad +\beta \mathrm{Tr}(\mathbf{H}^T\mathbf{EH}) + \gamma \mathrm{Tr}(\mathbf{SS}^T)
\end{aligned}
$$

$$(7)$$

We apply the matrix properties $\mathrm{Tr}(\mathbf{XY}) = \mathrm{Tr}(\mathbf{YX})$ and $\mathrm{Tr}(\mathbf{X}) = \mathrm{Tr}(\mathbf{X}^T)$. Let $\varPhi$, $\varPsi$ and $\varOmega$ be the Lagrange multiplier for $\mathbf{W}$, $\mathbf{H}$ and $\mathbf{S}$, respectively. Then the corresponding Lagrange function form of J is:

$$
\begin{aligned}
L_f &= 2\mathrm{Tr}(\mathbf{XX}^T) - 2\mathrm{Tr}(\mathbf{XH}^T\mathbf{W}^T) + \mathrm{Tr}(\mathbf{WHH}^T\mathbf{W}^T) \\
&\quad -2\mathrm{Tr}(\mathbf{XS}^T\mathbf{X}^T) + \mathrm{Tr}(\mathbf{XSS}^T\mathbf{X}^T) + \lambda \mathrm{Tr}(\mathbf{HLH}^T) \\
&\quad +\beta \mathrm{Tr}(\mathbf{H}^T\mathbf{EH}) + \gamma \mathrm{Tr}(\mathbf{SS}^T) + \mathrm{Tr}(\varPhi^T\mathbf{W}) + \mathrm{Tr}(\varPsi^T\mathbf{H}) + \mathrm{Tr}(\varOmega^T\mathbf{S})
\end{aligned}
$$

$$(8)$$

The partial derivatives of L_f with respect to $\mathbf{W}$, $\mathbf{H}$ and $\mathbf{S}$ respectively are:

$$\frac{\partial L_f}{\partial \mathbf{W}} = -2\mathbf{XH}^T + 2\mathbf{WHH}^T + \varPhi = 0 \tag{9}$$

$$\frac{\partial L_f}{\partial \mathbf{H}} = -2\mathbf{W}^T\mathbf{X} + 2\mathbf{W}^T\mathbf{WH} + 2\lambda\mathbf{HB} - 2\lambda\mathbf{HC} + 2\beta\mathbf{EH} + \varPsi = 0 \tag{10}$$

$$\frac{\partial L_f}{\partial \mathbf{S}} = -2\mathbf{X}^T\mathbf{X} + 2\mathbf{X}^T\mathbf{XS} + 2\gamma\mathbf{S} + \Omega = 0 \qquad (11)$$

From the KKT conditions $\Phi_{iq}\mathbf{W}_{iq} = 0$, $\Psi_{qj}\mathbf{H}_{qj} = 0$ and $\Omega_{jj}\mathbf{S}_{jj} = 0$, we can get the following equations:

$$(-2\mathbf{XH}^T + 2\mathbf{WHH}^T)_{iq}\mathbf{W}_{iq} + \Phi_{iq}\mathbf{W}_{iq} = 0 \qquad (12)$$

$$(-2\mathbf{W}^T\mathbf{X} + 2\mathbf{W}^T\mathbf{WH} + 2\lambda\mathbf{HB} - 2\lambda\mathbf{HC} + 2\beta\mathbf{EH})_{qj}\mathbf{H}_{qj} + \Psi_{qj}\mathbf{H}_{qj} = 0 \quad (13)$$

$$(-2\mathbf{X}^T\mathbf{X} + 2\mathbf{X}^T\mathbf{XS} + 2\gamma\mathbf{S})_{jj}\mathbf{S}_{jj} + \Omega_{jj}\mathbf{S}_{jj} = 0 \qquad (14)$$

Thus, the multiplicative update rules for $\mathbf{W}, \mathbf{H}, \mathbf{S}$ are defined as follows:

$$\mathbf{W}_{iq} \longleftarrow \mathbf{W}_{iq}\frac{(\mathbf{XH}^T)_{iq}}{(\mathbf{WHH}^T)_{iq}} \qquad (15)$$

$$\mathbf{H}_{qj} \longleftarrow \mathbf{H}_{qj}\frac{(\mathbf{W}^T\mathbf{X}+\lambda\mathbf{HC})_{qj}}{(\mathbf{W}^T\mathbf{WH}+\lambda\mathbf{HB}+\beta\mathbf{EH})_{qj}} \qquad (16)$$

$$\mathbf{S}_{jj} \longleftarrow \mathbf{S}_{jj}\frac{(\mathbf{X}^T\mathbf{X})_{jj}}{(\mathbf{X}^T\mathbf{XS}+\gamma\mathbf{S})_{jj}} \qquad (17)$$

$\mathbf{W}, \mathbf{H}$ and $\mathbf{S}$ are updated iteratively until the number of iteration exceed the maximum value or the objective value of (6) does not change. The procedure is summarized in Table 1.

Table 1. The Algorithm of Graph Learning Regularized Non-negative Matrix Factorization (GLNMF)

Input: Data matrix $\mathbf{X} \in \mathbb{R}^{m \times n}$, parameters λ, β, γ, t

Initialization: Randomly initialize non-negative matrices $\mathbf{W} \in \mathbb{R}^{m \times r}$, $\mathbf{H} \in \mathbb{R}^{r \times n}$. Similar to GNMF, use 0–1 weighting function to initialize $\mathbf{S} \in \mathbb{R}^{n \times n}$ where the number of nearest neighbors is set to 5. Calculate $\mathbf{C}$ and $\mathbf{B}$

Repeat

    1. Update $\mathbf{W}$ by rule (15)

    2. Update $\mathbf{H}$ by rule (16)

    3. Update $\mathbf{S}$ by rule (17)

    4. Keep the largest t elements in each column of $\mathbf{S}$ and set the remaining elements to zero

    5. Calculate $\mathbf{C} = (\mathbf{S} + \mathbf{S}^T)/2$ and $\mathbf{B} = diag(sum(\mathbf{C}, 2))$

Until Convergence

Output: Coefficient matrix $\mathbf{H}$

---

4   Experimental Results

In this part, we compare the proposed GLNMF algorithm with five typical algorithms, including K-Means, NMF, GNMF, CF and LCCF. Three face datasets are used, i.e., ORL, UMIST and PIE.

4.1   Data Sets

The statistical description of the three datasets are shown in Table 2. All the face images used in our experiments are manually aligned and cropped. Each face image is represented as a column vector and the features (pixel values) are then scaled to [0,1] (divided by 255).

Table 2. Statistics of the three datasets

Dataset	ORL	UMIST	PIE
Number of samples	400	575	1428
Dimension	1024	1600	1024
Number of classes	40	20	68
Number of samples in each class	10	19–48	21

4.2   Experiment Settings

In our experiment, the matrix X is used to denote the gray features of images. In the GLNMF model, there are four parameters, i.e., λ, β, γ and t. The best empirical choice is $\lambda = 30$, $\beta = 0.001$, $\gamma = 1$ and $t = 4$. Here, the parameter t is used to eliminate the interaction of cross subspace coefficients. To make a fair comparison, the best value of parameter λ appeared in GNMF and LCCF are set to 1 and 0.2 respectively. In addition, when we use the multiplicative update rule, we set the maximum number of iterations to 500. In the GNMF and LCCF, for each sample point x_j in X, we look for five sample points that are closest to it, and connect them with the edge. We use the $0 - 1$ weighting function to define the weight on the edge. In order to randomize the experiment, we use different clustering numbers to evaluate. For each given clustering number K, we conduct 20 rounds of random tests (except for the whole data set). The mean and standard error of the performance are reported in the Tables. All experiments are conducted in MATLAB, which is executed on a PC with an Intel Core i7-5500U CPU (2.40 GHz) and 8 GB RAM.

4.3   Comparative Analysis

The clustering result is evaluated by comparing the obtained sample label and the known label. Accuracy (AC) and normalized mutual information (NMI) are used to measure clustering performance respectively.

Table 3, 4, 5, 6, 7 and 8 are the clustering results on three face image datasets. Through these tables, we can see that the proposed GLNMF algorithm is always superior to the other five classic algorithms, and the best results are marked in bold. The experimental results also show that the performance of GNMF and LCCF is better than that of NMF and CF respectively, which is consistent with common sense.

Table 3. Clustering performance on ORL (ACC)

K	Accuracy (%)					
	K-Means	NMF	GNMF	CF	LCCF	GLNMF
5	81.9 ± 11.8	81.3 ± 13.6	84.1 ± 13.8	65.9 ± 9.5	82.8 ± 13.6	**85.9 ± 14.3**
10	65.5 ± 7.2	73.0 ± 6.7	75.8 ± 7.8	46.9 ± 7.6	61.4 ± 10.2	**75.9 ± 9.1**
15	59.6 ± 5.7	67.6 ± 5.7	70.5 ± 7.0	38.7 ± 3.9	56.4 ± 7.6	**73.1 ± 5.7**
20	59.0 ± 5.1	65.1 ± 4.2	66.7 ± 5.9	30.1 ± 2.5	49.2 ± 4.8	**68.4 ± 6.3**
25	57.2 ± 5.1	63.6 ± 3.8	66.2 ± 5.6	28.5 ± 2.0	48.5 ± 5.0	**66.8 ± 4.3**
30	55.4 ± 2.9	61.3 ± 3.2	63.2 ± 4.1	25.5 ± 1.8	46.7 ± 2.4	**64.6 ± 3.5**
35	53.7 ± 2.7	59.9 ± 2.9	60.9 ± 3.4	23.7 ± 1.1	43.5 ± 2.3	**62.5 ± 3.1**
40	53.5	57.5	60.5	24.5	42.0	**67.0**

Table 4. Clustering performance on ORL (NMI)

K	Normalized Mutual Information (%)					
	K-Means	NMF	GNMF	CF	LCCF	GLNMF
5	79.1 ± 12.4	80.0 ± 11.1	83.9 ± 11.9	56.8 ± 8.8	80.0 ± 15.5	**85.3 ± 13.1**
10	72.5 ± 6.3	77.8 ± 5.5	80.5 ± 6.3	50.0 + 8.0	65.8 ± 8.9	**81.2 ± 7.3**
15	70.8 ± 4.3	78.0 ± 3.7	79.2 ± 5.3	48.2 ± 4.9	65.9 ± 7.4	**82.2 ± 4.2**
20	71.4 ± 4.1	76.1 ± 2.9	77.4 ± 3.9	43.7 ± 2.6	62.5 ± 4.3	**79.7 ± 4.2**
25	71.4 ± 3.5	76.8 ± 2.8	78.3 ± 4.0	45.0 ± 2.2	64.0 ± 4.3	**80.1 ± 2.8**
30	71.3 ± 2.3	76.4 ± 1.9	77.7 ± 2.3	44.9 ± 2.1	64.1 ± 2.1	**79.5 ± 2.2**
35	71.5 ± 2.2	76.6 ± 1.9	76.6 ± 2.0	44.4 ± 1.2	62.8 ± 1.7	**78.3 ± 1.7**
40	71.8	74.6	75.7	46.4	60.5	**80.9**

Table 5. Clustering performance on UMIST (ACC)

K	Accuracy (%)					
	K-Means	NMF	GNMF	CF	LCCF	GLNMF
4	59.3 ± 12.1	58.7 ± 10.9	63.7 ± 13.4	56.2 ± 8.0	59.1 ± 11.1	**66.7 ± 14.7**
6	56.8 ± 7.2	54.7 ± 6.2	58.7 ± 8.1	53.0 ± 6.0	55.5 ± 6.9	**59.9 ± 10.0**
8	50.1 ± 7.3	49.7 ± 6.2	53.4 ± 8.4	48.2 ± 7.9	50.7 ± 7.6	**54.9 ± 6.6**
10	47.6 ± 4.0	46.7 ± 5.9	51.5 ± 4.5	46.2 ± 4.3	49.8 ± 4.4	**53.4 ± 5.4**
12	46.3 ± 4.4	45.8 ± 3.7	48.1 ± 4.8	44.4 ± 3.4	47.9 ± 4.4	**52.5 ± 4.9**
14	44.1 ± 3.3	42.3 ± 3.3	45.4 ± 4.5	40.0 ± 2.6	44.9 ± 3.6	**48.1 ± 3.9**
16	43.6 ± 3.3	41.0 ± 2.8	43.7 ± 2.6	40.1 ± 3.6	43.9 ± 3.4	**46.8 ± 4.0**
18	41.4 ± 3.3	41.2 ± 2.2	44.3 ± 2.5	38.4 ± 2.1	42.9± 2.3	**45.2 ± 2.7**
20	38.4	38.4	40.9	35.7	39.7	**43.3**

Table 6. Clustering performance on UMIST (NMI)

K	Normalized Mutual Information (%)					
	K-Means	NMF	GNMF	CF	LCCF	GLNMF
4	51.4 ± 12.6	48.4 ± 11.8	59.6 ± 13.8	45.3 ± 11.1	51.6 ± 11.8	**64.9 ± 16.1**
6	59.9 ± 5.8	54.7 ± 8.1	62.7 ± 7.4	52.9 ± 6.4	57.9 ± 5.7	**64.7 ± 8.1**
8	56.2 ± 7.6	55.7 ± 8.2	61.8 ± 8.0	53.4 ± 8.1	58.4 ± 7.1	**65.5 ± 7.9**
10	58.0 ± 4.5	55.7 ± 4.8	63.1 ± 5.7	54.1 ± 4.6	60.4 ± 4.1	**66.2 ± 5.0**
12	58.8 ± 4.3	57.0 ± 3.4	61.3 ± 4.9	54.6 ± 3.6	60.7 ± 3.3	**64.6 ± 5.1**
14	59.3 ± 3.1	55.6 ± 3.6	60.4 ± 4.1	53.1 ± 3.6	59.4 ± 4.2	**63.5 ± 4.2**
16	60.2 ± 3.1	56.7 ± 2.4	60.9 ± 3.4	54.5 ± 3.7	60.4 ± 3.5	**63.8 ± 3.0**
18	59.2 ± 3.0	58.0 ± 2.2	61.8 ± 2.2	54.7 ± 1.8	60.5 ± 2.1	**63.0 ± 2.4**
20	57.9	58.4	60.7	51.8	58.0	**61.4**

Table 7. Clustering performance on PIE (ACC)

K	Accuracy (%)					
	K-Means	NMF	GNMF	CF	LCCF	GLNMF
10	40.1 ± 4.3	79.5 ± 6.5	84.6 ± 7.1	52.5 ± 4.0	52.4 ± 4.5	**90.8 ± 7.6**
20	36.9 ± 2.8	80.7 ± 6.5	83.1 ± 6.6	40.7 ± 3.6	45.3 ± 3.6	**85.0 ± 4.5**
30	36.4 ± 2.6	77.2 ± 5.0	80.3 ± 3.6	34.9 ± 3.1	40.5 ± 3.8	**81.3 ± 3.6**
40	35.0 ± 1.5	75.1 ± 4.3	76.9 ± 3.0	30.5 ± 1.5	36.5 ± 2.0	**78.4 ± 2.5**
50	34.9 ± 1.7	76.3 ± 3.8	77.0 ± 4.1	27.7 ± 1.8	35.3 ± 2.0	**77.5 ± 3.7**
60	33.5 ± 1.5	75.4 ± 3.4	77.6 ± 3.4	25.4 ± 1.1	33.4 ± 1.5	**77.7 ± 2.5**
68	34.9	70.0	75.3	23.7	30.6	**77.0**

Table 8. Clustering performance on PIE (NMI)

K	Normalized Mutual Information (%)					
	K-Means	NMF	GNMF	CF	LCCF	GLNMF
10	52.4 ± 5.2	84.6 ± 3.3	91.2 ± 4.3	59.9 ± 4.2	64.7 ± 3.0	**94.5 ± 4.5**
20	58.0 ± 2.2	89.8 ± 3.9	92.3 ± 3.5	56.8 ± 3.6	67.7 ± 3.0	**93.7 ± 2.2**
30	61.5 ± 2.3	90.1 ± 2.4	92.2 ± 1.8	55.4 ± 3.3	66.2 ± 2.8	**92.7 ± 1.7**
40	63.4 ± 1.4	89.9 ± 2.1	91.0 ± 1.4	54.3 ± 1.5	65.1 ± 1.8	**91.9 ± 1.0**
50	64.4 ± 1.4	90.8 ± 1.6	91.5 ± 1.6	53.7 ± 1.8	66.0 ± 1.4	**91.7 ± 1.6**
60	65.3 ± 1.3	90.9 ± 1.2	91.8 ± 1.3	53.4 ± 1.4	66.1 ± 1.1	**92.0 ± 0.9**
68	67.2	89.0	91.0	53.5	63.5	91.2

5 Conclusions

By introducing the regularized term of self representation reconstruction error, we propose a new method of graph learning regularized non-negative matrix factorization. During our multiplicative update rules, the self representation coefficient is updated iteratively, and the weight matrix is calculated by the self representation coefficient. Clustering results on three face datasets indicate that GLNMF can obtain more higher performance than other clustering algorithms.

Acknowledgement. This work is supported in part by the National Natural Science Foundation of China Grant (No. 61906098, No. 61772284, No. 61701258), the National Key Research and Development Program of China (2018YFB1003702).

References

1. Lee, D.D., Seung, H.S.: Learning the parts of objects by non-negative matrix factorization. Nature **401**(6755), 788–791 (1999)
2. Cai, D., He, X., Han, J., Huang, T.S.: Graph regularized nonnegative matrix factorization for data representation. IEEE Trans. Pattern Anal. Mach. Intell. **33**(8), 1548–1560 (2011)
3. Peng, Y., Tang, R., Kong, W., Qin, F., Nie, F.: Parallel vector field regularized non-negative matrix factorization for image representation. In: IEEE International Conference on Acoustics, Speech and Signal Processing, pp. 2216–2220 (2018)
4. Long, X., Lu, H., Peng, Y., Li, W.: Graph regularized discriminative non-negative matrix factorization for face recognition. Multi. Tools Appl. **72**(3), 2679–2699 (2013). https://doi.org/10.1007/s11042-013-1572-z
5. Wang, Y.X., Zhang, Y.J.: Nonnegative matrix factorization: a comprehensive review. IEEE Trans. Knowl. Data Eng. **25**(6), 1336–1353 (2013)
6. Yi, Y., Wang, J., Zhou, W., Zheng, C., Qiao, S.: Non-negative matrix factorization with locality constrained adaptive graph. IEEE Trans. Circ. Syst. Video Technol. **30**(2), 427–441 (2020)
7. Peng, Y., Long, Y., Qin, F., Kong, W., Cichocki, A.: Flexible non-negative matrix factorization with adaptively learned graph regularization. In: IEEE International Conference on Acoustics, Speech and Signal Processing, pp. 3107–3111 (2019)

8. Coates, A., Andrew, Y.N.: Learning feature representations with k-means. Lect. Notes Comput. Sci. **7700**, 561–580 (2013)
9. Xu, W., Gong, Y.: Document clustering by concept factorization. In: International ACM SIGIR Conference on Research and Development in Information Retrieval, pp. 202–209 (2004)
10. Cai, D., He, X., Han, J.: Locally consistent concept factorization for document clustering. IEEE Trans. Knowl. Data Eng. **23**(6), 902–913 (2011)
11. You, C., Li, C. G., Robinson, D.P., Vidal, R.: Is an affine constraint needed for affine subspace clustering? In: IEEE International Conference on Computer Vision, pp. 9915–9924 (2019)

Identifying Task-Based Dynamic Functional Connectivity Using Tensor Decomposition

Wenya Liu[1,2], Xiulin Wang[1,2], Tapani Ristaniemi[2], and Fengyu Cong[1,2,3,4(✉)]

[1] School of Biomedical Engineering, Faculty of Electronic Information and Electrical Engineering, Dalian University of Technology, 116024 Dalian, China
wenyaliu0912@foxmail.com, xiulin.wang@foxmail.com, cong@dlut.edu.cn
[2] Faculty of Information Technology, University of Jyväskylä, Jyväskylä, Finland
tapani.e.ristaniemi@jyu.fi
[3] School of Artificial Intelligence, Faculty of Electronic Information and Electrical Engineering, Dalian University of Technology, 116024 Dalian, China
[4] Key Laboratory of Integrated Circuit and Biomedical Electronic System, Dalian University of Technology, 116024, Liaoning, Dalian, China

Abstract. Functional connectivity (FC) patterns in human brain are dynamic in a task-specific condition, and identifying the dynamic changes is important to reveal the information processing processes and network reconfiguration in cognitive tasks. In this study, we proposed a comprehensive framework based on high-order singular value decomposition (HOSVD) to detect the stable change points of FC using electroencephalogram (EEG). First, phase lag index (PLI) method was applied to calculate FC for each time point, constructing a 3-way tensor, i.e., connectivity × connectivity × time. Then a stepwise HOSVD (SHOSVD) algorithm was proposed to detect the change points of FC, and the stability of change points were analyzed considering the different dissimilarity between different FC patterns. The transmission of seven FC patterns were identified in a task condition. We applied our methods to EEG data, and the results verified by prior knowledge demonstrated that our proposed algorithm can reliably capture the dynamic changes of FC.

Keywords: Dynamic functional connectivity · HOSVD · EEG · Tensor decomposition

1 Introduction

Brain functional connectivity (FC) is essentially dynamic for different cognitive demands even in a task-specific condition, and identifying the changes of FC can help to understand the reconfiguration of brain network topology along cognitive tasks [3,6,11]. Electroencephalogram (EEG) can record the electrical brain activity in a millisecond timescale with low cost, and this temporal richness shines new light to the dynamic FC analysis in a specific cognitive task which presents short and repeated stimuli, like stimuli used in event-related potential (ERP) study. It is important to find the task-locked dynamic brain networks to

© Springer Nature Switzerland AG 2020
H. Yang et al. (Eds.): ICONIP 2020, CCIS 1333, pp. 361–369, 2020.
https://doi.org/10.1007/978-3-030-63823-8_42

explore the precise brain topology changes in information processing. For ERP study, traditional methods calculate static FC for the whole trial which can not accurately capture the real reconfiguration of brain networks regarding the stimuli. Based on the fact that moment-to-moment fluctuations in FC are more stable during task than rest [6], pinpointing the time intervals during which the FC is considered stationary is in line with reality under task-specific condition.

Existing methods for dynamic FC are mainly based on sliding window, which segment the whole time series into a number of overlapping time windows, then community detection, clustering and graph theory-based methods are applied to evaluate the FC evolutions across time windows [1,2,5,15]. But this kind of methods are sensitive to the choice of window length, overlapping and window shape [9]. Another category of commonly used methods are based on matrix factorization, like temporal principal component analysis (PCA) and temporal independent component analysis (ICA) [10,13], which decompose the data (time × connectivity) into connectivity components and the corresponding temporal profile. However, the uncorrelated or independent constraint imposed to connectivity components is not practical into use.

Recently, tensor decomposition methods are applied to dynamic FC analysis [11,12] for change point detection, which can take the multiway arrangement of connectivity along time, frequency and subject dimensions into consideration. Inspired by their works, which used high-order singular value decomposition (HOSVD) for the analysis of dynamic FC, in this study, we constructed a 3-way tensor formed by connectivity matrix along time (connectivity × connectivity × time), and proposed a comprehensive framework to detect the change points of brain networks in an ERP dataset. Our work is different from the previous studies in [11,12] with some new highlights. First, we proposed a stepwise HOSVD (SHOSVD) method to detect the dynamic changes sequentially and avoid spurious FC changes caused by outliers. Second, we combined the results from a range of parameters to obtain multiple sets of stable change points, allowing different dissimilarity between different pairs of FC patterns, so the results are not sensitive to the predefined threshold of FC dissimilarity measurement. Our proposed algorithm can efficiently track the dynamic changes of brain networks during task condition, and its feasibility is demonstrated by an ERP study.

2   Materials and Methods

2.1   Data Description

Our proposed framework was applied to EEG data which have been published in [7,16]. In this experiment, nineteen participants were informed to play a three-agent ("Self", another participant called "Other", and a computer called "Computer") gambling game, and two golden eggs were presented to choose by each agent. After the choice of a golden egg, a cue stimuli was presented which indicated whether the participants will be informed about the outcomes such that curiosity will be satisfied (CWS) or curiosity will not be satisfied (CWN), then the feedback of monetary gain or loss was given.

The data were collected at 64 scalp sites using the electrodes mounted in an elastic cap (Brain Product, Munich, Germany), and preprocessed using EEGLAB [4]. One participant was removed due to bad data quality, and data were down-sampled to 500 Hz and band-pass filtered to 1–40 Hz. Eye movements were rejected by ICA, and the cue-locked data were extracted from −200 ms to 1000 ms. Then any segment whose max amplitude exceeds 100 μV was removed.

According to the results of previous paper [16], we only analyzed the data of cue onset in Self and CWS condition, and 58 scalp channels were used in this study.

2.2 Phase Synchronization

The communication of brain regions or neural populations depends on phase interactions for electrophysiological neuroimaging techniques, like EEG [17]. Considering the volume conduction effect to sensor space connectivity, we calculated the pairwise synchronization using PLI which can avoid volume conduction effect by discarding zero-lag interactions [14].

For signal $x(t)$, $t = 1, 2, \cdots, T$, its analytical signal $z(t)$ can be constructed by Hilbert transform,

$$z(t) = x(t) + i\tilde{x}(t) = \frac{1}{\pi} PV \int_{-x}^{\infty} \frac{x(\tau)}{t - \tau} d\tau, \tag{1}$$

where $\tilde{x}(t)$ is the imaginary part and PV refers to the Cauchy principal value. Then the instantaneous phase $\varphi(t)$ can be computed as follows:

$$\varphi(t) = arctan\frac{\tilde{x}(t)}{x(t)}. \tag{2}$$

For an ERP dataset containing C channels, S subjects and N trials, the phase synchronization between channel i and channel j at time t for subject s can be computed by PLI:

$$PLI^s_{(i,j)}(t) = \frac{1}{N} \left| \sum_{n=1}^{N} sign(\Delta\varphi^s_{(i,j,n)}) \right|, \tag{3}$$

where $\Delta\varphi^s_{(i,j,n)} = \varphi^s_{(i,n)} - \varphi^s_{(j,n)}$ is the phase difference between channel i and channel j at time t for subject s. It should be noted that any 0 or $\pm\pi$ value of $\Delta\varphi^s_{(i,j,n)}$ is discarded here which is considered to be caused by volume conduction.

In our study, the PLI value is calculated by averaging across trials and subjects, because that phase synchrony can only be detected in a statistical sense. We also assume that the phases at time t are the same for all subjects due to the stimulus-locked EEG. Then we can get the time-varying adjacency matrix at time point t:

$$A_{(i,j)}(t) = \frac{1}{S} \sum_{s=1}^{S} PLI^s_{(i,j)}(t), \tag{4}$$

where $A(t) \in \mathbb{R}^{C \times C}$, and a nonnegative FC tensor of connectivity $\times$ connectivity $\times$ time can be constructed as $\mathcal{A} \in \mathbb{R}^{C \times C \times T}$.

2.3   Stepwise High-Order Singular Value Decomposition

HOSVD is a tensor generalization of singular value decomposition (SVD) with orthogonal factors in each mode. Each factor matrix is computed by the left singular vectors of SVD performed on the unfolded tensor along the corresponding mode, such as the factor in mode 3:

$$A_3 = U_{time} D V^T, \tag{5}$$

where $A_3 \in \mathbb{R}^{T \times CC}$ is mode 3 matricization of tensor $\mathcal{A}$, $D \in \mathbb{R}^{T \times CC}$ is the diagonal matrix, and $V \in \mathbb{R}^{CC \times CC}$ is the right singular vectors. The FC tensor $\mathcal{A} \in \mathbb{R}^{C \times C \times T}$ is fully decomposed using HOSVD:

$$\mathcal{A} = \mathcal{G} \times_1 U_{conn} \times_2 U_{conn} \times_3 U_{time}, \tag{6}$$

where $\mathcal{G} \in \mathbb{R}^{C \times C \times T}$ is the core tensor, $U_{conn} \in \mathbb{R}^{C \times C}$ and $U_{time} \in \mathbb{R}^{T \times T}$ are the factor matrices in connectivity space and time space, respectively. Note that the factor matrices in mode 1 and mode 2 are the same because of the symmetry of connectivity matrix $A(t)$, and the core tensor $\mathcal{G}$ represents the interactions between 3 modes.

Let $\mathcal{A}^{time}$ denote the multiplication of tensor $\mathcal{A} \in \mathbb{R}^{C \times C \times T}$ with the factor matrix $U_{time} \in \mathbb{R}^{T \times T}$ in mode 3, so we can get:

$$\mathcal{A}^{time} = \mathcal{A} \times_3 U_{time}^T, \tag{7}$$

Then we can get the first frontal slice:

$$A_{:,:,1}^{time} = \sum_{t=1}^{T} u_{t,1}^{time} A_{:,:,t}, \tag{8}$$

where $u_{t,1}^{time}$ denotes the tth element in the first column of factor matrix U_{time}, and $A_{:,:,t}$ means the tth frontal slice of the original tensor $\mathcal{A}$. Because factor matrix U_{time} is the left singular vectors of SVD performed on nonnegative matrix $A_{(3)}$, so elements of the first column $u_{:,1}^{time}$ are all positive or all negative, i.e., they have the same sign. So we can regard the first frontal slice $A_{:,:,1}^{time}$ as the weighted sum of connectivity across time, and this is also called the summarization of the stationary connectivity in a time interval [12]. On the other hand, $A_{:,:,1}^{time}$ captures most of the energy of time-varying connectivity patterns across the stationary time interval, due to that the corresponding singular value of $u_{:,1}^{time}$ is the largest one. Considering the superiority described above, we proposed a SHOSVD algorithm for dynamic FC change points detection, as illustrated below.

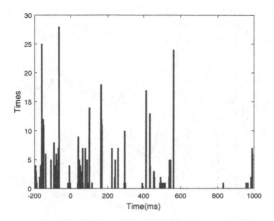

Fig. 1. The times of each time point detected as change point. 82 time points are detected as change points in 51 runs of SHOSVD.

Summary of the proposed SHOSVD algorithm:

Step 1: Set $t = 3$, and perform full HOSVD on the tensor $\tilde{\mathcal{A}} \in \mathbb{R}^{C \times C \times t}$ constructed by the first t frontal slices of original FC tensor $\mathcal{A}$.

Step 2: Compute the absolute value of the first frontal slice $\tilde{A}^{time}_{:,:,1}(t)$, and normalize it to $[0\ 1]$.

Step 3: Normalize the consequent three original FC matrices $\mathcal{A}_{:,:,t+1}$, $\mathcal{A}_{:,:,t+2}$ and $\mathcal{A}_{:,:,t+3}$ to $[0\ 1]$, respectively.

Step 4: Compute Euclidean distance ρ_1, ρ_2 and ρ_3 between $\tilde{A}^{time}_{:,:,1}(t)$ and $\mathcal{A}_{:,:,t+1}$, $\mathcal{A}_{:,:,t+2}$ and $\mathcal{A}_{:,:,t+3}$, respectively.

Step 5: Compare ρ_1, ρ_2 and ρ_3 with the predefined threshold λ.

Step 6: If $\rho_1 > \lambda$ & $\rho_2 > \lambda$ & $\rho_3 > \lambda$, save t as the change point for the sub-segment, remove $\tilde{\mathcal{A}} \in \mathbb{R}^{C \times C \times t}$ from original FC tensor $\mathcal{A}$, and go back to step 1. Else, set $t = t + 1$, and go back to step 1.

The detection will be terminated until all the time points are included to a stationary interval. Here we give some statements about the proposed SHOSVD algorithm. In step 1, we start the algorithm with $t = 3$ for the conduction of HOSVD, because we assume that the first three time points are in the same stationary segment. In step 2, the first frontal slice $\tilde{A}^{time}_{:,:,1}(t)$ should be all negative or all positive due to the uncertain sign of $u^{time}_{:,1}$, so here we take its absolute value for the following analysis. In step 2 and step 3, the normalization is necessary to constraint the matrices to the same scale, because we focus on the similarity between connectivity patterns which should not be affected by their amplitude scales. For a matrix X, the normalization is realized by $\tilde{x}_{ij} = \frac{x_{ij} - min(X)}{max - min(X))}$, so all the elements are constrained to $[0\ 1]$, which is the classical range of a FC matrix. In step 4, the Euclidean distance is computed by the L_2 norm of the difference between two matrices. In step 6, we test the distances for the consequent three time points to avoid spurious changes by outliers. In step 5, the predefined threshold λ is the only parameter to be determined in SHOSVD method, and its selection will be discussed in the next section.

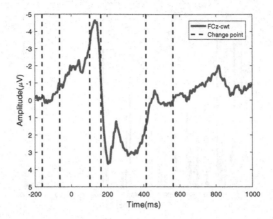

Fig. 2. The stable change points of dynamic functional connectivity. The red line represents the grand averaged data across trials and subjects of FCz channel. The blue dotted lines mean the change points located at -160 ms, -64 ms, 102 ms, 164 ms, 414 ms, and 562 ms. (Color figure online)

2.4 The Stability of Change Points

Considering the fact that the dissimilarity of various pairs of FC patterns may be different. For example, the distance ρ_{12} between connectivity patterns 1 and 2 is undoubtedly different from the distance ρ_{23} between connectivity patterns 2 and 3, because different connectivity patterns may share the same connections, like visual network and frontal-visual network, or share none connections, like visual network and frontal network. So we can not set a common threshold for the change point evaluation. Here we set a range of threshold $[\lambda_1 \ \lambda_2]$ which would be determined with experience by testing the performance of SHOSVD on the data, and perform SHOSVD for each threshold λ in the predefined range. After obtaining the multiple sets of change points, we take the most frequently appeared points as the final stable change points, which are considered to characterize the time-varying FC changes. Therefore, the results are not sensitive to the choice of threshold.

3 Results

3.1 Change Points Detection

First, PLI method was performed on the preprocessed data at each time point, constructing a 3-way FC tensor with dimensions of $58 \times 58 \times 600$. Then SHOSVD was applied for change points detection. Dissimilarity thresholds were selected between the range with a step of 0.1, so 51 sets of change points were obtained in this study. All the change points detected for the 51 runs of SHOSVD were shown in Fig. 1. Finally, we kept 10% of the most frequently appeared time points as the final stable change points which can characterize the dynamic FC

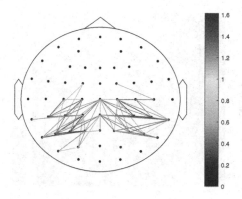

Fig. 3. The brain network summarization of stationary time interval (164–414) ms.

variety, as shown in Fig. 2. From the red line of Fig. 2, we can see that the cue stimuli induced a feedback-related negativity (FRN)-like component followed by a P300 component. Refer to [16] for a detailed explanation. According to Eqs. (6–8), we summarize the FC in time interval (164–414) ms. Figure 3 and Fig. 4 depicted the brain network and connectivity matrix of stationary time interval (164–414) ms which contained both FRN-like component and P300 component, respectively. We obtained a central-posterior network which was consistent with the previous findings [16].

3.2   Discussion

Previous studies have reported that curiosity is a type of reward anticipation which can induce a FRN-like component, and a following P300 component which is associated with context updating and behavioral adjustments [8,16,18]. In our results, we incorporated both FRN-like and P300 components into the same stable time interval (164–414) ms, and summarized a central-posterior functional connectivity. In the previous results, a central-posterior delta power was elicited by the cue stimuli within 200–350 ms, and the brain activation results were consistent with our findings [16]. From our results, we conclude that the curiosity satisfaction and behavioral adjustment may share the same brain topology configuration. However, this interpretation needs further verification which should take the FC variety across frequency domain into consideration. What's more, other stable time intervals also need to be deeply analyzed, which is our future extended work based on this study. The number of change points should be verified by prior knowledge which is important to the explanation of the results.

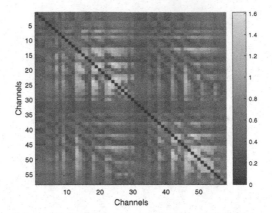

Fig. 4. The connectivity matrix summarization of stationary time interval (164–414) ms.

4   Conclusion

In this study, we proposed a comprehensive framework for the analysis of task-based dynamic FC. Tensor decomposition technique is applied considering the multiway arrangement of connectivity matrices across time, so both structure properties of FC and its variety information along time are considered for the change points detection. As we all know, it is hard and important to exactly lock the brain response to external stimuli and characterize the changes of brain states in a specific cognitive task. Our change points detection framework can efficiently separate different brain topology configurations in a task condition.

Acknowledgments. This work was supported by National Natural Science Foundation of China (Grant No. 91748105), National Foundation in China (No. JCKY2019110B009), the Fundamental Research Funds for the Central Universities [DUT2019] in Dalian University of Technology in China, and the scholarships from China scholarship Council (No. 201706060263 & No. 201706060262). The authors would like to thank Dr. Peng Li for the provide of EEG data and Guanghui Zhang for the preprocessing work.

References

1. Allen, E.A., Damaraju, E., Plis, S.M., Erhardt, E.B., Eichele, T., Calhoun, V.D.: Tracking whole-brain connectivity dynamics in the resting state. Cereb. Cortex **24**(3), 663–676 (2014)
2. Bassett, D.S., Wymbs, N.F., Porter, M.A., Mucha, P.J., Carlson, J.M., Grafton, S.T.: Dynamic reconfiguration of human brain networks during learning. Proc. Nat. Acad. Sci. **108**(18), 7641–7646 (2011)
3. Cohen, J.R.: The behavioral and cognitive relevance of time-varying, dynamic changes in functional connectivity. NeuroImage **180**, 515–525 (2018)

4. Delorme, A., Makeig, S.: Eeglab: an open source toolbox for analysis of single-trial eeg dynamics including independent component analysis. J. Neurosci. Methods **134**(1), 9–21 (2004)
5. Dimitriadis, S.I., Laskaris, N.A., Tsirka, V., Vourkas, M., Micheloyannis, S., Fotopoulos, S.: Tracking brain dynamics via time-dependent network analysis. J. Neurosci. Methods **193**(1), 145–155 (2010)
6. Gonzalez-Castillo, J., Bandettini, P.A.: Task-based dynamic functional connectivity: recent findings and open questions. Neuroimage **180**, 526–533 (2018)
7. Han, C., Li, P., Warren, C., Feng, T., Litman, J., Li, H.: Electrophysiological evidence for the importance of interpersonalcuriosity. Brain Res. **1500**, 45–54 (2013)
8. Kang, M.J., et al.: The wick in the candle of learning: epistemic curiosity activates reward circuitry and enhances memory. Psychol. Sci. **20**(8), 963–973 (2009)
9. Khambhati, A.N., Sizemore, A.E., Betzel, R.F., Bassett, D.S.: Modeling and interpreting mesoscale network dynamics. NeuroImage **180**, 337–349 (2018)
10. Leonardi, N., et al.: Principal components of functional connectivity: a new approach to study dynamic brain connectivity during rest. NeuroImage **83**, 937–950 (2013)
11. Leonardi, N., Van De Ville, D.: Identifying network correlates of brain states using tensor decompositions of whole-brain dynamic functional connectivity. In: 2013 International Workshop on Pattern Recognition in Neuroimaging, pp. 74–77. IEEE (2013)
12. Mahyari, A.G., Zoltowski, D.M., Bernat, E.M., Aviyente, S.: A tensor decomposition-based approach for detecting dynamic network states from EEG. IEEE Trans. Biomed. Eng. **64**(1), 225–237 (2016)
13. O'Neill, G.C., et al.: Measurement of dynamic task related functional networks using MEG. NeuroImage **146**, 667–678 (2017)
14. Stam, C.J., Nolte, G., Daffertshofer, A.: Phase lag index: assessment of functional connectivity from multi channel eeg and meg with diminished bias from common sources. Hum. Brain Mapp. **28**(11), 1178–1193 (2007)
15. Valencia, M., Martinerie, J., Dupont, S., Chavez, M.: Dynamic small-world behavior in functional brain networks unveiled by an event-related networks approach. Phys. Rev. E **77**(5), 050905 (2008)
16. Wang, J., et al.: To know or not to know? theta and delta reflect complementary information about an advanced cue before feedback in decision-making. Front. Psychol. **7**, 1556 (2016)
17. Womelsdorf, T., et al.: Modulation of neuronal interactions through neuronal synchronization. Science **316**(5831), 1609–1612 (2007)
18. Wu, Y., Zhou, X.: The p300 and reward valence, magnitude, and expectancy in outcome evaluation. Brain Res. **1286**, 114–122 (2009)

Improving Adaptive Bayesian Optimization with Spectral Mixture Kernel

Harsh Raj, Suvodip Dey$^{(\boxtimes)}$, Hiransh Gupta, and P. K. Srijith

Indian Institute of Technology Hyderabad, Hyderabad, India
{ma17btech11003,cs19resch01003,ma18btech11003,srijith}@iith.ac.in

Abstract. Bayesian Optimization has been successfully applied to find global optima of functions which are expensive to evaluate and without access to gradient information. Adaptive Bayesian Optimization extends it to dynamic problems where the functions over some space are assumed to evolve in a temporal dimension with temporally evolving optima. This requires the surrogate model used in Adaptive Bayesian Optimization to extrapolate correctly and accurately track optima with a minimum number of function evaluations. We propose to use Gaussian processes with a spectral mixture kernel to model the temporal dimension to accurately extrapolate and predict the optima. Spectral mixture kernel considers a mixture of Gaussian spectral density function which helps in quality extrapolation. We show the effectiveness of the proposed approach not only to various synthetic problems but also on a real-world problem of click-through rate prediction in an online learning setting. The experimental results demonstrate the superior performance of the proposed approach for Adaptive Bayesian Optimization.

Keywords: Bayesian Optimization · Adaptive Bayesian Optimization · Spectral mixture kernel

1 Introduction

Bayesian Optimization [3,8] is a powerful tool for black-box optimization problems when one does not have an analytical expression for the objective function or is expensive to evaluate or its derivatives are not available. It provides a gradient-free global optimization approach to find the optima with a minimum number of objective function evaluations. This is achieved in a sequential manner using a surrogate model (often Gaussian processes [7]) to represent the latent objective function and an acquisition function to suggest the parameter values to evaluate the objective function. A surrogate model incorporates prior belief about the objective function and updates it when samples are drawn from it to improve its posterior belief. The acquisition function uses the surrogate model to suggest the parameter values either to the areas where it believes the optima is located or to areas where exploration is required to improve the posterior.

The approaches to Bayesian Optimization assume the objective to be a function over some parameter space and does not consider a dynamic setting where

© Springer Nature Switzerland AG 2020
H. Yang et al. (Eds.): ICONIP 2020, CCIS 1333, pp. 370–377, 2020.
https://doi.org/10.1007/978-3-030-63823-8_43

the objective function and consequently the optima can vary over time. Consider the problem of tracking the location of minimum temperature in a building [1,2]. Since the temperature at a particular location can vary over time, the objective function should be time-dependent. Another example of such dynamism is hyper-parameter optimization in a streaming setting where the data can evolve over time. To model and address such temporal evolution of minima in dynamic environments, adaptive Bayesian optimization (ABO) was proposed by Nyikosa et al. [1,2]. They used a spatio-temporal Gaussian process (GP) as a surrogate model which considered a kernel over both the parameter space and time, and assumed it to be a product kernel over each of these dimensions. Both the kernels were modeled using a commonly used radial basis function (RBF) kernel. Though this kind of modeling helped to overcome the Markov assumption limitation of earlier work on sequential Bayesian Optimization [6] for dynamic optimization problems, the RBF kernel performs poorly in an extrapolation setting and fails to accurately track the optima.

In this work, we propose a more effective adaptive Bayesian optimization approach using a Gaussian process with spectral mixture kernel to model the temporal dimension. We show the effectiveness of this approach for adaptive Bayesian optimization on various synthetic and real-world experiments. The proposed approach is also found to be effective in hyper-parameter optimization of machine learning algorithms in an online learning setting.

2   Background of Adaptive Bayesian Optimization

Adaptive Bayesian Optimization (ABO) extends the framework of Bayesian Optimization to dynamic problems where the objective function value changes with time. Let $f(\mathbf{x})$ be an objective function where $\mathbf{x} \in \mathcal{S} \subset \mathcal{R}^D$ are the decision variables (or parameters to optimize). In ABO, the latent function f is assumed to vary over a time dimension t as well. So, the dynamic optimization problem is defined as follows

$$\underset{\mathbf{x}}{\mathrm{argmin}} f(\mathbf{x}, t) \quad s.t. \{\mathbf{x}, t\} \in \mathcal{F}(t) \subset \mathcal{S} \tag{1}$$

where, $\mathcal{S} \in \mathcal{R}^D$, $t \in \mathcal{T}$, and $f : \mathcal{S} \times \mathcal{T} \longrightarrow \mathcal{R}$. The objective is to discover and track the time-varying optima with minimum number of function evaluations.

Nyikosa et al. [1] proposed a spatio-temporal GP prior defined jointly over the parameter space and time i.e., $f(\mathbf{x}, t) \sim GP(\mu(\mathbf{x}, t), k_{ST}((\mathbf{x}, t), (\mathbf{x}', t')))$. The kernel defined jointly over parameter space and time is assumed to be product of kernels over parameter space and time, i.e., $k_{ST}((\mathbf{x}, t), (\mathbf{x}', t')) = k_{SE}(\mathbf{x}, \mathbf{x}') k_{SE}(t, t')$. They considered a squared exponential (SE) kernel, $k_{SE}(\mathbf{z}, \mathbf{z}') = \exp(-\frac{1}{2l^2}||\mathbf{z} - \mathbf{z}'||^2)$ (l being lengthscale), over both the parameter space and temporal space, with lengthscales l_s and l_t respectively. The function values exhibit high covariance not only if $\mathbf{x}$ values are closer in parameter space but also when they are closer in temporal dimension. The predictive mean $\mu(\mathbf{x}_*, t_*)$ and variance $\sigma^2(\mathbf{x}_*, t_*)$ are obtained following the standard GP prediction [7] with an additional time dimension. The next point to be evaluated is

---

Algorithm 1: Adaptive Bayesian Optimization Pseudocode

Place Gaussian Prior on objective function f.
Set N = Budget of Evaluations.
Observe f at n_0 points.
Set $n = n_0$, lower bound time as δ_t, and upper bound threshold ρ, $\rho \in (0, 1)$
while $n \leq N$ **do**
> Update Posterior using all available data
> Set current time t_c
> Set temporal lengthscale l_t from optimized hyper-parameters.
> Set Feasible Set for prediction $F(t_n) = \{S : t_c + \delta_t \leq t \leq t_c + \delta_t + \rho l_t\}$
> Find next evaluation point $(\mathbf{x}_n, t_n) = \underset{(\mathbf{X},t) \in F(t_n)}{\text{argmin}} \; a(\mathbf{x}, t)$
> Observe $y_n = f(\mathbf{x}_n, t_n)$
> Set n = n+1
end

---

decided by using the GP-LCB bound as the acquisition function. Thus, acquisition function is defined as $a(\mathbf{x}_*, t_*) = \mu(\mathbf{x}_*, t_*) - \beta \cdot \sigma(\mathbf{x}_*, t_*)$ which trades-off exploitation and exploration through the trade-off parameter $\beta > 0$ [5].

In ABO, one is always interested in finding minima in a temporally evolving space and consequently extrapolating over the temporal domain. The predictions become uncertain as we look too far into the future. So, we restrict the domain of the acquisition function a lengthscale (l_t) distance away from the last sample in the temporal dimension [1,7]. The pseudocode for the ABO is provided in Algorithm 1.

3   Proposed Approach

Adaptive Bayesian Optimization relies on extrapolating along the temporal dimension. However, standard kernels such as squared exponential (SE) fail poorly in extrapolation. The temporal SE kernel $k_{SE}(t, t') = \exp(-\frac{1}{2l_t^2}(t - t')^2)$, can be seen as a Gaussian centred at the last time of evaluation t and the value decreases exponentially to zero with lengthscale l_t. As we extrapolate beyond an interval, this becomes zero and the predictive mean falls back to the mean of the GP prior, affecting the predictive capability of the model. This can be fixed to some extent by setting the lengthscale to a large value. But increasing lengthscale smoothens the function making it incapable of capturing frequent fluctuations in the objective function. We propose to overcome this limitation by using a much more rich and flexible kernel for the temporal dimension, spectral mixture (SM) kernel, which can achieve quality extrapolation.

3.1   Spectral Mixture Kernel

Spectral mixture (SM) kernels are stationary kernels that perform exceptionally well for extrapolation tasks [4]. This is attributed to the fact that their spectral densities are modeled with a Gaussian mixture instead of coming from a single Gaussian distribution, unlike a squared exponential kernel. The spectral density completely determines the properties of a stationary and vanishing kernel. As spectral density and the kernel are Fourier duals of each other, we can get the spectral density as $S(s) = \int k(\tau)e^{-2\pi i s \tau} d\tau$ where, $\tau = t - t'$. For the SE kernel over the one dimensional temporal domain, $S_{SE}(s) = (2\pi l_t^2)^{1/2} exp(-2\pi^2 l_t^2 s^2)$, which is a single Gaussian centered at origin.

For the spectral mixture kernel, the spectral density is modeled as a mixture of Q Gaussians on $\mathbb{R}$, with q^{th} component having mean m_q and variance v_q. The Fourier dual of this spectral density leads to a spectral mixture (SM) kernel for the temporal dimension as

$$k_{SM}(\tau) = \int S(s)e^{2\pi i s \tau} ds = \sum_{q=1}^{Q} w_q exp(-2\pi^2 \tau^2 v_q) cos(2\pi \tau m_q) \qquad (2)$$

Thus, the SM kernel represents a mixture of functions trying to model the covariance. Each component in the mixture is a product of a Gaussian and cosine function. The Gaussian can be seen to represent the amplitude of the cosine function which decreases exponentially over time with lengthscale $\frac{1}{\sqrt{v_q}}$. The component period is given by $\frac{1}{m_q}$. The contribution of each mixture component is determined by weights w_q. The SM kernel can be seen to represent rich and varied covariance functions with the ability to extrapolate well into the future due to periodic and mixture components. They have been shown to forecast well for CO_2 concentration data and airline passenger data [4].

3.2 Spatio-Temporal Kernel

We applied the SM kernel to the time dimension, and SE kernel to the spatial dimension to get our desired spatio-temporal kernel k_{ST}^* where

$$k_{ST}^*((\mathbf{x}, t), (\mathbf{x}', t')) = k_{SE}(\mathbf{x}, \mathbf{x}')k_{SM}(t, t') \qquad (3)$$

We found that the product composition of SE and SM kernels performs better than using an additive composition or using any of the simple kernels directly. The lengthscale (l_t) along the time dimension is taken to be the weighted arithmetic mean of component lengthscales of the SM kernel, given by $l_t = \frac{\sum_{q=1}^{Q} \frac{w_q}{\sqrt{v_q}}}{\sum_{q=1}^{Q} w_q}$. This will give an estimate of how far ahead into the future we are confident of predicting our results.

4   Experiments

The primary objective of our experiment is to show the effectiveness of our proposed composite kernel (ABO-SE-SM) against the squared exponential kernel (ABO-SE) [1] for ABO framework. We have performed our experiments on both synthetic and real-world data. In all the experiments, we used GP-LCB [5] as the acquisition function and minimized it to find the next point. As suggested in [2], the trade-off parameter in the acquisition function was set to $\beta = \frac{1}{5}\sqrt{2\log(\frac{\pi^2 n^{\frac{D}{2}+2}}{3\delta})}$, where $\delta = 0.5$, $n = $ #past evaluations, and $D = $ dimensionality of k_{SM}. Here $D = 1$ since we have a single temporal dimension.

4.1   Synthetic Data

Data and Set Up: We follow [1] for the experimentation with synthetic data. Apart from a diverse set of continuously evolving standard test functions used in [1], we have added the Rastrigin function to test the effect on functions with a periodic structure. Rastrigin function is a non-linear multi-modal function. Due to a large number of local minima, tracking minima in this function is a challenging task. Since we want to find minima at fixed time intervals for this periodic function, we have limited the time interval in the search space below the lengthscale value. We limited the time interval to a threshold T, by replacing ρl_t with $min\{\rho l_t, T\}$ when creating the feasible set $F(t_n)$.

We considered a zero-mean GP as our surrogate function. The number of mixtures (Q) in k_{SM} was fixed to 4. For evaluation, we used an offline performance metric (B) [1], defined as $B(T) = \frac{1}{T}\sum_{t=1}^{T} b_t$ where $b_t = $ min $\{b_i : i = t, t-1, t-2, \ldots, t-w\}$, with window length $w = 3$. The window length was reduced from 5 (as used in [1]) to 3, to adapt to the improvement in the reduction of the total number of evaluations in our proposed approach. For each function, we fixed time variable t as the last dimension and treated the other dimensions as the spatial dimensions.

Results: Experiment results with synthetic functions are shown in Table 1and Fig. 1. Reported results are the mean B scores from 10 independent runs of each synthetic function. ABO-SE-SM outperformed both BO and ABO-SE in all of the 6 experiments in mean offline performance. In Table 1, the "%Change in Evaluations" column shows the average percentage change in the number of evaluations required by ABO-SE-SM over ABO-SE. We observe a superior performance of ABO-SE-SM with fewer evaluations in most cases. In cases where ABO-SE-SM used more evaluations than ABO-SE, we notice that ABO-SE-SM achieved a significant gain in offline performance. In these cases, function exhibits more complex temporal changes and needs closer temporal evaluations to keep track of the optima. Therefore, ABO-SE-SM provides a better balance between finding optima and minimizing the number of evaluations. Although the proposed kernel takes more time to train a single evaluation, it leads to a significant decrease in number of evaluations, and hence better in overall time taken. This is empirically supported by the experiment. We also note that, wherever ABO-SE-SM required fewer evaluations than ABO-SE, the lengthscale values of ABO-SE-SM exceed those of ABO-SE, suggesting that this enables ABO-SE-SM to extrapolate farther in time.

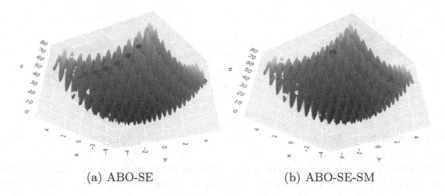

| (a) ABO-SE | (b) ABO-SE-SM |

Fig. 1. Illustration of training points (in yellow) and evaluation points (in red) of ABO applied on Rastrigin function using ABO-SE and ABO-SE-SM approaches. (Color figure online)

Table 1. ABO results for synthetic data

Function	Domain	Offline performance (B)			%Change in evaluations
		BO	ABO-SE	ABO-SE-SM	
6-hump Camelback	$[-3, 3] \times [-2, 2]$	13.73	10.57	**5.80**	+50%
Scaled Branin	$[0, 1]^2$	−0.45	−0.92	**−1.00**	−80%
Griewank	$[-5, 5]^2$	0.66	0.37	**0.32**	−56%
Rastrigin	$[-5.12, 5.12]^2$	36.99	37.09	**17.62**	−22%
Styblinski-Tang	$[-5, 5]^2$	−25.86	−24.19	**−38.25**	−72%
Hartmann	$[0, 1]^3$	−0.45	−0.97	**−1.16**	+75%

4.2   Real Data

Optimizing click-through rate (CTR) is a well-studied problem that is used extensively in industry to enhance sponsored search, advertising, recommendation systems, and so on. In Internet advertising, ads are required to change dynamically to adapt various temporal aspects like recency, seasonality, and so on. Apart from efficient modeling to capture the data dynamics, it is essential to update the hyper-parameters timely to get the best result. In this kind of scenario, hyper-parameters can evolve through time which is an ideal scenario for applying ABO. This motivated us to experiment on the Avazu Mobile Ads CTR data[1] and show the effectiveness of using ABO-SE-SM against ABO-SE to adjust the hyper-parameters of CTR models automatically.

Data and Set Up: We split the 10 days of Avazu CTR data into 240 hourly datasets, ordered chronologically in time as $D_1, D_2, \ldots D_t$. The task objective is to predict whether a given ad will be clicked, given its attributes, using model

---

[1] https://www.kaggle.com/c/avazu-ctr-prediction/data.

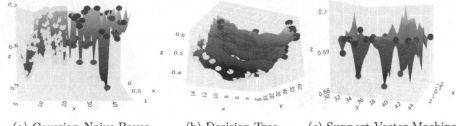

(a) Gaussian Naive Bayes	(b) Decision Tree	(c) Support Vector Machine

Fig. 2. Hyper-parameter optimization with ABO for different binary classification models on Avazu CTR data. Plot shows $z = -log(AUC)$ on test data, with model hyper-parameter θ on X axis, and time t on Y axis. Training points are shown in yellow. Optimal model hyper-parameters suggested by ABO-SE and ABO-SE-SM are shown in blue and red respectively. Note that the predictions for SVM have been compared after the first 8 unseen hours, as both kernels performed equally well for the first 8 h. (Color figure online)

$M(\theta_t)$, characterized by its hyper-parameters θ_t belonging to the parameter space Θ. At the time t, we use our ABO framework to predict the hyper-parameters θ_t of the model $M(\theta_t)$ that best fits the unseen data D_t, where "best fit" is determined by the model which gives highest ROC-AUC on test data. Let the test AUC Score of Model $M(\theta)$ on dataset D_t be $A(t, \theta)$. Then we train the GP surrogate model on the time indexed dataset of the model's performances, i.e., $\{(t, \theta_j, A(t, \theta_j)) : t \in \{1, 2, ...t_0\}, j \in \{1, 2, .., n_0\}, \theta_j \in \Theta\}$. For $t > t_0$, the goal is to predict $\hat{\theta}_t$ such that model $M(\hat{\theta}_t)$ has highest AUC on the unseen dataset D_t, i.e., $\hat{\theta}_t = \underset{\theta \in \Theta}{\operatorname{argmax}} A(t, \theta)$.

In this work, we have experimented with three different binary classification algorithms to model CTR data - (a) Gaussian Naive Bayes (GNB) with class priors $(\theta, 1 - \theta)$ as hyper-parameter where $\theta \in \Theta, \Theta = (0, 1)$, (b) Decision Tree (DT) with max depth (θ) as hyper-parameter where $\theta \in \Theta, \Theta = \{2,3,...,15\}$, and (c) SVM Classifier with L2 regularization parameter 10^θ as hyper-parameter where $\theta \in \Theta, \Theta = (-2,2)$.

Results: The results for the experiment on the real dataset is shown in Fig. 2 using a surface graph. We additionally examine the offline performance score (B) for the first ten evaluations in Table 2. We observe that ABO-SE-SM is able to model and predict the temporal change in class priors of the Gaussian Naive Bayes model (shown in Fig. 2a) to best fit the unseen future data, whereas ABO-SE could not. We observe a similar trend in Decision Tree where the depth hyper-parameter predicted by the ABO-SE-SM stays close to the best value (highest AUC being minima as shown in Fig. 2b) for all of the unseen datasets. For Decision Tree, we also notice that ABO-SE predicts only corner points for the unseen data as it chooses exploration over exploitation. This happens because the lengthscale of ABO-SE is too small to extrapolate effectively for unseen data. Similarly, ABO-SE-SM continues to perform better than ABO-SE while predicting the regularization hyper-parameter for the SVM classifier.

Table 2. Real data: Value of b_t on first 10 evaluations

Model	Approach	Value of b_t for first 10 Evaluations (t = 1,2, ..., 10)									Score(B)
GNB	ABO-SE	**0.59**	**0.59**	0.59	0.59	0.60	0.60	0.65	0.65	0.65	0.64	0.61
	ABO-SE-SM	0.60	0.60	**0.58**	**0.58**	**0.58**	**0.53**	**0.53**	**0.53**	**0.53**	**0.58**	**0.57**
DT	ABO-SE	**0.51**	**0.45**	**0.45**	0.45	0.45	0.46	0.49	0.51	0.55	0.56	0.49
	ABO-SE-SM	0.55	0.47	0.46	**0.42**	**0.42**	**0.42**	**0.42**	**0.46**	**0.45**	**0.44**	**0.45**
SVM	ABO-SE	0.69	0.69	0.69	0.69	0.69	0.69	0.69	0.69	0.69	0.69	0.69
	ABO-SE-SM	0.69	**0.68**	**0.68**	**0.68**	**0.68**	0.69	**0.67**	**0.67**	**0.67**	**0.67**	**0.68**

5   Conclusions

The spectral mixture (SM) kernel, when used along with adaptive Bayesian optimization (ABO), allows us the flexibility to predict minima that lie farther in the future. It extrapolates much better than the squared exponential (SE) kernel and can also exploit temporal patterns in the function. Higher lengthscales allow us to reach minima in a lesser number of evaluations, which is extremely useful when the objective function is expensive to evaluate. We suggest further experimenting with various machine learning models and temporally evolving datasets in order to exploit the usefulness of the spectral mixture kernel.

References

1. Nyikosa, F.M., Osborne, M.A., Roberts, S.J.: Bayesian optimization for dynamic problems. arXiv preprint arXiv:1803.03432 (2018)
2. Nyikosa, F.M.: Adaptive Bayesian optimization for dynamic problems. Ph.D. thesis, University of Oxford (2018)
3. Shahriari, B., Swersky, K., Wang, Z., Adams, R.P., De Freitas, N.: Taking the human out of the loop: a review of bayesian optimization. Proc. IEEE **104**(1), 148–175 (2015)
4. Wilson, A., Adams, R.: Gaussian process kernels for pattern discovery and extrapolation. In: International Conference on Machine Learning, pp. 1067–1075 (2013)
5. Srinivas, N., Krause, A., Kakade, S.M., Seeger, M.W.: Information-theoretic regret bounds for gaussian process optimization in the bandit setting. IEEE Trans. Inf. Theory **58**(5), 3250–3265 (2012)
6. Bogunovic, I., Scarlett, J., Cevher, V.: Time-varying gaussian process bandit optimization. In: Artificial Intelligence and Statistics, pp. 314–323 (2016)
7. Rasmussen, C.E., Williams, C.K.I.: Gaussian Processes for Machine Learning. The MIT Press, Cambridge (2006)
8. Mockus, J., Mockus, L.: Bayesian approach to global optimization and application to multiobjective and constrained problems. J. Optim. Theory Appl. **70**(1), 157–172 (1991)

Interpretability of Black Box Models Through Data-View Extraction and Shadow Model Creation

Rupam Patir$^{(\boxtimes)}$, Shubham Singhal, C. Anantaram, and Vikram Goyal

Indraprastha Institute of Information Technology, Delhi, India
{rupam13081,shubham18016,c.anantaram,vikram}@iiitd.ac.in

Abstract. Deep learning models trained using massive amounts of data, tend to capture one view of the data and its associated mapping. Different deep learning models built on the same training data may capture different views of the data based on the underlying techniques used. For explaining the decisions arrived by Black box deep learning models, we argue that it is essential to reproduce that model's view of the training data faithfully. This faithful reproduction can then be used for explanation generation. We investigate two methods for data-view extraction: Hill Climbing approach and a GAN-driven approach. We then use this synthesized data for explanation generation by using methods such as Decision-Trees and Permutation Importance. We evaluate these approaches on a Black box model trained on public datasets and show its usefulness in explanation generation.

Keywords: Interpretability · Data-view extraction · Data synthesis

1 Introduction

Machine Learning models, especially Deep Neural Networks (DNN), are being developed for various domains and are proving very effective. However, when such models are released as Black box models, where neither the training data nor the model details are published, the interpretability of these models becomes important to understand how the model arrives at its decisions. In this work, we focus on Black box ML models wherein the model's details such as its parameters, its mapping and representation details are not available. In such a scenario, we propose that it is important to faithfully extract the data-view captured in the model $\mathbf{M}$, in order to be able to build interpretable models for that Black box ML model $\mathbf{M}$. We define a notion of *data-view* of the target Black box model, using the set of data objects correctly classified by the model. Our method extracts the data-view via data synthesis to create a close approximation of the Target model's *data-view*. We propose two different techniques for this step. The first technique, inspired by Hill Climbing, is a query synthesis technique that generates a dataset such that the output probability vector has the least entropy as per the Target model. The second technique, inspired by GAN, learns

H. Yang et al. (Eds.): ICONIP 2020, CCIS 1333, pp. 378–385, 2020.
https://doi.org/10.1007/978-3-030-63823-8_44

a model for the data generation such that the target labels classified using the Black box model will have high accuracy. This is especially useful for synthesizing data for high dimensional datasets where the query synthesis technique becomes computationally expensive. Once the data-view is extracted, our approach builds a Decision Tree model based on this data-view, which is an interpretable Shadow model, and provides the interpretation for that Black box model. We also use Permutation Importance to dive deeper into the interpretation of the Target model. The main contributions in this paper are as follows:

- We show that the data-view extracted from a Black box model is a better reflection of the model's behaviour, and can be synthesized from the model.
- We show two synthesis methods for data-view extraction: a Hill Climbing approach, and an approach based on Generative Adversarial Networks (GAN).
- Using this synthesized dataset, we then interpret the Target model by creating a Shadow model in the form a Decision Tree. We also use Permutation Importance to give us a better understanding of the Target model.

2   State-of-the-Art

Broadly, prior work on interpretability [1,3,6,15] can be classified into:

Model-inspection methods: Class Activation Maps (CAM) and Gradient-based Class Activation Maps (GradCAM) [13] inspect the deep network and compute a feature-importance map by associating the feature maps in the final convolutional layer with particular classes. In GradCAM the correlation of the gradients of each class w.r.t. each feature map is done by weights of activations of the feature maps as an indication of which inputs are most important.

Shadow-model methods: LIME (Locally Interpretable Model-Agnostic Explanations) [11] assumes that the complex learned function can be approximated by a set of locally linear models while global interpretablity can be achieved via SP-LIME to give the Target model's global view on the data. Bastani et al. [2], propose a Shadow model approach on a global scale wherein they approximate the Target model in the form of an interpretable Shadow model that is generated after fitting a Gaussian distribution to the training data.

Data-based methods: Lakkaraju et al. [7] explain the global view using Decision Sets. Sangroya et al. [12] have used a Formal Concept Analysis based method to provide data based explanability.

In the above approaches either the availability of training data is essential or the details of the Target model are required, neither of which are available for a Black box model. Our approach differs in that we extract the data-view captured in the model and then build interpretable Shadow models for the Black box model.

3   Definitions

Definition 1. *Target Model: Target model M is a Black box machine learning model for which we only have access to the input space f and the output vec-*

tor of probabilities **p**. *However, no information is available regarding the model parameters.*

Definition 2. ***Shadow Model:*** *A Shadow model* **S** *is an interpretable model whose interpretations can be used to interpret the Target model* **M**.

Definition 3. ***Synthesized Dataset (D):*** *Synthesized Dataset is a set of data points with randomized feature values that belong to the input space* **f** *but follow the distribution learnt by model* **M**.

Definition 4. ***Data-View:*** *During the construction of model* **M** *the real-world features X_i and labels Y_i are projected to some X_i' and Y_i', respectively, in the model due to the way the model parameters, representation of the features, and labels are chosen and trained. Thus, instead of the original function f: $X \rightarrow Y$ what is learned is the function g: $X' \rightarrow Y'$. We call function g as the data-view captured by the model.*

Definition 5. ***Input Domain Knowledge:*** *The domain knowledge we have is the range of possible values the features X can take. We need this knowledge to generate data in a limited space rather than scanning for data records in an infinite space.*

Definition 6. ***Fidelity:*** *Fidelity is defined as the number of records that are predicted the same by both Black box model* **M** *and Interpretable model* **S**.

$$Fidelity = \sum_i \frac{C_i}{n} \tag{1}$$

where, $C_i = 0$ if $Classification(S, i) \neq Classification(M, i)$, and $C_i = 1$ if $Classification(S, i) = Classification(M, i)$ and n = total number of records.

4   Methodology

We use the Target model **M** itself to derive its data-view. By using query synthesis we are building the data-view of **M** in a bottom up approach using the model's data-view itself to synthesize records for our Shadow models. To explain the model **M** we create an interpretable Shadow model **S** that simulates the functionality of **M** in terms of decision making over input data instances. We use the following steps for the same. *Step 1*: Synthesize a data-view to use for training a Shadow model. *Step 2*: Train an interpretable Shadow model on the synthesized data-view. *Step 3*: Transform the model into a set of rules.

4.1   Data-View Generation Through Data Synthesis

As discussed earlier, model **M** captures a particular data-view of the original training data and models the mapping from input features to labels/predictions through some complex non-linear function. For a multi-class classification problem, this is viewed as classifying clearly positive instances in its appropriate class with some instances falling in the boundary regions between the classes. If we consider only the clearly positive instances being classified with a confidence threshold of 0.7 or more and disregard all instances that are very close to the borders of the classes with less confidence, then a simpler interpretable Shadow model can be constructed. We argue that it is better to synthesize data for model M than to take the original training data since the model M has captured a data-view from the original data. Thus, it is more appropriate to extract the data-view and use it to train an interpretable Shadow model S. We perform the data synthesis by generating data instances and posing these instances to M for classification/prediction and considering only those instances that have a positive classification/prediction beyond a threshold of 70% by the model. The generated dataset then reproduces the data-view of the model M.

We explore two different techniques for the data synthesis. The first technique generates a dataset whose output probability vector has the least entropy as per the Target model M. The second technique learns a model for the data generation process. With our synthesized dataset we train our Shadow model S.

Synthesis using Hill Climbing Method: To synthesize D, we use a query synthesis algorithm as proposed by Shokri et al. [14]. First, we generate a record by assigning random values for each feature in the model's input space. We then feed this record to the model M and get its class probability vector p. We accept a record as part of the dataset D only if the model is confident beyond a threshold (conf_{min}) that the record belongs to a class c. If the record does not meet this threshold we randomly reassign k features and repeat the process. Each time the record gets rejected we reduce the value of k and repeat the process. If there are no more features left to be re-assigned we discard the record and start again from the beginning. We repeat this process until we have a significant amount of records per class label to train our interpretable model S. We also limit the number of features we reassign with k_{max} and k_{min}. We use these limitations to speed up the process and consider only those records that will actually be admitted to the dataset. We reduce the number of features k in each revision so that the perturbations are localized to the record being considered.

Synthesis with GAN: The Hill Climbing Method would be costly when synthesizing highly dimensional datasets. We propose a method based on GAN to generate synthetic data which can be used for both low and high dimensional datasets. We first design a neural net architecture to be used as a generator for each of the dataset mentioned in Table 1. The goal of this generator is to generate a data point given to any corresponding noise. The number of input and output neurons of the generator is $noise\_size$ and number of features in the dataset, respectively. The steps for synthesizing the data are as follows:

1. For each class c we make a different generator G_c that takes a random noise of size $noise\_size$ as an input and generates a data sample as an output. Steps 2–4, as shown in Algorithm 1, are repeated for each generator G_c.

2. To train the generator, we replace what would normally be an original record discriminator in a standard GAN model with our Black box model **M**.
3. In the Forward pass, we use a random noise to generate a synthesized record and then pass it to the Black box model **M** to get output O_c.
4. We assign value 0.99 to neuron representing class c and 0 to the rest in an output array O_a, and assign error ϵ as cross entropy loss using O_a and O_c.
5. In the Backward pass, first freeze the weights $\mathbf{w}_{bbm}$ of the model **M** and then propagate the error ϵ. Using the error obtained at input layer of **M**, we update the weights $\mathbf{w}_{G_c}$ of the Generator G_c by making it the error obtained at the output layer of the generator G_c and back propagating it.
6. After training the generator G_c we can generate data by inputting any random noise of size *noise_size* and getting the output.

5   Experimental Analysis

Our goal is to investigate the effect of using a data-view of a Target model on the fidelity of Shadow model. To demonstrate this, we create two Shadow models; first, *OShadow*, that uses the original data that was used for training the Target model; and second, *SShadow*, that uses the data-view of the Target model for its training. We demonstrate through experiments that the *SShadow* model outperforms *OShadow* consistently in terms of fidelity.

5.1   Datasets and Target Model Learning

We use the datasets described in Table 1. Income dataset originally had 14 features which increased to 107 after binarization of the categorical features. We format the Purchase dataset as a user-product table which we then cluster using k-NN to get the class labels. We synthesize 10000 records for each class label for

Table 1. Datasets used for experiments

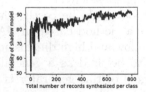

Fig. 1. Fidelity vs no. of records synthesized

Dataset	#objects	#features	Prediction type
Animal[a]	100	16	Classification
Diabetes[b]	768	8	Prob. of Diabetes
Mobile[c]	2000	20	Price range
Income[d]	32561	107	Income Bracket
Purchase[e]	9600	Variable	Variable

[a]https://archive.ics.uci.edu/ml/datasets/Zoo
[b]https://www.kaggle.com/uciml/pima-indians-diabetes-database
[c]https://www.kaggle.com/iabhishekofficial/mobile-price-classification
[d]https://www.kaggle.com/uciml/adult-census-income
[e]https://www.kaggle.com/c/acquire-valued-shoppers-challenge/data

each of our datasets using the approaches from Sect. 4.1. Figure 1 justifies why we chose 10000 since increasing the number of records doesn't negatively impact our fidelity. A confidence threshold of 0.7 was used in our experiments.

Table 2. Accuracy and fidelity (S: model trained with scaled data used for GAN)

Dataset	Acc. of Target Model	Fidelity *OShadow*	Fidelity *SShadow*		Accuracy of *SShadow*	
			Hill	GAN	Hill	GAN
Animal	95.23	95.23	95.23	95.23	90.47	90.47
Diabetes	69.48/74.67(S)	72.72/80.51(S)	84.41	81.81	71.42	74.67
Mobile	94	84.75	92.25	62.74	90.25	64.25
Income	84.24/84.75(S)	83.49/83.70(S)	98.66	93.59	74.5	76.4
Purchase30F2C	96.35	95.36	85.17	71.07	93.70	70.97
Purchase20F5C	95.31	90.94	93.96	58.63	93.65	58.68

5.2   Results

In Table 2, with the Hill Climbing algorithm, we see that the fidelity is higher when a Shadow model is trained on the target view. The only exception is the result for Purchase (30F & 2C) dataset which, in contrast to Purchase (20F & 5C), has lower *SShadow* model fidelity. It may be so because of the relatively higher number of features which affects the fidelity of our *SShadow* model. We can see from Table 2 that GAN algorithm does not work well for Mobile and Purchase datasets. This is because the generator is not able to generate data with much varying confidence thus reducing the variance in the generated data.

Table 3. Effect of the number of class labels

Classes	Fidelity	
	Hill	GAN
2	93.28	74.71
5	99.01	59.625
10	99.47	29.032
15	99.73	27.99

Table 4. Effect of the number of features

Features	Fidelity	
	Hill	GAN
20	85.01	72.94
40	75.91	73.08
50	67.58	72
75	52.13	71.59

Table 5. Time for synthesis per record (secs)

Dataset	Time taken	
	Hill	GAN
Diabetes	0.007	0.000075
Animal	0.05	0.000127
Purchase	0.02	0.00021
Mobile	0.01	0.0001
Income	0.03	0.00004

Effect of the number of Classes: For this study, we use the Purchase dataset with 15 features and generate 1000 records with 70% confidence threshold. From Table 3, we see that an increase in the number of classes does not negatively affect fidelity. This is so because the amount of information leaked by the Target model would not decrease with an increase in the number of classes.

Effect of the number of Dimensions: To study this, we use the Purchase dataset with 2 classes and generate 1000 records with 70% confidence threshold. From Table 4, we see that with the Hill Climbing method of data synthesis, increasing the dimensionality has a negative effect on fidelity. Meanwhile, the number of dimensions doesn't have much of an effect on the GAN algorithm as our generator's architecture also changes with respect to the number of dimensions. For more number of dimensions we tend to have a more complex model.

Effect of Synthesis Process: Although the GAN process of synthesizing data works better on a higher dimensional space as compared to the Hill Climbing algorithm (from Table 4), with the GAN approach there is less coverage of the input space by the synthesized data. As such, to induce better coverage within the synthesized data, we train multiple generators as each generator provides a different snippet of the view captured by our Target model. Table 5 shows that the GAN approach is faster, in terms of generating the data, as once the generator is fully learned we can generate data points quickly.

Interpreting our Shadow Models: Depending on the kind of interpretation we need the choice of Shadow model is open to the user, thereby making the approach agnostic to the type of Shadow model. To demonstrate effectiveness of the proposed approach for interpretation we chose to learn a Decision Tree and perform a Permutation Test (eli5[1]) on the data-view generated for Diabetes model. With the Decision Tree we found that Glucose is the root note and thus, it is one of the most important features in the data-view. With the Permutation Test we find that the important features are the same in both the Target model trained on the original data and our Shadow model trained on the synthesized data, with both models' most important features being Glucose, BloodPressure, Insulin and Age. As such, we infer that the approach gives a good approximation of the Target model in the form of an interpretable Shadow model.

6   Conclusion and Future Work

We presented a framework to explain a target Black box model when no training data or model details are available, by extracting the data-view to capture the Target model's functionality. This enables one to build good interpretable Shadow models. Experimental results show the proposed approach's efficacy in terms of improvement in the fidelity score. Future works include tackling the limitations of the algorithm such as its use in high dimensional datasets.

Acknowledgements. We thank the Infosys Center of Artificial Intelligence, IIIT-Delhi for support.

---

[1] https://eli5.readthedocs.io/en/latest/.

References

1. Adadi, A., Berrada, M.: Peeking inside the black-box: a survey on explainable artificial intelligence (xai). IEEE Access **6**, 52138–52160 (2018)
2. Bastani, O., Kim, C., Bastani, H.: Interpretability via model extraction. CoRR abs/1706.09773 (2017)
3. Chen, X., Duan, Y., Houthooft, R., Schulman, J., Sutskever, I., Abbeel, P.: Infogan: interpretable representation learning by information maximizing generative adversarial nets. In: Proceedings of the 30th International Conference on NIPS, pp. 2180–2188 (2016)
4. Friedman, J.H., Popescu, B.E.: Predictive learning via rule ensembles. Ann. Appl. Stat. **2**(3), 916–954 (2008)
5. Gilpin, L.H., Bau, D., Yuan, B.Z., Bajwa, A., Specter, M., Kagal, L.: Explaining explanations: an overview of interpretability of machine learning. In: 2018 IEEE 5th International Conference on Data Science and Advanced Analytics (DSAA), pp. 80–89 (2018)
6. Guo, W., Huang, S., Tao, Y., Xing, X., Lin, L.: Explaining deep learning models-a bayesian non-parametric approach. In: Neural Information Processing Systems. NIPS 2018 (2018)
7. Lakkaraju, H., Bach, S.H., Leskovec, J.: Interpretable decision sets: a joint framework for description and prediction. In: Proceedings of the 22Nd ACM SIGKDD. KDD'2016 (2016)
8. Lundberg, S.M., Lee, S.I.: A unified approach to interpreting model predictions. In: Neural Information Processing Systems (NIPS 2017), vol. 30 (2017)
9. Murdoch, W.J., Singh, C., Kumbier, K., Abbasi-Asl, R., Yu, B.: Definitions, methods, and applications in interpretable machine learning. In: Proceedings of the National Academy of Sciences (2019)
10. Puri, N., Gupta, P., Agarwal, P., Verma, S., Krishnamurthy, B.: MAGIX: model agnostic globally interpretable explanations. CoRR abs/1706.07160 (2017)
11 Ribeiro, M.T., Singh, S., Guestrin, C.: "Why should I trust you?": explaining the predictions of any classifier. In: SIGKDD (2016)
12. Sangroya, A., Anantaram, C., Rawat, M., Rastogi, M.: Using formal concept analysis to explain black box deep learning classification models. In: IJCAI-19 Workshop, FCA4AI, pp. 19–26 (2019)
13. Selvaraju, R.R., Cogswell, M., Das, A., Vedantam, R., Parikh, D., Batra, D.: Gradcam: visual explanations from deep networks via gradient-based localization. In: IJCV (2019)
14. Shokri, R., Stronati, M., Song, C., Shmatikov, V.: Membership inference attacks against machine learning models. In: 2017 IEEE Symposium on Security and Privacy (SP) (2017)
15. Shrikumar, A., Greenside, P., Kundaje, A.: Learning important features through propagating activation differences. CoRR abs/1704.02685 (2017)
16. Smilkov, D., Thorat, N., Kim, B., Viégas, F.B., Wattenberg, M.: Smoothgrad: removing noise by adding noise. CoRR abs/1706.03825 (2017)
17. Wang, F., Rudin, C.: Falling rule lists. In: AISTATS (2015)

Intra-domain Knowledge Generalization in Cross-Domain Lifelong Reinforcement Learning

Yiming Qian[1,2], Fangzhou Xiong[1,2,4], and Zhiyong Liu[1,2,3(✉)]

[1] State Key Lab of Management and Control for Complex Systems, Institute of Automation, Chinese Academy of Sciences, 100190 Beijing, China
{qianyiming2019,xiongfangzhou2015,zhiyong.liu}@ia.ac.cn
[2] School of Artificial Intelligence, University of Chinese Academy of Sciences (UCAS), 100049 Beijing, China
[3] CAS Centre for Excellence in Brain Science and Intelligence Technology, Chinese Academy of Sciences, 200031 Shanghai, China
[4] Alibaba Group, Hangzhou, China

Abstract. Lifelong reinforcement learning (LRL) is an important approach to achieve continual lifelong learning of multiple reinforcement learning tasks. The two major methods used in LRL are task decomposition and policy knowledge extraction. Policy knowledge extraction method in LRL can share knowledge for tasks in different task domains and for tasks in the same task domain with different system environmental coefficients. However, the generalization ability of policy knowledge extraction method is limited on learned tasks rather than learned task domains. In this paper, we propose a cross-domain lifelong reinforcement learning algorithm with intra-domain knowledge generalization ability (CDLRL-DKG) to improve generalization ability of policy knowledge extraction method from learned tasks to learned task domains. In experiments, we evaluated CDLRL-DKG performance on three task domains. And our results show that the proposed algorithm can directly get approximate optimal policy from given dynamical system environmental coefficients in task domain without added cost of computing time and storage space.

Keywords: Lifelong reinforcement learning · Knowledge generalization · Task domain

1 Introduction

Lifelong learning [1], which could continually accumulate and refine knowledge from learned tasks, then rapidly master new tasks by knowledge reuse [2], provides a feasible idea to solve artificial general intelligence. Lifelong learning algorithms have been researched in four main areas [1] including lifelong supervised

This work is fully supported by National Key Research and Development Plan of China grant 2017YFB1300202, NSFC, China grants U1613213, 61627808, and the Strategic Priority Research Program of Chinese Academy of Sciences under Grant XDB32050100.

© Springer Nature Switzerland AG 2020
H. Yang et al. (Eds.): ICONIP 2020, CCIS 1333, pp. 386–394, 2020.
https://doi.org/10.1007/978-3-030-63823-8_45

learning [3], lifelong unsupervised learning [4], lifelong semi-supervised learning [5], and lifelong reinforcement learning [6–8]. Lifelong reinforcement learning is an important approach to achieve continual lifelong learning of multiple reinforcement learning tasks. As LRL has rapid adaptability of new tasks and environments, the high expense cost in time and space of mastering new task in high dimensional continuous action spaces such as in areas of game and robotics will slump.

The two major methods to achieve knowledge reuse in lifelong reinforcement learning are task decomposition [8] reusing the same primitive sub-task model policy and policy knowledge extraction [6,7] reusing the shared prior policy knowledge of extraction. For policy knowledge extraction method, Cross-Domain Lifelong Reinforcement Learning (CDLRL) [7] is one of the typical algorithms. The core problem that CDLRL algorithm has solved is about how to refine shared knowledge in different task domains and in the same task domain to speed up new tasks' learning process without knowledge catastrophic forgetting. But for the new task with new system environmental coefficients in learned task domain, CDLRL algorithm still needs to compute task optimal policy solution and calculate task-specific coefficients. This means that CDLRL algorithm has knowledge generalization ability in learned tasks rather than in learned domains.

In this paper, we mainly concentrate on the problem of how to improve policy knowledge refinement methods' knowledge generalization ability from learned tasks to learned task domains. As task-specific coefficients in the same task domain correlate with given system environmental coefficients [9,10], we propose CDLRL-DKG to improve cross-domain lifelong reinforcement learning generalization ability from learned tasks to learned domains without added time and storage space cost.

The main contributions of this paper are two aspects. First, we propose CDLRL-DKG which could directly get approximate optimal policy of new task by given system environmental coefficients. Second, CDLRL-DKG could rapidly adapt new tasks in learned domains without added time and storage space cost. Section 2 gives a brief review on reinforcement learning and lifelong reinforcement learning algorithm, and Sect. 3 proposes the detailed algorithm. The experimental results are illustrated in Sect. 4, then Sect. 5 concludes this paper.

2 Background

2.1 Reinforcement Learning

In a reinforcement learning problem, an agent obtains optimal action strategy depending on interaction with environment system. As Markov decision processes (MDPs) could formally describe the environment system, reinforcement learning problems can be formalized as MDPs. The basic concept of MDPs could be represented by MDPs: $M = \langle X, A, P, R, \gamma \rangle$, where X is the set of possible states, A is the set of possible actions, $P : x_{n+1} \sim P(x_{n+1}|x_n, a_n) \in [0, 1]$ is the state transition function to describe the probability from current state x_n and selected action a_n to the next state x_{n+1}, $R : r_{n+1} = R(x_n, a_n, x_{n+1})$ is the reward function for state-action pairs to measure the agent performance, and $\gamma \in [0, 1)$ is the discount factor of future rewards. The policy $\pi = P(a_n | x_n)$ is the conditional probability distribution from current state x_n to execution action a_n. And trajectory $\tau = [x_{1:N}, a_{1:N}]$ is the sequence of state-action pairs over a horizon M.

The target of reinforcement learning is to find the optimal policy π which could make task get maximum reward in environment system. Policy gradient method (PG) [11] defines a vector $\theta \in \mathbb{R}^d$ to represent the policy π, then optimizes policy parameters θ by maximizing the expected average reward:

$$J(\theta) = E\left[\frac{1}{N}\sum_{n=1}^{N} r_{n+1}\right] = \int_{\mathbb{T}} p_\theta(\tau)\mathcal{R}(\tau)d\tau \tag{1}$$

where $\mathbb{T}$ is the set of possible trajectories, $\mathcal{R}(\tau) = \frac{1}{N}\sum_{n=1}^{N} r_{n+1}$ is the average reward of the trajectory τ, and $p_\theta(\tau)$ is the probability of trajectory τ.

2.2   Lifelong Reinforcement Learning

Comparing with policy gradient methods focusing on single-task learning, lifelong reinforcement learning algorithms focus on continual learning tasks from different task domains without catastrophic forgetting. We suppose that the agent needs to learn a series of reinforcement learning tasks $\mathcal{Z}^{(1)}, \mathcal{Z}^{(2)}, ..., \mathcal{Z}^{(T_{max})}$, and these tasks have different states and action spaces in different task domains. Then we could gather the tasks in the same domain to form task groups $\mathcal{G}^{(1)}, \mathcal{G}^{(2)}, ..., \mathcal{G}^{(G_{max})}$. Depending on the design of CDLRL algorithm framework in policy knowledge extraction method, CDLRL algorithm could be divided into two parts including knowledge acquisition and knowledge refinement. The first part is in charge of knowledge acquisition by PG algorithm such as Natural Actor-Critic (NAC) [11]. The acquired knowledge is optimal policy parameters set $\Theta^* = \{\theta^{(T_1)*}, \theta^{(T_2)*}, ..., \theta^{(T_{max})*}\}$ for optimal policy set $\Pi^* = \{\pi^*_{\theta(T_1)}, \pi^*_{\theta(T_2)}, ..., \pi^*_{\theta(T_{max})}\}$ of all trained tasks.

The second part is in charge of knowledge refinement by Cross-Domain Multi-Task Learning algorithm (CDMTL) [7]. Depending on knowledge acquisition, each task $t \in \mathcal{G}^{(g)}$ will get corresponding optimal policy parameters $\theta^{(t)} \in \mathbb{R}^{d^{(t)}}$. In order to get the shared knowledge $B^{(g)} \in \mathbb{R}^{d^{(t)} \times k}$ from optimal policy parameters set Θ^*, CDMTL algorithm assumes that each optimal policy parameters $\theta^{(t)} = B^{(g)} s^{(t)}$ is composed by shared knowledge base $B^{(g)}$ and task-specific coefficients $s^{(t)} \in \mathbb{R}^k$. As the tasks in different domains have different policy parameters spaces, shared knowledge base $B^{(g)}$ could not share knowledge in different task domains. In order to achieve cross-domain knowledge refinement, CDMTL introduces a repository of knowledge $L \in \mathbb{R}^{d \times k}$ to share knowledge for all tasks and a set of task group projection matrices $\Psi^{\mathcal{G}^{(1)}}, \Psi^{\mathcal{G}^{(2)}}, ..., \Psi^{\mathcal{G}^{(G_{max})}} \in \mathbb{R}^{d^{(t)} \times d}$ to share knowledge for tasks in the same task domain. As the results, each task optimal policy parameters could be represented as $\theta^{(t)} = \Psi^{\mathcal{G}^{(g)}} L s^{(t)}$.

Given task groups $\mathcal{G}^{(1)}, \mathcal{G}^{(2)}, ..., \mathcal{G}^{(G)}$, the all tasks could be represented as $T = \sum_{g=1}^{G} |\mathcal{G}^{(g)}|$. The loss function of CDMTL is:

$$
\begin{aligned}
& e_T\left(L, \Psi^{\mathcal{G}^{(1)}}, \Psi^{\mathcal{G}^{(2)}}, ..., \Psi^{\mathcal{G}^{(G)}}\right) \\
& = \sum_{g=1}^{G}\{\tfrac{1}{|\mathcal{G}^{(g)}|} \sum_{t \in \mathcal{G}^{(g)}} \min_{s^{(t)}} \left[-\mathcal{J}\left(\theta^{(t)}\right) + \mu_1 \|s^{(t)}\|_1\right] \\
& + \mu_2 \|\Psi^{\mathcal{G}^{(g)}}\|_F^2\} + \mu_3 \|L\|_F^2
\end{aligned}
\tag{2}
$$

where $\| \cdot \|_F$ is the Frobenius norm, and $\| \cdot \|_1$ is the L_1 norm. In experiments, loss function $e_T(\cdot)$ could be approximated by a second-order Taylor expansion of $\mathcal{J}_{\mathcal{L},\theta}\left(\widetilde{\theta}^{(t)}\right)$ ($\widetilde{\theta}^{(t)} = \Psi^{\mathcal{G}^{(g)}} L s^{(t)}$). The second derivative of $\mathcal{J}_{\mathcal{L},\theta}\left(\widetilde{\theta}^{(t)}\right)$ is:

$$
\Gamma^{(t)} = -E\left[\mathcal{R}^{(t)}(\tau) \sum_{n=1}^{N^{(t)}} \nabla_{\widetilde{\theta}^{(t)}, \widetilde{\theta}^{(t)}}^2 log \pi_{\widetilde{\theta}^{(t)}}\left(a_m^{(t)} | x_m^{(t)}\right)\right]_{\widetilde{\theta}^{(t)} = \alpha^{(t)}}
\tag{3}
$$

And the approximate loss function is:

$$
\begin{aligned}
& \widehat{e}_T\left(L, \Psi^{\mathcal{G}^{(1)}}, \Psi^{\mathcal{G}^{(2)}}, ..., \Psi^{\mathcal{G}^{(G)}}\right) \\
& = \sum_{g=1}^{G}\{\tfrac{1}{|\mathcal{G}^{(g)}|} \sum_{t \in \mathcal{G}^{(g)}} \min_{s^{(t)}} \left[\|\alpha^{(t)} - \Psi^{\mathcal{G}^{(g)}} L s^{(t)}\|_{\Gamma^{(t)}}^2 + \mu_1 \|s^{(t)}\|_1\right] \\
& + \mu_2 \|\Psi^{\mathcal{G}^{(g)}}\|_F^2\} + \mu_3 \|L\|_F^2
\end{aligned}
\tag{4}
$$

where $\|v\|_\Gamma$ is the Matrix norm and $\|v\|_\Gamma^2 = v^T \Gamma v$, and the task optimal policy solution $\alpha^{(t)}$ need to be solved by policy gradient algorithm.

3   The Proposed Method

We propose a cross-domain lifelong reinforcement learning algorithm with intra-domain knowledge generalization ability (CDLRL-DKG) to improve generalization ability from learned tasks to learned task domains. CDLRL-DKG algorithm could be divided into two parts including knowledge acquisition and knowledge refinement. For the first part, we use NAC algorithm to acquire knowledge of task optimal policy solution set. And for the second part, we use Cross-domain Multi-Task Learning algorithm with intra-domain knowledge generalization ability (CDMTL-DKG) to refine knowledge from task optimal policy solution set.

Depending on the CDMTL algorithm framework, we could reuse cross-domain shared knowledge L and task group projection matrix $\Psi^{\mathcal{G}^{(g)}}$ for a new task $t_{new} \in \mathcal{G}^{(g)}$ in learned task domain $\mathcal{D}^{(g)}$ ($\mathcal{G}^{(g)} \subset \mathcal{D}^{(g)}$). Although matrices L and $\Psi^{\mathcal{G}^{(g)}}$ ($\Psi^{\mathcal{G}^{(g)}} = \Psi^{\mathcal{D}^{(g)}}$) could be reused, the new task $t_{new} \in \mathcal{D}^{(g)}$ still needs to compute task optimal policy solution $\alpha^{(t_{new})}$ to calculate the new task-specific coefficient $s_{\mathcal{D}^{(g)}}^{(t_{new})}$ in CDMTL. Then the CDMTL's knowledge base will save the new task-specific coefficient $s_{\mathcal{D}^{(g)}}^{(t_{new})}$ to achieve generalization for next tasks with same specific dynamical system environmental coefficients $q_{\mathcal{D}^{(g)}}^{(t_{new})} \in Q_{\mathcal{D}^{(g)}}$. This means that the CDMTL algorithm has the generalization ability only in learned task-specific dynamical system environmental coefficients $q_{\mathcal{D}^{(g)}}^{(t)}$ $(t \in \mathcal{G}^{(g)})$ rather than in all possible dynamical system environmental coefficients' set $Q_{\mathcal{D}^{(g)}}$ of learned task domain $\mathcal{D}^{(g)}$.

In order to achieve the generalization ability in learned task domain $\mathcal{D}^{(g)}$, we assume task-specific dynamical system environmental coefficients $q_{\mathcal{D}^{(g)}}^{(t)}$ is correlated with task-specific coefficient $s_{\mathcal{D}^{(g)}}^{(t)}$. Then we construct the linear mapping relationship from $q_{\mathcal{D}^{(g)}}^{(t)}$ to $s_{\mathcal{D}^{(g)}}^{(t)}$ by matrix $W_{\mathcal{D}^{(g)}}$:

$$s_{\mathcal{D}^{(g)}}^{(t)} = W_{\mathcal{D}^{(g)}} q_{\mathcal{D}^{(g)}}^{(t)} \tag{5}$$

where $q_{\mathcal{D}^{(g)}}^{(t)} \in \mathbb{R}^p$, $s_{\mathcal{D}^{(g)}}^{(t)} \in \mathbb{R}^k$, and $W_{\mathcal{D}^{(g)}} \in \mathbb{R}^{k \times p}$. As approximate optimal policy parameters could be represented as $\widetilde{\theta}^{(t)} = \Psi^{\mathcal{D}^{(g)}} L s_{\mathcal{D}^{(g)}}^{(t)}$ in CDMTL, we could get:

$$\widetilde{\theta}^{(t)} = \Psi^{\mathcal{D}^{(g)}} L W_{\mathcal{D}^{(g)}} q_{\mathcal{D}^{(g)}}^{(t)} \tag{6}$$

As the task-specific dynamical system environmental coefficients $q_{\mathcal{D}^{(g)}}^{(t)}$ are set by experimental environmental information, Eq. (6) means that we could directly get the new task's approximate optimal policy just depending on given environmental information in the learned task domain without computing new task optimal policy solution $\alpha^{(t)}$ and calculating task-specific coefficient $s_{\mathcal{D}^{(g)}}^{(t_{new})}$.

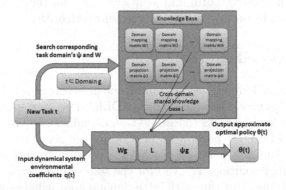

Fig. 1. The CDLRL-DKG framework to get new task's approximate optimal policy

Given task groups $\mathcal{G}^{(1)}, \mathcal{G}^{(2)}, ..., \mathcal{G}^{(G)}$, the all learned tasks could be represented as $T = \sum_{g=1}^{G} |\mathcal{G}^{(g)}|$. The task group $\mathcal{G}^{(g)}$ has all learned tasks and the corresponding task domain $\mathcal{D}^{(g)}$ has all possible tasks in this task domain $(\mathcal{G}^{(g)} \subset \mathcal{D}^{(g)})$. Depending on Eq. (3) and Eq. (4), we propose to learn cross-domain shared knowledge L, task domain projection matrix $\Psi^{\mathcal{D}^{(g)}}$, and task domain coefficient mapping matrix $W_{\mathcal{D}^{(g)}}$ as a whole in CDMTL-DKG. The approximate loss function of CDMTL-DKG is:

$$
\begin{aligned}
&\widehat{e}_T\left(L, \Psi^{\mathcal{D}^{(1)}}, \Psi^{\mathcal{D}^{(2)}}, ..., \Psi^{\mathcal{D}^{(G)}}, W_{\mathcal{D}^{(1)}}, W_{\mathcal{D}^{(2)}}, ..., W_{\mathcal{D}^{(G)}}\right) \\
&= \sum_{g=1}^{G}\{\tfrac{1}{|\mathcal{G}^{(g)}|}\sum_{t\in\mathcal{G}^{(g)}} \|\alpha^{(t)} - \Psi^{\mathcal{D}^{(g)}} L W_{\mathcal{D}^{(g)}} q_{\mathcal{D}^{(g)}}^{(t)}\|_{\Gamma^{(t)}}^2 \\
&\quad + \mu_1\|W_{\mathcal{D}^{(g)}}\|_F^2 + \mu_2\|\Psi^{\mathcal{D}^{(g)}}\|_F^2\} + \mu_3\|L\|_F^2
\end{aligned}
\tag{7}
$$

where $\|v\|_\Gamma$ is the Matrix norm and $\|v\|_\Gamma^2 = v^T\Gamma v$, and the task optimal policy solution $\alpha^{(t)}$ is acquired by NAC. We use gradient descent method to learn cross-domain shared knowledge L, task domain projection matrix $\Psi^{\mathcal{D}^{(g)}}$, and task domain coefficient mapping matrix $W_{\mathcal{D}^{(g)}}$. The gradient update of matrices L, $\Psi^{\mathcal{D}^{(g)}}$, and $W_{\mathcal{D}^{(g)}}$ in Eq. (7) are:

$$
\begin{aligned}
\triangle L = \eta_L\{\sum_g \frac{1}{|\mathcal{G}^{(g)}|}\sum_{t\in\mathcal{G}^{(g)}} \{-\Psi^{(\mathcal{D}^{(g)})^T}\Gamma^{(t)}\alpha^{(t)}\left(W_{(\mathcal{D}^{(g)})}q_{D^{(g)}}^{(t)}\right)^T \\
+\Psi^{(\mathcal{D}^{(g)})^T}\Gamma^{(t)}\Psi^{(\mathcal{D}^{(g)})}L\left(W_{(\mathcal{D}^{(g)})}q_{D^{(g)}}^{(t)}\right)\left(W_{(\mathcal{D}^{(g)})}q_{D^{(g)}}^{(t)}\right)^T\} + \mu_3 L\}
\end{aligned}
\tag{8}
$$

$$
\begin{aligned}
\triangle\Psi^{(\mathcal{D}^{(g)})} = \eta_{\Psi^{(\mathcal{D}^{(g)})}}\{\frac{1}{|\mathcal{G}^{(g)}|}\sum_{t\in\mathcal{G}^{(g)}} \{-\Gamma^{(t)}\alpha^{(t)}\left(LW_{(\mathcal{D}^{(g)})}q_{D^{(g)}}^{(t)}\right)^T \\
+\Gamma^{(t)}\Psi^{(\mathcal{D}^{(g)})}\left(LW_{(\mathcal{D}^{(g)})}q_{D^{(g)}}^{(t)}\right)\left(LW_{(\mathcal{D}^{(g)})}q_{D^{(g)}}^{(t)}\right)^T\} + \mu_2\Psi^{(\mathcal{D}^{(g)})}\}
\end{aligned}
\tag{9}
$$

$$
\begin{aligned}
\triangle W_{(\mathcal{D}^{(g)})} = \eta_{W_{(\mathcal{D}^{(g)})}}\{\frac{1}{|\mathcal{G}^{(g)}|}\sum_{t\in\mathcal{G}^{(g)}} \{-\left(\Psi^{(\mathcal{D}^{(g)})}L\right)^T\Gamma^{(t)}\alpha^{(t)}\left(q_{D^{(g)}}^{(t)}\right)^T \\
+\left(\Psi^{(\mathcal{D}^{(g)})}L\right)^T\Gamma^{(t)}\left(\Psi^{(\mathcal{D}^{(g)})}L\right)W_{(\mathcal{D}^{(g)})}q_{D^{(g)}}^{(t)}\left(q_{D^{(g)}}^{(t)}\right)^T\} + \mu_1 W_{(\mathcal{D}^{(g)})}\}
\end{aligned}
\tag{10}
$$

where η_L is the learning rate for L, $\eta_{\Psi^{(\mathcal{D}^{(g)})}}$ is the learning rate for $\Psi^{(\mathcal{D}^{(g)})}$, and $\eta_{W_{(\mathcal{D}^{(g)})}}$ is the learning rate for $W_{(\mathcal{D}^{(g)})}$. The proposed CDMTL-DKG algorithm is summarized in Algorithm 1.

4   Experimental Illustration

4.1   Experiment Setting

We accomplished the experiments in matlab (2012a) in windows 7 with 8.00 GB RAM. The three different dynamical environment systems, which are corresponding to three different task domains, for cross-domain lifelong reinforcement learning are Double Mass (DM), Cart-Pole (CP), and Double Cart-Pole (DCP).

Double Mass (DM): The double spring-mass-damper system has six environmental coefficients: two spring constants, damping constants, and masses. The target is to keep the first mass in a specific state by giving a force to the second mass.

Algorithm 1. CDMTL-DKG

Require:

all learning tasks' optimal policy solutions $\alpha^{(1)}, \alpha^{(2)}, ..., \alpha^{(T)}$

all learning tasks' dynamical system environmental coefficients $q^{(1)}, q^{(2)}, ..., q^{(T)}$

1: **while** not accomplish all tasks(1,2,...,T) **do**
2:     random select task t from (1,2,...,T)
3:     find task $t \in \mathcal{G}^{(g)}$
4:     update $L = L - \triangle L$
5:     update $\Psi^{(\mathcal{D}^{(g)})} = \Psi^{(\mathcal{D}^{(g)})} - \triangle \Psi^{(\mathcal{D}^{(g)})}$
6:     update $W_{(\mathcal{D}^{(g)})} = W_{(\mathcal{D}^{(g)})} - \triangle W_{(\mathcal{D}^{(g)})}$
7: **return** $L, \Psi^{\mathcal{D}^{(1)}}, \Psi^{\mathcal{D}^{(2)}}, ..., \Psi^{\mathcal{D}^{(G)}}, W_{\mathcal{D}^{(1)}}, W_{\mathcal{D}^{(2)}}, ..., W_{\mathcal{D}^{(G)}}$

Cart-Pole (CP): The inverted pendulum system has five environmental coefficients: cart mass, pole mass, pole's length, a inertia parameter, and a damping parameter. The target is to keep the pole upright.

Double Cart-Pole (DCP): The double-layer inverted pendulum system has seven environmental coefficients: cart mass, two pole masses, two pole's lengths, a inertia parameter, and a damping parameter. The target is to keep the double-layer pole upright.

The algorithms we have utilized in generalization performance of approximate optimal control policy are as follows:

PG [11]. Natural Actor-Critic in Policy Gradient.

CDLRL [7]. Cross-Domain Lifelong Reinforcement Learning.

CDLRL-DKG. Cross-Domain Lifelong Reinforcement Learning with Intra-domain knowledge generalization ability.

4.2   Experimental Results and Discussion

For each of these task domains, we generated 10 tasks with different environmental coefficients as training set, and then generated new 5 tasks with different environmental coefficients as test set. After learning CDLRL-DKG algorithm, we could directly use $\widetilde{\theta}^{(t_{new})} = \Psi^{\mathcal{D}^{(g)}} L W_{\mathcal{D}^{(g)}} q_{\mathcal{D}^{(g)}}^{(t_{new})}$ as new task's approximate control policy by given dynamical system environmental coefficients.

The Fig. 2 (a), (b), (c) are the average generalization performances of five new tasks' control policies in Double Mass task domain, Cart-Pole task domain, and Double Cart-Pole task domain. We can find that the policy performances of CDLRL-DKG and the policy performances of CDLRL are similar in these three task domains, and both of them are much better than policy gradient algorithm without prior knowledge. In Double Mass task domain, CDLRL-DKG is slightly lower than CDLRL. The possible reason is that linear mapping matrix $W_{\mathcal{D}(DM)}$ might not suit to reflect the non-linear mapping relationship from system environmental coefficients to task-specific coefficients.

Table 1 and Table 2 illustrate the new tasks' costs of computing time and storage space for CDLRL-DKG and CDLRL. We can find that the CDLRL-DKG

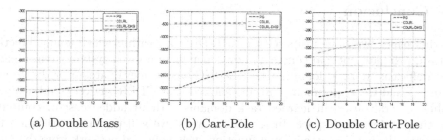

(a) Double Mass   (b) Cart-Pole   (c) Double Cart-Pole

Fig. 2. Average generalization performance of approximate optimal control policy for new tasks

Table 1. Cost of computing time

Model	New tasks	Double mass	Cart-pole	Double cart-pole
CDLRL-DKG	1	0.00099 sec	0.00091 sec	0.00093 sec
CDLRL	1	189.18 sec	250.93 sec	214.45 sec
CDLRL-DKG	3	0.0012 sec	0.0011 sec	0.0012 sec
CDLRL	3	765.27 sec	851.94 sec	755.70 sec
CDLRL-DKG	5	0.0013 sec	0.0016 sec	0.0013 sec
CDLRL	5	1181.29 sec	1347.19 sec	1256.83 sec

Table 2. Cost of storage space

Model	New tasks	Double mass	Cart-pole	Double cart-pole
CDLRL-DKG	1	$1 * W_{DM}$	$1 * W_{CP}$	$1 * W_{DCP}$
CDLRL	1	$1 * s_{DM}^{t_{new}}$	$1 * s_{CP}^{t_{new}}$	$1 * s_{DCP}^{t_{new}}$
CDLRL-DKG	3	$1 * W_{DM}$	$1 * W_{CP}$	$1 * W_{DCP}$
CDLRL	3	$3 * s_{DM}^{t_{new}}$	$3 * s_{CP}^{t_{new}}$	$3 * s_{DCP}^{t_{new}}$
CDLRL-DKG	5	$1 * W_{DM}$	$1 * W_{CP}$	$1 * W_{DCP}$
CDLRL	5	$5 * s_{DM}^{t_{new}}$	$5 * s_{CP}^{t_{new}}$	$5 * s_{DCP}^{t_{new}}$

almost does not need to consume computing time for new tasks in new system environmental coefficients, and not need to add new storage space. CDLRL needs to consume time to compute task optimal policy solution $\alpha^{(t_{new})}$ by policy gradient algorithm and then calculate the new task-specific coefficient $s_{\mathcal{D}(g)}^{(t_{new})}$ in new system environmental coefficients, and needs to consume storage space to save new task-specific coefficients $s_{\mathcal{D}(g)}^{(t_{new})}$. The costs of CDLRL of computing time and storage space are correlated with the number of new tasks. This shows that CDLRL-DKG has more highly efficient policy knowledge generalization ability than CDLRL in learned task domains.

5   Conclusion

In this paper, we have proposed CDLRL-DKG algorithm which could directly get approximate optimal control policy depending on given system environmental coefficients in task domain. CDLRL-DKG has been evaluated over three task domains and the experimental results showed that CDLRL-DKG could achieve policy generalization in learned task domains without added cost of computing time and storage space. In the future work, we will pay more attention to construct the non-linear mapping function such as neural network from dynamical system environmental coefficients to approximate optimal control policy in cross-domain lifelong policy gradient reinforcement learning.

References

1. Chen, Z., Liu, B.: Lifelong Machine Learning. Morgan & Claypool Publishers, San Rafael (2016)
2. Romera-Paredes, B., Torr, P.: An embarrassingly simple approach to zero-shot learning. In: Proceedings of the 32nd International Conference on Machine Learning, pp. 2152–2161 (2015)
3. Ruvolo, P., Eaton, E.: ELLA: An Efficient Lifelong Learning Algorithm. In: Proceedings of the 30th International Conference on Machine Learning, pp. 507–515 (2013)
4. Chen, Z., Liu, B.: Topic modeling using topics from many domains, lifelong learning and big data. In: Proceedings of the 31st International Conference on Machine Learning, pp. 703–711 (2014)
5. Mitchell, T., et al.: Never-ending learning. In: AAAI 2015 Proceedings of the Twenty-Ninth AAAI Conference on Artificial Intelligence, pp. 2302–2310 (2015)
6. Ammar, H.B., Eaton, E., Ruvolo, P., Taylor, M.: Online multi-task learning for policy gradient methods. In: Proceedings of the 31st International Conference on Machine Learning, pp. 1206–1214 (2014)
7. Ammar, H.B., Eaton, E., Luna, J.M., Ruvolo, P.: Autonomous cross-domain knowledge transfer in lifelong policy gradient reinforcement learning. In: IJCAI 2015 Proceedings of the 24th International Conference on Artificial Intelligence, pp. 3345–3351 (2015)
8. Wu, B., Gupta, J.K., Kochenderfer, M.J.: Model primitive hierarchical lifelong reinforcement learning. In: Proceedings of the 18th International Conference on Autonomous Agents and MultiAgent Systems, pp. 34–42 (2019)
9. Konidaris, G.D., Doshi-Velez, F.: Hidden parameter Markov decision processes: an emerging paradigm for modeling families of related tasks. In: AAAI Fall Symposia on Knowledge, Skill, and Behavior Transfer in Autonomous Robots (2014)
10. Isele, D., Rostami, M., Eaton, E.: Using task features for zero-shot knowledge transfer in lifelong learning. In: IJCAI'2016 Proceedings of the Twenty-Fifth International Joint Conference on Artificial Intelligence, pp. 1620–1626 (2016)
11. Peters, J., Schaal, S.: Natural actor-critic. Neurocomputing $71(7)$, 1180–1190 (2008)

Investigating Partner Diversification Methods in Cooperative Multi-agent Deep Reinforcement Learning

Rujikorn Charakorn[1], Poramate Manoonpong[1,2], and Nat Dilokthanakul[1(✉)]

[1] Bio-inspired Robotics & Neural Engineering Lab, School of Information Science & Technology, Vidyasirimedhi Institute of Science and Technology, Rayong, Thailand
{rujikorn.c_s19,poramate.m,natd_pro}@vistec.ac.th
[2] Embodied Artificial Intelligence and Neurorobotics Lab, The Mærsk Mc-Kinney Møller Institute, University of Southern Denmark, Odense, Denmark

Abstract. Overfitting to learning partners is a known problem, in multi-agent reinforcement learning (MARL), due to the co-evolution of learning agents. Previous works explicitly add diversity to learning partners for mitigating this problem. However, since there are many approaches for introducing diversity, it is not clear which one should be used under what circumstances. In this work, we clarify the situation and reveal that widely used methods such as partner sampling and population-based training are *unreliable* at introducing diversity under fully cooperative multi-agent Markov decision process. We find that generating pre-trained partners is a simple yet effective procedure to achieve diversity. Finally, we highlight the impact of diversified learning partners on the generalization of learning agents using cross-play and ad-hoc team performance as evaluation metrics.

Keywords: Coordination · Deep reinforcement learning · Multi-agent system · Generalization

1 Introduction

Working with novel partners is one of the goals of artificial intelligence [20]. This becomes crucial for the agent and its partners to achieve an objective when the agent is deployed to interact with unseen partners in the real world. For instance, an autonomous car must be able to handle various driver types on the road, including other autonomous vehicles and humans, to avoid accidents and to safely reach the intended destination. Deep reinforcement learning (DRL) has been used to solve complex tasks and domains in both single-agent and multi-agent environments. However, in fully cooperative games, agents that are trained together tend to exploit the common knowledge observed during training culminating in them, thus unable to coordinate with unseen agents [4,13].

Achieving robust agents is not trivial especially when the agents produced by DRL are very brittle [12]. A commonly used approach for alleviating this

© Springer Nature Switzerland AG 2020
H. Yang et al. (Eds.): ICONIP 2020, CCIS 1333, pp. 395–402, 2020.
https://doi.org/10.1007/978-3-030-63823-8_46

problem involves exposing the learning agent to a diverse set of partners during the training period. However, there are various methods for adding behavioral diversity to learning partners. In this work, we demonstrate that the methods widely used in competitive games do not apply to cooperative counterparts using a simplified two-player version of the Overcooked game. *Cross-play* [10] and *ad-hoc team* performance [20] are used to evaluate agents with unseen partners where agents have no prior joint experience and have to act without additional learning. This paper makes the following contributions:

1. We find that vanilla self-play, partner sampling and, surprisingly, population-based training (PBT) have the same diversity problem. This explains why PBT agents are not more robust than self-play agents and cannot play well with humans as reported in a recent work [4].
2. We illustrate that creating diversity by generating pre-trained partners is a simple but effective solution for fully cooperative environments.

2   Related Work

The ad-hoc teamwork problem has been proposed by Stone et al. [20] and, since then, has been tackled using classical methods [2,3]. Recent work involving MARL such as [5,9,17] focus on agent coordination whereby the agents are trained *together* to achieve the desired goal. Test-time performance (i.e., ad-hoc team), however, is largely ignored by methods proposed recently, which only consider the training performance. Many works [1,3,6,7] explicitly add diversity of training partners to improve the generalization of agents. Although they have the same goal of obtaining a diverse set of training partners, the methods they use are largely different. It is not clear which method is applicable in what circumstances since there is no documented comparison.

3   Materials and Methods

3.1   Overcooked as an Experimental Platform

The experiments in this paper are based on a simplified Overcooked game [4] to test the agent's ability to work with another agent (partner) under a fully cooperative environment. Here, we give a brief explanation of the game environment. There are only two players in this environment. The objective of the game is to cook and serve dishes of soup. There multiple collaborative subgoals before serving the soup. Doing so gives all players a reward of 20. This game is fully cooperative, meaning that all players share the total joint reward of the episode. Both players are supposed to work together in this environment, thus learning to coordinate and collaborate with their partner is crucial to achieving a high score. Figure 1 shows the layout of the game used in the experiments.

3.2   Diversification of Learning Partners

In competitive settings, [1] uses *partner sampling* (i.e., playing with uniformly sampled past versions of the partner) to help stabilize training. Instead of uniformly sampling from past versions, [18] samples learning partners based on the *quality score*. Furthermore, [16] use population-based training. Similarly, [21] introduces prioritized fictitious self-play (PFSP). On the other hand, in cooperative settings, various approaches have been used to acquire diversity during training, including using domain knowledge to generate diverse training partners [3,6], existing datasets [14,15] or a set of pre-trained agents [7].

Population-Based Training (PBT). PBT is a method for optimizing hyperparameters through concurrent learning agents by replacing weaker performers with the mutated hyperparameters of stronger ones along with their current (neural network) parameters. In each game, a learner π_θ and several partners π_{-i}, which are sampled from a population P, generate game trajectories. The learner's goal is to optimize the expected return, $G(\pi_i, \pi_{-i}) := \mathbb{E}_{\pi_{-i} \sim P}[\sum_{t=0}^{h} \gamma^t r | \pi_i, \pi_{-i}]$, where the policy π_i is played using the learner policy π_θ.

Self-play. The main idea of the algorithm is that the current learning agent will play with clones of itself to generate learning examples and then optimize their policies accordingly. Particularly, the learner's policy π_θ act as both π_i and π_{-i}. This approach does not apply diversity explicitly to learning partners since it exclusively learns from the current policy.

Partner Sampling. Instead of playing with the current policy like self-play, the policy will be saved periodically every k iterations, keeping only the last n versions. The learner then samples which partner to learn with from past versions of the policy. Effectively replacing the population P with past n versions of the policy.

Pre-trained Partners. This approach simply uses pre-trained self-play agents as partners to introduce diversity since different runs of a reinforcement learning algorithm usually yield different agent behaviors [8,11]. In similarity to partner sampling, it changes the population P with a set of pre-trained agents. The overall training scheme for each approach is shown in Fig. 2.

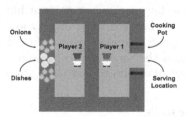

Fig. 1. The layout of Overcooked game used in the experiments.

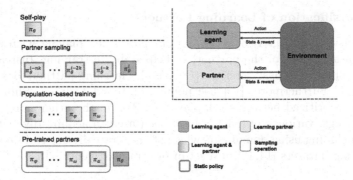

Fig. 2. Overview of each training procedure. The learning agent uses the trajectories to update its policy after playing with a partner. The static policy parameters will not be updated. The sampling operation is used when there is a set of possible agents to choose from.

4   Experiments

In this section, we investigate the source and impact of diversity using previously applied method. All methods are evaluated under the Overcooked environment. We consider the following hypotheses:

1. Does partner sampling introduce diversity to the learning partner?
2. Does PBT introduce diversity to the learning partner?
3. Does learning with a set of (diverse) pre-trained agents aid the generalization of learning agents?

There are four types of agents: self-play (SP), partner sampling (SP$_{past}$), population-based training (PBT), and agents that learn with pre-trained agents (PT). All agents in the experiments have the same network architecture and state representation, based on [4] and optimized with Proximal Policy Optimization [19].

To test the agents' generalization and diversity, the first evaluation method in this section will be *cross-play*, in which agents from different runs of the same type play together. This is a proxy of the ad-hoc performance, to establish whether or not the agents can play with their own type with the *only* deviation being the random seed. We note that the self-play scores reflect the competence of the agents while the cross-play scores show compatibility and diversity between agents. If the agents cannot play with their own type (potentially the minimum requirement of a robust agent), we also believe they do not generalize to other kinds of agents. However, if they manage to do well under cross-play, we then use a separate hold-out set of agents to test their ad-hoc performance.

4.1   Experimental Results

Self-play (SP). We evaluate SP agents using cross-play, resulting in the cross-play matrix shown in Fig. 3a. Since no diversity is explicitly introduced during training,

Table 1. Cross-play and self-play performance. The cross-play score is a mean of the off-diagonal entries (across populations in the case of PBT) while the self-play score is a mean of diagonal entries (within a population in the case of PBT) in each respective cross-play matrix as shown in Fig. 3.

Agent type	Cross-play	Self-play
Vanilla self-play (SP)	18.52 ± 42.38	190.06 ± 16.44
Partner sampling (SP_{past})	28.88 ± 46.64	186.80 ± 8.61
Population-based training (PBT)	25.27 ± 56.22	206.36 ± 25.79
Pre-trained partners: random seed (PT_{seeds})	112.51 ± 28.33	98.78 ± 39.04
Pre-trained partners: hyperparameters ($PT_{diverse}$)	175.67 ± 16.18	177.94 ± 13.05

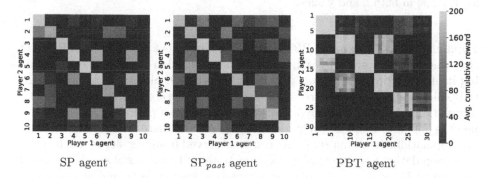

SP agent SP_{past} agent   PBT agent

Fig. 3. Cross-play matrix. The average game scores from agents of the same type. The x and y axes represent the first and second player, respectively. The diagonal shows the self-play performance of that particular agent. Off-diagonal entries visualize the cross-play performance. Each entry is evaluated by calculating the empirical episode reward mean of 100 game trajectories using a corresponding agent pair (a_x, a_y).

as expected, the cross-play scores of SP agents are relatively low compared to their self-play scores (see Table 1). This type of agent serves as our baseline for the cross-play performance. We note that the cross-play matrix shows that different runs produce diverse but incompatible behaviors.

Partner Sampling (SP_{past}.) This type of agent is identical to the SP except that it learns with uniformly sampled past versions of itself. While this method is widely used in previous competitive multi-agent environments, it fails to produce robust agents under cooperative environments. We further examine as to why this is the case. To this end, we visualize the cross-play performance of a single training run of this type, as shown in Fig. 4. We found that past versions of the same agents can play nicely with other past versions of themselves. This shows the lack of diversity in this training method since the past versions have similar behavior and are thus able to play with other versions of themselves but have low cross-play scores.

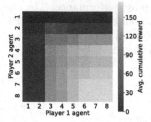

Fig. 4. Cross-play with past versions of an SP_{past} agent. The x and y axes represent the first and second player respectively. Agents from iteration [100,200,...800] represent as [1,2,...,8] in both x and y axes.

Population-Based Training (PBT). Here, we implement a round-robin PBT setting where, in an iteration, each agent in the population plays all agents, including itself, then updates its own policy just like the self-play type. After updating the policy, we replace the worst agent according to the cross-play score within the population by mutating the hyperparameters of the best performer. In this experiment, a population consists of five learning agents and there are a total of six different populations (training runs). As can be observed from Fig. 3c, agents from the same population are able to play together quite well (squares along the diagonal) but, surprisingly, their cross-play performance is similar to SP and SP_{past} agents. This result shows that PBT is not a reliable source of diversity, at least in the case of fully cooperative environments.

Using Pre-trained Agents as Learning Partners. In this experiment, we use a set of pre-trained self-play agents as learning partners during the training period. There are two types of pre-trained agents: (i) differ only in random seeds (PT_{seeds}); and (ii) differ in various hyperparameters ($PT_{diverse}$). Both types have 10 agents as training partners and another 10 hold-out test agents for the ad-hoc team. The cross-play scores of this experiment are visualized separately in Fig. 5 for clarity. It is clear from Table 1 that PT agents have significantly higher cross-play scores than other agent types. Confirming the fact that learning with a diverse set of (pre-trained) agents results in greater robustness, although the self-play performance of PT_{seeds} suffers. This also shows the significance of the diversity of behaviors generated by various sets of hyperparameters since both the self-play and cross-play scores of $PT_{diverse}$ are significantly higher than PT_{seeds}. Finally, we evaluate the PT agents with the unseen (pre-trained) partners under the ad-hoc team setting. The $PT_{diverse}$ agents perform better in both types of test partners as shown in Table 2.

Table 2. Ad-hoc team performance of PT agents. Each run is evaluated with 10 test agents over 100 game trajectories. The s.e.m is calculated from 10 different runs for each type of agent.

Agent type	Random seed test	Diverse test
PT_{seeds}	62.22 (s.e.m 15.89)	62.39 (s.e.m 10.18)
$PT_{diverse}$	**86.73** (s.e.m 15.44)	**98.36** (s.e.m 16.33)

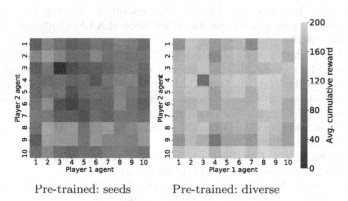

Pre-trained: seeds   Pre-trained: diverse

Fig. 5. Cross-play matrix of PT agents. Both PT_{seeds} and $PT_{diverse}$ have significantly better cross-play performance than displayed in other previous methods.

5   Conclusion

In this work, we show that learning with a diverse set of partners has a positive impact on the generalization of agents. We further investigate how such diversity can be achieved using various approaches. We find that widely used methods in competitive games do not reliably introduce diversity in cooperative games including PBT. The results suggest that obtaining partner diversity is not trivial. Then, we use separate training runs to produce a set of pre-trained partners, demonstrating that employing a diverse set of partners is better than just varying the random seeds in terms of generalization (both cross-play and ad-hoc team performance). Finally, the results of this paper highlight the importance of choosing the appropriate diversification method to ensure the required diversity for the desired task. We hypothesize that the diversity of partners will play a significant role in the robustness of agents in more complex tasks and bigger scale multi-agent environments. In future work, we would like to investigate further into these scenarios.

References

1. Bansal, T., Pachocki, J., Sidor, S., Sutskever, I., Mordatch, I.: Emergent complexity via multi-agent competition. arXiv preprint arXiv:1710.03748 (2017)

2. Barrett, S., Rosenfeld, A., Kraus, S., Stone, P.: Making friends on the fly: cooperating with new teammates. Artif. Intell. **242**, 132–171 (2017)
3. Canaan, R., Gao, X., Togelius, J., Nealen, A., Menzel, S.: Generating and adapting to diverse ad-hoc cooperation agents in Hanabi. arXiv preprint arXiv:2004.13710(2020)
4. Carroll, M., et al.: On the utility of learning about humans for human-AI coordination. In: Advances in Neural Information Processing Systems, pp. 5175–5186 (2019)
5. Foerster, J.N., Farquhar, G., Afouras, T., Nardelli, N., Whiteson, S.: Counterfactual multi-agent policy gradients. In: Thirty-Second AAAI Conference on Artificial Intelligence (2018)
6. Ghosh, A., Tschiatschek, S., Mahdavi, H., Singla, A.: Towards deployment of robust AI agents for human-machine partnerships. arXiv preprint arXiv:1910.02330 (2019)
7. Grover, A., Al-Shedivat, M., Gupta, J.K., Burda, Y., Edwards, H.: Learning policy representations in multiagent systems. arXiv preprint arXiv:1806.06464 (2018)
8. Henderson, P., Islam, R., Bachman, P., Pineau, J., Precup, D., Meger, D.: Deep reinforcement learning that matters. In: Thirty-Second AAAI Conference on Artificial Intelligence (2018)
9. Hu, H., Foerster, J.N.: Simplified action decoder for deep multi-agent reinforcement learning. arXiv preprint arXiv:1912.02288 (2019)
10. Hu, H., Lerer, A., Peysakhovich, A., Foerster, J.: "Other-play" for zero-shot coordination. arXiv preprint arXiv:2003.02979 (2020)
11. Islam, R., Henderson, P., Gomrokchi, M., Precup, D.: Reproducibility of benchmarked deep reinforcement learning tasks for continuous control. arXiv preprint-arXiv:1708.04133 (2017)
12. Justesen, N., Torrado, R.R., Bontrager, P., Khalifa, A., Togelius, J., Risi, S.: Illuminating generalization in deep reinforcement learning through procedural level generation. arXiv preprint arXiv:1806.10729 (2018)
13. Lanctot, M., et al.: A unified game-theoretic approach to multiagent reinforcement learning. In: Advances in Neural Information Processing Systems, pp. 4190–4203 (2017)
14. Le, H.M., Yue, Y., Carr, P., Lucey, P.: Coordinated multi-agent imitation learning. In: Proceedings of the 34th International Conference on Machine Learning-Volume 70, pp. 1995–2003. JMLR. org (2017)
15. Li, M.G., Jiang, B., Zhu, H., Che, Z., Liu, Y.: Generative attention networks for multi-agent behavioral modeling. In: AAAI, pp. 7195–7202 (2020)
16. Liu, S., Lever, G., Merel, J., Tunyasuvunakool, S., Heess, N., Graepel, T.: Emergent coordination through competition. arXiv preprint arXiv:1902.07151 (2019)
17. Lowe, R., Wu, Y., Tamar, A., Harb, J., Abbeel, O.P., Mordatch, I.: Multi-agent actor-critic for mixed cooperative-competitive environments. In: Advances in Neural Information Processing Systems, pp. 6379–6390 (2017)
18. OpenAI, Berner, C., et al.: Dota 2 with large scale deep reinforcement learning. arXiv preprint arXiv:1912.06680 (2019)
19. Schulman, J., Wolski, F., Dhariwal, P., Radford, A., Klimov, O.: Proximal policy optimization algorithms. arXiv preprint arXiv:1707.06347 (2017)
20. Stone, P., Kaminka, G.A., Kraus, S., Rosenschein, J.S.: Ad hoc autonomous agent teams: Collaboration without pre-coordination. In: Twenty-Fourth AAAI Conference on Artificial Intelligence (2010)
21. Vinyals, O., et al.: Grandmaster level in Starcraft II using multi-agent reinforcement learning. Nature **575**(7782), 350–354 (2019)

Learning Disentangled Representations with Attentive Joint Variational Autoencoder

Wen-tao Li, Jian-wei Liu$^{(\boxtimes)}$, Xiu-yan Chen, and Xiong-lin Luo

Department of Automation, College of Information Science and Engineering,
China University of Petroleum, Beijing Campus (CUP), Beijing 102249, China
liujw@cup.edu.cn

Abstract. Deep generative models for disentangled representation learning in unsupervised paradigm have recently achieved promising better performance. In this paper, we propose a novel Attentive Joint Variational Autoencoder (AJVAE). We generate intermediate continuous latent variables in the encoding process, and explicitly explore the underlying instinct varieties and diversities which are implicitly contain in training samples and fuse them by considering each variable's dynamic weight obtained by self-attention mechanism. Our method seeks to devise multiple intermediate latent variables, and comprehensively balance variation factors included in the samples to generate a final latent variable. The experimental results on several real-world data sets have demonstrated that the performance of our proposed framework outperforms current state of the art disentangling methods.

Keywords: Disentangled representation learning · Variational autoencoders · Varieties and diversities · Self-attention

1 Introduction

Now, more and more scholars realize that representation learning plays a critical role in machine learning research, and is the foundation for the recent success of neural network models. Disentanglement representation is defined as a representation in which the change of a single unit of representation corresponds to the change of a single variation factor of the data, while the other variables remain invariant [1].

Most initial attempts require supervised knowledge of data generative factors [2]. Then a number of unsupervised methods to learn disentangled factors have been proposed [3–5]. Recently, the research on learning the disentangled representation mainly focuses on the modeling of continuous variation factors. However, a large number of data sets contain inherently discrete generative factors, which are difficult to obtain by these methods. JointVAE [6] solved the problem by augmenting the continuous latent distribution of variational autoencoders with a relaxed discrete distribution. However, JointVAE has its own limitations. Especially in MNIST data set, the effect of disentanglement is better

© Springer Nature Switzerland AG 2020
H. Yang et al. (Eds.): ICONIP 2020, CCIS 1333, pp. 403–411, 2020.
https://doi.org/10.1007/978-3-030-63823-8_47

for discrete generation factor (type), but not for continuous generation factor (width, angle).

Based on the above facts, we analyze and summarize two leading reasons resulting in the performance that the effect of disentanglement for continuous latent variables is not pretty good as follows:

(1) One is that assuming the data is a variation of a fixed number of independent factors, all latent variables are actually conditionally independent. Thus it might result in the models failing to capture all dependencies in the data.

(2) Another major drawback is that the encoder for continuous variables in JointVAE directly generate a single continuous latent variable z for a sample data x, we don't think that this way is enough to fully grasp the instinct characteristics of the input data and lacks of pertinence for disentangled latent factors in the encoding process.

In this paper, to overcome aforementioned drawbacks and limitations, we proposed a framework. In the encoding process, we generate multiple intermediate continuous latent variables. By introducing the self-attention mechanism, the intermediate latent variables are weighted and summed to get a final latent variable, which will participate in the later model training process. We dub it as Attentive Joint Variational Autoencoders (AJVAE). AJVAE encourages disentanglement by extracting and integrating the rich multiple feature information of the original sample.

2   Related Work

2.1   VAE

VAE is a generative model, supposed that we define a joint distribution $p_\theta(x, z) = p_\theta(x|z)p(z)$, where x is a sample value that can be observed, z is a latent variable. The process from z to x is represented by the generative model $p_\theta(x|z)$, which is the decoding process. The process from x to z is represented by the recognitive model $q_\phi(z|x)$, which is the encoding process. The objective function of VAE is:

$$L(\theta, \phi) = E_{q_\phi(z|x)} \log(p_\theta(x|z)) - D_{KL}(q_\phi(z|x)||P(z)) \tag{1}$$

where, the first term is the log-likelihood of the reconstructed data sampled from the approximate posterior distribution $q_\phi(z|x)$, which can be measured by the reconstruction error; the second term is the Kullback-Leibler divergence between the approximate posterior distribution $q_\phi(z|x)$ and the prior distribution $p(z)$.

2.2 β−VAE

β−VAE is derived by modifying the VAE framework and augmenting it with a hyperparameter β. β−VAE models a joint distribution of the sample x and the latent variables z and learn continuous disentangled representations by maximizing the below objective function:

$$\mathcal{L}(\theta, \phi) = E_{q_\phi(z|x)}[\log p_\theta(x|z)] - \beta D_{KL}(q_\phi(z|x)||p(z)) \qquad (2)$$

Burgess et al. specifically proposed the objective function of controlling and gradually increasing the upper limit of mutual information during training process. The controlled information capacity is represented by C, and then the objective function is defined as:

$$\mathcal{L}(\theta, \phi) = E_{q_\phi(z|x)}[\log p_\theta(x|z)] - \gamma|D_{KL}(q_\phi(z|x)||p(z)) - C| \qquad (3)$$

where γ is a constant and constrains the Kullback-Leibler divergence term to match the C. Increasing C in the training process allows the model can encode the amount of information with control.

3   Attentive Joint Variational Autoencoder (AJVAE)

3.1   Network Architecture

The framework of our proposed AJVAE is shown in Fig. 1. Encoder generates latent variables $\mathbf{z}$ and $\mathbf{c}$ from sample data, respectively. And then decoder reconstructs them from latent variables $\mathbf{z}$ and $\mathbf{c}$. For the inferential process of continuous latent variables, we generate multiple intermediate latent variables:

$$\mathcal{F}(\mathbf{X^1}) = \{\mathbf{h}_c^1, \mathbf{h}_c^2, \mathbf{h}_c^3\} \qquad (4)$$

Assumed that the components of the intermediate latent variables are composed of **key** and *value* data pairs. We assume the **query** in self-attention mechanism follow the standard Gaussian distribution (Kingma 2014). Then we divide the transform process of generating the final latent variable by augmenting self-attention mechanism to intermediate latent variables into three stages.

Stage 1: We regard **query** vector $\mathbf{q}_c$ and each **key** vector $\mathbf{h}_c^i$ as concatenated vectors, which are derived from concatenating the mean value vector μ and vector $[\sigma_1^2, \cdots, \sigma_n^2]$ (n is denoted the dimension of the continuous latent variable) consisted of diagonal elements of covariance matrix $\sigma_i^2 I$ for some Gaussian distribution, respectively. And then we calculate the cosine similarity S_i between **query** vector $\mathbf{q}_c$ and **key** vector $\mathbf{h}_c^i$:

$$S_i = \frac{\mathbf{q}_c \cdot \mathbf{h}_c^i}{||\mathbf{q}_c|| \cdot ||\mathbf{h}_c^i||}, i = 1, 2, 3 \qquad (5)$$

Stage 2: In this stage, a calculation method similar to SoftMax is introduced to convert the similarity scores in the previous stage into alignment weights. The following identity is generally employed for calculation alignment weights:

$$\alpha_c^i = \frac{S_i}{\sum\limits_{i=1}^{3} S_i}, i = 1, 2, 3 \qquad (6)$$

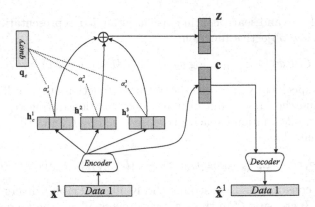

Fig. 1. Illustration of our AJVAE's Framework.

Stage 3: After obtained the alignment weight coefficient α_c^i corresponding to $\mathbf{h}_c^i$, and then the final latent continuous variable $\mathbf{z}$ can be obtained by weighted summation as follows:

$$\mathbf{z} = \sum_{i=1}^{3} \alpha_c^i \cdot \mathbf{h}_c^i, i = 1, 2, 3 \tag{7}$$

the final latent continuous variable $\mathbf{z}$ is also regarded as concatenating the mean value vector μ and matrix vectorization $[\sigma_1^2, \cdots, \sigma_n^2]$, which is consisted of diagonal elements of covariance matrix $\sigma_i^2 I$ for some Gaussian distribution.

3.2 Loss Function

Let $\mathbf{z}$ represent continuous latent variables and $\mathbf{c}$ represent categorical or discrete latent variables. With a posterior $q_\phi(\mathbf{z}, \mathbf{c}|\mathbf{x})$, prior $p(\mathbf{z}, \mathbf{c})$ and likelihood $p_\theta(\mathbf{x}|\mathbf{z}, \mathbf{c})$, the objective function of $\beta-$VAE can be written as follows:

$$\mathcal{L}(\theta, \phi) = E_{q_\phi(\mathbf{z}, \mathbf{c}|\mathbf{x})}[\log p_\theta(\mathbf{x}|\mathbf{z}, \mathbf{c})] - \beta D_{KL}(q_\phi(\mathbf{z}, \mathbf{c}|\mathbf{x})||p(\mathbf{z}, \mathbf{c})) \tag{8}$$

Assuming that continuous and discrete latent variables are conditionally independent, that is $q_\phi(\mathbf{z}, \mathbf{c}|\mathbf{x}) = q_\phi(\mathbf{z}|\mathbf{x})q_\phi(\mathbf{c}|\mathbf{x})$ and similarly for the prior $p(\mathbf{z}, \mathbf{c}) = p(\mathbf{z})p(\mathbf{c})$. Also we sub-divide the increased information capacity into two parts, control the capacity of discrete and continuous latent channels, respectively. Hence the final loss is:

$$\mathcal{L}(\theta, \phi) = E_{q_\phi(\mathbf{z}, \mathbf{c}|\mathbf{x})}[\log p_\theta(\mathbf{x}|\mathbf{z}, \mathbf{c})] - \gamma|D_{KL}(q_\phi(\mathbf{z}|\mathbf{x})||p(\mathbf{z})) \\ -C_z| - \gamma D_{KL}(q_\phi(\mathbf{c}|\mathbf{x})||p(\mathbf{c})) - C_c| \tag{9}$$

where C_z and C_c represent the capacity of controlled information of continuous channel and discrete channel, respectively, and the value of them are gradually increased in training process.

Table 1. Characteristics of the datasets.

Data	Type	Sample Number	Image Size(width-height)
MNIST	Handwriting	70,000	3232
FashionMNIST	Clothing	70,000	3232
CelebA	Faces	202,599	6464
dSprites	2D Shapes	737,280	6464

4 Experimental Results

4.1 Data Sets

MNIST: a data set includes a training set of 60,000 examples, and a test set of 10,000 examples.

FashionMNIST: a clothing data set contains 70,000 gray-scale images, and is divided into the following categories: T-shirt, trouser, pullover, dress, coat, sandal, shirt, sneaker, bag and ankle boot.

CelebA: a face data contains 202,599 face images with 10,177 celebrity identities, each of which is marked with features, including coordinates of 5 facial feature points and 40 attribute marks.

dSprites: a dataset of 2D shapes procedurally generated from 6 ground truth independent latent factors. These factors are color, shape, scale, rotation, x and y positions of a sprite.

In summary, the details information of each data are summarized in Table 1, including the types, sample numbers and image size, and the selection of hyperparameters can be seen in Table 2.

4.2 Baseline Methods

β-VAE: a state-of-the-art framework for automated discovery of interpretable factorized latent representations from raw image data in a completely unsuperivised manner.

CCβ-VAE: a framework with controlled capacity based on $\beta-$VAE. The C imposes the Kullback-Leibler divergence to be at a controllable value.

FactorVAE: a method that disentangles by encouraging the learned representation distribution to be factorial and hence independent across the dimensions.

β-TCVAE: a refinement and plug-in replacement of the $\beta-$VAE for learning disentangled representations, which is named as Total Correlation Variational Autoencoder.

InfoGAN: a learning disentangled representation by rewarding the mutual information between the samples and a subset of latent variables.

Table 2. Hyperparameters on each dataset.

Data	Data	γ	$\mathbf{C_z}$(range/iterations)	$\mathbf{C_c}$(range/iterations)
MNIST	5e-4	30	$0 - 5/100,000$	$0 - 5/100,000$
FashionMNIST	5e-4	100	$0 - 5/50,000$	$0 - 10/100,000$
CelebA	5e-4	100	$0 - 50/100,000$	$0 - 10/100,000$
dSprites	5e-4	150	$0 - 40/300,000$	$0 - 1.1/300,000$

4.3 Performance Evaluation

For Qualitative Aspects: the metric method of disentanglement is by inspecting latent traversals: visualizing the change of reconstruction while traversing one dimension of the latent space at a time.

For Quantitative Aspects: we quantitatively compare our framework with $\beta-$VAE, FactorVAE, InforGAN and $\beta-$TCVAE on the dSprites dataset employing the MIG [10].

4.4 Result and Analysis

MNIST. The disentanglement representation learning results and latent traversals on MNIST are shown in Fig. 3. We show the effect of the AJVAE model on the disentanglement of continuous and discrete potential variables (Fig. 2). It can be seen that AJVAE model has good disentanglement effect on continuous variables such as width, angle and stroke thickness of handwritten numerals and discrete variable of number type.

FashionMNIST. The latent traversal on FashionMNIST is shown in Fig. 3. We used 10 continuous and 1 discrete latent variable for this dataset. We compare the general representation without disentanglement with that of disentanglement. It can be seen that the former does not identify the potential change factors in the latent variable space of the original data sample, while for the representation of disentangled, continuous potential variables such as clothing size, color, and discrete latent variables including clothing type are found.

CelebA. We employed a model with 32 continuous latent variables and one 10 dimensional discrete latent variable. We compare the disentanglement results of AJVAE model with that of JointVAE model, as shown in Fig. 4. For the latent representation of joint disentanglement based on the introduction of self-attention mechanism, it can identify more potential change factors in the latent variable space, and the effect of dis entanglement is better.

dSprites. The results of the quantitative experiments are shown in Table 3. Our model is able to achieve scores close to the current best models and also better than most of the outstanding models proposed recently. It is believed that our model will have an outstanding advantage in disentanglement of continuous and discrete latent variables for data sets with significant discrete factors.

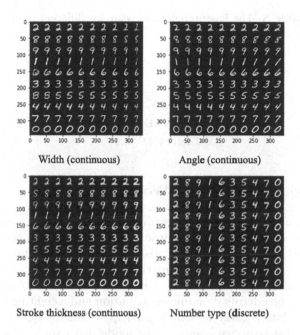

<table>
<tr><td>Width (continuous)</td><td>Angle (continuous)</td></tr>
<tr><td>Stroke thickness (continuous)</td><td>Number type (discrete)</td></tr>
</table>

Fig. 2. Representations of disentangled continuous and discrete variables of MNIST.

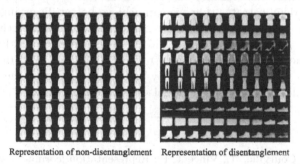

Representation of non-disentanglement   Representation of disentanglement

Fig. 3. Comparison of entangled and disentangled representations of FashionMNIST.

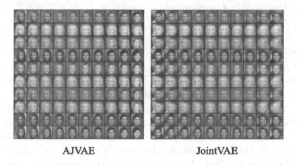

AJVAE   JointVAE

Fig. 4. Comparison of disentangled representations between AJVAE and JointVAE of CelebA.

Table 3. The Disentanglement score for different models.

Model	Score
AJVAE	0.34
β-VAE	0.33
InfoGAN	0.05
β-TCVAE	0.39
FactorVAE	0.18

5 Conclusion and Future Work

We proposed a novel framework of learning disentangled representations, which called Attentive Joint Variational Autoencoder (AJVAE). In the encoding process for continuous latent variables, we generate multiple intermediate latent representations, which deeply explore the underlying varieties and diversities included in training samples, and then introduce the self-attention mechanism to fuse them by considering dynamic contribution and weighting them to get the final continuous latent variable, which participate in subsequent model training procedure. Furthermore, we compare our model with some baselines of disentangled representations learning on several real-world datasets, and the experimental results demonstrates that we can achieve better disentangled effect.

In the future, it's interesting and meaningful to combine recently proposed models such as $\beta-$VAE [7], $CC\beta-$VAE [9], $\beta-$TCVAE [8] and FactorVAE [10] with our framework. More in-depth understanding of how disentanglement depends on the latent channel capacity and how to increase them will provide insights for building more stable models for the future work.

References

1. Bengio, Y., Courville, A., Vincent, P.: Representation learning: a review and new perspectives. IEEE Trans. Pattern Anal. Mach. Intell. **35**(8), 1798–1828 (2013)
2. Hinton, G.E., Krizhevsky, A., Wang, S.D.: Transforming auto-encoders. In: Honkela, T., Duch, W., Girolami, M., Kaski, S. (eds.) ICANN 2011. LNCS, vol. 6791, pp. 44–51. Springer, Heidelberg (2011). https://doi.org/10.1007/978-3-642-21735-7_6
3. Schmidhuber, J.: Learning factorial codes by predictability minimization. Neural Comput. **4**(6), 863–869 (1992)
4. Desjardins, G., Courville, A., Bengio, Y.: Disentangling factors of variation via generative entangling. arXiv preprint arXiv:1210.5474 (2012)
5. Chechik, G., Globerson, A., Tishby, N., Weiss, Y., Dayan, P.: Information bottleneck for Gaussian variables. J. Mach. Learn. Res. **6**, 165–188 (2005)
6. Dupont E: Learning disentangled joint continuous and discrete representations. In: NeurIPS 2018, 3–8 December 2018, Montréal, Canada, pp. 708–713 (2018)
7. Higgins, I., Matthey, L., Pal, A., et al.: Beta-VAE: learning basic visual concepts with a constrained variational framework. In: ICLR 2017, vol. 2, no. 5, pp. 1–6 (2017)

8. Chen, T.Q., Li, X., Grosse, R.B., et al.: Isolating sources of disentanglement in variational autoencoders. In: Advances in Neural Information Processing Systems, pp. 2610–2620 (2018)
9. Burgess, C.P., Higgins, I., Pal, A., et al.: Understanding disentangling in β-VAE. arXiv preprint arXiv:1804.03599 (2018)
10. Kim, H., Mnih, A.: Disentangling by factorising. arXiv preprint arXiv:1802.05983 (2018)

Minimum Variance Embedded Random Vector Functional Link Network

M. A. Ganaie[1], M. Tanveer[1(✉)], and P.N. Suganthan[2]

[1] Discipline of Mathematics, Indian Institute of Technology Indore, Simrol, Indore 453552, India
{phd1901141006,mtanveer}@iiti.ac.in
[2] School of Electrical and Electronic Engineering, Nanyang Technological University, Jurong West, Singapore
epnsugan@ntu.edu.sg

Abstract. In this paper, we propose an improved randomized based feed forward neural networks, known as Total variance minimization based random vector functional link network (Total-Var-RVFL) and intraclass variance minimization based random vector functional link network (Class-Var-RVFL). Total-Var-RVFL exploits the training data dispersion by minimizing the total variance while as Class-Var-RVFL minimizes the intraclass variance of the training data. The proposed classification models are evaluated on 18 datasets (UCI datasets). From the experimental analysis, one can see that the proposed classification models show better generalization performance as compared to the given baseline models.

Keywords: Extreme learning machine · Random vector functional link network · Class variance

1 Introduction

Randomization based neural networks have been successfully applied across a wide range of classification and regression problems due to their universal approximation ability [1–4]. Conventionally, back propagation based learning algorithms [5,6] are used for training these feed forward networks. However, problems like slow convergence, local minima problem and sensitive to learning rate setting make these iterative methods an ineffective choice. To avoid these issues, randomization based methods use closed form solutions [7–10] for training the network. They have shown better generalization performance and are faster to train [11–13]. Several models have been developed for classification tasks [14–17]. Among the randomization based algorithms, extreme learning machine [18] and random vector functional link network [19] are the mostly used methods. Random vector functional link network and extreme learning machine are the feed-forward single layer neural networks wherein the hidden layer weights and biases are randomly generated and kept fixed while as the output layer weights are optimized via closed form solution [19,20]. Although ELM is applied across many applications like action recognition [21] but the hidden layer output matrix

© Springer Nature Switzerland AG 2020
H. Yang et al. (Eds.): ICONIP 2020, CCIS 1333, pp. 412–419, 2020.
https://doi.org/10.1007/978-3-030-63823-8_48

is, usually, singular which limits the generalization of the ELM network. To overcome this issue, effective ELM [22] chooses proper network weights and biases by using the strictly diagonally dominant criterion. Optimization based regularized ELM method [18] overcame the full rank assumption and showed better generalization performance over a large number of classification problems. Minimum variance extreme learning machine (MVELM) for human action recognition [23] exploited the training data dispersion while optimizing the output layer weights. MVELM minimizes both the norm of the output layer weights and training data dispersion in the projection space. Among other variants of ELM, Hierarchical ELM (H-ELM) [24] is a multilayer framework wherein several randomly initialized autoencoders are stacked and trained independently and original ELM is used for the final classification. This multilayer architecture is also employed in semi-supervised [25] and unsupervised learning [26].

The presence of direct link from the input to output layer greatly improves the generalization performance of the randomization based neural networks like in RVFL model [27–29]. In randomization based algorithms, direct links regularize the network and hence RVFL shows better generalization performance than the ELM network [30,31]. The direct links also result in lower model complexity as the RVFL network is thinner and simpler in comparison to ELM network [32]. Based on Occam's Razor principle and PAC learning theory [33], the simpler and less complex models are better, hence, RVFL model is better than its counterpart ELM network.

Motivated by the simplicity and better generalization performance of the RVFL model [19] and minimum variance extreme learning machine [23], we propose novel multiclass classifiers known as Total variance minimization based random vector functional link network (Total-Var-RVFL) and intraclass variance minimization based random vector functional link network (Class-Var-RVFL) to optimize the output layer weights via minimization of both training data dispersion and norm of output layer weights.

The rest of the paper is organized as follows: Sect. 2 gives brief review of the related works. In Sect. 3, we discuss the proposed method. In Sect. 4, we present experimental results and comparison of the proposed methods with different classifiers. Finally, we present the conclusions in Sect. 5.

2 Related Work

Let $[X, Y]$ be the training set containing samples of the form $x_i, y_i, i = 1, 2, ..., N$, where $x_i \in \mathbb{R}^d$ is the feature vector and y_i is the corresponding class label of the ith training sample. Let J be the number of hidden neurons in the hidden layer of the feed forward neural networks.

2.1 Random Vector Functional Link Network

Random vector functional link network (RVFL) [19] is a single layer randomized feed forward network wherein the hidden layer weights and biases are generated randomly and kept fixed. The final layer receives input as the randomized projection based input features H and the original input features X. As the hidden layer weights and biases are kept fixed, only output layer weights are optimized. The objective function of the RVFL network is given as $O = \min_{\alpha}||M\alpha - Y||^2 + \lambda||\alpha||^2$ where $M = [H, X]$ is the concatenated matrix of non-linearly transformed features H and original sample features X, regularization parameter is λ and Y is the target label matrix.

The closed form solution of the objective function can be given either via regularized least squares (where $\lambda \neq 0$) or Moore-Penrose pseudoinverse (where $\lambda = 0$). Based on Moore-Penrose pseudoinverse, the optimized output layer weights are given by $\alpha = M^+Y$, where M^+ denotes the pseudoinverse. Using regularized least squares (or ridge regression), the optimized output layer weights are given by Primal Space: $\alpha = (M^TM + \lambda I)^{-1}M^TY$, and Dual Space: $\alpha = M^T(MM^T + \lambda I)^{-1}Y$.

3   Proposed Method

In this section, we discuss variance embedded variants of random vector functional link network. The proposed methods involve two step learning process wherein the first step requires the generation of enhanced features via randomized feature mapping. The second step involves incorporation of within class scatter matrix for generating the optimal output weights. In this paper, we exploit the training data dispersion for generating the optimal classifier. Unlike RVFL network, the proposed approach minimizes the output layer weights norm and the dispersion of the training data in the projected feature space and original feature space.

$$\underset{\alpha}{Min}\ \frac{1}{2}Tr(\alpha^TS\alpha) + \frac{\lambda}{2}||\alpha||_2^2 + \frac{C}{2}\sum_{i=1}^{N}||\xi_i||_2^2$$

$$s.t.\ \ h(x_i)\alpha = y_i^T - \xi_i^T, i = 1, 2, ..., N \tag{1}$$

where first term minimizes the variance of the training samples and second term of the objective function is the regularisation term and $h(.)$ is combination of original and randomized features. The variance term S is given as S_T for total variance and S_w for within class variance both are defined as follows:

The within class variance of the training data is given as: $S_w = \sum_{k=1}^{N}\sum_{i\in C_k}(x_i - m_k)(x_i - m_k)^T$, where m_k is the mean of kth class training data, C_k represents the kth class, $x_i \in \mathbb{R}^{(d+J)}$ is the training data sample.

The total variance of the training data is given as: $S_T = \sum_{i=1}^{N}(x_i - \mu)(x_i - \mu)^T$, where μ is the mean of the training data samples.

Substituting the constraints in the objective function (1) and taking the gradient with respect to α, we have $L = S\alpha + \lambda\alpha + CM^T(M\alpha - Y)$.

Setting the gradient to zero, we get $\alpha = (\frac{1}{C}S + \frac{\lambda}{C}I + M^TM)^{-1}M^TY$, where I is an identity matrix of appropriate dimensions. Testing data sample x is assigned the class based on the maximum probability as $f(x) = h(x)\alpha$.

4   Experimental Results

In this section, we analyze the experimental results of the given baseline models. We evaluate the performance of the given methods on the datasets available from the UCI repository [34]. We followed the same experimental setup and naming convention as given in the experimental study [35]. We used grid search approach to tune the optimal parameters corresponding to different given classification methods. The parameters are chosen from the range given as: $C = [10^{-6}, 10^{-5}, ..., 10^5, 10^6]$, $\lambda = [10^{-6}, 10^{-5}, ..., 10^5, 10^6]$ and number of hidden neurons $= 2 : 20 : 300$. We used relu activation function in the hidden layer. All experiments are performed on Windows-10 platform with 3-GB RAM and MATLAB-2019b.

Based on the previous discussion, variants of the proposed method include Total variance minimization based random vector functional link network (Total-Var-RVFL) and intraclass variance minimization based random vector functional link network (Class-Var-RVFL). The experimental results obtained by the given classification methods on different datasets is given in Table 1.

From the Table 1, the average accuracy of the classification models ELM, MVELM, MCVELM, RVFL, proposed Total-Var-RVFL and proposed Class-Var-RVFL are $75.83, 73.01, 74.97, 75.88, 77.94$, and 77.88, respectively. One can observe that the proposed Total-Var-RVFL and proposed Class-Var-RVFL classification models achieved better average accuracy in comparison to given baseline models. We use Friedman test [36] to analyze the statistical significance of the classification models. We assign rank R_i^j to the ith classifier of the p classifiers on the jth dataset with the best performing classifier getting the lower rank. Based on this evaluation, the average rank of the classification models ELM, MVELM, MCVELM, RVFL, proposed Total-Var-RVFL and proposed Class-Var-RVFL are $4.25, 4.22, 3.22, 4.06, 2.67$, and 2.58, respectively. Average rank of the jth classifier $R_j = \frac{1}{T} \sum_i r_i^j$ is used in Friedman test. Under the null-hypothesis, all classifiers are performing equally and hence their average ranks are equal, the Friedman statistic $\chi_F^2 = \frac{12T}{p(p+1)} [\sum_j R_j^2 - \frac{p(p+1)^2}{4}]$, is χ_F^2 distributed with $(p-1)$ degrees of freedom, here T is the total number of datasets and p is the number of classifiers. As Friedman's χ_F^2 is undesirably conservative and hence a better statistic $F_F = \frac{(T-1)\chi_F^2}{T(p-1)-\chi_F^2}$, follows $F-$distribution with $(p-1)(T-1)$ degrees of freedom. F_F is distributed with $F_F((p-1), (p-1)(T-1)) = F_F(5, 85) = 2.325$ at $\alpha = 0.05$. Here, we have $T = 18$ and $p = 6$. After simple calculations, we have $\chi_F^2 = 15.4707, F_F = 3.5289$. Hence, we reject the Null hypothesis. We use Nemenyi posthoc test to evaluate the significant difference among the models. The performance of the two classifiers is significantly better if the average ranks of the two models differ by at least critical difference, $cd = q_\alpha \sqrt{\frac{p(p+1)}{6T}}$, where q_α is the Studentized range statistic divided by $\sqrt{2}$. After simple calculations at $\alpha = 0.05$, one can see that Nemenyi test fails to detect the significant difference among the models, however, the proposed models achieved higher average accuracy and lower average rank as compared to the baseline models.

Table 1. Performance of ELM, MVELM, MCVELM, RVFL, proposed Total-Var-RVFL and proposed Class-Var-RVFL.

Dataset	ELM [18]	MVELM [23]	MCVELM [21]	RVFL [19]	Total-Var-RVFL	Class-Var-RVFL
	(Acc., Time(s))	(Acc., Time(s))	(Acc., Time(s))	(Acc., Time(s))	(Acc., Time(s))	(Acc., Time(s))
	(N, C)	(N, λ, C)	(N, λ, C)	(N, C)	(N, λ, C)	(N, λ, C)
arrhythmia	(68.81, 0.0108)	(71.46, 0.0387)	(70.35, 0.07)	(69.47, 0.0145)	(69.47, 0.0536)	(69.47, 0.067)
	(162, 0.1)	(202, 1000, 100)	(282, 100, 10)	(102, 1)	(142, 1000, 100)	(142, 1000, 100)
balloons	(75, 0.0002)	(50, 0.0003)	(50, 0.0005)	(75, 0.0003)	(81.25, 0.0006)	(81.25, 0.0006)
	(102, 0.000001)	(2, 0.000001, 1000)	(22, 0.000001, 100)	(2, 0.1)	(22, 0.000001, 0.001)	(22, 0.000001, 0.001)
blood	(78.61, 0.0073)	(76.47, 0.0261)	(79.28, 0.0031)	(77.81, 0.0218)	(79.01, 0.0174)	(79.01, 0.0188)
	(102, 10000)	(202, 0.001, 100)	(62, 0.000001, 100000)	(262, 100000)	(222, 0.1, 1000)	(222, 0.1, 1000)
breast-cancer	(69.37, 0.0041)	(69.37, 0.0153)	(70.77, 0.0044)	(68.66, 0.004)	(69.37, 0.0028)	(69.37, 0.0031)
	(122, 1000000)	(162, 100, 10000)	(82, 0.00001, 1)	(262, 100)	(102, 0.0001, 1)	(102, 0.0001, 1)
breast-cancer-wisc-prog	(81.12, 0.0023)	(83.16, 0.0104)	(80.61, 0.0272)	(76.53, 0.0021)	(82.14, 0.0071)	(81.12, 0.0013)
	(82, 1)	(142, 0.1, 0.1)	(242, 0.01, 0.01)	(142, 100)	(202, 0.1, 0.1)	(2, 10, 10000)
energy-y1	(85.16, 0.006)	(87.63, 0.0227)	(86.72, 0.0092)	(86.33, 0.024)	(87.11, 0.0078)	(87.37, 0.0316)
	(162, 10000)	(202, 0.00001, 1000)	(122, 0.0001, 100000)	(282, 1000000)	(122, 0.000001, 1000)	(282, 0.000001, 100)
glass	(68.87, 0.0023)	(62.26, 0.0153)	(60.38, 0.0045)	(66.04, 0.0026)	(64.15, 0.0046)	(66.04, 0.002)
	(242, 10)	(182, 1, 1000)	(82, 0.00001, 100000)	(222, 1000)	(142, 100, 100000)	(62, 0.00001, 1000)
heart-hungarian	(82.53, 0.0047)	(83.22, 0.0014)	(84.93, 0.0037)	(81.16, 0.0038)	(84.25, 0.0031)	(83.56, 0.0144)
	(182, 100)	(42, 0.000001, 100000)	(62, 10, 1)	(162, 100000)	(82, 1, 1000)	(282, 1000, 100000)
hepatitis	(78.21, 0.0007)	(73.72, 0.0206)	(78.21, 0.0336)	(78.85, 0.0012)	(82.05, 0.01)	(80.13, 0.0057)
	(62, 1000)	(222, 0.01, 10)	(282, 0.000001, 0.00001)	(82, 1000)	(282, 10, 1000)	(162, 0.1, 10)
hill-valley	(56.44, 0.0282)	(68.48, 0.0256)	(56.77, 0.0338)	(58.25, 0.0075)	(59.74, 0.0094)	(65.51, 0.009)
	(282, 10000)	(162, 0.0001, 0.1)	(202, 100, 1000000)	(62, 10000)	(22, 0.0001, 10)	(42, 0.00001, 0.1)
horse-colic	(66.18, 0.0078)	(61.76, 0.0207)	(63.24, 0.0299)	(64.71, 0.0012)	(66.18, 0.0011)	(66.18, 0.0169)
	(262, 0.1)	(202, 1, 0.1)	(242, 10, 1)	(22, 1)	(2, 0.01, 0.1)	(222, 100000, 10000)
lenses	(70.83, 0.0002)	(79.17, 0.0014)	(70.83, 0.0008)	(75, 0.0003)	(83.33, 0.0021)	(83.33, 0.0017)
	(22, 0.1)	(62, 10000, 1000)	(42, 10, 1)	(42, 0.1)	(122, 1000, 100)	(122, 100, 10)
mammographic	(81.35, 0.012)	(81.67, 0.0254)	(81.56, 0.0075)	(82.29, 0.0145)	(82.5, 0.0036)	(81.98, 0.0023)
	(182, 100000)	(182, 0.000001, 0.01)	(102, 0.0001, 10000)	(182, 1000)	(62, 0.1, 1000000)	(22, 0.001, 10000)
monks-3	(71.99, 0.0042)	(72.92, 0.0084)	(83.1, 0.0317)	(75.93, 0.0008)	(82.41, 0.0063)	(75.46, 0.0057)
	(122, 100000)	(142, 0.001, 100)	(262, 0.001, 0.01)	(42, 1000000)	(222, 0.001, 0.01)	(202, 0.00001, 0.01)
planning	(71.11, 0.0002)	(65.56, 0.009)	(71.67, 0.0129)	(71.11, 0.0004)	(71.11, 0.0005)	(71.11, 0.0006)
	(2, 1000000)	(142, 0.00001, 0.01)	(182, 0.000001, 0.001)	(2, 0.000001)	(2, 0.000001, 0.00001)	(2, 0.000001, 0.000001)
seeds	(94.23, 0.0005)	(65.38, 0.0007)	(95.19, 0.0038)	(94.23, 0.0022)	(94.71, 0.0008)	(95.67, 0.0008)
	(42, 10)	(22, 0.000001, 0.00001)	(82, 0.000001, 1000000)	(162, 100000)	(22, 0.00001, 1000000)	(22, 0.00001, 100)
statlog-german-credit	(77.1, 0.005)	(75.8, 0.0144)	(78.1, 0.0295)	(77.6, 0.0299)	(77.2, 0.0096)	(77.6, 0.0068)
	(102, 100)	(142, 0.1, 100000)	(202, 0.000001, 0.01)	(262, 10)	(102, 0.01, 100000)	(62, 1, 10000)
statlog-heart	(88.06, 0.0021)	(86.19, 0.0012)	(87.69, 0.0032)	(86.94, 0.0016)	(86.94, 0.0029)	(87.69, 0.0025)
	(122, 0.1)	(22, 1000, 1000)	(82, 10, 1)	(82, 0.1)	(82, 1, 0.1)	(82, 100, 10)
Average-Accuracy	75.83	73.01	74.97	75.88	77.94	77.88
Average-Rank	4.25	4.22	3.22	4.06	2.67	2.58

4.1 Analysis of the Number of Hidden Neurons

In this subsection, we analyze the significance of the number of hidden neurons on the generalization performance of the classification models. From Fig. 1a one can see that as the number of hidden neurons increase the generalization performance of the given baseline methods also increases. Also, the generalization performance of the proposed Class-Var-RVFL is better than the given baseline models. In Fig. 1b, it is visible that the generalization performance of the proposed models is almost consistent with varying number of hidden neurons. In Fig. 1c, it is evident that RVFL model initially performs better and its performance decreases with the increase of hidden neurons. However, the performance of the proposed Total-Var-RVFL is better than other baseline models.

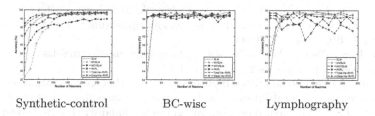

       Synthetic-control   BC-wisc   Lymphography

Fig. 1. Effect of enhanced features on the performance of the Classification models. (BC denotes Breast-cancer)

    Given the above analysis, it is imperative that the number of hidden neurons should be chosen properly to obtain better generalization performance across different classification datasets.

5 Conclusion

In this paper, we proposed total variance minimization based random vector functional link network (Total-Var-RVFL) and intraclass variance minimization based random vector functional link network (Class-Var-RVFL). The proposed methods exploit the training data dispersion in the original feature space as well as the randomized feature projection space while optimizing the output layer weights. From the experimental analysis, one can see that incorporation of total variance and class variance improved the generalization performance of the proposed models. In comparison to given baseline models, the proposed Total-Var-RVFL and Class-Var-RVFL models achieved better average accuracy. Also, the average rank of the proposed Class-Var-RVFL is better than other baseline models. In future, we will explore the deep architecture of these proposed classification methods to enhance the performance.

Acknowledgement. This work was supported by Science & Engineering Research Board (SERB) under Ramanujan fellowship Grant No. SB/S2/ RJN-001/2016 and

Early Career Research Award Grant No. ECR/2017/000053. It is also supported by Council of Scientific & Industrial Research (CSIR), New Delhi, INDIA under Extra Mural Research (EMR) Scheme Grant No. 22(0751)/17/ EMR-II. We gratefully acknowledge the Indian Institute of Technology Indore for providing facilities and support.

References

1. Hornik, K., Stinchcombe, M., White, H.: Multilayer feedforward networks are universal approximators. Neural Networks **2**(5), 359–366 (1989)
2. Igelnik, B., Pao, Y.-H.: Stochastic choice of basis functions in adaptive function approximation and the functional-link net. IEEE Trans. Neural Networks **6**(6), 1320–1329 (1995)
3. Leshno, M., Lin, V.Y., Pinkus, A., Schocken, S.: Multilayer feedforward networks with a nonpolynomial activation function can approximate any function. Neural Networks **6**(6), 861–867 (1993)
4. Park, J., Sandberg, I.W.: Universal approximation using radial-basis-function networks. Neural Comput. **3**(2), 246–257 (1991)
5. LeCun, Y., et al.: Handwritten digit recognition with a back-propagation network. In: Advances in Neural Information Processing Systems, pp. 396–404 (1990)
6. Denker, J.S., et al.: Neural network recognizer for hand-written zip code digits. In: Advances in Neural Information Processing Systems, pp. 323–331 (1989)
7. Schmidt, W.F., Kraaijveld, M.A., Duin, R.P.: Feed forward neural networks with random weights. In: International Conference on Pattern Recognition. IEEE Computer Society Press, pp. 1–1 (1992)
8. Te Braake, H.A., Van Straten, G.: Random activation weight neural net (rawn) for fast non-iterative training. Eng. Appl. Artif. Intell. **8**(1), 71–80 (1995)
9. Guo, P., Chen, C.P., Sun, Y.: An exact supervised learning for a three-layer supervised neural network. In: Proceedings of 1995 International Conference on Neural Information Processing, pp. 1041–1044 (1995)
10. Guo, P.: A vest of the pseudoinverse learning algorithm. arXiv preprint arXiv:1805.07828 (2018)
11. Widrow, B., Greenblatt, A., Kim, Y., Park, D.: The no-prop algorithm: a new learning algorithm for multilayer neural networks. Neural Networks **37**, 182–188 (2013)
12. White, H.: Approximate nonlinear forecasting methods. Handb. Econ. Forecast. **1**, 459–512 (2006)
13. Dash, Y., Mishra, S.K., Sahany, S., Panigrahi, B.K.: Indian summer monsoon rainfall prediction: a comparison of iterative and non-iterative approaches. Appl. Soft Comput. **70**, 1122–1134 (2018)
14. Ganaie, M.A., Tanveer, M., Suganthan, P.N.: Oblique decision tree ensemble via twin bounded SVM. Expert Syst. Appl. **143**, 113072 (2020)
15. Ganaie, M.A., Ghosh, N., Mendola, N., Tanveer, M., Jalan, S.: Identification of chimera using machine learning. Chaos: Interdisc. J. Nonlinear Sci. **30**(6), 063128 (2020)
16. Ganaie, M.A., Tanveer, M., Suganthan, P.N.: Regularized robust fuzzy least squares twin support vector machine for class imbalance learning. In: 2020 International Joint Conference on Neural Networks, IJCNN, pp. 1–8. IEEE (2020)

17. Tanveer, M., Rajani, T., Ganaie, M.A.: Improved sparse pinball twin SVM. In: 2019 IEEE International Conference on Systems, Man and Cybernetics (SMC), pp. 3287–3291. IEEE (2019)

18. Huang, G.-B., Zhou, H., Ding, X., Zhang, R.: Extreme learning machine for regression and multiclass classification. IEEE Trans. Syst. Man Cybern. Part B (Cybern.) **42**(2), 513–529 (2011)

19. Pao, Y.-H., Park, G.-H., Sobajic, D.J.: Learning and generalization characteristics of the random vector functional-link net. Neurocomputing **6**(2), 163–180 (1994)

20. Pao, Y.-H., Takefuji, Y.: Functional-link net computing: theory, system architecture, and functionalities. Computer **25**(5), 76–79 (1992)

21. Iosifidis, A., Tefas, A., Pitas, I.: Minimum class variance extreme learning machine for human action recognition. IEEE Trans. Circuits Syst. Video Technol. **23**(11), 1968–1979 (2013)

22. Wang, Y., Cao, F., Yuan, Y.: A study on effectiveness of extreme learning machine. Neurocomputing **74**(16), 2483–2490 (2011)

23. Iosifidis, A., Tefas, A., Pitas, I.: Minimum variance extreme learning machine for human action recognition. In: 2014 IEEE International Conference on Acoustics, Speech and Signal Processing (ICASSP), pp. 5427–5431. IEEE (2014)

24. Tang, J., Deng, C., Huang, G.-B.: Extreme learning machine for multilayer perceptron. IEEE Trans. Neural Networks Learn. Syst. **27**(4), 809–821 (2015)

25. Chang, P., Zhang, J., Hu, J., Song, Z.: A deep neural network based on ELM for semi-supervised learning of image classification. Neural Process. Lett. **48**(1), 375–388 (2018)

26. Sun, K., Zhang, J., Zhang, C., Hu, J.: Generalized extreme learning machine autoencoder and a new deep neural network. Neurocomputing **230**, 374–381 (2017)

27. Vuković, N., Petrović, M., Miljković, Z.: A comprehensive experimental evaluation of orthogonal polynomial expanded random vector functional link neural networks for regression. Appl. Soft Comput. **70**, 1083–1096 (2018)

28. Ganaie, M.A., Tanveer, M.: LSTSVM classifier with enhanced features from pretrained functional link network. Appl. Soft Comput., 106305 (2020)

29. Tang, L., Wu, Y., Yu, L.: A non-iterative decomposition-ensemble learning paradigm using rvfl network for crude oil price forecasting. Appl. Soft Comput. **70**, 1097–1108 (2018)

30. Henríquez, P.A., Ruz, G.A.: A non-iterative method for pruning hidden neurons in neural networks with random weights. Appl. Soft Comput. **70**, 1109–1121 (2018)

31. Mesquita, D.P., Gomes, J.P.P., Rodrigues, L.R., Oliveira, S.A., Galvão, R.K.: Building selective ensembles of randomization based neural networks with the successive projections algorithm. Appl. Soft Comput. **70**, 1135–1145 (2018)

32. Zhang, L., Suganthan, P.N.: A comprehensive evaluation of random vector functional link networks. Inf. Sci. **367**, 1094–1105 (2016)

33. Kearns, M.J., Vazirani, U.V., Vazirani, U.: An Introduction to Computational Learning Theory. MIT Press, Cambridge (1994)

34. Dua, D., Graff, C.: UCI machine learning repository (2017). http://archive.ics.uci.edu/ml

35. Fernández-Delgado, M., Cernadas, E., Barro, S., Amorim, D.: Do we need hundreds of classifiers to solve real world classification problems? J. Mach. Learn. Res. **15**(1), 3133–3181 (2014)

36. Demšar, J.: Statistical comparisons of classifiers over multiple data sets. J. Mach. Learn. Res. **7**, 1–30 (2006)

Non-norm-bounded Attack
for Generating Adversarial Examples

Ming Zhang, Hu Li[✉], Xiaohui Kuang, Yuanping Nie, Cheng Qian,
Zhendong Wu, and Gang Zhao

National Key Laboratory of Science and Technology on Information System Security,
Beijing 100101, China
lihu@nudt.edu.cn

Abstract. Recent studies have demonstrated that neural networks are
vulnerable to adversarial examples. Numerous attacks have been proposed for crafting various types of adversarial examples. However, almost
all the existing attacks adopt the L_p-norm or another distance metric to
bound the adversarial perturbations, which inadvertently facilitates the
implementation of some defenses. We present a novel non-norm-bounded
attack (NNBA) for generating adversarial examples. We formulate the
process of generating adversarial examples as an optimization problem,
which has just the objective of misclassifying the perturbed examples and
does not use the L_p-norm as the perturbation constraint. The examples
generated in this way naturally satisfy the requirements of adversarial
examples. Experimental results on the MNIST, CIFAR-10 and ImageNet
datasets show that NNBA can successfully generate adversarial examples
with small perturbations and high misclassification performance. Moreover, adversarial examples crafted by NNBA achieve high confidence,
good robustness and low computational cost. Our work sheds light on a
new type of adversarial attack, and we hope it will prompt research on
secure and robust machine learning models.

Keywords: Non-norm-bounded attack · Adversarial examples ·
Neural networks

1 Introduction

Machine learning has achieved great success in a wide range of applications,
such as image classification [6], speech recognition [5] and machine translation [3].
However, recent studies have demonstrated that machine learning especially deep
learning, is facing increasingly serious security problems, among which adversarial examples are one of the major threats. According to the current consensus
of researchers, adversarial examples are a kind of carefully perturbed examples that can not only be misclassified by the machine learning model, but can
also be imperceptible to humans [9,14]. Adversarial examples pose a great challenge to the application of machine learning in safety-critical scenarios and has

© Springer Nature Switzerland AG 2020
H. Yang et al. (Eds.): ICONIP 2020, CCIS 1333, pp. 420–428, 2020.
https://doi.org/10.1007/978-3-030-63823-8_49

drawn widespread attention from both academia and industry. There are various types of adversarial attacks that have been proposed for generating adversarial examples.

Generally, existing adversarial attacks each have their own unique attack algorithms to find the successfully misclassified adversarial examples, but with regard to guaranteeing the imperceptibility of the adversarial examples, these attacks almost adopt the same strategy—applying an L_p-norm to bound the perturbations. Therefore, such types of attacks are also called norm-bounded adversarial attacks. However, the L_p-norm has its limitations in measuring the similarity between two examples, and it seems that no one has challenged the need for an L_p-norm (or other distance metrics) as the constraint for perturbations in attack algorithms.

We propose a non-norm-bounded attack for generating adversarial examples to attack neural networks. Our attack just aims at generating perturbed examples that can be misclassified by the neural network. It does not contain an L_p-norm as the bound of perturbations. However, the perturbed examples generated by our non-norm-bounded attack naturally satisfy the requirements of adversarial examples: they are not only misclassified by the model, but also imperceptible to humans.

The rest of the paper is organized as follows. In Sect. 2, we first introduce some related work. In Sect. 3, we discuss the relationship between adversarial attacks and L_p-norm. In Sect. 4, we elaborate on our proposed non-norm-bounded attack. In Sect. 5, we present the experimental results. In Sect. 6, we conclude the work.

2   Related Work

Goodfellow et al. [4] proposed the fast gradient sign method (FGSM), which is a one-step algorithm and is formulated as: $\hat{x} = x + \epsilon \cdot \text{sign}(\nabla_x J(\theta, x, y))$. The original input x is updated by ϵ along the direction of the gradient of the adversarial loss $J(\theta, x, y)$ to obtain the adversarial example $\hat{x}$.

Papernot et al. [12] introduced an attack called the Jacobian-based saliency map approach (JSMA). The attack builds a saliency map to identify which features of the input most significantly impact the output.

Moosavi-Dezfooli et al. [11] proposed a method called DeepFool to find adversarial perturbations by searching for the closest distance from the original example to the hyperplane decision boundary.

Kurakin et al. [8] proposed the basic iterative method (BIM), which can be formulated as: $x_0^{adv} = x$, $x_{N+1}^{adv} = Clip_{x,\epsilon}\{x_N^{adv} + \alpha \cdot \text{sign}(\nabla_x J(x_N^{adv}, y_{true}))\}$. BIM can be regarded as an extension of FGSM. It takes a smaller step α in each iteration than FGSM and clips the updated adversarial example into the valid range ϵ.

Carlini and Wagner [2] introduced an optimization-based method (called CW in this article) to generate adversarial examples. CW is formulated as:

min $\|\boldsymbol{\delta}\|_p + c \cdot f(\boldsymbol{x} + \boldsymbol{\delta})$; s.t. $\boldsymbol{x} + \boldsymbol{\delta} \in [0, 1]^m$, where f is an objective function such that $C(\boldsymbol{x} + \boldsymbol{\delta}) = t$ if and only if $f(\boldsymbol{x} + \boldsymbol{\delta}) \leq 0$. In particular, when $\| \cdot \|_p$ is externalized as L_0, L_2 or L_∞, the attack can be denoted by CWL_0, CWL_2 or CWL_∞, respectively.

Madry et al. [10] presented a variation of BIM by performing projected gradient descent for randomly chosen starting points inside $\boldsymbol{x} + S$, called the PGD attack. PGD is formalized as: $\boldsymbol{x}^{t+1} = \prod_{\boldsymbol{x}+S}(\boldsymbol{x}^t + \alpha\mathrm{sign}(\nabla_{\boldsymbol{x}}L(\theta, \boldsymbol{x}, y)))$, where S is a fixed set of possible perturbations and serves as the boundary for the adversarial perturbations.

3   Adversarial Attacks and the L_p-Norm

Existing adversarial attacks usually utilize the L_p-norm to bound the perturbations to reach the imperceptibility. Table 1 lists some typical adversarial attacks and the L_p-norms (e.g., L_0, L_2 and L_∞) they utilize.

Table 1. Different attacks and the L_p-norms they utilize.

	FGSM	JSMA	DeepFool	BIM	CW			PGD
					CWL_0	CWL_2	CWL_∞	
L_0		✓			✓			
L_2			✓			✓		
L_∞	✓			✓			✓	✓

However, the L_p-norm is actually not a perfect choice for measuring the imperceptibility of adversarial examples. We give some examples in Fig. 1. In each subfigure, the first image is the clean image from the MNIST[1] database, the second is the adversarial image generated by CW [2], and the third is our manually perturbed image. In Fig. 1(a) and Fig. 1(b), the manually perturbed image is obtained by changing the value of all the background pixels from 0.0 to 0.1 (note that the raw pixel values are normalized to the range of $[0, 1]$). Compared with the adversarial image generated by CWL_0 or CWL_2, our manually perturbed image has a larger L_0 or L_2 value, but the difference between the manually perturbed image and the clean image is clearly more imperceptible to humans. In Fig. 1(c), the manually perturbed image is obtained by changing the value of the first nonzero pixel in the clean image from 0.329 to 1.0. It can be seen that the manually perturbed image has a larger L_∞ value, but the perturbations in it are more imperceptible than those in the adversarial image generated by CWL_∞.

---

[1] http://yann.lecun.com/exdb/mnist/.

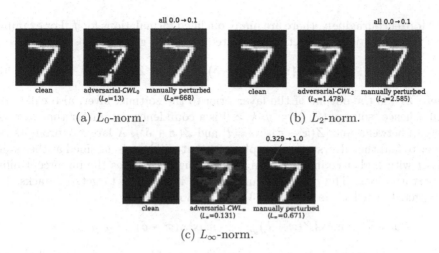

(a) L_0-norm.   (b) L_2-norm.

(c) L_∞-norm.

Fig. 1. L_p-norm and imperceptibility of the adversarial images generated by CW and our manually perturbed images.

4   Non-norm-bounded Attack

We now introduce our proposed non-norm-bounded attack for generating adversarial examples. First, we formally define the problem of finding an adversarial instance for the original example x as follows:

$$\text{obj } C(x + \delta) = t$$
$$\text{s.t. } x + \delta \in [l, \ h]^n \tag{1}$$

where C denotes the target neural network model, δ are the perturbations added to the original example x, $x + \delta$ denotes the adversarial example, and t is the target class label. If we want to perform an untargeted attack, we can just let $C(x + \delta) \neq y_{true}$. Equation (1) consists of only one objective function and one constraint. Therefore, the process of generating the adversarial example is to find the perturbations δ that can make the model misclassify the perturbed example to the target class such that the result is still in the valid range $[l, \ h]^n$. We do not adopt the L_p-norm as a constraint in (1). On the one hand, as mentioned above, the L_p-norm cannot accurately measure the imperceptibility; on the other hand, it is possible to find an attack method that satisfies the requirements of both misclassification and imperceptibility.

Inspired by the CW attack [2], if there is an objective function f such that $C(x + \delta) = t$ if and only if $f(x + \delta) \leq 0$, then we can externalize the problem (1) as:

$$\min f(x + \delta)$$
$$\text{s.t. } x + \delta \in [l, \ h]^n \tag{2}$$

More encouragingly, there are many qualified formulations for f. For example, the following objective function suggested in [2] is a good choice.

$$f(x + \delta) = \max\{\max[Z(x + \delta)_i : i \neq t] - Z(x + \delta)_t, \ -k\} \qquad (3)$$

where $Z(\cdot)$ is the output of the layer prior to the softmax layer, also called the logits; hence, softmax$(Z(\cdot)) = y$. $k \geq 0$ is a confidence parameter that controls the gap between $\max[Z(x + \delta)_i : i \neq t]$ and $Z(x + \delta)_t$. A larger k prompts the solver to find the adversarial example $x + \delta$ that will be misclassified as the target class t with higher confidence, which accordingly sacrifices the imperceptibility of perturbations. The objective function (3) is used for targeted attacks. For untargeted attacks, the function (3) can be modified as:

$$f(x + \delta) = \max\{Z(x + \delta)_{y_{true}} - \max[Z(x + \delta)_i : i \neq y_{true}], \ -k\} \qquad (4)$$

As is well known, (2) is an optimization problem over $\mathbb{R}^n$ with box constraints. There are some dedicated optimization approaches that handle box constraints, e.g., projected gradient descent and L-BFGS-B, i.e., L-BFGS with box constraints. For the following comparative study, we introduce an alternative approach, namely, change-of-variables, which was also used in [2].

Since $-1 \leq \tanh(w) \leq 1$, we can apply a nonlinear transformation to force $x + \delta$ to be in the box $[l, h]^n$. In particular, define a function g as:

$$g(w) = m \cdot \tanh(w) + p;$$
$$\text{where } m = \frac{h - l}{2}, \ p = \frac{h + l}{2} \qquad (5)$$

It is easy to confirm that $l \leq g(w) \leq h$. Therefore, just let $x + \delta = g(w)$, and (2) is equivalent to the following unconstrained optimization problem:

$$\min f(g(w)) \qquad (6)$$

We can then employ some commonly used optimization algorithms such as stochastic gradient descent, gradient descent with momentum and Adam [7] to solve the above unconstrained problem and are not limited to those that explicitly support box constraints. Note that the initial value for w is critical for finding the optimal solution, and also impacts the convergence speed of the optimization algorithm. As we know, the adversarial example may have a limited distance from the original one. Therefore, we can set the initial value for w as follows: let $x = g(w) = m \cdot \tanh(w_{init}) + p$, and w takes the initial value with $w_{init} = \text{arctanh}((x - p)/m)$.

Suppose w_{opt} is the optimal solution to the problem (6), then $x + \delta$, namely, the adversarial example, can be derived as:

$$x + \delta = m \cdot \tanh(w_{opt}) + p \qquad (7)$$

5   Experiments

We evaluate our non-norm-bounded attack (also sometimes abbreviated as NNBA) on three commonly used datasets: MNIST, CIFAR-10[2] and ImageNet[3]. We also compare NNBA with CW [2].

5.1   Experimental Setup and Evaluation Metrics

We trained two networks on the MNIST and CIFAR-10 datasets. The network architectures and the training approaches are identical to those presented in [2]. We achieve a 99.39% testing accuracy on MNIST and 78.17% on CIFAR-10. For the ImageNet dataset, we use the pre-trained Inception v3 network [13], which achieves approximately 96% top-5 accuracy.

To evaluate the attack comprehensively, we adopt the following evaluation metrics as presented in [9], namely MR (Misclassification ratio), AC_{adv} (Average confidence of the adversarial class), AC_{true} (Average confidence of the true class), R_{NT} (Robustness to noise tolerance), R_{GB} (Robustness to Gaussian blur), R_{IC} (Robustness to image compression) and ATC (Average time cost for generating one adversarial example).

5.2   Results on MNIST and CIFAR-10

Figure 2 illustrates some untargeted adversarial examples crafted by NNBA and CW on MNIST. The leftmost column is the original clean images, and the next four columns show the adversarial examples crafted by NNBA, CWL_0, CWL_2 and CWL_∞. We can see that the adversarial examples crafted by NNBA, CWL_2 and CWL_∞ achieve high imperceptibility, but the adversarial examples crafted by CWL_0 contain some visually noticeable perturbations. Figure 3 shows some untargeted adversarial examples on CIFAR-10. We can see that the adversarial examples crafted by NNBA, CWL_2 and CWL_∞ are visual indistinguishable from the clean ones, but obviously the perturbations made by CWL_0 are noticeable.

We then compare NNBA with CW based on the aforementioned evaluation metrics. We randomly select 1000 testing examples that are correctly classified by the corresponding model. For targeted attacks (TA), the target labels are randomly chosen from the remaining (non-original) classes. For metric R_{GB}, the radius of Gaussian blur is set to 0.5. For metric R_{IC}, we use Guetzli [1] as the image compression algorithm and the compression quality is set to 90%.

The comparison results are shown in Table 2. For MNIST dataset, we can see that for untargeted attacks (UA), in terms of the misclassification metrics, NNBA achieves the highest MR of 100%, the largest AC_{adv} of 0.522 and the smallest AC_{true} of 0.449; in terms of the robustness metrics, NNBA achieves the largest R_{NT} and R_{IC}, but with R_{GB} smaller than that of CWL_0. For targeted attacks (TA), NNBA performs the best in terms of MR, AC_{true}, R_{NT} and R_{IC},

---

[2] http://www.cs.toronto.edu/~kriz/cifar.html.
[3] http://www.image-net.org/.

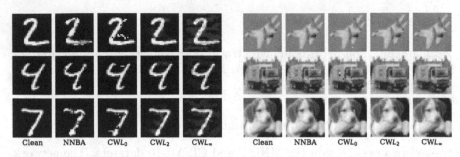

Fig. 2. Visual illustrations of *untargeted* adversarial examples crafted by NNBA and CW on MNIST.

Fig. 3. Visual illustrations of *untargeted* adversarial examples crafted by NNBA and CW on CIFAR-10.

but with AC_{adv} and R_{GB} smaller than those of CWL_0. Both NNBA and CW show a strong attack ability with very high misclassification rates of nearly 100%. Neither NNBA nor CW demonstrates robustness to Gaussian blur. However, only NNBA can resist the image compression by achieving an R_{IC} of 97.2% on untargeted attacks and 91.1% on targeted attacks. Moreover, the time cost of NNBA is lower than that of CW, and is especially lower by orders of magnitude than that of CWL_0 and CWL_∞.

Table 2. Comparisons between NNBA and CW on MNIST and CIFAR-10.

Dataset	Attack		Misclassification			Robustness			Time Cost
			MR	AC_{adv}	AC_{true}	R_{NT}	R_{GB}	R_{IC}	ATC/s
MNIST	NNBA	UA	100%	**0.522**	**0.449**	**0.072**	12.1%	**97.2%**	**0.288**
		TA	100%	0.370	**0.280**	**0.038**	5.2%	**91.1%**	**0.304**
	CWL_0	UA	100%	0.505	0.484	0.021	**12.6%**	88.3%	112.087
		TA	100%	**0.389**	0.352	0.016	**7.0%**	83.2%	109.334
	CWL_2	UA	99.8%	0.500	0.497	0.003	5.5%	34.6%	0.409
		TA	100%	0.381	0.374	0.003	1.4%	36.1%	0.443
	CWL_∞	UA	99.9%	0.501	0.496	0.006	5.6%	39.5%	88.389
		TA	100%	0.381	0.374	0.004	1.2%	36.2%	87.587
CIFAR-10	NNBA	UA	100%	**0.871**	**0.112**	**0.751**	46.6%	30.0%	**0.053**
		TA	100%	**0.686**	**0.083**	**0.496**	21.6%	7.0%	**0.049**
	CWL_0	UA	100%	0.502	0.483	0.019	31.4%	**39.6%**	13.837
		TA	100%	0.380	0.345	0.010	14.8%	**15.1%**	15.369
	CWL_2	UA	100%	0.527	0.463	0.064	21.9%	14.1%	0.059
		TA	100%	0.393	0.346	0.033	7.1%	2.0%	0.671
	CWL_∞	UA	100%	0.683	0.305	0.376	33.4%	22.3%	6.056
		TA	100%	0.487	0.249	0.184	11.0%	3.6%	7.639

For CIFAR-10 dataset, we find that both NNBA and CW achieves a MR of 100% for untargeted and targeted attacks. However, the adversarial examples crafted by NNBA have higher confidence than those crafted by CW since NNBA achieves a larger AC_{adv} and a smaller AC_{true}. The metric R_{NT} also corroborates this finding. On the CIFAR-10 dataset, neither NNBA nor CW can remain robust enough to Gaussian blur or image compression. NNBA just achieves an R_{GB} of 46.6% and an R_{IC} of 30.0% while conducting untargeted attacks. In terms of the time cost, NNBA obviously outperforms CW.

Therefore, we can conclude that our NNBA achieves a comparable and even better misclassification performance than CW; moreover, adversarial examples crafted by NNBA achieves higher confidence, more robustness and lower computational cost than those crafted by CW.

5.3   Results on ImageNet

We further evaluated NNBA on the ImageNet dataset. Due to the high computational cost, we just select 100 correctly classified images and randomly conduct untargeted or targeted attacks. The experimental results show that our NNBA can also be applied to attack large-scale networks such as Inception-v3. Additionally, attacks on ImageNet are particularly successful, and the misclassification rate can reach 100%. Figure 4 shows some adversarial examples crafted by NNBA on ImageNet. It can be seen that the perturbations generated by NNBA are so imperceptible that we cannot visually perceive the changes in the adversarial examples.

Fig. 4. Adversarial examples crafted by NNBA on ImageNet.

6   Conclusion

We propose a novel non-norm-bounded attack for generating adversarial examples to deceive neural networks. Our attack is apparently different from the existing adversarial attacks, which usually adopt the L_p-norm or other distance metrics to bound the adversarial perturbations. We systematically evaluated NNBA on the MNIST, CIFAR-10 and ImageNet datasets. The experimental results show that NNBA achieves comparable and even better misclassification performance than the state-of-the-art attacks. Additionally, adversarial examples crafted by NNBA achieve relatively higher confidence, more robustness and lower computational cost. As a new type of adversarial attack, our work poses grave challenges for some defenses, especially provable or certified defenses. Future work will concentrate on finding new types of non-norm-bounded attacks, explaining the reason for the existence of adversarial examples and improving the robustness of machine learning models.

References

1. Alakuijala, J., Obryk, R., Stoliarchuk, O., Szabadka, Z., Vandevenne, L., Wassenberg, J.: Guetzli: perceptually guided JPEG encoder. CoRR abs/1703.04421 (2017)
2. Carlini, N., Wagner, D.: Towards evaluating the robustness of neural networks. In: Proceedings of 2017 IEEE Symposium on Security and Privacy, pp. 39–57. IEEE (2017)
3. Gehring, J., Auli, M., Grangier, D., Yarats, D., Dauphin, Y.N.: Convolutional sequence to sequence learning. In: Proceedings of the 34th International Conference on Machine Learning, pp. 1243–1252 (2017)
4. Goodfellow, I.J., Shlens, J., Szegedy, C.: Explaining and harnessing adversarial examples. In: Proceedings of the 3rd International Conference on Learning Representations (2015)
5. Graves, A., Mohamed, A., Hinton, G.E.: Speech recognition with deep recurrent neural networks. In: IEEE International Conference on Acoustics, Speech and Signal Processing, pp. 6645–6649. IEEE (2013)
6. He, K., Zhang, X., Ren, S., Sun, J.: Deep residual learning for image recognition. In: Proceedings of 2016 IEEE Conference on Computer Vision and Pattern Recognition, pp. 770–778 (2016)
7. Kingma, D.P., Ba, J.: Adam: a method for stochastic optimization. In: Proceedings of the 3th International Conference on Learning Representations (2015)
8. Kurakin, A., Goodfellow, I., Bengio, S.: Adversarial machine learning at scale. In: Proceedings of the 5th International Conference on Learning Representations (2017)
9. Ling, X., Ji, S.: DEEPSEC: a uniform platform for security analysis of deep learning model. In: Proceedings of the 35th International Conference on Machine Learning, pp. 5283–5292 (2018)
10. Madry, A., Makelov, A., Schmidt, L., Tsipras, D., Vladu, A.: Towards deep learning models resistant to adversarial attacks. In: Proceedings of the 6th International Conference on Learning Representations (2018)
11. Moosavi-Dezfooli, S.M., Fawzi, A., Frossard, P.: DeepFool: a simple and accurate method to fool deep neural networks. In: Proceedings of 2016 IEEE Conference on Computer Vision and Pattern Recognition, pp. 2574–2582 (2016)
12. Papernot, N., McDaniel, P., Jha, S., Fredrikson, M., Celik, Z.B., Swami, A.: The limitations of deep learning in adversarial settings. In: Proceedings of 2016 IEEE European Symposium on Security and Privacy, pp. 372–387 (2016)
13. Szegedy, C., Vanhoucke, V., Ioffe, S., Shlens, J., Wojna, Z.: Rethinking the inception architecture for computer vision. In: Proceedings of 2016 IEEE Conference on Computer Vision and Pattern Recognition, pp. 2818–2826 (2016)
14. Szegedy, C., et al.: Intriguing properties of neural networks. In: Proceedings of the 2nd International Conference on Learning Representations (2014)

Sparse Asynchronous Distributed Learning

Dmitry Grischenko[1,2]($\boxtimes$), Franck Iutzeler[1], and Massih-Reza Amini[2]

[1] Department of Statistics (LJK), Université Grenoble Alpes, CNRS, Grenoble, France
dmitry.grischenko@univ-grenoble-alpes.fr,
franck.iutzeler@univ-grenoble-alpes.fr
[2] Department of Computer Science (LIG), Université Grenoble Alpes, CNRS, Grenoble, France
massih-reza.amini@univ-grenoble-alpes.fr

Abstract. In this paper, we propose an asynchronous distributed learning algorithm where parameter updates are performed by worker machines simultaneously on a local sub-part of the training data. These workers send their updates to a master machine that coordinates all received parameters in order to minimize a global empirical loss. The communication exchanges between workers and the master machine are generally the bottleneck of most asynchronous scenarios. We propose to reduce this communication cost by a sparsification mechanism which, for each worker machine, consists in randomly and independently choosing some local update entries that will not be transmitted to the master. We provably show that if the probability of choosing such local entries is high and that the global loss is strongly convex, then the whole process is guaranteed to converge to the minimum of the loss. In the case where this probability is low, we empirically show on three datasets that our approach converges to the minimum of the loss in most of the cases with a better convergence rate and much less parameter exchanges between the master and the worker machines than without using our sparsification technique.

Keywords: Asynchronous optimization · Sparsification

1 Introduction

Given the tremendous production of data and the ever growing size of collections, there is a surge of interest in both Machine Learning and Optimization communities for the development of efficient and scalable distributed learning strategies. In such context, training observations are generally split over different

Electronic supplementary material The online version of this chapter (https://doi.org/10.1007/978-3-030-63823-8_50) contains supplementary material, which is available to authorized users.

H. Yang et al. (Eds.): ICONIP 2020, CCIS 1333, pp. 429–438, 2020.
https://doi.org/10.1007/978-3-030-63823-8_50

computing nodes and learning is performed simultaneously where each node, also referred to as a *worker*, has its own memory and processing unit. Note that this is different from shared-memory parallel computing, where each worker machine can potentially have access to all available memory [9,17]. However, the bottleneck of distributed learning is the network bandwidth as for parameter tuning, information is exchanged across the nodes that are organized across a LAN. Most of the distributed algorithms perform parameter updates in a synchronized manner [2,4]. For these approaches, the slower worker machines may slow down the whole learning process as the faster ones have to wait all updates in order to terminate their computation and exchange information. Recently, many studies have focused on asynchronous distributed frameworks, where worker machines update their parameters simultaneously on a local sub-part of data and send their updated parameters to a master machine. The master integrates then all received parameters and broadcasts them back to each computing node for a new local update of their parameters [8,14]. The communication cost between workers and the master machine is generally prohibitive in asynchronous scenarios and most attention has been paid on reducing this cost [11,12,18]. In this way, asynchronous coordinate descent methods were proposed in [7,16]. These techniques are able to handle unbounded delays but they are based on decreasing stepsizes. To overcome this restriction, the recent works of [13,14] provide a delay-independent analysis technique that allows to integrate assumptions on the computing system with a constant stepsize and which was shown to outperform other asynchronous distributed strategies.

In this paper, we propose a first theoretically founded Sparse asynchrOnous Distributed leArning framework (called SODA). Our strategy aims to reduce the size of communications where just a part of the information is transmitted from a worker to the master in order to accelerate the convergence of delay-independent asynchronous distributed methods using a sparsification mechanism. This is done trough a sparsification mechanism that consists in choosing some local update entries that will not be transmitted to the master. Moreover, in the case of ℓ_1-regularized problems, we show that at the master level, update iterates identify some sparsity pattern in finite time with probability one, resulting in sparse downward communications from the master to the workers. Thus, communications in both directions (from the workers to the master and vice versa) become sparse. As a consequence, we leverage on this identification to improve our sparsification technique by preferably sampling the entries in the support of the master model. We show that in the case of strongly convex objectives, the convergence to the global empirical risk estimated over the whole training set is guaranteed when the probability of choosing such local entries is high. In the case where this probability is low, we empirically show on three datasets that our approach converges to the minimum of the loss in most of the cases with a better convergence rate than without using our sparsification strategy.

In the following section, we present our asynchronous distributed framework with sparse communication and prove in Sect. 3, that the approach is guaranteed to converge to the minimum of a strongly convex global empirical loss if entries of parameters transmitted to the master machine are randomly chosen with high probability. Section 4 describes experimental results that support this approach and Sect. 5 concludes this work by giving some pointers for some future work.

2   Asynchronous Distributed Learning with Sparsification

In this section we present our asynchronous distributed algorithm with sparse communications. Section 2.1 introduces the notation and problem formulation for asynchrony, and Sect. 2.2 presents the algorithm.

2.1   Notations and Framework

We consider the following distributed setup where there are M worker machines, $i \in \{1, \ldots, M\}$, each of which contains a subset $\mathcal{S}_i \subset \mathcal{S}$ of the training set (i.e. $\mathcal{S} = \sqcup_{i=1}^{M} \mathcal{S}_i$). Learning over such scattered data leads to optimization problems with composite objective of the form:

$$\min_{\boldsymbol{w} \in \mathbb{R}^n} \mathcal{L}(\boldsymbol{w}) = \sum_{i=1}^{M} \pi_i f_i(\boldsymbol{w}) + \lambda_1 \|\boldsymbol{w}\|_1, \tag{1}$$

where $\boldsymbol{w} \in \mathbb{R}^n$ are the parameters shared over all computing machines, $m = |\mathcal{S}|$ is the size of the training set, $\pi_i = |\mathcal{S}_i|/m$ is the proportion of observations locally stored in worker machine i, $f_i(\boldsymbol{w}) = \frac{1}{|\mathcal{S}_i|} \sum_{j \in \mathcal{S}_i} \ell_j(\boldsymbol{w})$ is the local empirical risk estimated on the subset $\mathcal{S}_i$ for machine i; ℓ_j is a smooth loss function for the training example $j \in \mathcal{S}_i$.

In this setting, our algorithm carries out computations without waiting for slower machines to finish their jobs. Each worker machine performs computations based on outdated versions of the main variable that it has. The master machine gathers the workers inputs, updates the parameters at each communication and sends back the updated versions to the current worker with which it is in interaction. We formalize this framework as :

- *For the master.* We define k, as the number of updates that the master has received from any of the worker machines. Thus, at time k, the master receives some input from a worker, denoted by i^k, updates its global variables, $\overline{\boldsymbol{w}}^k$ and $\boldsymbol{w}^k$; and sends $\boldsymbol{w}^k$ back to worker i^k.
- *For a worker $i \in \{1, \ldots, M\}$.* At time k, let d_i^k be the elapsed moment since the last time the master has communicated with worker i ($d_i^k = 0$ iff the master gets updates from worker i at exactly time k, i.e. $i^k = i$). We also consider D_i^k as the elapsed time since the second last update. This means that, at time k, the last two moments that the worker i has communicated with the master are $k - d_i^k$ and $k - D_i^k$.

Algorithm 1 SODA

Worker i	**Master**

Initialize $w_i = w_i^+ = \overline{w}^0$
 while not interrupted **do**
    Receive w from master
    Draw sparsity mask $\mathbf{M}_p$ as
 	
 $$\mathbb{P}[j \in \mathbf{M}_p] = \begin{cases} 1, & \text{if } j \in \text{supp}(w) \\ p, & \text{if } j \notin \text{supp}(w) \end{cases}$$
 	
    $w_i^+ = [w - \gamma \nabla f_i(w)]_{\mathbf{M}_p} + [w_i]_{\overline{\mathbf{M}_p}}$
    $\Delta = w_i^+ - w_i$
    $w_i = w_i^+$
    Send Δ to master
 end while
	Initialize $\overline{w}^0$
	 while not converged **do**
	    Receive Δ^k from agent i^k
	    $\overline{w}^k = \overline{w}^{k-1} + \pi_{i_k}\Delta^k$
	    $w^k = \text{prox}_{\gamma r}(\overline{w}^k)$
	    Send w^k to agent i^k
	 end while
	 Output w^k

2.2 Sparsity Mask Selection

Each worker independently computes a gradient step on its local loss for a randomly drawn subset of coordinates only. More specifically, the master machine keeps track of the weighted average of the most recent workers outputs, computes the proximity operator of the regularizer at this average point, and sends this result back to the updating worker i^k.

At iteration k, the randomly drawn subset of entries that worker i^k updates at time k is called *mask* and is denoted by $\mathbf{M}_p^k$ (in uppercase bold, to emphasize that it is the *only* random variable in the algorithm). We propose to select all the coordinates that are nonzero in the last parameter w received from the master machine, called $\text{supp}(w)$, and select some random zero entries of w with a fixed probability p (Algorithm 1). Without sparsification (i.e. $p = 1$ and $\mathbf{M}_1^k = \{1 \ldots, n\}$ at any time k), this iteration corresponds to the delay-independent asynchronous proximal-gradient algorithm proposed in [14].

The proposed algorithm SODA uses the following notation: for a vector of $w \in \mathbb{R}^n$ and a subset S of $\{1, .., n\}$, $[w]_S$ denotes the sparse vector where S is the set of non-null entries, for which they match those of w, i.e. $([w]_S)_{[i]} = w_{[i]}$ if $i \in S$ and 0 otherwise. In addition, we denote by $\overline{\mathbf{M}_p} = \{i \in \{1, \ldots, n\} : i \notin \mathbf{M}_p\}$.

In Algorithm 1, communications per iteration are (i) a blocking send/receive from a slave to the master (in blue) of size $|\mathbf{M}_p|$, and (ii) a blocking send/receive from the master to the last updating slave (in red) of the current iterate.

3 Theoretical Analyses

In this section, we first bound the expected deviation of the distance between a current solution found at iteration k and the true minimizer of the global loss (1) and then present our main result.

3.1 General Convergence Result

Lemma 1 (Expected deviation [6]). *Suppose all functions $\{f_i\}_{i=1,..,M}$ are μ-strongly convex and L-smooth (i.e. differentiable with Lipschitz continuous gradient). Let $\boldsymbol{w}^\star$ be the minimizer of the loss (1), and take $\gamma \in (0, 2/(\mu + L)]$, then for all $k \in [k_s, k_{s+1})$:*

$$\mathbb{E}\|\boldsymbol{w}^k - \boldsymbol{w}^\star\|^2 \leq (1 - \beta)^s \max_{i=1,..,M} \|\boldsymbol{w}_i^0 - \boldsymbol{w}_i^\star\|^2, \tag{2}$$

where $\boldsymbol{w}_i^\star = \boldsymbol{w}^\star - \gamma \nabla f_i(\boldsymbol{w}^\star); i \in \{1, \ldots, M\}$, and, the sequence of stopping times (k_s) defined iteratively as $k_0 = 0$ and

$$k_{s+1} = \min\left\{k : k - D_i^k \geq k_s \text{ for all } i\right\}, \tag{3}$$

and

$$\beta = 2\frac{\gamma\mu L}{\mu + L} - 1 + p.$$

This general result deserves several comments:

- The sequence (k_s) of stopping times is defined such that there are at least two updates of each worker between k_{s+1} and k_s. This sequence directly embeds the number of machines and the delays, and thus automatically adapts the various situations.
- Furthermore, we retrieve the convergence results of [13] in the case where there are no sparsification (i.e. $p = 1$), and if there is no delay, we recover the rate of vanilla proximal-gradient algorithm.
- Assuming that all machines are responsive (i.e. $s \to \infty$ when $k \to \infty$), the inequality (5) gives convergence if $\beta > 0$, i.e. $p > 1 - \alpha$. In other words, when we sample entries non-uniformly, we still have convergence if the probability of selection is big enough.
- Finally, when the problem is well-conditioned (i.e. $\mu \simeq L$ and thus $\alpha \simeq 1$), the algorithm is guaranteed to converge for any reasonable choice of p.

3.2 Sparsity Structure Identification and Effect on Communications

Recently, many studies have been conducted on introducing sparsity in the structure of parameters minimizing a learning objective with a ℓ_1-norm regularization term [1,3] and the identification of such sparsity structures with proximal gradient methods [5,15]. Unfortunately, proximal gradient algorithms with ℓ_1-norm regularization term featuring random values, as the mask that is used for sparsification of update, might not identify structure with probability one. However, as soon as an almost sure convergence is established, sparsity structure identification holds [10]. Taking into account that there is no almost sure convergence in our case let us adapt the identification result of [5] using the following Lemma.

Lemma 2 (Identification). *Suppose that that for any $\varepsilon > 0$ there exists iterate number K such that for any $k > K$ the average point $\|\overline{w}^k - \overline{w}^\star\|_2^2 < \varepsilon$ is ε-close to the final solution. Furthermore, let us assume that problem (1) is non-degenerate. That is :*

$$\left(\sum_{i=1}^{M} \pi_i \nabla f_i(w^\star)_{[j]} \right) < \lambda_1 \qquad \text{for all } j \in \text{supp}(w^\star). \tag{4}$$

Then for any $k > K$, we have: $\text{supp}(w^k) = \text{supp}(w^\star)$.

Now we are ready to present the following theoretical result that explains the practical interest of using the SODA algorithm in the case where the identification property takes place.

Theorem 1. *Suppose that all functions $\{f_i\}_{i=1,..,M}$ in (Eq. 1) are μ-strongly convex and L-smooth. Let $\gamma \in (0, 2/(\mu + L)]$, then in the case of identification of Lemma 2, $\text{supp}(w^k) = \text{supp}(w^\star)$, we have the following inequality:*

$$\|w^k - w^\star\|^2 \leq (1 - \alpha)^s C_i, \tag{5}$$

where $\alpha = 2\frac{\gamma\mu L}{\mu + L}$, $C_i = (1 - \alpha)^{-s_i}\|w^{k_{s_i}+1} - w^\star\|_2^2$, and $k_i \in [k_{s_i}, k_{s_i+1})$ be $k_i = \max\{k : \text{supp}(w^{k-1}) \neq \text{supp}(w^\star)\}$ with (k_s) the sequence of iterations defined in (3).

We can see from this theorem that after identification; the convergence rate does not depend on probability p. This means that communications become lessen with the same rate. On the other hand, as identification depends on this probability p, in practice, the selection of p should be a trade off between speed of identification and the size of sparsification.

4   Numerical Experiments

In the previous sections we proved the convergence of SODA in the case where the mask is formed with a high probability p. In this section, we present numerical results providing empirical evidence on a faster execution of SODA with lower communication cost than if the mask is not used.

4.1   Experimental Setup

In our experiments, we consider $\ell_1 - \ell_2$-regularized Logistic Regression surrogate loss that is common to many machine learning and signal processing applications and which can be minimized in a distributed way. With respect to our composite learning problem (1), that is:

$$\forall i \in \{1, \ldots, M\}, f_i(w) = \frac{1}{|S_i|} \sum_{(x_j, y_j) \in S_i} \left[\log\left(1 + e^{-y_j x_j^\top w}\right) + \frac{\lambda_2}{2}\|w\|_2^2 \right] \tag{6}$$

where $\mathcal{S}_i = (\mathbf{x}_j, y_j)_{j \in \{1,\ldots,|\mathcal{S}_j|\}} \in (\mathbb{R}^n \times \{-1, +1\})^{|\mathcal{S}_j|}$ is the sub-part of the training set stored in the worker machine $i \in \{1, \ldots, M\}$.

We performed experiments on three publicly available datasets[1]. Each dataset is normalized by dividing each feature characteristic by the maximum of the absolute value in the column using the scikit-learn Transformer API.[2] In Table 1, we present some statistics for these datasets as well as the percentage of no-zero entries of the final parameter (supp($\boldsymbol{w}^\star$)).

Table 1. Statistics of datasets used in our experiments: λ_1, λ_2 are respectively the hyperparmeters corresponding to ℓ_1 and ℓ_2 regularization terms, and the percentage of non-zero entries of the final solution w.r.t. this selection.

Dataset	m	n	λ_1	λ_2	$|\text{supp}(\boldsymbol{w}^\star)|$ in (%)
Madelon	2000	500	2×10^{-2}	10^{-3}	7
real-sim	72309	20958	10^{-4}	10^{-3}	8.6
rcv1_train	20242	47236	10^{-4}	10^{-3}	4.1

For the communications between the master and the workers, we used the message passing interface for Python (MPI4py)[3]. We compared our approach SODA with its direct competitor DAve-PG [14] which was shown to outperform other state-of-the-art asynchronous distributed algorithms. For comparisons, we plot objective values as their relative distance to the optimum, referred to as suboptimality, with respect to time, and also with respect to iterations and the number of exchanges for different values of the probability p used in the mask. We also present the dependence of sparsity of iterates to the number itcrates.

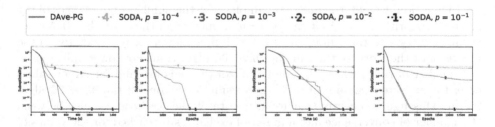

Fig. 1. Suboptimality versus time and epoch and the evolution of supp($\boldsymbol{w}^\star$) with respect to time for real-sim (left) and rcv1_train (right) datasets.

[1] https://www.csie.ntu.edu.tw/~cjlin/libsvmtools/datasets/.
[2] https://scikit-learn.org/stable/modules/generated/sklearn.preprocessing. normalize.html.
[3] https://mpi4py.readthedocs.io/en/stable/citing.html.

Speed of Convergence. Figure 1 presents suboptimality versus time and epochs for the DAve-PG algorithm [14], and the SODA algortihm with four values of probability p, to form the mask with $M = 20$ workers on real-sim and (top) rcv1_train (down) datasets. To this end, the minimum of the loss function (1), using (6), is first obtained with a precision $\epsilon = 10^{-15}$. As it can be observed, for larger values of the probability p; SODA converges much faster than DAve-PG (up to 2 times faster for $p = 10^{-1}$ on both datasets). This is mainly because that SODA passes through the whole data (epochs) in less time than DAve-PG.

Cost of Communication. We have computed the cost of communication, as the number of exchanges, between the master and the worker machines until convergence for different values of the probability p to form the mask. In the case where p is low, we know from the previous section that there is no guarantee that the algorithm SODA converges. However, note that as all workers are minimizing their local convex objectives, after one

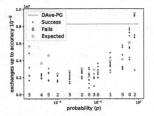

Fig. 2. Madelon dataset

round of communication between the master and all workers, it is easy to detect when the global objective (1) does not decrease at the master level and the algorithm can be stopped and restarted in this case. In Figure 2 we plot the amount of exchanges between the master and the workers for different values of the probability p used to form the mask on the madelon dataset. For each value of p; we run the algorithm 10 times. Blue dots correspond to successful runs where the algorithm converged to the minimum of the objective (1) up to the precision 10^{-15}. Red numbers at the bottom of the figure mention the number of times when the algorithm diverged and expected amount of exchanges are shown by orange stars.

In addition, we plot the line (in cyan blue) for the number of exchanges of the DAve-PG algorithm [14]. As it can be seen, in mostly all the cases the SODA algorithm converges to the minimum of (1) with much fewer exchanges between the master and the workers than in the DAve-PG algorithm. For lower values of p, the number of times where the algorithm converges is low and for larger values of p; the expected number of exchanges tends to the one of the DAve-PG algorithm. This figure suggests that for this dataset the best compromise between the number of convergence and number of exchanges is reached for the values of $p \in [0.01, 0.6]$.

Evolution of Sparsity. Let us now discuss the importance of sparsity, as the number of no-zero entries, of the final solution. Figure 3, shows the evolution of the percentage of no-zero entries of the parameter with respect to epochs on rcv1_train dataset for $M = 20$ workers and $\lambda_1 = 10^{-5}$. The sparsity of the solution increases over epochs for both DAve-PG and SODA algorithms.

This is mainly due to the use of the ℓ_1 in both algorithms. This sparsification is accentuated for SODA by the use of the mask. From previous plots, we observed that for higher values of the probability p, the proposed algorithm converges faster to the minimum of the composite objective. From this figure, it comes out that the SODA algorithm is able to identify the same set of informative non-zero entries, than DAve-PG, at convergence for higher values of the probability p.

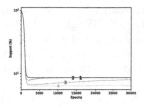

Fig. 3. rcv1_train dataset

5 Conclusion

In this paper, we proposed an asynchronous distributed learning algorithm with sparsification. The sparsification is induced through a mask that selects a sub-part of the model parameters constituted with all non-zero entries and some others chosen randomly with a fixed probability p. We have analyzed the convergence property of the algorithm by showing that when p is moderately high the algorithm is ensured to converge for strongly convex composite objectives. In the case of small values of p, we have empirically shown on three benchmarks that when the algorithm converges, it reaches faster the minimum with much less communications between the master and the worker machines than if the mask is not used.

References

1. Bach, F., Jenatton, R., Mairal, J., Obozinski, G., et al.: Optimization with sparsity-inducing penalties. Found. Trends® Mach. Learn. **4**(1), 1–106 (2012)
2. Boyd, S.P., Parikh, N., Chu, E., Peleato, B., Eckstein, J.: Distributed optimization and statistical learning via the alternating direction method of multipliers. Found. Trends Mach. Learn. **3**(1), 1–122 (2011)
3. Candes, E.J., Wakin, M.B., Boyd, S.P.: Enhancing sparsity by reweighted l 1 minimization. J. Fourier Anal. Appl. **14**(5–6), 877–905 (2008)
4. Chen, J., Monga, R., Bengio, S., Jozefowicz, R.: Revisiting distributed synchronous SGD. In: International Conference on Learning Representations Workshop Track (2016). https://arxiv.org/abs/1604.00981
5. Fadili, J., Malick, J., Peyré, G.: Sensitivity analysis for mirror-stratifiable convex functions. SIAM J. Optim. **28**(4), 2975–3000 (2018)
6. Grishchenko, D., Iutzeler, F., Malick, J., Amini, M.R.: Asynchronous distributed learning with sparse communications and identification. arXiv preprint arXiv:1812.03871 (2018)
7. Hannah, R., Yin, W.: On unbounded delays in asynchronous parallel fixed-point algorithms. J. Sci. Comput. **76**(1), 299–326 (2017). https://doi.org/10.1007/s10915-017-0628-z
8. Konečný, J., McMahan, H.B., Ramage, D., Richtárik, P.: Federated optimization: distributed machine learning for on-device intelligence. arXiv:1610.02527 (2016)

9. Kumar, V.: Introduction to Parallel Computing. Addison-Wesley Longman (2002)
10. Lee, S., Wright, S.J.: Manifold identification in dual averaging for regularized stochastic online learning. J. Mach. Learn. Res. **13**(1), 1705–1744 (2012)
11. Lin, Y., Han, S., Mao, H., Wang, Y., Dally, W.J.: Deep gradient compression: Reducing the communication bandwidth for distributed training. arXiv preprint arXiv:1712.01887 (2017)
12. Ma, C., Jaggi, M., Curtis, F.E., Srebro, N., Takáč, M.: An accelerated communication-efficient primal-dual optimization framework for structured machine learning. Optimization Methods and Software, pp. 1–25 (2019)
13. Mishchenko, K., Iutzeler, F., Malick, J.: A distributed flexible delay-tolerant proximal gradient algorithm. SIAM J. Optim. **30**(1), 933–959 (2020)
14. Mishchenko, K., Iutzeler, F., Malick, J., Amini, M.R.: A delay-tolerant proximal-gradient algorithm for distributed learning. In: Proceedings of the 35th International Conference on Machine Learning (ICML), vol. 80, pp. 3587–3595 (2018)
15. Nutini, J., Schmidt, M., Hare, W.: "active-set complexity" of proximal gradient: how long does it take to find the sparsity pattern? Optimization Lett. **13**(4), 645–655 (2019)
16. Sun, T., Hannah, R., Yin, W.: Asynchronous coordinate descent under more realistic assumptions. In: Advances in Neural Information Processing Systems (2017)
17. Valiant, L.G.: A bridging model for parallel computation. Commun. ACM **33**(8), 103–111 (1990)
18. Wangni, J., Wang, J., Liu, J., Zhang, T.: Gradient sparsification for communication-efficient distributed optimization. In: Advances in Neural Information Processing Systems, pp. 1306–1316 (2018)

Stable Training of Bellman Error
in Reinforcement Learning

Chen Gong[1], Yunpeng Bai[1], Xinwen Hou[1(✉)], and Xiaohui Ji[2]

[1] Institute of Automation, Chinese Academy of Sciences, Beijing, China
{gongchen2020,baiyunpeng2020}@ia.ac.cn, xwhou@nlpr.ia.ac.cn
[2] School of Information Engineering, China University of Geosciences in Beijing,
Beijing, China
xhji@cugb.edu.cn

Abstract. The optimization of Bellman error is the key to value function learning in principle. However, it always suffers from unstable training and slow convergence. In this paper, we investigate the problem of optimizing Bellman error distribution, aiming at stabilizing the process of Bellman error training. Then, we propose a framework that the Bellman error distribution at the current time approximates the previous one, under the hypothesis that the Bellman error follows a stationary random process if the training process is convergent, which can stabilize the value function learning. Next, we minimize the distance of two distributions with the Stein Variational Gradient Descend (SVGD) method, which benefits the balance of exploration and exploitation in parameter space. Then, we incorporate this framework in the advantage actor-critic (A2C) algorithms. Experimental results on discrete control problems, show our algorithm getting better average returns and smaller Bellman errors than both A2C algorithms and anchor method. Besides, it would stabilize the training process.

Keywords: Bellman error · Stein variational gradient descent · Value function optimization · Stationary random process · Kullback-leibler divergence

1 Introduction

While training a reinforcement learning (RL) model, the learning of value function is the key for the agent. However, RL algorithms are differently applicable for hard reality tasks, partially due to the slow convergence, unstable training, and other factors. A variety of solutions have been proposed to reduce the non-stationarity and incorrect updates, including experience replay, which stores the agent's data in an experience replay. The data can be batched [2,9–11,15,17] or randomly sampled from different time-steps [10]. However, experience replay requires more memory and it only applies to off-policy learning algorithms. Another approach from Bayesian inference constrains the distribution of network parameters with a posterior distribution to stabilize training

© Springer Nature Switzerland AG 2020
H. Yang et al. (Eds.): ICONIP 2020, CCIS 1333, pp. 439–448, 2020.
https://doi.org/10.1007/978-3-030-63823-8_51

[7,12]. However, there are too many network parameters, the complexity of the algorithm is very high, so it is necessary to reduce the instability of the algorithm from the Bellman error origin.

Our algorithm is inspired by the anchor method [12] and Stein Variational Gradient Descend (SVGD) [7], which constrain the distribution of network parameters. Actually, Bellman error follows a stationary random process. If the training process is convergent, Bellman error distribution on any time step will follow the same certain probability density distribution. Therefore, the Bellman error distribution can be considered consistent. Then, we propose a framework that the Bellman error distribution at the current time approximates the previous one to smooth the Bellman error distribution, in order to stabilize the value function learning stage, and further to stabilize the RL learning stage. What's more, we optimize our framework by utilizing SVGD, which benefits the balance of exploration and exploitation in parameter space.

2   Related Works

The Bellman error optimization is the key for deep RL learning. Deep Q-learning Network (DQN) [9] uses neural network to approximate the action state function. Dueling DQN [19] estimates the state value function and the advantage function instead of Q function. Schaul et al. propose the prioritized experience replay [14]. What's more, integrating the above algorithms, David et al. propose Rainbow [3].

Improving the training stability is a central topic in RL, there is a large body of related papers. By storing the agent's data in experience replay memory [2,9–11,15,17], agent uses this way to reduce non-stationarity and decorrelates updates. Trust Region Policy Optimization (TRPO) [15] and Proximal Policy Optimization (PPO) [16] use a simple distribution to approximate the complex state-action distribution. In Actor-Critic (AC) architecture [4], it combines the advantages of value based and policy gradient to increase the stability of the algorithm, and Asynchronous Advantage Actor-Critic (A3C) [8] runs multiple agents.

Prior work has also explored the use of network parameter distribution to RL learning. In anchor method [12] and Stein variational policy gradient (SVPG) [7] constrain the distribution of network parameters with a posterior distribution to stabilize training [7,12]. To our knowledge, we are firstly to optimal Bellman error distribution to stabilize the training stage in RL.

3   Preliminaries

3.1   Reinforcement Learning Background

Markov decision process (MDP) is a tuple, $(\mathcal{S}, \mathcal{A}, \mathcal{R}, \mathcal{P}, \eta)$, where $\mathcal{S}$ is a finite set of states, $\mathcal{A}$ is a finite set of actions, $\mathcal{R} : \mathcal{S} \times \mathcal{A} \times \mathcal{S} \to \mathcal{R}$ is the reward function, $\mathcal{P} : \mathcal{S} \times \mathcal{A} \times \mathcal{S} \to [0, 1]$ is the transition probability function, and $\eta \in [0, 1]$ is the discount factor.

The action value $Q^\pi(s,a) = \mathbb{E}_{\tau \sim \pi} \left[\sum_{i=0}^{\infty} \eta^i r_{t+i} | s_t = s, a_t = a \right]$ is the expected return for selecting action a in state s and following policy π. In policy π, $V^\pi(s) = \mathbb{E}_{\tau \sim \pi} \left[\sum_{i=0}^{\infty} \eta^i r_{t+i} | s_t = s \right]$ difines the state value function of s, which is the expected return for following policy π in state s.

Actor-Critic algorithm combines the benefits of policy gradient methods and value-based methods such as A2C [8]. Besides, A2C usually uses following equation as total objective function:

$$\mathcal{L}(\theta) = \mathbb{E}_{\tau \sim \pi} \left[\sum_{t=0}^{\infty} \log \pi \left(a_t | s_t; \theta \right) \left(R_t - b(s_t) \right) + \alpha \| R_t - V^\pi(s_t) \|^2 + \beta H \left(\pi \left(s_t | \cdot; \theta \right) \right) \right]$$

$$(1)$$

where $R_t = \sum_{i=1}^{\infty} \eta^{i-1} r_{t+i}$ is the accumulated reward from time step t; $H(\pi)$ is the entropy of policy and $b(s_t)$ is a baseline function. Usually $b(s_t)$ is replaced by value function $V^\pi(s_t)$; τ is a trajectory.

3.2 Stein Variational Gradient Descent (SVGD)

We describe the basic of the SVGD here, a method of approximate inference that integrates ideas from kernel method, Stein's method and variational inference. The readers can reference [5–7] for more details.

Assuming that $p(x)$ on $\mathcal{X} \subset \mathbb{R}^d$ is a positive and continuously differentiable probability density function (p.d.f), and $\phi(x) = [\phi_1(x), \cdots, \phi_d(x)]^\top$ is a smooth vector function. We aim to transport a set of initial points $\{x_i\}_{i=1}^n$ to approximate given target distribution $p(x)$.

SVGD achieves the approximation by iteratively updating a set of initial points $\{x_i\}_{i=1}^n$ with a deterministic gradient information: $x_i \leftarrow x_i + \epsilon \phi^*(x_i)$. ϵ is a small step size; $\phi^* : \mathbb{R}^d \rightarrow \mathbb{R}^d$ is a function chosen to maximumly decrease the KL divergence between the particle set and target distribution, and ϕ^* is defined as,

$$\phi^* = \arg\max_{\phi \in \mathcal{B}} \left\{ -\frac{d}{d\epsilon} \mathrm{KL} \left(q_{[\epsilon\phi]}(x) \| p(x) \right) \Big|_{\epsilon=0} \right\}$$

$$(2)$$

where $q_{[\epsilon\phi]}$ denotes the particles distribution updated using $x = x + \epsilon\phi(x)$ as $x \sim q$, and $\mathcal{B}$ is the unit ball of reproducing kernel Hilbert space (RKHS) $\mathcal{H}^d := \mathcal{H}_0 \times \mathcal{H}_0 \cdots \mathcal{H}_0$, $\mathcal{B} = \{ \phi \in \mathcal{H}^d : \ \|\phi\|_{\mathcal{H}^d} \leq 1 \}$. Liu & Wang prove that the objective in Eq. (2) can be transformed to a linear function of ϕ using Stein's method [5],

$$-\frac{d}{d\epsilon} \mathrm{KL} \left(q_{[\epsilon\phi]}(x) \| p(x) \right) \Big|_{\epsilon=0} = \mathbb{E}_{x \sim q(x)} \left[\mathrm{trace} \left(\mathcal{A}_p^\top \phi(x) \right) \right], \quad \mathcal{A}_p^\top \phi(x) = \nabla_x \log p(x)^\top \phi(x) + \nabla_x^\top \phi(x)$$

$$(3)$$

where $\mathcal{A}_p$ is called *Stein operator*; commonly, we consider $\mathcal{A}_p$ and the derivative operator ∇_x as $\mathbb{R}^d$ column vectors, so $\mathcal{A}_p^\top \phi$ and $\nabla_x^\top \phi$ are viewed as inner products, e.g., $\nabla_x^\top \phi = \sum_{i=1}^d \nabla_{x^i} \phi^i(x)$, and x^i and ϕ^i are the i-th variable of vector x and ϕ. Liu & Wang derive the solution of Eq. (3) [5],

$$\phi^*(\cdot) \propto \mathbb{E}_{x \sim q(x)} [\mathcal{A} k(x, \cdot)] = \mathbb{E}_{x \sim q(x)} \left[k(x, \cdot) \nabla_x \log p(x) + \nabla_x k(x, \cdot) \right]$$

$$(4)$$

where $k(x, \cdot)$ is a positive definite kernel associated with RKHS $\mathcal{H}$. Such we derive Stein variational gradient to make particles $\{x_i\}_{i=1}^n$ approximating $p(x)$.

4   Framework

4.1   Bellman Error in Reinforcement Learning

In actor network, state value function $V^\pi(s_t)$ denotes the expected return for following policy π in state s, which is the prediction of future rewards. We can derive the Bellman equation $V^\pi(s_t) = \mathbb{E}_{\tau \sim \pi}[r_{t+1} + \eta V^\pi(s_{t+1})]$ from state value function. Therefore, Bellman equation combines the $V^\pi(s_t)$ and $V^\pi(s_{t+1})$, which opens the door to value iterative method for calculating state value function.

In Deep RL, state value function is usually approximated using neural network: $V^\pi(s; \theta) \approx V^\pi(s)$. Let $V^\pi(s; \theta)$ be an approximate state value function with parameters θ. The parameters θ of the state value function $V^\pi(s; \theta)$ learned by iteratively minimizing a sequence of loss functions, which is called Bellman error, and the Bellman error distribution is defined as, $\mathcal{B}(X_t; \theta^{(T)}) = r_{t+1} + \eta V^\pi(s_{t+1}; \theta) - V^\pi(s_t; \theta)$, where X_t is a random variable which is equivalence to state s_t. $\mathcal{J}(X_t; \theta^{(T)})$ denotes the $p.d.f$ of Bellman error in time step T with state s_t.

Bellman error follows a stationary random process. When training process is convergent, $\mathcal{J}(X_t; \theta^{(T)})$ on any time step will follow the same probability density distribution. Naturally, we can use the $\mathcal{J}(X_t; \theta^{(T-1)})$ to restrict the $\mathcal{J}(X_t; \theta^{(T)})$, so that we can obtain more gradient information in time step T and get better training stability. In time step T, we formulate the optimization of $\mathcal{J}(X_t; \theta^{(T)})$ as the following regularized expected utility problem:

$$\min \left\{ \mathbb{E}_{\mathcal{J}(X_t; \theta^{(T)})} \left[\mathcal{B}(X_t; \theta^{(T)})^2 \right] + \gamma \mathbb{D}(\mathcal{J}(X_t; \theta^{(T)}) \| \mathcal{J}(X_t; \theta^{(T-1)})) \right\} \quad (5)$$

where $\mathcal{J}$ minimizes the expected utility, regularized by a KL divergence. By taking the derivative of the function in Eq. (5) and setting it to zero, we can show the optimal distribution of Bellman error distribution $\mathcal{J}(X_t; \theta^{(T)}) \propto \exp\{-\mathcal{B}(X_t; \theta^{(T)})^2\}$.

Merging the KL divergence and $\mathcal{L}(\theta)$, we derive the total objective function in this paper,

$$\mathcal{G}(\theta) = \mathcal{L}(\theta) + \gamma \mathbb{D}\left(\mathcal{J}(X_t; \theta^{(T)}) \| \mathcal{J}(X_t; \theta^{(T-1)}) \right) \quad (6)$$

4.2   Optimized with Stein Variational Gradient Descent

Obviously, the optimization of $\mathcal{L}(\theta)$ is simple, and we utilize Stein variational gradient descent (SVGD) [5] to optimize the $\mathbb{D}\left(\mathcal{J}(X_t; \theta^{(T)}) \| \mathcal{J}(X_t; \theta^{(T-1)}) \right)$.

SVGD is a non-parametric variational inference algorithm that leverages deterministic dynamics to transport a set of particles $\{x_i\}_{i=1}^n$ to approximate a target distribution. SVGD dose not confine the approximation in parametric families, and converges faster than MCMC because of the deterministic updates.

In our algorithm, SVGD updates the particles set $\{x_i\}_{i=1}^{n}$ via the direction function $\phi^*(\cdot)$, and $x_i = x_i + \epsilon\phi^*(x_i)$. $\phi^*(x_i)$ is the steepest direction to decrease the KL between the particle's distribution $\mathcal{J}(X_t; \theta^{(T)})$ and target distribution $\mathcal{J}(X_t; \theta^{(T-1)})$. The $\phi(x_i)$ is defined as [5],

$$\phi^*(x_i) = \mathbb{E}_{x_j \sim \mathcal{J}(X_t; \theta^{(T)})} \left[k(x_j, x_i) \nabla_{\hat{X}} \log \mathcal{J}(\hat{X}; \theta^{(T-1)})|_{\hat{X}=x_j} + \nabla_{\hat{X}} k(\hat{X}, x_i)|_{\hat{X}=x_j} \right] \tag{7}$$

where k is a positive kernel function. Notice that ϕ^* is the greedy direction that $\{x_i\}_{i=1}^{n}$ move towards $\mathcal{J}(X_t; \theta^{(T-1)})$. (Actually, $\phi^*(\cdot)$ is the maximization of directional derivative of $f(p) = \mathbb{D}(p\|q)$, which can be regarded as the gradient of $f(p)$.) Therefore, ϕ^* can be regarded as the gradient of $\frac{\partial \mathbb{D}\left(\mathcal{J}(x_i; \theta^{(T)})\|\mathcal{J}(x_i; \theta^{(T-1)})\right)}{\partial x_i}$.

However, our ultimate purpose is updating θ: $\frac{\partial \mathbb{D}\left(\mathcal{J}(x_i; \theta^{(T)})\|\mathcal{J}(x_i; \theta^{(T-1)})\right)}{\partial \theta}$. By chain rule,

$$\frac{\partial \mathbb{D}\left(\mathcal{J}(x_i; \theta^{(T)})\|\mathcal{J}(x_i; \theta^{(T-1)})\right)}{\partial \theta} = \frac{\partial \mathbb{D}\left(\mathcal{J}(x_i; \theta^{(T)})\|\mathcal{J}(x_i; \theta^{(T-1)})\right)}{\partial x_i} \frac{\partial x_i}{\partial \theta} \tag{8}$$

where $\phi^*(x_i)$ is defined in eq. (7). In our algorithm, the policy-value parameter θ is updated by common policy gradient algorithm. Therefore, the $\nabla_\theta \mathcal{G}(\theta)$ is concluded as,

$$\frac{\partial \mathcal{G}(\theta)}{\partial \theta} = \mathbb{E}_{\tau \sim \pi} \left[\frac{\partial \mathcal{L}(\theta)}{\partial \theta} \right] + \gamma \mathbb{E}_{x_i \sim P(s_{t-1}, a_t)} \left[\phi^*(x_i) \frac{\partial x_i}{\partial \theta} \right] \tag{9}$$

4.3 Exploration and Exploitation in Parameter Space

In fact, our algorithm also has advantages, which can explore and exploit the parameter space Θ better than original A2C. In Eq. (7), $\phi^*(\cdot)$ can be divided into two terms that play different roles in the exploitation and exploration respectively.

The first term is $k(x_j, x_i) \nabla_{\hat{X}} \log \mathcal{J}(\hat{X}; \theta^{(T-1)})|_{\hat{X}=x_j}$, which develops the exploitation in Θ. In the first term, the gradient $\nabla_{\hat{X}} \log \mathcal{J}(\hat{X}; \theta^{(T-1)})$ drives the θ towards the high probability regions of $\mathcal{J}(\hat{X}; \theta^{(T-1)})$ with information sharing across similar particles.

The second term $\nabla_{\hat{X}} k(\hat{X}, x_i)$ pushes the particles away from each other, and it likes a repulsive force that prevents all particles collapsing together into a local modes of $\mathcal{J}(\hat{X}; \theta^{(T-1)})$. For example, considering the RBF kernel: $k(x_i, x_j) = \exp\left(-\frac{1}{h}\|x_i - x_j\|^2\right)$. The second term is $\sum_j \frac{2}{h}(x_i - x_j)k(x_j, x_i)$. It derives x_i away form its neighboring x_j that have large $k(x_j, x_i)$. Actually, if we just utilize one particle ($n = 1$) and make $\nabla_{\hat{X}} k(\hat{X}, x_i) = 0$, Algorithm 1 will reduce to a single chain of typical gradient ascent for maximum a posterior (MAP) method.

Algorithm 1: Optimization of Bellman Error based on Stein

---

1   $\theta \leftarrow$ initialize network parameter
2   $\gamma \leftarrow$ initialize hyper-parameter
3   $\epsilon \leftarrow$ learning rate
4   $M \leftarrow$ the number of particles that samples form $\mathcal{J}(\hat{X}; \theta^{(T-1)})$
5   $s \leftarrow$ initial state
6   $T \leftarrow$ the counter
7   **repeat**
8   Draw a batch of data $\{s_t, a_t, r_t, s_{t+1}\}_{t=1}^n$ from enviroment
9   **for** *each* $s_t \in \{s_t\}_{t=1}^n$ **do**
10 | Draw M samples $\{x^i\}_{i=1}^M$ from $\mathcal{J}(\hat{X}; \theta^{(T-1)})$
11   **end**
12   Get the batch of data $\mathcal{X} = \{s_t, \{x_t^i\}_{i=1}^M, a_t, r_t, s_{t+1}\}_{t=1}^n$
13   **for** $i = 1, 2, \cdots, n$ **do**
14   **for** *particle* $j = 1, 2, \cdots, M$ **do**
15       $\phi^*(x_i) =$
       $\frac{1}{M} \left[k(x_i^j, x_i) \nabla_{\hat{X}} \log \mathcal{J}(\hat{X}; \theta^{(T-1)})|_{\hat{X}=x_i^j} + \nabla_{\hat{X}} k(\hat{X}, x_i)|_{\hat{X}=x_i^j} \right]$
16   x_i^j denotes the jth particle in $\{x_i^j\}_{j=1}^n$
17   **end**
18      $\triangle\theta \leftarrow \frac{1}{n} \sum_{i=1}^n [\nabla_\theta \mathcal{L}(\theta) + \gamma\phi^*(x_i)]$
19      $\theta \leftarrow \theta + \epsilon\triangle\theta$
20   **end**
21    $T \leftarrow T + 1$
22 **until** $T > T_{max}$;

---

5   Experiments

In this section, we design the experiments from 3 aspects as follow. The code of SVA2C can be found in this anonymized link:[1]

5.1   RL Algorithm in Our Framework

In our algorithm, we sample Bellman error by the embedding network [18] with the noise $\epsilon \sim \mathcal{N}(0, 0.1)$: $\eta(X, \epsilon)$, and the number of particles from each state s is 32. The Bellman error distribution in time step: $\mathcal{J}(X_t; \theta^{(T)})$ is assumed to be Gaussian distribution, which is defined as: sample a batch of $\{x_j^i\}_{j=1}^{n=32}$ from a given state s_i, $\mathcal{J}(X_t; \theta^{(T)}) = \mathcal{N}(X_t; \mu = \frac{1}{n} \sum_{j=1}^n x_j^i, \sigma^2 = \frac{1}{n} \sum_{j=1}^n (x_j^i - \mu)^2)$. In our experiments, the kernel function is RBF kernel $k(x_i, x_j) = \exp\left(-\frac{1}{h}\|x_i - x_j\|^2\right)$, where $h = \text{med}^2/\log n$, med is the median

---

[1] https://github.com/2019ChenGong/SVA2C.

of pairwise distances between the current particles $\{x_j^i\}_{j=1}^{n=32}$ [5]. Notice that in this way, the h changes adaptively across the iterations. As for the other hyper-parameters in RL, they are consistent with the parameters in OpenAI-baselines[2].

For comparisons, we implement our algorithm and two relevant algorithm: the original A2C method [8] and anchor method [12]. In anchor method, the loss function is defined as $\text{Loss}_{\text{anchor}} = \mathcal{L}(\theta) + \frac{\lambda}{N}\|\theta - \theta_0\|^2$, where θ_0 denotes the prior distribution of network parameters and θ is the current distribution of network. Anchor method is also a kind of Bayesian inference method. In our experiment, we combine the A2C algorithm and anchor method, and the hyper-parameters of RL framework are consistent with OpenAI-baseline. Besides, the hyper-parameters of anchor method are simply choosen the default parameters in follow link[3]. In conclusion, we implement the follow three algorithms:

Regular A2C: Basic A2C algorithm reference in OpenAI-Baselines, implemented $\eta(X)$ as the embedding network.

Stein variational A2C: Use $\eta(X, \epsilon)$ as the embedding network to sample the particles set from Bellman error distribution. Pseudo code of our algorithm is presented in Algorithm 1.

Anchor A2C: Use $\eta(X)$ as the embedding network. The settings of parameters are referenced the link[3] for details.

Figure (1) (a)–(h) show the performance of three A2C-based algorithm in gym Atari games (NoFrameskip-v4) [1]. We can see that our algorithm improves both sample-efficient and average return than A2C and anchor method in most environments.

5.2   Compared with Bellman Error

In Fig. (2) (a)–(h), we compare the Bellman error performance of our algorithm and A2C in eight games. What's more, all the hyper-parameter settings stay the same with the experimental setting in Sect. 5.1.

In ideal situation, the change in Bellman errors always is large in early stage of the training, due to the agent mainly focuses on exploration. Besides, in later stage of the training, the agent mainly focuses on exploitation. Obviously, our algorithm is more in line with the ideal situation in most games, because our algorithm can smooth the value function, obtain more gradient information in training stage.

5.3   The Balance of Exploration and Exploitation in Our Algorithm

In Eq. (7), the $\nabla_{x_j} k(x_j, x_i)$ equals to $\sum_j \frac{2}{h}(x_i - x_j)k(x_j, x_i)$ in ours experiment setting with $k(x_i, x_j) = \exp\left(-\frac{1}{h}\|x_i - x_j\|^2\right)$. Therefore, the bandwidth h regulates the weight of exploration in our algorithm to balance the exploration

---

[2] https://github.com/openai/baselines/tree/master/baselines/a2c.
[3] https://github.com/TeaPearce.

and exploitation. The larger h is, the more emphasis should be focued on exploration in our algorithm, and vice versa. We record the bandwidth h in Pong and
Seaquest games. In Fig. (3)(a)-(b), we can see that the h is large in early training
but decreasing gradually. It means that our algorithm emphasizes exploration
in the early training stage and exploitation in the later, which conforms to the
ideal training process of RL.

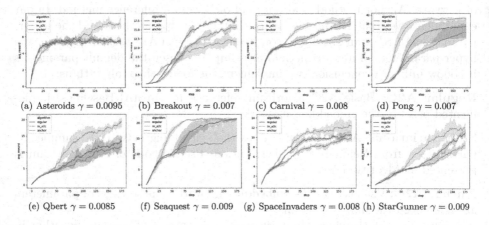

(a) Asteroids $\gamma = 0.0095$ (b) Breakout $\gamma = 0.007$ (c) Carnival $\gamma = 0.008$ (d) Pong $\gamma = 0.007$

(e) Qbert $\gamma = 0.0085$ (f) Seaquest $\gamma = 0.009$ (g) SpaceInvaders $\gamma = 0.008$ (h) StarGunner $\gamma = 0.009$

Fig. 1. Learning curves by SVA2C and two baselines.

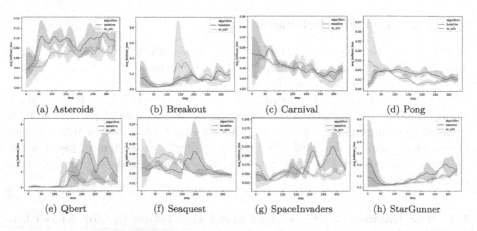

(a) Asteroids   (b) Breakout   (c) Carnival   (d) Pong

(e) Qbert   (f) Seaquest   (g) SpaceInvaders   (h) StarGunner

Fig. 2. Result of Bellman error by SVA2C and A2C.

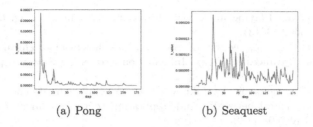

(a) Pong   (b) Seaquest

Fig. 3. Bandwidth h learning curves by our algorithm.

6   Conclusion

In this paper, we investigate the influence of optimizing Bellman error distribution, aiming at stabilizing the process of training. Then, we propose the framework restraining the Bellman error distribution. Therefore, we analysis the target distribution generated with historical data for current Bellman error distribution, and minimizing the distance of current distribution and target distribution using Stein variational gradient descent. We experimentally prove that compared with vanilla RL and anchor method our algorithm can improve the performance and reduce the Bellman error. Finally, we discuss that the reason that our algorithm fail to work in a few games, because the target distribution can not fit all games, which gives directions for our further work.

References

1. Bellemare, M.G., Naddaf, Y., Veness, J., Bowling, M.: The arcade learning environment: an evaluation platform for general agents. J. Artif. Intell. Res. **47**, 253–279 (2013)
2. Espeholt, L., Soyer, H., Munos, et al.: Impala: scalable distributed deep-rl with importance weighted actor-learner architectures. arXiv preprint arXiv:1802.01561 (2018)
3. Hessel, M., Modayil, J., Hasselt, V., et al.: Rainbow: combining improvements in deep reinforcement learning. In: Thirty-Second AAAI Conference on Artificial Intelligence (2018)
4. Konda, V.R., Tsitsiklis, J.N.: Actor-critic algorithms. In: Advances in neural information processing systems, pp. 1008–1014 (2000)
5. Liu, Q., Wang, D.: Stein variational gradient descent: a general purpose Bayesian inference algorithm. Adv. Neural Inf. Process. Syst. **29**, 2378–2386 (2016)
6. Liu, Q., Wang, D.: Stein variational gradient descent as moment matching. Adv. Neural Inf. Process. Syst. **31**, 8854–8863 (2018)
7. Liu, Y., et al.: Stein Variational Policy Gradient. arXiv:1704.02399 (2017)
8. Mnih, V., Badia, A.P., Mirza, M., et al.: Asynchronous methods for deep reinforcement learning. In: International conference on machine learning, pp. 1928–1937 (2016)
9. Mnih, V., Kavukcuoglu, K., Silver, et al.: Human-level control through deep reinforcement learning. Nature **518**(7540), 529–533 (2015). https://doi.org/10.1038/nature14236

10. Mnih, V., et al.: Playing atari with deep reinforcement learning. arXiv preprint arXiv:1312.5602 (2013)
11. Nachum, O., Gu, S.S., Lee, H., Levine, S.: Data-efficient hierarchical reinforcement learning. In: Advances in Neural Information Processing Systems, pp. 3303–3313 (2018)
12. Pearce, T., Anastassacos, N., Zaki, M., Neely, A.: Bayesian inference with anchored ensembles of neural networks, and application to reinforcement learning. arXiv preprint arXiv:1805.11324 (2018)
13. Pearce, T., Zaki, M., Brintrup, A., Anastassacos, N., Neely, A.: Uncertainty in neural networks: Bayesian ensembling. arXiv preprint arXiv:1810.05546 (2018)
14. Schaul, T., Quan, J., Antonoglou, I., Silver, D.: Prioritized experience replay. arXiv preprint arXiv:1511.05952 (2015)
15. Schulman, J., Levine, S., Abbeel, P., Jordan, M., Moritz, P.: Trust region policy optimization. In: International conference on machine learning, pp. 1889–1897 (2015)
16. Schulman, J., Wolski, F., Dhariwal, P., Radford, A., Klimov, O.: Proximal policy optimization algorithms. arXiv preprint arXiv:1707.06347 (2017)
17. Silver, D., Lever, G., Heess, N., Degris, T., Wierstra, D., Riedmiller, M.: Deterministic policy gradient algorithms (2014)
18. Tang, J., Qu, M., Wang, M., et al.: Line: Large-scale information network embedding. In: Proceedings of the 24th international conference on world wide web, pp. 1067–1077 (2015)
19. Wang, Z., Schaul, T., Hessel, M., Van Hasselt, H., Lanctot, M., De Freitas, N.: Dueling network architectures for deep reinforcement learning. arXiv preprint arXiv:1511.06581 (2015)

Supervised Level-Wise Pretraining for Sequential Data Classification

Dino Ienco[1]([⊠]), Roberto Interdonato[2], and Raffaele Gaetano[2]

[1] INRAE, UMR TETIS, LIRMM, Univ. Montpellier, Montpellier, France
dino.ienco@irstea.fr
[2] CIRAD, UMR TETIS, Montpellier, France
{roberto.interdonato,raffaele.gaetano}@cirad.fr

Abstract. Recurrent Neural Networks (RNNs) can be seriously impacted by the initial parameters assignment, which may result in poor generalization performances on new unseen data. With the objective to tackle this crucial issue, in the context of RNN based classification, we propose a new supervised layer-wise pretraining strategy to initialize network parameters. The proposed approach leverages a data-aware strategy that sets up a taxonomy of classification problems automatically derived by the model behavior. To the best of our knowledge, despite the great interest in RNN-based classification, this is the first data-aware strategy dealing with the initialization of such models. The proposed strategy has been tested on five benchmarks coming from three different domains, i.e., Text Classification, Speech Recognition and Remote Sensing. Results underline the benefit of our approach and point out that data-aware strategies positively support the initialization of Recurrent Neural Network based classification models.

Keywords: Supervised pretraining · Recurrent neural network · Multi-class classification · RNN initialization

1 Introduction

Deep Learning based approaches are commonly adopted to cope with a broad variety of signal analysis scenarios: Convolutional Neural Networks (CNN) have demonstrated their effectiveness in a plethora of different image analysis tasks [12] while Recurrent Neural Networks (RNN) have exhibited impressive results in one dimensional signal processing tasks such as Natural language processing and understanding, Speech Recognition and Remote sensing analysis [8,11,13]. Despite the fact that new neural network architectures are constantly proposed [2,7], the success of such approaches is a result of many advances in basic elements such as activation functions and initialization strategies. During the training process, neural networks are sensitive to the initial weights [14]. In particular, RNNs can suffer from "vanishing gradient" or instability if they are not correctly initialized [6]. In the context of RNN, few initialization approaches were proposed [3] which are generally task or data agnostic. Other strategies initialize network weights by exploiting pretrained models

© Springer Nature Switzerland AG 2020
H. Yang et al. (Eds.): ICONIP 2020, CCIS 1333, pp. 449–457, 2020.
https://doi.org/10.1007/978-3-030-63823-8_52

learned on big datasets [4,5] but such pretrained networks are not available in general cases. As shown in [14] for supervised classification tasks, neural network initialization is a critical issue that can prejudice good generalization performances on new unseen data.

With the aim to deal with RNN initialization, in this paper we propose a data/task-aware supervised pretraining strategy to initialize network parameters. Differently from existing approaches [3], where RNN models are initialized in a data agnostic setting, here we propose to leverage the basic RNN model behavior on the task at hand to set up a taxonomy of nested classification problems, ranked by increasing order of complexity. Following such hierarchy of classification tasks, weights are learnt and transferred through the different levels in a top-down fashion by means of sequential fine-tuning. Finally, the weights derived by such sequence of successive discrimination problems will be used to initialize the RNN based model dealing with the original classification task. Our approach can be seen as a self-pretrain/fine-tuning pipeline, which is adaptively built based on the specific task and dataset under analysis. To the best of our knowledge, the only work that tackles the issue of weight initialization considering a supervised data-aware setting is the one presented in [14]. Here, the authors propose a strategy to initialize a multi-layer perceptron model using a supervised pretraining involving the discrimination between real vs shuffled data, with no adaptation with respect to the specific task (data-aware but not task-aware).

To assess the performance and the behavior of our proposal, we conduct experiments on five benchmarks coming from three different domains, comparing our strategy with several baseline and competing approaches.

2   TAXO: Supervised Level-Wise Pretraining for Sequential Classification Based on RNN

In this section we introduce our supervised level-wise pretraining procedure to initialize the model weights of a generic Recurrent Neural Network dealing with multi-class classification tasks. We denote with $X = \{X_i\}_{i=1}^n$ the set of multivariate time series data. We underline that X can contain time-series with different lengths. We can divide the set of examples X in three disjoint sets: training set X^{train}, validation set X^{valid} and test set X^{test} where $X^{train} \cap X^{valid} = \emptyset$, $X^{train} \cap X^{test} = \emptyset$ and $X^{valid} \cap X^{test} = \emptyset$. Associated to X^{train} and X^{valid} we also have a class information: Y^{train} and Y^{valid}, respectively. Y^{train} and Y^{valid} are defined on the same set of classes: $Y_i^{train} \in C$ and $Y_i^{valid} \in C$ where $C = \{C_j\}_{j=1}^{|C|}$ is the set of classes and $|C|$ is the number of different classes. The supervised level-wise pretraining process has three steps driven by the task at hand in conjunction with the behavior of the model on the associated data:

Step 1. Given a training and a validation set (X^{train} and X^{valid}) with the corresponding class set (Y^{train} and Y^{valid}), the Recurrent Neural Network model is trained on (X^{train}, Y^{train}) while (X^{valid}, Y^{valid}) is used to perform an unbiased evaluation of the model while tuning the model weights. The model that achieves the best performances on X^{valid} across a fixed number of training epochs is retained. Here, the classification task is performed on the original set of classes C. The RNN model generated at this step is named M_0.

Step 2. Given the retained model M_0, we compute the confusion matrix between the prediction of M_0 on X^{valid} and Y^{valid}. Successively, for each class C_j, we compute the entropy associated to the prediction of that class:

$$Entropy(C_j) = -\sum_{k=1}^{|C|} p_{jk} \times \log p_{jk}$$

where p_{jk} is the probability of the class j to be misclassified with the class k. Such probability is obtained from the confusion matrix after it has been row-normalized to obtain a probability distribution with row-sums equal to 1. The entropy quantifies the uncertainty of the model M_0 on each class, i.e., a class that is misclassified with many other ones is associated with a bigger uncertainty value than a class that is always misclassified with just another class. Given that higher entropy values correspond to higher classifier uncertainty, the classes C_j are then ranked in decreasing order w.r.t. their uncertainty, producing the ranking R.

Step 3. We exploit the ranking R to produce a taxonomy of different classification problems on which the RNN will be pretrained for the multi-class classification tasks defined on the set of classes C. Given a depth parameter d, we proceed level-wise: we pick the first class of the ranking R, $C_{R(1)}$, and we build a binary classification task in which the training and validation examples (X^{train} and X^{valid}) associated to the class $C_{R(1)}$ have the label 1 while all the other examples have the label 0. We hence train the model (from scratch at this level), and generate the current model M_1. Then, we select the class in the second position of the ranking, $C_{R(2)}$, and add another class to the classification problem (3 classes at level 2). We fine-tune the model M_1 on the new three-class classification task obtaining the model M_2. The procedure continues level-wise until the level d is reached.

Generally speaking, the model M_t is trained (fine-tuned for $t > 1$) on a multi-class problem involving $t+1$ classes, where the first t classes are those in the set $\bigcup_{j=1}^{t} C_{R(j)}$ with the higher values of entropy and the last class groups together all the others original classes ($C \setminus \{\bigcup_{j=1}^{t} C_{R(j)}\}$). At the end of this process, the weights of the model M_d are employed to initialize the final RNN model that will tackle the original multi-class classification task defined on the set of classes C. Note that we deliberately choose to leave the maximum depth d as a free parameter, as a mean to control the computational burden of the method, but ideally the whole depth inferred by the total number of classes ($d = |C| - 1$) might be explored.

In practice, each classification stage is achieved by connecting the Recurrent Neural Network unit (LSTM or GRU) directly with an output layer with as many neurons as the number of involved classes. The decision is obtained via a SoftMax layer. Considering the main step of our approach, in which the different models ($M_1, ..., M_d$) are learnt, we only modify the output layer at each different level with a dense output layer with a number of neurons equal to the corresponding number of classes. The model weights that are transferred from one level of the taxonomy to another are the weights associated to the RNN unit.

The rationale behind our strategy is that it supports the weight learning exploration to focus on classes that are difficult to predict, modifying in a second time the previous weights to integrate the discrimination of "easier" classes in the model decision. In other words, it forces the learning trajectory to deal as soon as possible with the hard classes of the dataset with the aim to avoid biasing the final model towards the recognition of the easy (separable, representative) classes.

3   Experimental Evaluation

In this section we evaluate our supervised pretraining strategy on five real-world sequential datasets coming from three different domains: Text Classification, Speech Recognition and Remote Sensing (Satellite Image Time Series). In all such domains, RNNs are the common state of the art strategy to perform supervised classification [1,8,11]. For the first two domains Long-Short Term Memory (LSTM) is the RNN model that is usually employed [11] while Gated Recurrent Unit have demonstrated their ability to well fit remote sensing data analysis [8,10]. Considering both LSTM and GRU, we equipped the RNN models with an attention mechanism [1], a widely used strategy to allow RNN models to focus on the most informative portions of the input sequences. We name the RNN models equipped with our supervised level-wise pretraining strategy $LSTM_{taxo}$ and GRU_{taxo}. As baseline competitors, we take into account the following approaches: i) An RNN approach without any supervised pretraining, named $LSTM$ (GRU resp.) for Text Classification and Speech Recognition (Remote Sensing resp.) tasks. ii) An RNN approach with a supervised pretraining inspired by [14]. First, a copy of the dataset is created by independently shuffling, for each sample, the order of its elements in the sequence to break sequential dependencies. Then a binary classification task is set up to discriminate between examples coming from the original dataset and examples coming from the shuffled dataset. The network is firstly trained to solve the binary task. Finally, the weights of the network that have dealt with the binary task are employed as initialization of the RNN network dealing with the original multiclass task. We name such a competitor $LSTM_{sh}$ (GRU_{sh} resp.). iii) A variant of the proposed supervised pretraining approach in which the loss function, at the different levels of pretraining, is weighted using class cardinalities in order to cope with class unbalance (larger weights to classes with fewer samples). We name such competitor $LSTM_{taxo}^{W}$ (GRU_{taxo}^{W} resp.).

To assess the performances of the different methods we consider two standard metrics: Accuracy and F-Measure. The metrics are computed performing a train, validation and test evaluation considering 50%, 20% and 30%, respectively, of the original data. For each dataset and method, we repeat the procedure 5 times and we report average and standard deviation for each metric. LSTM models involve 256 hidden units and they are trained for 250 epochs while GRU models are deployed with 512 hidden units and trained for 1 000 epochs. We use Adam as optimizer to learn the model weights with a learning rate of 5×10^{-4} and a batch size of 32. For all the experiments we set the value of the d parameter to 3.

3.1 Text Classification

We consider a well known text classification dataset: the 20 Newsgroup text collection[1] (*20News*) that contains approximately 20 000 newsgroup documents, partitioned across 20 different newsgroups. In our evaluation, we consider a subset of the 20 Newsgroup dataset involving nine classes (*comp.graphics, comp.windows.x, rec.autos, rec.sport.hockey, sci.electronics, sci.space, sci.med, talk.politics.misc, talk.religion.misc*) for a total of 7 481 documents. The minimum, maximum and average document length are 18, 500 and 195, respectively. According to recent literature [16], each word is associated to the corresponding word embedding used as input to feed the Recurrent Neural Network model. To this end, we use Glove word embeddings [15] pretrained on Wikipedia 2014 with vector dimension equals to 100^{2}.

Table 1. F-Measure and Accuracy, average and std. deviation, on the 20Newsgroups classification task considering the different competing methods.

	20Newsgroups	
	F-Measure	Accuracy
LSTM	91.65 ± 0.60	91.65 ± 0.6
LSTM$_{Sh}$	92.13 ± 0.46	92.14 ± 0.45
LSTM$_{taxo}^{W}$	91.76 ± 0.97	91.77 ± 0.99
LSTM$_{taxo}$	$\mathbf{92.26 \pm 0.78}$	$\mathbf{92.27 \pm 0.79}$

Table 1 reports the F-Measure and Accuracy of the different competing methods on the 20 Newsgroup text collection. We can note that LSTM$_{taxo}$ achieves the best performances. Generally, all the data-aware strategy perform slightly better than the base approach without any pretraining (*LSTM*) on the textual classification task.

3.2 Speech Recognition Tasks

We consider two well known speech recognition tasks: Japanese Vowel (*JapVowel*) and Arabic Digits (*ArabDigits*) (cf. Table 2). The former sets up a classification task to distinguish among nine male speakers by their utterances

---

[1] http://qwone.com/jason/20Newsgroups/.
[2] https://nlp.stanford.edu/projects/glove/.

Table 2. Speech Recognition datasets characteristics

Dataset	# Samples	# Dims	Min/Max/Avg Length	# Classes
JapVowel	640	12	7/29/15	9
ArabDigits	8 800	13	4/93/39	10

of two Japanese vowels while the latter involves 88 different speakers (44 males and 44 females) pronouncing digits in Arabic language. For each benchmark, Frequency Cepstral Coefficients (MFCCs) are firstly extracted and, successively, multi-variate time series are constructed for each sample in the dataset.

Table 3. F-Measure and Accuracy, average and std. deviation, on the Speech Recognition tasks considering the different competing methods.

	JapVowel		ArabDigits	
	F-Measure	Accuracy	F-Measure	Accuracy
LSTM	94.53 ± 1.82	94.61 ± 1.74	99.42 ± 0.16	99.42 ± 0.16
$LSTM_{Sh}$	94.82 ± 1.67	94.84 ± 1.67	**99.69 ± 0.23**	**99.69 ± 0.23**
$LSTM_{taxo}^{W}$	**95.53 ± 1.61**	**95.53 ± 1.60**	99.58 ± 0.09	99.58 ± 0.09
$LSTM_{taxo}$	94.91 ± 2.80	95.05 ± 2.60	99.60 ± 0.10	99.60 ± 0.10

Table 3 reports on the Accuracy and F-Measure of the different competing methods on the two Speech Recognition datasets. We can observe that all the supervised pretraining methods ($LSTM_{Sh}$, $LSTM_{taxo}^{W}$ and $LSTM_{taxo}$) generally achieve higher performances than the baseline (LSTM). On the *JapVowel* benchmark, the two variants of our proposal obtain the best results, with $LSTM_{taxo}^{W}$ being the best performing method. This can be explained by the fact that, on such small sized dataset (640 samples), random sampling produces train, validation and test subsets with slightly different class distributions, making the loss weighting strategy more appropriate for generalization. On the *ArabDigits* speech recognition task, the best performances are obtained by the $LSTM_{Sh}$ approach with a very limited gain in terms of both F-Measure and Accuracy w.r.t. the competitors. Nevertheless, although the baseline strategy ($LSTM$) already achieves high discrimination performances on this dataset, we can see that $LSTM_{taxo}^{W}$ and $LSTM_{taxo}$ reach comparable scores, while slightly reducing the classification uncertainty compared to $LSTM_{Sh}$.

3.3 Remote Sensing Data Analysis

We consider two Satellite Image Time Series (SITS) land cover classification datasets: *Gard* and *Reunion* Island (cf. Table 4). Both datasets are preprocessed as done in [9]: starting from a suitable object layer, the spectral information is aggregated at segment level for each available timestamp, hence generating the multi-variate time series. The first dataset (*Gard*) [10], concerns a zone in the South of France, while the second one (*Reunion*) [9], focuses on Reunion Island, a French overseas department located in the Indian Ocean.

Table 4. Satellite Image Time Series datasets characteristics.

Dataset	# Samples	# Dims	Length	# Classes
Gard	1 673	16	37	7
Reunion	7 462	5	34	13

For both datasets, source imagery is acquired via the ESA Sentinel-2 (S2) mission[3]. The first dataset *Gard* uses a larger spectral information (10 bands from S2 at 10 and 20 m resolution, all resampled at 10 m) plus six radiometric indices [10] for a total of 16 channels for each timestamps, while the second dataset *Reunion* only includes four radiometric bands at 10 m of resolution plus the Normalized Differential Vegetation Index [9] for a total of 5 channels for each timestamps.

Table 5. F-Measure and Accuracy, average and std. deviation, on the Satellite Image Time Series datasets considering the different competing methods.

	Gard		Reunion	
	F-Measure	Accuracy	F-Measure	Accuracy
GRU	85.59 ± 1.35	85.74 ± 1.36	68.34 ± 0.52	70.46 ± 0.27
GRU_{Sh}	84.00 ± 1.10	84.00 ± 1.05	66.45 ± 2.08	68.66 ± 1.52
GRU_{taxo}^{W}	89.64 ± 1.64	89.74 ± 1.52	73.03 ± 2.81	74.33 ± 2.41
GRU_{taxo}	**90.84 ± 1.49**	**90.89 ± 1.48**	**76.77 ± 4.41**	**77.67 ± 3.84**

Results of the evaluation are reported in Table 5. It can be noted how in this case the proposed methods (GRU_{taxo} and GRU_{taxo}^{W}) significantly outperform the baseline (GRU). Differently from the previous experiments, we can note that the competitor based on timestamps shuffle (GRU_{Sh}) degrades the performances w.r.t. the baseline approach. This is not surprising due to the strong temporal dependencies that characterize such kind of data [10]. Here, the supervised level-wise pretraining clearly ameliorates the performances of the RNN approach and GRU_{taxo} demonstrated to be more effective that its variant involving the weighting loss mechanism (i.e., GRU_{taxo}^{W}). Note also that, differently to what happened on *JapVowel*, the SITS benchmarks are characterized by a strong class unbalance, with very close distributions on both training and test sets, which makes the unweighted loss strategy more effective.

---

[3] https://sentinel.esa.int/web/sentinel/missions/sentinel-2.

4   Conclusion

In this paper we have presented a new supervised level-wise pretraining strategy to support RNN-based classification. To the best of our knowledge, no previous work was proposed to deal with data/task-aware RNN initialization for classification tasks. Our strategy has been assessed on benchmarks coming from three different domains, i.e., Text Classification, Speech Recognition and Remote Sensing. On all domains, our proposal has achieved better or comparable performances w.r.t. the competing methods. Future research will be devoted to transfer the proposed strategy to other neural models, i.e. CNN, as well as to compress the level-wise taxonomy avoiding the choice of the depth parameter d.

References

1. Britz, D., Guan, M.Y., Luong, M.: Efficient attention using a fixed-size memory representation. In: EMNLP, pp. 392–400 (2017)
2. Cai, H., Zhu, L., Han, S.: Proxylessnas: direct neural architecture search on target task and hardware. In: ICLR (2019)
3. Choromanski, K., Downey, C., Boots, B.: Initialization matters: orthogonal predictive state recurrent neural networks. In: ICLR (2018)
4. Devlin, J., Chang, M., Lee, K., Toutanova, K.: BERT: pre-training of deep bidirectional transformers for language understanding. In: NAACL-HLT, pp. 4171–4186 (2019)
5. Ge, W., Yu, Y.: Borrowing treasures from the wealthy: deep transfer learning through selective joint fine-tuning. In: CVPR, pp. 10–19 (2017)
6. Glorot, X., Bengio, Y.: Understanding the difficulty of training deep feedforward neural networks. In: AISTATS, pp. 249–256 (2010)
7. Huang, G., Liu, Z., van der Maaten, L., Weinberger, K.Q.: Densely connected convolutional networks. In: CVPR, pp. 2261–2269 (2017)
8. Ienco, D., Gaetano, R., Dupaquier, C., Maurel, P.: Land cover classification via multitemporal spatial data by deep recurrent neural networks. IEEE Geosci. Remote Sensing Lett. **14**(10), 1685–1689 (2017)
9. Ienco, D., Gaetano, R., Interdonato, R., Ose, K., Minh, D.H.T.: Combining sentinel-1 and sentinel-2 time series via RNN for object-based land cover classification. In: IGARSS, pp. 3930–3933 (2019)
10. Interdonato, R., Ienco, D., Gaetano, R., Ose, K.: A dual view point deep learning architecture for time series classification. ISPRS J. Photogrammetry Remote Sensing **149**, 91–104 (2019)
11. Khalil, R.A., Jones, E., Babar, M.I., Jan, T., Zafar, M.H., Alhussain, T.: Speech emotion recognition using deep learning techniques: a review. IEEE Access **7**, 117327–117345 (2019)
12. Liu, W., Wang, Z., Liu, X., Zeng, N., Liu, Y., Alsaadi, F.E.: A survey of deep neural network architectures and their applications. Neurocomputing **234**, 11–26 (2017)
13. Mou, L., Ghamisi, P., Zhu, X.X.: Deep recurrent neural networks for hyperspectral image classification. IEEE Trans. Geosci. Remote Sensing **55**(7), 3639–3655 (2017)
14. Peng, A.Y., Koh, Y.S., Riddle, P., Pfahringer, B.: Using supervised pretraining to improve generalization of neural networks on binary classification problems. In: ECML/PKDD, pp. 410–425 (2018)

15. Pennington, J., Socher, R., Manning, C.D.: Glove: global vectors for word representation. In: EMNLP, pp. 1532–1543 (2014)
16. Wang, J., Wang, Z., Zhang, D., Yan, J.: Combining knowledge with deep convolutional neural networks for short text classification. In: IJCAI, pp. 2915–2921 (2017)

Toward an Ensemble of Object Detectors

Truong Dang, Tien Thanh Nguyen$^{(\boxtimes)}$, and John McCall

School of Computing, Robert Gordon University, Aberdeen, UK
t.nguyen11@rgu.ac.uk

Abstract. The field of object detection has witnessed great strides in recent years. With the wave of deep neural networks (DNN), many break-throughs have achieved for the problems of object detection which previously were thought to be difficult. However, there exists a limitation with DNN-based approaches as some architectures are only suitable for particular types of object. Thus it would be desirable to combine the strengths of different methods to handle objects in different contexts. In this study, we propose an ensemble of object detectors in which individual detectors are adaptively combine for the collaborated decision. The combination is conducted on the outputs of detectors including the predicted label and location for each object. We proposed a detector selection method to select the suitable detectors and a weighted-based combining method to combine the predicted locations of selected detectors. The parameters of these methods are optimized by using Particle Swarm Optimization in order to maximize mean Average Precision (mAP) metric. Experiments conducted on VOC2007 dataset with six object detectors show that our ensemble method is better than each single detector.

Keywords: Object detection · Ensemble method · Ensemble learning · Evolutionary computation · Particle swarm optimization

1 Introduction

Object detection is a problem in which a learning machine has to locate the presence of objects with a bounding box and types or classes of the located objects in an image. Before the rise of Deep Neural Networks (DNN), traditional machine learning methods using handcrafted features [13,22] were used with only modest success since these extracted features are not representative enough to describe many kinds of diverse objects and backgrounds. With the successes of DNN in image classification [11], researchers began to incorporate insights gained from Convolutional Neural Networks (CNN) to object detection. Some notable results in this direction include Faster RCNN [7] or You Look Only Once (YOLO) [16]. However, some object detectors are only suitable for specific types of objects. For example, YOLO struggles with small objects due to strong spatial constraints imposed on bounding box predictions [15]. In this study, we propose to combine several object detectors into an ensemble system. By combining multiple learners for the collaborated decision, we can obtain better results than using a single learner [20]. The key challenge of building ensembles of object

© Springer Nature Switzerland AG 2020
H. Yang et al. (Eds.): ICONIP 2020, CCIS 1333, pp. 458–467, 2020.
https://doi.org/10.1007/978-3-030-63823-8_53

detectors is to handle multiple outputs so that the final output can determine what objects are in a given image and where they are located.

The paper is organized as follows. In Sect. 2, we briefly review the existing approaches relating to object detection and ensemble learning. In Sect. 3, we propose a novel weight-based ensemble method to combine the bounding box predictions of selected base detectors. The bounding boxes for combination are found by a greedy process in which boxes having Intersection-over-Union (IoU) values with each other higher than a predetermined threshold are grouped together. We consider an optimisation problem in maximizing the mean Average Precision (mAP) metric of the detection task. The parameters of combining method are found by using an evolutionary computation-based algorithm in solving this optimisation problem. The details of experimental studies on the VOC2007 dataset [6] are described in Sect. 4. Finally, the conclusion is given in Sect. 5.

2 Background and Related Work

2.1 Object Detectors

Most early object detection systems were based on extracting handcrafted features from given images then applying a a conventional learning algorithm such as Support Vector Machines (SVM) or Decision Trees [13,22] on those features. The most notable handcrafted methods were the Viola-Jones detector [21] and Histogram of Oriented Gradients (HOG) [5]. However, these methods only managed to achieve modest accuracy while requiring great expertise in handcrafting feature extraction. With the rise of deep learning, in 2014 Girshick et al. proposed Regions based on Convolutional Neural Network (CNN) features (called RCNN), the first DNN-based approach for object detection problem [8]. This architecture extracts a number of object proposals by using a selective search method and then each proposal is fed to a CNN to extract relevant features before being classified by a linear SVM classifier. Since then, object detection methods have developed rapidly and fall into two groups: two-stage detection and one-stage detection. Two-stage detection such as Fast-RCNN [7] and Faster-RCNN [17] follows the traditional object detection pipeline, generating region proposals first and then classifying each proposal into each of different object categories. Even though these networks give promising results, they still struggle with objects which have a broad range of scales, less prototypical images, and that require more precise localization. One-stage detection algorithms such as YOLO [15] and SSD [12] regard object detection as a regression or classification problem and adopt a unified architecture for both bounding box localization and classification.

2.2 Ensemble Methods and Optimization

Ensemble methods refer to the learning model that combines multiple learners to make a collaborated decision [18,20]. The main premise of ensemble learning is that by combining multiple models, the prediction of a single learner will likely be compensated by those of others, thus making better overall predictive performance. Nowadays, many ensemble methods have been introduced and they are categorized into two main groups, namely homogeneous ensembles and heterogeneous ensembles [20]. The first group includes ensembles generated by training one learning algorithm on many schemes of the original training set. The second group includes ensembles generated by training several different learning algorithms on the original training set.

Research on ensemble methods focuses on two stages of building an ensemble, namely generation and integration. For the generation stage, approaches focus on designing novel architectures for the ensemble system. Nguyen et al. [19] designed a deep ensemble method that involves multiple layers of ensemble of classifiers (EoC). A feature selection method works on the output of a layer to obtain the selected features as the input for the next layer. In the integration stage, besides several simple combining algorithms like Sum Rule and Majority Vote [10], Nguyen et al. [20] represented the predictions of the classifiers in the form of vectors of intervals called granule prototypes by using information granules. The combining algorithm then measures the distance between the predictions for a test sample and the granule prototypes to obtain the predicted label. Optimization methods have been applied to improve the performance of existing ensemble systems in terms of ensemble selection (ES) which aims to search for a suitable EoC that performs better than using the whole ensemble. Chen et al. [2] used ACO to find the optimal EoC and the optimal combining algorithm.

3   Proposed Method

3.1   General Description

In this study, we introduce a novel ensemble of object detectors to obtain higher performance than using single detectors. Assume that we have T base object detectors, denoted by $OD_i (i = 1, ..., T)$. Each detector works on an image to identify the location and class label of objects in the form of prediction results $\mathbf{R_i} = \{R_{i,j}\}, R_{i,j} = \left(BB_{i,j}, (l_{i,j}, conf_{i,j}) \right), (i = 1, ..., T; j = 1, ..., r_i$ where r_i is the number of objects detected by OD_i). The elements of $R_{i,j}$ are detailed as:

- Bounding box $BB_{i,j} = (x_{i,j}, y_{i,j}, w_{i,j}, h_{i,j})$ identifies the location of a detected object where $x_{i,j}, y_{i,j}, w_{i,j}$ and $h_{i,j}$ are the top-coordinates and the width and height of the bounding box
- Prediction $(l_{i,j}, conf_{i,j})$ where $l_{i,j}$ is the predicted label and $conf_{i,j}$ is the confidence value, which is defined as the probability for the prediction of this label

Our proposed ensemble algorithm deals with the selection of suitable detectors among all given ones, as well as combining the bounding boxes of the selected detectors. In order to select suitable detectors, we introduce a number of selection variables $\alpha_j \in \{0,1\}, j = 1, ..., T$ with each binary variable α_j representing whether detector OD_j is selected or not. The combining process is conducted after the selection process. To combine the bounding boxes made by the selected detectors, we need to know which bounding box of each detector predicts the same object. Our proposed method consists of two steps:

- Step 1: Measure the similarity between pairs of bounding boxes between the detection results from different detectors to create groups of similar bounding boxes
- Step 2: For each group, combine the bounding boxes

The similarity between bounding boxes is measured using Intersection over Union (IoU), which is very popular in object detection research [22]. With two bounding boxes $BB_{i,j}$ and $BB_{p,q}$, the IoU measure between them is given by:

$$IoU(BB_{i,j}, BB_{p,q}) = \frac{area(BB_{i,j} \cap BB_{p,q})}{area(BB_{i,j} \cup BB_{p,q})} \tag{1}$$

This measure is compared to a threshold θ ($0 \le \theta \le 1$). If the $IoU > \theta$ then they are grouped together, eventually forming a number of box groups $G = (g_1, g_2, ..., g_K)$, where K is the number of groups. Note that we do not consider the IoUs between boxes made by the same detector ($i \ne p$) since we combine bounding boxes of different detectors. We also combine bounding boxes that have the same predicted label. For each group, we perform combination of the bounding boxes. Let $W_i^x, W_i^y, W_i^w, W_i^h \in [0,1]$ be the weights of detector $OD_i (i = 1, ..., T)$. Then the combined bounding box for group g_k will be $BB_k = (x_k, y_k, w_k, h_k)$ in which:

$$coord_k = \frac{\sum_{BB_{p_l(k),q_l(k)} \in g_k} \mathbb{I}[\alpha_{p_l(k)} = 1] W_{p_l(k)}^{coord} coord_{p_l(k),q_l(k)}}{\sum_{BB_{p_m(k),q_m(k)} \in g_k} W_{p_m(k)}^{coord}}, \tag{2}$$

where $\mathbb{I}[.]$ is the indicator function, and $coord_k \in \{x_k, y_k, w_k, h_k\}$. Therefore, our ensemble is completely determined by the following parameters: $(W_i^x, W_i^y, W_i^w, W_i^h, \alpha_j, \theta), i, j = 1, ..., T$.

3.2 Optimisation

The question that arises from the proposed method is how to search for the best parameters $(W_i^x, W_i^y, W_i^w, W_i^h, \alpha_j, \theta), i, j = 1, ..., T$ for each situation, where $W_i^x, W_i^y, W_i^w, W_i^h$ are the bounding box weights, α_j are the selection variables, and θ is the IoU threshold. We formulate an optimisation problem which we can solve to find the optimal value for these parameters. The fitness function is chosen to be the mean Average Precision (mAP), which is defined as the

---

Algorithm 1. Combining object detectors

Input: Bounding box results by the detectors (BB_i), the prediction labels (l_i), confidence values $(conf_i)$, index of detector (det_i) $(i = 1, ..., nbb)$ with nbb being the total number of bounding boxes, bounding box weights for each detector $(W_j^x, W_j^y, W_j^w, W_j^h)$, the threshold for choosing each detector α_j and IoU threshold θ

Output: The combined bounding boxes
1: Remove detectors that does not satisfy $\alpha_j \geq 0.5$. Sort the bounding boxes in descending order of confidence value. Set $G \leftarrow \{\}, E \leftarrow \{\}, Assign \leftarrow \{assign_1, assign_2, ..., assign_{nbb}\}$ where $assign_i$ is the group which BB_i is assigned to, and initialize $assign_i$ to 0. Set $group\_idx \leftarrow 1$.
2: **for** $i \leftarrow 1$ to nbb **do**
3:     **if** $assign_i \neq 0$ **then**
4:         continue
5:     $assign_i \leftarrow group\_idx$
6:     **for** $j \leftarrow i + 1$ to nbb **do**
7:         **if** $assign_j \neq 0$ or $det_i == det_j$ or $l_i \neq l_j$ **then**
8:             continue
9:         **if** $IoU(BB_i, BB_j) > \theta$ **then**
10:            $assign_j \leftarrow group\_idx$
11:    $group\_idx \leftarrow group\_idx + 1$
12: $K \leftarrow groupd\_idx - 1$
13: $G \leftarrow \{g_1, g_2, ..., g_K\}$ where $g_k = \{BB_i\}$ such that $assign_i == k$
14: **for** $k \leftarrow 1$ to K **do**
15:    Combine boxes in g_k to get $BB_k = (x_k, y_k, w_k, h_k)$ by using Eq. 2,
16:    $E.insert(BB_k)$
17: **return** E

---

average of Average Precision for each class. In order to calculate AP_c, we need to calculate the precision and recall. Precision and recall are defined as follows:

$$Precision = \frac{TP}{TP + FP}, Recall = \frac{TP}{TP + FN} \tag{3}$$

where TP (True Positive) is the number of correct cases, FP (False Positive) is the number of cases where a predicted object does not exist, FN (False Negative) is the number of cases where an object is not predicted. The IoU measure between a predicted bounding box and a ground truth box determines whether the ground truth box is predicted by the algorithm. The AP summarises the shape of the precision/recall curve, and is evaluated by firstly computing a version of the measured precision/recall curve with precision monotonically decreasing, by setting the precision for recall r to the maximum precision obtained for any recall $r' \geq r$. Then the AP is calculated as the area under this curve by numerical integration. This is done by sampling at all unique recall value at which the maximum precision drops. Let p_{interp} be the interpolated precision values. Then the average precision is calculated as follows:

$$AP = \sum_n (r_{n+1} - r_n)p_{interp}(r_{n+1}), p_{interp}(r_{n+1}) = max_{r_1 \geq r_{n+1}}(p_1) \qquad (4)$$

Thus with T detectors, the optimisation problem is given by:

$$max_{\mathbf{w}=(W_i^x, W_i^y, W_i^w, W_i^h, \alpha_j, \theta)} mAP(\mathbf{w})$$
$$\text{s.t. } W_i^x, W_i^y, W_i^w, W_i^h \in [0,1], \alpha_j \in \{0,1\}, \theta \in [0,1], i, j = 1, \cdots, T \qquad (5)$$

We use PSO [3,9] to find the optimal values for $(W_i^x, W_i^y, W_i^w, W_i^h, \alpha_j, \theta)$. Compared to other optimisation algorithms, PSO offers some advantages. Firstly, as a member of the family of evolutionary computation methods, it is well suited to handle non-linear, non-convex spaces with non-differentiable, discontinuous objective functions. Secondly, PSO is a highly-efficient solver of continuous optimisation problems in a range of applications, typically requiring low numbers of function evaluations in comparison to other approaches while still maintaining quality of results [14]. Finally, PSO can be efficiently parallelized to reduce computational cost. To work with continuous variables in PSO, we convert each α_j into a continuous variable belonging to $[0, 1]$. If α_j is higher than 0.5, the corresponding detector is added to the ensemble. The average mAP value in a 5-fold cross-validation procedure is used as the fitness value.

The combining and training procedures are described in Algorithm 1. Algorithm 1 receives inputs including the bounding boxes made by the detectors (BB_i), confidence values $(conf_i)$, prediction labels (l_i) and the parameters $(W_i^x, W_i^y, W_i^w, W_i^h, \alpha_j, \theta)$. Each bounding box (BB_i) also has an associated variable (det_i) which delineates the index of the detector responsible for (BB_i). For example, if (BB_i) is predicted by the detector (OD_j) then $det_i = j$. Line 1 sorts the selected bounding boxes in decreasing order of confidence value. Line 3–10 assigns each bounding box to a group. For each bounding box BB_i we first check if it has been assigned to one of the existing groups before assigning it to the new group $group\_idx$ (line 3–5). Then with each unassigned bounding box BB_j that is not made by the same detector as that of BB_i and have the same prediction we add BB_j to group $group\_idx$ if its IoU value with BB_i is greater than θ (line 6–10). After all boxes are grouped, lines 12 to 17 combine the boxes in each group and returns the combined bounding boxes.

4   Experimental Studies

4.1   Experimental Setup

In the experiments, we used a number of popular object detection algorithms as base detectors for our ensemble method. The base detectors used are SSD Resnet50, SSD InceptionV2, SSD MobilenetV1 [12], FRCNN InceptionV2,

Table 1. Left: mAP result for the base detectors and the proposed method. Right: Weights for the bounding boxes of each base detectors (x, y, w, h, α)

Detector	mAP (%)	Detector	Weights				
RFCN-Resnet101	64.67		x	y	w	h	α
FRCNN-InceptionV2	62.02	RFCN-Resnet101	0.77	0.56	0.32	0.33	0.76
SSD-InceptionV2	41.96	FRCNN-InceptionV2	0.77	1.00	1.00	0.71	0.53
SSD-Mobilenet-V1	38.4	SSD-InceptionV2	0.49	0.71	0.22	0.30	0.93
SSD-Resnet50	39.93	SSD-Mobilenet-V1	0.35	0.93	0.25	0.00	0.42
FRCNN-Resnet50	64.34	SSD-Resnet50	0.00	0.00	0.94	0.58	0.73
Proposed method	**67.23**	FRCNN-Resnet50	0.89	0.80	0.29	1.00	0.99

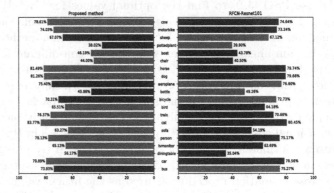

The red or blue color means better or poorer performance on an object

Fig. 1. A comparison of AP result for each class between the proposed method and RFCN-Resnet101. (Color figure online)

FRCNN Resnet50 [17], and RFCN Resnet101 [4]. We used the default configuration for all of these methods. Training process was done for 50000 iterations. For the PSO algorithm, the inertial weight a was set to 0.9 while two parameters C_1 and C_2 were set to 1.494. The number of iterations was set to 100 while the population size was set to 50. The dataset VOC2007 was used in this paper containing 5011 images for training and validation, and 4952 images for testing. The evaluation metric used in the paper was mAP (mean Average Precision). Among the 9963 images in the VOC2007 dataset, there are 2715 images having at least one object of difficult tag. Because we focus on the improvements of combining the results of bounding boxes from each detector, the difficult examples have been included into the evaluation.

4.2   Result and Discussion

Table 1 (left) shows the mAP result of the proposed method and the base detectors. The proposed method has mAP value of 67.23%, which outperforms the best base detector RFCN-Resnet101 by 2.56%. Figure 1 shows a detailed comparison of AP values between the two methods for each class. It can be seen

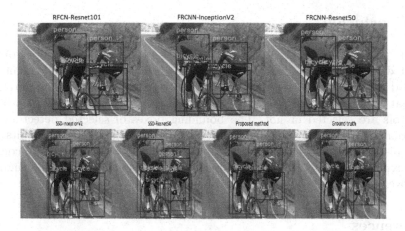

Fig. 2. Example result of selected base detectors and proposed method

that the proposed method achieves a remarkable increase for the "dining table" object, from 35.04% to 56.17%. This is followed by "sofa" with an increase of 9.08% from 54.19% to 63.27%. Other objects such as "dog" or "train" also saw a modest increase. On the other hand, "bicycle" and "bottle" saw a decrease, from 72.73% to 70.31% and from 49.26% to 45.98% respectively. It should be noted that ensemble methods ensure that the overall result is better, even though some cases might be worse than the base learners. In total, there are 14 object types that saw an increase due to the proposed method. Table 1 (right) shows the weights for the bounding boxes for each of the base detectors. The first and second columns show the weights of the top-left coordinates, while the third, fourth and fifth columns show the width, height weights and selection threshold respectively. From the table, it is clear that the algorithm automatically chooses the better base detectors for combining the bounding boxes, since most of the contributions of weights are from RFCN-Resnet10 (64.67%), FRCNN-InceptionV2 (62.02%) and FRCNN-Resnet50 (64.34%).

Figure 2 provides a comparison between the selected base detectors (those with $\alpha_i \geq 0.5$ after optimisation) and the proposed method. It can be seen that RFCN-Resnet101, SSD-Resnet50, and FRCNN-Resnet50 correctly identify two bicycles, but wrongly predicts another bicycle that spans the two real bicycles. On the other hand, FRCNN-Resnet50 wrongly predicts three person objects in the image. Due to the combination procedure, the redundant bicycle and person objects have been removed. Also, the bounding box for the left person by SSD-InceptionV2 is slightly skewed to the right, but after applying weighted sum of bounding boxes of the base detectors, the combined box has been positioned more accurately.

5   Conclusion

In this paper, we presented a novel method for combining a number of base object detectors into an ensemble that achieves better results. The combining method is constructed using PSO algorithm to search for a defining parameter set that optimise mAP. Parameters are selective indicators which show whether detectors are selected or not. The bounding boxes of selected detectors then are combined based on a weights-based combining method. Our results on a benchmark dataset show that the proposed ensemble method is able to combine the strengths and mitigate the drawbacks of the base detectors, resulting in an improvement compared to each individual detector.

References

1. Banfield, R., Hall, L., Bowyer, K., Kegelmeyer, W.: Ensemble diversity measures and their application to thinning. Information Fusion **6**, 49–62 (2005)
2. Chen, Y., et al.: Applying ant colony optimization to configuring stacking ensembles for data mining. Expert Syst. Appl. **41**(6), 2688–2702 (2014)
3. Clerc, M., Kennedy, J.: The particle swarm - explosion, stability, and convergence in a multidimensional complex space. Trans. Evol. Comp **6**(1), 58–73 (2002)
4. Dai, J., Li, Y., He, K., Sun, J.: R-FCN: object detection via region-based fully convolutional networks. In: Proceedings of NIPS, pp. 379–387 (2016)
5. Dalal, N., Triggs, B.: Histograms of oriented gradients for human detection. Proc. CVPR. **1**, 886–893 (2005)
6. Everingham, M., et al.: The PASCAL Visual Object Classes Challenge 2007 (VOC2007). http://host.robots.ox.ac.uk/pascal/VOC/
7. Girshick, R.: Fast R-CNN. In: Proceedings of ICCV, pp. 1440–1448 (2015)
8. Girshick, R., Donahue, J., et al.: Rich feature hierarchies for accurate object detection and semantic segmentation. In: Proceedings of CVPR, pp. 580–587 (2014)
9. Kennedy, J., Eberhart, R.: Particle swarm optimization. Proc. IJCNN **4**, 1942–1948 (1995)
10. Kittler, J., Hatef, M., et al.: On combining classifiers. IEEE Trans. Pattern Anal. Mach. Intell. **20**(3), 226–239 (1998)
11. Krizhevsky, A., Sutskever, I., Hinton, G.E.: ImageNet classification with deep convolutional neural networks. In: Proceedings of NIPS, Curran Associates, pp. 1097–1105 (2012)
12. Liu, W., et al.: SSD: single shot multibox detector. In: Leibe, B., Matas, J., Sebe, N., Welling, M. (eds.) ECCV 2016. LNCS, vol. 9905, pp. 21–37. Springer, Cham (2016). https://doi.org/10.1007/978-3-319-46448-0_2
13. Lowe, D.G.: Distinctive image features from scale-invariant keypoints. Int. J. Comput. Vision **60**(2), 91–110 (2004)
14. Perez, R., Behdinan, K.: Particle swarm approach for structural design optimization. Comput. Struct. **85**, 1579–1588 (2007)
15. Redmon, J., et al.: You only look once: unified, real-time object detection. In: Proceedings of CVPR, pp. 779–788 (2016)
16. Redmon, J., Farhadi, A.: YOLOv3: an Incremental Improvement. arXiv:1804.02767 [cs] (Apr 2018)

17. Ren, S., He, K., Girshick, R., Sun, J.: Faster R-CNN: towards real-time object detection with region proposal networks. IEEE Trans. Pattern Anal. Mach. Intell. **39**(6), 1137–1149 (2015)
18. Nguyen, T., Nguyen, M., Pham, C., Liew, C., Witold, P.: Combining heterogeneous classifiers via granular prototypes. Appl. Soft Comput. **73**, 795–815 (2018)
19. Nguyen, T., et al: Deep heterogeneous ensemble. In: Proceedings of ICONIP, pp. 1–9 (2019)
20. Nguyen, T., Luong, V., Dang, T., Liew, C., McCall, J.: Ensemble selection based on classifier prediction confidence. Pattern Recogn. **100**, 107104 (2020)
21. Viola, P., Jones, M.: Rapid object detection using a boosted cascade of simple features. Proc. CVPR. **1**, 511–518 (2001)
22. Zhao, Z.Q., Zheng, P., Xu, S.T., Wu, X.: Object detection with deep learning: a review. In: IEEE Transactions on Neural Networks and Learning Systems, pp. 1–21 (2019)

Transfer Learning for Semi-supervised Classification of Non-stationary Data Streams

Yimin Wen[1(✉)], Qi Zhou[1], Yun Xue[2], and Chao Feng[1]

[1] Guangxi Key Laboratory of Image and Graphic Intelligent Processing,
Guilin University of Electronic Technology, Guilin, China
ymwen2004@aliyun.com, zqguidian@163.com, henryfung01@126.com
[2] School of Municipal and Surveying Engineering, Hunan City University,
Yiyang, China
yunxue1209@163.com

Abstract. In the scenario of data stream classification, the occurrence of recurring concept drift and the scarcity of labeled data are very common, which make the semi-supervised classification of data streams quite challenging. To deal with these issues, a new classification algorithm for partially labeled streaming data with recurring concept drift is proposed. CAPLRD maintains a pool of concept-specific classifiers and utilizes historical classifiers to label unlabeled data, in which the unlabeled data are labeled by a weighted-majority vote strategy, and concept drifts are detected by automatically monitoring the threshold of classification accuracy on different data chunks. The experimental results illustrate that the transfer learning from historical concept-specific classifiers can improve labeling accuracy significantly, the detection of concept drifts and classification accuracy effectively.

Keywords: Concept drift · Semi-supervised learning · Transfer learning

1 Introduction

In the era of big data, data streams are very common, examples include financial transaction of credit cards, network intrusion information, and so on. Concept drift [1] often occurs in these data streams, in which the distribution of data is not stationary and makes the traditional classification methods not applicable to data stream [2,3]. Recurring concept drift is a special type of concept drift, referring to the phenomenon that concepts appeared in the past may reoccur in the future [4]. However, some algorithms like [5–7] don't consider the occurrence of recurring concept. Furthermore, in many real applications, the labeled

---

The original version of this chapter was revised: The typesetting errors in Tables 2–5 were corrected. The correction to this chapter is available at https://doi.org/10.1007/978-3-030-63823-8_95

instances are always scarce, and the cost of labeling unlabeled instances is high. Therefore, using transfer learning and semi-supervised methods to solve these problems are promising.

In this paper, a new Classification Algorithm for Partially Labeled data stream with Recurring concept Drift (CAPLRD)[1] is proposed. CAPLRD can be employed as a framework for semi-supervised classification of data stream with recurring concept drifts. The main contributions of CAPLRD are as follows: (1) a new algorithm of Semi-Supervised Learning with Node Ensemble (SSLNE) is proposed to label unlabeled instances, which employs labeled instances to locate the similar local areas among historical classifiers, and then employs these local areas to assist labeling unlabeled instances. (2) A new simple method of Recurring Concept Drift Detection (RCDD) is proposed. RCDD mainly finds the classifier that has the best classification accuracy on the current data chunk in the ensemble classifiers. If the highest accuracy exceeds the preset threshold, the current data chunk corresponds to a recurring concept, otherwise corresponds to a new concept. It is very interesting that the threshold can be automatically adjusted according to the number of labeled instances.

2   Related Work

This paper is related to semi-supervised classification of data stream and transfer learning, therefore, we briefly discuss them.

The approaches for semi-supervised classification of data stream can be broadly divided into recurring-concept-based and non-recurring-concept-based. ReaSC [8] and SUN [9] are non-recurring-concept-based method. ReaSC utilizes both labeled and unlabeled instances to train and update the classification model and maintains a pool of classifiers. Each classifier is built over a data chunk as a collection of micro-clusterings which are generated through semi-supervised clustering, and an ensemble of these cluster-based classifiers is used to classify instances. SUN employs a clustering algorithm to produce concept clusters at leaves in an incremental decision tree. If a concept drift is detected, the trained decision tree is pruned to adapt to the new concept.

SPASC [10] and REDLLA [11] are recurring-concept-based approaches. SPASC maintains a pool of historical classifiers and detects the recurring concept drifts by the similarity between the current data chunk with the best classifier. REDLLA adopts decision tree as its classification model, and it detects concept drift by deviations between history and new concept clusters.

Transfer learning is an important learning method and employed to address data stream classification in recent years. Condor [12] reuses historical models to build new model and update model pool, by making use of the biased regularization technique for multiple model reuse learning. SCBELS [13] utilizes the local structure mapping strategy [14] to compute local similarity around each sample and combines with semi-supervised Bayesian method to perform concept detection which borrows idea from transfer learning.

---

[1] Source code: https://gitee.com/ymw12345/caplrdsrc.git.

3   The Proposed Algorithm

3.1   The Framework of CAPLRD

Without loss of generality, this paper assumes that a data stream is processed batch by batch in which some of them are randomly selected to be labeled by a supervisor. For convenience, $B^t = (x_1^t, x_2^t, ..., x_m^t)$ is used to denote a batch of instances collected in the time t. $B_L^t = (x_1^t, x_2^t, ..., x_n^t)$ and $Y_L^t = (y_1^t, y_2^t, ..., y_n^t)$ denote the labeled samples in B^t and their labels, respectively, whereas $B_U^t = (x_{n+1}^t, x_{n+2}^t, ..., x_m^t)$ denotes the remaining unlabeled instances.

CAPLRD is described in the Algorithm 1. CAPLRD employs VFDT (very fast decision tree) [15] as the base model, and many concept-specific classifiers are maintained in a pool. For each coming data chunk, the pool selects a classifier as an "active classifier" to classify the current data chunk. And then, SSLNE is employed to label the unlabeled instances. Next, RCDD is employed to detect concept drifts. If a new concept is detected, a new model is trained and added into the pool, otherwise, a historical model is updated.

Algorithm 1: CAPLRD

    Input: a streaming data in the form of batches: B^t, B_L^t, Y_L^t, B_U^t; the parameter: θ

    Output: the predicted labels of all the instances in B^t

1 Initialization: $activeClf$=NULL; E=NULL; B^t=NULL;

2 $activeClf$=createTree(B_L^1);

3 $E = E \cup activeClf$; $r=0$; $act=r$; $t=2$;

4 **while** *a new data batch is available* **do**

5   B^t=read_next_batch(); $activeClf$.classify(B^t);

6   (B', Y_L')=SSLNE(B_L^t, Y_L^t, B_U^t, E, θ);

7      $index$=RCDD(B', Y_L', E, act);

8   **if** $index == -1$ **then**

9          $curClf$=createTree(B', Y_L');

10        $curClf.highestAcc$=0; $E = E \cup curClf$; r++;

11        $activeClf$=$curClf$; $act=r$;

12   **else**

13   acc=E_{index}.classify(B');

14        $E_{index}.highestAcc$=max(acc, $E_{index}.highestAcc$);

15   E_{index}.update(B', Y_L'); $activeClf$=E_{index}; $act=index$;

16   B'=NULL; Y_L'=NULL; B^t=NULL; t++;

3.2   Employing Historical Classifiers for Transfer Learning

SSLNE are described in the Algorithm 2. SSLNE is proposed to expand the labeled instances in the current data batch and hence alleviate the scarcity of labeled data. There are many semi-supervised learning methods like the well-known self-training [16] and tri-training [17] methods. However, in these methods, if the wrongly classified samples are added to the original training set, the errors will be accumulated in the subsequent training process. SSLNE is based on the facts that even two data batches corresponding to different concepts, their distributions may be similar in some subregions. A trained decision tree can divide an instance space into many subregions, and hence we can use the similar subregions among the historical trees to label the unlabeled instances.

Algorithm 2: SSLNE

Input: the pool of historical classifiers: E, the current data batch: B_L, $\quad\quad$ Y_L, B_U and the threshold θ

Output: the expanded labeled data chunk: B'

1   B'=NULL; $B' = B' \cup B_L$; Y'_L=NULL; $Y'_L = Y'_L \cup Y_L$;

2   **for** *each E_i in E* **do**

3      $E_i.lnode.N$=0; $E_i.lnode.CN$=0;

4   **for** *each x_i^l in B_L* **do**

5          $E_i.lnode$=E_i.sort_into_leaf(x_i^l); $E_i.lnode.N$++;

6   **if** *x_i^l is classified correct* **then**

7             $E_i.lnode.CN$++;

8   **for** *each x_i^u in B_U* **do**

9   **for** $1 \leq j \leq labelNum$ **do**

10   each class WS_j=0;

11   **for** *each E_i in E* **do**

12        $E_i.lnode$=E_i.sort_into_leaf(x_i^u);

13   **if** *$E_i.lnode.N$==0* **then**

14   go to step 11;

15   **else**

16   label x_i^u with $E_i.lnode$ and obtain the predicted label c;

17          $acc - E_i.lnode.CN/E_i.lnode.N$; $T = acc - 1.0/labelNum$;

18   **if** $T > \theta/labelNum$ **then**

19             $WS_c = WS_c + T$;

20   WS_k=max$\{WS_1, WS_2, ..., WS_{labelnum}\}$;

21   **if** $WS_k > \theta/labelNum$ **then**

22   x_i^u is labeled with the label k; $B' = B' \cup x_i^u$; $Y'_L = Y'_L \cup k$;

23   **return** (B', Y'_L);

More specifically, for each historical classifier, all the labeled instances in the current data batch are sorted into its leaves. In the process of traversing the decision tree, $lnode.N$ is saved for counting the number of instances that are sorted into its corresponding leaf, while $lnode.CN$ is saved for counting the number of correct classified instances among them. Then, for each historical classifier, each unlabeled instance in the current data batch is sorted into a leaf of it. The value of $lnode.CN/lnode.N$ to this leaf node can be used to present the classification confidence of the historical classifier for this unlabeled instance. The larger the value of $lnode.CN/lnode.N$, the higher the local similarity is between the historical classifier and the current data batch. At last, the historical trees with the value of $lnode.CN/lnode.N$ are ensembled to give the classification result for the unlabeled instances, then the unlabeled instance with its predicted class label is added into the set of labeled instances in the current data batch.

3.3   Recurring Concept Drift Detection

RCDD is described in the Algorithm 3. In RCDD, if the classification accuracy of a historical classifier E_i on the current data batch is higher than the threshold β ($\beta = E_i.highestAcc - \delta$, $\delta = \sqrt{\frac{2.0}{w}}$, w means the number of labeled instances in B'), then the current data batch is considered include the same concpet with E_i. The larger w means there are more labeled instances in the current data chunk, and a classifier will be evaluated more accurately with more labeled instances. And hence, we set the smaller the w and the larger the δ, even the δ is empirical.

Algorithm 3: RCDD

Input: the expanded labeled data batch: B', the label: Y, the pool of
  classifiers: E, the index of active classifier in E: r;
Output: the index of classifier that corresponds to the same concept as
  B' in E or -1 which means B' corresponds to a new concept

1 Compute the classification accuracy acc of E_r in B';
2 **if** $acc > (E_r.highestAcc - \delta)$ **then**
3 $\quad$⌊ return r;

4 $maxAcc=0$; $index=-1$;
5 **for** each $E_i \in E$ except E_r **do**
6 $\quad$ Compute the classification accuracy acc of E_i in B';
7 $\quad$ **if** $acc > (E_i.highestAcc - \delta)$ and $acc > maxAcc$ **then**
8 $\quad\quad$⌊ $maxAcc = acc$; $index = i$;

9 return $index$;

---

4   Experiments

To evaluate the performance of SSLNE, the first group is conducted to compare SSLNE with the self-training and tri-training algorithms under the framework of CAPLRD. That is, in CAPLRD, SSLNE is replaced by the self-training and tri-training algorithm in turn while the other codes remain the same.

To evaluate the performance of RCDD, the second group is conducted to compare RCDD with CCPRD which is the recurring concept drift detection method of CCP [4] under the framework of CAPLRD. That is, in CAPLRD, RCDD is replaced by CCPRD while the other codes remain the same.

To evaluate the performance of CAPLRD, the third group is conducted to compare CAPLRD with REDLLA and SPASC.

To evaluate the sensitiveness of θ to CAPLRD, in the fourth group, the values of θ is set as 0, 0.2, 0.4, 0.5, 0.6, 0.8, and 0.9, respectively.

In this paper, The size of the pool is unlimited. The unlabeled ratio is set as 0.9, which means 90% of labels are not available. These experiments are repeated 50 times for the synthetic datasets and 20 times for the real datasets. The parameters of CCPRD are set as follows: $\theta = 0.5$, $Cmax = 3$. The paired t-test at 95% confidence level has been conducted to detect whether the differences between our approach and other compared methods are statistically significant.

4.1 Datasets

In Table 1, the synthetic datasets of sea and cir are generated by MOA [18], the definition of sine is if $a * sin(b * x_1 + \theta) + c > x_2$, the label is 0, otherwise is 1. While the electricity dataset is collected from the Australia New South Wales electricity market, the weather dataset comes from an air force base with a 50-year time span and diverse weather patterns and the spam dataset is collected from various kinds of email about advertisements for products/web sites etc.

Table 1. Datasets with concept drifts.

Datasets	Drift value	Instances	Dim	Class	Chunk size
Cir	A:a = 0 b = 0 R = 2, B:a = 0 b = 0 R = 3 C:a = 2 b = 2 R = 2, D:a = 2 b = 2 R = 3 A-B-C-D-A-B-C-D	40,000	2	2	200
Sea	θ = 5-8-12-15-5-8-12-15	40,000	3	2	200
Sine	b = 1-π-3π-1-π-3π, θ = 0, a = 1, c = 0	30,000	3	2	200
Electricity	Unknown	45,312	14	2	200
Spam	Unknown	4,601	57	2	100
Weather	Unknown	18,159	8	2	200

4.2 Experimental Results

From Table 2, it can be observed that the accumulative accuracy of CAPLRD based on SSLNE is significantly better than it based on self-training or tri-training in all synthetic and real datasets. These results illustrate that the transfer learning from historical classifiers can bring effective improvement for semi-supervised learning.

From Table 3, it can be observed that the accumulative accuracy of CAPLRD based on RCDD is better than it based on CCPRD on all the datasets, except slightly worse than on the weather dataset. The reason why RCDD is better than CCPRD may be that CCPRD uses the distance between the concept vector and the concept cluster to judge whether is it a recurring concept, which has a certain

Table 2. The accumulative accuracy (%) of CAPLRD on each dataset when its module for semi-supervised learning is replaced with SSLNE, self-training, and tri-training, respectively. •/∘ indicates CAPLRD based on SSLNE is significantly better/worse than the compared methods.

Datasets	Cir	Sea	Sine	Electricity	Spam	Weather
Self-training	77.03±0.10•	78.39±0.08•	66.16±0.15•	65.66±0.19•	60.22±0.32•	60.49±0.23•
Tri-training	80.66±0.09•	81.94±0.11•	69.18±0.15•	68.49±0.19•	63.40±0.43•	66.52±0.20•
SSLNE	**82.47±0.22**	**87.76±0.12**	**81.46±0.18**	**73.70±0.21**	**71.93±0.87**	**68.45±0.12**

Table 3. The accumulative accuracy (%) of CAPLRD on each dataset when its module for concept drift detection is set as RCDD and CCPRD, respectively. •/∘ indicates CAPLRD based on RCDD is significantly better/worse than it based on CCPRD.

Datasets	Cir	Sea	Sine	Electricity	Spam	Weather
CCPRD	81.45±0.16•	80.02±0.23•	77.76±0.26•	72.70±0.29•	70.65±1.03•	**68.76±0.30**∘
RCDD	**82.47±0.22**	**87.76±0.12**	**81.46±0.18**	**73.70±0.21**	**71.93±0.87**	68.45±0.12

ambiguity. For CCPRD, the effect of the classifier corresponding to this concept is that the classification of current data chunk cannot be optimal. RCDD is to find a corresponding classifier with the highest classification accuracy in the ensemble model, so RCDD is more accurate than CCPRD detection.

From Table 4, it can be observed that CAPLRD achieves higher accumulative accuracy than SPASC and REDLLA on the synthetic datasets, and performs better than SPASC on real datasets. From Fig. 1, it can be observed that CAPLRD can track concept drifts more accurately, and recover to a high classification accuracy quickly on the first four datasets, REDLLA performs better than CAPLRD on the weather and spam datasets. The reason for this phenomenon may be that it is impossible to determine where the concept drift occurs for real data steams, and the artificially dividing the data streams to chunks may cause the current data chunk to be impure, that is it may contain other concepts.

Table 4. The accumulative accuracies (%) of CAPLRD, SPASC, and REDLLA. •/∘ indicates CAPLRD is significantly better/worse than SPASC and REDLLA.

Datasets	Cir	Sea	Sine	Electricity	Spam	Weather
SAPSC	78.00±0.20•	66.13±0.41•	67.63±0.23•	58.68±0.17•	63.22±0.36•	65.31±0.28•
REDLLA	81.74±0.12•	66.05±0.24•	71.67±0.11•	66.50±0.50•	**75.26±0.35**∘	**72.16±0.19**∘
CAPLRD	**82.47±0.22**	**87.76±0.12**	**81.46±0.18**	**73.70±0.21**	71.93±0.87	68.45±0.12

Table 5 is about the influence of θ on the CAPLRD algorithm when the value of θ was set to 0, 0.2, 0.4, 0.5, 0.6, 0.8, and 0.9, respectively. From Table 5, it can be observed that the accumulative accuracy of CAPLRD is not sensitive to θ.

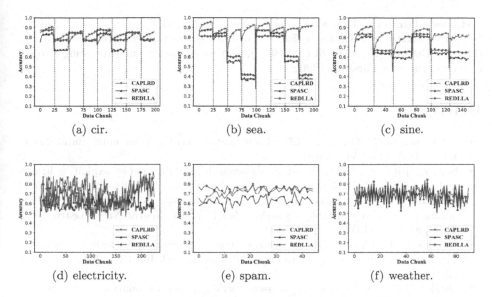

(a) cir.   (b) sea.   (c) sine.

(d) electricity.   (e) spam.   (f) weather.

Fig. 1. Drift tracking of CAPLRD, SPASC, and REDLLA on each dataset.

Table 5. Accumulative accuracy (%) of CAPLRD on all datasets with different θ.

Datasets	Cir	Sea	Sine	Electricity	Spam	Weather
$\theta = 0$	81.71±0.23	86.78±0.15	79.98±0.18	73.08±0.25	74.69±0.93	68.77±0.15
$\theta = 0.2$	82.16±0.20	87.09±0.15	80.27±0.16	73.28±0.17	73.50±1.25	69.08±0.17
$\theta = 0.4$	82.40±0.19	87.26±0.14	80.90±0.19	73.70±0.21	72.20±1.09	68.78±0.20
$\theta = 0.5$	82.46±0.23	87.76±0.12	81.45±0.17	73.70±0.21	71.93±0.87	68.45±0.12
$\theta = 0.6$	82.30±0.23	87.61±0.15	81.08±0.19	73.11±0.18	73.47±1.13	68.94±0.20
$\theta = 0.8$	83.01±0.23	88.06±0.13	81.35±0.15	73.61±0.16	72.77±1.03	68.38±0.12
$\theta = 0.9$	82.88±0.21	88.17±0.14	81.76±0.17	73.33±0.21	74.89±1.07	68.66±0.15

5   Conclusion

The innovation of the proposed CAPLRD lies in that it includes two components of SSLNE and RCDD. The experimental results demonstrate that the proposed SSLNE can utilizes historical classifiers to label the unlabeled instances effectively, which can expand the set of limited labeled instances and improve the generalization ability. The proposed RCDD is sensitive to the recurring concept drift detection and responds fast due to the threshold can be automatically adjusted according to the number of labeled instances. Besides, CAPLRD performs much better than REDLLA and SPASC. However it has the limitation that the base learner has to be decision tree model. How to extend the semi-supervised classification method so that any type of supervised classification model can be adopted as base learner is still challenging and interesting for future work.

Acknowledgments. This work was partially supported by the National Natural Science Foundation of China (61866007, 61662014), Natural Science Foundation of Guangxi District (2018GXNSFDA138006), and Image Intelligent Processing Project of Key Laboratory Fund (GIIP2005).

References

1. Schlimmer, J.C., Granger, R.H.: Incremental learning from noisy data. Mach. Learn. **1**(3), 317–354 (1986)
2. Sun, Y., Tang, K., Zhu, Z.X., et al.: Concept drift adaptation by exploiting historical knowledge. IEEE Trans. Neural Netw. Learn. Syst. **29**(10), 4822–4832 (2017)
3. Brzezinski, D., Stefanowski, J.: Reacting to different types of concept drift: the accuracy updated ensemble algorithm. IEEE Trans. Neural Netw. Learn. Syst. **25**(1), 81–94 (2013)
4. Katakis, I., Tsoumakas, G., Vlahavas, I.: Tracking recurring contexts using ensemble classifiers: an application to email filtering. Knowl. Inf. Syst. **22**(3), 371–391 (2010)
5. Ditzler G, Polikar R.: Semi-supervised learning in nonstationary environment. In: Proceedings of the 2011 International Joint Conference on Neural Networks, Piscataway, NJ, pp. 2741–2748. IEEE (2011)
6. Bertini, J.R., Lopes, A.D., Zhao, L.: Partially labeled data stream classification with the semi-supervised k-associated graph. J. Braz. Comput. Soc. **18**(4), 299–310 (2012)
7. Dyer, K.B., Capo, R., Polikar, R.: Compose: a semi-supervised learning framework for initially labeled nonstationary streaming data. IEEE Trans. Neural Netw. Learn. Syst. **25**(1), 12–26 (2014)
8. Masud, M.M., Woolam, C., Gao, J.: Facing the reality of data stream classification: coping with scarcity of labeled data. Knowl. Inf. Syst. **33**(1), 213–244 (2012)
9. Wu, X.D., Li, P.P., Hu, X.G.: Learning from concept drifting data streams with unlabeled data. Neurocomputing **92**, 145–155 (2012)
10. Hosseini, M.J., Gholipour, A., Beigy, H.: An ensemble of cluster-based classifiers for semi-supervised classification of non-stationary data streams. Knowl. Inf. Syst. **46**(3), 567–597 (2016)
11. Li, P.P., Wu, X.D., Hu, X.G.: Mining recurring concept drifts with limited labeled streaming data. ACM Trans. Intell. Syst. Technol. **3**(2), 1–32 (2012)
12. Zhao, P., Cai, L.W., Zhou, Z.H.: Handling concept drift via model reuse. Mach. Learn. **109**(3), 533–568 (2018)
13. Wen, Y.M., Liu, S.: Semi-supervised classification of data streams by BIRCH ensemble and local structure mapping. J. Comput. Sci. Technol. **35**(2), 295–304 (2020)
14. Gao, J., Fan, W., Jiang, J.: Knowledge transfer via multiple model local structure mapping. In: Proceedings 14th ACM SIGKDD International Conference on Knowledge Discovery and Data Mining, New York, pp. 283–291. ACM (2008)
15. Domingos, P., Hulten, G.: Mining high-speed data streams. In: Proceedings of the 6th ACM SIGKDD international conference on Knowledge discovery and data mining, New York, pp. 71–80. ACM (2000)

16. Zhu, X.J., Goldberg, A.B.: Introduction to semi-supervised learning. Synth. Lect. Artif. Intell. Mach. Learn. **3**(1), 1–130 (2009)
17. Zhou, Z.H., Li, M.: Tri-training: exploiting unlabeled data using three classifier. IEEE Trans. Knowl. Data Eng. **17**(11), 1529–1541 (2005)
18. Bifet, A., Holmes, G., Kirkby, R.: MOA: massive online analysis. J. Mach. Learn. Res. **11**(2), 1601–1604 (2010)

Neural Network Models

A Supervised Learning Algorithm for Learning Precise Timing of Multispike in Multilayer Spiking Neural Networks

Rong Xiao(iD) and Tianyu Geng[(✉)](iD)

Sichuan University, Chengdu 610065, People's Republic of China
{rxiao,tygeng}@scu.edu.cn

Abstract. Biological evidence shows that precise timing spikes can more accurately describe the activity of the neuron and effectively transmit spatio-temporal patterns. However, it is still a core challenge to trigger multiple precise timing spikes in each layer of multilayer spiking neural network (SNN), since the complexity of the learning targets increases significantly for multispike learning. To address this issue, we propose a novel supervised, multispike learning method for multilayer SNNs, which can accomplish the complex spatio-temporal pattern learning of spike trains. The proposed method derives the synaptic weight update rule from the Widrow-Hoff (WH) rule, and then credits the network error simultaneously to preceding layers using backpropagation. The algorithm has been successfully applied to the benchmark datasets from the UCI dataset. Experimental results show that the proposed method can achieve comparable classification accuracy with classical learning methods and a state-of-the-art supervised algorithm. In addition, the training framework effectively reduces the number of connections, thus improving the computational efficiency of the network.

Keywords: Spiking neural network · Supervised learning · Multilayer neural network · Multiple precise timing spikes

1 Introduction

Research evidence shows that the precise spatio-temporal firing pattern of groups of neurons can convey relevant information [1], which enables us to use time as a communication and computing resource in spiking neural networks (SNNs). In recent years, learning methods focusing on how to deal with spatio-temporal spikes by a supervised way have also been explored [2]. This scheme can train single or multilayer networks to fire the required output spike train. For single-layer networks, different spike-timing based learning rules have been developed [3,4]. Theses rules adopt either an error function minimized by gradient descent or an

This work is supported by National Natural Science Foundation of China under Grant No. 61906126.

analog of the Widrow-Hoff (WH) rule. Remote supervised method (ReSuMe) [5] is an outstanding method due to its effectiveness. It uses Spike-Timing-Dependent Plasticity (STDP) and anti-STDP window to finish the learning process. All of these existing single-layer algorithms can successfully finish the training, while the efficiency of them is low, especially for complex tasks. Therefore, training a hierarchical SNN in the closest way to the brain is required.

To further improve the learning performance, the Quick Propagation, Resilient Propagation [6] and the SpikeProp [7] are studied. However, due to the sudden jump or discontinuity of error function, the gradient learning method may lead to learning failure. Another thread of research is to use the revised version of the WH learning rule for SNNs. ReSuMe is extended to the Multi-layer Remote Supervised Learning Method (Multi-ReSuMe) in [8], where multiple pulses are considered in each layer. The delay of spike propagation is a vital feature in the real biological nervous system [9]. Combining ReSuMe and delay learning, [10] further puts forward a new algorithm for multiple neurons. Although many efforts have been made for SNN structure design and learning, in most of the existing learning methods, the transformation of relevant information is realized by using rate coding or single spike of neurons [11] due to the discontinuous nature of neuronal spike timing. Thus, it remains as one of the challenging problems to build an SNN that can learn such spike pattern-to-spike pattern transformations.

In this paper, a novel supervised learning method is presented, which trains the multilayer SNN for transmitting spatio-temporal spike patterns. In this work, the error function from Widrow Hoff (WH) rule, based on the difference between the actual and expected output spike trains, is first introduced to change the synaptic weights, and then is applied to neurons triggering multispike in each layer through a backpropagation learning rule. The main innovations of this method consist in: 1) extending the WH rule-based PSD rule to learn spatio-temporal spike patterns in multilayer SNNs and 2) effectively reducing the number of connections, thus improving the computational efficiency of the network. Finally, our method is evaluated thoroughly on the benchmark datasets. Experimental results show this algorithm can achieve high learning accuracy and have a significant improvement in the computational efficiency of the network.

2　Neuron Model

Firstly, we define a spike train as a series of impulses triggered by a specific neuron at its firing time, which is given as the following form: $S(t) = \sum_f \delta(t-t^f)$, where t^f is the f-th firing time, and $\delta(x)$ is the Dirac function: $\delta(x) = 1$ (if x = 0) or 0 (otherwise). Then a linear stochastic neuron model is introduced in continuous time for constructing a relation between the input and output impulse trains as used in [8]. The instantaneous firing rate $R(t)$ of a postsynaptic neuron i is the probability density of firing at time t and is determined by the instantaneous firing rates of its presynaptic neurons j: $R_i(t) = \frac{1}{k}\sum_j w_{ij} R_j(t)$ where k is the number of presynaptic neurons. In a single calculation, we only

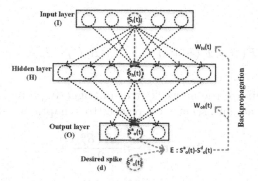

Fig. 1. Multilayer network structure. Input neurons are connected to the output neuron by hidden neurons. w_{oh} represents the weight between an output neuron o and hidden neuron h. w_{hi} represents the weight between an hidden neuron h and input neuron i.

get a concrete spike train $S(t)$ instead of a direct $R(t)$ of the neuron. However, $R(t)$ can be defined as the expectation over $S(t)$ for an infinite number of trials.

$$R(t) = \langle S(t) \rangle = \lim_{M \to \infty} \frac{1}{M} \sum_{k=1}^{M} S_k(t) \tag{1}$$

where M is the number of trials, and $S_k(t)$ is the concrete spike train for each trial. In this paper, we use $R(t)$ to derive the learning method because of its smoothness. In a single run, $R(t)$ will be replaced by $S(t)$ at a suitable point.

For simplicity, the leaky integrate-and-fire (LIF) model [12] is considered. For a postsynaptic neuron, the input synaptic current is calculated as:

$$I_{syn} = \sum_{t} w_i I_{PSC}^i(t) \tag{2}$$

where w_i is the synaptic efficacy of the i-th afferent neuron, and I_{PSC}^i is the un-weighted postsynaptic current (PSC) from the corresponding afferent.

$$I_{PSC}^i(t) = \sum_{t^j} K(t - t^j)H(t - t^j) \tag{3}$$

where t^j is the time of the j-th impulse triggered from the i-th afferent neuron, $H(t)$ represents the Heaviside function, and K is the normalized kernel: $K(t - t^j) = V_0 \cdot (exp(\frac{-(t-t^j)}{\tau_m}) - exp(\frac{-(t-t^j)}{\tau_s}))$. V_0 is the normalization factor. τ_m and τ_s are slow and fast decay constants, respectively. Their proportion is fixed as $\tau_m/\tau_s = 4$. When V_m crosses the firing threshold ϑ, the neuron will emit an output spike, and the membrane potential is reset to V_r.

2.1   Learning Algorithm

The instantaneous training error is computed according to the difference between the actual instantaneous triggering rate $R_o^a(t)$ and the desired instantaneous triggering rate $R_o^d(t)$:

$$E(t) = E\left(R_o^a(t)\right) = \frac{1}{2} \sum_{o \in O} \left[R_o^a(t) - R_o^d(t)\right]^2 \tag{4}$$

Our goal is to minimize the network error in triggering a required output spike pattern through gradient ascent with respect to synaptic weights,

$$\Delta w_{oh}(t) = -\eta \frac{\partial E\left(R_o^a(t)\right)}{\partial w_{oh}} \tag{5}$$

where η is the learning rate. The derivative of the error function can be further expanded by introducing the chain rule. Since $R(t)$ can be replaced at a suitable point by an estimate for a single run $S(t)$, the weights is updated according to

$$\Delta w_{oh}(t) = \frac{1}{n_h} \left[S_o^d(t) - S_o^a(t)\right] S_h(t) \tag{6}$$

Following PSD learning rule derived by the WH rule, we replace the nonlinear product by the spike convolution method, $\tilde{s}_h(t) = s_h(t) * K(t)$. Hence,

$$\frac{dw_{oh}(t)}{dt} = \eta \left[s_o^d(t) - s_o^a(t)\right] \left[s_h(t) * K(t)\right] \tag{7}$$

In PSD, weight adaptation only relies on the current states, which is different from the rules involving STDP, where both the pre- and post-synaptic spiking times are stored and used for adaptation [13]. By combining Eq. 7, we finally get the total weight update:

$$\begin{aligned}
\Delta w_{oh} &= \eta \int_0^T \Delta w_{oh}(t) dt \\
&= \eta [\sum_m \sum_f K\left(t_d^m - t_h^f\right) H\left(t_d^m - t_h^f\right) \\
&\quad - \sum_n \sum_f K\left(t_a^n - t_h^f\right) H\left(t_a^n - t_h^f\right)]
\end{aligned} \tag{8}$$

The weight modifications for hidden layer neurons are computed similarly:

$$\begin{aligned}
\Delta w_{hi}(t) &= -\frac{\partial E\left(R_o^a(t)\right)}{\partial w_{hi}} \\
&= -\frac{\partial E\left(R_o^a(t)\right)}{\partial R_h(t)} \frac{\partial R_h(t)}{\partial w_{hi}}
\end{aligned} \tag{9}$$

The weight modification formula of hidden neurons becomes

$$\Delta w_{hi}(t) = \frac{1}{n_h n_i} \sum_{o \in O} \left[S_o^d(t) - S_o^a(t)\right] S_i(t) w_{oh} \tag{10}$$

To modify synaptic weights in the same gradient direction, we use the modulus $|w_{oh}|$ as mentioned in [8]:

$$\Delta w_{hi}(t) = \frac{1}{n_h n_i} \sum_{o \in O} [S_o^d(t) - S_o^a(t)] S_i(t) |w_{oh}| \tag{11}$$

The total weights for the hidden neurons are changed

$$\Delta w_{hi} = \eta [\sum_{o \in O} \sum_m \sum_f K\left(t_d^m - t_i^f\right) H\left(t_d^m - t_i^f\right)$$
$$- \sum_{o \in O} \sum_n \sum_f K\left(t_a^n - t_i^f\right) H\left(t_a^n - t_i^f\right)] |w_{oh}| \tag{12}$$

The weights further are changed by synaptic scaling [8],

$$w_{ij} = \begin{cases} (1+f)w_{ij}, & w_{ij} > 0 \\ (\frac{1}{1+f})w_{ij}, & w_{ij} < 0 \end{cases} \tag{13}$$

where f is the scaling factor. We set $f > 0$ when the firing rate $r < r_{min}$, and $f < 0$ for $r > r_{max}$. The sensitivity of the network to its initial state is reduced by keeping the postsynaptic neuron firing rate within a particular range $[r_{min}, r_{max}]$. We introduce the van Rossum metric [13] with a filter function to measure the distance between two spike trains, written as:

$$Dist = \frac{1}{\tau} \int_0^\infty [f(t) - g(t)]^2 dt \tag{14}$$

$f(t)$ and $g(t)$ are filtered signals of the two pulse trains. τ is the free parameter.

3   Simulations

3.1   Learning Sequences of Spikes

There are N input neurons, and each input neuron sends out a random pulse train which has a uniform distribution over a time interval T. The hidden layer contains H neurons, and the output layer contains only M neurons. The default parameters used in the following experiments are set to $N = 100$, $H = 200$, $M = 1$ and $T = 0.2$ s. The time step is set as $dt = 0.01$. The initial synaptic weight can be randomly selected from a Gaussian distribution of mean value 0 and standard deviation 0.1. The spike threshold $\vartheta = 1$, and the reset potential is 0. The refectory time is set to $t_{ref} = 0$. We set the parameters $\eta = 0.01$, $\tau_m = 10$ ms, and $\tau_s = 2.5$ ms. The target spike sequence is specified as [40, 80, 120, 160] ms. For each run, the training process is performed for up to 500 epochs or until the distance equals 0. 20 independent runs is repeated for averaging our experimental results. Figure 2 shows the learning process. During the time window T, we use van Rossum Dist to present the training error. Initially, the neuron can trigger a spike at any arbitrary time, which causes a large distance

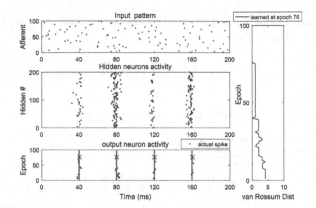

Fig. 2. The training process of spike sequences is illustrated. The output neuron is trained to reproduce pulses at the target time (light red bars at the bottom). The input spike pattern is displayed at the top. The middle and bottom show the actual triggering spikes for hidden and output neurons after learning, respectively (given by the blue dots). The right figure displays the distance between the target spike sequence and the actual output spike sequence. (Color figure online)

value. During the training phase, the neuron gradually is trained to fire spikes at the desired time, which is represented by the decrease of distance. After the last 76 learning epochs, the firing time of the output spikes matches the target spikes, and the error function value is reduced to 0. This experiment shows our method can successfully allow the neuron to fire a target pulse sequence within several training epochs.

3.2   Classification on the UCI Dataset

Iris. A basic benchmark dataset for plant classification. It contains 3 types of iris plants. Each category contains 50 samples and each of which is represented by 4 variables. There are 150 instances. 50% samples are chosen from each class to build the training set, and the rest for testing. We use population coding, as described in [14], to convert the Iris data features into spike times. As a result, each feature value is encoded by 6 identically shaped overlapping Gaussian functions, then $4 \times 6 = 24$ input spikes are obtained as the input of 24 synapses. In addition, all patterns have 5 additional input synapses with input spikes at fixed times [2, 4, 6.5, 7.5, 10] to ensure that the target spikes can be launched. The total number of input neurons is $4 \times 6 + 5 = 29$. There are 50 hidden neurons and 3 output neurons. The total time duration for the input pattern is set to $T = 10$ ms. The network is trained to trigger a desired train of [6.5, 7.5] ms corresponding to the correct input category, and to keep silent for other categories.

Our approach can achieve comparable or even higher accuracy (reported $96 \pm 1.3\%$ accuracy) compared with the traditional neural network [15,16] in Table 1. This result shows our method is successful in training temporal SNNs.

Table 1. Comparison with other methods on the Iris dataset

Method	Epochs	Testing accuracy (%)
Spiking Methods		
SpikeProp (2002) [16]	1000	96.1 ± 0.1
SWAT (2010) [11]	500	95.3
MSGD (2013) [17]	241	94.4
Multi-ReSuMe (2013) [8]	174	94.0 ± 0.79
Xie et al. (2016) [18]	18	96.0
Xie et al. (2017) [19]	2	95.0
Taherkhani et al. (2018) [10]	100	95.7
BP-STDP (2019) [20]	120	96.0
Proposed method	80	96.0 ± 1.3
Non-Spiking Methods		
SVM and Bayesian (2014) [15]	–	96.0
Matlab BP (2010) [16]	$2.6 \cdot 10^6$	95.5 ± 0.1
Matlab LM (2010) [16]	3750	95.7 ± 0.1

Our method is compared with other spike-based methods. In Table 1, SpikeProp [16], Xie et al. [18,19], BP-STDP [20] and the proposed method achieve a similar high accuracy on the Iris dataset. However, compared with SpikeProp [16] which requires 1000 convergent epochs, the proposed method only needs 120 convergent epochs. Although Xie et al. [18,19] have improved the training efficiency and reduced the training epochs from 18 to 2 training epochs, their method is not a real multilayer SNN, where only synaptic weights from input to hidden neurons are adjusted, whereas all synaptic weights from hidden to output neuron are set to 1. For BP-STDP and Multi-ReSuMe, about 75% of the total Iris dataset for each class is used as the training set, but we only use 50% of the total Iris dataset for training and the classification performance can be significantly improved in the testing set. In addition, different from Taherkhani et al. [8,10,16], the proposed method does not need sub-connections and thus reduces the number of weight modification.

4   Conclusion

This paper proposes a novel supervised, multispike learning algorithm for multilayer SNNs, which can trigger multiple spikes at precise desired times for each layer. The proposed method derives weight update rule from the WH rule, and then credits the network error simultaneously to previous layers by using back-propagation. Experimental results show our method achieve high learning accuracy with a significant improvement in computational efficiency of the network.

References

1. Butts, D.A., et al.: Temporal precision in the neural code and the timescales of natural vision. Nature **449**(7158), 92 (2007)
2. Knudsen, E.I.: Instructed learning in the auditory localization pathway of the barn owl. Nature **417**(6886), 322 (2002)
3. Pfister, J.P., Toyoizumi, T., Barber, D., Gerstner, W.: Optimal spike-timing-dependent plasticity for precise action potential firing in supervised learning. Neural Comput. **18**(6), 1318–1348 (2006)
4. Gardner, B., Grüning, A.: Supervised learning in spiking neural networks for precise temporal encoding. PloS one **11**(8), e0161335 (2016)
5. Ponulak, F., Kasiński, A.: Supervised learning in spiking neural networks with resume: sequence learning, classification, and spike shifting. Neural Comput. **22**(2), 467–510 (2010)
6. McKennoch, S., Liu, D., Bushnell, L.G.: Fast modifications of the spikeprop algorithm. In: The 2006 IEEE International Joint Conference on Neural Network Proceedings, pp. 3970–3977. IEEE (2006)
7. Shrestha, S.B., Song, Q.: Adaptive learning rate of spikeprop based on weight convergence analysis. Neural Netw. **63**, 185–198 (2015)
8. Sporea, I., Grüning, A.: Supervised learning in multilayer spiking neural networks. Neural Comput. **25**(2), 473–509 (2013)
9. Taherkhani, A., Belatreche, A., Li, Y., Maguire, L.P.: Dl-resume: a delay learning-based remote supervised method for spiking neurons. IEEE Trans. Neural Netw. Learn. Syst. **26**(12), 3137–3149 (2015)
10. Taherkhani, A., Belatreche, A., Li, Y., Maguire, L.P.: A supervised learning algorithm for learning precise timing of multiple spikes in multilayer spiking neural networks. IEEE Trans. Neural Netw. Learn. Syst. **99**, 1–14 (2018)
11. Wade, J.J., McDaid, L.J., Santos, J.A., Sayers, H.M.: Swat: a spiking neural network training algorithm for classification problems. IEEE Trans. Neural Netw. **21**(11), 1817–1830 (2010)
12. Gerstner, W., Kistler, W.M.: Spiking Neuron Models: Single Neurons, Populations. Cambridge University Press, Plasticity (2002)
13. Yu, Q., Tang, H., Tan, K.C., Li, H.: Precise-spike-driven synaptic plasticity: learning hetero-association of spatiotemporal spike patterns. Plos one **8**(11), e78318 (2013)
14. Snippe, H.P.: Parameter extraction from population codes: a critical assessment. Neural Comput. **8**(3), 511–529 (1996)
15. Wang, J., Belatreche, A., Maguire, L., Mcginnity, T.M.: An online supervised learning method for spiking neural networks with adaptive structure. Neurocomputing **144**, 526–536 (2014)
16. Bohte, S.M., Kok, J.N., La Poutre, H.: Error-backpropagation in temporally encoded networks of spiking neurons. Neurocomputing **48**(1), 17–37 (2002)
17. Xu, Y., Zeng, X., Han, L., Yang, J.: A supervised multi-spike learning algorithm based on gradient descent for spiking neural networks. Neural Netw. **43**, 99–113 (2013)

18. Xie, X., Qu, H., Liu, G., Zhang, M., Kurths, J.: An efficient supervised training algorithm for multilayer spiking neural networks. PloS one **11**(4), e0150329 (2016)
19. Xie, X., Qu, H., Yi, Z., Kurths, J.: Efficient training of supervised spiking neural network via accurate synaptic-efficiency adjustment method. IEEE Trans. Neural Netw. Learn. Syst. **28**(6), 1411–1424 (2017)
20. Tavanaei, A., Maida, A.: BP-STDP: approximating backpropagation using spike timing dependent plasticity. Neurocomputing **330**, 39–47 (2019)

A Term and Phase Invariant Neural Network for Fault Signal Diagnosis

Yong Zhou[1], Haoyu Li[1], and Li Lin[2(✉)]

[1] School of Software, Dalian University of Technology, Dalian, China
{kevinzh,378130873}@dlut.edu.cn
[2] College of Locomotives and Rolling Stock, Dalian Jiaotong University,
Dalian, China
julandalili@126.com

Abstract. Since the industrial production is becoming more and more large-scale, producing a large number of signal data. Which make it difficult for traditional methods to effectively and accurately extract and analyze the signals. In this paper, a novel Term and phase invariant neural network (TPINN) based on one-dimensional convolution neural network combined and timing analysis is proposed, which can solve the problem effectively. In the first stage, the improved one-dimensional big kernel convolution network is used to extract the phase invariant features of the original signal. In the second stage, the collected features are analyzed in time domain combined with timing analysis layer. This model can extract the phase invariant features when facing the random initial sampling point, and then combine the timing analysis to get the final classification result. Compared with the traditional methods, this method can accurately extract the signal features without deliberately selecting the sampling points, improve the efficiency, and analyze the characteristics of the signal in the time domain, improve the final classification accuracy.

Keywords: Convolutional neural network · Feature learning · Fault diagnosis · Timing analyze

1 Introduction

Nowadays large-scale mechanical equipment is widely used in modern industry, bearing is the most basic and easily worn component under the harsh working conditions. And the fault will cause enormous potential safety hazards and economic losses. Therefore, automatically and timely fault diagnosis of the health status of bearing has become a hot topic and attract more and more attention [3,12].

As a new branch of mechanical fault detection technology, intelligent fault diagnosis technology can effectively analyze the collected data and obtain reliable diagnosis results.There are two main problems in the existing methods:

© Springer Nature Switzerland AG 2020
H. Yang et al. (Eds.): ICONIP 2020, CCIS 1333, pp. 490–497, 2020.
https://doi.org/10.1007/978-3-030-63823-8_56

1. Shallow structural models, such as Support vector machine (SVM), Back-propagation neural network (BPNN), etc. [2,8,14] when faced with a large number of data cant accurately extract the input feature information, which limits the ability to diagnose faults [1,10,15].
2. The common deep model learning features can't overcome the errors caused by the phase(Because of the randomness of sampling position, there will be phase difference in the same sampling period), which ultimately leads to inaccurate diagnosis results of bearing health status. And too complex network model and data processing will bring high time cost, and can not get timely diagnosis results. For example in [13], the model ignore the phase difference and the method in [11] need to process the raw data which reduce the efficiency.

In this paper, a novel intelligent fault diagnosis model TPINN based on deep convolution and timing is proposed. The model can extract phase invariant features from the original vibration signal data, and then the features can be analyzed in timing analysis layer. There are two layers in feature extraction part. In the first layer, a big convolution kernel is used to ensure that there are enough receptive fields to contain phase information. In the second layer, we use a small convolution kernel to ensure sufficient time resolution. After each layer, the data is compressed by the maximum pooling operation, and we can obtain the invariant features. In the part of feature analysis, considering the time characteristics of the vibration signal, we replace the full connection layer with the cells which have time characteristics to give full play to its memory function of the past information. Finally we can get the final diagnosis result.

The results show that the proposed method is more accurate and effective than other methods, and can be adopted to more working environment. The main contributions of the model are as follows:

1. By the use of big kernel and small kernel, we can get rid of the influence of phase difference and automatically extract the phase invariant features.
2. In the feature analysis layer, considering the time characteristic of vibration signal, we design a time sequence analysis layer to replace full connection layer. So that we can consider the time characteristics of features and get more accurate results.

2   The Proposed Methods in This Paper

In this paper, we propose a novel intelligent fault diagnosis method for rolling bearing. This method includes two main parts: one-dimensional convolution layer and feature analysis layer with time characteristics.

2.1   Extract Phase Invariant Features with Big Kernel Convolution

Convolutional neural network (CNN) was proposed by Yann Lecun in 1989 [7]. The model designed in this paper is used to process one-dimensional vibration signal, so this section will focus on one-dimensional convolution structure [5,6]. The key of convolution layer is convolution kernel. Through the convolution of the input signal, the corresponding characteristics can be obtained.

Here we use a big convolution kernel to convolute the original signal. In this case, the convolution operation can be regarded as the feature detector at different positions. In a large convolution window, the feature information in the window can be extracted, and then combined with the Maximum Pooling operation, the feature information in the window can be filtered again. Even if the feature position in the window moves, the most important information can be obtained, and finally the phase invariant feature can be obtained. That is whenever the detection is carried out for the same fault, which means that there may be signals with different initial phases, and the same output response will be obtained. In the second convolution layer, we use a small convolution kernel to improve the time resolution. Finally, in the whole feature extraction process, the effect of phase difference can be greatly reduced by the overlay of the big and small convolution kernels and the Max Pooling layer, so that the phase invariant features can be extracted. As shown in Fig. 1, two input signals with different phases from the same fault can obtain the same fault characteristics after feature extraction by convolution layer.

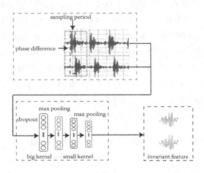

Fig. 1. The process of phase invariant features extraction.

Recurrent neural network (RNN) is mainly used to process time series data and shows good performance [4], but it can't solve the long-term dependence problem. In order to make the model more effective in maintaining long-term memory, Hochreiter and Jrgen Schmidhuber propose a long short term memory (LSTM) neural network. The key structures of LSTM are "forget gate" and "input gate". For the time sequence analysis layer used in this paper, the input data is the phase invariant features, which greatly reduces the scale of the original data, and doesn't need the complex cell structure, so we optimize the structure of the traditional one-dimensional LSTM [9].

The essence of forgetting gate is the probability of transferring the previous state information. Here we can set a truncation function, and we can directly take zero for information without memory value; at the same time, we can couple forgetting gate and input gate, which can simplify cell structure (integrate two gates into one) and make decisions on forgetting content and input content at the same time. As shown in Fig. 2 and the process can be described as follows:

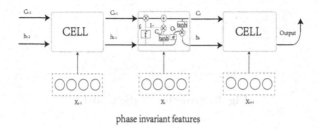

phase invariant features

Fig. 2. The cell in time sequence analysis layer.

$$f_t = f(w_f * [h_{t-1}, X_t] + b_f) \tag{1}$$

$$C_t = tanh(w_c * [h_{t-1}, X_t] + b_f) \tag{2}$$

$$C_t = f_t * C_{t-1} + (1 - f_t) * C_t \tag{3}$$

$$O_t = \sigma(w_o * [h_{t-1}, X_t] + b_o) \tag{4}$$

$$h_t = O_t * tanh(C_t) \tag{5}$$

where f_t represents the probability of forgetting the memory in forgetting gate, C_t is the state at time t, h_t is the output at time t. f is the truncation activation function. For the information with weight less than 0.5, the weight is set to 0 directly, and if the weight more than 0.5, f represents the *Sigmoid* function, which can reduce the calculation cost of the model on the premise of keeping important information.

The structure of the model proposed in this paper is shown in Fig. 3 and the parameters are shown in Table 1.

Table 1. Parameters of the model.

Parameter description	Value
The units of the input layer	384
The number of hidden layers in CNN	2
The units of first convolution layer	32
The kernel size of first convolution layer	13
The units of second convolution layer	16
The number of cells in timing analysis layer	128

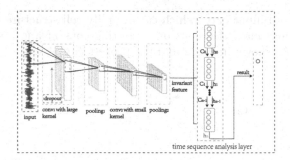

Fig. 3. Structure of the model.

3   Experiment and Analysis

3.1   Experimental Data Description

In this paper, the experimental data of rolling bearings in the laboratory of Case Western Reserve University (CWRU) are used as the experimental samples. The data collection platform is mainly composed of induction motor, torque sensor and power meter, as shown in Fig. 4.

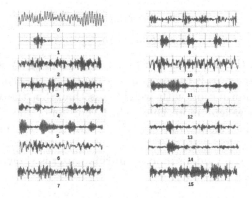

Fig. 4. The samples of signals used in this paper.

We use 16 kinds of fault samples collected at the maximum power speed of 1797, which have different fault direction, fault type and fault severity. Each sample contained 384 data points. 4032 samples were randomly selected as training data, and 1355 samples were selected as training data. More parameters in this experiment are available in Table 2.

3.2   Comparison with Traditional Methods

In order to prove that the method proposed in this paper is superior to the traditional method, four traditional intelligent models are used in the experiment.

Table 2. Parameters of the rolling bearing.

Parameter description	Value
Bearing specs	SKF6205
Rotating speed	12 point, bold
Sampling frequency	5.4152 Hz, 3.5848 Hz, 4.7135 Hz
Fault location	Inner ring, outer ring, ball
Faulty diameter	0.007 in, 0.014 in, 0.021 in

All methods use 384 data points as input, without data preprocessing, and simulate the real working environment. Figure 5 shows the detailed experimental results of each experiment on the data. It can be seen from the figure that the method proposed in this paper can achieve 96% accuracy.

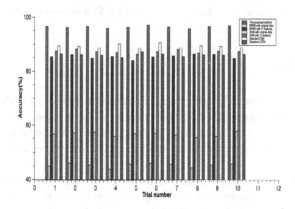

Fig. 5. Phase difference between the same signals.

From the comparison, we can see that:

1. The diagnostic performance of shallow model depends largely on the extraction of artificial features. When the most sensitive features can be extracted as input, the performance will be greatly improved. However, in the face of a large and varied number of data, the diagnostic efficiency will be seriously affected.
2. Although a single deep learning method can obtain more accurate results than the traditional model, it is difficult to extract multifaceted features in the face of complex original signal input.

3.3   The Effectiveness of the Proposed Model

After selecting the appropriate parameters, the following Fig. 6 and Fig. 7 show the loss and accuracy curve of the method proposed in the training process.

From the figure, we can find that the model converges with the training to about 250 steps. Although the model contains the characteristics of phase invariance and time, the structure complexity is relatively high, and the convergence speed is slightly slow, but it shows high test accuracy and model stability in the test data.

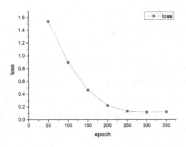

Fig. 6. The variation curve of loss.   **Fig. 7.** The variation curve of accuracy.

4   Conclusion

In this paper we propose a bearing fault diagnosis method TPINN. The method consists of two main steps: firstly, the original data is taken as input directly, phase invariant features are extracted through feature extraction layer. The features are used as the input of time sequence analysis layer and the diagnosis result is obtained.

Compared with the traditional shallow model and standard depth model method, this method overcomes the dependence on artificial feature and can fully extract the features of phase invariance and time relationship, so that can achieve higher diagnostic accuracy. At the same time, it opens up a new direction to diagnose the original signal. With further research, more accurate and effective methods will be found.

References

1. Bengio, Y.: Courville, aaron, vincent, pascal: Representation learning: a review and new perspectives. IEEE Trans. Pattern Anal. Mach. Intell. **35**(8), 1798–1828 (2013)
2. Feng, J., Lei, Y., Jing, L., Xin, Z., Na, L.: Deep neural networks: a promising tool for fault characteristic mining and intelligent diagnosis of rotating machinery with massive data. Mech. Syst. Sign. Process. **72–73**, 303–315 (2016)
3. Guo, L., Li, N., Jia, F., Lei, Y., Lin, J.: A recurrent neural network based health indicator for remaining useful life prediction of bearings. Neurocomputing **240**, 98–109 (2017)
4. Hermans, M., Schrauwen, B.: Training and analyzing deep recurrent neural networks. In: Advances in Neural Information Processing Systems (2013)

5. Janssens, O., Slavkovikj, V., Bram, V.S.: Convolutional neural network based fault detection for rotating machinery. J. Sound Vib. **377**, 331–345 (2016)
6. Jia, F., Lei, Y., Guo, L., Lin, J., Xing, S.: A neural network constructed by deep learning technique and its application to intelligent fault diagnosis of machines. Neurocomputing **272**, 619–628 (2018)
7. Lecun, Y., et al.: Backpropagation applied to handwritten zip code recognition. Neural Comput. **1**(4), 541–551 (1989)
8. Lei, Y., Jia, F., Lin, J., Xing, S., Ding, S.: An intelligent fault diagnosis method using unsupervised feature learning towards mechanical big data. IEEE Trans. Ind. Electron. **63**, 1 (2016). https://doi.org/10.1109/TIE.2016.2519325
9. Sak, H., Senior, A., Beaufays, F.: Long short-term memory based recurrent neural network architectures for large vocabulary speech recognition (2014)
10. Shao, H., Jiang, H., Wang, F., Zhao, H.: An enhancement deep feature fusion method for rotating machinery fault diagnosis. Knowl. Based Syst. **119**, 200–220 (2017)
11. Shao, H., Jiang, H., Zhang, H., Duan, W., Liang, T., Wu, S.: Rolling bearing fault feature learning using improved convolutional deep belief network with compressed sensing. Mech. Syst. Sign. Process. **100**, 743–765 (2018)
12. Wei, Z., Wang, Y., He, S., Sao, J.: A novel intelligent method for bearing fault diagnosis based on affinity propagation clustering and adaptive feature selection. Knowl. Based Syst. **116(C)**, 1–12 (2017)
13. Wei, Z., Li, C., Peng, G., Chen, Y., Zhang, Z.: A deep convolutional neural network with new training methods for bearing fault diagnosis under noisy environment and different working load. Mech. Syst. Sig. Process. **100**, 439–453 (2018)
14. Xiao, Y., Wang, H., Lin, Z., Xu, W.: Two methods of selecting gaussian kernel parameters for one-class SVM and their application to fault detection. Knowl. Based Syst. **59**, 75–84 (2014)
15. Zhao, M., Jia, X.: A novel strategy for signal denoising using reweighted SVD and its applications to weak fault feature enhancement of rotating machinery. Mech. Syst. Sig. Process. **94**, 129–147 (2017)

Adaptive Skewness Kurtosis Neural Network : Enabling Communication Between Neural Nodes Within a Layer

Yifeng Wang, Yang Wang, Guiming Hu, Yuying Liu, and Yi Zhao$^{(\boxtimes)}$

Harbin Institute of Technology, Shenzhen, China
zhao.yi@hit.edu.cn

Abstract. The statistical properties of neural networks are closely associated with their performance. From this perspective, the training process of deep learning models can be divided into two stages corresponding to the procedures of feature extraction and integration. In the feature extraction stage, the mean and variance of the hidden layer changes; during the feature integration stage, the mean and variance remain relatively stable, while the skewness and kurtosis change considerably. Meanwhile, constructing intra-layer connections may improve the performance of neural networks. Consequently, a novel Adaptive Skewness Kurtosis (ASK) structure is proposed, which enables deep learning networks to connect within a layer. On the basis of stabilizing the mean and variance of the layer, the ASK structure adaptively adjusts the skewness and kurtosis of the layer by communicating the connections between neuron nodes in the layer to improve the feature integration ability of the model ultimately. Based on the ASK structure, we propose an ASK neural network (ASKNN) where the ASK structure designed to a standard BP neural network (BPNN) to adjust the high order moments. Compared with the standard BPNN, ASKNN performs better especially when dealing with the data contaminated with noise.

Keywords: Skewness · Kurtosis · Deep learning · Intra-layer connection · Feature integration

1 Introduction

Images can also be viewed as certain probability distributions of pixel values [1,2]. Taking image classification as an example, the type of image data set determines the distribution of pixels [3]. As for neural networks, if we regard the neuron nodes in each layer as a feature map formed by extracting features from

Supported by an Innovative Research Project of Shenzhen under Project No. KQJSCX20180328165509766, National Natural Science Foundation of Guangdong Province under Project No.2020A1515010812 and the National Key R&D Program of China under Grant No. 2018YFB1003800, 2018YFB1003805.

H. Yang et al. (Eds.): ICONIP 2020, CCIS 1333, pp. 498–507, 2020.
https://doi.org/10.1007/978-3-030-63823-8_57

the preceding layer, then the pixel values of the feature map correspond to the values of neuron nodes in the layer [4,5]. Therefore, the probability distribution of neuron nodes in each layer is closely associated with the issue the model aims to address. It implies that neuron nodes in each layer need successive modifications in training to gradually grasp certain distribution and statistical properties. Layer Normalization improves the performance of deep learning networks by applying normalization to every layer [6,7]. This operation not only changes the mean and variance of neuron nodes of each layer but also changes their kurtosis and skewness. It concludes that making shifts to the statistical properties of neural networks may contribute to their better performance.

Artificial neural network (ANN) is an algorithmic model that imitates the behavioral characteristics of animal neural networks and utilizes structures similar to synaptic connections of neurons for information processing [8–10]. Actually the communication and transmission of information between neurons in the same neural network layer are of great importance, especially the brain nerves that process large amounts of information. However, the calculations between neurons in the layer may destroy the statistical properties of the layer and ruin the information extracted from the previous layer, which may be the main reason why there is no such architecture in deep learning models so far.

For all those reasons, we design an adaptive skewness-kurtosis neural network (ASKNN), which can adaptively modify its skewness and kurtosis without changing the mean value and variance of the neural network layer, and at the same time this model ensures effective information communication and exchange between neurons without significantly changing its statistical properties in a layer.

2 The Construction of Adaptive Skewness Kurtosis Neural Network (ASKNN)

Three-layers BP neural network is selected as the research basis. In order to stabilize the mean and variance of the neural network layer, we achieve the operation by two steps: *Cut* and *Supply*. Starting from the first node of the hidden layer, the value of the first node is cut, and we add the *Cut* value to the second node, naturally, the variance of the entire hidden layer fluctuates. To make the variance back to the origin, the second node is supplied, and the *Supply* value that is computed according to the *Cut* value and variance variation is added to the third node. By analogy, the entire hidden layer is executed. Consequently, the variance of the hidden layer stays unchanged. Moreover, the *Cut* and *Supply* confirm the invariance of the mean. It is worth noting that the *Cut* value is set as parameters in the deep learning model, which is adaptively adjusted during the training procedure, and the *Supply* value is directly calculated by statistical rules. Wherefore, training parameters and the network scale will not dramatically increase.

2.1 The Mathematical Model of ASKNN

Let the number of nodes in the hidden layer be N, the mean of the hidden layer be m, and the initial variance be var_0, then the hidden layer can be represented as a $1 \times N$ array h:

$$h = (h_0, h_1, h_2 \cdots h_{N-1}) \tag{1}$$

Let Cut be a $1 \times \lfloor \frac{N}{2} \rfloor$ array of truncated values; let $Supply$ be a $1 \times \lfloor \frac{N}{2} \rfloor$ array of compensation values. The architecture of the model is exhibited in Fig. 1.

The mathematical representation of the model is as follows:

Let the hidden layer neuron node value be h_i, the value of the neuron node after one step and two steps respectively be h_i', h_i''. An operation cycle is completed when i moves from an even to the next even (that is to say, a Cut step and a $Supply$ step constitute an operation cycle). Suppose i is even, then we have:

$$
\begin{aligned}
h_i' &= h_i - Cut_{i/2} & h_{i+1}' &= h_{i+1} + Cut_{i/2} \\
h_{i+1}'' &= h_{i+1}' - Supply_{i/2} & h_{i+2}' &= h_{i+2} + Supply_{i/2}
\end{aligned}
\tag{2}
$$

Assume that the variance of the hidden layer of the $\frac{i}{2}$ cycle equals to the initial variance var_0, that is:

$$var_0 = [\sum_{j=0}^{i-1} (h_j - m)^2 + (h_i - m)^2 + (h_{i+1} - m)^2 + \sum_{j=i+2}^{N-1} (h_j - m)^2] \tag{3}$$

After the Cut step, the variance becomes var_1:

$$
\begin{aligned}
var_1 = \frac{1}{N-1} [&\sum_{j=0}^{i-1} (h_j - m)^2 + (h_i - Cut_{i/2} - m)^2 \\
&+ (h_{i+1} + Cut_{i/2} - m)^2 + \sum_{j=i+2}^{N-1} (h_j - m)^2]
\end{aligned}
\tag{4}
$$

Thus, variance variation is obtained:

$$
\begin{aligned}
\Delta var = \frac{1}{N-1} [&(h_i - Cut_{i/2} - m)^2 - (h_i - m)^2 \\
&+ (h_{i+1} + Cut_{i/2} - m)^2 - (h_{i+1} - m)^2]
\end{aligned}
\tag{5}
$$

Performing the $Supply$ step, suppose the supplied variance is var_0', we have:

$$
\begin{aligned}
var_0' = \frac{1}{N-1} [&\sum_{j=0}^{i-1} (h_j - m)^2 + (h_i - Cut_{i/2} - m)^2 + \sum_{j=i+3}^{N-1} (h_j - m)^2 \\
&+ (h_{i+1} + Cut_{i/2} - Supply_{i/2} - m)^2 + (h_{i+2} + Supply_{i/2} - m)^2]
\end{aligned}
\tag{6}
$$

To make var_0' equal to var_0, the below equation should be satisfied:

$$\Delta var = var_1 - var_0 = var_1 - var_0' \tag{7}$$

So, we conclude that :

$$
\begin{aligned}
Supply_{i/2} = \frac{1}{2}[&-(h_{i+2} - h_{i+1} - Cut_{i/2}) \\
\pm &((h_{i+2} - h_{i+1} - Cut_{i/2})^2 + 2[(h_i - m)^2 \\
&+ (h_{i+1} - m)^2 - (h_0 - Cut_{i/2} - m)^2 \\
&- (h_{i+1} + Cut_{i/2} - m)^2])^{\frac{1}{2}}]
\end{aligned}
\tag{8}
$$

However, this equation may not have real number solutions for that if the Cut step of the last operation cycle varies the variance such largely that the $Supply$ step of this cycle can not smooth the alteration anyhow. Against this situation, the model algorithm has been improved.

2.2 Improved Mathematical Model of ASKNN

In the case where it is impossible to supply the variance at one time, we develop the variance accumulation approach:

Under this circumstance, this inequation holds:

$$
|var_1 - var_0| > |var_1 - var_0'| \tag{9}
$$

Minimize this function, the solution is as below:

$$
Supply_{i/2} = \frac{1}{2}(h_{i+1} + Cut_{i/2} + h_{i+2}) \tag{10}
$$

Thus, it gets the minimum which is also the residual unsupplied variance, denoted as remain:

$$
\begin{aligned}
remain = \frac{1}{2}&((h_i - Cut_{i/2} - m)^2 + (h_{i+1} + Cut_{i/2} - m)^2 \\
&- (h_i - m)^2 - (h_{i+1} - m)^2) - \frac{1}{4}(h_{i+2} - h_{i+1} - Cut_{i/2})^2
\end{aligned}
\tag{11}
$$

Accordingly, the following relations hold:

$$
\begin{aligned}
var_0 = \frac{1}{N-1}[&\sum_{j=0}^{i-1}(h_j - m)^2 + (h_i - m)^2 \\
&+ (h_{i+1} - m)^2 + \sum_{j=i+2}^{N-1}(h_j - m)^2] - remain
\end{aligned}
\tag{12}
$$

$$
\begin{aligned}
\Delta var = \frac{1}{N-1}[&(h_i - Cut_{i/2} - m)^2 - (h_i - m)^2 \\
&+ (h_{i+1} + Cut_{i/2} - m)^2 - (h_{i+1} - m)^2] + remain
\end{aligned}
\tag{13}
$$

Finally, the $Supply$ value is attained. Via fusing the remaining unsupplied variance into the next operation cycle, the variance can return to the initial value in the case of variance changes can not be supplied to the initial value at one time.

Nevertheless, the variance accumulation approach may make variances of subsequent operation rounds more difficult to be supplied. To ensure the whole variance to be stable, some last nodes only employ *Supply* steps without *Cut* steps. The number of these nodes named tail retention N_{tail} is the hyper-parameter of the algorithm model. In this way, the length of the *Cut* array is $N_{Cut} = \lfloor \frac{N - N_{tail}}{2} \rfloor - 1$, and the length of the supplied array is $N_{Supply} = N_{Cut} + N_{tail}$. In this case, the structure of ASKNN is shown in Fig. 2.

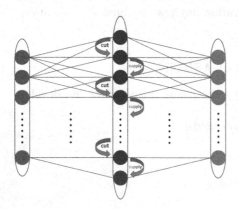

Fig. 1. Schematic diagram of adaptive skewness-kurtosis neural network architecture.

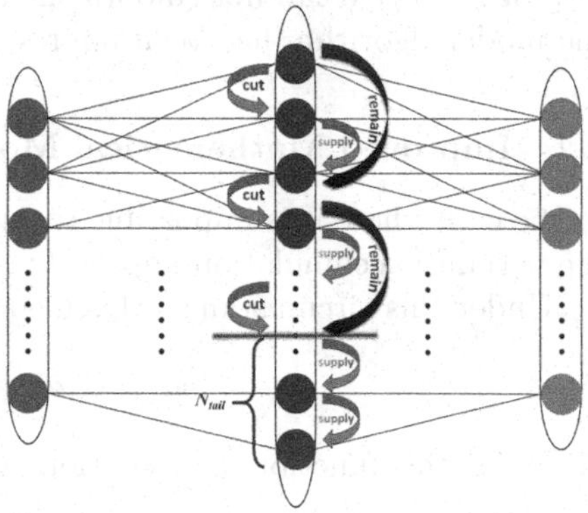

Fig. 2. Schematic diagram of improved adaptive skewness-kurtosis neural network architecture

3   Experiments and Results

Experiments are conducted on MNIST handwritten digit recognition Dataset and the dataset with 20% salt-and-pepper noise which can well verify the noise resistance ability and the generalization ability of ASKNN. For comparison, ASKNN and BP neural network which share the same parameters.

The bootstrap method is adopted to extract data to train models. Bootstrap is a kind of resampling approach [11]. Batches produced via using the Bootstrap method can better reflect the statistical properties of the training dataset without damaging the data distribution. Since the training data input during each training is similar in statistical nature, it is more helpful to compare the performance of different models in the training process. Table 1 documents some experimental results of BPNN and ASKNN trained multiple times with different combinations of training times, the number of hidden neuron nodes, and the tail retention N_{tail}.

Based on the experimental results, findings are summarized as follows:

• Compared with BPNN with the same training times and the number of neuron nodes in the hidden layer, the training parameters of ASKNN only increased by less than 1%.

• Experimental results also suggest that over-fitting is more likely to happen to BPNN than ASKNN when they both have massive hidden nodes.

• On the MNIST data with 20% salt-and-pepper noise, the standard BP neural network performs evidently worse in that the accuracy on the test set is ever lower than 11%. In contrast, the accuracy of ASKNN on the test set is steadily increased.

We subsequently designed some targeted experiments, and applied the ASK structure proposed in this article to the more advanced VGG network, GoogLeNet, and ResNet in the field of image recognition. We found that in the face of normal data sets, these deep learning models can show very good performance. At this time, the ASK structure hardly works. However, when the data set contains various noises and the process of feature extraction and integration is no longer smooth, the ASK structure will play its role. Take the VGG network as an example. When faced with the noise-free data set, the recognition accuracy of the VGG network can reach 97% or even higher. At this time, the *Cut* value and *Supply* value in the ASK structure are both close to 0, which also means that the ASK structure hardly works, and the *Cut* value is adjusted by itself during the training process. Therefore, as long as the training strategy is appropriate, the performance of the deep learning model with the ASK structure is generally better than the performance before the addition. However, in the face of various noise data, the performance of the deep learning model with the ASK structure has been significantly improved.

4   Performance Analysis

In terms of probability theory and mathematical statistics, language can be considered as specific probability distributions of letters; image data can also be regarded as specific probability distributions of pixel values which depend on the image type in the data set. Given that the forward propagation of the neural network is a structure that continuously extracts and processes information and features from data, then the hidden layer can be interpreted as a feature map whose distribution conceals the information that the classification or regression task relies on. Therefore, the statistic nature of the feature map is closely related to the performance of the neural network. Since the standard BP neural network model has no intra-layer connection structure, the modification of the feature map during the training process is achieved indirectly through adjusting the values of the weight and bias connected to the preceding layer. By this means, it is sometimes tough to adjust the feature map to the best state. When the feature map is adjusted to a suboptimal state, it is difficult to continue to adjust, so the accuracy of the model on the test set cannot continue to improve after reaching the bottleneck.

Table 1. Experimental results of different networks on MNIST with 20% salt-and-pepper noise

	N_hidden	N_step	BPNN			ASKNN		
			Parameters number	Training loss	Test accuracy	Parameters number	Training loss	Test accuracy
MNIST	400	0.1 k	318010	**2.204**	**24.04%**	318195	2.278	23.73%
		0.3 k		**1.991**	**58.22%**		2.205	34.56%
		0.6 k		1.643	71.87%		2.106	50.38%
		1.2 k		**1.185**	**78.90%**		1.817	67.70%
		2.0 k		**0.866**	**83.02%**		1.281	76.90%
		5.0 k		0.485	87.89%		0.537	**88.45%**
		10.0 k		0.368	89.86%		**0.336**	**90.17%**
		15.0 k		0.329	90.81%		**0.294**	**92.35%**
	1569	0.1 k	1247365	**2.099**	**52.03%**	1248134	2.262	24.23%
		1.0 k		**1.045**	**81.85%**		1.802	69.31%
		10.0 k		**0.238**	**92.37%**		0.256	91.42%
		50.0 k		0.154	92.98%		**0.138**	**95.79%**
Add 20% Pepper Noise	400	0.1 k	318010	6.659	10.09%	318195	**5.228**	9.98%
		1.0 k		2.371	**10.93%**		**2.337**	10.81%
		10.0 k		2.574	10.80%		**2.325**	**10.97%**
		50.0 k		13.267	9.89%		**2.296**	**13.42%**
		100.0 k		15.119	9.92%		**2.287**	**16.97%**
		200.0 k		16.501	9.78%		**2.273**	**21.48%**
	1569	0.1 k	1247365	12.775	**10.31%**	1248134	6.256	10.03%
		10.0 k		**4.842**	**10.46%**		5.345	10.38%
		20.0 k		9.749	10.43%		**3.786**	**11.98%**
		100.0 k		12.259	9.99%		**2.306**	**14.74%**

Therefore, aiming at studying the evolution of the feature map and the change of statistical properties within the training process, we visually analyze the hidden layer of the BPNN and the ASKNN which both have 400 neuron nodes in their hidden layers. The ASKNN models trained at different times are saved, including from models in the under-fitted state to models in the somewhat nice state. Samples in the test set are input to these models, and the hidden layer is visually captured as 20 × 20 feature maps, as shown in Fig. 4.

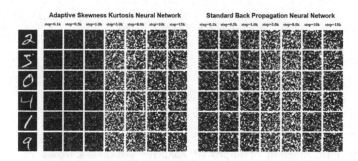

Fig. 3. Visualization of hidden layers of ASK neural network and BP neural network trained under different samples and training times.

As shown in Fig. 3, the training procedure can be divided into two stages. The first stage is from the beginning of training to around steps = 3 k. The main features of this stage are that the mean and variance of the hidden layer gradually increase, which manifested in that the visualized maps turn to white from black. It is depicted that the primary work of this stage is to extract rough features and shallow rules from the data. Meanwhile, a large number of neuron nodes in the hidden layer are activated. But since at this stage the training is insufficient, the features derived are pretty trivial some of which may even be meaningless. In this sense, the subsequent training stage can be viewed as when the features are filtered, refined and integrated.The second stage is from about steps = 3 k to the end of training characterized by that the value of neuron nodes fluctuates around the steady-state. This stage can be further subdivided into two phases: the first phase is from steps = 3 k to steps = 10 k, during this period, with the increase and decrease of different neuron values, the mean value of the hidden layer decreased slightly; the second phase is from steps = 10 k to steps = 15 k, during this period the mean and variance of the hidden layer almost stay unchanged and the value of neuron nodes shift one to another which makes the skewness and kurtosis of the hidden layer change accordingly.

It can be seen from Fig. 3 that in the first stage of the training process in which the mean of the hidden layer increases and the feature map turns to white from black, ASKNN models lag behind BPNN models as the feature maps of ASKNN models turn to white slower than those of BPNN models. On the contrary, in the second stage especially in its second phase, the ASK-structure reveals its strength that it builds up the feature selection ability and the feature integration ability of deep learning models through maintaining the stability of the mean and variance of the hidden layer and automatically modifying the distribution, such as skewness and kurtosis, of the feature map with establishing connections between neuron nodes in the same layer. Experimental results finalized under diverse combinations of batch size, Ntail and the number of neuron nodes in the hidden layer also confirmed the above analysis, as shown in Fig. 4.

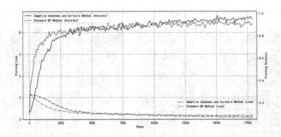

Fig. 4. Schematic diagram of improved adaptive skewness-kurtosis neural network architecture.

5   Conclusions

In this paper, we found that during the training process, the mean and variance of the hidden layer changes greatly in the phase of feature extraction while the feature integration phase is related to the changes of the kurtosis and skewness of the hidden layer. Therefore, ASKNN is proposed, which adaptively adjusts the kurtosis and skewness of hidden layers to improve the feature integration and pattern extraction ability of DPNN. ASKNN even performs better on the noisy data. Concentrated on the inter-layer communication manner, the advantages of ASKNN primarily result from the stability of the statistical properties of the hidden layer. Note that, the inter-layer connection method established in this paper may not enable the most effective communication among neuron nodes in the same layer. The future study shall make efforts to find a balance between sufficient interaction among neuron nodes and preserving the basic statistic properties of neural networks. To do so, there requires lots of mathematical theoretical research and contains much room for improvement in the future.

References

1. Chang, J.H., Shin, J.W., Kim, N.S., Mitra, S.K.: Image probability distribution based on generalized gamma function. IEEE Sig. Process. Lett. **12**(4), 325–328 (2005)
2. Cheng, L., Dong-jian, H.: Efficient method for object contour extraction based on probability distribution image. J. Comput. Appl. **10**, 52 (2008)

3. Masmoudi, A., Puech, W., Bouhlel, M.S.: Efficient adaptive arithmetic coding based on updated probability distribution for lossless image compression. J. Electron. Imaging **19**(2), 023014 (2010)
4. Li, X., Xiong, H., Wang, H., Rao, Y., Liu, L., Huan, J.: Delta: Deep learning transfer using feature map with attention for convolutional networks. arXiv preprint arXiv:1901.09229 (2019)
5. Jain, S., Zaveri, T., Prajapati, K., Patel, S.: Deep learning feature map for content based image retrieval system for remote sensing application. Int. J. Image Min. (2016)
6. Yoshida, Y., Karakida, R., Okada, M., Amari, S.I.: Statistical mechanical analysis of learning dynamics of two-layer perceptron with multiple output units. J. Phys. Math. Theor. **52**(18), 184002 (2019)
7. Yoshida, Y., Karakida, R., Okada, M., Amari, S.I.: Statistical mechanical analysis of online learning with weight normalization in single layer perceptron. J. Phys. Soc. Jpn. **86**(4), 044002 (2017)
8. Aizenberg, I., Moraga, C.: Multilayer feedforward neural network based on multi-valued neurons (MLMVN) and a backpropagation learning algorithm. Soft Comput. **11**(2), 169–183 (2007)
9. Zhang, Z., Zhang, K., Khelifi, A.: Multivariate Time Series Analysis in Climate and Environmental Research. Springer, Berlin (2018)
10. Deng, L., Yu, D.: Deep learning: methods and applications. Found. Trends Sig. Process. **7**(3–4), 197–387 (2014)
11. Johnson, R.W.: An introduction to the bootstrap. Teach. Stat. **23**(2), 49–54 (2001)

Channel Pruning via Optimal Thresholding

Yun Ye[1]([✉]), Ganmei You[1], Jong-Kae Fwu[2], Xia Zhu[2], Qing Yang[1], and Yuan Zhu[1]

[1] Intel, Beijing, China
{yun.ye,ganmei.you,qing.y.yang,yuan.y.zhu}@intel.com
[2] Intel, Santa Clara, USA
{jong-kae.fwu,xia.zhu}@intel.com

Abstract. Structured pruning, especially channel pruning is widely used for the reduced computational cost and compatibility with off-the-shelf hardware devices. Among existing works, weights are typically removed using a predefined global threshold, or a threshold computed from a predefined metric. These designs ignore the variation among different layers and weights distribution, therefore, they may often result in sub-optimal performance caused by over-pruning or under-pruning. In this paper, we present a simple yet effective method, termed Optimal Thresholding (OT), to prune channels with layer dependent thresholds that optimally separate important from negligible channels. By using OT, negligible channels are pruned to achieve high sparsity while minimizing performance degradation. Since most important weights are preserved, the pruned model can be further fine-tuned and quickly converge with very few iterations. Our method demonstrates superior performance, especially when compared to the state-of-the-art designs at high levels of sparsity.

Keywords: Structured pruning · Convolutional neural networks.

1 Introduction

The heavy computation of deep neural networks always poses challenges when deploying them to devices with limited hardware resources. Among the extensive researches to tackle the challenges, network pruning is popular for the ability to reduce the complexity of a model without or with moderate harm to performance [3,8]. It can be divided into unstructured pruning and structured pruning. Unstructured pruning [3] directly removes weights without any structural constraints and usually requires specialized hardware or libraries [3]. Structured pruning [8,12] works by removing structured weights, such as filters, layers, or branches. It is advantageous in many practical applications because it is friendly to GPU, CPU, and many other commonly seen acceleration cards.

In most existing structured pruning methods, a predefined global threshold is used to determine which part of weights to discard based on an importance metric.

© Springer Nature Switzerland AG 2020
H. Yang et al. (Eds.): ICONIP 2020, CCIS 1333, pp. 508–516, 2020.
https://doi.org/10.1007/978-3-030-63823-8_58

For example, Liu *et al.* proposed Network Slimming (NS) [8] to impose sparsity constraints on the scaling factors of batch normalization (BN) [6] layers. Then, the global threshold is calculated from the sorted scaling factors for pruning a predefined percentage of channels. Such a predefined threshold often results in either under-pruning due to the retention of unimportant weights, or over-pruning due to the discarding of important weights. In the left plot of Fig. 1, we show the distribution of the scaling factors from the 8th BN layer in a VGG-14 which is trained with L_1 penalty following [8] on CIFAR-10 [7]. VGG-14 is modified from VGG-16 [11] by replacing the classifier by a fully-connected layer. The scaling factors follow a bimodal distribution, which was also observed in previous works but not carefully discussed [8]. In such a distribution, we assume that the group with larger magnitudes is important, while the other weights are negligible. Under this assumption, the optimal threshold should fall in between the important and negligible weights as shown in Fig. 1. Furthermore, layers in a neural network are generally not equally important to the final performance [12]. Therefore, it is natural to expect the pruning threshold is layer dependent.

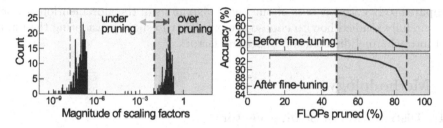

Fig. 1. Illustration of over/under-pruning. **left:** Histogram of the scaling factors from a BN layer trained with sparsity constraint. The green dashed line depicts the optimal threshold separating the under- and over-pruning region by our method. The orange and red lines are examples of under- and over-pruning respectively. **right:** The corresponding accuracy of the left plot before & after fine-tuning, obtained by scaling the optimal thresholds of all layers by certain amounts.

In this paper, we propose a very simple, flexible, and efficient approach, termed Optimal Thresholding (OT), to prune channels with layer dependent thresholds. For each layer, we use the cumulative sum of squares as the criterion to find the threshold that optimally separating the scaling factors to prune as many as possible channels with minimal impact on performance. By avoiding over-pruning, OT makes minimal damages to the original model. Therefore the fine-tuning can converge with relatively very few training iterations. Note that though we apply OT layer-wise, it can be naturally extended to more general structures as long as scaling factors are used.

The effectiveness of OT is verified on CIFAR-10/100 [7] and ILSVRC-2012 [10] with several popular network architectures. It has shown that OT provides even better performance in moderately pruned networks. It can also extend the pruned model to very high sparsity with minimal performance degradation. Compared to the latest state-of-the-art, OT achieves better performance under the same computation budget, especially at the very high sparsity. One-shot pruned models by using OT achieve even better performance than the iteratively pruned models by using NS [8].

2   Related Works

Liu *et al.* [8] proposed Network Slimming (NS), which first enforces sparsity on the scaling factors of BN, and then prune channels by a threshold calculated from a predefined drop ratio. The method is very simple to implement but suffers from over/under-pruning which we will demonstrate in Sect. 3.1. Ye *et al.* [12] studied the same idea and pointed out that enforcing sparsity on the scaling factors of BN is more reasonable because each scaling factor multiplies a normalized input thus the channel importance becomes comparable across layers. Ye adopted ISTA [1] for optimization. To speed up and stabilize the optimization using ISTA, they used a re-scaling trick which is much more complicated to train and implement compared to NS. To the best of our knowledge, none of the aforementioned work has carefully studied how to choose the pruning threshold considering the inter- and intra-channel distribution of scaling factors.

3   Methodology

3.1   Distribution of Scaling Factors

We first solve the following sparsity constrained problem:

$$\hat{\theta} = \arg\min_{\theta} \mathcal{L}\left(\theta\right) + \lambda \sum_{\gamma \in \Gamma} |\gamma|, \tag{1}$$

where $\mathcal{L}$ and θ are loss function and trainable parameters. Γ is a set of scaling factors, while λ controls the degree of sparsity. Such a regularization acts like soft-thresholding that the γs without strong gradients against it will be close to zero (around or smaller than $lr \times \lambda$) after training. Other γs with strong gradients will remain much larger values. Thus after training the γs tend to be bimodally distributed. As pointed out by [12], the importance of channels can be measured by γs. We assume that the group of larger γs is important, while others are negligible.

In addition to the under/over-pruning problem we demonstrated in Sect. 1, the difference in distribution between layers is also a problem for the predefined threshold. As shown in the left part of Fig. 2, the groups of important weights are not aligned. By using a global threshold, it will be problematic for layers with smaller scaling factors. For example, if we want to prune 73% of the channels following NS [8], the calculated threshold (the red dashed line) is too big for the 10th layer resulting in over-pruning.

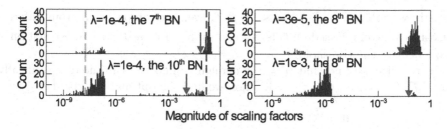

Fig. 2. Distributions of BN scaling factors in VGG-14. **left:** The orange and red dashed lines represent the thresholds for pruning 30% and 73% percent of channels respectively. For both **left** and **right:** The green arrows are the thresholds identified by the proposed method.

To determine the optimal threshold for a specific L_1 penalty, we also studied the distribution of γs under different intensities of L_1. We observed that in the range from very weak to strong L_1 penalty, the important γs are always several orders of magnitude larger than the negligible ones. An example is shown in the right part of Fig. 2.

3.2 Optimal Thresholding for Pruning

For a given set of scaling factors Γ, we denote Γ_N as the subset of negligible γs, and Γ_I as the subset of important γs. Here, we consider the most common case that both $|\Gamma_I|$ and $|\Gamma_N|$ are not empty. Ideally the optimal threshold is a γ_{th} such that $\sup \Gamma_N < \gamma_{th} \leq \inf \Gamma_I$. For $p \geq 0$, the following inequalities hold:

$$\sum_{\gamma \in \Gamma_N} |\gamma|^p \leq |\Gamma_N| \, |\sup \Gamma_N|^p \tag{2}$$

$$|\Gamma_I| \, |\inf \Gamma_I|^p \leq \sum_{\gamma \in \Gamma_I} |\gamma|^p \leq |\Gamma_I| \, |\sup \Gamma_I|^p. \tag{3}$$

Then we have

$$\frac{\sum_{\gamma \in \Gamma_N} |\gamma|^p}{\sum_{\gamma \in \Gamma} |\gamma|^p} \leq \frac{\sum_{\gamma \in \Gamma_N} |\gamma|^p}{\sum_{\gamma \in \Gamma_I} |\gamma|^p} \leq \frac{|\Gamma_N| \, |\sup \Gamma_N|^p}{|\Gamma_I| \, |\inf \Gamma_I|^p} = \frac{|\Gamma_N|}{|\Gamma_I|} \alpha^{-p}, \tag{4}$$

$$\frac{\sum_{\gamma \in \Gamma_N} |\gamma|^p + |\inf \Gamma_I|^p}{\sum_{\gamma \in \Gamma} |\gamma|^p} \geq \frac{|\inf \Gamma_I|^p}{\sum_{\gamma \in \Gamma} |\gamma|^p} \geq \frac{|\inf \Gamma_I|^p}{|\Gamma| \, |\sup \Gamma_I|^p} = \frac{1}{|\Gamma|} \beta^{-p}, \tag{5}$$

where $\alpha = \frac{\inf \Gamma_I}{\sup \Gamma_N}$, and $\beta = \frac{\sup \Gamma_I}{\inf \Gamma_I}$. If there is a δ such that $\frac{|\Gamma_N|}{|\Gamma_I|} \alpha^{-p} \leq \delta \leq \frac{1}{|\Gamma|} \beta^{-p}$, it can be used to separate important and negligible γs. In our experiments, by ignoring the very small portion of outliers falling in between the two subsets, we observed that α ranges from 10^5 to 10^6 and β ranges from 2 to 100 typically, and the higher λ is the lower β is. The term $\frac{|\Gamma_N|}{|\Gamma_I|}$ and $\frac{1}{|\Gamma|}$ are bounded by the design of the network, and they do not change with p. Therefore, as long as p is large enough, we will have $\frac{|\Gamma_N|}{|\Gamma_l|}\alpha^{-p} << \frac{1}{|\Gamma|}\beta^{-p}$, even for comparing Γ from different convolution layers. Based on this, we can simply use $\frac{1}{|\Gamma|}\beta^{-p}$ as an estimation of δ to calculate the threshold.

In practice we find that $p = 2$ is enough to find the threshold. Specifically, define $\Gamma_<(x) = \{\gamma | \gamma \in \Gamma, \gamma < x\}$. Then we find the optimal threshold as

$$\gamma_{th} = \gamma' \in \Gamma,$$

$$\text{s.t.} \sum_{\gamma \in \Gamma_<(\gamma')} \gamma^2 < \delta \sum_{\gamma \in \Gamma} \gamma^2 \leq \sum_{\gamma \in \Gamma_<(\gamma')} \gamma^2 + \gamma'^2. \tag{6}$$

γ_{th} can be easily calculated by finding the first γ with a cumulative sum of squares larger than or equal to δ from the ascendingly sorted Γ. We observed that this algorithm can reliably find the threshold in various situations. For examples, the optimal thresholds found by Eq. 6 are shown as the green dashed line in Fig. 1, and the arrows in Fig. 2. In addition to avoiding over-/under-pruning, another advantage of OT over NS is that OT does not suffer from breaking a network by pruning the entire layer.

Dealing with Skip Connections. To handle the possible redundant branch in architectures with skip connections, we first calculate a global optimal threshold γ_g by applying Eq. 6 to all the scaling factors of the network. Then, for all the branches with BN layers, we remove the entire branch if the scaling factors of the last BN layer are smaller than γ_g. For BN layers that share input channels with other branches, we follow NS [8] to mask out the negligible channels by channel selection.

4   Experiments

Our method was evaluated on CIFAR-10/100 [7] and ILSVRC-2012 [10] with popular network architectures. For simplicity, we use $\delta = 1e-3$, which is estimated from the typical values based on our experimental settings, for all the experiments.

We follow the same setup of NS [8] for CIFAR. For OT, we train the base models with different λs. Note that it does not imply that OT requires more computations on training than NS. For NS, the optimal λ is obtained by performing a grid search [8]. In addition to VGG-14, we evaluated ResNet-50 [4] and DenseNet-121 [5]. After pruning, the models are fine-tuned for 40 epochs with a lr of $1e-3$. We found this to be sufficient for both NS and OT to converge. Especially for OT, we observed that it converges in 3 epochs for most cases. We also conducted experiments by train-from-scratch (TFS) for the pruned models, following the experimental settings from [9].

For ILSVRC-2012, we follow the official example from PyTorch and the sparsity settings from NS [8]. In addition to the accuracy on the validation set, we also report the accuracy after 1 epoch fine-tuning to check if the model converges quickly.

4.1 Verifying the Optimal Thresholds

For a VGG-14, after trained on CIFAR-10 with $\lambda = 1e-4$, we calculate the thresholds of all layers by OT. Then, we shift the thresholds of all layers simultaneously by a number in log10 scale. The results are shown in the right part of Fig. 1. The upper graph is the test accuracy before fine-tuning, we can see that in the under-pruning region (pale orange), the pruned percentage of FLOPs increases without any degradation in accuracy. This indicates that the pruned channels are all negligible for the final performance. When the threshold shifts into the over-pruning region (pale red), a distinct performance drop is observed, implying that important weights are removed. A similar trend can also be observed in the lower graph, which is the result of fine-tuning. Although fine-tuning can partially recover the accuracy, the performance is lower in the over-pruning region than the performance with the optimal threshold.

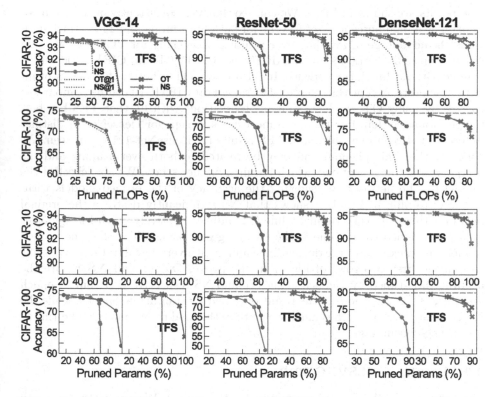

Fig. 3. Results on CIFAR-10/100, compared with NS. In each column, the left plots are results by fine-tuning and the right plots are results by TFS. The green dashed line represents the baseline accuracy. The dotted line represents the accuracy fine-tuned by 1 epoch. All plots share the same legend as in the left top plot.

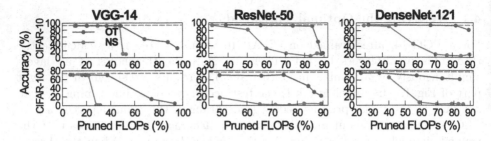

Fig. 4. Accuracy vs. pruned FLOPs without any further training. All plots share the same legend as in the left top plot. The green dashed line represents the accuracy of the baseline model.

4.2   Results on CIFAR-10/100

The results are shown in Fig. 3. We can see that OT consistently outperform NS in pruning a high percentage of FLOPs for both fine-tuning and TFS, which indicates the advantage of avoiding over-pruning. Especially for VGG-14, by using NS only up to 53% FLOPs for CIFAR-10 and 31% FLOPs for CIFAR-100 can be pruned without break the network. In most cases, OT is better than NS in pruning parameters, except that ResNet-50 trained on CIFAR-10 can be comparable to NS. By using OT, we have similar observations with [9] that TFS has better performance than fine-tuning in most cases, except for DenseNet. A distinct difference between fine-tuned and TFS results for DenseNet-121 is not seen. We conclude that this phenomenon may be related to both over-pruning and the ubiquity of skip-connections, which requires further study. We also checked the impact on the networks by showing the accuracy of the pruned models without any training in Fig. 4. It shows that NS significantly destroys the original networks through over-pruning, while OT induces relatively much less damage.

As mentioned earlier, one of the advantages of using OT is that the pruned model can quickly converge during fine-tuning with very few iterations. We show this in the first two rows of Fig. 3. In the figure, **OT@1** and **NS@1** are the accuracy fine-tuned by 1 epoch using OT and NS respectively. By only 1 epoch training, OT is very close to the result obtained by training 40 epochs, while the NS accuracy after 1 epoch is much worse than the final result, making fine-tuning more time-consuming.

4.3   Results on ILSVRC-2012

The results on ILSVRC-2012 are summarized in Table 1. We can see that for both VGG-16 and PreResNet-50, OT outperforms NS with less computation budget. Particularly, we find that by using OT, for VGG-16 the accuracy after only 1 epoch fine-tuning almost achieves the best accuracy, and for PreResNet-50 the accuracy after 3 epochs almost achieves the best accuracy. While by using NS the results after a few epochs fine-tuning are not good enough. For large scale data like ILSVRC-2012, OT significantly saves time for fine-tuning compared to NS.

Table 1. Results on ILSVRC-2012. p represents the percentage of pruned channels for NS. In the column of "Accuracy", for NS and OT, from the left to right are the results fine-tuned by 1 epoch, 3 epochs and all the 15 epochs respectively. M and G represent 10^6 and 10^9 respectively

Architecture	Method	Accuracy (%)	GFLOPs
VGG-16	Baseline	74.09	15.66
	NS ($p = 0.415$)	65.47/68.66/71.02	8.33
	OT ($\lambda = 2e-4$)	72.02/71.98/72.16	7.71
PreResNet-50	Baseline	75.04	4.14
	NS ($p = 0.375$)	63.32/66.79/69.60	1.95
	OT ($\lambda = 2e-4$)	69.56/70.01/70.40	1.84

4.4 Iterative Pruning

Iterative pruning often outperforms one-shot pruning [2] or extend the percentage of pruned FLOPs to the region that cannot be achieved by one-shot pruning [8]. Interestingly, in this section we find that iterative pruning is not suitable for OT; however, we also show in Fig. 5 that OT outperforms the iteratively pruned model by NS, even without the time-consuming procedure. The probable reason may be that by using OT, the pruned model is very stable and does not lose important weights.

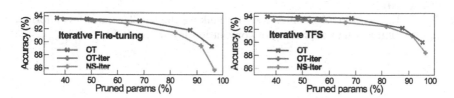

Fig. 5. Results of iterative pruning. OT-iter and NS-iter are results by iteratively pruning using OT and NS respectively. OT represents the result by one-shot pruning.

5   Conclusion

We have presented channel pruning design by layer-wise calculating the optimal thresholds to avoid both under- and over-pruning. To find the optimal threshold, we proposed an algorithm that preserves the cumulative sum of squares of the scaling factors from the BN layer. Our method is extremely simple yet effective and has been validated to outperforming state-of-the-art designs in extensive experiments. For the first time, the distribution of scaling factors in pruning and its relationship to under- and over-pruning is carefully studied by this work. We hope that further research based on our work can provide inspiration for finding more efficient networks.

References

1. Daubechies, I., Defrise, M., De Mol, C.: An iterative thresholding algorithm for linear inverse problems with a sparsity constraint. Commun. Pure Appl. Math. **57**(11), 1413–1457 (2004)
2. Frankle, J., Carbin, M.: The lottery ticket hypothesis: finding sparse, trainable neural networks. In: International Conference on Learning Representations (2019)
3. Han, S., Pool, J., Tran, J., Dally, W.: Learning both weights and connections for efficient neural network. In: Advances in Neural Information Processing Systems, vol. 28 (2015)
4. He, K., Zhang, X., Ren, S., Sun, J.: Deep residual learning for image recognition. In: CVPR June 2016
5. Huang, G., Liu, Z., van der Maaten, L., Weinberger, K.Q.: Densely connected convolutional networks. In: CVPR July 2017
6. Ioffe, S., Szegedy, C.: Batch normalization: accelerating deep network training by reducing internal covariate shift. In: ICML, pp. 448–456 (2015)
7. Krizhevsky, A.: Learning multiple layers of features from tiny images. Technical report (2009)
8. Liu, Z., Li, J., Shen, Z., Huang, G., Yan, S., Zhang, C.: Learning efficient convolutional networks through network slimming. In: ICCV (2017)
9. Liu, Z., Sun, M., Zhou, T., Huang, G., Darrell, T.: Rethinking the value of network pruning. In: International Conference on Learning Representations (2019)
10. Russakovsky, O., et al.: Imagenet large scale visual recognition challenge. Int. J. Comput. Vis. **115**(3), 211–252 (2015). https://doi.org/10.1007/s11263-015-0816-y
11. Simonyan, K., Zisserman, A.: Very deep convolutional networks for large-scale image recognition. In: 3rd International Conference on Learning Representations, ICLR (2015)
12. Ye, J., Lu, X., Lin, Z., Wang, J.Z.: Rethinking the smaller-norm-less-informative assumption in channel pruning of convolution layers. In: ICLR (2018)

Concatenated Tensor Networks for Deep Multi-Task Learning

Maolin Wang[1], Zeyong Su[1], Xu Luo[1], Yu Pan[1], Shenggen Zheng[2],
and Zenglin Xu[1,2,3(✉)]

[1] University of Electronic Science and Technology of China, Chengdu, China
morin.w98@gmail.com, octsven@gmail.com, 1x81666316@gmail.com,
perryupan@gmail.com, zenglin@gmail.com
[2] Pengcheng Lab, Shenzhen, China
[3] Harbin Institute of Technology(Shenzhen), Shenzhen, China

Abstract. Deep Multi-Task Learning has achieved great success in a
number of domains. However, the enormous number of parameters results
in extremely large storage costs for current deep Multi-Task models.
Several methods based on tensor networks were proposed to address this
problem. However, the tensor train format based methods only share
the information of one mode. The huge central core tensor of the tucker
format is hard to be stored and optimized. To tackle these problems, we
introduce a novel Concatenated Tensor Network structure, in particular,
Projected Entangled Pair States (PEPS) like, into multi-task models. We
name the resulted multi-task models as Concatenated Tensor Multi-Task
Learning (CT-MTL).

Keywords: Multi-task learning · Tensor networks · Neural networks

1 Introduction

Multi-Task Learning (MTL)[19,20] aims to improve the accuracy of each individual learning task by exploiting useful information from different but related
tasks and learn them simultaneously. From the perspective of deep learning,
learning tasks simultaneously can be seen as adding a common prior knowledge
to each of the task, which could improve the learning result if prior is correct. So,
how to design appropriate sharing strategies to obtain effective prior information
is an important problem for Deep Multi-Task Learning.

Hard parameter sharing is adapted to solve this problem in some previous
work [16]. An early deep multi-task structure [16] is constructed by a Deep Neural
Network architecture whose sharing layers share all information and sharing
and independent layers structure is designed manually. However, this kind of
structure needs a careful design on lots of hyper-parameters such as numbers of
layers in both sharing and independent layers. And the hard sharing architecture

This work was partially supported by the National Key Research and Development
Program of China (No. 2018AAA0100204).

H. Yang et al. (Eds.): ICONIP 2020, CCIS 1333, pp. 517–525, 2020.
https://doi.org/10.1007/978-3-030-63823-8_59

can be harmful when learning high-level task-specific features and will also lead to the negative transfer among tasks [2, 14].

Another kind of work partially avoids these problems by using soft parameter sharing [14]. In this way, one sharing DNN is learned for each task, while other individual DNNs are related by limiting the aligned weights. Different regularization methods are used, including the l_2 norm regularization [4], the trace norm regularization [14] and tensor norm priors [18]. A disadvantage of the soft-sharing models is the difficulty of training an extremely large number of parameters and storing them during the learning process while it is adopted on small devices such as mobile phones [2, 14].

In order to tackle these problems, Yang et al. [13] first propose the multi-task models with tensor networks. Tensor networks represent a higher-order tensor as sparsely interconnected low-order tensors. Yang et al. [13] employ the Tensor Train format on Deep Multi-Task Learning models and encode the final node in the tensor train format as the shared knowledge. Yang et al. [13] also propose multi-task models based in a Tucker format. They encode one factor as the shared knowledge, but the huge central core tensor is hard to be stored and optimized [2]. More specifically, the Tucker Multi-Task layer can be viewed as one hard shared layer, one soft shared layer and another hard shared layer. Tensor Train can be viewed as one hard shared layer and another soft shared layer which only considered the information of one dimension. Such pattern sharing strategies are vulnerable to the negative transfer of the features.

To address these problems and also inspired by the powerful ability of 2-d tensor network: Projected entangled pair(PEPS), we propose our Multi-Task Learning model with PEPS-like Concatenated Tensor Networks (CTN)[6]. The key idea of concatenated tensor networks is that the small tensors in an original tensor network are replaced by another tensor network [3]. The influence of shared environment tensor will be naturally equal to each core by carefully designing the structure [6]. This can also be useful to reduce the size (volume) of core tensors and can make tensor-network benefit from distributed storage and computation [3, 6].

We have conducted the experiment on MNIST, FasionMnist, AdienceFacesis and Omniglot, with outstanding performance over TT [13] and Tucker [13].

2   Background

2-D Tensor Networks. A tensor network structure with different typologies and higher dimensional connections can also be considered. Projected entangled pair state (PEPS) [5, 9, 11] in Fig. 1(a) is one high dimensional tensor network which generalizes MPS. PEPS provides a natural structure which can capture more information from high dimensionality [5]. The PEPS has polynomial correlation decay with the separation distance, by contrast, MPS has exponential correlation decay. This indicates that PEPS has more powerful representation ability because it strengthens the interaction between different tensor modes. This indicates that the representation ability of PEPS is better than that of MPS. [3, 5]

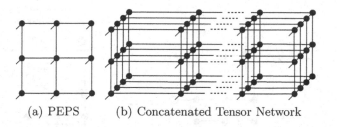

(a) PEPS   (b) Concatenated Tensor Network

Fig. 1. Graphical representation of some classical tensor networks. Figure 1(a) shows one 3×3 PEPS tensor network. Figure 1(b) shows one 3D structure Concatenated Tensor Network based on PEPS.

Concatenated Tensor Networks (CTN) [6] is one common way to generalize the dimensions of tensor-network. Given a tensor network, we can replace the individual tensor in the network by another tensor network. Figure 1(b) shows the concatenated tensor network structure which generalize the PEPS.

Tensor Based Deep Learning. Inspired by the good properties of tensor networks, they are now been widely applied into the deep learning models. This leads to the great reduction of parameters while improving the performance. Among these methods, A. Novikov et al. [8] impose the tensor train decomposition (TTD) to the fully-connected layers in both CNNs and RNNs, which solves these problems occurred in CP and Tucker decomposition. J. Ye et al. [15,17] use the Block-Term tensor decomposition in RNNs and have obtained a better performance. However, Tucker core tensor is hard to be stored and optimized. C. Chen et al. [1] presents the matrix product operator RBM (MPORBM) that both of the visible and hidden layers are tensor train format, and result in higher expressive power. Compared with the block-term model and tensor train decomposition, Y. Pan et al. [10] and M. Wang et al. [12] utilize the tensor ring structure to improve the performance of RNNs and RBMs with fewer parameters recently.

3   Model

The basic soft sharing strategy of the matrix based sharing model is shown in Figure 2. If we have T linear models (tasks) parameterized by $I \times O$ weight matrices, the collection of all those matrices can be viewed as a $\mathcal{W} \in \mathbb{R}^{I \times O \times T}$ tensor. We can factorize each task's parameter $\mathcal{W}_{\cdot,\cdot,i}$ as shared factor $L \in \mathbb{R}^{I \times O \times K}$ and a task-specific factor $S_i \in \mathbb{R}^K$. Each task's parameter is linear combination of latent basis with task-specific information:

$$W^{(i)} : \mathcal{W}_{\cdot,\cdot,i} = \sum_{k=1}^{K} \mathcal{L}_{\cdot,\cdot,k} S_{k,i}$$

The above matrix based sharing model is a kind of soft-sharing multi-task models. Compared to the hard sharing strategy, this strategy can avoid the

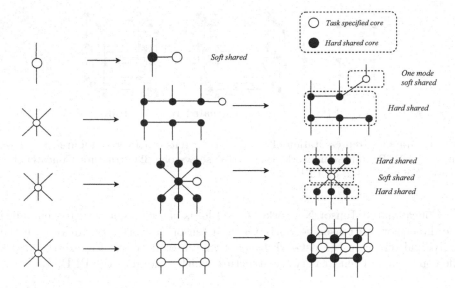

Fig. 2. Neural network parameters' sharing strategies of soft-shared, Tucker, Tensor Train and ours. Black cores are hard shared cores and white cores are task specified cores.

negative transfer among tasks. But such typically involve enormous number of trainable parameters and require extremely large storage and memory.

To solve these problems, Yang et al. [13] employ the Tensor Train format and encode the final nodes in the tensor train format as the shared knowledge. Tensor train format only shares the information of one dimension. More specifically, we can first tensorize input-output weight $W \in \mathbb{R}^{I \times O}$ into $\mathcal{W} \in \mathbb{R}^{I_1 \times I_2 \times, ..., \times I_n \times O_1 \times O_2, ..., \times O_m}$ and employ the Tensor Train format, and $\mathcal{S}$ is the task-specific factor:

$$
\begin{aligned}
\mathcal{W}_{l_1, l_2, ..., l_{n+m}} &= \mathcal{G}_{l_1}^{(1)} \mathcal{G}_{l_2}^{(2)} ... \mathcal{G}_{l_{n+m}}^{(n+m)} \mathcal{S} \\
&= \sum_{r_0, r_1, ..., r_{n+m}} \mathcal{G}_{r_0, l_1, r_1}^{(1)} ... \mathcal{G}_{r_{n+m-1}, l_{n+m}, r_{n+m}}^{(d)} \mathcal{S}_{r_{n+m}}
\end{aligned}
$$

Yang et al. [13] also propose multi-task models based in a Tucker format. They encode one factor as the shared knowledge, and $\mathcal{S}$ is the task-specific factor::

$$
\mathcal{W}_{l_1, l_2, ..., l_{n+m}} = \sum_{k_1 ... k_{n+m+1}} \mathcal{G}_{k_1, k_2, ..., k_{n+m+1}} U_{d_1, k_1}^{(1)} ... U_{d_N, k_N}^{(n+m)} \mathcal{S}_{k_{n+m+1}} \tag{1}
$$

Tensor Train and Tucker format share almost all factors of layer-wise weights as common factors. As shown in Fig. 2, the TT format shares the last core as a common factor. The TT layer can be viewed as one hard shared layer combined with another soft shared layer. The Tucker format encodes one factor as the shared knowledge. The Tucker Multi-Task layer can be viewed as one hard shared layer, one soft shared layer and another hard shared layer. And the huge central core tensor is hard to be stored and optimized. Such pattern sharing strategies are vulnerable to the negative transfer of the features.

And for ours, inspired by the powerful expression ability of PEPS, we use the PEPS-like format and each node can be viewed as soft shared via Concatenated Tensor Network. We generalize our multi-task model represents the tensorized input-output weight $\mathcal{W} \in \mathbb{R}^{I_1 \times I_2 \times, \dots, \times I_n \times O_1 \times O_2, \dots, \times O_n}$ as follows:

$$
\mathcal{D}_{i_{1,1} \cdots i_{1,N}; i_{M,1} \cdots i_{M,N}} = \sum_{h^{(R1)}, h^{(C1)}} \sum_{h^{(R2)}, h^{(C2)}} \sum_{m,n} \sum_{q_{mn}}
$$

$$
\mathcal{A}^{(m,n)}_{i_{mn}; h^{(R1)}_{l_{mn}}, h^{(R1)}_{r_{mn}}, h^{(C1)}_{u_{mn}}, h^{(C1)}_{d_{mn}}, q_{mn}} \mathcal{S}^{(m,n)}_{h^{(R2)}_{l_{mn}}, h^{(R2)}_{r_{mn}}, h^{(C2)}_{u_{mn}}, h^{(C2)}_{d_{mn}}, q_{mn}} \quad (2)
$$

where

$$
\begin{cases}
\mathcal{A}^{(m,n)} \in \mathbb{R}^{I_{mn} \times R^{(R1)}_{l_{mn}} \times R^{(R1)}_{r_{mn}} \times R^{(C1)}_{u_{mn}} \times R^{(C1)}_{d_{mn}} \times R^Q_q} \\
\mathcal{S}^{(m,n)} \in \mathbb{R}^{R^{(R2)}_{l_{mn}} \times R^{(R2)}_{r_{mn}} \times R^{(C2)}_{u_{mn}} \times R^{(C2)}_{d_{mn}} \times R^Q_q} \\
I_{mn} = 1 \quad when \quad m \neq 1, m \neq M
\end{cases}
$$

And $\forall i, R_i^{(R1)} \in \mathbf{R}^{(R1)}, R_i^{(C1)} \in \mathbf{R}^{(C1)}, R_i^{(R2)} \in \mathbf{R}^{(R2)}, R_i^{(C2)} \in \mathbf{R}^{(C2)}, R_i^{(Q)} \in \mathbf{R}^{(Q)}$. The indices definitions are almost the same as Equation (??).

$\mathbf{R}^{(R1)}, \mathbf{R}^{(C1)}, \mathbf{R}^{(R2)}, \mathbf{R}^{(C2)}$ and $\mathbf{R}^{(Q)}$ are the rank sets. $\mathbf{R}^{(Q)}$ affects the impact of $\mathcal{S}^{(m,n)}$ on $\mathcal{A}^{(m,n)}$.

In our model, we consider tensor $\mathcal{S}$ as the common environment among all tasks. We make it as sharing knowledge and the influence of shared environment tensor will be naturally equal to each core. Compared with TT format sharing strategies, our model may not suffer from the correlation's decay of tensor cores. Compared with Tucker format, our model also doesn't have the huge central core tensor which is hard to store and optimize.

4 Experiment

Our method is implemented with Pytorch. We compare our model with single-task learning (STL), tensor train multi-task model(TT-MTL), and Tucker based multi-task model. To be fair, all the methods are adopted with the same network architecture. Our experiments are conducted on the following datasets: **MNIST**, **FashionMNIST**, **AdienceFaces** and **Omniglot**.

4.1 Homogeneous Multi-task Learning

The MNIST 10-class classification problem can be converted into ten 1-vs-all binary classification problems. This conversion constructs a mult-task classification problem with homogeneous 10-tasks. In this experiment, we are concerned about two performance metrics: average accuracy of binary classification problems and multi-class classification accuracy. We use a simple CNN architecture

Table 1. Average Accuracy of Binary and Multi-class Classification of MNIST

Fraction	STL	Tucker	TT	CTN
	Bin., Multi	Bin., Multi	Bin., Multi	Bin., Multi.
1%	0.886, 0.773	0.901, 0.823	0.918, 0.839	**0.929, 0.856**
10%	0.960, 0.921	0.977, 0.947	0.971, 0.949	**0.981, 0.953**
50%	0.974, 0.950	0.986, 0.966	0.980, 0.959	**0.989, 0.969**
100%	0.986, 0.972	0.990, 0.979	0.985, 0.970	**0.993, 0.983**

Table 2. Accuracy of the gender and age classification in face analysis

Fraction	STL	Tucker	TT	CTN
	Gender, Age	Gender, Age	Gender, Age	Gender, Age
1%	0.533, 0.221	0.564, 0.252	0.535, 0.230	**0.576, 0.259**
10%	0.672, 0.299	0.710, 0.345	0.671, 0.323	**0.727, 0.364**
50%	0.742, 0.452	0.771, 0.467	0.756, 0.460	**0.785, 0.479**
100%	0.757, 0.466	0.802, 0.489	0.788, 0.488	**0.813, 0.501**

LeNet5 and FC layers are converted into a different multi-task tensor-network model format. We test the model with different fractions of the training dataset. From the Table 1 we can see that the proposed method CTN outperforms all other methods including STL, Tucker, and TT.

4.2   Heterogeneous MTL: Face Analysis

We use the AdienceFace data set to evaluate the performance of heterogeneous MTL models. There are two tasks: the gender classification task and the age group classification task. For the gender classification task, we choose 10945 images for training and 3558 for testing; while for the age classification task, we choose 11868 images for training and 3754 for testing.

We use the same CNN architecture as [13]. Convolution layers are also hard shared in all MTL models, and FC layers (except the last one) are converted into different multi-task tensor-network model formats.

Table 2 shows the accuracy of the gender classification task and the age group classification task, respectively. From Table 2 we see that Tucker outperforms TT. All other methods surpass the STL baseline in all cases. Our proposed CTN method performs better than Tucker and TT, especially in the age group classification task.

4.3   Heterogeneous MTL: Multi-alphabet Recognition

Omniglot contains 50 alphabets. We divided the data set into 50 tasks, and each task corresponds to an alphabet. And the goal of each task is to recognize characters in the alphabet. We choose 10% of all images as the test dataset and 10%...90% of images for training. We use a simple CNN architecture LeNet5 and FC layers are converted into a different multi-task tensor-network model format.

Table 3. Accuracy of the alphabet classification

Fraction	STL	Tucker	TT	CTN
90%	0.701	0.747	0.745	**0.779**
70%	0.671	0.714	0.713	**0.744**
50%	0.568	0.655	0.653	**0.672**
30%	0.479	0.527	0.515	**0.540**
20%	0.391	0.422	0.420	**0.433**
10%	0.232	0.244	0.241	**0.246**

Table 3 reports the average accuracy across 50 tasks of all methods. In this Multi-alphabet recognition task we find that: (1) All MTL methods outperform the STL method, (2) our proposed method invariably outperforms any other methods especially when the training set is large, and (3) we see that the performance between the Tucker and TT is nearly the same.

Table 4. Results of the multi-datasets analysis

Samples A vs B	STL	TT	CTN
100vs100	0.733, 0.690	0.712, 0.622	0.742, 0.707
1000vs100	0.875, 0.690	0.877, 0.675	0.880, 0.716
100vs1000	0.733,0.787	0.738, 0.782	0.774, 0.788
1000vs1000	0.875, 0.787	0.897, 0.790	0.899, 0.801

4.4 Tasks from Loosely Related Datasets

In this experiment, we want to test the multiple datasets situation where the tasks are loosely related. There are two tasks: task A is assigned to recognize 10 digits in MNIST and task B is to recognize 10 types of fashion product in FasionMNIST.

We use four FC layers in this experiment and the first three layers are converted into the multi-task tensor-network model format. Table 4 shows the average accuracy result of two tasks with the different sample size. From this table, we find that the fasion recognition task and the digit recognition task can promote each other in the TT model and the CTN model. TT performs slightly worse than STL when the amount of training data is not enough. Our CTN method consistently outperforms the STL and TT models.

5   Conclusion

In this paper, we propose the multi-task model architecture based on the PEPS-like Concatenated Tensor Network and design appropriate sharing strategies. Our model design discards the huge central core tensor which is notorious for high-cost storage and tricky optimization as in the Tucker model. Our model achieve better performance than the TT model and the Tucker model among all datasets. In future work, it is promising to explore the generalization of our model to other neural network architectures(like RNNs).

References

1. Chen, C., Batselier, K., Ko, C.Y., Wong, N.: Matrix product operator restricted Boltzmann machines. In: 2019 International Joint Conference on Neural Networks(IJCNN), Budapest, pp. 1–8. IEEE (2019)
2. Chen, X., Hou, M., Zhou, G., Zhao, Q.: Tensor ring nets adapted deep multi-tasklearning (2018). https://openreview.net/forum?id=BJxmXhRcK7
3. Cichocki, A., Lee, N., Oseledets, I.V., Phan, A.H., Zhao, Q., Mandic, D.P.: Tensornetworks for dimensionality reduction and large-scale optimization: part 1 low-rank tensor decompositions. Found. Trends Mach. Learn. **9**(4–5), 249–429 (2016)
4. Duong, L., Cohn, T., Bird, S., Cook, P.: Low resource dependency parsing: cross-lingual parameter sharing in a neural network parser. In: ACL 2015, Short Papers, pp. 845–850, Beijing (2015)
5. Huang, H., Liu, Y., Zhu, C.: Low-rank tensor grid for image completion. https://arxiv.org/pdf/1903.04735v3.pdf arXivpreprint arXiv:1903.04735 (2019)
6. Hübener, R., Nebendahl, V., Dür, W.: Concatenated tensor network states. New J. Phys. **12**(2), 025004 (2010)
7. Long, M., Cao, Z., Wang, J., Philip, S.Y.: Learning multiple tasks with multilinear relationship networks. In: Advances in Neural Information Processing Systems, pp. 1594–1603, Long Beach (2017)
8. Novikov, A., Podoprikhin, D., Osokin, A., Vetrov, D.P.: Tensorizing neural networks. In: Cortes, C., Lawrence, N.D., Lee, D.D., Sugiyama, M., Garnett, R. (eds.) Advances in Neural Information Processing Systems, pp. 442–450, Montreal (2015)
9. Oseledets, I.V.: Tensor-train decomposition. SIAM J. Sci. Comput. **33**(5), 2295–2317 (2011)
10. Pan, Y., et al.: Compressing recurrent neural networks with tensor ring for action recognition. In: AAAI, pp. 4683–4690. AAAI Press (2019)
11. Verstraete, F., Wolf, M.M., Perez-Garcia, D., Cirac, J.I.: Criticality, the area law, and the computational power of projected entangled pair states. Phys. Rev. Lett. **96**(22), 220601 (2006)
12. Wang, M., Zhang, C., Pan, Y., Xu, J., Xu, Z.: Tensor ring restricted Boltzmann machines. In: IJCNN 2019, pp. 1–8. IEEE (2019)
13. Yang, Y., Hospedales, T.M.: Deep multi-task representation learning: a tensor factorisation approach. In: ICLR 2017
14. Yang, Y., Hospedales, T.M.: Trace norm regularised deep multi-task learning. In: Proceedings of ICLR 2017, Workshop Track (2017)
15. Ye, J., et al.: Learning compact recurrent neural networks with block-term tensor decomposition. In: CVPR 2018, Salt Lake City, pp. 9378–9387 (2018)

16. Zhang, Z., Luo, P., Loy, C.C., Tang, X.: Facial landmark detection by deep multi-task learning. In: Fleet, D., Pajdla, T., Schiele, B., Tuytelaars, T. (eds.) ECCV 2014. LNCS, vol. 8694, pp. 94–108. Springer, Cham (2014). https://doi.org/10.1007/978-3-319-10599-4_7
17. Ye, J., Li, G., Chen, D., Yang, H., Zhe, S., Xu, Z.: Block-term tensor neural networks. Neural Netw. **11–21**(130), 0893–6080 (2020)
18. Long, M., Cao, Z., Wang, J., Philip, S.Y.: Learning multiple tasks with multi linear relationship networks. In: NIPS, pp. 1594–1603 (2017)
19. Liu, B., et al.: Learning from semantically dependent multi-tasks. In: IJCNN, pp. 3498–3505. IEEE (2017)
20. Ren, Y., Yan, X., Hu, Z., Xu, Z.: Self-paced multi-task multi-view capped-norm clustering. In: Cheng, L., Leung, A.C.S., Ozawa, S. (eds.) ICONIP 2018. LNCS, vol. 11304, pp. 205–217. Springer, Cham (2018). https://doi.org/10.1007/978-3-030-04212-7_18

Consensus Driven Self-Organization: Towards Non Hierarchical Multi-Map Architectures

Noémie Gonnier[1]([✉]), Yann Boniface[2], and Hervé Frezza-Buet[1]

[1] Université de Lorraine, CentraleSupélec, CNRS, LORIA, 57000 Metz, France
`noemie.gonnier@loria.fr, herve.frezza-buet@centralesupelec.fr`
[2] Université de Lorraine, CNRS, LORIA, 54000 Nancy, France
`yann.boniface@loria.fr`

Abstract. This paper introduces CxSOM, a model to build modular architectures based on self-organizing maps (SOM). An original consensus driven approach enables to adress non-hierarchical architectures where SOMs get organized jointly. The paper aims at showing how the modules are able to store the association between data, and evaluating, by a mutual information criterion, the resulting organization. These results stand as preliminary work to study bigger architectures.

Keywords: Neural network models · Self-organizing maps · Multi-modal architecture

1 Introduction

Artificial neural networks are an illustration of how computer science can benefit from biologically-inspired paradigms. Deep learning [5] is an example of advances in computer science that has a biological flavor, since it is based on the formal neuron, which is an abstraction of actual nervous cells. Nevertheless, bringing a biological concept up to operative computational techniques usually overcomes the biological side. In deep learning, sophisticated gradient-based techniques and many other refinements do not really have identified counterparts in biology. The present paper follows the same kind of path, from biology to computer algorithms, but rather in the field of self-organizing substrates observed in the cerebral cortex of mammals. The cortex is described as a tiling of similar [14] elementary circuits over a neural surface that get topologically organized by adaptive processes. The cerebral cortex as a whole is understood as an architecture involving numerous interconnected self-organizing modules, handling different modalities and their associations [2,15]. Self-organizing feature maps (SOMs) introduced by Kohonen [9] model one of such modules. It is nowadays a vector quantization machine learning technique thanks to tricks like argmax computation, decreasing winner-take-all kernel width, decreasing learning rates, that needed to be introduced.

© Springer Nature Switzerland AG 2020
H. Yang et al. (Eds.): ICONIP 2020, CCIS 1333, pp. 526–534, 2020.
https://doi.org/10.1007/978-3-030-63823-8_60

Although the topographical aspect of self-organization observed on the cortex surface has successfully been transposed to machine learning context, the modular aspect of the cortical organization has lesser been explored in this perspective. This motivates the work presented in this paper, since materials and methods are proposed in order to build up modular architectures from self organizing computational modules. On a rather biological side, some models of hierarchical cortically-inspired modular architectures have been proposed [10,16]. Robotics or computer vision are generally addressed as proofs of concept in such approaches, since the focus is rather on biological plausibility than on the SOM algorithm itself: in [10] the SOM is quite small, in [13] it is used beforehand for initialization and in [16] it is replaced by another vector quantization paradigm close to growing neural gas.

On the machine learning side, some approaches address modular self-organization. A variety of them, reviewed in [17], are based on the ART paradigm, initially inspired from biology. Self-organization addressed in these works is not topographic and are therefore out of the scope of this paper. Approaches involving several self-organizing maps are not necessary a modular architecture either. For example, in [18], the input space is split into several subset so that several SOMs handle a specific subset. Hierarchical SOMs may also be confusing since hierarchy is involved in the computation of a *single* SOM, as clearly explained in [3]. In the end, quite a few works address modular and topographical self-organization. Let us mention [7] which is an algorithmical approach oriented toward letter-phoneme integration as well as A-SOM [8] which introduces associative SOMs. The present work is in line with these two, with a higher stress on computational homogeneity between the modules and scalability for architectures with many modules. The architecture proposed in this paper relies on a dynamical process leading to a global *consensus* among all the modules. This consensus drives the self-organization in each module so that they perform a joint self-organization. This is the extension of previous work involving a cellular paradigm closer to the biological side [11,12] and leading to an abstraction of the neural field toward SOM-like structures, as initiated in [1]. This paper introduces self-organizing modules as well as a methodology for grouping them into an architecture. Moreover, an original method based on mutual information is introduced to measure how self-organization arises. The paper is organized as follows. First, a reformulation of the SOM algorithm is introduced, enabling the connection of modules as non-hierarchical architectures and allowing the definition of an original measure of organization. Then experiments on 2D data are presented.

2   Model: CxSOM

The main goal of the study is to set-up rules to build up a SOM architecture which achieves vector quantization tasks, as conventional SOM does, while learning relationship between associated data. The model has to be applicable to any structure and particularly non-hierarchical ones, and unlike A-SOM where some maps are specifically designed to connect other standard SOMs, all the modules are designed to be of the same type, eventually differing by some parameters.

2.1   SOMs as Blocks of an Architecture

Each module i is a slightly modified version of Kohonen's self organizing map [9]. First, let us introduce the standard model: a map is a graph with a fixed size and fixed topology. The input space is noted $\mathcal{D}$, the map being fed by inputs $\xi \in \mathcal{D}$. In this study, for plotting considerations, the graph is a one-dimensional line of N units, where each one is indexed by a position $p = \frac{i}{N-1}, 0 \leq i \leq N$. To each of those units is associated a weight vector $\omega_e(p) \in \mathcal{D}$, also referred to as *prototype*, randomly initialized. The algorithm performs vector quantization by creating a mapping of the input space over the N prototypes, with the specificity that the prototypes of two close units in the map are also close in $\mathcal{D}$, creating a continuity in the mapping. At each learning iteration, a new input $\xi \in \mathcal{D}$ is presented to the map. The BMU is found as the position having the maximal *activity* where

$$a(\xi, p) = \exp[\frac{\|\xi - \omega_e(p)\|^2}{2\sigma^2}] \tag{1}$$

Learning is realized by moving each unit towards ξ relatively to how close it is from Π:

$$\forall p, \omega_e(p, t+1) = \omega_e(p, t) + \alpha \times H_e(\Pi, p) \times (\xi - \omega_e(p, t)) \tag{2}$$

$H(\Pi, p)$ is a linearly decreasing function around Π in map positions space, reaching 0 at a distance h_e. In our approach, the learning rate α and the neighborhood radius h_e are constant, as opposed to most SOM-based works.

2.2   CxSOM Architecture Model

Let us now consider the architecture of n modules connected as a directed graph G. A module (i.e., a map) i takes an external input from $\mathcal{D}^i$, and a set of BMU from all the other maps connected to this one. SOM model is then extended to handle these multiple inputs. As G may present cycles, modifying Π in a map then modifies the activity and thus the BMU of already computed maps; the search for BMU must be a *consensus* between maps.

The notations of the model are summarized in Fig. 1 for an example of two maps connected one to another. Let us note ξ the external input of a map, and $\gamma_1, ..., \gamma_K$ its set of contextual inputs which are the BMU Π of all the other maps connected to this one in G. Taking the BMU as the only information transmitted between maps, encoding a state, brings homogeneity in the model: regardless of the dimension of the prototypes of a map, the transmitted information is a position. This encoding has already been used successfully as the information being transmitted between computational steps within a map, in models like SOMSD [6]. It is used here as well as a compact representation of remote map's state. Each unit is associated to $K+1$ weight vectors, each vector being associated to an input: ω_e is relative to the external input and $\omega_{c1}, \omega_{c2}, ..., \omega_{cK}$ are relative to the contextual inputs. Hence, the contextual weights are mappings over remote map position space. Learning is performed online by presenting a set of inputs to the architecture. A learning iteration is described in Algorithm 1: inputs are presented to each map in the architecture, and each set of weights ω_{ck} computes its activity distribution a_{ck} from a Gaussian matching, relatively to its input. These activities are merge into a global matching a_g.

$$a_g(p) = \sqrt{a_e(\xi, p) \times (\beta a_e(\xi, p) + (1 - \beta)a_c(p))}, \quad \text{with} \quad a_c(p) = \frac{1}{K} \sum_{k=1}^{K} a_{ck}(\gamma_k, p)$$

$$(3)$$

β is a merge factor, set to 0.5 in all the experiments. Notice that a map may have only contextual inputs; its global matching is then a_c, and map activity is driven by the behavior of other maps in the architecture. A spatial gaussian convolution is then applied on a_g, for stability issues not detailed here. Then, a *relaxation* is realized to find a ensemble $(\Pi_0, \cdots, \Pi_N)$ so that each BMU is situated at the maximum of its map's activity . This search is performed by small displacements of Π in each map until a stable state is reached.Once the BMU is found, each set of weights ω_{ck} is separately updated according to Eq. 2, relatively to the corresponding input. External neighborhood radius h_e is taken superior to the contextual ones h_c, see Fig. 1. Equation 3 ensures the global matching is mainly driven by the external inputs, and the difference between neighborhood radius keeps learning process on a smaller and more local scale for contexts compared to external weights. Both properties contribute to learning stability and convergence.

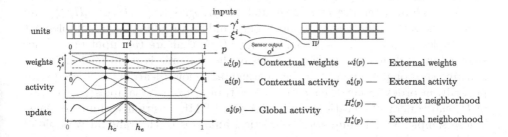

Fig. 1. Notations for a map in a CxSOM architecture, taking one contextual input.

3   Experiments and Results

3.1   Experiments Formalization

In order to exhibit what is learnt during self-organization and to quantify the progression of that learning, the formalization of experiments rely on random

Input: $\xi^1, ..., \xi^K \leftarrow (o^1, \cdots, o^K) \in \mathcal{D}^1 \times \cdot \times \mathcal{D}^K$
$t \leftarrow 0$
$\forall i, \Pi^i \leftarrow \arg\max_p a_e(\xi^i, p)$
while $\Pi(t) \neq \Pi(t-1)$ **do**
  forall the *Map i* **do**
    $\gamma_1^i, ... \gamma_k^i \leftarrow$ BMUs from connected maps
    Computation of a_g^i (Eq. 3)
    $p\star^i \leftarrow \arg\max_p a_g^i(p)$
    $\Pi^i \leftarrow \Pi^i + min(\Delta, |p\star^i - \Pi^i|) \times \mathrm{sgn}(p\star^i - \Pi^i)$
  end
  $t \leftarrow t+1$
end
$\forall i, \omega_e^i(p) \leftarrow \omega_e^i(p) + H_e(\Pi^i, p)(\omega_e^i(p) - \xi^i)$
$\forall i, \forall k, \omega_{ck}^i(p) \leftarrow \omega_{ck}^i(p) + H_c(\Pi^i, p)(\omega_{ck}^i(p) - \gamma^i)$

Algorithm 1: Learning iteration with relaxation process

variables. Let us consider that the data given to the learning process are sampled independently and identically (i.i.d.) from a random variable. Here, that random variable, denoted by U, does not directly feed the learning process. U is rather "seen" through a set of observation functions $s^1, \cdots, s^n$ so that the input samples are realizations of the joint random variable $(O^1, \cdots, O^n) = (s^1(U), \cdots, s^n(U)) \in \mathcal{D}^1 \times \cdots \mathcal{D}^n$. In our architectural approach, each observation feeds the external input of a dedicated map. As SOMs work online, $(O^1, \cdots, O^n)$ samples are provided one by one, learning being performed at each time step t from the realization $(o_t^1, \cdots, o_t^n)$ of the variable $(O^1, \cdots, O^n)$. Moreover, at time t, each map i computes a BMU Π^i, so that $(\Pi_t^1, \cdots, \Pi_t^n)$ is the state of the whole architecture at t. The tuples $\{(u_t, o_t^1, \cdots, o_t^K, \Pi_t^1, \cdots, \Pi_t^n)\}_t$ can then be viewed as samples of a global joint random variable. Let us complement such tuples with the values $\omega_e^1(\Pi_t^1) \cdots, \omega_e^n(\Pi_t^n)$, that are the input prototypes selected by each map at t. The analysis of the dynamic is performed after last learning step or periodically during learning as follows: learning is freezed temporarily, in order to get a collection of N tuples, from N samples $\{u_n\}_{1 \leq n \leq N}$ of U, subsequent observations and subsequent BMU position within the maps. These samples enable numerical statistical analyzes of the random variable of which they are realizations.

Another use of the collected tuples is to evaluate how well a map i has "discovered" the existence of U. If the map has captured the existence of U, its BMU values should be informative about the corresponding U values. The pairs $\{(u_n, \Pi_n^i)\}_{1 \leq n \leq N}$ should draw an actual *function* $u = f(\Pi)$. This is what further plots in Fig. 4 actually show. In statistical terms, the samples should show that U depends on the random variable Π^i. This dependency can be evaluated from samples by computing *mutual information* between Π^i and U: $I(\Pi^i, U)$, representing in information theory how much information a realization of Π^i

carries about U probability. It's defined from entropy H as:

$$I(\Pi^i, U) = H(U) - H(U|\Pi^i) \tag{4}$$

In our results, I is then normalized by $H(U)$, which is the maximum value $I(\Pi^i, U)$ can reaches when u is an actual function of Π. Although this property can be visually evaluated on one dimensional maps and one dimensional data, it gets harder in larger dimensions, in which cases such an indicator is useful. Estimation is realized by discretizing the variables through binning and probabilities estimated by counting the samples. As the datasets are artificial and as big as needed, the estimation is not a problem. In the following, this is performed periodically, while learning takes place, in order to exhibit an increase of the mutual information between Π^i and U as the map gets jointly self-organized. This is illustrated further in Fig. 5. To sum up, modelling the input as well as the status of the architecture as joint random variables facilitates an illustration and evaluation of what is actually learnt within the maps. This is used further to analyze the experimental setup presented in this paper.

3.2   Evaluation of the Model on Two Maps

This experiment aims at understanding which mecanisms are involved in the organization by analyzing 2 maps connected one to another and therefore developing a methodology to that end. The external inputs (O_1, O_2) are the (X, Y) coordinates of a point on a circle centered in $(0.5, 0.5)$, radius 0.5, both depending on the hidden variable U as $(X, Y) = (\frac{1+cos(2\pi U)}{2}, \frac{1+sin(2\pi U)}{2})$. The architecture is trained on 2000 iterations, U being uniformly drawn in $[0, 1[$ on each one. α is set to 0.1, $h_e = 0.2$, $h_c = 0.07$, $\Delta = 0.01$. After training, learning is freezed and U, thus (X, Y), and (Π^X, Π^Y) after relaxation, are sampled 1000 times in order to build plots in Figs. 2, 3, 4. Two samples S_1 and S_2, whose elements are referred to as $(x_1, y_1, u_1, \Pi_1, ...)$ and $(x_2, y_2, u_2, \Pi_2, ...)$ in the following, are highlighted in the plots. They correspond to $x_1 = x_2 = 0.6$, $y_1 = 0$ and $y_2 = 1$, $u_1 = 0.8$ and $u_2 = 0.2$.

The relation ship between $w_e^X(\Pi^X)$ and ξ is plotted in Fig. 3 to evaluate if vector quantization is achieved: it should be close to identity. Even if some accuracy is lost compared to a standard map, vector quantization is correctly achieved within each map. Figure 2 presents the weights repartition in each map after training. It can be seen that the weights are globally disposed according to the external inputs: if two nodes have close external prototypes, then they are close in the map. Within this overall repartition, weights are disposed according to U in a reduced number of "zones", in gray in the figure. For example, S_1 and S_2 share their X value, but have different U. BMUs are thus in two consecutive "zones" on the map according on Fig. 2, making the distinction between the U value, but keeping the BMU prototype close to the input value. These zones also correspond to the steps in Fig. 3: as w_e is smooth, two areas winning for a same interval of X have slightly different w_e, both still close to X, but corresponding to different U. The right graphic in Fig. 2 shows on a same plot the center region of map X and the pairs (Π^X, X). It is noticeable that entire zones of map units never win: BMUs are actually located at the extrema of contextual weights, two consecutive zones corresponding to a same range of external inputs, but different U. The context is thus introducing a discontinuity in the map, which is unexpected in topology preserving self-organization. In Fig. 4, U value is plotted according to the corresponding BMU position. It shows that U can be deduced from Π in each map.

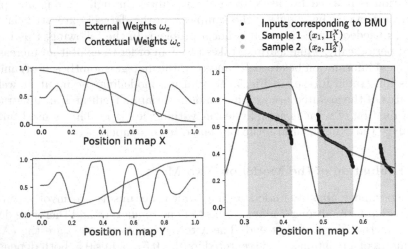

Fig. 2. Weights disposition of a 2-map structure after learning. Inputs corresponding to winning positions on a segment of map X are plotted in the right graphic. The disposition of contextual weights resulting of joint self-organization allows the map to find the BMU for a sample according to U and not only the external input value.

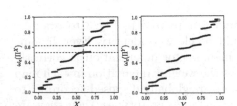

Fig. 3. BMU weight distribution according to inputs. It should be close to identity.

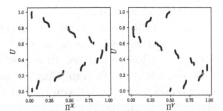

Fig. 4. U distribution according to BMU position. U can be deduced from Π in each map.

The ability to make a distinction in each map's state depending on U is measured by a mutual information criterion. For sake of comparison between maps which are learning independently on X and Y and joint maps, Fig. 5 shows normalized mutual information between U and Π in both maps during learning, as described in Sect. 3.1. Every 20 learning iterations, 5000 samples are computed and mutual information evalutated on them. The curves are a mean of 30 runs of the experiment. Estimation is realized though binning. U bin size is set to 0.02, whereas Π are already discrete variables taking 500 values. To allow comparison, the bin size is the same for the estimation of normalized mutual information on both independent and joint maps. First, the figure shows that mutual information increases from initial random weights to final state; more interestingly, it shows a significant enhancement between independent maps and joint maps. So, while oberving Π in independent maps gives a good precision on X value but lets U uncertain, observing Π in joint maps may lose a bit of accuracy on X but ensures a BMU also carries information about the whole state of observations, and has "discovered" U.

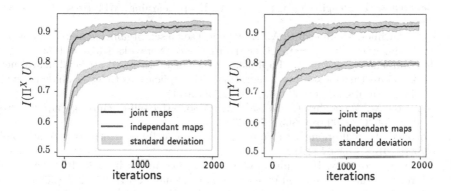

Fig. 5. Mutual information evolution between BMU positions and U.

4 Conclusion

This paper introduces an extension of self-organizing maps usable as module in non-hierarchical architectures. Each of those modules performs vector quantization, as standard SOM does, but the learning process is also driven by a consensus between modules, allowing them to share and store information about remote map's state. This information sharing has been measured by a mutual information based evaluation. As BMUs, i.e., positions, are transmitted between maps as representation of a map's state, the model is scalable to any architecture, unrelated to each module's input space dimension. The experiments on two maps depict the organization created by this information transmission: each module organizes itself in regard of its external inputs, but also differentiates the BMUs depending on the global state of observations. This behavior is particularly interesting considering the simplicity of the information shared between maps. This work can be related to the one carried in [4] on recurrent SOM for temporal sequence processing. The basic architecture behavior brought to light in this paper enables forthcoming work on larger architectures, two-dimensional SOMs and integration of recurrent processes.

References

1. Baheux, D., Fix, J., Frezza-Buet, H.: Towards an effective multi-map self organizing recurrent neural network. In: Proceedigs ESANN'2014, pp. 201–206 (2014)
2. Ballard, D.H.: Cortical connections and parallel processing: structure and function. Behav. Brain Sci. **9**, 67–129 (1986)
3. Dittenbach, M., Rauber, A., Merkl, D.: Uncovering hierarchical structure in data using the growing hierarchical self-organizing map. Neurocomputing **48**(1), 199–216 (2002)
4. Fix, J., Frezza-Buet, H.: Look and feel what and how recurrent self-organizing maps learn. In: Vellido, A., Gibert, K., Angulo, C., Martín Guerrero, J.D. (eds.) WSOM 2019. AISC, vol. 976, pp. 3–12. Springer, Cham (2020). https://doi.org/10.1007/978-3-030-19642-4_1
5. Goodfellow, I., Bengio, Y., Courville, A.: Deep Learning. MIT Press, Cambridge (2016)
6. Hagenbuchner, M., Sperduti, A.: Ah Chung Tsoi: a self-organizing map for adaptive processing of structured data. IEEE Trans. Neural Networks **14**(3), 491–505 (2003)
7. Jantvik, T., Gustafsson, L., Papliński, A.P.: A self-organized artificial neural network architecture for sensory integration with applications to letter-phoneme integration. Neural Comput. **23**(8), 2101–2139 (2011)
8. Johnsson, M., Balkenius, C., Hesslow, G.: Associative self-organizing map. In: Proceedings IJCCI'2009, pp. 363–370 (2009)
9. Kohonen, T.: Self-organized formation of topologically correct feature maps. Biol. Cybern. **43**(1), 59–69 (1982)
10. Lallee, S., Dominey, P.: Multi-modal convergence maps: from body schema and self-representation to mental imagery. Adapt. Behav. **21**(4), 274–285 (2013)
11. Lefort, M., Boniface, Y., Girau, B.: SOMMA: Cortically Inspired Paradigms for Multimodal Processing, pp. 1–8 (2013)
12. Ménard, O., Frezza-Buet, H.: Model of multi-modal cortical processing: coherent learning in self-organizing modules. Neural Networks **18**(5–6), 646–655 (2005)
13. Miikkulainen, R., Bednar, J.A., Choe, Y., Sirosh, J.: Computational Maps in the Visual Cortex. Springer, New York (2005)
14. Miller, K.D., Simons, D.J., Pinto, D.J.: Processing in layer 4 of the neocortical circuit: new insights from visual and somatosensory cortex. Curr. Opin. Neurobiol. **11**, 488–497 (2001)
15. Mountcastle, V.B.: The columnar organization of the neocortex. Brain **120**, 701–722 (1997)
16. Parisi, G.I., Tani, J., Weber, C., Wermter, S.: Emergence of multimodal action representations from neural network self-organization. Cogn. Syst. Res. **43**, 208–221 (2017)
17. Tan, A.H., Subagdja, B., Wang, D., Meng, L.: Self-organizing neural networks for universal learning and multimodal memory encoding. Neural Networks **120**, 58–73 (2019)
18. Wan, W., Fraser, D.: Multisource data fusion with multiple self-organizing maps. IEEE Trans. Geosci. Remote Sens. **37**(3), 1344–1349 (1999)

Continuous Boundary Approximation from Data Samples Using Bidirectional Hypersphere Transformation Networks

Prayook Jatesiktat[1]($\boxtimes$), Guan Ming Lim[2], and Wei Tech Ang[1,2]

[1] Rehabilitation Research Institute of Singapore, Nanyang Technological University,
11 Mandalay Road, Singapore 308232, Singapore
prayook001@e.ntu.edu.sg, wtang@ntu.edu.sg
[2] School of Mechanical and Aerospace Engineering, Nanyang Technological
University, 50 Nanyang Avenue, Singapore 639798, Singapore
guanming001@e.ntu.edu.sg

Abstract. Given a set of multidimensional data samples, we propose
a way to approximate a continuous boundary that compactly contains
all the samples. The method optimizes two residual neural networks to
transform a unit hypersphere surface to a continuous boundary in the
data space and vice versa. The networks are trained by shrinking the
boundary while containing all the training samples inside through a loss
function. The learning results in a bidirectional relationship, where the
mapping from the data space to the spherical space can be used for one-
class classification, while the inverse mapping can be used for generative
tasks. The method is tested on 2D toy datasets, 3D, and 6D human joint
pose to illustrate the results. The source code and the data are made
publicly available.

Keywords: Concave hull · Implicit representation · Residual network

1 Introduction

Among many goals of machine learning algorithms, one of them is to approximate
the probability distribution of data from collected data samples. Knowing an
accurate underlying distribution structure of a specific data class can yield the
capabilities to generate a new data sample or to estimate how likely a query
sample belongs to the class. However, the collected data samples might not
always be densely packed throughout the region and can contain gaps and void
regions that should also be included in the class region. One way to include those
void areas in the modelling is to wrap all those samples with one continuous
boundary because it is common in nature that a class may have continuous

Supported by Agency for Science, Technology and Research (A*STAR), Nanyang Technological University (NTU) and the National Healthcare Group (NHG). Project code:
RFP/19003.

variation in some dimensions that form one continuous hypervolume in its high-dimensional space. Implicit representation of this boundary from a collection of samples is the central focus of this paper.

Traditionally, convex and concave hulls can be seen as a collection of linear boundaries that links a subset of samples together to contain all the other points. Although the convex hull method can provide the simplicity of solution uniqueness, the solution is often not tight-fit and can leave some large void areas between a boundary and some internal points. Even if this void area can be solved by a concave hull, the existing n-dimensional concave hull algorithm [5] can only provide piecewise construction of the boundary without a fast way to check if a new sample is inside or outside the boundary. This inefficiency causes these tools to perform badly in both classification and generation tasks. In addition, most of the concave hull algorithms do not support over 3 dimensions.

One-class support vector machine (OCSVM) is a well-known method that can be used to perform a fast classification after learning from a collection of samples from one class. However, OCSVM does not guarantee that the learned boundary will be connected as one piece. Because it does not assume one class of continuous volume, hyperparameters have to be carefully selected to generate the desired single-region result [7]. If an application needs to obey the single-region constraint or try to avoid holes in the classification volume, OCSVM is not a suitable option. Also, its formulation mainly focuses on performing a fast classification rather than a fast generation of new samples.

Generative Adversarial Networks (GAN) can also be modified to approximate a compact boundary from a set of data samples for anomaly detection [4]. However, similarly to OCSVM, it does not have the single-region constraint.

In this work, we propose a new representation of the continuous boundary with a unique set of following characteristics. 1) The boundary will split the space into one continuous internal volume and one continuous external volume. 2) The representation of the boundary is learned from a collection of data samples which can be in a high dimensional space. 3) The representation allows a fast calculation to test if a new sample is inside or outside the class region. 4) The representation allows a fast generation of new samples from the learned boundary.

2   Method

According to Jordan–Brouwer separation theorem, any compact, connected hypersurface in $\mathbb{R}^n$ will divide $\mathbb{R}^n$ into two connected regions; the "outside" and the "inside" [6]. If the surface of a unit hypersphere is morphed into a new hypersurface that tightly contains data samples, this new hypersurface can be used to define the boundary of the class. With this idea, the boundary can be represented by the morphing functions that transform between the unit hypersphere and the boundary in the data space. An artificial neural network is chosen as a universal approximator for both directions of morphing functions as it can provide non-linear space transformation with continuity.

Numerical optimization is used to search for the morphing functions. The optimization process searches for a non-linear transformation that morphs the surface of a unit hypersphere in N-dimensional space into a boundary in data space which is also N-dimensional. This deformed boundary should wrap tightly around all the samples in the training data. At the same time, we also need to find an inverse function that transforms the hypersurface in the data space back to the original unit hyper-spherical space. This inverse function allows a fast computation to check whether a sample is inside or outside the boundary as the internal area in the unit spherical space is simply defined by "Euclidean norm lesser than one". On the other hand, the direct transformation from the unit hypersphere allows a quick generation of the data by randomly sampling a point inside the unit hypersphere and transforming it into the data space.

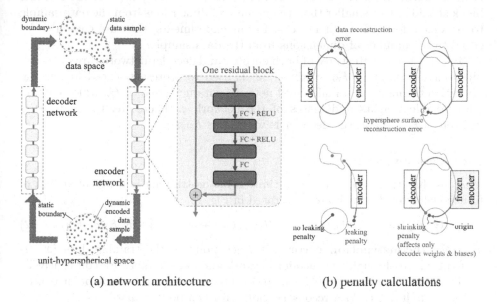

(a) network architecture   (b) penalty calculations

Fig. 1. (a) The proposed architecture for continuous boundary learning. During the optimization, the dynamic boundary in data space will gradually morph to wrap around the static training data points. In contrast, the dynamic cluster of encoded data samples will gradually change the formation to compactly fit inside the static unit hypersphere. **(b)** How the data flow in the calculation of four penalties in the cost function. Note that the shrinking penalty (bottom right) is calculated using current weights and biases of the encoder but the error gradient from the shrinking penalty will not be used to update the encoder. This trick encourages the boundary in data space to constantly move inward perpendicularly to the current surface tangent.

2.1   Neural Network Architecture

The network architecture is shown in Fig. 1a. It is composed of two architecturally identical networks named as encoder and decoder. The encoder network will transform the data space into the spherical space and the decoder network will do the opposite. This encoding-decoding structure is similar to autoencoder but without any dimensional bottleneck in the data flow. Each network is a long series of modified residual blocks [1]. All these residual blocks are initialized as a nearly identical function at the beginning of the training process to force the initialized encoder and decoder chain to be a nearly identical function. This residual network structure and the nearly identical initialization allow the network to become very deep (e.g., 50 residual blocks or more) and still converge to a good solution. Each residual block in our experiments can be formulated as

$$ResBlock(g) = g + W_3 Relu(W_2 Relu(W_1 g + b_1) + b_2) + b_3 \qquad (1)$$

given that W_i and b_i are weights and biases of that block and $Relu(\cdot)$ is a rectified linear unit. The number of hidden nodes in every layer of the residual block should not be smaller than the number of dimensions from the data sample to prevent information bottlenecks. In our experiments, they are chosen to be equal to the number of dimensions from the data sample.

Because the architectures of both encoder and decoder networks are identical, one function notation $F_{\Theta_q} : \mathbb{R}^n \mapsto \mathbb{R}^n$ is used to represent a feed forwarding operation through a residual neural network parameterized by Θ_q which contain all learnable weights and biases of the network q. Therefore, the encoder is written as $F_{\Theta_e}(\cdot)$ and the decoder is written as $F_{\Theta_d}(\cdot)$.

2.2   Cost Function

The cost function (Eq. 2) to be optimized in the training is a weighted sum of four penalty terms which are illustrated in Fig. 1b.

$$J(\Theta_e, \Theta_d) = w_r R(\Theta_e, \Theta_d) + w_h H(\Theta_e, \Theta_d) + w_l L(\Theta_e) + w_s S(\Theta_e, \Theta_d) \qquad (2)$$

1. **Data reconstruction error** (R): Each point in the training data (x_i) is fed forward through the encoder network and decoder network consecutively. The squared difference between the output point and the input point is used as a penalty. The data reconstruction error can be formulated as

$$R(\Theta_e, \Theta_d) = \frac{1}{a} \sum_i^a ||F_{\Theta_d}(F_{\Theta_e}(x_i)) - x_i||^2 \qquad (3)$$

where a is the training data size, and $|| \cdot ||$ is the Euclidean norm.

2. **Hypersphere surface reconstruction error** (H): Similar to the data reconstruction error, but using uniformly sampled points on the surface of the unit hypersphere. Each point (s_i) is fed forward through the decoder and encoder network consecutively. The squared difference between the output and the input point is the penalty. The term can be formulated as

$$H(\Theta_e, \Theta_d) = \frac{1}{c} \sum_i^c ||F_{\Theta_e}(F_{\Theta_d}(s_i)) - s_i||^2 \qquad (4)$$

where c is the number of samples. The larger the dimension of the hypersphere, the greater the number of samples is needed to ensure sufficient surface coverage.

3. **Leaking penalty** (L): Each point in the training data (x_i) is fed forward through the encoder network. The penalty will be activated when the Euclidean norm of the encoded vector is larger than one (i.e., the encoded vector is outside the boundary of the unit hypersphere). The term can be formulated as

$$L(\Theta_e) = \frac{1}{a} \sum_i^a \max(0, ||F_{\Theta_e}(x_i)||^2 - 1) \tag{5}$$

Although the leaking penalty is calculated in the hyperspherical space, it also creates an indirect effect of leaking prevention in the data space boundary with the support from the two reconstruction terms. Because of the two reconstruction terms, we can assume that if a point stays in the "inside" region of the hyperspherical space, the associated decoded point in data space is likely to also stay in the "inside" region. Therefore, forcing a point to move "inside" the unit hypersphere will indirectly force its associated point in data space to also stay "inside" (via boundary expansion done by changes in the decoder).

4. **Shrinking term** (S): Points on the surface of the unit hypersphere are sampled uniformly. Each point (s_i) is fed forward through the decoder network and the frozen version of the encoder network $(\bar{\Theta}_e)$ consecutively. Euclidean norm of the output vector is used directly as a penalty term. The error gradient of this shrinking term will be backpropagated to only weights and biases in the decoder network but not the encoder network. This will encourage the boundary in data space to keep shrinking while having the leaking penalty to prevent it from shrinking too much beyond the outer shell of training data. The term can be formulated as

$$S(\Theta_e, \Theta_d) = \frac{1}{c} \sum_i^c ||F_{\bar{\Theta}_e}(F_{\Theta_d}(s_i))|| \tag{6}$$

While the first three terms are expected to be minimized to some near-zero values, the shrinking term is expected to keep fluctuating around a value slightly below one even after the convergence.

These four terms are designed to work together. Missing one of the terms could lead to an undesired result. Removing one or both of the reconstruction error terms will cause a failure in maintaining the reversible connection between two networks. Removing the leaking penalty alone will cause the surface in data space to shrink infinitely. Removing the shrinking term alone will cause the boundary to stop evolving when all the data points are contained within the boundary regardless of the shape or how big the boundary is.

One important feature of this cost function design is the flexibility in terms of data dimension. As the data space boundary is not shrunk by minimizing the volume, we can circumvent the issue of formulating the volume term to be differentiable and general for any high dimensional space. Since the target space can be in any number of dimensions, the proposed method is designed to potentially support them all. To investigate the potential of this proposed technique, experiments with 2-, 3-, and 6-dimensional data are conducted.

2.3 Initialization and Optimization

By initializing all the weights to a near-zero value (e.g., sampling from Gaussian distribution with zero mean and 0.1 standard deviation in our experiments) and biases to zero, all the residual blocks in both encoder and decoder will act as virtually identical functions because of the skip connections. The volume of the unit hypersphere will stay in roughly the same shape after it is decoded and encoded again. The encoder and decoder will start close to an inverse of each other and they will evolve together while maintaining this inversion property since the beginning. This way of initialization together with the residual network architecture is crucial for the successful convergence of this technique. If the weights are initialized with large random values the optimization is not likely to converge to a useful solution. Our experiments are implemented in TensorFlow. The cost function are minimized with ADAM optimizer [3] with default learning parameters (i.e., $learning\_rate=0.001$, $beta1=0.9$, $beta2=0.999$, and $epsilon=10^{-8}$).

3 Experiments and Results

3.1 Two-Dimensional Toy Datasets

To better visualize the generalization capability of the proposed method and observe the stability of the training, we first test with two manually generated 2D datasets. In this 2D case, the unit hypersphere is represented by a unit circle. Both the encoder and the decoder contain 15 residual blocks. The size of the boundary samples (c) are set to 100 for the surface reconstruction error and the shrinking term. The weights for the cost function are $w_r = 50$, $w_h = 50$, $w_l = 100$, and $w_s = 1$. Figure 2 shows the transformation of the boundary through the training from the initialization to the moment it converges and how the unit circle space will be like if it is deformed through the decoder to the data space.

3.2 Three-Dimensional Joint Pose Datasets

The method is tested on 3D joint pose data. Motion capture data from nine upper-limb tasks of one subject is used to extract 3D shoulder pose (orientation of the upper arm relative to the thorax) and 3D elbow pose (orientation of the forearm relative to the upper arm). Those nine tasks related to upper limb rehabilitation include box-and-block test, towel folding, grasping, sideway cylinder shifting, hand-to-mouth, hand-to-head, hand-to-back, key turning in sitting pose, and key turning in standing pose. All the tasks are recorded by Qualisys motion capture system with 16 cameras. One frame in the record gives one pose sample for each joint. Each orientation is represented by a 3D rotation vector. The direction is the axis of rotation and the magnitude is the amount of rotation in radian. For the shoulder joint, this representation jointly combines flexion/extension, abduction/adduction, and internal/external rotation. For the

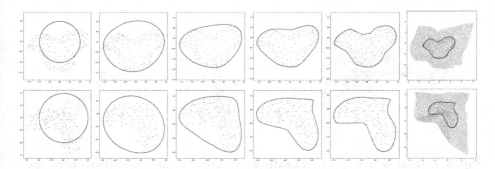

Fig. 2. Each row is the learning results from one dataset. The leftmost plots show the boundary in data space at the initialization. The subsequent plots on the right side show the results after 256, 2000, 5000, and 20000 iterations of training respectively. The boundary can gradually adjust itself while maintaining small differences between the original sample (black points) and the reconstructed sample (red points). The rightmost column visualizes how a square grid with a blue unit circle will look like if it is transformed through the learned decoder network. One small square grid has the original size of 0.1 by 0.1 units. The original size of the big square sheet is 2 by 2 units. (Color figure online)

elbow joint, this representation jointly combines elbow flexion/extension and forearm pronation/supination. Both the encoder and the decoder contain 60 residual blocks. The size of the boundary samples (c) are set to 1,000 for the surface reconstruction error and the shrinking term. The weights for the cost function are $w_r = 17$, $w_h = 17$, $w_l = 100$, and $w_s = 1$. The learned boundary for both shoulder and elbow pose can be seen in Fig. 3.

3.3   Six-Dimensional Combined Joint Pose Datasets

The experiment is expanded further to 6D space by combining 3D shoulder pose with 3D elbow pose from the same motion-capture frame together. Both the encoder and the decoder contain 60 residual blocks. The size of the boundary samples (c) are set to 100,000 for the surface reconstruction error and the shrinking term. The weights for the cost function are $w_r = 17$, $w_h = 17$, $w_l = 100$, and $w_s = 1$. However, the 6D boundary is not visualizable on a 2D screen. To validate the result, a high-dimensional boundary slicer is built to visualize a sliced boundary in three dimensions at a time (with rotatable interaction) while keeping the values of the other 3 dimensions constant. The generated boundary seems to generally follow the shape of the data points. The software code and the pre-trained networks to generate the interactive graphical user interface of the slicer are available in the supplementary repository [2].

3.4   Computation Cost

The optimization in all the experiments are executed on an Intel Core i7-6850K CPU (3.60 GHz) and one NVIDIA GeForce GTX 1080 Ti GPU. It takes about

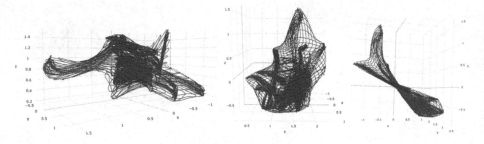

Fig. 3. Left: 3D shoulder pose. **Middle and right**: 3D elbow pose from two perspectives. In both cases, the method can generate a 3D boundary (blue) that can compactly contain data points (gray) as expected. These blue lines on the boundary are generated by feeding parallels of latitude from a unit circle to the trained decoder. The samples from elbow pose are aligned in a nearly flat 2D sheet with a little bit of twist as the elbow joint naturally has only two degrees of freedom (i.e., elbow flexion/extension and forearm pronation/supination). The interactive versions of these 3D plots are also available in the supplementary repository [2]. (Color figure online)

12 min, 2 h, and 18 h for the optimization to converge in the case of 2D, 3D, and 6D data respectively.

4   Discussions

4.1   Potential Applications

In general, the proposed method is highly suitable for modelling a data class where the data samples are intrinsically connected in one continuous region. One of them is the human joint range of motion (ROM) whether it is from one specific joint, from a limb, or the whole body. This section describes some potential applications in physical rehabilitation and human-robot interaction by having this new representation of joint ROM as the center of the discussion.

Joint Range-of-Motion Monitoring. Range of motion (ROM) is commonly used to diagnose and track the progress in physical rehabilitation. Conventional clinical practice measures each ROM component separately. For example, the shoulder ROM is split into 1) flexion/extension 2) adduction/abduction and 3) internal/external rotation. Each component is measured independently to retrieve the minimum and the maximum angles. However, in reality, the ROM in one specific component depends on the state of other components. For instance, the range of right shoulder internal/external rotation can be as large as almost 180 degrees when the right upper arm is pointing to the right side or downward, but when the upper arm points forward, the range of the shoulder internal/external rotation will reduce to around 110 degrees. This kind of conditional ROM can become even more complicated in patients with neurological conditions such as stroke. Tracking their progress during a rehabilitation program with the traditional active ROM could miss some useful information that limits the effectiveness of intervention or exercise prescription. Therefore, an obvious application of this technique is progress tracking in physical rehabilitation through the growth of the active range of motion (AROM) boundary. By overlaying the AROM boundary of a patient against that of healthy subjects, a specific exercise can be tailored by a therapist to induce the expansion of the boundary toward the area of missing ability.

Safety Boundary for Wearable Robots. Wearable assistive robots that interface with user's body parts (e.g., exoskeleton, collaborative robot arm) need to have an understanding of a safety boundary in the user's motion space to prevent the device from moving beyond what the user can do and cause an injury. If this boundary is determined heuristically, it requires knowledge and experience to apply the appropriate heuristics effectively. However, using the proposed method, a precise boundary could be learned automatically from the data pool of healthy subjects. Besides, the encoder network allows fast computation and checking of whether the robot's trajectory falls outside the safety boundary, thus allowing the robot to plan a safe and responsive motion.

4.2   Limitation and Future Work

This technique is suitable for data distribution that can be wrapped by a surface of genus-zero. If the formation of data samples has a more complicated topology, the fundamental shape used in one end of the bidirectional mapping can be changed for more accurate modelling. For example, if the data are clustered as a ring, a hypertorus should be used instead of a hypersphere and the penalty terms should be redesigned. Automatic prediction of the underlying manifold and a proper selection of the fundamental shape is a challenging research direction.

To make this technique even more useful, the architecture can be modified to make the boundary morph according to some continuous conditions. One suggested way is to concatenate the multi-dimensional condition information to every layer of the networks. This concept has been tested primarily with lower limb pose under gait-phase condition and it works as expected. This conditional boundary should be explored further with other types of applications.

References

1. He, K., Zhang, X., Ren, S., Sun, J.: Identity mappings in deep residual networks. In: Leibe, B., Matas, J., Sebe, N., Welling, M. (eds.) ECCV 2016. LNCS, vol. 9908, pp. 630–645. Springer, Cham (2016). https://doi.org/10.1007/978-3-319-46493-0_38
2. Jatesiktat, P., Lim, G.M.: Boundary learning: Supplementary materials. https://github.com/ntu-rris/bound-learning-supplementary/
3. Kingma, D.P., Ba, J.: Adam: A method for stochastic optimization. CoRR abs/1412.6980 (2014). http://arxiv.org/abs/1412.6980
4. Ngo, P.C., Winarto, A.A., Kou, C.K.L., Park, S., Akram, F., Lee, H.K.: Fence GAN: towards better anomaly detection. In: 2019 IEEE 31st International Conference on Tools with Artificial Intelligence (ICTAI), pp. 141–148 (2019)

5. Park, J.S., Oh, S.J.: A new concave hull algorithm and concaveness measure for n-dimensional datasets. J. Inf. Sci. Eng. **28**(3), 587–600 (2012)
6. Schmaltz, W.: The jordan-brouwer separation theorem (2009). https://math.uchicago.edu/may/VIGRE/VIGRE2009/REUPapers/Schmaltz.pdf
7. Wang, S., Liu, Q., Zhu, E., Porikli, F., Yin, J.: Hyperparameter selection of one-class support vector machine by self-adaptive data shifting. Pattern Recogn. **74**, 198–211 (2018). https://doi.org/10.1016/j.patcog.2017.09.012

Convergence of Mini-Batch Learning
for Fault Aware RBF Networks

Ersi Cha, Chi-Sing Leung$^{(\boxtimes)}$, and Eric Wong

Department of Electrical Engineering, City University of Hong Kong,
Hong Kong, China
ersicha2-c@my.cityu.edu.hk, {eeleungc,e.wong}@cityu.edu.hk

Abstract. In between online and batch modes, there is a mini-batch concept that takes a subset of the training samples for updating the weights at each iteration. Traditional analysis of mini-batch is based on the stochastic gradient descent in which we assume that the process of taking mini-batches is performed in a random manner. In fact, practically, the mini-batch process is not in a random manner. In the last decade, many online and batch learning algorithms for fault aware radial basis function (RBF) networks. However, not much works on mini-batch for fault aware RBF networks are reported. This paper proposes a mini-batch learning algorithm for fault aware RBF networks. In our approach, rather than using the assumptions of the stochastic gradient descent, we consider that the partitions of mini-batches are fixed, and that those mini-batches are presented in a fixed order. Even with the above fixed arrangement, we are still able to prove that the training weight vector converges to the fault aware batch mode solution. In addition, we present the sufficient condition for the convergence.

Keywords: Mini-batch · Weight fault · Convergence

1 Introduction

In realization of a neural network, flaw and imperfection cannot be avoided. Multiplicative weight noise and open weight faults [1–3] are common fault/noise model to describe the imperfection. There were some fault/noise aware batch mode algorithms for RBF networks [4,5]. However, the disadvantage of using the batch mode learning is that it needs to store the entire input-output history. One way to solve this problem is to develop an online algorithm. However, current CPU/GPU architectures do not efficiently handle for online data.

In between online and batch modes, there is a mini-batch concept. Many traditional analyzes of mini-batch are based on the stochastic gradient descent [6]. Practically, for ease of implementation, the mini-batches process is in a determinism manner. Hence there is a gap between the practical implementation and the theoretical analysis.

This paper proposes a mini-batch learning algorithm for fault aware RBF networks in which weight noise and weight fault appear concurrently. In our

© Springer Nature Switzerland AG 2020
H. Yang et al. (Eds.): ICONIP 2020, CCIS 1333, pp. 545–553, 2020.
https://doi.org/10.1007/978-3-030-63823-8_62

approach, the partitioning process and the presentation order are in a determinism manner. We prove that the training weight vector converges to the optimal batch mode solution. In addition, we present the sufficient conditions for convergence.

The organization of this paper is as follows. Section 2 reviews the concept of RBF networks. Section 3 presents our fault aware mini batch algorithm and the convergent analysis. The experimental result is shown in Sect. 4. Conclusion is made in Sect. 5.

2   RBF Networks with Concurrent Fault

We use a regression problem as an example to show our mini-batch results. The regression problem is with N training sample pairs $(\boldsymbol{x}_k, o_k)$'s. The dimension of input vectors $\boldsymbol{x}_k$'s is D and the expected outputs o_k's are scalers. The RBF approach uses a weighted sum of L RBF nodes to describe the training data, given by

$$f(\boldsymbol{x}) \approx \sum_{l=1}^{L} \alpha_l h_l(\boldsymbol{x}), \tag{1}$$

where $\boldsymbol{\alpha} = [\alpha_1, \cdots, \alpha_L]^{\mathrm{T}}$ is the weight vector, $h_l(\boldsymbol{x}) = \exp\left(-\frac{\|\boldsymbol{x} - \boldsymbol{c}_l\|^2}{w}\right)$ is the output of the l-th RBF node, $\boldsymbol{c}_l$ is the corresponding RBF center, and w is used to define the spread of the RBF function. In this paper, we set the same spread for all RBFs. We can write the network output in a vector form:

$$f(\boldsymbol{x}, w) = \boldsymbol{h}^{\mathrm{T}}(\boldsymbol{x})\boldsymbol{\alpha}, \text{where } \boldsymbol{h}(\boldsymbol{x}) = [h_1(\boldsymbol{x}), \cdots, h_L(\boldsymbol{x})]^{\mathrm{T}}. \tag{2}$$

The conventional training criterion is

$$\mathcal{J}_l(\boldsymbol{\alpha}) = \sum_{k=1}^{N} (o_k - \boldsymbol{h}^{\mathrm{T}}(\boldsymbol{x}_k)\boldsymbol{\alpha})^2. \tag{3}$$

Based on simple matrix inverse, the optimal solution is

$$\boldsymbol{\alpha}_{ls} = (\boldsymbol{H})^{-1} \sum_{k=1}^{N} \boldsymbol{h}(\boldsymbol{x}_k) o_k, \text{where } \boldsymbol{H} = \sum_{k=1}^{N} \boldsymbol{h}(\boldsymbol{x}_k) \boldsymbol{h}^{\mathrm{T}}(\boldsymbol{x}_k). \tag{4}$$

In real situation, an RBF network may suffer from multiplicative weight noise and open weight fault at the same time [4,5]. This fault situation can be modelled as

$$\tilde{\alpha}_l = (\alpha_l + a_l\alpha_l)b_j \ \forall \ l = 1, \cdots, L, \tag{5}$$

where $\tilde{\alpha}_l$ is the implemented weight. Variables a_l's are the normalized noise factors that describe the effect of multiplicative noise. This paper assumes that they are zero mean symmetric random variables with the same distribution and are independent. Their variance is equal to σ_a^2. In addition, variables b_l's are open fault factors that describe the connection statuses of the weights. If the α_l is opened, b_l is equal to zero. Otherwise, it is equal to one. This paper assumes that they are binary random variables and are independent. Their probability mass function is $\text{Prob}(b_l = 0) = p_b$ and $\text{Prob}(b_l = 1) = 1 - p_b$.

From [4,5], the fault aware objective function is

$$\mathcal{J}(\boldsymbol{\alpha}) = \sum_{k=1}^{N}(o_k - \boldsymbol{h}^{\mathrm{T}}(\boldsymbol{x}_k)\boldsymbol{\alpha})^2 + \boldsymbol{\alpha}^{\mathrm{T}}\boldsymbol{R}\boldsymbol{\alpha}, \tag{6}$$

where $\boldsymbol{R} = (p_b + \sigma_a^2)\boldsymbol{G} - p_b\boldsymbol{H}$, $\boldsymbol{G}$ is a diagonal matrix whose elements are extracted from $\boldsymbol{H}$, i.e., $[\boldsymbol{G}]_{ll} = [\boldsymbol{H}]_{ll}$, for $l = 1, \cdots, L$. The optimal solution for (6) is

$$\boldsymbol{\alpha}_* = [\boldsymbol{H} + \boldsymbol{R}]^{-1}\sum_{k=1}^{N}\boldsymbol{h}(\boldsymbol{x}_k)o_k. \tag{7}$$

3   Mini-Batch and its Convergence

For the mini-batch case, we divide the N samples into N_{min} mini-batches in the non-overlaying manner. The j-th mini-batch has n_j samples, where $n_1 + n_2 + \cdots + n_{N_{min}} = N$. Let V_j be an index set that contains the indices referring to the training samples in the j-th mini-batch. That is, if the k-th training sample belongs to the j-th mini-batch, then k is an element of V_j.

Unlike the stochastic gradient descent [6] in which we assume that the process of taking subset is performed in a random manner, we present the mini-batches and perform subsetting in a determinism manner. In a learning cycle, each mini-batch is presented exactly once in a fixed order. At the m-th iteration, we consider the j-th mini-batch. From (6), the instantaneous cost is given by

$$\mathcal{J}_j(\boldsymbol{\alpha}) = \sum_{p\in V_j}(o_p - \boldsymbol{h}^{\mathrm{T}}(\boldsymbol{x}_p)\boldsymbol{\alpha})^2 + \boldsymbol{\alpha}^{\mathrm{T}}\boldsymbol{R}_j\boldsymbol{\alpha}, \tag{8}$$

where

$$\boldsymbol{R}_j = (p_b + \sigma_a^2)\boldsymbol{G}_j - p_b\boldsymbol{H}_j, \boldsymbol{H}_j = \sum_{p\in V_j}\boldsymbol{h}(\boldsymbol{x}_p)(\boldsymbol{h}(\boldsymbol{x}_p))^{\mathrm{T}}, \tag{9}$$

and $\boldsymbol{G}_j$ is diagonal matrix obtained from the main diagonal of $\boldsymbol{H}_j$. Note that

$$\boldsymbol{R} = \sum_{j=1}^{N_{mini}}\boldsymbol{R}_j, \text{ and } \boldsymbol{H} = \sum_{j=1}^{N_{mini}}\boldsymbol{H}_j. \tag{10}$$

Since $\boldsymbol{H}_j$ is a sum of outer products of a number of pairs of identical vectors., $\boldsymbol{G}_j$ must be positive definite.

The gradient of $\mathcal{J}_j(\boldsymbol{\alpha})$ is

$$\frac{\partial \mathcal{J}_j}{\partial \boldsymbol{\alpha}} = -2\sum_{p\in V_j}\boldsymbol{h}(\boldsymbol{x}_p)o_p + 2(\boldsymbol{H}_j + \boldsymbol{R}_j)]\boldsymbol{\alpha}, \tag{11}$$

Let $\alpha_{m,j}$ be the weight vector at the m-th iteration after presenting the j-th mini-batch. At the m-th iteration, the j-th mini-batch leads to the following update:

$$\alpha_{m,j} = (I - \mu Z_j)\alpha_{m,j-1} + \mu \sum_{p \in V_j} h(x_p)o_p, \tag{12}$$

where μ is the learning rule, and

$$Z_j = H_j + R_j. \tag{13}$$

We will prove the following theorem to show that the proposed mini-batch algorithm stated in (12) converges the inverse solution.

Theorem 1. *There are sufficient convergent conditions for the mini-batch algorithm stated in (12), given by*

1. *Z_j is a symmetric and positive definite matrix for all j.*
2. *$0 < \mu < 2/\rho_{max}$, where ρ_{max} is $\max\{\rho_1, \rho_2, \cdots, \rho_{N_{mini}}\}$ and ρ_j is the largest eigenvalue of Z_j.*

If both conditions hold, we have following results,

1. *$\alpha_{m,j} \longrightarrow \alpha_{*,j}$, as $m \longrightarrow \infty$, for all j.*
2. *If $\mu \longrightarrow 0$, then $\alpha_{*,j} \longrightarrow \alpha^*$.*

Proof: The logic of our proof is similar to [9]. To simplify the proof, we first introduce some notations:

$$W_j = (I - \mu Z_j), \tag{14}$$

$$d_j = \sum_{p \in V_j} h(x_p)o_p. \tag{15}$$

With those notations, (12) is rewritten as

$$\alpha_{m,j} = W_j\alpha_{m,j-1} + d_j. \tag{16}$$

We apply (16) for one whole cycle. Then we have

$$\alpha_{m,j} = \tilde{W}_j\alpha_{m-1,j} + \tilde{d}_j \tag{17}$$

where

$$\tilde{W}_j = W_j W_{j-1} \cdots W_1 W_{N_{mini}} \cdots W_{j+1} \tag{18}$$

$$\tilde{d}_1 = \mu\,(d_j + W_j d_{j-1} + W_j W_{j-1} d_{j-2} + \cdots). \tag{19}$$

In order to ensure that (17) converges we should ensure that the norm of $\tilde{W}_j$ is less than one for all j. If all the norms of $W_{j'}$'s are less than one for all $j' = 1, \cdots, N_{mini}$, then the norm of $\tilde{W}_j$ is less than one for $j = 1, \cdots, N_{mini}$ and (17) converges.

Let $\boldsymbol{\beta}$ be a unit vector such that

$$\|\boldsymbol{W}_{j'}\| = \|\boldsymbol{W}_{j'}\boldsymbol{\beta}\|_2. \tag{20}$$

We consider

$$\|\boldsymbol{W}_{j'}\boldsymbol{\beta}\|_2^2 = \boldsymbol{\beta}^{\mathrm{T}}(\boldsymbol{I} - \mu\boldsymbol{Z}_{j'})^{\mathrm{T}}(\boldsymbol{I} - \mu\boldsymbol{Z}_{j'})\boldsymbol{\beta}. \tag{21}$$

Since $\boldsymbol{\beta}$ is a unit vector,

$$\|\boldsymbol{W}_{j'}\boldsymbol{\beta}\|_2^2 = 1 - 2\mu\boldsymbol{\beta}^{\mathrm{T}}\boldsymbol{Z}_{j'}\boldsymbol{\beta} + \mu^2\boldsymbol{\beta}^{\mathrm{T}}\boldsymbol{Z}_{j'}^{\mathrm{T}}\boldsymbol{Z}_{j'}\boldsymbol{\beta}. \tag{22}$$

From the condition stated in the theorem, $\boldsymbol{Z}_{j'}$'s are symmetric and positive definite. **Note that for the fault aware case and weight decay case, $\boldsymbol{Z}_{j'}$'s must symmetric and positive definite.**
Hence we have

$$1 - 2\mu\boldsymbol{\beta}^{\mathrm{T}}\boldsymbol{Z}_{j'}\boldsymbol{\beta} + \mu^2\boldsymbol{\beta}^{\mathrm{T}}\boldsymbol{Z}_{j'}^{\mathrm{T}}\boldsymbol{Z}_{j'}\boldsymbol{\beta} \leq 1 - 2\mu\boldsymbol{\beta}^{\mathrm{T}}\boldsymbol{Z}_{j'}\boldsymbol{\beta} + \rho_j\mu^2\boldsymbol{\beta}^{\mathrm{T}}\boldsymbol{Z}_{j'}\boldsymbol{\beta}. \tag{23}$$

where $\rho_{j'}$ is the largest eigenvalue of $\boldsymbol{Z}_{j'}$. Clearly, if μ is less than $\frac{2}{\rho_{j'}}$, then

$$1 - 2\mu\boldsymbol{\beta}^{\mathrm{T}}\boldsymbol{Z}_{j'}\boldsymbol{\beta} + \mu^2\boldsymbol{\beta}^{\mathrm{T}}\boldsymbol{Z}_{j'}^{\mathrm{T}}\boldsymbol{Z}_{j'}\boldsymbol{\beta} \leq 1 - 2\mu\boldsymbol{\beta}^{\mathrm{T}}\boldsymbol{Z}_{j'}\boldsymbol{\beta} + \rho_j\mu^2\boldsymbol{\beta}^{\mathrm{T}}\boldsymbol{Z}_{j'}\boldsymbol{\beta} \leq 1. \tag{24}$$

Hence, if μ is less than $\frac{2}{\rho_{j'}}$, then the norm of $\boldsymbol{W}_{j'}$ is less than one. Furthermore if μ is less than $\frac{2}{\rho_{max}}$, then the norm of $\tilde{\boldsymbol{W}}_j$ is less than one for all j, where ρ_{max} is $\max\{\rho_1, \rho_2, \cdots, \rho_{N_{mini}}\}$. That means, $\boldsymbol{\alpha}_{m,j} \longrightarrow \boldsymbol{\alpha}_{*,j}$, as $m \longrightarrow \infty$, for all j.
Since $\boldsymbol{\alpha}_{m,j} \longrightarrow \boldsymbol{\alpha}_{*,j}$ as m tends to infinity, from (17), we have

$$(\boldsymbol{I} - \tilde{\boldsymbol{W}}_j)\boldsymbol{\alpha}_{*,j} = \tilde{\boldsymbol{d}}_j, \forall j \tag{25}$$

$$\boldsymbol{\alpha}_{*,j} = (\boldsymbol{I} - \tilde{\boldsymbol{W}}_j)^{-1}\tilde{\boldsymbol{d}}_j, \forall j. \tag{26}$$

From (10), (13–15), (18), and (19), $\tilde{\boldsymbol{W}}_j$ and $\tilde{\boldsymbol{d}}$ can be rewritten as

$$\tilde{\boldsymbol{W}}_j = \boldsymbol{I} - \mu \sum_{j=1}^{N_{mini}} \boldsymbol{Z}_j + \boldsymbol{\Omega}(\mu^2) = \boldsymbol{I} - \mu(\boldsymbol{H} + \boldsymbol{R}) + \boldsymbol{\Omega}(\mu^2) \tag{27}$$

$$\tilde{\boldsymbol{d}}_1 = \mu \sum_{k=1}^{N} \boldsymbol{h}(\boldsymbol{x}_k)o_k + \boldsymbol{\Phi}(\mu^2), \tag{28}$$

where the orders of all the elements in $\boldsymbol{\Omega}(\mu^2)$ and $\boldsymbol{\Phi}(\mu^2)$ are greater than μ^2. Therefore, when μ tends to zero, (26) becomes

$$\boldsymbol{\alpha}_{*,j} \rightarrow (\boldsymbol{H} + \boldsymbol{R})^{-1} \sum_{k=1}^{N} \boldsymbol{h}(\boldsymbol{x}_k)o_k = \boldsymbol{\alpha}_*. \tag{29}$$

It is the optimal solution stated in (10). The proof is completed. ∎

Table 1. Properties of the five data sets.

Dataset	Number of features	Size of training set	Size of test set	RBF width	No. of RBF (by OLS)
Abalone	7	2000	2177	0.1	65
Housing	13	400	106	2.0	60
Concrete	9	500	530	0.5	200
MG	6	700	685	1.0	75

4   Simulation

Since the noise resistant ability of the fault aware batch mode algorithm is nearly the best [4,5], this section aims at verifying our theoretical results of the proposed fault aware mini-batch algorithm.

4.1   Data Sets and Setting

We use four datasets [9,10] which are commonly used in the research area of RBF to verify our theoretical results. They are Abalone, Housing price, Concrete, and Mackey-Glass (MG). The RBF centers are obtained from the orthogonal least squares (OLS) concept [8]. After applying OLS, a number of samples are chosen as the RBF centers. The detailed settings of those datasets are shown in Table 1. The mini-batch size is set to 50.

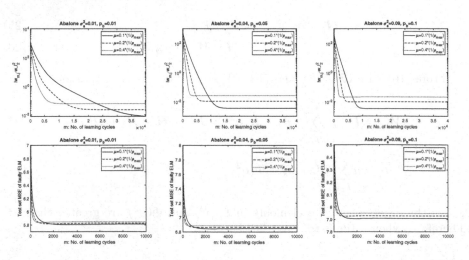

Fig. 1. First row: Difference between the trained weight vector and the batch mode solution versus the number m of learning cycles. Second row: Test set MSE of faulty networks verse the number m of learning cycles.

4.2   Convergence

This section investigates the convergence of the fault aware mini-batch algorithm. We would like to check whether the experiment results matches our theoretical results. We consider the Abalone dataset and three fault scenarios: $\{\sigma_a^2 = 0.01, p_b = 0.01\}$, $\{\sigma_a^2 = 0.04, p_b = 0.05\}$, and $\{\sigma_a^2 = 0.09, p_b = 0.1\}$. Three learning rate values are used: $\mu \in \{\frac{0.1}{\rho_{max}}, \frac{0.2}{\rho_{max}}, \frac{0.4}{\rho_{max}}\}$.

The first result, shown in the first row of Fig. 1, illustrates the convergence to the batch mode optimal weight vector α_*. From the figure, in terms of the weight difference, the algorithm converges. Also, if we decrease the learning rate μ, a better converged value is obtained. As μ tends to zero, the weight vector tends to the fault aware batch mode solution.

One may argue that the convergence is very slow, especially for the Abalone dataset. However, from the second row of Fig. 1, **the test set error converges in a much fast way.** For Abalone dataset with $\{\sigma_a^2 = 0.01, p_b = 0.01\}$ and $\mu = \frac{0.1}{\rho_{max}}$, the weight vector difference needs more 40,000 learning cycles to converge. However, from the test set MSE point of view, the algorithm converges within 2,000 learning cycles.

4.3   Performance Comparison

The proposed fault aware mini-batch algorithm is compared with other algorithm. Since there are few results on the fault aware mini-batch algorithm, we compare our algorithm with the optimized weight decay algorithm. As the weight decay regularizer is capable to restrict the magnitude of the output weights, the weight decay algorithm has certain capability to tackle the noise situation. In the weight decay concept, one tuning parameter is the weight decay constant. Since there is no theoretical way to select weight decay constant, for each setting, we use the trial-and-error method to select the best weight decay constant from the range of $[10^{-6}, 10^{-1}]$.

We consider three fault scenarios: $\{\sigma_a^2 = 0.01, p_b = 0.01\}$, $\{\sigma_a^2 = 0.04, p_b = 0.05\}$, and $\{\sigma_a^2 = 0.09, p_b = 0.10\}$. The learning rate value is set to $\mu = \frac{0.1}{\rho_{max}}$.

Also, the four datasets are randomly partition 20 times. That means, for each setting, we run the two algorithms 20 times. Table 2 summarizes the statistics of these 20 runs. It also show the mean differences and the paired-t results. It should be noticed that for 20 runs, the critical one-tail t-value is 1.729.

From the table, the average MSE values of our fault aware mini-batch algorithm is better than those of the optimized weight decay algorithm. For instance in the Abalone dataset, when the noise characteristics is $\{\sigma_a^2 = 0.01, p_b = 0.01\}$, the average MSE of the optimized weight decay is 5.9348. With our algorithm, the average MSE is reduced to 5.82716.

For another case, when the noise characteristics is $\{\sigma_a^2 = 0.09, p_b = 0.10\}$, the average MSE of the optimized weight decay is 9.68017. With our algorithm, the average MSE is reduced to 7.99358.

In the table, we also show the t-statistics. For 20 samples, the critical one-tail t-value is 1.729. From the table, all the t values are greater than that critical value. Hence there is strong evidence to confirm that our proposed fault aware mini-batch algorithm is superior to the optimized weight decay method.

Table 2. Comparison between the proposed fault aware mini-batch algorithm and optimized weight decay algorithm. The table shows the average MSE over 20 runs. The value inside the bracket is the standard deviation. For 20 runs, the critical one-tail t-value is 1.729.

Data set	Fault level	Optimized weight decay avg (std)	Fault aware mini batch avg (std)	Average improvement	t-value
Abalone	$\sigma_a^2 = 0.01, p_b = 0.01$	5.93479(0.26957)	5.82716(0.34682)	0.107622	3.335
	$\sigma_a^2 = 0.04, p_b = 0.05$	7.63324(0.35532)	6.88492(0.46183)	0.748329	12.922
	$\sigma_a^2 = 0.09, p_b = 0.10$	9.68017(0.43063)	7.99358(0.59954)	1.686589	17.987
MG	$\sigma_a^2 = 0.01, p_b = 0.01$	0.02346(0.00114)	0.02336(0.00121)	0.000101	2.642
	$\sigma_a^2 = 0.04, p_b = 0.05$	0.03177(0.00140)	0.02952(0.00145)	0.002259	11.888
	$\sigma_a^2 = 0.09, p_b = 0.10$	0.04454(0.00192)	0.03607(0.00161)	0.008462	26.004
Concrete	$\sigma_a^2 = 0.01, p_b = 0.01$	0.01652(0.00070)	0.01643(0.00074)	0.000095	3.495
	$\sigma_a^2 = 0.04, p_b = 0.05$	0.02128(0.00112)	0.02029(0.00099)	0.000986	11.939
	$\sigma_a^2 = 0.09, p_b = 0.10$	0.02595(0.00173)	0.02336(0.00150)	0.002588	17.593
Housing	$\sigma_a^2 = 0.01, p_b = 0.01$	0.01794(0.00319)	0.01776(0.00303)	0.000183	2.184
	$\sigma_a^2 = 0.04, p_b = 0.05$	0.02415(0.00447)	0.02322(0.00404)	0.000925	5.626
	$\sigma_a^2 = 0.09, p_b = 0.10$	0.02941(0.00559)	0.02705(0.00478)	0.002367	9.244

5   Conclusion

This paper theoretically investigates the convergence of mini-batch for the fault aware case. In our approach, subsets of the training samples and the presentation order of the subsets are fixed. Even with the above fixed arrangement, we are still able to theoretically prove that the training weight vector converges to the batch mode solution. In addition, we derive the sufficient condition for the convergence. Our simulation results confirm our theoretical findings and show that our proposed fault aware mini-batch algorithm is superior to the optimized weight decay.

Acknowledgments. The work was supported by a research grant from City University of Hong Kong (9610431).

References

1. Liu, B., Kaneko, T.: Error analysis of digital filters realized with floating-point arithmetic. Proc. IEEE **57**(10), 1735–1747 (1969)

2. Martolia, R., Jain, A., Singla, L.: Analysis survey on fault tolerance in radial basis function networks. In: 2015 IEEE International Conference on Computing, Communication Automation (ICCCA), pp. 469–473 (2015)
3. Murakami, M., Honda, N.: Fault tolerance comparison of IDS models with multi-layer perceptron and radial basis function networks. In: International Joint Conference on Neural Networks, pp. 1079–1084 (2007)
4. Leung, C.S., Wan, W.Y., Feng, R.: A regularizer approach for RBF networks under the concurrent weight failure situation. IEEE Trans. Neural Networks Learn. Syst. **28**(6), 1360–1372 (2017)
5. Feng, R., Han, Z.F., Wan, W.Y., Leung, C.S.: Properties and learning algorithms for faulty RBF networks with coexistence of weight and node failures. Neurocomputing **224**, 166–176 (2017)
6. Konečný, J., Liu, J., Richtárik, P., Takac, M.: Mini-batch semi-stochastic gradient descent in the proximal setting. IEEE J. Sel. Top. Signal Process. **10**(2), 242–255 (2016)
7. Wang, Z.Q., Manry, M.T., Schiano, L.: LMS learning algorithms: misconceptions and new results on converence. IEEE Trans. Neural Networks **11**(1), 47–56 (2000)
8. Chen, S.: Local regularization assisted orthogonal least squares regression. Neurocomputing **69**(4–6), 559–585 (2006)
9. Lichman, M.: UCI machine learning repository (2013). http://archive.ics.uci.edu/ml
10. Chang, C.C., Lin, C.J.: LIBSVM: a library for support vector machines. ACM Trans. Intell. Syst. Technol. **2**, 1–27 (2011)

Convolutional Neural Network Architecture with Exact Solution

Toshi Sinha$^{(\boxtimes)}$ and Brijesh Verma$^{(\boxtimes)}$

Central Queensland University, Brisbane, Qld 4000, Australia
{t.sinha,b.verma}@cqu.edu.au

Abstract. Convolutional Neural Networks (CNNs) have been explored rigorously, due to their complex image classification capabilities and applied in many real-world applications. In majority of such applications, training of CNN using a back-propagation type iterative learning has become a standard practice, but this makes training of CNN very inefficient and uncertain because of various problems such as local minima and paralysis. Other iterative and non-iterative learning including exact solution-based learning might be more efficient in terms of accuracy and certainty in training, however, potential of this type of combined learning has not been fully explored by CNN researchers. Therefore, in this paper an exact solution based new convolutional neural network architecture is proposed. In proposed architecture, a novel concept is introduced in which the weights of CNN layers are updated using iterative process for a fixed number of epochs and then the weights of fully connected layer are calculated using an exact solution process. Both iterative and calculated weights are then used for training the full architecture. The proposed approach has been evaluated on three benchmark datasets such as CIFAR-10, MNIST and Digit. The experimental results have demonstrated that the proposed approach can achieve higher accuracy than the standard CNN. Statistical significance test was carried out to prove the efficacy of proposed approach.

Keywords: Neural networks · Non-iterative learning · Image classification

1 Introduction

Convolutional neural network has been researched by computer vision community since 1980s [1, 2, 3]. The Neocognitron [3] was probably the first CNN that had a deep structure and was first to incorporate neurophysiological insights. Several supervised and unsupervised learning algorithms have been proposed to train the weights of CNN in over decades. In 1986, backpropagation algorithm [4] was introduced to train the neural networks by computing gradients of loss function with respect to the weights of the network. However, due to lack of proper hardware and software training deep architecture was a nightmare. In 2012, ImageNet competition brought AlexNet [1] in limelight, having efficient use of graphics processing units (GPUs), new dropout regularization [5], rectified linear units [6] and effective data augmentation [1]. Since then CNN based models have been popular and widely used to solve various computer vision problems across various applications including complex image recognition [9], object detection [1],

© Springer Nature Switzerland AG 2020
H. Yang et al. (Eds.): ICONIP 2020, CCIS 1333, pp. 554–562, 2020.
https://doi.org/10.1007/978-3-030-63823-8_63

optical character recognition [2], hyperspectral image processing [7], natural language processing [4], visual tracking system [8] and identifying different radiographic images [11, 12].

CNN consists of convolutional and pooling layers called as blocks, stacked on each other followed by one or more fully connected layer. Convolution is a linear transformation, element-wise matrix multiplication and addition. To add non-linearity Rectifier Linear Unit (ReLu) is added in each block of CNN [10]. Pooling layer is used for downsampling of feature maps by combining outputs of group of neurons to a single neuron in next layer [10]. Further in fully connected layer every neuron in one layer to every neuron in another layer. In past few years, the concept of deeper the network better the classification and recognition accuracies [11] has given, 8-layer AlexNet [1], 16-layer VGG [12], and 152-layer ResNet [13]. However, the performance improvement by increasing the network depth has reached saturation.

In all these architectures end to end training of CNN is carried out using iterative method such as back propagation algorithm. However, back propagation suffers from slow convergence, not guaranteed to find global minimum, getting trapped in a local minimum and being sensitive to the learning rate configurations. Therefore, new types of learning strategies should be introduced and investigated. This paper introduces some new strategies which combine best of iterative and exact solution methods. The original contributions of this paper are as follows. (1) A new convolutional neural network architecture that can use two types of learning strategies is proposed. (2) A new learning strategy by combining iterative and exact solution for the training of whole network is introduced. (3) A comparative analysis and impact of introducing new learning strategy on accuracy and consistency is presented.

The rest of the paper is organized as follows. Section 2 reviews related literature. Section 3 describes the proposed approach. Section 4 presents experimental results and comparative analysis. A conclusion is drawn in Sect. 5.

2 Related Work

In this section, we review recently published relevant papers. Several CNN based classification studies are carried out to improve the accuracy and reduce the training time.

The true power of neural network lies in their capability of learning important and complicated features from images and numeric data [14]. CNNs are good at grasping invariant features but not always best at classification [15]. Whereas, provided with a good feature vector, Gaussian-kernel Support Vector Machines (SVMs) are good at producing decision surfaces. Better systems can be designed by combining features derived from CNNs with auxiliary classification models like L1-SVM [14], L2-SVM [15], k-Nearest Neighbor [18] or Extreme Learning Machine (ELM) [20]. In many cases, it was found that such combinations significantly improved the capabilities of SVMs, KNNs or ELMs compared to running these algorithms on the raw data, and in some cases also surpass the performance of the neural network alone [14–20].

Features extracted from fully connected layer are mostly used for transfer learning, these features suffer from lack of description of local patterns, which is critical when occlusion or truncation exists. When translation and occlusion are severe, features extracted from last convolution or pooling layer gives better accuracy than the features extracted from fully connected layers [21]. Further combining features from different CNN layers, improves the object recognition accuracy. Concatenation and addition fusion methods are used to integrate multilayer features in CNN [22]. It is also found that large sized images are better than resized ones, as a feed for CNN. Convolutional bag-of-features layer [23], inspired by Bag-of-Features layer (BoF) was introduced before the fully connected layer and the model was trained using backpropagation algorithm, however, number of parameters were reduced only in the first fully connected layer. Training a deep convolutional neural network using back propagation algorithm, takes several hours even when advanced software and hardware is used. It takes many iterations to adjust network parameters such as weights and biases of each layer. As the network depth and width increases the number of parameters increases [11], and enlarged networks are prone to overfitting. Also, the computational cost increases.

3 Proposed Approach

This section describes our proposed approach, which is called deep convolutional network with exact solution. A novel architecture is introduced that uses iterative and exact solution strategies for training the whole network.

3.1 Proposed Architecture

The proposed architecture of the deep convolutional network with exact solution is presented in Fig. 1.

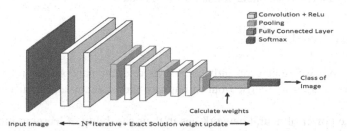

Fig. 1. Proposed architecture of convolutional neural network with exact solution

The proposed architecture consists of input layer, convolutional layers, pooling layers, fully connected layer and lastly the output layer. The input layer containing the raw pixel values of input image (resized square image) is passed to convolutional layer. Convolutional layer consists of set of learnable filters, these filters span along width (w) and height (h) and extends through full depth (d) of the input volume. Based on number of filters (p) the activation maps are created. These activation maps have got activations of different part of the input image. Further these maps are passed to convolutional layer or pooling layer to learn several discriminative features at different level of abstraction.

Pooling layer is used for down-sampling and to reduce the number of parameters. Then comes the fully connected layer, where the output from pooling layer, a single vector of values is multiplied with weights to determine the probability of input class using softmax activation function. The entire network is trained using new learning strategy, by combining iterative and exact solution algorithms. The network weights are updated using iterative learning algorithm for N number of times, and then using exact solution the weights of fully connected layer W_{fc} are calculated. Further the entire network is updated using these new weights.

The overall network is a combination of function composition and matrix multiplication and can be represented as

$$Y_{nm} := f_L(W_L f_{L-1}(W_{L-1} f_{L-2}(W_{L-2} \ldots f_1(W_{conv} X_{ns}) \ldots))) \tag{1}$$

where Y_{nm} is network output, L is number of layers in the network, W_L is weight of last layer, W_{conv} is weight of first convolutional layer and X_{ns} is input image data, n is number of training records and s size of input record. During model training, set of input and output pairs are passed through the network, the difference between the network output Y_{nm} and target output T_{nm}, is the loss of the model; cost function, can be stated as follows

$$C(T_{nm}, Y_{nm}) = C\ (T_{nm}, f_L(W_L f_{L-1}(W_{L-1} f_{L-2}(W_{L-2} \ldots f_1(W_{conv} X_{ns}) \ldots)))) \tag{2}$$

The main aim of training a network is to reduce the cost function. The proposed new learning strategy combines iterative and exact solution for the training of whole network. Firstly, the network is trained using backpropagation algorithm for N number of iterations (epochs), hence the weights are updated, and the cost function reduces

$$C^N\left(T_{nm}, Y_{nm}^N\right) = C^N\left(T_{nm}, f_L\left(W_L^N f_{L-1}\left(W_{L-1}^N f_{L-2}\left(W_{L-2}^N \ldots f_1(W_{conv} X_{ns}) \ldots\right)\right)\right)\right) \tag{3}$$

After N iterative learning, the cost function lies between zero and C. $0 \leq C^N < C$.

Secondly, after N iterations, the weights of fully connected layer are calculated using non-iterative Moore-Penrose inverse strategy. The convolutional and pooling layers convert the input image into a feature vector represented as $F_{[k_{ns}]}$. Feature vector $F_{[k_{ns}]}$ can be modeled as a vector of real numbers and can be represented as

$$F_{[k_{ns}]} \in \mathbb{R}^n \tag{4}$$

$$F_{[k_{nc}]} = \begin{bmatrix} k_{11} & & k_{1s} \\ k_{21} & \overset{..}{} & k_{2s} \\ . & \overset{..}{} & . \\ . & \overset{..}{} & . \\ k_{n1} & \overset{..}{} & k_{ns} \end{bmatrix} \tag{5}$$

Where $k_{11} .. k_{1s}$ is a row vector of matrix $F_{[k_{nc}]}$ that represents the number of training records and $k_{11} .. k_{n1}$ is a column vector of matrix $F_{[k_{nc}]}$ and represents the number of convolutional features. The network output after N iterations can be written as

$$Y_{nm}^N = F_{[k_{ns}]} * W_{fc}^N \tag{6}$$

Using Moore-Penrose inverse strategy the weight of fully connected layer can be calculated as

$$W_{fc}^N = W_{L-1}^N = \begin{bmatrix} k_{11} & & k_{1s} \\ k_{21} & \cdot\cdot & k_{2s} \\ \cdot & & \cdot \\ \cdot & \cdot\cdot & \cdot \\ \cdot & & \cdot \\ k_{n1} & \cdot\cdot & k_{ns} \end{bmatrix}^{-1} * Y_{nm}^N \tag{7}$$

After applying both iterative and non-iterative training strategies, the network output can be formulated as Eq. (8), further system is tested, and accuracy is calculated.

$$Y_{nm}^N = f_L(W_L^N f_{L-1} \left(\begin{bmatrix} k_{11} & & k_{1s} \\ k_{21} & \cdot\cdot & k_{2s} \\ \cdot & & \cdot \\ \cdot & \cdot\cdot & \cdot \\ \cdot & & \cdot \\ k_{n1} & \cdot\cdot & k_{ns} \end{bmatrix}^{-1} * Y_{nm} \right) f_{L-2}(W_{L-2}^N \ldots f_1(W_{conv}X_{ns})\ldots))))$$

$$\tag{8}$$

3.2 Proposed Training and Testing Algorithms

Algorithms for training and testing of the proposed convolutional neural network with exact solution are shown in Fig. 2 and Fig. 3 respectively.

Algorithm: Training of CNN with Exact Solution

Input: Training dataset $[X_{train}, T_{train}]$
Output: Trained network
    Begin
        Step 1: Initialize CNN model (network layers, filters and weights)
                Initialize training algorithm parameters (learning rate μ, optimizer and momentum mo)
        Step 2: for each training epoch ep in $[1, 2, \ldots N]$ **do**
              a.   Pass training data (X_{train}, T_{train}) to the network.
              b.   Train network using SGDM optimizer
              c.   Update network weights while iterative training
        end
        Step 3: Calculate the weights of fully connected layer W_{fc}^N using equation (7).
        Step 4: Update the network with new weights W_{fc}^N
    End

Fig. 2. Algorithm for training convolutional neural network with exact solution

4 Experimental Results and Discussion

4.1 Benchmark Datasets Used for Experiments

Three benchmark datasets are used in this study: Digit [24], MNIST [25] and CIFAR-10 [26]. The main reason behind using these datasets is that these datasets have real world examples with a wide variety of images and widely used by other researchers in this field.

Algorithm: Testing of CNN with Exact Solution
Input: Testing dataset $X = [X_{test}, T_{test}]$ and Trained network

Output: Classification accuracy
 Begin
    Step 1: Pass test data (X_{test}, T_{test}) to the trained network and obtain the network output using equation (8)
    Step 2: Calculate classification accuracy on test dataset
 End

Fig. 3. Algorithm for testing convolutional neural network with exact solution

Table 1. Test accuracy on Digit dataset

Weights	576		1152		2304	
Epochs	CNN	ES	CNN	ES	CNN	ES
1	33.77	95.23	62.70	**99.33**	72.57	**99.93**
2	45.57	97.43	84.53	99.73	87.10	99.90
3	63.23	97.97	90.60	99.47	94.43	99.90
4	76.57	**99.00**	93.27	99.47	96.87	99.87
5	76.93	96.95	95.47	99.93	97.77	**100.00**
6	87.40	98.80	97.33	99.70	98.43	99.97
7	85.13	98.47	97.97	99.93	98.83	99.97
8	91.57	99.10	97.63	99.87	99.03	99.97
9	96.10	99.20	98.80	99.90	99.07	99.93
10	95.03	99.50	99.03	99.77	99.57	100.00
15	**98.60**	99.77	**99.37**	99.83	**99.97**	99.97
20	**98.60**	99.40	99.60	99.93	99.98	100.00

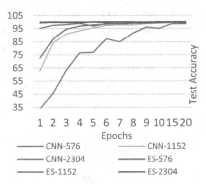

Fig. 4. Test accuracy graph for CNN and ES for digit dataset.

4.2 Experimental Setup

MATLAB R2018b is used for implementing and testing the proposed approach. The network architecture used had 3 convolutional layers and 3 pooling layers. Between each convolutional and pooling layer, ReLu and batch normalisation was present. A fully connected layer with softmax function was used at the end of architecture. The same architecture was used for both standard CNN and proposed architecture with exact solution.

4.3 Results and Discussion

The proposed approach is evaluated, and results are presented in Table 1, Table 2 and Table 3 for Digit, MNIST and CIFAR-10 datasets respectively. Testing is carried out with different network weights of fully connected layer and different training iterations. The respective graphs are presented in Fig. 4, Fig. 5 and Fig. 6.

Table 2. Test accuracy on MNIST dataset

Weights	576		1152		2304	
Epochs	CNN	ES	CNN	ES	CNN	ES
1	97.19	98.13	97.80	98.57	97.76	98.84
2	98.19	**98.57**	98.15	98.70	98.67	**98.96**
3	98.23	98.39	98.41	98.70	98.57	98.92
4	98.41	98.44	98.74	**98.90**	98.64	98.96
5	98.41	98.62	98.78	98.77	98.75	98.97
6	98.55	98.67	98.77	98.86	98.93	98.94
7	**98.57**	98.69	98.78	98.74	**98.95**	98.97
8	98.54	98.38	98.84	98.84	99.00	99.05
9	98.60	98.61	**98.94**	98.83	99.02	99.08
10	98.61	98.30	98.98	98.98	99.15	99.10
15	98.70	98.58	99.00	98.67	99.05	99.04

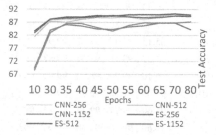

Fig. 5. Test accuracy graph for CNN and ES for MNIST dataset.

Table 3. Test accuracy on CIFAR-10 dataset

Weights	256		512		1152	
Epochs	CNN	ES	CNN	ES	CNN	ES
10	81.60	82.89	81.40	83.6	68.61	69.36
30	87.87	88.18	87.40	88.2	83.01	83.93
35	88.05	88.56	87.00	89.00	86.53	**86.10**
40	88.12	88.71	88.10	89.00	86.52	85.58
45	88.88	89.20	88.80	89.6	84.99	84.43
50	89.42	**89.66**	88.70	89.40	83.64	84.27
55	89.02	89.14	89.20	89.90	85.80	85.24
60	88.07	88.74	89.00	**90.00**	86.83	85.72
65	88.92	88.89	89.40	**90.00**	86.81	86.80
70	89.59	89.48	**90.10**	**90.30**	86.81	86.80
80	**89.65**	89.30	89.42	89.88	**87.22**	84.26

Fig. 6. Test accuracy graph for CNN and ES for CIFAR-10 dataset.

In Table 1, the test accuracy achieved by proposed approach is always higher than the standard CNN. For number of weights as 1152 and 2304, exact solution achieves test accuracy of 99.33% and 99.93% respectively, after very first epoch, whereas standard CNN achieves same accuracy after 15 epochs. Even for 576 weights, after 4 epochs the proposed approach achieves accuracy of 99% and even after 20 epochs CNN achieves 98.6%, which is 0.4% lesser. In Fig. 4, line graph shows that exact solution reaches and remains at higher accuracy from very first epoch and the network converges in very few iterations.

In Table 2, it is visible that for almost every epoch the test accuracy achieved by proposed approach is higher than standard CNN. For 576 and 2304 weights, the test accuracy achieved by proposed approach after two epochs is 98.57% and 98.96% respectively, whereas for standard CNN the same results are achieved after 7 epochs. However, for 1152 weights, exact solution gives good accuracy after 4 epochs whereas CNN gives close accuracy after 9 epochs. Figure 5 shows that the proposed approach has achieved high accuracy in very early stage and remains higher or close to the standard CNN for all tested network weights.

In Table 3, for 256 weights, test accuracy obtained by proposed approach is higher than the standard CNN for initial epochs 10, 30, 40 till 65 epochs and after that it remains almost close to standard CNN. Also, test accuracy of 89.66% is achieved by proposed approach after 50 epochs, whereas for CNN similar accuracy is obtained after 80 epochs. For 512 weights, proposed approach always has achieved higher accuracy than CNN. However, when 1152 weights are tested with different epochs, both approaches gave almost similar accuracies. This dataset is complex as compare to the previous two datasets; however, as shown in Fig. 6, the proposed approach has shown similar trend.

5 Conclusion

A novel concept of convolutional neural network architecture with exact solution was presented and investigated in this paper. The weights of CNN layers are updated using iterative process for a certain number of epochs and then the weights of fully connected layer are calculated using an exact solution method. Both iterative learning and exact solution strategies are used to calculate the weights. Further these updated weights are used for training the full architecture. The evaluation of the proposed concept was conducted on three benchmark datasets which showed that the proposed approach can perform much better than the standard CNN. In few iterations, the proposed architecture reaches highest accuracy, however standard CNN takes higher number of iterations to reach same accuracy. Experimental results prove that the proposed network converges faster than the standard CNN network, hence computation cost is low. The reason behind faster converges is due to use of two weight calculation/updating strategies while training the entire architecture.

References

1. Krizhevsky, A., Sutskever, I., Hinton, G.E.: ImageNet classification with deep convolutional neural networks. In: Advances in Neural Information Processing Systems, pp. 1097–1105 (2012)
2. LeCun, Y., Bengio, Y., Hinton, G.: Deep learning. Nature **521**, 436–444 (2015)
3. Fukushima, K.: Neocognitron: a self-organizing neural network for a mechanism of pattern recognition unaffected by shift in position. Biol. Cybern. **36**(4), 193–202 (1980)
4. LeCun, Y., Boser, B., Denker, J.S., Henderson, D., Howard, R.E., Hubbard, W., Jackel, L.: Backpropagation applied to handwritten zip code recognition. Neural Comput. **1**, 541–551 (1989)
5. Hinton, G., Srivastava, N., Krizhevsky, A., Sutskever, I., Salakhutdinov, R.: Dropout: a simple way to prevent neural networks from overfitting. J. Mach. Learn. Res. **15**, 1929–1958 (2014)
6. Glorot, X., Bordes, A., Bengio, Y.: Deep sparse rectifier neural networks. In: Proceedings 14th International Conference on Artificial Intelligence and Statistics, pp. 315–323 (2011)

7. Fabelo, H., et al.: Deep learning-based framework for in vivo identification of glioblastoma tumor using hyperspectral images of human brain. Sensors (Basel), **19**(4) (2019)
8. Le, Z., Suganthan, P.N.: Visual tracking with convolutional random vector functional link network. IEEE Trans. Cybern. **47**(10), 3243–3253 (2017)
9. Simonyan, K., Zisserman, A.: Very deep convolutional networks for large-scale image recognition. In: Proceedings International Conference on Learning Representations. http://arxiv.org/abs/1409.1556 (2014)
10. LeCun, Y., Bottou, L., Bengio, Y., Haffner, P.: Gradient-based learning applied to document recognition. Proc. IEEE **86**, 2278–2324 (1998)
11. Szegedy, C., et al.: Going deeper with convolutions. In: IEEE Conference on Computer Vision and Pattern Recognition, pp. 1–9 (2015)
12. Chatfield, K., Simonyan, K., Vedaldi, A., Zisserman, A.: Return of the devil in the details: delving deep into convolutional nets. In: British Machine Vision Conference (2014)
13. Liang, M., Hu, X.: Recurrent convolutional neural network for object recognition. In: IEEE Conference on Computer Vision and Pattern Recognition, pp. 3367–3375 (2015)
14. Notley, S., Magdon-Ismail, M.: Examining the use of neural networks for feature extraction: A comparative analysis using deep learning, support vector machines, and k-nearest neighbor classifiers. https://arxiv.org/abs/1805.02294 (2018)
15. Huang, F.J., LeCun, Y.: Large-scale learning with SVM and convolutional for generic object categorization. In: IEEE Conference on Computer Vision and Pattern Recognition, pp. 284–291 (2006)
16. Niu, X.X., Suen, C.Y.: A novel hybrid CNN–SVM classifier for recognizing handwritten digits. Pattern Recogn. **45**(4), 1318–1325 (2011)
17. Sharif Razavian, A., Azizpour, H., Sullivan, J., Carlsson, S.: CNN features off-the-shelf: an astounding baseline for recognition. In: CVPR Workshops (2014)
18. Ren, W., Yu, Y., Zhang, J., Huang, K., Learning convolutional nonlinear features for K nearest neighbor image classification. In: Proceedings of the IEEE International Conference on Pattern Recognition (ICPR), Stockholm, Sweden, 24–28 August 2014
19. Sinha, T., Verma, B.: A non-iterative radial basis function based quick convolutional neural network. In: Proceedings of the International Joint Conference on Neural Networks (IJCNN) 2020
20. Pang, S., Yang, X.: Deep convolutional extreme learning machine and its application in handwritten digit classification. In: Computational Intelligence and Neuroscience, pp. 1–10 (2016)
21. Zheng, L., et.al.: Good practice in CNN feature transfer. arXiv:1604.00133 (2016)
22. Ma, C., Mu, X., Sha, D.: Multi-layers feature fusion of convolutional neural network for scene classification of remote sensing. IEEE Access **7**, 121685–121694 (2019)
23. Passalis, N., Tefas, A.: Training lightweight deep convolutional neural networks using bag-of-features pooling. IEEE Trans. Neural Networks Learn. Syst. **30**(6), 1705–1715 (2019)
24. Digit dataset from Matlab Toolbox
25. The MNIST Database of handwritten digits. http://yann.lecun.com/exdb/mnist/
26. CIFAR-10 dataset. https://www.cs.toronto.edu/kriz/cifar.html

Deep Learning for Classification of Cricket Umpire Postures

WJ Samaraweera[1(✉)], SC Premaratne[2], and AT Dharmaratne[1]

[1] School of Information Technology, Monash University, Bandar Sunway, Malaysia
{wishma.samaraweera,anuja}@monash.edu
[2] Faculty of Information Technology, University of Moratuwa, Moratuwa, Sri Lanka
samindap@uom.lk

Abstract. Among various multimedia resources on Internet, videos are the most popular among humans since they require less active brain power compared with static images, text and audio. With the exponential growth of videos available online, solutions for automatic content analysis in different contexts have attracted the attention of researchers. In diverse types of videos, generating highlights of sports videos is a highly considered segment by recent researchers. This research is focused on examining the existing deep learning architectures to analyze the feasibility of combining prevailing network models with classifiers while checking which combination gives the highest performance. A novel combination is presented to automatically detect the cricket umpire postures under five events (Six, No Ball, Out, Wide, None) using Convolutional Neural Networks (CNNs) and standard classifiers. The proposed method utilizes VGG16, ResNet50V2 and MobileNetV2 CNN architectures to extract the features and SVM and Naïve Bayes to classify the identified features into umpire postures. A new dataset has been constructed for this research which contains a total of 350 cricket umpire images. The results demonstrate that ResNet50V2 model in combination with SVM classifier gives the highest classification performance for the proposed dataset.

Keywords: Image classification · CNN · Umpire postures

1 Introduction

According to the statistics, within every minute 300 h of videos are uploaded to YouTube and each month 3.25 billion hours of video are watched on YouTube [1]. These videos can be categorized into various types such as entertainment, sports, news, etc. Video data on the Internet has a rapid growth in areas like video conferencing, multimedia authoring systems, education and video on demand systems. Most of these videos can be searched and accessed later if anyone is interested in them. This proves the significance in paying attention on Video Retrieval or Video Highlights Retrieval.

© Springer Nature Switzerland AG 2020
H. Yang et al. (Eds.): ICONIP 2020, CCIS 1333, pp. 563–570, 2020.
https://doi.org/10.1007/978-3-030-63823-8_64

From all the different types of videos mentioned above, sports videos take a prominent place due to the high number of fans around the world. Therefore, generating highlights of sports videos is highly recognized as a research area. Among different sports, cricket is famous all around the world and there is a large pool of fan base. Furthermore, cricket is not a few hours game as it has different formats which can last from one to five days. Therefore, detecting highlights of a cricket match is much needed in the present days. To extract highlights of a sport video, visual features can be taken into consideration. Visual features of these games can be commonly identified as shot classification, scene classification, shot-boundary detection, and action recognition or motion recognition [2]. Using umpire postures to identify the main events of a cricket match can be considered highly appropriate because the umpire is the key person who gives decisions in a match. Further, it will not lead to any faulty identification due to the smaller number (two) of umpires in the field.

Using Convolutional Neural Networks (CNN) to address this issue is an effective way among the state-of-the-art methods. This research is focused on identifying the best amalgamation of CNNs and classifiers to detect umpire postures in a cricket match. A combination of pre-trained CNNs and standard classifiers has been used to analyze the performance of them in identifying umpire postures. VGG16 [3], ResNet50V2 [4] and MobileNetV2 [5], are used here with Support Vector Machine (SVM) and Naïve Bayes classifiers. Umpire's movements and hand movements are basically utilized to identify postures under five main events; Six, No Ball, Wide, Out and Non-event which represents all other events outside the four main events.

2   Literature Review

Due to the well-established fan base around the world, analyzing sports videos has played a key role in decision making in the recent past [6]. Although numerous methods have been used to summarize sports videos, lots of them were focused on single sport summarization based on highlights and other key events. To extract highlights of a sports video visual features can be taken into consideration. Gong et al. [7] extracted highlights of soccer using penalty, midfield, corner kick, shot at goal etc. Zhou et al. [8] summarized and extracted highlighted scenes of basketball using fast break, dunk, close up shots etc. Statistics show that 97% of highlights of a game usually have close up shot of that specific player who did score, got a wicket, tried to get a wicket etc. [9] Furthermore, identifying other special features of a game such as pitch view, excitement clips, crowd view etc. is very important in event detection [9]. Shot Ontology is a different type of research area under summarization of sports videos [10] which includes some shot management such as detecting and classifying shots, detecting scoreboard and motion statistics.

The development of detecting highlights of a cricket video is a very active area of research [11,12], in which subsets of frames called key frames are selected. Further most of the state-of-the-art methods utilized to detect highlights of a cricket video have moved towards neural networks. A novel method was proposed by A Ravi et al. [11], which is getting the results for umpire pose detection in cricket videos using machine learning. Highlights of the cricket videos are automatically extracted using two pre-trained CNNs, InceptionV3 and VGG19 which were trained on ImageNet dataset. The Support Vector Machine classifier is trained on the features extracted by the CNNs to identify the umpire poses. A shot classification of sports video has been conducted by Minhas et al. [13] using AlexNet CNN to classify shots in Cricket and Soccer videos. They have compared different classification models such as Support Vector Machine (SVM), Extreme Learning Machine (ELM), K-Nearest Neighbors (KNN), and standard Convolution Neural Network (CNN) with AlexNet. Another research that uses a similar technology has been conducted by Rafiq et al. [2] and to classify scenes in Cricket videos, they have used AlexNet CNN comparing the performance with other CNN modules named Inception V3, VGG16, VGG19 and ResNet50. Since these distinct methods were trained on different datasets, comparing these results to decide the maximum performance is a tricky point.

3   Proposed Method

The base of the proposed method is the pre-trained VGG16 [3], ResNet50V2 [4] and MobileNetV2 [5] CNNs which are trained using ImageNet database that emerged through ImageNet Large-Scale Visual Recognition Challenge (ILSVRC) [14]. VGG16 has two fully connected layers with 4096 nodes in each and the classification is done by softmax. The ResNet utilizes skip connection concept which adds the output from a specific layer to a later layer. MobileNetV2 has an initial convolution layer with 32 filters and 19 residual bottleneck layers which is built upon the architecture of MobileNetV1 [15]. The Depth wise Separable Convolution (DSC) in MobileNetV2 empowers high accuracy and performance. Further, this DSC helps to decrease the complexity cost and model size of MobileNetV2. This feature enables the model to work with mobile devices or any other device with low computational power.

The proposed method can be considered as a modified combination of two state-of-the-art techniques. CNNs are utilized to get the advantage of transfer learning and classification algorithms are utilized to obtain a strong classification. Transfer learning is used to optimize the output and get a speedy progress in the applied model.

In the proposed work, a new dataset was prepared for training and testing as a substitute to a publicly available database called SNOW [11]. SNOW dataset was prepared by Ravi et al. to detect umpire poses in cricket videos a couple of years ago. Nevertheless, with the intention of getting a more balanced and well-adjusted input to the proposed method, the new dataset was prepared with the help of SNOW dataset. Images for the new dataset were collected through cricket videos from YouTube and Google images. The new dataset contains five event classes identified as Six, No ball, Out, Wide and one additional event class for No action. This No action class includes images where the umpire is showing any other action beside the four main events or simply when umpire is not doing a specific action. The database contains 350 images in total, 70 images each for the five classes. From the new image set, 80% of images are used as the training set and the remaining 20% of images are used as the testing images. From the training image set, 20% of images were used as the validation image set.

Image Pre-processing

All the images were re-scaled to 224 * 224 size to fit into the models. Then these images were imported to a numpy array which provides a platform to manipulate the image data easily. After that the image data in the array were converted to different formats required by the relevant model using the preprocess_input function. Finally, the outputs from this function are fed to CNN for feature extraction.

Proposed Models

Figure 1 represents the Network Model Architectures of Proposed Method.

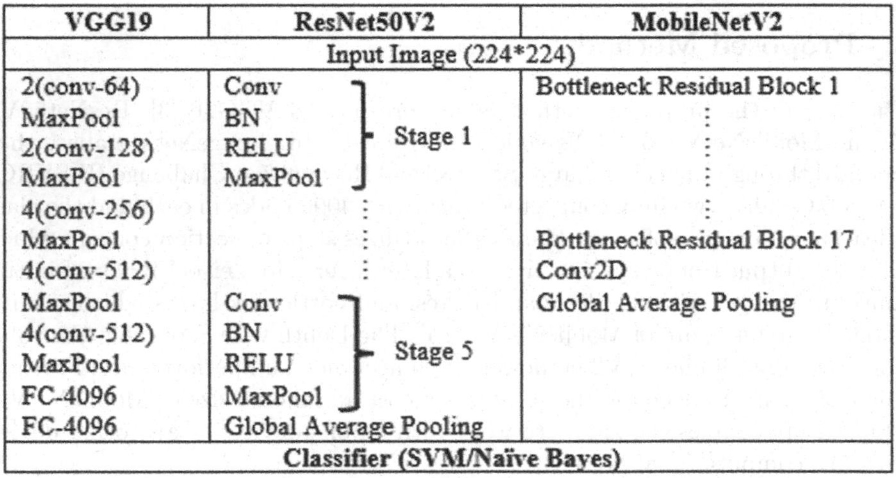

VGG19	ResNet50V2	MobileNetV2
Input Image (224*224)		
2(conv-64) MaxPool 2(conv-128) MaxPool	Conv ⎤ BN ⎥ Stage 1 RELU ⎥ MaxPool ⎦	Bottleneck Residual Block 1 ⋮ ⋮ ⋮
4(conv-256) MaxPool 4(conv-512)	⋮ ⋮ ⋮	⋮ Bottleneck Residual Block 17
MaxPool 4(conv-512) MaxPool FC-4096 FC-4096	Conv ⎤ BN ⎥ Stage 5 RELU ⎥ MaxPool ⎦ Global Average Pooling	Conv2D Global Average Pooling
Classifier (SVM/Naïve Bayes)		

Fig. 1. Neural network model architectures.

Method 1 – VGG16, ResNet50V2 and MobileNetV2 models were used to extract features of the umpire images and final classification layer of the CNN has been modified with standard Support Vector Machine (SVM) classifier to get the classifications. VGG16 utilized the standard 13 convolutional layers and two dense or fully connected layers. The final dense layer has been replaced with the SVM classifier to get the classifications. Five max pooling layers are present in the CNN which follow 2, 4, 7, 10 and 13 convolutional layers as in the standard VGG16 architecture [3]. ResNet50V2 contains 50 deep layers. These 50 layers are under 5 stages each having a convolutional block and identity block. Both convolutional block and identity block have 3 convolutional layers each [4]. Final prediction layer has been replaced with a standard linear SVM to get strong classifications. MobileNetV2 model has 53 layers which uses depth wise separable convolution as efficient building blocks [5]. The last prediction layer of this model is also substituted with linear SVM classifier. Features are extracted from the last fully connected layers of each VGG16, ResNet50V2 and MobileNetV2 models. To get classifications through SVM, a linear kernel has been used with a regularization parameter of 10.

Method 2 – VGG16, ResNet50V2 and MobileNetV2 models were used exactly as in the Method 1 with Naïve Bayes classifier to get the classifications instead of SVM classifier. In both Methods 1 and 2, the models adapted from VGG16, ResNet50V2 and MobileNetV2 are employed using the pretrained weights. After that classifiers are added on to the CNN to get strong classifications.

4   Experimental Results

Under this section, the performance of the proposed method is evaluated based on the task of classifying umpire postures in cricket. Evaluation was done in two stages. In the first evaluation, results are validated on a 10-Fold Cross validation test and a Leave-One-Out validation test. Table 1 summarizes the validation results for all three CNN models.

Table 1. Training and validation accuracy.

CNN	Classifier	Validation method (%)	
		10-fold cross	Leave-one-out
VGG16	SVM	66.67	63.33
	Naïve Bayes	53.33	46.67
ResNet50V2	SVM	60.00	64.58
	Naïve Bayes	70.00	58.75
MobileNetV2	SVM	80.00	70.83
	Naïve Bayes	61.67	57.92

The highest accuracy is achieved by MobileNetV2 model with SVM classifier. Both VGG16 and ResNet50V2 models when combined with SVM, shows almost similar results in Leave-One-Out validation.

These results were compared with the classifier 2 of the method conducted by Ravi et al. [11] which uses InceptionV3 and two fully connected layers of VGG19 model. The compared validation results show that MobileNetV2 with SVM can demonstrate results almost similar to InceptionV3, VGG19 – FC1 and VGG19 – FC2 layer.

Objective metrics were employed to measure the performance of the proposed methods. Precision Recall and F1 Score are the objective measures that were considered. These three measures were calculated considering the classification of umpire postures correctly and incorrectly by the models. Table 2 depicts the tabulated results of the metrics which were used to measure the performance of each event in each model of the proposed method. Model No.s refer as follows: (i) VGG16 & SVM (ii) VGG16 & Naive Bayes (iii) ResNet50V2 & SVM (iv) ResNet50V2 & Naive Bayes (v) MobileNet50 & SVM (vi) MobileNet50 & Naive Bayes.

Table 2. Precision, Recall, F1 Score values of all models in five events.

Metric	Event	(i)	(ii)	(iii)	(iv)	(v)	(vi)
Precision	Six	0.88	0.71	0.87	0.88	0.75	1.00
	NoBall	0.55	0.33	0.53	0.44	0.50	0.36
	Out	0.55	0.38	0.64	0.40	0.50	0.42
	Wide	0.50	0.33	0.57	0.62	0.55	0.66
	None	0.46	0.33	0.87	0.66	0.72	0.50
Recall	Six	0.80	0.50	0.70	0.80	0.60	0.70
	NoBall	0.50	0.30	0.70	0.40	0.40	0.40
	Out	0.50	0.50	0.90	0.60	0.70	0.80
	Wide	0.40	0.40	0.40	0.50	0.50	0.20
	None	0.70	0.30	0.70	0.60	0.80	0.50
F1 Score	Six	0.84	0.58	0.77	0.84	0.66	0.82
	NoBall	0.52	0.31	0.60	0.42	0.44	0.38
	Out	0.52	0.43	0.75	0.48	0.58	0.55
	Wide	0.44	0.36	0.47	0.55	0.52	0.30
	None	0.56	0.31	0.77	0.63	0.76	0.50

These results show that as an average, all models can identify event Six with a high precision, recall and F1 score values compared to other events. Further, according to the results, all models tends to give higher results with SVM classifier than Naïve Bayes classifier.

According to Table 3, it highlights that ResNet50V2 model in combination with SVM classifier gives the highest result on the new dataset. MobileNetV2 and VGG16 models also have considerably decent results with SVM classifier. Further, it shows that compared to Naïve Bayes classifier, SVM gives better results.

Figure 2 shows some classification results by the proposed model. The first five images (blue color labels) display the correctly classified images and the second five images (red color labels) display misclassified images by ResNet50V2 and SVM classifier.

The proposed architecture is designed to support five event classes of umpire postures named Six, Out, No ball, Wide and None in cricket. In the proposed method VGG16, ResNet50V2 and MobileNetV2 CNN deep-learning architectures are employed to extract the features and SVM and Naïve Bayes are used to classify the results.

Table 3. Performance measurements.

CNN	Classifier	Metrics (%)		
		Precision	Recall	F1 score
VGG16	SVM	59.33	58.00	57.98
	Naïve Bayes	41.97	40.00	40.36
ResNet50V2	SVM	70.05	68.00	67.69
	Naïve Bayes	60.50	58.00	58.60
MobileNetV2	SVM	60.65	60.00	59.65
	Naïve Bayes	59.02	52.00	51.27

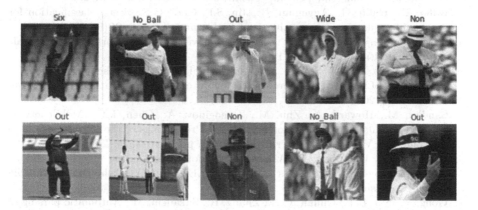

Fig. 2. Classification results of ResNet50V2 with SVM.

5 Conclusion

This paper proposed a combined CNN model to classify five different poses of cricket umpires with the use of transfer learning and deep learning architecture. Three main pre-trained keras models named VGG16, ResNet50 and MobileNet were used as the main models in the research. Added to the CNN modules two machine learning classification algorithms; SVM and Naïve Bayes were used as classifiers. A new dataset was created with a total of 350 images belonging to five different event classes. According to the classification results ResNet50V2 model gives the highest performance based on the new dataset. These proposed models can be used to analyze cricket video contents automatically. As future work, improvements can be made in the combination of deep learning architectures and classifiers. Another improvement that can be looked in to is modifying the existing layers of the CNNs and adding custom designed layers based on the scenario. For the enhancement of the dataset, data augmentation can be used to regenerate images utilizing the existing images.

Moreover, with the results obtained for MobileNetV2 model, further research can be conducted directing the sports video summarization into mobile devices.

Considering the lightweight feature of MobileNet compared to other models, the research can be extended to develop a mobile application which will be more convenient in today's world.

Acknowledgments. We thank JMDGCM Dodandeniya for his contribution during the preparation of this research paper.

References

1. Cvety, 2020. 37 Mind Blowing YouTube Facts, Figures and Statistics-2020. MerchDope. https://merchdope.com/youtube-stats, Accessed 22 May 2020
2. Rafiq, M., Rafiq, G., Agyeman, R., Jin, S.I., Choi, G.S.: Scene classification for sports video summarization using transfer learning. Sensors 20(6), 1702 (2020)
3. Simonyan, K., Zisserman, A.: Very deep convolutional networks for large-scale image recognition. arXiv:1409.1556 (2014)
4. He, K., Zhang, X., Ren, S., Sun, J.: Deep residual learning for image recognition. In: Proceedings of the IEEE Conference on Computer Vision and Pattern Recognition, pp. 770–778 (2016)
5. Sandler, M., Howard, A., Zhu, M., Zhmoginov, A., Chen, L.C.: Mobilenetv 2: inverted residuals and linear bottlenecks. In: Proceedings of the IEEE Conference on Computer Vision and Pattern Recognition, pp. 4510–4520 (2018)
6. Kokaram, A., Delacourt, P.: A new global motion estimation algorithm and its application to retrieval in sports events. In: IEEE Ffourth Workshop on Multimedia Signal Processing, pp. 251–256 (2001)
7. Gong, Y., Sin, L.T., Chuan, C.H., Zhang, H., Sakauchi, M.: Automatic parsing of TV soccer programs. In: Proceedings IEEE International Conference Multimedia Computing and System, pp. 167–174 (1995)
8. Zhou, W., Vellaikal, A., Kuo, C.C.J.: Rule-based video classification system for basketball video indexing. In: ACM Workshops on Multimedia, Los Angeles, California, United States. ACM (2000)
9. Chowdhury, M.R.: Cricket delivery detection and processing. IN/PA, 496 (2015)
10. Deng, L.Y., Liu, Y.: Semantic analysis and video event mining in sports video. In: 22nd International Conference on Advanced Information Networking and Applications-Workshops (aina workshops 2008), Okinawa, pp. 1517–1522 (2008). https://doi.org/10.1109/WAINA.2008.167
11. Ravi, A., Venugopal, H., Paul, S., Tizhoosh, H.R.: A Dataset and Preliminary Results for Umpire Pose Detection Using SVM Classification of Deep Features. arXiv:1809.06217 (2018)
12. Islam, M.N.A., Hassan, T.B., Khan, S.K.: A CNN-based approach to classify cricket bowlers based on their bowling actions. arXiv:1909.01228 (2019)
13. Minhas, R.A., Javed, A., Irtaza, A., Mahmood, M.T., Joo, Y.B.: Shot classification of field sports videos using alexnet convolutional neural network. Appl. Sci. 9(3), 483 (2019)
14. Russakovsky, O., et al.: Imagenet large scale visual recognition challenge. Int. J. Comput. Vis. 115(3), 211–252 (2015)
15. Howard, A.G., et al.: MobileNets: Efficient Convolutional Neural Networks for Mobile Vision Applications. arXiv:1704.04861 (2017)

Detection of Web Service Anti-patterns Using Neural Networks with Multiple Layers

Sahithi Tummalapalli[1], Lov kumar[2(✉)], N. L. Bhanu Murthy[1], and Aneesh Krishna[2]

[1] BITS Pilani Hyderabad, Hyderabad, India
{P20170433,lovkumar,bhanu}@hyderabad.bitspilani.ac.in
[2] Curtin University, Perth, Australia
a.krishna@curtin.edu.au

Abstract. Anti-patterns in service-oriented architecture are solutions to common issues where the solution is ineffective and may end up in undesired consequences. It is a standard exercise that initially seems like the best solution; however, it finally ends up having bad results that outweigh any benefits. Research revealed that the presence of anti-patterns leads to the demeaning of the quality and design of the software systems, which makes the process of detecting anti-patterns in web services very crucial. In this work, we empirically investigate the effectiveness of three feature sampling techniques, five data sampling techniques, and six classification algorithms in the detection of web service anti-patterns. Experiment results revealed that the model developed by considering metrics selected by Principal Component Analysis (PCA) as the input obtained better performance compared to the model developed by other metrics. Experimental results also showed that the neural network model developed with two hidden layers has outperformed all the other models developed with varying number of hidden layers.

Keywords: Machine learning · SOA · Anti-patterns · Web services

1 Introduction:

Service Oriented Architecture (SOA) is developing as the prime integration and architectural framework in the present mind-boggling and heterogeneous computing environment. Web services are the favored standard-based approach to acknowledge SOA. Like Object-oriented programming, Web services also suffer from the deterioration of the design and Quality of Software (QoS), which leads to a poor solution called Anti-patterns. An anti-pattern is a repeated application of code or design that leads to a bad outcome. Research revealed that the presence of anti-patterns hinders the progress and maintenance of the software system. Several web service anti-patterns are discovered over time [1] and in this paper, we considered the following four anti-patterns: **GOWS**: God Object Web Service (AP1), **FGWS**: Fine-Grained Web Service (AP2), **CWS**: Chatty Web Service (AP3), and **DWS**: Data Web Service (AP4).

© Springer Nature Switzerland AG 2020
H. Yang et al. (Eds.): ICONIP 2020, CCIS 1333, pp. 571–579, 2020.
https://doi.org/10.1007/978-3-030-63823-8_65

The primary motivation of this study is to prove that the source code metrics teamed up with the machine learning framework plays a pivotal role in the detection of web service anti-patterns. The secondary objective of this research is to develop models for the automatic detection of web service anti-patterns with the best predictive capability. Area Under a ROC Curve (AUC) and hypothesis testing approach are used to examine the relative execution of the different variations of data sampling technique: SMOTE, different feature selection techniques, and machine learning algorithms in the detection of SOA anti-patterns. In this work, we attempt to answer the following research questions:

RQ1: What is the impact of the application of data sampling techniques for developing anti-pattern prediction models?
RQ2: Is there any critical distinction between the exhibition of the models produced using a subset of features selected by applying various feature selection techniques?
RQ3: Does there exist a neural network model that outperforms all others?

2   Related Work:

Palma et al. [2] proposed a framework SODA-W for specifying and detecting the 10 anti-patterns present in the weather and finance-related data. This proposed framework achieved an accuracy of 75% and a recall of 100%. Ouni et al. [3] has used cooperative parallel evolutionary algorithms (P-EA), an automated approach to detect the anti-patterns. The idea behind their innovation is the combination of several detection algorithms executing in parallel optimization processes would give better results. Settas et al. [4] used the Protege platform, a web-based environment, to facilitate collaborative ontology editing. The model rectifies the false and imprecise information in SPARSE (using anti-pattern ontology as the knowledge base), an intelligent system that can detect anti-patterns existing in a software project. The statistical results confirm that the proposed technique outperforms other existing techniques.

3   Experimental Dataset

The data set with 226 publicly available web services that are shared by Ouni et al. on GitHub[1] are used for experiments in this paper. The dataset is of high quality, as Ouni et al. [5] who shared the dataset publicly in GitHub has manually validated the anti-patterns. The raw data that is available in the dataset is of WSDL format. A close observation of the dataset revealed that the percentage of anti-patterns present in the is varying from 5.75% to 10.62% i.e., GOWS exists in 21 out of 226 WSDL files. Similarly, FGWS, DWS, and CWS anti-patterns are present in 13, 14, and 21 out of 226 anti-patterns.

---

[1] https://github.com/ouniali/WSantipatterns.

4   Research Framework

Figure 1 illustrates the methodology for the anti-patterns prediction in web services. As discussed in Sect. 3, the dataset has a collection of web services from various domains in WSDL format. CKJM metrics are computed for each java file (A WSDL file has multiple java files) using CKJM extended tool. Further, the aggregation measures are applied on the CKJM metrics computed at the file level to obtain metrics at the system level which forms the dataset. After the formulation of the dataset, we apply different variants of SMOTE, i.e., SMOTE, BSMOTE, SVMSMOTE, SMOTEENN, and SMOTETOMEK, to address the class imbalance problem. Then we apply two different feature selection techniques, i.e., PCA and RSA, for selecting the significant features in the dataset. Further, we use the subset of features selected using PCA, RSA along with the essential metrics (SM) selected in our previous paper [6] to generate the models for the prediction of web service anti-patterns. In this paper, we use different variants of the neural network along with the ensemble technique to generate the models. Lastly, the execution of the models is evaluated using different evaluation metrics and the impact of various techniques used for generating models are speculated based on the results of hypothesis testing.

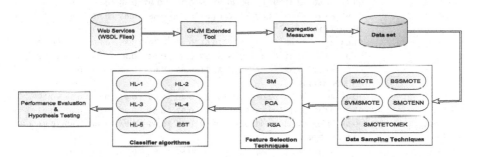

Fig. 1. Research framework for web service anti-pattern prediction

5   Experimental Results

Artificial Neural Networks (ANN) are known for their ability to learn and model non-linear and complex relationships. A neural network is a collection of interconnected nodes. The input patterns are collected by the unit nodes in the input layer and are mapped to the target variables in the output layer. In this work, we apply five different variants of neural network (NN) by changing the number of hidden k hidden layers (HL), i.e., NN with 1 HL (HL−1), NN with 2 HL (HL−2), NN with 3 HL (HL−3), NN with 4 HL (HL−4) and NN with 5 HL (HL−5). The feature matrix sets selected from different feature selection techniques are taken as input to each of the models. In addition to these models, we are also using an ensemble technique for the prediction of anti-patterns. The output of the previous models are given as input to the ensemble technique.

A five-fold cross-validation technique is applied to validate the results of the generated models. The models were trained using the original (imbalanced) dataset as well as the balanced dataset obtained after applying the data sampling techniques. Table 1 depicts the results of the models generated for the prediction of GOWS anti-pattern using five-fold cross-validation. The information present in Table 1 shows that the model developed using the neural network with 2 or 3 hidden layers have a good predictive aptness as compared to others. Similarly, the models trained using balanced data have good potential in predicting anti-patterns as compared to models generated using the original data.

Table 1. Accuracy & AUC values for GOWS anti-pattern

Feature Selection	Accuracy						AUC					
	ORG											
	HL-1	HL-2	HL-3	HL-4	HL-5	EST	HL-1	HL-2	HL-3	HL-4	HL-5	EST
SM	50.44	82.74	89.38	78.32	77.88	90.71	0.47	0.61	0.59	0.65	0.74	0.59
PCA	92.04	90.71	91.59	92.04	91.15	90.71	0.86	0.81	0.77	0.80	0.76	0.75
RSA	91.15	92.04	91.15	91.15	90.71	90.71	0.82	0.85	0.86	0.87	**0.88**	0.72
	SMOTE											
SM	55.61	62.93	53.17	36.59	71.22	58.54	0.56	0.63	0.53	0.37	0.84	0.47
PCA	90.73	92.68	93.41	92.68	92.20	91.95	0.96	**0.97**	0.96	0.96	0.95	0.93
RSA	81.95	85.12	79.02	84.39	81.46	64.88	0.90	0.88	0.85	0.87	0.86	0.71
	BSMOTE											
SM	44.63	48.29	88.05	67.80	47.07	79.51	0.45	0.49	0.88	0.68	0.36	0.87
PCA	92.93	92.93	93.41	93.41	92.68	81.95	0.96	**0.97**	**0.97**	0.96	0.96	0.91
RSA	84.39	83.17	87.32	84.88	85.85	39.51	0.89	0.87	0.89	0.89	0.88	0.59
	SVMSMOTE											
SM	40.49	69.27	59.27	82.68	80.49	65.85	0.40	0.65	0.53	0.82	0.94	0.77
PCA	91.71	93.17	93.17	92.44	94.15	76.59	0.97	**0.98**	0.97	0.97	0.97	0.92
RSA	90.98	90.98	92.93	91.95	93.41	75.37	0.94	0.94	0.96	0.95	0.95	0.91
	SMOTEENN											
SM	86.35	89.16	78.31	83.53	91.16	28.11	0.87	0.89	0.79	0.84	0.91	0.49
PCA	88.58	91.64	93.04	92.76	80.50	86.63	0.96	**0.98**	0.96	0.97	0.93	0.86
RSA	96.81	96.45	95.04	97.52	95.39	62.77	1.00	1.00	1.00	1.00	0.99	0.84
	SMOTETOMEK											
SM	46.72	53.28	39.62	71.31	74.04	67.49	0.47	0.53	0.40	0.66	0.71	0.54
PCA	90.49	90.24	91.46	91.95	93.17	74.63	0.95	**0.96**	0.94	0.94	0.96	0.91
RSA	85.57	89.18	87.11	71.91	90.46	65.21	0.92	0.92	0.90	0.87	0.92	0.83

6 Comparative Analysis

In this section, we have discussed and analyzed the results obtained by applying various data sampling, feature selection, and machine learning classifiers on the considered dataset for the anti-patterns prediction. The empirical analysis of the results is carried out methodically by answering the research questions defined in Sect. 1.

RQ1: What is the impact of the application of data sampling techniques for developing anti-pattern prediction models?

The impact of data sampling techniques is evaluated by analyzing the performance measures (AUC, Accuracy, and F-Measure) of anti-pattern prediction models developed before and after the application of data sampling techniques. In this paper, we employed Box-plots, and Statistical hypothesis testing to evaluate the significance and reliability of the models generated.

Comparison of the data sampling techniques based on Descriptive Statistics and Box-plots: Figure 2 depicts the box-plots for the data sampling techniques and the original data. These are useful for comparing the minimum, maximum, median, and inter-quartile range (Q1; Q3) of the various developed models. Figure 2 shows that the mean value of the model developed using the sampling technique **SMOTENN** is higher than the corresponding values of the other models. From Fig. 2, it is observed that the inter-quartile range for model generated using SMOTE is comparatively taller when compared to the models generated using other sampling techniques which indicates that the performance parameters computed from multiple executions are showing more variations.

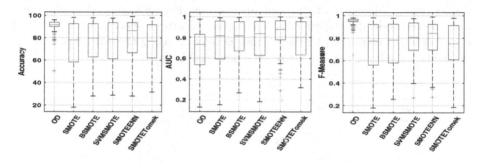

Fig. 2. Box-plot for accuracy and AUC: data sampling techniques

Comparison of the data sampling techniques based on Statistical hypothesis: We used Wilcoxon signed-rank test to evaluate the performance of the data sampling techniques statistically. The null hypothesis investigated by the Wilcoxon signed-rank test is defined as below:

Null-Hypothesis: The AUC performance value of the models commenced for web service anti-pattern prediction using various data sampling techniques is not significantly different.

The null hypothesis is accepted if the pair-wise value is greater than the considered threshold value of 0.05. From Table 2, it is noticed that most of the comparison points are having P-value, which is higher than 0.05. Hence we conclude that the null hypothesis is accepted, which means that there is no significant difference between the execution of the models generated employing various sampling techniques.

RQ2: Is there any critical distinction between the exhibition of the models produced using a subset of features selected by applying various feature selection techniques?

Table 2. Wilcoxon signed test: Data sampling techniques

	ORG	SMOTE	BSMOTE	SVMSMOTE	SMOTENN	SMOTETOMEK
ORG	1.00	0.01	0.00	0.00	0.00	0.01
SMOTE	0.01	1.00	0.65	0.57	0.05	0.99
BSMOTE	0.00	0.65	1.00	0.81	0.08	0.64
SVMSMOTE	0.00	0.57	0.81	1.00	0.20	0.51
SMOTEENN	0.00	0.05	0.08	0.20	1.00	0.03
SMOTETOMEK	0.01	0.99	0.64	0.51	0.03	1.00

The impact of the models developed by using the subset of features selected by applying various feature selection techniques is evaluated by analyzing the performance measures (AUC, Accuracy, and F-measure) on the considered dataset.

Comparison of the feature selection techniques based on Descriptive Statistics and Box-plots: Figure 3 shows the box-plots for the models trained using selected features and all features. Figure 3 show that the mean value of the model developed using the subset of features selected applying **PCA** is higher when compared to the models developed using the subset of features selected by applying other feature selection techniques.

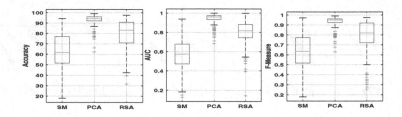

Fig. 3. Box-plot for accuracy and AUC: Feature selection techniques

Comparison of the feature selection techniques based on Statistical hypothesis: In this paper, Wilcoxon signed-rank test is used for evaluating the performance of the models generated using various feature selection techniques. From Table 3, it is observed that many of the comparison points are having P-value which is less than 0.05. Hence we conclude that the null-hypothesis is rejected, which means that, there is a noticeable difference between the performance of the models generated using the subset of features selected by applying various feature selection techniques.

RQ3: Does there exists a neural network model that outperforms all others?
The impact of the models generated using the neural network with different number of hidden layers and ensemble technique is evaluated by analyzing the performance measures (Accuracy, AUC, and F-measure) on the considered dataset.

Table 3. Wilcoxon signed test: Feature selection techniques

	SM	PCA	RSA
SM	1	4.73E-46	8.98E-26
PCA	4.73E-46	1	9.31E-28
RSA	8.98E-26	9.31E-28	1

Comparison of the classifier techniques based on Descriptive Statistics and Box-plots: Figure 4 shows the box-plots for the models generated using a neural network with a varying number of hidden layers and ensemble technique. Figure 4 show that the mean value of the model developed using the neural network with two hidden layers (HL−2) is showing preferable execution when compared to the models developed using a neural network with other numbers of hidden layers. HL−2 is showing greater performance when compared to the model generated using the ensemble technique (EST).

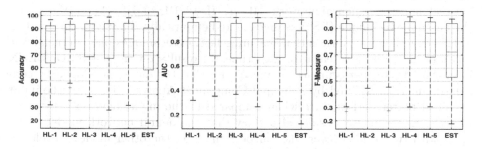

Fig. 4. Box-plot for accuracy and AUC: Classifier techniques

Comparison of the classifier techniques based on Statistical hypothesis: In this paper, Wilcoxon signed-rank test is used to evaluate the performance of the models developed using neural network with varying number of hidden layers and the ensemble technique. Considering only the models developed using the neural network with varying number of hidden layers, we notice from Table 4, that many of the comparison points are having P-value, which is higher than 0.05, from which we conclude that the null-hypothesis is accepted, which means that, there is no significant variation between the performance of the models generated using a neural network with varying number of hidden layers. If we consider the model developed by applying neural networks with any number of hidden layers and ensemble technique, it is observed that most of the comparison points are having a p-value of less than 0.05. Hence we conclude that the null-hypothesis is rejected and infer that there is a significant variation between the execution of the models generated using neural network (HL−1, HL−2, HL−3, HL−4 and HL−5) and the ensemble technique (EST).

Table 4. Wilcoxon signed test: Classifier techniques

	HL-1	HL-2	HL-3	HL-4	HL-5	EST
HL-1	1.00	0.53	1.00	0.92	0.95	0.00
HL-2	0.53	1.00	0.62	0.62	0.58	0.00
HL-3	1.00	0.62	1.00	0.99	0.97	0.00
HL-4	0.92	0.62	0.99	1.00	0.84	0.00
HL-5	0.95	0.58	0.97	0.84	1.00	0.00
EST	0.00	0.00	0.00	0.00	0.00	1.00

7 Conclusion

The principle inference of this work is that neural network with less number of hidden layers can be used for the effective prediction of web service anti-patterns. In this paper, the application of five data sampling techniques along with the original data, three feature selection techniques and six machine learning classifier techniques, i.e., neural network ($HL-1$, $HL-2$, $HL-3$, $HL-4$ and $HL-5$) and the ensemble technique (EST) is investigated empirically. The significant finding of this experimental work is that feature selection techniques play a crucial role in removing irrelevant features. Experimental results reveal that SMOTEENN is showing better performance. We also infer that the model developed by considering metrics selected by Principal Component Analysis (PCA) as the input obtained better performance when compared to the model developed by other metrics. Experimental results also show that the neural network model developed with two hidden layers has outperformed all the other models developed with varying number of hidden layers.

References

1. Dudney, B., Asbury, S., Krozak, J.K., Wittkopf, K.: J2EE Antipatterns. John Wiley & Sons, Hoboken (2003)
2. Palma, F., Moha, N., Tremblay, G., Guéhéneuc, Y.-G.: Specification and detection of SOA antipatterns in web services. In: Avgeriou, P., Zdun, U. (eds.) ECSA 2014. LNCS, vol. 8627, pp. 58–73. Springer, Cham (2014). https://doi.org/10.1007/978-3-319-09970-5_6
3. Ouni, A., Kessentini, M., Inoue, K., Cinnéide, M.O.: Search-based web service antipatterns detection. IEEE Trans. Serv. Comput. **10**(4), 603–617 (2017)
4. Settas, D., Meditskos, G., Bassiliades, N., Stamelos, I.G.: Detecting antipatterns using a web-based collaborative antipattern ontology knowledge base. In: International Conference on Advanced Information Systems Engineering, pp. 478–488. Springer (2011). https://doi.org/10.1007/978-3-642-22056-2_50

5. Ouni, A., Kessentini, M., Inoue, K., Cinnéide, M.O.: Search-based web service antipatterns detection. IEEE Trans. Serv. Comput. **10**(4), 603–617 (2015)
6. Tummalapalli, S., Kumar, L., Neti, L.B.M.: An empirical framework for web service anti-pattern prediction using machine learning techniques. In: 2019 9th Annual Information Technology, Electromechanical Engineering and Microelectronics Conference (IEMECON), pp. 137–143. IEEE (2019)

Fractional Backpropagation Algorithm – Convergence for the Fluent Shapes of the Neuron Transfer Function

Zbigniew Gomolka[⊠]

College of Natural Sciences, University of Rzeszow,
Pigonia St. 1, 35-959 Rzeszow, Poland
zgomolka@ur.edu.pl

Abstract. The classic algorithm of backpropagation of errors requires that the neural transfer function is differentiable and usually the algebraic form of this derivative determines the implementation of the algorithm minimizing the SSE error function. The paper extends the idea of homogeneous ANNs of the feed-forward type, which can be designed with the use of calculus of finite differences. We present a novel model of a neural network which uses a fractional order derivative mechanism. It has been shown that by using numerical approximation of a fractional order derivative, it is possible to smoothly model the dynamics of the transfer function of a single neuron without the need to modify the algebraic form of its base functions like sigmoid. This approach universalizes the neural network model, and enhance the area of possible applications.

Keywords: Back propagation · Fractional derivative

1 Introduction

Neural networks are one of the powerful tools of modern artificial intelligence and have been used for many years. The feed-forward model of neural networks learned by the supervised method is the subject of research of many scientific centers all over the world. Algorithms allowing for the intelligent selection of weighting factors and effective and efficient conduct of the learning process are an attractive subject of many research works [1, 3, 7–9]. As an example presenting one of many variations of network learning algorithms, a homogeneous network model was developed which allows the construction of a homogeneous network enabling the realization of a given transformation of a non-linear input signal. This paper presents a model of the Fractional Backpropagation (FBP) neural network which uses various methods of fractional order derivative approximation. It has been shown experimentally that it is possible to search for a minimum error function (SSE) for non-integer derivatives of basic functions. It is presented how different methods of selection of non-integer order coefficients for the determination of the Grunwald-Letnikov (GL) and Riemann-Liouville (RL) derivatives in the FBP network have influence on the accuracy of approximation

© Springer Nature Switzerland AG 2020
H. Yang et al. (Eds.): ICONIP 2020, CCIS 1333, pp. 580–588, 2020.
https://doi.org/10.1007/978-3-030-63823-8_66

of the derivative and consequently on the convergence of learning process. The results presented in the experimental part show that it is possible to conduct a convergent learning process not only for the total values of the derivative of the SSE error function.

2 Fusion of Fractional Calculus and Neural Nets

Actually there are a few mathematical models that enable the determination of a discrete approximation of the fractional order derivative [2]. Here and later we use known direct and reverse Grunwald-Letnikov (GL) definitions respectively:

$$D_d^\nu f(x) = \lim_{h \to 0+} \frac{\sum_{i=0}^{\infty} (-1)^i \binom{\nu}{i} f(x - ih)}{h^\nu} \tag{1}$$

$$D_r^\nu f(x) = (-1)^\nu \lim_{h \to 0+} \frac{\sum_{i=0}^{\infty} (-1)^i \binom{\nu}{i} f(x + ih)}{h^\nu} \tag{2}$$

where $\binom{\nu}{i}$ means Newton's binomial, while ν is the fractional order of the derivative function $f(x)$, x_0 - states the range of differentiation, h - is real number. In the direct mode the consecutive coefficients are real while in the reverse mode the fractional coefficients are complex. On the basis of solutions works [5,6], which were devoted to homogeneous networks, a network structure was proposed which uses the measurement of the discrete difference of non-integer order. A fragment of such a network is shown in Fig. 1.

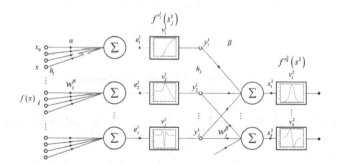

Fig. 1. Feed forward homogeneous network with fractional difference measurement.

The input signal measurement in the first layer of the presented network is carried out according to the following relation:

$$_{x_0}D_x^\alpha f(x) = \lim_{h_1 \to 0} \frac{1}{h_1^\alpha} \sum_{i=0}^{\lfloor (x-x_0)/h_1 \rfloor} (-1)^i \binom{\alpha}{i} f(x - ih_1) \tag{3}$$

where: α means the non-integer order of the derivative in the first layer of the network, h_1 - the step of discretization in layer one, β means the fractional order of the derivative in the second layer of the network and h_2 - the step of discretization in layer two. Turning to discrete notation, we assume that for a given discrete function $f(x)$ of the real variable x which is defined on the interval $\langle x_0, x \rangle$ where $0 \leq x_0 \leq x$, the backward difference of the non-integer order α will be expressed in the following form: $_{x_0}\Delta_x^\alpha$ (fractional or integer), where $\alpha \in IR^+$:

$$_{x_0}\Delta_x^\alpha f(x) = \sum_{i=0}^{\lfloor (x-x_0)/h \rfloor} w_i^\alpha f(x - ih) \qquad (4)$$

where individual weighting factors w_i^α are defined as:

$$w_i^\alpha = \begin{cases} 1 & i = 0 \\ (-1)^i \frac{\alpha(\alpha-1)(\alpha-2)...(\alpha-i+1)}{i!} & i = 1, 2, 3, ..., N \end{cases} \qquad (5)$$

where N is a number of measurements. Alternatively, using the Γ function directly we can get:

$$w_i^\alpha = (-1)^i \frac{\Gamma(\alpha+1)}{\Gamma(i+1)\Gamma(\alpha-i+1)} \qquad (6)$$

Assuming that $x_0 = 0$, we have:

$$_0\Delta_x^\alpha f(x) = \sum_{i=0}^{\lfloor x/h \rfloor} w_i^\alpha f(x - ih) \qquad (7)$$

The ordinary progressive difference we can define as

$$_x\Delta_\infty^\alpha f(x) = \sum_{i=0}^{\infty} w_i^\alpha f(x + ih) \qquad (8)$$

Weighting factors may be determined by several exemplary methods (in Matlab notation):

Listing 1.1. Fractional coefficients of v order and length of k

```
function y=coef(v,k)
    k=1:k-1;
    k= [1    (1-((v+1)./k))];
    y= (-1^v).*non_int_coef(v,k);
end
function y= non_int_coef(n,k)
    k=1:length(k)-1;
    y= cumprod([1,  1 - ((n+1) ./ k)]);
end
```

In the presented form, non-integer order coefficients can be determined with the use of a factorial. The Gamma function form can also be used for this purpose:

Listing 1.2. Fractional coefficients of v order and length of k computed with the use of Gamma function

```
function  y= coef(v,k)
% v- nonintegral derivaive order
% k- the number of nonzero coefficients
    k=0:k-1;
    y= (-1).^k.*gamma(v+1)
       ./(gamma(k+1).*gamma(v-k+1));
```

Considering sigmoid as an exemplary transfer function which most often appear in the ANN learning algorithms [6], a sigmoid-like base function has been adopted:

$$f_B(x) = log(1 + e^x) \tag{9}$$

It is worth noting that if $\nu = 1$ the first and second derivative of this function equals:

$$f_B^{\nu+1}(x) = f_B^\nu(x)(1 - f_B^\nu(x)) \tag{10}$$

which is discrete approximation of the classic algebraic form. In addition, for any given shape of such a function it is possible to calculate its derivative to obtain information about the gradient of error function. This is a key advantage of the proposed approach, which allows us to use those functions for which it is not possible to determine the algebraic derivative of the fractional order.

3   Fractional Backpropagation Network Model

Let us assume the following model of L layered neural network for which a model with a fractional order derivative mechanism will be given (see Fig. 2). Except for the transfer function, this model resembles the classic Back-Prop (BP) network model where the input signal is presented by an input vector matrix: $P = [p^1, \ldots, p^q]$ where q denotes consecutive vectors in the training set, e and a denotes entry signal to the neuron and it's activation respectively.

The flow of the signal within the network regarding it's feed-forward type has been proposed in details in [6]. Briefly the flow of the signal within the network can be described as following. The input signal e to the neurons in the first layer equals:

$$e_1(j) = \sum_{i=1}^{K} w_1(i,j) p(i) + b_1(j) \tag{11}$$

$$a_1(j) = f(e_1(j)) \tag{12}$$

where: $w_1(i,j)$ standard matrix of the randomized weights connecting the receptor layer with the first layer of neurons, $a_1(j)$ - activation of neuron. Similarly,

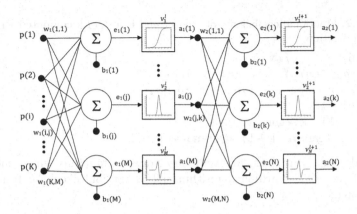

Fig. 2. Presumed FBP model of the network

the input signal for neurons in the second layer is equal to:

$$e_2(k) = \sum_{j=1}^{M} w_2(j,k) a_1(j) + b_2(k) \tag{13}$$

Typically, the bias vector might be placed in the weight matrix and the notation changes respectively:

$$a_2(k) = f\left(\sum_{j=0}^{M} w_2(j,k) f\left(\sum_{i=0}^{K} w_1(i,j) p(i)\right)\right) \tag{14}$$

In the presented model (differently than in the classic approach), the transition function of a single neuron is taken as a Grunwald-Letnikov fractional derivative (FGL) of *log* base function. Based on the definition of the integer derivative and the fractional derivative, the FGL derivative is denoted by the formula:

$$_{e_0}D_e^{\nu} f(e) = \lim_{h \to 0} \frac{1}{h^{\nu}} \sum_{n=0}^{\lfloor (e-e_0)/h \rfloor} (-1)^n \binom{\nu}{n} f_B(e - nh) \tag{15}$$

where ν - order of the fractional derivative of basis function $f_B(x)$, e_0 - the interval range, h-step of discretization. Another examples of the possible basis functions as well as their retrieval have been shown in [6]. When $h \to 0$ and $\nu = 1$ this GL derivative of $f_B(e)$ becomes:

$$_{e_0}D_e^1 f_B(e) = \frac{1}{1 + e^{-s}} \tag{16}$$

For $\nu = 1$ and $n \to 0$, regarding additivity property of derivatives [4] we have:

$$_{e_0}D_e^{\nu+1} f_B(e) = {}_{e_0}D_e^{\nu}\left({}_{e_0}D_e^1 f_B(e)\right) = {}_{e_0}D_e^1 f_B(e)\left(1 - {}_{e_0}D_e^1 f_B(e)\right) \tag{17}$$

or directly:

$$e_0 D_e^{\nu+1} f_B(e) = e_0 D_e^2 f_B(e) \tag{18}$$

Based on the presented considerations, the general formula for weight modification for L layered neural network with transition function obtained by fractional derivative of the base function can be given:

$$w_1^q(i,j) = w_1^{q-1}(i,j) + \eta \delta_j^l a_i^l \tag{19}$$

where the value δ_j^i, while presenting the $q - th$ pattern, will be written as:

$$\delta_j^i = \begin{cases} (t_j - a_j^l) \; _{e_0} D_e^{\nu+1} f_B(e) & l = L \\ _{e_0} D_e^{\nu+1} f_B(e) \sum_{k=0}^{N^{l+1}} \delta_k^{l+1} w_{l+1}(j,k) & l < L \end{cases} \tag{20}$$

where: l - means the number of the considered layer, j - the number of the neuron in layer l, k - is the number of neurons in the layer $l+1$, N - is the number of neurons in layer l, η - learning rate. In the above considerations, it was assumed that in the presented network architecture the parameter ν has non integral value and is the same in each layer as well as for individual neurons transfer function retrival.

4   FBP Convergence Under the XOR Problem

The XOR problem was assumed as the input task for the fractional backpropagation neural network (FBP). The diagram of the network designed for this purpose is shown in Fig. 3.

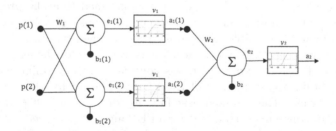

Fig. 3. FBP network architecture for the XOR problem.

It has been assumed that for a randomly selected set of weights and bias $S\{w_1, b_1, w_2, b_2\}$ a learning process will be performed for successive smoothly changing values of parameter ν in the presumed range $0 \leq \nu \leq 1.2$ for comparisons in series of tests. The network uses a discrete approximation of the fractional GL derivative of the log base function f_B in case of shape ν and derivative $\nu + 1$ acquiring respectively:

$$e_0 D_e^{(\nu)} f_B\,(e) = \lim_{\substack{h \to \nu \\ e - e_0 = kh}} \frac{1}{h^\nu} \begin{bmatrix} a_0^{(\nu)} & \cdots & a_k^{(\nu)} & \cdots & a_N^{(\nu)} \end{bmatrix} \begin{bmatrix} f_B\,(e) \\ f_B\,(e-h) \\ \vdots \\ f_B\,(e-kh) \end{bmatrix} \tag{21}$$

In formula 21 the coefficients of the fractional order of GL derivative have been denoted as a_k^ν, to avoid collision of symbols with the notation of the ordinary weight matrices used in the FBP architecture. The initial values of weights $\{w_1, b_1, w_2, b_2\}$ have been shown in Table 1 and these values are common to each subsequent learning process. Those values have been obtained with standard randomizing procedure within the Matlab environment.

Table 1. Randomized values of weights

Initial set	w_1	b_1	w_2	$b2$
1	$\begin{bmatrix} -0.9416 & 0.4607 \\ 0.8577 & -0.0228 \end{bmatrix}$	$\begin{bmatrix} 0.1571 \\ -0.5254 \end{bmatrix}$	$\begin{bmatrix} -0.0823 \\ 0.9262 \end{bmatrix}$	$\begin{bmatrix} 0.0936 \end{bmatrix}$
2	$\begin{bmatrix} 0.0424 & 0.8743 \\ -0.2554 & 0.6591 \end{bmatrix}$	$\begin{bmatrix} 0.6982 \\ -0.2549 \end{bmatrix}$	$\begin{bmatrix} -0.1864 \\ 0.7451 \end{bmatrix}$	$\begin{bmatrix} 0.08670 \end{bmatrix}$

5   Results

In the experimental part of the work, it was assumed that the proposed FBP model would be tested in order to solve the linearly not separable problem. This is a task in which it is possible to demonstrate both the network's ability to solve non-linearly separable tasks and to test the convergence of the learning process. In the initial phase, an experiment was conducted to determine whether it is possible to obtain a convergence of the FBP algorithm for the values of non-integer derivatives of the assumed base function or not. The left part of Fig. 4 a) shows the three consecutive trainings for a FBP algorithm carried out with a first set of initial weights and biases defined in the Table 1. The FBP network uses a momentum and an adaptive change of weights mechanism. The right side of the graph shows the functions of neuron transition in the network for the assumed order of fractional derivative ν. The green circles indicate the initial values of the SSE error for each of the three consecutive learning cycles. The red circles indicate the final values of the SSE error at the end of each cycle, respectively. As we can see, the learning process of FBP networks converges not only for $\nu = 1$ but also for fractional values of the order of the derivative, i.e. $\nu = 0.7$ and $\nu = 1.1$. This is novel and important result indicating that it is possible to conduct an effective learning process for FBP networks for a fractional order

ν of derivative. In subsequent experiments, it was assumed that the learning process would be conducted taking into account different lengths of the fractional coefficient vectors. Figure 4 b) show in the form of 3D chart the successive 25 learning cycles with the "Initial set 1" weight matrix set (see Table 2) for length of fractional coefficients: $N = 100$.

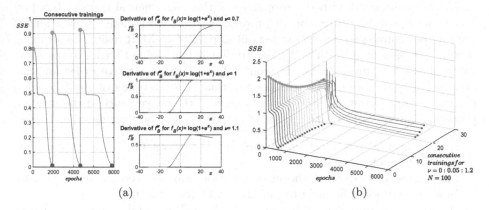

(a)   (b)

Fig. 4. FBP training convergence with exemplary ν order of fractional derivative of transfer functions f_B^{ν} (a) and convergence with given number of derivative approximation vector length in the 3D view form (b) respectively.

Table 2. Final weight sets 1 and 2 achieved with different number of fractional coefficients

Initial set		w_1	b_1	w_2	$b2$
1	Trained successfully	$\begin{bmatrix} -3.1385 & 2.9420 \\ 2.9045 & -2.8780 \end{bmatrix}$	$\begin{bmatrix} -0.9229 \\ -1.0435 \end{bmatrix}$	$\begin{bmatrix} 4.7210 \\ 4.8499 \end{bmatrix}$	$\begin{bmatrix} -4.5251 \end{bmatrix}$
	Failed training	$\begin{bmatrix} -5.1796 & 4.9263 \\ 5.1184 & -4.8662 \end{bmatrix}$	$\begin{bmatrix} -0.5648 \\ -0.6089 \end{bmatrix}$	$\begin{bmatrix} 8.1876 \\ 8.2542 \end{bmatrix}$	$\begin{bmatrix} -3.2366 \end{bmatrix}$
2	Trained successfully	$\begin{bmatrix} -6.3314 & 3.1741 \\ -6.3129 & 3.1738 \end{bmatrix}$	$\begin{bmatrix} 0.3541 \\ -1.5682 \end{bmatrix}$	$\begin{bmatrix} -7.6391 \\ -1.7631 \end{bmatrix}$	$\begin{bmatrix} 3.3676 \end{bmatrix}$
	Failed training	$\begin{bmatrix} 0.0378 & 0.8435 \\ -0.2592 & 0.6284 \end{bmatrix}$	$\begin{bmatrix} 0.6917 \\ -0.2876 \end{bmatrix}$	$\begin{bmatrix} 0.0595 \\ 0.6320 \end{bmatrix}$	$\begin{bmatrix} 0.5826 \end{bmatrix}$

As can be seen, the convergent learning process is achieved for subsequent orders of the fractional derivative, i.e. for a smooth change in the shape of the transition function of a single neuron. The insufficient coefficient vector length to approximate the discrete derivative clearly limits the convergence range of the network in the considered range of variation of the ν factor.

6   Conclusion

In the presented paper the model of FBP network which uses a fractional-order GL derivative mechanism to approximate the SSE error derivative function and the transfer function of a single neuron in each layer has been presented. The proposed model of the learning algorithm is a new approach that eliminates the limitations associated with the properties of the single neural transfer function known in current literature. For the proposed FBP network model, simulations of the network convergence were carried out as part of an XOR task. The resulting weight sets presented in Table 2 indicate that it is possible to achieve the same value of the SSE function for different values of the derivative order and the assumed shapes of the basis transfer function. The accuracy of the fractional derivative approximation has a key influence on the convergence of the training process. Final remarks for the presented studies might be formulated as follow:

- fractional derivative mechanism can be fused into neural network structure and training algorithm,
- minimizing procedure of the error function can be used for different base functions without the need to modify the IT model of network,
- the proposed approach can be used in both shallow and deep neural networks architectures. This important contribution is a key achievement of this work.

References

1. Bao, C., Pu, Y., Zhang, Y.: Fractional-order deep backpropagation neural network. Comput. Intell. Neurosci. (2018)
2. Garrappa, R.: Numerical evaluation of two and three parameter Mittag-Leffler functions. SIAM J. Numer. Anal. **53**, 1350–1369 (2015)
3. Ghosh, U., Sarkar, S., Das, S.: Solution of system of linear fractional differential equations with modified derivative of Jumarie type. Am. J. Math. Anal. **3**(3), 72–84 (2015)
4. Giusti, A.: A comment on some new definitions of fractional derivative. Nonlinear Dyn. **93**(3), 1757–1763 (2018). https://doi.org/10.1007/s11071-018-4289-8
5. Gomolka, Z., Dudek-Dyduch, E., Kondratenko, Y.P.: From homogeneous network to neural nets with fractional derivative mechanism. In: Rutkowski, L., Korytkowski, M., Scherer, R., Tadeusiewicz, R., Zadeh, L.A., Zurada, J.M. (eds.) ICAISC 2017. LNCS (LNAI), vol. 10245, pp. 52–63. Springer, Cham (2017). https://doi.org/10.1007/978-3-319-59063-9_5
6. Gomolka, Z.: Neurons'transfer function modeling with the use of fractional derivative. In: DepCoS-RELCOMEX 2018, AISC, vol. 761. Springer (2019). https://doi.org/10.1007/978-3-319-91446-6_21
7. Moret, I.: Shift-and-invert Krylov methods for time-fractional wave equations. Numer. Func. Anal. Optim. **36**(1), 86–103 (2015)
8. Tarasov, V.: No nonlocality. No fractional derivative. Commun. Nonlinear Sci. Numer. Simul. **62**, 157–163 (2018)
9. Wang, J., Wen, Y., Gou, Y., Ye, Z., Chen, H.: Fractional-order gradient descent learning of BP neural networks with Caputo derivative. Neural Networks, **89**, 19–30

FTR-NAS: Fault-Tolerant Recurrent Neural Architecture Search

Kai Hu, Dong Ding, Shuo Tian, Rui Gong, Li Luo, and Lei Wang[✉]

College of Computer Science and Technology, National University of Defense Technology,
Changsha, China
{hukai18,leiwang}@nudt.edu.cn

Abstract. With the popularity of the applications equipped with neural networks on edge devices, robustness has become the focus of researchers. However, when deploying the applications onto the hardware, environmental noise is unavoidable, in which errors may cause applications crash, especially for the safety-critic applications. In this paper, we propose *FTR-NAS* to optimize recurrent neural architectures to enhance the fault tolerance. First, according to real deployment scenarios, we formalize computational faults and weight faults, which are simulated with Multiply-Accumulate (MAC)-independent and identically distributed (i.i.d) Bit-Bias (MiBB) model and Stuck-at-Fault (SAF) model, respectively. Next, we establish a multi-objective NAS framework powered by the fault models to discover high-performance and fault-tolerant recurrent architectures. Moreover, we incorporate fault-tolerant training (FTT) in the search process to further enhance the fault tolerance of the recurrent architectures. Experimentally, C-FTT-RNN and W-FTT-RNN we discovered on PTB dataset have promising fault tolerance for computational and weight faults. Besides, we further demonstrate the usefulness of the learned architectures by transferring it to WT2 dataset well.

Keywords: Recurrent neural network · Neural architecture search · Fault tolerance

1 Introduction

RNNs have been overwhelmingly successful in many natural language processing (NLP) tasks. However, there exist many challenges in deploying safety-critical RNN applications onto neural network accelerators based on various hardware platforms, e.g., FPGA, ASIC, Resistive Random Access Memory (RRAM). For instance, cosmic radiation and humidity variations are common factors that could lead to errors. Even worse, circuits become more sensitive to these environmental noises due to the down-scaling of CMOS technology. Besides, the emerging metal-oxide RRAM devices suffer from many types of permanent hard faults, such as Stuck-at-Faults (SAFs), which result in performance degradation and could not be easily relieved.

In this paper, we propose *FTR-NAS* to optimize RNN architectures to enhance the fault tolerance capability. To verify the feasibility, we accomplish a preliminary experiment, and the perplexity of two baseline models under Gaussian noise are shown in

© Springer Nature Switzerland AG 2020
H. Yang et al. (Eds.): ICONIP 2020, CCIS 1333, pp. 589–597, 2020.
https://doi.org/10.1007/978-3-030-63823-8_67

Table 1. Although Gaussian noise could not simulate the real hardware faults well, the experiments on PTB dataset show that the fault tolerance vary among neural architectures. In addition, Li et al. [1] propose the feature faults and weight faults based on actual hardware deployment, and find fault-tolerant CNN architectures. This further proves that neural architectures have an important impact on fault tolerance.

Table 1. Perplexities of two baseline models under Gaussian noise on PTB dataset. The experimental results are obtained by retraining for only 50 epochs.

RNN model	Perplexity with Gaussian noise			Params(M)
	0	10^{-6}	10^{-4}	
ENAS [2]	89	203.2	986.3	24M
DARTS [3]	88.3	347.3	1278.2	23M

† $0/10^{-6}/10^{-4}$ denotes variances of Gaussian noise. The larger the variance, the greater the amplitude of oscillation of per-MAC.

Neural architecture search (NAS) focuses on automating the architecture optimization process, however, early NAS methods search for high-performance architectures without taking hardware deployment into consideration. High latency and high fault rate in the inference process make it difficult to deploy the discovered architectures to real hardware devices. Therefore, in order to discover high-performance and fault-tolerant recurrent neural architectures, we establish a multi-objective NAS framework where incorporates the simulated hardware signal feedback into the search process. Experiments show the discovered architectures achieve a promising fault tolerance against computational faults and weight faults while maintaining high-performance.

The main contributions of the paper follow as: **(1)** We classify two types of faults for RNNs considering the computational flow of RNNs and real deployment scenarios, namely computational faults and weight faults. Moreover, we apply Multiply-Accumulate (MAC)-i.i.d Bit-Bias (MiBB) and Stuck-at-Fault (SAF) fault model to formalize these two types of faults, respectively; **(2)** We establish FTR-NAS to discover high-performance and fault-tolerance architectures. To our best knowledge, it's the first to enhance fault tolerance of RNNs by NAS. Moreover, we accomplish fault-tolerant training (FTT) [4] in searching and training process, which further improves fault-tolerance of the discovered architectures; **(3)** Experiments on PTB show that C-FTT-RNN discovered under the computational faults achieves the test perplexity of 67.6, which is lower than DARTS by 13.8, while W-FTT-RNN discovered under the weight faults achieves the test perplexity of 71.3, which is lower than ENAS by 12.8. Besides, we further demonstrate the usefulness of the learned architectures by transferring it to WT2 well.

2 Background

RNN: The structure of basic RNN is simple, however, the gradient flow in RNNs often leads to exploding and vanishing. Therefore the slight deviation of weights or computation will easily lead to the fault of the entire system. Hence our recurrent cell is enhanced with a highway bypass [5]. The accomplishment is as follows:

$$
\begin{cases}
c_0 = sigmoid\left(W_{xc}\, x_t + W_{hc}\, h_{prev}\right), \\
h_0 = c_0\, tanh\left(W_{xh}\, x + W_{hh}\, h_{prev}\right) + (1 - c_0)\, h_{prev}, \\
c_t = sigmoid\left(W_c\, c_{t-1}\right), \\
h_t = c_t f\left(W_h\, h_{t-1}\right) + (1 - c_t)\, h_{t-1},
\end{cases}
\tag{1}
$$

where W_{xc}, W_{hc}, W_{xh}, W_{hh}, W_c, W_h denote parameter matrices; h_{prev} indicates the output of the previous hidden layer; c, h denote cell state vector and hidden layer vector, respectively. $f(.)$ refers to the activation function selected for each node of the cell.

Fault Analysis: Both FPGAs and ASICs belong to CMOS-based platforms. Circuits become more sensitive to computational errors due to the down-scaling of CMOS technology. Specifically, LUT-based computational logic in FPGAs, Gate-based computational logic in ASICs are easy to induce accumulated bias errors. Besides, RRAM-based accelerators with immature technology suffer from much higher hard fault error rates, such as SAF faults. As reported by [6], the overall SAF ratio could be larger than 10% ($p_1 = 9.04\%$ for SAF1 and $p_0 = 1.75\%$ for SAF0) in a fabricated RRAM device.

3   Related Work

Fault Tolerance: Triple Modular Redundancy (TMR) and sensitivity analysis are the common fault-tolerant methods. From the algorithmic perspective, FTT is to train the neural network injected faults, which can enhance fault tolerance of the network [4].

NAS: Early NAS methods are computing-intensive, however, ENAS [2] proposes to speed up the performance estimation process by sharing weights among all models. Hu et al. [7] applies the randomness-enhanced tabu algorithm as a controller to sample candidate architectures in the reduced search space on the basis of weight sharing, which further enhances the efficiency of NAS. Recently, Cai et al. [8] integrate the latency term into the architecture searching process to meet the needs of edge devices, which are able to improve hardware inference efficiency. Li et al. [1] takes the faults in the hardware deploying process into consideration and discovers fault-tolerant CNNs.

4   Method

4.1   Fault Injection

In this paper, our fault simulations apply 8-bit fixed-point quantization for the computation and weights following [1]. The section will show how to inject the two types of faults into the RNN model.

Computational Faults. For CMOS-based platforms, the occurring probability of hard errors and memory buffer errors are much smaller than accumulated bias errors. Therefore, we focus on accumulated bias errors (abbreviated as computational faults), which randomly occur in per-MAC during the computation process. We apply MAC-i.i.d Bit-Bias (MiBB) fault model [1] to simulate computational faults in the RNN inference process. The RNN inference process with MiBB fault injection can be written as:

$$
\begin{aligned}
b &= \theta\, 2^{\alpha-1}\,(-1)^{\beta} \\
c_0 &= sigmoid\left(W_{xc}\, x_t + W_{hc}\, h_{prev} + b_1\right), \\
h_0 &= c_0\, tanh\left(W_{xh}\, x + W_{hh}\, h_{prev} + b_2\right) + (1 - c_0)\, h_{prev}\,, \\
c_t &= sigmoid\left(W_c\, c_{t-1}\right), \\
h_t &= c_t\, f\left(W_h\, h_{t-1}\right) + (1 - c_t)\, h_{t-1} + b_3\,, \\
s.t. \quad \theta &\sim Bernoulli\,(p)^{H\times W}\,, \\
\alpha &\sim U\,\{0, ..., Q-1\}^{H\times W}\,, \\
\beta &\sim U\,\{0, 1\}^{H\times W}
\end{aligned}
\tag{2}
$$

where b is to bit-bias and b_1, b_2, b_3 are generated independently, θ is the mask indicating whether an error occurs at each position of matrix, α indicates the bit position of the accumulated bias, β represents the bias sign. The dimension of the intermediate result tensor is denoted as (H, W).

Weight Faults. RRAM cells containing SAF faults get stuck at high-resistance state (HRS) or low-resistance state (LRS). HRS causes the corresponding logical weight would be stuck at 0, namely SAF0; LRS leads to SAF1 fault, causing the weight to be stuck at $-R^w$ if it's negative, or R^w otherwise. As described in Eq. 3, $-R^w$ and R^w indicate the lowest or highest magnitudes of the representation range, respectively.

$$
[-R^w, R^w] = [-2^{-l}(2^{Q+1} - 1), 2^{-l}(2^{Q+1} - 1)]
\tag{3}
$$

where Q and l denote bit-width and fraction length of a tensor.

Here we use the c_t term in Eq. 2 as an example, the c_t' with SAF fault injection [1] is written as follow:

$$
\begin{aligned}
c_t &= sigmoid\left(W_c\, c_{t-1}\right), \\
s.t. \quad W_c &= (1 - \theta)\, W_c + \theta\, e\,, \\
\theta &\sim Bernoulli\,(p_0 + p_1)^{H\times W}\,, \\
m &\sim Bernoulli\,(\frac{p_1}{p_0 + p_1})^{H\times W} \\
e &= R^w\, sgn(W)\, m
\end{aligned}
\tag{4}
$$

where R^w refers to the representation bound in Eq. 3, θ is the mask indicating whether fault occurs at each weight position, m is the mask representing the SAF types (SAF0 or SAF1) at faulty weight positions, e is the mask representing the faulty target values (0 or $\pm R^w$). Every single weight has an i.i.d probability of p_0 to be stuck at 0, and p_1 to be stuck at the positive or negative bounds of the representation range.

SAF faults will directly lead to the weights deviation, so we classify it as weight faults. In our implementation, all the six matrices (W_{xc}, W_{hc}, W_{xh}, W_{hh}, W_c, and W_h) in Eq. 1 are injected with weight faults.

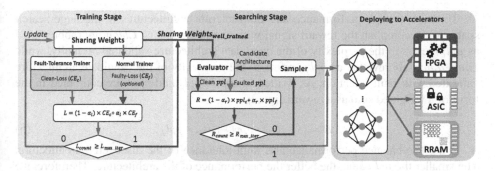

Fig. 1. The framework of multi-objective architecture search.

4.2 Deriving Fault-Tolerant Recurrent Neural Architectures

FTR-NAS. The overall framework for deriving fault-tolerant recurrent neural architectures is illustrated in Fig. 1. Below we will explain in detail. We use and modify the NAS framework of [7]. As shown in Algorithm 1, the sampler applies the randomness-enhanced tabu strategy to sample candidate architectures constantly. Evaluator evaluates each candidate architecture and generates a reward signal to encourage the sampler to discover a better architecture.

The recurrent cell is employed a single directed acyclic graph (DAG) with 12 nodes. We allow 2 activation functions (namely $ReLU$ and $tanh$), then the search space has $2^{12} \times 12! \approx 2 \times 10^{12}$ candidate models.

Algorithm 1. FTR-NAS

1: **function FT-NAS(** $tabu\_list, tabu\_size, R, S, f, p_{valid}$ **)**
2: $\quad arch =$ INITIALARCHGENERATOR( )
3: $\quad tabu\_list.append(model.arch)$
4: $\quad$ **for** $round = 1 \rightarrow R$ **do** $\qquad\qquad\qquad\qquad$ ▷ explore new architectures
5: $\qquad arch =$ RANDOMARCH( )
6: $\qquad$ **for** $step = 1 \rightarrow S$ **do** $\qquad\qquad$ ▷ exploit current architecture for S steps
7: $\qquad\quad arch =$ ARCHMUTATE$(arch)$
8: $\qquad\quad$ **if** $arch \notin tabu\_list$ **then**
9: $\qquad\qquad ppl_c =$ ARCHEVALUATE$(arch)$ $\qquad\qquad$ ▷ ppl_c: clean perplexity
10: $\qquad\qquad ppl_f =$ ARCHEVALUATE$(arch, f, p_{valid})$ ▷ ppl_c: faulty perplexity
11: $\qquad\qquad Reward = (1 - \alpha_r) * ppl_c + \alpha_r * ppl_f$
12: $\qquad\quad$ **end if**
13: $\qquad\quad$ **while** $Reward < Tbest$ **do**
14: $\qquad\qquad$ **if** $len(tabu\_list) < tabu\_size$ **then**
15: $\qquad\qquad\quad tabu\_list.append(arch)$
16: $\qquad\qquad\quad Tbest = Reward$
17: $\qquad\qquad$ **end if**
18: $\qquad\quad$ **end while**
19: $\qquad\quad arch = tabu\_list[-1]$
20: $\qquad$ **end for**
21: $\quad$ **end for**
22: **end function**

To discover high-performance and fault-tolerant architectures in the huge search space, we accomplish the reward signal with two components. *Clean ppl* (abbreviated as ppl_c) refers to the perplexity of the candidate architecture validated normally, while *Faulted ppl* (abbreviated as ppl_f) refers to the perplexity of the candidate architecture validated with fault injection. As written in Eq. 5, ppl_c and ppl_f are combined in the form of a weighted sum as a reward signal:

$$R = (1 - \alpha_r) \times ppl_c + \alpha_r \times ppl_f \tag{5}$$

α_r is used to balance performance and fault tolerance of the discovered architecture. The smaller the *ppl* value, the better the performance of the architecture. Therefore, we expect to get a smaller reward. The whole search process is summarized as Algorithm 1. The parameters R in line 4 and S in line 6 balance the global exploration and local exploitation for sampling candidate architectures. Parameter f in line 10 refers to the type of fault model, and p_{valid} is the proportion to inject faults in the searching process.

Fault-Tolerant Training (FTT). After finish the architecture searching process, we apply FTT to enhance the fault resilience capability of the discovered recurrent neural architecture. Moreover, we introduce FTT to the architecture searching process.

Algorithm 2. FTT

1: **function FTT(** $(x_t, y_t), f, p_{train}$ **)**
2:     $arch = $ RANDOMARCH( )   ▷ randomly sample a candidate architecture
3:     $CE_c = CE(\mathbf{RNN}(arch; w; x_t), y_t)$ ▷ the clean loss
4:     $CE_f = CE(\mathbf{RNN}(arch; w; x_t; f; p_{train}), y_t)$ ▷ the faulted loss
5:     $L = (1 - \alpha_l) * CE_c + \alpha_l * CE_f$
6:     $w = w - \eta_w \nabla_w L$ ▷ w: sharing weights
7: **end function**

In particular, sharing weights [2] are applied in the neural architecture searching process to reduce search cost. To further enhance the fault tolerance of discovered architectures, we use fault-tolerant trainer to train the sharing weights (shown in Fig. 1), in which random faults are injected in the training process. When searching with FTT, we balance the clean cross-entropy loss CE_c and the cross entropy-loss with fault injection CE_f with the coefficient α_l[1]:

$$L = (1 - \alpha_l) \times CE_c + \alpha_l \times CE_f \tag{6}$$

The specific implementation is illustrated in Algorithm 2. Parameter p_{train} in line 4 is the proportion to inject faults in the sharing weights updating process. The updated sharing parameters w will be used in the fault-tolerant architecture search process.

The complete pseudo-code searching for fault-tolerant recurrent architecture with FTT technology is shown in Algorithm 3. This algorithm is finished in two stages.

---
[1] α_l keeps consistent in both architecture searching and training process.

First, sharing weights are trained for 150 epochs with fault injection (EPOCH = 150 in line 2). Next, we search for the fault-tolerant architectures with the trained sharing weights w.

Algorithm 3. FTR-NAS with FTT

1: **Input:** (x_t, y_t), f, p_{train}, $tabu\_list \leftarrow \emptyset$, $tabu\_size$, R, S, p_{valid}, EPOCH
2: **for** epoch < EPOCH **do**   ▷ EPOCH:the epochs of trainning sharing weights
3:     $w = $ **FTT**$((x_t, y_t), f, p_{train})$
4: **end for**
5: $Bset_arch = $ **FT-NAS**$(tabu\_list, tabu\_size, R, S, f, p_{valid}, w)$
6: **Return** $Bset\_arch$

---

5 Experiments and Results

We apply our method to a language modeling task on PTB dataset. To further demonstrate transferability of *FTR-NAS*, we perform extended experiments to transfer the cells we discover to a larger WT2 dataset. All the experiments are implemented in PyTorch framework with four Tesla V100 GPUs. In FTR-NAS, an 8-bit fixed-point representation is used throughout the search and training process. The main baselines are the two recurrent architectures discovered by ENAS [2] and DARTS [3], respectively.

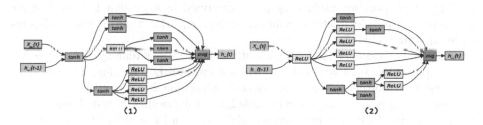

Fig. 2. The recurrent cells we discover in PTB dataset. (1): The recurrent cell we discover to defend against MiBB computational fault model; (2): The recurrent cell we discover to defend against SAF weight fault model.

In our experiments, all the recurrent architectures consist of 12 nodes following the setting of ENAS. Besides, we apply the reduced search space to obtain a high-performance recurrent architecture with less time. Specifically, the activation functions only contain $ReLU$ and $tanh$. In the architecture search process, we search for 30,000 different recurrent architectures in total (R_{max_iter} = 30,000 in Fig. 1). In particular, the parameters R and S in Algorithm 1 are set to 1000 and 30. That means we first exploit 30 neighborhood solutions for a current candidate architecture and then samples a random architecture for global exploration [7]. In addition, we use SGD optimizer to train the sharing weights for 150 epochs (L_{max_iter} = 150 in Fig. 1).

Table 2. Comparison of different architectures under the MiBB computational fault model.

Architecture	Training	ppl with MiBB faults (PTB)				ppl with MiBB faults (WT2)			
		0	3e−5	1e−4	3e−4	0	3e−5	1e−4	3e−4
ENAS [2]	Clean	58.3	89.1	101.9	113.5	69.4	97.5	112.9	129.8
DARTS [3] †	Clean	58.6	92.7	106.6	121.3	69.6	103.4	116.5	128.7
C-FT-RNN	Clean	**57.8**	**77.4**	**83.4**	**92.6**	**69.1**	**86.3**	**94.1**	**105.8**
ENAS [2]	p = 3e−4	–	76.7	89.3	104.3	–	88.6	99.7	120.6
DARTS [3] †	p = 3e−4	–	81.4	94.3	110.3	–	92.5	103.4	117.6
C-FTT-RNN	p = 3e−4	–	**67.6**	**72.3**	**85.3**	–	**76.4**	**80.6**	**94.3**

† Obtained by training the corresponding architecture using our codes and setup. The corresponding architecture is publicly released by the authors in the paper.

Table 3. Comparison of different architectures under the SAF weight fault model.

Architecture	Training	ppl with SAF faults (PTB)				ppl with SAF faults (WT2)			
		0	0.08	0.10	0.12	0	0.08	0.10	0.12
ENAS [2]	Clean	58.3	98.7	113.9	128.5	69.4	107.5	121.6	136.8
DARTS [3]	Clean	58.6	92.3	109.6	127.3	69.6	102.5	118.9	138.3
W-FT-RNN	Clean	**57.9**	**83.4**	**87.6**	**108.6**	**69.1**	**93.6**	**96.5**	**103.7**
ENAS [2]	p = 0.10	–	84.1	88.6	117.3	–	96.5	109.4	123.5
DARTS [3]	p = 0.10	–	82.4	91.3	110.8	–	94.3	103.6	119.4
W-FTT-RNN	p = 0.10	–	**71.3**	**73.9**	**90.2**	–	**81.8**	**83.1**	**97.5**

5.1 Tolerate MiBB Computational Faults

We implement the recurrent cell based on the description of Eq. 1. Following [1], the per-MAC fault injection probability p_{valid} described in Algorithm 1 is 10^{-4} in the search process. Besides, both the reward coefficients α_r in Eq. 5 and the loss coefficients α_l in Eq. 6 are set to 0.5.

Besides, we conduct FTR-NAS without/with fault-tolerant training. Meanwhile, we also train two baselines with both normal and fault-tolerant training. The per-MAC fault injection probability p_{train} described in Algorithm 2 is 3×10^{-4} in the fault-tolerant training process. As shown in Table 2, when the models are tested under MiBB faults, we try per-MAC fault injection probability p_{test} in $\{3 \times 10^{-5}, 10^{-4}, 3 \times 10^{-4}\}$. As shown in Fig. 2(1), C-FT-RNN is the discovered recurrent cell to defend against computational faults. We can find in Table 2 that C-FT-RNN has better computational fault tolerance than the baselines. Meanwhile, our cell can also achieve the lower test ppl without faults. Results show that the fault tolerance of each architecture could be improved after FTT. When p_{test} is 3×10^{-5}, the ppl of C-FTT-RNN is 67.6, which is lower than DARTS by 13.8. To further demonstrate the usefulness of *FT-NAS*, we perform extended experiments to transfer C-FT-RNN to a larger WT2 dataset. The results on WT2 dataset show that our architecture is more scalable than the two baselines.

5.2 Tolerate SAF Weight Faults

In the fault-tolerant training and architecture searching process, the overall SAF ratio $p_{train} = p_{valid} = p_0 + p_1$ (described in Algorithm 1, 2) is set to 10%, where the proportion of SAF0 and SAF1 is 83.7% and 16.3%, respectively ($p_0 = 8.37\%$,

$p_1 = 1.63\%$). When each model is tested under SAF faults, we successively try weight fault injection probability p_{test} in $\{0.08, 0.10, 0.12\}$. After a simple grid search, the reward coefficient α_r is set to 0.4 and the loss coefficient α_l is set to 0.6.

As shown in Fig. 2(2), W-FT-RNN is the recurrent cell we discover to defend against SAF weight faults. Table 3 shows the detailed experimental results. Compared with baselines, W-FT-RNN has a better performance without injecting SAF weight faults. Meanwhile, W-FT-RNN still has better weight fault tolerance capability when injected various degrees of faults. Moreover, the fault tolerance of W-FTT-RNN is further improved through fault-tolerant training. When p_{test} is 0.08, the perplexity of W-FTT-RNN is 71.3, which is lower than ENAS by 12.8. Equally, we perform extended experiments to transfer W-FT-RNN to WT2 dataset. W-FTT-RNN has a strong fault tolerance to defend against weight faults in more complex tasks.

6   Conclusion

In the paper, we propose *FTR-NAS* to optimize the architecture to improve fault-tolerant capability. First, we find computational and weight faults are the main reason to induce the application crashes in different platforms. Next, we establish a multi-objective fault-tolerant NAS framework. Experiments show that the discovered architectures on PTB can transfer to larger WT2 dataset well. In the future, we will explore the more complex relationship between architecture optimization and fault tolerance.

Acknowledgments. This work is founded by National Key R&D Program of China [grant numbers 2018YFB2202603].

References

1. Li, W., Ning, X., Ge, G., Chen, X., Wang, Y., Yang, H.: FTT-NAS: discovering fault-tolerant neural architecture. In: 2020 25th Asia and South Pacific Design Automation Conference (ASP-DAC), pp. 211–216. IEEE (2020)
2. Pham, H., Guan, M.Y., Zoph, B., Le, Q.V., Dean, J.: Efficient neural architecture search via parameter sharing. arXiv preprint arXiv:1802.03268 (2018)
3. Liu, H., Simonyan, K., Yang, Y.: Darts: Differentiable architecture search. arXiv preprint arXiv:1806.09055 (2018)
4. He, Z., Lin, J., Ewetz, R., Yuan, J.S., Fan, D.: Noise injection adaption: end-to-end reram crossbar non-ideal effect adaption for neural network mapping. In: Proceedings of the 56th Annual Design Automation Conference 2019, pp. 1–6 (2019)
5. Zilly, J.G., Srivastava, R.K., Koutník, J., Schmidhuber, J.: Recurrent highway networks. In: Proceedings of the 34th International Conference on Machine Learning-Volume 70. pp. 4189–4198. JMLR. org (2017)
6. Chen, C.Y., et al.: RRAM defect modeling and failure analysis based on march test and a novel squeeze-search scheme. IEEE Trans. Comput. **64**(1), 180–190 (2014)
7. Hu, K., Shuo, T., Shasha, G., Nan, L., Li, L., Wang, L.: Recurrent neural architecture search based on randomness-enhanced Tabu algorithm (2020, in press)
8. Cai, H., Zhu, L., Han, S.: Proxylessnas: direct neural architecture search on target task and hardware. arXiv preprint arXiv:1812.00332 (2018)

Generating Random Parameters in Feedforward Neural Networks with Random Hidden Nodes: Drawbacks of the Standard Method and How to Improve It

Grzegorz Dudek[✉][iD]

Electrical Engineering Faculty, Czestochowa University of Technology,
Czestochowa, Poland
dudek@el.pcz.czest.pl

Abstract. The standard method of generating random weights and biases in feedforward neural networks with random hidden nodes selects them both from the uniform distribution over the same fixed interval. In this work, we show the drawbacks of this approach and propose new methods of generating random parameters. These methods ensure the most nonlinear fragments of sigmoids, which are most useful in modeling target function nonlinearity, are kept in the input hypercube. A new method generating sigmoids with uniformly distributed slope angles demonstrated the best performance on the illustrative examples.

Keywords: Feedforward neural networks · Neural networks with random hidden nodes · Randomized learning algorithms

1 Introduction

Single-hidden-layer feedforward neural networks with random hidden nodes (FNNRHN) have become popular in recent years due to their fast learning speed, good generalization performance and ease of implementation. Additionally, these networks do not use a gradient descent method for learning, which is time consuming and sensitive to local minima of the error function (which is nonconvex in this case). In randomized learning, weights and biases of the hidden nodes are selected at random from any interval $[-u, u]$, and stay fixed. The optimization problem becomes convex and the output weights can be learned using a simple, scalable standard linear least-squares method [7]. The resulting FNN has a universal approximation capability when the random parameters are selected from a symmetric interval according to any continuous sampling distribution [5]. But how to select this interval and which distribution to use are open questions, and considered to be the most important research gaps in randomized learning [2,11].

Supported by Grant 2017/27/B/ST6/01804 from the National Science Centre, Poland.

H. Yang et al. (Eds.): ICONIP 2020, CCIS 1333, pp. 598–606, 2020.
https://doi.org/10.1007/978-3-030-63823-8_68

Typically, the hidden node weights and biases are both selected from a uniform distribution over the fixed interval, $[-1, 1]$, without scientific justification, regardless of the data, problem to be solved, and activation function type [8]. Some authors optimize the interval looking for u to ensure the best model performance [1,6,9,10]. Recently developed methods [3,4] propose more sophisticated approaches for generating random parameters, where the distribution of the activation functions in space is analyzed and their parameters are adjusted randomly to the data.

In this work we show the drawbacks of a standard method of random parameters generation and propose its modification. We treat the weights and biases separately due to their different functions. The biases are generated on the basis of the weights and points selected from the input space. The resulting sigmoids have their nonlinear fragments, which are most useful for modeling the target function (TF) fluctuations, inside the input hypercube. Moreover, we show how to generate the weights to produce sigmoids with the slope angles distributed uniformly.

2   Generating Sigmoids Inside the Input Hypercube

Let us consider an approximation problem of a single-variable TF of the form:

$$y(x) = \sin(20 \cdot \exp x) \cdot x^2 \tag{1}$$

To learn FNNRHN we create a training set Φ containing $N = 5000$ points (x_l, y_l), where $x_l \sim U(0, 1)$ and y_l are calculated from (1) and then distorted by adding noise $\xi \sim U(-0.2, 0.2)$. A test set of the same size is created in the same manner but without noise. The output is normalized in the range $[-1, 1]$.

Figure 1 shows the results of fitting when using FNNRHN with 100 sigmoid hidden nodes which weights and biases are selected from $U(-1, 1)$ and $U(-10, 10)$. The bottom charts show the hidden node sigmoids whose linear combination forms the function fitting data. This fitted function is shown as a solid line in the upper charts. As you can see from the figure, for $a, b \in [-1, 1]$ the sigmoids are flat and their distribution in the input interval $[0, 1]$ (shown as a grey field) does not correspond to the TF fluctuations. This results in a very weak fit. When $a, b \in [-10, 10]$, the sigmoids are steeper but many of them have their steepest fragments, which are around their inflection points, outside of the input interval. The saturated fragments of these sigmoids, which are in the input interval, are useless for modeling nonlinear TFs. So, many of the 100 sigmoids are wasted. From this simple example it can be concluded that to get a parsimonious flexible FNNRHN model, the sigmoids should be steep enough and their steepest fragments, around the inflection points, should be inside the input interval.

Let us analyze how the inflection points are distributed in space when the weights and biases are selected from a uniform distribution over the interval $[-u, u]$. The sigmoid value at its inflection point χ is 0.5, thus:

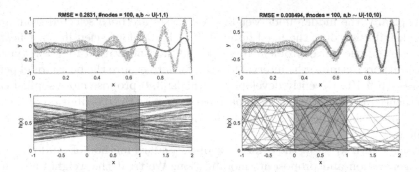

Fig. 1. TF (1) fitting: fitted curves and the sigmoids constructing them for $a, b \sim U(-1, 1)$ (left panel) and for $a, b \sim U(-10, 10)$ (right panel).

$$\frac{1}{1 + \exp(-(a \cdot \chi + b))} = 0.5 \tag{2}$$

From this equation we obtain:

$$\chi = -a/b \tag{3}$$

The distribution of the inflection point is a distribution of the ratio of two independent random variables having both the uniform distribution, $a, b \sim U(-u, u)$. In such a case, the probability density function (PDF) of χ is:

$$f(\chi) = \int_{-\infty}^{\infty} |a| f_A(a) f_B(a\chi) da = \begin{cases} \int_{-u}^{u} |a| f_A(a) f_B(a\chi) da & \text{for } |\chi| < 1 \\ \int_{-\frac{u}{|\chi|}}^{\frac{u}{|\chi|}} |a| f_A(a) f_B(a\chi) da & \text{for } |\chi| \geq 1 \end{cases}$$

$$= \begin{cases} \dfrac{1}{4} & \text{for } |\chi| < 1 \\ \dfrac{1}{4|\chi|^2} & \text{for } |\chi| \geq 1 \end{cases} \tag{4}$$

where f_A and f_B are the PDFs of weights and biases, respectively.

The left panel of Fig. 2 shows the PDF of χ. The same PDF can be obtained when $a \sim U(-u, u)$ and $b \sim U(0, u)$ (case sometimes found in the literature). As you can see from Fig. 2, the probability that the inflection point is inside the input interval (shown as a grey field) is 0.25. This means that most sigmoids have their steepest fragments, which are most useful for modeling TF fluctuations, outside of this interval. For the multivariable case, when we consider n-dimensional sigmoids, the situation improves – see the right panel of Fig. 2. For $n = 2$ almost 46% of sigmoids have their inflection points in the input rectangle. This percentage increases to more than 90% for $n \geq 7$.

To obtain an n-dimensional sigmoid with one of its inflection points χ inside the input hypercube $H = [x_{1,\min}, x_{1,\max}] \times ... \times [x_{n,\min}, x_{n,\max}]$, first, we generate

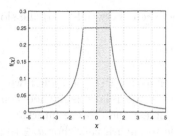 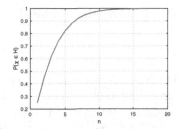

Fig. 2. PDF of χ when $a, b \sim U(-u, u)$ (left panel) and probability that χ belongs to $H = [0, 1]^n$ depending on n (right panel).

weights $\mathbf{a} = [a_1, ..., a_n]^T \subset \mathbb{R}^n$. Then we set the sigmoid in such a way that χ is at some point $\mathbf{x}^*$ from H. Thus:

$$h(\mathbf{x}^*) = \frac{1}{1 + \exp\left(-\left(\mathbf{a}^T \mathbf{x}^* + b\right)\right)} = 0.5 \tag{5}$$

From this equation we obtain:

$$b = -\mathbf{a}^T \mathbf{x}^* \tag{6}$$

Point $\mathbf{x}^* = [x_1^*, ..., x_n^*]$ can be selected as follows:

- this can be some point randomly selected from H: $x_j^* \sim U(x_{j,\min}, x_{j,\max})$, $j = 1, ..., n$. This method is suitable when the input points are evenly distributed in H.
- this can be some randomly selected training point: $\mathbf{x}^* = \mathbf{x}_\xi \in \Phi$, where $\xi \sim U\{1, ..., N\}$. This method distributes the sigmoids according to the data density, avoiding empty regions.
- this can be a prototype of the training point cluster: $\mathbf{x}^* = \mathbf{p}_i$, where $\mathbf{p}_i$ is a prototype of the i-th cluster. This method groups the training points into $m = \#$nodes clusters. For each sigmoid a different prototype is taken as $\mathbf{x}^*$.

3 Generating Sigmoids with Uniformly Distributed Slope Angles

It should be noted that weight a translates nonlinearly into the slope angle of a sigmoid. Let us analyze sigmoid S which has its inflection point χ in $x = 0$. In such a case $b = 0$. A derivative of S in $x = 0$ is equal to the tangent of its slope angle α in χ:

$$\tan \alpha = ah(x)\left(1 - h(x)\right) = \frac{a}{1 + \exp(-(a \cdot 0 + 0))}\left(1 - \frac{1}{1 + \exp(-(a \cdot 0 + 0))}\right) \tag{7}$$

From (7) we obtain the relationship between the weight and the slope angle:

$$\alpha = \arctan \frac{a}{4} \tag{8}$$

This relationship is depicted in Fig. 3 as well as the PDF of α when weights a are generated from different intervals. Note that the relationship between a and α is highly nonlinear. Interval $[-1, 1]$ for a corresponds to the interval $[-14°, 14°]$ for α, so only flat sigmoids are obtainable in such a case. For $a \in [-10, 10]$ we obtain $\alpha \in [-68.2°, 68.2°]$, and for $a \in [-100, 100]$ we obtain $\alpha \in [-87.7°, 87.7°]$. For narrow intervals for a, such as $[-1, 1]$, the distribution of α is similar to a uniform one. When the interval for a is extended, the shape of PDF of α changes – larger angles, near the bounds, are more probable than smaller ones. When $a \in [-100, 100]$, more than 77% of sigmoids are inclined at an angle greater than $80°$, so they are very steep. In such a case, there is a real threat of overfitting.

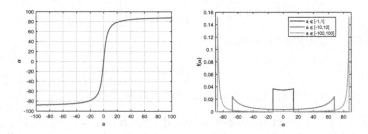

Fig. 3. Relationship between a and α (left panel) and PDF of α for different intervals for a (right panel).

To generate sigmoids with uniformly distributed slope angles, first we generate $|\alpha| \sim U(\alpha_{min}, \alpha_{max})$ individually for them, where $\alpha_{min} \in (0°, 90°)$ and $\alpha_{max} \in (\alpha_{min}, 90°)$. The border angles, α_{min} and α_{max}, can both be adjusted to the problem being solved. For highly nonlinear TFs, with strong fluctuations, only α_{min} can be adjusted, keeping $\alpha_{max} = 90°$. Having the angles, we calculate the weights from (8):

$$a = 4 \tan \alpha \tag{9}$$

For the multivariable case, we generate all n weights in this way, independently for each of m sigmoids. This ensures random slopes (between α_{min} and α_{max}) for the multidimensional sigmoids in each of n directions.

The proposed methods of generating random parameters of the hidden nodes are summarized in Algorithm 1. In this algorithm weights a can be generated randomly from $U(-u, u)$ or optionally, to ensure uniform distribution of the sigmoid slope angles, they can be determined based on the slope angles generated randomly from $U(\alpha_{min}, \alpha_{max})$. The bounds: u, α_{min} and α_{max} should be selected in cross-validation.

Algorithm 1. Generating Random Parameters of FNNRHN

Input:

Number of hidden nodes m

Number of inputs n

Bounds for weights, $u \in \mathbb{R}^+$, or optionally bounds for slope angles, $\alpha_{\min} \in (0°, 90°)$ and $\alpha_{\max} \in (\alpha_{\min}, 90°)$

Set of m points $\mathbf{x}^* \in H$: $\{\mathbf{x}_1^*, ..., \mathbf{x}_m^*\}$

Output:

$$\text{Weights } \mathbf{A} = \begin{bmatrix} a_{1,1} & \cdots & a_{m,1} \\ \vdots & \ddots & \vdots \\ a_{1,n} & \cdots & a_{m,n} \end{bmatrix}, \quad \text{biases } \mathbf{b} = [b_1, \ldots, b_m]$$

Procedure:

for $i = 1$ **to** m **do**

  for $j = 1$ **to** n **do**

    Choose randomly $a_{i,j} \sim U(-u, u)$ or optionally

    choose randomly $\alpha_{i,j} \sim U(\alpha_{\min}, \alpha_{\max})$ and calculate

$$a_{i,j} = (-1)^q \cdot 4 \tan \alpha_{i,j}, \text{ where } q \sim U\{0, 1\}$$

  end for

  Calculate $b_i = -\mathbf{a}_i^T \mathbf{x}_i^*$

end for

---

4   Simulation Study

The results of TF (1) fitting when using the proposed method is shown in Fig. 4. In this case the weights were selected from $U(-10, 10)$ and biases were determined according to (8). As you can see from this figure, all sigmoids have their inflection points inside H. The number of hidden nodes to achieve $RMSE = 0.0084$ is 35. To obtain a similar level of error we need over 60 nodes when using the standard method for generating the parameters.

The following experiments concern multivariable function fitting. TF in this case is defined as:

$$g(\mathbf{x}) = \sum_{j=1}^{n} \sin(20 \cdot \exp x_j) \cdot x_j^2 \tag{10}$$

TF (10) is depicted in the upper left panel of Fig. 5. The training set contains N points $(\mathbf{x}_l, y_l)$, where $x_{l,j} \sim U(0, 1)$ and y_l are calculated from (10), then normalized in the range $[-1, 1]$ and distorted by adding noise $\xi \sim U(-0.2, 0.2)$. A test set of the same size is created in the same manner but without noise.

The experiments were carried out for $n = 2$ ($N = 5000$), $n = 5$ ($N = 20000$) and $n = 10$ ($N = 50000$), using:

- SM – the standard method of generating both weights and biases from $U(-u, u)$,

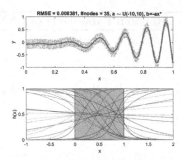

Fig. 4. TF (1) fitting: fitted curve and the sigmoids constructing it for the proposed method.

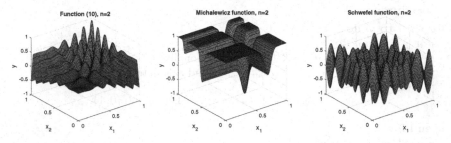

Fig. 5. Target functions.

- PMu – the proposed method of generating weights from $U(-u, u)$ and biases according to (8),
- PMα – the proposed method of generating slope angles from $U(\alpha_{min}, 90°)$, then calculating weights from (9), and biases from (8).

Figure 6 shows the mean test errors over 100 trials for different node numbers. For each node number the optimal value of u or α_{min} was selected from $u \in \{1, 2, ..., 10, 20, 50, 100\}$ and $\alpha_{min} \in \{0°, 10°, ..., 80°\}$, respectively. As you can see from Fig. 6, PMα in all cases leads to the best results. For $n = 2$ it needs less nodes to get a lower error (0.0352) than PMu and SM. Interestingly, for higher dimensions, using too many nodes leads to an increase in the error for SM and PMu. This can be related to the overfitting caused by the steep nodes generated by the standard method. In the same time, for PMα, where the node slope angles are distributed uniformly, a decrease in the error is observed.

Similar experiments were performed using the following highly nonlinear TFs:

- Michalewicz function:

$$g(\mathbf{x}) = -\sum_{i=1}^{n} \sin(x_i) \sin^{2m}\left(\frac{ix_i^2}{\pi}\right), \text{where } m = 10, x_i \in [0, \pi] \qquad (11)$$

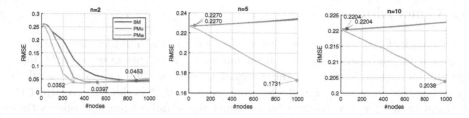

Fig. 6. RMSE depending on the number of nodes for function (10).

– Schwefel function:

$$g(\mathbf{x}) = 418.9829n - \sum_{i=1}^{n} x_i \sin(\sqrt{|x_i|}), \text{where } x_i \in [-500, 500] \quad (12)$$

These TFs after normalization in the range $[0,1]$ for all x_i and $[-1,1]$ for y are shown in Fig. 5. The training and test points are generated in the same way as for TF (10) and the training points are distorted by adding noise $\xi \sim U(-0.2, 0.2)$.

Figures 7 and 8 show the mean test RMSE over 100 trials for different methods of generating random parameters, different number on nodes, and $n = 2$, 5 or 10. Note that PMα in all cases leads to the best results.

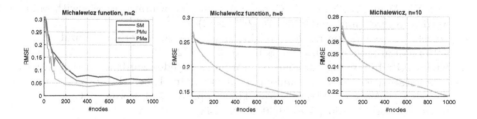

Fig. 7. RMSE depending on the number of nodes for Michalewicz function.

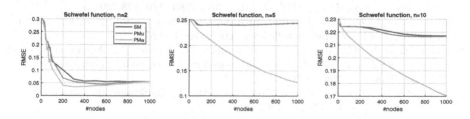

Fig. 8. RMSE depending on the number of nodes for Schwefel function.

5   Conclusion

A drawback of the standard method of generating random hidden nodes in FNNs is that many sigmoids have their most nonlinear fragments outside of the input hypercube, especially for low-dimensional cases. So, they cannot be used for modeling the target function fluctuations. Moreover, it is difficult to adjust the optimal values for weights and biases when the standard method selects these both parameters from the same interval.

In this work, we propose methods of generating random parameters which ensure that all the sigmoids have their steepest fragments inside the input hypercube. In addition, we show how to determine the weights to ensure the sigmoids have uniformly distributed slope angles. This prevents overfitting which can happen when weights are generated in a standard way, especially for highly nonlinear target functions. The proposed methods treat weights and biases separately due to their different functions. The weights are determined first and then biases are determined on the basis of weights and data distribution. The basic conclusions of this work can serve as general guidelines for designing FNNs with random hidden nodes for regression.

References

1. Cao, F., Wang, D., Zhu, H., Wang, Y.: An iterative learning algorithm for feedforward neural networks with random weights. Inf. Sci. **328**, 546–557 (2016)
2. Cao, W., Wang, X., Ming, Z., Gao, J.: A review on neural networks with random weights. Neurocomputing **275**, 278–287 (2018)
3. Dudek, G.: Generating random weights and biases in feedforward neural networks with random hidden nodes. Inf. Sci. **481**, 33–56 (2019)
4. Dudek, G.: Improving randomized learning of feedforward neural networks by appropriate generation of random parameters. In: Rojas, I., Joya, G., Catala, A. (eds.) IWANN 2019. LNCS, vol. 11506, pp. 517–530. Springer, Cham (2019). https://doi.org/10.1007/978-3-030-20521-8_43
5. Husmeier, D.: Random vector functional link (RVFL) networks. In: Husmeier, D. (ed.) Neural Networks for Conditional Probability Estimation: Forecasting Beyond Point Predictions, pp. 87–97. Springer, London (1999). https://doi.org/10.1007/978-1-4471-0847-4_6
6. Li, M., Wang, D.: Insights into randomized algorithms for neural networks: practical issues and common pitfalls. Inf. Sci. **382–383**, 170–178 (2017)
7. Principe, J., Chen, B.: Universal approximation with convex optimization: gimmick or reality? IEEE Comput. Intell. Mag. **10**(2), 68–77 (2015)
8. Scardapane, S., Comminiello, D., Scarpiniti, M., Uncini, A.: A semi-supervised random vector functional-link network based on the transductive framework. Inf. Sci. **364–365**, 156–166 (2016)
9. Wang, D., Li, M.: Stochastic configuration networks: fundamentals and algorithms. IEEE Trans. Cybern. **47**(10), 3466–3479 (2017)
10. Zhang, L., Suganthan, P.: A comprehensive evaluation of random vector functional link networks. Inf. Sci. **367–368**, 1094–1105 (2016)
11. Zhang, L., Suganthan, P.: A survey of randomized algorithms for training neural networks. Inf. Sci. **364–365**, 146–155 (2016)

Image Captioning Algorithm Based on Sufficient Visual Information and Text Information

Yongqiang Zhao, Yuan Rao$^{(\boxtimes)}$, Lianwei Wu, and Cong Feng

Xi'an Jiaotong University, Xi'an 710049, China
`yongqiang1210@stu.xjtu.edu.cn, yuanrao@163.com`

Abstract. Most existing attention-based methods on image captioning focus on the current visual information and text information at each step to generate the next word, without considering the coherence between the visual information and the text information itself. We propose sufficient visual information (SVI) module to supplement the existing visual information contained in the network, and propose sufficient text information (STI) module to predict more text Words to supplement the text information contained in the network. Sufficient visual information module embed the attention value from the past two steps into the current attention to adapt to human visual coherence. Sufficient text information module can predict the next three words in one step, and jointly use their probabilities for inference. Finally, this paper combines these two modules to form an image captioning algorithm based on sufficient visual information and text information model (SVITI) to further integrate existing visual information and future text information in the network, thereby improving the image captioning performance of the model. These three methods are used in the classic image captioning algorithm, and have achieved achieve significant performance improvement compared to the latest method on the MS COCO dataset.

Keywords: Image captioning · Sufficient visual information · Sufficient text information

1 Introduction

The purpose of image captioning is to generate the corresponding text captioning sentence from the visual content of the image. Image captioning is a difficult task. First, it needs to understand the feature information contained in the image well, and it needs to efficiently extract the salient feature information contained in the image to apply to the text generation content. Second, it needs to use the language model identifies specific information from the extracted visual features and generates corresponding captioning sentences.

In the past few years, researchers have proposed many deep learning-based "encoding-decoding" models [1,2] to solve this problem. Among them, the

© Springer Nature Switzerland AG 2020
H. Yang et al. (Eds.): ICONIP 2020, CCIS 1333, pp. 607–615, 2020.
https://doi.org/10.1007/978-3-030-63823-8_69

encoder based on convolutional neural network is responsible for extracting visual feature information from the image. The decoder is responsible for generating the corresponding text captioning sentence by using the existing visual feature information. The Show, Attend and Tell algorithm introduces the attention mechanism to image captioning tasks for the first time. The algorithm shows a huge improvement in all evaluation indicators. The attention module focuses on establishing a connection between the current image feature information and the corresponding word. Although the attention module in the decoder can provide accurate and effective visual information for text generation, the existing attention methods only take the hidden state h_t of the current word as input and calculate only for the output result h_{t+1}, this attention mechanism ignores the visual correlation between adjacent words. At the same time, the words in the captioning sentence of the existing image captioning algorithm are generated one by one, and the predicted word y'_{t+1} is highly dependent on the previous word y_t, which can easily bring cumulative errors in the final generated text. In order to solve the above problems, we propose an image captioning algorithm based on sufficient visual information and text information to make full use of the visual and text information contained in the image captioning model, thereby improving the overall performance of the image captioning model.

2   Relate Work

So far, many deep learning image captioning algorithms based on the "encoding-decoding" framework [3,4] have been proposed. Oriol [5] first proposed the Show and Tell algorithm, which uses a pre-trained CNN to encode image information into feature vectors, and at the same time decodes the feature vectors as input to the LSTM to obtain corresponding captioning sentences. Mao [6] associate the feature vector of the image with each word in order to retain visual information for the words generated later. Lisa [7] separated the first language information from the LSTM language and used it only at the logistic regression layer. Xu [8] introduced the attention mechanism to the image captioning task for the first time, and initialized the hidden state of LSTM using visual feature vectors. It turns out that the attention mechanism has made great progress in image captioning, and has been applied to almost all the latest image captioning algorithms.

Attention-based image captioning algorithms usually need to use pre-trained CNN models on additional datasets to extract the visual features of the image. With the emergence of a new data set Visual Genome [9], detection-based encoders can more efficiently extract the visual features of images. Although the existing related algorithms [10] have significantly improved the performance of image captioning algorithms, all these efforts have focused on embedding more information into the encoded features and neglecting the relevance of visual attention. A visual information module that fully considers the effect of previous attention vectors on the current attention vector.

In addition to the attention mechanism, solutions to cumulative errors also play an important role in image captioning. Samy [11] proposed scheduling sampling for RNN sequence prediction, which uses the sampled y_t' instead of the true y_t during the training phase, it can reduce the cumulative error caused by the maximum sampling. Chen [12] introduced an automatic reconstruction network to regulate transitions between adjacent hidden states. All these methods still stay in the verbatim generation process and do not consider how to improve the prediction process to reduce the cumulative error caused by the maximum sampling. Therefore, we make predictions during both the training and testing phases, and actively use future information to adjust the current selection, so that we can make fuller use of textual information in the network and generate image captioning sentences more efficiently.

3   Method

3.1   Sufficient Visual Information Module

The conventional attention module uses the attention function $f_{att}(V, h_t)$ to calculate the weighted average vector att_t. The attention mechanism usually connects the calculated att_t directly with h_t to predict the next word y_{t+1}'. However, this attention mechanism does not have visual coherence, att_t cannot be used in subsequent predictions. Therefore, we propose a sufficient visual information module, which can take the existing attention results into account and make full use of the visual information in the network. As shown in Fig. 1. We introduce att_{t-1} and att_{t-2} and concatenate them with the current hidden state h_t as the input of f_{att}. The new att_t is expressed as:

$$att_t = f_{att}(V, h_t * att_{t-1} * att_{t-2}) \tag{1}$$

where * means concatenation, $h_t * att_{t-1} * att_{t-2}$ can be expressed as H_t. This paper uses H_t to distinguish the importance of different feature vectors v_i. The weight calculation formula is as follows:

$$u_{i,t} = w_u tanh(W_{vu}v_i + W_{hu}H_t) \tag{2}$$

where W_{vu}, W_{hu} and w_u are parameters in f_{att}, $\alpha_t = softmax(u_t)$, $\alpha_t = \{\alpha_{1,t}, \alpha_{2,t}, ..., \alpha_{k,t}\} \in R^k$ is a k-dimensional vector, The total is 1. The final attention calculation formula is $att_t = \sum_{i=1}^{k} \alpha_{i,t}v_i$. It is worth noting that we consider att_{t-1} and att_{t-2} as areas that have participated in the attention mechanism and use them for current attention generation.

3.2   Sufficient Text Information Module

In the prediction stage, the prediction result y_{t+1}' largely depends on y_t'. An incorrect sampling result will generate a cumulative error during the sequence generation process. Therefore, we have proposed a sufficient text information

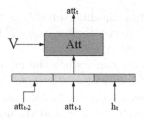

Fig. 1. Sufficient visual information module

module, using multiple prediction methods of y'_{t+1}, y'_{t+2}, and y'_{t+3} to ease the problem.

The input information in the sufficient text information module is the hidden state h_t^1 and the visual feature V. We use the attention module to obtain att_t^1 and enter them together in LSTM2. The specific information is shown in Fig. 2. Here we represent the attention function as f_{att}, the mathematical operation of LSTM2 as F2, and the series operation as *, then the calculation formula of h_t^2 is as follows:

$$h_t^2 = f_{att}(h_t^1 * att_t^1 h_{t-1}^2) \tag{3}$$

where $att_t^1 = f_{att}(V, h_t^1)$, h_t^2 is the hidden state of LSTM2 output. Usually, h_t^2 is input to the logistic regression layer and the probability p_{t2} of y'_{t+1} is obtained. We represent the logistic regression layer of p_t^2 as logit1 and calculate p_t^2:

$$p_t^2 = softmax(logit1(h_t^2)) \tag{4}$$

As the training progresses, h_t^2 will get more accurate information to generate the word y_{t+1}, which provides us with sufficient information support. So we treat h_t^2 as a special input of y_{t+1}, and we can predict the next word by historical information and h_t^2. As shown in Fig. 2, h_t^2 also passes the attention module (Att) and LSTM2 to predicts h_t^3. The same color indicates that the attention module and LSTM2 use the same operation as h_t^1. The main difference from the original method is that the hidden state of LSTM2 is updated to h_t^2, while h_{t-1}^2 is used for h_t^1, and then h_t^3 is generated by:

$$h_t^3 = F_2(h_t^2 * att_t^2, h_t^2) \tag{5}$$

where $att_t^2 = f_{att}(V, h_t^2)$, Next, connect h_t^3 to another logistic regression layer logit2 to predict the probability p_t^3 of y'_{t+2}. The specific formula is:

$$p_t^3 = softmax(logit2(h_t^3)) \tag{6}$$

Similarly, we use the method of generating y'_{t+2} to generate y'_{t+3}, and its corresponding hidden state h_t^4 and probability p_t^4, The specific information is shown in Fig. 2. The specific formula is as follows: In the training phase with cross entropy loss, a T-sufficient text information module is executed, where T represents the length of the words in the captioning sentence. This process will generate three prediction sequences: $Y^{1'} = \{y_1^{1'}, y_2^{1'}, ..., y_T^{1'}, EOS\}$, and $Y^{2'} = \{y_2^{2'}, y_3^{2'}, ..., y_T^{2'},$ EOS, EOS\}$ and $Y^{3'} = \{y_3^{3'}, ..., y_T^{3'}, EOS, EOS, EOS\}$, where $Y1'$ corresponds to h_t^2, $Y2'$ corresponds to h_t^3, $Y3'$ corresponds to h_t^4, EOS represents the end of the training and testing process. The input in the training phase usually starts with a zero vector sentence, and the prediction sequence ends with an EOS sentence. h_t^3 depends on h_t^2, so there is no $y_1^{2'}$ in $Y^{2'}$, h_t^4 depends on h_t^3, so there is no $y_1^{3'}$ in $Y^{3'}$. When h_t^2 yields EOS, we also give up the last EOS in $Y^{2'}$. Similarly, we also give up the last EOS in $Y^{3'}$. We define the loss as:

$$loss_1 = -\frac{1}{T} \sum_{t=1}^{T} log(p_t^2(y_t|y_{1:t-1})) \tag{7}$$

$$loss_2 = -\frac{1}{T-1} \sum_{t=2}^{T} log(p_t^3(y_t|y_{1:t-2})) \tag{8}$$

$$loss_3 = -\frac{1}{T-2} \sum_{t=3}^{T} log(p_t^4(y_t|y_{1:t-3})) \tag{9}$$

$$loss = loss_1 + loss_2 + loss_3 \tag{10}$$

The loss treats $Y^{1'}$, $Y^{2'}$, and $Y^{3'}$ equally, so that the model can accurately predict y'_{t+1}, y'_{t+2} and y'_{t+3}. To take advantage of this, we combine the predicted probabilities of y'_{t+1}, y'_{t+2}, and y'_{t+3} by $p'_t = p_t^2 + \lambda_1 p_{t-1}^3 + \lambda_2 p_{t-2}^4$, Where p_t^2 is calculated from h_t^2, p_{t-1}^3 is calculated from h_{t-1}^3, and p_{t-2}^4 is calculated from h_{t-2}^4 It is obtained that λ_1 and λ_2 are trade-off coefficients for balancing p_t^2, p_{t-1}^3, and p_{t-2}^4. During training, p_t^2, p_{t-1}^3, and p_{t-2}^4 all improve the authenticity of y_{t+1}, thereby effectively reducing the accumulation due to incorrect sampling error.

3.3   Sufficient Visual and Textual Information Model

Sufficient visual information module takes the first two layers of attention as input, which can improve the visual information contained in the model. Sufficient text information module makes full use of the hidden state and also predicts the next three words at a time, which can improve the text information contained in the model. We combine these two modules together, and only need to keep three attention results for the next time step in one time step (att_t^1, att_t^2, and att_t^3), As shown in Fig. 3. our model can more accurately predict the next word based on sufficient visual and textual information, thereby significantly improving the image captioning effect of the model.

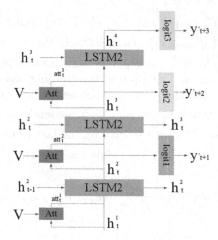

Fig. 2. Sufficient text information module

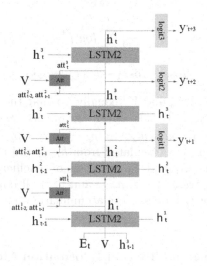

Fig. 3. Sufficient visual and textual information model

4   Experiments

4.1   Experimental Details

In the encoding phase, we use Bottom-up and Top-down as the basic model, and use the detection vectors it proposes as features. Our decoding phase also uses the Bottom-up and Top-down attention model as the basic model. In order to make a fair comparison with existing related algorithms, we directly use the same hyperparameters proposed in Bottom-up and Top-down.

4.2 Experimental Results

1) Selection of Parameter in the Model

In STI model and SVITI model, we combine the three generated sequences with the trade-off parameters λ_1 and λ_2 for model selection. During the training process, we noticed that the convergence loss of $Y^{2'}$ is slightly larger than the convergence loss of $Y^{1'}$, and the convergence loss of $Y^{3'}$ is slightly larger than $Y^{2'}$. The convergence loss of λ_1 increases from 0 to 1 and gradually increases the importance of $Y^{2'}$, and λ_2 increases from 0 to 1 and gradually increases the importance of $Y^{3'}$. In the experiment, we use the cluster search algorithm to sample the output sequence, which can effectively cover the best words in the three sequences, and set the values of λ_1 and λ_2 to less than 1. Table 1 shows the experimental results of STI model and SVITI model under the condition of $\lambda_2 = 0$. Table 2 shows the result under the optimal value of λ_1.

The results in Table 1 show that both the STI model and the SVITI model achieve the best performance when $\lambda_1 = 0.5$. This is reasonable, because if λ_1 is

Table 1. Comparison of performance results between STI model and SVITI model at different λ_1 values when $\lambda_2 = 0$

STI Model/SVITI Model					
λ_1	B-1	B-4	M	R	C	S
0.1	76.4/76.6	36.2/36.6	27.6/27.8	56.6/56.9	112.5/113.7	20.6/20.7
0.3	76.8/76.8	36.5/36.8	27.6/27.8	56.8/57.0	113.1/114.0	20.6/20.7
0.4	76.9/77.1	36.5/36.9	27.6/27.8	56.9/57.1	113.4/114.1	20.7/20.8
0.5	76.9/77.1	36.6/37.0	27.7/27.8	57.0/57.2	113.7/114.2	20.8/20.9
0.6	77.0/77.0	36.6/36.7	27.6/27.8	57.0/57.1	113.6/114.2	20.8/20.8
0.7	77.1/77.1	36.6/36.6	27.6/27.7	56.9/57.0	113.5/114.1	20.7/20.8
0.9	77.3/77.2	36.5/36.5	27.5/27.7	56.9/56.9	113.3/113.8	20.7/20.8

Table 2. Comparison of performance results between SVI model and SVITI model under different values of λ_2 when $\lambda_1 = 0.5$

STI Model/SVITI Model					
λ_1	B-1	B-4	M	R	C	S
0.1	76.6/76.8	36.4/36.8	27.7/27.8	56.7/57.0	112.9/114.1	20.7/20.7
0.3	76.9/76.9	36.6/37.0	27.7/27.9	57.0/57.0	113.6/114.2	20.7/20.8
0.4	77.1/77.4	36.8/37.1	27.9/28.0	57.2/57.3	114.0/114.4	20.0/21.1
0.5	77.1/77.3	36.7/37.0	27.8/27.9	57.1/57.2	113.9/114.3	20.9/20.0
0.6	77.1/77.3	36.6/36.9	27.8/27.9	57.1/57.1	113.8/114.1	20.8/20.9
0.7	77.3/77.3	36.6/36.8	27.7/27.8	57.1/57.0	113.8/114.0	20.8/20.9
0.9	77.5/77.4	36.6/36.7	27.7/27.7	57.0/56.9	113.6/113.9	20.8/20.9

too small, the sequence $Y^{2'}$ may not work on the final sampling. On the contrary, if λ_1 is too large, the sequence $Y^{2'}$ may eventually be sampled. The effect is too large, and the training loss shows that $Y^{1'}$ converges slightly better than $Y^{2'}$, so we finally set λ_1 to 0.5. The results in Table 2 show that the STI model and the SVITI model achieve the best experimental results at $\lambda_1 = 0.5$ and $\lambda_2 = 0.4$. The reason why λ_2 is smaller than λ_1 is that $Y^{3'}$ will affect the final result, but its effect is not as great as the $Y^{2'}$ sequence. Our STI model will generate three sequences of $Y^{1'}$, $Y^{2'}$, and $Y^{3'}$. In the training phase, we use λ_1 and λ_2 to balance the contributions of the three sequences.

2) Ablation Experiment

After determining the values of λ_1 and λ_2, we evaluated our method on the MS COCO dataset. SVI module, STI module, and SVITI model are independently trained and verified every 0.5 cycles. Finally, the weights that perform best on the validation data set are selected for testing, and the validation program also uses a cluster search method. All three models have undergone cross-entropy loss. The self-critical learning starts from the best weights stored during training and has cross-entropy loss. The experimental results of the three models are shown in Table 3. As can be seen from Table 3, these three methods want to significantly improve the baseline model. In the case of cross-entropy loss, the CIDEr score of the SVI model increased by 0.8%. The STI module showed better performance than the SVI module, the CIDEr score increased by 2.1%. The SVITI method combines the SVI method and the STI method. In the case of cross entropy loss, the CIDEr scores increased by 2.7%. The experimental results can fully prove the effectiveness of our models.

Table 3. Experimental results of SVI model, STI model and SVITI model on MS COCO dataset

Models	BLEU-1	BLEU-4	Meteor	ROUGE-L	CIDEr	SPICE
SCST:Att2in	–	31.3	26.0	54.3	101.3	–
SCST:Att2all	–	30.0	25.9	53.4	99.4	–
ARnet	74.0	33.5	26.1	54.6	103.4	19.0
Up-Down	77.2	36.2	27.0	56.4	113.5	20.3
Ours:SVI	77.5	36.8	27.7	57.1	114.4	20.9
Ours:STI	77.5	37.1	28.0	57.3	115.9	21.0
Ours:SVITI	77.9	37.5	28.2	57.6	116.6	21.4

5   Conclusion and Feature Works

We propose sufficient visual information methods to embed previous visual information, and propose sufficient text information methods to predict the next two words. Our SVI method inputs the attention values of the first two steps into the cur-rent attention module, which satisfies human visual coherence. The STI method can predict the next three words generated in one step. This method uses the continuity of language and integrates future information to satisfy the adequacy of text information. The SVITI method combines the SVI and STI methods, and can achieve significant performance improvement compared to the latest method on the MS COCO dataset. All three methods can be easily applied to most attention-based "encoding-decoding" image captioning models. In future work, we will further make full use of the visual and text information in the image captioning model, continuously improve the overall performance of the image captioning model, and tap their potential in the application field.

References

1. Yin, G., Sheng, L., Liu, B., et al.: Context and attribute grounded dense captioning. In: Proceedings of the IEEE Conference on Computer Vision and Pattern Recognition, pp. 6241–6250 (2019)
2. Yang, X., Tang, K., Zhang, H., et al.: Auto-encoding scene graphs for image captioning. In: Proceedings of the IEEE Conference on Computer Vision and Pattern Recognition, pp. 10685–10694 (2019)
3. Anderson, P., He, X., Buehler, C., et al.: Bottom-up and top-down attention for image captioning and visual question answering. In: Proceedings of the IEEE Conference on Computer Vision and Pattern Recognition, pp. 6077–6086 (2018)
4. Xu, Y., Wu, B., Shen, F., et al.: Exact adversarial attack to image captioning via structured output learning with latent variables. In: Proceedings of the IEEE Conference on Computer Vision and Pattern Recognition, pp. 4135–4144 (2019)
5. Vinyals, O., Toshev, A., Bengio, S., Erhan, D.: Show and tell: a neural image caption generator. In: CVPR, pp. 3156–3164 (2015)
6. Mao, J., Xu, W., Yang, Y., Wang, J., Huang, Z., Yuille, A.: Deep captioning with multimodal recurrent neural networks (M-RNN). In: ICLR (2015)
7. Hendricks, L.A., Venugopalan, S., Rohrbach, M., Mooney, R., Saenko, K., Darrell, T.: Deep compositional captioning: describing novel object categories without paired training data. In: CVPR, pp. 1–10 (2016)
8. Xu, K., et al.: Show, attend and tell: neural image caption generation with visual attention. In: ICML, pp. 2048–2057 (2015)
9. Krishna, R., et al.: Visual genome: connecting language and vision using crowd-sourced dense image annotations. IJCA 123(1), 32–73 (2017)
10. Anderson, P., He, X., Buehler, C., et al.: Bottom-up and top-down attention for image captioning and visual question answering. In: Proceedings of the IEEE Conference on Computer Vision and Pattern Recognition, 6077–6086 (2018)
11. Bengio, S., Vinyals, O., Jaitly, N., et al.: Scheduled sampling for sequence prediction with recurrent neural networks. In: Advances in Neural Information Processing Systems, pp. 1171–1179 (2015)
12. Chen, X., Ma, L., Jiang, W., et al.: Regularizing RNNs for caption generation by reconstructing the past with the present. In: Proceedings of the IEEE Conference on Computer Vision and Pattern Recognition, pp. 7995–8003 (2018)

Mutual Information Decay Curves and Hyper-parameter Grid Search Design for Recurrent Neural Architectures

Abhijit Mahalunkar$^{(\boxtimes)}$ and John D. Kelleher

ADAPT Research Center, Technological University Dublin, Dublin, Ireland
{abhijit.mahalunkar,john.d.kelleher}@tudublin.ie

Abstract. We present an approach to design the grid searches for hyper-parameter optimization for recurrent neural architectures. The basis for this approach is the use of mutual information to analyze long distance dependencies (LDDs) within a dataset. We also report a set of experiments that demonstrate how using this approach, we obtain state-of-the-art results for DilatedRNNs across a range of benchmark datasets.

Keywords: Long Distance Dependencies · Recurrent neural architectures · Hyper-parameter tuning · Vanishing gradients

1 Introduction

Recurrent neural networks trained using backpropagation through time suffer from exploding or vanishing gradients [1,7,8,10]. This problem presents a specific challenge in modeling sequential datasets which exhibit long distance dependencies (LDDs) [13]. LDDs describe an interaction between two (or more) elements in a sequence that are separated by an arbitrary number of positions. This results in the decay of statistical dependence of two points with increasing distance between them. Building recurrent neural architectures that are able to model LDDs is an open research problem and much of the current research on the topic focuses on designing new neural architectures. Early work in this direction proposed a hierarchical recurrent neural network that introduced several levels of state variables, working at different time scales [5]. This work inspired other architectures, such as DilatedRNN [3], Skip RNN [2], etc. Other well-known approaches to address this challenge are [4,6,9,14,16,17]. In this paper, we argue that a key step in designing recurrent neural architectures is to understand the decay of dependence in sequential data and to use this understanding to inform the setting of the relevant hyper-parameters of the architecture. In previous work, we developed an algorithm to compute and visualize the decay of dependence of the symbols within the dataset [12]. In this paper, we build on this previous work and show how this type of analysis can inform the selection of hyper-parameters of existing recurrent neural architectures. In this regard, we use DilatedRNNs [3] as a test model, and for several benchmark datasets, we

© Springer Nature Switzerland AG 2020
H. Yang et al. (Eds.): ICONIP 2020, CCIS 1333, pp. 616–624, 2020.
https://doi.org/10.1007/978-3-030-63823-8_70

study the decay of dependence of a dataset and then design a set of dilations tailored to that dataset. With this approach, we achieve better performance as compared to the technique mentioned in the original implementation [3].

2   Dilated Recurrent Neural Networks

In this paper, we demonstrate how the analysis of the decay of dependence is a useful source of information to guide the selection of hyper-parameters to model the sequential data. We have chosen DilatedRNNs [3] as test model for our experiments because of the relatively transparent relationship between some of the hyper-parameters of this architecture and the ability of the network to model LDDs. The DilatedRNN architecture is a multi-layer and cell-independent architecture characterized by multi-resolution dilated recurrent skip-connections. This alleviates the gradient problems and extends the range of temporal dependencies. Upon stacking multiple dilated recurrent layers with increasing skip-connections, these networks can learn temporal dependencies at different scales. DilatedRNN architecture and the dilations are described in [3]. The size of dilations per layer and the number of layers are supplied using the *dilations* hyper-parameter. This hyper-parameter controls the gradient flow and memory capacity of the DilatedRNNs. We hypothesize that to optimize the performance of a DilatedRNN on a dataset, the set of dilations should be tailored to match LDDs within the dataset. In particular: 1) the max dilation should match the span of LDDs present in the dataset (i.e. the dilation length should not extend to distances where there is low mutual information), 2) the increase in the size of dilation per layer should match the decay of dependence observed in the dataset (i.e. in regions where there is a rapid decay of dependence, there should be dense set of skip-connections capturing the dependence).

The process we propose for fitting the dilations hyper-parameter of these networks to a dataset is as follows: 1) plot the dependency decay curve [12], 2) design a grid search over the hyper-parameter space using the framework presented in this paper, 3) fit the model to the data and evaluate. To demonstrate this approach, we train DilatedRNNs on MNIST and Penn Treebank (PTB).

3   Interpreting Dependency Decay Curve to Inform Hyper-parameter Optimization

In [12], we proposed an algorithm to analyze the decay of dependence in sequential datasets. This analysis can be visualised by plotting this decay on a log-log axis, where the x-axis describes the distance d between two observations in the sequence and the y-axis describes the mutual information (MI) at that d (in *nats*). We call these plots dependency decay curves and this paper focuses on how the analysis of these plots can be used to guide hyper-parameter selection. The decay of dependence either follows exponential decay, indicating the absence of LDDs, or power-law decay, indicating the presence of LDDs. Furthermore, the influence of various phenomena on LDDs can lead to decay curve following: 1) power-law decay, 2) power-law decay with a periodicity present, or 3) broken power-law. A broken power-law is made up of multiple power-laws joined at inflection point. Figure 1 illustrates how these different types of decay are exhibited in an dependency decay curve plot. As dependency decay curves are plotted on a log-log axis a curve that follows a straight line represents a power-law decay (e.g. Fig. 1(a)).

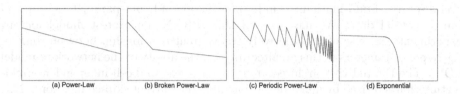

Fig. 1. Dependency decay curve framework which displays standard LDD curves

In the context of DilatedRNNs the best dilation hyper-parameters to model a dataset exhibiting power-law decay are: 1) max dilation should be equal to d where the dependency decay curve crosses $MI = 10^{-5}$ (this threshold is informed by [11] as MI below this is assumed to be noise); and 2) the set of dilations should be designed such that the density of skip-connections in a region should increase when the slope is high and decrease when it is low. The standard progression of dilations used for DilatedRNNs is $1, 2, 4, 8, \ldots$ and these dilations are a good guide for reasonable rates of dependency decay (similar to the slope in Fig. 1(a)). However, if the line gets steeper the spacing between the skip-connections should become smaller and denser e.g. $1, 2, 3, 4, 5, \ldots$. Figure 2 illustrates the design pattern we use to connect the slope of the decay of dependence to the density of the skip-connections in a DilatedRNN. In Fig. 2(a) and (b), we see two power-law decays in two plots. In each plot we have drawn a sequence of equidistant horizontal lines representing hidden layers. We use the density of the x-intercept of every horizontal line to inform the patterning of the skip-connections for every layer in the network.

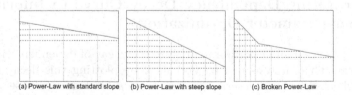

Fig. 2. Mapping set of dilations to dependency decay curve

Figure 1(b) is an dependency decay curve plot that exhibits a broken power-law [15]. The hyper-parameter selection for such plots follow the same rules as that of the power-law decay curve, with one major difference being that the presence of multiple power-laws will require different patterning of the dilations in different segments of the broken power-law in order to model the different rates of MI decay. Figure 2(c), shows that when the steeper power-law changes to a shallower power-law, the dilations become more sparse. Figure 1(c) is a dependency decay curve plot that is exhibiting a power-law decay with periodicity. The presence of periodicity within the decay indicates that the max dilation parameter should be set to the period of the MI peaks. The set of dilations can still follow the standard pattern for DilatedRNNs. An exponential decay involves a rapid decay in mutual information, such as that shown in Fig. 1(d). Such a rapid decay indicates the absence of LDDs. So in order to model such datasets, the max dilation should be set to where the dependency decay curve crosses the MI $= 10^{-5}$. It can follow the standard set of dilations of the DilatedRNNs.

4 Dependency Decay Curves of Benchmark Datasets

4.1 Sequential MNIST

Sequential MNIST is widely used to evaluate recurrent neural architectures. It contains 240000 training and 40000 test images. Each of these is 28×28 pixels in size, and each pixel can take one of 256 pixel values. In order to use them in a sequential task, the 2D images are converted into a 1D vector of 784 pixels by concatenating all the rows of the pixels. This transformation results in pixel dependencies which span up to approximately 28 pixels. These dependencies arise due to high correlation of a pixel with its neighboring pixels. The structure of the Sequential MNIST dataset is such that its dependency decay curve is likely to contain regular peaks and troughs. We plot the dependency decay curve of the unpermuted and permuted sequential MNIST datasets in Fig. 3(a).

Standard sequential MNIST exhibits high MI at $D = 1$ indicating strong dependencies at close proximity. The dependencies then decay as a function of power-law. Hence, in-order to fully capture these dependencies, the recurrent neural architectures should maintain gradients/attention across multiple timescales as a function of power-law to accurately model these dependencies. However, we see peaks of MI at intervals of 28 due to pixel dependencies. The regular peaks in the decay curve indicate that the span of the dependencies lie within $D \approx 28$.

We generated *permuted* versions of the sequential MNIST dataset with multiple seeds for use as a comparator with the unpermuted sequential MNIST. When we examine the dependency decay curves of permuted MNIST datasets, we observe that the dependencies are substantially less between close-by symbols (pixels in this case), e.g. for $D = 1$ the green, red and purple lines are much lower than the blue line. This is a result of permutations applied to the data which disrupt spatial dependencies. Another impact of this disruption is the relatively flat curve for $D < 300$ which indicates an absence of spatial dependencies. In-order to model these datasets that exhibit a relatively flat curve, the recurrent neural architectures requires uniform distribution of attention/gradients across all time scales. However, beyond $D > 300$, we observe exponential decay of dependence, where the value of MI falls below 10^{-5} indicating no further dependencies. This point ($D \approx 780$) indicates the span of the dependencies and the limit on the memory capacity of recurrent neural architectures.

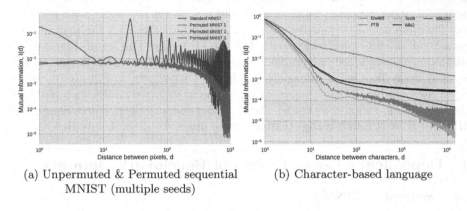

(a) Unpermuted & Permuted sequential   (b) Character-based language
MNIST (multiple seeds)

Fig. 3. Dependency decay curves

4.2   Character-Based Datasets

There are a number of natural language datasets that are frequently used to benchmark recurrent neural architectures, such as the Penn TreeBank (PTB), Wiki2, Wiki103, Text8 and Enwik8. These datasets can either be analysed at the word or character level. In this section we focus our analysis at the character level. Figure 3(b) shows the dependency decay curve of these character-based datasets. These plots follow a power-law decay function. Except Enwik8, which follows a single power-law decay, all the other datasets (PTB, Wiki2, Wiki103 and Text8) follow multiple *power-laws* with an inflection point[1]. The character-based datasets exhibit two distinct decay curves i) single power-law decay (Enwik8), and ii) broken power-law decay (the rest of the curves). The optimal hyper-parameters are selected based on the framework discussed in Sect. 3.

5   Optimising Hyper-parameters of Recurrent Neural Architectures

5.1   Experiments with Sequential MNIST

In this experiment, we trained DilatedRNNs with unpermuted and permuted sequential MNIST datasets in a classification task (classify digits 0–9 from their

---

[1] Enwik8 exhibits a single power-law due to the presence of XML code (strict markup grammar and long contextual dependencies). Consequently, the dependency decay curve of Enwik8 are different from the rest of the character-based datasets.

images). The original paper that introduced DilatedRNNs [3] used the same max dilation hyper-parameter for both of these datasets i.e. 256, and a standard set of dilations (i.e., $1, 2, 4, 8, \dots$). The best results reported by [3] for these two datasets were: unpermuted sequential MNIST 99.0/99.2 and permuted sequential MNIST 95.5/96.1. However, our analysis of these datasets has revealed different max dependencies across these dataset. For unpermuted sequential MNIST we identified a periodicity of 28 and so we expected the max dilation value to be near 28 to deliver better performance. In permuted sequential MNIST we identified that the dependencies extend up to 780 and so we would expect better performance by extending the max dilation up to this value.

Table 1. Results for sequential MNIST using GRU cells

# of layers	Set of dilations	Hidden per layer	Accuracy
4	$1, 2, 4, 8$	20/50	98.96/99.18
5	$1, 2, 4, 8, 16$	20/50	98.94/99.21
6	$1, 2, 4, 8, 16, 32$	20/50	**99.17/99.27**
7	$1, 2, 4, 8, 16, 32, 64$	20/50	99.05/99.25
8	$1, 2, 4, 8, 16, 32, 64, 128$	20/50	99.15/99.23
9	$1, 2, 4, 8, 16, 32, 64, 128, 256$	20/50	98.96/99.17

Table 2. Results for permuted sequential MNIST using RNN cells

# of layers	Set of dilations	Hidden per layer	Accuracy
7	$1, 2, 4, 8, 16, 32, 64$	20/50	95.04/95.94
8	$1, 2, 4, 8, 16, 32, 64, 128$	20/50	95.45/95.88
9	$1, 2, 4, 8, 16, 32, 64, 128, 256$	20/50	95.5/96.16
10	$1, 2, 4, 8, 16, 32, 64, 128, 256, 512$	20/50	95.62/96.4
11	$1, 2, 4, 8, 16, 32, 64, 128, 256, 512, 780$	20/50	**95.66/96.47**

To test these hypotheses we trained DilatedRNNs with various sets of dilations. To keep our results comparable with those reported in [3] the original code[2] was kept unchanged except for the max dilation hyper-parameter. The test results of these experiments are in Tables 1 and 2. For unpermuted task, the model delivered best performance for max dilation of 32. Focusing on the results of the permuted sequential MNIST, the best performance was delivered with the max dilation of 780. These results confirm that the best performance is obtained when the max dilation is similar to the span of the LDDs of a given dataset.

---

[2] https://github.com/code-terminator/DilatedRNN.

5.2   Experiments with Character-Based Datasets

In this experiment, we trained DilatedRNN with PTB dataset in a language modeling task. The standard evaluation metric of language models is perplexity and it is a measure of the confusion of the model when making predictions. The original DilatedRNNs paper [3] reported best performance on PTB with a perplexity of 1.27 using GRU cells and max dilation of 64. However, the original DilatedRNN implementations used for this task has not been released. Hence we used another implementation of DilatedRNN[3]. Having done multiple experiments with this new implementation, including using the same hyper-parameters as those reported in [3], we found that the perplexity was always higher than the original implementation. We attribute this to the fact that [3] does not report all the hyper-parameter settings they used and so we had to assume some of the hyper-parameters (other than the dilations) used for this task. The test perplexity results of these experiments are in Table 3.

Table 3. Results for character-based datasets (PTB) using GRU cells

Model #	# of layers	Set of dilations	Hidden per layer	# of parameters	Test perplexity (bpc)
1.	7	$1, 2, 4, 8, 16, 32, 64$	256	2660949	1.446
2.	8	$1, 2, 4, 8, 16, 32, 64, 128$	256	3055701	1.471
3.	12	$1, 2, 4, 8, 16, 32, 64, 128, 256, \ldots 512, 1024, 2048$	256	4634709	1.561
4.	7	$1, 2, 3, 4, 5, 6, 8$	256	2660949	1.416
5.	8	$1, 2, 4, 8, 16, 32, 73, 240$	256	3055701	1.456
6.	12	$1, 2, 3, 4, 5, 6, 8, 11, 18, 32, 73, 240$	256	4634709	**1.386**

Recall from Sect. 4.2, that the character-based PTB dataset exhibits a broken power-law dependency decay. Consequently, following the framework we presented, we expect that a model that has set of dilations that follow the pattern that we have proposed for broken power-laws (with different densities of connections on either side of the inflection point) should outperform a model that uses a standard set of dilations. This experiment was designed to test this hypothesis while controlling the model size. We designed six different model architectures (listed in Table 3), three using the standard dilations (model# 1, 2, and 3) and three using dilation patterns informed by the dependency decay curve analysis of PTB dataset (model# 4, 5, and 6). Furthermore, in designing these architectures we controlled for the effect of model size on performance by ensuring that for each of the 3 models whose dilations were fitted to the dependency decay curve there was an equivalent sized model in the set of models using the standard pattern of dilations. Following the analysis of the PTB dataset we observe the inflection point of the broken power-law decay to be ≈12. We designed one model (model# 4) with a dense set of dilations up to the inflection point and two using

---

[3] https://github.com/zalandoresearch/pytorch-dilated-rnn.

patterns of dilations that follow the broken power-law pattern. Of these two, one model (model# 5) used standard set of dilations up to the inflection point and sparse dilations beyond and the second model (model# 6) used the dilation patterns that we believe most closely fits the broken power-law dependence decay of PTB dataset. The results of these six models are listed in Table 2.

One finding from these experiments is that larger models do not always outperform smaller models, for example models 1 and 4 outperform models 2, 3, and 5. More relevantly, however, if we compare models of the same size but with different patterns of dilations i.e. comparing model 1 with 4, model 2 with 5, and model 3 with 6, we find that in each case the model that uses pattern of dilations suggested by our framework (models 4, 5, and 6) outperforms the corresponding standard dilations model (models 1, 2, and 3). Furthermore, the best overall performance is achieved by model 6 which uses a broken-power law pattern of dilations. The custom set of dilations used by model 6 maximizes it's memory capacity over the steeper region of the dependency decay curve before the inflection point by introducing dense dilations. However, beyond the inflection point the dilations are sparse allowing for longer dependencies to be modeled by using less memory capacity. We interpret these results as confirming that best model performance is obtained when the pattern of dilations is customized to fit the dependency decay curve of the dataset being modeled.

6   Discussion and Conclusion

In this paper, we have set out an approach to the design the hyper-parameter search space for recurrent neural architectures. The basis of this work is to use mutual information to analyse the dependency decay of a dataset. The dependency decay curve of a dataset is indicative of the presence of a specific dependency decay pattern in the dataset. For example, our analysis of sequential MNIST and character-based datasets indicate that the dependency decay of sequential MNIST is very different from character-based datasets. Understanding the properties of the underlying grammar that produces a sequence can aid in designing the grid-search space for the hyper-parameters to model a given dataset. In this work, we have used DilatedRNNs to illustrate our approach, and have demonstrated how customising the dilations to fit the dependency decay curve of a dataset improves the performance of the DilatedRNNs. However, we believe that the core idea of this approach can be more generally applied. Different neural architectures use different mechanisms to model LDDs, however these mechanisms have hyper-parameters that control how they function and we argue that it is useful to explicitly analyse the dependency decay curve of a dataset when selecting these hyper-parameters for the network.

Acknowledgments. The research is supported by TU Dublin Scholarship Award. This research is also partly supported by the ADAPT Research Centre, funded under the SFI Research Centres Programme (Grant 13/ RC/2106) and is co-funded under the European Regional Development Funds. We also gratefully acknowledge the support of NVIDIA Corporation with the donation of the Titan Xp GPU under NVIDIA GPU Grant used for this research.

References

1. Bengio, Y., Simard, P., Frasconi, P.: Learning long-term dependencies with gradient descent is difficult. IEEE Trans. Neural Netw. **5**(2), 157–166 (1994)
2. Campos, V., Jou, B., Giró-i Nieto, X., Torres, J., Chang, S.F.: Skip RNN: learning to skip state updates in recurrent neural networks. In: International Conference on Learning Representations (2018)
3. Chang, S., et al.: Dilated recurrent neural networks. Adv. Neural Inf. Process. Syst. **30**, 77–87 (2017)
4. Dai, Z., Yang, Z., Yang, Y., Carbonell, J., Le, Q., Salakhutdinov, R.: Transformer-XL: attentive language models beyond a fixed-length context. In: Proceedings of the 57th Annual Meeting of the Association for Computational Linguistics (2019)
5. El Hihi, S., Bengio, Y.: Hierarchical recurrent neural networks for long-term dependencies. In: Proceedings of the 8th International Conference on Neural Information Processing Systems, pp. 493–499. MIT Press, Cambridge (1995)
6. Graves, A., Wayne, G., Danihelka, I.: Neural Turing Machines. ArXiv e-prints, October 2014
7. Hochreiter, S.: Untersuchungen zu dynamischen neuronalen Netzen. Master's thesis, TU Munich (1991)
8. Hochreiter, S., Bengio, Y., Frasconi, P.: Gradient flow in recurrent nets: the difficulty of learning long-term dependencies. In: Kolen, J., Kremer, S. (eds.) Field Guide to Dynamical Recurrent Networks. IEEE Press (2001)
9. Hochreiter, S., Schmidhuber, J.: Long short-term memory. Neural Comput. **9**(8), 1735–1780 (1997)
10. Kelleher, J.D.: Deep Learning. MIT Press, Cambridge (2019)
11. Lin, H.W., Tegmark, M.: Critical behavior in physics and probabilistic formal languages. Entropy **19**(7), 299 (2017)
12. Mahalunkar, A., Kelleher, J.D.: Understanding recurrent neural architectures by analyzing and synthesizing long distance dependencies in benchmark sequential datasets. arXiv e-prints arXiv:1810.02966, October 2018
13. Mahalunkar, A., Kelleher, J.D.: Using regular languages to explore the representational capacity of recurrent neural architectures. In: Kůrková, V., Manolopoulos, Y., Hammer, B., Iliadis, L., Maglogiannis, I. (eds.) ICANN 2018. LNCS, vol. 11141, pp. 189–198. Springer, Cham (2018). https://doi.org/10.1007/978-3-030-01424-7_19
14. Merity, S., Xiong, C., Bradbury, J., Socher, R.: Pointer sentinel mixture models. CoRR abs/1609.07843 (2016). http://arxiv.org/abs/1609.07843
15. Rhoads, J.E.: The dynamics and light curves of beamed gamma-ray burst afterglows. Astrophys. J. **525**(2), 737–749 (1999)
16. Salton, G.D., Ross, R.J., Kelleher, J.D.: Attentive language models. In: Proceedings of the Eighth International Joint Conference on Natural Language Processing (Volume 1: Long Papers), pp. 441–450 (2017)
17. Vaswani, A., et al.: Attention is all you need. In: Guyon, I., et al. (eds.) Advances in Neural Information Processing Systems 30, pp. 5998–6008 (2017)

RCNN for Region of Interest Detection in Whole Slide Images

Anupiya Nugaliyadde[1(✉)], Kok Wai Wong[1], Jeremy Parry[1,2], Ferdous Sohel[1], Hamid Laga[1], Upeka V. Somaratne[1], Chris Yeomans[3], and Orchid Foster[3]

[1] Discipline of Information Technology, Mathematics and Statistics, Murdoch University, Perth, Western Australia
{a.nugaliyadde,k.wong}@murdoch.edu.au
[2] Western Diagnostic Pathology, Perth, Western Australia
[3] Pathwest Laboratory Medicine, Perth, Western Australia

Abstract. Digital pathology has attracted significant attention in recent years. Analysis of Whole Slide Images (WSIs) is challenging because they are very large, i.e., of Giga-pixel resolution. Identifying Regions of Interest (ROIs) is the first step for pathologists to analyse further the regions of diagnostic interest for cancer detection and other anomalies. In this paper, we investigate the use of RCNN, which is a deep machine learning technique, for detecting such ROIs only using a small number of labelled WSIs for training. For experimentation, we used real WSIs from a public hospital pathology service in Western Australia. We used 60 WSIs for training the RCNN model and another 12 WSIs for testing. The model was further tested on a new set of unseen WSIs. The results show that RCNN can be effectively used for ROI detection from WSIs.

Keywords: RCNN · Whole Slide Images · Region of Interest

1 Introduction

Medical image processing is a complex task which requires complex image processing approaches [1]. Medical images are larger and complex than many non-medical images used for image processing. However, often contain smaller variations in colour, hue and contours to an untrained human eye, making them challenging for computation because feature engineering is mostly based on general human perception of images [2]. Many image processing approaches have been applied for medical image processing for examples like X-Ray, magnetic, scopes, and thermal imaging [1,3]. Whole Slide Image (WSI)s have been used extensively in digital pathology [4]. However, WSI presents unique challenges when compared to X-ray, CT scans and other medical images. WSIs have high

This project is funded by a Research Translation Grant 2018 by the Department of Health, Western Australia.

H. Yang et al. (Eds.): ICONIP 2020, CCIS 1333, pp. 625–632, 2020.
https://doi.org/10.1007/978-3-030-63823-8_71

dimensions, show variation in stains between different WSIs, and often lacks label data, especially for ROI detection [5]. WSIs are very large, ranging from 3000 pixels × 4000 pixels to 55000 pixels × 60000 pixels, and the stains contrast between WSI can be substantial. Besides, WSIs often have a large area of background which are not of interest to pathologists [6]. Filtering out the background and the unwanted sections of WSI is an important step to assist pathologists in analysing the important regions of the image. The step can allow the pathologists to identify the Regions of Interest (ROI)s and perform more focused diagnosis using the identified ROIs [7]. The identification of ROIs is important and beneficial for further processing and analysis of images because it will act as a filter to pass only the ROIs to the pathologists, thus reducing the time spent on analyzing and processing of the images [8].

Segmentation on WSI to identify ROI is a common approach that has been developed over the last few years [9,10]. Most of the ROI detection methods are unsupervised because the number of training data is limited to WSI ROI detection [11]. Segmentation requires the image to have similar variations throughout each WSI. However, in real-world WSIs, the staining is different and therefore, the segmentation parameters change from WSI to WSI [9]. Machine learning approaches require the use of feature engineering to facilitate identification tasks. However, most features in WSI are not easily visible or explainable by the experts. Therefore, a deep learning approach which learns features automatically show high potential [4,13]. Convolutional Neural Network (CNN)s have a high potential in learning features without feature engineering in images [4]. RCNN has emerged as a successful approach to learn and identify ROIs in images of many application domains [14,15]. However, the variations in colour, hue and contour in most images are much higher and more apparent than WSI [5,16]. Furthermore, most applications in other domains using RCNN to identify ROIs require the use of a large number of training data for learning [17]. The purpose of this paper is to investigate the use of RCNN for ROI detection by using a small number of labelled WSIs for training.

The ROI selected for this study were Germinal Centres (GC) within normal and benign lymph nodes. GC are organized collections of activated lymphocytes and other immune cells that develop within follicles in response to immune stimulation. Before becoming stimulated, follicles lack GC and are called primary follicles. After stimulation, they develop GC and are called secondary follicles. Distinguishing primary and secondary follicles can be challenging for a pathologist, who may have to revert to using special antibody stains such as BCL6, which highlights key GC cells. This study aimed to develop and test an algorithm that can support a pathologist in identifying GC without using special stains. The real WSIs of patients used in this study is provided by a public hospital pathology service in Western Australia, and pathologists validate results.

2   Methodology

The RCNN proposed by Girshick et al. was used for the experiment [14]. Figure 1 provided an illustration of the RCNN used for ROI detection in WSI. First, the large WSIs were patched, and the patches were passed through selective search to identify regions of proposals as described more in Sect. 2.1. The candidate region proposals were moved onto a CNN. VGG16 pre-trained on ImageNet was used for the CNN because it is capable of capturing the basic features such as colour, hue, contours, etc. of any image. This feature extraction supports a model in learning features from a limited number of training data because the base of the feature extracted is already learnt, and only fine-tuning of the model is required. The CNN extracts the features (colour, hue and con-tours) of candidate regions, and the last layer is a dense layer which classifies the ROI and background. The proposed candidate regions and the ground truth calculate the intersection over union and label them. The model consists of two sections, which are sequentially connected to each other. The first section comprises of independent region proposal, which is used to extract the regions of an image. The second section is a large CNN, which extracts feature vectors and uses the feature vectors to classify the regions. The RCNN model in this paper learns to classify two classes; ROI and background. Although the general architecture and structure of the RCNN were used, adjustments were made to improve the ROI detection in WSIs.

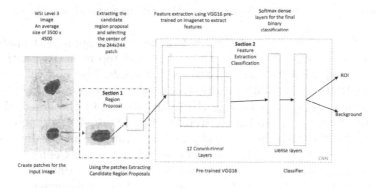

Fig. 1. Illustration of the flow of the RCNN method

2.1   Region Proposal

Region proposal was used to avoid selecting many regions as potential ROIs for feature extraction. In the model, the region proposal generates candidate region proposal areas irrespective of any category. The patches are passed through a selective search, which is used to identify the candidate region proposals. The selective search will generate initial sub-segmentation for the initial candidate region proposals after which the similar regions are combined recursively to create larger candidate region proposals using the greedy algorithm. Finally, the generated regions are used to create the final candidate region proposals to be used for feature extraction and classification, which is the CNN, as shown in Fig. 1.

2.2   Feature Extraction and Classification

Adjustment of the original RCNN in this paper focus on the feature extraction and classification layers. The candidate region proposals were passed to the CNN, and the CNN extracted 4096-dimensional features vector from each candidate proposal region. A 224 × 224 RGB image patch from the WSI was passed through 5 convolutional layers and two fully connected layers. The CNN used was based on the pre-trained VGG 16 model from ImageNet. The first 15 layers were frozen during the training process. The last-second layer was removed and replaced by a 2-unit softmax dense layer to predict the background and the ROIs. Adam optimizer was used with a learning rate of 0.0001. Categorical cross-entropy was used as the loss function. The final model had a total of 126,633,474 trainable parameters and 7,635,264 non-trainable parameters.

3   Experimentation and Results

In this paper, WSIs of patients from a public hospital pathology service in Western Australia are used in the study. We used 60 WSIs for training the RCNN model and another 12 WSIs for testing. The ROI that need to identify for this study were regions that could contain GC within normal and benign lymph nodes.

The first step of using the RCNN is to generate the appropriate patches. A sliding window which moved from left to right and top to bottom without any overlap was used to create patches of 244 × 244 pixels. These patches contained the marked ROIs by the pathologists. One of the objectives of this study was to find the best process of feeding the information into the designed RCNN model. Therefore, two experiments were set up. The first case, named as the Base Case, fed the entire patch (244 × 244) generated from the ROI into the RCNN to learn and predict. The second case, named as the Center Case, made use of the extracted version of the patch by taking 199 × 199 from the entire patch (244 × 244). The Center Case using 199 × 199 was selected after a trial had been performed to find the optimum centre patch size, in which 199 × 199 provided the best performance. The following summarizes the two cases shown in this paper:

1. Base Case RCNN: The model used the entire patch (244 × 244) from the ROI to learn and predict.
2. Center Case RCNN: The model used the centre patch of 199 × 199 patch extracted from the centre patch of 244 × 244 to learn and train the model.

Table 1 shows a comparison between the two different approaches of RCNN models that are used for the ROI detection based on the test data set (12 WSIs). Intersection Over Union (IOU) is used to compare the model's results [18]. The Center Case RCNN outperformed the Base Case RCNN model for ROIs identification. The same training and testing data were used for both the models. The improved results demonstrate that considering the centre of the patch can

Fig. 2. The comparison of the ROIs generated from Base Case (yellow), Centre Case (blue) and the ground truth marked by pathologist (red) of a testing WSI. (Color figure online)

support better ROI detection in WSIs used in the experiment. Figure 2 presents the comparison of the ROIs identified by the Base Case RCNN and the Centre Case RCNN with the ground truth ROI of a testing WSI.

Table 1. IOU comparison between the different RCNN models used for ROI detection

Base case RCNN	Centre case RCNN
0.61	0.92

4 Unseen Data Testing

After the RCNN model has been established and finalised from the previous experiment, the model was further tested on unseen data consist of 6 WSIs from the hospital. The 6 WSIs were given to a technical assistant and the trained RCNN model. The technical assistant and the RCNN model both annotated ROIs for the given WSIs independently. After which, a senior pathologist will evaluate and compare both annotations. The senior pathologist compared and evaluated the results, as shown in Table 2. The established RCNN identified a total of 112 from the 115 ROIs from the 6 WSIs, including some which were missed by the technical assistant. The discrepancy was estimated visually by directly comparing human ROI identification and RCNN ROI identification. Figure 3 shows a comparison of the RCNN identification with the human identified ROIs, and this shows both the model and human was able to locate all the ROIs.

From Table 2, it can be observed that specimen 2 and 6 were labelled as identical to those by the technical assistant, and validated visually by the senior pathologist. The results demonstrated that the RCNN model is capable of learning the features of the ROIs in WSIs from the 60 WSIs used in training and perform well for the testing set and the unseen dataset.

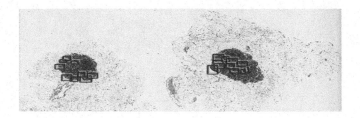

Fig. 3. This compares human annotations and the model annotations for Specimen 6. The model has predicted all the ROIs. Blue ROIs are marked by the RCNN model and red ROIs are marked by the technical assistant. (Color figure online)

Table 2. Comparison of the results of the human technical assistant and the established RCNN.

Specimen	Total ROI by human	Total ROI by RCNN	Discrepant ROI
1	44	44	4
2	8	8	0
3	12	12	4
4	14	14	1
5	17	14	8
6	20	20	0
Total	**115**	**112**	**17**

5   Discussions

Table 1 shows that the Centre Case performs better than the Base Case by obtaining an IOU of 0.92 (base case 0.61) for the RCNN that has been established in this paper. From observation, it was found that in the case of the Centre Case, the patch used to give a feature-rich area for the RCNN to learn ROI specific features. The use of the centre of a patch provided the model with a clearer ROI particular features. Therefore, the model was able to extract and learn the features of the ROIs accurately. In the unseen data test, the RCNN performed well as validated by the senior pathologist. The senior pathologist makes the decision by considering whether the ROIs identified have included the GC and its boundary. Therefore, even if the technical assistant's annotations and the RCNN's annotations were not 100% matching, the senior pathologist would consider that the ROIs have correctly been identified. In this case, the exact alignment of the ROIs identified by the technical assistant and the RCNN is not required. In the unseen data testing, as evaluated by the senior pathologist, the established RCNN was capable of performing similarly to the technical assistant in Specimen 3 and Specimen 6, as shown in Fig. 4 (Specimen 6) and Table 2. Furthermore, the proposed method was capable of identifying ROIs which were not identified by a human, technical assistant but missed ROIs that the technical

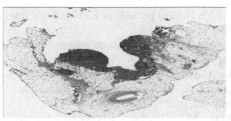

Fig. 4. The comparison between the technical assistant missing ROI and the RCNN model missing ROI in Specimen 4. The red cross indicates the ROI that the technical assistant missed, and the yellow cross indicates what the model missed. (Color figure online)

assistant can identify (Fig. 4). From Table 2, the differences are small as validated by the senior pathologist for other specimens.

6 Conclusion

In this paper, an investigation of the application for RCNN for WSI ROI identification is presented. RCNN's feature extraction and classification were modified for ROI detection in WSI using a limited number of training data. A public hospital pathology service in Western Australia provided the labelled WSIs. 60 WSIs and 12 WSIs were used to train and test the RCNN, respectively. Patches were made from the gigapixel images. The centres of the patches were used to train and test the RCNN. The use of the centre patch enabled the RCNN to learn features of the ROI well. Selective search, with the use of the greedy algorithm, was used to generate the candidate region proposal, and features were extracted using VGG 16 pre-trained on ImageNet, with the final softmax dense layer used to generate the classification. Results show that the established RCNN can be used to identify ROI on WSI, which could assist pathologists in the detection of regions that could contain GC within normal and benign lymph nodes. Further work is underway to use a special protein maker stain to establish definitive ground truth for the germinal centre identification. This stain can be used for a comparison of human versus computer identification of the ROIs.

References

1. Bankman, I.: Handbook of Medical Image Processing and Analysis. Elsevier, Amsterdam (2008)
2. Gibson, E., et al.: NiftyNet: a deep-learning platform for medical imaging. In: Computer Methods and Programs in Biomedicine, vol. 158, pp. 113–122. Elsevier (2018)
3. Semmlow, J.L., Griffel, B.: Biosignal and Medical Image Processing. CRC Press, Hoboken (2014)

4. Niazi, M.K.K., Parwani, A.V., Gurcan, M.N.: Digital pathology and artificial intelligence. Lancet Oncol. **20**, 253–261 (2019)
5. Bejnordi, B.E., et al.: Stain specific standardization of whole-slide histopathological images. IEEE Trans. Med. Imag. **35**, 404–415 (2015)
6. Sertel, O., Kong, J., Shimada, H., Catalyurek, U.V., Saltz, J.H., Gurcan, M.N.: Computer-aided prognosis of neuroblastoma on whole-slide images: classification of stromal development. Pattern Recognit. **42**, 1093–1103 (2009)
7. Kothari, S., Phan, J.H., Stokes, T.H., Wang, M.D.: Pathology imaging informatics for quantitative analysis of whole-slide images. J. Am. Med. Inform. Assoc. **20**, 1099–1108 (2013)
8. Brunyé, T.T., Mercan, E., Weaver, D.L., Elmore, J.G.: Accuracy is in the eyes of the pathologist: the visual interpretive process and diagnostic accuracy with digital whole slide images. J. Biomed. Inform. **66**, 171–179 (2017)
9. Li, R., Huang, J.: Fast regions-of-interest detection in whole slide histopathology images. In: International Workshop on Patch-Based Techniques in Medical Imaging, pp. 120–127. Elsevier (2015)
10. Mehta, S., Mercan, E., Bartlett, J., Weaver, D., Elmore, J., Shapiro, L.: Learning to segment breast biopsy whole slide images. In: 2018 IEEE Winter Conference on Applications of Computer Vision (WACV), pp. 663–672. IEEE (2018)
11. Cruz-Roa, A., et al.: Automatic detection of invasive ductal carcinoma in whole slide images with convolutional neural networks. In: Medical Imaging 2014: Digital Pathology, vol. 9041, p. 904103. International Society for Optics and Photonics (2014)
12. Sharma, H., Zerbe, N., Klempert, I., Hellwich, O., Hufnagl, P.: Deep convolutional neural networks for automatic classification of gastric carcinoma using whole slide images in digital histopathology. Comput. Med. Imag. Graph. **61**, 2–13 (2017)
13. Nugaliyadde, A., Wong, K.W., Sohel, F., Xie, H.: Language modeling through Long-Term memory network. In: International Joint Conference on Neural Networks (IJCNN), pp. 1–6. IEEE (2019)
14. Girshick, R., Donahue, J., Darrell, T., Malik, J.: Rich feature hierarchies for accurate object detection and semantic segmentation. In: Proceedings of the IEEE Conference on Computer Vision and Pattern Recognition, pp. 580–587 (2014)
15. Girshick, R.: Fast R-CNN. In: Proceedings of the IEEE International Conference on Computer Vision, pp. 1440–1448 (2015)
16. Somaratne, U.V., Wong, K.W., Parry, J., Sohel, F., Wang, X., Laga, H.: Improving follicular lymphoma identification using the class of interest for transfer learning. In: Digital Image Computing: Techniques and Applications (DICTA), pp. 1–7 (2019)
17. Agarwal, M., Al-Shuwaili, T., Nugaliyadde, A., Wang, P., Wong, K.W., Ren, Y.: Identification and diagnosis of whole body and fragments of Trogoderma granarium and Trogoderma variabile using visible near infrared hyperspectral imaging technique coupled with deep learning. Comput. Electron. Agric. **173**, 105438 (2020)
18. Ding, J., Xue, N., Long, Y., Xia, G.S., Lu, Q.: Learning RoI transformer for oriented object detection in aerial images. In: Proceedings of the IEEE Conference on Computer Vision and Pattern Recognition, pp. 2849–2858 (2019)

Real-Time Probabilistic Approach for Traffic Prediction on IoT Data Streams

Sanket Mishra[✉], Raghunathan Balan, Ankit Shibu, and Chittaranjan Hota

Department of Computer Science and Information Systems,
Birla Institute of Technology and Science Pilani, Hyderabad Campus,
Jawahar Nagar, Hyderabad 500078, India
{p20150408,f20170703,f20170297,hota}@hyderabad.bits-pilani.ac.in

Abstract. IoT data analytics refers to the analysis of voluminous data captured by connected devices. These devices interact with the environment and capture the details which are streamed to a central repository where the processing of this data is done. This collected data may be heterogeneous in nature, as research has identified weather, social, and pollution data as key players in traffic prediction in smart cities, making the analytics challenging. In this work, we propose Unir, an event driven framework for analyzing heterogeneous IoT data streams. In the first step, we ingest the data from Twitter, weather and traffic APIs and store it in a persistent data store. Later, this data is preprocessed and analyzed by deep learning models to forecast future data points. In the second step, a supervised Hidden Markov Model consumes the sequence of predicted data points from the first layer. The HMM is trained using the ground truth labels obtained from TomTom API to find the likelihood values of a congestion event. The likelihood for congestion and non-congestion sequences is learned by a Logistic regression which assigns a confidence to the occurrence of an event. The proposed approach displays a 77% overall accuracy in comparison to the baseline approach on experiments.

Keywords: Deep learning · Long Short Term Memory networks · Complex Event Processing · Hidden Markov Models · Probabilistic approach

1 Introduction

Internet of Things (IoT) depicts a world of interconnected 'things' that has led to a significant rise in the number of devices connected to Internet. Presently, sensors range from generic sensing devices attached to embedded IoT boards to embedded sensors in the smartphone. In Intelligent Transportation Systems (ITS) scenarios, data is often of large order and poses a big data problem. ITS applications gather large data for inferring patterns from these data streams. Depending upon the underlying application, the complex patterns can be transformed to complex events using a Complex Event Processing (CEP) engine.

© Springer Nature Switzerland AG 2020
H. Yang et al. (Eds.): ICONIP 2020, CCIS 1333, pp. 633–641, 2020.
https://doi.org/10.1007/978-3-030-63823-8_72

This research area involves data processing, fusion and generation of complex events from various univariate data streams for real-time congestion prediction in ITS scenarios. In this work, the CEP engine is augmented with Unir[1] that represents a fusion of Long Short Term Memory (LSTM) networks and a probabilistic Hidden Markov Model (HMM). The intuition behind the consideration of a fused approach in Unir is that we need to predict events using a deep regression approach and analyze this sequence on a supervised HMM-LR approach to identify the confidence in congestion sequences and non-congestion sequences. Further, we assign a probability to the occurrence of the complex event.

Akbar et al. [1] developed a predictive CEP that uses Adaptive Moving Window Regression (AMWR) to predict simple events. The regression approaches ingest data using an adaptive window based on the Mean Absolute Percentage Error (MAPE) that increases or decreases to contain the error within 5%–20%. The predicted data points were sent to the CEP engine which fuses them to form complex "congestion" events well before their occurrence. However, it is found in the presence of noise and non-stationarity in data, the performance of the model is poor. Mishra et al. [4] identified this shortcoming and proposed an end to end solution using LSTM approach for forecasting future points and merging them in a CEP to generate complex "congestion" events. The authors [1] improved their work [3] and formulated advanced scenarios for congestion prediction with the inclusion of social data from Twitter. The Twitter data was used to formulate Large Crowd Concentration (LCC) events which signify large density of people in certain locations. The authors analyzed the impact of such social data in congestion prediction and enhanced it [2] using Complex Event Processing to create probabilistic events concerning congestion prediction.

This paper is an improvement over the work [2] that employs a Bayesian Belief Network (BBN) for identifying causal relationships between traffic data, weather data, temporal data and social data through their conditional probabilities.

Our major contributions in this work are as follows:

- Our significant contribution in this work is the formulation of Unir, modular probabilistic framework to address uncertainty in detection of complex events in CEP with the help of sensor data fusion. We also merge HMM-LR (Hidden Markov Model-Logistic Regression) to identify probability of occurrence of a complex event by analyzing sequences.
- We validate the effectiveness of the proposed approach on a real world ITS use-case against a Bayesian Belief Network approach proposed in an earlier work [2].

2   Dataset Description and Pre-processing

The data is taken from the city of Madrid from September 2019 to November 2019. The traffic data is acquired through a REST (REpresentational State

---

[1] 'Unir' is a Spanish word which means merge or join.

Transfer) API (Application Program Interface)[2], the weather data from an API web service[3] and Twitter data[4] to aggregate the count of tweets coming from considered locations.

The dataset comprises of 24000 data points out of which 17000 points are considered for training and 7000 points for testing the model. The traffic, weather and social data are collected and stored in a time series database. The traffic data has a 5 min interval and tweets were arriving every second. Tweets were aggregated every 5 min for creating the 'tweet count' variable and the weather data was grouped into 'cloudy', 'rainy' and 'clear' classes. The weather data was down sampled from 15 min to 5 min. The data is initially segregated on the basis of timestamps to represent different "contexts" of the day. The data is initially grouped on the basis of weekday and weekend. Then on the basis of time, the data is divided into morning, afternoon, evening and late evening times. The intuition behind the inclusion of tweets in the congestion prediction for a certain region is indicative of the density of people in a particular location.

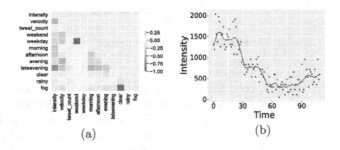

(a)   (b)

Fig. 1. a) Pearson correlation coefficient b) loess smoothed intensity data

Figure 1(a) shows the Pearson Correlation technique to identify linear relationships amongst the features used in the concocted work. From Fig. 1(a), we conclude that *intensity* and *tweet count* are positively correlated and *intensity* and *velocity* are negatively correlated. Even *weekday-weekend* and *fog-clear* are negatively correlated. The advantage of using this analysis is to validate that the predictions are accurate and not erroneous owing to correlation between features. In real world data, noise occurs randomly due to faults in sensor or data loss which can be detrimental for a forecasting model. The imputation of missing values is done using mice library. For removal of noise, we incorporate a locally estimated scatterplot smoothing (loess) technique to smoothen the raw IoT data. The smoothing mechanism eliminates noise and irregularities in the raw data and thus forms better quality continuous data. Figure 1(b) illustrates the smoothed data for 10 neighbors on intensity attribute. We use Min-Max normalization approach for feature scaling in this work.

---

[2] http://informo.munimadrid.es/informo/tmadrid/pm.xml.

[3] https://api.darksky.net/forecast/.

[4] https://api.twitter.com/1.1/search/tweets.json.

In the next section, we describe the various modules of Unir and outline their functionalities.

3   Unir: Deep Fusion Statistical Framework

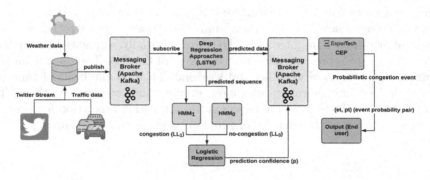

Fig. 2. Proposed framework

Figure 2 presents our proposed framework Unir for probabilistic event generation using CEP. First, the data acquisition, preprocessing and ingestion are handled by Kafka and subsequently sent to the CEP engine. Secondly, the framework handles the probabilistic inference mechanism on simple events and predictions for formulating probabilistic events. In the following section, we elaborate the working mechanism of Unir.

We have made use of Apache Kafka as the message broker for real time publishing and subscribing to data between the different modules. The predictions from the regression module are sent to the CEP for event processing. The Kafka broker is deployed on one thread while the CEP executes concurrently on another thread. This concurrent execution using different threads avoids starvation of the CEP engine which may hamper event generation and ML predictions.

The proposed solution, Unir, is a practical and feasible framework for handling prediction on real-world IoT applications. It consists of modules that can be easily integrated to form an event processing framework. The IoT data streams are sent to the CEP engine where the higher order events are identified and fused to form complex events. In real world situations, data is heterogeneous in nature and there can be sudden events or phenomenon, such as, a sudden accident or ambulance causing road jam. This scenario cannot be justified, as the dependency of a complex event depends upon a multitude of factors, such as, time of day, time of week, weather conditions, etc. along with generic traffic information. In this work, we counter the de facto standard of the CEP engines and propose a probabilistic CEP which can not only handle heterogeneity in IoT streams but also predict events with a greater accuracy.

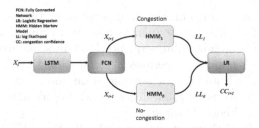

Fig. 3. Proposed approach

In the proposed methodology, our predictive analytics module has three parts. Figure 3 depicts the proposed model. In the first part, we employ a Kafka consumer which fetches the aggregated data from the databases and feeds it to the regression models. We employ a dense LSTM regression for predicting future data points on the traffic attributes. The LSTM model is trained on weather data, time of day and time of week to forecast the value of intensity, velocity and tweet counts. The context in which a prediction takes place may change over the time. This leads to a phenomenon called "data drift". As the models predict on IoT streams, we handle data drift by using a heuristic proposed in our earlier work [4].

The model is trained on the new data instances by sliding the window. The performance of the LSTM is validated using Mean Absolute Percentage Error (MAPE). Based on the magnitude of the error, the model is retrained. Once the model generates the predictions, it is ingested via a Kafka consumer into the CEP. Then the CEP fuses these data instances using Event Processing Language (EPL) queries to predict a complex event much before its occurrence. But because of the uncertainty in real world datasets and heterogeneity in data [2], the inference of sequences that depict 'congestion' patterns is required.

In the regression part, we use FCN (fully connected network) and LSTM with dropout layers for regularization. Formally, given an input sequence $X = [x_{t-1}, x_{t-2}, .., x_{t-k}]$, k represents the look-back window size and $x_i \in R^d$ with d features. We compute h_t using the standard equations governing the LSTM cell. FCN is used to compute $y_{t+1} = W_r h_t + b_r$, $y_{t+1} \in R^3$ corresponding to *intensity, velocity* and *tweet count*. Apart from these three dynamic features, all other features like time of day, time of week and weather conditions are static for a given context window. Hence, x_{t+1} is derived using y_{t+1} and x_t. Further, y_{t+1} is fed as input to HMMs for traffic congestion prediction.

The second part of our framework comprises of a supervised HMM model. We train two different HMM models, S_0 and S_1, that are trained on "no congestion" and "congestion" sequences respectively. The HMMs use Gaussian emission function to learn the underlying probability distributions of traffic conditions in both scenarios. We use TomTom API for fetching the true "congestion" events in the city of Madrid. This is a necessary step for identification of the true congestion events not considered in the baseline approach [2].

As the HMMs are trained on the input sequences, they are able to infer the probabilistic distribution of the sequences relevant to congestion and no congestion scenarios. When a new input sequence Y arrives, S_0 gives the probability $P(no-congestion|Y)$ and S_1 generates $P(congestion|Y)$. Thus, S_0 and S_1 give "output confidence" C_0 and C_1 for no-congestion and congestion events respectively. These values are not probabilities rather log likelihood values obtained using Maximum Likelihood Estimation.

For a dataset D, with input sequences $Y_1, Y_2, Y_3, ..., Y_N$ ($N = |D|$), where $Y_i \in R^{l \times 3}$ and l is the sequence length of HMM, we obtain corresponding confidence pairs $< C_{11}, C_{12} >, < C_{21}, C_{22} >, ..., < C_{N1}, C_{N2} >$ from HMMs. Using TomTom API, we obtain the ground truth labels $g_1, g_2, g_3, ..., g_N$ where $g_i = 0$ and $g_i = 1$ representing no-congestion and congestion respectively. For obtaining probabilities from the log likelihood values, we employ a logistic regression approach. The logistic regression trains on the confidence pairs with target labels to learn the probabilities with respect to the likelihoods of the two events. This helps in identifying the probability output p given any new input sequence from its corresponding confidence pairs which are computed by the HMMs. The output of the logistic regression represents the confidence of a congestion event.

3.1   Evaluation Metrics

The LSTM regression approach consumes the data streams and is trained on traffic features, climate data, social data and temporal data. LSTM forecasts the traffic attributes, intensity and velocity and social data, that is, tweet counts for a particular region. To verify the performance of the forecasting task, we use Mean Absolute Percentage Error (MAPE) metric, which is defined as follows:

$$MAPE = \frac{1}{n} \sum_{i=1}^{n} \frac{|y_i - y_i'|}{y_i} \tag{1}$$

where y_i is the observed value and y_i' is the predicted value.

For validating the performance of the proposed HMM-LR approach, we consider the "accuracy" metric[5].

$$Accuracy = \frac{TP + TN}{TP + FP + TN + FN} \tag{2}$$

where, TP, FP, TN and FN represent True Positive, False Positive, True Negative and False Negative.

The next section exhibits various experiments conducted to identify the optimal parameters for LSTM and HMM. It also presents the sensitivity analysis on the HMM approach to find the optimal set of features and sequence length for best performance.

---

[5] We have also evaluated the HMM-LR approach on other evaluation metrics, such as, precision, recall, F-measure and AUC (Area Under Curve) that is not exhibited in this work.

4   Experimental Results and Discussion

Various experiments are executed to discover the optimal parameters of LSTM and HMM. For identifying the optimal hyperparamaters of the LSTM, the HyperOpt library is used. The optimal hyperparameters are marked at points where the metric exhibits best performance. We consider four different regression approaches as baselines for comparing our proposed approach, such as, Bidirectional LSTM, Adaptive Moving Window Regression [1], Stacked LSTM and CNN-LSTM.

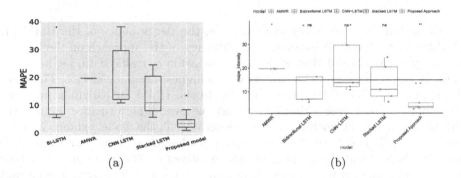

(a)   (b)

Fig. 4. a) MAPE performance on various regression approaches on intensity b) Statistical significance testing comparing the performance of the regression approaches

We follow a similar training and evaluation protocol for all models, using HyperOpt to determine hyper-parameters, such as, learning rate, number of hidden layers, etc. We use a learning rate of 1e−3 for all neural networks. For BiLSTM and stacked LSTM, we include 3 hidden layers and 16 hidden nodes along with a dropout of 0.25. For CNN-LSTM, we use 1D convolutional layer and 1D max pooling layer with 64 filters of kernel size 5, which is followed by a LSTM layer. We use a ReLU function (Rectified Linear Unit) as the activation function in hidden layers and linear in output layer. For AMWR [1], we use initial training window of 15, radial basis function as the kernel for the SVR regressor and gamma of 0.1. For the proposed LSTM regression, we use 4 hidden layers with 8 hidden nodes each with a lookback of 5.

The performance of the considered approaches on the basis of MAPE metrics are depicted in Fig. 4(a). The proposed technique gives the best performance using MAPE metric and it also surpasses the performance of the baselines including the approach [1]. We implement a Kruskal-Wallis significance test to verify the statistical significance between the regression approaches. From Fig. 4(b), it is inferred that the alternate hypothesis is rejected and thus it indicates no statistical significance between considered regression techniques.

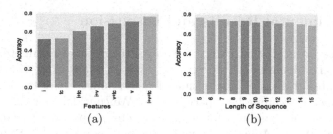

Fig. 5. a) Performance evaluation of HMM on various feature combinations b) Performance evaluation of HMM over varying sequence lengths

Figure 5(a) represents the evaluation on the performance of the HMM-LR on different features[6]. It evaluates the efficiency of the approach on the basis of accuracy[7]. It is noticed that with the combination of traffic data, i.e, intensity, velocity and tweet count, the model exhibits highest accuracy of 77%. The input sequence of predicted data points are fed to the HMM for assigning probability to the complex events that can impact the overall performance. Figure 5(b) exhibits that with an optimal sequence length of '5', the model exhibits a better performance. It is noticed that with a sequence length of '5', the number of true positives is 534 and the number of false positives is 309. The number of false positive subsequently increases with an increase in length leading to a significant loss of accuracy. When sequence is of length 12, we notice 494 true positives and 413 false positives but the accuracy drops to 71%. The sequence length affects the classification accuracy as smaller sequences result in faster predictions. The smaller sequences also hold the most recent data points on which the models are trained for classification.

Figure 6 presents the comparison in performance between the proposed approach and a baseline approach Bayesian Belief Network (BBN) [2]. The BBN computes the conditional probability of each of the traffic features, that is, intensity, velocity and tweet count and constructs a Bayesian Network. It also considers external factors like weather and time for predicting congestion. We have bench-marked our approach against the Bayesian network [2]. Our model performance is comparatively better than the performance of the Bayesian Network in similar settings. The underlying reason behind this rise in performance is the HMM-LR in our approach is assigning probabilities to predicted data points and BBN is computing conditional probabilities of the features and then assigning probabilities. Figure 6(b) depicts the statistical significance results of both the considered approaches executed using 10-fold cross-validation. From Fig. 6(b), it is inferred that the alternate hypothesis is rejected and thus it indicates no statistical significance between both the approaches.

---

[6] i, v and tc represent intensity, velocity and tweet counts respectively.
[7] Similar results are obtained for precision, recall, F-measure and AUC.

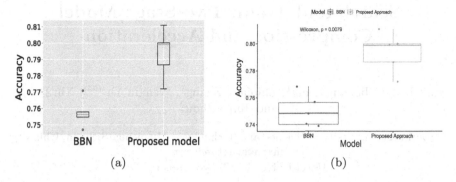

Fig. 6. Performance evaluation of proposed approach over Bayesian Belief Network [2] on the basis of evaluation metrics of accuracy metric b) Statistical significance test of proposed approach and baseline approach

5   Conclusion

This paper outlines the implementation of Unir, a fused deep learning and probabilistic based approach for event processing on IoT data streams. We investigated the data and identified the variations over different times of day and week. We identified the environmental, social and temporal features that are important factors in predicting congestion in an ITS scenario. Hypothesis tests exhibited the statistical significance between considered approaches and our approach. The better performance of the proposed approach makes it a suitable model for CEP integration in real-time congestion predictions on IoT streams.

References

1. Akbar, A., Khan, A., Carrez, F., Moessner, K.: Predictive analytics for complex IoT data streams. IEEE Internet Things J. **4**(5), 1571–1582 (2017)
2. Akbar, A., et al.: Real-time probabilistic data fusion for large-scale IoT applications. IEEE Access **6**, 10015–10027 (2018)
3. Kousiouris, G., et al.: An integrated information lifecycle management framework for exploiting social network data to identify dynamic large crowd concentration events in smart cities applications. Future Gener. Comput. Syst. **78**, 516–530 (2018)
4. Mishra, S., Jain, M., Siva Naga Sasank, B., Hota, C.: An ingestion based analytics framework for complex event processing engine in internet of things. In: Mondal, A., Gupta, H., Srivastava, J., Reddy, P.K., Somayajulu, D.V.L.N. (eds.) BDA 2018. LNCS, vol. 11297, pp. 266–281. Springer, Cham (2018). https://doi.org/10.1007/978-3-030-04780-1_18

Search-and-Train: Two-Stage Model Compression and Acceleration

Ning Jiang[1], Jialiang Tang[1], Zhiqiang Zhang[1], Wenxin Yu[1(✉)], Xin Deng[1], and Jinjia Zhou[2]

[1] Southwest University of Science and Technology, Mianyang, Sichuan, China
yuwenxin@swust.edu.cn
[2] Hosei University, Tokyo, Japan

Abstract. Convolutional neural networks have achieved great success in many fields. However, the practical application of convolutional neural networks is hindered due to the high consumption of memory and computational. In this paper, we propose a two-stage method for model compression and acceleration. More specifically, the training process mainly includes the search stage and train stage, the approach is abbreviated as ST. In the search stage, we first search and remove the unnecessary parts of a large pre-trained network (named supernet) by certain evaluation criteria to get a pruned network. Then the weights in the pruned network are initialized to get a small network (called a subnet). During the training stage, the supernet is untrainable, and the subnet will be trained under the supervision of the supernet. The knowledge extracted from the supernet will be transmitted to the subnet, then the subnet will be able to learn from the dataset and the knowledge at the same time. We have proved the effectiveness of our method through implement extensive experiments on several state-of-the-art CNN models (including VGGNet, ResNet, and DenseNet). The subnet only with 1/10 parameters and 1/2 calculations achieves more significant performance than the supernet.

Keywords: Convolutional neural networks · Model compression and acceleration · Two-stage · Supernet · Subnet

1 Introduction

In recent years, convolutional neural networks (CNNs) have greatly promoted the development of artificial intelligence. And the CNNs have achieved excellent results in many computer vision tasks. Overall, with the continuous improvement of the CNNs performance, its depth and width are also increasing. However, these large-scale CNNs with superior performance often with huge memory and computational burdens. The great memory and computing resource consumption of CNNs are unaffordable for these resource-limited intelligent devices such as autonomous vehicles, smart speakers, and smartphones.

© Springer Nature Switzerland AG 2020
H. Yang et al. (Eds.): ICONIP 2020, CCIS 1333, pp. 642–649, 2020.
https://doi.org/10.1007/978-3-030-63823-8_73

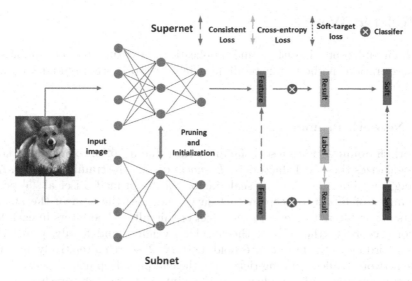

Fig. 1. The total structure of our proposed method. The subnet will be learned under the supervision of the truth labels and the knowledge from the supernet.

Many approaches have been proposed to compress and accelerate these large CNNs, mainly include network pruning [6], knowledge distillation [4]. Network pruning first selects and prunes unimportant parts of the CNNs by specific criteria, and then fine-tunes the pruned network on the dataset. The performance of CNNs is unsatisfactory when the pruning rate is higher. Knowledge distillation transfers knowledge from a large teacher network to a small student network to promote the small student network to get better performance. So, the student network can meet practical applications, with fewer parameters and calculations. But knowledge distillation requires a network with a specific optimized structure as a student network.

In this paper, we propose a two-stage model compression and acceleration method to solve these problems. An optimized structure is crucial for the CNNs to use fewer parameters and calculations to achieve excellent performance. Our method is divided into the search stage and the training stage. Figure 1 is the overall framework of our proposed approach ST. We will first search for an optimized small network (called subnet) from a big network (called supernet). The input image will be input to the supernet and subnet respectively to obtain the features, classification results, and soft labels of the supernet and subnet. Then the consistency loss, cross-entropy loss, and soft-target loss are calculated in turn. Then the optimized subnet will achieve significant accuracy. In the training process, same as [8], the sub-network will be initialized and trained from scratch. Extensive experiments on the benchmark dataset demonstrate that the subnet with much fewer parameters and calculations trained by our proposed ST can achieve higher accuracy than the supernet.

2   Related Work

Based on different algorithm and applications, existing model compression and acceleration methods can be divided into network pruning and knowledge distillation.

2.1   Network Pruning

Network slimming [7] adds a scale factor to each channel of the convolution kernel and regularizes these scale factors by $L1\text{-}norm$ during the training process. After training, the channels with low scale factor will be pruned. Li et al. [5] presets the number of filters to keep in each layer and uses the sum of the absolute weights of the filters to measure the effect of this filter. The filters in each layer will sort accord to the sum of the absolute weights, and finally, prune these filters according to the preset threshold. Lottery [2] search a relatively optimized sparse network (called winning tickets) in the complex deep neural network. The parameter amount and complexity of the winning tickets are much lower, but it achieves an inference accuracy similar to the original network. Dong et al. [1] uses the neural architecture search to perform network pruning, and similar to us, the original network is used to transfer knowledge to the pruned network. But their search phase is time-consuming, and the accuracy of the pruned network is reduced to some extent.

2.2   Knowledge Distillation

Knowledge distillation utilizes a teacher network with more parameters and calculations to transfer knowledge to a student network with fewer parameters and calculations to improving the performance of the student network. The concept of knowledge distillation was first proposed by Hinton et al. [4]. Them input the output of the network to the softmax function to get the soft-target, the student network will learn from the soft-target and realize knowledge transfer. CCKD [9] introduced the correlation congruence for knowledge distillation, in the progress of knowledge transfer, the instance-level information and the correlation between instances are transferred together.

3   Approach

In this section, we will explain how to implement our proposed method. The purpose of our proposed method is to find an optimized small subnet and train the subnet to gets performance beyond the supernet.

3.1   Search the Subnet

The fundamental process of network pruning is to find and remove the part that contributes less to the final result from a CNNs and then fine-tune it.

The pruned network has fewer parameters and calculations while retaining as much accuracy as possible. However, recent research [8] shows that the reason why the pruned network achieves well results is that the network pruning can search for a small network with superior performance, not because the valuable weight is retained in the pruned network. Therefore, in this paper, we use the approach of network pruning to searching for a suitable network structure and take the network slimming [6] as an example to elaborate how to search the subnet. Different from network slimming that contains the weight in the pruned network to fine-tune, we initialize the weights in the pruned network to obtain an optimized subnet. More specifically, we will add a trainable scale factor γ to each channel of the neural network. During the training process, the weights of the network and these scale factors will be jointly trained. After training, each scale factor of the channel represents their final contribution to the network, and these channels with small scale factors will be removed. To reduce the parameters in the training process, we use batch normalization (BN) to act as a scale layer. BN is a basic unit of CNNs and is widely applied in existing neural networks, the transformation progress can be written as follows:

$$\hat{x} = \frac{x_{in} - \mu}{\sqrt{\sigma^2 + \epsilon}}; \quad x_{out} = \gamma\hat{x} + \beta \tag{1}$$

The x_{in} and x_{out} are the input and output of BN, σ and μ are the standard deviation and mean values of x_{in}, ϵ is a minimum to prevent division by zero errors. The γ is multiplied with the x_{in}, it is equivalent to the scale factor of the x. So, the γ in BN is used as the scale factor and the $L1$-$norm$ is applied to the γ to promote it to zero. After training, these channels in each layer will sort by the γ. Then we will prune the channels with a lower γ according to the preset prune ratio. For example, when using the 19-layers VGGNet19 [10] as a supernet, we will prune 70% of the channels and initialize the weight of the remaining channels to get a supernet.

3.2   Train the Subnet

Different from the network pruning, which improves the performance of the pruned network through fine-tuning, in the paper, the subnet will train from scratch. Figure 1 shows the train process of the subnet. The input image is first input into the supernet and subnet to obtain the feature of the supernet $F_p = \{f_{p1}, f_{p2}, \cdots, f_{pn}\}$ and the feature of subnet $F_b = \{f_{b1}, f_{b2}, \cdots, f_{bn}\}$, n is the number of feature. Because the supernet is a pre-trained neural network with excellent performance, we assume that if the feature of the subnet is more consistent with those of the supernet, then the subnet also has a similar performance. To enhance the consistency of the feature of supernet and subnet, the Euclidean distance is used to calculate the consistency loss of their feature. The consistency loss function is formula as:

$$\mathcal{L}_{cs} = \frac{1}{n} \sum_{i=1}^{n} \left\| F_{bi} - F_{pi} \right\|_2 \tag{2}$$

Then, the feature of the supernet and subnet will input into the classification layer to obtain the classification result of the supernet $T_p = \{t_{p1}, t_{p2}, \cdots, t_{pn}\}$ and the classification result of the subnet $T_b = \{t_{b1}, t_{b2}, \cdots, t_{bn}\}$. Specifically, the classification result of CNNs is the one-hot vector, such as $o = [0,1,0...0]$. There is only one value is one and others are zero. The one-hot vector o only contains the information of the class that the corresponding value is 1. However, there are often many similar pictures in the dataset. To utilize these similar information, Hinton et al. [4] proposed to input the classification result to the softmax function to get the soft-target example as $s = [0.1,0.8,...,0.05]$ to transfer knowledge. There are many non-zero values in the soft-target, which means the soft-target s contains more information than one-hot vector o. So, in our proposed approach, the soft-target is used to transfer knowledge from the supernet to the subnet. For the classification result $T = \{t_1, t_2, \cdots, t_n\}$ of neural network, the soft-target can be get as follows:

$$s^i = \frac{\exp\left(t^i / Temp\right)}{\sum_j \exp\left(t^j / Temp\right)} \tag{3}$$

The Temp is the temperature to soft the output neural network, a bigger Temp can get a bigger soft-target. By utilizing the Eq. 3, the soft-target of supernet and subnet can be get as $S_p = \{s_{p1}, s_{p2}, \cdots, s_{pn}\}$ and $S_b = \{s_{b1}, s_{b2}, \cdots, s_{bn}\}$ respectively. And the loss function of soft-target is elaborated as:

$$\mathcal{L}_{st} = \frac{1}{n} \sum_i \mathcal{H}_{KLdiv}\left(s_p^i, s_b^i\right) \tag{4}$$

The $\mathcal{H}_{KLdiv}$ is the KL divergence.

In the train process of CNNs, the network will be trained under the supervision of the ground-truth label. To promote the subnet classification more accurately, the classification result will calculate the cross-entropy loss with the ground-truth label through the following formula:

$$\mathcal{L}_{label} = \frac{1}{n} \sum_i \mathcal{H}_{cross}\left(y_T^i, t^i\right) \tag{5}$$

The $\mathcal{H}_{cross}$ is the cross-entropy loss function.

By combining these loss functions proposed above, our final objective function is:

$$\mathcal{L}_{Total} = \alpha \mathcal{L}_{cs} + \beta \cdot T^2 \mathcal{L}_{st} + \gamma \mathcal{L}_{label} \tag{6}$$

The α, β and γ are the hyperparameter to adjust the three term in Eq. 6.

4   Experiments

In this section, we will chose three pruning algorithms to search the network model for extensive experiments. We use the automatic structure pruning [7] to search the subnet. We use the CIFAR-10 and CIFAR-100 datasets for training.

Table 1. Results for using network slimming to search subnet.

Dataset	Model	Original	Prune ratio	Fine-tuned	Accuracy
CIFAR-10	VGGNet-19	93.53%	70%	93.60%	**94.27%**
	PreResNet-164	95.04%	40%	94.77%	**95.69%**
	DenseNet-40	94.10%	60%	94.00%	**94.33%**
CIFAR-100	VGGNet-19	72.63%	70%	72.32%	**73.94%**
	PreResNet-164	76.80%	40%	76.22%	**77.24%**
	DenseNet-40	73.82%	60%	73.35%	**73.98%**

The training set has 50,000 pictures, and the test set has 10,000 pictures. The CIFAR datasets consist of 32×32 pixel images in multiple categories, CIFAR-10 contains ten categories, and CIFAR-100 contains 100 categories. In all experiments, the parameters in the total objective function Eq. 6 are set to: $\alpha = 0.1$, $\beta = 0.9$ and $\gamma = 0.1$.

4.1 Automatic Structure Pruning

Automatic structure pruning [7] automatically performs structured pruning by adding scale factors to each channel. Section 3.1 describes the specific implementation steps. The training sets are set as follows, the batch size is 64, the learning rate is 0.1 and divide by 10 every 80 times epoch, the weight is 1e-4, the momentum is 0.9, and the SGD is used as the optimizer. When using the 19-layers VGGNet-19 as supernet, we will prune 70% channels of the VGGNet-19 to get the subnet. When taking the 164-layers pre-activation PreResNet-164 as supernet, there are 40% parameters be pruned. And when the 40-layers DenseNet is set as supernet, we will cut off 60% channels of it.

Table 1 shows the experimental results of taking automatic structure pruning to search the subnet. The accuracy of these small subnets trained by ST is significantly higher than that of training subnets by fine-tuning. Even compared with the original large supernet, the subnet trained by our method still has more superior performance. These experimental results show that our proposed ST can automatically search and train an optimal network, and achieve better performance than the supernet with only fewer memory and computational burden.

4.2 Various Pruned Ratio to Search Subnet

To prove the effectiveness of our proposed ST more extensively, there are different pruned ratios for experiments. The 19-layers VGGNet-19 is selected as supernet, and the automatic structure pruning network slimming is used to search the subnet. The pruned ratio are set as 30%, 50% and 70%. Table 2 displays the experiment results. The subnet trained by our ST achieved better results than the subnet fine-tuning on the dataset when using all pruning ratios, and also

Table 2. Results for using various pruned ration to search subnet. The FLOPs mean floating-point operations per second, which is used to represent the amount of calculation. The pruned ratio is 0% means the network unpruned and without the accuracy of fine-tuned and ST.

Dataset	Original	Pruned ratio	Parameter	FLOPs	Fine-tuned	ST
CIFAR-10	93.46%	0%	20.8M	7.97×10^8	-	-
		50%	5.01M	5.01×10^8	93.55%	**94.01%**
		60%	3.70M	3.98×10^8	93.48%	**94.13%**
		70%	2.31M	3.91×10^8	93.52%	**94.21%**
CIFAR-100	72.51%	0%	20.8M	7.97×10^8	-	-
		50%	5.01M	5.01×10^8	72.37%	**73.30%**
		60%	3.70M	3.98×10^8	72.21%	**73.58%**
		70%	2.31M	3.91×10^8	72.17%	**73.93%**

Table 3. Results for the subnet trained by ST compare to other method. Scratch represents the accuracy of the pruned network train from scratch.

Dataset	Model	Original	PR	Scratch	Fine-tuned	KD	ST
CIFAR-10	VGGNet-19	93.53%	70%	93.30%	93.52%	91.94%	**94.27%**
	PreResNet-164	95.04%	40%	94.70%	94.68%	94.06%	**95.69%**
CIFAR-100	VGGNet-19	72.63%	70%	71.86%	72.17%	69.21%	**73.94%**
	PreResNet-164	76.80%	40%	76.36%	76.10%	72.15%	**77.24%**

achieved better performance than the supernet. Especially when the pruning rate is 70%, the subnet trained by ST only has about 1/10 parameters and 1/2 calculations of the supernet achieve the accuracy of 94.21% and 73.93% on the CIFAR-10 and CIFAR-100 datasets, respectively, which are significantly higher than the accuracy of supernet.

4.3   Comparison with Various Approach

In this section, the subnet trained by ST will compare to the subnet trained from scratch, the subnet trained by fine-tuned and the subnet trained by knowledge distillation [4]. When the subnet trained from scratch, the pruned will be initialized and without the supernet to transfer knowledge. When using knowledge distillation for training, the subnet is obtained by directly reducing the number of channels in the supernet according to the corresponding pruning ratio. We chose the 19-layers VGGNet-19, the 164-layers pre-activation PreResNet-164, and the 40-layers DenseNet-40 as supernets. The experimental results is exhibits in Table 3. The PR means pruned ratio and the KD means knowledge distillation. When using different structures as supernets, the corresponding subnets trained by our ST all obtain the highest accuracy and the subnets trained by knowledge distillation cannot achieve well performance due to the lack of an optimized structure. The experimental results prove that the search and train phases of ST jointly promote the subnet to achieve better results.

5   Conclusion

Convolutional Neural Networks (CNNs) are generally over-parameterize, and their huge memory and computational burden hinder their application to practical applications. In this paper, we propose a two-stage model compression and acceleration approach. We first search for an optimized small subnet from a large supernet. Then the subnet is trained from scratch and the knowledge is transformed from supernet to the subnet. Extensive experiments prove that our proposed method can be widely applied to existing advanced CNNs to compress the size of the network and improving the performance of the network. In future work, we will further explore more effective network search and knowledge transfer methods. And train the more compact and efficient network model.

Acknowledgements. This research is supported by Sichuan Provincial Science and Technology Program (No.2019YFS0146).

References

1. Dong, X., Yang, Y.: Network pruning via transformable architecture search. In: Wallach, H.M., Larochelle, H., Beygelzimer, A., d'Alché-Buc, F., Fox, E.B., Garnett, R. (eds.) Advances in Neural Information Processing Systems 32: Annual Conference on Neural Information Processing Systems 2019, NeurIPS 2019, 8–14 December 2019, Vancouver, BC, Canada, pp. 759–770 (2019)
2. Frankle, J., Carbin, M.: The lottery ticket hypothesis: Finding sparse, trainable neural networks. arXiv preprint arXiv:1803.03635 (2018)
3. He, K., Zhang, X., Ren, S., Jian, S.: Deep residual learning for image recognition. In: 2016 IEEE Conference on Computer Vision and Pattern Recognition (CVPR) (2016)
4. Hinton, G., Vinyals, O., Dean, J.: Distilling the knowledge in a neural network. Comput. Sci. **14**(7), 38–39 (2015)
5. Li, H., Kadav, A., Durdanovic, I., Samet, H., Graf, H.P.: Pruning filters for efficient convnets (2016)
6. Liu, Z., Li, J., Shen, Z., Huang, G., Yan, S., Zhang, C.: Learning efficient convolutional networks through network slimming. In: IEEE International Conference on Computer Vision, ICCV 2017, Venice, Italy, 22–29 October 2017, pp. 2755–2763. IEEE Computer Society (2017). https://doi.org/10.1109/ICCV.2017.298
7. Liu, Z., Li, J., Shen, Z., Huang, G., Yan, S., Zhang, C.: Learning efficient convolutional networks through network slimming. In: Proceedings of the IEEE International Conference on Computer Vision, pp. 2736–2744 (2017)
8. Liu, Z., Sun, M., Zhou, T., Huang, G., Darrell, T.: Rethinking the value of network pruning. In: 7th International Conference on Learning Representations, ICLR 2019, New Orleans, LA, USA, 6–9 May 2019. OpenReview.net (2019). https://openreview.net/forum?id=rJlnB3C5Ym
9. Peng, B., et al.: Correlation congruence for knowledge distillation (2019)
10. Simonyan, K., Zisserman, A.: Very deep convolutional networks for large-scale image recognition. Computer Science (2014)

Shallow VAEs with RealNVP Prior can Perform as Well as Deep Hierarchical VAEs

Haowen Xu[1,2] , Wenxiao Chen[1,2] , Jinlin Lai[1] , Zhihan Li[1,2] ,
Youjian Zhao[1,2] , and Dan Pei[1,2(✉)]

[1] Department of Computer Science and Technology, Tsinghua University,
Beijing, China
{xhw15m,chen-wx17,laijl16,lizhihan17}@mails.tsinghua.edu.cn,
{zhaoyoujian,peidan}@tsinghua.edu.cn
[2] Beijing National Research Center for Information Science and Technology
(BNRist), Beijing, China

Abstract. Learn the prior of VAE is a new approach to improve the
evidence lower-bound. We show that using learned RealNVP prior and
just one latent variable in VAE, we can achieve test NLL comparable
to very deep state-of-the-art hierarchical VAE, outperforming many previous works with complex hierarchical VAE architectures. We provide
the theoretical optimal decoder for Benoulli $p(\mathbf{x}|\mathbf{z})$. We demonstrate
that, with learned RealNVP prior, β-VAE can have better rate-distortion
curve than using fixed Gaussian prior.

1 Introduction

Variational auto-encoder (VAE) [12] is a powerful deep generative model, trained
by variational inference, which demands the intractable true posterior to be
approximated by a learned distribution, thus many different variational posteriors have been proposed [11,12,16]. Alongside, some previous works further
improved the variational lower-bound by learning the prior [2,9,10,17].

Despite the achievements of these previous works on posteriors and priors,
the state-of-the-art VAE models with continuous latent variables all rely on deep
hierarchical latent variables[1], although some of them might have used complicated posteriors/priors as components in their architectures. Most latent variables in such deep hierarchical VAEs have no clear semantic meanings, just a
technique for reaching good lower-bounds. We thus raise and answer a question: **with the help of learned priors, can shallow VAEs achieve performance comparable or better than deep hierarchical VAEs?** This
question is important because a shallow VAE would be much more promising

---

[1] The term "hierarchical latent variables" refers to multiple layers of latent variables,
while "one latent variable" refers to just one $\mathbf{z}$ in standard VAEs. "deep" refers to
many hierarchical latent variables, while "shallow" refers to few latent variables.

© Springer Nature Switzerland AG 2020
H. Yang et al. (Eds.): ICONIP 2020, CCIS 1333, pp. 650–659, 2020.
https://doi.org/10.1007/978-3-030-63823-8_74

to scale to more complicated datasets than deep hierarchical VAEs. To answer this question, we conduct comprehensive experiments on several datasets with learned RealNVP priors and just one latent variable, which even shows advantage over some deep hierarchical VAEs with powerful posteriors. In summary, our contributions are:

- We conduct comprehensive experiments on four binarized datasets with four different network architectures. Our results show that VAE with RealNVP prior consistently outperforms standard VAE and RealNVP posterior.
- We are the first to show that using learned RealNVP prior with just one latent variable in VAE, it is possible to achieve test negative log-likelihoods (NLLs) comparable to very deep state-of-the-art hierarchical VAE on these four datasets, outperforming many previous works using complex hierarchical VAE equipped with rich priors/posteriors.
- We provide the theoretical optimal decoder for Bernoulli $p(\mathbf{x}|\mathbf{z})$.
- We demonstrate that, with learned RealNVP prior, β-VAE can have better rate-distortion curve [1] than using fixed Gaussian prior.

2   Preliminaries

2.1   Variational Auto-Encoder

Variational auto-encoder (VAE) [12] uses a latent variable $\mathbf{z}$ with prior $p_\lambda(\mathbf{z})$, and a conditional distribution $p_\theta(\mathbf{x}|\mathbf{z})$, to model the observed variable $\mathbf{x}$. $p_\theta(\mathbf{x}) = \int_{\mathcal{Z}} p_\theta(\mathbf{x}|\mathbf{z}) p_\lambda(\mathbf{z}) \, d\mathbf{z}$, where $p_\theta(\mathbf{x}|\mathbf{z})$ is derived by a neural network with parameter θ. $\log p_\theta(\mathbf{x})$ is bounded below by evidence lower-bound (ELBO):

$$\log p_\theta(\mathbf{x}) \geq \mathcal{L}(\mathbf{x}; \lambda, \theta, \phi) = \mathbb{E}_{q_\phi(\mathbf{z}|\mathbf{x})} \left[\log p_\theta(\mathbf{x}|\mathbf{z}) \right] - D_{\mathrm{KL}}(q_\phi(\mathbf{z}|\mathbf{x}) \| p_\lambda(\mathbf{z})) \quad (1)$$

where $q_\phi(\mathbf{z}|\mathbf{x})$ is the variational posterior to approximate $p_\theta(\mathbf{z}|\mathbf{x})$, derived by a neural network with parameter ϕ. Optimizing $q_\phi(\mathbf{z}|\mathbf{x})$ and $p_\theta(\mathbf{x}|\mathbf{z})$ w.r.t. empirical distribution $p^\star(\mathbf{x})$ can be achieved by maximizing the expected ELBO w.r.t. $p^\star(\mathbf{x})$:

$$\mathcal{L}(\lambda, \theta, \phi) = \mathbb{E}_{p^\star(\mathbf{x})} \mathbb{E}_{q_\phi(\mathbf{z}|\mathbf{x})} \left[\log p_\theta(\mathbf{x}|\mathbf{z}) + \log p_\lambda(\mathbf{z}) - \log q_\phi(\mathbf{z}|\mathbf{x}) \right] \quad (2)$$

A hyper-parameter β can be added to $\mathcal{L}(\lambda, \theta, \phi)$, in order to control the trade-off between reconstruction loss and KL divergence, known as β-VAE [1,8]:

$$\mathcal{L}_\beta(\lambda, \theta, \phi) = \mathbb{E}_{p^\star(\mathbf{x})} \mathbb{E}_{q_\phi(\mathbf{z}|\mathbf{x})} \left[\log p_\theta(\mathbf{x}|\mathbf{z}) + \beta \left(\log p_\lambda(\mathbf{z}) - \log q_\phi(\mathbf{z}|\mathbf{x}) \right) \right] \quad (3)$$

[9] suggested an alternative decomposition of Eq. 2:

$$\mathcal{L}(\lambda, \theta, \phi) = \underbrace{\mathbb{E}_{p^\star(\mathbf{x})} \mathbb{E}_{q_\phi(\mathbf{z}|\mathbf{x})} \left[\log p_\theta(\mathbf{x}|\mathbf{z}) \right]}_{\textcircled{1}} - \underbrace{D_{\mathrm{KL}}(q_\phi(\mathbf{z}) \| p_\lambda(\mathbf{z}))}_{\textcircled{2}} - \underbrace{\mathbb{I}_\phi[Z; X]}_{\textcircled{3}} \quad (4)$$

where $\mathbb{I}_\phi[Z; X] = \iint q_\phi(\mathbf{z}, \mathbf{x}) \log \frac{q_\phi(\mathbf{z}, \mathbf{x})}{q_\phi(\mathbf{z}) \, p^\star(\mathbf{x})} \, d\mathbf{z} \, d\mathbf{x}$ is the *mutual information*. Since $p_\lambda(\mathbf{z})$ is only in $\textcircled{2}$, ELBO can be enlarged if $p_\lambda(\mathbf{z})$ is trained to match $q_\phi(\mathbf{z})$.

2.2 RealNVP Prior

As a universal density estimator, RealNVP [6] can be readily adopted to derive a learnable prior $p_\lambda(\mathbf{z})$ from a simple prior $p_\xi(\mathbf{w})$ (*e.g.*, unit Gaussian) as follows:

$$p_\lambda(\mathbf{z}) = p_\xi(\mathbf{w}) \left| \det\left(\frac{\partial f_\lambda(\mathbf{z})}{\partial \mathbf{z}} \right) \right|, \quad \mathbf{z} = f_\lambda^{-1}(\mathbf{w}) \tag{5}$$

where $\det(\partial f_\lambda(\mathbf{z})/\partial \mathbf{z})$ is the Jacobian determinant of $f_\lambda(\mathbf{z}) = (f_K \circ \cdots \circ f_1)(\mathbf{z})$, with each f_k being invertible. [6] introduced the *affine coupling layer* as f_k, while [13] further introduced *actnorm* and *invertible* 1×1 *convolution*.

3   The Optimal Decoder for Bernoulli $p(\mathbf{x}|\mathbf{z})$

Proposition 1. *Given a finite number of discrete training data, i.e.,* $p^\star(\mathbf{x}) = \frac{1}{N} \sum_{i=1}^N \delta(\mathbf{x} - \mathbf{x}^{(i)})$, *if* $p_\theta(\mathbf{x}|\mathbf{z}) = \mathrm{Bernoulli}(\boldsymbol{\mu}_\theta(\mathbf{z}))$, *where the Bernoulli mean* $\boldsymbol{\mu}_\theta(\mathbf{z})$ *is produced by the decoder, and* $0 < \mu_\theta^k(\mathbf{z}) < 1$ *for each of its k-th dimensional output, then the optimal decoder* $\boldsymbol{\mu}_\theta(\mathbf{z})$ *is:*

$$\boldsymbol{\mu}_\theta(\mathbf{z}) = \sum_i w_i(\mathbf{z}) \, \mathbf{x}^{(i)}, \quad where \; w_i(\mathbf{z}) = \frac{q_\phi(\mathbf{z}|\mathbf{x}^{(i)})}{\sum_j q_\phi(\mathbf{z}|\mathbf{x}^{(j)})} \; and \; \sum_i w_i(\mathbf{z}) = 1 \tag{6}$$

Proof. See [18] due to page limitations.

4   Experiments

4.1   Setup

Datasets. We use statically and dynamically binarized MNIST (denoted as *StaticMNIST* and *MNIST* in our paper), FashionMNIST and Omniglot.

Models. We perform systematically controlled experiments, using the following models: (1) **DenseVAE**, with dense layers; (2) **ConvVAE**, with convolutional layers; (3) **ResnetVAE**, with ResNet layers; and (4) **PixelVAE** [7], with several PixelCNN layers on top of the ResnetVAE decoder. For RealNVP [6], we use K blocks of invertible mappings (K is called *flow depth* hereafter), while each block contains an *invertible dense*, a dense *coupling layer*, and an *actnorm* [13]. The dimensionality of $\mathbf{z}$ are 40 for StaticMNIST and MNIST, while 64 for FashionMNIST and Omniglot.

Training and Evaluation. Unless specified, all experiments are repeated for 3 times to report metric means. We perform early-stopping using negative log-likelihood (NLL), to prevent over-fitting on StaticMNIST and on all datasets with PixelVAE. We use 1,000 samples to compute various metrics on test set.

4.2 Quantitative Results

In Tables 1 and 2, we compare ResnetVAE and PixelVAE with RealNVP prior to other approaches on StaticMNIST and MNIST. Due to page limitations, results on Omniglot and FashionMNIST are omitted, but they have a similar trend. All models except ours and that of [10] used at least 2 latent variables. Notice that, although [10] also adopted RealNVP prior, we have better test NLLs than their work, as well as solid analysis on our experimental results.

Our ResnetVAE with RealNVP prior is second only to BIVA among all models without PixelCNN decoder, and ranks the first among all models with PixelCNN decoder. On MNIST, the NLL of our model is very close to BIVA, while the latter used 6 latent variables and very complicated architecture. Meanwhile, our ConvVAE with RealNVP prior has lower test NLL than ConvHVAE with *Lars prior* and *VampPrior*. Since the architecture of ConvVAE is simpler than ConvHVAE (which has 2 latent variables), it is likely that our improvement comes from the RealNVP prior rather than the different architecture.

Tables 1 and 2 show that using RealNVP prior with just one latent variable, it is possible to achieve NLLs comparable to very deep state-of-the-art VAE (BIVA), ourperforming many previous works (including works on priors, and works of complicated hierarchical VAE equipped with rich posteriors like VAE + IAF). **This discovery shows that shallow VAEs with learned prior and a small number of latent variables is a promising direction.**

Table 1. Test NLL on StaticMNIST. "†" indicates a hierarchical model with 2 latent variables, while "‡" indicates at least 3 latent variables. $K = 50$ in our models.

Model	NLL
Models without PixelCNN decoder	
ConvHVAE + Lars prior[†] [2]	81.70
ConvHVAE + VampPrior[†] [17]	81.09
ResConv + RealNVP prior [10]	81.44
VAE + IAF[‡] [11]	79.88
BIVA[‡] [14]	**78.59**
Our ConvVAE + RNVP $p(z)$	80.09
Our ResnetVAE +RNVP $p(z)$	79.84
Models with PixelCNN decoder	
VLAE[‡] [4]	79.03
PixelHVAE + VampPrior[†] [17]	79.78
Our PixelVAE + RNVP $p(z)$	**79.01**

Table 2. Test NLL on MNIST. "†" and "‡" has the same meaning as Table 1.

Model	NLL
Models without PixelCNN decoder	
ConvHVAE + Lars prior[†] [2]	80.30
ConvHVAE + VampPrior[†] [17]	79.75
VAE + IAF[‡] [11]	79.10
BIVA[‡] [14]	**78.41**
Our ConvVAE +RNVP $p(z)$	78.61
Our ResnetVAE + RNVP $p(z)$	78.49
Models with PixelCNN decoder	
VLAE[‡] [4]	78.53
PixelVAE[†] [7]	79.02
PixelHVAE + VampPrior[†] [17]	78.45
Our PixelVAE + RNVP $p(z)$	**78.12**

4.3 Qualitative Results

Figure 1 samples images from ResnetVAE with/without RealNVP prior. Compared to standard ResnetVAE, ResnetVAE with RealNVP prior produces fewer digits that are hard to interpret. The last column of each 6 × 6 grid shows the training set images, most similar to the second-to-last column in pixel-wise L2 distance. There are differences between the last two columns, indicating our model is not just memorizing the training data.

4.4   Ablation Study

RealNVP prior leads to substantially lower NLLs than standard VAE and RealNVP posterior Table 3 shows the NLLs of DenseVAE, ResnetVAE and PixelVAE with $K = 20$. We see that RealNVP prior consistently outperforms standard VAE and RealNVP posterior in test NLL, with as large improvement as about 2 nats (compared to standard ResnetVAE) or 1 nat (compared to ResnetVAE with RealNVP posterior) on ResnetVAE, and even larger improvement on DenseVAE. The improvement is not so significant on PixelVAE, likely because less information is encoded in the latent variable of PixelVAE [7].

Using RealNVP prior only has better NLL than using both RealNVP prior and posterior, or using RealNVP posterior only, with the same total number of RealNVP layers, as shown in Table 4.

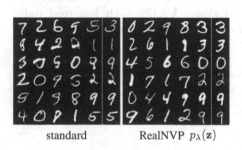

Fig. 1. Sample means from $p_\lambda(\mathbf{z})$ of ResnetVAE with: (left) Gaussian prior; (right) RealNVP prior. The last column of each 6 × 6 grid shows the training set images, most similar to the second-to-last column in pixel-wise L2 distance.

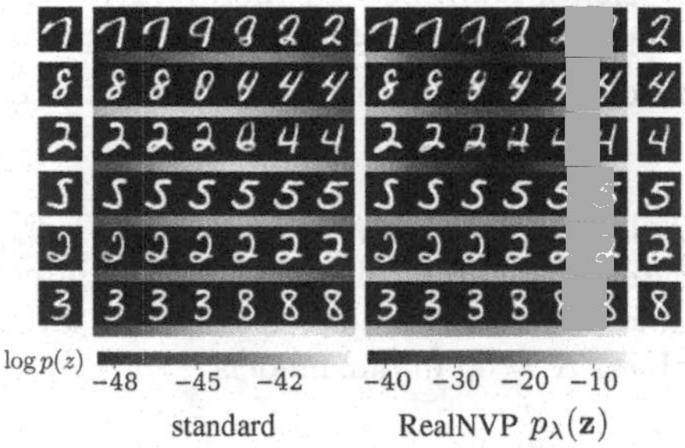

Fig. 2. Interpolations of $\mathbf{z}$ from Resnet-VAE, between the centers of $q_\phi(\mathbf{z}|\mathbf{x})$ of two training points, and heatmaps of $\log p_\lambda(\mathbf{z})$. The left- and right-most columns are the training points.

Table 3. Average test NLL (lower is better) of different models, with Gaussian prior & Gaussian posterior ("normal"), Gaussian prior & RealNVP posterior ("RNVP $q(z|x)$"), and RealNVP prior & Gaussian posterior ("RNVP $p(z)$"). $K = 20$.

Datasets	DenseVAE			ResnetVAE			PixelVAE		
	Normal	RNVP $q(z\|x)$	RNVP $p(z)$	Normal	RNVP $q(z\|x)$	RNVP $p(z)$	Normal	RNVP $q(z\|x)$	RNVP $p(z)$
StaticMNIST	88.84	86.07	**84.87**	82.95	80.97	**79.99**	79.47	79.09	**78.92**
MNIST	84.48	82.53	**80.43**	81.07	79.53	**78.58**	78.64	78.41	**78.15**
FashionMNIST	228.60	227.79	**226.11**	226.17	225.02	**224.09**	224.22	223.81	**223.40**
Omniglot	106.42	102.97	**102.19**	96.99	94.30	**93.61**	89.83	89.69	**89.61**

Table 4. Test NLL of Resnet-VAE on MNIST, with RealNVP posterior ("$q(z|x)$"), RealNVP prior ("$p(z)$"), and RealNVP prior & posterior ("both"). Flow depth K is $2K_0$ for the posterior or the prior in "$q(z|x)$" and "$p(z)$", while K_0 for both the posterior and the prior in "both".

ResnetVAE &	K_0			
	1	5	10	20
$q(z|x)$, $K = 2K_0$	80.29	79.68	79.53	79.49
both, $K = K_0$	79.85	79.01	78.71	78.56
$p(z)$, $K = 2K_0$	**79.58**	**78.75**	**78.58**	**78.51**

Table 5. Average number of *active units* of ResnetVAE, with standard prior & posterior ("normal"), RealNVP posterior ("RNVP $q(z|x)$"), and RealNVP prior ("RNVP $p(z)$").

Dataset	ResnetVAE		
	Normal	RNVP $q(z|x)$	RNVP $p(z)$
StaticMNIST	30	40	40
MNIST	25.3	40	40
FashionMNIST	27	64	64
Omniglot	59.3	64	64

Table 6. Average test ELBO ("*elbo*"), reconstruction loss ("*recons*"), $\mathbb{E}_{p^*(x)}D_{KL}(q_\phi(\mathbf{z}|\mathbf{x})\|p_\lambda(\mathbf{z}))$ ("*kl*"), and $\mathbb{E}_{p^*(x)}D_{KL}(q_\phi(\mathbf{z}|\mathbf{x})\|p_\theta(\mathbf{z}|\mathbf{x}))$ ("*$kl_{z|x}$*") of ResnetVAE with different priors.

Dataset	Standard				RealNVP $p(z)$			
	elbo	recons	kl	$kl_{z|x}$	elbo	recons	kl	$kl_{z|x}$
StaticMNIST	−87.61	−60.09	**27.52**	4.67	**−82.85**	**−54.32**	28.54	**2.87**
MNIST	−84.62	−58.70	**25.92**	3.55	**−80.34**	**−53.64**	26.70	**1.76**
FashionMNIST	−228.91	−208.94	**19.96**	2.74	**−225.97**	**−204.66**	21.31	**1.88**
Omniglot	−104.87	−66.98	**37.89**	7.88	**−99.60**	**−61.21**	38.39	**5.99**

Active Units. Table 5 counts the *active units* [3] of different ResnetVAEs, which quantifies the number of latent dimensions used for encoding information from input data. We can see that, both RealNVP prior and posterior can make all units of a ResnetVAE to be active (which is in sharp contrast to standard VAE). This in conjunction with Tables 3 and 4 indicates that, the good regularization effect, "a learned RealNVP prior can lead to more active units than a fixed prior" [2, 17], is not the main cause of the huge improvement in NLLs, especially for the improvement of RealNVP prior over RealNVP posterior.

4.5 Reconstruction Loss and Posterior Overlapping

Better Reconstruction Loss. In Table 6, *ELBO* and *reconstruction loss* ("*recons*", which is ① in Eq. 4) of ResnetVAE with RealNVP prior are substantially higher than standard ResnetVAE, just as the trend of test log-likelihood (LL) in Table 3. On the contrary, $\mathbb{E}_{p^*(x)}D_{KL}(q_\phi(\mathbf{z}|\mathbf{x})\|p_\lambda(\mathbf{z}))$ ("*kl*", which is ② + ③) happens to be larger. Since ELBO equals to ① − (② + ③), this suggests that in our experiments, the improvement in ELBO (and also NLL) of ResnetVAE with RealNVP prior all comes from the improved reconstruction loss.

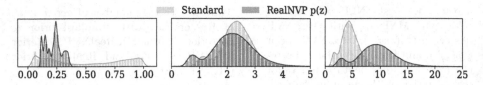

Fig. 3. Histograms of: (left) per-dimensional stds of $q_\phi(\mathbf{z}|\mathbf{x})$; (middle) distances between closest pairs of $q_\phi(\mathbf{z}|\mathbf{x})$; and (right) *normalized distances*. See Appendix A.

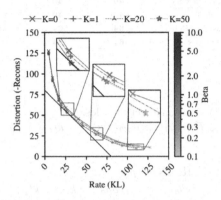

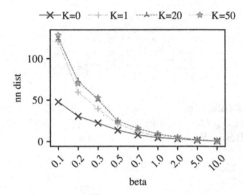

Fig. 4. Rate $(D_{\mathrm{KL}}(q_\phi(\mathbf{z}|\mathbf{x})\|p_\theta(\mathbf{z})))$ and distortion (*i.e.*, the negate of *reconstruction loss*) of β-ResnetVAE trained with different β and prior flow depth K.

Fig. 5. Average *normalized distance* of β-ResnetVAE trained with different β and prior flow depth K.

Smaller Standard Deviation of Gaussian Posterior with RealNVP Prior. In Fig. 3, we plot the histograms of per-dimensional stds of $q_\phi(\mathbf{z}|\mathbf{x})$, as well as the distances and *normalized distances* (which is roughly distance/std) between each closest pair of $q_\phi(\mathbf{z}|\mathbf{x})$ (see Appendix A for formulations). The stds of $q_\phi(\mathbf{z}|\mathbf{x})$ with RealNVP prior are substantially smaller, and the *normalized distances* are larger. Larger *normalized distances* indicate less density of $q_\phi(\mathbf{z}|\mathbf{x})$ to be overlapping. We discussed one possible theoretical reason of this phenomenon in [18], on the basis of our Proposition 1.

Appropriate Overlapping Among $q_\phi(\mathbf{z}|\mathbf{x})$ with Learned Prior. To demonstrate that the stds of $q_\phi(\mathbf{z}|\mathbf{x})$ with RealNVP prior are reduced according to the dissimilarity between $\mathbf{x}$ rather than being reduced equally (*i.e.*, $q_\phi(\mathbf{z}|\mathbf{x})$ exhibits "appropriate overlapping"), we plot the interpolations of $\mathbf{z}$ between the centers of $q_\phi(\mathbf{z}|\mathbf{x})$ of two training points, and $\log p_\lambda(\mathbf{z})$ of these interpolations in Fig. 2, We visualize $p_\lambda(\mathbf{z})$, because it is trained to match $q_\phi(\mathbf{z})$, and can be computed much more reliable than $q_\phi(\mathbf{z})$; and because the density of $q_\phi(\mathbf{z})$ between $\mathbf{z}$ corresponding to two $\mathbf{x}$ points can be an indicator of how $q_\phi(\mathbf{z}|\mathbf{x})$ overlap between them. The RealNVP $p_\lambda(\mathbf{z})$ scores the interpolations of $\mathbf{z}$ between the centers of $q_\phi(\mathbf{z}|\mathbf{x})$ of two training points, giving low likelihoods to hard-to-interpret interpolations between two dissimilar **x** (the first three rows), while giving high likelihoods to good interpolations between two similar **x** (the last three rows). In contrast, the unit Gaussian prior assigns high likelihoods to all interpolations, even to hard-to-interpret ones. This suggests that the posterior overlapping is "more appropriate" with RealNVP prior than with unit Gaussian prior.

Learned Prior Influences the Trade-Off Between Reconstruction Loss and KL Divergence. We plot the rate-distortion curve (RD curve) [1] of β-ResnetVAE trained with different β and flow depth K in Fig. 4. Rate is $D_{\mathrm{KL}}(q_\phi(\mathbf{z}|\mathbf{x})\|p_\theta(\mathbf{z}))$, while distortion is negative reconstruction loss. Each connected curve with the same shape of points in Fig. 4 correspond to the models with the same K, but different β. We can see that the curves of $K = 1$ is closer to the boundary formed by the green line and the x & y axes than $K = 0$, while $K = 20$ & 50 are even closer. According to [1], points on the RD curve being closer to the boundary suggests that the corresponding models are closer to the theoretical optimal models on a particular dataset, when traded between reconstruction loss and KL divergence. Given this, we conclude that learned prior can lead to a "better" trade-off from the perspective of RD curve.

We also plotted the average *normalized distance* of β-ResnetVAE trained with different β and flow depth K in Fig. 5. Learned prior can encourage less posterior overlapping than unit Gaussian prior for various β, not only for $\beta = 1$.

5   Related Work

Learned priors, as a natural choice for the conditional priors of intermediate variables, have long been unintentionally used in hierarchical VAEs [11,14]. A few works were proposed to enrich the prior, *e.g.*, Gaussian mixture priors [5], and auto-regressive priors [4,7], without the awareness of its relationship with the *aggregated posterior*, until [9]. Since then, attempts have been made in matching the prior to *aggregated posterior*, by using RealNVP [10], variational mixture of posteriors [17], and learned accept/reject sampling [2]. However, none of these works recognized the improved reconstruction loss induced by learned prior. Moreover, they did not show that learned prior with just one latent variable can achieve comparable results to those of many deep hierarchical VAEs.

The trade-off between reconstruction loss and KL divergence was discussed in the context of β-VAE [1,8,15], however, they did not further discuss the impact of a learned prior on this trade-off. [15] also discussed the posterior overlapping, but only within the β-VAE framework, thus was only able to control the degree of overlapping globally, without considering the local dissimilarity between **x**.

6   Conclusion

In this paper, using learned RealNVP prior with just one latent variable in VAE, we managed to achieve test NLLs comparable to very deep state-of-the-art hierarchical VAE, outperforming many previous works of complex hierarchical

VAEs equipped with rich priors/posteriors. We provide the theoretical optimal decoder for Benoulli $p(\mathbf{x}|\mathbf{z})$. We showed that with learned RealNVP prior, β-VAE can have better rate-distortion curve [1] than with fixed Gaussian prior. We believe this paper is an important step towards shallow VAEs with learned prior and a small number of latent variables, which potentially can be more scalable to large datasets than those deep hierarchical VAEs.

Acknowledgments. This work has been supported by National Key R&D Program of China 2019YFB1802504 and the Beijing National Research Center for Information Science and Technology (BNRist) key projects.

A   Formulation of Closest Pairs of $q_\phi(\mathbf{z}|\mathbf{x})$ and Others

$q_\phi(\mathbf{z}|\mathbf{x}^{(j)})$ is the *closest neighbor* of $q_\phi(\mathbf{z}|\mathbf{x}^{(i)})$ if $j = \arg\min_{j\neq i} \|\boldsymbol{\mu}_\phi(\mathbf{x}^{(j)}) - \boldsymbol{\mu}_\phi(\mathbf{x}^{(i)})\|$. Such pairs of $q_\phi(\mathbf{z}|\mathbf{x}^{(i)})$ and $q_\phi(\mathbf{z}|\mathbf{x}^{(j)})$ are called *closest pairs of* $q_\phi(\mathbf{z}|\mathbf{x})$. The *distance* d_{ij} and the *normalized distance* $\widetilde{d_{ij}}$ of a closest pair $q_\phi(\mathbf{z}|\mathbf{x}^{(i)})$ and $q_\phi(\mathbf{z}|\mathbf{x}^{(j)})$ are defined as $\mathbf{d}_{ij} = \boldsymbol{\mu}_\phi(\mathbf{x}^{(j)}) - \boldsymbol{\mu}_\phi(\mathbf{x}^{(i)})$, $d_{ij} = \|\mathbf{d}_{ij}\|$, and $\widetilde{d_{ij}} = \frac{2d_{ij}}{\mathrm{Std}[i;j]+\mathrm{Std}[j;i]}$ Roughly speaking, the *normalized distance* $\widetilde{d_{ij}}$ can be viewed as "distance/std" along the direction of $\mathbf{d}_{ij}$, which indicates the scale of the "hole" between $q_\phi(\mathbf{z}|\mathbf{x}^{(i)})$ and $q_\phi(\mathbf{z}|\mathbf{x}^{(j)})$.

References

1. Alemi, A., et al.: Fixing a Broken ELBO. In: ICML, pp. 159–168 (2018)
2. Bauer, M., Mnih, A.: Resampled priors for variational autoencoders. In: The 22nd International Conference on Artificial Intelligence and Statistics, pp. 66–75 (2019)
3. Burda, Y., Grosse, R.B., Salakhutdinov, R.: Importance weighted autoencoders. In: ICLR 2016, Conference Track Proceedings (2016)
4. Chen, X., et al.: Variational lossy autoencoder. In: ICLR (2017)
5. Dilokthanakul, N., et al.: Deep unsupervised clustering with gaussian mixture variational autoencoders. arXiv preprint arXiv:1611.02648 (2016)
6. Dinh, L., Sohl-Dickstein, J., Bengio, S.: Density estimation using real NVP. In: 5th International Conference on Learning Representations, ICLR (2017)
7. Gulrajani, I., et al.: Pixelvae: a latent variable model for natural images. In: ICLR 2017, Conference Track Proceedings (2017)
8. Higgins, I., et al.: Beta-VAE: learning basic visual concepts with a constrained variational framework. In: ICLR 2017, vol. 3 (2017)
9. Hoffman, M.D., Johnson, M.J.: Elbo surgery: yet another way to carve up the variational evidence lower bound. In: Workshop in Advances in Approximate Bayesian Inference, NIPS (2016)
10. Huang, C.W., et al.: Learnable Explicit Density for Continuous Latent Space and Variational Inference. arXiv:1710.02248 (2017)
11. Kingma, D.P., et al.: Improved variational inference with inverse autoregressive flow. NIPS **2016**, 4743–4751 (2016)
12. Kingma, D.P., Welling, M.: Auto-encoding variational bayes. In: ICLR (2014)

13. Kingma, D.P., Dhariwal, P.: Glow: generative flow with invertible 1x1 convolutions. NIPS **2018**, 10215–10224 (2018)
14. Maaløe, et al.: BIVA: a very deep hierarchy of latent variables for generative modeling. arXiv:1902.02102 (2019)
15. Mathieu, E., Rainforth, T., Siddharth, N., Teh, Y.W.: Disentangling disentanglement in variational autoencoders. ICML **2019**, 4402–4412 (2019)
16. Rezende, D., Mohamed, S.: Variational inference with normalizing flows. In: ICML-15, pp. 1530–1538 (2015)
17. Tomczak, J., Welling, M.: VAE with a VampPrior. In: International Conference on Artificial Intelligence and Statistics, pp. 1214–1223 (2018)
18. Xu, H., et al.: On the necessity and effectiveness of learning the prior of variational auto-encoder. http://arxiv.org/abs/1905.13452

Software Defect Prediction with Spiking Neural Networks

Xianghong Lin[1(✉)], Jie Yang[1], and Zhiqiang Li[2]

[1] College of Computer Science and Engineering, Northwest Normal University,
Lanzhou 730070, China
linxh@nwnu.edu.cn, yang15769392975@163.com
[2] College of Computer Science, Shaanxi Normal University, Xian 710119, China
lizq@snnu.edu.cn

Abstract. Software defect prediction is one of the most active research areas in software engineering and plays an important role in software quality assurance. In recent years, many new defect prediction studies have been proposed. There are four main aspects of research: machine learning-based prediction algorithms, manipulating the data, effor-softaware prediction and empirical studies. The research community is still facing many challenges in constructing methods, and there are also many research opportunities in the meantime. This paper proposes a method of applying spiking neural network to software defect prediction. The software defect prediction model is constructed by feedforward spiking neural networks and trained by spike train learning algorithm. This model uses the existing project data sets to predict software defects projects. Extensive experiments on 28 public projects from five data sources indicate that the effectiveness of the proposed approach with respect to the considered metrics.

Keywords: Spiking neural networks · Classification techniques · Software defect prediction · Software quality assessment

1 Introduction

As one of the most popular research topics in software engineering, software defect prediction (SDP) has attracted a lot of attention and was studied exensively in recent years [1]. SDP aims to identify more likely defectprone modules (functions, classes, files, changes, etc.) to help with the prioritization of software quality assurance efforts such as testing or code review. It is especially important when the organization's quality assurance resource is limited [1,2].

In the past few decades, more and more research works pay attention to the software defect prediction and a lot of papers have been published [2]. There have already been several excellent systematic review works for the software defect prediction [3,4]. Catal and Diri [4] reviewed 74 defect prediction papers in 11 journals and several conference proceedings by focusing on software metrics,

© Springer Nature Switzerland AG 2020
H. Yang et al. (Eds.): ICONIP 2020, CCIS 1333, pp. 660–667, 2020.
https://doi.org/10.1007/978-3-030-63823-8_75

data sets and meth-ods to build defect prediction models. They mainly survey machine learning and statistical analysis-based methods for defect prediction [2]. The research community is still facing a number of challenges for building methods and many research opportunities exist.

Spiking neural networks (SNNs) that composed of biologically plausible spiking neurons are usually known as the third generation of artificial neural networks (ANNs) [5]. The spike trains are used to represent and process the neural information in spiking neurons, which can integrate many aspects of neural information, such as time, space, frequency, and phase, etc. [6,7]. As a new brain-inspired computational model of the neural network, SNN has more powerful computing power compared with a traditional neural network model [8]. Thus, it is valuable to study SNN method to deal with SDP problems.

2   Related Work

2.1   Defect Prediction Process

To build a defect prediction model, the first step is to create data instances from software archives such as version control systems (e.g. SVN, CVS, GIT), issue tracking systems and so on. The version control systems contain the source codes and some commit messages, while the issue tracking systems include some defect information. According to prediction granularity, each instance can represent a method, a class, a source code file, a package or a code change. The instance usually contains a number of defect prediction metrics (features), which are extracted from the software archives. The metric values represent the complexity of software and its development process. An instance can be labelled as defective or nondefective according to whether the instance contains defects or not. Then, based on the obtainedrd metrics and labels, the defect prediction models can be built by using a set of training instances. Finally, the prediction model can classify whether a new test instance is defective or not. The overview of software defect prediction process based on SNN model is shown in Fig. 1.

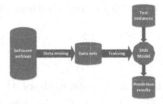

Fig. 1. Software defect prediction on SNN model

3   Research Methodology

3.1   The Learning Algorithm of Multilayer SNNs

The Error Function of Spike Trains

The spike train $s = \{t_i \epsilon \Gamma : i = 1, \cdots, N\}$, represents the ordered sequence of spike times fired by the spiking neuron in the interval $\Gamma = [0, T]$ and can be expressed formally as:

$$s(t) = \sum_{i=1}^{N} \delta(t - t_i) \tag{1}$$

In order to facilitate the analysis and calculation, we can choose a specific smoothing function h, using the convolution to convert the discrete spike train to a unique continuous function:

$$f_s(t) = s * h = \sum_{i=1}^{N} h(t - t_i) \tag{2}$$

The multilayer SNNs used in this study are fully connected feed forward networks. All neurons in the subsequent layer. In order to simplify the learning rule for simpler description, the network only contains one hidden layer. The feed forward SNNs contain three layers, including the input layer, hidden layer and output layer, and the number of neurons in each layer is N_i, N_h and N_o respectively.

The input and output signals of spike neurons are expressed in the form of spike trains; that is, spike trains encode neural information or external stimuli. The computation performed by single spiking neurons can be defined as a mapping from the input spike trains to the appropriate output spike train. For a given spiking neuron, we assume that the input spike trains are $s_i \epsilon S(\Gamma), i = 1, \cdots, N$ and the output spike train is $s_o \epsilon S(\Gamma)$. In order to analyze the relationship between the input and output spike trains, we use the linear Poisson neuron model [14]. This neuron model outputs a spike train, which is a realization of a Poisson process with the underlying intensity function estimation. The spiking activity of the postsyaptic neuron is defined by the estimated intensity functions of the presynaptic neurons. The contributions of all input spike trains are summed up linearly:

$$f_{s_o}(t) = \sum_{i=1}^{N} w_{oi} f_{s_i}(t) \tag{3}$$

where the weights w_{oi} represent the strength of the connection between the presynaptic neuron i and the postsynaptic neuron o. There are two reasons for this simplification. (1) Although dendritic trees of neurons have complex structures for information processing, the linear summation of inputs has been observed both in hippocampal pyramidal neurons [15] and cerebellar Purkinje cells [16]. (2) The linear summation of smoothed spike trains will be used for the derivation of the corresponding learning rule, in accordance with the preliminary results reported by Carnell and Richardson [17].

The goal of supervised learning for SNN is that for a given input spike train pattern, the output neurons eventually fire the desired spike trains by adjusting the synaptic weights. Therefore, the key of the supervised learning algorithm for multilayer feed-forward SNN is to define the spike train error function and the learning rule of synaptic weights.

In order to compute the network error, we first convert the actual spike train $s_o^a \in S(\Gamma)$ and the desired spike train $s_o^d \in S(\Gamma)$ of the output neuron to continuous functions using Eq. (3). The instantaneous network error is formally defined in terms of the square difference between the corresponding smoothed functions $f_{s_o^a}(t)$ and $f_{s_o^d}(t)$ at time t for all output neurons. It can be represented as:

$$E(t) = \frac{1}{2} \sum_{o=1}^{N_0} \left[f_{s_o^a}(t) - f_{s_o^d}(t) \right]^2 \tag{4}$$

The total error of the network in the time interval Γ is:

$$E = \int_\Gamma E(t)\, dt \tag{5}$$

Thus, the spike train error function in the network can be computed by the spike train inner products.

The Learning Rule of Multilayer SNNs

According to multiple spikes error backpropagation algorithm, the delta update rule is employed to adjust all synaptic weights. The weight adjustment for the i synapse from the presynaptic neuron to the postsynaptic neuron is calculated as:

$$\Delta w_i = -\eta \bigtriangledown E_i \tag{6}$$

where η is the learning rate and ΔE_i is the gradient of the multiple spikes error function for the weight of the w_i. It can be expressed as the integral in the time interval of the derivative of the error function $E(t)$ with respect to the weight W_i:

$$\Delta E_i = \int_\Gamma \frac{\partial E(t)}{\partial w_i} dt \tag{7}$$

Using the multiple spikes error function and the chain rule, According to the derivative of the error function E with respect to the synaptic weight w_i at time t, it can be obtained:

$$\frac{\partial E(t)}{\partial w_i} = \frac{\partial E(t)}{\partial f_{s_a}} \frac{\partial f_{s_a}}{\partial w_i} = [f_{s_a}(t) - f_{s_d}(t)]f_{s_i}(t) \tag{8}$$

where $s_i(t) \in S(\Gamma)$ Represents the spike train emitted by the input neuron i. The calculated value of the gradient of the synaptic weight w by the error function E is as follows:

$$\Delta E_i = \int_\Gamma [f_{s_a}(t) - f_{s_d}(t)]f_{s_i}(t) dt$$
$$= F(s_a, s_i) - F(s_d, s_i)) \tag{9}$$

where $F(s_i, s_j)$ is the inner product of two spikes trains. In Multi-STIP, the adjustment rule for synaptic weight between a neuron in the output layer and a neuron in the hidden layer is

$$
\begin{aligned}
\Delta w_{oh} &= -\eta \left[F\left(s_a^o(t), s_h(t)\right) - F\left(s_d^o(t), s_h(t)\right) \right] \\
&= -\eta \left[\sum_{g=1}^{F_d^o} \sum_{k=1}^{F_h} k\left(t_d^g, t_h^k\right) - \sum_{j=1}^{F_a^o} \sum_{k=1}^{F_h} k\left(t_a^j, t_h^k\right) \right]
\end{aligned}
\tag{10}
$$

and the adjustment rule for synaptic weight between a neuron in the hidden layer and a neuron in the input layer is

$$
\begin{aligned}
w_{hi} &= -\eta \sum_{o=1}^{N_o} \left[F\left(s_a^o(t), s_i(t)\right) - F\left(s_d^o(t), s_i(t)\right) \right] w_{oh} \\
&= -\eta \sum_{o=1}^{N_o} \left[\sum_{g=1}^{F_d^o} \sum_{f=1}^{F_i} k\left(t_d^g, t_i^f\right) - \sum_{j=1}^{F_a^o} \sum_{f=1}^{F_i} k\left(t_a^j, t_i^f\right) \right] w_{oh}
\end{aligned}
\tag{11}
$$

Where N_o is the number of output neurons, t_i^f and t_h^k are spike firing times in the input spike train $s_i(t)$ and hidden neuron spike train $s_h(t)$, respective, t_a^j and t_d^g are actual and desired spikes corresponding to an output neuron, and F_i, F_h, F_a^o and F_d^o are the numbers of spikes in s_i, s_h, $s_a^o(t)$, and $s_d^o(t)$ respectively.

4   Experimental Design

4.1   Experimental Datasets

In experiment, we employ 28 publicly available and commonly used projects from five different data sources including NASA [20], SOFTLAB [21], ReLink [22], AEEEM [23] and MORPH [24,25] as the experiment data. We select one project as the target data in turn, and separately use other projects as source data.

4.2   Evaluation Measures

In experiment, we employ four commonly used measures to evaluate the performance of defect prediction models, including recall rate (Pd), false positive rate (Pf), F-Measure (FM), G-Mean (GM). Pd and Pf are two widely used measures for SDP. These measures can be defined by using true positive (TP), false negative (FN), false positive (FP) and true negative (TN). Here, TP, FN, FP and TN are the number of defective instances that are predicted as defective, the number of defective instances that are predicted as defectfree, the number of defectfree instances that are predicted as defective, and the number of defectfree instances that are predicted as defectfree, respectively [19].

4.3 Parameter Settings

In this experiment we adopted spike response model. Some basic data remain unchanged during the experiment: The number of input layer neurons is 37, the number of hidden layer neurons is 14, and the number of output layer neurons is 1. The simulation time duration of each neuron is 100 ms, the time step is 0.1 ms. The learning rate is set as 0.006 and the maximum iteration number in a training processw is 20. We repeat the learning process 100 trails, each trail uses the 90% samples of the available training data. We compare the SNN method to the BPNN, Because BPNN and SNN are both artificial neural networks. We implement BPNN based on java programming followed the settings of the corresponding papers. To be fair, we applied z-score normalization to all of training and test data before running those algorithms.

5 Experimental Results

5.1 Comparison Result with Baselines

Figures 2, 3, 4 and 5 show the mean results of Pd, Pf, FM and GM for each target project. From these results, we can observe that SNN obtains the highest Pd, FM, GM. For the 28 target projects from five data sources, there are 600 possible prediction combinations in total. Thus, this way of setting may be suitable for some prediction combinations, but not suitable for the other combinations. From figures, we can see that SNN can obtain desirable prediction results. This shows that the effectiveness and feasibility of the proposed SNN approach.

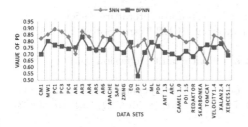

Fig. 2. Comparison results in Pd for each target

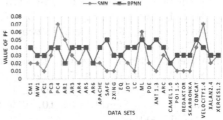

Fig. 3. Comparison results in Pf for each target

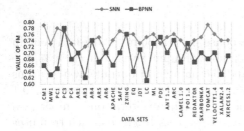 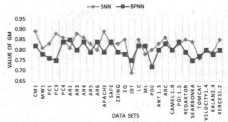

Fig. 4. Comparison results in FM for each target

Fig. 5. Comparison results in GM for each target

6 Conclusion

Software defect prediction with spiking neural networks, The software defect prediction model is constructed by feed-forward spiking network and trained by Spike train convolution algorithms, Extensive experiments on 28 public projects from five data sources indicate that the effectiveness of the proposed SNN approach with respect to the considered metrics. There are still many opportunities and challenges in the future work.

References

1. Li, Z., Jing, X.Y., Zhu, X., et al.: Heterogeneous defect prediction with two-stage ensemble learning. Autom. Softw. Eng. **26**(3), 599–651 (2019)
2. Zhiqiang, L., Xiao-Yuan, J., Xiaoke, Z.: Progress on approaches to software defect prediction. Iet Softw. **12**(3), 161–175 (2018)
3. Hall, T., Beecham, S., Bowes, D., et al.: A systematic literature review on fault prediction per-formance in software engineering. IEEE Trans. Softw. Eng. **38**(6), 1276–1304 (2012)
4. Catal, C., Diri, B.: A systematic review of software fault prediction studies. Expert Syst. Appl **36**(4), 7346–7354 (2009)
5. Maass, W.: Networks of spiking neurons: the third generation of neural network models. Neural Netw. **10**, 1659–1671 (1997). https://doi.org/10.1016/S0893-6080(97)00011-7
6. Whalley, K.: Neural coding: timing is key in the olfactory system. Nat. Rev. Neurosci. **14**, 458–458 (2013). https://doi.org/10.1038/nrn3532
7. Walter, F., Röhrbein, F., Knoll, A.: Computation by time. Neural Process. Lett. **44**(1), 103–124 (2015). https://doi.org/10.1007/s11063-015-9478-6
8. Wang, X., Lin, X., Dang, X.: A delay learning algorithm based on spike train kernels for spiking neurons. Front. Neurosci. **13**, 252 (2019)
9. Wang, X., Lin, X., Dang, X.: Supervised learning in spiking neural networks: a review of algorithms and evaluations. Neural Netw. **125**, 258–280 (2020)
10. Wang, X.: supervised learning in spiking neural networks with inner product of spike trains (2015)
11. Carnell, A., Richardson, D.: Linear algebra for time series of spikes. In: ESANN, pp. 363–368 (2005)

12. Park, I.M., Seth, S., Rao, M., Príncipe, J.C.: Strictly positive-definite spike train kernels for point-process divergences. Neural Comput. **24**(8), 2223–2250 (2012)
13. Paiva, A.R., Park, I., Príncipe, J.C.: A reproducing kernel hilbert space framework for spike train signal processing. Neural Comput. **21**(2), 424–449 (2009)
14. Gütig, R., Aharonov, R., Rotter, S., Sompolinsky, H.: Learning input correlations through nonlinear temporally asymmetric hebbian plasticity. J. Neurosci. **23**(9), 3697–3714 (2003)
15. Cash, S., Yuste, R.: Linear summation of excitatory inputs by CA1 pyramidal neurons. Neuron **22**(2), 383–394 (1999)
16. Brunel, N., Hakim, V., Isope, P., Nadal, J.P., Barbour, B.: Optimal information storage and the distribution of synaptic weights: perceptron versus purkinje cell. Neuron **43**(5), 745–757 (2004)
17. Carnell, A., Richardson, D.: Linear algebra for time series of spikes. In: ESANN, pp. 363–368 (2004)
18. Lin, X., Wang, X., Hao, Z.: Supervised learning in multilayer spiking neural networks with in-ner products of spike trains. Neurocomputing **237**, 59–70 (2017)
19. Li, Z., Jing, X.Y., Wu, F., et al.: Cost-sensitive transfer kernel canonical correlation analysis for heterogeneous defect prediction. Autom. Softw. Eng. **25**, 201–245 (2017)
20. Shepperd, M., Song, Q., Sun, Z., Mair, C.: Data quality: some comments on the nasa software defect datasets. IEEE Trans. Softw. Eng. **39**(9), 1208–1215 (2013)
21. Menzies, T., Krishna, R., Pryor, D.: The Promise Repository of Empirical Software Engineering Data (2016). http://openscience.us/repo
22. Wu, R., Zhang, H., Kim, S., Cheung, S.C.: Relink: recovering links between bugs and changes. In: ESEC/FSE'11, pp. 15–25 (2011)
23. D'Ambros, M., Lanza, M., Robbes, R.: Evaluating defect prediction approaches: a benchmark and an extensive comparison. Empir. Softw. Eng. **17**(4–5), 531–577 (2012)
24. Peters, F., Menzies, T., Gong, L., Zhang, H.: Balancing privacy and utility in cross-company defect prediction. IEEE Trans. Softw. Eng. **39**(8), 1054–1068 (2013a)
25. Nam, J., Kim, S.: Heterogeneous defect prediction. In: ESEC/FSE 2015, pp. 508–519 (2015)

Spatial Graph Convolutional Networks

Tomasz Danel[1]([✉])(iD), Przemysław Spurek[1](iD), Jacek Tabor[1](iD),
Marek Śmieja[1](iD), Łukasz Struski[1](iD), Agnieszka Słowik[2](iD),
and Łukasz Maziarka[1](iD)

[1] Faculty of Mathematics and Computer Science, Jagiellonian University,
Łojasiewicza 6, 30-428 Krakow, Poland
tomasz.danel@ii.uj.edu.pl
[2] Department of Computer Science and Technology, University of Cambridge,
15 JJ Thomson Ave, Cambridge CB3 0FD, UK

Abstract. Graph Convolutional Networks (GCNs) have recently become the primary choice for learning from graph-structured data, superseding hash fingerprints in representing chemical compounds. However, GCNs lack the ability to take into account the ordering of node neighbors, even when there is a geometric interpretation of the graph vertices that provides an order based on their spatial positions. To remedy this issue, we propose Spatial Graph Convolutional Network (SGCN) which uses spatial features to efficiently learn from graphs that can be naturally located in space. Our contribution is threefold: we propose a GCN-inspired architecture which (i) leverages node positions, (ii) is a proper generalization of both GCNs and Convolutional Neural Networks (CNNs), (iii) benefits from augmentation which further improves the performance and assures invariance with respect to the desired properties. Empirically, SGCN outperforms state-of-the-art graph-based methods on image classification and chemical tasks.

Keywords: Graph convolutional networks · Convolutional neural networks · Chemoinformatics

1   Introduction

Convolutional Neural Network (CNNs) use trainable filters to process images or grid-like objects in general. They have quickly overridden feed-forward networks in computer vision tasks [9,13], and later also excelled in parsing text data [7]. However, CNNs can only be used to analyze tensor data in which local patterns are prominent. One of the data structures that does not conform to this requirement is graph, which can be used to represent, e.g., social networks, neural networks, and chemical compounds. In these applications, local patters may also play a key role in processing big graph structures. Borrowing from CNNs, Graph Convolutionl Networks (GCNs) use local filters to aggregate information from neighboring nodes [2,3]. However, most of these networks do not distinguish node neighbors and apply the same weights to each of them, sometimes modified by node degrees [8], edge attributes, or trainable attention weights [15].

© Springer Nature Switzerland AG 2020
H. Yang et al. (Eds.): ICONIP 2020, CCIS 1333, pp. 668–675, 2020.
https://doi.org/10.1007/978-3-030-63823-8_76

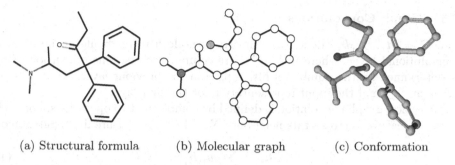

(a) Structural formula   (b) Molecular graph   (c) Conformation

Fig. 1. Representation of small molecules. (a) shows the structural formula of a compound (methadone); (b) presents the molecular graph constructed from the structural formula. (c) depicts an exemplary molecular conformation (one of the energetic minima), which is a 3D embedding of the graph.

In many cases, graphs are coupled with spatial information embedded in their nodes. For example, images can be transformed to graphs where nodes correspond to image pixels (color channels). In this case, each pixel has 2-dimensional coordinates, which define its position in the image. In chemical applications, molecules can be represented as graphs (Fig. 1). Standard GCNs do not take spatial positions of the nodes into account, which is a considerable difference between GCNs and CNNs. Moreover, in the case of images, geometric features allow to augment data with translation or rotation and significantly enlarge the given dataset, which is crucial when the number of examples is limited.

In this paper, we propose Spatial Graph Convolutional Networks (SGCN), a variant of GCNs, which is a proper generalization of CNNs to the case of graphs. In contrast to existing GCNs, SGCN uses spatial features of nodes to aggregate information from the neighbors. On one hand, this geometric interpretation is useful to model many real examples of graphs, such as graphs of chemical compounds. In this case, it is possible to perform data augmentation by rotating a given graph in a spatial domain and, in consequence, improve network generalization when the amount of data is limited. On the other hand, a single layer of SGCN can be parametrized so that it returns an output identical to a standard convolutional layer on grid-like objects, such as images (see Theorem 1).

The code is available at github.com/gmum/geo-gcn.

2 Spatial Graph Convolutional Network

We use the following notation throughout this paper: let $\mathcal{G} = (V, \boldsymbol{A})$ be a graph, where $V = \{v_1, \ldots, v_n\}$ denotes a set of nodes (vertices) and $\boldsymbol{A} = [a_{ij}]_{i,j=1}^{n}$ represents edges. Let $a_{ij} = 1$ if there is a directed edge from v_i to v_j, and $a_{ij} = 0$ otherwise. Each node v_i is represented by a d-dimensional feature vector $\boldsymbol{x}_i \in \mathbb{R}^d$. Typically, graph convolutional neural networks transform these feature vectors over multiple subsequent layers to produce the final prediction.

2.1   Graph Convolutions

Let $H = [h_1, \ldots, h_n]$ denote the matrix of node features being an input to a convolutional layer, where $h_i \in \mathbb{R}^{d_{in}}$ are column vectors. The dimension of h_i is determined by the number of filters used in the previous layer. We denote as $X = [x_1, \ldots, x_n]$ the input representation for the first layer.

A typical graph convolution is defined by combining two operations. For each node v_i, feature vectors of its neighbors $N_i = \{j : a_{ij} = 1\}$ are first aggregated:

$$\bar{h}_i = \sum_{j \in N_i} u_{ij} h_j, \tag{1}$$

which could be also written in a matrix form as $\bar{H} = U H^T$. Where the weights $U \in \mathbb{R}^{n \times n}$ are either trainable (e.g. [15] applied attention mechanism) or determined by adjacency matrix A (e.g. [8] motivated their selection using spectral graph theory).

Next, a standard MLP is applied to transform the intermediate representation $\bar{H} = [\bar{h}_1, \ldots, \bar{h}_n]$ into the final output of a given layer:

$$\text{MLP}(\bar{H}; W) = \text{ReLU}(W^T \bar{H} + b), \tag{2}$$

where $W \in \mathbb{R}^{d_{in} \times d_{out}}$ is a trainable weight matrix and $b \in \mathbb{R}^{d_{out}}$ is a trainable bias vector (added column-wise). A typical graph convolutional neural network is composed of a sequence of graph convolutional layers (described above), see Fig. 2. Next, its output is aggregated to the final response depending on a given task, e.g. node or graph classification.

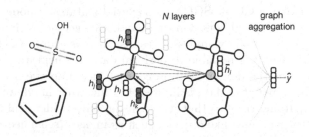

Fig. 2. An overview of the full network. A molecule is transformed to the graph representation and fed to the N consecutive (spatial) graph convolutional layers. In the figure, the convolution is demonstrated at the grey node – feature vectors of the adjacent nodes h_j, h_k, and h_l are aggregated together with the central node h_i to create a new feature vector $\bar{h}_i$ for the grey node. In the proposed spatial variant, the relative positions of the neighbors are used in the aggregation (see Eq. 3). At the end, all the node vectors are averaged, and the final prediction $\hat{y}$ is produced.

2.2   Spatial Graph Convolutions

In this section, the spatial graph convolutions are defined. The basic assumption is that each node v_i is additionally identified by its coordinates $p_i \in \mathbb{R}^t$. In the case of images, p_i is the vector of two dimensional pixel coordinates, while for chemical compounds, it denotes location of the atom in thr two or three dimensional space (depending on the representation of chemical compound). In contrast to standard features x_i, p_i is not changed across layers, but only used to construct a better graph representation. For this purpose, (1) is replaced by:

$$\bar{h}_i(U, b) = \sum_{j \in N_i} \text{ReLU}(U^T(p_j - p_i) + b) \odot h_j, \tag{3}$$

where $U \in \mathbb{R}^{t \times d}, b \in \mathbb{R}^d$ are trainable parameters, d is the dimension of h_j and $\odot$ is element-wise multiplication. The pair U, b plays a role of a convolutional filter which operates on the neighborhood of v_i. The relative positions in the neighborhood are transformed using a linear operation combined with non-linear ReLU function. This scalar is used to weigh the feature vectors h_j in a neighborhood.

By the analogy with classical convolution, this transformation can be extended to multiple filters. Let $U = [U^{(1)}, \ldots, U^{(k)}]$ and $B = [b^{(1)}, \ldots, b^{(k)}]$ define k filters. The intermediate representation $\bar{h}_i$ is then a vector defined by:

$$\bar{h}_i(U, B) = \bar{h}_i(U^{(1)}, b^{(1)}) \oplus \cdots \oplus \bar{h}_i(U^{(k)}, b^{(k)}), \tag{4}$$

where $\oplus$ denotes the vector concatenation. Finally, MLP transformation is applied in the same manner as in (2) to transform these feature vectors into new representation.

Equation 3 can be easily parametrized to obtain graph convolution presented in Eq. 1. If all spatial features p_i are put to 0, then (3) reduces to:

$$\bar{h}_i(U, b) = \sum_{j \in N_i} \text{ReLU}(b) h_j.$$

This gives a vanilla graph convolution, where the aggregation over neighbors does not contain parameters. Different $b = u_{ij}$ can also be used for each pair of neighbors, which allows to mimic many types of graph convolutions.

2.3   Data Augmentation

In practice, the size of training data is often insufficient for generalization. To overcome this problem, one can perform data augmentation. The introduction of spatial features allow us to perform data augmentation in a natural way, which is not feasible using only the graph adjacency matrix.

The formula (3) is invariant to the translation of spatial features, but its value depends on rotation of graph. In consequence, the rotation of the geometrical graph leads to different values of (3). Since in most domains the rotation does not affect the interpretation of the object described by such a graph, this property can be used to produce more instances of the same graph. This reasoning is exactly the same as in the classical view of image processing.

3   Relation Between SGCN and CNNs

In contrast to typical GCNs, which consider graphs as relational structures, SGCN assumes that a graph can be coupled with a spatial structure. In particular, SGCN is capable of imitating the behavior of CNNs. In other words, the formula (3) can parametrize any convolutional filter in classical CNNs. In this section, we first describe this fact formally and next confirm this observation in an experimental study.

Theoretical Findings. Let us introduce a notation concerning convolutions in the case of images. For simplicity only convolutions without pooling and with odd mask size are considered. In general, given a filter $F = [f_{i'j'}]_{i',j'\in\{-k..k\}}$ its result on the image $H = [h_{ij}]_{i\in\{1..N\},j\in\{1..K\}}$ is given by $F * H = G = [g_{ij}]_{i\in\{1..N\},j\in\{1..K\}}$, where

$$g_{ij} = \sum_{\substack{i'=-k..k:\, i+i'\in\{1..N\},\\ j'=-k..k:\, j+j'\in\{1..K\}}} f_{i'j'} h_{i+i',j+j'}.$$

Theorem 1. *Let $H \in \mathbb{R}^{N\times K}$ be an image. Let $F = [f_{i'j'}]_{i',j'\in\{-k..k\}}$ be a given convolutional filter, and let $n = (2k+1)^2$ (number of elements of F). Then there exist SGCN parameters: $U \in \mathbb{R}^{2\times 1}$, $b_1,\ldots,b_n \in \mathbb{R}$, and $w \in \mathbb{R}^n$ such that the image convolution can be represented as SGCN, i.e.*

$$F * H = \sum_{i=1}^{n} w_i \bar{H}(U, b_i).$$

We prove Theorem 1 in the extended version of the paper [1].

Experimental Verification. To demonstrate the correspondence between CNNs and SGCN, we consider the MNIST dataset. To build the graph representation, each pixel is mapped to a graph node, making a regular grid with connections between adjacent pixels. We also consider an alternative representation [11], in which nodes are constructed from an irregular grid of 75 superpixels. The edges are determined by spatial relations

Table 1. Classification accuracy on two graph representations of MNIST.

Method	Grid	Superpixels
CNN	99.21%	-
ChebNet	99.14%	75.62%
MoNet	99.19%	91.11%
SplineCNN	99.22%	95.22%
GAT	99.26%	95.83%
SGCN	**99.61%**	**95.95%**

between nodes using k-nearest neighbors. We report the results by state-of-the-art methods used to process geometrical shapes: ChebNet [2], MoNet [11], SplineCNN [4], and GAT [15]. For the first representation, SGCN is also compared to CNN with an analogical architecture.

The results presented in Table 1 show that SGCN outperforms comparable methods. Its performance is slightly better than SplineCNN, which reports state-of-the-art results on this task. We also get higher accuracy than CNN, which confirms that SGCN is its proper generalization.

4 Experiments: A Case Study in Predicting Molecular Properties of Chemical Compounds

Experimental Setting. Three datasets of small molecules were chosen from the MoleculeNet [16] benchmark: BBBP is a binary classification task, and ESOL and FreeSolv have continuous targets. To predict 3D atom positions, we use universal force field (UFF) method from the RDKit package. We run this procedure up to 30 times and augment the data with random rotations. Datasets are split according to the MoleculeNet standards. A random search is run for all models testing 100 hyperparameter sets for each of them. All runs are repeated 3 times.

We compare popular chemical models: graph models (Graph Convolution [3], Weave [6], MPNN [5]), RF and SVM using ECFP fingerprints [12] of size 1024, and attention models (EAGCN [14], MAT [10]). Our method used train- and test-time data augmentation[1]. In order to investigate the impact of the positional features, we add the atom positions to the atom representation of GCN, and apply the same augmentation. We name this model pos-GCN.

Table 2. Performance measured with ROC AUC for BBBP and RMSE for ESOL and FreeSolv. Best mean results and intervals overlapping with them are bolded. For the first column higher is better, for the second and the third lower is better.

Method	BBBP	ESOL	FreeSolv
SVM	0.603 ± 0.000	0.493 ± 0.000	0.391 ± 0.000
RF	0.551 ± 0.005	0.533 ± 0.003	0.550 ± 0.004
GC	0.690 ± 0.015	0.334 ± 0.017	0.336 ± 0.043
Weave	0.703 ± 0.012	0.389 ± 0.045	0.403 ± 0.035
MPNN	0.700 ± 0.019	0.303 ± 0.012	$\mathbf{0.299 \pm 0.038}$
EAGCN	0.664 ± 0.007	0.459 ± 0.019	0.410 ± 0.014
MAT	0.711 ± 0.007	0.330 ± 0.002	$\mathbf{0.269 \pm 0.007}$
pos-GCN	0.696 ± 0.008	0.301 ± 0.011	$\mathbf{0.278 \pm 0.024}$
SGCN	$\mathbf{0.743 \pm 0.004}$	$\mathbf{0.270 \pm 0.005}$	$\mathbf{0.299 \pm 0.033}$

Results. The results in Table 2 show that for the first two datasets, SGCN outperforms all the tested models by a significant margin, i.e. the difference between SGCN and other methods is statistically significant. In the case of FreeSolv, the mean result obtained by SGCN is slightly worse than MAT and pos-GCN, but this difference is not statistically significant due to the high variance.

Ablation Study of the Data Augmentation. We examined how removing predicted positions, and thus setting all positional vectors to zero in Eq. 3, affects the scores achieved by our model on chemical tasks. The results are depicted in Fig. 3. It

---

[1] For all datasets, slight improvements can be observed with the augmented data.

clearly shows that even predicted node coordinates improve the performance of the method. In the same plot we also show the outcome of augmenting the data with random rotations and 30 predicted molecule conformations, which were calculated as described above. It occurs that the best performing model uses all types of position augmentation. More ablation studies on data augmentation can be found in the extended version of the paper [1].

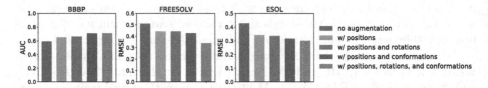

Fig. 3. Comparison of different augmentation strategies on three chemical datasets. No augmentation is a pure GCN without positions. In the conformation variant multiple conformations were precalculated and then sampled during training. Rotation augmentation randomly rotates molecules in batches. For the first bar-plot higher is better, for the second and the third lower is better.

5   Conclusion

We proposed SGCN which is a general model for processing graph-structured data with spatial features. Node positions are integrated into our convolution operation to create a layer which generalizes both GCNs and CNNs. In contrast to the majority of other approaches, our method can effectively use added information about location to construct self-taught feature masking, which can be augmented to achieve invariance with respect to the desired properties. Furthermore, we provide a theoretical analysis of our spatial graph convolutions. The experiments confirm the strong performance of our method.

Acknowledgements. The work of T. Danel was supported by the National Science Centre (Poland) grant no. 2018/31/B/ST6/00993. The work of P. Spurek was supported by the National Centre of Science (Poland) Grant No. 2019/33/B/ST6/00894. The work of J. Tabor was supported by the Foundation for Polish Science Grant No. POIR.04.04.00-00-14DE/18-00 co-financed by the European Union under the European Regional Development Fund. The work of M. Śmieja was supported by the grant no. LIDER/37/0137/L-9/17/NCBR/2018 from the Polish National Centre for Research and Development. The work of Ł. Struski was supported by the National Science Centre (Poland) grant no. 2017/25/B/ST6/01271. The work of Ł. Maziarka was supported by the National Science Centre (Poland) grant no. 2019/35/N/ST6/02125.

References

1. Danel, T., et al.: Spatial graph convolutional networks. arXiv preprint arXiv:1909.05310 (2019)

2. Defferrard, M., Bresson, X., Vandergheynst, P.: Convolutional neural networks on graphs with fast localized spectral filtering. In: Advances in Neural Information Processing Systems, pp. 3844–3852 (2016)

3. Duvenaud, D.K., et al.: Convolutional networks on graphs for learning molecular fingerprints. In: Advances in Neural Information Processing Systems, pp. 2224–2232 (2015)

4. Fey, M., Lenssen, J.E., Weichert, F., Müller, H.: SplineCNN: fast geometric deep learning with continuous B-spline kernels. In: Proceedings of the IEEE Conference on Computer Vision and Pattern Recognition, pp. 869–877 (2018)

5. Gilmer, J., Schoenholz, S.S., Riley, P.F., Vinyals, O., Dahl, G.E.: Neural message passing for quantum chemistry. In: Proceedings of the 34th International Conference on Machine Learning, vol. 70, pp. 1263–1272 (2017). JMLR.org

6. Kearnes, S., McCloskey, K., Berndl, M., Pande, V., Riley, P.: Molecular graph convolutions: moving beyond fingerprints. J. Comput. Aided Mol. Des. 30(8), 595–608 (2016). https://doi.org/10.1007/s10822-016-9938-8

7. Kim, Y.: Convolutional neural networks for sentence classification. arXiv preprint arXiv:1408.5882 (2014)

8. Kipf, T.N., Welling, M.: Semi-supervised classification with graph convolutional networks. arXiv preprint arXiv:1609.02907 (2016)

9. Krizhevsky, A., Sutskever, I., Hinton, G.E.: Imagenet classification with deep convolutional neural networks. In: Advances in Neural Information Processing Systems, pp. 1097–1105 (2012)

10. Maziarka, Ł., Danel, T., Mucha, S., Rataj, K., Tabor, J., Jastrzębski, S.: Molecule-augmented attention transformer. In: Workshop on Graph Representation Learning, Neural Information Processing Systems 2019 (2019)

11. Monti, F., Boscaini, D., Masci, J., Rodola, E., Svoboda, J., Bronstein, M.M.: Geometric deep learning on graphs and manifolds using mixture model CNNs. In: Proceedings of the IEEE Conference on Computer Vision and Pattern Recognition, pp. 5115–5124 (2017)

12. Rogers, D., Hahn, M.: Extended-connectivity fingerprints. J. Chem. Inf. Model. 50(5), 742–754 (2010)

13. Seferbekov, S.S., Iglovikov, V., Buslaev, A., Shvets, A.: Feature pyramid network for multi-class land segmentation. In: CVPR Workshops, pp. 272–275 (2018)

14. Shang, C., et al.: Edge attention-based multi-relational graph convolutional networks. arXiv preprint arXiv:1802.04944 (2018)

15. Veličković, P., Cucurull, G., Casanova, A., Romero, A., Lio, P., Bengio, Y.: Graph attention networks. arXiv preprint arXiv:1710.10903 (2017)

16. Wu, Z., Ramsundar, B., Feinberg, E.N., Gomes, J., Geniesse, C., Pappu, A.S., Leswing, K., Pande, V.: Moleculenet: a benchmark for molecular machine learning. Chem. Sci. 9(2), 513–530 (2018)

STM-GAN: Sequentially Trained Multiple Generators for Mitigating Mode Collapse

Sakshi Varshney[✉], P. K. Srijith, and Vineeth N. Balasubramanian

Computer Science and Engineering, Indian Institute of Technology, Hyderabad,
Hyderabad, India
{cs16resch01002,srijith,vineethnb}@iith.ac.in

Abstract. Generative adversarial networks have shown promise in generating images and videos. However, they suffer from the mode collapse issue which prevents it from generating complex multi-modal data. In this paper, We propose an approach to mitigate the mode collapse issue in generative adversarial networks (GANs). We propose to use multiple generators to capture various modes and each generator is encouraged to learn a different mode through a novel loss function. The generators are trained in a sequential way to effectively learn multiple modes. The effectiveness of the proposed approach is demonstrated through experiments on a synthetic data set, image data sets such as MNIST and fashion MNIST, and in multi-topic document modelling.

Keywords: Generative Adversarial Network · Mode collapse · Topic modelling

1 Introduction

Generative adversarial networks(GANs) [1] have shown to be useful to generate complex high dimensional data such as images and videos. GANs are successfully deployed in many real-world applications such as, Synthesizing super-resolution images [2], 3D object generation [3], interactive image generation [4]. Generative adversarial networks try to learn the unknown data distribution P_{data} implicitly using the model distribution P_{model}. The GAN framework consists of two networks: a discriminator network which receives samples from both the real distribution P_{data} and the model distribution P_{model}, and a generator network which generates samples from the model distribution P_{model}. The objective of the discriminator network is to efficiently differentiate the real samples and the generated samples. On the contrary, the objective of the generator is to generate samples close to the real samples which can fool the discriminator. Thus the training procedure of GAN involves the discriminator and generator network in a zero-sum game playing against each other. This process of training the networks in an alternative manner to achieve a state of equilibrium is highly unstable which results in mode collapse issue. Recently, few works were proposed to address mode collapse issue in GANs [6,7,9,10]. Some approaches focus on

© Springer Nature Switzerland AG 2020
H. Yang et al. (Eds.): ICONIP 2020, CCIS 1333, pp. 676–684, 2020.
https://doi.org/10.1007/978-3-030-63823-8_77

improving the objective function to achieve better convergence. On the contrary, some explicitly force the model to learn various modes present in the true distribution. In our work, we use multiple generator approach to learn the various modes present in the data distribution. Each generator is encouraged to learn different mode from the other generator through sequential training and a novel loss function. The generated sample from one of the trained generator is selected as the final output. We demonstrate the effectiveness of this approach on multi-modal image datasets as well as text documents. Our main contributions can be summarized as follows.

* A sequential training approach on multiple generators to mitigate mode collapse problem in GAN.
* A sequentially trained mixture of generators model for document generation and topic modelling of text data.
* Demonstrating the effectiveness of the proposed approaches in both the image data and text data.

2   Related Work

There are few works which make changes in the objective function to address mode collapse issue. WGAN [6] is a recent method which uses a probability metric based on earth mover distance to reflect the difference between true and modelled distribution. LSGAN [7] adopt least squares loss function for the discriminator and show that minimizing the objective function of LSGAN yields minimizing the Pearson χ^2 divergence.

An alternative approach is to have multiple generators instead of using one. Coupled GAN [8] framework consists of a tuple of GANs, each for different data domain. It trains generator with shared parameters to learn the joint distribution of multi-domain images. MAD-GAN [9] is a multi-agent architecture, consists of multiple generators and single discriminator. It makes changes in the discriminator architecture such that in addition to classifying real or fake samples, it also identify the generator that generates the sample. Mixture of generators(MGAN) [10] also proposed a GAN architecture consists of multiple generators. It minimises the Jenson-Shannon divergence(JSD) between the generators distribution and the true distribution while it maximises the JSD among generators.

3   Background

GAN is an implicit generative model, GAN framework consists of two networks which are trained using minmax game: the generator network learns optimal parameter θ_g which generate samples $G(z; \theta_g)$ that emulates data points $\mathcal{D} = (x_i)_{i=1}^n$ from real distribution P_{data}, where $z \sim p(z)$ is a prior input noise. Discriminator $D(x, \theta_d)$ learns to distinguish real samples $x \sim P_{data}$ from the generated samples $x = G(z; \theta_g) \sim P_{model}$. The overall GAN objective is:

$$\min_{\theta_g} \max_{\theta_d} V(\theta_g, \theta_d) = E_{x \sim P_{data}} [\log D(x; \theta_d)] + E_{z \sim p_z(z)} [\log(1 - D(G(z; \theta_g); \theta_d))]$$

(1)

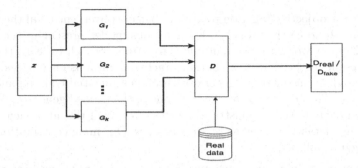

Fig. 1. Multilple generator GAN architecture

The training of discriminator and generator is performed in an alternate manner. The discriminator $D(x; \theta_d) \in [0, 1]$ provides the estimated probability that
sample x comes from the true data distribution. The objective of discriminator is to maximize the score $D(x; \theta_d)$ for samples coming from real distribution
$x \sim P_{data}$ while minimizing it for the generated samples ($x \sim P_{model}$). The
objective of the generator network is to improve the generated sample by maximizing the discriminator probability. The theoretical proof of convergence shows
that generator learns true data distribution. However, practically convergence
is hard to achieve as the training procedure of GAN involves training two networks in an alternative manner. This causes the network to suffer from mode
collapse issue. GAN shows mode collapse issue while trained for data consisting
of samples from various modes.

4   Sequentially Trained Multiple Generative Adversarial Networks

We propose an approach to address the mode collapse issue associated with the
standard GAN training. The proposed approach is motivated by the observations
resulting from the standard training of GAN when applied to multi-modal data.
In the standard approach, Discriminator is trained to provide high probability
to high-density regions associated with real data. Generator focus on any of the
modes for which discriminator provides higher probability and starts generating
data from this mode while ignoring other modes.   Our idea is to use a new
generator to cover the modes for which discriminator is giving a high probability rather than letting the existing generator to move to an alternate mode. We
train different generators for capturing different modes in the data. To achieve
this we consider a GAN framework with multiple generators as in Fig. 1. Our
architecture consists of K generators and a single discriminator. The standard
GAN loss function does not encourage diversity among the multiple generators.
We propose a novel loss function and a sequential training algorithm which will
allow our multiple generator framework to cover all the modes. To encourage
each generator to capture different mode, appropriate changes have to be made

---

Algorithm 1: Sequential training of multiple generators

Require: $K, z \sim p_z(z), x \sim P_{data}$

   while Not converged **do**

      Generator update

      for $(i = 1, \ldots, K)$ **do**

         $\max_{\theta_{g_i}} E_{z \sim p_z(z)}[D(G_i(z; \theta_{g_i})) \times H.M.((1 - D(G_{i-1}(z; \theta_{g_{i-1}}))), ..., (1 - D(G_1(z; \theta_{g_1}))))]$

      end for

      Discriminator update

         $\max_{\theta_d} E_{x \sim P_{data}}[\log D(x; \theta_d)] + \sum_{k=1}^{K} E_{z \sim p_z(z)}[\log(1 - D(G_k(z; \theta_{g_k}); \theta_d))]$

   end while

   return $\theta_d, \theta_{g_i}, i = 1, ..K$

---

in the objective function of each generator. We propose to train the generators in a sequential manner with the loss function of the first generator similar to the vanilla generator loss function i.e. $\max_{\theta_{g_1}} E_{z \sim p_z(z)}[D(G_1(z; \theta_{g_1}))]$. The objective function of remaining generators is updated sequentially based on previously trained generators. For the second generator, we want it to focus on region or mode not covered by the first generator. To achieve this, objective function for i^{th} generator is updated based on all the generators $G_1, \ldots, G_{i-1}$ as follows.

$$\max_{\theta_{g_i}} E_{z \sim p_z(z)}[D(G_i(z; \theta_{g_i})) \times H.M.((1 - D(G_{i-1}(z; \theta_{g_{i-1}}))), ..., (1 - D(G_1(z; \theta_{g_1}))))]$$

(2)

where H.M. represents the harmonic mean. The objective function ensures that the current generator focus on the samples belonging to the modes ignored by previous generators. Thus, this approach pushes each generator to learn different modes from the previous generators. The gradient of the current generator is controlled by the output of the discriminator for previously trained generators. The harmonic mean of the probabilities ensure the current generator learn modes where the probabilities $(D(G_i(z)))$ for all the previous generator is low, i.e. $(1 - D(G_i(z)))$ is high. The arithmetic mean and geometric mean are not desirable when one of the generator value is high and other is low. Algorithm 1 provides a pseudo-code of the sequential training process. After training, the images are generated from one of the trained generators.

4.1 Document Modelling Using Sequentially Trained Multiple GAN

Document collection (corpus) contain documents talking about multiple topics such as politics, sports, entertainment etc. Documents can be seen to represent multi-modal data with each mode corresponding to a topic distribution. The topic distribution, i.e. distribution over words is different for every topic. Topics such as politics have a higher distribution of words like minister and party while topic on sports has a higher distribution on football, player etc. We can model such a collection of documents using the GAN framework described in Sect. 4.

We assume there are K generators, with each generator $G_k(z)$ possibly representing a topic k and generating the representation of the document from that topic. Thus, the mixture of generators model for modelling the documents can be represented as follows.

$$p(\boldsymbol{w}) = \sum_k p(k)p(\boldsymbol{w}|k) = \sum_k p(k)G_k(\boldsymbol{w}) \tag{3}$$

The advantage of a GAN based approach is that it can model and generate any representation of the document (TF, TF-IDF and other sentence embeddings). Moreover, it can capture complex relationship (correlations) across different dimensions in the document representations using the generator neural network. The generators are trained using the sequential training process proposed in Algorithm 1.This allows generators to focus on different topics and generate from it leading to a better document generation model.

5   Experiments and Results

We perform experiments on various synthetic as well as real-world datasets including image and text to demonstrate the effectiveness of the proposed approach sequentially trained multiple GAN (STM-GAN). We show experimental results for 1D Gaussian dataset, Fashion MNIST and 20 newsgroup dataset. For synthetic and Fashion-MNIST experiment comparison, we use the popular state-of-the-art Wasserstein GAN (WGAN) [6] and another generative modelling approach based on mixture of generators (MGAN) [10]. For document modelling, we use adversarial neural topic model (ATM) [5], a recently proposed approach for topic modelling using GAN, for performance comparison.

5.1   Synthetic Experiments

We first perform simple experiments over synthetic dataset created using a mixture of Gaussian distribution which is having multiple modes. The data used for this experimental setup is generated using Gaussian mixture distribution having six mixture components with mean at 10,15,25,60, 90 and 110, and variance 3,3,2,2 5 and 5. Training data consists of 20,000 samples generated using the Gaussian mixture distribution. Figure 2 plots the synthetic training data (blue line) and the data generated by the trained STM-GAN model (green line) and WGAN and MGAN. We can observe that STM-GAN with $K = 4$ generators were able to cover all the modes of the Gaussian mixture and is sufficient. On further increasing the number of generators, more than one generator starts capturing similar mixture components. It is clear from the Fig. 2 our approach captures all the modes available in the dataset and provides a better approximation of true data distribution than WGAN and MGAN.

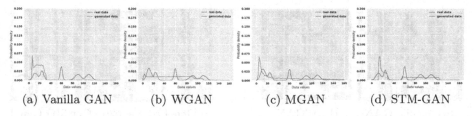

(a) Vanilla GAN   (b) WGAN   (c) MGAN   (d) STM-GAN

Fig. 2. 1-D mixture of 4 Gaussians modelled using Vanilla GAN, WGAN, MGAN, and STM-GAN with 4 generators.

5.2 Image Generation

We performed experiments over Fashion-MNIST [11]dataset. We have shown perceptual results as well quantitative results of the image dataset. We consider inception score [12] to provide the quantitative results. The perceptual results are shown in Fig. 3. It is clear as we increase the number of generators to four in the proposed approach STM-GAN, it generates more diverse images from the dataset. Each generator focuses on a particular mode and generates images from that mode. It is visible from the figure that our approach provides more diverse images than Vanilla GAN and WGAN framework. The inception scores are shown in Table 1. For calculating inception score we have considered 20,000 images generated using Vanilla GAN, WGAN and STM-GAN. We also compared inception score of the generated images against the real images. We can observe that the inception score of STM-GAN is higher than that of WGAN showing the effectiveness of the proposed approach.

5.3 Document Modelling

We conduct experiments to study the ability of our models to generate documents and learn latent topics in an unsupervised manner. We consider 20 newsgroup dataset to perform experiments. We select documents of 5 distinct topics(science,computer,religion,automobiles,sports) from this 20 newsgroup dataset based on the domain associated with each topic to form dataset for our experiments. It consists of total 4742 documents. We first pre-process the data by removing punctuation, common stop-words, performing stemming. We consider 1960 most frequent words, and consequently a word vector of size 1960. We consider the bag-of-words representation of documents weighted by TF-IDF. We assume the topics are unknown to us and use five generator STM-GAN to model the documents and learn the latent topics. The generators used in the STM-GAN for document modelling framework uses the same architecture.

We use cosine similarity to evaluate the quality of generated documents and discovered topics. Higher values of cosine similarity show the model is able to generate documents similar to training data. We compare our results with Vanilla GAN and Adversarial neural topic model (ATM) [5] which provides topic distribution sampled using Dirichlet prior as input to the generator and generates the

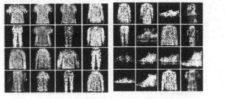 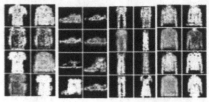

(a) Vanilla GAN   (b) WGAN   (c) Gen 1 (d) Gen 2(e) Gen 3(f) Gen 4

Fig. 3. Fashion MNIST images generated using a) Vanilla GAN b) WGAN c–f) 4 generators of STM-GAN

Table 1. Inception score for Fashion-MNIST dataset

	Real data	Vanilla GAN	WGAN	STM-GAN
Mean	4.4450	1.9528	2.2814	**2.6480**
Variance	0.0690	0.1282	0.0388	0.1062

corresponding document. Table 3 shows the cosine similarity computed between the documents generated by different generators in the STM-GAN model and the training documents from each topic. We find that each topic has a high cosine similarity to one of the generators in the STM-GAN and this is higher than that for ATM and vanilla GAN.

We create a TSNE plot of the documents generated using generators of STM-GAN. It is shown in the Fig. 4, which reflects different clusters formed by the documents of different generators. Table 2 shows the most frequent words generated by different generators in STM-GAN. It exhibits that different generators capture document belonging to different topic distribution.

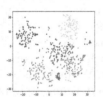

Fig. 4. TSNE plot of STM-GAN generated documents.

Table 2. Top words generated using individual generators of STM-GAN trained on 20 newsgroup data.

	Top Keywords
Gen 1	Game, Coverage,lost,judge,games,penalty,pittsburgh,goal
Gen 2	Fans, winning, training,owner,team,washington, player,cup
Gen 3	Natural,child,faith, believe,situation, thought,morality
Gen 4	Systems,frame,electronic,image,video,fax,conferencing
Gen 5	Windows,programs,color,file,vga,cs,interface,pc,bit

Table 3. Cosine similarity with training documents on 20 newsgroup dataset

		Topic 1	Topic 2	Topic 3	Topic 4	Topic 5
STM-GAN	Generator 1	0.1167	0.1521	0.1651	**0.2825**	0.1629
	Generator 2	0.1193	0.1202	0.1830	0.1982	0.1223
	Generator 3	**0.2106**	0.1228	**0.2051**	0.1188	0.1384
	Generator 4	0.1256	**0.2601**	0.1595	0.1244	0.1847
	Generator 5	0.1800	0.2165	0.1633	0.1308	**0.1987**
	Vanilla GAN	0.1794	0.1791	0.1584	0.1877	0.1648
	ATM	0.1953	0.1884	0.1767	0.2015	0.1849

6 Conclusion

In this paper, we have proposed a novel approach to address mode collapse issue in GAN. The idea is to train multiple generators to capture various modes present in the data distribution. We train the generators in a sequential manner such that each generator is encouraged to focus on the modes ignored by the previous generator. To achieve this objective, the loss function of the subsequent generator is updated based on previous generators. We perform experiments on synthetic, image and text datasets to demonstrate the performance of our model for various domain datasets. We present perceptual as well as quantitative results to show the effectiveness of our approach in capturing various modes as well as generating good quality samples. In future work, we aim to use our model with different GAN loss functions such as Wasserstein distance and we would also like to improve document generation by incorporating text-specific loss functions in our framework.

References

1. Goodfellow, I., et al.: Generative adversarial nets. In: NIPS (2014)
2. Ledig, C., et al.: Photo-realistic single image super-resolution using a generative adversarial network. In: CVPR (2017)
3. Wu, J., Zhang, C., Xue, T., Freeman, B., Tenenbaum, J.: Learning a probabilistic latent space of object shapes via 3D generative adversarial modeling. In: NIPS (2016)
4. Zhu, J.-Y., Kröhenbühl, P., Shechtman, E., Efros, A.A.: Generative visual manipulation on the natural image manifold. In: Leibe, B., Matas, J., Sebe, N., Welling, M. (eds.) Computer Vision – ECCV 2016. Lecture Notes in Computer Science, vol. 9909, pp. 597–613. Springer, Cham (2016). https://doi.org/10.1007/978-3-319-46454-1_36
5. Wang, R., Zhou, D., He, Y.: ATM: Adversarial-neural Topic Model. arXiv:1811.00265
6. Arjovsky, M., Chintala, S., Bottou, L.: Wasserstein GAN. In: ICLR (2017)
7. Mao, X., Li, Q., Xie, H., Raymond, Y.K., Lau, Z.W., Smolley, S.P.: Least squares generative adversarial networks. In: IEEE ICCV (2017)

8. Liu, M.-Y., Tuzel, O.: Coupled generative adversarial networks. In: NIPS (2016)
9. Ghosh, A., Kulharia, V., Namboodiri, V., Torr, P.H.S., Dokania, P.K.: Multi-agent diverse generative adversarial networks. In: CVPR (2018)
10. Hoang, Q., Nguyen, T.D., Le, T., Phung, D.: MGAN: training generative adversarial nets with multiple generators. In: ICLR (2018)
11. Xiao, H., Rasul, K., Vollgraf, R.: Fashion-MNIST: a novel image dataset for benchmarking machine learning algorithms (2017)
12. Salimans, T., Goodfellow, I., Zaremba, W., Cheung, V., Radford, A., Chen, X.: Improved techniques for training GANs. In: NIPS (2016)

Variable-Depth Convolutional Neural Network for Text Classification

Ka-Hou Chan[✉], Sio-Kei Im, and Wei Ke

School of Applied Sciences, Macao Polytechnic Institute, Macao, China
{chankahou,marcusim,wke}@ipm.edu.mo

Abstract. This article introduces a recurrent CNN based framework for the classification of arbitrary length text in natural sentence. In our model, we present a complete CNN design with recurrent structure to capture the contextual information as far as possible when learning sentences, which allows arbitrary-length sentences and more flexibility to analyze complete sentences compared with traditional CNN based neural networks. In addition, our model greatly reduces the number of layers in the architecture and requires fewer training parameters, which leads to less memory consumption, and it can reach $O(\log n)$ time complexity. As a result, this model can achieve enhancement in training accuracy. Moreover, the design and implementation can be easily deployed in the current text classification systems.

Keywords: Recurrent · Convolutional neural network · Text classification · Machine learning

1 Introduction

Sentiment analysis [19], as opinion mining [15], is a key Natural Language Processing (NLP) task that has received widespread attention in recent years. It refers to the process of computationally identifying and classifying ideas expressed in text to determine whether the user's attitude toward product is positive, negative, or neutral [2]. However, traditional feature representation methods for sentiment analysis often ignore contextual information of word order in text or perceptual patterns. Compared to those approaches, depth learning has the ability to perform sentiment analysis tasks because it has the ability to deal with the challenges faced by sentiment analysis, which can seriously affect the accuracy of classification. Recently, the rapid development of pre-trained word embedding and depth neural networks has brought new inspiration to various NLP tasks. Many researchers have attempted to combine the concepts of traditional machine learning with depth learning to develop more accurate sentiment classifiers, thereby improving the task of classifying any text content with minimal constraints, with pre-trained word embedding method [1], and neural networks have demonstrated their outstanding performance in sentiment analysis and many other NLP tasks [17]. However, for any sequence data that earlier

© Springer Nature Switzerland AG 2020
H. Yang et al. (Eds.): ICONIP 2020, CCIS 1333, pp. 685–692, 2020.
https://doi.org/10.1007/978-3-030-63823-8_78

information will always be weakened by newer one, which contradicts the equivalence of information. The key components are often reduced the efficacy when they are used to capture the semantics of a whole document. In this way, when using CNN to deal with long sentences, it is difficult to analyze the contextual information of the entire sentence. In practice, they are using more complex architecture to overcome this issue, and requiring stacking many layers in order to capture long-term dependencies.

1.1   Related Work

With the popular model Recurrent Neural Network (RNN) model [18], which allows variable-length data sizes being acceptable, and thus it is more flexible for perceived data. It enables better capture of the contextual information that analyzes text word-by-word in the order of sequence data, and preservation of the semantic of all of the previous text in a fix-sized hidden layer [4]. In [7], it introduced Long Short-Term Memory (LSTM) to develop and to achieve well performance, and in [24], it proposed attention-based LSTM model for aspect-level sentiment classification. In [26], it proposed to capture the influence of the surrounding words while performing sentiment classification of entities. On the other hand, sentiment analysis of language can always be determined by certain words in a sentence. Thus, Convolutional Neural Network (CNN) model can better capture the semantic of texts [13], with the ability to filter out feature patterns from a set of perceived data. There are a series of filters applied to the perceived data to obtain and to learn the identified features, and especially, for pattern analysis within regions, for which excel at learning of meaningful representations of features and concepts within the perceived data [3]. CNN-based model for NLP achieved excellent results in semantic parsing [25], and sentence modeling [9]. These capabilities make CNN extremely valuable for solving problems in the classification domain. Recently, in [5], it introduced a novel CNN model based on effective CNN by using word embedding to encode text. These capabilities as well make CNN extremely valuable for solving problems in the classification domain [12]. In addition, many researchers are also devoted to combine CNN and RNN models for text classification [8,14]. In [23], it proposed a regional CNN-LSTM model, and in [6], it presented a CNN- and LSTM- based depth neural network model for short texts analysis, and in [11], it combined contextual information with word embedding as an effective way to represent a word in CNN-based recurrent architectures. These methods first filter the features through several CNN layers, and then the results passed to the RNN for analyzing the results. There is no doubt that these methods can take advantage of CNN and RNN networks, but the number and the size of the layers which they used are always fixed.

In this work, the purpose is to decrease the parameters allocated for training and to reduce complex architectures. We investigated CNN as a recurrent module that can be re-used multiple times like the concept of RNN. First, we follow [10] to achieve convolutional layer for embedding vectors (words), which may capture the contextual information when learning word representations, and then reserving a larger range of the word ordering while learning representations of texts. Second, in order to hand over the feature size between CNN modules, we employed a set of adapt layers for the recovery from pooling layer to convolutional layer. It is worth mentioning that our model combining with the recurrent structure but we no longer used RNN module, and our model utilizes the advantage of both recurrent neural models and convolutional neural models. Furthermore, our model exhibits a time complexity of $O(\log n)$, which is logarithmic correlated with the length of the sentence.

1.2 Outline

The rest of this article is organized as follows: Sect. 2 discusses the design of Variable-Depth CNN. An architecture is indicated to give an analysis of training parameters allocation and performance, including how the source sentences go through the neural network which will result in classification. Next, in Sect. 3, we give the idea of how this approach can be implemented, which will be followed by the configurations of our experiments and evaluation of corresponding environments. The results and improvements will be illustrated and be discussed further in details in Sect. 4 as well. Finally, Sect. 5 concludes this paper.

2   Variable-Depth Convolutional Neural Network

In this section, we present the details of the network architecture. As shown in Fig. 1, it indicates that our model consists of CNN and AdaptConnect. The input of the network is a sentence or a paragraph, which is a sequence of words. The output of the network contains class elements. From the beginning, we use word embedding as the input vector, and bring them into the convolutional and pooling layers for learning to extract and capture high-level features. Its output is provided to an adaptive network for dimension and size regulation to the next CNN. Then, we determine whether the adapted data are sent to the CNN recurrently or output to perform the classification layer.

2.1   Size of Convolutional Kernel

CNN is an unbiased network, which can effectively analyze the contextual information of the entire sentence based on the kernel range (K_r), but it is difficult to determine the size: small K_r may result in the loss of some critical information, whereas large K_r results in an enormous parameter space (which is difficult to achieve). Our proposed model can overcome this problem. Since we would like to reuse the same convolutional layer in each recurrent, instead of stacking more layers, the number of training parameters will not increase in proportion to the depth of the network. Therefore, our model allows worry-free parameter allocation, and the recommended size is the same as the average of the sentence length. Furthermore, each vocabulary is encoded to the embedding vector, and the size must cover an entire vector, then each vector produces a convolutional result with the output feature and must be kept in the sentence length for consistency.

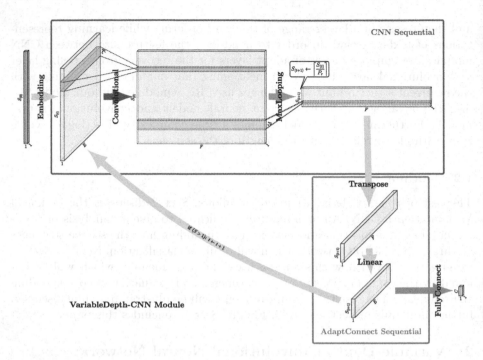

Fig. 1. The design of VariableDepth-CNN module. This figure indicates the complete data flow (with dimension size), layer sequential and recurrent conditions. This CNN sequential is a traditional CNN architecture, another sequential named as AdaptConnect transposes the convolutional data into a suitable size for the next CNN operation.

2.2 Recurrent Condition

The convolutional result is passed to the pooling layer, we use max-pooling over the feature with pooling range (P_r). The max-pooling layer can capture the most important feature in the context and ignore the others. By repeating this pooling, at the end we obtain the most important feature in a sentence. In our model, the length of the sentence (S) will only be updated through the max-pooling layer as follows:

$$S_{(t+1)} = \left\lceil \frac{S_{(t)}}{P_r} \right\rceil \tag{1}$$

where S is reduced in each recurrent if $(P_r > 1)$, t means the number of times. Thus, we also select this S as our recurrent condition as $(S > 1)$, instead of the recurrent that finishes at the end of the sentence. Furthermore, it is found out that the number of times of recurrent is reduced to $\log_{P_r}(S_{(0)})$. Therefore, increasing P_r is good for the overall performance when satisfying $(P_r \leq K_r)$, and our model can reach to $O(\log n)$ time complexity, which is logarithmic correlated with the length of the sentence.

3   Implementation

Since the ideas and algorithms have been determined and decided, our architecture can be implemented as shown in Fig. 1. It should be well noted that there are four major parts in the whole network, they are **Embedding, CNN, AdaptConnect** and **FullyConnect**. In order to achieve our desired network, we make use of the scientific depth learning framework PyTorch [20] for our implementation. These four parts can be achieved in the *Sequential* container and the *Forward* function in Algorithm 2, which are the implementation interface provided by PyTorch.

Algorithm 1: *Sequential* container for **Embedding, CNN, AdaptConnect** and **FullyConnect**.

---

1   **Sequential** Embedding :
2   │   Embedding.from_pretrained(*embeddings* ← "glove.6B.300d")   ▷ [21]
3   │   Dropout(*probability* ← 0.2)
4   **end Sequential**
5
6   **Sequential** CNN :
7   │   Conv2d(*in* ← 1, *out* ← F, *kernel_size* ← (K_r, E), *padding* ← $(\lfloor \frac{K_r}{2} \rfloor, 1)$)
8   │   ReLU()
9   │   MaxPool2d(*kernel_size* ← $(P_r, 1)$, *padding* ← $(\lfloor \frac{P_r}{2} \rfloor, 1)$)
10 **end Sequential**
11
12 **Sequential** AdaptConnect :
13 │   Transpose(*dim0* ← 1, *dim1* ← 3)
14 │   Linear(*in* ← F, *out* ← E)
15 │   Softsign()
16 **end Sequential**
17
18 **Sequential** FullyConnect :
19 │   Flatten(*start_dim* ← 1)
20 │   Linear(*in* ← E, *out* ← C)
21 **end Sequential**

Based on these *Sequential* containers, we propose to construct a simple and efficient model. This VariableDepth-CNN model can be achieved by a while-loop instead of stacking many layers. Furthermore, since only one CNN layer is recurrently used, the result becomes more stable and predictable. As shown in Algorithm 2, we can now present a variable-depth network, and the depth comprehension will pass through the CNN for each recurrent dynamically. The expected depth is $\lceil \log_{P_r} \left(S_{(0)} \right) \rceil$.

Algorithm 2: Pseudo code for the whole architecture of VariableDepth-CNN.

```
1 def forword :
2   ...                                        ▷ text.shape : [batch_size, S_(0)]
3      feature ← Embedding(text)              ▷ feature.shape : [batch_size, S_(0), E]
4      feature ← feature.unsqueeze(1)                    ▷ [batch_size, 1, S_(0), E]
5      t ← 0
6
7      while feature.S_(t) > 1 do
8          feature ← CNN(feature)                    ▷ [batch_size, F, S_(t+1), 1]
9          feature ← AdaptConnect(feature)           ▷ [batch_size, 1, S_(t+1), E]
10         t ← t + 1
11     end
12
13     return FullyConnect(feature)                      ▷ [batch_size, C]
14 end def
```

---

4 Experiment Results and Discussion

In this section, we evaluate our presented network architecture on standard environment of text classification. The performance of the proposed model was evaluated on two benchmark sentiment analysis datasets: **IMDB** [16] and **SST** [22]. All our experiments were conducted on an NVIDIA GeForce GTX 1080 with 8.0GB of video memory. We evaluated the classification performance on the same environment with and without the usage of our model. In order to avoid the divergence, we used the adaptive gradient related optimizer, the Adagrad [27] method and the learning rate was set to 0.01. For further details, the complete Python source codes are provided, and they can be found at, github.com/ChanKaHou/VariableDepth-CNN

Table 1. The best accuracy of various experiments for two benchmark sentiment analysis datasets.

	CNN [10]	CNN+LSTM [23]	Our proposed
IMDB	0.8593	0.8661	0.8929
SST	0.6403	0.6511	0.6629

As indicated in Table 1, we found out that the test accuracy after 200 epochs. Our proposed approach has improved the performance. This illustrates that our proposed unbiased model is more suitable for constructing the semantic representation of texts compared with previous neural networks. Note that contextual information is captured by the kernel range, thus the performance of a CNN is influenced by the K_r. The convergence becomes faster with increasing K_r, and we consider that the best K_r should be the same as the average sentence length, because the result with large K_r becomes stagnate or even worse in our experiments.

5 Conclusion

We propose a novel unbiased model, which is a text classification model by processing one CNN layer recurrently. Our model allows arbitrary-length sentence which is not requiring fixed-length pre-processing work on sentences. It can guarantee the integrity of the sentence. Compared with typical models, our report is competitive in terms of accuracy. The results of the experiments show that our proposed framework can achieve similar or even better performance on sentiment analysis tasks compared to the most popular CNN-based methods. In addition, our model greatly reduces the number of layers in the architecture and requires fewer training parameters, leading to less memory consumption. Furthermore, NLP tasks, such as machine translating or multi-label text classification, can be investigated by this model.

Acknowledgment. The article is part of the research project funded by The Science and Technology Development Fund, Macau SAR (File no. 0001/2018/AFJ).

References

1. Bengio, Y., Courville, A.C., Vincent, P.: Representation learning: A review and new perspectives. IEEE Trans. Pattern Anal. Mach. Intell. **35**(8), 1798–1828 (2013)
2. Collobert, R., Weston, J., Bottou, L., Karlen, M., Kavukcuoglu, K., Kuksa, P.P.: Natural language processing (almost) from scratch. J. Mach. Learn. Res. **12**, 2493–2537 (2011)
3. Conneau, A., Schwenk, H., Barrault, L., LeCun, Y.: Very deep convolutional networks for text classification. In: EACL, vol. 1, pp. 1107–1116. Association for Computational Linguistics (2017)
4. Elman, J.L.: Finding structure in time. Cogn. Sci. **14**(2), 179–211 (1990)
5. Georgakopoulos, S.V., Tasoulis, S.K., Vrahatis, A.G., Plagianakos, V.P.: Convolutional neural networks for toxic comment classification. In: SETN, pp. 35:1–35:6. ACM (2018)
6. Guggilla, C., Miller, T., Gurevych, I.: CNN- and lSTM-based claim classification in online user comments. In: COLING, pp. 2740–2751. ACL (2016)
7. Hochreiter, S., Schmidhuber, J.: Long short-term memory. Neural Comput. **9**(8), 1735–1780 (1997)
8. Huang, Q., Chen, R., Zheng, X., Dong, Z.: Deep sentiment representation based on CNN and lSTM. In: 2017 International Conference on Green Informatics (ICGI), pp. 30–33. IEEE (2017)
9. Kalchbrenner, N., Grefenstette, E., Blunsom, P.: A convolutional neural network for modelling sentences. In: ACL, vol. 1, pp. 655–665. The Association for Computer Linguistics (2014)

10. Kim, Y.: Convolutional neural networks for sentence classification. In: EMNLP, pp. 1746–1751. ACL (2014)
11. Lai, S., Xu, L., Liu, K., Zhao, J.: Recurrent convolutional neural networks for text classification. In: AAAI, pp. 2267–2273. AAAI Press (2015)
12. Lakshmi, B.S., Raj, P.S., Vikram, R.R., et al.: Sentiment analysis using deep learning technique CNN with K means. Int. J. Pure Appl. Math. 114(11), 47–57 (2017)
13. LeCun, Y., Bottou, L., Bengio, Y., Haffner, P.: Gradient-based learning applied to document recognition. Proc. IEEE 86(11), 2278–2324 (1998)
14. Liang, M., Hu, X.: Recurrent convolutional neural network for object recognition. In: CVPR, pp. 3367–3375. IEEE Computer Society (2015)
15. Liu, B.: Sentiment Analysis and Opinion Mining. Synthesis Lectures on Human Language Technologies. Morgan & Claypool Publishers, Vermont (2012)
16. Maas, A.L., Daly, R.E., Pham, P.T., Huang, D., Ng, A.Y., Potts, C.: Learning word vectors for sentiment analysis. In: ACL, pp. 142–150. The Association for Computer Linguistics (2011)
17. Mikolov, T.: Statistical language models based on neural networks. In: Presentation at Google, Mountain View, 2nd April 2012
18. Mikolov, T., Karafiát, M., Burget, L., Cernocký, J., Khudanpur, S.: Recurrent neural network based language model. In: INTERSPEECH, pp. 1045–1048. ISCA (2010)
19. Nasukawa, T., Yi, J.: Sentiment analysis: Capturing favorability using natural language processing. In: K-CAP, pp. 70–77. ACM (2003)
20. Paszke, A., Gross, S., Chintala, S., Chanan, G., Yang, E., DeVito, Z., Lin, Z., Desmaison, A., Antiga, L., Lerer, A.: Automatic differentiation in PyTorch (2017)
21. Pennington, J., Socher, R., Manning, C.D.: Glove: Global vectors for word representation. In: EMNLP, pp. 1532–1543. ACL (2014)
22. Socher, R., Perelygin, A., Wu, J., Chuang, J., Manning, C.D., Ng, A.Y., Potts, C.: Recursive deep models for semantic compositionality over a sentiment treebank. In: EMNLP, pp. 1631–1642. ACL (2013)
23. Wang, J., Yu, L., Lai, K.R., Zhang, X.: Dimensional sentiment analysis using a regional CNN-LSTM model. In: ACL, vol. 2. The Association for Computer Linguistics (2016)
24. Wang, Y., Huang, M., Zhu, X., Zhao, L.: Attention-based LSTM for aspect-level sentiment classification. In: EMNLP, pp. 606–615. The Association for Computational Linguistics (2016)
25. Yih, W., He, X., Meek, C.: Semantic parsing for single-relation question answering. In: ACL, vol. 2, pp. 643–648. The Association for Computer Linguistics (2014)
26. Zhang, M., Zhang, Y., Vo, D.: Gated neural networks for targeted sentiment analysis. In: AAAI, pp. 3087–3093. AAAI Press (2016)
27. Zhou, Z., Chen, S., Chen, Z.: FANNC: A fast adaptive neural network classifier. Knowl. Inf. Syst. 2(1), 115–129 (2000)

Robotics and Control

Adaptive Neural Control for Efficient Rhythmic Movement Generation and Online Frequency Adaptation of a Compliant Robot Arm

Florentijn Degroote[1,2], Mathias Thor[3], Jevgeni Ignasov[3],
Jørgen Christian Larsen[3], Emilia Motoasca[1], and Poramate Manoonpong[3,4(✉)]

[1] Faculty of Engineering Technology, Technologiecampus Ghent,
Ku Leuven, Leuven, Belgium
florentijn.degroote@gmail.com, emilia.motoasca@kuleuven.be
[2] ML6, Esplanade Oscar Van De Voorde 1, 9000 Ghent, Belgium
florentijn.degroote@ml6.eu
[3] Embodied AI and Neurorobotics Lab, SDU Biorobotics, The Mærsk Mc-Kinney
Møller Instituttet, University of Southern Denmark, Odense, Denmark
{mathias,jeign14,jcla,poma}@mmmi.sdu.dk
[4] BRAIN Lab, School of Information Science and Technology, Vidyasirimedhi
Institute of Science and Technology, Rayong, Thailand

Abstract. In this paper, we propose an adaptive and simple neural control approach for a robot arm with soft/compliant materials, called GummiArm. The control approach is based on a minimal two-neuron oscillator network (acting as a central pattern generator) and an error-based dual integral learning (DIL) method for efficient rhythmic movement generation and frequency adaptation, respectively. By using this approach, we can precisely generate rhythmic motion for GummiArm and allow it to quickly adapt its motion to handle physical and environmental changes as well as interacting with a human safely. Experimental results for GummiArm in different scenarios (e.g., dealing with different joint stiffnesses, working against elastic loads, and interacting with a human) are provided to illustrate the effectiveness of the proposed adaptive neural control approach.

Keywords: Adaptive robot behavior · Soft robot · Human-machine interaction · Artificial intelligence

1 Introduction

Since robots are being used more extensively for service duties, exploring inaccessible areas and handling emergency and security tasks, the field of robotics is moving toward more autonomous and intelligent systems. As a result, easy and flexible cooperation between humans and robots is becoming increasingly important and must be considered during development of modern robots [10].

© Springer Nature Switzerland AG 2020
H. Yang et al. (Eds.): ICONIP 2020, CCIS 1333, pp. 695–703, 2020.
https://doi.org/10.1007/978-3-030-63823-8_79

Trajectory tracking for traditional robot arms works well for determined tasks due to stiff joints without passive compliance. While the use of stiff joints avoids the coupling effect between joints [1], this conventional approach does not permit humans to interact with the robot safely.

To address this problem, Stoelen et al. (2016) [5] have developed a new type of robot arm with soft/compliant materials, called GummiArm. To mimic human-like muscle compliance, GummiArm is designed in such a way that it inherently involves passive compliance and in turn increases the coupling effects, which require a more sophisticated control approach in order to move efficiently and in an adaptable manner.

In this work, we propose a simple and adaptive neural control approach for GummiArm. The control approach is based on 1) a minimal two-neuron oscillator network (acting as a central pattern generator (CPG)) for efficient rhythmic movement generation and 2) an error-based dual integral learning (DIL) mechanism for online frequency adaptation. The DIL makes sure the arm is able to follow the entire given trajectory, generated by the CPG, by adapting the frequency. As a result, we reduce the loss of precision, avoid unwanted movement, and in the worst-case scenario, motor collapse in various manipulation tasks.

The adaptive neural control approach uses only motor positions as sensory feedback and does not require the kinematic or dynamic model of the arm as is often needed in classical arm control techniques [8]. This approach allows us to treat the coupling effects between the compliant robot joints as unknown while achieving good shock tolerance, low reflected inertia, little damage during inadvertent contact, and automatic frequency adaptation of the arm. Recent related works in the field of rhythmic movement generation and frequency adaptation include the use of the Rowat-Selverston oscillating neuron model (CPG) with dynamic Hebbian learning for human-robot handshaking [2]. However, this work evaluates the control method on a simulated Kinova Mico robot with stiff joints. Another work proposes a new framework based on a combination of several components, including the Matsuoka neural model (CPG), feature processing, neural networks, and signal filtering, for adaptive locomotion of the NAO humanoid robot with stiff joints [9]. While these recent works are impressive in their own right, they do not deal with the control of compliant joints and real-time adaption with uncertainty of arm properties, loads and external disturbances as proposed here.

This study is a continuation of our previous works [6,7] which proposed the control method and mainly applied it to control legged robots with stiff joints and one of the works briefly introduced compliant arm control. Here, we present the complete technical details, analysis, and experimental results of compliant arm control in various scenarios which have not been previously published. Furthermore, compared to related works in the field of rhythmic movement generation and frequency adaptation, the work goes beyond the existing works [2,9] by demonstrating real-time online adaptation in the real compliant robot arm system with uncertainty of arm properties, loads, and external disturbance which has not been shown by others.

2   Bio-inspired Compliant Robot Arm (GummiArm)

2.1   Technical Specification of GummiArm

To mimic the compliant property of a human arm, each joint of GummiArm is driven indirectly through tendons by two or three motors. The tendons are made of FilaFlex filament, which is an elastic material, and provides the arm with passive compliance. The robot has seven degrees of freedom (DOFs) and is equivalent to a 50th percentile female right arm (see [5] for more details). Each motor in GummiArm is a digital DC servo of the AX-12A or AX-18A type, from Dynamixel, equipped with a PID controller for position control.

2.2   Simulation of GummiArm

We simulated GummiArm using the robot simulation framework V-REP and used the Robot Operating System (ROS) to interface between our adaptive neural control and the real and simulated GummiArm robots. This makes it possible to have direct communication between both real-world and simulated entities. These two communicating entities are depicted in Fig. 1.

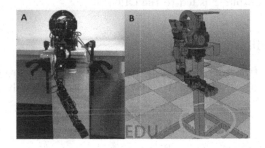

Fig. 1. A) Real GummiArm robot in a resting position. **B)** Simulated arm in V-REP.

3   Adaptive Neural Control

In this study, an artificial neural network is used to develop the adaptive neural control of GummiArm. It consists of two main mechanisms, as shown in Fig. 2A. The first mechanism is a recurrent neural network which is formed as the SO(2)-oscillator [4]. The oscillator, which functions as a CPG, is used to generate the rhythmic movements of GummiArm. The second mechanism is an error-based DIL method. It is used for quickly adapting the frequency of the generated rhythmic movements to match the performance of GummiArm.

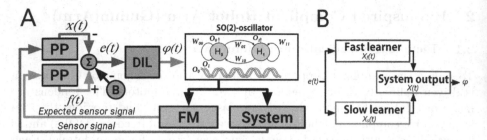

Fig. 2. A) The combination of the DIL [6] and the SO(2)-oscillator [4] based CPG model for robot control (modified from [6]), which outputs the motor commands as periodic patterns for both the shoulder roll joint motor and the elbow joint motor. The error feedback $e(t)$ is the subtraction of the (preprocessed/PP) low-pass filtered measured joint angle amplitude (x(t), sensor signal) and the (preprocessed/PP) low-pass filtered expected joint angle amplitude (f(t), expected sensor signal). The expected joint angle is obtained from the transformation of a CPG output through a forward model (FM). $\varphi(t)$ is a frequency control parameter (Eq. 3) of the SO(2)-oscillator. B denotes a bias term. The system refers to the GummiArm robot. **B)** Schematic representation of the DIL. $x(t)$ denotes the system output and is the sum of the outputs from the slow and fast learners ($x_f(t)$ and $x_s(t)$, respectively). $e(t)$ denotes the error and is the difference between the preprocessed signals from the forward model and the system. The DIL's output φ is fed to the CPG.

3.1   SO(2)-Oscillator (CPG)

The oscillator has two fully interconnected neurons with four synapses w_{00}, w_{01}, w_{10}, and w_{11} (see Fig. 2A). The activity in each neuron evolves as:

$$a_i(t+1) = \sum_{j=1}^{N} w_{ij} o_j(t) \; ; \; i = 1, ..., N, \tag{1}$$

where N denotes the number of units and w_{ij} is the synaptic strength of the connection from neuron j to neuron i. Equation 2 shows the neuron output o_i, given by a hyperbolic tangent (tanh) transfer function:

$$o_i = tanh(a_i) = \frac{2}{1 + e^{-2a_i}} - 1. \tag{2}$$

The network can act as a CPG if the weights are set according to the special orthogonal group SO(2) as:

$$\begin{pmatrix} w_{00}(t) & w_{01}(t) \\ w_{10}(t) & w_{11}(t) \end{pmatrix} = \alpha. \begin{pmatrix} \cos(\varphi(t)) & \sin(\varphi(t)) \\ -\sin(\varphi(t)) & \cos(\varphi(t)) \end{pmatrix}, \tag{3}$$

with $-\pi < \varphi < \pi$ and $\alpha = 1.01$, the CPG generates periodic outputs $o_{\{0,1\}}$ of the neurons $H_{\{0,1\}}$, shown in Fig. 2A, where φ defines the frequency of the output signals. The outputs (i.e., o_0 and o_1) are linearly translated to the position motor commands of the shoulder roll joint and the elbow joint of GummiArm. Only the shoulder roll joint angle information is used as feedback in this study. This is to show that using only one feedback is enough for adaption. More feedback (e.g., position errors from other joints) can be included and might result in better error calculation and in turn reduce the adaption times.

3.2   Error-Based Dual Integral Learning (DIL)

In order to adapt the frequency of the CPG during runtime such that Gum-miArm can efficiently perform its movements with a low tracking error under different conditions, the error based DIL from [6] is used as a plug-in to the CPG. In principle, the DIL relies on error feedback, given as the difference between the low-pass filtered motor command amplitude for the shoulder roll joint of the CPG and the measured low-pass filtered motor position amplitude of the shoulder roll joint of GummiArm. The DIL combines slow and fast learners in parallel for fast and stable error reduction [6], as depicted in Fig. 2B.

Each learner receives exactly the same error and assimilates part of it using the rules in Eq. 4 to alter the estimate of the perturbation.

$$x_f(t) = A_f.x_f(t-1) + B_f.e(t) + C_f. \int e(t),$$

$$x_s(t) = A_s.x_s(t-1) + B_s.e(t) + C_s. \int e(t), \tag{4}$$

$$x(t) = x_s(t) + x_f(t) \ , \ e(t) = f(t) - x(t),$$

where $x_s(t)$ and $x_f(t)$ are the outputs of the slow and fast learners, respectively. $x(t)$ denotes the sum of the two outputs, $e(t)$ denotes the error feedback given as the tracking error between the low-pass filtered expected joint angle amplitude $f(t)$ and the low-pass filtered actual joint angle amplitude of GummiArm $x(t)$.

The expected joint angle amplitude is calculated from a CPG output through a forward model (FM). The FM here is modeled as a simple gain. This makes it possible to compare the CPG output with the actual joint angle sensory feedback from GummiArm. B_f and B_s are the learning rates, and A_f and A_s are the retention factors. The selection of the parameters is constrained so that $B_f > B_s$ and $A_f < A_s$. The last part of the equation also takes the accumulated error into account under the constraint that $C_f > C_s$. This term thrusts the learning process to minimize any constant error. The slow learner consequently learns more slowly as indicated by the lower learning rates of B_s and C_s but remembers for longer as indicated by a higher retention factor A_s. B is a small threshold bias term which allows for increasing and decreasing the frequency of the CPG during the learning process to find a proper level. In this study, we empirically tuned the parameters based on the mentioned assumption as such we can almost guarantee the stability. However, we will further investigate the parameter analysis for the adaptation stability in future work. For implementation, the DIL directly changes the frequency of the CPG (i.e., $\varphi(t) = x(t)$) based on error feedback. The advantage of implementing the DIL is that the CPG is coupled with the physical world via sensory feedback from the joint angle of the shoulder roll joint. This means that the DIL offers the possibility that the tracking error can be minimized by enabeling GummiArm to quickly adapt its movements and stabilize itself. The use of two learners in parallel has several desirable properties such as fast and stable learning, savings in relearning, tracking error reduction, and spontaneous recovery of previously learned parameters (see [6] for more details of the learning mechanism).

4   Experimental Results

In this section, we present the performance of the proposed adaptive neural control for efficient rhythmic movement generation and online frequency adaptation of GummiArm. Only feedback from the real-world shoulder joint motor was provided to the DIL. The parameters of the DIL were $A_s = 0.992$, $A_f = 0.59$, $B_s = 0.0036$, $B_f = 0.1$, $C_s = 0.00018$, $C_f = 0.007$, and $B = 0.05$.

Four main experiments were conducted to show the online adaptation of the control to deal with different joint stiffnesses, elastic loads, and human-robot interaction. In each experiment, real-world circumstances were altered, and the robot arm was set to perform a rhythmic back and forth horizontal end effector movement. As mentioned before, this motion is fundamental for sawing and cutting applications as well as pick and place conveyor belt operations.

In each experiment, the DIL was activated after a short period of time because GummiArm needs to come from a resting position to its moving state. GummiArm was also initialized with a value of the SO(2)-oscillator parameter φ to generate initial high frequency movements. An arbitrary frequency of 0.64 Hz was chosen for the first two experiments and GummiArm's stable frequency of 0.265 Hz was chosen for the last two experiments.

Figure 3A shows the result of the first experiment. The control automatically adapted its frequency to GummiArm to minimize tracking error and as a result, GummiArm could follow the generated rhythmic movement. The stable working frequency of 0.265 Hz was reached after 90 s   For applications such as sawing wood or cutting objects, traction results in an opposing force to the rhythmic motion. In the following experiments, we show that GummiArm is able to stabilize itself in such conditions. Figure 3B shows the result of the second experiment where the control automatically adapted its frequency to deal with a high shoulder joint stiffness in GummiArm. The tension was altered by changing the offset positions of the two motors in the shoulder joint (see red arrows in Fig. 3B). In this case, the steady-state stability frequency was approached after 70 s; about 20 s earlier in comparison to the original state adaptation time. Another test with a lower tension applied to the shoulder roll joint can be seen at vimeo.com/362777822 (password is QCNXngC0YQ).

Figure 4A shows the result of the third experiment in which the arm started with an initial frequency of 0.265 Hz. In this experiment, the end effector of GummiArm was connected to an elastic load (i.e., elastic rubber band) having a pulling force of 3 N. This elastic rubber bands has a stiffness of 0.7 N/cm. The working frequency in this case was lower at 0.240 Hz, compared to the stable

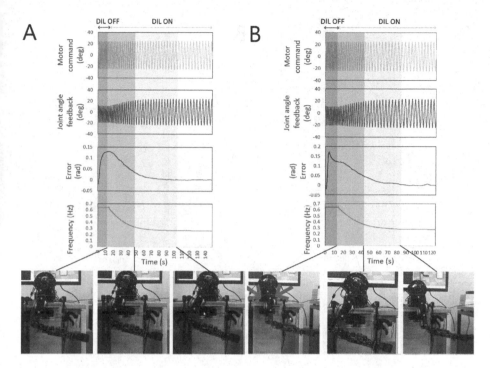

Fig. 3. A) First experiment: starting point configuration (normal joint stiffness). The supplementary video of this experiment can be seen at vimeo.com/362777732. **B)** Second experiment (high joint stiffness). The supplementary video of this experiment can be seen at vimeo.com/362777903. The password for the videos is QCNXngC0YQ.

frequency. Another test with an elastic load of up to 5 N attached to the end-effector can be seen at vimeo.com/362778130 (password is QCNXngC0YQ). The experimental result shows that the control automatically adapted its frequency to deal with different elastic loads attached to GummiArm and that stiffness is negatively correlated with the working frequency.

Figure 4B shows the result of the last experiment in which the control automatically adapted its frequency to deal with a variety of external human perturbations to see how GummiArm reacts to human intervention. These perturbations include encumbering and encouraging GummiArm's movement twice after having reached a zero steady-state error (see 1 and 3), and once while reaching zero steady-state error (see 2). It takes around 100 s to recover from a 4.7 s lasting total obstruction (see 1), around 35 s to recover from a forced frequency of 0.343 Hz (see 2) and around 80 s to recover from a semi obstruction lasting 9.3 s (see 3). This experiment shows that dealing with perturbations is time-invariant and that GummiArm adapts at a moderate speed, which might be suitable for maintenance or non-critical intervention applications.

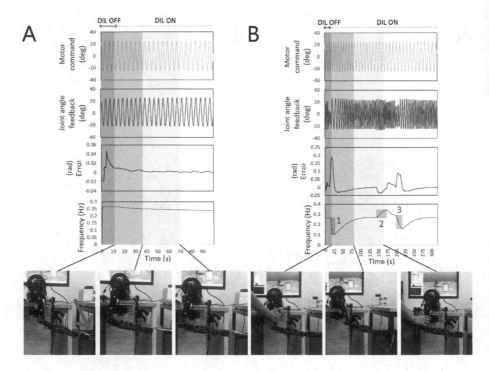

Fig. 4. A) Third experiment: an elastic load of up to 3 N is attached to the end-effector. The supplementary video of this experiment can be seen at vimeo.com/362778000. **B)** Fourth experiment: a human subject interacting with the robot three times (see (1), (2), and (3)). The supplementary video of this experiment can be seen at vimeo.com/362778423. The password for the videos is QCNXngC0YQ.

5   Conclusions

In this paper, we used an adaptive neural control mechanism consisting of a CPG and DIL to let a robot arm, called GummiArm, perform the rhythmic end effector movements necessary for pick-and-place tasks, sawing wood, cutting objects, etc. We showed that the control entity effectively curtails the tracking error between desired and actual joint movements. It is also important to emphasize that the adaptive neural control works online and can achieve multiple adaptations (including adapting the arm property with different joint stiffnesses, elastic loads, and unexpected human interaction) by relying only on a tracking error feedback-based objective function which is more simple than using multiple complex objective functions or robot kinematic control. The proposed mechanism makes sure that the CPG frequency stabilizes and matches the performance of GummiArm, in real-time.

This adaptive neural control is well suited to enable a robot to operate safely around humans and can be potentially applied to other robotic systems. Future extensions of this work include 1) introducing a motor pattern shaping mechanism [3] to transform the primitive rhythmic CPG signals into complex motor signals for complicated manipulation tasks, 2) using more sensory feedback for better error calculation to speed up the adaption time, and 3) applying the control framework as a basis for soft/compliant robot control in terms of "closed-loop control with online adaptation" which remains one of the challenges in soft robotics research.

Acknowledgements. We thank Martin Stoelen to provide the technical details of GummiArm. This research was supported by Center for BioRobotics at the University of Southern Denmark and VISTEC-research funding on Bio-inspired Robotics.

References

1. Dallali, H., Medrano-Cerda, G., Kashiri, N., Tsagarakis, N., Caldwell, D.: Decentralized feedback design for a compliant robot arm. In: Modelling Symposium (EMS), 2014 European, pp. 269–274. IEEE (2014)
2. Jouaiti, M., Caron, L., Hénaff, P.: Hebbian plasticity in CPG controllers facilitates self-synchronization for human-robot handshaking. Front. Neurorobotics **12**, 29 (2018)
3. Kulvicius, T., Ning, K., Tamosiunaite, M., Wörgötter, F.: Joining movement sequences: Modified dynamic movement primitives for robotics applications exemplified on handwriting. IEEE Trans. Robot. **28**(1), 145–157 (2012)
4. Pasemann, F., Hild, M., Zahedi, K.: SO(2)-networks as neural oscillators. In: Mira, J., Álvarez, J.R. (eds.) IWANN 2003. LNCS, vol. 2686, pp. 144–151. Springer, Heidelberg (2003). https://doi.org/10.1007/3-540-44868-3_19
5. Stoelen, M.F., Bonsignorio, F., Cangelosi, A.: Co-exploring actuator antagonism and bio-inspired control in a printable robot arm. In: Tuci, E., Giagkos, A., Wilson, M., Hallam, J. (eds.) SAB 2016. LNCS (LNAI), vol. 9825, pp. 244–255. Springer, Cham (2016). https://doi.org/10.1007/978-3-319-43488-9_22
6. Thor, M., Manoonpong, P.: Error-based learning mechanism for fast online adaptation in robot motor control. IEEE Trans. Neural Networks Learn. Syst. **31**, 1–10 (2019). https://doi.org/10.1109/TNNLS.2019.2927737
7. Thor, M., Manoonpong, P.: A fast online frequency adaptation mechanism for CPG-based robot motion control. IEEE Rob. Autom. Lett. **4**(4), 3324–3331 (2019)
8. Wang, R., Dai, Y.: The anthropomorphic robot arm joint control parameter tuning based on Ziegler Nichols PID. In: 2015 3rd International Conference on Mechanical Engineering and Intelligent Systems. Atlantis Press (2015). https://doi.org/10.2991/icmeis-15.2015.27
9. Wang, Y., Xue, X., Chen, B.: Matsuoka's CPG with desired rhythmic signals for adaptive walking of humanoid robots. IEEE Trans. Cybern. **50**, 1–14 (2018). https://doi.org/10.1109/TCYB.2018.2870145
10. Weiss, A., Buchner, R., Tscheligi, M., Fischer, H.: Exploring human-robot cooperation possibilities for semiconductor manufacturing. In: 2011 International Conference on Collaboration Technologies and Systems (CTS), pp. 173–177. IEEE (2011)

An Ensemble Learning Approach to Improve Tracking Accuracy of Multi Sensor Fusion

Anoop Karnik Dasika$^{(\boxtimes)}$ (ID) and Praveen Paruchuri (ID)

International Institute of Information Technology, Hyderabad, Telangana, India
anoop.dasika@research.iiit.ac.in, praveen.p@iiit.ac.in

Abstract. Finding or tracking the location of an object accurately is a key problem in defence applications as well as the problem of object localization in the fields of robotics and computer vision. Radars fall into the spectrum of high-end defence sensors or systems on which the security and surveillance of the entire world depends. There is much focus on the topic of Multi Sensor Fusion (MSF) in recent years with radars as the sensors. In this paper, we focus on the problem of asynchronous observation of data which can reduce the tracking accuracy of an MSF system comprised of radars of different types at different locations. Our solution utilizes a machine learning approach to train models on hundreds of hours of (anonymized real) Multi Sensor Fusion data provided by radars performing tracking activity across the Indian airspace. Our approach comprises of 3 steps: In step 1, we train an ensemble model of logistic regression and Xgboost to predict Splitting error. In step 2, we use Xgboost to predict the second type of error, namely Merging error to improve the tracking accuracy further. The third step uses nearest neighbour search to compensate for the predicted errors by retaining the data points removed in the first step while maintaining the tracking accuracy. Our experimental results show that the trained models provide reasonable predictions of errors and increase the accuracy of tracking by 15% while retaining 100% of the data.

Keywords: Radars · Multi Sensor Fusion · Object tracking

1 Introduction

Determining or tracking the location of objects is an important problem in robotics [1], computer vision [12] and for defence applications in general [9]. Radars are generally used in defence applications when we need to locate objects over long distances and fall into the category of high-end security systems on which surveillance of entire world depends in current times. Radar is an electromagnetic system [15] which is useful for detection and location of target objects such as aircraft, ships, spacecraft, vehicles, people and natural environment [10]. Radars work in all kinds of weather, and this all-weather capability

© Springer Nature Switzerland AG 2020
H. Yang et al. (Eds.): ICONIP 2020, CCIS 1333, pp. 704–712, 2020.
https://doi.org/10.1007/978-3-030-63823-8_80

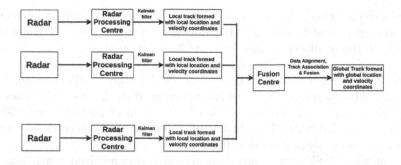

Fig. 1. Working of Multi Sensor Fusion system

has contributed to their extensive use in various commercial applications such as autonomous robotics and mobile systems and defence applications such as tracking, surveillance and detection of targets in air, naval and ground.

The topic of **Multi Sensor Fusion (MSF)** has received much attention in the recent years [15] due to the increasing automation across the world which resulted in a significant increase in the number of information collection devices. MSF in Radars has also received significant attention. Generally, they have overlapping regions they monitor, which can result in detection or collection of varying data on the same aspect of an issue or for the same target being tracked, which makes MSF a necessity. Through the integration of data obtained from different sensors, the results can in general, be optimized better and made continuous in terms of having a complete picture rather than having individual snapshots of a scenario obtained using multiple independent radars. Considering the fact that newer radars with different properties may replace some of the older ones over time, defence organizations would in general need to perform multi sensor fusion for a heterogeneous multi radar system.

Due to the differences in sampling rate of sensors, the communication delay between sensors and the overlapping regions of observations for the various sensors, there can be asynchronicity in sensors' observations which can significantly reduce the tracking accuracy of an MSF system. Most of the works in literature [3] on multi sensor fusion process operate on small domain settings. Among the ones that involve the usage of machine learning (ML) techniques, ML is used during the fusion process. However, our work involves monitoring the Indian air space, which is a vast area with lots of objects to track in real-time, needing a scalable solution. In addition, our proposed solution uses data obtained from the output of the MSF process and improves upon it, so the work would be useful to any organization where sharing know-how of the MSF process itself may not be feasible due to privacy issues.

2   Problem Description

The Indian Air Force uses a multi radar system to detect flights pan India. These radars are located in different parts of the country, and each radar has its own processing center. Measurement data is processed by each radar resulting in multi-target local tracks L_t. The processing involves usage of Kalman and advanced Kalman filters to compute the 3d location (in the form of distance from the sensor) and velocity of the above tracks. The processed information is then sent to fusion center of the system which performs Multi Sensor Fusion (MSF) for data alignment, data interconnection, track filtering and association and track fusion to obtain the position in the form of latitude, longitude and altitude. The global track $\mathbf{G_t}$ is then computed using the local track information. Figure 1 captures the process flow involved.

A real-world MSF system has a lot of engineering involved apart from track association and alignment algorithms, which typically include human-generated rules tailored to specific use cases. As the use cases expand, as heterogeneous radars get added, as the nature of targets change and as the requirements for accuracy increase, the system gets more prone to errors due to limitations in the MSF logic. Consider a scenario in which there are say 4 air targets. Sensors gather data from these air targets and generate Air Situation Picture (ASP) displaying 4 air targets with relevant attributes. However, there will be times where the actual number of air targets are shown as 4+/4− for a certain period and then again shown as 4. If the MSF system observes 4+ air targets, we call the error as a **Splitting error $\mathbf{E_s}$**, i.e. sensing multiple targets when only a single one is present. When it observes 4− air targets, we call the error as **Merging error $\mathbf{E_m}$** (sensing a single target when multiple targets are present). $\mathbf{E_s}$ can lead to the system assuming that there is an enemy flight in the air even though there is not any. $\mathbf{E_m}$ can lead to the system assuming that there is no enemy flight in the air even though there may be one (or more). Both these errors in air surveillance can result in errors in threat evaluation which can result in wrong action getting taken, leading to severe threats and security issues.

3   Our Proposed Solution

Figure 2 presents a block diagram of our proposed solution to improve the tracking accuracy by using a machine learning approach using the data obtained from output of MSF. The MSF data is collected daily and is stored as a history dump (one week of past data which we refer to as dataset in the paper) to train two separate models that classify Splitting and Merging respectively. Please note that

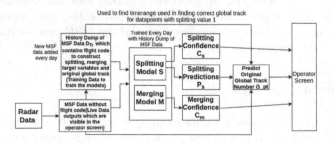

Fig. 2. Proposed AI model

the dataset includes flight code that helps with getting the target variables for Splitting and Merging models, while the real-time data does not contain flight code. The Splitting model **S** would provide Splitting confidence $\mathbf{C_s}$, i.e. probability of Splitting. When a data point has a high $\mathbf{C_s}$, it is classified as Splitting else it is real. We find the original Global Track number $\mathbf{G_t}$ of all the data points classified as Splitting. Similar to Splitting model **S**, the trained Merging model **M** provides Merging confidence $\mathbf{C_m}$, i.e. probability of Merging.

Our approach comprises of 3 steps as described below: In the first step, we train an ensemble model of logistic regression and Xgboost to classify all data points into Splitting and real which can help to improve the accuracy of tracking. In the second step, we use Xgboost to classify all data points into Merging and real, which can improve the accuracy of tracking further. The third step uses nearest neighbour search to modify data points classified as Splitting into real ones, i.e. correct the false global track assigned to it. Figure 3 presents a block diagram of these three steps.

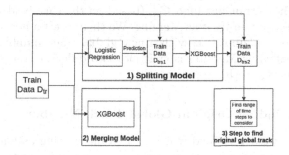

Fig. 3. Models training methodology

3.1   Step 1: Splitting Classification Model

Based on our understanding of the dataset, we identified the following features to use for development of Splitting model **S** – latitude, longitude, altitude, speed and direction of an object detected by MSF system at each time step precise to a millisecond, number of radars and a unique id depicting the specific combination of radars used in the MSF system for the creation of individual data points. MSF performed on the data provided by individual radars leads to the assignment of global track number $\mathbf{G_t}$ to each of the newly detected objects. If for a particular flight, a new $\mathbf{G_t}$ is assigned even though there is an existing one, all the data points detected with this new $\mathbf{G_t}$ are a result of Splitting from the original $\mathbf{G_t}$ of the flight and will be classified as **Splitting** (data points created as a result of Splitting Error $\mathbf{E_s}$). We denote the training dataset with features mentioned above as $\mathbf{D_{tr}}$ and test dataset as $\mathbf{D_t}$. As part of the ensemble model, we first use a parametric ML algorithm Logistic regression and train it with $\mathbf{D_{tr}}$. We add the predictions obtained using the logistic regression to our train set $\mathbf{D_{tr}}$ and test set $\mathbf{D_t}$ and denote these new datasets as $\mathbf{D_{trs1}}$ and $\mathbf{D_{ts1}}$ respectively. Next, we use a non-parametric ML algorithm XGBoost and train it with the new train dataset D_{trs1}. We obtain Splitting confidence C_s from the above model. If the output has high C_s (based on the threshold which gives the highest f1 score), we classify it as Splitting. We add the predictions obtained by using the XGBoost model to both our train set D_{trs1} and test set D_{ts1} and denote these new data sets as D_{trs2} and D_{ts2} respectively.

3.2   Step 2: Merging Classification Model

We use the initial training set D_{tr}, and the initial test set D_t for purposes of developing this model. If for a particular global track number G_t, a new flight number gets associated to it by MSF system, all the data points detected with this G_t and the new flight number are a result of Merging of 2 different flights and will be classified as Merging (data points are a combination of multiple flights merging after MSF at some time step). We use a non-parametric machine learning algorithm XGBoost and train it with D_{tr} to obtain the Merging confidence C_d. If the output has high C_m (based on the threshold which gives the highest f1-score), we classify it as Merging. We then insert a new data point with the same features as input but with a new global track number. Hence, every data point classified as Merging is split into two different tracks which in turn leads to a reduction of Merging error E_m.

3.3   Step 3: Finding Original Global Track Number

In the first step, we determined which data point is being assigned global track G_t accurately and which is not. However, we cannot just delete the data points which have splitting issues as we may lose important tracking information of targets. The third step, therefore, helps in correcting/retaining the data points, which were classified as Splitting. First, we create a new train dataset D_{trgt} and test dataset D_{tgt} from our train D_{trs2} and test dataset D_{ts2} obtained by Splitting model S by retaining entries predicted as Splitting. Every data point in our dataset forms at a particular time precise to a millisecond. In the dataset D_{trgt}, for every data point, we construct a small new dataset (using data points from original train dataset D_{tr}) which includes all the data points that are in the immediate past of this data point dp. For each data point in the new train dataset D_{trgt}, we find its correct G_t as follows: We compute the Euclidean distance between the features latitude, longitude and altitude of each data point in the constructed dataset with dp. We then set G_t of the data point dp with the G_t of the data point with the lowest Euclidean distance computed.

4   Experiments and Results

As part of our experimentation, we compare the performance of our Splitting S and Merging M models with the following algorithms: Logistic regression

[7], Gaussian Naive Bayes [14], Support Vector Machines [16], Gaussian Nearest Neighbour [2], Random Forest Classifier [8], XGBoost [4], Stacking Logistic regression with XGBoost [13] and Artificial Neural Networks [6].

Dataset: Our dataset contains 3.3 million data points obtained as part of 1 week of MSF history dump. It is post-processed by us as per the method provided in Sects. 4.1 and 4.2, as it does not contain Splitting and Merging values which we obtain using the flight code provided in the MSF data. After post-processing of MSF data, we obtain around 653 k (k = 1000) data points classified as **Splitting** (i.e., formed as a result of Splitting error) and around 73 k data points classified as **Merging** (i.e., formed as a result of Merging error). This translates to an error rate of 22% (i.e., tracking accuracy of 78%), 20% due to Splitting error and 2% due to Merging error. Due to this imbalance in data, instead of using accuracy or mean squared error as the criterion, we use f1-score, which is the harmonic mean of precision and recall. From the dataset, 3.2 million data points are selected randomly as our test dataset D_t while the other 100k data points are used as train dataset D_{tr} (a small train dataset was found to be sufficient from experimentation since a bigger set either led to overfitting or no further increase in accuracy).

4.1 Splitting Classification Model

Table 1 presents prediction results for eight different techniques (including our technique Stacking Logistic regression with XGBoost). The results are obtained using comparison of Splitting prediction P_S and **Splitting** (target variable) value in the test dataset D_t. Please note **Splitting** value is obtained using post-processing of MSF history dump containing flight code, which is not available in real-time testing. Dataset D_{tr} was used for training the Splitting model **S** along with hyperparameter tuning. A number of structures were considered for designing the neural network that provides best feasible performance.

Table 1. Results of Splitting model

Sr. No.	Algorithm	F1 Score	Recall
1)	Logistic regression	0.55	0.68
2)	Gaussian Naive Bayes	0.49	0.69
3)	Support vector machines	0.49	0.37
4)	K nearest neighbours	0.38	0.38
5)	Random forest classifier	0.86	0.81
6)	XGBoost	0.89	0.84
7)	Stacking logistic regression with XGBoost	0.94	0.94
8)	Artificial neural networks	0.64	0.81

Table 1 shows that a stacking model which ensembles Logistic regression with an XGBoost classifier has the best performance predicting the Splitting errors

$\mathbf{E_s}$. We obtain the following scores from this model when applied to our test dataset $\mathbf{D_t}$: Accuracy = 0.98, Precision = 0.95, Recall = 0.94, F1 Score = 0.94. Hence, the tracking accuracy of the test dataset $\mathbf{D_t}$ can be increased from the previous 78% in the first model to around 95%, if we delete the data points classified as Splitting. We observed the following order of importance for the features namely logistic regression predictions followed by Flight type, global track number, no of radars used (the no of radars used to get this data point) and location parameters.

4.2   Merging Classification Model

Table 2 presents prediction results for seven different techniques (including our technique XGBoost) obtained using comparison of Merging prediction $\mathbf{P_M}$ and **Merging** (target variable) value (obtained using post-processing of MSF history dump data containing flight code, which is not available in real-time), in the test dataset $\mathbf{D_t}$. Note that the dataset $\mathbf{D_{tr}}$ was used for training and hyperparameter tuning the Merging model $\mathbf{M}$. As with Splitting model $\mathbf{S}$, a number of structures were considered for the design of a neural network to obtain the best feasible performance. Table 2 shows that XGBoost classifier has the best performance in predicting the Merging Errors $\mathbf{E_m}$. We obtain the following scores from this model when applied to our test dataset $\mathbf{D_t}$: Accuracy = 1, Precision = 0.92, Recall = 0.89, F1 Score = 0.91. Hence, tracking accuracy of the test dataset $\mathbf{D_t}$ can be increased from previous 95% in the second model to around 97%, if we add an extra data point with new G_t for every $\mathbf{P_m}$ = 1. We observed the following order of importance for the features namely, Flight type, global track number, no of radars used (the no of radars used to get this data point) and location parameters.

Table 2. Results of Merging model

Sr. No.	Algorithm	F1 Score	Recall
1)	Logistic regression	0.1	0.19
2)	Gaussian Naive Bayes	0.04	1
3)	Support vector machines	0.12	0.4
4)	K nearest neighbours	0.11	0.11
5)	Random forest classifier	0.45	0.35
6)	XGBoost	0.91	0.89
7)	Stacking logistic regression with XGBoost	0.88	0.85
8)	Artificial neural networks	0.51	0.62

4.3   Finding Original Global Track Number

For finding the original track number, we first look into clustering algorithms [5] as we want to cluster all the data points classified as Splitting with real data points. As cluster locations (i.e. feature values of data points classified as Splitting) are fixed, there was no need for learning using clustering algorithms, hence a simple Euclidean distance was considered. Via experimentation with our training data $\mathbf{D_{trgt}}$, we found that a time range of 20 s provides the highest accuracy in terms of predicting G_t, which we used to obtain the predicted global track number $\mathbf{G_{pt}}$ for our test dataset $\mathbf{D_{tgt}}$. By comparing $\mathbf{G_t}$ and $\mathbf{G_{pt}}$, we observe an accuracy of 61% for $\mathbf{D_{tgt}}$. This means that due to the compensation of errors performed using Step 3, we have a 61% chance of being able to identify the correct global track $\mathbf{G_{pt}}$ of a flight which was classified as Splitting. Hence, our final accuracy without the third step is 97% but with only around 78% retention of data while after the third step, our accuracy reduces to 91% but with 100% data retention.

4.4 Summary of Results

Among the 3.2 million data points in the test dataset $\mathbf{D_t}$, with around 20% having **Splitting** value 1 (formed due to Splitting error $\mathbf{E_s}$) and 2% having **Merging** value 1 (formed due to Merging error) $\mathbf{E_m}$, we are able to predict 98% of the data points that have Splitting error and 99% of the data points that have Merging error. If we delete the data points with Splitting error we obtain a tracking accuracy increase from 78% to almost 95% but a reduction of data points from 3.2 million data points to 2.6 million in test dataset $\mathbf{D_t}$. Using step 3, we can add back all the data points to the test dataset $\mathbf{D_t}$, but tracking accuracy reduces to 91%, which is still a 13% increase from MSF. As merging is predicted with near 100% accuracy, we correct the 2% Merging error and increase total tracking accuracy to 93% which boils down to a total of 15% increase in tracking accuracy over the output of MSF with 100% data retention.

5 Conclusions and Future Work

In this paper, we focused on the issue of improving the accuracy of the output of an existing Multi Sensor (Radar) Fusion System used in the context of tracking flights across the Indian airspace. Due to the asynchronous observation of targets by the radars as well as overlapping regions of observation, several errors happen during the fusion process primarily categorized into Merging and Splitting errors. We, therefore, introduced a three-step ML approach to train models to predict Splitting (step 1), Merging of tracks in data (step 2) and use nearest neighbour search (step 3) to compensate for the identified errors that would help to improve the tracking accuracy while retaining all of the data. Using this three-step process, we are able to improve the accuracy of tracking from 78% to about 93% while retaining 100% of the data. Along with high performance, we also score well on explainability, which is an important criterion for the deployment of intelligent systems of this nature.

While our algorithm can potentially help with identifying and compensating for errors in tracking, given the sensitive nature of defence operations there can still be uncertainty in the mind of an operator overseeing this system. We, therefore, plan to explore the usage of a formal planning model like Partially Observable Markov Decision Process (POMDP) [11], which can enable tracking of belief over the current situation and influence the actions that follow.

Acknowledgments. We would like to thank BEL (Bharat Electronics Limited), Ghaziabad for their generous support on this work.

References

1. Andreopoulos, A., Hasler, S., Wersing, H., Janssen, H., Tsotsos, J.K., Korner, E.: Active 3d object localization using a humanoid robot. IEEE Trans. Rob. **27**(1), 47–64 (2010)
2. Brownlee, J.: Master Machine Learning Algorithms: Discover How they Work and Implement them from Scratch. Machine Learning Mastery (2016)
3. Chandrasekaran, B., Gangadhar, S., Conrad, J.M.: A survey of multisensor fusion techniques, architectures and methodologies. In: SoutheastCon 2017, pp. 1–8. IEEE (2017)
4. Chen, T., Guestrin, C.: Xgboost: A scalable tree boosting system. In: Proceedings of the 22nd ACM SIGKDD International Conference on Knowledge Discovery and Data Mining, pp. 785–794 (2016)
5. Hartigan, J.A., Wong, M.A.: Algorithm as 136: A k-means clustering algorithm. J. R. Stat. Soc. Ser. c (Appl. Stat.) **28**(1), 100–108 (1979)
6. Hassoun, M.H., et al.: Fundamentals of Artificial Neural Networks. MIT Press, Cambridge (1995)
7. Kleinbaum, D.G., Dietz, K., Gail, M., Klein, M., Klein, M.: Logistic Regression. Springer, New York (2002)
8. Liaw, A., Wiener, M.: Classification and regression by randomforest. R News **2**(3), 18–22. [SPSurl1urlSPS] (2002)
9. Lyon, D.: Theorizing Surveillance. Routledge, New York (2006)
10. Ma, K., Zhang, H., Wang, R., Zhang, Z.: Target tracking system for multi-sensor data fusion. In: 2017 IEEE 2nd Information Technology, Networking, Electronic and Automation Control Conference (ITNEC), pp. 1768–1772. IEEE (2017)
11. Ong, S.C., Png, S.W., Hsu, D., Lee, W.S.: POMDPs for robotic tasks with mixed observability. In: Robotics: Science and Systems, vol. 5, p. 4 (2009)
12. Ozuysal, M., Lepetit, V., Fua, P.: Pose estimation for category specific multiview object localization. In: 2009 IEEE Conference on Computer Vision and Pattern Recognition, pp. 778–785. IEEE (2009)
13. Polikar, R.: Ensemble learning. In: Ensemble Machine Learning, pp. 1–34. Springer, New York (2012)
14. Rish, I., et al.: An empirical study of the naive Bayes classifier. In: IJCAI 2001 Workshop on Empirical Methods in Artificial Intelligence, vol. 3, pp. 41–46 (2001)
15. Ruotsalainen, M., Jylhä, J.: Learning of a tracker model from multi-radar data for performance prediction of air surveillance system. In: 2017 IEEE Congress on Evolutionary Computation (CEC), pp. 2128–2136. IEEE (2017)
16. Scholkopf, B., Smola, A.J.: Learning with Kernels: Support Vector Machines, Regularization, Optimization, and Beyond. Adaptive Computation and Machine Learning Series. The MIT Press, Cambridge (2018)

Composition and Analysis of Pareto Optimal Compromise Solutions for Multiobjective Robust Controller Using GPC and CAN2s

Hironobu Nakayama, Ko Ogi, Kazuya Matsuo, and Shuichi Kurogi[✉]

Kyushu Institute of Technology, Tobata, Kitakyushu, Fukuoka 804-8550, Japan
{nakayama.hironobu605,oogi.kou568}@mail.kyutech.jp,
{matsuo,kuro}@cntl.kyutech.ac.jp
http://kurolab.cntl.kyutech.ac.jp/

Abstract. So far, we have developed a multiobjective robust controller using GPC (generalized predictive controller) and CAN2s (competitive associative neural nets) to learn and approximate Jacobian matrices of nonlinear dynamics of the plant to be controlled. Here, the CAN2 is an artificial neural net for learning efficient piecewise linear approximation of nonlinear function. In our recent research study, we have clarified a significant property of the controller that it achieves the closed loop transfer function to have unstable poles for quick response during transient period and to have stable poles during steady state. Here, the controller for multiobjective control usually has conflicting multiple control objectives, such as reducing settling time and overshoot, and then the control strategy has to adjust weighted objectives. Thus, in this paper, we focus on Pareto optimal compromise solutions of the proposed controller, where the controller should achieve reasonable Pareto solutions for a wide range of weighted control objectives. By means of numerical experiments, we show that the controller can achieve a reasonable Pareto solutions by using integrated CAN2s consisting of two primitive CAN2s, each trained for one of the multiple objectives.

Keywords: Multiobjective robust control · Pareto optimal compromise solution · Primitive and integrated CAN2 · Generalized predictive control

1 Introduction

So far, we have developed a multiobjective robust controller using GPC (generalized predictive controller) [1] and multiple CAN2s (competitive associative nets) [2–5]. Here, a single CAN2 is an artificial neural net introduced for learning efficient piecewise linear approximation of nonlinear function by means of competitive and associative schemes [6–8]. We have constructed a multiobjective robust controller using multiple CAN2s to learn to approximate nonlinear

© Springer Nature Switzerland AG 2020
H. Yang et al. (Eds.): ICONIP 2020, CCIS 1333, pp. 713–722, 2020.
https://doi.org/10.1007/978-3-030-63823-8_81

dynamics of plants (specifically, overhead traveling crane models) with several parameter values and two control objectives to reduce settling time and overshoot. Our method enables the controller to cope with those objectives and the plants with different parameter values by means of switching multiple CAN2s [2–4]. In our recent study [9], by means of employing a simplified linear model of the overhead traveling crane, we have clarified a significant property of the controller that it switches CAN2s for the closed loop transfer function to have unstable poles for quick response during transient period and to have stable poles during steady state. Here, a multiobjective robust controller usually has conflicting multiple control objectives, such as reducing settling time and overshoot, and then the control strategy has to adjust weighted control objectives. Thus, in this paper, we focus on Pareto optimal compromise solutions, or Pareto front, of the proposed controller, where the controller should achieve reasonable Pareto solutions for a wide range of weighted control objectives.

From a review of multiobjective optimization [11], there are two approaches called Pareto method and scalarization method, respectively. The latter uses a scalar function of a fixed weighted sum of objectives, and applies metaheuristic algorithms, such as GA (genetic algorithm), PSO (particle swarm optimization), to obtain the optimal solution. On the other hand, this paper examines our controller from the point of view of Pareto method. Especially, we are going to integrate a number of CAN2s for multiobjective robust controller to compose and analyze a sufficient number of Pareto optimal solutions. Here, note that our previous studies, such as [9], have obtained several Pareto optimal compromise solutions to analyze the behavior of the controller, especially the properties in robust control. From another point of view, a survey of multiobjective optimal control [12] gives an overview of recent mathematical developments in accelerating multiobjective optimal control because the Pareto set generally consists of an infinite number of solutions and the computational effort is challenging. However, those developments cannot be applied to the present controller using the CAN2s, while we have the similar problem where the controller needs a combinatorial (huge) number of CAN2s to obtain all Pareto optimal solutions and we manage to compose a reasonable number of CAN2s.

The rest of the paper is organized as follows. In Sect. 2, we show the multiobjective robust controller using GPC and CAN2s, and shows a method to compose Pareto optimal compromise solutions. In Sect. 3, we show numerical experiments and examine the Pareto optimal solutions, followed by the conclusion in Sect. 4.

2   Multiobjective Robust Controller Using GPC and CAN2s

We execute multiobivjecte robust controller using GPC and CAN2s shown in Fig. 1(a). In this section, we show the procedure to achieve multiobjective robust control and compose Pareto solutions, while we omit to describe GPC and CAN2 owing to the space limit (see [9] for details).

2.1 Primitive and Integrated CAN2s for Single-Objective Robust Control

For all test plants θ in $\Theta^{[\mathrm{tst}]} = \{\theta_1, \theta_2, \cdots\}$ and a control objective O, we execute single-objective robust control by means of the following three procedures:

1. **Training CAN2s:** Let $\mathrm{CAN2}_N^{[\theta]}$ be a CAN2 for training the plant $\theta \in \Theta^{[\mathrm{tr}]}$, where $N \in \mathcal{N}^{[\mathrm{unit}]} = \{N_1, N_2, \cdots, N_{|\mathcal{N}|}\}$ represents the number of units of the CAN2, and $\Theta^{[\mathrm{tr}]}$ represents the set of training plants. We execute the iterations of the following two phases to obtain $\mathrm{CAN2}_{N,i}^{[\theta]}$ for the iteration number $i \in \mathcal{I}^{[\mathrm{it}]} = \{1, 2, \cdots, |\mathcal{I}^{[\mathrm{it}]}|\}$.

   (1) **control phase:** At the first ($i = 1$) iteration, a default control sequence (see Sect. 3.2 for details) is applied to control the plant, while at the ith iteration for $i \geq 2$, control the plant by means of the GPC with $\mathrm{CAN2}_{N,i-1}^{[\theta]}$ obtained in the previous training phase.

   (2) **training phase:** Obtain $\mathrm{CAN2}_{N,i}^{[\theta]}$ by training a CAN2 with the dataset $D_i = \{(\Delta x_t^{[\mathrm{p}]}, \Delta y_t^{[\mathrm{p}]}) \mid t = 1, 2, \cdots, |D_i|\}$ obtained in the above control phase. Here, see [9] for details of $\Delta x_t^{[\mathrm{p}]}$ and $\Delta y_t^{[\mathrm{p}]}$ consisting of the differential input $\Delta u_t^{[\mathrm{p}]}$ and output $\Delta y_t^{[\mathrm{p}]}$ of the plant owing to the space limit.

2. **Integration of CAN2s for single-objective robust control:** Among $\mathrm{CAN2}_{N,i}^{[\theta]}$ ($i \in \mathcal{I}^{[\mathrm{it}]}$, $N \in \mathcal{N}^{[\mathrm{unit}]}$), we obtain the one with the best performance with respect to a control objective O, which we call primitive CAN2 and denote $\mathrm{CAN2}_N^{[\theta \cdot O]}$. Furthermore, let us denote $\mathrm{CAN2}_N^{[\Theta^{[\mathrm{tr}]} \cdot O]} = \left\{ \mathrm{CAN2}_N^{[\theta \cdot O]} \mid \theta \in \Theta^{[\mathrm{tr}]} \right\}$ which we call integrated CAN2.

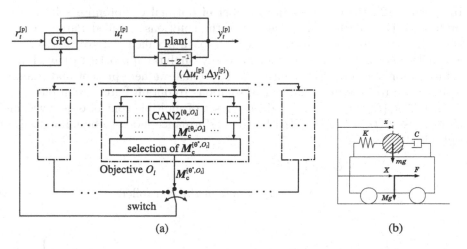

Fig. 1. Schematic diagram of (a) multiobjective controller and (b) plant model of a car and load.

3. **Single-objective robust control using integrated CAN2:** Single-objective robust control is applied to all test plants θ in $\Theta^{[\text{tst}]} = \{\theta_1, \theta_2, \cdots\}$, and the control to a test plant $\theta \in \Theta^{[\text{tst}]}$ is executed by the following steps at each discrete time t:

step 1: The weight vector $\boldsymbol{w}_c$ closest to $\Delta\boldsymbol{x}_t^{[\text{p}]}$ is selected and the corresponding $\boldsymbol{M}_c^{[\theta \cdot O]}$ is obtained for all $\text{CAN2}_N^{[\theta \cdot O]} \in \text{CAN2}_N^{[\Theta^{[\text{tr}]} \cdot O]}$.

step 2: From all selected $\boldsymbol{M}_c^{[\theta \cdot O]} \in \boldsymbol{M}_c^{[\Theta^{[\text{tr}]} \cdot O]} \equiv \{\boldsymbol{M}_c^{[\theta \cdot O]} \mid \theta \in \Theta^{[\text{tr}]}\}$, we obtain $\boldsymbol{M}_c^{[\theta^* \cdot O]}$ with the smallest prediction error for the recent plant output, i.e.

$$\boldsymbol{M}_c^{[\theta^* \cdot O]} = \operatorname*{argmin}_{\boldsymbol{M}_c^{[\theta \cdot O]} \in \boldsymbol{M}_c^{[\Theta^{[\text{tr}]} \cdot O]}} \frac{1}{N_e} \sum_{l=0}^{N_e-1} \left\| \Delta y_{t-l}^{[\text{p}]} - \boldsymbol{M}_c^{[\theta \cdot O]} \Delta\boldsymbol{x}_{t-l}^{[\text{p}]} \right\|^2 . \quad (1)$$

step 3: The GPC switches the prediction model as $\boldsymbol{M}_c = \boldsymbol{M}_c^{[\theta^* \cdot O]}$ to obtain the predictive input $\widehat{\Delta u}_t^{[\text{p}]}$ which is used for the operational input to the plant at t (see [9] for details of the predictive input).

In [9], we have shown that the controller achieves the closed loop transfer function to have unstable poles for quick response during transient period and to have stable poles during steady state. Furthermore, the controller using the integrated $\text{CAN2}_N^{[\Theta^{[\text{tr}]} \cdot O]}$ has achieved better control performance than the controller with a primitive $\text{CAN2}_N^{[\theta \cdot O]}$ owing that the integrated CAN2 involves rich information to control the plants more than each primitive CAN2 and the above model switching method has worked effectively.

2.2   Multiobjective Robust Control and Pareto Optimal Solutions

In general [12], there are infinite number of optimal compromise solutions for multiobjective control, where the set of the solutions is called Pareto set and the corresponding points in the objective space is called Pareto front. For the controller shown above, we do not have any analytic approach to have Pareto solutions for multiobjective control, so far. Thus, we here present and examine a procedure to generate a number of solutions to obtain Pareto solutions.

Let $\Omega = \{O_1, O_2, \cdots, O_{|\Omega|}\}$ denote a set of multiple control objectives, and J_l for $O_l \in \Omega$ ($l = 1, 2, \cdots, |\Omega|$) be the performance index to be minimized (or optimized):

$$O_l : \min_{x \in \mathcal{X}} J_l(x)$$

$$\text{s.t.} \quad \text{constraints of the controller}, \quad (2)$$

where

$$\mathcal{X} = \left\{ \bigcup_{\theta \in \Theta, N \in \mathcal{N}, O \in \mathcal{O}} \left\{ \text{CAN2}_N^{[\theta \cdot O]} \right\} \; \middle| \; (\Theta, \mathcal{N}, \mathcal{O}) \in 2^{\Theta^{[\text{tr}]} \times \mathcal{N}^{[\text{unit}]} \times \Omega} \right\} \quad (3)$$

indicates the set of all possible integrated CAN2s, and 2^X the power set of X. Although we would like to obtain Pareto solutions of the controller, there are a huge number of integrated CAN2s in $\mathcal{X}$. Thus, for a reasonable number of Pareto optimal compromise solutions to be examined, we compose a set of integrated CAN2s obtained from the combination of two primitive CAN2s given by

$$\text{CAN2}^{[\{\theta_s,\theta_{s'}\}\cdot O_l]} \equiv \left\{ \text{CAN2}^{[\theta_s\cdot O_l]}, \text{CAN2}^{[\theta_{s'}\cdot O_l]} \right\}, \tag{4}$$

$$\text{CAN2}^{[\theta_s\cdot O_l,\theta_{s'}\cdot O_{l'}]} \equiv \left\{ \text{CAN2}^{[\theta_s\cdot O_l]}, \text{CAN2}^{[\theta_{s'}\cdot O_{l'}]} \right\}, \tag{5}$$

where $\theta_s, \theta_{s'} \in \Theta^{[\text{tst}]}$, $O_l, O_{l'} \in \Omega$, $s' \neq s$ and $l' \neq l$. Then, we execute the control with these integrated CAN2s and obtain Pareto solutions for the objectives in Ω.

In addition, for the robust control of all test plants in $\Theta^{[\text{tst}]}$, we use $\Theta^{[\text{tr}]} = \Theta^{[\text{tst}]}$ although we have used smaller number of training plants than the number of test plants to show the generalization ability of the controller in [9].

3   Numerical Experiments and Analysis

3.1   Plant Model of a Car and a Load

We examine a linear plant model of a car and a load shown in Fig. 1(b) (see [5] for details) obtained by replacing the crane on a overhead traveling crane shown in [4] by a load (mass) with a spring and a damper in order to analyze the present control method analytically. From the figure, we have motion equations given by

$$m\ddot{x} = -K(x - X) - C(\dot{x} - \dot{X}) \tag{6}$$

$$M\ddot{X} = F + K(x - X) \tag{7}$$

where x and X are the positions of the load and the car, respectively, m and M are the weights of the load and the car, respectively, K the spring constant, C the damping coefficient, and F is the driving force of the car.

3.2   Parameter Settings and Control Objectives

The parameters of the plant have been set as follows; weight of the car $M = 100$ kg, spring constant $K = 15$ kg/s^2, damping coefficient $C = 10$ kg/s, and the maximum driving force $F_{\max} = 30$ N. We obtain discrete signals by $u_t^{[\text{p}]} = F(tT_s)$ and $y_t^{[\text{p}]} = x(tT_s)$ with sampling period $T_s = 0.01$ s, where the index [p] represents the input and output signals of the plant to distinguish those of the CAN2s.

The controller has to move the load on the car from $x = 0$ to the target (destination) position $x_d = 5$ m by means of operating F, where we consider two control objectives $O_1, O_2 \in \Omega = \{\text{ST}, \text{OS}\}$. Here, $O_1 = \text{ST}$ and $O_2 = \text{OS}$ denote the control objectives to minimize (optimize) the settling time $J_1 = t_{\text{ST}}$ [s], and the overshoot $J_2 = x_{OS}$ [s], respectively. For the iteration of the control and training phases shown in Sect. 2.1, we have employed $|\mathcal{I}^{[it]}| = 10$ iterations and the set of the number of units being $\mathcal{N}^{[unit]} = \{2, 3, \cdots, 11\}$. The default control sequence for the control phase at the fist iteration is as $F(t) = 0.8F_{max}$ for $0 \leq t < 5$ [s], 0 for $5 \leq t < 10$ [s] and $-0.8F_{max}$ for $10 \leq t < 15$ [s], which moves and stops the car at a certain position. We have used the same parameter values of GPC and CAN2 as shown in [9].

As described in Sect. 2.2, we use the same set of plants for training and test $\theta = m \in \Theta^{[tr]} = \Theta^{[tst]} = \{10\,kg, 20\,kg, \cdots, 60\,kg\}$, where m indicates the weight of the load on the car, and we have $CAN2^{[\{\theta_s, \theta_{s'}\} \cdot O_l]}$ and $CAN2^{[\theta_s \cdot O_l, \theta_{s'} \cdot O_{l'}]}$ for $\theta_s, \theta_{s'} \in \Theta^{[tst]}$, $O_l, O_{l'} \in \{ST, OS\}$, $s' \neq s$, $l' \neq l$.

3.3 Results and Analysis

Numerical Results: We have applied the controller to all test plants θ in $\Theta^{[tst]}$ and obtained the control performance for two control objectives, settling time and overshoot. We show the mean performance of the controller using the primitive $CAN2^{[\theta \cdot O]}$, the integrated $CAN2^{[\{\theta_s, \theta_{s'}\} \cdot O_l]}$ and $CAN2^{[\theta_s \cdot O_l, \theta_{s'} \cdot O_{l'}]}$, in Tables 1, 2 and 3, respectively. We can see that there are one or more Pareto solutions indicated by boldface figures in each table for both primitive and integrated CAN2s.

Table 1. Result of the performance of the controller with primitive $CAN2_N^{[\theta \cdot O]}$ for the objective $O \in \{ST, OS\}$. The value of t_{ST} [s] and x_{OS} [mm] indicates the mean of the control result for the test plant $\theta = m \in \Theta^{[tst]} = \{10\,kg, 20\,kg, \cdots, 60\,kg\}$. The boldface figures indicate Pareto optimal solutions among all solutions in Tables 1, 2, and 3.

	$O = ST$			$O = OS$		
	N	t_{ST}	x_{OS}	N	t_{ST}	x_{OS}
$CAN2_N^{[10kg \cdot O]}$	4	22.90	129.8	11	25.23	57.0
$CAN2_N^{[20kg \cdot O]}$	4	23.28	127.3	6	28.47	1.7
$CAN2_N^{[30kg \cdot O]}$	8	23.83	125.7	7	26.22	2.2
$CAN2_N^{[40kg \cdot O]}$	6	19.88	68.8	6	29.08	1.5
$CAN2_N^{[50kg \cdot O]}$	6	30.65	303.8	5	30.25	16.3
$CAN2_N^{[60kg \cdot O]}$	4	**21.83**	**4.8**	5	75.17	0.5

Pareto Solutions in the Object Space: In order to examine the Pareto solutions in detail, we depict the Pareto optimal solutions and nonoptimal solutions on the objective space in Fig. 2(a), while we also show the CAN2s corresponding to the Pareto solutions in (b). In (a), we can see that the Pareto solutions depicted with red open circles connected by red line show that they cover a wide range of weighted control objectives. Namely, for a certain weight pair

Table 2. Result of the performance of the controller with integrated $\text{CAN2}_N^{[\{(\theta_s,\theta_{s'})\}\cdot O_l]}$ for $\theta_s, \theta_{s'}(\neq \theta_s) \in \Theta^{[\text{tst}]}$, $O_l \in \{\text{ST}, \text{OS}\}$. See Table 1 for the meaning of the values.

	$O = \text{ST}$		$O = \text{OS}$	
	t_{ST}	x_{OS}	t_{ST}	x_{OS}
$\text{CAN2}_N^{[\{10\text{kg},20\text{kg}\}\cdot O]}$	20.70	98.7	25.93	1.8
$\text{CAN2}_N^{[\{10\text{kg},30\text{kg}\}\cdot O]}$	29.18	183.5	24.33	12.8
$\text{CAN2}_N^{[\{10\text{kg},40\text{kg}\}\cdot O]}$	**18.30**	**68.0**	22.40	44.5
$\text{CAN2}_N^{[\{10\text{kg},50\text{kg}\}\cdot O]}$	25.12	197.3	27.02	31.7
$\text{CAN2}_N^{[\{10\text{kg},60\text{kg}\}\cdot O]}$	22.20	13.20	35.57	13.5
$\text{CAN2}_N^{[\{20\text{kg},30\text{kg}\}\cdot O]}$	20.50	66.7	28.50	1.0
$\text{CAN2}_N^{[\{20\text{kg},40\text{kg}\}\cdot O]}$	22.75	128.2	**25.18**	**0.5**
$\text{CAN2}_N^{[\{20\text{kg},50\text{kg}\}\cdot O]}$	22.77	72.8	28.12	0.8
$\text{CAN2}_N^{[\{20\text{kg},60\text{kg}\}\cdot O]}$	**18.58**	**39.3**	**28.53**	**0.3**
$\text{CAN2}_N^{[\{30\text{kg},40\text{kg}\}\cdot O]}$	23.73	81.7	26.67	2.0
$\text{CAN2}_N^{[\{30\text{kg},50\text{kg}\}\cdot O]}$	26.63	144.5	28.30	0.8
$\text{CAN2}_N^{[\{30\text{kg},60\text{kg}\}\cdot O]}$	22.67	20.7	27.45	11.8
$\text{CAN2}_N^{[\{40\text{kg},50\text{kg}\}\cdot O]}$	23.88	172.8	28.83	2.5
$\text{CAN2}_N^{[\{40\text{kg},60\text{kg}\}\cdot O]}$	22.03	36.5	38.47	5.8
$\text{CAN2}_N^{[\{50\text{kg},60\text{kg}\}\cdot O]}$	24.77	24.5	32.32	129.7

$w = (w_{\text{ST}}, w_{\text{OS}})$ for two objectives (ST, OS) and the set of Pareto solutions, $P = \{p_i = (t_{\text{ST}}, x_{\text{OS}})_i \mid i = 1, 2, \cdots\}$, we can select a Pareto solution given by

$$p_{i^*} = \underset{p_i \in P}{\operatorname{argmin}} \left| \frac{w}{\|w\|} - \frac{p_i}{\|p_i\|} \right|, \tag{8}$$

and then, the controller with the integrated CAN2 corresponding to p_{i^*} can be effectively used for the objectives weighted by w.

From another point of view, one of the important properties of Pareto solutions is the convexity of the Pareto front, where [11] states that the convex MOO (multiobjective optimization) problem is easier than non-convex problem, and if the MOO problem is convex, then there are many algorithms that can be used to solve the problem. We can see that the Pareto front in Fig. 2(a) depicted in red line seems convex. However, the problem here to obtain the controller or the integrated CAN2 which achieves intermediate Pareto solution does not seem so easy.

Relationship Between Pareto Solutions and CAN2s: From the above point of view to obtain intermediate Pareto solution, let us examine the relationship between Pareto solutions and the CAN2 used for the control shown in Fig. 2(b). We can see that the Pareto solutions p_1 and p_2 corresponding to large weights of the objective ST are achieved with integrated CAN2s for ST, and p_7 and p_8 corresponding to large weights of the objective OS are achieved

Table 3. Result of the performance of the controller with integrated $CAN2_N^{[\theta_s \cdot O_l, \theta_{s'} \cdot O_{l'}]}$ for $\theta_s, \theta_{s'}(\neq \theta_s) \in \Theta^{[tst]}$, $O_l, O_{l'}(\neq Q_l) \in \{ST, OS\}$. See Table 1 for the meaning of the values.

	$(O_l, O_{l'}) = (ST, OS)$		$(O_l, O_{l'}) = (OS, ST)$	
	t_{ST}	x_{OS}	t_{ST}	x_{OS}
$CAN2_N^{[10kg \cdot O_l, 20kg \cdot O_{l'}]}$	**22.68**	3.3	27.23	139.2
$CAN2_N^{[10kg \cdot O_l, 30kg \cdot O_{l'}]}$	23.50	6.0	24.43	105.2
$CAN2_N^{[10kg \cdot O_l, 40kg \cdot O_{l'}]}$	**21.00**	**15.8**	21.97	78.5
$CAN2_N^{[10kg \cdot O_l, 50kg \cdot O_{l'}]}$	22.63	41.7	23.70	17.8
$CAN2_N^{[10kg \cdot O_l, 60kg \cdot O_{l'}]}$	23.95	39.0	21.27	23.8
$CAN2_N^{[20kg \cdot O_l, 30kg \cdot O_{l'}]}$	22.08	28.0	22.42	21.5
$CAN2_N^{[20kg \cdot O_l, 40kg \cdot O_{l'}]}$	19.13	49.0	22.88	6.3
$CAN2_N^{[20kg \cdot O_l, 50kg \cdot O_{l'}]}$	24.22	146.5	24.58	31.0
$CAN2_N^{[20kg \cdot O_l, 60kg \cdot O_{l'}]}$	22.77	86.7	26.02	0.7
$CAN2_N^{[30kg \cdot O_l, 40kg \cdot O_{l'}]}$	21.33	56.3	23.48	10.3
$CAN2_N^{[30kg \cdot O_l, 50kg \cdot O_{l'}]}$	28.72	149.5	25.42	1.5
$CAN2_N^{[30kg \cdot O_l, 60kg \cdot O_{l'}]}$	25.05	58.8	23.37	11.7
$CAN2_N^{[40kg \cdot O_l, 50kg \cdot O_{l'}]}$	26.23	23.8	26.23	78.3
$CAN2_N^{[40kg \cdot O_l, 60kg \cdot O_{l'}]}$	25.50	28.2	25.22	1.8
$CAN2_N^{[50kg \cdot O_l, 60kg \cdot O_{l'}]}$	27.12	52.7	**25.12**	**2.0**

with integrated CAN2s for OS. And p_3, p_5 and p_6 corresponding to intermediate weights are achieved with the integrated CAN2s involving primitive CAN2s for ST and OS. However, p_4 is achieved with the primitive CAN2 for ST. The above correspondence between Pareto solutions and integrated CAN2s indicates that we may have a better Pareto solution than p_4 by means of using integrated CAN2 for ST and OS.

From another point of view, there are multiple-use primitive CAN2s in the integrated CAN2s for Pareto solutions, i.e. $CAN2^{[10kg \cdot ST]}$ are used for p_1, p_3, p_5, $CAN2^{[20kg \cdot OS]}$ are used for p_5, p_7, p_8, $CAN2^{[60kg \cdot ST]}$ are used for p_2, p_4, p_6, and $CAN2^{[40kg \cdot OS]}$ are used for p_3, p_7. These multiple-use primitive CAN2s are considered to play essentially important roles for the control objectives.

From different point of view, we can see that p_3 in Fig. 2 (the third red open circle from the top) seems to have small degree of convexity, which indicates that there will be a better solution with other CAN2s. Furthermore, one may want to have a Pareto solution near $(t_{ST}, x_{OS}) \simeq (20.0\,s, 20.0\,mm)$, say $p_{3'}$, as an intermediate point between p_2 and p_3, or p_2 and p_4. From the above examinations, we may be able to improve the performance of p_3 and achieve $p_{3'}$ by means of combining $CAN2^{[60kg \cdot ST]}$ and other integrated CAN2s because it is in between p_2 and p_4 both using $CAN2^{[60kg \cdot ST]}$. We would like to examine these properties much more and develop a method to compose intermediate Pareto solutions in our future research study.

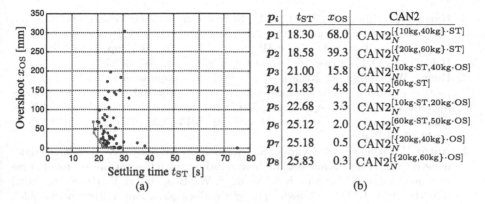

Fig. 2. (a) Obtained Pareto optimal compromise solutions depicted by red open circles connected by red line, and nonoptimal solutions depicted by black open circles. (b) The CAN2s corresponding to the Pareto solutions $p_i = (t_{ST}, x_{OS})_i$ for $i = 1, 2, \cdots, 8$. (Color figure online)

4   Conclusion

We have composed and analysed Pareto optimal solutions for the multiobjective robust controller using GPC and CAN2s. In order to analyze whether the controller can adjust a wide range of weighted objectives, we have proposed a method to compose a set of integrated CAN2s for the controller to achieve reasonable set of Pareto optimal solutions. By means of numerical experiments, we have shown that a reasonable set of Pareto optimal solutions are obtained and the controller with the integrated CAN2s corresponding to the solutions can adjust weighted objectives widely. In order to obtain intermediate Pareto solutions, we have examined and clarified several properties on the relationship between Pareto solutions and integrated CAN2s. We would like to examine these properties much more and develop a method to compose intermediate Pareto solutions in our future research study. We could not have enough time to analyze the number of units N of the CAN2s, which is for our future research study. Furthermore, this paper evaluated only the mean performance indices for the robust control to test plants, we would like to evaluate other statistical values, such as the minimum, the maximum, the standard deviation, which is also for our future research study.

References

1. Clarki, D.W., Mohtadi, C.: Properties of generalized predictive control. Automatica **25**(6), 859–875 (1989)
2. Kurogi, S., Yuno, H., Nishida, T., Huang, W.: Robust control of nonlinear system using difference signals and multiple competitive associative nets. In: Lu, B.-L., Zhang, L., Kwok, J. (eds.) ICONIP 2011. LNCS, vol. 7064, pp. 9–17. Springer, Heidelberg (2011). https://doi.org/10.1007/978-3-642-24965-5_2

3. Huang, W., Kurogi, S., Nishida, T.: Robust controller for flexible specifications using difference signals and competitive associative nets. In: Huang, T., Zeng, Z., Li, C., Leung, C.S. (eds.) ICONIP 2012. LNCS, vol. 7667, pp. 50–58. Springer, Heidelberg (2012). https://doi.org/10.1007/978-3-642-34500-5_7

4. Huang, W., Kurogi, S., Nishida, T.: Performance improvement via bagging competitive associative nets for multiobjective robust controller using difference signals. In: Lee, M., Hirose, A., Hou, Z.-G., Kil, R.M. (eds.) ICONIP 2013. LNCS, vol. 8226, pp. 319–327. Springer, Heidelberg (2013). https://doi.org/10.1007/978-3-642-42054-2_40

5. Huang, W., Ishiguma, Y., Kurogi, S.: Properties of multiobjective robust controller using difference signals and multiple competitive associative nets in control of linear systems. In: Loo, C.K., Yap, K.S., Wong, K.W., Beng Jin, A.T., Huang, K. (eds.) ICONIP 2014. LNCS, vol. 8836, pp. 58–67. Springer, Cham (2014). https://doi.org/10.1007/978-3-319-12643-2_8

6. Kurogi, S., Ren, S.: Competitive associative network for function approximation and control of plants. In: Proceedings of NOLTA 1997, pp. 775–778 (1997)

7. Kohonen, T.: Associative Memory. Springer, Heidelberg (1977). https://doi.org/10.1007/978-3-642-96384-1

8. Ahalt, A.C., Krishnamurthy, A.K., Chen, P., Melton, D.E.: Competitive learning algorithms for vector quantization. Neural Netw. 3, 277–290 (1990)

9. Nakayama, H., Matsuo, K., Kurogi, S.: Stability analysis of multiobjective robust controller employing switching of competitive associative nets. In: Gedeon, T., Wong, K.W., Lee, M. (eds.) ICONIP 2019. CCIS, vol. 1143, pp. 365–375. Springer, Cham (2019). https://doi.org/10.1007/978-3-030-36802-9_39

10. Kurogi, S., Sawa, M., Ueno, T., Fuchikawa, Y.: A batch learning method for competitive associative net and its application to function approximation. In: Proceedings of SCI 2004, vol. 5, pp. 24–28 (2004)

11. Guanantara, N.: A review of multi-objective optimization: methods and its applications. Cogent Eng. 5 (2018). https://doi.org/10.1080/23311916.2018.1502242

12. Peitz, S., Dellniz, M.: A survey of recent trends in multi-objective optimal control - surrogate models, feedback control and objective reduction. Math. Comput. Appl. 23, 30 (2018). https://doi.org/10.3390/mca23020030

13. Yoshimi, M., Nishimoto, K., Hiroyasu, T., Miki, M.: Discussions of Pareto solutions for visualization multi-objective optimization problems using spherical self-organizing maps - case study discussions through diesel engine design problems. In: Proceedings of IPSJ 2010, vol. 3, pp. 166–174 (2010)

14. Sakawa, M., Ishii, H., Nishizaki, I.: Soft Optimization. Asakura Publishing, Tokyo (1995)

15. Sannomiya, N., Kita, H., Tamaki, H., Iwamoto, T.: Genetic Algorithms and Optimization. Asakura Publishing, Tokyo (1998)

Part-Boundary-Aware Networks for Surgical Instrument Parsing

Jiaqi Liu[1,2], Yu Qiao[2], Jie Yang[1,2], and Yun Gu[1,2(✉)]

[1] Institute of Medical Robotics, Shanghai Jiao Tong University, Shanghai, China
geron762@sjtu.edu.cn
[2] Institute of Image Processing and Pattern Recognition, Shanghai Jiao Tong University, Shanghai, China

Abstract. Semantic parsing of surgical instruments provides essential information for further control. Due to the visual variations in surgery scenes, it challenging for automate segmentation task of instruments. In this paper, we proposed PBANet, which is short for Part-Boundary-Aware Networks, decomposing the instrument segmentation into two sub-tasks. An encoder-decoder architecture is adopted to predict the part-aware distance map that highlights the spatial structure of instruments. The segmentation mask is then obtained via the sigmoid function. We further propose to use a multi-scale dilation loss to reduce the boundary confusion. Empirical evaluations are performed on EndoVis2017 sub-challenge, demonstrating that the proposed method achieves superior performance compared to baseline methods.

Keywords: Boundary-aware dice · Surgical instrument parsing · Signed distance map

1 Introduction

Robotic-assisted minimal invasive surgery (MIS) has drawn wide attention in recent decades due to its effectiveness in clinical practice. The increasing levels of autonomy in MIS requires the automation of surgical subtask, particularly those are tedious and repetitive during the surgery. As a pivotal task of autonomous surgery, semantic parsing of surgical instruments provides essential information for further control. In this paper, we focus on the problem of instrument segmentation that separates the instruments from the tissue background and identify the specific parts. A typical task is to recognize the parts of instruments including shafts, wrists and clasper. Compared to the segmentation of natural images, instrument segmentation only involves limited numbers of semantic classes and the patterns are also fixed. However, this task is also challenging due to the visual variations such as illumination changes, tissue and instrument occlusion, shadows and specular reflections.

Recently, deep neural networks have achieved promising performance in medical semantic segmentation task. Most of the research works are based on

© Springer Nature Switzerland AG 2020
H. Yang et al. (Eds.): ICONIP 2020, CCIS 1333, pp. 723–730, 2020.
https://doi.org/10.1007/978-3-030-63823-8_82

the encoder-decoder structure. In order to extract rich information from the image, stronger architectures, including astrous convolution [3], attention mechanism [13] and contextual affinity [5], are proposed which significantly boosted the semantic segmentation.

For surgical instrument segmentation, García-Peraza-Herrera et al. [6] proposed ToolNet based on holistically-nested networks; TernausNet [12] utilized a UNet-like structure and won the EndoVis2017 grand-challenge [1]. Ni et al. [8] proposed a refined-attention mechanism to highlight the discriminative regions; Qin et al. [10] generated multiple samples with rotation augmentations and added the contour-based constraints to improve the fine-grained results. Considering the segmentation tasks of surgical instruments, the challenges lie in two folds: (1) A instrument is composed with a specific number of individual parts of which the shape and spatial relationships are relatively fixed. Although recent works indicate that these information can be learned via data-driven methods, the limited size of dataset in surgery scenes requires explicit modeling of the features; (2) The visual artifacts including illumination changes and occlusion lead to poor performance, especially the regions around the boundary of objects. Although the boundary-aware constraints have been considered in previous works [10], an extra decoder is added for contour estimation which involves more parameters to learn.

In this paper, we proposed PBANet, which is short for Part-Boundary-Aware Networks, decomposing the instrument segmentation into two sub-tasks. As shown in Fig. 1, an encoder-decoder architecture is adopted to predict the part-aware distance map that highlights the spatial structure of instruments. The segmentation mask is then obtained via the sigmoid function. We further propose to use a multi-scale dilation loss to reduce the boundary confusion. Empirical evaluations are performed on EndoVis2017 sub-challenge, demonstrating that the proposed method achieves superior performance compared to baseline methods.

2   Methodology

2.1   Method Overview

The main workflow of the proposed method is illustrated in Fig. 1. An encoder-decoder architecture is deployed for instrument segmentation. In this work, we use ResNet-34 [7] as the encoder network followed by five deconvolution layers as the decoder network. The numbers of output channels of deconvolution layers are set to $\{256, 128, 64, 32, 16\}$. To further extract the contextual information, the skip-connections similar to UNet are added between the encoder and the decoder[1]. We learn the parameters of the network considering the part-aware distance described in Sect. 2.2 and the multi-scale dilated boundary in Sect. 2.3.

---

[1] The main contribution of this paper is not the network architecture. Therefore, it can be adapted to other encoder-decoder networks.

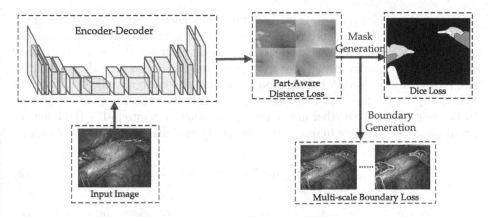

Fig. 1. The main framework of the proposed method: The input image is firstly fed into an encoder-decoder network to generate the part-aware distance map.

Fig. 2. Examples of surgical instrument segmentation.

2.2 Learning for Part-Aware Distance Map

The class-wise binary mask has been widely-used to represent the semantic region of objects. However, it lacks the awareness of the feasible shape, especially for the geometrical relationship of surgical instruments. Although this information can be extracted via the data-driven methods, effective learning is challenged by the limited size of dataset, leading to poor performance. To highlight the part-aware structure, we regress the pixel-to-boundary distance of each class, which is also known as signed distance map in 3D vision [9]. Let $x = \{x_{i,j}\}$ denote the image and $y = \{y_{i,j}^{(0)}, \ldots, y_{i,j}^{(c)}\}$ denote the class-wise segmentation mask where $y_{i,j}^{(k)} = 1$ indicates that $x_{i,j}$ belongs to class k. Otherwise, $y_{i,j}^{(k)} = 0$. Given a specific pixel $x_{i,j}$ in the image, the signed distance function $\phi^{(k)}(\cdot)$ maps the coordinates of pixel to a real value as follows:

$$\phi^{(k)}(x_{i,j}) = \begin{cases} 0, & \text{if } y_{i,j}^{(k)} = 1 \quad \text{and} \quad x_{i,j} \in \mathbf{C}^{(k)}, \\ -\inf_{\forall z \in \mathbf{C}}^{(k)} \|x_{i,j} - z\|, & \text{if } y_{i,j} = 1 \quad \text{and} \quad x_{i,j} \notin \mathbf{C}^{(k)}, \\ +\inf_{\forall z \in \mathbf{C}}^{(k)} \|x_{i,j} - z\|, & \text{if } y_{i,j} = 0. \end{cases} \tag{1}$$

where $\mathbf{C}^{(k)}$ is the set pixels of contour[2] in class k. Therefore, the part-aware distance is set to zero if the pixels are from the contour. For pixels within the

---

[2] The width of contour is set to 1 in this section.

background, $\phi^{(k)}(x_{i,j})$ is set to the coordinate distance between the pixel and the closest one from the contour. To distinguish the foreground and background, the sign function is used to indicate whether inside or outside the contour. Figure 2 presents the examples of distance map. Four images in the second row indicate the part-aware distance for each class (including the background). Compared to the binary mask, the distance map introduces more explicit geometry of each instrument parts. We further normalize the distance map into $[-1, +1]$. Given the groundtruth of distance map $\phi^{(k)}(x)$, we firstly optimize the following problem:

$$\mathcal{L}_{part} = \sum_{\forall x} \sum_{k=1}^{c} \|(\hat{\phi}^{(k)}(x) - \phi^{(k)}(x))\|_{L_{1,\text{Smooth}}} \tag{2}$$

where $\hat{\phi}^{(k)}(x)$ is the predicted distance map for class k. $\| \cdot \|_{L_{1,\text{Smooth}}}$ is the Smoothed L_1 loss.

Previous work [4] used multiple outputs that simultaneously predicts the mask and distance map. This will introduce more parameters to learn. In this work, we use a sigmoid function, $\sigma(-k\phi(x)) = \frac{1}{1+e^{-k\phi(x)}}$, to generate the approximated mask. When k is set to large positive number, the positive values of distance map will be pushed to zeros while the negative values will be pushed to ones. Therefore, we learn the binary mask for each class as follows:

$$\mathcal{L}_{dice} = -\sum_{\forall x} \sum_{k=1}^{c} \frac{2\sigma(-k\phi(x_i))y_i}{\sigma(-k\phi(x_i))\sigma(-k\phi(x_i)) + y_i y_i} \tag{3}$$

which is the standard DiceLoss between the groundtruth mask and the approximated mask generated by the distance map.

2.3   Learning for Multi-scale Boundary-Aware Dilation

The visual artifacts including illumination changes and occlusion are common in surgery scenes. This will significantly affect the accuracy of instrument segmentation especially for the region closed to the boundary. To address this problem, Qin et al. [10] added extra channels to predict the contour. However, this strategy involves more parameters and, more importantly, only estimates the contour of fixed width. For contours of smaller width, it focuses more on the region closed to the region of interest while the contextual information is limited. In this case, it is preferred for high sensitivity to highlight the fine-grained structures. For contours of larger width, both intra-class and inter-class regions are covered, leading to richer contextual information. In this case, it is preferred for high specificity to reduce further mis-classification. Instead of adding extra channels for contours, we use max-pooling operators of various kernel sizes MaxPool$^{(s)}$ to generate the contours from masks as follows:

$$C^{(s)} = \text{MaxPool}^{(s)}(y) - y \tag{4}$$

Based on Eq. (4), we defined the multi-scale dilation loss as follows:

$$\mathcal{L}_{boundary} = -\sum_{s}(1 + \beta(s)^2)\frac{\hat{C}^{(s)}C^{(s)}}{\beta(s)^2\hat{C}^{(s)}\hat{C}^{(s)} + C^{(s)}C^{(s)}} \tag{5}$$

where $\hat{C}^{(s)}$ and $C^{(s)}$ are prediction and groundtruth of contour with specific width s. This is a F_β metric for all s. In this paper, $\beta(s)$ is also a sigmoid function $\beta(s) = \frac{1}{1+e^{-s}}$. With larger s, the F_β metric focuses more on precision of contour estimation while the smaller s emphasizes more on sensitivity.

2.4 Overall Optimization

The overall optimization problem is the integration of part-aware loss in Eq. (2), DiceLoss in Eq. (3) and boundary-aware loss in Eq. (5) as follows:

$$\mathcal{L} = \mathcal{L}_{dice} + \lambda(\mathcal{L}_{part} + \mathcal{L}_{boundary}) \tag{6}$$

where λ is the balancing weight. We empirically set it to 0.01 in this paper. Since all items in Eq. (6) is fully differentiable, the parameters of the neural networks can be learned via back-propagation strategy [11].

3 Experiments

In this section, experiments are performed to evaluate to proposed method via both qualitative and quantitative results. The critical parameters are also discussed.

3.1 Dataset and Experiment Settings

The EndoVis2017 dataset [1] is made up of eight sequences of abdominal porcine procedures recorded using da Vinci Xi systems. Each sequence has 225 frames with the resolution 1280×1024. The endoscope image is labeled by four classes including background and three individual parts of instrument. Among them, six sequences are used for training and the remaining two sequences are used for testing. During training, the data is augmented via vertical and horizontal clipping.

To learn the parameters of the neural networks, we use the Adam solver with a batch size of 2. The learning rate is set to 0.0001 which is decayed via CosineAnnealing scheduler at the first 10 epochs and kept fixed in next 40 epochs. The PyTorch[3] framework is adopted to implement the deep convolution neural networks and the hardware platform used is a standard workstation with Intel i7-8700 CPU and NVIDIA GeForce 1080Ti.

---

[3] https://github.com/pytorch/pytorch.

Table 1. Quantitative results of the baselines and proposed method. 'Ours' represent the proposed method.

Methods	Mean DSC	Mean IoU
TernausNet [12]	0.8224	0.7315
LinkNet [2]	0.8053	0.7084
ResUNet [7]	0.8682	0.7814
ResUNet-Contour [10]	0.8733	0.7875
ResUNet-SDF [4]	0.8702	0.7825
Ours-S{5}	0.8699	0.7841
Ours-S{7}	0.8731	0.7869
Ours-S{5, 7}	0.8779	0.7943
Ours-S{3, 5, 7}	0.8773	0.7940
Ours	0.8801	0.7986

3.2   Quantitative Results

We firstly present the quantitative results of instrument segmentation on EndoVis2017 dataset. The standard Dice similarity coefficient (DSC) and intersection of union (IOU) were used as the overall metrics to evaluate the segmentation performance. Several baselines are adopted in this paper for comparison including *TernausNet* [12], *LinkNet* [2], *ResUNet* [7], *ResUNet-Contour* [10] and *ResUNet-SDF* [4]. Among them, TernausNet and LinkNet are participants of EndoVis2017 grand-challenge; ResUNet is the basic network of the proposed method that only uses DiceLoss; ResUNet-Contour adds an extra decoder for contour estimation of each class while ResUNet-SDF uses extra decoder for distance map estimation. Table 1 presents the mean DSC and mean IoU over all classes. The result demonstrates that the proposed method outperforms baseline methods by achieving the mean DSC of 0.8801 and the mean IoU of 0.7986. Although ResUNet-Contour and ResUNet-SDF used multi-task learning can improve the accuracy of the segmentation, they introduced more parameters to learn compared to the proposed method.

We also present brief discussions of the key parameters. As shown in Table 1, *Ours-S{·}* denotes different setups of MaxPooling kernels used in boundary-aware loss. *Ours-S{5}* indicates only $s = 5$ is used while *Ours-S{5, 7}* indicates both $s = 5$ and $s = 7$ are used. We removed the part-aware loss for fair comparisons. The results indicates that the combination of multiple sizes of kernels can improve the segmentation accuracy and the smaller kernels are not helpful compared to larger ones.

3.3   Qualitative Results

We also present the qualitative results of baselines and the proposed methods in Fig. 3. For simple cases in the first row, most of the method can provide promis-

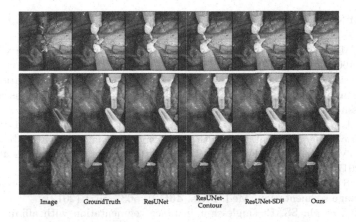

Fig. 3. Examples of surgical instrument segmentation.

ing segmentation results of instrument parts. When the background object is similar to the shafts as shown in the second row, the baseline methods obtain small false-positive regions at the bottom. However, the proposed method can effectively avoid this situation due to part-aware distance loss. For cases with strong illumination variations in third row, the proposed method can preserve better shape completeness compared to baselines. Moreover, the fine-grained contours of the proposed are also clearer. These results demonstrate the promising performance contributed from the part-aware loss and boundary-aware loss.

4   Conclusion

Semantic parsing of surgical instruments provides essential information for further control. Due to the visual variations in surgery scenes, it challenging for automate segmentation task of instruments. In this paper, we proposed PBANet, which is short for Part-Boundary-Aware Networks, decomposing the instrument segmentation into two sub-tasks. An encoder-decoder architecture is adopted to predict the part-aware distance map that highlights the spatial structure of instruments. The segmentation mask is then obtained via the sigmoid function. We further propose to use a multi-scale dilation loss to reduce the boundary confusion. Experiments on EndoVis2017 demonstrate the two advantages of the proposed method: (1) The part-aware distance map can provide better representation of the geometrical structure of instruments; (2) The multi-scale boundary dilation can preserve clearer segmentation of contour regions. Therefore, the proposed method achieves superior mean DSC and IoU scores compared to baseline methods.

Acknowledgement. This work was partly supported by the National Key R&D Program of China (2019YFB1311503), NSFC (61375048,61661010,61977046,62003208), Committee of Science and Technology, Shanghai, China (19510711200) and Shanghai Sailing Program (20YF1420800).

References

1. Allan, M., et al.: 2017 robotic instrument segmentation challenge. arXiv preprint arXiv:1902.06426 (2019)
2. Chaurasia, A., Culurciello, E.: LinkNet: exploiting encoder representations for efficient semantic segmentation. In: 2017 IEEE Visual Communications and Image Processing (VCIP), pp. 1–4. IEEE (2017)
3. Chen, L.C., Papandreou, G., Kokkinos, I., Murphy, K., Yuille, A.L.: DeepLab: semantic image segmentation with deep convolutional nets, atrous convolution, and fully connected CRFs. IEEE Trans. Pattern Anal. Mach. Intell. **40**(4), 834–848 (2017)
4. Dangi, S., Linte, C.A., Yaniv, Z.: A distance map regularized CNN for cardiac cine MR image segmentation. Med. Phys. **46**(12), 5637–5651 (2019)
5. Gao, N., et al.: SSAP: single-shot instance segmentation with affinity pyramid. In: Proceedings of the IEEE International Conference on Computer Vision, pp. 642–651 (2019)
6. García-Peraza-Herrera, L.C., et al.: ToolNet: holistically-nested real-time segmentation of robotic surgical tools. In: 2017 IEEE/RSJ International Conference on Intelligent Robots and Systems (IROS), pp. 5717–5722. IEEE (2017)
7. He, K., Zhang, X., Ren, S., Sun, J.: Deep residual learning for image recognition. In: Proceedings of the IEEE Conference on Computer Vision and Pattern Recognition, pp. 770–778 (2016)
8. Ni, Z.L., Bian, G.B., Xie, X.L., Hou, Z.G., Zhou, X.H., Zhou, Y.J.: RASNet: segmentation for tracking surgical instruments in surgical videos using refined attention segmentation network. In: 2019 41st Annual International Conference of the IEEE Engineering in Medicine and Biology Society (EMBC), pp. 5735–5738. IEEE (2019)
9. Park, J.J., Florence, P., Straub, J., Newcombe, R., Lovegrove, S.: DeepSDF: learning continuous signed distance functions for shape representation. In: Proceedings of the IEEE Conference on Computer Vision and Pattern Recognition, pp. 165–174 (2019)
10. Qin, F., Lin, S., Li, Y., Bly, R.A., Moe, K.S., Hannaford, B.: Towards better surgical instrument segmentation in endoscopic vision: multi-angle feature aggregation and contour supervision. arXiv preprint arXiv:2002.10675 (2020)
11. Rumelhart, D.E., Hinton, G.E., Williams, R.J.: Learning representations by back-propagating errors. Nature **323**(6088), 533–536 (1986)
12. Shvets, A.A., Rakhlin, A., Kalinin, A.A., Iglovikov, V.I.: Automatic instrument segmentation in robot-assisted surgery using deep learning. In: 2018 17th IEEE International Conference on Machine Learning and Applications (ICMLA), pp. 624–628. IEEE (2018)
13. Zhang, H., et al.: Context encoding for semantic segmentation. In: Proceedings of the IEEE conference on Computer Vision and Pattern Recognition, pp. 7151–7160 (2018)

Time Series Analysis

A Contextual Anomaly Detection Framework for Energy Smart Meter Data Stream

Xiufeng Liu[1]([⊠]), Zhichen Lai[2]([⊠]), Xin Wang[3], Lizhen Huang[4], and Per Sieverts Nielsen[1]

[1] Technical University of Denmark, 2800 Lyngby, Denmark
xiuli@dtu.dk
[2] Sichuan University, Chengdu, China
ryanlai.cs@gmail.com
[3] Southwest Jiaotong University, Chengdu, China
[4] Norwegian University of Science and Technology, Trondheim, Norway

Abstract. Monitoring abnormal energy consumption is helpful for demand-side management. This paper proposes a framework for contextual anomaly detection (CAD) for residential energy consumption. This framework uses a sliding window approach and prediction-based detection method, along with the use of a concept drift method to identify the unusual energy consumption in different contextual environments. The anomalies are determined by a statistical method with a given threshold value. The paper evaluates the framework comprehensively using a real-world data set, compares with other methods and demonstrates the effectiveness and superiority.

Keywords: Contextual · Anomaly detection · Data stream · Concept drift

1 Introduction

According to the EU energy in figures [3], households account for 27% of total energy consumption and 16% carbon emissions. Several studies [8,10,11] have shown that thermal renovation often does not deliver the expected energy savings. This is because household energy consumption is largely dependent on household characteristics and occupant behaviour. Therefore, an effective approach is to monitor user energy consumption, in particular, to detect and diagnose abnormal consumption. This now become possible with the use of smart meters. By analysing smart meter data, utilities can then provide personalised services and energy-efficiency suggestions.

Anomaly detection refers to the process of identifying unusual observations that do not meet expectations, also known as outlier detection [7]. Contextual factors often play an important role in influencing energy consumption, which must be taken into account when detecting anomalies. We call it contextual

© Springer Nature Switzerland AG 2020
H. Yang et al. (Eds.): ICONIP 2020, CCIS 1333, pp. 733–742, 2020.
https://doi.org/10.1007/978-3-030-63823-8_83

anomaly detection in this paper. For example, the increase in electricity consumption in summer may not need to be considered as anomalies if we consider the effects of weather temperature. This is because people usually use more energy in summer due to air conditioning for cooling. However, if the temperature is mild and no air conditioning is used, the high consumption should be detected as an anomaly. This is also true in other contexts, such as changes in consumption patterns, thermal renovation of buildings or changes in occupants, which may cause the general consumption pattern shifts. Therefore, contextual anomaly detection consists of identifying individual observations or patterns that differ from the masses in the same context. In this paper, the consumption trend or pattern changes due to variations in the contextual environment are considered as *concept drift*, which means that the overall pattern or trend may change abruptly or gradually. The anomalies will be detected accordingly in each context.

Depending on how the streaming data are processed, the methods can be divided into batch and stream data anomaly detection. This paper focuses on the latter. Compared to the detection of anomalies in batch data, the detection of anomalies in data streams consists of additional challenges due to their complex nature and data stream evolving. These challenges include high velocity, the presence of noisy data, and concept drift. The model trained on static data may not be suitable for detection on a data stream because the time series may drift, e.g., the data distribution changes. Therefore, the detection models should be retrained if a concept drift occurs. To remedy this, our earlier work [7] updates the detection models iteratively using a lambda system and uses the latest model to detect anomalies of a data stream. This approach runs in a cluster environment and requires a large amount of computing capacity. It is therefore not an ideal solution for stream data mining in an environment with limited computing resources such as IoT devices.

In this paper, we implement a contextual anomaly detection framework, called *CAD*. It integrates with a concept drift detector to identify each context and trains the detection model when a concept drift occurs. It can be integrated into a building energy management system or a building information management platform (BIM) to enable automation of energy performance monitoring or design of building energy systems. This paper makes the following contributions: (1) We propose an algorithm of detecting contextual anomalies for high-frequent energy consumption data streams; (2) We propose an unsupervised concept drift detection method for contextual detection; (3) We evaluate the proposed framework comprehensively, and compare with other approaches using a real-world energy consumption data set.

2   The Framework

The proposed framework for contextual anomaly detection is presented in Fig. 1. This framework detects anomalies on the streaming data from smart meters. First, it uses online concept drift detection to identify different contexts representing the change of energy consumption environment. The reason is that context-dependent factors are often difficult to determine. Then, the framework uses an algorithm to predict short-term energy consumption values. In the end, the predicted value is compared with the actual value by calculating the distance which is used to determine an anomaly or not according to a given threshold value. The anomaly can be used for notification purposes or control signal in smart energy systems.

Figure 2 shows an illustrating example using synthetic data to explain when and how an anomaly is detected. In this time series, two concept drifts are first identified, and the prediction model is retrained when a concept drift is determined. Thus, the concept drifts are used to identify the context shifts and the consumption values are predicted using the retrained model in each context (see the red line). Anomaly scores are calculated based on prediction errors, and those with anomaly scores above a threshold value are classified as anomalies. The concept drift detection, short-term prediction, and anomaly classifier are described in greater detail in the following.

2.1   Context Shift Detection

The concept drift detection can be formalised as follows. For a data stream, $\mathcal{D} = \{(X_1, y_1), (X_2, y_2), \ldots, (X_t, y_t), \ldots\}$, where X is the vector of features and y is the class, the concept drift can be defined as the distribution shift detection, i.e., $p(X_t, y_t) \neq p(X_{t-1}, y_{t-1})$, where p represents the probability of concept drift. The entire data stream is divided into the segments in which the drifts of the underlying distributions are detected accordingly. We perform the model update only when a drift is detected. The algorithm is called $CAD\text{-}D3$, derived from the Discriminative Drift Detector (D3) [5] (see Algorithm 1). It detects a drift by comparing the divergence of data statistics between two segments in a time window.

Figure 3 shows the architecture. A fixed-length time window, W, slides on a time series with two segments partitioned by a ratio of p, w and pw, used to hold old and new data respectively. The separability of the two segments is determined by an AUC value ranging from 0.5 to 1. 1 means that the two classes can be perfectly separated and 0.5 means that they overlap completely. With a given threshold τ, if the AUC value is greater than or equal to τ, the old data will be dropped and the new data will be moved into it (the lower left); otherwise, the pw elements at the tail of the sliding window will be dropped and the remaining data in the sliding window will be shifted to the left (see Algorithm 1 for details). Therefore, this method can identify different contexts of energy consumption.

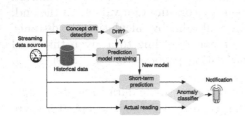

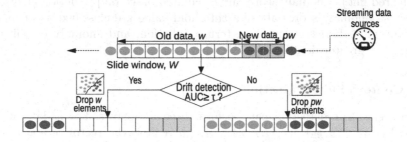

Fig. 1. Architecture overview

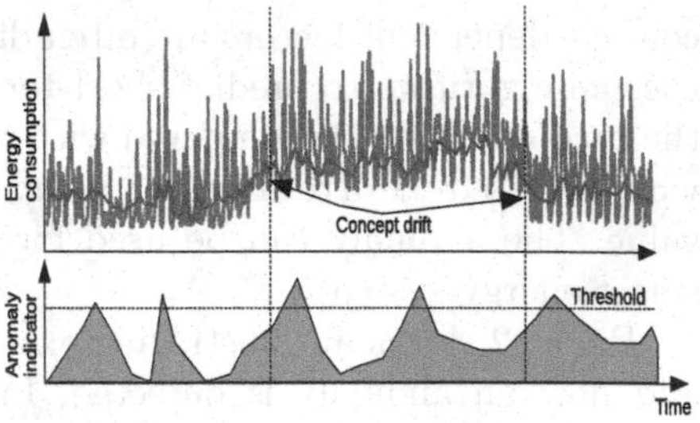

Fig. 2. Contextual anomaly detection overview (Color figure online)

Fig. 3. Concept drift detection architecture of CAD-D3

2.2 Consumption Prediction

We now present how to predict short-term energy consumption. The energy consumption pattern of residential households typically has a periodicity characteristics, e.g., with low consumption during the night and high consumption during the day with morning and evening peaks. The yearly pattern has a seasonality (or seasonal periodicity), e.g., with higher consumption in both summer and winter, due to electrical cooling and heating. The fluctuations with a long range of time are considered as contextual shifts in this paper, e.g., weather temperature changes. We choose the LSTM (Long Short-Term Memory) model which has shown good performance in time series prediction [12]. LSTM is a deep learning method with numerous hidden layers, which has a gate structure and a memory cell to manage the temporal correlation of time series. A LSTM model can be seen as the function $\mathcal{F}(\cdot)$ that maps a sequence of past observations to an output as the predicted value. It is defined as: $X'_t = \mathcal{F}(X_{t-1}, X_{t-2}, \cdots, X_{t-24})$, where X'_t is the predicted value, and $X_{t-1}, X_{t-2}, \cdots, X_{t-24}$ are the past values, representing the last 24 h energy consumption that constitute a daily periodicity.

2.3 Aggregated for Contextual Anomaly Detection

We now aggregate the above concept drift detection and the LSTM prediction model to detect contextual anomalies for energy consumption time series. The aggregated model is presented in Algorithm 1. The input includes an individual consumption time series $\mathcal{TS}$, the period d ($d = 24$ as the default for daily periodicity), the size of window holding old data w, the window ratio for holding new data p, and the drift threshold τ. The algorithm is for online concept drift detection, $\mathcal{C}$ and anomaly detection $\mathcal{AD}$, as well as retraining the prediction model, $\mathcal{AP}$.

This algorithm first divides the elements in the sliding window W into multiple groups according to the period d (line 16), then extracts the group statistics as the features to train the concept drift detection model, including mean, standard deviation, and range. The drift discriminative classifier is a logistic regression model trained by the extracted features (lines 21–22), then a concept drift is detected (lines 23–24). The group statistical characteristics is used as the features for training the classifier. The AUC is then used as the measure to determinate the separability between the old and new data. This is done by introducing a slack variable s, which labels old data as 1 and new data as 0 (line 19–20). If the AUC is greater than or equal to the user-specified drift threshold value τ, a concept drift is determined. In the end, the auto-regressive predictor $\mathcal{AP}$ (i.e., the LSTM model) is retrained to predict energy consumption in the next context after the concept drift (lines 30–31).

The following describes the anomaly classifier $\mathcal{AD}$. For the input X_t at the time t, the corresponding prediction error $err_t = |X_t - X'_t|$ is calculated (line 8). The error represents the prediction capability of the generated model. Instead of directly thresholding the error to identify an anomaly, the error distribution is used as the indirect metric for calculating anomaly score. At the time t with N_t data points, the errors are modeled as a rolling normal distribution, $\mathcal{N}(\mu_t, \sigma_t^2)$, where:

$$\mu_t = \frac{\sum_{i=1}^{N_t} err_i}{N_t}, \quad \sigma_t^2 = \frac{\sum_{i-1}^{N_t} (err_i - \mu_t)^2}{N_t}, \quad S(err) = 1 - \frac{1}{\sigma_t \sqrt{2\pi}} e^{-\frac{(err - \mu_t)^2}{2\sigma_t^2}}$$

(1)

If the anomaly score, S, is greater than or equal to a user-defined threshold value, ϵ, i.e. $S(err) \geq \epsilon$, the corresponding data point is classified as an anomaly.

3   Evaluation

The experiments were conducted on an HP laptop, configured with an Intel(R) Core(TM) i7-8700 processor (3.20 GHz, 6 Cores), 16 GB RAM, and a Western Digital Hard driver (1TB, 6 Gb/s, 64 MB Cache and 7200 RPM), running Windows 10 Professional edition. The LSTM network is implemented with Keras 2.3.1 [2].

The Irish Commission for Energy Regulation (CER) data set [6] is used, with time series of 4,182 households from July 2009 to December 2010, a resolution of 30 min. We made the following pre-processing: aggregate to an hourly resolution and concatenate multiple time series to obtain a longer time series. The concatenations of different time series with statistical significance in values can be seen as a context shift, as well as the changes due to weather temperatures.

Algorithm 1: Contextual anomaly detection model

---

1 **function CAD**(*TimeSeries* TS, *WindowSize* w, *Period* d, *NewDataRatio* p, *DriftThreshold* τ)

2   Initialize window W where $|W| = w(1 + p)$;

3   Discriminative classifier C;

4   Auto-regressive predictor AP;

5   Statistical anomaly detector AD;

6   **while** TS *generates a new sample* X **do**

7          $X' = AP(W[|W| - d, |W|])$;

8          $err = |X - X'|$;

9   **if** $AD(err)$ *alarms* **then**

10             $Anomaly = True$;

11   **else**

12             $Anomaly = False$;

13   **end**

14   **if** W *is not full* **then**

15             $W \leftarrow W \cup X$;

16   **else**

17             $G = \{G_1, ..., G_{|W|/d}\} \leftarrow$ Split W into $|W|/d$ groups, each of which G_i has d elements, $i \in [1, |W|/d]$;

18             $F = \{F_1, ..., F_{|W|/d}\} \leftarrow$ Calculate mean, standard deviation and range as the classification feature F_i of G_i;

19   S is vector of $s = \{0, 1\}$, $|S| = |W|/d$, label for old data (0) and new data (1);

20             $s = 0$ for old data $F[1, (w/d)]$;

21             $s = 1$ for new data $F[(w/d) + 1, |W|/d]$;

22             $(F_{train}, S_{train}), (F_{test}, S_{test}) \leftarrow$ Split classification feature F into train and test set with S;

23   Train the discriminative classifier $C(F_{train}, S_{train})$ on the train set;

24             $AUC(F_{test}, S_{test}) \leftarrow$ Test $C(F_{test}, S_{test})$ on the test set;

25   **if** $AUC(F_{test}, S_{test}) \geq \tau$ **then**

26                 $Drift = True$;

27   Drop w elements from the tail of W;

28   **else**

29                 $Drift = False$;

30   Drop wp elements from the tail of W;

31   **end**

32   **end**

33   **if** $Drift$ *is True* **then**

34   Retrain AP model;

35   **end**

36   **end**

37 **end**

The following subsections will first investigate the optimal hyperparameters for the CAD model, then evaluate the concept drift model and the influence of the model update frequency on the prediction accuracy, and finally evaluate the anomaly detection.

3.1 Hyperparameter Investigation for the CAD Model

The hyperparameters include the LSTM units of the time series predictor, the sliding window size and the AUC threshold of the concept drift detector. The following studies will be based on the performance evaluated by mean square

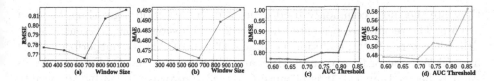

Fig. 4. Impact of sliding window size and AUC threshold on prediction

Table 1. Different LSTM units in CAD

No. LSTM units	RMSE	MAE
5	0.963	0.557
10	0.842	0.512
25	0.766	0.471
50	0.792	0.496

Table 2. Concept drift on prediction

Model	RMSE	MAE
DDM	1.117	0.694
ADWIN	1.101	0.674
D3	0.826	0.558
CAD-D3	0.766	0.471

error (RMSE) and mean absolute error (MAE).

$$RMSE = \sqrt{\sum_{i=1}^{N} \frac{(X_i' - X_i)^2}{N}}, \qquad MAE = \frac{\sum_{i=1}^{N} |X_i' - X_i|}{N} \qquad (2)$$

where X' is the predicted value, X is the observation (actual reading) and N is the number of observations.

We first investigate the optimal number of LSTM units by varying the number of LSTM units. The corresponding RMSE and MAE values are in Table 1, which shows that the CAD model performs the best when the number of units is set to 25.

We next investigate the optimal sliding window size W by varying from 288 (corresponding to the hourly readings of 6 days) to 1,056 (corresponding to the hourly readings of up to 44 days). The results are shown in Fig. 4a and b, in which the lines both have a "V" shape, with the lowest value at $W = 672$ (corresponding to the hourly readings of 28 days). We then investigate the AUC threshold of the concept drift detector, and use a fixed window size $W = 672$, but vary the threshold value from 0.6 to 0.85. The results are shown in Fig. 4c and d, showing that the AUC threshold of $\tau = 0.7$ has the best result. Therefore, the window size $W = 672$ and the concept drift threshold $\tau = 0.7$ are used as the default parameters.

3.2 Comparison with Other Drift Detection Models

We now compare CAD-D3 with other baselines, including the original D3, and DDM [1] and ADWIN [4]. The reason for choosing DDM and ADWIN is that they are the most commonly used concept drift detection algorithms for data stream. The results are presented in Table 2, which shows how different concept drift detectors affect prediction accuracy. D3 and CAD-D3 outperform DDM and ADWIN according to the RMSE and MAE values, and CAD-D3 performs slightly better than D3. It is because CAD-D3 improves the D3 by taking into account the statistical features in its classifier, including mean, standard deviation and range of daily consumption data. This results in greater accuracy, but also allows more updates to be triggered for predictions.

3.3   Evaluation of Model Update Frequency

In this study, we compare the model without update (static model), the model with regular updates (regular model) and the model update triggered by concept drift (CAD model). We randomly select a time series for the experiment. Figure 5a–c show the results of the three models, while Fig. 5d shows the original time series for better visual comparison. The results show that the static model predicts electricity consumption with a relatively fixed pattern because it was trained by the early data and is not able to adapt well to data variations in different contextual environments. In Fig. 5b, the regular model shows a similar result to the static model in Fig. 5a. Note that the prediction accuracy is related to the freshness of the model used. Here we specify the update frequency for every 4,000 h for the regular model, which does not obtain the same prediction accuracy as the CAD model. In contrast, the CAD model is more adaptable. The model is updated according to the contextual environment variation, which maintains the freshness of the model.

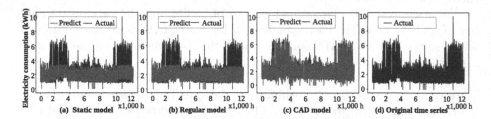

Fig. 5. Prediction by the models with different update frequency

We calculate the corresponding RMSE and MAE values in Table 3. The static model has the highest RMSE and MAE values, followed by the regular model. However, we can see that the regular model has improved the RMSE value by 27.3% and the MAE value by 26.9% compared to the static model. In this case, the CAD model gives the best result, i.e., it can achieve good prediction accuracy in contextual environments.

Table 3. Impact by update frequency

Model	RMSE	MAE
Static model	1.203	0.722
Regular model	0.918	0.528
CAD model	0.766	0.471

Table 4. Comparison between models

Model	Precision	Recall	F1-score
Tukey BP	0.544	0.831	0.564
Static model	0.557	0.671	0.537
Regular model	0.580	0.793	0.585
CAD model	0.584	0.844	0.636

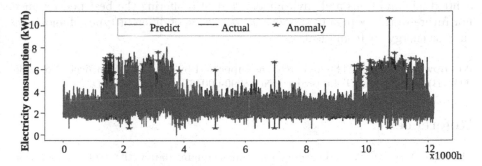

Fig. 6. A showcase of anomaly detection using the CAD model (Color figure online)

3.4 Evaluation of Anomaly Detection

Since there are no ground-truth anomalies, we label the data manually, aided by a time series visualisation tool and a Python program. Again, we compare the CAD model with the static model and the regular model. We also introduce *Tukey Boxplot (BP)* [9] as an additional baseline to evaluate the proposed framework.

Figure 6 is a showcase of anomaly detection by the CAD model, with detected anomalies marked with a red star. Note that the ϵ anomaly detection threshold is set to 0.6. Table 4 summarises the performance of anomaly detection based on the metrics including precision, recall and F1 score. According to the F1 score, the static model has the lowest accuracy in anomaly detection. It is noteworthy that there is a big difference between the static model and the other models in terms of recall value. The accuracy of the regular model is better than the static model, but its recall value is lower than the Tukey BP. The CAD model outperforms others in all metrics, which means that our model outperforms others in detecting contextual anomalies. The others, like the static model, have not taken into account contextual shifts because their models are fixed, which makes it less accurate. Although the regular model performs better than the static model, blind updates may not help to obtain better accuracy because a concept drift can occur exactly after the model is updated. Because Tukey BP analyses the overall statistical characteristics without considering the periodicity and drift of the data, its performance is not superior. In contrast, the contextual CAD model is well suited for detecting anomalies for time series with periodicity and drifts, such as energy consumption data, as it can maintain model freshness.

4   Conclusions and Future Work

This paper proposed a framework for online contextual anomaly detection for the data stream from smart meters. Concept drift was used to signal the refreshing of the prediction model. In this paper, the errors between the actual and predicted values were modeled into a rolling normal distribution and used to calculate the score for identifying anomalies. We have conducted extensive experiments to evaluate the framework, and the results verified the superiority of the proposed CAD model over other baselines, being better able to adapt to changes in contextual conditions and environment, but also offering the best performance. For future work, we plan to support the detection of different types of anomalies such as energy theft and leakage.

Acknowledgement. This research was supported by the CITIES project (No. 1035-00027B) and the HEAT 4.0 project (No. 8090-00046B) funded by IFD.

References

1. Bifet, A., Gavalda, R.: Learning from time-changing data with adaptive windowing. In: Proceedings of the 2007 SIAM International Conference on Data Mining, pp. 443–448. SIAM (2007)
2. Chollet, F., et al.: Keras. https://github.com/keras-team/kerasas. Accessed 10 Sept 2020
3. EU Energy in Figures: Statistical pocketbook 2018. European Union (2018)
4. Gama, J., Medas, P., Castillo, G., Rodrigues, P.: Learning with drift detection. In: Bazzan, A.L.C., Labidi, S. (eds.) SBIA 2004. LNCS (LNAI), vol. 3171, pp. 286–295. Springer, Heidelberg (2004). https://doi.org/10.1007/978-3-540-28645-5_29
5. Gözüaçık, Ö., Büyükçakır, A., Bonab, H., Can, F.: Unsupervised concept drift detection with a discriminative classifier. In: Proceedings of CIKM, pp. 2365–2368 (2019)
6. ISSDA: Irish social science data archive. http://www.ucd.ie/issda/data/commissionforenergyregulationceras. Accessed 10 Sept 2020
7. Liu, X., Nielsen, P.S.: Scalable prediction-based online anomaly detection for smart meter data. Inf. Syst. **77**, 34–47 (2018)
8. Lundström, L., Wallin, F.: Heat demand profiles of energy conservation measures in buildings and their impact on a district heating system. Appl. Energy **161**, 290–299 (2016)
9. Mosteller, F., Tukey, J.W., et al.: Data Analysis and Regression: A Second Course in Statistics. Addison-Wesley Publishing Company, Boston (1977)
10. Passer, A., Ouellet-Plamondon, C., Kenneally, P., John, V., Habert, G.: The impact of future scenarios on building refurbishment strategies towards plus energy buildings. Energy Build. **124**, 153–163 (2016)
11. Risholt, B., Time, B., Hestnes, A.G.: Sustainability assessment of nearly zero energy renovation of dwellings based on energy, economy and home quality indicators. Energy Build. **60**, 217–224 (2013)
12. Siami-Namini, S., Tavakoli, N., Namin, A.S.: A comparison of ARIMA and LSTM in forecasting time series. In: Proceedings of ICMLA, pp. 1394–1401 (2018)

A New Time Series Forecasting Using Decomposition Method with SARIMAX Model

Chalermrat Nontapa[1]([✉]), Chainarong Kesamoon[1], Nicha Kaewhawong[1], and Peerasak Intrapaiboon[2]

[1] Department of Mathematics and Statistics, Faculty of Science and Technology, Thammasat University, Pathum Thani 12120, Thailand
`chalermrat.non@dome.tu.ac.th`, {`chainarong,nicha`}`@mathstat.sci.tu.ac.th`
[2] Corporate Innovation Office, Siam Cement Group, Bangkok, Thailand
`peerasai@scg.com`

Abstract. In this paper, we present a new method for forecasting time series data, namely decomposition method with SARIMA and decomposition method with SARIMAX models. The proposed technique starts with decomposing time series data into trend-cycle-irregular and seasonality components by multiplicative decomposition method. Both of SARIMA and SARIMAX are applied to the trend-cycle-irregular part to find the model that best describes it. Each of SARIMA trend-cycle-irregular and SARIMAX trend-cycle-irregular are then combined with seasonal index to make series of forecast value. These proposed forecasting methods are applied to four real monthly data sets such that the electricity consumption in provincial area of Thailand, the number of international tourists in Thailand, the US\$/THB exchange rate and the SET index. The proposed methods are compared to SARIMA and SARIMAX models. The result shows that the decomposition method with SARIMAX trend-cycle-irregular can perform well. The best method has reduced average error rate for 3 months and 12 months lead time forecasting of 39.9622% and 10.4992%, respectively. In addition, the decomposition method with SARIMAX model has the lowest average MAPE of 1.8364% for 3 months and 2.9575% for 12 months lead time forecasting, respectively.

Keywords: Time series · Decomposition method · SARIMAX

1 Introduction

Time series forecasting is a dynamic research area which has attracted attentions of researcher's community over last few decades. One of the most popular and frequently used stochastic time series models is the Autoregressive Integrated Moving Average (ARIMA) [3,6] model. The basic assumption made to implement this model is that the considered time series is linear and follows a particular known statistical distribution, such as the normal distribution.

© Springer Nature Switzerland AG 2020
H. Yang et al. (Eds.): ICONIP 2020, CCIS 1333, pp. 743–751, 2020.
https://doi.org/10.1007/978-3-030-63823-8_84

ARIMA model has subclasses of other models, such as the Autoregressive (AR) [6], Moving Average (MA) [6] and Autoregressive Moving Average (ARMA) [6] models. For seasonal time series forecasting, Box and Jenkins [5] had proposed a quite successful variation of ARIMA model, viz. the Seasonal ARIMA (SARIMA) [2]. When an ARIMA model includes other time series as input variables, the model is sometimes referred to as an ARIMAX model. Pankratz [1] refers to the ARIMAX model as dynamic regression. The ARIMA procedure provides a comprehensive set of tools for univariate time series: model identification, parameter estimation, diagnostic checking and forecasting and it offers great flexibility in the kinds of ARIMA or ARIMAX models that can be analyzed [4,5]. This model may also have seasonal fluctuations we also called this case in Seasonal Autoregressive Integrated Moving Average (SARIMA) and Seasonal Autoregressive Integrated Moving Average with Exogenous Variables (SARIMAX). Decomposition method is the one of classical time series forecasting method, which estimates trend component by mathematical functions. This approach is not appropriate because it has many errors in time series forecasting. Since, the mathematical models cannot explain behavior of nature of trend component. One way to describe the trend component in a time series data, we will fit the trend-cycle-irregular component using higher efficiency model.

In this paper, we present a new idea of time series forecasting using decomposition method with SARIMA trend-cycle-irregular and decomposition method with SARIMAX trend-cycle-irregular. The seasonal component is still estimated by ratio-to-moving average method. This method is used to detect seasonality for four real monthly data sets such as the electricity consumption in provincial area of Thailand, the number of international tourists in Thailand, the US$/THB exchange rate and the SET index. The rest of this paper is organized as follows: In the following section, we review the decomposition method, SARIMA model, SARIMAX model and proposed method. Sections 3 explains data preparation and model evaluation criteria. Empirical results for comparing the forecasting techniques from four monthly real data sets are illustrated in Sect. 4. The final section provides the conclusion and future research.

2   Methodology

2.1   Decomposition Method

An important goal in time series analysis is the decomposition of a series into a set of non-observables components that can be associated to different types of temporal variations such as trend, seasonal, cycle and irregular. The most common forms are known as additive and multiplicative decompositions, which are expressed in Eqs. (1) and (2), respectively.

$$y_t = (T_t + S_t + C_t + I_t) + \varepsilon_t \tag{1}$$

$$y_t = (T_t \times S_t \times C_t \times I_t) + \varepsilon_t \tag{2}$$

2.2 Seasonal Autoregressive Integrated Moving Average (SARIMA) Model

Seasonal Autoregressive Integrated Moving Average (SARIMA) Model is an extension of ARIMA that explicitly supports univariate time series data with a seasonal component. It adds three new hyperparameters to specify the autoregression (AR), differencing (I) and moving average (MA) for the seasonal component of the series, as well as an additional parameter for the period of the seasonality. A Seasonal ARIMA model is formed by including additional seasonal terms in the SARIMA$(p, d, q)(P, D, Q)_s$.

SARIMA$(p, d, q)(P, D, Q)_s$ model:

$$\phi_p(B) \Phi_P(B^S)(1 - B)^d (1 - B^S)^D y_t = \theta_q(B) \Theta_Q(B^S) \varepsilon_t \tag{3}$$

$$\left(1 - \sum_{i=1}^p \phi_i B^i\right)\left(1 - \sum_{k=1}^P \Phi_k B^{kS}\right) z_t = \left(1 - \sum_{j=1}^q \theta_j B^j\right)\left(1 - \sum_{l=1}^Q \Theta_l B^{lS}\right) \varepsilon_t \tag{4}$$

y_t is the observation at time t.
ε_t is a random error at time t.; $\varepsilon_t \sim NID\left(0, \sigma_\varepsilon^2\right)$
$\phi_p(B)$ is the Non-Seasonal Autoregressive operator of p-order.
$\theta_q(B)$ is the Non-Seasonal Moving Average operator of q-order.
$\Phi_P(B^S)$ is the Seasonal Autoregressive operator of P-order.
$\Theta_Q(B^S)$ is the Seasonal Moving Average operator of Q-order.

2.3 Seasonal Autoregressive Integrated Moving Average with Exogenous Variables (SARIMAX) Model

Seasonal Autoregressive Integrated Moving Average with Exogenous Variables (SARIMAX) Model is a SARIMA model with Exogenous Variables (X), called SARIMAX$(p, d, q)(P, D, Q)_s$ where X is the vector of exogenous variables. The exogenous variables can be modeled by multiple linear regression equation is expressed as follows:

$$y_t = \beta_0 + \beta_1 X_{1,t} + \beta_2 X_{2,t} + \cdots + \beta_k X_{k,t} + \omega_t \tag{5}$$

where β_0 is constant parameter and $\beta_1, \beta_2, \ldots, \beta_k$ are regression coefficient parameters of exogenous variables, $X_{1,t}, X_{2,t}, \ldots, X_{k,t}$ are observations of k number of exogenous variables corresponding to the dependent variable y_t; ω_t is a stochastic residual, i.e. the residual series that is independent of input series.

$$\omega_t = \frac{\theta_q(B) \Theta_Q(B^S)}{\phi_p(B) \Phi_P(B^S)(1 - B)^d (1 - B^S)^D} \varepsilon_t \tag{6}$$

The general SARIMAX model equation can be obtained by substituting Eq. (6) in Eq. (5) [4].

SARIMAX(p, d, q) $(P, D, Q)_s$ model:

$$y_t = \beta_0 + \sum_{i=1}^{k} \beta_i X_{i,t} + \frac{\theta_q(B) \Theta_Q(B^S)}{\phi_p(B) \Phi_P(B^S)(1 - B)^d (1 - B^S)^D} \varepsilon_t \tag{7}$$

2.4 Proposed Method

Decomposition Method with SARIMA and SARIMAX Models

The proposed method start by decomposing in time series data into four parts such that irregular (I) trend-cycle (TC) trend-cycle-irregular (TCI) and seasonality (S) components by using multiplicative decomposition. SARIMA and SARIMAX are applied to the trend-cycle-irregular part to find the model that best describes it. After that, each of SARIMA and SARIMAX trend-cycle-irregular are then combined with seasonal index to make series of forecast values.

$$y_t = (T \times C \times I)_{t,SARIMA} \times S_t + \varepsilon_t \tag{8}$$

$$y_t = (T \times C \times I)_{t,SARIMAX} \times S_t + \varepsilon_t \tag{9}$$

3 Data Preparation and Model Evaluation Criteria

3.1 Data Descriptions and Data Preparation

In this paper, we have four real monthly data sets, which are used to demonstrate the effective of proposed methods such that the electricity consumption in provincial area of Thailand [7], the number of international tourists in Thailand [8], the US\$/THB exchange rate [9] and the SET index [10]. To assess the forecasting performance of different models, each data set is divided into two samples of training and testing. The training data is used exclusively for model development and then, the test sample for 3 months and 12 months are used to evaluate the established model. The data compositions for the four data sets are given in Table 1.

Table 1. Details of the time series data sets.

Series	Sample size	Training set	Test set	
			3 months	12 months
Electric	216	2002 – 2018 (204)	2019	2019
Tourists	276	1997 – 2018 (264)	(January - March)	(January - December)
USD/THB	216	2002 – 2018 (204)		
SET	264	1998 – 2018 (252)		

3.2   Model Evaluation Criteria

Mean Absolute Percentage Error (MAPE) is a measure of prediction accuracy of a forecasting method in statistics. It usually expresses the accuracy as a ratio. MAPE is defined by the formula:

$$MAPE\% = \frac{1}{n} \sum_{t=1}^{n} \left| \frac{y_t - \hat{y}_t}{y_t} \right| \times 100 \tag{10}$$

Reduce Error Rate (RER) is a measure of reduce errors for proposed model when compares with original model as a ratio. If the RER equals 100% then forecasting by proposed method is the highest accuracy to the original method. Otherwise, If the RER equals 0% then accuracy of proposed method is not different from original method. RER is defined by the formula:

$$RER\% = \left(1 - \frac{MAPE_{Proposed}}{MAPE_{Original}} \right) \times 100 \tag{11}$$

4   Empirical Results and Discussion

The forecasting results for four real monthly data sets using SARIMA, SARIMAX, Decomposition method with SARIMA and SARIMAX for 3 months and 12 months lead time forecasting were showed in Table 2 and Table 3. We have conducted experiments on RStudio and SPSS package.

Table 2. MAPE and average MAPE of four datasets for 3 months lead time forecasting.

Method	Electric	Tourist	USD/THB	SET	Avg. MAPE (3 months)
SARIMA	2.8308	1.7868	2.6639	4.3900	2.9179
SARIMAX	1.6829	0.5919	1.7672	4.0506	2.0232
DEC-SARIMA	1.2400	1.3114	1.6784	3.3090	1.8847
DEC-SARIMAX	1.5601	0.8215	1.7606	3.2035	**1.8364***

Table 3. MAPE and average MAPE of four datasets for 12 months lead time forecasting.

Method	Electric	Tourist	USD/THB	SET	Avg. MAPE (12 months)
SARIMA	2.8440	2.2795	4.2617	3.7751	3.2901
SARIMAX	2.5369	2.7287	4.1052	3.6173	3.2470
DEC-SARIMA	2.1757	2.6162	3.9803	3.5516	3.0810
DEC-SARIMAX	2.1200	2.2099	4.0211	3.4791	**2.9575***

Tables 2 and 3 show average MAPE of four time series forecasting methods for 3 months and 12 months lead time forecasting. It found that decomposition method with SARIMAX model has the lowest average MAPE of 1.8364% and 2.9575%, respectively. Moreover, the decomposition method with SARIMAX model fitting was adequate for four real monthly data sets with the Portmanteau Statistic Q of Box-Ljung. This model has been checked by using residual analysis. We conclude that the random errors are normally distributed, no autocorrelated, zero mean and constant variance.

Table 4. R^2 and average R^2 of Training Model.

Method	Electric	Tourist	USD/THB	SET	Avg. R^2%
SARIMA	98.8709	98.3914	98.7996	98.9149	98.7442
SARIMAX	98.7918	98.2553	98.9005	98.9559	98.7259
DEC-SARIMA	99.2708	98.6639	98.8386	98.9075	98.9202
DEC-SARIMAX	99.2863	98.6853	99.2184	98.9304	**99.0301***

Table 4 shows that the average coefficient of determination (R^2) of four real monthly data sets are 98.7442%, 98.7259%, 98.9202%, 99.0301% for SARIMA, SARIMAX, decomposition method with SARIMA and decomposition method with SARIMAX, respectively. The average R^2 of decomposition method with SARIMAX is the best fit model for four real monthly data sets.

Table 5 shows average Reduce Error Rates (RER) of the decomposition method with SARIMAX model for four real monthly data sets in 3 months and 12 months lead time forecasting. It found that the proposed model has average RER of 39.9622% and 10.4992%, respectively. Moreover, the proposed model for 3 months lead time forecasting is more accurate than for 12 months lead time forecasting. In addition, the decomposition method with SARIMAX model had the highest average R^2 of 99.0301%.

5   Conclusion and Future Research

5.1   Conclusion

Time series forecasting is one of the very demanding subjects over the last few decades, since can be applied for financial, economics, engineering and scientific modeling. The standard statistical technique from the literature, namely decomposition method and Box-Jenkins method are well known for many researchers. The aim of this research are prefer new method, namely decomposition method with SARIMA and decomposition method with SARIMAX models with application to four real monthly data sets such that the electricity consumption in provincial area of Thailand, the number of international tourists in Thailand, the

Table 5. Decomposition method with SARIMAX model and RER% for 3 months and 12 months lead time forecasting.

Decomposition method with SARIMAX model	RER% (3 months)	RER% (12 months)
data set 1: Electric	44.8884	25.4571
SARIMAX$((13), 0, (2, 15, 44, 47, 51))(0, 0, 0)_{12}$ TCI with TCI_{t-1} and TCI_{t-12} $\left(R^2\% = 99.2863\right)$ $y_t = [\beta_0 + \beta_1\left(TCI_{t-1}\right) + \beta_2\left(TCI_{t-12}\right) + \phi_{13}\omega_{t-13} - \theta_2\varepsilon_{t-2}$ $-\theta_{15}\varepsilon_{t-15} - \theta_{44}\varepsilon_{t-44} - \theta_{47}\varepsilon_{t-47} - \theta_{51}\varepsilon_{t-51} + \varepsilon_t] \times S_t + \varepsilon'_t$ $\hat{y}_t = [119.9010 + 0.8468\left(TCI_{t-1}\right) + 0.1486\left(TCI_{t-12}\right)$ $-0.2896\omega_{t-13} - 0.2338\varepsilon_{t-2} - 0.1924\varepsilon_{t-15}$ $-0.1738\varepsilon_{t-44} - 0.2690\varepsilon_{t-47} + 0.1908\varepsilon_{t-51}] \times \hat{S}_t$		
data set 2: Tourist	54.0240	3.0533
SARIMAX$((1, 9), 0, (9, 23, 42))(1, 0, (1, 5))_{12}$ TCI with TCI_{t-1} and TCI_{t-12} $\left(R^2\% = 98.6853\right)$ $y_t = [\beta_1\left(TCI_{t-1}\right) + \beta_2\left(TCI_{t-12}\right) + \phi_1\omega_{t-1}$ $+\phi_9\omega_{t-9} + \Phi_1\omega_{t-12} - \phi_1\Phi_1\omega_{t-13} - \phi_9\Phi_1\omega_{t-21}$ $-\theta_9\varepsilon_{t-9} - \theta_{23}\varepsilon_{t-23} - \theta_{42}\varepsilon_{t-42} - \Theta_1\varepsilon_{t-12}$ $+\theta_9\Theta_1\varepsilon_{t-21} + \theta_{23}\Theta_1\varepsilon_{t-35} + \theta_{42}\Theta_1\varepsilon_{t-54} - \theta_5\varepsilon_{t-60}$ $+\theta_9\Theta_5\varepsilon_{t-69} + \theta_{23}\Theta_5\varepsilon_{t-83} + \theta_{42}\varepsilon_{t-102} + \varepsilon_t] \times S_t + \varepsilon'_t$ $\hat{y}_t = [0.8557\left(TCI_{t-1}\right) + 0.1517\left(TCI_{t-12}\right) + 0.1497\omega_{t-1}$ $+0.4261\omega_{t-9} + 0.3387\omega_{t-12} - 0.0507\omega_{t-13} - 0.1443\omega_{t-21}$ $-0.4034\varepsilon_{t-9} + 0.1430\varepsilon_{t-23} - 0.1683\varepsilon_{t-42} - 0.4890\varepsilon_{t-12}$ $+0.1973\varepsilon_{t-21} - 0.0699\varepsilon_{t-35} + 0.0823\varepsilon_{t-54} + 0.2599\varepsilon_{t-60}$ $-0.1032\varepsilon_{t-69} + 0.0366\varepsilon_{t-83} - 0.0431\varepsilon_{t-102}] \times \hat{S}_t$		
data set 3: USD/THB	33.9089	5.6456
SARIMAX$((25), 0, (9))(0, 0, 1)_{12}$ TCI with TCI_{t-1} and TCI_{t-12} $\left(R^2\% = 99.2184\right)$ $y_t = [\beta_0 + \beta_1\left(TCI_{t-1}\right) + \beta_2\left(TCI_{t-12}\right)$ $+\phi_{25}\omega_{t-25} - \Theta_1\varepsilon_{t-12} - \theta_9\Theta_1\varepsilon_{t-21} + \varepsilon_t] \times S_t + \varepsilon'_t$ $\hat{y}_t = [0.4004 + 1.3529\left(TCI_{t-1}\right) - 0.3654\left(TCI_{t-12}\right)$ $-0.1512\omega_{t-25} - 0.1613\varepsilon_{t-12} - 0.0339\varepsilon_{t-21}] \times \hat{S}_t$		
data set 4: SET	27.0273	7.8409
SARIMAX$(0, 0, (33))(0, 0, 0)_{12}$ TCI with TCI_{t-1} $\left(R^2\% = 98.9301\right)$ $y_t = [\beta_1\left(TCI_{t-1}\right) - \theta_{33}\varepsilon_{t-33}\varepsilon_t] \times S_t + \varepsilon'_t$ $\hat{y}_t = [1.0037\left(TCI_{t-1}\right) - 0.1689\varepsilon_{t-33}] \times \hat{S}_t$		
Average	39.9622	10.4992

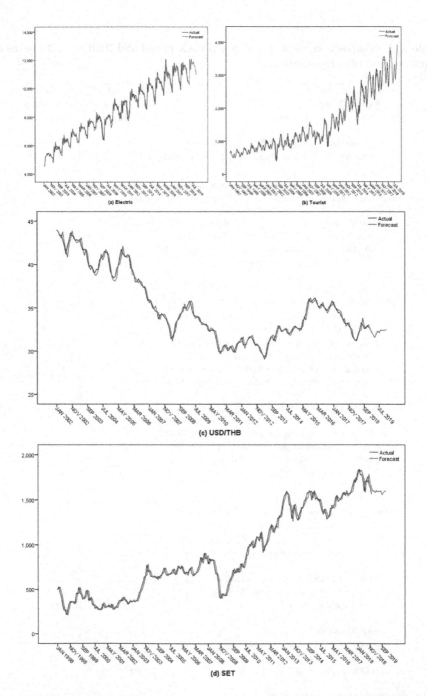

Fig. 1. The time plots of actual value (blue line) and forecast value (red line) for four real monthly data sets: (a) Electric, (b) Tourist, (c) USD/THB exchange rate and (d) SET index using decomposition method with SARIMAX model. (Color figure online)

US\$/THB exchange rate and the SET index. The proposed methods are compared to SARIMA and SARIMAX models. The performance evaluation results indicated that the decomposition method with SARIMAX model can perform well. In addition, the decomposition method with SARIMAX model have average reduced error rate of 39.9622% and 10.4992% for 3 months and 12 months lead time forecasting, respectively which are compared to SARIMA model and we can see the RER in each data sets.

5.2 Future Research

We can try to use trend-cycle-irregular (TCI) in Exponential Smoothing method, Holt-Winters method or Neural Network (NN) by applying this technique to some other problems and big data sets with various numbers of features.

Acknowledgments. This work was supported by the Government of Canada, Canada-ASEAN Scholarships and Educational Exchanges for Development (SEED 2019–2020).

References

1. Pankratz, A.: Forecasting with dynamic regression models. Int. J. Forecast. **8**(4), 647–648 (1991)
2. Hamzacebi, C.: Improving artificial neural networks performance in seasonal time series forecasting. Inform. Sci. **178**(23), 4550–4559 (2008)
3. Zhang, P.G.: Time series forecasting using a hybrid ARIMA and neural network model. Neurocomputing **50**, 159–175 (2003)
4. Cools, M., Moons, E., Wets, G.: Investigating variability in daily traffic counts using ARIMAX and SARIMA (X) models: assessing impact of holidays on two divergent site locations. J. Transp. Res. Board **10**(1), 1–22 (2009)
5. Peter, Ď., Silvia, P.: ARIMA vs. ARIMAX - which approach is better to analyze and forecast macroeconomic time series?. In: Jaroslav, R., Daniel, S. (eds.) Proceedings of 30th International Conference Mathematical Methods in Economics 2012, MME, pp. 136–140. Karviná, Czech Republic (2012). http://ies.fsv.cuni.cz/default/file/download/id/21584
6. Hipel, K.W., McLeod, A.I.: Time Series Modelling of Water Resources and Environmental Systems, 1st edn. Elsevier, Amsterdam (1994)
7. Energy Policy and Planning Office (EPPO) Ministry of Energy, Electricity Consumption in the Provincial Area of Thailand, http://www.eppo.go.th/index.php/en/en-energystatistics/summary-statistic?orders[publishUp]=publishUp&issearch=1. Accessed 1 Mar 2020
8. Bank of Thailand, Number of International Tourists in Thailand, www.bot.or.th/App/BTWS_STAT/statistics/ReportPage.aspx?reportID=875&language=th. Accessed 8 Mar 2020
9. Bank of Thailand, US\$/THB exchange rate, https://www.bot.or.th/English/Statistics/Pages/default.aspx. Accessed 12 Mar 2020
10. Stock Exchange of Thailand, the SET Index, https://www.set.or.th/en/market/market_statistics.html. Accessed 15 Mar 2020

Adversarial Attacks on Deep Learning Systems for User Identification Based on Motion Sensors

Cezara Benegui and Radu Tudor Ionescu[✉]

University of Bucharest, 14 Academiei, Bucharest, Romania
cezara.benegui@fmi.unibuc.ro, raducu.ionescu@gmail.com

Abstract. For the time being, mobile devices employ implicit authentication mechanisms, namely, unlock patterns, PINs or biometric-based systems such as fingerprint or face recognition. While these systems are prone to well-known attacks, the introduction of an explicit and unobtrusive authentication layer can greatly enhance security. In this study, we focus on deep learning methods for explicit authentication based on motion sensor signals. In this scenario, attackers could craft adversarial examples with the aim of gaining unauthorized access and even restraining a legitimate user to access his mobile device. To our knowledge, this is the first study that aims at quantifying the impact of adversarial attacks on machine learning models used for user identification based on motion sensors. To accomplish our goal, we study multiple methods for generating adversarial examples. We propose three research questions regarding the impact and the universality of adversarial examples, conducting relevant experiments in order to answer our research questions. Our empirical results demonstrate that certain adversarial example generation methods are specific to the attacked classification model, while others tend to be generic. We thus conclude that deep neural networks trained for user identification tasks based on motion sensors are subject to a high percentage of misclassification when given adversarial input.

Keywords: Adversarial attacks · Adversarial examples · Signal processing · Motion sensors · User authentication · Convolutional neural networks

1 Introduction

Nowadays, usage of mobile devices has grown exponentially, becoming the first choice for most users. Since personal devices allow manipulation and access to private data, security is one of the most important factors to consider. Whereas all operating systems and applications allow for standard security configuration, such as unlock patterns, PINs or facial recognition, it is well known that they are prone to attacks such as smudge [1], reflection [25] and video capture attacks [20,26]. With the advancement of technology, different sensors were introduced in mobile devices, among others being motion sensors. Recent works [2,15,21,22] proposed continuous and unobtrusive authentication systems that

© Springer Nature Switzerland AG 2020
H. Yang et al. (Eds.): ICONIP 2020, CCIS 1333, pp. 752–761, 2020.
https://doi.org/10.1007/978-3-030-63823-8_85

use motion sensors, such as the gyroscope and the accelerometer, to silently identify users, employing machine learning models, e.g. convolutional neural networks. Unobtrusive authentication methods, based on motion sensor data, are best used for enhancing implicit authentication systems (such as facial detection algorithms and fingerprint scanners). Due to recent scientific progress, implicit methods require fewer steps for the registration phase. As shown in literature [2], machine learning models based on motion sensor data are great candidates for the aforementioned process, taking into consideration their capability to register users in as less as 20 steps.

In this study, our objectives are (i) to determine if adversarial examples can be crafted for deep learning models based on motion sensor signals, and (ii) to evaluate the impact and the universality of adversarial examples for deep learning models based on motion sensor signals. In an adversarial setting, data samples are crafted by an attacker and fed as input to a classifier, with the aim of inducing a different output, other than the expected label. Although deep neural networks used in image recognition and computer vision tasks are known to be prone to adversarial attacks [4,7,13], to our knowledge, there is no research conducted on deep neural networks trained on motion signals collected from mobile devices. Therefore, we are the first to experiment with various adversarial attack generation methods on different neural network architectures, that are trained to identify users based on motion sensor signals. Within this frame of reference, we seek to gather empirical evidence on how different neural networks architectures are affected by the generated adversarial examples. Our approach is to employ convolutional neural models trained for user identification [2], using samples from HMOG data set [21]. Rauber et al. [18] released a Python-based toolbox used for model robustness benchmarking, called Foolbox. We use the built-in Foolbox attack strategies to generate adversarial examples for our convolutional neural networks.

In summary, our aim is to answer the following research questions (RQs) in the context of adversarial example generation on motion sensor data:

- RQ1: Can we generate adversarial examples to attack deep learning models for user identification based on motion sensor data?
- RQ2: Are the adversarial examples universal or specific to certain neural architectures?
- RQ3: What generative methods produce the most damaging adversarial attacks?

2 Related Work

There are many works that conducted research on user identification on mobile devices using motion sensor data [11,12,15,19,21–24]. Among the broad range of explored methods, some rely on voice and accelerometer-based user recognition [23], while others perform human movement tracking based on motion sensors [21]. The most recent and best-performing approaches are based on deep learning [2,15]. So far, researchers explored recurrent neural networks [15] and convolutional neural networks [2]. However, none of the previous works investigated the possibility of generating adversarial attacks by adding indistinguishable perturbations to the motion signals recorded on mobile devices. In this paper, we focus on convolutional neural networks (CNNs), which were shown to outperform Long Short-Term Memory networks in the recent work of Benegui et al. [2]. The approach proposed in [2] consists in converting motion sensor signals into images that are provided as input to a convolutional neural network. Although CNN models provide outstanding results on various computer vision tasks [5, 8, 9], some recent studies [4, 17] showed that adversarial examples can generate sizeable misclassification error rates, indicating that CNNs are not robust to adversarial attacks. For instance, Chen et al. [4] showed that adversarial attacks induce an error rate of 95.80% in CNNs trained for image classification. Simple black-box tools used to generate adversarial samples, e.g. Foolbox [18], represent practical ways of crafting attacks without requiring any prior knowledge related to the attacked model. Papernot et al. [17] noted that generator models for adversarial examples can be universal, i.e. examples optimized on a classification model can easily produce misclassification errors for other classification models with different architectures. We note that the aforementioned studies targeted neural networks for objects and image classification problems. To our knowledge, we are the first to study adversarial attacks on neural networks used in user identification tasks based on motion sensor signals recorded on mobile devices.

3   Method

3.1   Convolutional Neural Networks

With the aim of answering our research questions, we implement three CNN models, with the same design and configuration proposed by Benegui et al. [2], starting from a shallower 6-layer CNN architecture and increasing the depth gradually to 9 layers and 12 layers, respectively. Each model consists of different convolutional (conv) layers followed by max pooling and fully-connected (fc) layers. All layers are activated by Rectified Linear Units (ReLU), except for the classification layer. Each fc layer has a dropout rate of 0.4 to prevent overfitting. Max pooling layers have a pool size of 2×2 and are applied at stride 2. Since our models are trained for multi-class classification, Softmax activation is preferred in the last layer, since it outputs the probability of each class. Network training is performed using the Adam optimizer [10] with the categorical cross-entropy loss function. In all models, the final layer is composed of 50 neurons, equal to the number of classes.

In the 6-layer CNN, we employ 3 conv layers, 2 fc layers and one Softmax classification layer. The second architecture, with a depth of 9 layers, is built as follows: 6 conv layers, 2 fc layers and the classification layer. Lastly, our 12-layer CNN is composed of 9 conv layers, 2 fc layers and the Softmax classification layer. While the three models share some architectural elements, each model is trained independently, having no weights in common with any of the other models.

3.2   Adversarial Example Generation Strategies

Adversarial examples represent scarcely modified data samples that, when provided as input to neural networks, determine incorrect predictions. Starting from the assumption that different methods of generating adversarial examples can provide different results, we propose to experiment with four different gradient-based or decision-based attack methods. The goal of crafting an adversarial example from a real example is to produce a misclassification error, i.e. the adversarial attack is about inducing incorrect predictions. This is achieved by maximizing the categorical cross-entropy loss. In order to craft a realistic adversarial example, we also aim at minimizing the mean squared error with respect to the original example used as starting point for the optimization. Therefore, our second goal is to create adversarial samples as similar as possible to the originals. By jointly maximizing the categorical cross-entropy and minimizing the mean squared error between two inputs (the original and the adversarial example), we can obtain an adversarial example with a high percentage of similarity to the original, unnoticeable for humans, that is wrongly classified by the neural network. We note that the generator might not always converge to an adversarial example having both properties, i.e. not all attacks are successful. Next, we briefly present the considered attacks.

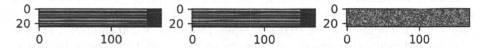

Fig. 1. An original and an adversarial example generated by the Boundary Attack. The left-most image represents the original motion sensor signals. The second image is the adversarial example. The right-most image depicts an exaggerated map of differences between the original and the adversarial image. Best viewed in color. (Color figure online)

Boundary Attack. The Boundary Attack [3] method is a simple and efficient attack that starts from a randomly generated perturbation vector. In each iteration, the method regenerates the adversarial sample until the difference to the original input becomes smaller, yet still recognized as adversarial, by minimizing the L_2-norm of perturbations. Figure 1 shows a comparison between an original example and an adversarial example generated by the Boundary Attack.

Fast Gradient Sign Attack. This attack perturbes the input sample given to a classification model considering the gradient of the loss, gradually amplifying the gradient magnitude until the model misclassifies the generated example [6].

DeepFool L_2 Attack. Introduced by Moosavi-Dezfooli et al. [14], the DeepFool L_2 attack takes an original sample and generates a perturbation vector that is added to the adversarial sample. For each class, the algorithm computes the smallest distance required to reach the class boundary using a linear classifier.

Once the smallest distance has been computed, a corresponding move towards the direction of the class boundary is made. Using this attack, a perturbation vector that misleads the classifier can be identified in as less as three iterations.

Jacobian-Based Saliency Map Attack. Papernot et al. [16] introduced a targeted attack based on gradients, that computes a score, called the saliency score, for each feature available in the original sample. The computations are performed in an iterative manner. Therefore, in each iteration the saliency score can change the prediction of the model from the original class to a different class.

4   Experiments

4.1   Data Set

We use the HMOG data set [21], which is composed of discrete signals, gathered from the accelerometer and gyroscope motion sensors, while 50 users perform tap gestures on a mobile device screen. While each user is performing a tap gesture, signals are recorded for a period of 1.5 s, as follows: values are captured starting with 0.5 s before the tap, continuing for another second after the tap was performed. Sensor sample values are arranged on 3 spatial coordinates, namely (x, y, z). Since the values are recorded at an approximate frequency 100 Hz, we commonly obtain around 150 values for the signal corresponding to one axis. For our experiments, we recorded signals associated with 200 gestures per user, thus obtaining a data set of 10.000 samples (50 users × 200 samples). For the training and evaluation process, we employ an 80%–20% train-test split, hence, 160 samples per user are used for training, while the other 40 samples are used for testing.

4.2   Evaluation Metrics

In our experiments, we employ the misclassification error as evaluation metric. Since adversarial samples are crafted to fool the deep CNNs, the goal of the attack is to increase the misclassification rate. We also calculate the misclassification error of the deep networks on the original test samples, thus providing a measure of the impact of the adversarial attacks.

4.3   Parameter Tuning and Implementation Details

Benegui et al. [2] described the optimal hyperparameters for the CNN models trained on the HMOG data set. Hence, we employ the same hyperparameters, obtaining similar results. The learning rate is 10^{-3} and the mini-batch size is 32. Furthermore, we use dropout layers with a rate of 0.4 after each fully-connected layer. We train each CNN model using the Adam optimizer [10] for a total of 50 epochs. We use the Foolbox library [18] to generate adversarial samples. Foolbox provides out-of-the-box implementations for state-of-the-art gradient-based and decision-based attacks. We employ the four example generation methods presented in Sect. 3 using the default Foolbox hyperparameters, except for the Boundary Attack method, where we employ a batch size equal to 20 and run the algorithm for a maximum of 5 iterations on each original sample.

4.4 Experimental Setup

After neural network training on 160 samples per user, the remaining 40 data samples are used for both testing and adversarial generation. Since our data set contains 50 users in total, we generate 2.000 adversarial samples (40 test samples × 50 users) with each generative method, namely the Fast Gradient Sign Attack, the DeepFool L_2 Attack, the Jacobian-Based Saliency Map Attack and the Boundary Attack. Thus, we obtain a total of 8.000 adversarial examples. In our experiments, we employ three CNN architectures of different depths, particularly of 6 layers, 9 layers and 12 layers. To answer RQ2, we test the adversarial examples generated for one CNN model on the other CNN models.

Lastly, we explore an ensemble classification method, by combining all the proposed CNNs through a weight voting scheme, using the classification accuracy rates of the independent models as weights. In this context, an attack is universal if the majority vote predicted by the ensemble is not equal to the ground-truth label. Adversarial samples are given as input to the ensemble, with the aim of further exploring their universality.

Table 1. Empirical results obtained by distinct neural network architectures under various adversarial attacks, in the user identification task. The results are reported in terms of the misclassification error (lower values indicate higher robustness to adversarial attacks). The model for which the adversarial examples were generated is marked with an asterisk.

Adversarial generation strategy	Misclassification error		
	6-layer CNN	9-layer CNN	12-layer CNN
None	8.20%	4.45%	5.80%
Boundary Attack on 6-layer CNN	100.00%*	48.60%	42.30%
DeepFool L_2 Attack on 6-layer CNN	100.00%*	6.20%	8.00%
Gradient Sign Attack on 6-layer CNN	99.95%*	16.90%	25.20%
Saliency Map Attack on 6-layer CNN	100.00%*	66.55%	43.30%
Boundary Attack on 9-layer CNN	67.10%	99.95%*	47.40%
DeepFool L_2 Attack on 9-layer CNN	5.25%	100.00%*	8.85%
Gradient Sign Attack on 9-layer CNN	17.90%	100.00%*	22.05%
Saliency Map Attack on 9-layer CNN	85.55%	100.00%*	53.95%
Boundary Attack on 12-layer CNN	72.05%	64.55%	100.00%*
DeepFool L_2 Attack on 12-layer CNN	5.30%	6.65%	100.00%*
Gradient Sign Attack on 12-layer CNN	18.20%	11.55%	99.8%*
Saliency Map Attack on 12-layer CNN	89.35%	83.60%	100.00%*

4.5   Results

In Table 1, we present the empirical results obtained by distinct neural network architectures in the user identification task, under various adversarial attacks. One by one, each CNN model is selected as the attacked model. Since we are interested in the universality of the adversarial examples, we feed the adversarial examples generated for a specific model to all other models. To allow a better estimation of the impact of each adversarial attack, we report the misclassification error rates on the original test samples.

Observations. Considering the overall results, we observe that the adversarial examples generated using the Jacobian-Based Saliency Map are the most effective across CNN models. In general, the attacks seem to have a higher degree of universality as the adversarial examples are optimized for deeper networks. Among the considered attacks, it appears that the DeepFool L_2 Attack exhibits the least degree of universality. We also observe that the depth of the network under attack is strongly correlated to the robustness to adversarial examples optimized on other CNN models, i.e. deeper models are more robust. However, each CNN model can be easily attacked when the adversarial examples are optimized on the respective model, proving that no model is robust to targeted attacks. In this context, we next seek to find out if an ensemble formed of the four CNN models is robust to all adversarial attacks.

Adversarial attacks on CNN ensemble. In our last experiment, we feed the adversarial examples to an ensemble of CNN models, presenting the corresponding results in Table 2. First, we note the ensemble attains improved results on

Table 2. Empirical results obtained by the CNN ensemble based on weighted majority voting under various adversarial attacks, in the user identification task. The results are reported in terms of the misclassification error (lower values indicate higher robustness to adversarial attacks).

Adversarial generation strategy	Misclassification error of CNN ensemble
None	2.45%
Boundary Attack on 6-layer CNN	46.09%
DeepFool L_2 Attack on 6-layer CNN	2.95%
Gradient Sign Attack on 6-layer CNN	15.04%
Saliency Map Attack on 6-layer CNN	59.15%
Boundary Attack on 9-layer CNN	59.25%
DeepFool L_2 Attack on 9-layer CNN	3.10%
Gradient Sign Attack on 9-layer CNN	15.84%
Saliency Map Attack on 9-layer CNN	77.40%
Boundary Attack on 12-layer CNN	65.94%
DeepFool L_2 Attack on 12-layer CNN	3.04%
Gradient Sign Attack on 12-layer CNN	11.05%
Saliency Map Attack on 12-layer CNN	86.75%

original test samples, the error rate being 2% lower than that of the best individual model, namely the 9-layer CNN. While DeepFool L_2 and Fast Gradient Sign do not seem to break the ensemble, it appears that the CNN ensemble is not robust to the Boundary Attack and the Jacobian-Based Saliency Map Attack. The misclassification error rates are typically higher as the adversarial attacks are targeted on deeper and deeper networks. This is consistent with the results presented in Table 1. We conclude that combining the CNNs into an ensemble is not effective for blocking certain adversarial attacks.

5   Conclusion

In this paper, we studied different methods of generating adversarial examples for deep models trained on motion sensor signals. We conducted a series of user identification experiments, considering different CNN architectures using both original and adversarial examples. The evaluation led to conclusive empirical results, enabling us to answer the proposed research questions. We hereby conclude our work by answering the research questions:

- RQ1: Can we generate adversarial examples to attack deep learning models for user identification based on motion sensor data?
  Answer: Generating adversarial attacks is possible, producing misclassification error rates of nearly 100%, irrespective of the CNN architecture. The answer to RQ1 is affirmative.
- RQ2: Are the adversarial examples universal or specific to certain neural architectures?
  Answer: After experimenting with four adversarial attack strategies, we observed that some attacks are specific, namely the DeepFool L_2 Attack and the Fast Gradient Sign Attack, while others are rather universal, namely the Boundary Attack and the Jacobian-Based Saliency Map Attack. In conclusion, it really depends on the attack strategy. It is perhaps important to mention here that the degree of universality grows with the depth of the target CNN used to optimize the adversarial examples.
- RQ3: What generative methods produce the most damaging adversarial attacks?
  Answer: All the consider adversarial attack methods induce misclassification error rates of nearly 100% when the optimization and the evaluation is performed on the same CNN model. However, considering the universality of the attack strategies, the most damaging adversarial attack is definitely the one based on the Jacobian-Based Saliency Map.

In summary, we conclude that deep neural networks for user identification are affected by adversarial examples, even in the cross-model evaluation setting. In most cases, the misclassification error rates grow by substantial margins. In future work, we aim to design novel deep neural networks that are robust to adversarial examples, perhaps by introducing a way to identify adversarial examples.

References

1. Aviv, A.J., Gibson, K., Mossop, E., Blaze, M., Smith, J.M.: Smudge attacks on smartphone touch screens. In: Proceedings of WOOT, pp. 1–7 (2010)
2. Benegui, C., Ionescu, R.T.: Convolutional neural networks for user identification based on motion sensors represented as images. IEEE Access 8(1), 61255–61266 (2020)
3. Brendel, W., Rauber, J., Bethge, M.: Decision-Based adversarial attacks: reliable attacks against black-box machine learning models. In: Proceedings of ICLR (2018)
4. Chen, H., Zhang, H., Chen, P.Y., Yi, J., Hsieh, C.J.: Attacking visual language grounding with adversarial examples: a case study on neural image captioning. In: Proceedings of ACL, pp. 2587–2597 (2018)
5. Georgescu, M.I., Ionescu, R.T., Popescu, M.: Local learning with deep and hand-crafted features for facial expression recognition. IEEE Access 7, 64827–64836 (2019)
6. Goodfellow, I.J., Shlens, J., Szegedy, C.: Explaining and harnessing adversarial examples. In: Proceedings of ICLR (2015)
7. Gragnaniello, D., Marra, F., Poggi, G., Verdoliva, L.: Analysis of adversarial attacks against CNN-based image forgery detectors. In: Proceedings of EUSIPCO, pp. 967–971 (2018)
8. He, K., Zhang, X., Ren, S., Sun, J.: Deep residual learning for image recognition. In: Proceedings of CVPR, pp. 770–778 (2016)
9. Ionescu, R.T., Alexe, B., Leordeanu, M., Popescu, M., Papadopoulos, D., Ferrari, V.: How hard can it be? Estimating the difficulty of visual search in an image. In: Proceedings of CVPR, pp. 2157–2166 (2016)
10. Kingma, D.P., Ba, J.: Adam: a method for stochastic optimization. In: Proceedings of ICLR (2015)
11. Ku, Y., Park, L.H., Shin, S., Kwon, T.: Draw it as shown: behavioral pattern lock for mobile user authentication. IEEE Access 7, 69363–69378 (2019)
12. Li, H., Yu, J., Cao, Q.: Intelligent walk authentication: implicit authentication when you walk with smartphone. In: Proceedings of BIBM, pp. 1113–1116 (2018)
13. Li, Y., Tian, D., Bian, X., Lyu, S., et al.: Robust adversarial perturbation on deep proposal-based models. In: Proceedings of BMVC (2018)
14. Moosavi-Dezfooli, S.M., Fawzi, A., Frossard, P.: DeepFool: a simple and accurate method to fool deep neural networks. In: Proceedings of CVPR, pp. 2574–2582 (2016)
15. Neverova, N., et al.: Learning human identity from motion patterns. IEEE Access 4, 1810–1820 (2016)
16. Papernot, N., et al.: Technical Report on the CleverHans v2.1.0 Adversarial Examples Library. arXiv preprint arXiv:1610.00768v6 (2018)
17. Papernot, N., McDaniel, P., Goodfellow, I.: Transferability in Machine Learning: from Phenomena to Black-Box Attacks using Adversarial Samples. arXiv preprint arXiv:1605.07277 (2016)
18. Rauber, J., Brendel, W., Bethge, M.: Foolbox: a python toolbox to benchmark the robustness of machine learning models. In: Proceedings of ICML Reliable Machine Learning in the Wild Workshop (2017)
19. Shen, C., Yu, T., Yuan, S., Li, Y., Guan, X.: Performance analysis of motion-sensor behavior for user authentication on smartphones. Sensors 16(3), 345 (2016)
20. Shukla, D., Kumar, R., Serwadda, A., Phoha, V.V.: Beware, your hands reveal your secrets. In: Proceedings of CCS, pp. 904–917 (2014)

21. Sitová, Z., et al.: HMOG: new behavioral biometric features for continuous authentication of smartphone users. IEEE Trans. Inf. Forensics Secur. **11**(5), 877–892 (2016)
22. Sun, L., Wang, Y., Cao, B., Philip, S.Y., Srisa-An, W., Leow, A.D.: Sequential keystroke behavioral biometrics for mobile user identification via multi-view deep learning. In: Proceedings of ECML-PKDD, pp. 228–240 (2017)
23. Vildjiounaite, E., et al.: Unobtrusive multimodal biometrics for ensuring privacy and information security with personal devices. In: Fishkin, K.P., Schiele, B., Nixon, P., Quigley, A. (eds.) Pervasive 2006. LNCS, vol. 3968, pp. 187–201. Springer, Heidelberg (2006). https://doi.org/10.1007/11748625_12
24. Wang, R., Tao, D.: Context-aware implicit authentication of smartphone users based on multi-sensor behavior. IEEE Access **7**, 119654–119667 (2019)
25. Xu, Y., Heinly, J., White, A.M., Monrose, F., Frahm, J.M.: Seeing double: reconstructing obscured typed input from repeated compromising reflections. In: Proceedings of CCS, pp. 1063–1074 (2013)
26. Ye, G., et al.: Cracking android pattern lock in five attempts. In: Proceedings of NDSS (2017)

An LSTM Based Deep Learning Method for Airline Ticket Price Prediction

Ke Du[1], Jiaxing Yan[1], Zhou Hang[1], Zhihao Chen[2], and Lulu Wu[1(✉)]

[1] School of Science, Shandong Jianzhu University, Jinan 250101, China
`wululu176224@126.com`
[2] FEMTO-ST Institute, UMR 6174 CNRS, Univ. Bourgogne Franche-Comté, 90000 Belfort, France
`zhihao.chen@femto-st.fr`

Abstract. Airline ticket prices are changing all the time dynamically. Booking tickets with the lowest costs is a challenging task. In this paper, we propose a multi-layer convolution long short-term memory network model (MLC-LSTM) and associated time series based data processing method for airline ticket price prediction. In our model, the parallel fully connected LSTM blocks extract the independent historical data from different flights and the following convolution layers merge and decode the inter and intra-information. From the results of experiment, the proposed model outperforms many existing models such as the basic LSTM, and the efficiency of the data processing method is also proved.

Keywords: LSTM · Airline ticket · Deep learning · Price prediction.

1 Introduction

Airplanes have become an indispensable way of transportation. How to buy tickets with lower prices is an important concern. Researchers mainly focus on two points: ticket price prediction [1–3] and optimal purchase time determination [4,5]. Traditional statistical or machine learning methods are employed to make predictions on both tasks. For ticket price prediction, researchers work on regression methods by selecting multiple features, such as linear regression, support vector regression, random forest regression, gradient ascent regression, etc. [3,6]. These methods have become the current mainstream price prediction tools. In [2], K. Tziridis et al. make a comparison between several basic machine learning models for ticket price prediction. The effects of different features on ticket prices are also examined in the experiments. The prediction accuracies of these models are not satisfying. With the evolution of machine learning, more advanced models for prediction emerged, such as long short-term memory networks (LSTM) [7]. Therefore, the airfare prediction should be investigated in more detail.

In this paper, a novel deep learning model based on LSTM and convolutional neural network (CNN) is proposed for airline ticket price prediction through integrated learning. Multi-layer convolutions and multiple parallel fully connected LSTM blocks work together to make the model better to analyze and extract the

© Springer Nature Switzerland AG 2020
H. Yang et al. (Eds.): ICONIP 2020, CCIS 1333, pp. 762–769, 2020.
https://doi.org/10.1007/978-3-030-63823-8_86

internal and external influences on ticket prices. Besides the neural network, we propose a new time series data processing method that considers historical prices as a part of the input vector and guarantees the invariance of the original data in the time dimension. The combination of novel data processing methods and deep learning model has made our prediction model performance significantly improved than traditional ticket price prediction models.

The rest of this paper is organized as follows. In Sect. 2, the proposed MLC-LSTM model and its working process are presented. The description of experiments and result analysis are shown in Sect. 3. Finally, we draw the conclusion and make the perspectives in Sect. 4.

2   The Proposed Method

2.1   Data Preparation

Based on the truth that airline ticket prices can be regarded as time series, we prepare the data with time series characteristics to feed the networks. The raw data can not be used as input directly because there are at least three time dimensions for each flight: time of flight departure, date of ticket purchased and the number of days to departure. Experiments indicate that setting the date of flight departure as the first time series, and the number of days to departure (far to near) as the second time series is a good choice. In this way, the ticket price sequence of a flight can be structured as in Fig. 1. The bottom line is a series of departure date numbered from 1 to N. And for each date, it is a sub-sequence of the ticket prices of the flight. On the top line, there are 30 values ($p_{1,30}$ to $p_{1,1}$) in the sub-sequence representing the ticket prices of one flight booked 30 days to 1 day before departure. Thus, the data for N dates can be reshaped as a sequence with a length of $30 \times N$ where each value represents the ticket price booked certain days before departure. For example, $p_{1,30}$ means the ticket price for the flight on the first departure date and booked 30 days before departure.

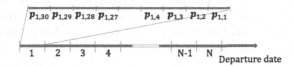

Fig. 1. The ticket prices arranged in time series sequence.

As discussed in [2], lots of features are usually taken into account for ticket price prediction. Based on the data we can obtain, 6 attributes have significant impacts on the ticket price changing are counted, shown in Table 1. Departure and arrival time are transformed from 24 h to decimal (e.g., 19.50 means 19:30). The attributes constitute a part of the 36-dimensional input vector, marked as a_1 to a_6 in Fig. 2. And the following 30 values come from the reshaped ticket price sequence in Fig. 1. If a price $p_{i,j}$ is chosen as the output of the model, b_1 to b_{30} are the nearest 30 values in front of which in the sequence as the bottom in Fig. 2. For example, when the output is $p_{32,30}$, the corresponding b_1 to b_{30} are $p_{31,30}$ to $p_{31,1}$; when the output is $p_{32,29}$, b_1 to b_{30} correspond to $p_{31,29}$ to $p_{31,1}$ and $p_{32,30}$.

Table 1. The selected features of flights

Attributes	Ranges	Descriptions
Departure time	$0.00 \sim 24.00$	The departure time in 24 h
Arrival time	$0.00 \sim 24.00$	The departure time in 24 h
Departure date	$1 \sim N$	A certain date in the days investigated
Days to departure	$1 \sim 30$	Number of days booking tickets before departure
Day of week	$1 \sim 7$	7 days in one week
Holiday	1, 0	Yes/No

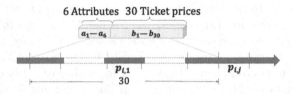

Fig. 2. The data structure of the input.

2.2 MLC-LSTM Model

As shown in Fig. 3, the model includes three parts: the parallel fully connected LSTM for the extraction of single flight's information, the one-dimensional convolutions for the inter-flight information fusion and the fully connected layer for the decoding of the final prediction.

Five Independent LSTM Blocks. As illustrated on the top part of Fig. 3, five independent deep fully connected LSTM blocks are employed to deal with the ticket price data of five flights. These flights have the same routine, booking dates and departure dates, but the departure times are chronological in one day. Their information can refer to each other to enhance the prediction accuracy of the target flight because of the similar internal and timing characteristics. The middle flight in Fig. 3 is the one needed to be predicted. x_1, x_2, x_3, x_4, and x_5 are the input vectors of five flights. For each flight, x_i represents a vector of 36 components: $(a_1, a_2, ..., a_6, b_1, b_2, ..., b_{30})$. With these data, the information of

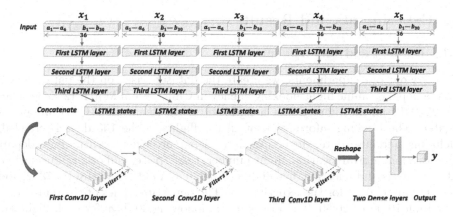

Fig. 3. The architecture of the MLC-LSTM model.

each flight is trained independently to a fully connected LSTM block to extract the information for price prediction. During this step, each LSTM block does not affect each other. Here, each flight is subjected to a block with three LSTM layers for local and temporal information extraction. Based on a large number of experiments, three is the appropriate depth of layers. Through the five independent LSTM blocks, the output of each block is a vector of length 64. The length is the number of nodes in the last layer of each block. It contains the status information extracted from the 6 attributes at the time of departure and the 30 ticket prices in the sequence.

Multi-layer Convolutions. Since the five vectors represent the status information that can be obtained in the order of departure date as elaborated above, we can concatenate them as a long sequence with a length of 320 (64×5). Then, the multi-layer convolution stack is used for information extraction by sections where the stack includes three one-dimensional convolutions as shown in Fig. 3. In each layer of convolutions, a window slides from the beginning to the end through the sequence. The outputs layers are matrices with the size of $320 \times filters$, where $filters$ is the number of kernels in a convolution layer. Here the size is 32 for the first convolution and 16 for the last two. By this means, the interaction of chronologically adjacent flights is contained in output matrices.

Fully Connected Layers. Fully connected layers are put at the end of the model to decode the concatenated outputs. The output of the final fully connected layer for prediction is the ticket price **y**. For this network, the depth of which is two and the input is a sequence of 5120 (320×16) values reshaped from the output of the multi-layer convolutional neural network stack. The MSE loss function calculates the similarity between the predicted prices and the ground truths, and then the gradient descent algorithm is used for backpropagation and get the optimal parameter setting of the model.

3   Experiments and Results

3.1   Dataset and Experiments

To carry out our experiments, we create the dataset based on the data crawled from a popular online flight booking agency in China. From March 12 to September 25, 2019, all the flights from Chengdu (CTU) to Guangzhou (CAN) are investigated. The booking information of all the flights in the 165 days is crawled, including purchase date, departure date, departure time, arrival time, departure location, arrival location, flight number, ticket price, and other information. After analysis and selection, five flights (3U8735, CA4309, CA3418, HU7352, and JD5162) are chosen for the experiments. The departure times of them are adjacent from 19:00 to 20:50. The prices in the following 30 days for each flight are originally crawled every day. With the method described in Sect. 2.1, we get the valid data of 135 days, totally of 20250 pieces of the 5 flights.

24 groups of experiments are carried out based on the different amounts of data used for training. The partitions of the data are listed in Table 2.

Table 2. Experimental data partition

No.	Training set	Validation set	Test set
1	4020×0.8	4020×0.2	30
2	3990×0.8	3990×0.2	60
3	3960×0.8	3960×0.2	90
...			...
24	3330×0.8	3330×0.2	720

Each flight consists of 4050 pieces of valid data. For the first experiment, the first 4020 pieces of data are used for training. 80% of them are training set, and the other 20% are left for validation. The last 30 pieces consist the test set. There is no overlap between different sets. We set the batch_size as 256, the learning rate is 0.00002. Adam and Rectified Linear Unit (ReLU) are chosen as optimizer and activation function respectively. To evaluate the training and optimize the model, mean squared error (MSE) is chosen as the loss function.

After the training, the 36-dimensional vector in the test set is used to predict the prices in the sequence. In the iteration, the output consists of the next input vector. We only use the 30 prices in the prediction representing the prices of the flight booking 30 days to 1 day before departure. For the 24 groups of experiments, we can get 720 predicted prices.

The other five groups of experiments are carried out for comparison. Three models were used in other research of ticket price prediction, including linear regression [2, 6], random forest regression [3], and support vector regression (SVR). In these models, the inputs are the 6 attributes we talked in Sect. 2.1, and the outputs are corresponding ticket prices. Based on our model, the multi-dimensional input fully connected LSTM (FC-LSTM) neural network is tested in two ways. One with the 6 attributes, and the other with the 36-dimensional vectors, the same as our model, which includes 6 attributes and 30 historical ticket prices.

To evaluate the effectiveness of our model, root mean square error (RMSE) and prediction accuracy (ACC) are used. The formulations are as the follows:

$$RMSE = \sqrt{\frac{\sum_{i=1}^{n}(p_{r,i} - p_{p,i})^2}{n}} \tag{1}$$

$$ACC = 1 - \frac{\sum_{i=1}^{n}(\frac{|p_{r,i}-p_{p,i}|}{p_{r,i}})}{n} \tag{2}$$

where $p_{r,i}$ and $p_{p,i}$ represent the actual ticket price and the predicted one respectively. The number of prices predicted is n.

3.2   Results and Analysis

The same data sets are used in experiments on our model and the three existing regression models to get the performances. And, also we conducted sufficient experiments and parameters adjustment on the proposed model and five groups of experiments in comparison to ensure to the stable loss value. For each model, we calculate RMSE and ACC of 24 groups of experiments for ticket price prediction in the following 30 days. And then, the average values of 1, 7, and 30 days are evaluated. The results are shown in Table 3 and the best values are marked bold.

It can be seen from the results that the linear regression model performs the worst in ticket price prediction. When it comes to the SVR model, the

Table 3. Experimental results evaluated by RMSE and ACC

Model	Metrics	Days predicted		
		1	7	30
Linear regression	RMSE	0.1162	0.1479	0.2910
	ACC(%)	78.07	73.64	59.98
SVR	RMSE	0.0850	0.0826	0.1480
	ACC(%)	84.80	85.36	84.22
Random forest	RMSE	0.0735	0.0847	0.1184
	ACC(%)	85.32	86.06	85.96
FC-LSTM (6-D input)	RMSE	0.1434	0.1452	0.2457
	ACC(%)	82.02	81.69	71.57
FC-LSTM (36-D input)	RMSE	0.0767	**0.0801**	0.1618
	ACC(%)	89.30	87.62	80.92
MLC-LSTM	RMSE	**0.0638**	0.0867	**0.1323**
	ACC(%)	**91.20**	**90.11**	**86.55**

performance has been greatly improved compared with the linear regression model, and the prediction accuracies of the three terms are all about 85%. The random forest model is similar to SVR. Its prediction accuracies for all terms exceed 85%. The performance of FC-LSTM model with 6-dimensional input vectors is better than linear regression but weaker than SVR and random forest models. The ACC even drops to 71% in long-term prediction. In contrast, using the data set obtained by our new data processing method and establishing an LSTM model with the 36-dimensional input vectors can greatly improve the performance. Experiments show that accuracies of the model in both short-term and medium-term predictions exceed SVR and random forest models. It is evident that the new data processing method we proposed is effective. But the LSTM model shows the weakness in long-term ticket price prediction even the 36-dimensional input vectors are employed. The MLC-LSTM model proposed in this paper outperforms the other five groups of experiments. The average accuracies exceed 90% in both the short-term and medium-term predictions, and the long-term prediction accuracy also reaches a satisfying value of 88%. Compared with the LSTM model, the stability of our model has been improved. The declination of accuracy in long-term prediction is only 2%, which is much lower than other models tested.

Figure 4 shows the average accuracies of experiments at each departure day. As can be seen from the figure, the accuracies of the 6 prediction methods decrease gradually as the longer the booking is made in advance. Among them, accuracies of linear regression and LSTM with the 6-dimensional input vectors are relatively low. The accuracies of SVR and random forest are similar on all the days and relatively stable in the short and medium-term predictions. But in the long-term prediction, especially near to 30 days, the performances go worse greatly. The FC-LSTM with the 36-dimensional input vectors has an advantage in the short-term prediction of the first five days, because the input vector contains more historical price information, which allows it to grasp the

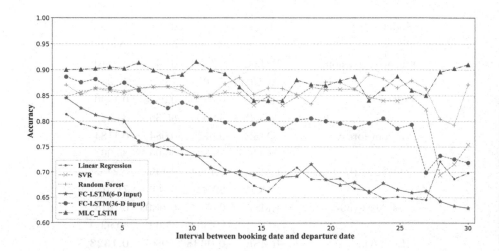

Fig. 4. Prediction accuracy of the flights in the following 30 days.

short-term change trend well. But in the medium and long-term predictions, the accuracy gradually declines for the accumulation of errors caused by constant iterations. Compared with the other five methods, the proposed MLC-LSTM model shows superior performance in short, medium, and long-term predictions. Although the fluctuation after 15 days making its performance close to SVR and random forest models, the accuracy can reach 90% and above over the first 12 days. In addition, the results also indicate that one-dimensional convolution can reduce the error propagation caused by the iteration process.

4   Conclusion and Perspectives

In this paper, we improve the prediction accuracy of airfare by proposing an MLC-LSTM model. The information of multiple flights is extracted independently and fused by multi-layer convolutions. Therefore, the internal and external influences of the target flight are well described. We also propose a data arrangement method to reduce the dimensionality of the data with multiple time dimensions. The experimental results show that our method performs well.

Although the overall performance of our method is better than the methods in comparison, there is a notable gap between the predicted prices and the true values on some dates. In future works, we will optimize the arrangement of the data to better express the characteristics in the time dimension and show more obvious features for training. With more long-term historical data, we can also modify the model to further improve the performance for long-term predictions.

References

1. Chen, Y., Cao, J., Feng, S., Tan, Y.: An ensemble learning based approach for building airfare forecast service. In: IEEE International Conference on Big Data, Santa Clara, CA, USA, pp. 964–969 (2015)
2. Tziridis, K., Kalampokas, T., Papakostas, G. A., Diamantaras, K. I.: Airfare prices prediction using machine learning techniques. In: 25th European Signal Processing Conference (EUSIPCO), Kos, Greece, pp. 1036–1039 (2017)
3. Vu, V.H., Minh, Q.T., Phung, P.H.: An airfare prediction model for developing markets. In: 32nd International Conference on Information Networking (ICOIN), Chiang Mai, Thailand, pp. 765–770 (2018)
4. Chawla, B., Kaur, M.C.: Airfare analysis and prediction using data mining and machine learning. Int. J. Eng. Sci. Invent. 6(11), 10–17 (2017)
5. Xu, Y., Cao, J.: OTPS: a decision support service for optimal airfare ticket purchase. In: International Conference on Big Data, Boston, USA , pp. 1265–1270. IEEE (2017)
6. Abdella, J., A., Zaki, N., Shuaib, K.: Automatic detection of airline ticket price and demand: a review. In: 13th International Conference on Innovations in Information Technology, Al Ain, UAE, pp. 169–174 (2018)
7. Hochreiter, S., Bengio, Y., Frasconi, P., Schmidhuber, J.: Gradient flow in recurrent nets: the difficulty of learning long-term dependencies. in: A Field Guide to Dynamical Recurrent Neural Networks. IEEE, New York (2001)

Attention-Based Multi-component LSTM for Internet Traffic Prediction

Qian Xu[1(✉)], Zhenjie Yao[1,2], Yanhui Tu[1,3], and Yixin Chen[4]

[1] Purple Mountain Laboratories, Nanjing 211111, China
xuqian@pmlabs.com.cn, yanhui.tu@gmail.com
[2] Institute of Microelectronics, Chinese Academy of Sciences, Beijing 100029, China
yaozhenjie@gmail.com
[3] Nanjing Future Network Industry Innovation Co., LTD., Nanjing 211111, China
[4] Washington University in St. Louis, St. Louis, USA
chen@cse.wustl.edu

Abstract. With the rapid development of Internet technology, various kinds of electronic products such as mobile phones and laptops become widely available and our daily lives rely more and more on the Internet. Increasing network access brings a series of problems for *Internet Service Provider (ISP)*, such as network congestion and network resource allocation. Effective network traffic prediction can alleviate the aforementioned problems by estimating future traffic based on historical data. In this paper, we propose a novel model named Attention-based Multi-Component LSTM (AMC-LSTM) for Internet traffic prediction. The proposed model is composed of three independent LSTM components, including hour component, day component and week component, to jointly forecast future network traffic with historical data. Moreover, attention mechanism is incorporated into each component to capture the most informative time steps. Experimental results on real-world datasets demonstrate the effectiveness of our model.

Keywords: Internet traffic prediction · LSTM · Multi-component · Attention

1 Introduction

In recent years, the volume of Internet traffic is increasing rapidly with the widely usage of diverse web applications, which brings forward higher requirements for network planning and network security. Hence, Internet traffic prediction is attracting more attention for the ability of estimating future network traffic with historical traffic data [8]. With accurate and timely Internet traffic forecasting, bandwidth resource can be allocated in advance to avoid network congestion and anomaly attack can be detected when significant deviation from the expected behavior occurs [5,17].

Due to the importance of Internet traffic prediction, great efforts have been devoted for more accurate forecasting results [8,11]. The main solutions of Internet traffic prediction can be classified into two categories, i.e. linear prediction and nonlinear prediction. Linear prediction methods such as Holt-Winters [3] and ARIMA [2] concentrate on statistical characteristics, but are unable to meet high accuracy requirement for nonlinear traffic data. Thus, *Neural Network (NN)* based nonlinear prediction methods are

© Springer Nature Switzerland AG 2020
H. Yang et al. (Eds.): ICONIP 2020, CCIS 1333, pp. 770–777, 2020.
https://doi.org/10.1007/978-3-030-63823-8_87

becoming mainstream solutions. Paulo *et. al* applied *Multi-Layer Perceptron (MLP)* to Internet traffic forecasting and achieved competitive results compared with conventional linear methods [5–7]. Zhuo *et al.* proposed to add a DNN network after the common LSTM to model the characteristics of network traffic autocorrelation [20]. Zhao *et al.* proposed to forecast traffic volume for traffic matrix based on deep LSTM RNNs and a linear regression model [19]. Tokuyama *et al.* devised a RNN-VTD method by applying both timestamp and day of the week information as extra attribute input to LSTM [16]. Lazaris *et al.* developed a novel LSTM model with a clustering-based preprocessing step for fine-grained network traffic forecasting [12]. Andreoletti *et al.* proposed to use *Diffusion Convolutional Recurrent Neural Network (DCRNN)*, which is a graph-based algorithm, to forecast traffic on the links of a real backbone network [1].

Some researchers suggest that Internet traffic data exhibits the characteristic of auto-correlation [5,20], which means time series data repeats itself periodically. Guo *et al.* designed a novel multi-component graph convolutional network, called ASTGCN, for highway traffic forecasting involved with *Intelligent Transportation System (ITS)* [9]. This model consists of three components, including recent component, daily-periodic component and weekly-periodic component. The three components are first trained separately to model recent, daily, and weekly patterns, respectively. Then, the outputs of them are integrated to get the final forecasting targets.

Motivated by the effectiveness of ASTGCN [9], we propose to apply multi-component LSTM for Internet traffic prediction associated with a single network link. Our approach has three components: hour component, day component, and week component, which handle hourly, daily, and weekly predictions, respectively. LSTM is utilized to model temporal characteristics and long-term dependencies of the time series. Considering that LSTM is insufficient in paying different extent of attention on historical time steps, we incorporates the attention mechanism into each LSTM component by assigning different weight coefficients for previous time steps.

2 AMC-LSTM MODEL

2.1 Problem Statement

Denote $X = \{x_1, \cdots, x_T\}$ as the time series. x_i represents the traffic value at time i and T is the total number of time slots. As for Internet traffic prediction, the input of the model is historical network traffic volume, and the output is the predicted traffic volume in next n timestamps from $T + 1$ to $T + n$. And we expect to learn the nonlinear mapping function from the historical time series to the target values.

The main challenge for Internet traffic prediction lies in how to model the inherent nonlinear relationship among the network traffic data. Conventional LSTM uses the historical time series as input, and learns the nonlinear mapping function via its repeated memory cells. However, LSTM has limitation in that, while it captures intra-hour dependencies, it tends to ignore intra-day and intra-week ones to a large extent due to its memory structure. Moreover, for LSTM, it is hard to assign different degree of attention to different segments of the time series [13,14]. To tackle these problems, we propose to capture periodicity at different scales with multi-component LSTM, and focus on more informative parts by adopting an attention mechanism.

2.2   Attention-Based Multi-component LSTM (AMC-LSTM)

To address the limitations of single LSTM, we propose an attention-based multi-component LSTM (AMC-LSTM) model.

Multi-component LSTM. AMC-LSTM is composed of three independent LSTM components, including an hour component, a day component and a week component. Denote m as the number of sampling points per day, t_0 as current time and T_p as the size of predicting window. As shown in Fig. 1, T_h, T_d and T_w represent the length of hourly, daily and weekly time series corresponding to hour, day and week component, respectively. We require T_h, T_d and T_w to be integral multiples of T_p. The three components aim to model recent, daily and weekly trends of the historical data, respectively.

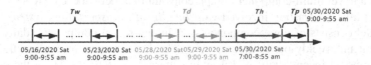

Fig. 1. Input time series of AMC-LSTM (suppose T_p is 1 hour, T_h, T_d and T_w are twice of T_p).

- Hour component
  $$X_h = (x_{t_0-T_h+1}, x_{t_0-T_h+2}, \cdots, x_{t_0})$$
  X_h is the input of the hour component, which represents the traffic flow generated in recent past few hours. Generally speaking, future traffic tends to go on based on recent past pattern and would not change suddenly in most circumstances.
- Day component
  $$X_d = (x_{t_0-(T_d/T_p)*m+1}, \cdots, x_{t_0-(T_d/T_p)*m+T_p},$$
  $$x_{t_0-(T_d/T_p-1)*m+1}, \cdots, x_{t_0-(T_d/T_p-1)*m+T_p},$$
  $$\cdots, x_{t_0-m+1}, \cdots, x_{t_0-m+T_p})$$
  Day component takes the sequences from past few days at the same time periods with the predicted window as input. Intra-day trends and routine patterns due to people's working and living habits are also very important and appear frequently.
- Week component
  $$X_w = (x_{t_0-7*(T_w/T_p)*m+1}, \cdots, x_{t_0-7*(T_w/T_p)*m+T_p},$$
  $$x_{t_0-7*(T_w/T_p-1)*m+1}, \cdots, x_{t_0-7*(T_w/T_p-1)*m+T_p},$$
  $$\cdots, x_{t_0-7*m+1}, \cdots, x_{t_0-7*m+T_p})$$
  X_w is the input series of week component. Similar to intra-day trends, Internet traffic appears to have intra-week trends during weekdays and weekends.

Attention Mechanism. When generating the output value at time t, LSTM only takes the nearest hidden state h_{t-1} into consideration, and ignores the other previous states. However, as we analyzed before, the generation probability of the output can be affected by multiple historical hidden states.

Suppose h_i is a hidden state at time i generated by LSTM. With the one-layer MLP, we can get the hidden representation u_i by

$$u_i = \tanh(W h_i + b) \tag{1}$$

Here, W and b are learnable parameters. Denote v as the time-level context vector. The correlation coefficient between u_i and context vector v is computed as $u_i^T v$. It can be transformed into attention coefficient by the softmax function:

$$\alpha_i = \frac{\exp(u_i^T v)}{\sum_i \exp(u_i^T v)} \tag{2}$$

Here, the attention coefficient α_i reveals the importance of previous hidden states. The new weighted representation of hidden state at time t can be calculated by the weighted sum of the attention coefficient α_i and the original hidden state h_i.

$$h_t' = \sum_i \alpha_i h_i \tag{3}$$

The new weighted hidden state h_t' considers multiple historical hidden states by assigning different weights on them. Such an attention mechanism has two advantages. First, it allows the model to automatically pay attention to more informative time steps for the prediction task. Second, it allows us to extend the training data to include a long time frame, allowing us to utilize more network data.

Multi-component Fusion. Hour, day and week component tend to capture recent, intra-day and intra-week trends, respectively. To take all these aspects into account simultaneously, the results generated by three independent LSTM components are fused to get the final prediction targets. The final prediction volume can be represented by:

$$\hat{Y} = W_h \odot \dot{Y}_h + W_d \odot \ddot{Y}_d + W_w \odot \hat{Y}_w \tag{4}$$

where $\odot$ is the Hadamard product. W_h, W_d and W_w are learnable parameters, reflecting different importance of the hour, day and week components on prediction task. Figure 2 gives the overall architecture of the proposed AMC-LSTM.

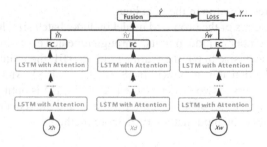

Fig. 2. Framework of the proposed AMC-LSTM.

3   Experimental Analysis

3.1   Datasets and Evaluation Metrics

In this paper, two real-world Internet traffic datasets from different ISPs are used for experiments. Dataset A comes from a private ISP involved with 11 European cities [5]. The data was recorded every 30 s from 6:57am on June 7, 2005 to 11:17am on July 29, 2005 corresponding to a transatlantic link. Dataset B belongs to the UK academic network backbone (UKERNA), which was collected every five minutes from 9:30am on November 19, 2004 to 11:11am on January 27, 2005 [6]. For more efficient prediction, original data points are aggregated by summing all data points within five minutes. Then we have the aggregated datasets A5M and B5M. Here, two standard evaluation metrics including RMSE and MSE are used to measure the performance.

3.2   Comparison Methods

To validate the effectiveness of the proposed AMC-LSTM, we conduct comparison with five baseline algorithms, including HA, ARIMA, SVR, LSTM and GRU.

– HA: History Average model, which gives the prediction value by calculating the average Internet traffic volume of the historical time series.
– ARIMA [18]: Auto-Regressive Integrated Moving Average model, which is one of the most common methods for time series forecasting.
– SVR [15]: Support Vector Regression model, which estimates future Internet traffic based on the idea of Support Vector Machine.
– LSTM [10]: Long Short Term Memory network, which predicts future behaviour by memory blocks.
– GRU [4]: Gated Recurrent Unit model is one of the most popular variants of LSTM, which has a relatively simple structure and faster training ability.

3.3   Parameter Setting

In this paper, we mainly consider short-term Internet traffic prediction and set $T_h = 12$, $T_d = 12$, $T_w = 12$ and $T_p = 12$. The proposed AMC-LSTM takes the recent past one hour data, the same hour in previous days and the same hour in previous weeks as input, and predicts the Internet traffic in the next hour.

The main parameters of the proposed model include: batch size, learning rate, training epoch and the number of hidden units. Through repeated experiments, we manually adjust and set the batch size to 64, the learning rate to 0.01, the training epoch to 3000, and the number of hidden units to be within $\{8, 16, 32, 64, 128\}$. And we set the number of layers in hidden layers to two. The proposed AMC-LSTM is optimized by the Adam optimizer. 80% of the overall data is used for training and the remaining for testing. In addition, we normalize the input data with Z-Score method.

3.4   Internet Traffic Prediction Results

We conduct experiments on two real-world Internet traffic datasets and the results are listed in Table 1. From the experimental results, it is obvious that conventional linear prediction methods including HA, ARIMA and SVR, did not perform well. While deep learning based methods including LSTM, GRU, MC-LSTM (multi-component LSTM without attention) and AMC-LSTM, achieve relatively better performance via modelling nonlinear mapping with multiple neurons. LSTM and GRU obtain stable and satisfactory performance to a certain extent by capturing long-term dependencies with repeated memory cells. Moreover, we can find that MC-LSTM and AMC-LSTM consistently outperform LSTM and GRU. This implies that recent, daily and weekly patterns do contribute to the task of future prediction. To mining the effectiveness of attention mechanism, we further make comparisons with MC-LSTM and AMC-LSTM. We can observe that AMC-LSTM, with its effective attention mechanism, can consistently outperform MC-LSTM across all datasets.

Table 1. Evaluation on datasets A5M and B5M.

Method	A5M		B5M	
	RMSE	MAE	RMSE	MAE
HA	19.69	13.06	168.02	111.30
ARIMA	19.76	13.32	165.08	107.29
SVR	9.79	6.76	85.96	53.29
LSTM	7.70	5.56	69.29	46.62
GRU	7.68	5.43	68.98	45.56
MC-LSTM (ours)	7.59	5.37	60.72	43.32
AMC-LSTM (ours)	**7.42**	**5.28**	**54.81**	**40.61**

We visualize the predicting results of AMC-LSTM within one day and one week compared with the ground truth in Fig. 3. Regardless of the negligible deviation from ground truth, we can observe that AMC-LSTM can not only capture the variation trends of network traffic, but also detect the peak and bottom accurately.

To find out the influence of different components, we define a average amplitude of weight matrices (AAWM) associated with hour, day and week components in the process of multi-component fusion, which is defined as $\frac{1}{m*n}\sum_{i=1}^{m}\sum_{j=1}^{n}|W_{ij}|$. Here, $\mathbf{W} \in \mathbb{R}^{m \times n}$ is denoted as the weight matrix. This indicator can measure the impact of different components to a certain extent. We further visualize the different AAWMs on dataset A5M and B5M in Fig. 4. As shown in the figure, it is obvious that all the three components contribute much to the predicting results on A5M, which is associated with 11 European cities and the Internet traffic comes from residents' network access needs for daily life, working and entertainment. For the strong routine patterns, future traffic can be well estimated by hour, day and week components. As for dataset B5M, we can find that week component and hour component play a more important role on future prediction, while day component seems to be less informative. Dataset B5M belongs to the

UK academic network backbone, and the network traffic mainly involves with online courses and academic activities on the basis of weekly plans. Actually, network traffic data from different sources have different patterns and characteristics. The proposed AMC-LSTM, whose three independent components focus on intra-hour, intra-day and intra-week trends of the historical data, can capture the data characteristics by assigning different weights on different components, and improve the prediction results.

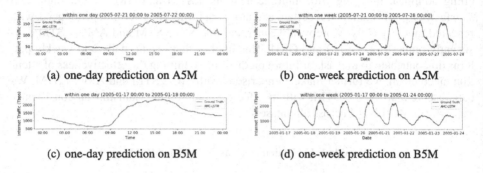

(a) one-day prediction on A5M   (b) one-week prediction on A5M

(c) one-day prediction on B5M   (d) one-week prediction on B5M

Fig. 3. Internet traffic predicting results

Fig. 4. AAWMs of hour, day and week components on dataset A5M (left) and B5M (right).

4   Conclusions and Future Work

In this paper, we proposed an attention-based multi-component LSTM (AMC-LSTM) method for short-term Internet traffic prediction. Three independent LSTM components take historical data from recent hours, the same periods in last few days and the same time periods in previous few weeks as input, and capture intra-hour, intra-day, and intra-week trends, respectively. Then, the results generated by these three components are fused to get the final predicting results. In addition, attention mechanism is incorporated into every component to identify and focus on more informative factors. Experimental results on real-world Internet traffic datasets validate the effectiveness of AMC-LSTM.

The proposed AMC-LSTM forecasts Internet traffic associated with a single network link based on historical data. Actually, the network traffic of one link is associated with multiple links in the network, especially the links with close topological distances. In the future, we plan to extend this work by considering the network topology to predict the traffic volume of the entire network.

References

1. Andreoletti, D., Troia, S., Musumeci, F., Giordano, S., Maier, G., Tornatore, M.: Network traffic prediction based on diffusion convolutional recurrent neural networks. In: IEEE Conference on Computer Communications Workshops, INFOCOM WKSHPS (2019)
2. Box, G.E.P., Jenkins, G.M.: Time Series Analysis: Forecasting and Control. Holden-Day, Incorporated, Raleigh (1990)
3. Chatfield, C., Yar, M.: Holt-winters forecasting: some practical issues. Stat. **37**(2), 129–140 (1988)
4. Cho, K., Van Merrienboer, B., Bahdanau, D., Bengio, Y.: On the properties of neural machine translation: encoder-decoder approaches. arXiv:1409.1259. Computation and Language (2014)
5. Cortez, P., Rio, M., Rocha, M., Sousa, P.: Internet traffic forecasting using neural networks. In: International Joint Conference on Neural Network (2006)
6. Cortez, P., Rio, M., Rocha, M., Sousa, P.: Multi-scale internet traffic forecasting using neural networks and time series methods. Expert Syst. **29**(2), 143–155 (2010)
7. Cortez, P., Rio, M., Sousa, P., Rocha, M.: Forecasting internet traffic by neural networks under univariate and multivariate strategies, pp. 61–70 (2008)
8. Feng, H., Shu, Y.: Study on network traffic prediction techniques. In: International Conference on Wireless Communications (2005)
9. Guo, S., Lin, Y., Feng, N., Song, C., Wan, H.: Attention based spatial-temporal graph convolutional networks for traffic flow forecasting. In: Proceedings of the AAAI Conference on Artificial Intelligence, vol. 33, pp. 922–929 (2019)
10. Hochreiter, S., Schmidhuber, J.: Long short-term memory. Neural Comput. **9**(8), 1735–1780 (1997)
11. Joshi, M., Hadi, T.H.: A review of network traffic analysis and prediction techniques. arXiv:1507.05722. Networking and Internet Architecture (2015)
12. Lazaris, A., Prasanna, V.K.: An LSTM framework for modeling network traffic. Immunotechnology, pp. 19–24 (2019)
13. Li, Y., Zhu, Z., Kong, D., Han, H., Zhao, Y.: EA-LSTM: evolutionary attention-based LSTM for time series prediction. Knowl. Based Syst. **181**, 104785 (2019)
14. Qin, Y., Song, D., Cheng, H., Cheng, W., Jiang, G., Cottrell, G.W.: A dual-stage attention-based recurrent neural network for time series prediction, pp. 2627–2633 (2017)
15. Smola, A.J., Scholkopf, B.: A tutorial on support vector regression. Stat. Comput. **14**(3), 199–222 (2004)
16. Tokuyama, Y., Fukushima, Y., Yokohira, T.: The effect of using attribute information in network traffic prediction with deep learning, pp. 521–525 (2018)
17. Wang, S., Sun, Q., Hua, Z., Yang, F.: Detecting SYN flooding attacks based on traffic prediction. Secur. Commun. Netw. **5**(10), 1131–1140 (2012)
18. Williams, B.M., Hoel, L.A.: Modeling and forecasting vehicular traffic flow as a seasonal arima process: theoretical basis and empirical results. J. Transp. Eng. **129**(6), 664–672 (2003)
19. Zhao, J., Qu, H., Zhao, J., Jiang, D.: Towards traffic matrix prediction with lstm recurrent neural networks. Electron. Lett. **54**(9), 566–568 (2018)
20. Zhuo, Q., Li, Q., Han, Y., Yong, Q.: Long short-term memory neural network for network traffic prediction. In: 2017 12th International Conference on Intelligent Systems and Knowledge Engineering (ISKE) (2017)

Entropy of LOO Predictable Horizons to Select a Learning Machine and a Representative Prediction of Chaotic Time Series

Daichi Miyazaki, Kazuya Matsuo, and Shuichi Kurogi(✉)

Kyushu Institute of technology, Tobata, Kitakyushu, Fukuoka 804-8550, Japan
miyazaki.daichi304@mail.kyutech.jp,
{matsuo,kuro}@cntl.kyutech.ac.jp
http://kurolab.cntl.kyutech.ac.jp/

Abstract. Recently, we have presented several methods to select representative predictions of chaotic time series. Here, the methods employ strong learners capable of making predictions with small error, where usual ensemble mean does not work well owing to an ensemble member with short term predictable horizon because the ensemble prediction error of chaotic time series grows exponentially after the smallest predictable horizon of the ensemble member. Here, we refer to 'predictable horizon' as the first point in time after which the prediction error exceeds a certain error threshold. So far, we have developed several methods to select representative predictions from a set of many predictions by means of using a LOOCV (leave-one-out cross-validation) measure to estimate predictable horizon. From the analysis of the methods showing that the method works well with sufficiently large number of predictions generated by sufficiently strong learning machines, this paper presents a method to generate a large number of predictions and select a learning machine and a representative prediction using the entropy of LOO predictable horizons. By means of numerical experiments, we show and examine the effectiveness of the present method.

Keywords: Representative prediction of chaotic time series · Entropy of leave-one-out predictable horizons · Long-term unpredictability

1 Introduction

So far, a number of methods for time series prediction have been studied [1–3], where our methods awarded 3rd and 2nd places in the competitions held at IJCNN'04 [4] and ESTSP'07 [5], respectively. Our methods and many other methods utilize model selection techniques evaluating the mean square prediction error (MSE) for holdout and/or cross-validation datasets. Although those methods select the models with good predictions for validation dataset, they cannot always provide good predictions for test dataset. This is because the prediction error of chaotic time series increases exponentially with the increase of time and the MSE of a set of predictions is largely affected by a small number of predictions with short predictable horizons even if the most of the predictions have long predictable horizons. Here, we refer to 'predictable horizon' as the first

ⓒ Springer Nature Switzerland AG 2020
H. Yang et al. (Eds.): ICONIP 2020, CCIS 1333, pp. 778–787, 2020.
https://doi.org/10.1007/978-3-030-63823-8_88

point in time after which the prediction error exceeds a certain error threshold, and note that there are similar notions on the horizon of prediction: the notion of 'predictability horizon' is specified slightly differently with the correlation of time series in [6], 'prediction horizon' is refered to as the number of time steps for the cost of prediction error in model predictive control research area [7], and the present notion of 'predictable horizon' has almost the same meaning as 'the critical time of decoupling' in the research studies on numerical chaotic solutions [8–10], where they do not use prediction but numerical solution.

From another point of view of [11,12], the probabilistic prediction has come to dominate the science of weather and climate forecasting, mainly because the theory of chaos at the heart of meteorology shows that for a simple set of nonlinear equations (or Lorenz's equations shown below) with initial conditions changed by minute pertur bations, there is no longer a single deterministic solution and hence all forecasts must be treated as probabilistic. Although most of the methods shown in [11] use ensemble mean to obtain representative forecast, we recently have presented several methods to select representative predictions of chaotic time series [13,14] because our methods employ strong learners capable of making predictions with small error, where usual ensemble mean does not work well owing that ensemble prediction error of chaotic time series grows exponentially after the smallest predictable horizon of the ensemble member, while there are individual predictions showing better performance than ensemble mean. Precisely, we have introduced LOOCV (leave-one-out cross-validation) measure to estimate predictable horizon to select a representative prediction from a number of predictions generated by strong learning machines. Comparing with our previous methods embedding model selection techniques using MSE [4,5], the LOOCV method has an advantage that it selects a representative prediction for each start time of test time series because the prediction error depends not only on validation time series but also test time series. In [14], we have clarified that the method using LOOCV predictable horizon works reasonably when a cluster of predictions has sufficiently large number of predictions generated by sufficiently strong learning machines. This paper focuses on this condition, and proposes a method to select a learning machine and a representative prediction by means of introducing the entropy of LOO predictable horizons of a large number of predictions generated by learning machines (or CAN2s) trained with different initial weight vectors.

The rest of the paper is organized as follows. Section 2 describes the method to generate a large number of predictions, and then select a learning machine and a representative prediction expected to have large predictable horizon. Section 3 shows numerical experiments and the analysis, followed by the conclusion in Sect. 4.

2   Generation and Selection of Predictions of Chaotic Time Series

2.1   IOS Prediction of Chaotic Time Series

Let y_t ($\in \mathbb{R}$) denote a chaotic time series for a discrete time $t = 0, 1, 2, \cdots$ fulfilling $y_t = r(\boldsymbol{x}_t) + e(\boldsymbol{x}_t)$. Here, $r(\boldsymbol{x}_t)$ is a nonlinear function of a vector $\boldsymbol{x}_t = (y_{t-1}, y_{t-2}, \cdots, y_{t-k})^T$ generated by the delay embedding with dimension k from a chaotic differential dynamical system (see [1] for chaotic time series), and an error

$e(\boldsymbol{x}_t)$ owing to an executable finite calculation precision is added since y_t is obtained not analytically but numerically. In general, a time series generated with higher precision has small prediction error for longer duration of time from the prediction start time. Thus, with respect to a ground truth time series $y_t^{[\mathrm{gt}]}$ generated with a sufficiently high precision (see Sect. 3 for details), we execute prediction shown below with standard 64 bit precision.

Let $y_{t:h} = y_t y_{t+1} \cdots y_{t+h-1}$ denote a time series with the initial time t and the horizon h. For a given and training time series $y_{t_g:h_g} (= y_{t_g:h_g}^{[\mathrm{train}]})$, we are supposed to predict succeeding time series $y_{t_p:h_p}$ for $t_p \geq t_g + h_g$. Then, we make the training dataset $D^{[\mathrm{train}]} = \{(\boldsymbol{x}_t, y_t) \mid t \in I^{[\mathrm{train}]}\}$ for $I^{[\mathrm{train}]} = \{t \mid t_g \leq t < t_g + h_g\}$ to train a learning machine. After the learning, the machine executes IOS (iterated one-step ahead) prediction by $\hat{y}_t = f(\boldsymbol{x}_t)$ for $t = t_p, t_{p+1}, \cdots$, recursively, where $f(\boldsymbol{x}_t)$ denotes prediction function of $\boldsymbol{x}_t = (x_{t1}, x_{t2}, \cdots, x_{tk})^T$ whose elements are given by

$$x_{tj} = \begin{cases} y_{t-j} \ (t - j < t_p) \\ \hat{y}_{t-j} \ (t - j \geq t_p). \end{cases} \tag{1}$$

Here, $y_t \ (t < t_p)$ is supposed to be known as the initial state for the prediction $\hat{y}_{t_p:h_p}$.

2.2 Single and Bagging CAN2 for Generating Large Number of IOS Predictions

From the analysis of LOOCV predictable horizon in [13], the LOOCV predictable horizon is expected to work when there are sufficiently large number of sufficiently strong learning machines. To have this done, we make a large number of predictions by means of CAN2s and a number of seeds of random generators as follows.

A single CAN2 has N units. The jth unit has a weight vector $\boldsymbol{w}_j \triangleq (w_{j1}, \cdots, w_{jk})^T \in \mathbb{R}^{k \times 1}$ and an associative matrix (or a row vector) $\boldsymbol{M}_j \triangleq (M_{j0}, M_{j1}, \cdots, M_{jk}) \in \mathbb{R}^{1 \times (k+1)}$ for $j \in I^N \triangleq \{1, 2, \cdots, N\}$. The CAN2 after learning the training dataset $D^{[\mathrm{train}]} = \{(\boldsymbol{x}_t, y_t) \mid t \in I^{[\mathrm{train}]}\}$ approximates the target function $r(\boldsymbol{x}_t)$ by

$$\hat{y}_t = \tilde{y}_{c(t)} = \boldsymbol{M}_{c(t)} \tilde{\boldsymbol{x}}_t, \tag{2}$$

where $\tilde{\boldsymbol{x}}_t \triangleq (1, \boldsymbol{x}_t^T)^T \in \mathbb{R}^{(k+1) \times 1}$ denotes the (extended) input vector to the CAN2, and $\tilde{y}_{c(t)} = \boldsymbol{M}_{c(t)} \tilde{\boldsymbol{x}}_t$ is the output value of the $c(t)$th unit of the CAN2. The index $c(t)$ indicates the unit who has the weight vector $\boldsymbol{w}_{c(t)}$ closest to the input vector $\boldsymbol{x}_t$, or $c(t) \triangleq \underset{j \in I^N}{\operatorname{argmin}} \|\boldsymbol{x}_t - \boldsymbol{w}_j\|$. The above prediction performs piecewise linear approximation of $y = r(\boldsymbol{x})$ and N indicates the number of piecewise linear regions.

We use the learning algorithm introduced in [15] whose high performance in regression problems has been shown in several applications, e.g. Evaluating Predictive Uncertainty Challenge [16]. The prediction performance after the learning varies depending on the initial weight vectors $\boldsymbol{w}_j$ which are selected randomly from $\boldsymbol{x}_t \ (t \in I^{[\mathrm{train}]})$ in training data set $D^{[\mathrm{train}]}$. In the following, let $\theta_{N,s}$ denote the learning machine or the CAN2 with the number of units $N \in \mathscr{N}$ and trained with the seed $s \in \mathcal{S}$ of the random generator, and $\Theta_{\mathscr{N},\mathcal{S}}^{[\mathrm{single}]} \triangleq \{\theta_{N,s} \mid N \in \mathscr{N}, s \in \mathcal{S}\}$.

The bagging method is usually employed for reducing the variance of single learning machines [17], and we use bagging CAN2s obtained as follows (see [17,18] for details); let $D^{[n\alpha^\sharp,j]} = \{(\boldsymbol{x}_t, y_t) \mid t \in I^{[n\alpha^\sharp,j]})\}$ be the jth bag (multiset, or bootstrap sample set) involving $n\alpha$ elements, where the elements in $D^{[n\alpha^\sharp,j]}$ are resampled randomly with replacement from the training dataset $D^{[\text{train}]}$ involving $n = |D^{[\text{train}]}|$ elements. Here, α (> 0) indicates the bag size ratio to the given dataset, and $j \in J^{[\text{bag}]} \triangleq \{1, 2, \cdots, b\}$. Here, note that $\alpha = 1$ is used in many applications (see [18,19]), but we use $\alpha = 2.3$ in the experiments shown below after the tuning of α (see [18] for validity and effectiveness of using variable α). Here, statistically, the data in $D^{[\text{train}]}$ is out of the bag $D^{[n\alpha^\sharp,j]}$ with the probability $(1 - 1/n)^\alpha \simeq e^{-\alpha}$. Inversely, the data in D^n is in $D^{n\alpha^\sharp,j}$ with the probability $1 - e^{-\alpha} \simeq 0.632$ for usual $\alpha = 1$ and 0.90 for $\alpha = 2.3$. Thus, with $\alpha = 2.3$, we use 90% data in $D^{[\text{train}]}$ for training a learning machine, and then the variance of the prediction is expected to be smaller than with using smaller α.

Let $\theta_{N,s}^{[j]}$ denote the (single) CAN2 after leaning the bag $D^{[n\alpha^\sharp,j]}$, and $\Theta_{\mathcal{N},\mathcal{S}}^{[\text{bag}]} \triangleq \{\theta_{N,s}^{[j]} \mid j \in J^{[\text{bag}]}, N \in \mathcal{N}, s \in \mathcal{S}\}$. Then, with $\Theta_{\mathcal{N},\mathcal{S}}^{[\text{bag}]}$, the bagging for predicting the target value $r_{t_c} = r(\boldsymbol{x}_{t_c})$ is done by

$$\hat{y}_t^{\left[\theta_{N,s}^{[\text{bag}]}\right]} \triangleq \frac{1}{b} \sum_{j \in J^{[\text{bag}]}} \hat{y}_t^{[j]} \equiv \left\langle \hat{y}_t^{[j]} \right\rangle_{j \in J^{[\text{bag}]}} \tag{3}$$

where $\hat{y}_{t_c}^{[j]} \triangleq \hat{y}^{[j]}(\boldsymbol{x}_{t_c})$ denotes the prediction by the learning machine $\theta_{N,s}^{[j]}$. The angle brackets $\langle \cdot \rangle$ indicate the mean, and the subscript $j \in J^{[\text{bag}]}$ indicates the range of the mean. For simple expression, we sometimes use $\langle \cdot \rangle_j$ instead of $\langle \cdot \rangle_{j \in J^{[\text{bag}]}}$ in the following.

2.3   LOOCV Predictable Horizon for Selecting a Representative Prediction

As shown in [13], we execute a prepossessing of removing implausible predictions in $\hat{y}_{t_p:h_p} = y_{t_p:h_p}^{[\theta]}$ for $\theta \in \Theta = \Theta_{\mathcal{N},\mathcal{S}}^{[\text{single}]}$ or $\Theta_{\mathcal{N},\mathcal{S}}^{[\text{bag}]}$, and we obtain a set of plausible predictions $Y_{t_p:h_p}^{[\Theta_S]} \triangleq \left\{ y_{t_p:h_p}^{[\theta]} \mid \theta \in \Theta_S \subset \Theta \right\}$ by means of examining the similarity of attractors. Due to the space limit, see [13] for details. Next, as a measure of predictable horizon, we define predictable horizon between two predictions $y_{t_p:h_p}^{[\theta]}$ and $y_{t_p:h_p}^{[\theta']}$ in $Y_{t_p:h_p}^{[\Theta_S]}$ as

$$h_{t_p}^{[\theta,\theta']} = h\left(y_{t_p:h_p}^{[\theta]}, y_{t_p:h_p}^{[\theta']} \right) = \max\left\{ h \mid \forall s \leq h \leq h_p; \left| y_{t_p+s}^{[\theta]} - y_{t_p+s}^{[\theta']} \right| \leq e_y \right\}, \tag{4}$$

where e_y indicates a threshold. Next, we introduce LOO (leave-one-out) predictable horizon given by

$$h_{t_p}^{[\theta,\Theta_S]} = \left\langle h_{t_p}^{[\theta,\theta']} \right\rangle_{\theta' \in \Theta_S \setminus \theta}. \tag{5}$$

Then, we have the longest LOO prediction as $h_{t_p}^{[\Theta_S]} = \max \left\{ h_{t_p}^{[\theta,\Theta_S]} \mid \theta \in \Theta_S \right\}$, which we call LOOCV predictable horizon as introduced in [13]. We refer to $y_{t_p}^{[\Theta_S]}$ as the representative prediction that has the LOOCV predictable horizon $h_{t_p}^{[\Theta_S]}$.

2.4 Hierarchical Clustering for Multiple Representative Predictions

In order to obtain multiple representative prediction involved in $Y_{t_p:h_p}^{[\Theta_S]}$, we execute hierarchical binary clustering of $Y_{t_p:h_p}^{[\Theta_S]}$ into $Y_{t_p:h_p}^{\left[\Theta_S^{[L,c]}\right]}$ for $L = 0, 1, \cdots, L_{\max}$ and $c = 0, 1, 2, \cdots, 2^L - 1$. Owing to the space limit, see [13] for details.

2.5 Entropy of LOO Predictable Horizons for Model Selection

In our previous research in [14], we have shown that the bagging CAN2 shows a good performance in making IOD predictions, while we could not have developed a method to select the best number of units, N, of the CAN2s. From the point of view of the condition that sufficiently large number of sufficiently strong learning machines for the LOOCV predictable horizon to work well (see [13] for details), we need to have a large number of different predictions near ground truth time series. Then, the LOO predictable horizons $h_{t_p}^{[\theta,\Theta_S]}$ corresponding to the actual predictable horizons $h_{t_p}^{[\theta,\mathrm{gt}]}$ should have almost the same values. Then, as a measure for the uniform distribution of the LOO predictable horizons, we introduce the entropy given by

$$H_{t_p}^{[N,L,c]} = - \sum_{\theta \in \Theta_N^{[L,c]}} \frac{h_{t_p}^{\left[\theta,\Theta_N^{[L,c]}\right]}}{\sum_{\theta' \in \Theta_N^{[L,c]}} h_{t_p}^{\left[\theta',\Theta_N^{[L,c]}\right]}} \log \frac{h_{t_p}^{\left[\theta,\Theta_N^{[L,c]}\right]}}{\sum_{\theta' \in \Theta_N^{[L,c]}} h_{t_p}^{\left[\theta',\Theta_N^{[L,c]}\right]}} \tag{6}$$

where $\Theta_N^{[L,c]}$ represents the set of learning machine (CAN2s with N units) which generate the set of predictions $Y_{t_p:h_p}^{\left[\Theta_S^{[L,c]}\right]}$ in the cluster c at the hierarchical level L. Here, from the analysis of the hierarchical method in [13], a cluster in the highest level, $L = L_{\max}$, is expected to achieve better performance. Furthermore, from the supposition that a good CAN2 generates a large number of good predictions, the cluster

$$c = \tilde{c} = \underset{c \in \mathcal{C}}{\mathrm{argmax}} \left| Y_{t_p:h_p}^{\left[\Theta_S^{[L,c]}\right]} \right|$$ is expected to achieve better performance. Finally, for the

set of prediction start time $t_p = T_p$, we select $N = \tilde{N}$ to maximize the entropy as

$$\tilde{N} = \underset{N \in \mathcal{N}}{\mathrm{argmax}} \left\langle H_{t_p}^{[N,L,c]} \right\rangle_{t_p \in T_p} \Bigg|_{L=L_{\max}, c=\tilde{c}}. \tag{7}$$

Here, we expect that the CAN2 with $\tilde{N}$ units provides a large number of predictions (hopefully) near the ground truth, while it is not guaranteed. Actually, we can imagine a bad learning machine which provides almost the same bad predictions. Thus, the above method will not work for different kind of learning machines, but we hope that it works for the CAN2s as good learning machines.

3   Numerical Experiments and Analysis

3.1   Experimental Settings

We use the Lorenz time series, as shown in [13], obtained from the original differential dynamical system given by

$$\frac{dx_c}{dt_c} = -\sigma x_c + \sigma y_c, \quad \frac{dy_c}{dt_c} = -x_c z_c + r x_c - y_c, \quad \frac{dz_c}{dt_c} = x_c y_c - b z_c, \quad (8)$$

for $\sigma = 10$, $b = 8/3$, $r = 28$. Here, we use continuous time t_c and discrete time $t \, (= 0, 1, 2, \cdots)$ related by $t_c = tT$ with sampling time T. Actually, we have generated the ground truth time series $y(t) = x_c(tT)$ for $t = 1, 2, \cdots, 5500$ from the initial state $(x_c(0), y_c(0), z_c(0)) = (-8, 8, 27)$ with $T = 0.025$LTS (Lorenz time step) via Runge-Kutta method with 256 bit precision and step-size $h = 10^{-8}$LTS implemented by GMP (GNU multi-precision library). We use $y_{0:h_{tr}} = y_{0:2000}$ for training learning machines, and execute IOS prediction of $y_{t_p:h_p}$ with the initial input vector $\boldsymbol{x}_{t_p} = (y(t_p - 1), \cdots, y(t_p - k))$ for prediction start time $t_p \in \mathcal{T}_p = \{2000 + 100i \mid i = 0, 1, 2, \cdots, 29\}$ and prediction horizon $h_p = 500$. We use the embedding dimension $k = 10$, and make the training dataset $D^{[\text{train}]} = \{(\boldsymbol{x}_t, y_t) \mid t \in I^{[\text{train}]}\}$ for $I^{[\text{train}]} = \{10, 11, \cdots, 1999\}$ from $y_{0:2000}$. For the bagging CAN2, we have used $b = 20$ bags.

3.2   Results and Analysis

Model Selection and Example of Representative Prediction: We have obtained $50(= |\mathcal{S}|)$ predictions $y_{t_p}^{[\theta]}$ for each single CAN2, $\theta \in \Theta_{\mathcal{N},\mathcal{S}}^{[\text{single}]}$, and bagging CAN2, $\theta \in \Theta_{\mathcal{N},\mathcal{S}}^{[\text{bag}]}$, and prediction start time $t_p \in \mathcal{T}_p$. Then, for each set of 50 predictions, we have applied the hierarchical clustering upto $L_{\max} - 2$ hierarchical level, and obtained the entropy $H_{t_p}^{[N,L,c]}$ for $L = 0, 1, 2$, $N \in \mathcal{N}$, $c = 0, 1, \cdots, 2^L - 1$, and $t_p \in \mathcal{T}_p$. Finally, from (7), we have selected the number of units $N = \tilde{N} = 90$ and 50 for the single CAN2 and the bagging CAN2, respectively.

In Fig. 1, we show example of the representative predictions depicted by the thick blue line for the selected single and bagging CAN2s and $t_p = 2400$, where we also show superimposed predictions $y_{t_p:h_p}^{[\theta]}$ generated by the selected CAN2s and the ground truth time series depicted by the thick red line.

Relationship Between the Entropy and the Predictable Horizon: In order to analyze the validity of the present method, we first examine the relationship between the entropy $H^{[N,L]} = \left\langle H_{t_p}^{[N,L,\tilde{c}]} \right\rangle_{t_p \in \mathcal{T}_p}$ of the LOO predictable horizons and the mean (actual) predictable horizon in the cluster, $h^{[N,L,\text{gt}]} = \left\langle h_{t_p}^{[\theta,\text{gt}]} \right\rangle_{t_p \in \mathcal{T}_p, \theta \in \Theta_{N}^{[L,\tilde{c}]}}$, shown in Fig. 2(a). We can see that $N = 90$ for the single CAN2 and $N = 50$ for the bagging CAN2 has the largest entropy for $L = 2$, respectively. Here, we can see that the

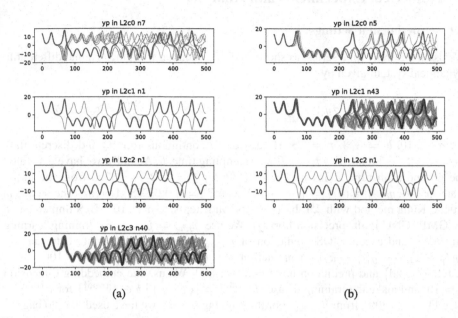

(a)   (b)

Fig. 1. For the prediction start time $t_p = 2400$ and the hierarchical level $L = 2$, superimposed predictions $y_{t_p:h_p}^{[\theta]}$ generated by (a) the selected single CAN2 with $N = 90$ and (b) the selected bagging CAN2 with $N = 50$ in the clusters $c = 0, 1, 2, 3$ are displayed from the top to the bottom. The representative prediction in the cluster $c = \tilde{c} = 3$ and 1 in (a) and (b), respectively, is depicted by thick blue line, while the ground truth time series $y_{t_p:h_p}^{[gt]}$ with the thick red line is superimposed in each cluster. The predictable horizon of the representative predictions is $h_{t_p}^{[\theta,gt]} = 237$ and 385 for (a) and (b), respectively, for the error threshold $e_y = 15$. Note that we have 50 original predictions but one prediction for (a) and (b), and one cluster in (b) are eliminated through the clustering process.

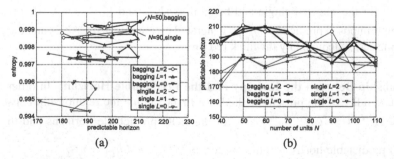

(a)   (b)

Fig. 2. (a) The entropy $H^{[N,L]}$ vs. the predictable horizon $h^{[N,L,gt]}$, and (b) the predictable horizon $h^{[N,L,gt]}$ vs. the number of units N. In (a), the entropy $H^{[N,L]}$ for all $N \in \mathcal{N}$ with the same L is connected with line.

data for larger L has larger entropy, which indicates that the hierarchical clustering has worked well. Furthermore, it is desirable that the entropy and the predictable horizon have a positive correlation, and we may say that all data points of the entropy and the predictable horizon for $L = 0, 1, 2$ and single and bagging CAN2s have a weak but positive correlation.

Relationship Between the Predictable Horizon and the Number of Units: Next, we examine the predictable horizon $h^{[N,L,\text{gt}]}$ vs. the number of units N of the CAN2s in Fig. 2(b). We can see that the relationship is not smooth, but the largest predictable horizon is achieved with the selected models, i.e. $N = 90$ and 50 for the single and bagging CAN2, respectively. It is remarkable that we have selected the above models without using the information of the predictable horizon but only with the entropy.

From another point of view, the bagging CAN2s have larger predictable horizons for $N \leq 70$ than the single CAN2s. However, the comparison for $N \geq 80$ is difficult while we have shown the improvement of the bagging in [14]. These facts seem to contradict. One of the reason is considered that the performance of a single CAN2 with large N may have large variance, but it is not so clear and we would like to examine this phenomena in our future research studies.

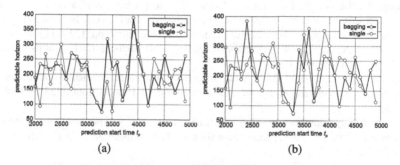

(a)   (b)

Fig. 3. The predictable horizons $h_{t_p}^{[\theta,\text{gt}]}$ for $t_p \in \mathcal{T}_p$, $\theta \in \Theta_{N=90}^{[L,\tilde{c}]}$ of the selected single CAN2 and $\theta \in \Theta_{N=50}^{[L,\tilde{c}]}$ of the selected bagging CAN2, and the hierarchical level (a) $L = 0$ and (b) $L = 2$.

Relationship Between the Predictable Horizon and the Prediction Start Time: Next, for the selected single CAN2 with $N = 90$ and the bagging CAN2 with $N = 50$, we examine not the mean but the constituent predictable horizons $h_{t_p}^{[\theta,\text{gt}]}$ for $t_p \in \mathcal{T}_p$ and $L = 0, 2$ in Fig. 3. In (a) and (b), we can see that the bagging CAN2 does not always have larger $h_{t_p}^{[\theta,\text{gt}]}$ than single CAN2, although the mean performance $h^{[N,L,\text{gt}]}$ of the bagging CAN2 with $N = 50$ is larger than the single CAN2 with $N = 90$.

4   Conclusion

We have presented a method to generate a large number of predictions and select a learning machine and a representative prediction using the entropy of LOO predictable horizons. By means of numerical experiments, we show and examine the effectiveness of the present method. We would like to examine and analyze the details of the present method much more, and compare with other methods in our future research studies.

References

1. Aihara, K.: Theories and Applications of Chaotic Time Series Analysis. Sangyo Tosho, Tokyo (2000)
2. Lendasse, A., Oja, E.: Time series prediction competition: the cats benchmark. In: Proceedings of IJCNN2004, pp. 1615–1620 (2004)
3. Ty, A.J.A., Fang, Z., Conzalez, R.A., Rozdeba, P.J., Abarbanel, H.D.I.: Machine learning of time series using time-delay embedding and precision annealing. Neural Comput. 31(10), 2004–2024 (2019)
4. Kurogi, S., Ueno, T., Sawa, M.: Time series prediction of the CATS benchmark using Fourier bandpass filters and competitive associative nets. Neurocomputing 70(13–15), 2354–2362 (2007)
5. Kurogi, S., Tanaka, S., Koyama, R.: Combining the predictions of a time series and the first-order difference using bagging of competitive associative nets. In: Proceedings of the European Symposium on Time Series Prediction, ESTSP 2007, pp. 123–131 (2007)
6. Kravtsov, Y.A.: Limits of Predictability. Springer, Heidelberg (2012). https://doi.org/10.1007/978-3-642-51008-3
7. Lucia, S., Finkler, T., Rngell, S.: Multi-stage nonlinear model predictive control applied to a semi-batch polymerization reactor under uncertainty. J. Process Control 23(9), 1306–1319 (2013)
8. Teixeira, J., Reynolds, C.A., Judd, K.: K: time step sensitivity of nonlinear atmospheric models: numerical convergence, truncation error growth, and ensemble design. J. Atmos. Sci. 64, 175–189 (2007)
9. Wang, P., Li, J., Li, Q.: Computational uncertainty and the application of a high-performance multiple precision scheme to obtaining the correct reference solution of Lorenz equations. Numer. Algorithms 59(1), 147–159 (2011)
10. Liao, S., Wang, P.: On the mathematically reliable long-term simulation of chaotic solutions of Lorenz equation in the interval [0, 1000]. Sci. China Phys. Mech. Astron. 57(2), 330–335 (2014)
11. Slingo, J., Palmer, T.: Uncertainty in weather and climate prediction. Phil. Trans. R. Soc. A 369, 4751–4767 (2011)
12. WMO: Guidelines on Ensemble Prediction Systems and Forecasting, WMO-No.1091, World Meteorological Organization, Geneva, Switzerland (2012)
13. Kurogi, S., Shimoda, N. Matsuo, K.: Hierarchical clustering of ensemble prediction using LOOCV predictable horizon for chaotic time series. In: Proceedings of IEEE-SSCI 2017, pp. 1789–1795 (2017)
14. Kurogi, S., Toidani, M., Shigematsu, R., Matsuo, K.: Performance improvement via bagging in probabilistic prediction of chaotic time series using similarity of attractors and LOOCV predictable horizon. Neural Comput. Appl. 29(9), 341–349 (2018)
15. Kurogi, S.: Asymptotic optimality of competitive associative nets and its application to incremental learning of nonlinear functions. Syst. Comput. Jpn. 38(9), 85–96 (2007)

16. Quiñonero-Candela, J., Rasmussen, C.E., Sinz, F., Bousquet, O., Schölkopf, B.: Evaluating predictive uncertainty challenge. In: Quiñonero-Candela, J., Dagan, I., Magnini, B., d'Alché-Buc, F. (eds.) MLCW 2005. LNCS (LNAI), vol. 3944, pp. 1–27. Springer, Heidelberg (2006). https://doi.org/10.1007/11736790_1
17. Breiman, L.: Bagging predictors. Mach. Learn. **26**, 123–140 (1996)
18. Kurogi, S.: Improving generalization performance via out-of-bag estimate using variable size of bags. J. Japan. Neural Netw. Soc. **16**(2), 81–92 (2009)
19. Efron, B., Tbshirani, R.: Improvements on cross-validation: the.632+ bootstrap method. J. Am. Stat. Assoc. **92**, 548–560 (1997)

Improving the Stability of a Convolutional Neural Network Time-Series Classifier Using SeLU and Tanh

Melanie Renkin[✉] and Jessica Sharmin Rahman

Research School of Computer Science, Australian National University,
Canberra, Australia
{melanie.renkin,jessica.rahman}@anu.edu.au

Abstract. Emotion recognition by machine learning methods has been a topic of interest for many years. This paper presents an analysis in stabilising a time-series, emotional response classifier. The network uses six convolutional layers to perform feature extraction on time-series data before passing the features into a fully connected classifier. To increase the stability of the network, SeLUs were used to prevent training failure and introduce internal normalisation, and a tanh activation function in the final fully connected layer helps to regularise the output. This network was able to classify emotional responses to music from physiological data with relatively high performance in the evaluation measures and stability in the loss values. Classification of excitement in response to music was performed with 98.9% (±1.1) accuracy in the training set, 91.3% (±10.8) in the validation set and 90.6% in the test set.

Keywords: Emotion recognition · Convolutional Neural Network · Stability · Electrodermal activity · Time-series classification · Scaled exponential linear units · Tanh

1 Introduction

Researchers have been studying the recognition of human emotions for decades, primarily focusing on recognizing emotions via facial expressions or vocal cues [4,9]. Emotion recognition has applications in human-computer interfacing [8], software engineering [6] and support systems for people with impaired emotion recognition abilities [14]. In the early 2000's researchers began to use physiological signals such as electrodermal activity in emotion recognition [10]. Electrodermal activity (EDA) refers to the electrical signals that are present in the skin. Research has shown that EDA can reflect psychological responses and states [7]. This physiological data has been used in neural networks and deep learning models to predict and classify human emotional responses. These models can produce high levels of accuracy, however, there are some reports of

© Springer Nature Switzerland AG 2020
H. Yang et al. (Eds.): ICONIP 2020, CCIS 1333, pp. 788–795, 2020.
https://doi.org/10.1007/978-3-030-63823-8_89

poor generalization on unseen participants, perhaps, due to the wide variety of physiological responses participants may experience [1,2].

Unlike other tools used in emotion detection, such as electroencephalograms and facial monitoring systems, electrodermal activity monitors are generally unobtrusive and able to be worn long term to monitor EDA [11]. These monitors frequently output time-series data, which can be pre-processed and used in fully connected neural networks [13] or used in the original sequential format in convolutional or recurrent neural network feature extractors [16]. Convolutional Neural Networks (CNNs) have been found to be perform well on feature extraction in emotion recognition tasks [16], however, as with many neural networks, can become unstable as the architecture deepens [15].

This paper presents an analysis in stabilising the performance of a feature extracting, time-series classifier using the self normalising features of scaled exponential linear units and the regularising features of the tanh function. The classifier is trained on a small, physiological, time-series dataset and is used in binary emotional response classification. The paper is organized as follows. Following this introduction, Sect. 2 describes the methods used in this study including the dataset, classifier architecture development and evaluation measures used to assess the model. Section 3 presents the results of the architecture development process, the final performance of the model and presents a discussion of these results. Section 4 concludes the paper and discusses future work.

2   Methods

2.1   Data and Data Encoding

For this study two datasets were used, both from a study by Rahman et al. [13]. The first was the pre-processed dataset used in the publication, which included both physiological data obtained from an EDA monitor and emotional response data collected from 24 participants. The physiological data has been preprocessed into 14 variables which were not used in this study. The second dataset was the time series data prior to preprocessing. Both datasets contain information on 24 participants over 12 songs. Each participant listened to 8 of the 12 songs while 4 physiological readings per second were collected. The two datasets were joined on participant and song identification numbers to produce a single dataset on 24 participants which includes time-series physiological data collected while the participant listened to music and their emotional response to the music.

The target variable was designed by Rahman et al. to contain three classes: Depressing, Unsure and Exciting. For this analysis, the aim was to classify the participants emotional response as being excited or not, as such, the target variable was converted to a binary response; 1 for excited or 0 otherwise. The same encoding was used to encode the remaining emotional responses, Comforting, Pleasant, Soothing, Relaxing, Happy and Attention as 1 for each of these responses or 0 otherwise. These variables were used to test the network architectures generalisability to different emotional responses.

2.2   Time-Series Classifier Architecture

A feature extractor was built with 6 convolutional layers. The initial inputs were padded with zeros to the length of the longest time-series in the data set, in this case, 1103 time-steps. First, a convolution was performed with 4 feature maps, a kernel size of 4, stride length of 1, and was padded to avoid data loss. Next a pooling layer reduced the length of the sequences by half to 552. The second layer used the same settings to produce 8 feature maps pooled to a length of 226. A third layer repeated the process to produce 12 feature maps of length 138. The final three layers again all used a kernel size of 4, stride length of 1 and were padded to avoid data loss. They produced 16, 20 and 24 feature maps respectively. Each of these three layers were pooled to reduce the length by 4 times to lengths of 34, 8 and 2 values respectively. The final layer was pooled again to produce a single value per pattern in each of the 24 feature maps. After each pooling step in all six layers, an activation layer was introduced using various activation functions as discussed in Sect. 2.3. The 24 feature maps were passed into the fully connected layer as input.

Two fully connected layers were used to classify the data. First a 24 unit input layer followed by a hidden layer of 12 units. The output of the fully connected layers were two values for classification. A softmax function was used to obtain probabilities for classification into each class.

2.3   Stability

To improve the stability of the classifier, various activation functions were tested after each pooling step and in the fully connected classifier. Rectified linear units (ReLU), Leaky ReLU and scaled exponential linear unit (SeLU) activation functions were trialled after the max-pooling layers and first fully connected layer, while a tanh function was also introduced to the final fully connected layer. An Adam optimisation algorithm was used.

The network was initially trialled using 500 epochs and a learning rate of 0.01. Once the activation functions had been selected, the number of epochs was dropped to 200 and the learning rate was tested at intervals of 0.0025 beginning at 0.01 and stopping at 0.001. In the final trial a learning rate scheduler was implemented which reduced the learning rate from 0.01 by 0.75 times every 25 epochs.

2.4   Evaluation Measures

To evaluate the performance of the classifier, the data was separated into a training set and a testing set using an 80:20 ratio. The training set was then split into a training set and validation set using leave one out cross validation due to the small size of the dataset. All splits were made after grouping the data by participant in order to evaluate the model on new unseen participants. For selection of all activation functions and hyperparameter settings, five evaluation measures were used to analyse the performance of the network. These included accuracy, precision, sensitivity, specificity and f measure, only accuracy and f measure are reported in this paper.

3 Results and Discussion

3.1 Results

Stability. Using standard ReLU activation in the convolutional and fully connected layers showed a high level of variability in stability and performance of the network. This was seen in the large loss spikes during training (Fig. 1A) and spread of the evaluation measures (Fig. 2). Training failure was seen in multiple runs. Changing to Leaky ReLUs saw improvements in the variability of the evaluation metrics (Fig. 2), however, larger spikes were seen in the loss values during training (Fig. 1B). Using the tanh activation function in the last fully connected layer produced an increase in stability (Fig. 1C) with marginal improvements in the evaluation measures. The mean validation accuracy increased from 86.3% (±11.4) with a Leaky ReLU activation function to 87.5% (±11.5) with tanh. While the stability was improved, large loss spikes were still seen during training (Fig. 1C). SeLU activation in the convolutional layers and the first fully connected layer reduced the loss spikes (Fig. 1D) and improved the validation accuracy to 93.8% (±6.4).

Lowering of the learning rate showed little change in the evaluation metrics (Table 1), however, the stability of the loss showed increasing improvement as the learning rate decreased (Fig. 1C, D and E). A learning rate of 0.001 showed very small fluctuations in the loss but often failed to avoid a local minimum just below 0.7. Implementing a learning rate scheduler to decrease the learning rate by 0.75 times every 25 steps allowed the network to bypass the local minimum while still preventing loss spikes and potentially reducing the number of epochs required for the network to converge (Fig. 1F).

Emotional Response Classification. The final test accuracy of the classifier was 90.6%, precision was 94.7%, sensitivity was 90.0%, specificity was 91.7% and f measure was 92.3%. When the classifier was trained on other emotional responses it performed well, with evaluation measures comparable to those for the excitement classification (Table 2), provided the class distribution was balanced. In the presence of significant class imbalance, the network failed to learn.

Table 1. Evaluation Measures by Learning Rate. Accuracy and F measures reported are the mean across 20-fold cross validation performed on the training data. The standard deviation of this mean is reported in brackets.

Learning rate	Epochs	Set	Accuracy (%)	F measure (%)
0.001	200	Training	95.9 (±1.4)	96.5 (±1.3)
		Validation	90.0 (±7.7)	91.8 (±6.8)
LR scheduler	200	Training	98.9 (±1.1)	99.0 (±0.9)
		Validation	91.3 (±10.8)	92.7 (±9.2)

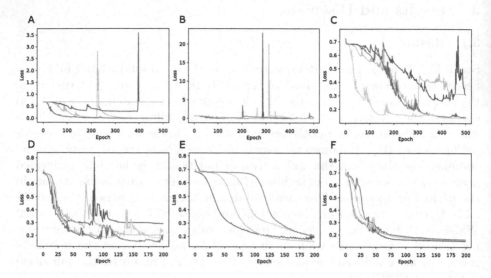

Fig. 1. Plots of training losses by epoch for four randomly selected cross validation folds. Scales in Figs. 1A and 1B are adjusted for better visualisation. **A:** Initial settings of ReLU activation in both the convolutional and FC layers with 500 epochs and a learning rate of 0.01. **B:** Leaky ReLUs in both the convolutional and FC layers with the same hyper parameters as A. **C:** Leaky ReLU activation in the convolution layers and Tanh activation in the last FC layer with the same hyper parameters as A. **D:** SeLU activation in the convolutional layers and tanh activation in the last FC layer, 200 epochs and a learning rate of 0.005. **E:** SeLU activation in the convolutional layers and tanh activation in the last FC layer, 200 epochs and a learning rate of 0.001. **F:** SeLU activation in the convolutional layers and tanh activation in the last FC layer, 200 epochs with a learning rate scheduler.

Table 2. Performance of Classifier Architecture on Various Emotions. Accuracy and F measures reported for training and validation sets are the mean across 20-fold cross validation performed on the training data. The standard deviation is reported in brackets.

Emotion	Set	Accuracy (%)	F measure (%)
Excited	Training	98.9 (±1.1)	99.0 (±0.9)
	Validation	91.3 (±10.8)	92.7 (±9.2)
	Testing	90.6	92.3
Happy	Training	98.1 (±3.2)	98.7 (±2.3)
	Validation	95.0 (±11.8)	95.4 (±11.5)
	Testing	100	100
Attention	Training	97.4 (±6.3)	99.3 (±4.1)
	Validation	96.9 (±6.9)	98.0 (±4.5)
	Testing	100	100

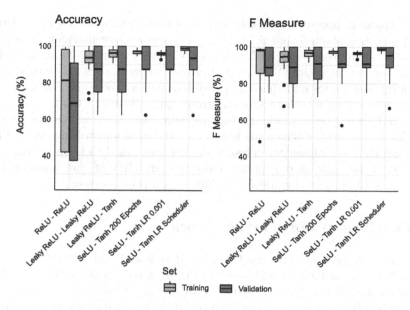

Fig. 2. Boxplots of the distribution of the evaluation measures. Thick horizontal line represents the median value. **ReLU - ReLU** – ReLU activation functions used in both the convolutional and FC layers. **Leaky ReLU - Leaky ReLU** – Leaky ReLUs in both the convolutional and FC layers. **Leaky ReLU - Tanh** – Tanh activation function in the last FC layer. **SeLU - Tanh 200 Epochs** – Number of epochs reduced from 500 to 200. **SeLU - Tanh LR 0.001** – LR reduced from 0.01 to 0.001. **SeLU -Tanh LR Scheduler** – LR scheduler used.

3.2 Discussion

Given that this study was performed on a small dataset containing long sequences dying ReLUs were observed from very early in training, resulting in training failure. The use of leaky ReLUs prevented training failure and based on the evaluation measures the model appeared to perform quite well across the board. However, large, spiking loss values could be seen during training and the performance of the network relied on ending training before or after the loss spikes, which was often down to chance. Similar to methods used in generative adversarial networks [12], adding a bounded activation function such as tanh in the final fully connected layer helped to stabilise the network and spiking loss values were brought under control, though not eliminated. Replacing the leaky ReLUs with SeLUs [5] led to both improved stability and higher performance.

SeLUs combine a scaled log curve to prevent dying ReLUs with internal normalisation to prevent shifts in the mean and variance of the outputs between layers [5]. Using SeLUs between the convolutional layers allowed for improvement in both the stability and performance of the network. Lowering the learning rate further stabilised the network, however, a low learning rate had difficulty navigating around local minima. The learning rate scheduler allowed the network to avoid the local minima early in training and reduce variability in the loss later in training, providing a stable and consistent classification system. Huang et al. [3] recently showed that SeLUs can effectively replace shortcut connections and batch normalisation in ResNet-50, allowing very deep CNNs to be trained without the use of residual learning. Here, we show that SeLUs can stabilise fluctuating loss values and thus the performance of a time-series classifier.

The network architecture showed strong generalisability when trained and tested on the additional emotional response data, high performance was obtained in evaluation measures across the board for validation and testing data. Where significant class imbalance was present the network failed to learn, demonstrating, that despite the strong performance and stability of the classifier, class imbalance still needs to be addressed during data pre-processing.

4   Conclusions and Further Work

This paper has presented a deep CNN based time-series classifier trained on a small physiological dataset and stabilised using a combination of dying ReLU prevention and internal normalisation provided by SeLU, bounded activation provided by the tanh function and fine control of the learning rate provided by the learning rate scheduler. These features prevented significant spiking of the loss value and allowed for stable and repeatable training. The classifier was thus able to obtain 98.9% ($\pm$1.1) accuracy in classifying excitement in the training set, 91.3% ($\pm$10.8) in the validation set and 90.6% in the test set. The results presented here are comparable to those presented by Rahman et al. who used a pre-processed form of the data along with genetic algorithms for feature selection to classify musical genre, and emotional response from the physiological data. The network architecture was generalisable to different emotional responses provided they had relatively balanced class distributions.

This work along with the work of Huang et al. [3] adds to the evidence that SeLU activation functions can effectively replace ReLU activation functions with additional self normalising benefits to the resulting network. Further work should be done on this classifier to test the level of resistance to class imbalance, and determine the networks performance on multiclass-classification and other physiological time-series datasets and emotion recognition tasks. More generally, further work should be done to examine the mechanisms behind this technique and its use in stabilising both CNNs in general as well as other deep learning algorithms.

References

1. Al Machot, F., Elmachot, A., Ali, M., Al Machot, E., Kyamakya, K.: A deep-learning model for subject-independent human emotion recognition using electrodermal activity sensors. Sensors **19**(7), 1659 (2019)
2. Ganapathy, N., Swaminathan, R.: Emotion recognition using electrodermal activity signals and multiscale deep convolution neural network. Stud. Health Technol. Inform. **258**, 140 (2019)

3. Huang, Z., Ng, T., Liu, L., Mason, H., Zhuang, X., Liu, D.: SNDCNN: self-normalizing deep CNNs with scaled exponential linear units for speech recognition. In: 2020 IEEE International Conference on Acoustics, Speech and Signal Processing (ICASSP), ICASSP 2020, Barcelona, Spain, pp. 6854–6858 (2020)
4. Johnson, W.F., Emde, R.N., Scherer, K.R., Klinnert, M.D.: Recognition of emotion from vocal cues. Arch. Gen. Psychiatry **43**(3), 280–283 (1986)
5. Klambauer, G., Unterthiner, T., Mayr, A., Hochreiter, S.: Self-normalizing neural networks. In: 31st Conference on Neural Information Processing Systems, Long Beach, CA, USA, pp. 972–981 (2017)
6. Kołakowska, A., Landowska, A., Szwoch, M., Szwoch, W., Wróbel, M.: Emotion recognition and its application in software engineering. In: 6th International Conference on Human System Interactions, Sopot, Poland, pp. 532–539 (2013)
7. Kreibig, S.D.: Autonomic nervous system activity in emotion: a review. Biol. Psychol. **84**(3), 394–421 (2010)
8. Gavrilova, M.L., Tan, C.J.K., Sourin, A., Sourina, O. (eds.): Transactions on Computational Science XII. LNCS, vol. 6670. Springer, Heidelberg (2011). https://doi.org/10.1007/978-3-642-22336-5
9. Padgett, C., Cottrell, G.W.: A simple neural network models categorical perception of facial expressions. In: Proceedings of the 20th Annual Conference of the Cognitive Science Society, Madison USA, pp. 806–811 (1998)
10. Picard, R.W., Vyzas, E., Healey, J.: Toward machine emotional intelligence: analysis of affective physiological state. IEEE Trans. Pattern Anal. Mach. Intell. **23**(10), 1175–1191 (2001)
11. Poh, M., Swenson, N.C., Picard, R.W.: A wearable sensor for unobtrusive, long-term assessment of electrodermal activity. IEEE Trans. Biomed. Eng. **57**(5), 1243–1252 (2010)
12. Radford, A., Metz, L., Chintala, S.: Unsupervised Representation Learning with Deep Convolutional Generative Adversarial Networks, vol. 57, no. 5. arXiv e-prints arXiv:1511.06434 (2015)
13. Rahman, J.S., Gedeon, T., Caldwell, S., Jones, R., Hossain, M.Z., Zhu, X.: Melodious micro-frissons: detecting music genres from skin response. In: 2019 International Joint Conference on Neural Networks (IJCNN), Budapest, Hungary, pp. 1–8 (2019)
14. White, S.W., Abbott, L., Wieckowski, A.T., Capriola-Hall, N.N., Aly, S., Youssef, A.: Feasibility of automated training for facial emotion expression and recognition in autism. Behav. Ther. **49**(6), 881–888 (2018)
15. Zheng, S., Song, Y., Leung, T., Goodfellow, I.: Improving the robustness of deep neural networks via stability training. In: 2016 IEEE Conference on Computer Vision and Pattern Recognition (CVPR), Las Vegas, NV, pp. 4480–4488 (2016)
16. Zheng, Y., Liu, Q., Chen, E., Ge, Y., Zhao, J.L.: Time series classification using multi-channels deep convolutional neural networks. In: Li, F., Li, G., Hwang, S., Yao, B., Zhang, Z. (eds.) WAIM 2014. LNCS, vol. 8485. Springer, Cham (2014). https://doi.org/10.1007/978-3-319-08010-9_33

Proposing Two Different Feature Extraction Methods from Multi-fractal Detrended Fluctuation Analysis of Electroencephalography Signals: A Case Study on Attention-Deficit Hyperactivity Disorder

Zahra Roozbehi[1] , Mahsa Mohaghegh[1] , Hossein Lanjanian[2] ,
and Peyman Hassani Abharian[3]([☒])

[1] Auckland University of Technology, Auckland, New Zealand
{zahra.roozbehi,mahsa.mohaghegh}@aut.ac.nz
[2] Institute of Biochemistry and Biophysics, University of Tehran, Tehran, Iran
H.Lanjanian@ut.ac.ir
[3] Brain and Cognition Clinic, Institute for Cognitive Science Studies, Tehran, Iran
abharian@iricss.org

Abstract. This study presents two pipelines of extracting multi-fractal detrended fluctuation analysis (MFDFA) features, to diagnose ADHD in children of age 7–13 thorough application of feature vectors and an auto-regression on the features. The features are q-order Hurst exponent, classical scaling exponent, and singularity spectrum. The MFDFA features of Electroencephalography (EEG) signals in the rest state of 16 ADHD and 16 normal children were extracted. Beside the calculated feature matrix (A), a second matrix (B) consisting of auto-regression coefficients of A was produced. Prominent features of A and B were selected and then classified using a linear support vector machine (SVM) algorithm, resulting in 94% and 97% accuracy respectively. Channels 16 and 2 in the EEG played the most important roles in discriminating the two groups, as it was proved in the literature. This study, though, depicted the individual differences in fractal properties of these two regions for the first time, which could be used as a bio-marker or a diagnosis tool for ADHD.

Keywords: Features selection · Machine learning · Multi-fractal detrended fluctuations analysis · Non-linear analysis of EEG signals · Attention-deficit hyperactivity disorder

1 Introduction

ADHD is a disorders that not only has a relatively high prevalence of 9.4% in children in US, but also its damaging effects continues up to the adulthood [1].

© Springer Nature Switzerland AG 2020
H. Yang et al. (Eds.): ICONIP 2020, CCIS 1333, pp. 796–803, 2020.
https://doi.org/10.1007/978-3-030-63823-8_90

To be labelled as an ADHD, the most common practice relies on clear symptoms outlined in Diagnostic and Statistical Manual of Mental Disorders (DSM-5) [9]. However, due to its observation-based approach, misdiagnose occurs around 20% [3]. Therefore, improving diagnosis tools is of importance.

In the past 40 years, scholars have been exploring the use of neuroimaging to provide the quantitative data needed to develop a diagnostic tool. Among these EEG has been used extensively. Theta/Beta Ratio (TBR) is the most promising quantitative assessment tool so far that has been approved by FDA in 2013 for ADHD clinical assessment. However, studies report inconclusive clinical efficacy of TBR.

As a result of three EEG attributes, chaotic, complex and self-similar, chaos theory springs to mind for analysis. And Out of many possible methods, to explore chaotic and complex systems, fractal geometry is proved to be the most promising approach [7].

Multi fractal detrended fluctuation analysis [4] is specifically useful in identifying fractal properties including scaling characteristics and correlations in noisy, non-stationary time-series. Scaling components of the method are used as features to study more complex dynamics of the data.

To date, only two studies have applied MFDFA on ADHD and non-ADIID children for diagnosis, which are done by Khoshnoud [5] and Spröhnle [8]. In the former, done in rest mode, the multifractal spectra, along with another two nonlinear features were applied to gain 83% of accuracy. Despite the decent accuracy attained, this is not a holistic investigation of MFDFA capacity for ADHD discrimination; rather it is more of a general chaos theory evaluation, for all three features are of chaos, but not necessarily MFDFA.

The latter study has applied a different feature set, merely including multifractals for classification. This study was performed in a task mode in order to prove that dynamics of human inferential processes are responsible for executive dysfunctions, such as ADHD. While in order to detect metabolic regular operation of the cortex it is decent to record EEG in either eyes-closed or open in a relaxed mode. Because, ADHD is a constantly present disorder, not just a momentary reaction to a particular stimulus. Therefore, the rest mode would show more of the related dynamics, instead of the unwanted reactions.

Exploring both previous studies, a gap exists in knowledge at the nexus of full range MFDFA measures and the rest mode EEG recording. As this approach not only investigates exclusively MFDFA ability as an independent diagnosis tool, but it also surmounts achieving an unrealistic high accuracy out of the classifier's probable bias toward undesired reactions to stimuli.

Two new pipelines are presented herein with an exhaustive use of MFDFA features to assess ADHD in rest mode. In particular, the objectives are to (1) describe the fractal behavior of the EEG data and (2) to discriminate two classes of ADHD and normal using Support vector machine (SVM) classifier. The core of this proposal lies in a unique calculus estimation of multifractal measures.

2   Method and Materials

This research, which is conducted in pilot method with a control group, consists of three stages, data collection, pre-processing and main analysis. All are aimed at achieving three goals: an accuracy for discriminating ADHD children, contributing regions of the brain in this discrimination and fractal properties of these regions.

2.1   Data Collection and Pre-processing

The primary statistical population of this study was 80 ADHD and 35 normal children aged 7–13 years old. However, we ended up 16 ADHD and 16 normal cases after a primarily 6-step filter and pre-processing. Disorder children were the clients who visited Behjou Psychiatry Clinic in Tehran, Iran, that their disorder was confirmed by the clinic's neurologist. Control subjects, whose clinical diagnosis report was negative to any psychiatric disorder, have been chosen from random schools in Tehran, Iran. Subjects of each group were sorted based on the defined scores of six criteria including age, intelligence, education, gender, parents' educational level and an IQ between 85 and 120. A rest mode with eyes closed EEG data of each subject was recorded in 19 channels, according to 10–20 International system (Fp1, Fp2, F3, F4, C3, C4, P3, P4, O1, O2, F7, F8, T3, T4, T5, T6, Fz, Cz and Pz). The average duration of recording was 2 min, 250 Hz frequency and 16-bit resolution. All 19 channels of each participant were pre-processed in MatlabR2013a, according to the steps in [2]. After a visual artefact Detection and removal, the general and the line noise were suppressed using a finite impulse response filter of 1–60 Hz and a notch filter 50 Hz respectively. And Common average of all channels used for re-referencing.

2.2   Main Analysis

The pre-processing outputs which are the inputs of the main analysis are now 32 matrices (one per sample) with 19 columns (channels) and 7500 rows (5 Min. * 60 s * 250 Hz). In order to explore differences among the two groups of subjects, primarily their salient features were extracted by MFDFA as it is explained in Sect. 2.2. Hereafter, we had two feature matrices A and B, as a byproduct of A. Both matrices have 32 rows, each represents one subject. Extracted features are $h(q), \tau(q)$ and $f(\alpha)$. B, however, is a compact form of A, made of only auto-regressed coefficients of each one of three feature vectors.

Next, the a most essential columns of A, and the b most important columns of B were chosen, resulting in $32 * a$ and $32 * b$ matrices. Finally, all 32 rows of the just attained tables were classified.

Feature Extraction. In order to describe MFDFA features, first monofractal detrended fluctuation analysis (DFA) is illustrated: Suppose we have a time-series: $X(i) = 1, 2, \ldots, N$.

$Y(i)$ is calculated as follow, where $\langle x \rangle$ is the mean of $X(i)$

$$Y(i) = \sum_{k=1}^{i}[x_k - \langle x \rangle], \qquad\qquad i = 1, 2, \ldots, N \qquad (1)$$

The whole length of the signal (N) is divided into N_s number of segments consists of certain number of samples (s).

$$N_s = int(\frac{N}{s}) \qquad (2)$$

The local RMS variation for any sample size s is the function $F(s, \nu)$. This function can be written as follows:

$$F^2(s, \nu) = \frac{1}{s}\sum_{i=1}^{N_s}\{Y[(\nu - 1)s + i] - y_\nu(i)\}^2 \qquad (3)$$

Finally, the fluctuation function is defined as:

$$F_q(s) = \{\frac{1}{N_s}\sum_{\nu=1}^{N_s}F^2(s, \nu)\}^{\frac{1}{2}} \sim s^H \qquad (4)$$

Which is speculated to scale as s^H, where H is a non-negative value, named Hurst exponent. It determines the correlativity of $X(i)$. to generalize monofractal DFA to multifractal DFA, an inclusive fluctuation function is required. Here, scaling exponent is not just a constant; instead it is a function of a newly defined symmetric variable, q. Bringing q into the equation, expands the interpretation, from only different lengths of intervals to both small and large fluctuations, that in DFA where not clear. For MFDFA, the last step in DFA is changed to below:

$$F_q(s) = \{\frac{1}{N_s}\sum_{\nu=1}^{N_s}[F^2(s, \nu)]^{\frac{q}{2}}\}^{\frac{1}{q}} \sim s^{h(q)} \qquad (5)$$

As a result, MFDFA provides multiple magnifiers $(s^{h(q)})$ for each length (s) of intervals. q, which can be any real value, determines which fluctuations are $h(q)$ describing. In particular, when it is positive, $h(q)$ is describing periods of time with large fluctuations and vice versa.

To have a better description of the multifractality, the generalized Hurst exponent $h(q)$ of MFDFA is related to the classical scaling exponent $\tau(q)$ by the relation:

$$\tau(q) = qh(q) - 1 \qquad (6)$$

Then the singularity spectrum $f(\alpha)$, that is related to $\tau(q)$ via a Legendre transform is defined:

$$\alpha = \tau^{'}(q) \qquad (7)$$

and

$$f(\alpha) = q\alpha - \tau(q) \qquad (8)$$

Where α denotes the strength of a singularity spectrum or Holder exponent, and $f(\alpha)$ is the fractal dimension of a pointset with particular α. The wealth of multifractality is evaluated by the width of its spectrum:

$$\Delta\alpha = \alpha_{max} - \alpha_{min} \tag{9}$$

In this study vectors of $h(q), \tau(q)$ and $f(\alpha)$ were features with the length of 100. So, we have a $32 * 19 * 3 \times 100$ feature matrix A. Next, the calculated degrees of auto-regression that were 6 for $hq, 3$ for αq and 3 for $f(\alpha)$ formed features of matrix B.

$$h(q) = A_h + B_h q + C_h q^2 + D_h q^3 + E_h q^4 + F_h q^5 \tag{10}$$
$$\tau(q) = A_\tau + B_\tau q + C_\tau q^2 \tag{11}$$
$$f(\alpha) = A_f + B_f \alpha + C_f \alpha^2 \tag{12}$$

As there are $19 * 12$ features for every participant, we ended up a matrix of size $32 \times (19 * (6 + 3 + 3)) = 32 \times 228$.

Feature Selection and Classification. Only the most important columns of feature matrices were selected by SVM method, introduced by Vapnik [11], to be classified as being ADHD or normal.

3   Results

Once two feature matrices A and B were calculated, SVM feature selection algorithm chose 13 features for method A and 7 features for method B. Table 2 presents contributing channels along with associated regions of the brain for auto-regression method (B), and important channels found by spectrum of value method (A) plus respective q values and the corresponding accuracy.

4   Discussion

The result of this study is interpreted in three categories: accuracy, crucial regions and fractal characteristics.

Accuracy. Two visual measures to plot multifractality are the broader singularity width along with less linear classical scaling exponent [4]. Both these indicators are evident in Fig. 1. It illustrates multi-fractal spectrum $[f(\alpha)$ vs $\alpha]$ and exponent function spectrum $[\tau(q)$ vs $q]$ for data acquired from channel 16, as this channel is the boldest channel in the selected features. The top row shows the spectrum of each participant independently, whereas the bottom row plots are the average of each. Normal subjects (blue lines) in a and c show a broader width; and ADHD subjects (red lines) show a less linear curve in b and d. $f(\alpha)$ and τ_q, could distinguish the study groups quite reliably, 97% and 94% accuracy by method A and B respectively. And these findings are significant in both methods, as both P-values were less than 0.001 for a test of the null hypothesis that the groups are not distinguishable.

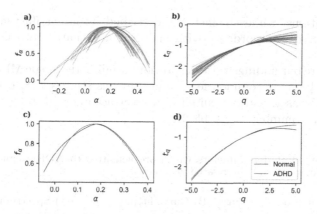

Fig. 1. Left) Multifractal spectrum [$f(\alpha)$ vs α] and Right) exponent function spectrum [$\tau(q)$ vs q] for channel 16 of EEG, the salient channel in discriminating groups. In figures, a, and b the spectrum of each participant has been shown independently (all 32 subjects), in figures c and d the average of each class has been plotted

Regions. The contributing regions in classification task were P4 in parietal cortex and FP2 in frontal cortex, which were mapped from channel 16 and 2 [6]. Interestingly, physiological, anatomical and biochemical dysfunctions within these parts of cortex circuits have been explicitly (via neuroimaging) and implicitly (via behavioral studies) shown to be associated with ADHD [10], and this result clearly supports both the parietal and the frontal lobe theories of ADHD.

Table 1. Main features of MFDFA and their significant properties. MF: multifractal

Features	Multifractality	Correlations
H	$h_q(q = 2)$	$0 < H < 0.5$ long-range anti-correlated
		$H = 0.5$ uncorrelated
		$0.5 < H < 1$ long-range correlated
h_q	$q > 0$	Larger $h(q)$ in large fluctuations
	$q < 0$	Smaller $h(q)$ in small fluctuations
$\tau(q)$		The more linear, the les MF
$f(\alpha)$	$f(\alpha)$ inverted parabola	The wider, the more MF
$\Delta\alpha = \alpha_{max} - \alpha_{min}$	Multifractality index	The more, the more MF

Fractality. What this study adds to our understanding of the parietal and the frontal lobe theories of ADHD, is the EEG fluctuations difference in these regions. As in Table 2, q, manifests two completely distinguishable behaviors for each of the selected regions. Channel 16 always appears with the negative q, mostly around -4, while channel 2 mostly is along with positive q, roughly 2 (Table 2). This means that in channel 16 and 2, two different types of fluctuations are affected by ADHD (correlations of h(q) in Table 1). The first one is revealing small fluctuations, while channel 2 is described by larger fluctuations. These findings are also in accordance with multifractality nature of the variation in ADHD signals [8].

To compare our findings with the previous studies, the single MFDFA feature, $\Delta\alpha$, that is the most common feature in previous studies [5,8] is evaluated on the existing dataset, which resulted in a lower accuracy (65.6%), but the same crucial channel, number 16 (Table 2).

Table 2. The selected parameters which are sensitive to ADHD conditions for all categories of features and the related accuracy

C) Previous method			Curve	B) Curve fitting				A) Spectrum of value			
Selected features		Acc%		Selected features			Acc%	Selected features			Acc%
Para	Ch			EEG	Ch	Coeff		Spect	Ch	q	
$\Delta(\alpha)$	16	65.6	$f(\alpha)$	P4	16	A_f	96.8	hq	16	−3.713	94.3
				Pz	15	A_f			2	4.208	
				C4	11	C_f			16	−3.812	
				F3	4	A_f			5	4.109	
				Cz	10	B_f			16	−3.91	
			τq	Pz	16	A_t			2	3.911	
									16	−3.614	
								τq	16	−3.713	
									2	4.406	
			hq	Fz	5	A_h			16	−3.812	
								$f(\alpha)$	16	−1.733	
								α	16	−2.327	
									2	1.931	

5 Conclusion

Two accurate and simple pipelines were suggested for applying three nonlinear features of MFDFA technique (q-order Hurst exponent, classical scaling exponent and singularity spectrum) to discriminate ADHD versus healthy children of age 7–13. The accuracies of 97% and 94% has been achieved by these methods respectively. Furthermore, not only did the study show that channel 16 and channel 2 are the most important ones in differentiating ADHD from normal children, but it also illustrates significant differences in their fluctuations. The future step of this study could be a comparative investigation of these two channels, in terms of fractal properties and biological functionality. Signals recorded by channel 16 (P4 region) present large fluctuations, while those of recorded by channel 2 (FP2 region) are affected by small fluctuations. This result differentiates between the contribution of parietal lobe and frontal lobe, that have been proved to be involved in causing ADHD. Another instrumental role of this study was to find polynomials coefficients to fit calculus curves on fractal products in ADHD diagnosis.

Acknowledgment. We would like to thank the staff of Behju clinic for their assistance with the collection of data.

References

1. Danielson, M.L., Bitsko, R.H., Ghandour, R.M., Holbrook, J.R., Kogan, M.D., Blumberg, S.J.: Prevalence of parent-reported ADHD diagnosis and associated treatment among U.S. children and adolescents, 2016. J. Clin. Child Adolesc. Psychol. **47**(2), 199–212 (2018). https://doi.org/10.1080/15374416.2017.1417860
2. Delorme, A., et al.: EEGLAB, SIFT, NFT, BCILAB, and ERICA: new tools for advanced EEG processing. Comput. Intell. Neurosci. **2011**, 130714 (2011)
3. Elder, T.E.: The importance of relative standards in ADHD diagnoses: evidence based on exact birth. J. Chem. Inf. Model. **53**(9), 1689–1699 (2013). https://doi.org/10.1017/CBO9781107415324.004
4. Kantelhardt, J.W., et al.: Multifractal detrended fluctuation analysis of nonstationary time series. Physica A Stat. Mech. Appl. **316**(1–4), 87–114 (2002)
5. Khoshnoud, S., Nazari, M.A., Shamsi, M.: Functional brain dynamic analysis of ADHD and control children using nonlinear dynamical features of EEG signals. J. Integr. Neurosci. **17**(1), 17–30 (2018). https://doi.org/10.3233/JIN-170033
6. Klem, G.H., Lüders, H.O., Jasper, H.H., Elger, C.: The ten-twenty electrode system of the international federation. The international federation of clinical neurophysiology. Electroencephalogr. Clin. Neurophysiol. **Suppl. 52**, 3–6 (1999)
7. Kumar, D., Arjunan, S.P., Aliahmad, B.: Fractals: Applications in Biological Signalling and Image Processing. CRC Press, Boca Raton (2017)
8. Labra-Spröhnle, F., et al.: Predictive Modelling of The Dynamic Patterns of Thinking in Attention-Deficit/Hyperactivity Disorder: Diagnostic Accuracy of Spatiotemporal Fractal Measures. bioRxiv, p. 420513 (2018). https://doi.org/10.1101/420513
9. Thomas, R., Mitchell, G.K., Batstra, L.: Attention-deficit/hyperactivity disorder: are we helping or harming? BMJ **347**, f6172 (2013). https://doi.org/10.1136/bmj.f6172
10. Ting, W., Guozheng, Y., Banghua, Y.: EEG feature extraction in brain computer interface based on wavelet packet decomposition. Chin. J. Sci. Instrum. **28**(12), 2230 (2007)
11. Vapnik, V.: The Nature of Statistical Learning Theory. Springer, New York (2013). https://doi.org/10.1007/978-1-4757-3264-1

Recursive Maximum Correntropy Criterion Based Randomized Recurrent Broad Learning System

Yinuo Wang[1(✉)], Yu Guo[2], and Fei Wang[1]

[1] College of Artificial Intelligence, Xi'an Jiaotong University, Xi'an, China
wynkingdom@stu.xjtu.edu.cn, wfx@mail.xjtu.edu.cn
[2] School of Software Engineering, Xi'an Jiaotong University, Xi'an, China
yu.guo@xjtu.edu.cn

Abstract. Recurrent broad learning system (RBLS) is an effective way for complex dynamic system modeling. However, the typical RBLS is optimized under the minimum mean square error criterion, which is sensitive to large outliers and impulsive noise. Furthermore, the auto-encoder RBLS uses needs pre-training, making it's impossible for RBLS to be used in online learning tasks.

In this paper, we propose an efficient robust randomized RBLS for online learning. In this method, we adopt randomly weighted networks as input feature extracting part, while random recurrent network with sparsely connected nodes as dynamic characteristics capturing part. Recursive maximum correntropy criterion is used to enhance the robustness of randomized RBLS for online learning. With the randomized structure and online robust learning method, the system can be updated efficiently and shows better performance against the outliers and impulsive noise.

Keywords: Randomized · Recurrent broad learning system · Time series · Recursive maximum correntropy criterion · Robustness

1 Introduction

Time series prediction aims to predict the future observations of a dynamic system using the historical data collected from the system. Due to the development of neural networks (NNs), especially deep neural networks, many methods based on NNs have been used on time series prediction. Though deep NNs are powerful, they suffer from time-consuming training process, gradient explosion or

This work is partially supported by the National Key Research and Development Program of China under grant number 2017YFC0803905, National Major Science and Technology Projects of China under grant number 2019ZX01008103, the program of introducing talents of discipline to university B13043 and the Fundamental Research Funds for the Central Universities.

H. Yang et al. (Eds.): ICONIP 2020, CCIS 1333, pp. 804–812, 2020.
https://doi.org/10.1007/978-3-030-63823-8_91

vanishing and being trapped in local optimums due to their deep structures and the gradient-based learning algorithms.

Random vector functional link networks (RVFLNs) are proposed to overcome the drawbacks of traditional NNs. RVFLN is a multi-layer perceptron (MLP), of which only the output weights are adaptable parameters, while the remaining parameters are fixed random values independently generated in advance [6]. This allows RVFLN to use linear regression to analytically determine the output weights. Compared with traditional NN learning algorithms like backpropagation, many RVFLNs such as extreme learning machine [5] and broad learning system [3], have achieved a much faster learning speed and obtained better generalization performance.

The RVFLNs discussed above can only map the static relations between inputs and outputs, when used in time series prediction, sliding window method is often adopted. The window size of this method is a hyper-parameter that cannot be trained, which makes the network hard to tune. This often leads to a less satisfying result. Some random networks with internal feedback such as echo state network (ESN) [7] and recurrent broad learning system (RBLS) [12] are proposed to avoid such drawback. Though RBLS achieves better results in time series analysis, the sparse auto-encoder (SAE) it uses makes it unsuitable for online learning tasks.

The methods discussed above are based on mean square error criterion, which is sensitive to outliers and performs badly in non-Gaussian situations. In recent years, advance in information theoretic learning (ITL) yields maximum correntropy criterion (MCC) [9]. Correntropy is a nonlinear and local similarity measure that is insensitive to outliers [1,2]. Due to its simplicity and robustness, MCC has drawn increasing attention and has been successfully applied to various tasks [8,10], including time series analysis [4,11].

In this work, we use sparse reservoirs of ESNs as the enhancement nodes in RBLS. The feature nodes are also randomly weighted networks instead of SAEs. We name this system randomized RBLS, which demands less computational resources than typical RBLS due to its randomness and sparseness and doesn't require pre-training. Then we use a recursive MCC (RMCC) to enhance the robustness of randomized RBLS. In this way, the RBLS obtains the merit of online learning and the insensitivity to the outliers for sequential data analysis.

The rest of this paper is organized as follows. In Sect. 2, the details of recursive MCC based randomized RBLS (randomized RBLS-RMC) are given. In Sect. 3, we present experiment results, then in Sect. 4, conclusions are drawn.

2 Randomized Recurrent Broad Learning System Based on Recursive Maximum Correntropy

2.1 Randomized Recurrent Broad Learning System

The structure of randomized RBLS is shown in Fig. 1. Randomized RBLS consists of input, feature nodes, enhancement nodes, and output. The input is first mapped to feature nodes, which are then concatenated as the input of enhancement nodes. Finally, the feature nodes and the enhancement nodes are concatenated and connected to the output.

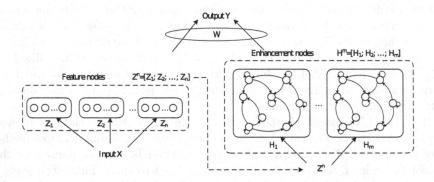

Fig. 1. Structure of randomized RBLS

The n feature nodes are generated as

$$Z_i(t) = \phi_i(W_{ei}^{\mathrm{T}}X(t) + \beta_{ei}), \ i = 1, 2, \dots, n \tag{1}$$

where $Z_i(t) \in \mathbb{R}^{k_i \times 1}$ is the i th group of feature node at time t, while $X(t) \in \mathbb{R}^{M \times 1}$ is the input vector at time t. W_{ei} and β_{ei} are randomly generated, and ϕ_i is tanh activation function. The concatenated feature nodes are denoted as $Z^n(t) = [Z_1(t); Z_2(t); \dots; Z_n(t)] \in \mathbb{R}^{(\sum_{i=1}^{n} k_i) \times 1}$.

Then the m enhancement nodes are generated in a recurrent way as

$$H_j(t) = \xi_j(W_{hj}^{\mathrm{T}}Z^n(t) + W_{xj}^{\mathrm{T}}H_j(t-1)), \ j = 1, \dots, m \tag{2}$$

where $H_j(t) \in \mathbb{R}^{p_j \times 1}$ is the j group of enhancement node at time t. W_{hj} and W_{xj} are randomly generated and ξ_j is sigmoid activation function. The concatenated feature nodes are denoted as $H^m(t) = [H_1(t); H_2(t); \dots; H_m(t)] \in \mathbb{R}^{(\sum_{j=1}^{m} p_j) \times 1}$. Note that the enhancement nodes are reservoirs of ESNs. The recurrent connections W_{xj} in reservoir are sparse with a lot of zeros. Such structure can reduce the computational complexity compared with a fully connected recurrent one.

Finally, the feature nodes and the enhancement nodes are concatenated and the output is calculated as

$$Y(t) = W^{\mathrm{T}}[Z^n(t); H^m(t)] = W^{\mathrm{T}}A(t). \tag{3}$$

2.2 Recursive Maximum Correntropy

Correntropy is a nonlinear and local similarity measure between two random variables X and Y, which is defined by

$$V(X,Y) = E_{XY}[\kappa(X,Y)] = \iint \kappa(X,Y)p_{X,Y}(x,y)\mathrm{d}x\mathrm{d}y \tag{4}$$

where $\kappa(\cdot, \cdot)$ is a kernel function satisfying Mercers theory, and $p_{X,Y}(x, y)$ denotes the joint PDF of X and Y. In practice, however, the joint PDF of X and Y is usually unknown, and the amount of samples can be used is limited. We use

$$\hat{V}(X, Y) = \frac{1}{N} \sum_{i=1}^{N} \kappa(x_i, y_i) \tag{5}$$

to estimate correntropy instead, where x_i and y_i are samples of X and Y.

In this work, we use correntropy with Gaussian kernel as training criterion. Concretely, we optimize the output weights of the randomized RBLS by maximizing the correntropy recursively, which is called recursive maximum correntropy. The weighted regularized cost function with an exponentially weighted mechanism is defined as

$$J = \max_{\boldsymbol{W}_t} \sum_{j=1}^{t} \beta^{t-j} G_\sigma(d_j - \boldsymbol{W}_t^{\mathrm{T}} \boldsymbol{A}_j) - \frac{1}{2} \beta^t \gamma \|\boldsymbol{W}_t\|^2 \tag{6}$$

where β is the forgetting factor, which can put more weight on recent data and less on past data. γ is the regularization factor and G_σ is Gaussian kernel. The desired output at time j is denoted as d_j, the output weights of randomized RBLS is denoted as $\boldsymbol{W}_t$ and the concatenated feature at time j is $\boldsymbol{A}_j$.

Setting the gradient of J with respect to $\boldsymbol{W}_t$ as zero, we can obtain the solution to $\boldsymbol{W}_t$ as follows,

$$\boldsymbol{W}_t = [\sum_{j=1}^{t} \beta^{t-j} \boldsymbol{A}_j \boldsymbol{A}_j^{\mathrm{T}} e_j + \sigma^2 \beta^t \gamma \boldsymbol{I}]^{-1} [\sum_{j=1}^{t} \beta^{t-j} \boldsymbol{A}_j d_j e_j] = \boldsymbol{R}_D^{-1}(t) \boldsymbol{P}_D(t) \tag{7}$$

where $\boldsymbol{P}_D(t) = \sum_{j=1}^{t} \beta^{t-j} \boldsymbol{A}_j d_j e_j$, $\boldsymbol{R}_D(t) = \sum_{j=1}^{t} \beta^{t-j} \boldsymbol{A}_j \boldsymbol{A}_j^{\mathrm{T}} e_j + \sigma^2 \beta^t \gamma \boldsymbol{I}$ and $e_j = \exp(-(d_j - \boldsymbol{W}_t^{\mathrm{T}} \boldsymbol{A}_j)/(2\sigma^2))$. Considering that $\boldsymbol{W}_t$ will not change significantly after one iteration, we can replace $\boldsymbol{W}_t$ with $\boldsymbol{W}_{t-1}$, yielding a recursive form of $\boldsymbol{R}_D(t)$ and $\boldsymbol{P}_D(t)$ as follows,

$$\begin{aligned} \boldsymbol{R}_D(t) &= \beta \boldsymbol{R}_D(t-1) + \boldsymbol{A}_t \boldsymbol{A}_t^{\mathrm{T}} \exp(-\frac{(d_t - \boldsymbol{W}_{t-1}^{\mathrm{T}} \boldsymbol{A}_t)^2}{2\sigma^2}) \\ \boldsymbol{P}_D(t) &= \beta \boldsymbol{P}_D(t-1) + \boldsymbol{A}_t d_t \exp(-\frac{(d_t - \boldsymbol{W}_{t-1}^{\mathrm{T}} \boldsymbol{A}_t)^2}{2\sigma^2}) \end{aligned} \tag{8}$$

We use matrix inversion lemma to compute $\boldsymbol{R}_D^{-1}(t)$, yielding

$$\boldsymbol{S}_D(t) = \boldsymbol{R}_D^{-1}(t) = \frac{1}{\beta} \left[\boldsymbol{S}_D(t-1) - \frac{\boldsymbol{S}_D(t-1) \boldsymbol{A}_t \boldsymbol{A}_t^{\mathrm{T}} \boldsymbol{S}_D(t-1)}{\boldsymbol{A}_t^{\mathrm{T}} \boldsymbol{S}_D(t-1) \boldsymbol{A}_t + \beta \exp(-\frac{(d_t - \boldsymbol{W}_{t-1}^{\mathrm{T}} \boldsymbol{A}_t)^2}{2\sigma^2})} \right]. \tag{9}$$

Based on (8) and (9), the procedure of randomized RBLS-RMC is summarized in Algorithm 1.

Algorithm 1: Recursive Maximum Correntropy Based Randomized Recurrent Broad Learning System

---
Input: $X(j)$, d_j
Output: W_t
1 **Initialization:** $S_D(0) = \frac{1}{\gamma\sigma^2}I$, $P_D(0) = [0, 0, \ldots, 0]^T$, $W_0 = [0, 0, \ldots, 0]^T$;
2 **while** $t \geq 1$ **do**
3   Calculate the output of randomized RBLS according to (1)(2)(3);
4   Update $S_D(t)$ according to (9);
5   Update $P_D(t)$ according to (8);
6   Update W_t according to (7);
7      $t = t + 1$;
8 **end**

---

3   Experiments

3.1   Experiment Setup

To evaluate the robustness of proposed method, outliers and noise added to training data are modeled using gross error model:

$$D_p = \{D|D = (1 - p)F + pG, 0 \leq p \leq 1\}, \tag{10}$$

where G and F are stochastic variables which occur with probabilities p and $1 - p$ respectively. In this experiment, F and G follow Gaussian distribution with standard deviation of 0.1 and 4 respectively, and $p = 0.35$. The performance is assessed by the root mean square error (RMSE) between the predicted signal $\hat{y}(t)$ and the target signal $y(t)$. All the experiments are conducted on a computer with Intel Core i5-8300H CPU and 16 GB RAM, and the results are averaged over 50 independent Monte Carlo runs.

The compared models are: BLS, ESN and RBLS. Recursive least square (RLS) is applied to ESN, RBLS and randomized RBLS. The network settings are listed in Table 1. Since the network size of the tested methods are the same, the difference in performance is due to network structures and training methods.

The hyper-parameters in RLS and RMC are decided using grid search. In RLS, we search for the forgetting factor β and the regularization factor γ. The search range for β is $\{0.01, 0.1, 1, 10, 100\}$. Since forgetting factor β is multiplied repeatedly, a small change might lead to a relatively great change of the result, so we use a two-step grid-search to find β. First, we narrow it down to $[0.990, 1.000]$, then we use grid search to decide $\beta = 0.997$. As for RMC, the kernel size $\sigma = 0.2$ is selected based on experience, and the forgetting factor β as well as the regularization factor γ are selected the same as those in RLS.

The compared models are tested in the following tasks.

Chaotic Time Series Prediction: Mackey-Glass time series, as a widely used benchmark task for nonlinear dynamic system modeling, is generated by

$$\frac{\mathrm{d}x}{\mathrm{d}y} = ax(t) + \frac{bx(t - \tau)}{1 + x(t - \tau)^{10}} \tag{11}$$

Table 1. Parameter settings in evaluated models

Method	Settings
ESN	Reservoir size: 500
	Spectral radius: 0.95
	Sparsity: 0.5
BLS	Feature nodes: 20 nodes per group × 4 groups
	Enhancement nodes: 200 nodes per group × 2 groups
	Window size: 5
RBLS	Feature nodes: 20 nodes per group × 4 groups
	Enhancement nodes: 200 nodes per group × 2 groups
Randomized RBLS	Feature nodes: 20 nodes per group × 4 groups
	Enhancement nodes: 200 nodes per group × 2 groups
	Spectral radius: 0.95
	Sparsity: 0.5

where $x(t)$ denotes the state signal at time step t. The parameters in (11) is selected as $a = -0.1$, $b = 0.2$, $\tau = 17$, and $x(0) = 1.2$. The goal is to predict the state signal $x(t+1)$ using historical information. The length of contaminated training sample is 2000, and the length of clean testing sample is 1000.

Nonlinear Dynamic System Identification: The nonlinear dynamic system [13] is given as

$$y(k+1) = 0.72y(k) + 0.025y(k-1)u(k-1) + 0.01u^2(k-2) + 0.2u(k-3), \quad (12)$$

where $u(k)$ is the control signal and $y(k)$ is the output signal. The training data are generated with $u(k) = 1.05\sin(k/5)$, $y(1) = y(2) = y(3) = y(4) = 0$. 1000 contaminated samples are used as training data. The test data are generated with $u(k)$ as follows,

$$u(k) = \begin{cases} \sin(\pi k/25), & 0 < k < 250 \\ 1.0, & 250 \le k < 500 \\ -1.0, & 500 \le k < 750 \\ 0.6\sin(\pi k/10) + 0.1\sin(\pi k/32) + 0.3\sin(\pi k/25) & 750 \le k < 1000. \end{cases}$$
$$(13)$$

1000 clean samples are chosen as testing data. The goal is to build an identification model of system equation (12). The input of the system is $x(k) = [y(k), u(k)]$, and the output is $y(k+1)$.

3.2   Experiment Results

Table 2 shows the RMSE of the prediction results of different methods. It can be observed that in an environment with noise and large outliers, our proposed randomized RBLS-RMC can obtain better performance in testing errors.

Table 2. Comparison of RMSE on Mackey-Glass series prediction and system identification with noise and outliers

Method		ESN	BLS	RBLS	ESN-RLS	RBLS-RLS	Randomized RBLS-RLS	**Randomized RBLS-RMC**
Macky-Glass series prediction	Avg.	1.1501E-1	1.0146E-1	1.2293E-1	1.4384E-1	8.8856E-2	8.9249E-2	**4.5000E-2**
	Std.	3.1352E-2	2.0237E-2	2.1263E-2	3.6302E-2	3.0783E-2	2.8553E-2	**1.5180E-3**
Nonlinear dynamic system identification	Avg.	6.7881E-1	5.4590E-1	8.5652E-1	1.7944E-1	1.2203E-1	1.1501E-1	**3.5904E-2**
	Std.	2.3386E-1	2.6596E-2	3.1802E-1	6.4102E-2	5.3002E-2	5.0727E-2	**8.7807E-3**

The convergence curves of different algorithms are presented in Fig. 2, and the prediction and error curves are presented in Fig. 3. It can be seen that randomized RBLS trained with RMC outperforms other algorithms with faster convergence speed while keeping lower RMSE.

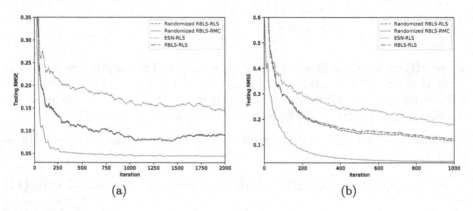

(a)   (b)

Fig. 2. Convergence curves of different algorithms for (a) Mackey-Glass time series prediction with noise and outliers and (b) nonlinear dynamic system identification with noise and outliers

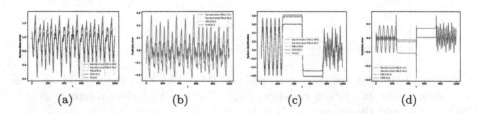

(a)   (b)   (c)   (d)

Fig. 3. Prediction and error curve of different algorithms for Mackey-Glass time series prediction with noise and outliers and nonlinear dynamic system identification with noise and outliers

Furthermore, due to the sparseness of our proposed model, the inference time is reduced compared with RBLS [12]. In time series prediction and system identification, the inference time is reduced from 0.9 s to 0.5 s, indicating our proposed model demands less computational resources.

4 Conclusion

In this paper, we propose a recursive maximum correntropy based randomized recurrent broad learning system, called randomized RBLS-RMC. The randomly weighted structure enables fast extracting both spatial and temporal features of time series, and the RMC algorithm improves the robustness of the randomized RBLS while enabling the online learning capacity of the model. Experiment results show that randomized RBLS-RMC can achieve better performance against the outliers and impulsive noise.

References

1. Chen, B., Wang, J., Zhao, H., Zheng, N., Príncipe, J.C.: Convergence of a fixed-point algorithm under maximum correntropy criterion. IEEE Sig. Process. Lett. **22**(10), 1723–1727 (2015)
2. Chen, B., Xing, L., Liang, J., Zheng, N., Principe, J.C.: Steady-state mean-square error analysis for adaptive filtering under the maximum correntropy criterion. IEEE Sig. Process. Lett. **21**(7), 880–884 (2014)
3. Chen, C.P., Liu, Z.: Broad learning system: an effective and efficient incremental learning system without the need for deep architecture. IEEE Trans. Neural Netw. Learn. Syst. **29**(1), 10–24 (2017)
4. Guo, Y., Wang, F., Chen, B., Xin, J.: Robust echo state networks based on correntropy induced loss function. Neurocomputing **267**, 295–303 (2017)
5. Huang, G.B., Zhu, Q.Y., Siew, C.K., et al.: Extreme learning machine: a new learning scheme of feedforward neural networks. Neural Netw. **2**, 985–990 (2004)
6. Husmeier, D.: Neural Networks for Conditional Probability Estimation: Forecasting Beyond Point Predictions. Springer, London (2012). https://doi.org/10.1007/978-1-4471-0847-4
7. Jaeger, H.: The "echo state" approach to analysing and training recurrent neural networks-with an erratum note. GMD Rep. **148**(34), 13 (2001). German National Research Center for Information Technology GMD Technical Report, Bonn, Germany
8. Li, M., Huang, C., Wang, D.: Robust stochastic configuration networks with maximum correntropy criterion for uncertain data regression. Inf. Sci. **473**, 73–86 (2019)
9. Liu, W., Pokharel, P.P., Príncipe, J.C.: Correntropy: properties and applications in non-Gaussian signal processing. IEEE Trans. Sig. Process. **55**(11), 5286–5298 (2007)
10. Qi, Y., Wang, Y., Zheng, X., Wu, Z.: Robust feature learning by stacked autoencoder with maximum correntropy criterion. In: 2014 IEEE International Conference on Acoustics, Speech and Signal Processing (ICASSP), pp. 6716–6720. IEEE (2014)
11. Wu, Z., Shi, J., Zhang, X., Ma, W., Chen, B.: Kernel recursive maximum correntropy. Sig. Process. **117**, 11–16 (2015)

12. Xu, M., Han, M., Chen, C.P., Qiu, T.: Recurrent broad learning systems for time series prediction. IEEE Trans. Cybern. **50**, 1405–1417 (2018)
13. Yang, C., Qiao, J., Han, H., Wang, L.: Design of polynomial echo state networks for time series prediction. Neurocomputing **290**, 148–160 (2018)

Time and Incentive-Aware Neural Networks for Life Insurance Premium Prediction

Xinrui Li, Liang Zhao, Xi Yin$^{(\boxtimes)}$, Yinxin Zhu, Jianping Shen, and Wei Tong

Ping An Life Insurance Company of China, Ltd., Futian, Shenzhen, China
{lixinrui598,zhaoliang425,yinxi445,zhuyinxin903,shenjianping324,
tongwei002}@pingan.com.cn

Abstract. Life insurance premium analysis is significant because it can assess the market conditions and formulate development strategies for the companies. However, this task is less explored, because it is too difficult to capture the intricacy of life insurance products and it is highly influenced by both regulatory policies and social welfare. By thoroughly examining the life insurance premium gained by all insurance companies in China from 2001 to 2019, we find that the premium is greatly affected by two factors, time and the incentive mechanism that yields the "Good-Start" phenomenon. We, therefore, propose a novel Time and Incentive-aware Long-Short-Term-Memory (LSTM-TI) network to exploit the effectiveness of LSTM in modeling highly non-linear sequential data while incorporating the time effect and the incentive signals essentially. Empirical evaluation on the dataset shows that our LSTM-TI model attains significantly better performance than the strong baseline methods.

Keywords: Insurance premium prediction · "Good-Start" · LSTM

1 Introduction

Life insurance premium analysis is of practical importance because it can assess the market conditions and formulate development strategies for life insurance companies [1]. The analysis can also provide regulatory authorities with prospective information, which helps to conduct pro-cyclical regulations for developing stable and healthy insurance markets [2].

Recently, only several pieces of research, e.g., autoregressive integrated moving average (ARIMA), or seasonal ARIMA (SARIMA) [3] and Hodrick–Prescott (HP) filtering [4], have been exploited to analyze the seasonal fluctuations of insurance premium. However, ARIMA and SARIMA can only model the linear relationships in the data, while HP filtering is limited to analyzing purely historical and static time series data in a closed domain. Generally, the exploration

---

X. Li and L. Zhao—make equal contributions to this work under the guidance of H. Yang.

H. Yang et al. (Eds.): ICONIP 2020, CCIS 1333, pp. 813–821, 2020.
https://doi.org/10.1007/978-3-030-63823-8_92

of life insurance premium is inadequate [5] because the life insurance products are usually designed with complex premium calculation mechanisms. This makes the premium prediction very difficult.

In this paper, by carefully analyzing the monthly premium of all life insurance companies in China from 2001 to 2019[1], we observe that the "Good-Start" phenomenon, a large amount of life insurance policies sold in January of each year, appears since 2013. By further investigating the underlying reasons, we understand that this phenomenon is caused by the incentive mechanism, i.e., relatively high price discounts, sales commission, and channel commission.

To model the "Good-Start" phenomenon, we propose a novel Time and Incentive-aware LSTM model, namely LSTM-TI. LSTM-TI extends a vanilla LSTM by converting the month(time) information into the month(time) embedding and including the incentive mechanism through a switching gate. By only considering the absolute time information, we can derive the LSTM-T model accordingly.

We highlight our contributions as follows:

- We are the first to effectively model the "Good-Start" phenomenon by deep neural networks for life insurance premium prediction.
- We propose a flexible framework named LSTM-TI, which not only exploits the power of the vanilla LSTM in capturing non-linear sequential data, but also elegantly integrates an absolute time feature and an incentive switch.
- By conducting adequate experiments on the monthly premium data from 2001 to 2019, we demonstrate that our proposed LSTM-TI model can significantly reduce the prediction errors compared to strong baseline methods.

2   Related Work

2.1   Time Series Forecasting by Deep Neural Networks

Deep neural networks (DNN) have been introduced to model non-linearity among data due to their effective data representations [6]. Several pieces of related work have been proposed to investigate the financial data [7,12]. As an early attempt to model the asset price movement, DNN has demonstrated strong evidence against the Efficient Market Hypothesis (EMH) [8]. Later, LSTM has been widely employed in time-series prediction [9,11] as well as in financial data analytics [12]. The vanilla LSTM is adopted to predict the monthly premium of life insurance in China [13]. However, the existing studies overlook the unique characteristics of life insurance premium, e.g., the "Good-Start" phenomenon.

2.2   Research on the "Good-Start" Phenomenon

The "Good-Start" phenomenon has been mainly investigated in qualitative research [2,14,15]. Some researchers target at analyzing the deficiencies of

---

[1] https://www.wind.com.cn/NewSite/edb.html.

the phenomenon [14], while others focus on exploring the impact of the phenomenon [2] and the corresponding regulation policies [15]. Currently, only a piece of work on quantitative research [16] is proposed to study this phenomenon by SARIMA. However, SARIMA can only model the linear data relationships and cannot explain the impact of "Good-Start" from the business perspective.

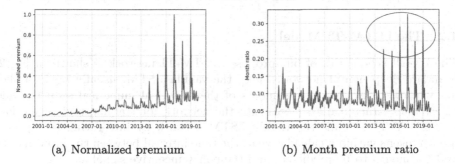

(a) Normalized premium   (b) Month premium ratio

Fig. 1. An illustration of (a) the total premium from all life insurance companies in China from 2001 to 2019 normalized by the overall max-min normalization and (b) the month premium to the total premium in the corresponding year.

3   Data and the Characteristics

We crawl available life insurance data, the gross premium of all life insurance companies of China from 2001 to 2019. Figure 1 illustrates the trend of the data and shows that the insurance premium contains two significant characteristics:

- The premium changes in an annual cycle with an overall upward trend, and depends strongly on the specific month. See Fig. 1a for an illustration.
- The premium is highly affected by the policy incentives, as demonstrated by the "Good-Start" phenomenon appearing significantly after 2013. In Fig. 1b, there are several noticeable spikes after 2013, which shows that a large amount, over 30%, of life insurance policies are sold in January of each year.

The fluctuation of the premium reveals the difficulty of the prediction task, which cannot be directly resolved by the existing deep neural networks.

4   Our Proposal

In this section, we first define the task formulation. After that, we present our proposed Time and Incentive-aware LSTM (LSTM-TI) model.

4.1   Task Formulation

Premium prediction can be formulated as a regression task, or a task of time series prediction, which can be defined as follows: Given a set of training data, $\{x_i, y_i\}_{i=1}^N$, where $x_i \in \mathbb{R}^d$ usually takes d components, or premiums of the last d months, and N is the number of the training samples. The objective is to learn a mapping function $f(x)$, which predicts well for the future premium y.

4.2   The LSTM-TI Model

The overall schematics of our proposed LSTM-TI network is shown in Fig. 2. Standard deep neural networks, e.g., the vanilla LSTM, usually apply a sliding window to extract the segments of the historical numerical sequence and insert the extracted data pieces into the network for training and prediction. Our LSTM-TI extends the vanilla LSTM network by integrating the specific month tokens within a calendar year, the time interval between the input month and the month to be predicted, and the policy incentive signal as well.

The Vanilla LSTM Network. The vanilla LSTM network was first introduced by [10] via the gate mechanism to solve the notorious gradient exploding and vanishing issues faced in training the vanilla recurrent neural networks. A typical LSTM consists of three controlling gates: the forget gate f_t, the input gate i_t, and the output gate o_t, respectively; see the upper part in Fig. 2. These gates determine the information flow at the current time step. The mathematical cell representations can be given as follows:

$$c_t = f_t \odot c_{t-1} + i_t \odot \tilde{c} \tag{1}$$

$$h_t = o_t \odot \tanh(c_t), \tag{2}$$

where c_t and h_t represent the current cell state and hidden output, respectively. c_{t-1} is the last cell state, and $\tilde{c}$ is a variable shown in Fig. 2. $\odot$ indicates the element-wise multiplication.

The Absolute Month Feature. Since the vanilla LSTM cannot encode the absolute time instance of the input sequence, a critical factor for life insurance premium prediction, our LSTM-TI aims to add such features and provide complementary information. Thus, we add a time-instance state T_t in addition to the cell state and hidden state at each time step; see the bottom left component in Fig. 2. Specifically, we convert the absolute predicted month and the month interval between the predicted month and the current month into two embeddings, and combine them to create another gate g_t (termed time gate). The time gate is used to help selecting the input information relevant to the specific month to add to the time-instance state.

$$g_t = \sigma(W_m([EM(m_{tp} - m_t), EM(m_{tp})]) + b_m) \tag{3}$$

$$T_t = [(W_n(g_t \odot x_t) + b_n), T_{t-1}], \tag{4}$$

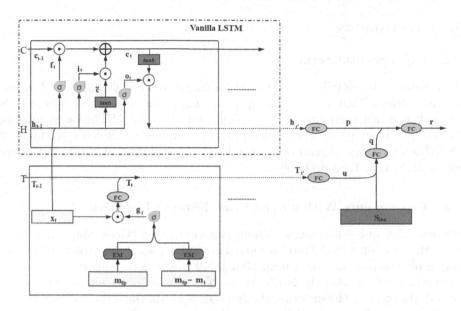

Fig. 2. The architecture of our LSTM-TI model. "FC" represents a fully-connected layer. "EM" represents embedding of a vector. tanh is the hyperbolic tangent activation function. σ defines the sigmoid function. $\oplus$ means vector sum and $\odot$ indicates the element-wise multiplication.

where x_t represents the current input, σ is the sigmoid function, and EM represents embedding of the month tokens. m_{tp} denotes the month to be predicted and m_t is the current month.

The Incentive Switch for Modeling the "Good-Start" Phenomenon. Another important component of LSTM-TI is to model the "Good-Start" by a policy incentive switch s_{inc}; see the orange box in Fig. 2. Suppose the month to be predicted is January, the switch is turned on to generate an incentive signal, simulating the "Good-Start" occurrence. For the rest of months without incentive, the switch is kept off. As another absolute month feature, this incentive signal is incorporated into the time-instance state of our model, see Eq. (5). Information accumulated from all time-instance states is merged with the hidden output at the last time step p to obtain the final prediction r as follows:

$$q = W_S([u, s_{inc}]) + d_s \tag{5}$$
$$r = W_r([p, q]) + d_r \tag{6}$$

The standard metric, Mean Square Error (MSE), is applied to measure the loss of the real premium r_i and the predicted premium $\hat{r}_i$ by our proposed LSTM-TI:

$$\text{MSE} = \frac{1}{k} \sum_{i=1}^{k} (r_i - \hat{r}_i)^2 \tag{7}$$

where k is the size of the training batch.

5   Experiments

5.1   Experimental Setup

We construct the paired data by the historical premium splitting in a 12-month sliding window. That is, $x_i = [p_i, p_{i+1}, \ldots, p_{i+12}]$ and $y_i = p_{i+13}$, where p_i is the i-th month's premium in the training set. For the LSTM-based models, ADAM [17] is adopted as the optimizer. The number of hidden layer units of LSTM is set to 64 and numbers of the five FC layer units, shown in Fig. 2, are set to 32, 8, 1, 1, 1, respectively.

5.2   Experiments Without the "Good-Start" Incentive

We first carry out experiments without considering the "Good-Start" incentive. Since the onset of "Good-Start" occurred in 2013, we set the splitting ratio to 3:1 and apply the premium data from 2001 to 2009 as the training data to predict the premium from 2010 to 2012. As no "Good-Start" was introduced in this period, this part of the experiments does not activate the incentive switch.

Figure 3(a) shows the predicted premium vs. the real premium:

- The vanilla LSTM network (the green dashed line) cannot follow the trend of the real premium well and yields a large MSE error of 8.5e−4.
- Our LSTM-T model (the magenta dotted line) follows the trend of the real premium more closely and yields a smaller MSE of 2.6e−4, 69% reduction, than the vanilla LSTM. More specifically, the vanilla LSTM's prediction lag in the beginning of each year fades away since LSTM-T absorbs the time feature effectively and reduces the dependence on the last month's premium.

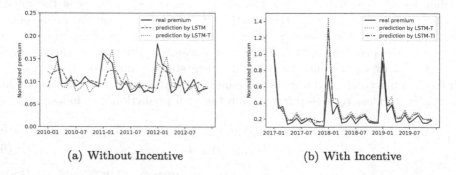

(a) Without Incentive   (b) With Incentive

Fig. 3. Comparisons of LSTM, LSTM-T, and LSTM-TI in the predicted period: (a) years without the "Good-Start" phenomenon (2010–2012) and (b) years with the "Good-Start" phenomenon (2017–2019).

5.3   Experiments on the "Good-Start" Incentive

Effect of the "Good-Start" incentive is investigated by training the premium from 2001 to 2016 and predicting the premium from 2017 to 2019. In other words, we include additional 4 years of the incentive signals (2013–2016) in the training data. Figure 3(b) shows the predicted premium vs. the real premium:

– Though LSTM-T (the magenta dotted line) demonstrates a strong prediction capability, it still yields a large MSE from December to February of each year, especially in 2018. This is due to the fact that LSTM-T cannot sufficiently capture the incentive signal and thus is difficult to accurately forecast the stimulus in January and the surrounding months.
– Remarkably, due to introduction of the incentive switch as well as the proper feature fusion design, our LSTM-TI (blue dash-dotted line) can predict the premium well around January of each year. The overall MSE has been further reduced from 1.87e−2 to 0.95e−2, 49% decrease, compared to LSTM-T.

5.4   Comparison with Traditional Algorithms

We compare LSTM-T and LSTM-TI with the vanilla LSTM and three traditional linear time-series prediction models, AR, ARIMA, and SARIMA. All the models are predicted in three representative years: 2012, 2016, and 2019. Here, 2012 is selected because it is the last year before the occurrence of the "Good-Start". We select 2019 for premium prediction because it is the most recent year while 2016 is selected because it is in the middle.

Table 1. The MSE comparison and the improvement percentage of our LSTM-TI model over its variants and three strong baselines for the years of 2012, 2016, and 2019. The order of magnitude of all MSE values is 10^{-4} due to data normalization.

Model	2012		2016		2019	
	MSE	LSTM-T improvement	MSE	LSTM-TI improvement	MSE	LSTM-TI improvement
LSTM	12.8	78%	289.9	93%	353.3	98%
LSTM-T	**2.8**	0	58.6	65%	14.8	51%
LSTM-TI	-	-	**20.3**	0	**7.3**	0
AR	4.0	30%	61.2	67%	27.2	73%
ARIMA	3.8	26%	81.3	75%	30.2	76%
SARIMA	**2.8**	0	34.5	41%	22.7	68%

Table 1 reports the overall results. We can observe that

– In 2012, without considering the "Good-Start" phenomenon, our LSTM-T and SARIMA attain the same minimum MSE. This shows the effectiveness of our proposal in including the month information.
– In 2016 and 2019, our proposed LSTM-TI yields 41% and 68% improvement over those of the best linear model, SARIMA. The gain is tremendous and demonstrates LSTM-TI is effective in absorbing the incentive information.

6   Conclusion

In this paper, we focus on the life insurance premium prediction and investigate the impact of incentive mechanisms, e.g., the "Good-Start" phenomenon, on the gross monthly premium of China. We propose a novel LSTM-based model to include the time and incentive information directly. Thorough experiments show that our LSTM-TI model significantly outperforms the strong baseline methods.

References

1. Swiss Re: World insurance in 1998: Deregulation, overcapacity and financial crises curb premium growth. Sigma No. 7/1999 (1998)
2. Huang, S.C., Yang, J.C.: Viewing "grey rhino" in insurance from the negative growth of "good start" in 2018. Taxpaying **10**, 195 (2018)
3. Schmidhuber, J.: Deep learning in neural networks: an overview. Neural Netw. **61**, 85–117 (2015)
4. Zhang, Y.C., Wang, Y.T., Wan, L.H.: A comparative study on insurance cycle and economic cycle in China. Insur. Stud. **6**, 40–47 (2016)
5. Wu, J., Su, F.: Cyclicity of nonlife insurance products and a comparative analysis of influencing factors - based on insurance cycles and underwriting cycle theory. Insur. Stud. **9**, 29–41 (2014)
6. Goodfellow, I., Bengio, Y., Courville, A.: Deep Learning. MIT Press, Cambridge (2016). http://www.deeplearningbook.org
7. Nikou, M., Mansourfar, G., Bagherzadeh, J.: Stock price prediction using deep learning algorithm and its comparison with machine learning algorithms. Int. Syst. Account. Financ. Manage. **26**(4), 164–174 (2019)
8. White, H.: Economic prediction using neural networks: the case of IBM daily stock returns. In: ICNN, vol. 2, pp. 451–458 (1988)
9. Brownlee, J.: Time series prediction with LSTM recurrent neural networks in Python with Keras, p. 18 (2016). machinelearningmastery.com
10. Hochreiter, S., Schmidhuber, J.: Long short-term memory. Neural Comput. **9**(8), 1735–1780 (1997)
11. Liu, W., Liu, W.D., Gu, J.: Forecasting oil production using ensemble empirical model decomposition based long short-term memory neural network. J. Petrol. Sci. Eng. **189**, 107013 (2020)
12. Cao, J., Li, Z., Li, J.: Financial time series forecasting model based on CEEMDAN and LSTM. Physica A Stat. Mech. Appl. **519**, 127139 (2019)
13. Diao, L., Wang, N.: Research on premium income prediction based on LSTM neural network. Adv. Soc. Sci. Res. J. **6**(11), 256–260 (2019)
14. Ren, B.T., Yun, Y.Q.: Phenomenon analysis of "good start" in Chinese life insurance companies. J. Insur. Prof. Coll. **31**(1), 28–30 (2017)
15. Wu, J.: The significant impact of file no. 134 on "good start" in 2018. China Insurance, vol. 1, p. 3 (2018)

16. Liu, Y.H.: Breakpoint analysis of life insurance premium time series based on SARIMA model. Collect. Essays Finan. Econ. **2**, 71–79 (2013)
17. Kingma, D.P., Ba, J.: Adam: a method for stochastic optimization. In: Bengio, Y., LeCun, Y. (eds.) 3rd International Conference on Learning Representations (Conference Track Proceedings), ICLR 2015, San Diego, CA, USA, 7–9 May 2015 (2015)

To Augment or Not to Augment? Data Augmentation in User Identification Based on Motion Sensors

Cezara Benegui and Radu Tudor Ionescu[✉]

University of Bucharest, 14 Academiei, Bucharest, Romania
cezara.benegui@fmi.unibuc.ro, raducu.ionescu@gmail.com

Abstract. Nowadays, commonly-used authentication systems for mobile device users, e.g. password checking, face recognition or fingerprint scanning, are susceptible to various kinds of attacks. In order to prevent some of the possible attacks, these explicit authentication systems can be enhanced by considering a two-factor authentication scheme, in which the second factor is an implicit authentication system based on analyzing motion sensor data captured by accelerometers or gyroscopes. In order to avoid any additional burdens to the user, the registration process of the implicit authentication system must be performed quickly, i.e. the number of data samples collected from the user is typically small. In the context of designing a machine learning model for implicit user authentication based on motion signals, data augmentation can play an important role. In this paper, we study several data augmentation techniques in the quest of finding useful augmentation methods for motion sensor data. We propose a set of four research questions related to data augmentation in the context of few-shot user identification based on motion sensor signals. We conduct experiments on a benchmark data set, using two deep learning architectures, convolutional neural networks and Long Short-Term Memory networks, showing which and when data augmentation methods bring accuracy improvements. Interestingly, we find that data augmentation is not very helpful, most likely because the signal patterns useful to discriminate users are too sensitive to the transformations brought by certain data augmentation techniques. This result is somewhat contradictory to the common belief that data augmentation is expected to increase the accuracy of machine learning models.

Keywords: Data augmentation · Signal processing · User authentication · Motion sensors · Deep neural networks

1 Introduction

Nowadays, mobile devices have become the most utilized digital devices in our daily activities, replacing personal computers. Usage of our personal devices and access to all applications require strong authentication systems. Albeit all mobile operating systems grant users the possibility to set up secure passwords,

© Springer Nature Switzerland AG 2020
H. Yang et al. (Eds.): ICONIP 2020, CCIS 1333, pp. 822–831, 2020.
https://doi.org/10.1007/978-3-030-63823-8_93

PINs or unlock patterns, it is well known that such protection mechanisms are not fully secure and are prone to physical attacks such as fingerprint attacks [1,18], or security breaches caused by internal audio or video signal hacking [13]. A potential solution to avoid such attacks is to rely on an additional implicit authentication system. Some recent works [2,9,14,16] proposed such unobtrusive authentication systems based on analyzing data captured by motion sensors, e.g. accelerometer and gyroscope, using machine learning methods.

In a realistic setting, in which implicit authentication factors (based on motion sensors) support explicit authentication factors (based on face recognition or fingerprint scanning), the registration process necessary for the implicit authentication system is expected to be short, i.e. the number of samples collected during registration must be reduced to a bare minimum. This requirement is imposed by the fact that explicit authentication systems are typically based on a fast registration process. Hence, an implicit authentication system should not represent an additional burden to the end user. In this context, machine learning models based on motion sensors should deliver good performance results in a few-shot learning context, as also noticed by Benegui et al. [2].

In this paper, we aim to find out if the accuracy of few-shot learning models based on motion sensors can be improved through data augmentation. Although data augmentation is a commonly-used approach to enhance image [12] and signal [7] processing systems, to our knowledge, we are the first to study data augmentation techniques for user authentication based on signals collected from motion sensors. We note that we cannot trivially borrow data augmentation techniques from computer vision. For example, in computer vision, flipping an image horizontally will contain the same objects in a different yet realistic pose, which should help the machine learning system to generalize better. In motion signal analysis, flipping a signal on the temporal axis will invert any patterns that belong to a user, thus having a negative effect on the machine learning model. Even the addition of random noise might be problematic, since the signal patterns specific to a user can be very sensitive and the added noise might simply cover them. In this work, we propose a set of data augmentation methods for motion signals, that represent more plausible ways of improving the generalization capacity of machine learning models for motion sensor data. In order to make sure that the original signals are not affected by excessively strong augmentation, we empirically experiment with parameters that control the degree of augmentation, finding optimal values for these parameters. In summary, our aim is to find answers to the following research questions (RQs) in the context of few-shot user identification based on motion sensor signals:

- RQ1: Can data augmentation bring accuracy improvements?
- RQ2: Which of the proposed data augmentation methods brings accuracy improvements?
- RQ3: Are the data augmentation methods generic or specific to certain machine learning models?

We hereby note that RQ1 and RQ2 are strongly related, although RQ1 is more generic. If at least one of the proposed data augmentation methods brings accuracy improvements, we can provide a positive answer to RQ1. If none of the proposed data augmentation methods work, we cannot be sure of a negative answer to RQ1, i.e. there might be a data augmentation method that can bring accuracy improvements and we did not think of it. To minimize this risk, we propose a broad range of plausible data augmentation techniques.

In order to answer RQ1 and RQ2, we experiment with several data augmentation methods, namely adding random noise, temporal scaling, intensity scaling and warping, comparing the results with and without data augmentation. In order to answer RQ3, we consider to augment two independent deep learning models, namely a convolutional neural network (CNN) and a convolutional Long Short-Term Memory (ConvLSTM) network.

2   Related Work

Different studies explore the user identification task on mobile devices using various techniques. For example, Sitová et al. [14] approached the problem by analyzing human movement captured by different motion sensors, apprehending two specific sets of features: stability features and resistance features. During a tap gesture on the screen, motion data is collected and transformed into statistical features, which are given as input to a machine learning model. Recent research [4,6,9,11,14,16,17] shows that machine learning models generally attain better accuracy rates in the user identification process, compared to models based on statistical features. Among these machine learning models, a recent trend is to employ deep learning approaches [2,9,16]. Neverova et al. [9] presented an approach based on recurrent neural networks by combining the two essential steps of machine learning (feature extraction and classification) into a single step. This is achieved through end-to-end learning. The method presented in [9] requires a longer period of data gathering in order to produce optimal results. However, as noted by Benegui et al. [2], a user can also be identified from motion sensors by training a model on as few as 20 taps on the screen. This enables a fast registration and allows the coupling with explicit authentication systems based on face recognition or fingerprint scanning. We hereby note that none of the methods designed for user identification based on motion sensor data study data augmentation. Nonetheless, we acknowledge that in related fields, e.g. human activity recognition, recent studies have shown that augmentation methods applied to time-series data can enhance classification results [7,15]. To our knowledge, we are the first to study data augmentation on discrete motion sensor values used for user identification on mobile devices.

3   Methods

3.1   Learning Models

In order to answer our research questions, we conducted experiments with two deep learning models, a CNN and a ConvLSTM, on the HMOG data set [14].

We follow the experimental setting of Benegui et al. [2], (i) training the deep learning models on a subset of 50 users in a multi-way classification task and (ii) employing the pre-trained models in a few-shot user identification task on the other 50 users. A complete description of the CNN and the ConvLSTM architectures is given in [2]. We further utilize the embeddings resulting from either neural model as inputs to a Support Vector Machines (SVM) classifier, modeling the few-shot user identification task as a binary classification problem. Benegui et al. [2] showed the benefits of modeling the user identification task as a binary classification problem with SVM instead of an outlier detection task with one-class SVM.

3.2 Data Augmentation

Starting with the assumption that data augmentation can have a positive impact on the accuracy of the user identification system, we propose to experiment with different data augmentation techniques in order to assess their benefits.

Adding Random Noise. The first augmentation is to add a Gaussian noise signal ϑ that is randomly generated from a normal distribution $\mathcal{N}(\mu, \nu)$, where μ is the mean μ and σ is the standard deviation. Given a motion sensor signal S of length $|S| = n$, the addition of the Gaussian noise is formally expressed as follows:

$$S_i = \vartheta_i + S_i, \; \vartheta_i \sim \mathcal{N}(\mu, \nu), \; \forall i \in \{1, \ldots, n\}. \tag{1}$$

We note that the amplitude of the noise signal and the degree to which it affects our signal S are controlled through the parameter σ. In the experiments, we try out different values for σ.

Temporal Scaling. The second augmentation method scales the signal in the temporal domain based on a scaling factor f_T. When the scaling factor f_T is greater than 1, the length of the signal S increases and the resulting signal is equally cropped on both sides to preserve the original signal length. When f_T has a value lower than 1, the original signal gets contracted and the resulting signal is zero-padded at both ends in order to keep the initial signal length. In order to rescale the discrete signal, we apply linear interpolation [8].

Signal Intensity Scaling. Given a signal S and an intensity scale factor f_I, the augmented signal is obtained by multiplying each signal value S_i with the scale factor. Formally, the intensity scaling augmentation of a signal S is given by:

$$S_i = f_I \cdot S_i, \; \forall i \in \{1, \ldots, n\}. \tag{2}$$

In the experiments, we try out different values for f_I.

Left-to-Right Warping. We propose an augmentation procedure in which the original signal is warped in the temporal domain by contracting the right side of the signal and expanding its left side. Given a motion sensor signal S of length $|S| = n$, we first select two cutting points t_1 and t_2, randomly, as follows:

$$t_1 \sim \mathcal{U}(\lfloor n/4 \rfloor, \lfloor n/2 \rfloor), \; t_2 \sim \mathcal{U}(\lfloor n/2 \rfloor, \lfloor 3 \cdot n/4 \rfloor), \tag{3}$$

where $\lfloor \cdot \rfloor$ is the flooring function and $\mathcal{U}(a, b)$ generates an integer value that is uniformly distributed between a and b. The left part of the signal is stretched from t_1 to t_2. In the same time, the right part of the signal is contracted from t_1 to t_2. The discrete values are computed through linear interpolation. The resulting signal has the same length as the input signal.

Right-to-Left Warping. An analogous warping augmentation procedure is to contract the left side of the signal, while stretching its right side. We call this type of augmentation right-to-left warping. As for the left-to-right warping, we rely on the randomly-generated cutting points t_1 and t_2 to establish exactly how the signal is warped.

4 Experiments

4.1 Data Set

We experiment on the HMOG [14] data set, which consists of discrete signals from mobile device motion sensors (gyroscope and accelerometer). Motion sensors yield values for three axes (x, y, z) at 100 Hz. We record values for 1.5 s during tap gestures on the screen, resulting in discrete signals of approximately 150 values. Signals are collected for 100 users, considering the first 200 tap events for each user. Hence, the resulting data set consists of 20,000 signal samples. Further, we divide the users in half, using the first half (50 users) to train the neural networks in a 50-way classification task and the second half for the few-shot user identification experiments. In the 50-way classification task, we employ an 80%–20% train-validation split, thus having 160 samples per user for training and 40 samples per user for validation. In the few-shot user identification experiments, we have 50 binary classification problems (one per user) in which the training set is composed of 20 positive and 100 negative samples and the test set is composed of another 100 positive and 100 negative samples. It is important to note that the 100 negative training samples are gathered from one subset of users and the 100 negative test samples are gathered from another (disjoint) subset of users. By adopting disjoint sets of users, we ensure that features representative for the attackers are not seen during training, resulting a in realistic scenario for our experiments.

4.2 Experimental Setup

Evaluation Metrics. We compute the accuracy, the false acceptance rate (FAR) and the false rejection rate (FRR) for each user. We then report the values averaged over the 50 users selected for the few-shot user identification experiments.

Parameter Tuning for Learning Models. For the CNN model, we use the hyperparameters described in [2], which provided optimal results on the validation set. We thus fix the learning rate to 10^{-3} and use mini-batches of 32 samples. The model is trained using Adam [5] for 50 epochs. To avoid overfitting, each fully-connected layer uses dropout at a rate of 0.4. For the ConvLSTM architecture, we use the same hyperparameter settings as for the CNN model. Therefore, we set the learning rate to 10^{-3} and train the model for 50 epochs on mini-batches of 32 samples. Each fully-connected layer employs a dropout rate of 0.4. In the few-shot user identification task, we adopt binary SVM classifiers based on either a linear kernel or an RBF kernel [10]. Throughout the experiments, we try out different values for the regularization parameter C of the SVM, considering values in the set $\{1, 10, 100\}$. In order to compare the various SVM models in a balanced and fair setting, we automatically adjust the bias value of each SVM such that the difference between the FAR and the FRR is less than 1%.

Baselines. We consider as baselines, the results attained by the SVM based on CNN or ConvLSTM embeddings, respectively, without data augmentation.

Data Augmentation Scenarios. We note that the degree of augmentation is not only reflected by the hyperparameter choices for the data augmentation methods, but also by the number of augmented samples. Therefore, in our experiments, we explore two different ratios between the number of original samples and the number of augmented samples, as follows. In the first augmentation scenario, we employ an augmentation ratio of 1×, so that during the training phase, each original data sample is copied and augmented once. This results in a training set with 40 positive samples (20 original and 20 augmented) and 200 negative samples (100 original and 100 augmented). In the second augmentation scenario, we employ an augmentation ratio of 0.5×, so that during the training phase, one in every two original data samples is copied and augmented once. This results in a training set with 30 positive samples (20 original and 10 augmented) and 150 negative samples (100 original and 50 augmented). We hereby note that we do not use data augmentation during the testing phase, i.e. we keep the same number of test samples, 100 positive and 100 negative per user.

Parameter Tuning for Data Augmentation Methods. We tune the parameters of each augmentation method in order to assess which configuration provides the highest improvements in terms of identification accuracy. We carry out the augmentation based on random Gaussian noise using different values for the standard deviation value σ, considering $\sigma \in \{0.0125, 0.025, 0.05, 0.1, 0.2, 0.3, 0.4, 0.5\}$. We note that the amplitude of the Gaussian noise is directly proportional to the value of σ, so greater values result in larger deviations from the original signal. For temporal scaling, the degree to which a signal is stretched or contracted is controlled by the parameter f_T, which represents the temporal scaling factor. In our experiments, we select f_T within a range of values that results in either stretching (when $f_T > 1$) or contracting (when $f_T < 1$) the original signals. For f_T, we considered values in the set $\{0.8, 0.9, 0.95, 0.975, 0.9875, 1.0125, 1.025, 1.05, 1.1, 1.2\}$. For intensity scaling, the degree to which the amplitude of a signal is exaggerated or flattened is controlled by the parameter f_I, which represents the intensity scaling factor. For f_I, we considered values in the set {0.8, 0.9, 0.95, 0.975, 0.9875, 1.0125, 1.025, 1.05, 1.1, 1.2}. For signal warping, we consider the direction of the warp, left-to-right $(L \rightarrow R)$ or right-to-left $(L \leftarrow R)$, as the only parameter that requires tuning. In the subsequent experiments, we report accuracy rates only for the optimal parameter values, specifying in each case the corresponding hyperparameter value. The parameters are validated by fixing the data representation to the embeddings provided by the CNN. We then use the same parameters for the ConvLSTM, in order to avoid overfitting in hyperparameter space.

4.3   Results

In Table 1, we present the empirical results obtained by various SVM classifiers based on CNN or ConvLSTM features for different augmentation scenarios. For each type of augmentation, we include the scores attained only for the best performing parameters.

Table 1. Results for the few-short user identification task with various SVM classifiers trained on embeddings provided by pre-trained CNN or ConvLSTM models, with and without data augmentation. Each augmentation procedure is evaluated in two augmentation scenarios. In each case, results are reported only for the optimal hyperparameter values. Accuracy, FAR and FRR scores represent the average values computed on 50 users. Results that exceed the baseline accuracy rates are marked with asterisk.

Augmentation method	Parameter value	SVM+CNN embeddings					SVM+ConvLSTM embeddings				
		Kernel	C	Accuracy	FAR	FRR	Kernel	C	Accuracy	FAR	FRR
No augmentation											
-	-	RBF	1	96.37%	3.30%	3.96%	RBF	1	96.18%	4.00%	3.64%
Augmentation of all samples with ratio 1×											
Random noise	$\sigma = 0.025$	Linear	100	96.54%*	3.46%	3.45%	Linear	1	95.63%	4.30%	4.44%
Temporal scaling	$f_T = 0.975$	Linear	100	96.48%*	4.01%	3.83%	Linear	10	96.77%*	3.30%	3.15%
Intensity scaling	$f_I = 0.95$	Linear	1	96.50%*	3.58%	3.41%	Linear	1	93.63%	6.60%	6.14%
Warping	$L \leftarrow R$	RBF	1	94.87%	4.96%	5.29%	Linear	1	95.94%	3.98%	4.14%
Augmentation of all samples with ratio 0.5×											
Random noise	$\sigma = 0.05$	Linear	1	96.54%*	3.42%	3.49%	Linear	10	96.48%*	3.96%	3.07%
Temporal scaling	$f_T = 1.05$	Linear	100	96.77%*	3.26%	3.19%	Linear	1	94.89%	5.08%	5.13%
Intensity scaling	$f_I = 1.0125$	Linear	1	96.41%*	3.42%	3.76%	Linear	10	95.35%	4.74%	4.57%
Warping	$L \rightarrow R$	RBF	1	94.49%	5.24%	5.79%	Linear	10	95.56%	4.36%	4.53%

Augmentation of All Samples with Ratio 1×. When we copy and augment all training samples exactly once, we observe that the SVM based on CNN embeddings performs better than the baseline SVM for three independent augmentation techniques: random noise addition, temporal scaling and intensity scaling. However, the differences between the baseline SVM based on CNN embeddings and the SVM based on CNN embeddings with data augmentation are slim, the maximum improvement being +0.17%. The random noise and the temporal scaling augmentation methods yield their best accuracy rates using an SVM based on a linear kernel and a regularization of $C = 100$. The intensity scaling augmentation works better with an SVM based on a linear kernel with $C = 1$. With respect to the SVM based on ConvLSTM embeddings, we observe accuracy improvements (+0.59%) only when the data is augmented through temporal scaling. We notice that none of the observed improvements are statistically significant. We also note that warping is the only augmentation technique that seems to degrade performance for both CNN and ConvLSTM embeddings.

Augmentation of All Samples with Ratio 0.5×. If the number of augmented samples was too high in the first augmentation scenario, we should be able to observe this problem in the second augmentation scenario, in which the augmentation ratio is 0.5×. Considering the comparative results presented in Table 1, we notice moderate changes in terms of accuracy rates. As in the first scenario, the same three data augmentation methods bring performance improvements over the baseline SVM based on CNN embeddings. Temporal scaling generates an accuracy improvement of +0.40% for the linear kernel and $C = 100$, becoming the best augmentation method, followed by the random noise augmentation with an increase of +0.17% (just as in the first augmentation scenario). With respect to the SVM based on ConvLSTM embeddings, we observe that the baseline is surpassed only when the data is augmented with random noise. Considering that we attained better results with temporal scaling for the augmentation ratio 1×, we conclude that the results reported for the SVM based on ConvLSTM embeddings are inconsistent.

5   Conclusion

In this paper, we have studied different augmentation strategies for signals generated by motion sensors, with the intention of answering a set of research questions regarding the usefulness of data augmentation for the few-shot user identification problem. We performed a set of experiments with various data augmentation approaches using two state-of-the-art neural architectures, a CNN and a ConvL-STM, allowing us to answer the proposed research questions. We conclude our work by answering our research questions below:

- RQ1: Can data augmentation bring accuracy improvements?
  Answer: In order to answer this question, we tried out multiple augmentation methods such as adding random noise, temporal scaling, intensity scaling and warping. We observed performance improvements (under 0.6%) for all methods, besides warping (see Table 1). In summary, the answer to RQ1 is affirmative, although the improvements are not statistically significant.
- RQ2: Which of the proposed data augmentation methods brings accuracy improvements?
  Answer: Among the considered augmentation methods, we discovered that

adding random noise, temporal scaling and intensity scaling can bring performance improvements. However, these improvements are not consistent across
machine learning models and augmentation scenarios (see Table 1).

– RQ3: Are the data augmentation methods generic or specific to certain
machine learning models?
Answer: We considered to augment the data for two models, one based on
CNN embeddings and one based on ConvLSTM embeddings. In most cases,
we observed performance gains for the SVM model based on CNN embeddings (see Table 1). In very few cases, we noticed improvements for the SVM
based on ConvLSTM embeddings (see Table 1). We thus conclude that the
data augmentation methods do not generalize across different models.

Looking at the overall picture, we conclude that data augmentation is not
useful for few-shot user identification based on motion sensor data. We also notice
that the augmentation hyperparameters (σ, f_T and f_I) that provided the best
results tend to correspond to the smallest changes on the original signals. This
indicates that data augmentation is rather harmful, distorting or covering the
patterns useful for discriminating registered users from attackers. In this context,
we do not recommend data augmentation on discrete signals recorded by motion
sensors. In future work, we aim to explain [3] why the plain models (without
augmentation) obtain such good results. Our intuition is that the models rely
on features that are sensitive to changes brought by data augmentation.

Acknowledgment. The research leading to these results has received funding from
the EEA Grants 2014-2021, under Project contract no. EEA-RO-NO-2018-0496.

References

1. Andriotis, P., Tryfonas, T., Oikonomou, G., Yildiz, C.: A pilot study on the security
   of pattern screen-lock methods and soft side channel attacks. In: Proceedings of
   WiSec, pp. 1–6 (2013)
2. Benegui, C., Ionescu, R.T.: Convolutional neural networks for user identification
   based on motion sensors represented as images. IEEE Access **8**(1), 61255–61266
   (2020)
3. Bărbălău, A., Cosma, A., Ionescu, R.T., Popescu, M.: A generic and model-agnostic
   exemplar synthetization framework for explainable AI. In: Proceedings of ECML-
   PKDD (2020)
4. Ehatisham-ul Haq, M., Azam, M.A., Naeem, U., Amin, Y., Loo, J.: Continuous
   authentication of smartphone users based on activity pattern recognition using
   passive mobile sensing. J. Netw. Comput. Appl. **109**, 24–35 (2018)
5. Kingma, D.P., Ba, J.: Adam: a method for stochastic optimization. In: Proceedings
   of ICLR (2015)
6. Ku, Y., Park, L.H., Shin, S., Kwon, T.: Draw it as shown: behavioral pattern lock
   for mobile user authentication. IEEE Access **7**, 69363–69378 (2019)
7. Le Guennec, A., Malinowski, S., Tavenard, R.: Data augmentation for time series
   classification using convolutional neural networks. In: Proceedings of AALTD
   Workshop (2016)

8. Meijering, E.: A chronology of interpolation: from ancient astronomy to modern signal and image processing. Proc. IEEE **90**(3), 319–342 (2002)
9. Neverova, N., et al.: Learning human identity from motion patterns. IEEE Access **4**, 1810–1820 (2016)
10. Shawe-Taylor, J., Cristianini, N.: Kernel Methods for Pattern Analysis. Cambridge University Press, Cambridge (2004)
11. Shen, C., Yu, T., Yuan, S., Li, Y., Guan, X.: Performance analysis of motion-sensor behavior for user authentication on smartphones. Sensors **16**(3), 345 (2016)
12. Shorten, C., Khoshgoftaar, T.M.: A survey on image data augmentation for deep learning. J. Big Data **6**(1), 60 (2019)
13. Simon, L., Anderson, R.: PIN skimmer: inferring PINs through the camera and microphone. In: Proceedings of SPSM, pp. 67–78 (2013)
14. Sitová, Z., et al.: HMOG: new behavioral biometric features for continuous authentication of smartphone users. IEEE Trans. Inf. Forensics Secur. **11**(5), 877–892 (2016)
15. Steven Eyobu, O., Han, D.S.: Feature representation and data augmentation for human activity classification based on wearable IMU sensor data using a deep LSTM neural network. Sensors **18**(9), 2892 (2018)
16. Sun, L., Wang, Y., Cao, B., Philip, S.Y., Srisa-An, W., Leow, A.D.: Sequential keystroke behavioral biometrics for mobile user identification via multi-view deep learning. In: Proceedings of ECML-PKDD, pp. 228–240 (2017)
17. Wang, R., Tao, D.: Context-aware implicit authentication of smartphone users based on multi-sensor behavior. IEEE Access **7**, 119654–119667 (2019)
18. Zhang, Y., Xia, P., Luo, J., Ling, Z., Liu, B., Fu, X.: Fingerprint attack against touch-enabled devices. In: Proceedings of SPSM, pp. 57–68 (2012)

Unsupervised Visual Time-Series Representation Learning and Clustering

Gaurangi Anand[✉] and Richi Nayak

School of Computer Science, Queensland University of Technology,
Brisbane, Australia
gaurangianand@hdr.qut.edu.au, r.nayak@qut.edu.au

Abstract. Time-series data is generated ubiquitously from Internet-of-Things (IoT) infrastructure, connected and wearable devices, remote sensing, autonomous driving research and, audio-video communications, in enormous volumes. This paper investigates the potential of unsupervised representation learning for these time-series. In this paper, we use a novel data transformation along with novel unsupervised learning regime to transfer the learning from other domains to time-series where the former have extensive models heavily trained on very large labelled datasets. We conduct extensive experiments to demonstrate the potential of the proposed approach through time-series clustering. Source code available at https://github.com/technophyte/LDVR.

Keywords: Unsupervised learning · Time-series clustering

1 Introduction

Time-series data is generated ubiquitously in enormous amounts from sensors and IoT. With the prior knowledge about labels, it can be observed that the samples have minor to major shape variations across pre-defined labels, as seen in Fig. 1. These variations can be incorporated in feature representation and learning. However, a large-scale time-series labelling is expensive and requires domain expertise, paving way for unsupervised tasks for time-series [12].

Time-series clustering is an unsupervised task with data representation and a suitable similarity measure as its core components. Some methods propose sophisticated similarity measures applied to raw time-series data, while others propose effective representations suitable to simpler similarity measures like Euclidean Distance (ED). Both the approaches define the means for unsupervised estimation of the extent of resemblance between the samples utilizing characteristics such as their shape [14], shapelets [7], alignment [3] and structure [13]. This extent is guided by the information acquired through supervised or unsupervised learning. In the absence of labels, transfer learning (TL) is one of the solutions [2] where the model learned on source task, rich with labelled information, is fine-tuned for a target task. Typically the source and target datasets are related with the latter being comparatively small. The recent success of deep

© Springer Nature Switzerland AG 2020
H. Yang et al. (Eds.): ICONIP 2020, CCIS 1333, pp. 832–840, 2020.
https://doi.org/10.1007/978-3-030-63823-8_94

BeetleFly	CBF	FISH	ShapeletSim	Trace

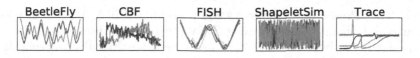

Fig. 1. Five sample datasets from UCR [4] with one sample per cluster

learning has brought advancements to TL methods in the fields of Natural Language Processing and Computer Vision (CV) with large datasets like *Wikipedia*, and *ImageNet* [10] for fine-tuning various related data-scarce tasks. However, no such labelled time-series corpus of a similar scale exists.

In this paper, we propose a novel approach of leveraging the large-scale training from a popular CV-based dataset [5] to the time-series data in an unsupervised manner. The relatedness of ImageNet data and time-series has not been explored earlier, providing an opportunity to use visual recognition for time-series as commonly done for images. It facilitates representing time-series from a visual perspective inspired by human visual cognition, involving 2-D convolutions, unlike the 1-D convolutional approaches popular in time-series domain [7]. We utilize the shifted variants of the original time-series to train a model to isolate the distinct local patterns of the time-series irrespective of their location within the overall layout, and evaluate the approach for time-series clustering. More specifically, the contributions of this paper are as follows:

1. We approach the problem of time-series analysis as the human visual cognitive process by transforming the 1-D time-series data into 2-D images.
2. We leverage the training of the very large dataset available in the CV field to the unsupervised representation learning for time-series through a pre-trained 2-D deep Convolutional Neural Network (CNN) model.
3. We propose a novel unsupervised learning regime using triplet loss for time-series data using 2-D convolutions and shift-invariance.
4. The resultant time-series representation has fixed length regardless of the variable length time-series that enables pairwise comparison of time-series data in linear time using Euclidean distance.

2 Related Literature

With the availability of unlabelled datasets, several unsupervised learning methods have emerged ranging from conventional algorithms [1, 19] to stacked deep architectures [6, 12], for obtaining a representation based on the end task. These representations can be data adaptive like Symbolic Aggregate Approximation (SAX) [13] or non-data adaptive like Discrete Fourier Transform (DFT), Discrete Wavelet Transform (DWT) and Piecewise Aggregate Approximations (PAA). A model-based representation is generated by identifying the model parameters through training based on the relevant properties. Once trained, a model is used as a feature extractor [7] for the end task.

Similarity PreservIng RepresentAtion Learning (SPIRAL) [11] preserves the similarity of Dynamic Time Warping (DTW) distance in the approximated similarity matrix, to be then used for conventional partitional clustering like k-means. k-shape [14] adapts the clustering algorithm to the distance measure for cross-correlation while assigning clusters. Unsupervised Salient Subsequence Learning (USSL) [19] identifies the salient subsequences from the time-series and performs clustering based on shapelet learning and spectral analysis. Deep Embedding for Clustering (DEC) [18] and Improved Deep Embedding Clustering (IDEC) [8] are deep learning based non-time-series clustering. Unsupervised triplet loss training has been proposed for time-series [7] where representations are learned and evaluated for time-series classification using 1-D dilated causal convolutions. Deep Temporal Clustering Representation (DTCR) [12] is a deep learning-based end-to-end clustering for time-series clustering that jointly learns time-series representations and assigns cluster labels using k-means loss.

Existing deep learning-based time-series representation methods do not use pre-trained networks due to 1) the latter not being tailored to time-series and 2) the popularity of 1-D convolutions for sequential data. Bridging this gap by utilizing a 2-D pre-trained CNN not only helps to leverage large-scale training but also provides a local pattern-based time-series representation. To the best of our knowledge, this is the first time-series representation approach combining visual perception with unsupervised triplet loss training using 2-D convolutions.

3   Proposed Approach

We propose to first transform time-series into images to leverage the large-scale training from a 2-D deep CNN pre-trained with ImageNet. This CNN is then modified and re-trained for feature extraction in unsupervised setting utilizing a novel triplet loss training.

1-D to 2-D Feature Transformation (f_T). The 1-D time-series dataset is transformed into 2-D image dataset, achieved by simply *plotting* a 1D time-series as a time-series image, and used as 2D matrix to take advantage of 2-D convolution operations [9,10] through pre-trained 2-D CNNs. This emulation of human visual cognition to inspect/cluster time-series data using this transformation enables the vision-inspired systems to interpret the time-series visually.

CNN Architecture. We use ResNet50 [9] as our pre-trained CNN, trained on the large-scale ImageNet dataset [5] for the task of object classification. It consists of residual connections that add depth to the vanilla CNN architecture [10] useful for highly complex CV tasks. ImageNet [5] comprises millions of images with 1000 classes. CNN learned on this data provides visual local pattern based representations extracted as 3-D feature tensors from each of its composite layers. These feature tensors, called *feature maps*, have the local spatial pattern mapping with respect to each of the input images. ImageNet allows the network to learn lots of variations in local shape patterns. With that as a premise, we argue that when using visual representations of 1-D time-series most of their shape patterns would be easily represented through a pre-trained 2-D CNN. The subsequent fine-tuning helps to add the time-series bias to shape patterns. As a result, relevant shape patterns are obtained for 2-D time-series matrices.

The modified ResNet is depicted in Fig. 2. ResNet is retained up to its last convolution layer by removing the fully connected layer trained for the object classification task. The local spatial patterns in the form of activations for each of the time-series images are retrieved within the feature maps. A 2-D convolution layer is then appended to it, followed by the Global Max Pooling (GMP) layer [17]. This layer leverages the local patterns within different feature maps irrespective of their actual activation location in an image for introducing shift-invariance. It helps matching time-series images where the observed local patterns may not exactly align spatially. We then append a $l2$-normalization layer to improve the network training by providing stability to it.

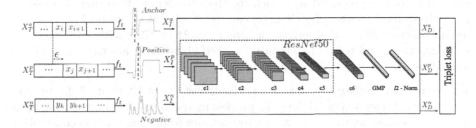

Fig. 2. Overview of the proposed learning framework with $c1\ldots6$ convolution layers of the CNN followed with GMP and $l2$-normalization layer

Let X_T be the set of 1-D univariate time-series that is transformed into an equivalent set of 2-D time-series images, X_I. X_D refers to the representations obtained from this deep network. Using the $l2$-normalized representation for each individual time-series, we generate unsupervised triplets as described below. Once trained, the $l2$-normalized output is used as the Learned Time-series Representation, called as Learned Deep Visual Representation (LDVR).

Triplet Selection. Triplet loss training helps to ensure that similar instances obtain similar representations, while the dissimilar ones are pushed apart with a margin, α. Unlike the usual supervision-based triplet selection [7,16], we propose a novel unsupervised triplet selection for 2-D time-series images. A positive pair consists of an original instance with its shifted variant, and its pairing with any other sample forms the negative pair. This training helps identifying the patterns that can be isolated from the layout and modify the representations such that the *anchor* and *positive* are brought closer and separated from *negative*.

We address the challenge of unsupervised triplet selection by considering a pool of time-series across a large number of datasets. From this pool, two time-series samples, X_{T_a} and X_{T_n} as anchor and negative respectively, are selected randomly from a dataset and a random shift to X_{T_a} is added by introducing a circular shift of randomly chosen ϵ time-steps to obtain X_{T_p}, called positive. The feature transformation is applied to the triplet set to obtain X_{I_a}, X_{T_p}, and X_{I_n}. Figure 2 depicts the process of triplet selection with X_{T_a}, X_{T_p} and X_{T_n} as the triplets, where X_{T_p} is obtained by introducing a shift of ϵ to X_{T_a}.

Clustering. The modified ResNet trained with the unsupervised Triplet loss produces a fixed length representation, X_D, called LDVR for each time-series image. Assuming the compact feature representation to be separable in Euclidean space, a distance based clustering algorithm likes k-means can be applied.

4   Experiments

Extensive experiments are conducted to evaluate the accuracy of the LDVR generated by the proposed approach for the time-series clustering. We use the publicly available time-series UCR repository [4] with 85 datasets. The sequences in each dataset have equal length ranging from 24 to 2709, with 2 to 60 classes, split into train and test. The already assigned class labels are treated as cluster identifiers and only used in evaluation.

Experimental Setup. We use the previous version of UCR of 47 datasets for unsupervised selection of triplets. To prevent memorization and overfitting of the network training, we randomly select 100 samples from them[1]. For each iteration, we perform 10 circular shifts each time with randomly chosen ϵ varying between 0.6 and 1.0, representing the percentage of time-series length. A total of 3056 distinct instances were added to the pool for triplet selection. The inclusion of shifted samples forces the network to learn local patterns isolated from the layout, and use them for matching independent of their actual location across samples. All the time-series of variable length were transformed into images of 640 × 480 resolution. This value was derived from UCR where 80% of datasets have length below 640; to keep aspect ratio as standard 4:3, height set to 480.

The batch-size and learning rate for training was 32 and 0.05 respectively, trained for 200 epochs with filter size of 3 × 3 with the stride of 1 and margin $\alpha = 1.0$. The pre-trained *ResNet50* network was frozen up to $c5$ layer and randomly initialized for next layers for triplet loss training. The best number of feature maps for $c6$ layer was estimated to be 4096. Once trained, the representation of dimension $d = 4096$ is obtained on which clustering is performed. Figure 4 (left) shows the sensitivity of LDVR with varying margin values and number of $c6$ feature maps w.r.t. average NMI scores.

Benchmarking Methods. We benchmarked the LDVR for time-series clustering (i.e. k-means with euclidean distance) with several methods. First, we include the Pre-trained Deep Visual Representation (PDVR) i.e., the representations extracted from the c5 layer before the Triplet loss training. We use deep learning based two non time-series clustering methods, DEC [18] and IDEC [8]

---

[1] Datasets that do not contain enough samples, we chose 60% of the total samples.

to cluster 2-D matrix time-series image data. Three traditional distance measure based methods include *SPIRAL* [11], k-shape [14] and ED with k-means (ED) applied on raw time-series. Additionally, we include the two common time series representation methods, SAX (1d-SAX) [13] and DWT [15].

Two recent time-series clustering approaches: DTCR [12] and USSL [19] have partial results published and have not made their source-codes available for them to be included in benchmarking. We provide a short analysis in the end.

All methods are evaluated with Normalized Mutual Information (NMI) and Rand Index (RI), the most common metrics to evaluate time-series clustering.

The network training is done on SGI Altix XE cluster with an Intel(R) Xeon(R) 2.50 GHz E5-2680V3 processor running SUSE *Linux*. We use Keras 2.2.2 with Tensorflow backend and Python 3.5.

5   Results: Clustering Accuracy Performance

We first compute the cumulative ranking for both the NMI and RI scores, with the lower rank indicative of a better score. For each dataset, LDVR, PDVR and other methods are ranked based on their performance from 1 to 9, considering ties. The total rank across all datasets is computed for each method cumulatively and then averaged across all datasets, as shown in Table 1.

Table 1. Average cumulative ranks and average scores for NMI and RI for 85 datasets

	LDVR	PDVR	DEC	IDEC	SPIRAL	ED	k-shape	SAX	DWT
Avg. Rank (NMI)	**2.74**	3.36	5.25	5.66	**2.66**	3.08	3.98	3.81	3.12
Avg. Score (NMI)	**0.36**	0.32	0.23	0.19	0.30	0.29	0.25	0.29	0.29
Avg. Rank (RI)	**2.42**	3.02	4.66	5.16	3.09	3.35	4.22	3.51	3.40
Avg. Score (RI)	**0.73**	0.72	0.66	0.60	0.69	0.69	0.63	0.70	0.69

As seen in Table 1, the average cumulative NMI ranks for LDVR and SPIRAL are lowest, however LDVR gets maximum wins and the maximum average NMI score, by winning in 28 datasets. SPIRAL and PDVR win on 17 and 16 datasets. Moreover, the high average RI score and lowest cumulative average RI rank indicate the promising performance of LDVR, with winning on 26 datasets for RI, followed by PDVR and SPIRAL with 18 and 14 wins, respectively.

The poor results of DEC and IDEC indicate that 2-D matrix image data is not sufficient for effective clustering. PDVR is the pre-trained representation, which when fine-tuned to LDVR, helps in achieving a performance boost in more than 50% of the datasets. This validates that the unsupervised fine-tuning proposed in this paper adds a bias thereby improving the clustering.

Table 2 shows the comparative performance of LDVR with DTCR [12] and USSL [19]. In the absence of their source code, we compare first on their published 36 UCR datasets in the first three columns, the reason for selection of

Table 2. Performance comparison (Average RI Score) of LDVR, DTCR and USSL

M_1 (#36)	M_2 (#36)	M_3 (#36)	M_3 (#**Top 36**)	M_3 (#Top 73)	M_3 (#All 85)
0.77	0.76	0.70	**0.90**	0.77	0.73
M1: DTCR [12]			**M2**: USSL [19]	**M3**: LDVR	

these datasets is undisclosed. It can be observed that LDVR comes very close to DTCR and USSL. However, the average RI values on LDVR's top 36 datasets is significantly higher than that published for the two methods. The next columns show it takes as high as 73 UCR datasets to maintain the RI score of 0.77, and drops only to 0.73 when considering all 85 datasets.

Though many methods have been proposed for time-series analysis, shape-based clustering still appears to be challenging. The combined performance evaluation through NMI and RI establishes LDVR as the leading state-of-the-art method capable of attaining accurate time-Series representation and clusters while considering the shape of the time-series.

5.1 Comparative Performance

Figure 3 shows the performance of distance-measure and representation-based methods used for benchmarking compared against LDVR using NMI scores on all 85 datasets. The larger numbers of points in yellow triangle indicate the goodness of LDVR against all of its competitors. The comparison with the leading algorithm, k-shape, ascertains that not many datasets require cross-correlation distance to be used as a shape similarity measure, with LDVR winning on 57 out of 85 datasets. Similarly, DTW based SPIRAL is not as effective and accurate as LDVR, losing on total 50 datasets.

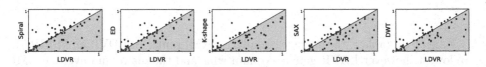

Fig. 3. Pairwise performance comparison of LDVR against traditional methods, with each dot as a dataset. The dots appearing in yellow triangle indicate LDVR performs better for that dataset. (Color figure online)

These methods end up having false matches due to the forced alignment of time-series which is not always needed. On the other hand, k-means provide better clusters on LDVR versus ED, proving that the learned visual representations are stronger and accurate for point-to-point comparison than the raw 1-D time-series values.

We also report the performance of all the methods with respect to the varying length time-series of the UCR repository. We group the UCR datasets into 3

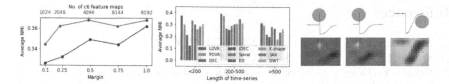

Fig. 4. Left: Sensitivity analysis with respect to number of c6 feature maps (red) and margin for triplet loss (blue). Middle: Variations in average NMI performance with respect to different time-series length bins. Right: Visualization of c6 feature map activations and local feature patterns that led to correct time-series matching (Color figure online)

categories based on the sequence lengths; (1) 31 datasets with length <200, (2) 29 datasets with length 200 to 500, and (3) 25 datasets with length >500. It can be observed from Fig. 4 (middle), that LVDR performs best in all the categories and does not depend on the time-series length. Despite the variable length of input time-series, the feature representation vector size in LDVR remains constant, depending on the number of feature maps in c6 layer, that is, 4096.

Qualitative Analysis with Visualization. Figure 4 (right most) shows a triplet from the Trace dataset from UCR. The first 2 instances are anchor and positive, with the third one as negative. The discriminant pattern (marked as red in top row), observed in anchor, is slightly shifted in positive pair. The corresponding feature maps (in bottom row) show similar activations for the anchor-positive pair. However, the discriminant pattern is not seen in the negative instance which belongs to a different cluster. As a result, the feature maps corresponding to the absent patterns have different activation distribution. This proves how the local pattern based visual representation is useful and helps in identifying patterns which are similar within instances of the same cluster and discriminative across instances of different clusters.

6 Conclusion

We propose a novel way of generating representations for time-series using visual perception and unsupervised triplet loss training. The proposed approach has explored the relatedness of CV datasets to the time-series where the latter is expressed as 2-D image matrices, unlike the usual 1-D manner. Additionally, we utilize an existing pre-trained 2-D CNN with certain modifications to obtain an effective time-series representation, LDVR. Extensive experiments demonstrated that LDVR outperforms existing clustering methods without requiring dataset-specific training. This establishes LDVR as the leading state-of-the-art model-based representation learning method, suitable for time-series clustering. Neither being fixed to any pre-trained network, nor tied to downstream task of clustering or classification, this makes the proposed approach highly flexible and adaptable to any target task.

References

1. Aghabozorgi, S., Shirkhorshidi, A.S., Wah, T.Y.: Time-series clustering-a decade review. Inf. Syst. **53**, 16–38 (2015)
2. Bengio, Y.: Deep learning of representations for unsupervised and transfer learning. In: Proceedings of ICML Workshop on Unsupervised and Transfer Learning, pp. 17–36 (2012)
3. Berndt, D.J., Clifford, J.: Using dynamic time warping to find patterns in time series. In: KDD Workshop, Seattle, WA, vol. 10, pp. 359–370 (1994)
4. Chen, Y., et al.: The UCR time series classification archive (2015)
5. Deng, J., Dong, W., Socher, R., Li, L.J., Li, K., Fei-Fei, L.: ImageNet: a large-scale hierarchical image database. In: 2009 IEEE Conference on Computer Vision and Pattern Recognition, pp. 248–255. IEEE (2009)
6. Fawaz, H.I., Forestier, G., Weber, J., Idoumghar, L., Muller, P.A.: Deep learning for time series classification: a review. Data Min. Knowl. Disc. **33**(4), 917–963 (2019)
7. Franceschi, J.Y., Dieuleveut, A., Jaggi, M.: Unsupervised scalable representation learning for multivariate time series. In: Advances in Neural Information Processing Systems, pp. 4652–4663 (2019)
8. Guo, X., Gao, L., Liu, X., Yin, J.: Improved deep embedded clustering with local structure preservation. In: IJCAI (2017)
9. He, K., Zhang, X., Ren, S., Sun, J.: Deep residual learning for image recognition. In: Proceedings of the IEEE Conference on Computer Vision and Pattern Recognition, pp. 770–778 (2016)
10. Krizhevsky, A., Sutskever, I., Hinton, G.E.: ImageNet classification with deep convolutional neural networks. In: Advances in Neural Information Processing Systems, pp. 1097–1105 (2012)
11. Lei, Q., Yi, J., Vaculin, R., Wu, L., Dhillon, I.S.: Similarity preserving representation learning for time series clustering. In: IJCAI 2019, pp. 2845–2851 (2019)
12. Ma, Q., Zheng, J., Li, S., Cottrell, G.W.: Learning representations for time series clustering. In: Advances in Neural Information Processing Systems (2019)
13. Malinowski, S., Guyet, T., Quiniou, R., Tavenard, R.: 1d-SAX: a novel symbolic representation for time series. In: Tucker, A., Höppner, F., Siebes, A., Swift, S. (eds.) IDA 2013. LNCS, vol. 8207, pp. 273–284. Springer, Heidelberg (2013). https://doi.org/10.1007/978-3-642-41398-8_24
14. Paparrizos, J., Gravano, L.: Fast and accurate time-series clustering. ACM Trans. Database Syst. (TODS) **42**(2), 8 (2017)
15. Popivanov, I., Miller, R.J.: Similarity search over time-series data using wavelets. In: IEEE Proceedings 18th International Conference on Data Engineering (2002)
16. Schroff, F., Kalenichenko, D., Philbin, J.: FaceNet: a unified embedding for face recognition and clustering. In: Proceedings of the IEEE Conference on Computer Vision and Pattern Recognition, pp. 815–823 (2015)
17. Tolias, G., Sicre, R., Jégou, H.: Particular object retrieval with integral max-pooling of CNN activations. In: International Conference on Learning Representations (2016)
18. Xie, J., Girshick, R., Farhadi, A.: Unsupervised deep embedding for clustering analysis. In: International Conference on Machine Learning (2016)
19. Zhang, Q., Wu, J., Zhang, P., Long, G., Zhang, C.: Salient subsequence learning for time series clustering. IEEE Trans. Pattern Anal. Mach. Intell. **41**(9), 2193–2207 (2018)

Correction to: Transfer Learning for Semi-supervised Classification of Non-stationary Data Streams

Yimin Wen, Qi Zhou, Yun Xue, and Chao Feng

Correction to:
Chapter "Transfer Learning for Semi-supervised
Classification of Non-stationary Data Streams"
in: H. Yang et al. (Eds.): *Neural Information Processing*,
CCIS 1333, https://doi.org/10.1007/978-3-030-63823-8_54

The originally published version of the chapter 54 consisted typesetting errors in Tables 2–5. This has been corrected.

The updated version of this chapter can be found at
https://doi.org/10.1007/978-3-030-63823-8_54

Author Index

Printed in the United States
By Bookmasters